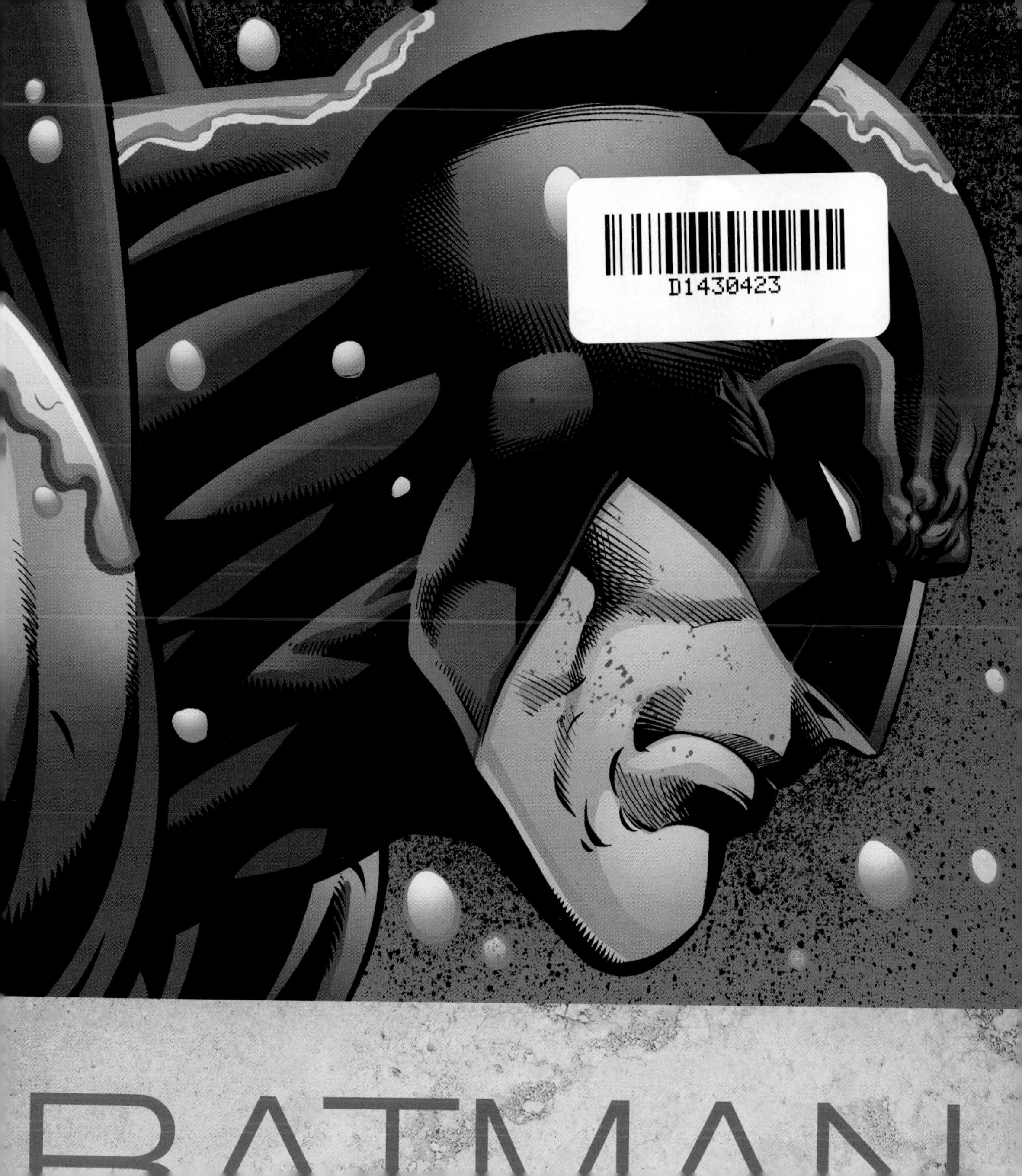

BATMAN

TABLE OF CONTENTS

BATMAN CREATED BY BOB KANE

COLLECTION COVER BY ALEX MALEEV AND BILL SIENKIEWICZ

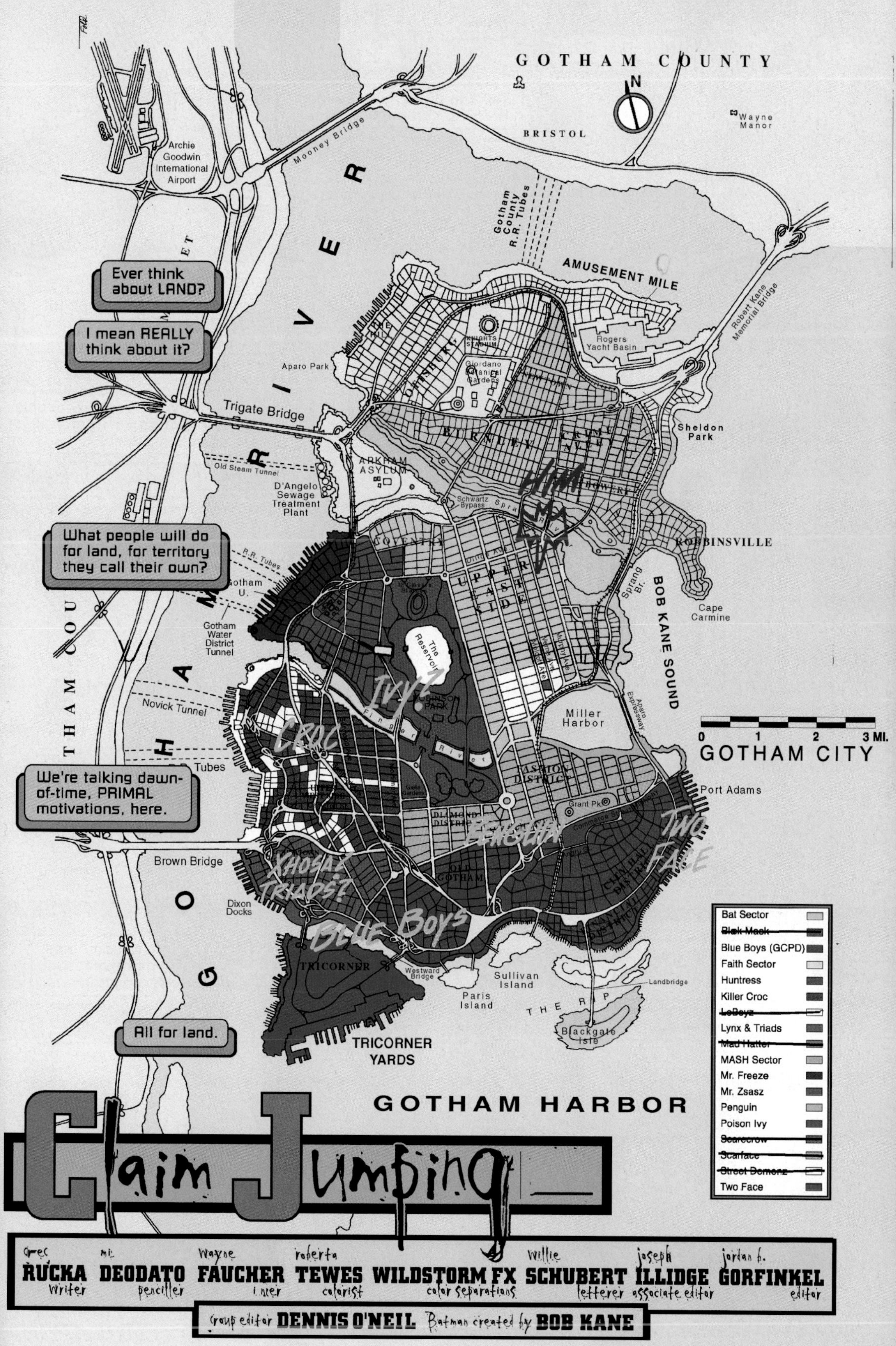

Ever think about LAND?
I mean REALLY think about it?
What people will do for land, for territory they call their own?
We're talking dawn-of-time, PRIMAL motivations, here.
All for land.
GOTHAM COUNTY
N
BRISTOL
Wayne Manor
Archie Goodwin International Airport
Mooney Bridge
Gotham County R.R. Tubes
AMUSEMENT MILE
Robert Kane Memorial Bridge
Rogers Yacht Basin
Aparo Park
Giordano Botanical Gardens
Trigate Bridge
Sheldon Park
BURNLEY
ARKHAM ASYLUM
Old Steam Tunnel
D'Angelo Sewage Treatment Plant
Schwartz Bypass
BOWERY
ROBBINSVILLE
COVENTRY
R.R. Tubes
Gotham U.
UPPER EAST SIDE
Sprang Br.
BOB KANE SOUND
Cape Carmine
Gotham Water District Tunnel
The Reservoir
Robinson Park
Ivy?
Novick Tunnel
CROC
Finger River
Miller Harbor
Aparo Expressway
0 1 2 3 MI.
GOTHAM CITY
Tubes
FASHION DISTRICT
Port Adams
Grant Pk
DIAMOND DISTRICT
Commerce St.
ENGLISH
TWO FACE
Brown Bridge
OLD GOTHAM
XHOSA? TRIADS?
Dixon Docks
BLUE BOYS
TRICORNER
Westward Bridge
Sullivan Island
Paris Island
Landbridge
THE RAP
Blackgate Isle
TRICORNER YARDS
GOTHAM HARBOR
GOTHAM RIVER
Bat Sector
Black Mask
Blue Boys (GCPD)
Faith Sector
Huntress
Killer Croc
LeBoyz
Lynx & Triads
Mad Hatter
MASH Sector
Mr. Freeze
Mr. Zsasz
Penguin
Poison Ivy
Scarecrow
Scarface
Street Demonz
Two Face
Claim Jumping
greg RUCKA writer
mr. DEODATO penciller
wayne FAUCHER inker
roberta TEWES colorist
WILDSTORM FX color separations
willie SCHUBERT letterer
joseph ILLIDGE associate editor
jordan b. GORFINKEL editor
group editor DENNIS O'NEIL
Batman created by BOB KANE

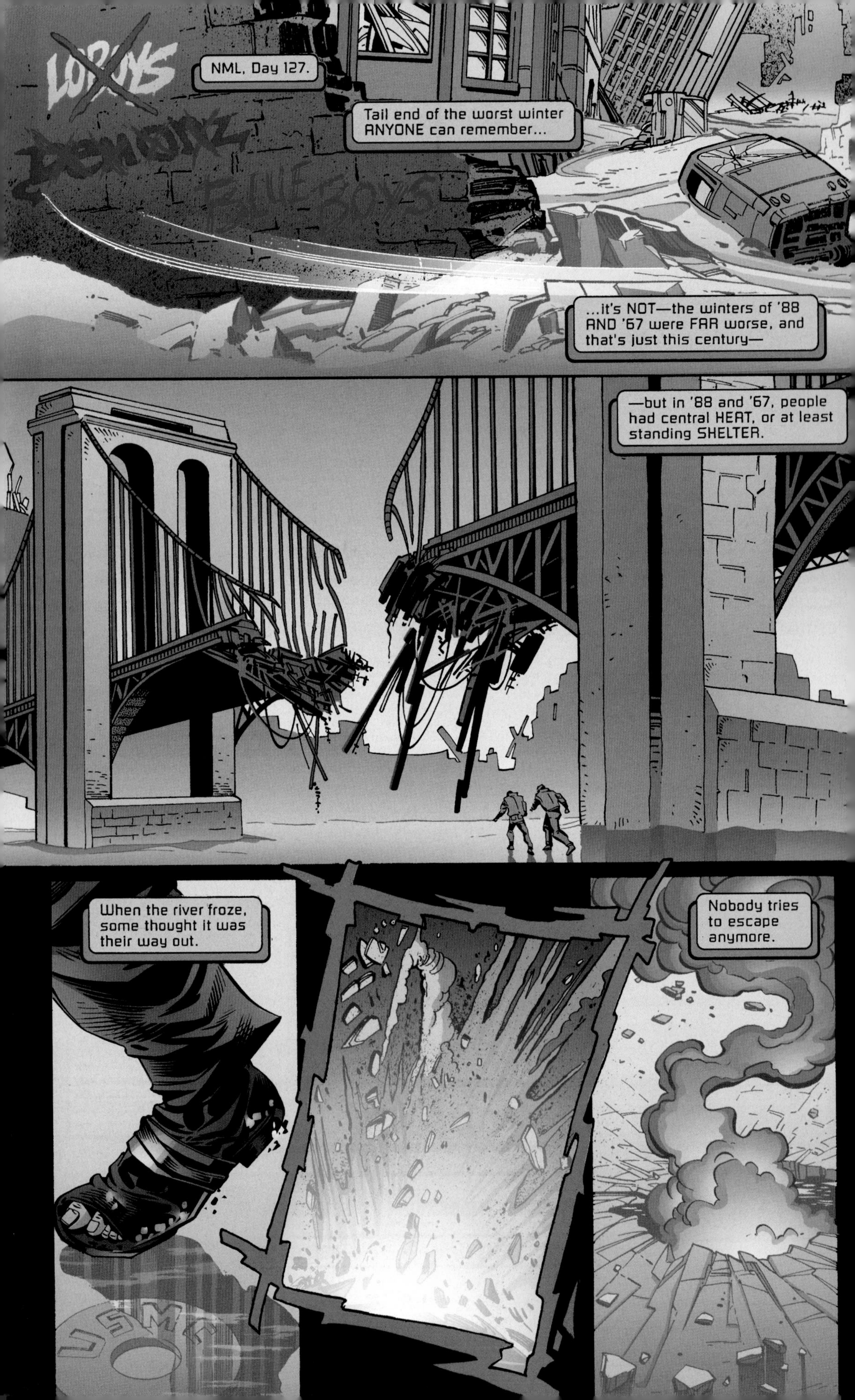
NML, Day 127.
Tail end of the worst winter ANYONE can remember...
...it's NOT—the winters of '88 AND '67 were FAR worse, and that's just this century—
—but in '88 and '67, people had central HEAT, or at least standing SHELTER.
When the river froze, some thought it was their way out.
Nobody tries to escape anymore.

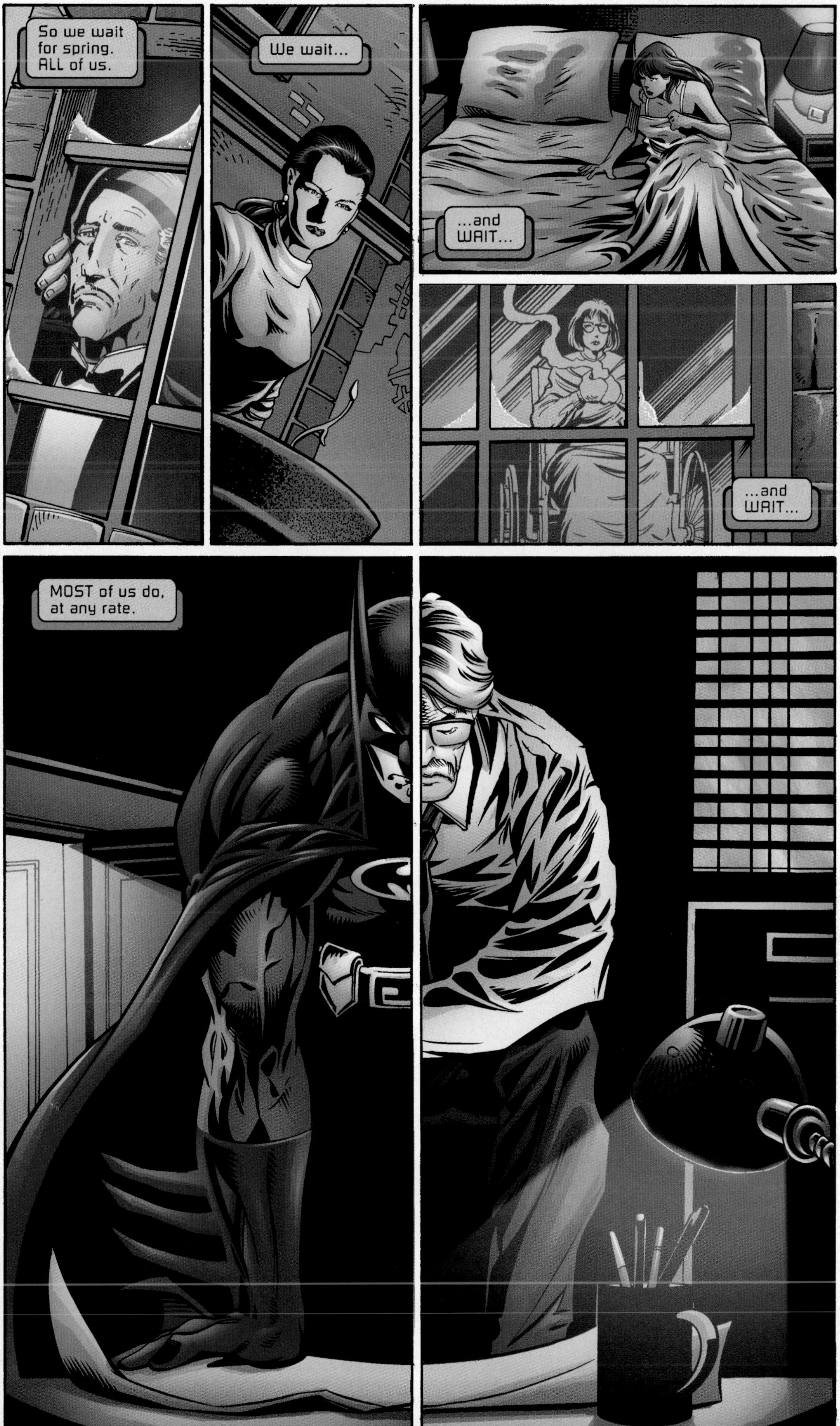
So we wait for spring. ALL of us.
We wait...
...and WAIT...
...and WAIT...
MOST of us do, at any rate.

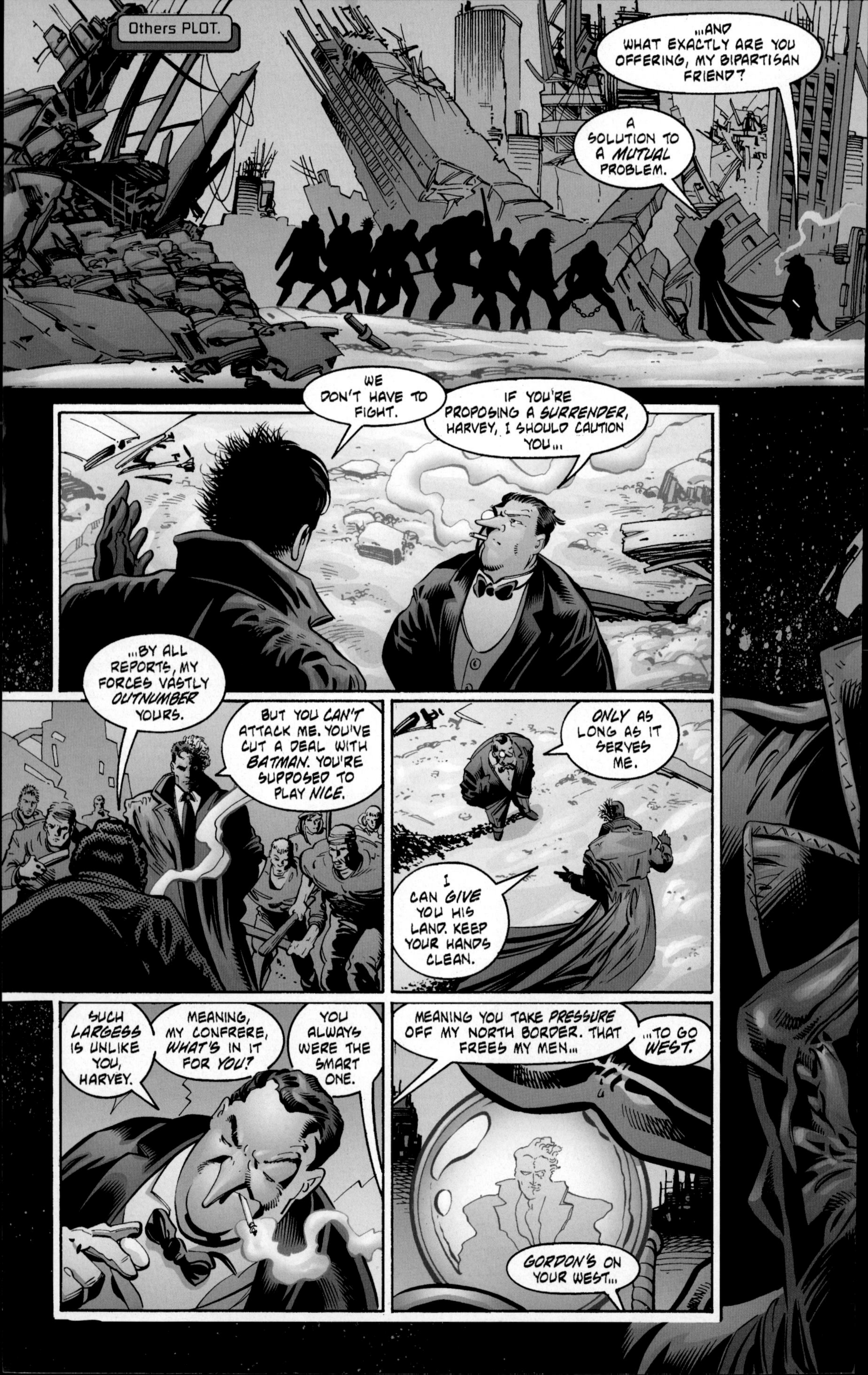

Others PLOT.
...AND WHAT EXACTLY ARE YOU OFFERING, MY BIPARTISAN FRIEND?
A SOLUTION TO A MUTUAL PROBLEM.
WE DON'T HAVE TO FIGHT.
IF YOU'RE PROPOSING A SURRENDER, HARVEY, I SHOULD CAUTION YOU...
...BY ALL REPORTS, MY FORCES VASTLY OUTNUMBER YOURS.
BUT YOU CAN'T ATTACK ME. YOU'VE CUT A DEAL WITH BATMAN. YOU'RE SUPPOSED TO PLAY NICE.
ONLY AS LONG AS IT SERVES ME.
I CAN GIVE YOU HIS LAND. KEEP YOUR HANDS CLEAN.
SUCH LARGESS IS UNLIKE YOU, HARVEY.
MEANING, MY CONFRERE, WHAT'S IN IT FOR YOU?
YOU ALWAYS WERE THE SMART ONE.
MEANING YOU TAKE PRESSURE OFF MY NORTH BORDER. THAT FREES MY MEN...
...TO GO WEST.
GORDON'S ON YOUR WEST...

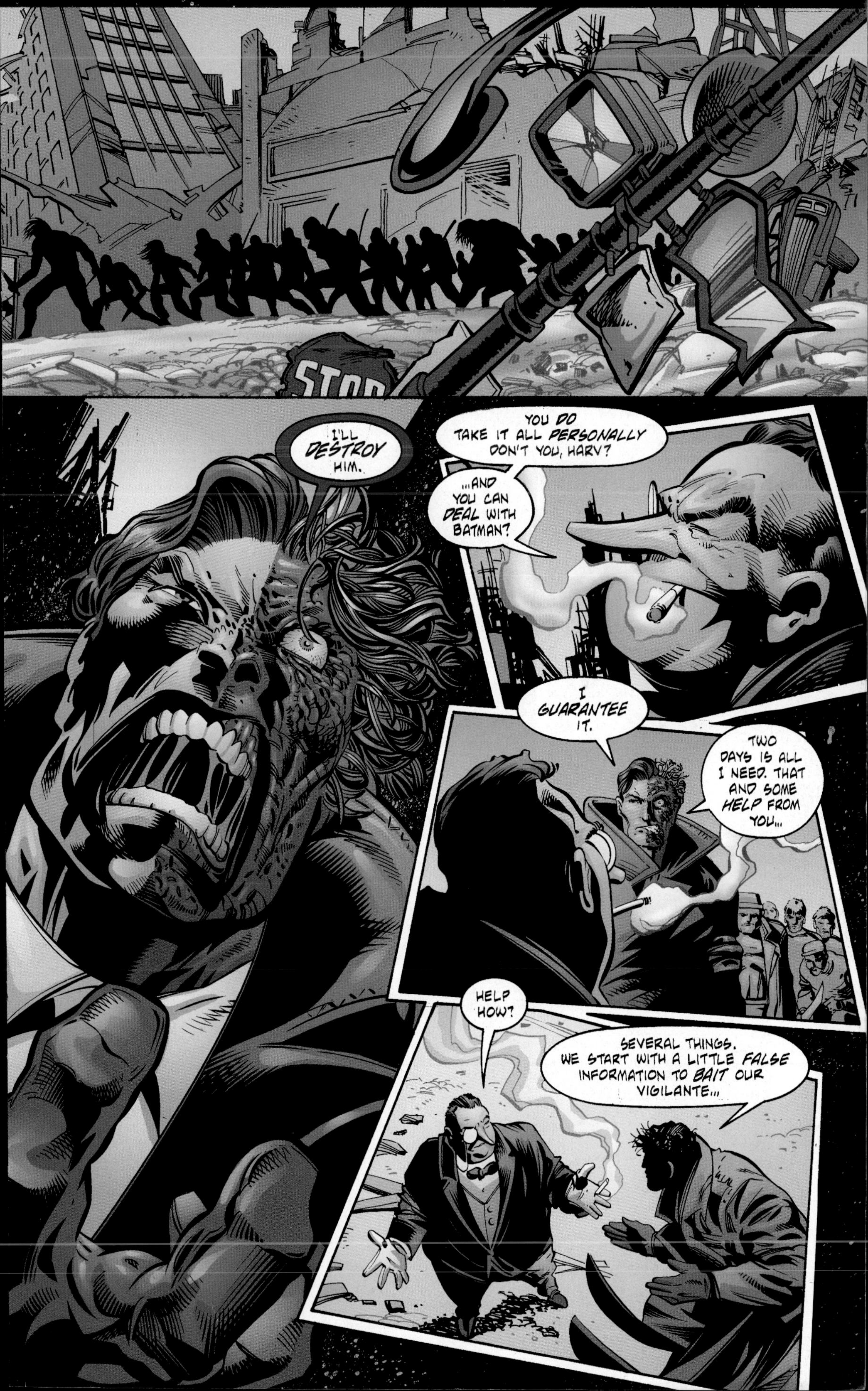
STOP
I'LL DESTROY HIM.
YOU DO TAKE IT ALL PERSONALLY DON'T YOU, HARV?
...AND YOU CAN DEAL WITH BATMAN?
I GUARANTEE IT.
TWO DAYS IS ALL I NEED. THAT AND SOME HELP FROM YOU...
HELP HOW?
SEVERAL THINGS. WE START WITH A LITTLE FALSE INFORMATION TO BAIT OUR VIGILANTE...

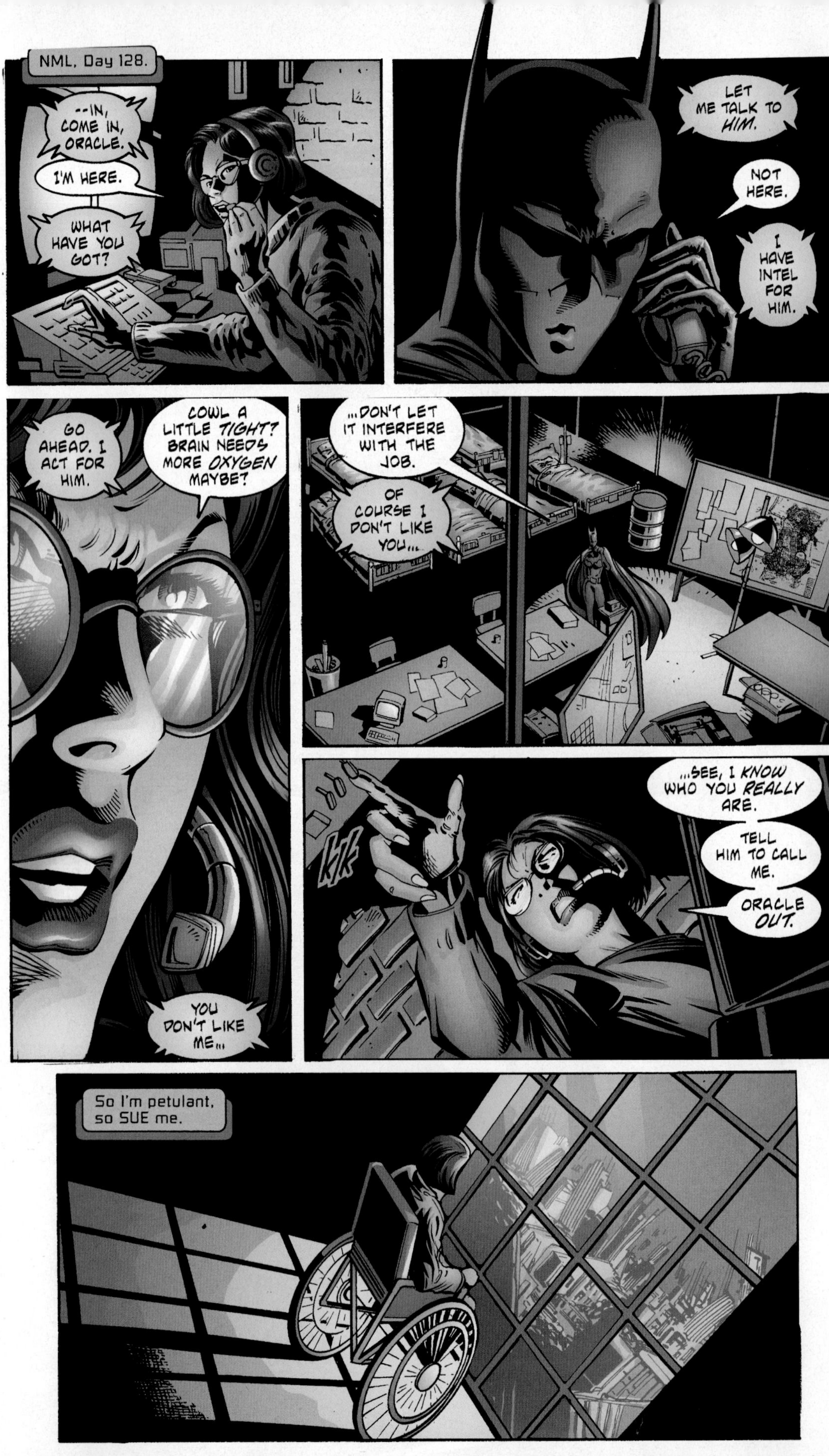
NML, Day 128.
--IN, COME IN, ORACLE.
I'M HERE.
WHAT HAVE YOU GOT?
LET ME TALK TO HIM.
NOT HERE.
I HAVE INTEL FOR HIM.
GO AHEAD. I ACT FOR HIM.
COWL A LITTLE TIGHT? BRAIN NEEDS MORE OXYGEN MAYBE?
YOU DON'T LIKE ME...
...DON'T LET IT INTERFERE WITH THE JOB.
OF COURSE I DON'T LIKE YOU...
...SEE, I KNOW WHO YOU REALLY ARE.
TELL HIM TO CALL ME.
ORACLE OUT.
KLIK
So I'm petulant, so SUE me.

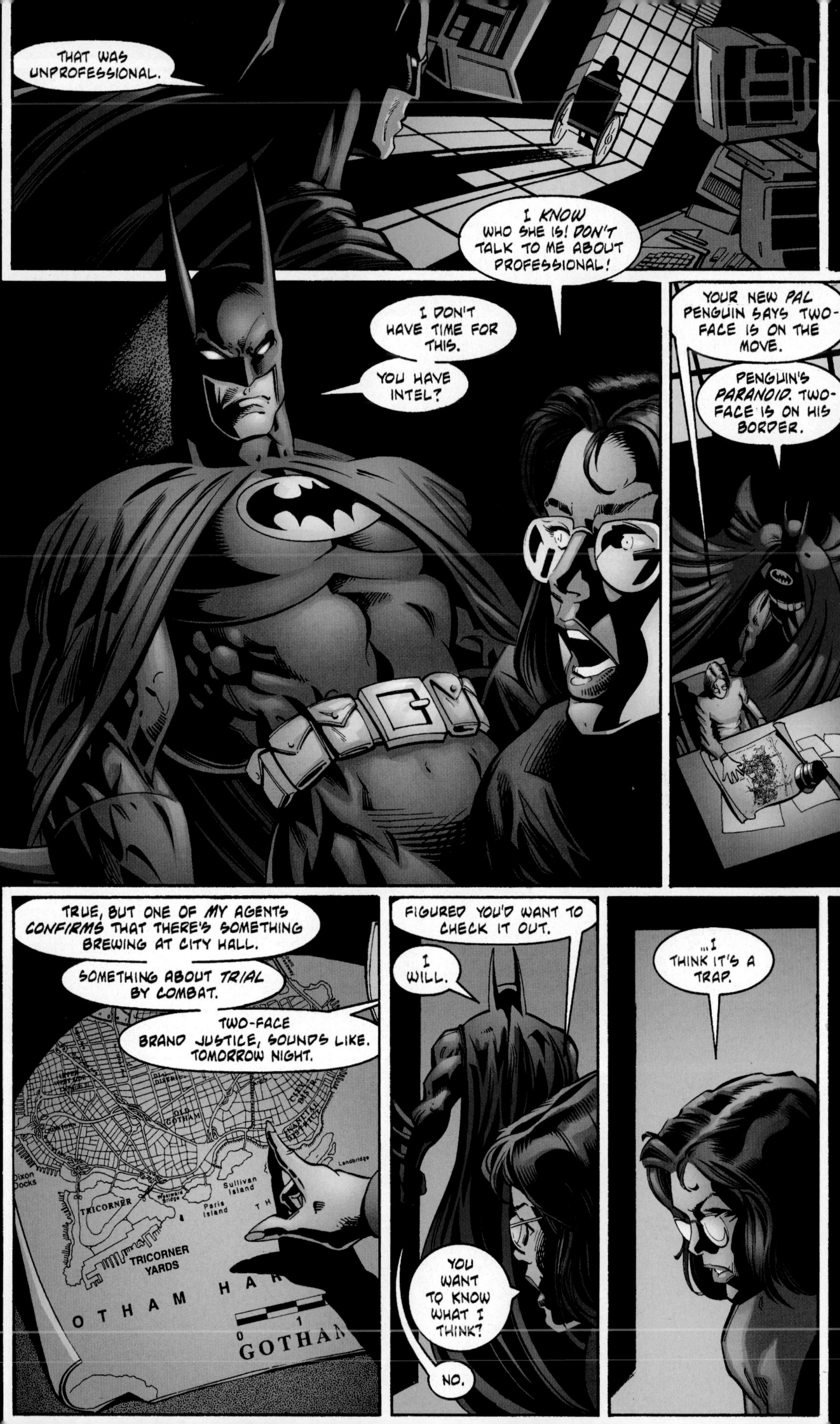
THAT WAS UNPROFESSIONAL.
I KNOW WHO SHE IS! DON'T TALK TO ME ABOUT PROFESSIONAL!
I DON'T HAVE TIME FOR THIS.
YOU HAVE INTEL?
YOUR NEW PAL PENGUIN SAYS TWO-FACE IS ON THE MOVE.
PENGUIN'S PARANOID. TWO-FACE IS ON HIS BORDER.
TRUE, BUT ONE OF MY AGENTS CONFIRMS THAT THERE'S SOMETHING BREWING AT CITY HALL.
SOMETHING ABOUT TRIAL BY COMBAT.
TWO-FACE BRAND JUSTICE, SOUNDS LIKE. TOMORROW NIGHT.
OLD GOTHAM
Dixon Docks
TRICORNER
Sullivan Island
Paris Island
Landbridge
TRICORNER YARDS
GOTHAM HAR
OTHAM
0
1
GOTHAM
FIGURED YOU'D WANT TO CHECK IT OUT.
I WILL.
YOU WANT TO KNOW WHAT I THINK?
NO.
...I THINK IT'S A TRAP.

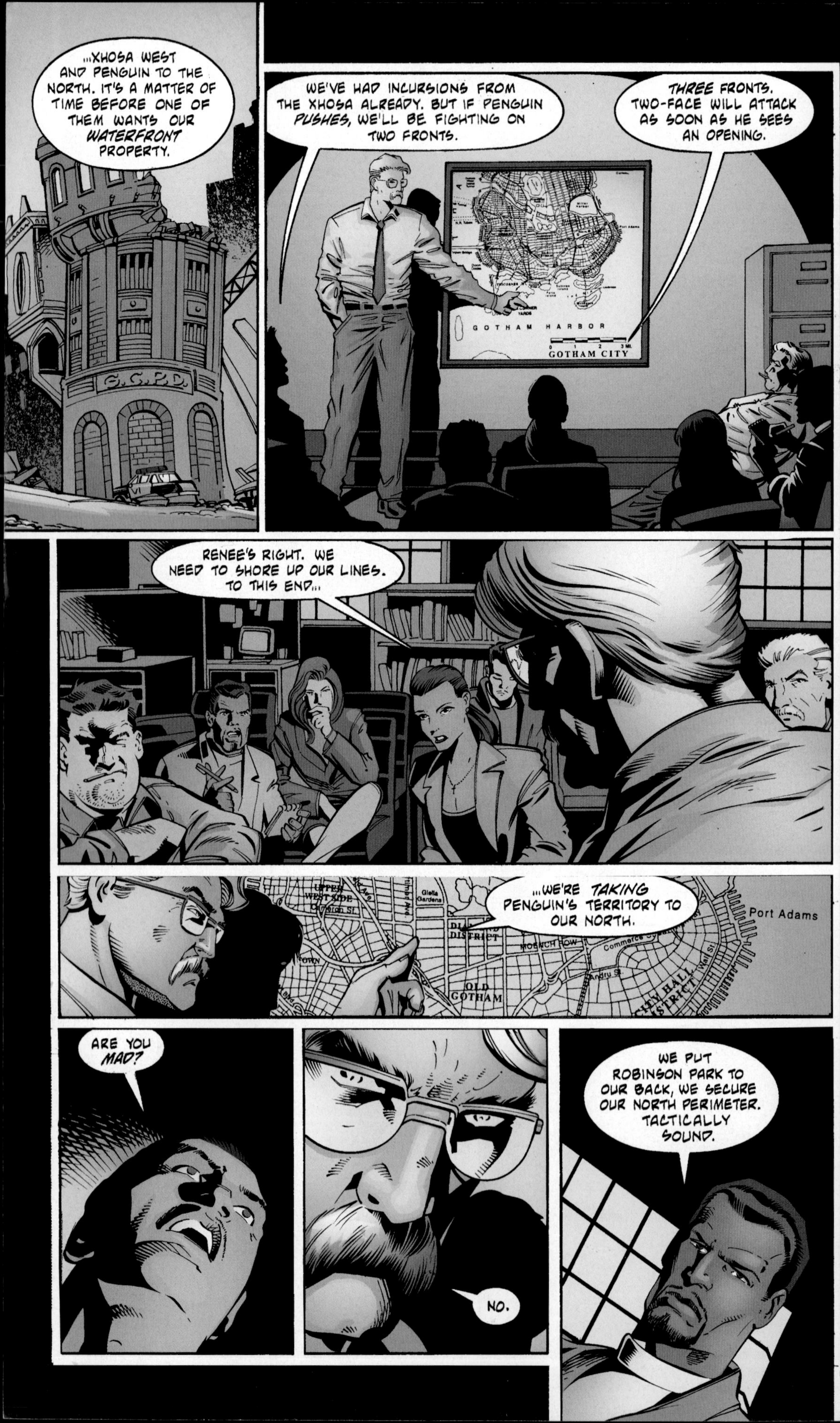
...XHOSA WEST AND PENGUIN TO THE NORTH. IT'S A MATTER OF TIME BEFORE ONE OF THEM WANTS OUR WATERFRONT PROPERTY.
G.C.P.D.
WE'VE HAD INCURSIONS FROM THE XHOSA ALREADY. BUT IF PENGUIN PUSHES, WE'LL BE FIGHTING ON TWO FRONTS.
THREE FRONTS. TWO-FACE WILL ATTACK AS SOON AS HE SEES AN OPENING.
GOTHAM HARBOR
GOTHAM CITY
RENEE'S RIGHT. WE NEED TO SHORE UP OUR LINES. TO THIS END...
...WE'RE TAKING PENGUIN'S TERRITORY TO OUR NORTH.
UPPER WEST SIDE
Port Adams
OLD GOTHAM
ARE YOU MAD?
NO.
WE PUT ROBINSON PARK TO OUR BACK, WE SECURE OUR NORTH PERIMETER. TACTICALLY SOUND.

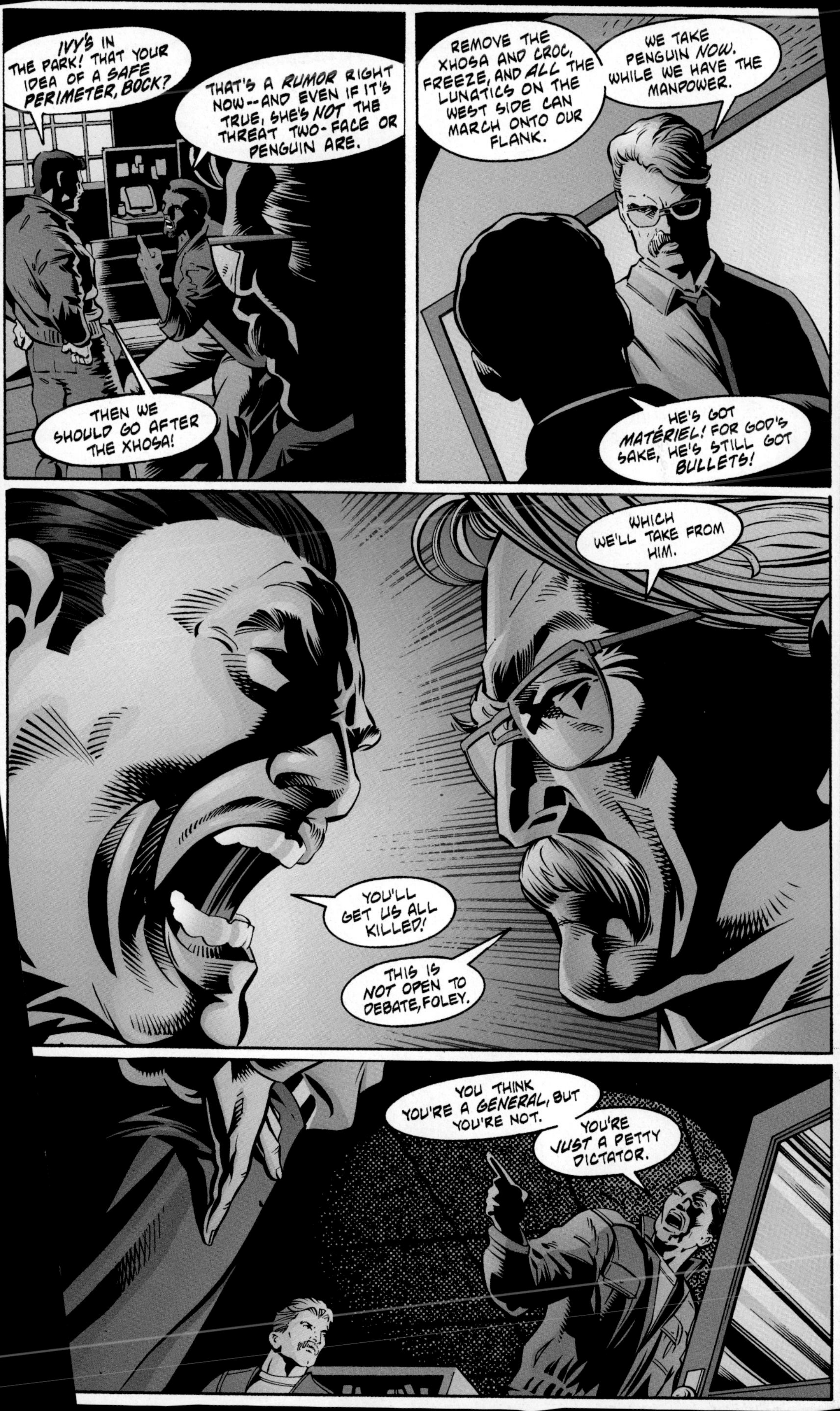
IVY'S IN THE PARK! THAT YOUR IDEA OF A SAFE PERIMETER, BOCK?
THAT'S A RUMOR RIGHT NOW--AND EVEN IF IT'S TRUE, SHE'S NOT THE THREAT TWO-FACE OR PENGUIN ARE.
THEN WE SHOULD GO AFTER THE XHOSA!
REMOVE THE XHOSA AND CROC, FREEZE, AND ALL THE LUNATICS ON THE WEST SIDE CAN MARCH ONTO OUR FLANK.
WE TAKE PENGUIN NOW. WHILE WE HAVE THE MANPOWER.
HE'S GOT MATÉRIEL! FOR GOD'S SAKE, HE'S STILL GOT BULLETS!
WHICH WE'LL TAKE FROM HIM.
YOU'LL GET US ALL KILLED!
THIS IS NOT OPEN TO DEBATE, FOLEY.
YOU THINK YOU'RE A GENERAL, BUT YOU'RE NOT.
YOU'RE JUST A PETTY DICTATOR.

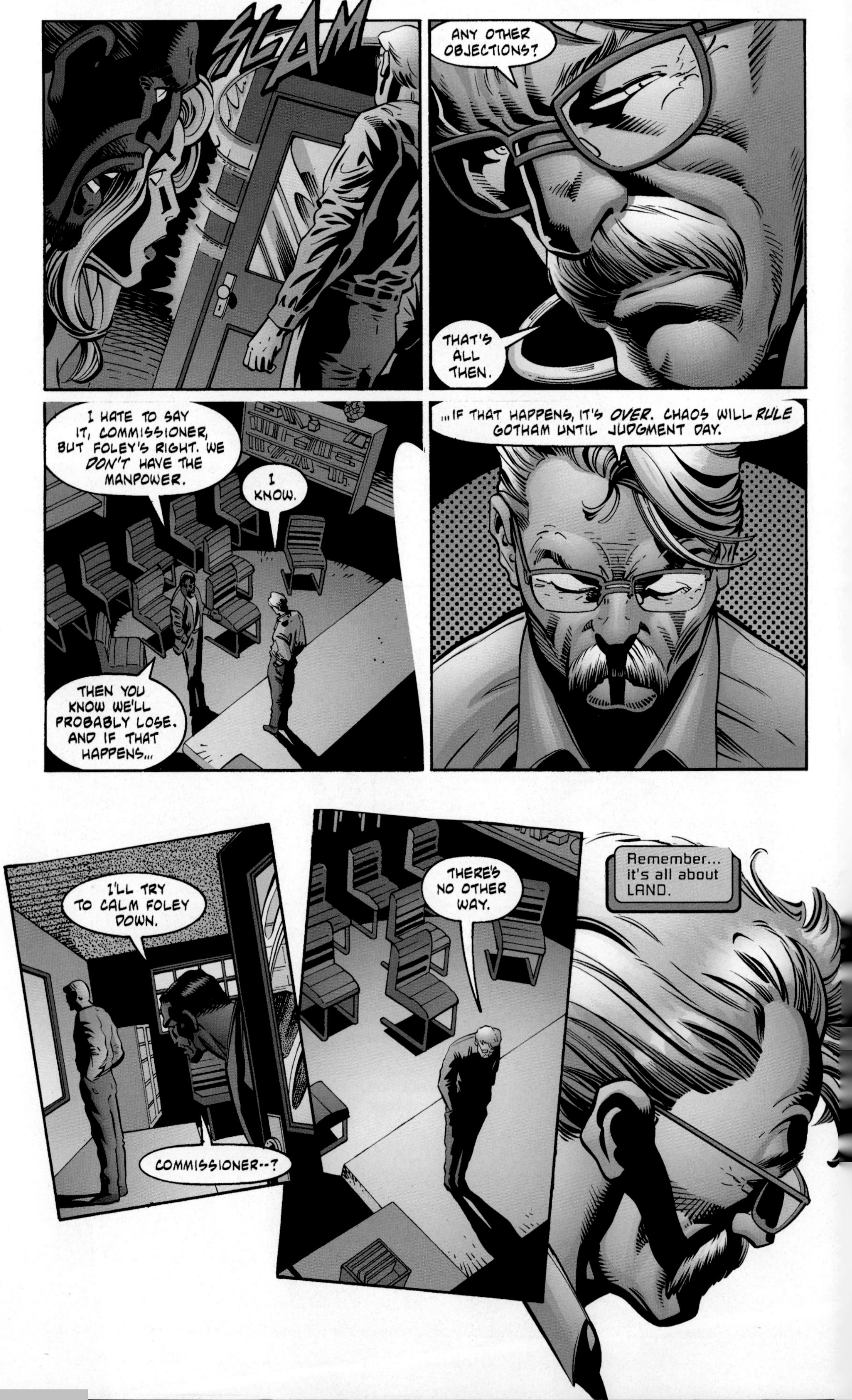
SLAM
ANY OTHER OBJECTIONS?
THAT'S ALL THEN.
I HATE TO SAY IT, COMMISSIONER, BUT FOLEY'S RIGHT. WE DON'T HAVE THE MANPOWER.
I KNOW.
THEN YOU KNOW WE'LL PROBABLY LOSE. AND IF THAT HAPPENS...
...IF THAT HAPPENS, IT'S OVER. CHAOS WILL RULE GOTHAM UNTIL JUDGMENT DAY.
I'LL TRY TO CALM FOLEY DOWN.
COMMISSIONER--?
THERE'S NO OTHER WAY.
Remember... it's all about LAND.

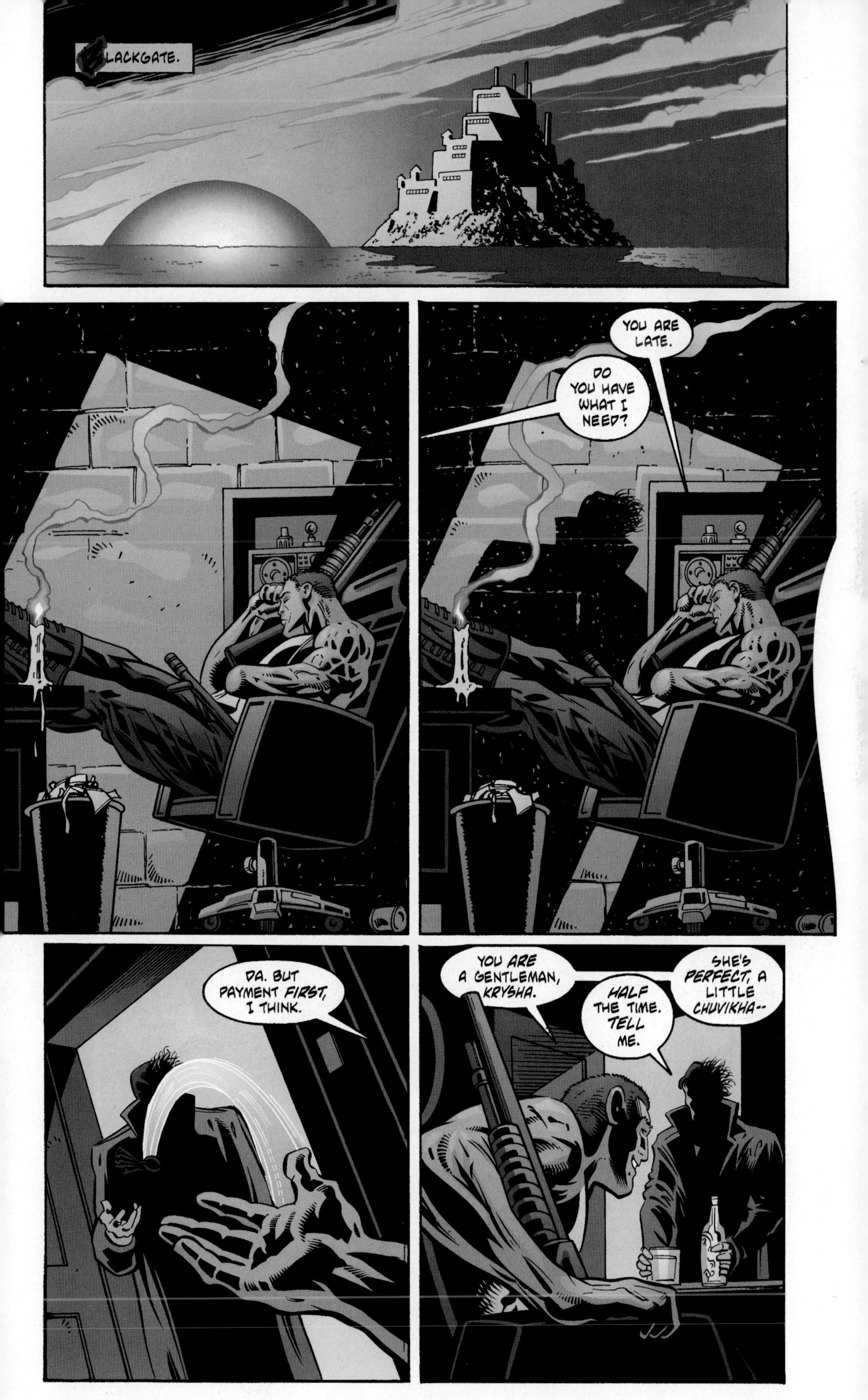
BLACKGATE.
YOU ARE LATE.
DO YOU HAVE WHAT I NEED?
DA. BUT PAYMENT FIRST, I THINK.
YOU ARE A GENTLEMAN, KRYSHA.
HALF THE TIME. TELL ME.
SHE'S PERFECT, A LITTLE CHUVIKHA--

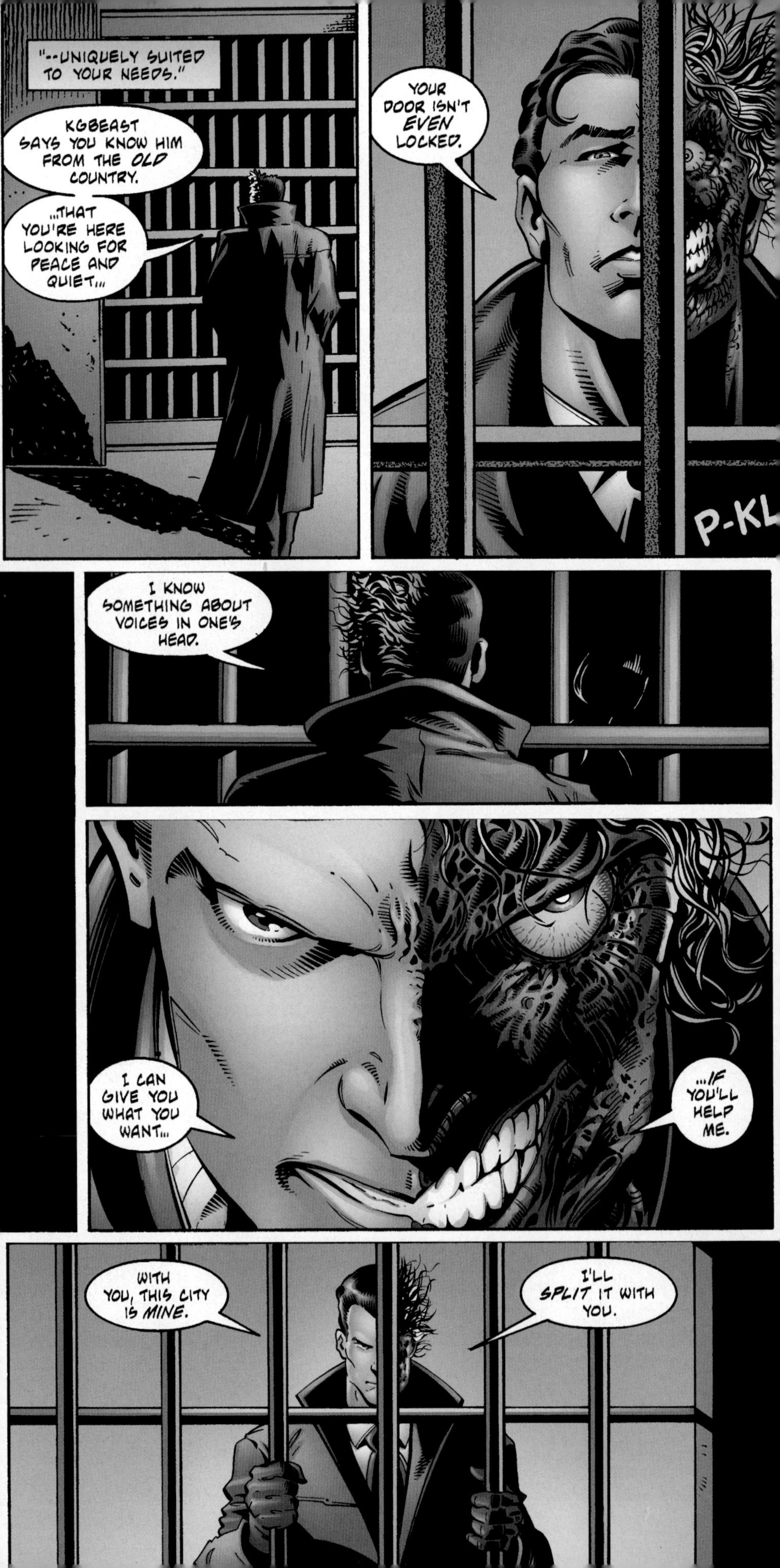
"--UNIQUELY SUITED TO YOUR NEEDS."
KGBEAST SAYS YOU KNOW HIM FROM THE OLD COUNTRY.
...THAT YOU'RE HERE LOOKING FOR PEACE AND QUIET...
YOUR DOOR ISN'T EVEN LOCKED.
P-KL
I KNOW SOMETHING ABOUT VOICES IN ONE'S HEAD.
I CAN GIVE YOU WHAT YOU WANT...
...IF YOU'LL HELP ME.
WITH YOU, THIS CITY IS MINE.
I'LL SPLIT IT WITH YOU.

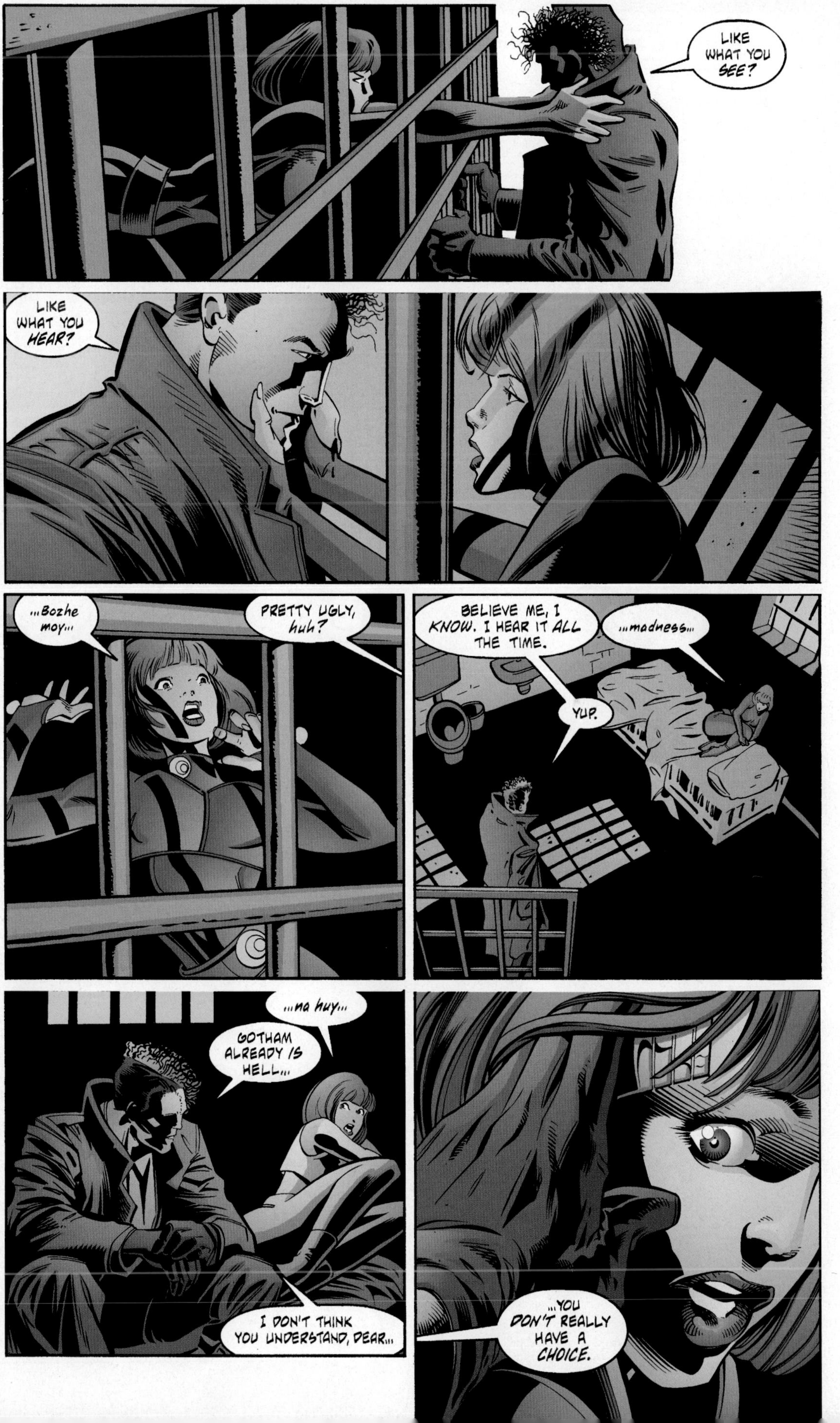

LIKE WHAT YOU SEE?
LIKE WHAT YOU HEAR?
...Bozhe moy...
PRETTY UGLY, huh?
BELIEVE ME, I KNOW. I HEAR IT ALL THE TIME.
...madness...
YUP.
...na huy...
GOTHAM ALREADY IS HELL...
I DON'T THINK YOU UNDERSTAND, DEAR...
...YOU DON'T REALLY HAVE A CHOICE.

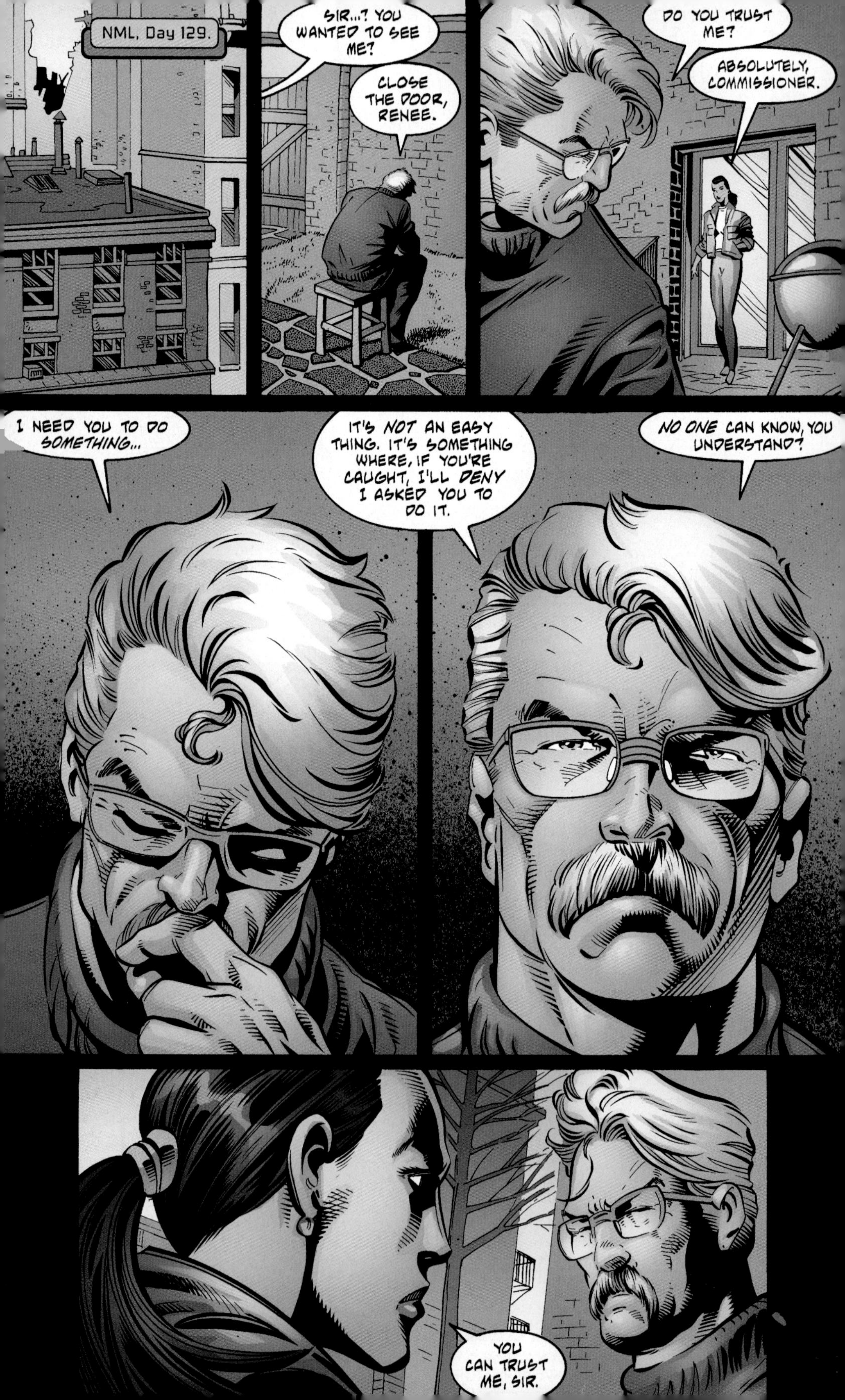

NML, Day 129.
SIR...? YOU WANTED TO SEE ME?
CLOSE THE DOOR, RENEE.
DO YOU TRUST ME?
ABSOLUTELY, COMMISSIONER.
I NEED YOU TO DO SOMETHING...
IT'S NOT AN EASY THING. IT'S SOMETHING WHERE, IF YOU'RE CAUGHT, I'LL DENY I ASKED YOU TO DO IT.
NO ONE CAN KNOW, YOU UNDERSTAND?
YOU CAN TRUST ME, SIR.

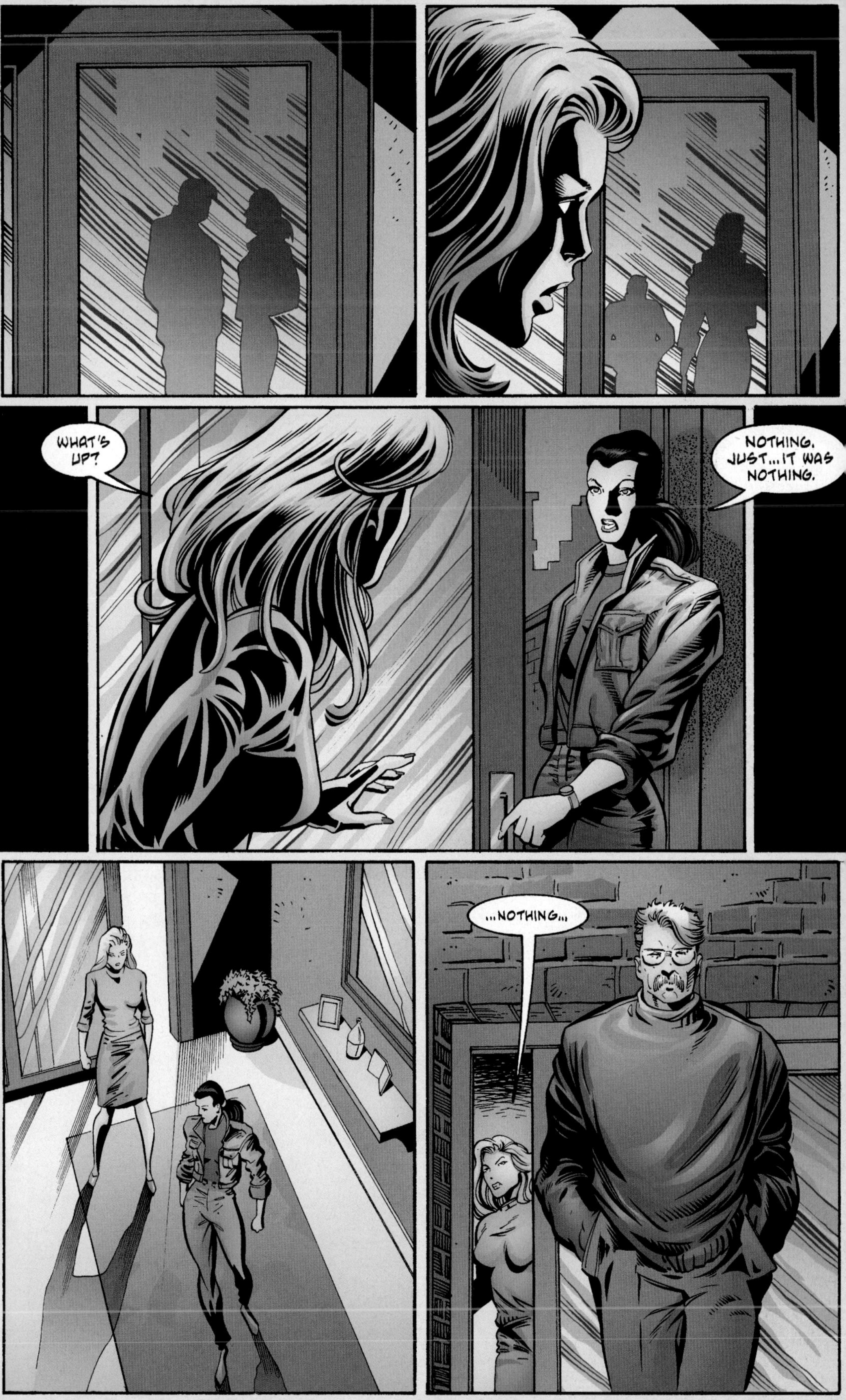
WHAT'S UP?
NOTHING. JUST...IT WAS NOTHING.
...NOTHING...

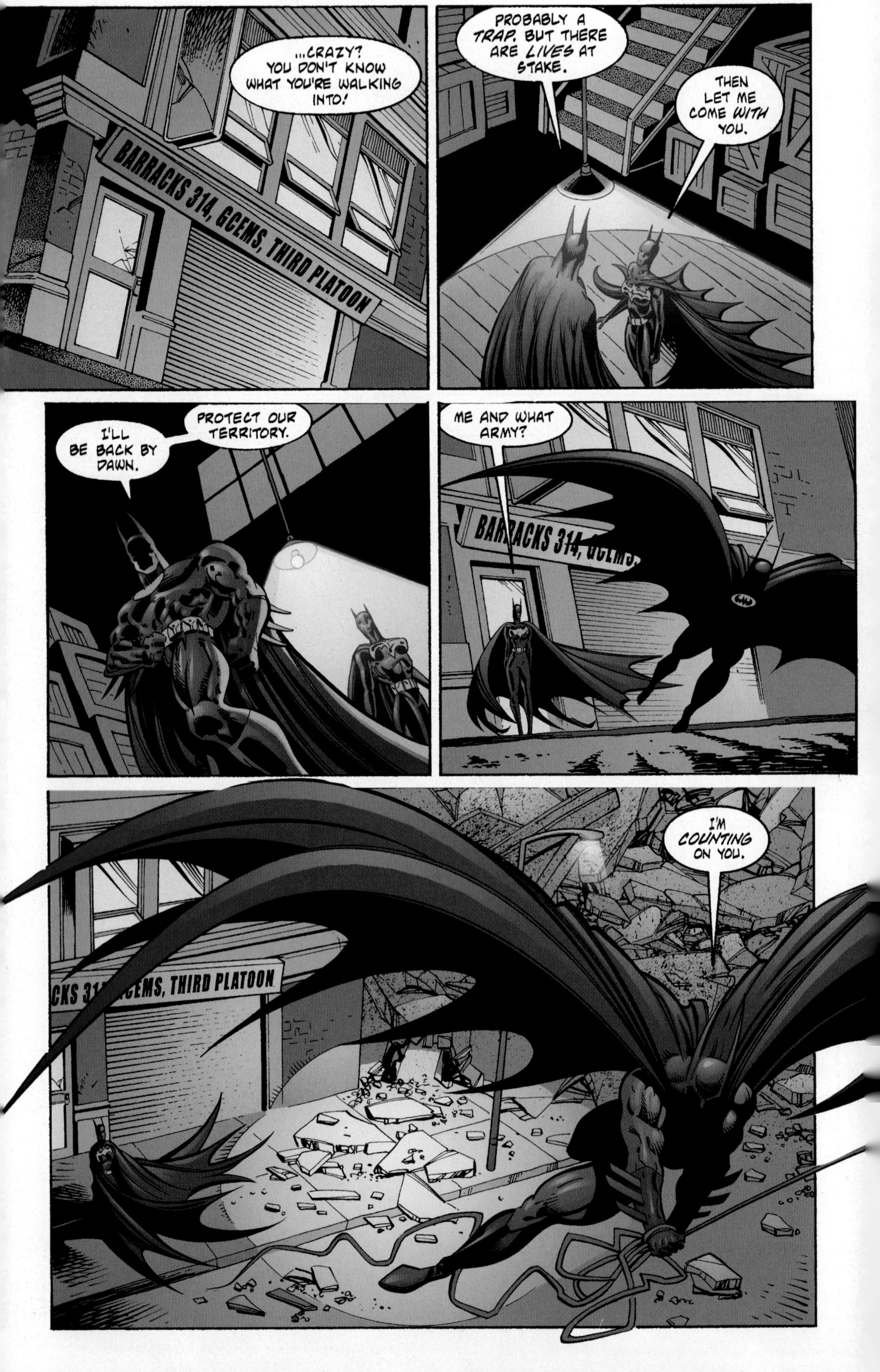
...CRAZY? YOU DON'T KNOW WHAT YOU'RE WALKING INTO!
BARRACKS 314, GCEMS, THIRD PLATOON
PROBABLY A TRAP. BUT THERE ARE LIVES AT STAKE.
THEN LET ME COME WITH YOU.
PROTECT OUR TERRITORY.
I'LL BE BACK BY DAWN.
ME AND WHAT ARMY?
I'M COUNTING ON YOU.
CKS 31 GCEMS, THIRD PLATOON

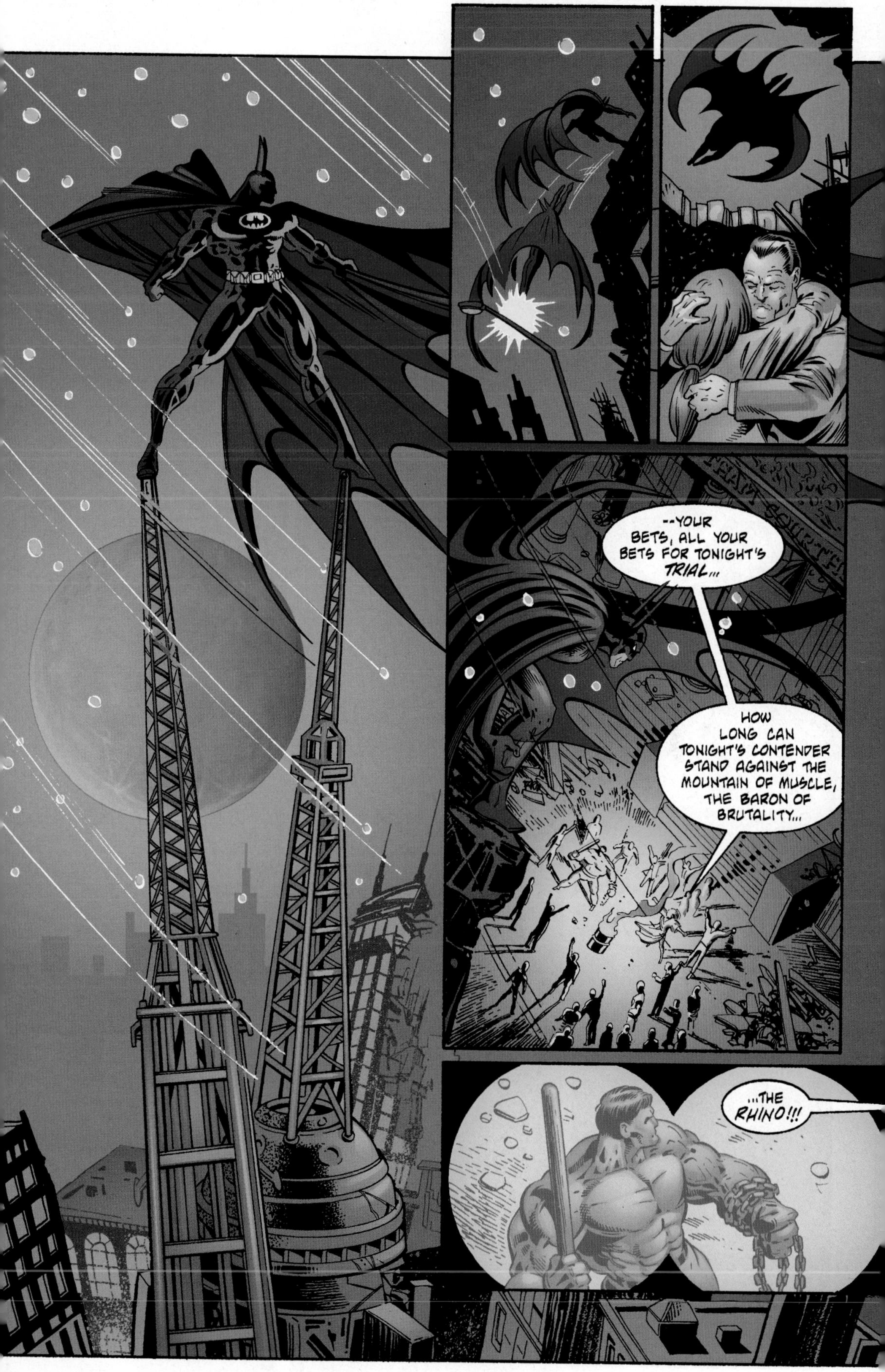
--YOUR BETS, ALL YOUR BETS FOR TONIGHT'S *TRIAL*...
HOW LONG CAN TONIGHT'S CONTENDER STAND AGAINST THE MOUNTAIN OF MUSCLE, THE BARON OF BRUTALITY...
...THE *RHINO!!!*

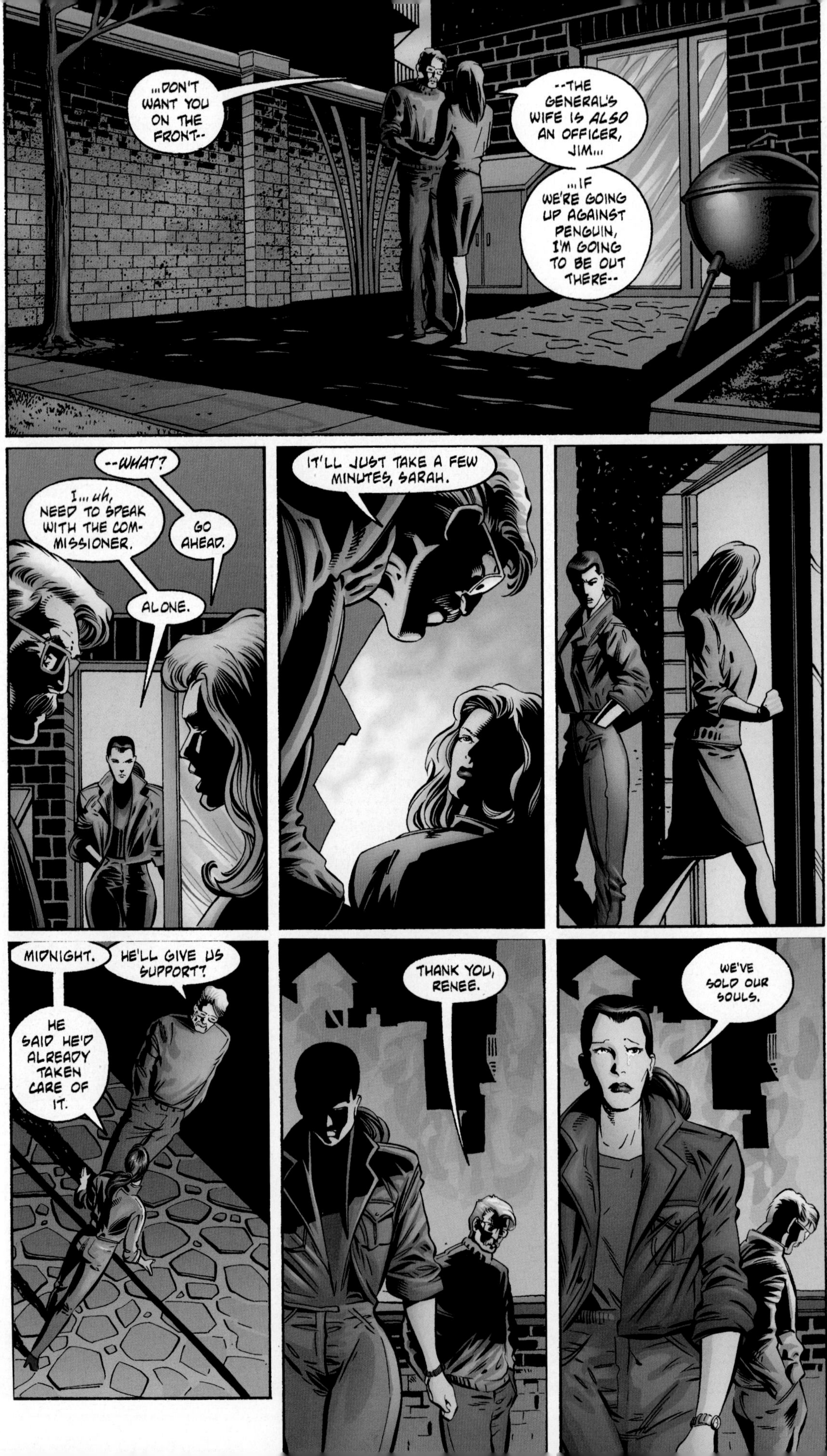
...DON'T WANT YOU ON THE FRONT--
--THE GENERAL'S WIFE IS ALSO AN OFFICER, JIM...
...IF WE'RE GOING UP AGAINST PENGUIN, I'M GOING TO BE OUT THERE--
--WHAT?
I... uh, NEED TO SPEAK WITH THE COM-MISSIONER.
GO AHEAD.
ALONE.
IT'LL JUST TAKE A FEW MINUTES, SARAH.
MIDNIGHT.
HE'LL GIVE US SUPPORT?
HE SAID HE'D ALREADY TAKEN CARE OF IT.
THANK YOU, RENEE.
WE'VE SOLD OUR SOULS.

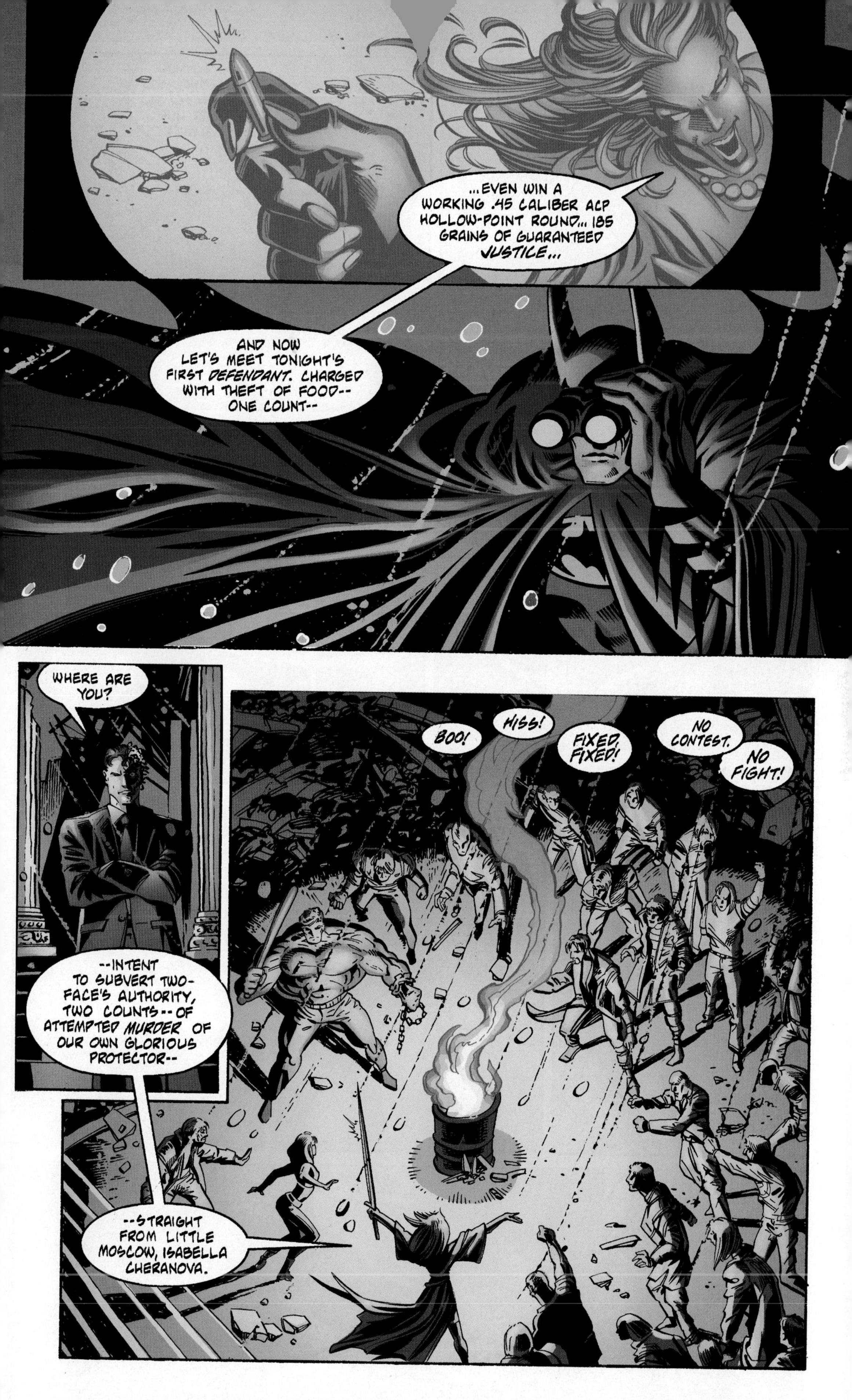
...EVEN WIN A WORKING .45 CALIBER ACP HOLLOW-POINT ROUND... 185 GRAINS OF GUARANTEED JUSTICE...
AND NOW LET'S MEET TONIGHT'S FIRST DEFENDANT. CHARGED WITH THEFT OF FOOD-- ONE COUNT--
WHERE ARE YOU?
BOO!
HISS!
FIXED, FIXED!
NO CONTEST.
NO FIGHT!
--INTENT TO SUBVERT TWO-FACE'S AUTHORITY, TWO COUNTS--OF ATTEMPTED MURDER OF OUR OWN GLORIOUS PROTECTOR--
--STRAIGHT FROM LITTLE MOSCOW, ISABELLA CHERANOVA.

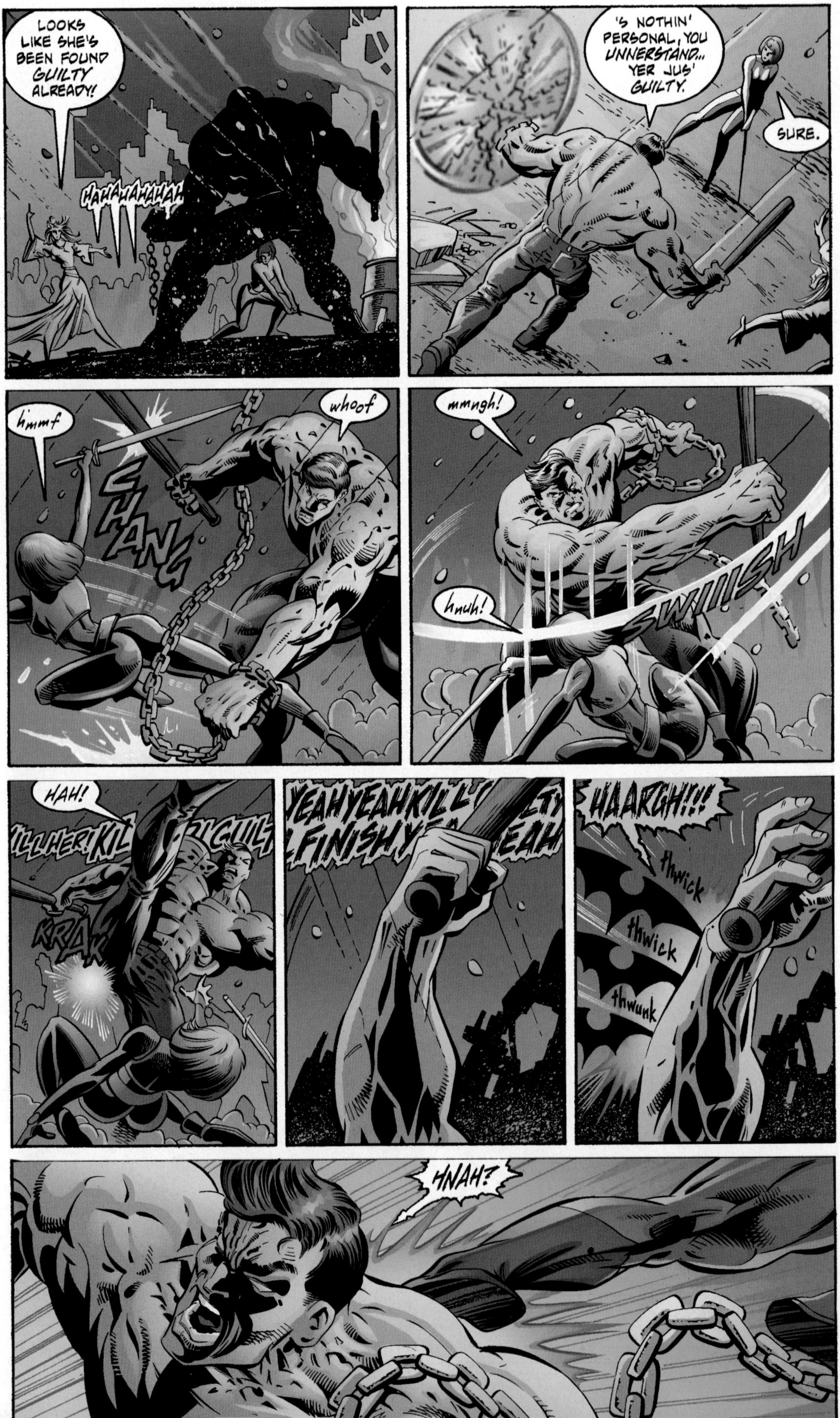

LOOKS LIKE SHE'S BEEN FOUND GUILTY ALREADY!
HAHAHAHAHAH
'S NOTHIN' PERSONAL, YOU UNNERSTAND... YER JUS' GUILTY.
SURE.
hmmf
whoof
CHANG
mmngh!
hnuh!
SWIIISH
HAH!
KRAK
HAARGH!!!
thwick
thwick
thwunk
HNAH?

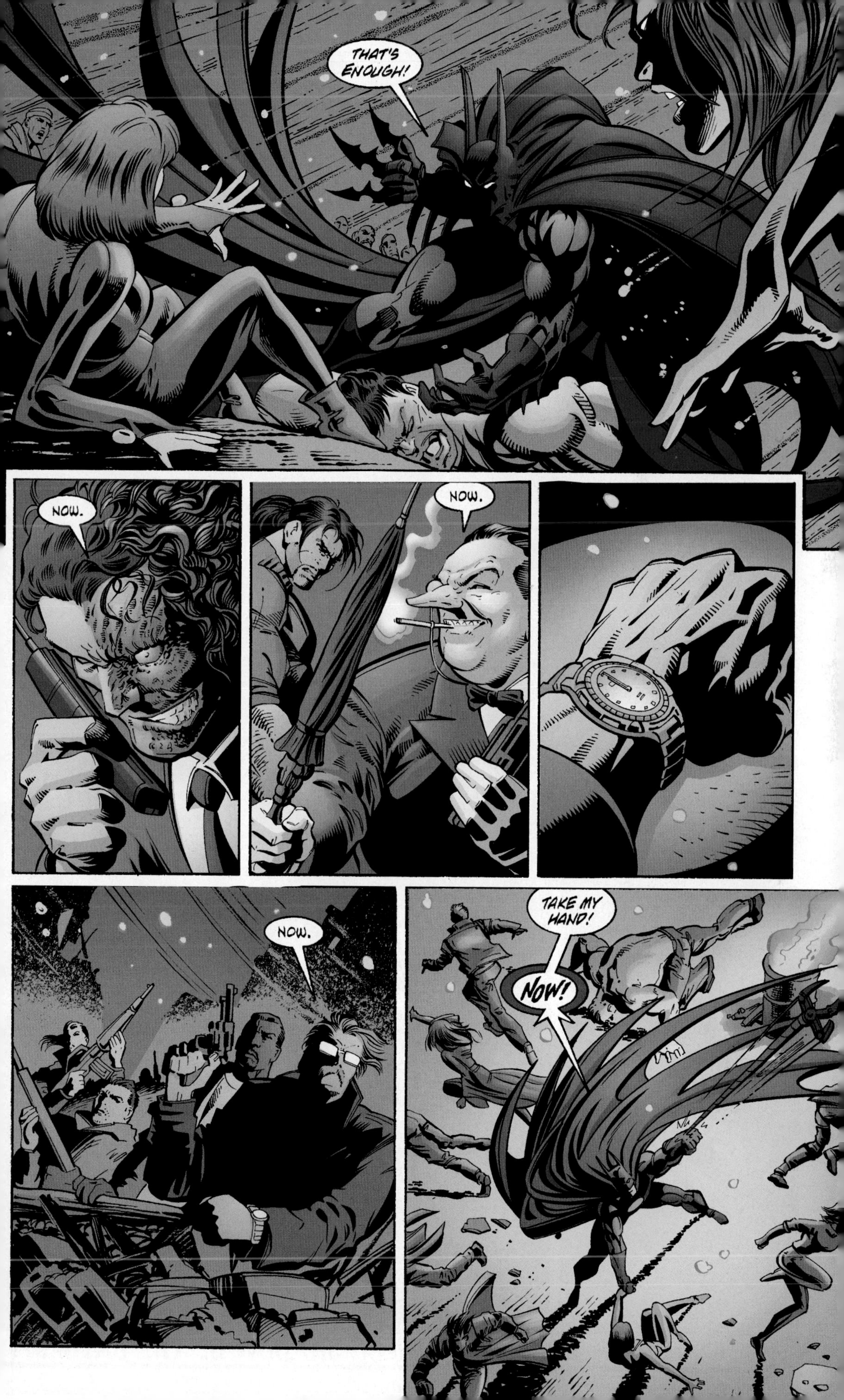
THAT'S ENOUGH!
NOW.
NOW.
NOW.
TAKE MY HAND!
NOW!

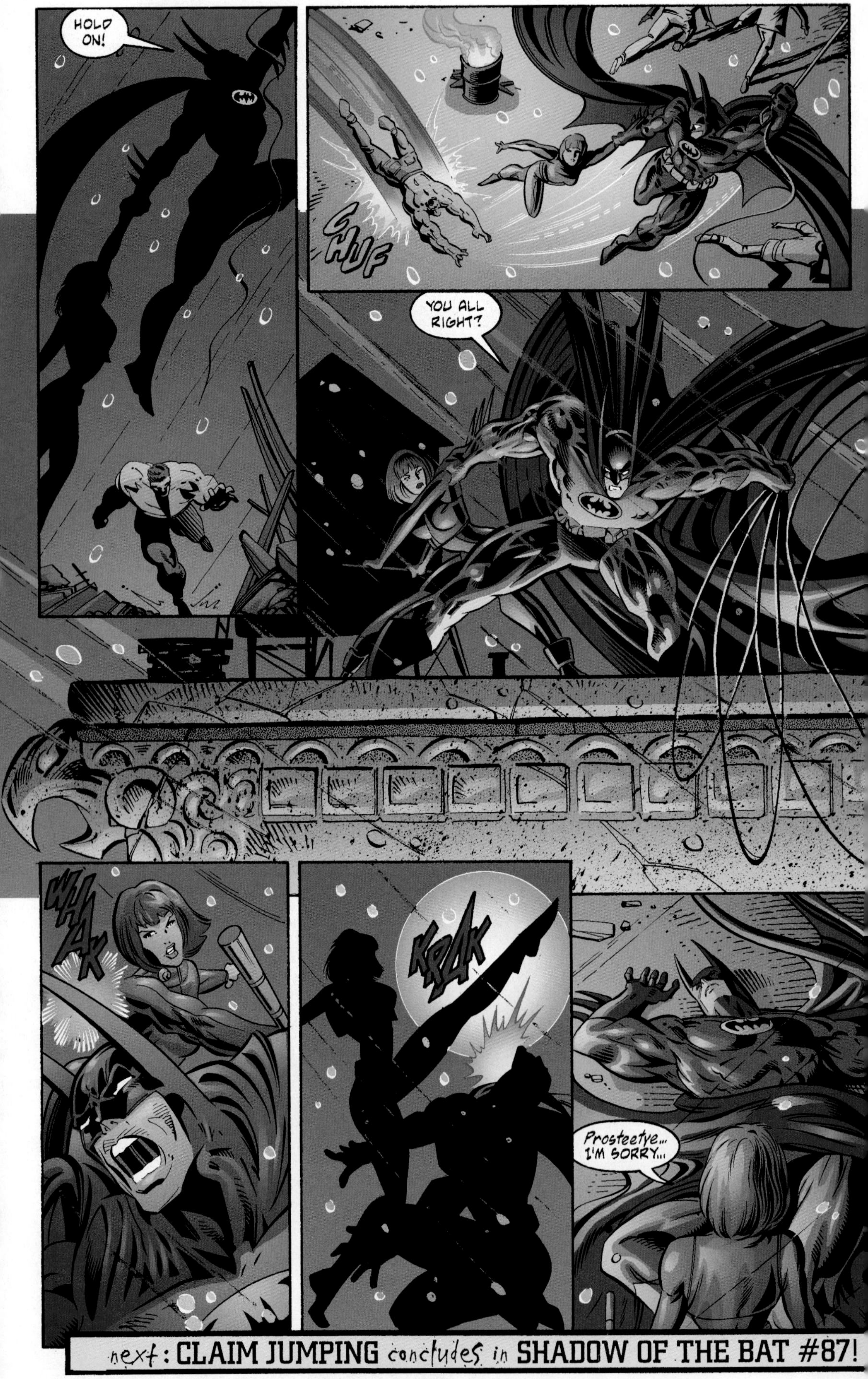
HOLD ON!
CHUF
YOU ALL RIGHT?
WHAK
KRAK
Prosteetye... I'M SORRY...
next: CLAIM JUMPING concludes in SHADOW OF THE BAT #87!

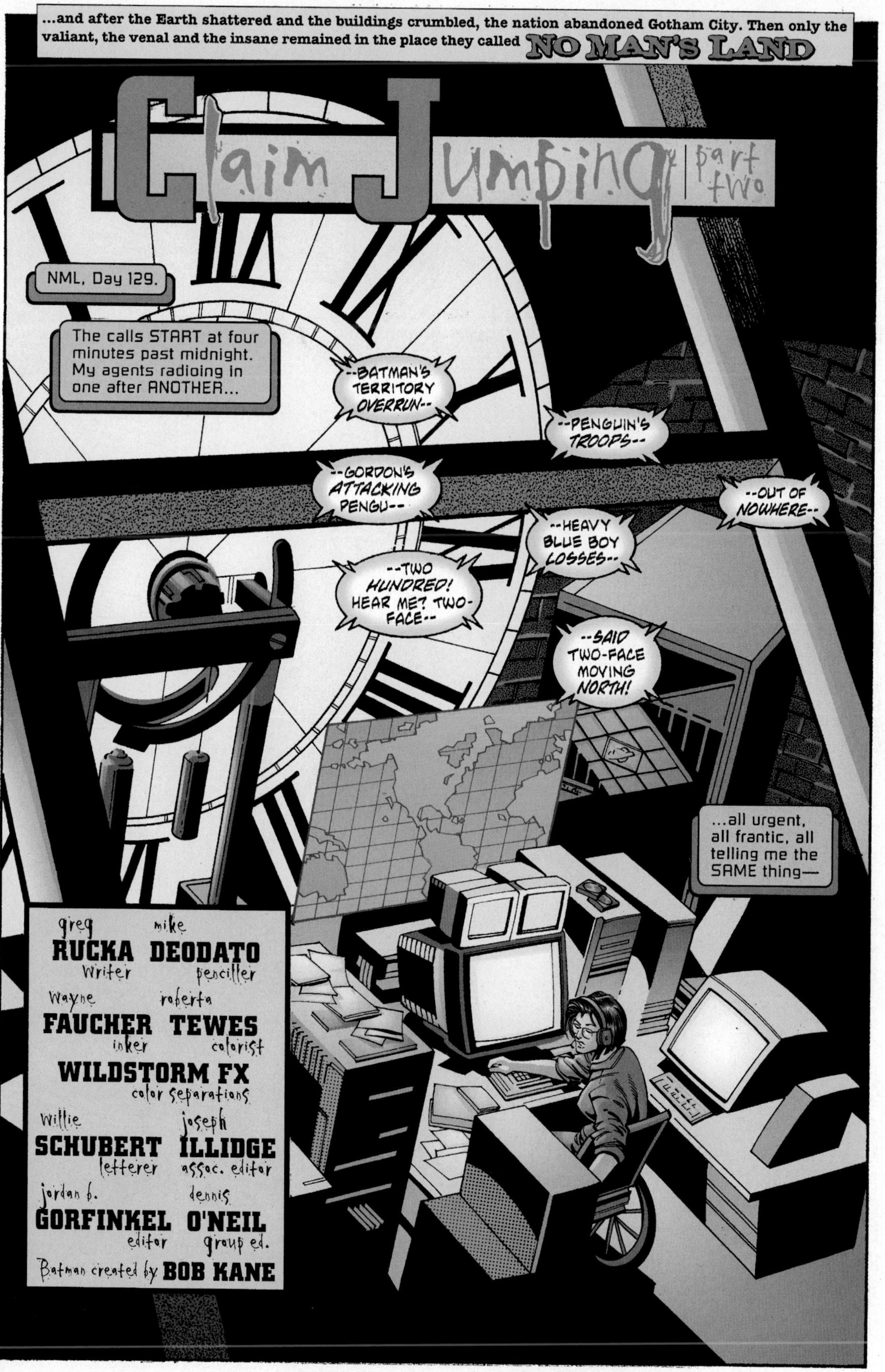
...and after the Earth shattered and the buildings crumbled, the nation abandoned Gotham City. Then only the valiant, the venal and the insane remained in the place they called NO MAN'S LAND
Claim Jumping part two
NML, Day 129.
The calls START at four minutes past midnight. My agents radioing in one after ANOTHER...
--BATMAN'S TERRITORY OVERRUN--
--PENGUIN'S TROOPS--
--GORDON'S ATTACKING PENGU--
--OUT OF NOWHERE--
--HEAVY BLUE BOY LOSSES--
--TWO HUNDRED! HEAR ME? TWO-FACE--
--SAID TWO-FACE MOVING NORTH!
...all urgent, all frantic, all telling me the SAME thing—
greg RUCKA writer
mike DEODATO penciller
wayne FAUCHER inker
roberta TEWES colorist
WILDSTORM FX color separations
willie SCHUBERT letterer
joseph ILLIDGE assoc. editor
jordan b. GORFINKEL editor
dennis O'NEIL group ed.
Batman created by BOB KANE

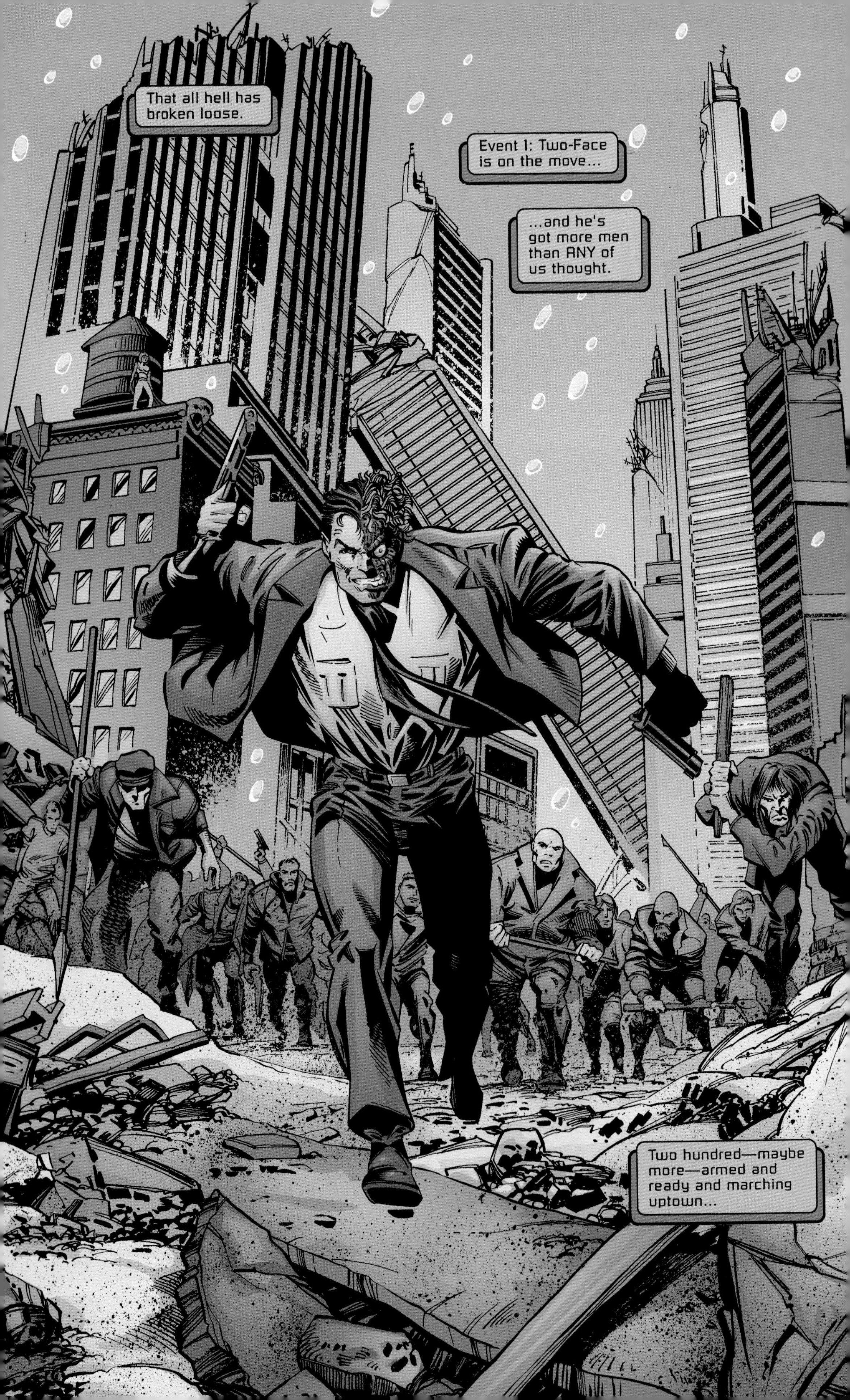
That all hell has broken loose.
Event 1: Two-Face is on the move...
...and he's got more men than ANY of us thought.
Two hundred—maybe more—armed and ready and marching uptown...

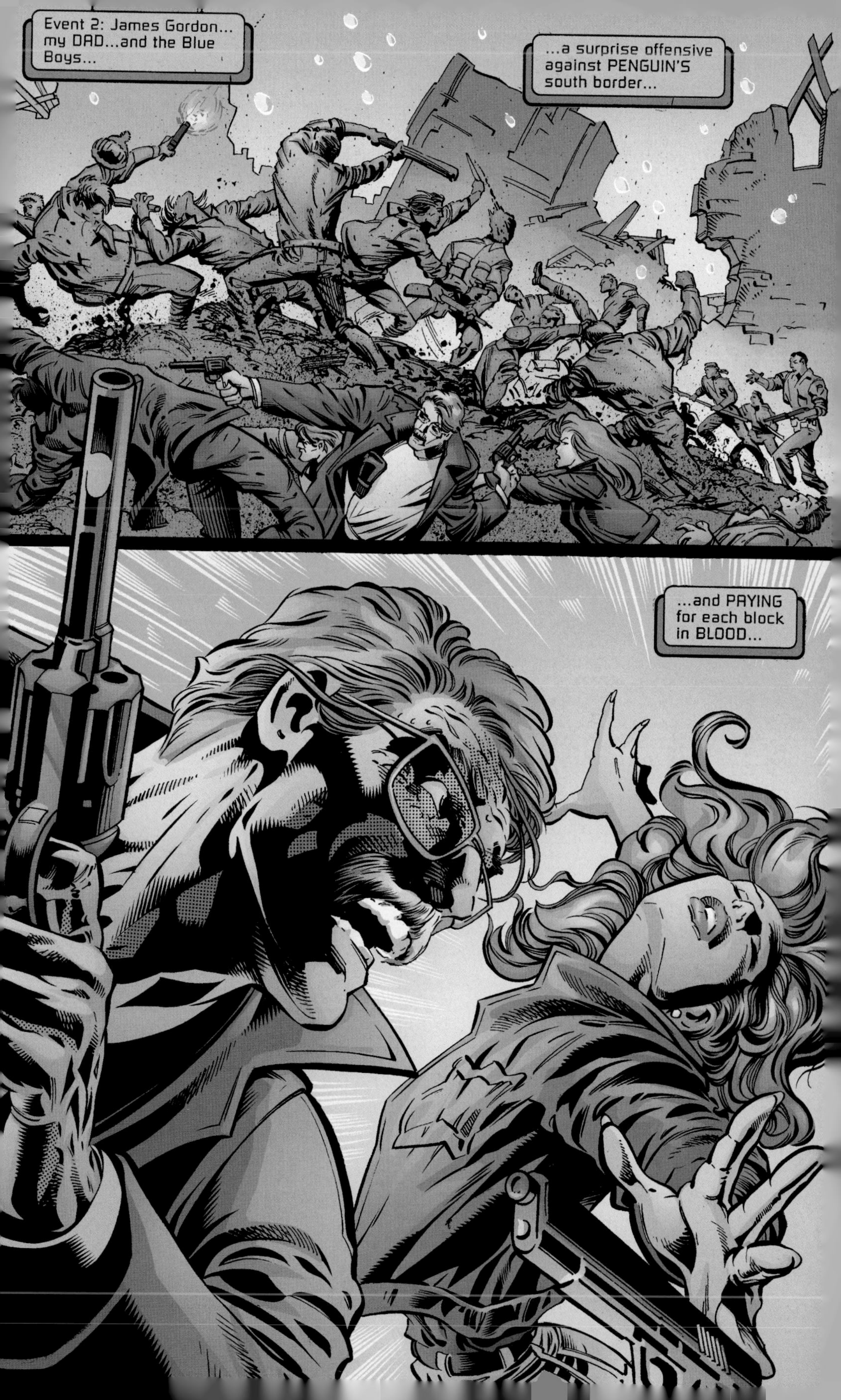

Event 2: James Gordon... my DAD...and the Blue Boys...
...a surprise offensive against PENGUIN'S south border...
...and PAYING for each block in BLOOD...

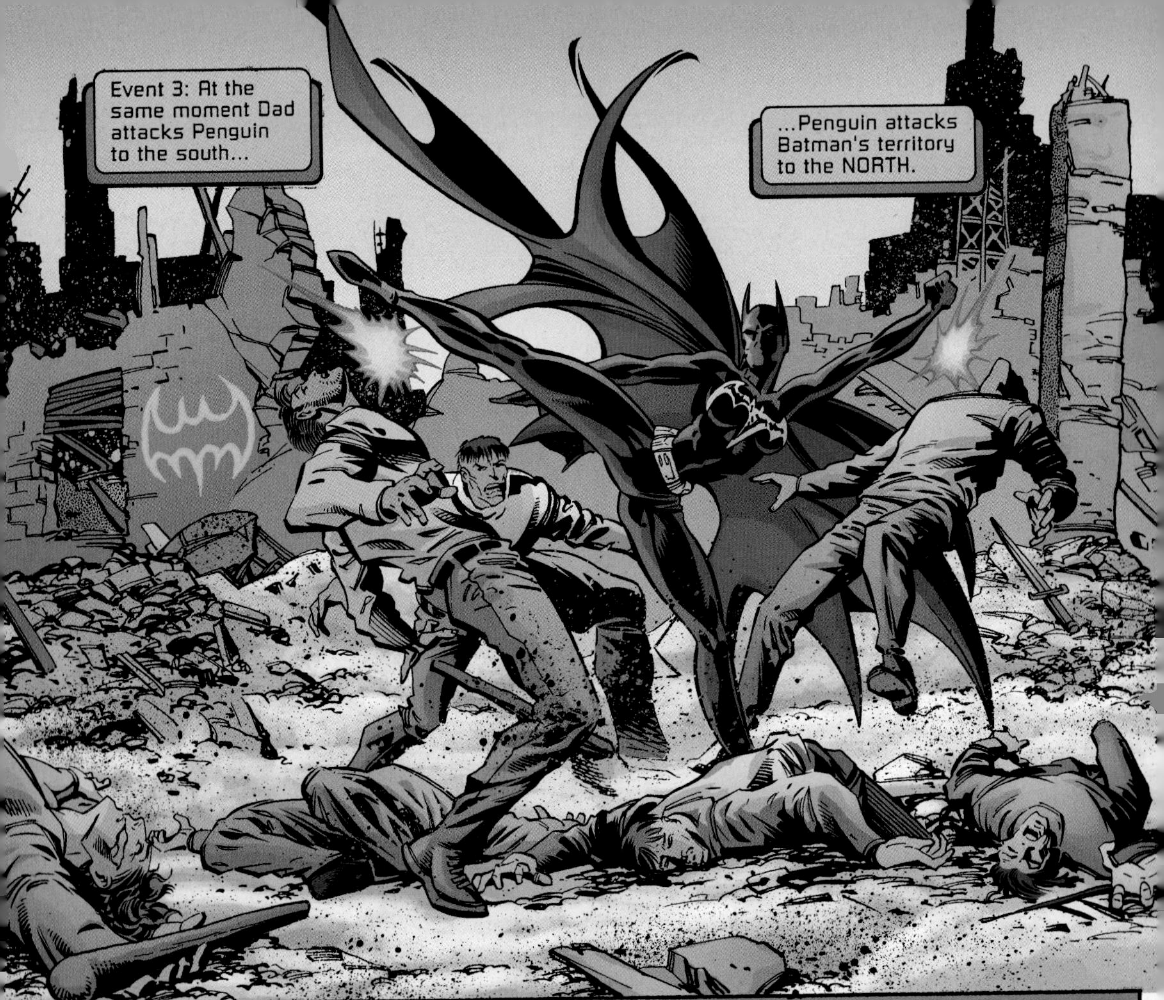
Event 3: At the same moment Dad attacks Penguin to the south...
...Penguin attacks Batman's territory to the NORTH.

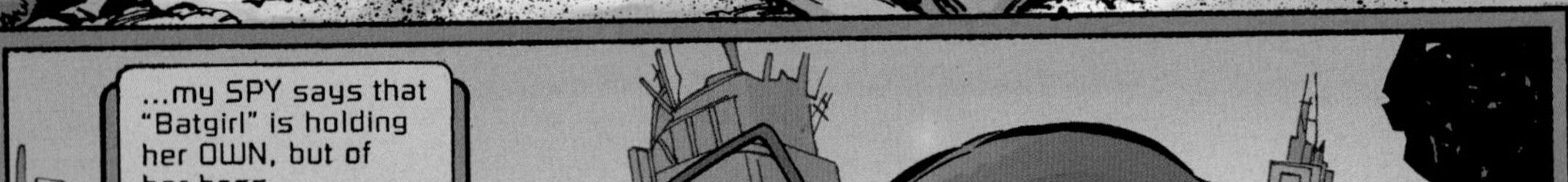
...my SPY says that "Batgirl" is holding her OWN, but of her boss...

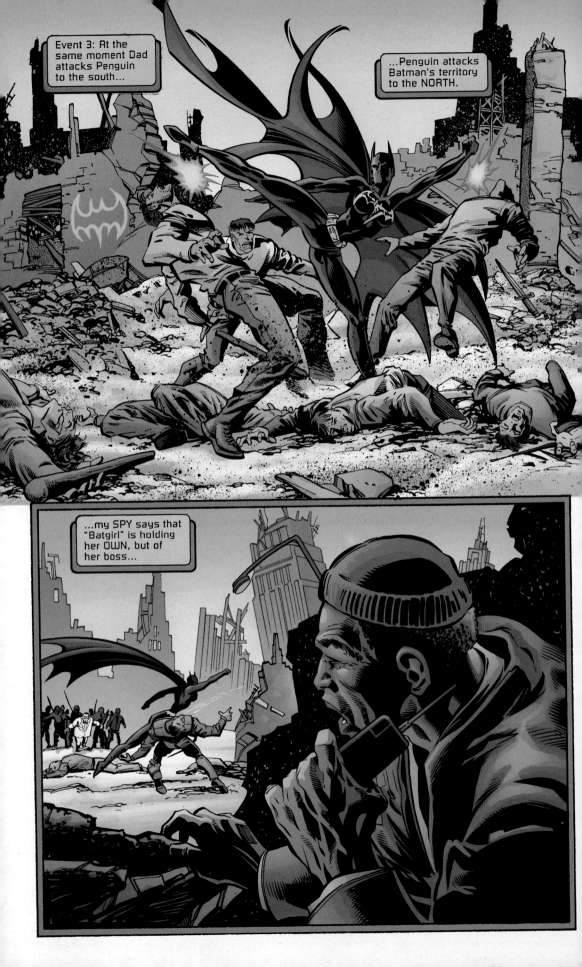

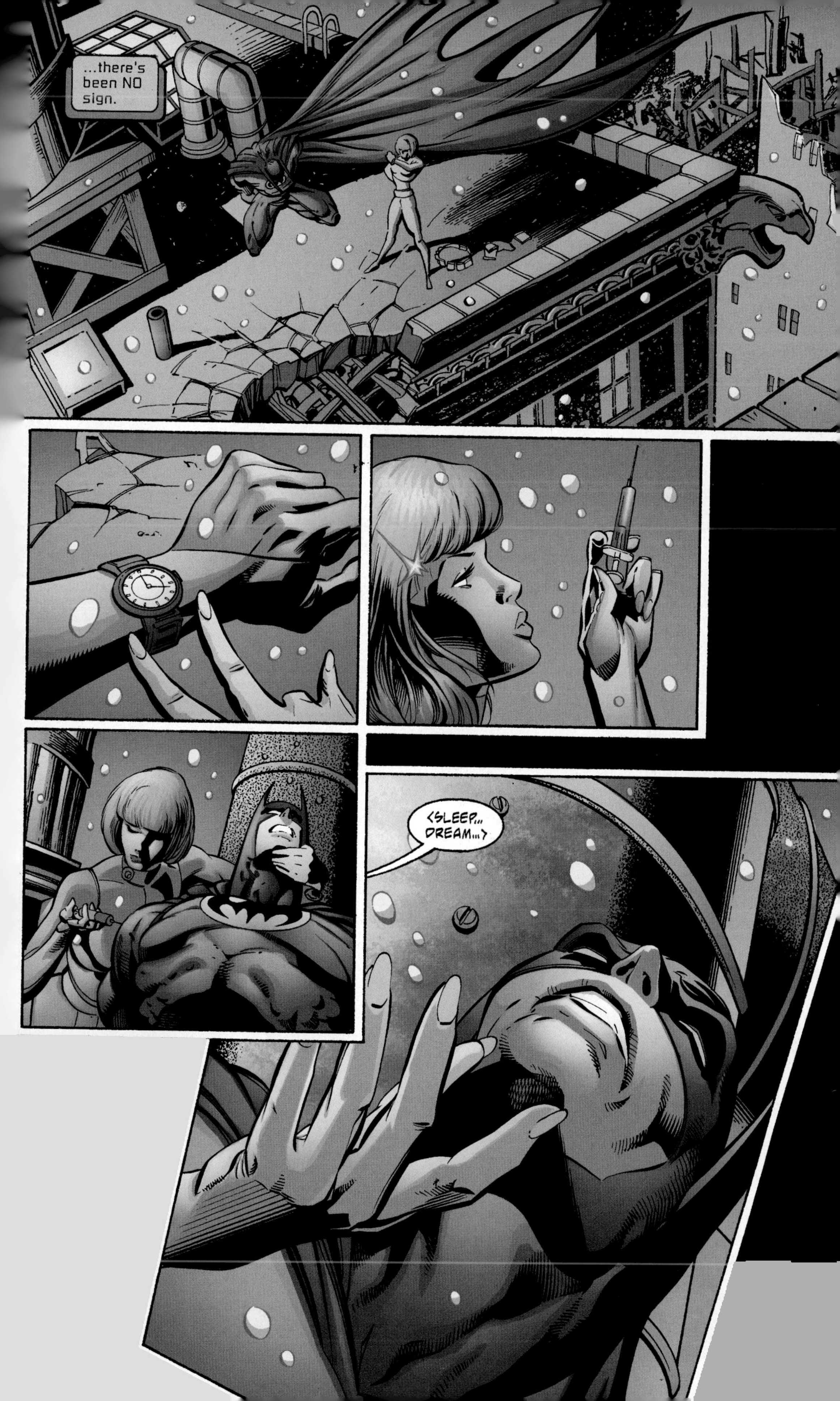
...there's been NO sign.
<SLEEP... DREAM...>

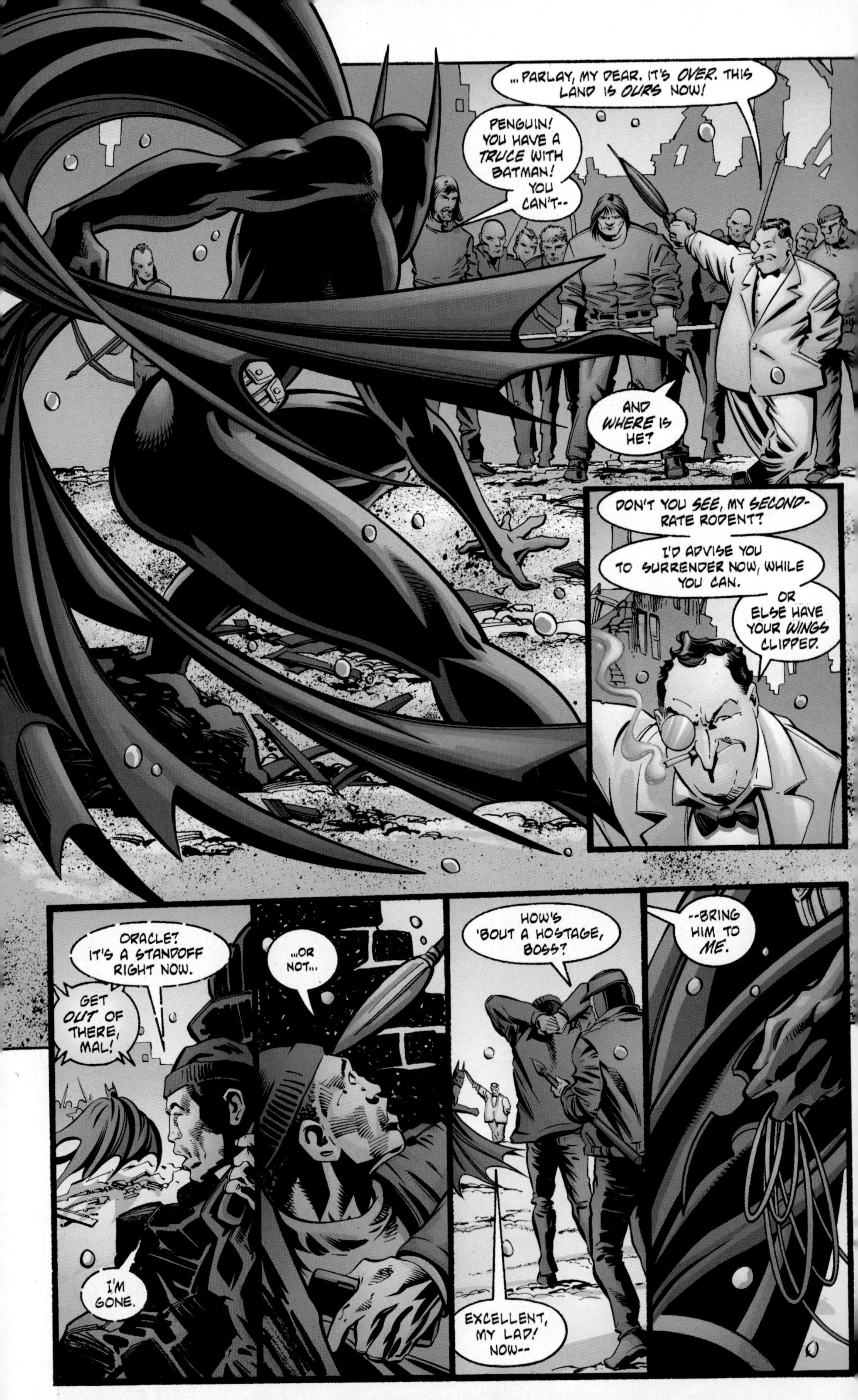
...PARLAY, MY DEAR. IT'S OVER. THIS LAND IS OURS NOW!
PENGUIN! YOU HAVE A TRUCE WITH BATMAN! YOU CAN'T--
AND WHERE IS HE?
DON'T YOU SEE, MY SECOND-RATE RODENT?
I'D ADVISE YOU TO SURRENDER NOW, WHILE YOU CAN.
OR ELSE HAVE YOUR WINGS CLIPPED.
ORACLE? IT'S A STANDOFF RIGHT NOW.
GET OUT OF THERE, MAL!
I'M GONE.
...OR NOT...
HOW'S 'BOUT A HOSTAGE, BOSS?
EXCELLENT, MY LAD! NOW--
--BRING HIM TO ME.

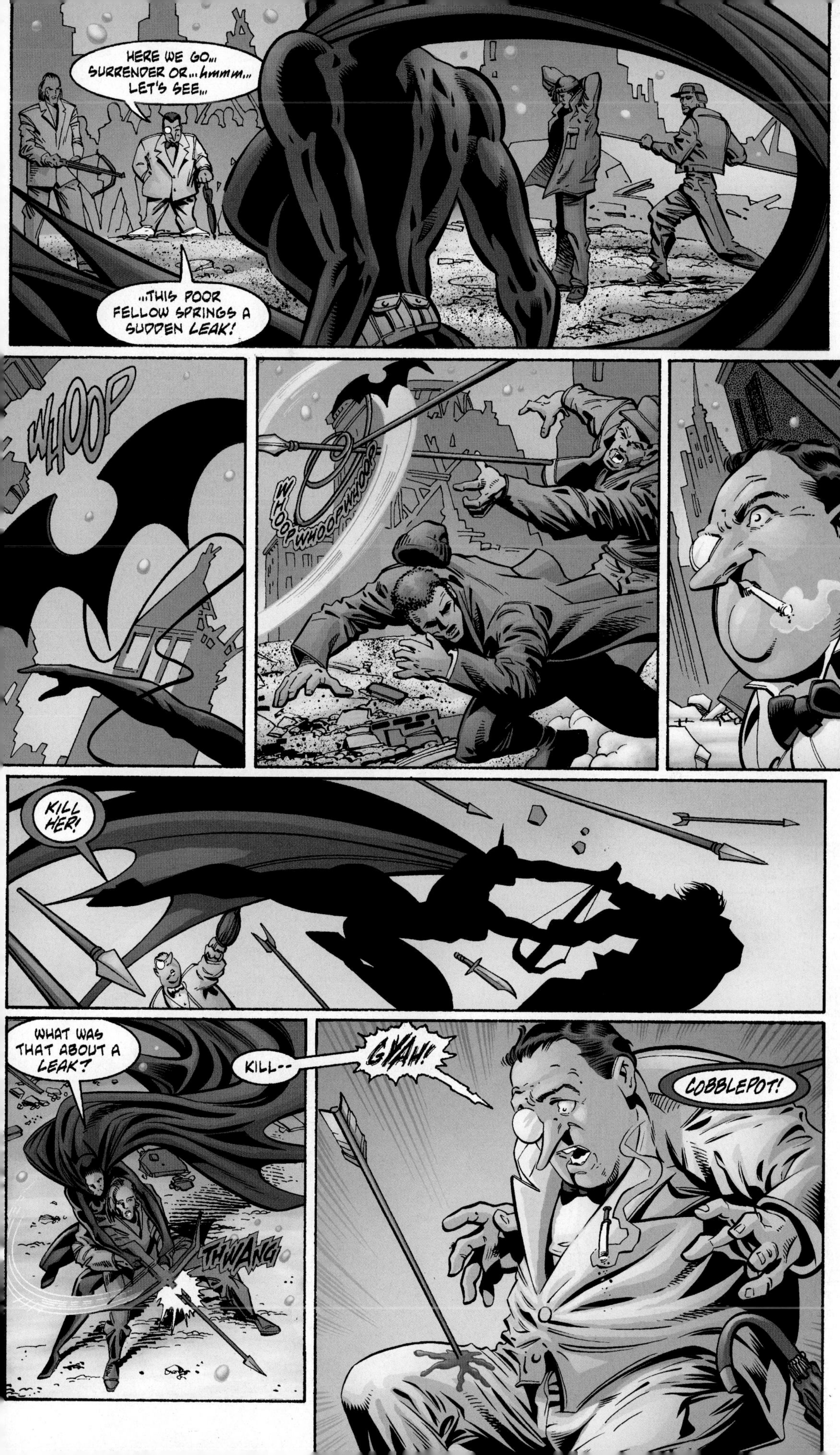
HERE WE GO... SURRENDER OR... hmmm... LET'S SEE...
...THIS POOR FELLOW SPRINGS A SUDDEN LEAK!
WHOOP
WHOOPWHOOPWHOOP
KILL HER!
WHAT WAS THAT ABOUT A LEAK?
THWANG
KILL--
GYAH!
COBBLEPOT!

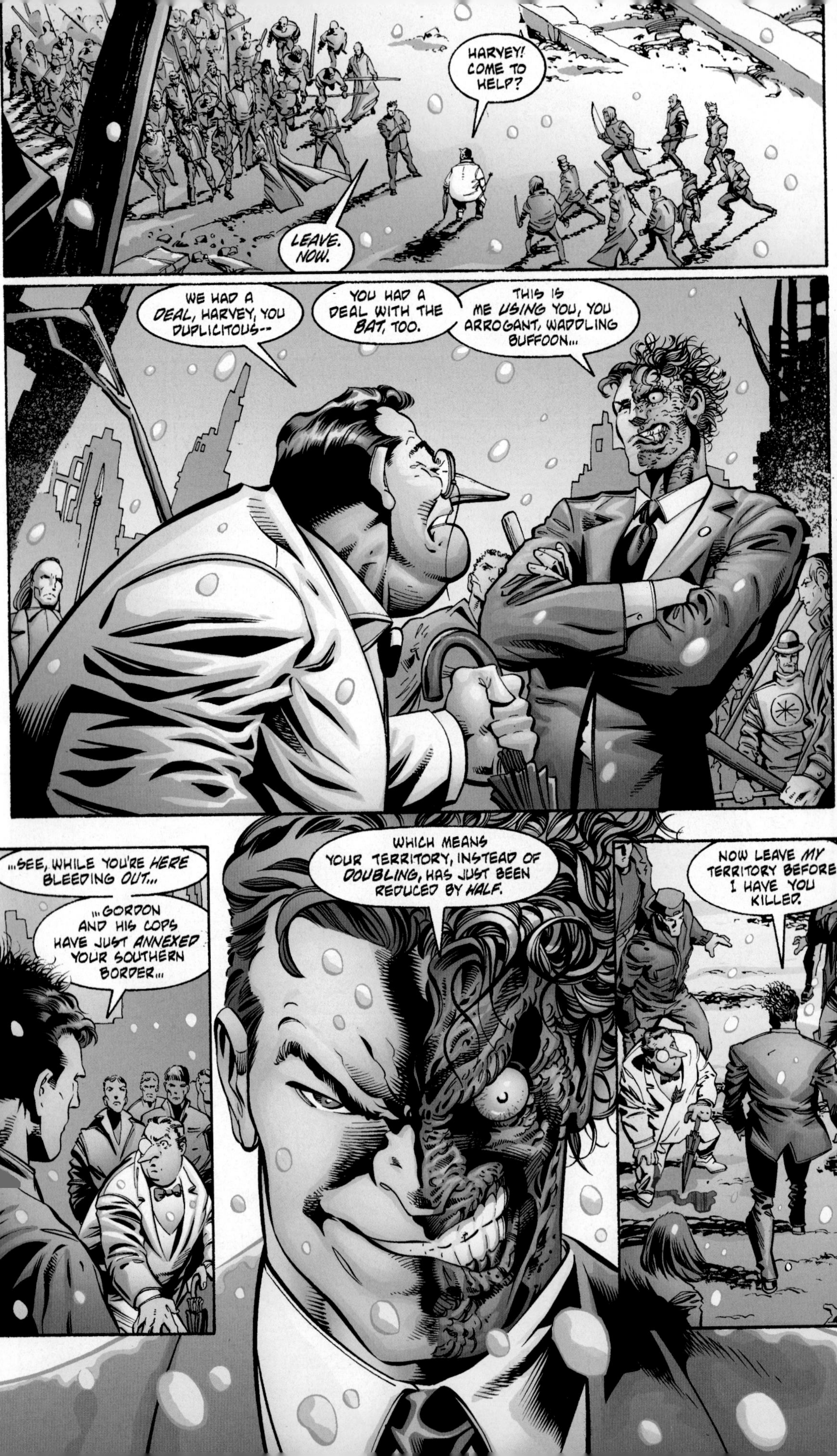
HARVEY! COME TO HELP?
LEAVE. NOW.
WE HAD A DEAL, HARVEY, YOU DUPLICITOUS--
YOU HAD A DEAL WITH THE BAT, TOO.
THIS IS ME USING YOU, YOU ARROGANT, WADDLING BUFFOON...
...SEE, WHILE YOU'RE HERE BLEEDING OUT...
...GORDON AND HIS COPS HAVE JUST ANNEXED YOUR SOUTHERN BORDER...
WHICH MEANS YOUR TERRITORY, INSTEAD OF DOUBLING, HAS JUST BEEN REDUCED BY HALF.
NOW LEAVE MY TERRITORY BEFORE I HAVE YOU KILLED.

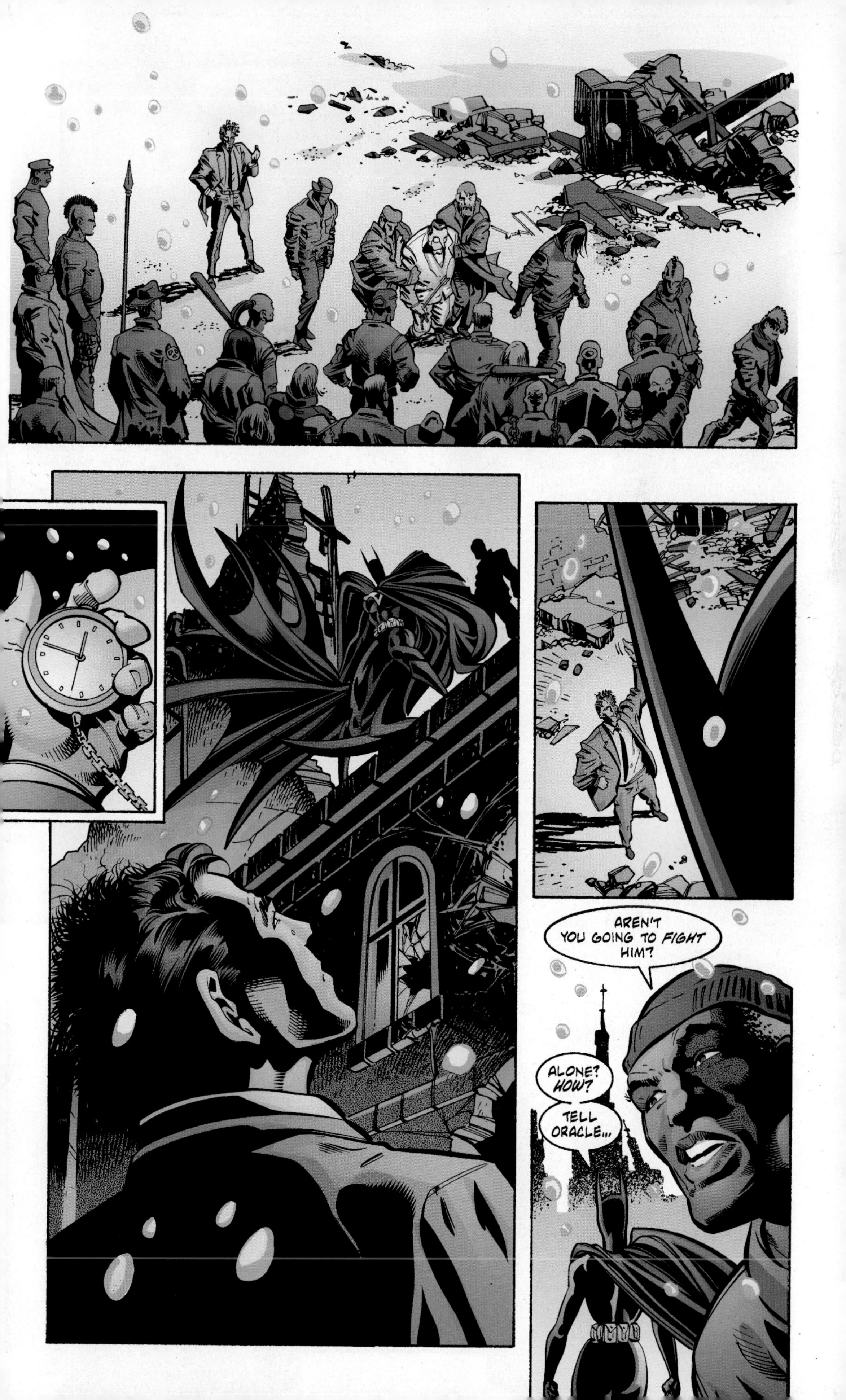
AREN'T YOU GOING TO FIGHT HIM?
ALONE? HOW?
TELL ORACLE...

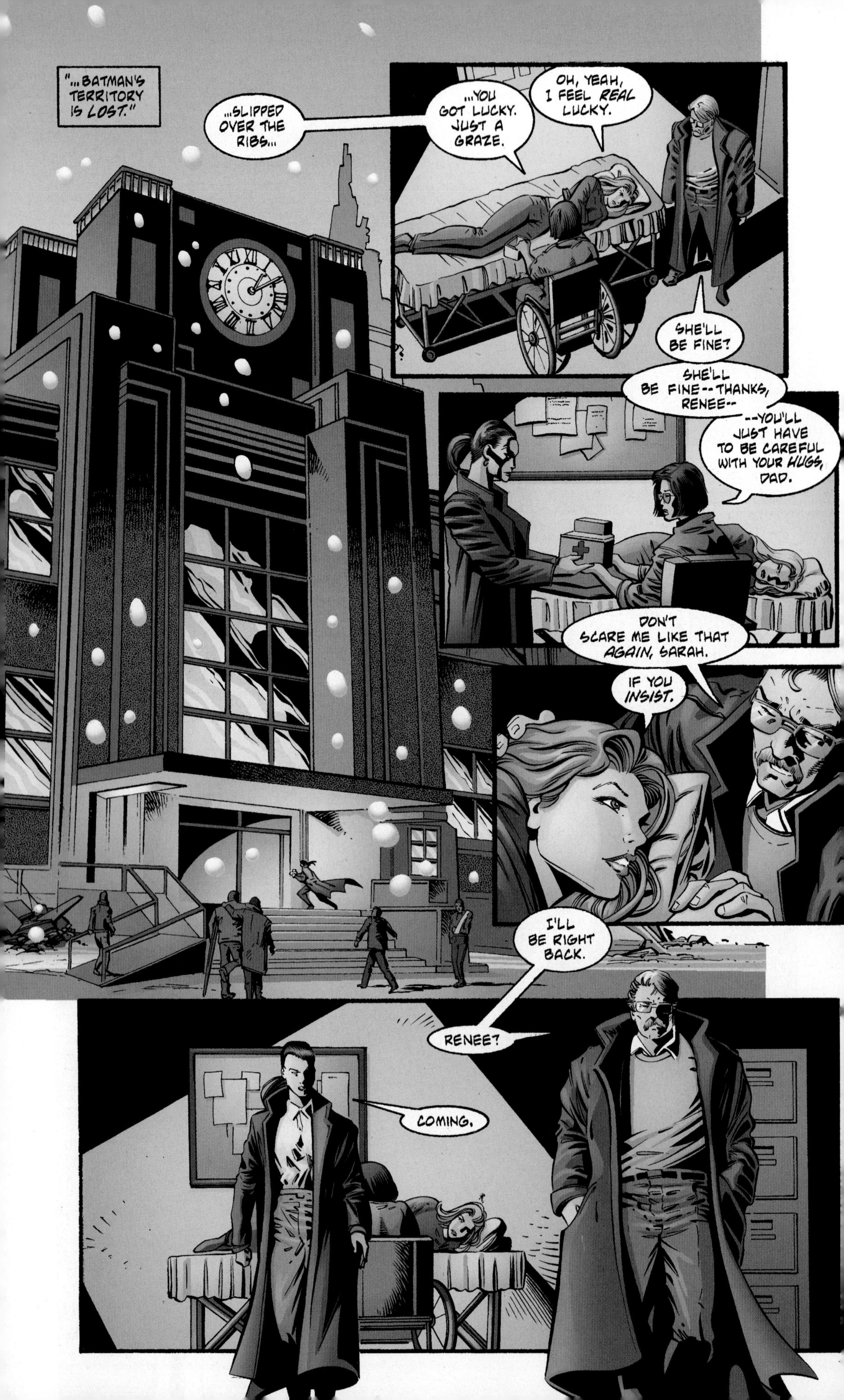
"...BATMAN'S TERRITORY IS LOST."
...SLIPPED OVER THE RIBS...
...YOU GOT LUCKY. JUST A GRAZE.
OH, YEAH, I FEEL REAL LUCKY.
SHE'LL BE FINE?
SHE'LL BE FINE--THANKS, RENEE--
--YOU'LL JUST HAVE TO BE CAREFUL WITH YOUR HUGS, DAD.
DON'T SCARE ME LIKE THAT AGAIN, SARAH.
IF YOU INSIST.
I'LL BE RIGHT BACK.
RENEE?
COMING.

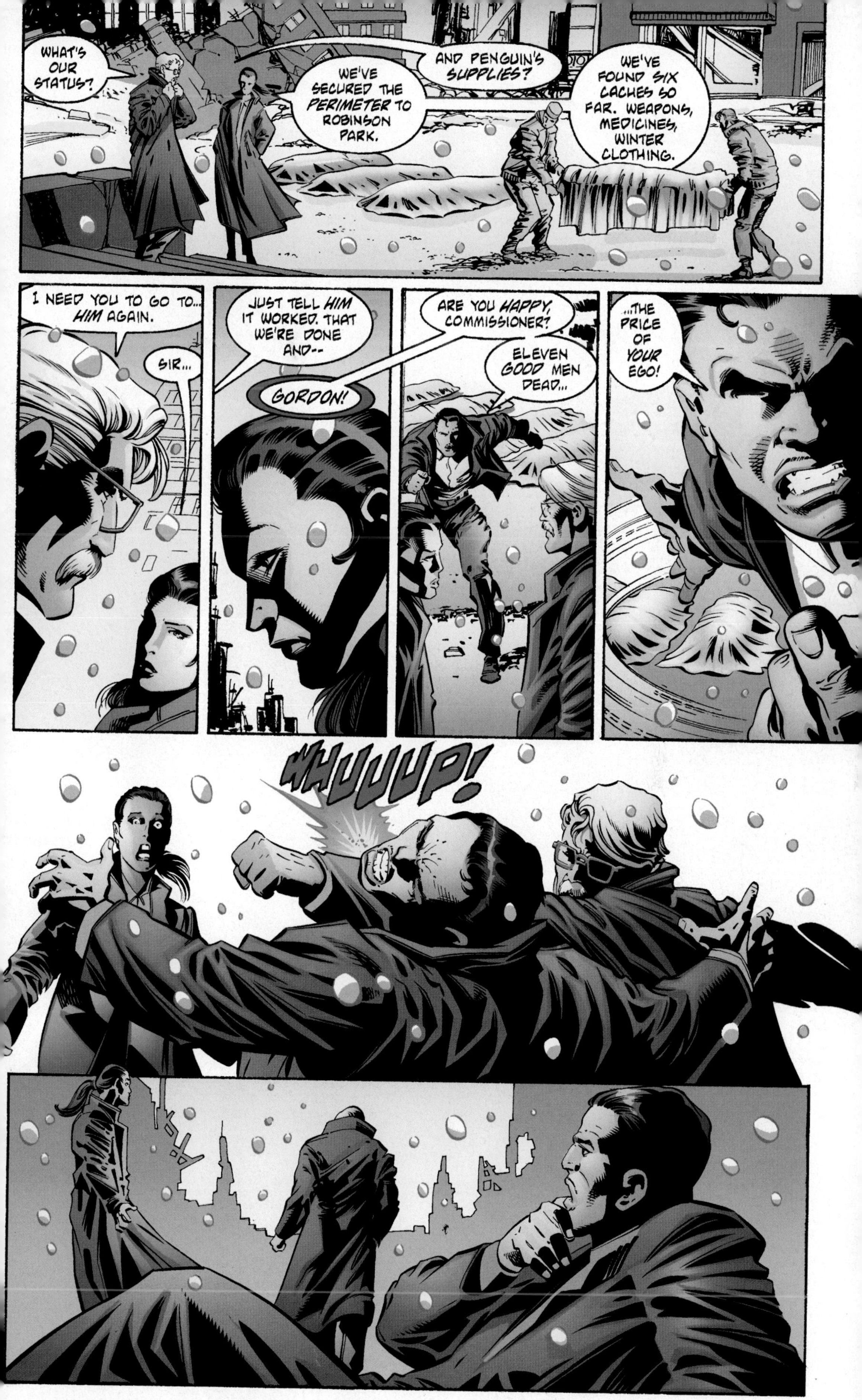
WHAT'S OUR STATUS?
WE'VE SECURED THE PERIMETER TO ROBINSON PARK.
AND PENGUIN'S SUPPLIES?
WE'VE FOUND SIX CACHES SO FAR. WEAPONS, MEDICINES, WINTER CLOTHING.
I NEED YOU TO GO TO... HIM AGAIN.
SIR...
JUST TELL HIM IT WORKED. THAT WE'RE DONE AND--
GORDON!
ARE YOU HAPPY, COMMISSIONER?
ELEVEN GOOD MEN DEAD...
...THE PRICE OF YOUR EGO!
WHUUUP!

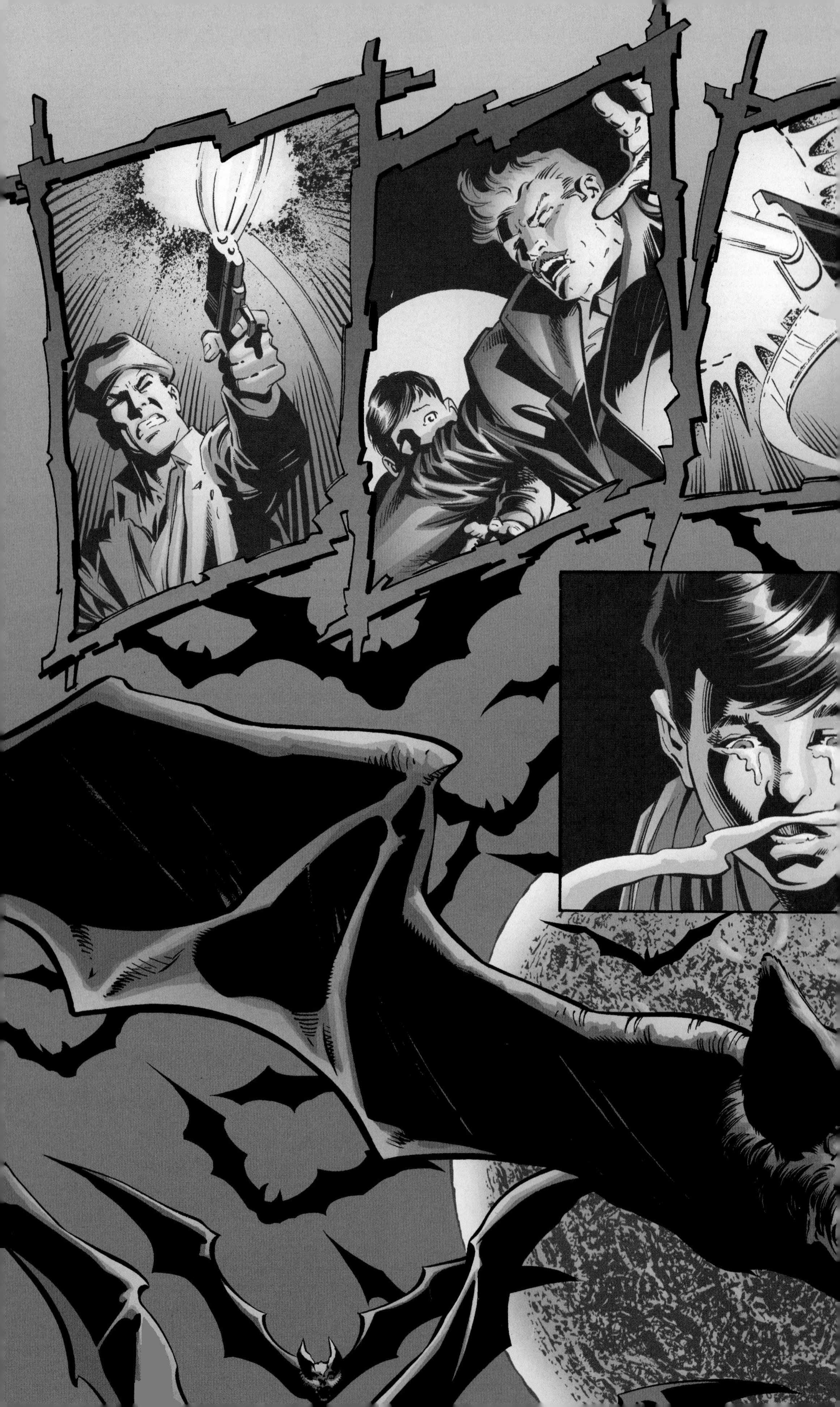

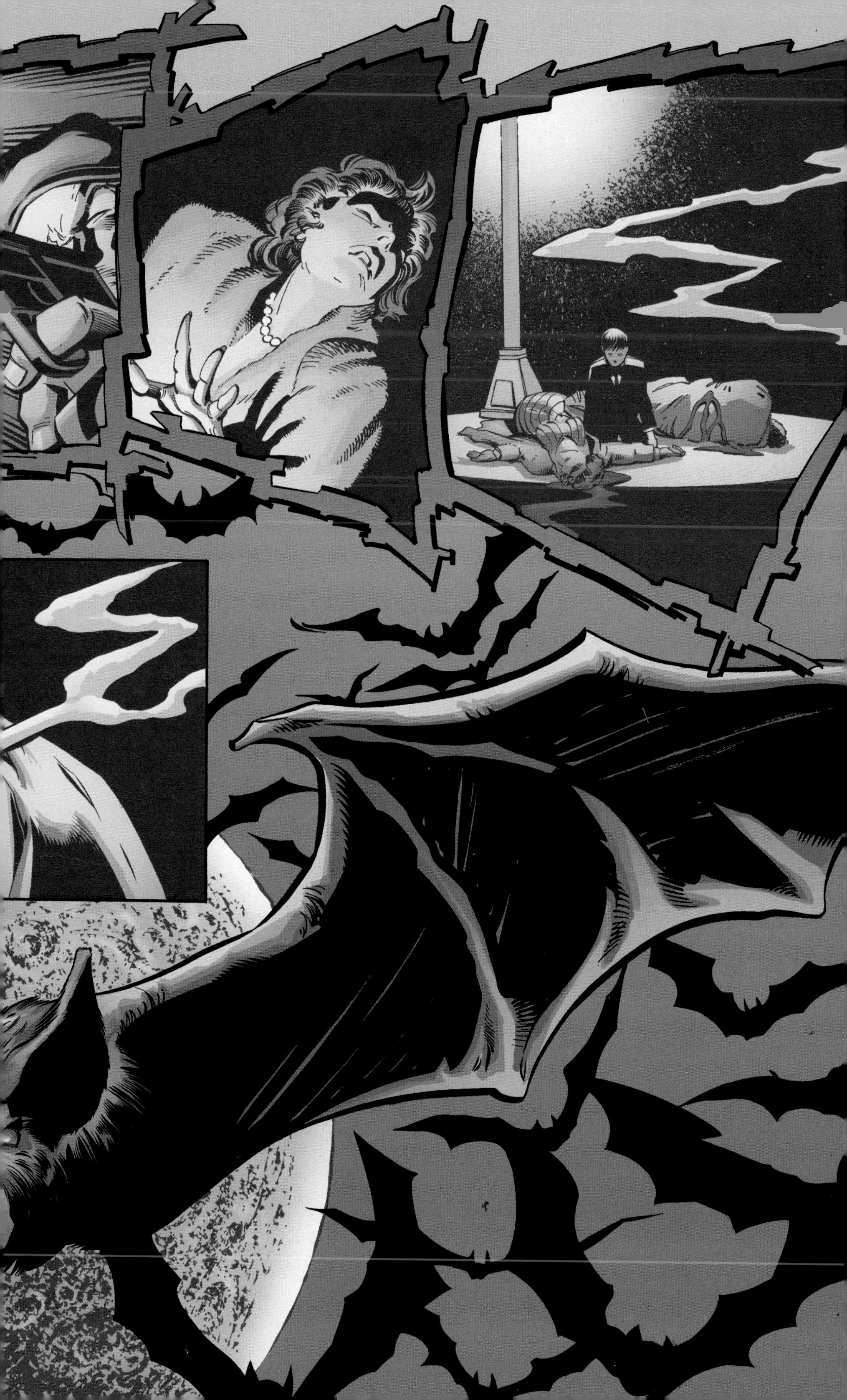

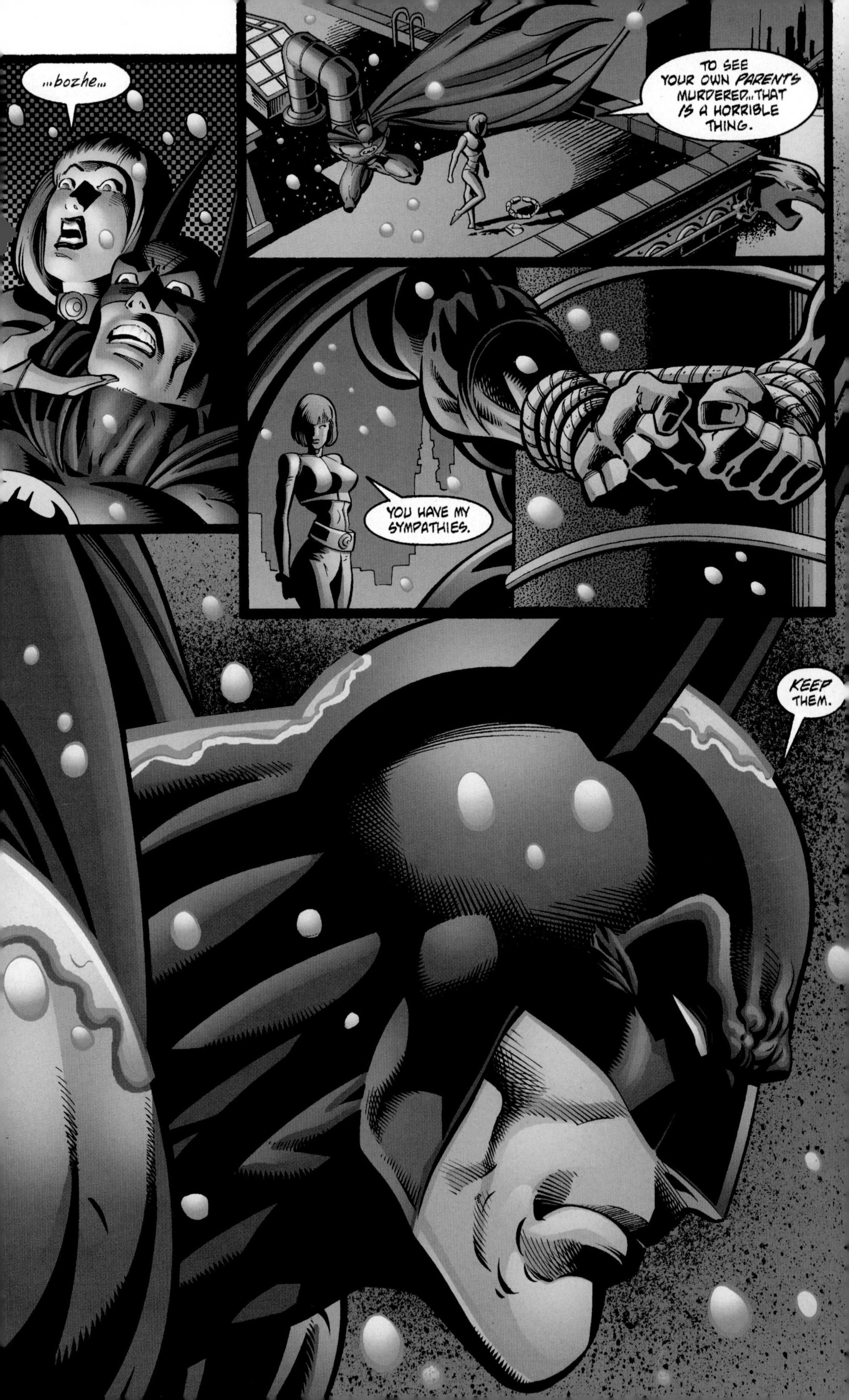
...bozhe...
TO SEE YOUR OWN PARENTS MURDERED...THAT IS A HORRIBLE THING.
YOU HAVE MY SYMPATHIES.
KEEP THEM.

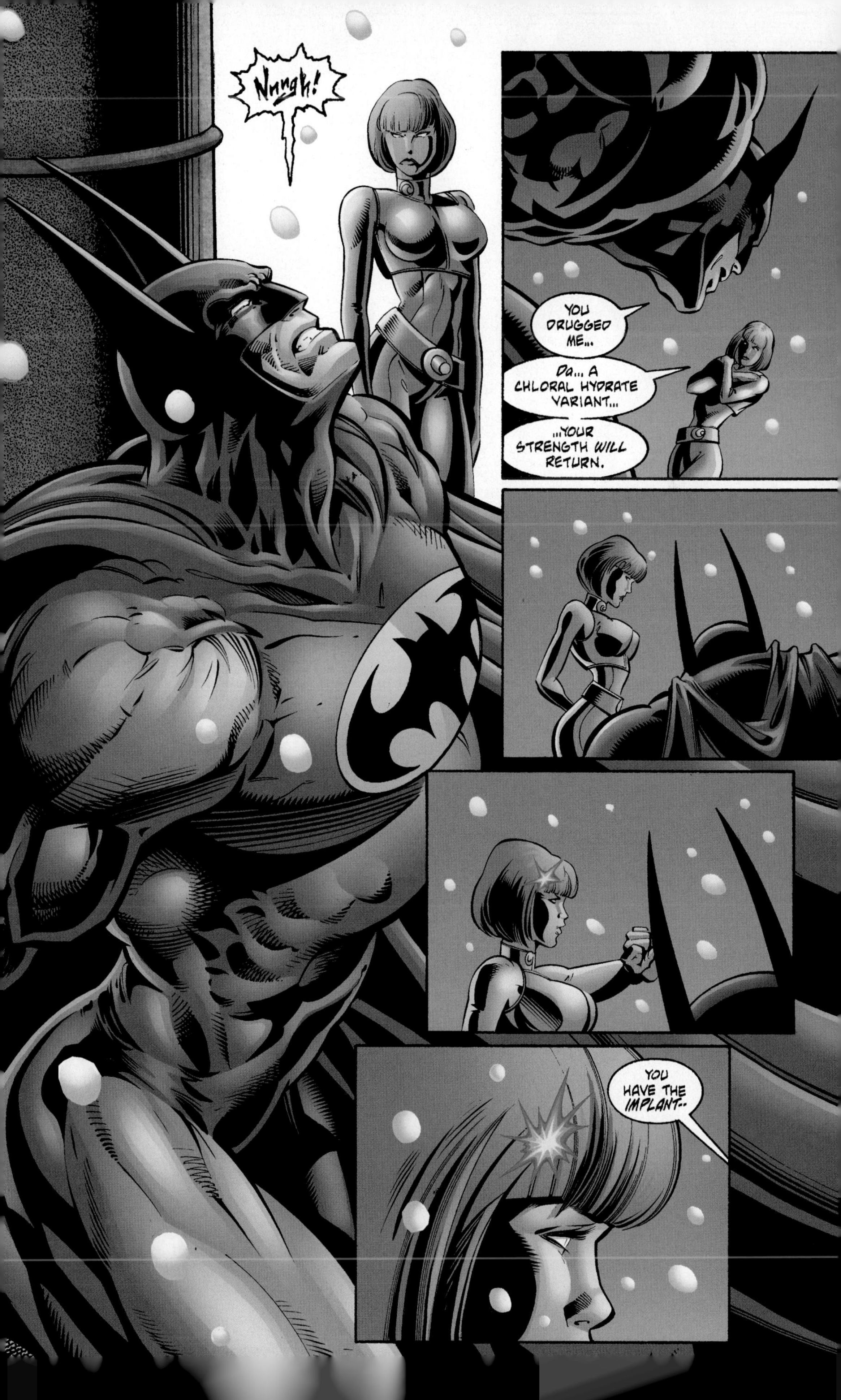
Nnngh!
YOU DRUGGED ME...
Da... A CHLORAL HYDRATE VARIANT...
...YOUR STRENGTH WILL RETURN.
YOU HAVE THE IMPLANT..

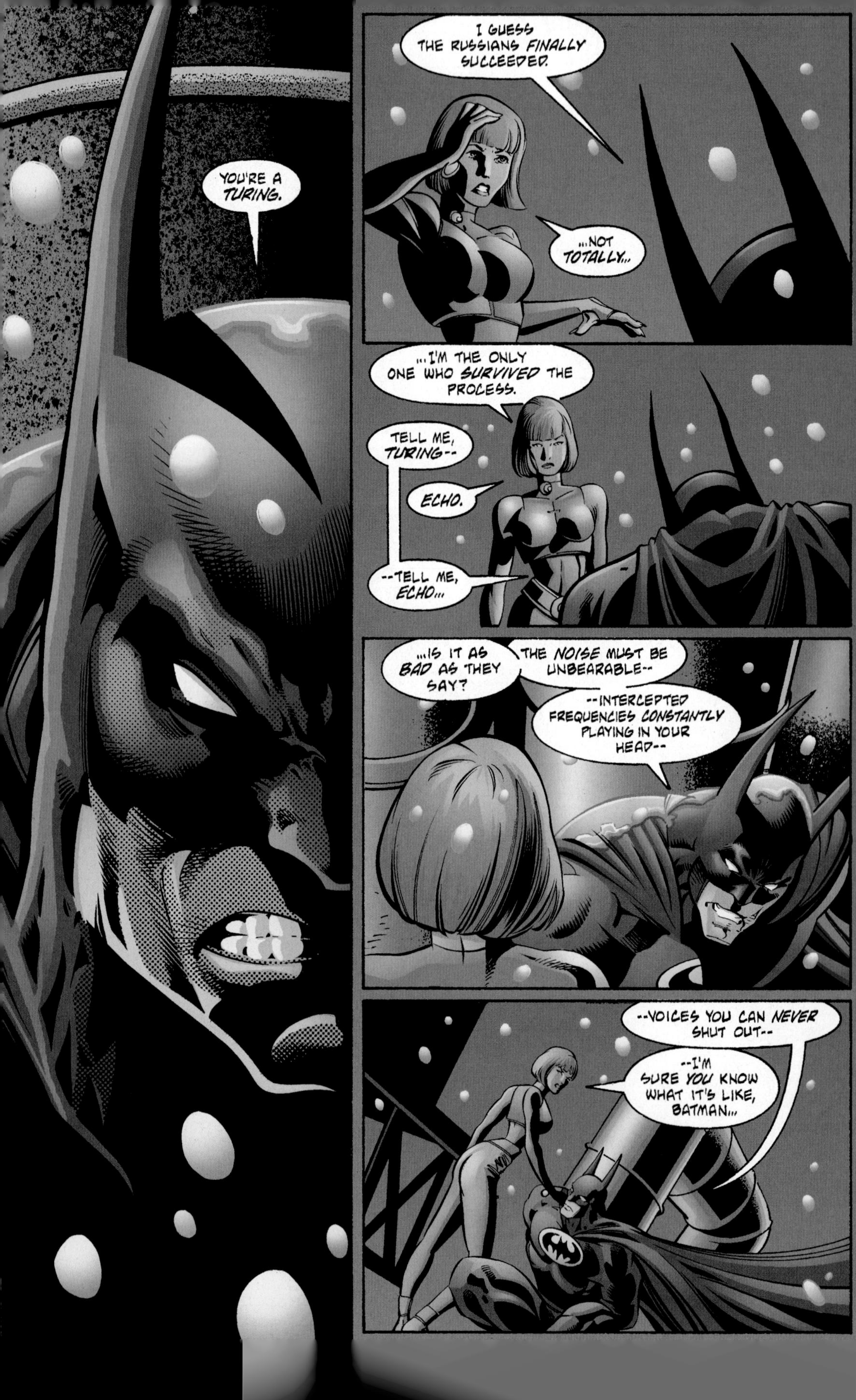
YOU'RE A TURING.
I GUESS THE RUSSIANS FINALLY SUCCEEDED.
...NOT TOTALLY...
...I'M THE ONLY ONE WHO SURVIVED THE PROCESS.
TELL ME, TURING--
ECHO.
--TELL ME, ECHO...
...IS IT AS BAD AS THEY SAY?
THE NOISE MUST BE UNBEARABLE--
--INTERCEPTED FREQUENCIES CONSTANTLY PLAYING IN YOUR HEAD--
--VOICES YOU CAN NEVER SHUT OUT--
--I'M SURE YOU KNOW WHAT IT'S LIKE, BATMAN...

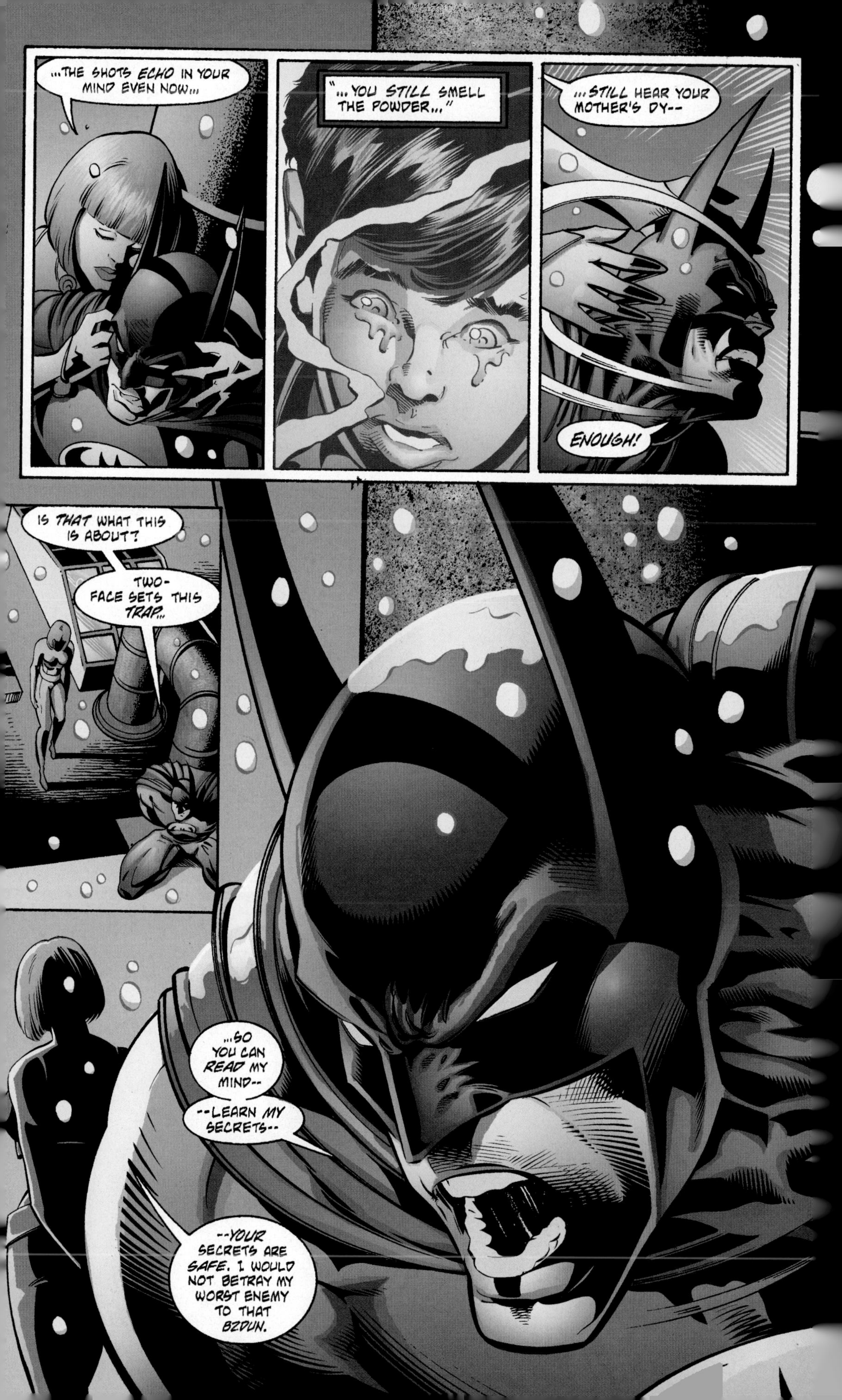
...THE SHOTS ECHO IN YOUR MIND EVEN NOW...
"...YOU STILL SMELL THE POWDER..."
...STILL HEAR YOUR MOTHER'S DY--
ENOUGH!
IS THAT WHAT THIS IS ABOUT?
TWO-FACE SETS THIS TRAP...
...SO YOU CAN READ MY MIND--
--LEARN MY SECRETS--
--YOUR SECRETS ARE SAFE. I WOULD NOT BETRAY MY WORST ENEMY TO THAT BZDUN.

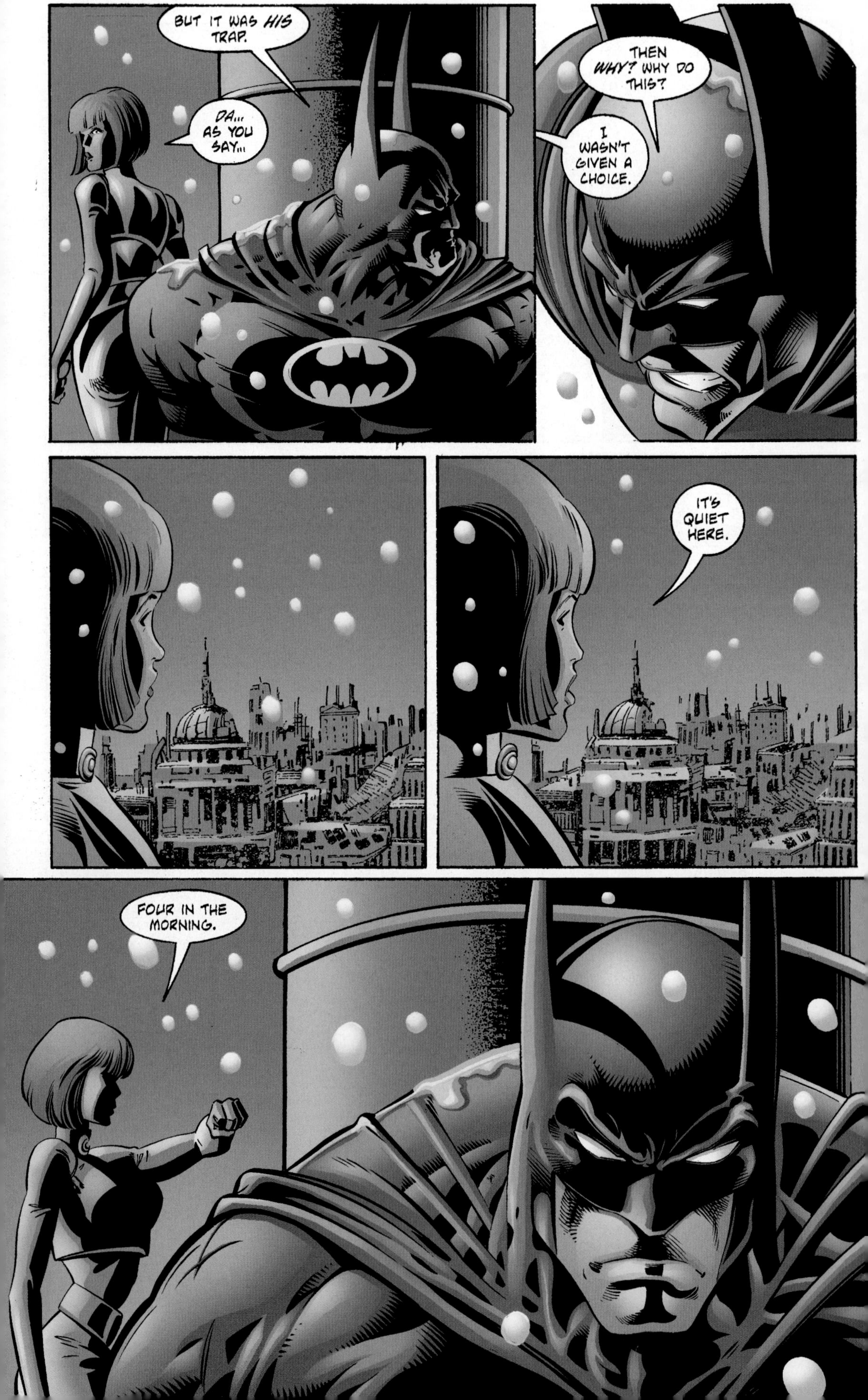
BUT IT WAS HIS TRAP.
DA... AS YOU SAY...
THEN WHY? WHY DO THIS?
I WASN'T GIVEN A CHOICE.
IT'S QUIET HERE.
FOUR IN THE MORNING.

I HAVE KEPT YOU HERE FOR FOUR HOURS...

TIME ENOUGH FOR TWO-FACE TO TAKE WHAT WAS YOURS.

I AM TRULY SORRY FOR YOUR LOSS.

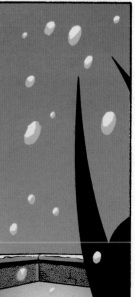

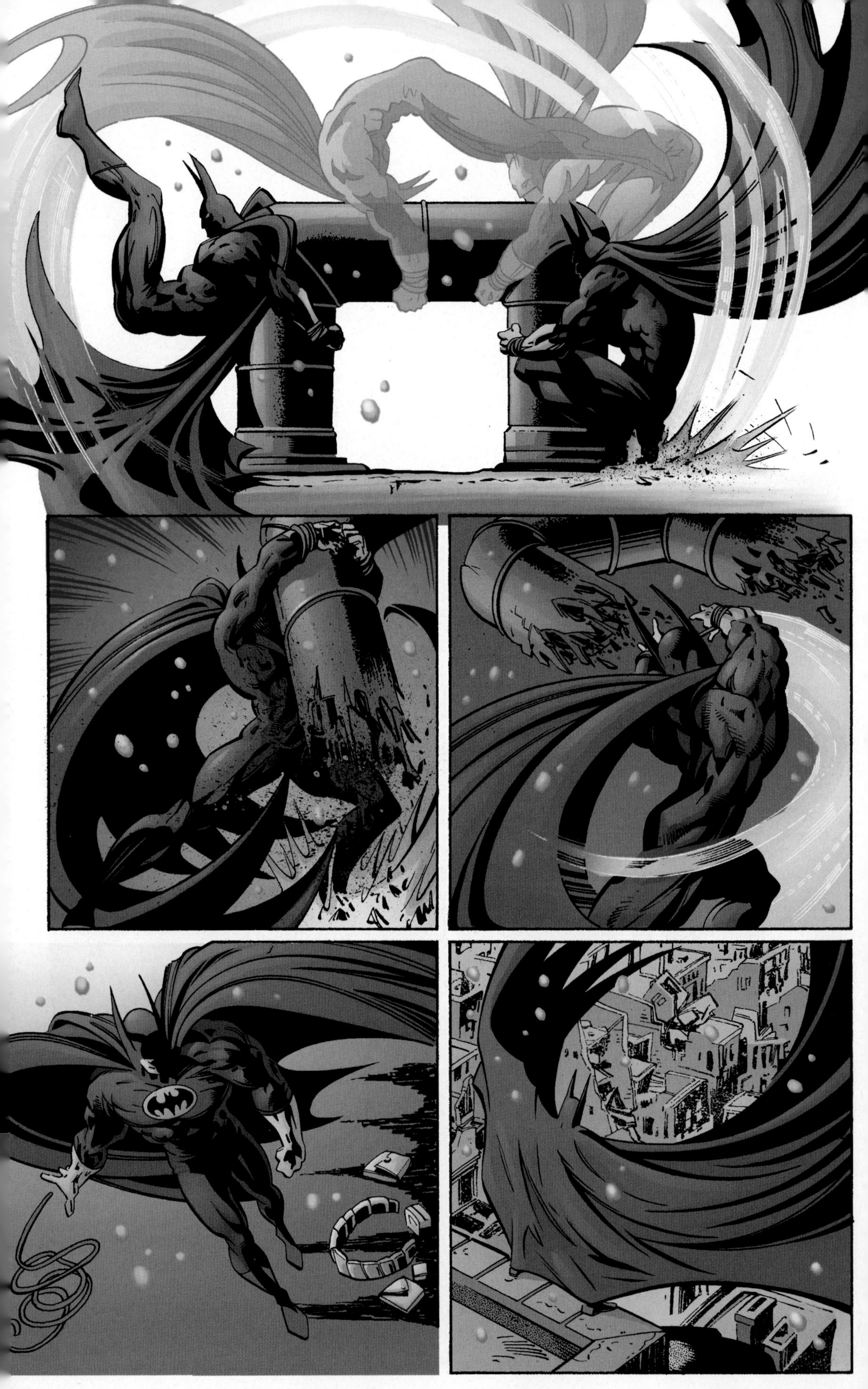

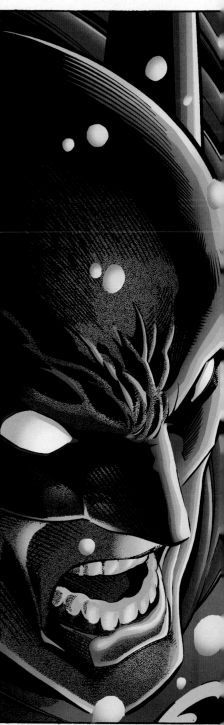

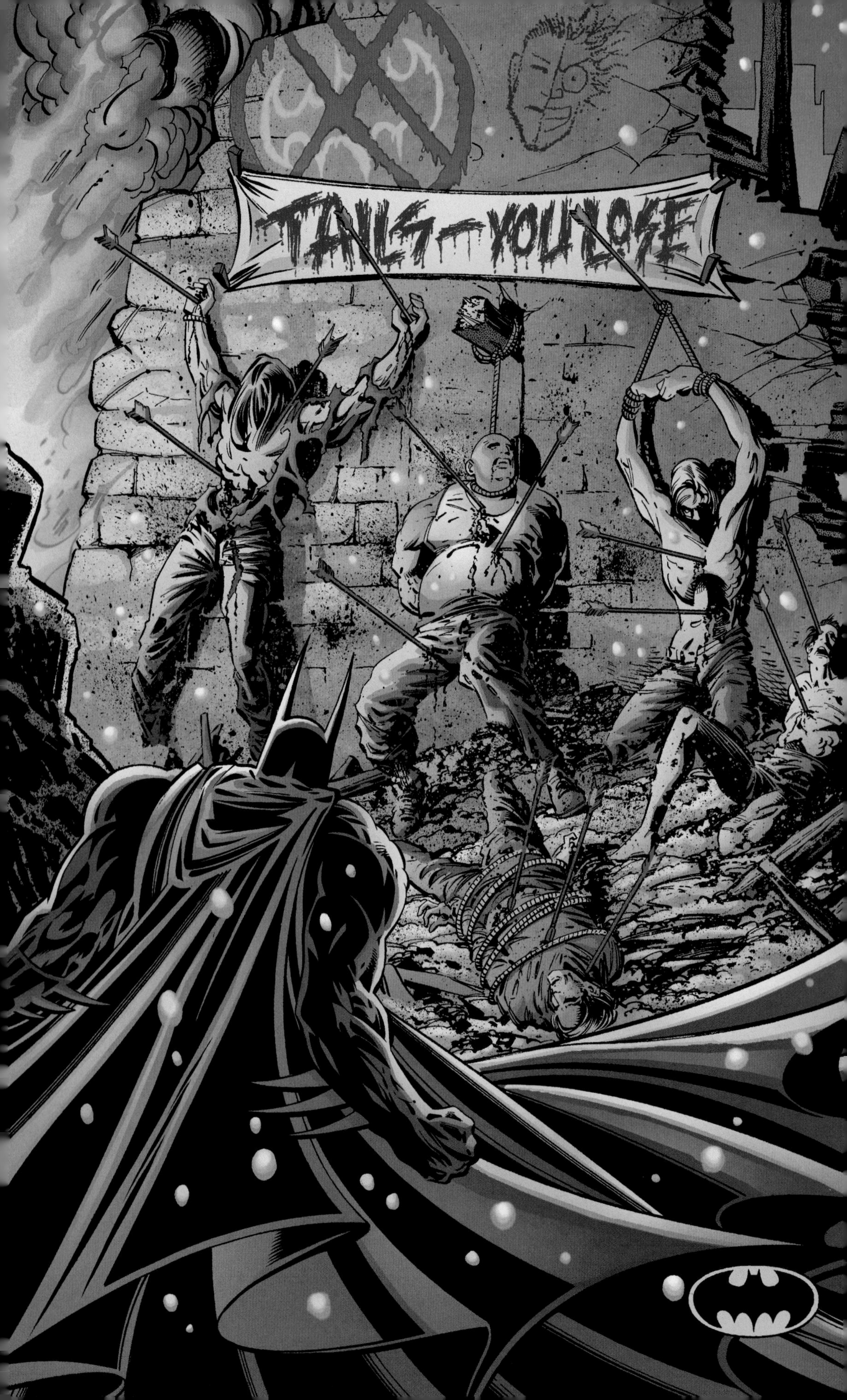
TAILS — YOU LOSE

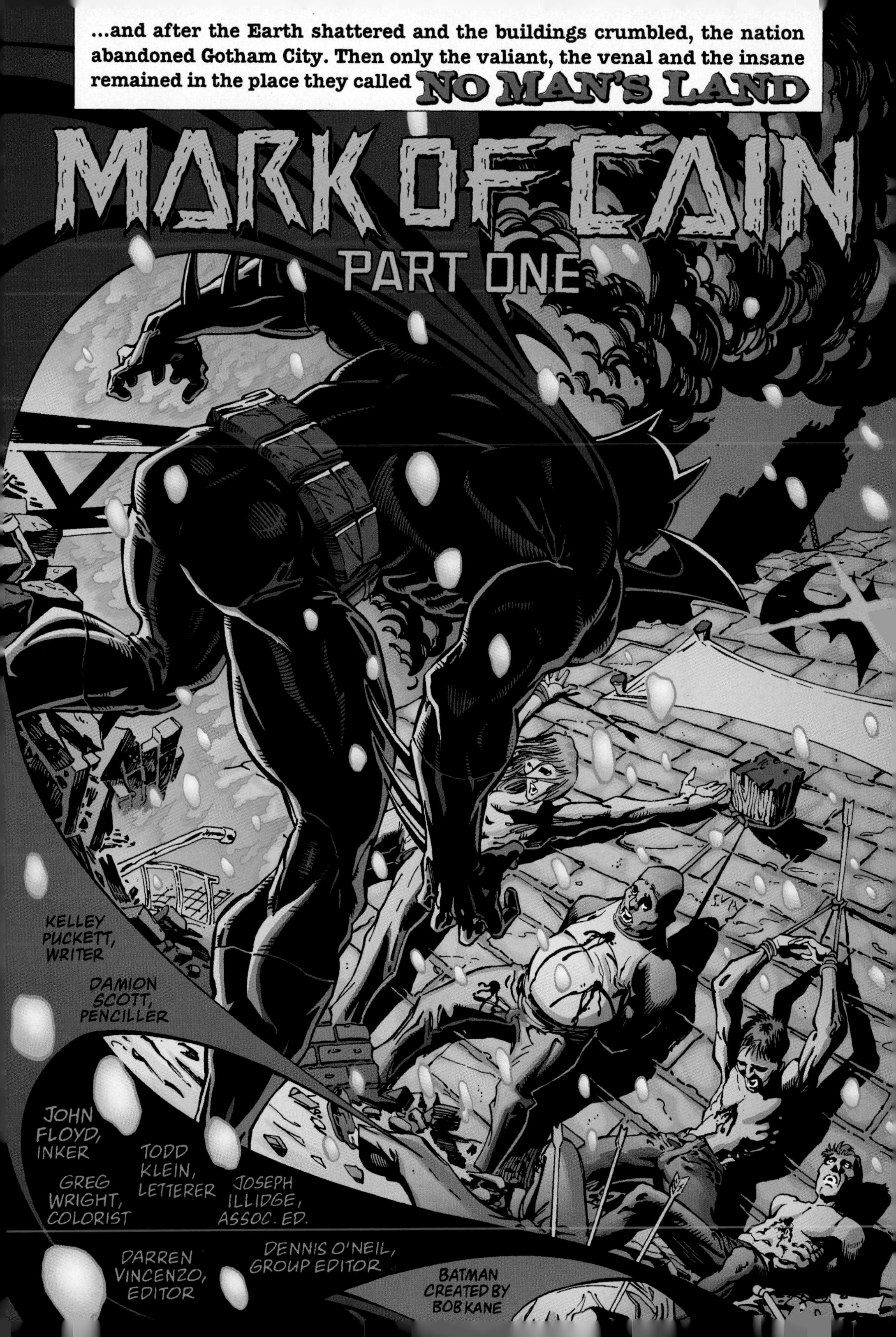
...and after the Earth shattered and the buildings crumbled, the nation abandoned Gotham City. Then only the valiant, the venal and the insane remained in the place they called NO MAN'S LAND
MARK OF CAIN
PART ONE
KELLEY PUCKETT, WRITER
DAMION SCOTT, PENCILLER
JOHN FLOYD, INKER
TODD KLEIN, LETTERER
GREG WRIGHT, COLORIST
JOSEPH ILLIDGE, ASSOC. ED.
DARREN VINCENZO, EDITOR
DENNIS O'NEIL, GROUP EDITOR
BATMAN CREATED BY BOB KANE

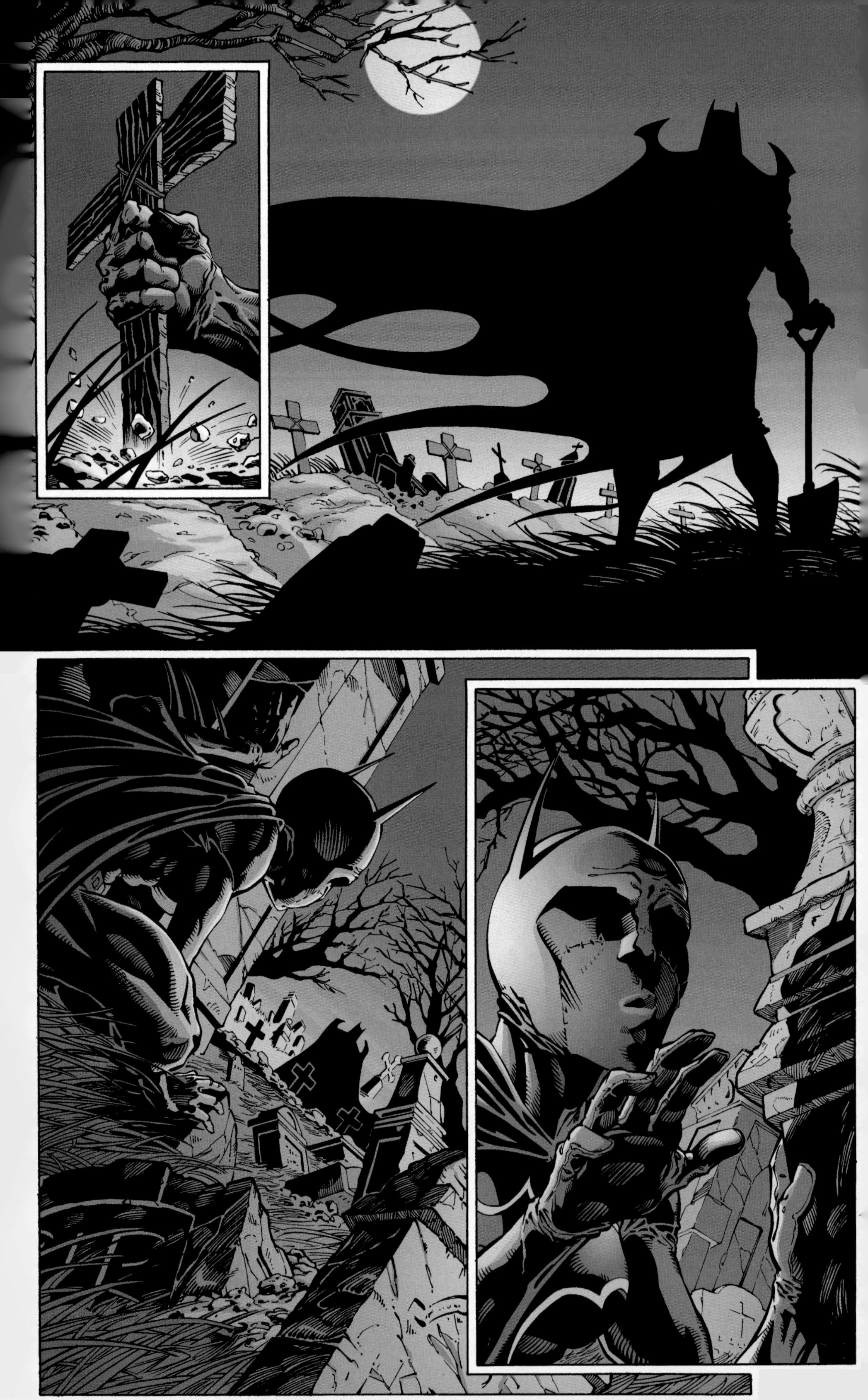

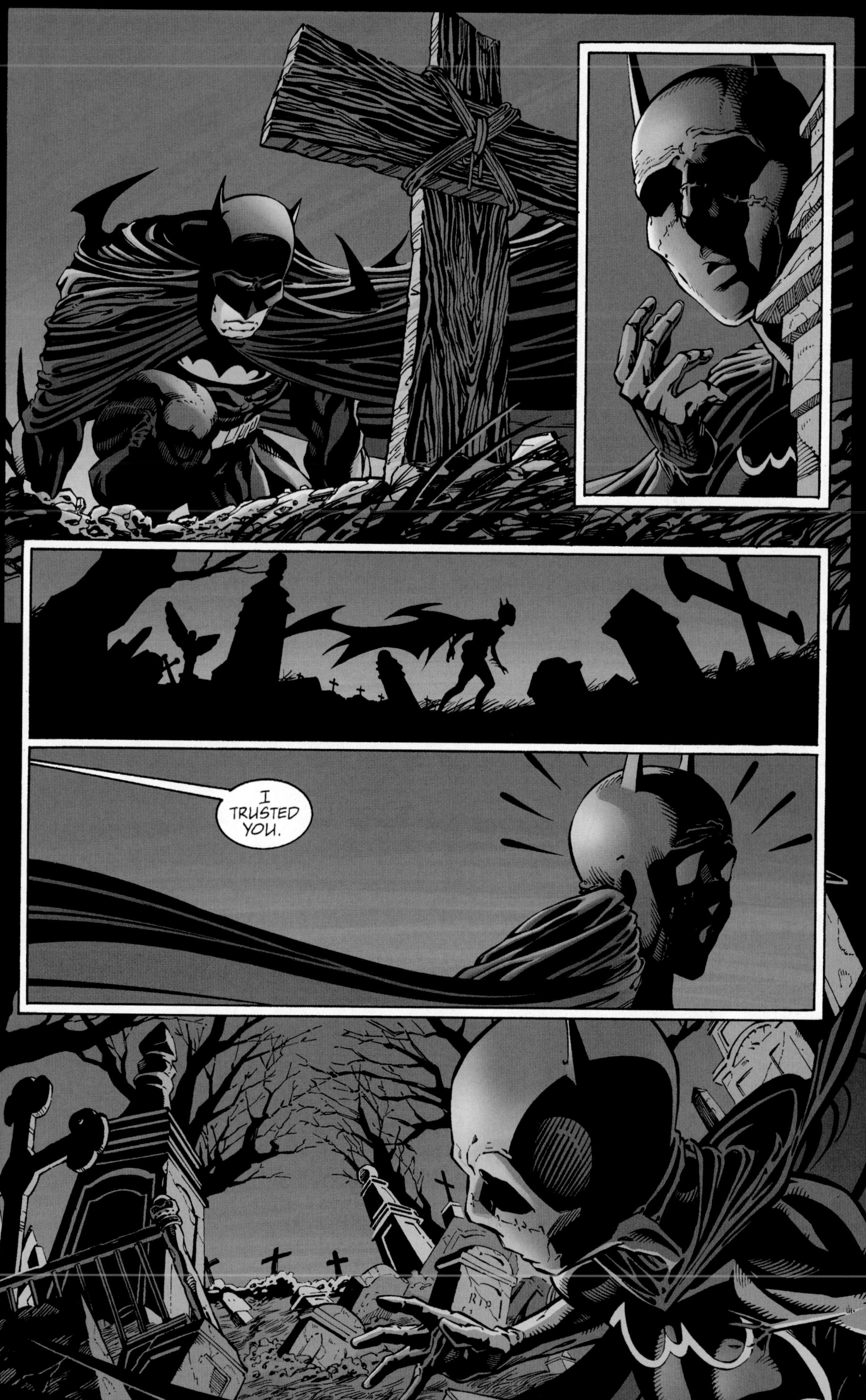
I TRUSTED YOU.

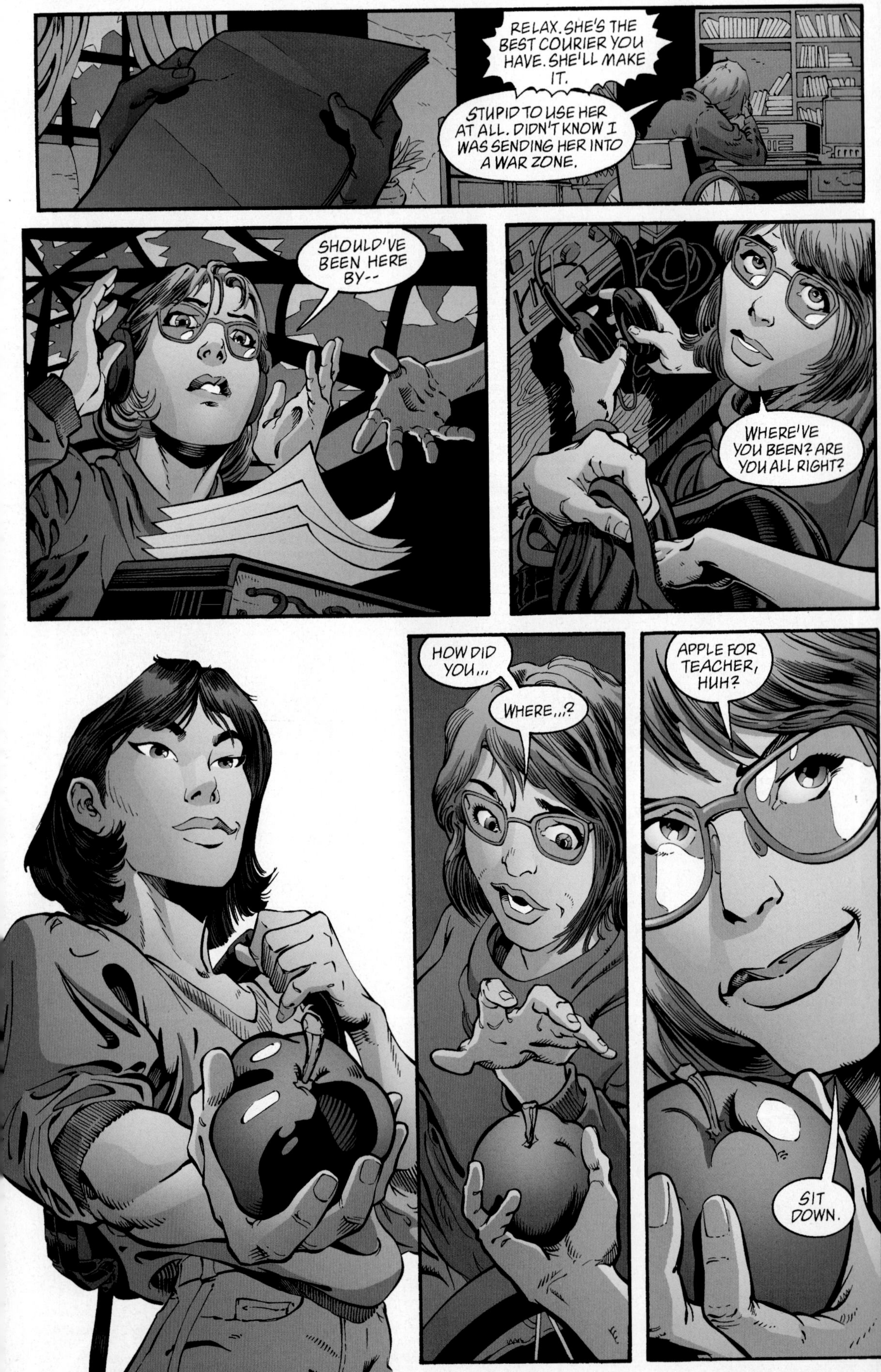
RELAX. SHE'S THE BEST COURIER YOU HAVE. SHE'LL MAKE IT.
STUPID TO USE HER AT ALL. DIDN'T KNOW I WAS SENDING HER INTO A WAR ZONE.
SHOULD'VE BEEN HERE BY--
WHERE'VE YOU BEEN? ARE YOU ALL RIGHT?
HOW DID YOU...
WHERE...?
APPLE FOR TEACHER, HUH?
SIT DOWN.

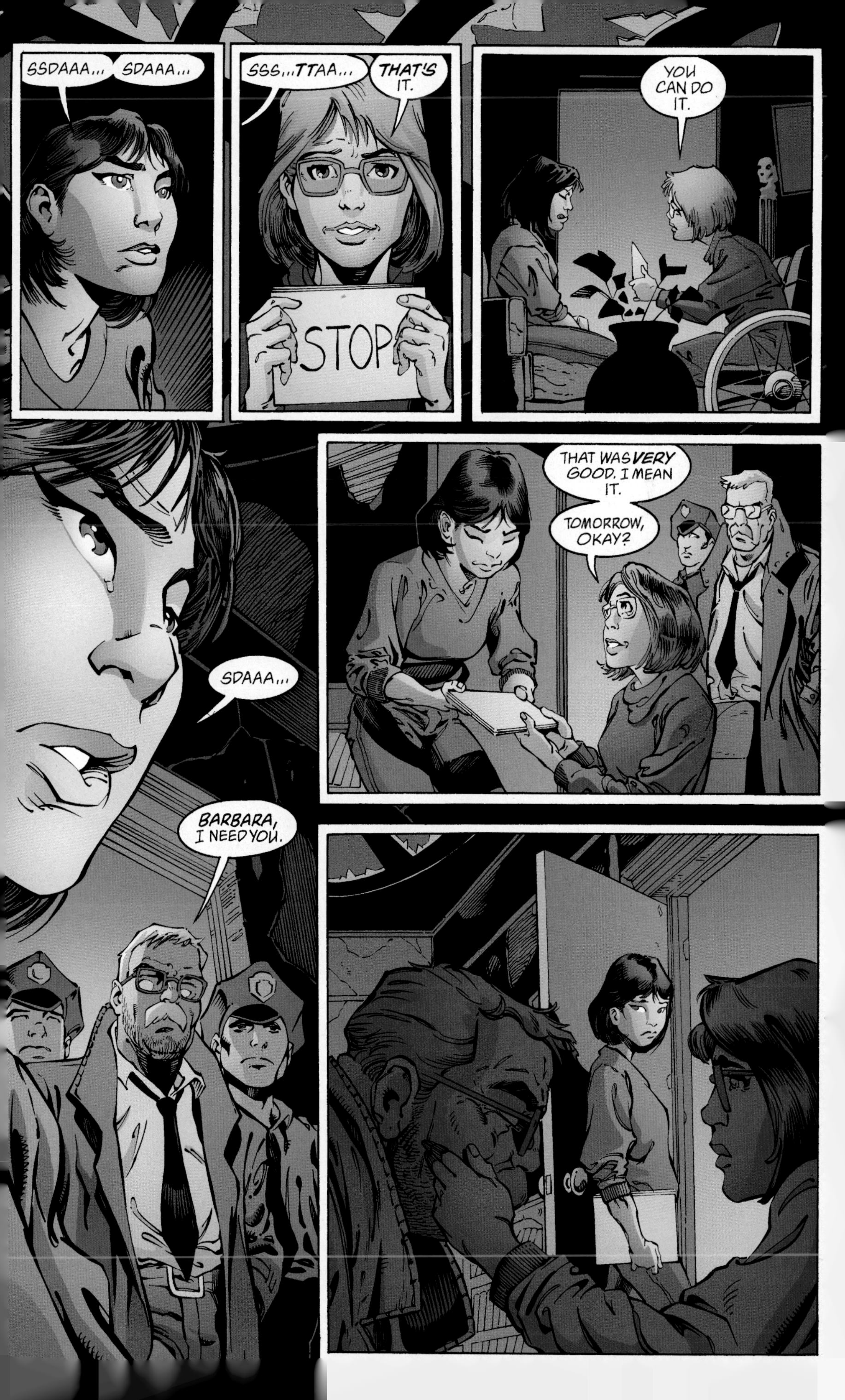
SSDAAA...
SDAAA...
SSS...TTAA...
THAT'S IT.
STOP
YOU CAN DO IT.
SDAAA...
THAT WAS VERY GOOD. I MEAN IT.
TOMORROW, OKAY?
BARBARA, I NEED YOU.

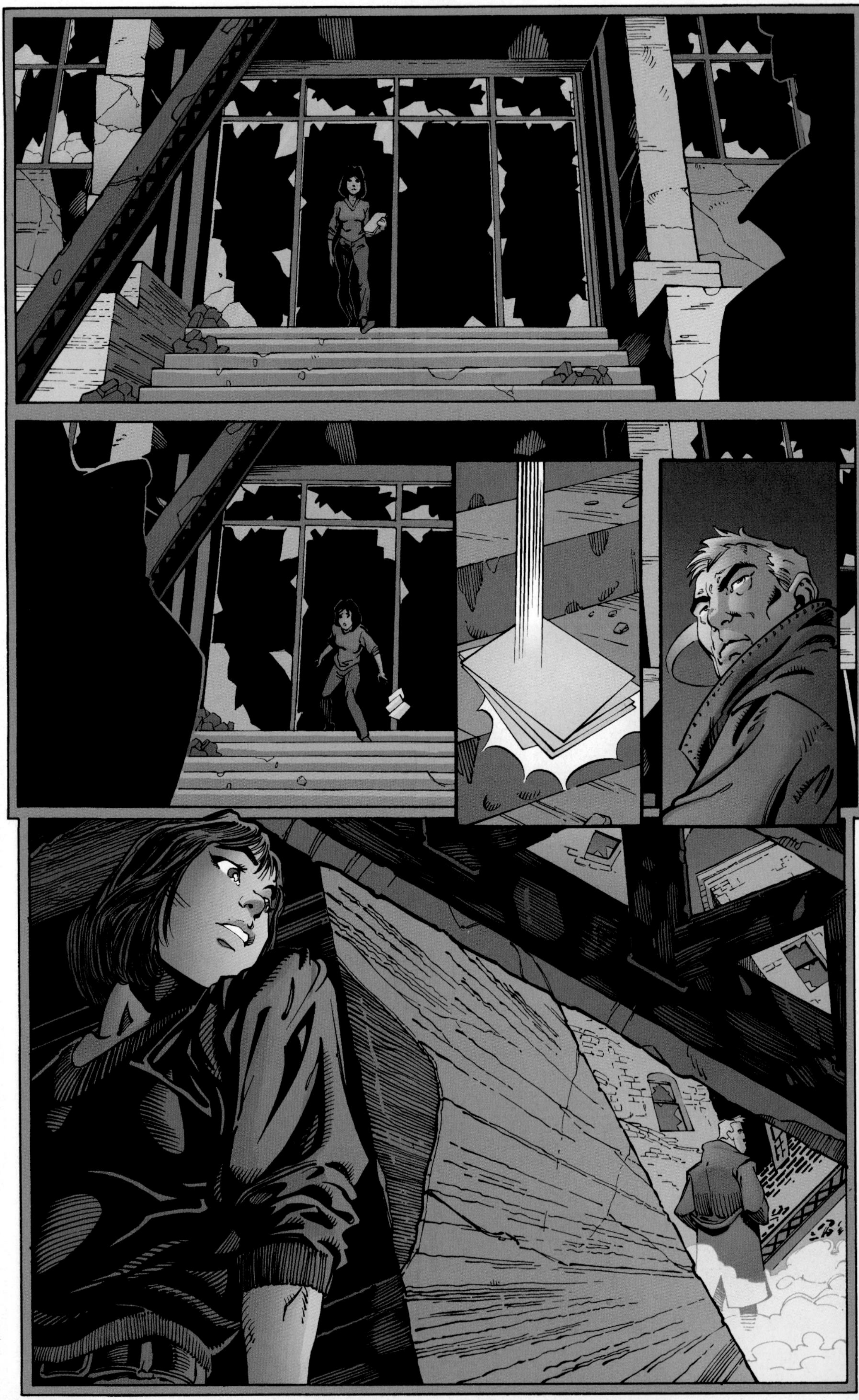

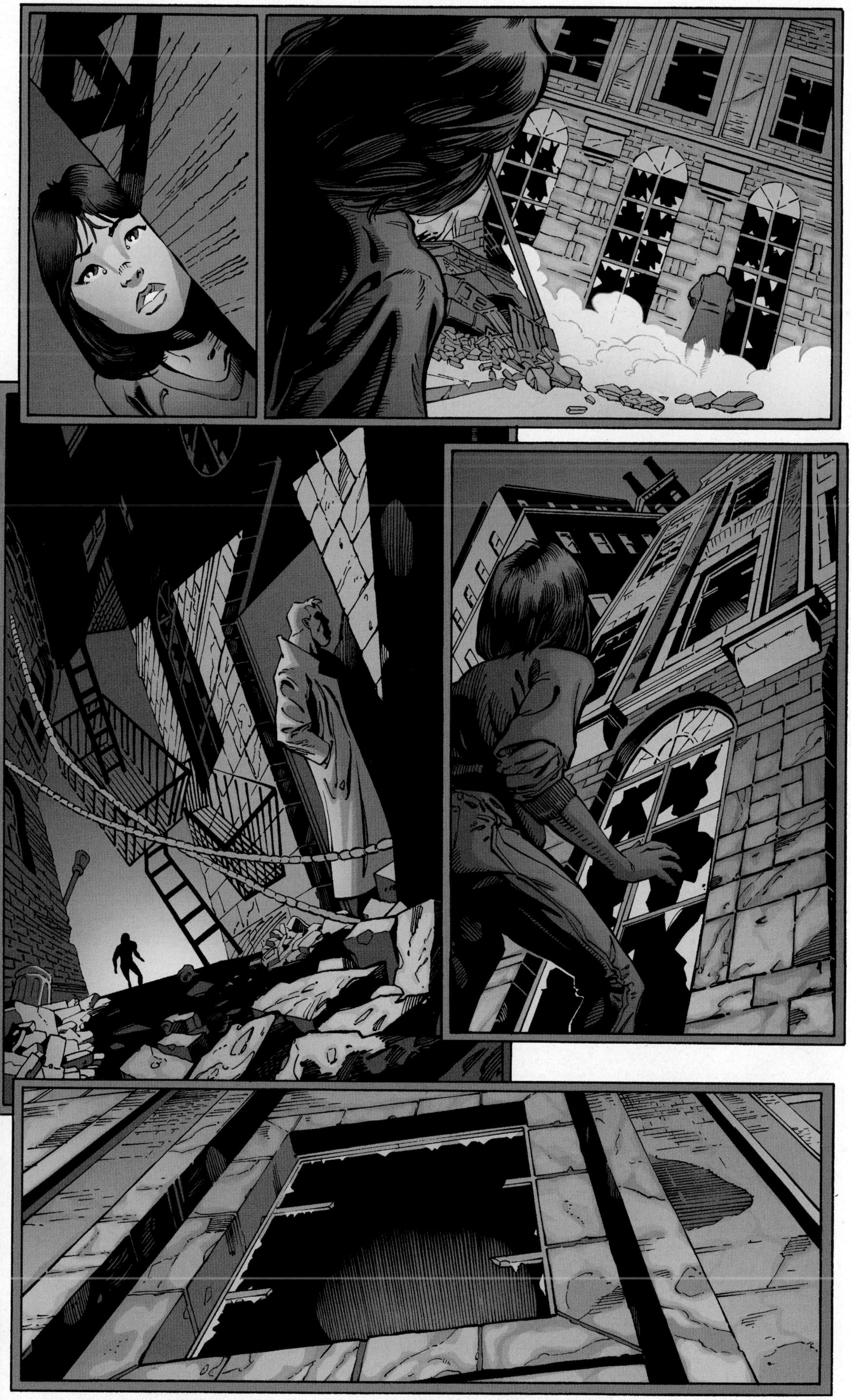

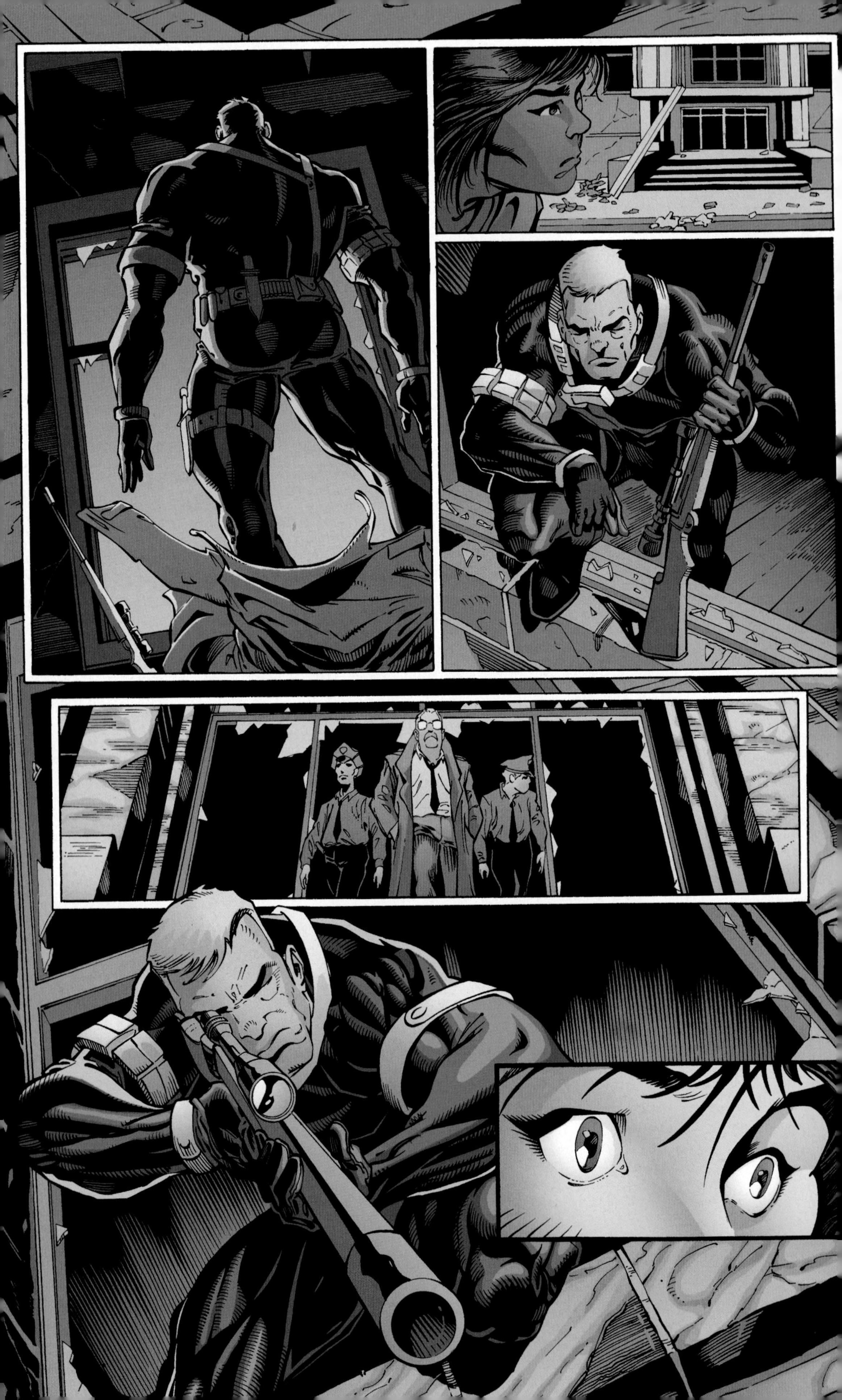

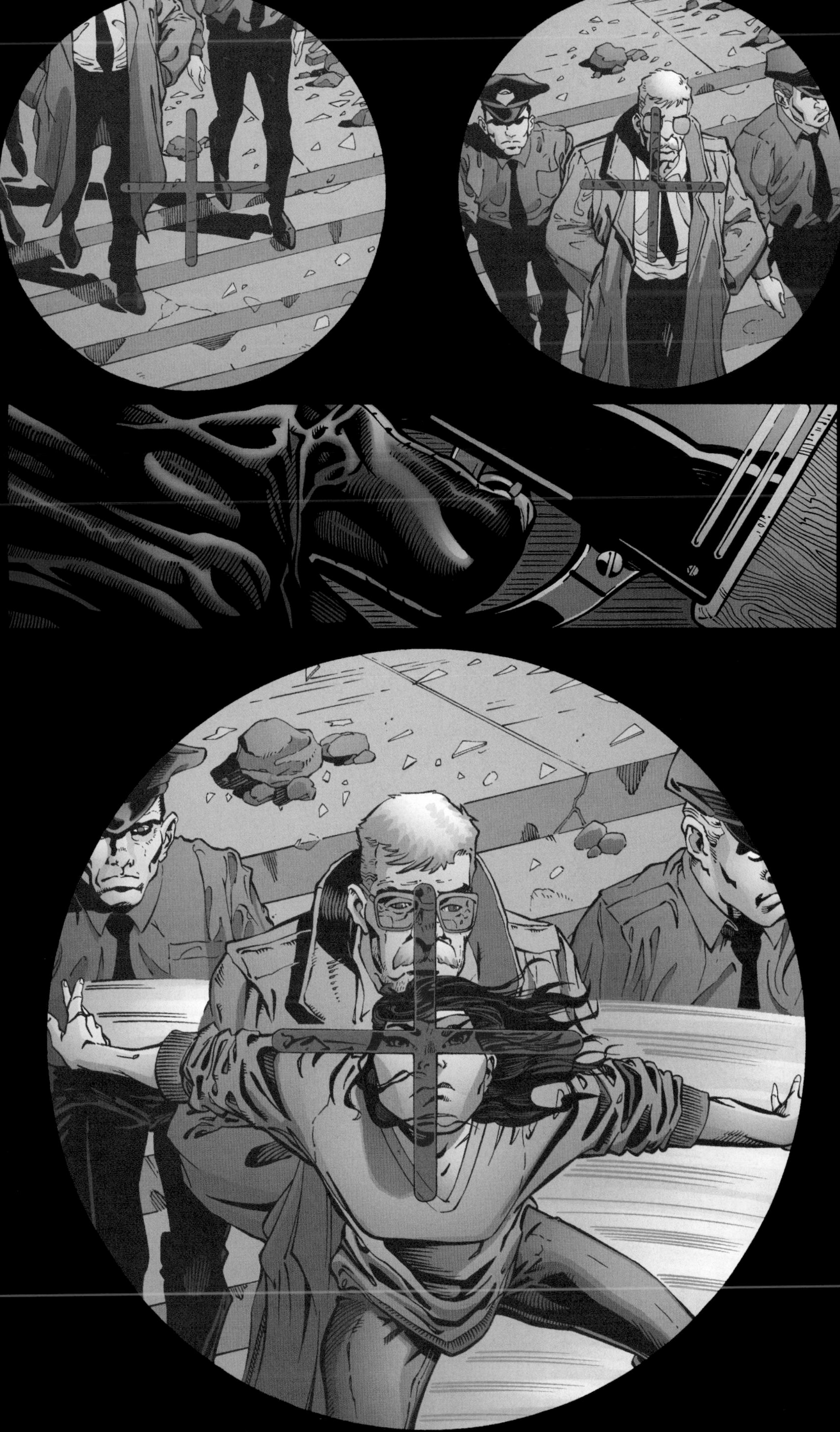

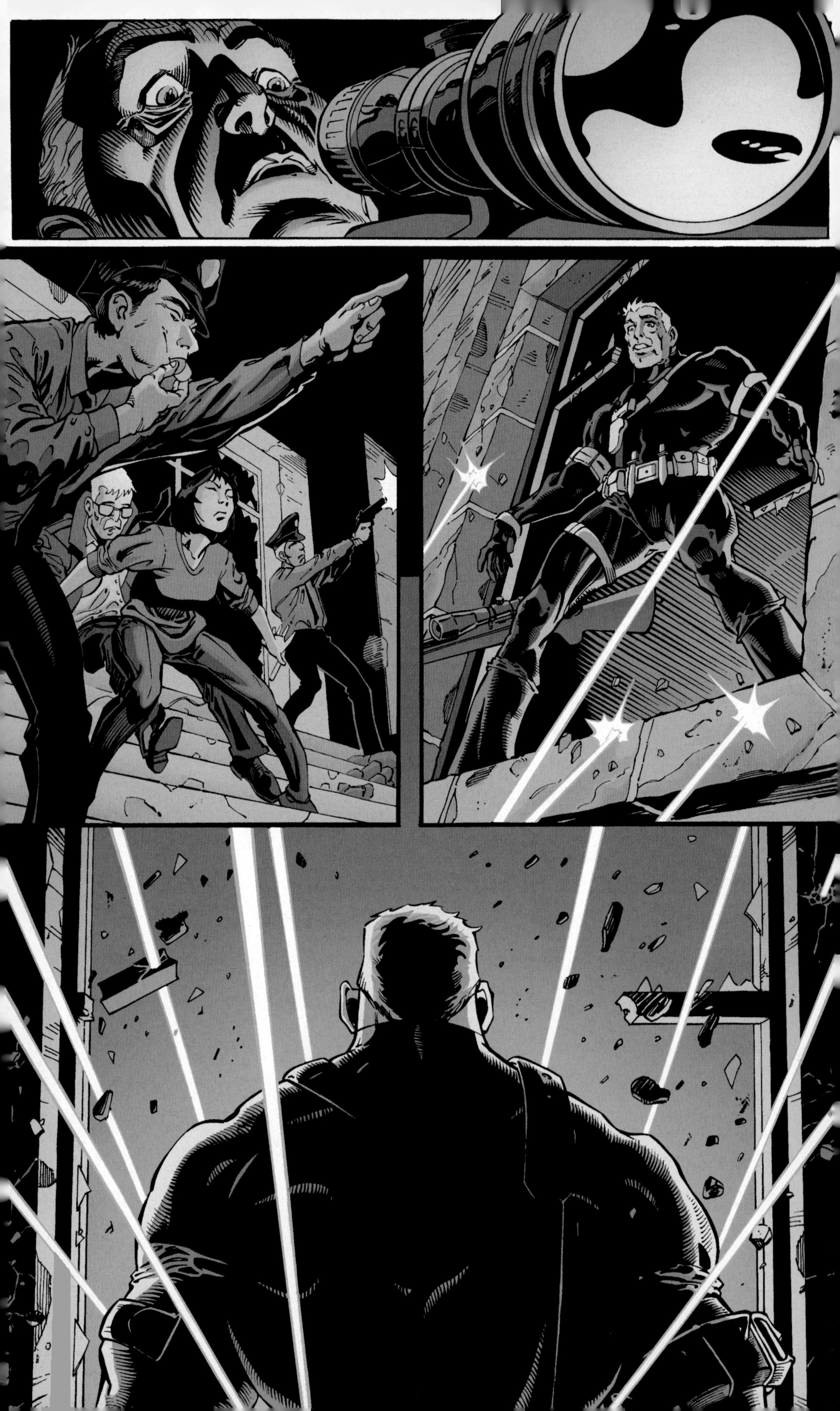

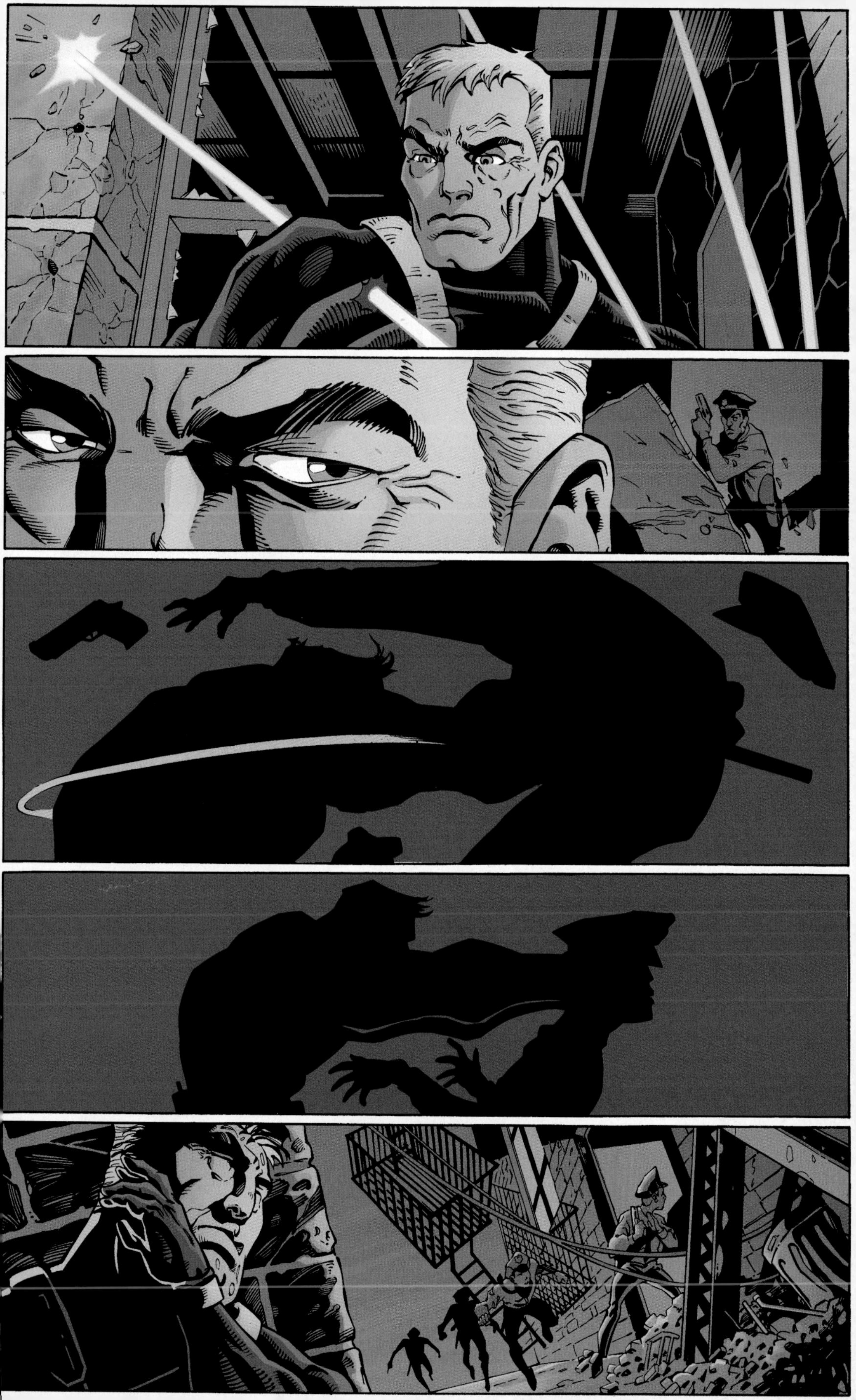

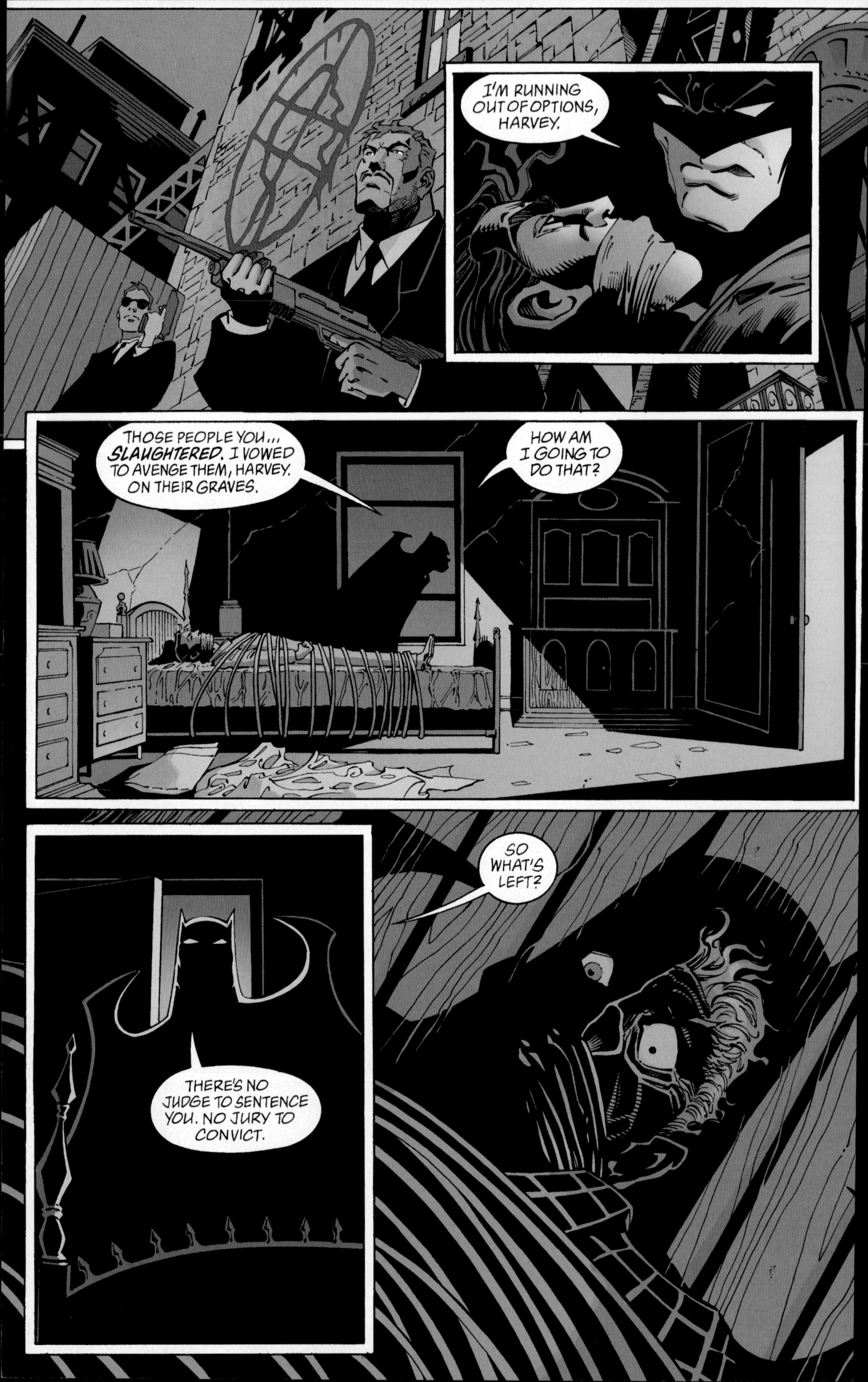
I'M RUNNING OUT OF OPTIONS, HARVEY.
THOSE PEOPLE YOU... SLAUGHTERED. I VOWED TO AVENGE THEM, HARVEY. ON THEIR GRAVES.
HOW AM I GOING TO DO THAT?
SO WHAT'S LEFT?
THERE'S NO JUDGE TO SENTENCE YOU. NO JURY TO CONVICT.

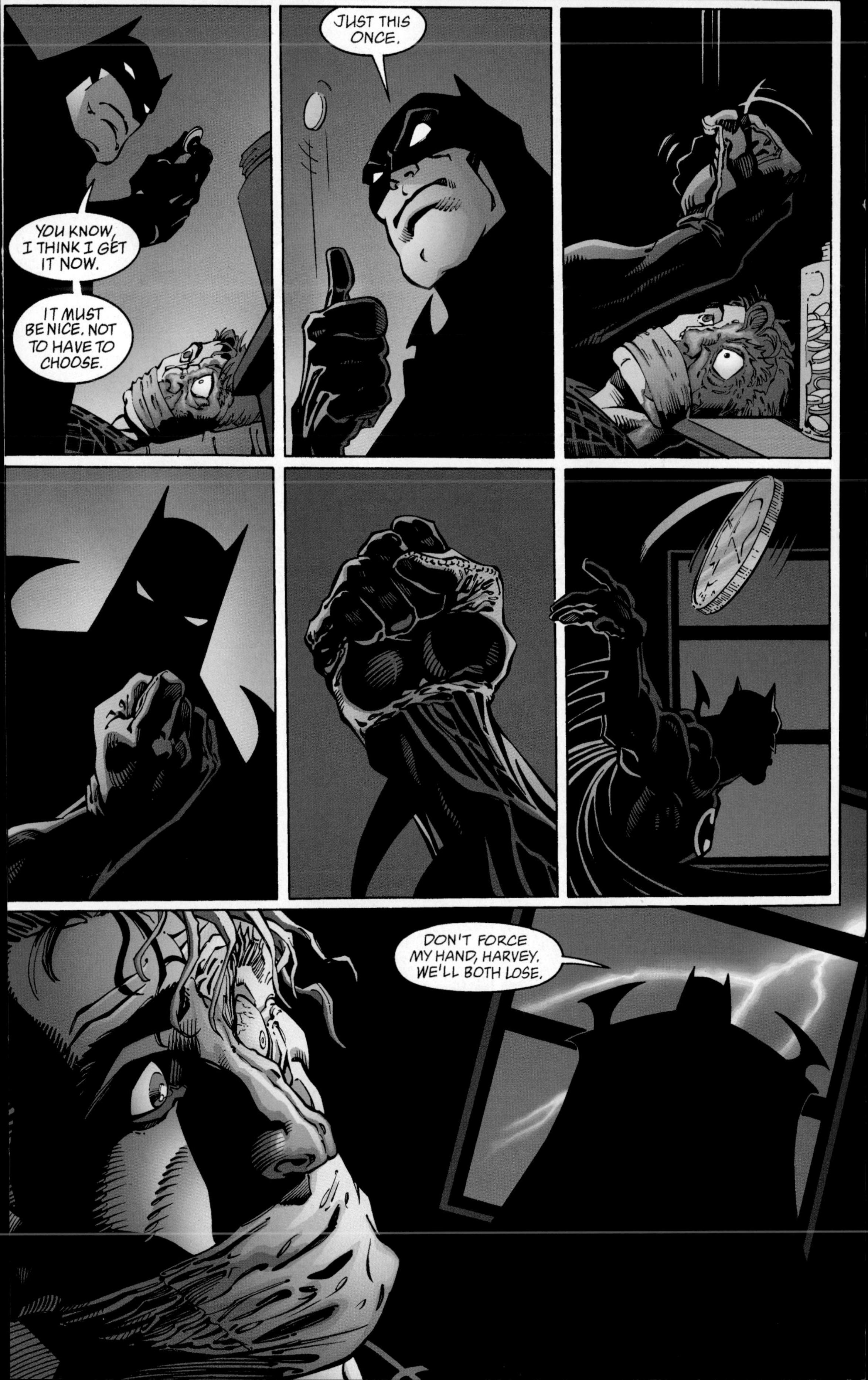
YOU KNOW, I THINK I GET IT NOW.
IT MUST BE NICE. NOT TO HAVE TO CHOOSE.
JUST THIS ONCE.
DON'T FORCE MY HAND, HARVEY. WE'LL BOTH LOSE.

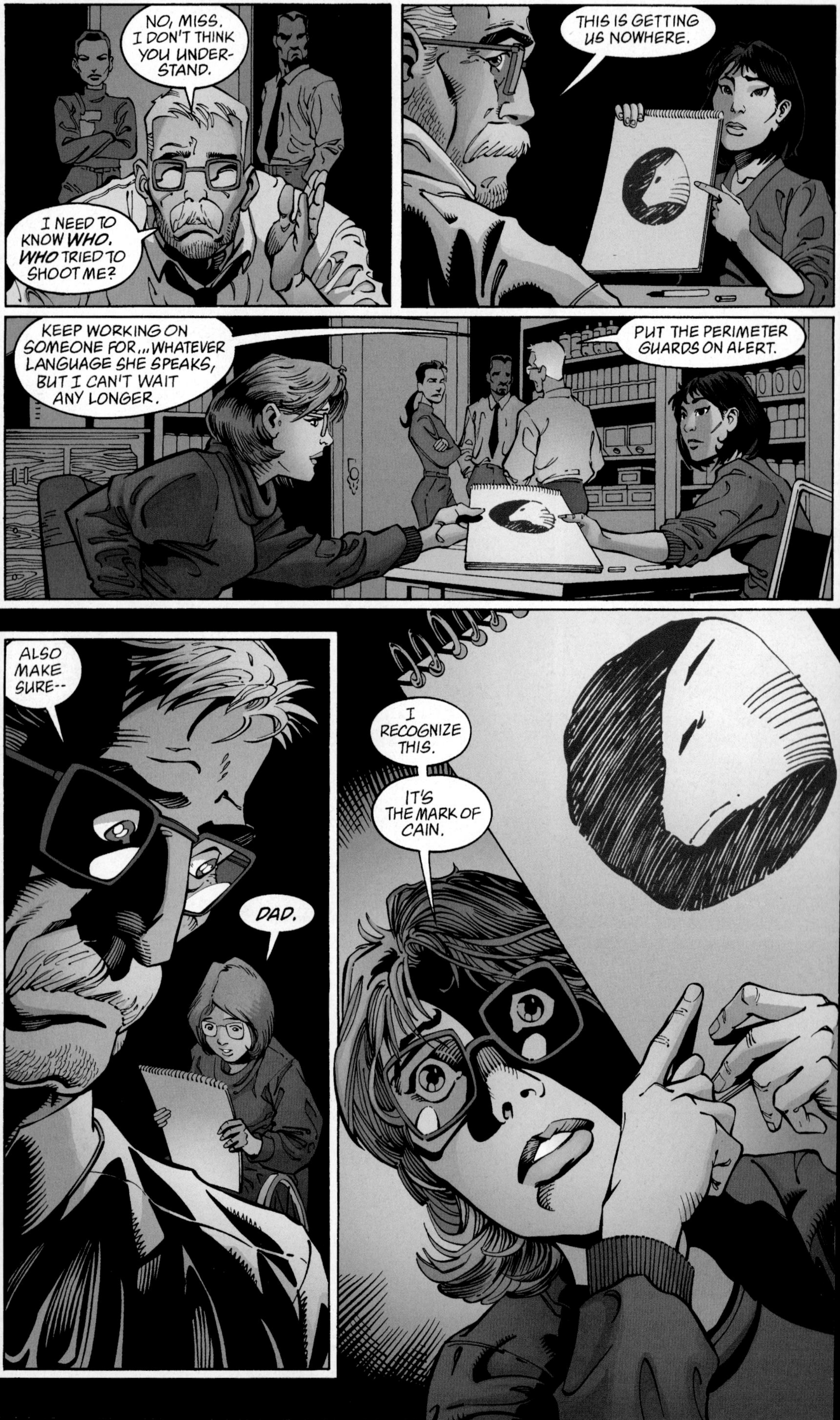
NO, MISS. I DON'T THINK YOU UNDER-STAND.
I NEED TO KNOW **WHO**. **WHO** TRIED TO SHOOT ME?
THIS IS GETTING US NOWHERE.
KEEP WORKING ON SOMEONE FOR... WHATEVER LANGUAGE SHE SPEAKS, BUT I CAN'T WAIT ANY LONGER.
PUT THE PERIMETER GUARDS ON ALERT.
ALSO MAKE SURE--
DAD.
I RECOGNIZE THIS.
IT'S THE MARK OF CAIN.

CAIN?

DAVID... CAIN?

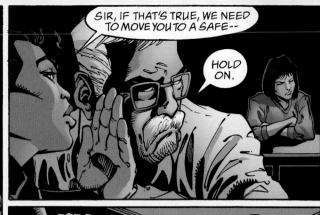

SIR, IF THAT'S TRUE, WE NEED TO MOVE YOU TO A SAFE--

HOLD ON.

CAIN SHOOTS GIRLS. HE DIDN'T SHOOT YOU. WHY?

YOU KNOW HIM. DON'T YOU.

YOU'RE HIS DAUGHTER?

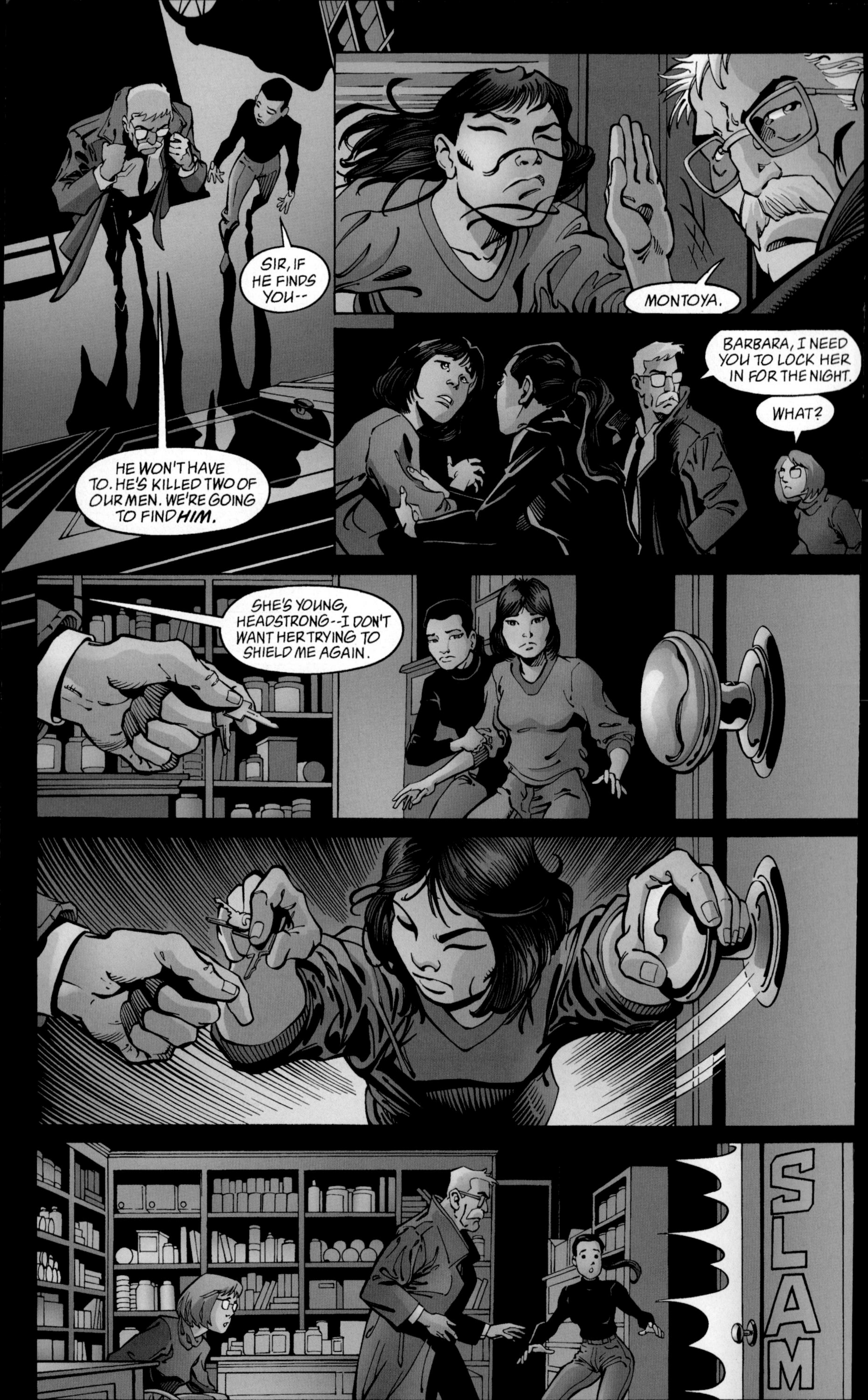
SIR, IF HE FINDS YOU--
HE WON'T HAVE TO. HE'S KILLED TWO OF OUR MEN. WE'RE GOING TO FIND HIM.
MONTOYA.
BARBARA, I NEED YOU TO LOCK HER IN FOR THE NIGHT.
WHAT?
SHE'S YOUNG, HEADSTRONG--I DON'T WANT HER TRYING TO SHIELD ME AGAIN.
SLAM

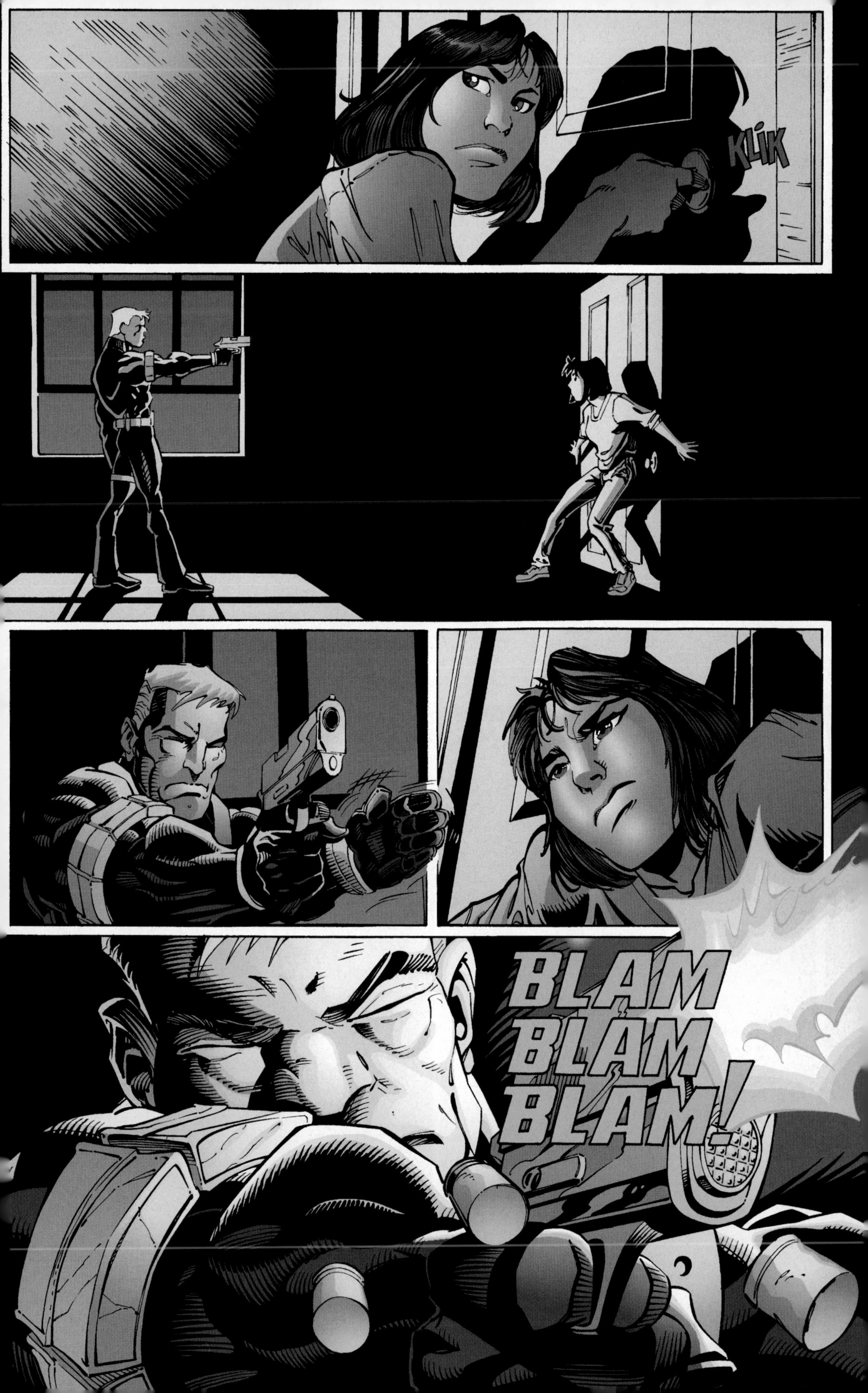
KLIK
BLAM
BLAM
BLAM!

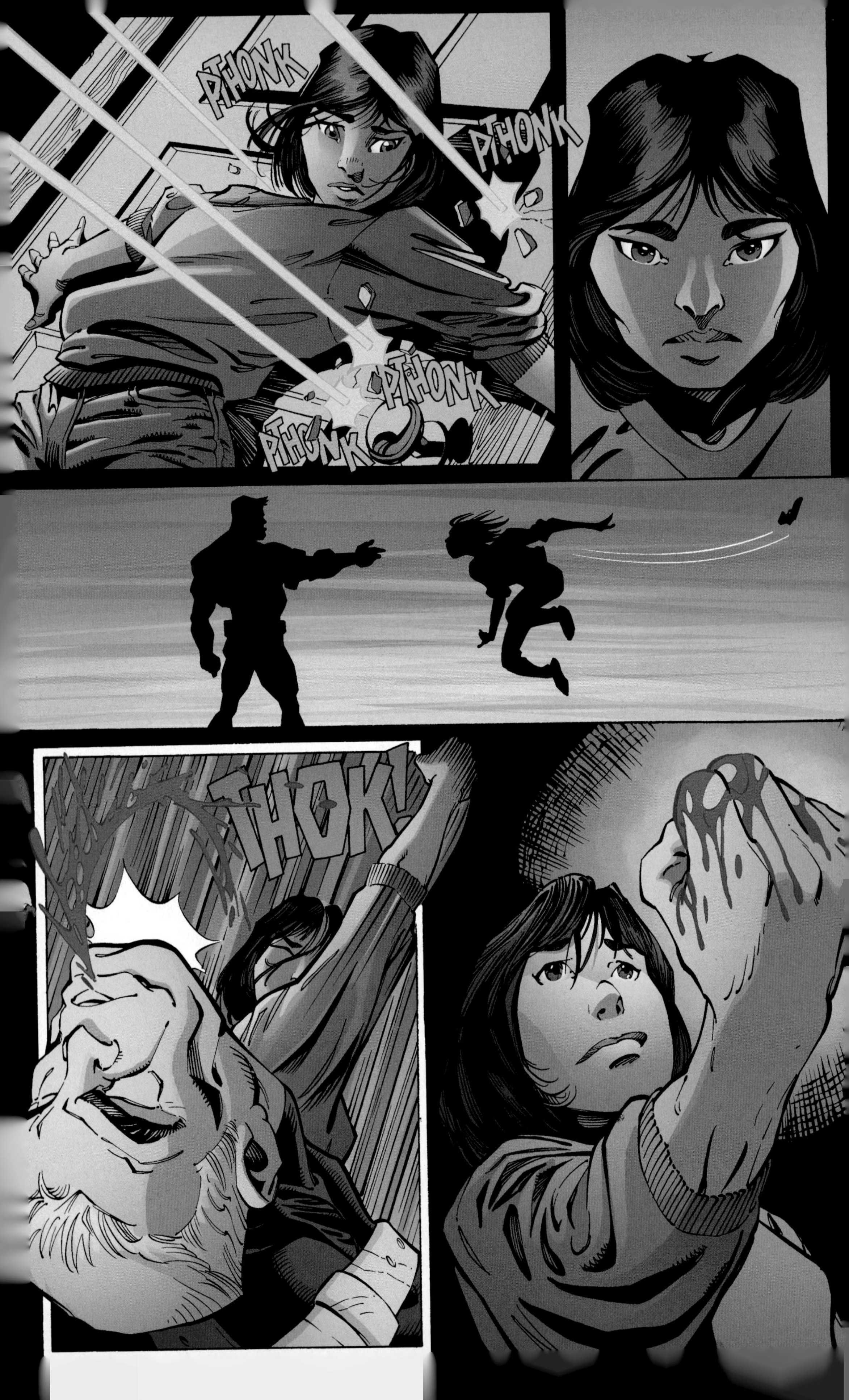
PTHONK
PTHONK
PTHONK
PTHONK
THOK!

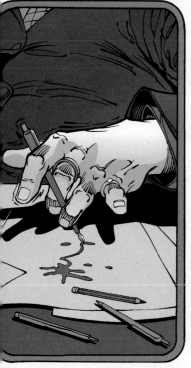
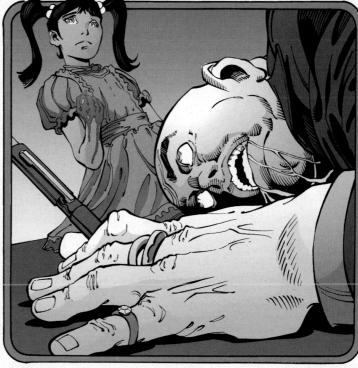

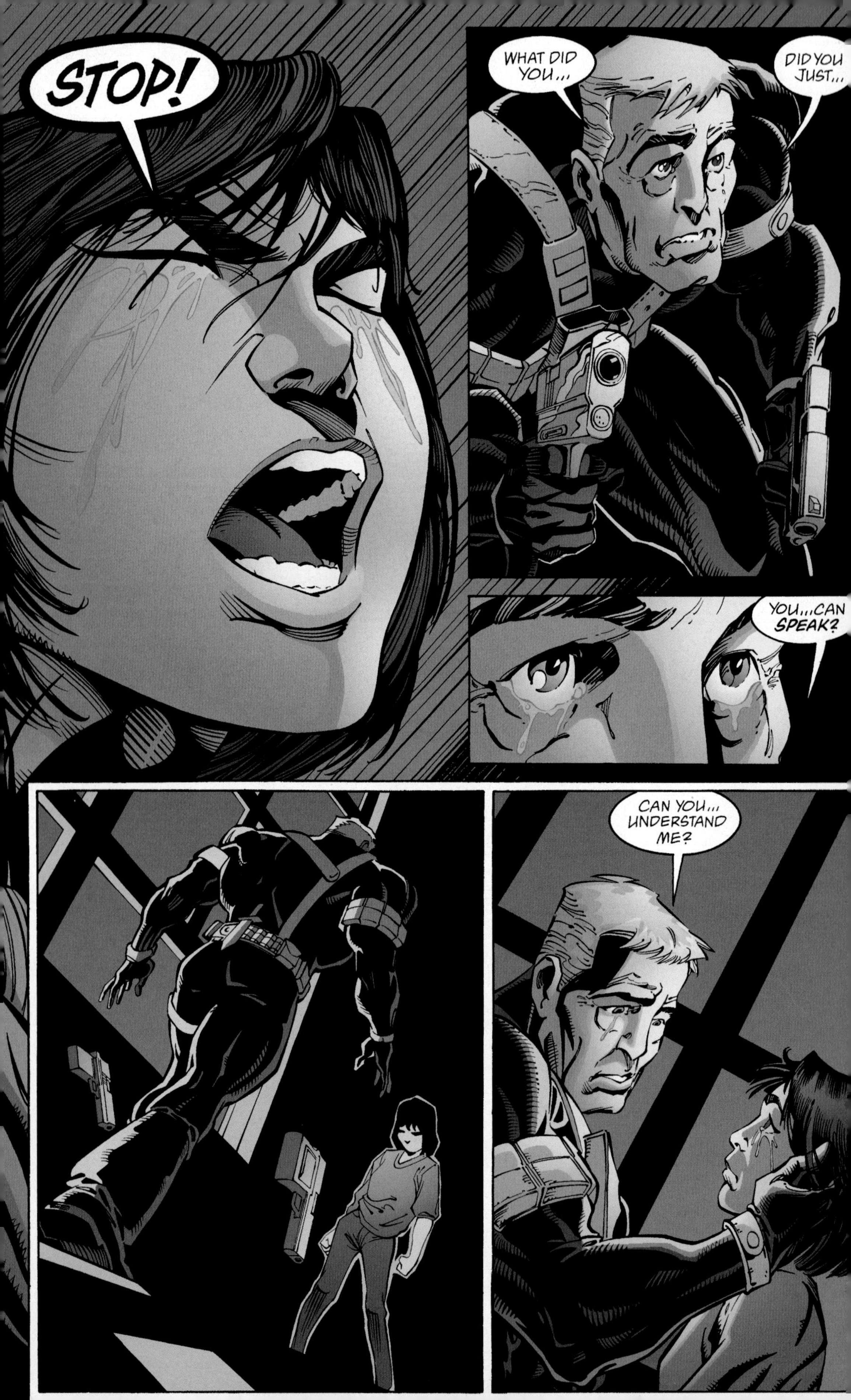
STOP!
WHAT DID YOU...
DID YOU JUST...
YOU...CAN SPEAK?
CAN YOU... UNDERSTAND ME?

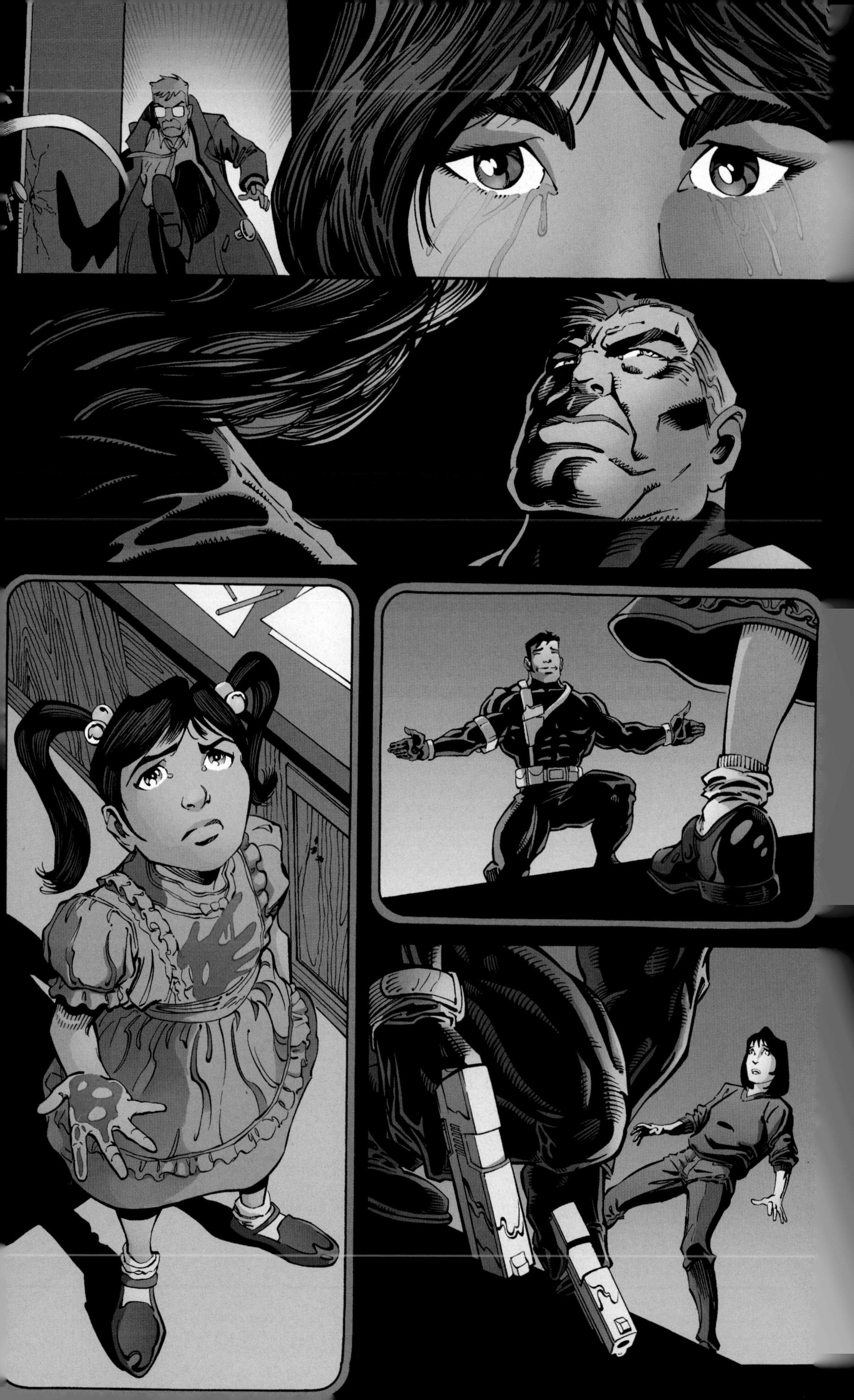

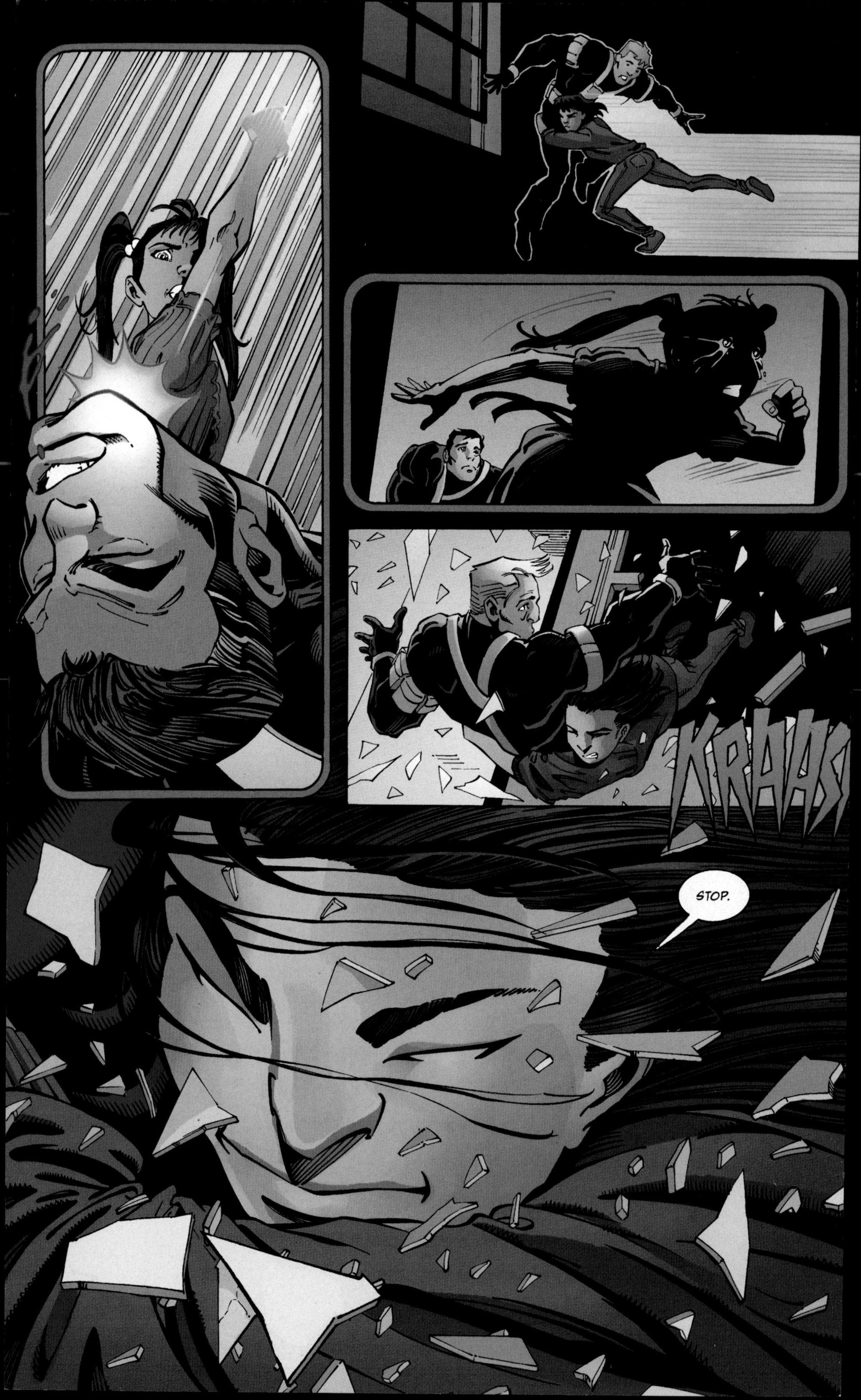
KRAAS
STOP.

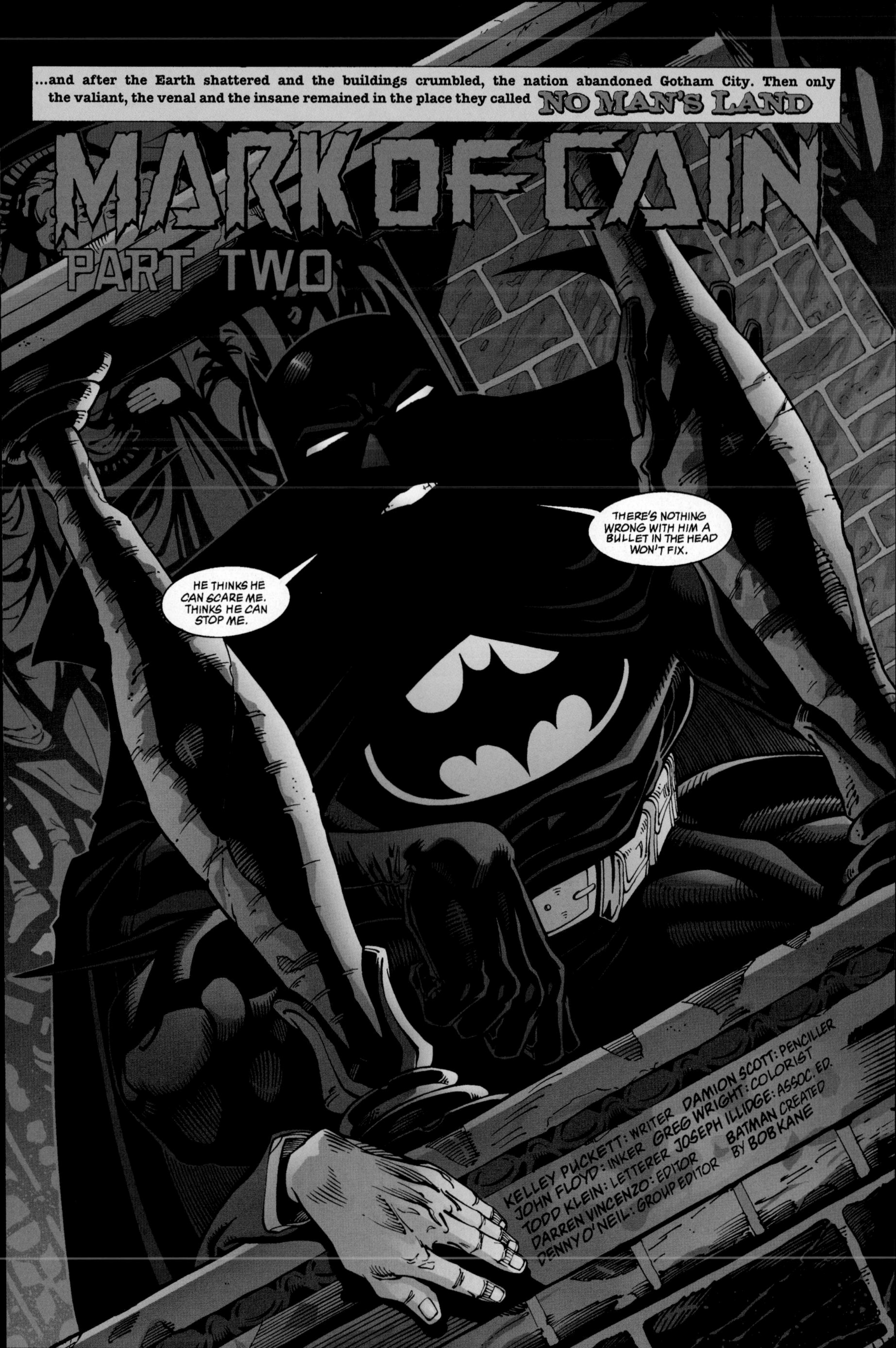

...and after the Earth shattered and the buildings crumbled, the nation abandoned Gotham City. Then only the valiant, the venal and the insane remained in the place they called NO MAN'S LAND
MARK OF CAIN
PART TWO
HE THINKS HE CAN SCARE ME. THINKS HE CAN STOP ME.
THERE'S NOTHING WRONG WITH HIM A BULLET IN THE HEAD WON'T FIX.
KELLEY PUCKETT: WRITER DAMION SCOTT: PENCILLER
JOHN FLOYD: INKER GREG WRIGHT: COLORIST
TODD KLEIN: LETTERER JOSEPH ILLIDGE: ASSOC. ED.
DARREN VINCENZO: EDITOR BATMAN CREATED
DENNY O'NEIL: GROUP EDITOR BY BOB KANE

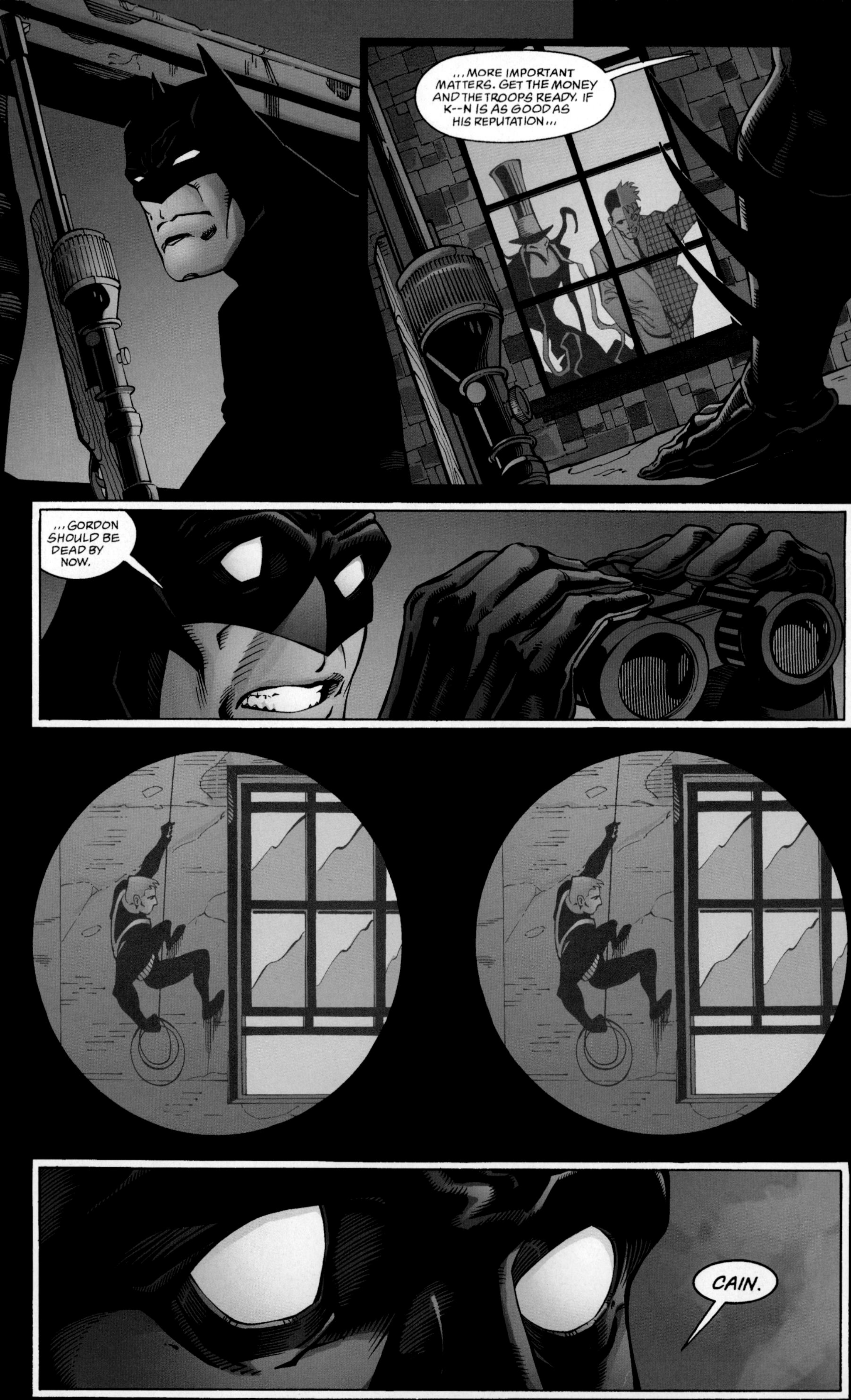
...MORE IMPORTANT MATTERS. GET THE MONEY AND THE TROOPS READY. IF K--N IS AS GOOD AS HIS REPUTATION...
...GORDON SHOULD BE DEAD BY NOW.
CAIN.

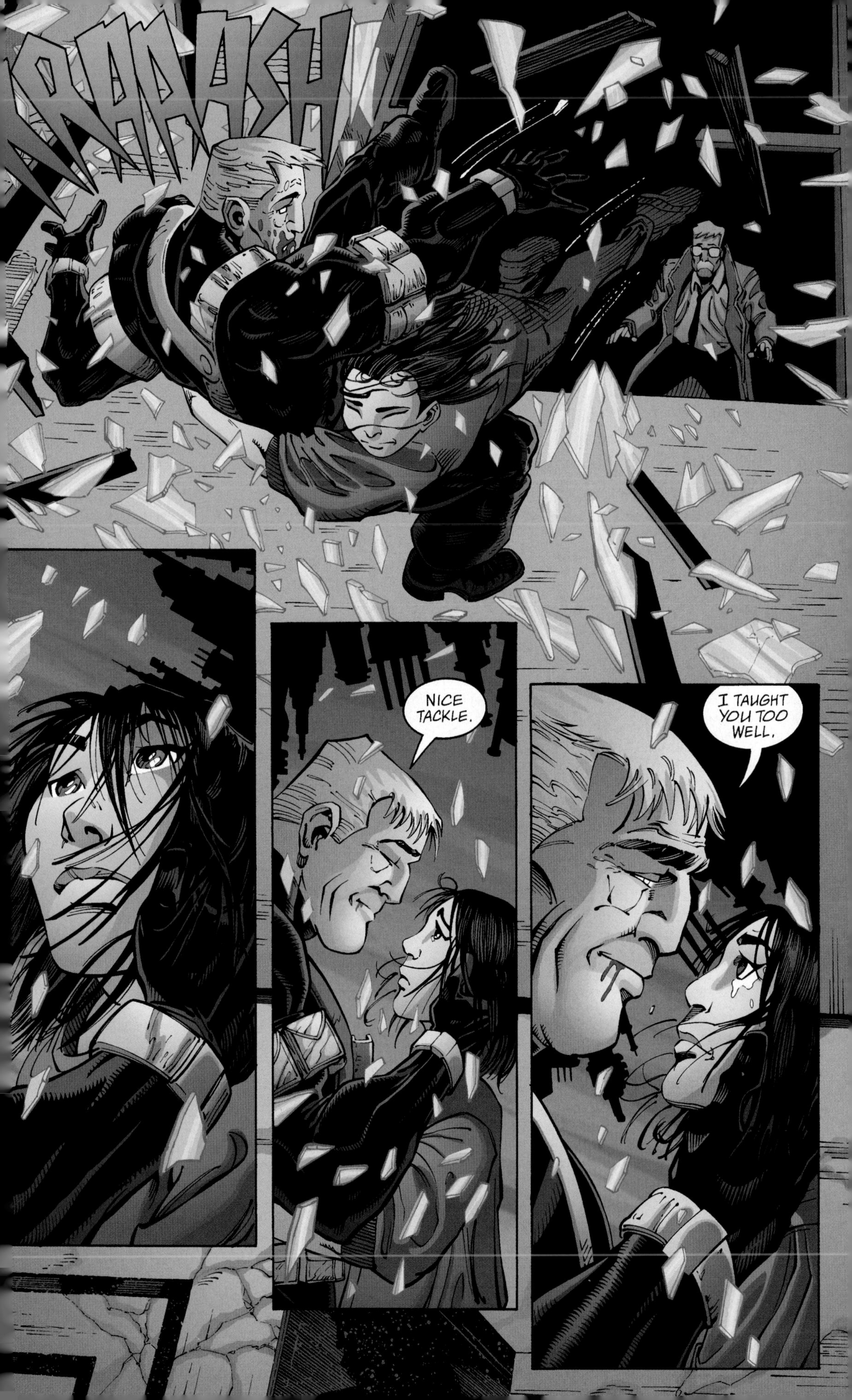
KRAAASH
NICE TACKLE.
I TAUGHT YOU TOO WELL.

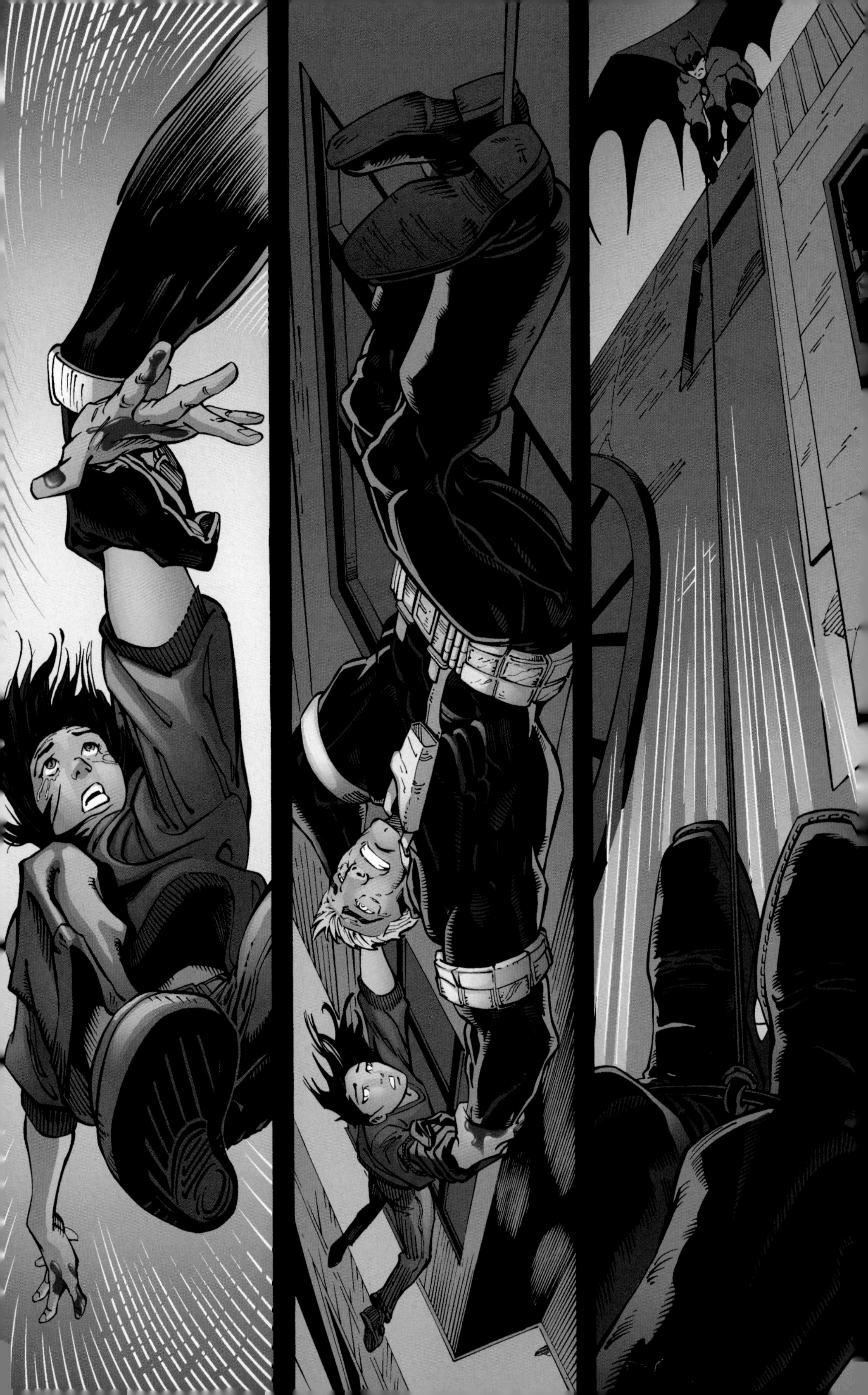

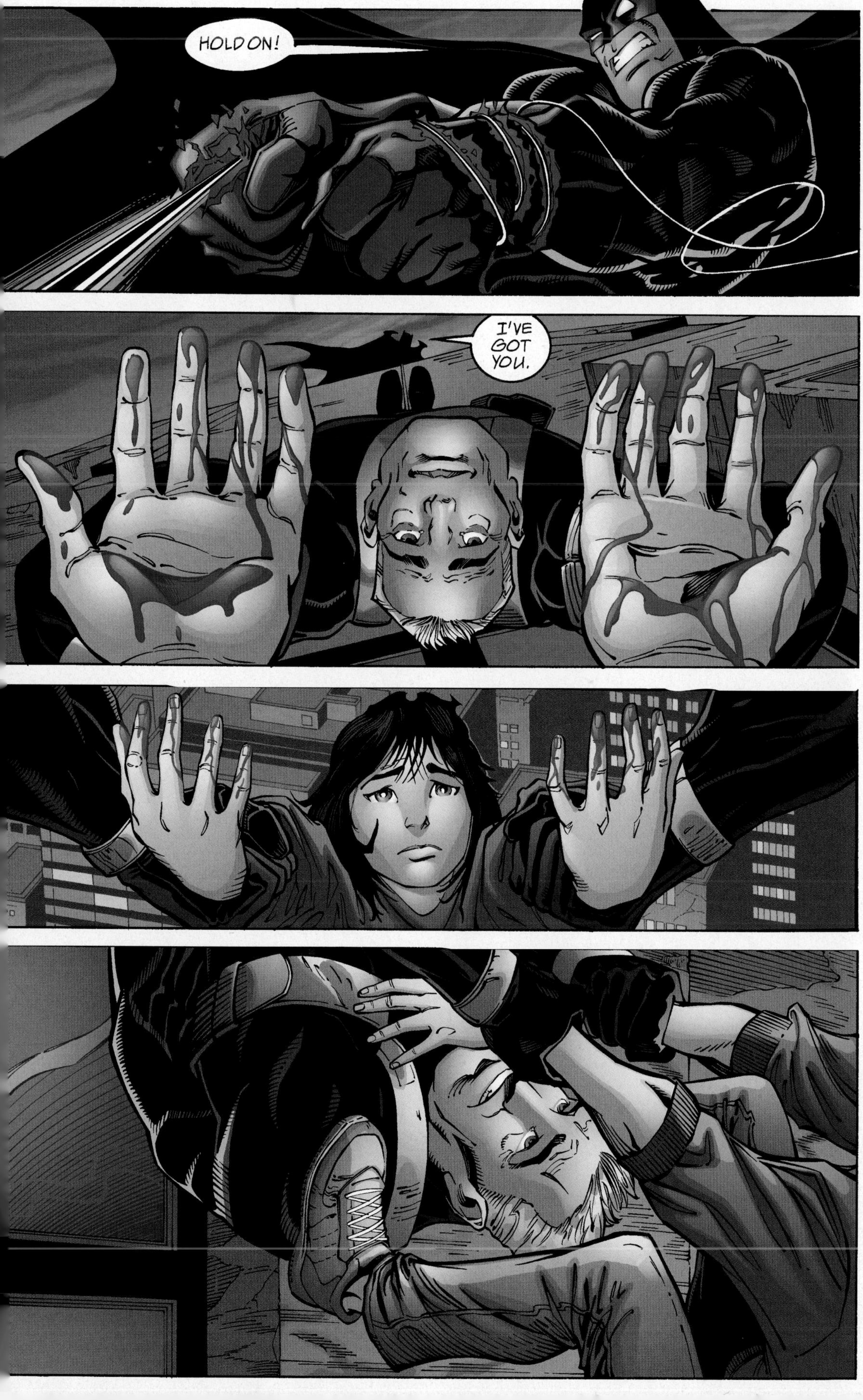
HOLD ON!
I'VE GOT YOU.

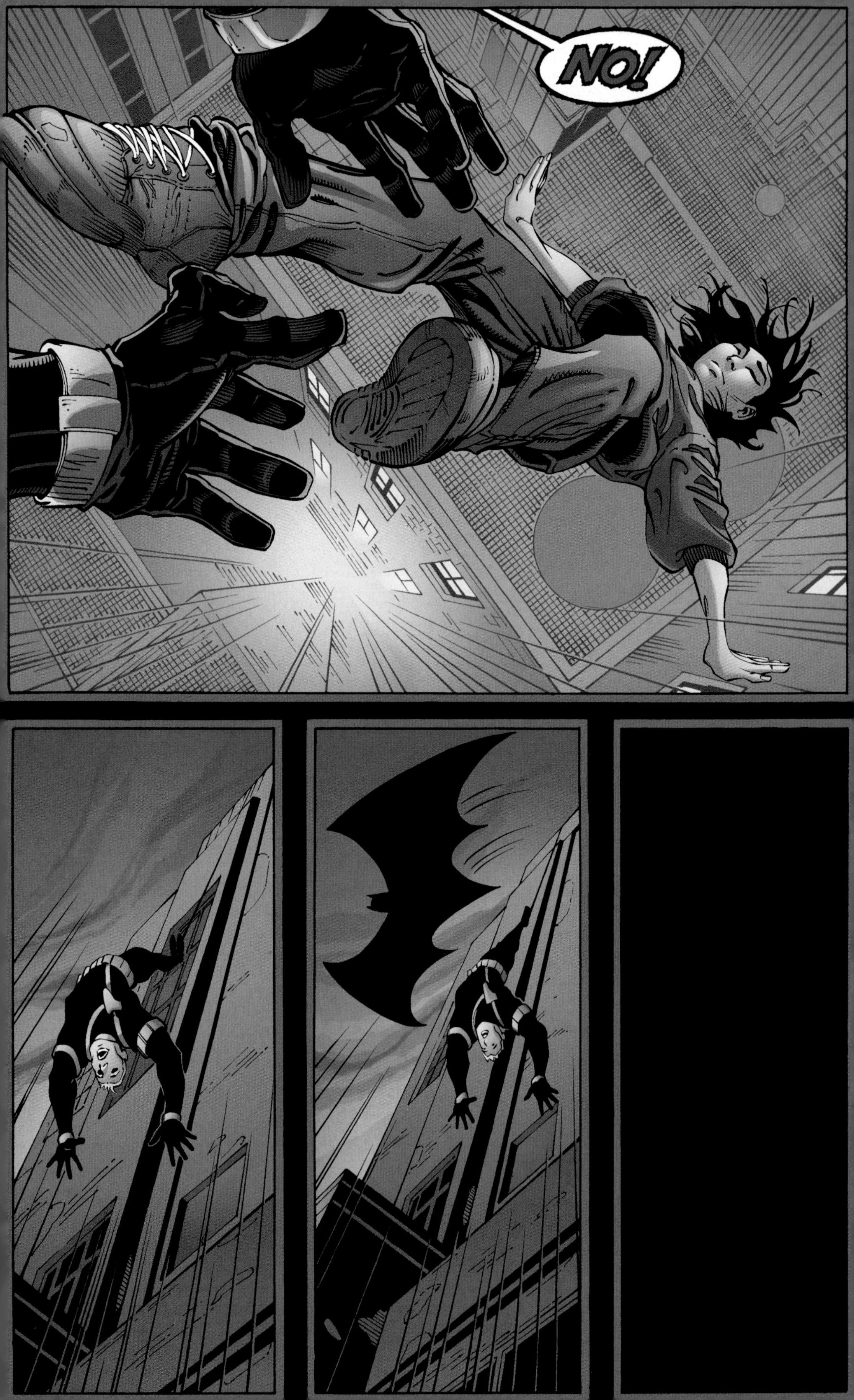
NO!

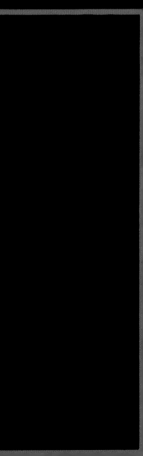

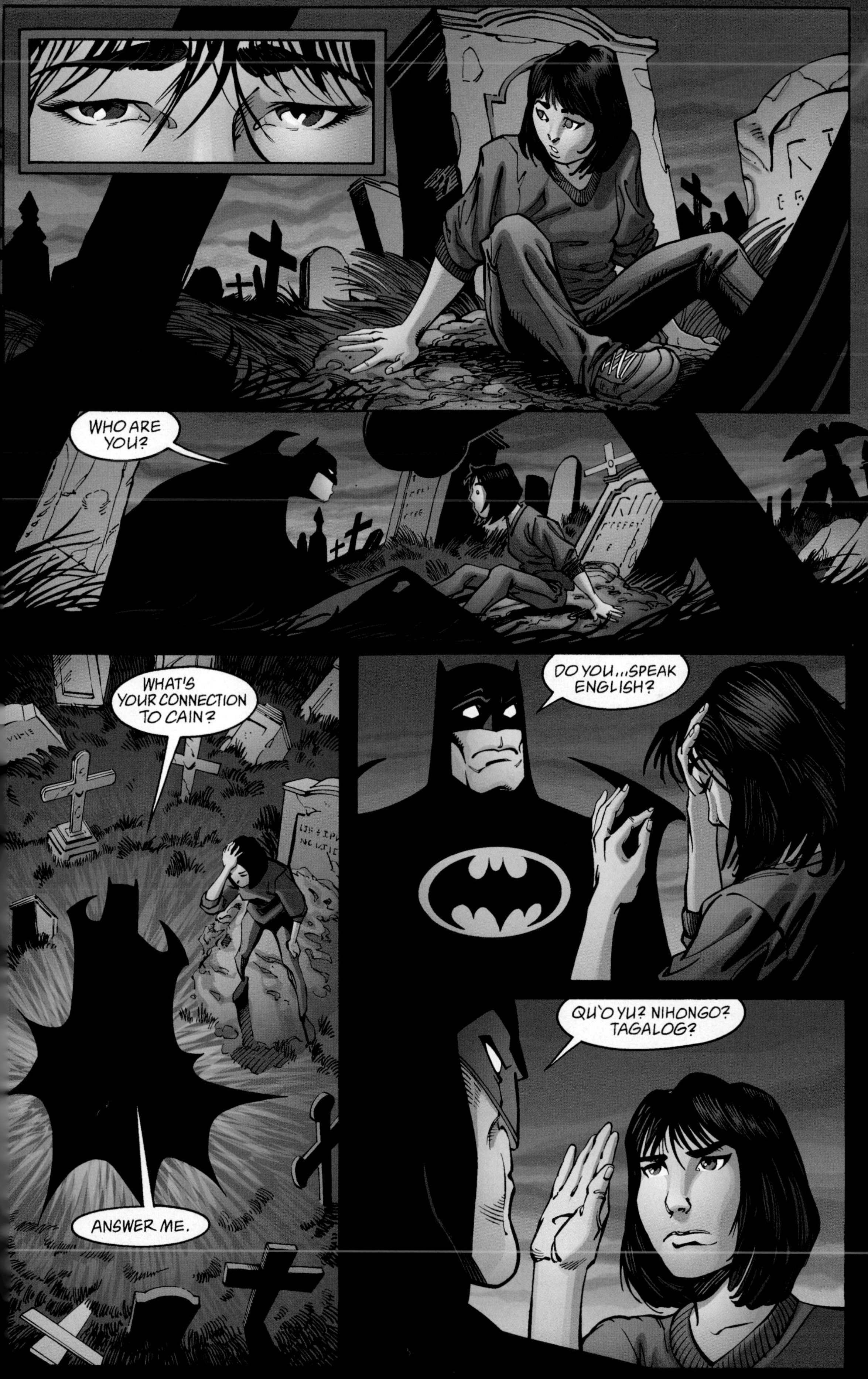
WHO ARE YOU?
WHAT'S YOUR CONNECTION TO CAIN?
ANSWER ME.
DO YOU...SPEAK ENGLISH?
QU'O YU? NIHONGO? TAGALOG?

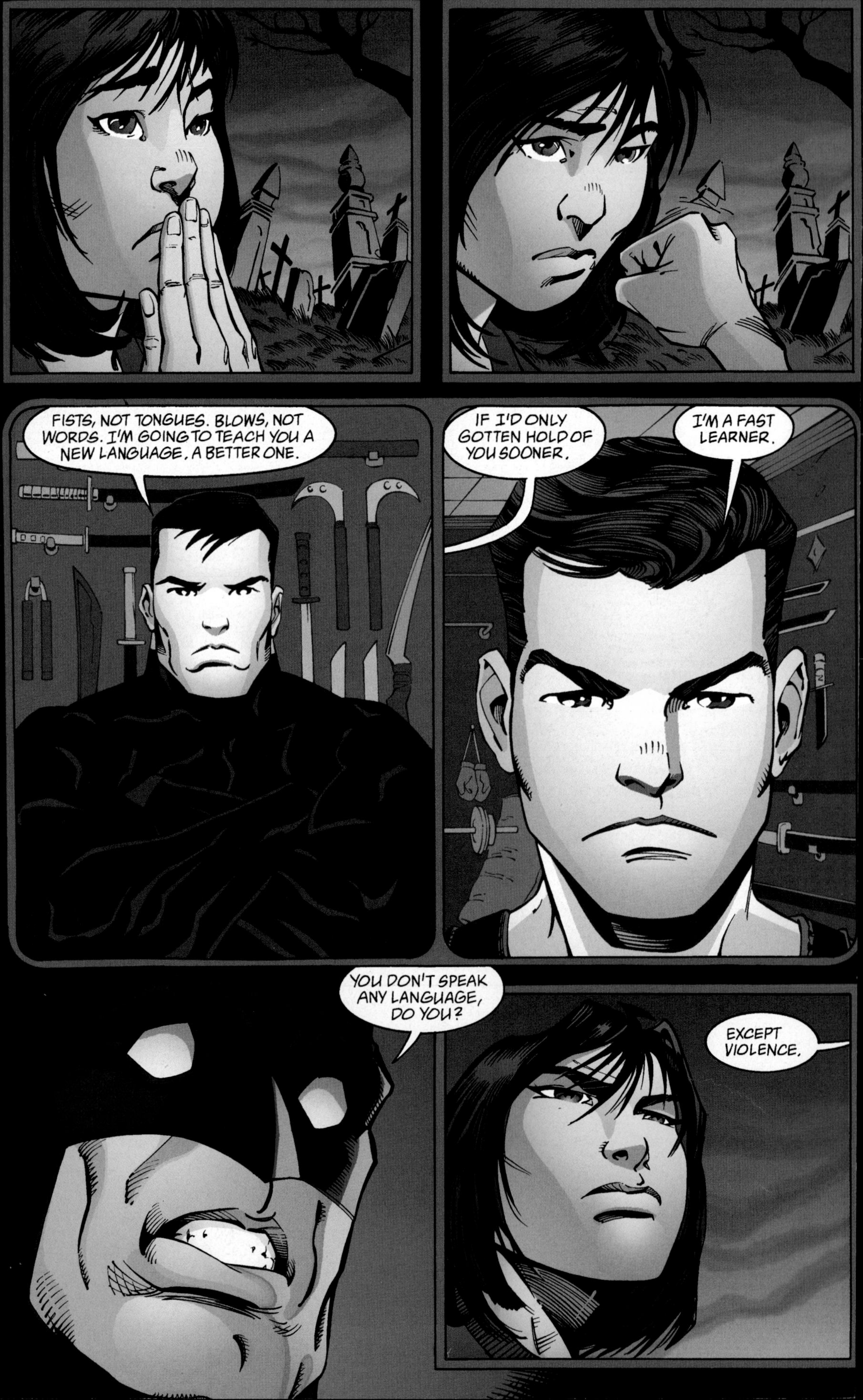
FISTS, NOT TONGUES. BLOWS, NOT WORDS. I'M GOING TO TEACH YOU A NEW LANGUAGE, A BETTER ONE.
IF I'D ONLY GOTTEN HOLD OF YOU SOONER.
I'M A FAST LEARNER.
YOU DON'T SPEAK ANY LANGUAGE, DO YOU?
EXCEPT VIOLENCE.

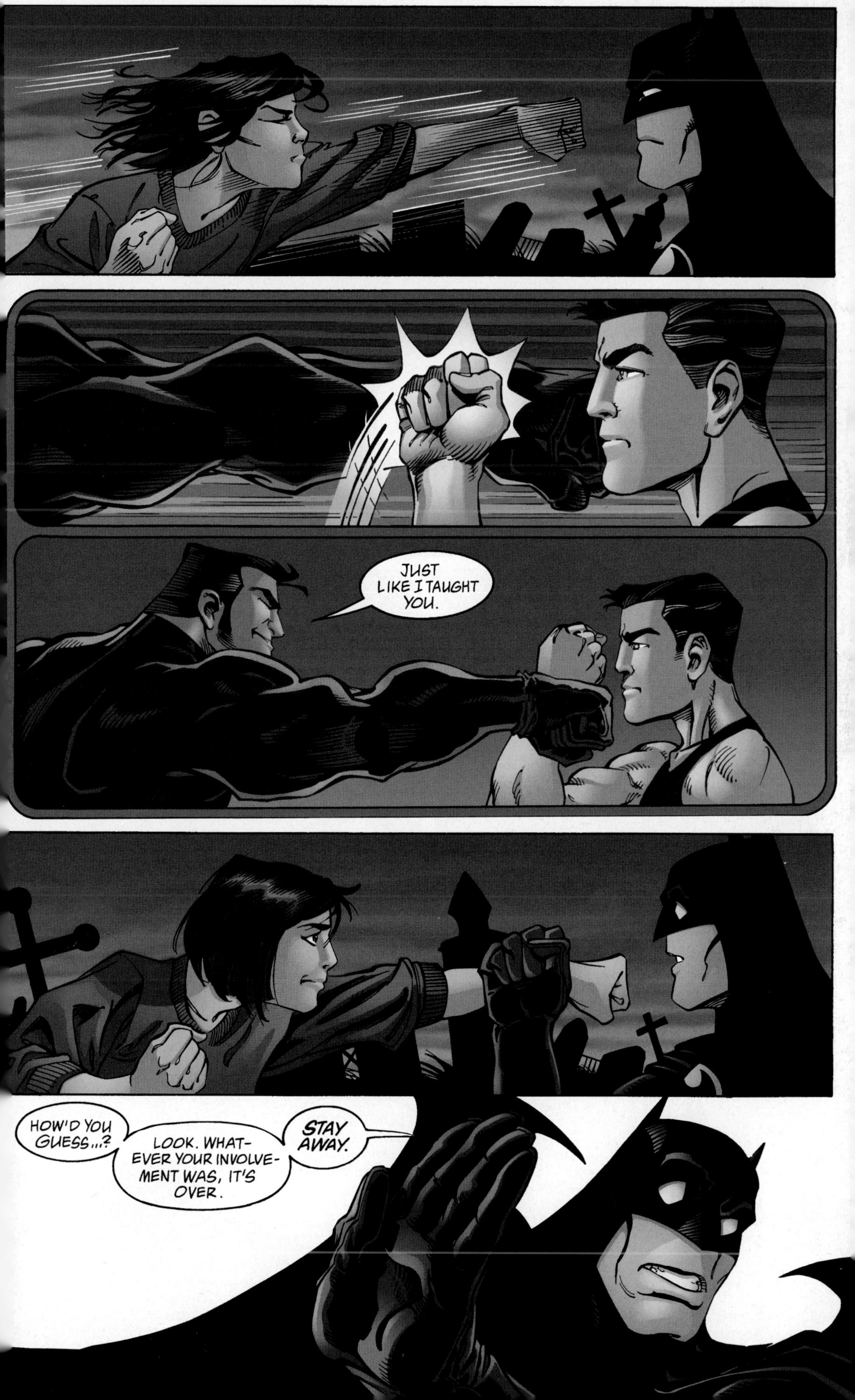
JUST LIKE I TAUGHT YOU.
HOW'D YOU GUESS...?
STAY AWAY.
LOOK. WHATEVER YOUR INVOLVEMENT WAS, IT'S OVER.

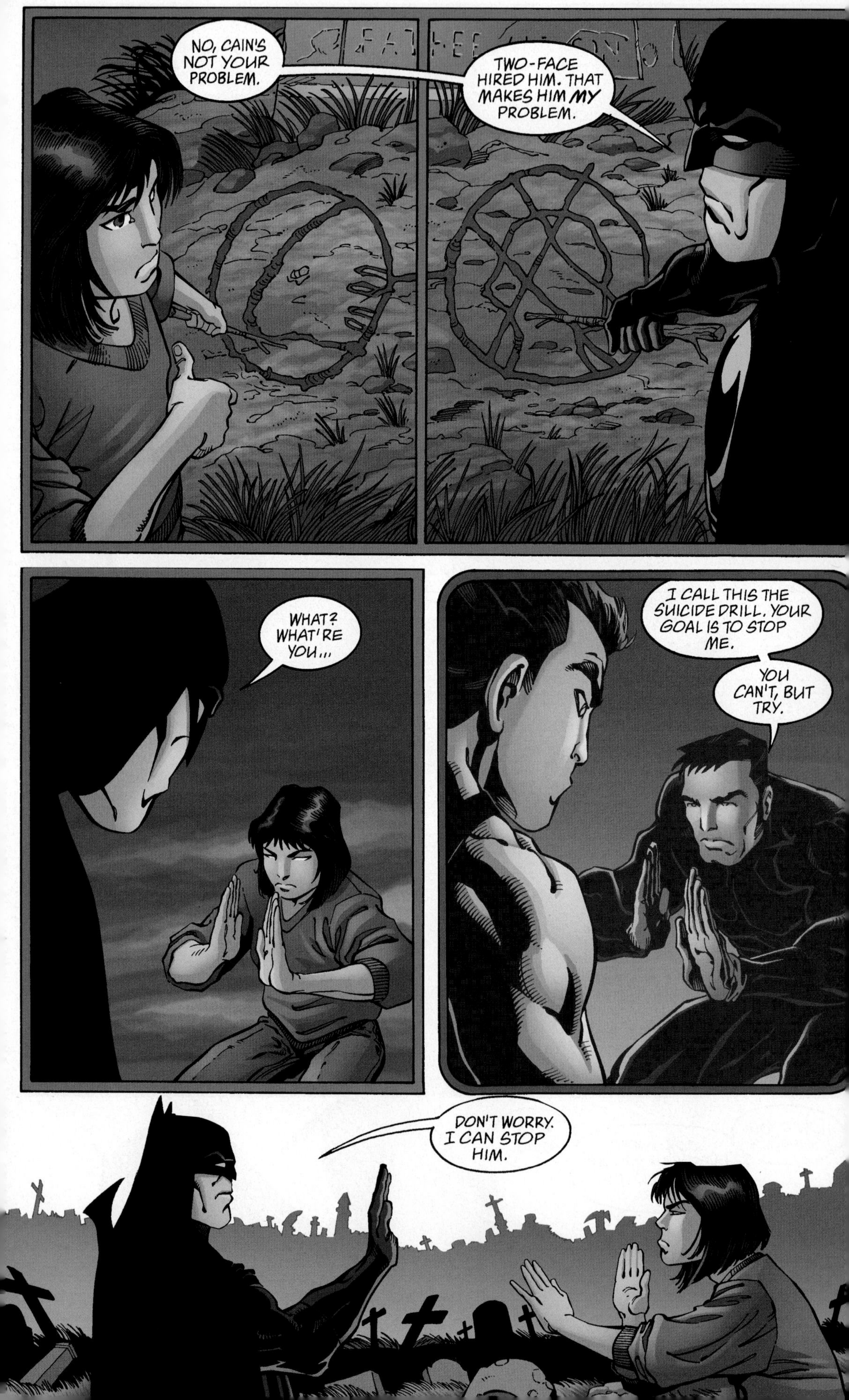
NO, CAIN'S NOT YOUR PROBLEM.
TWO-FACE HIRED HIM. THAT MAKES HIM MY PROBLEM.
WHAT? WHAT'RE YOU...
I CALL THIS THE SUICIDE DRILL. YOUR GOAL IS TO STOP ME.
YOU CAN'T, BUT TRY.
DON'T WORRY. I CAN STOP HIM.

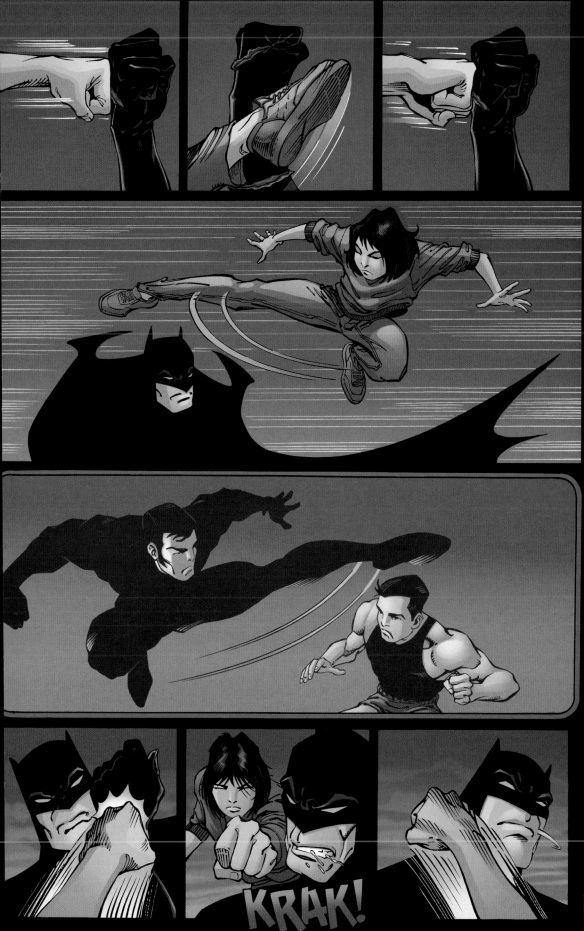

KRAK!

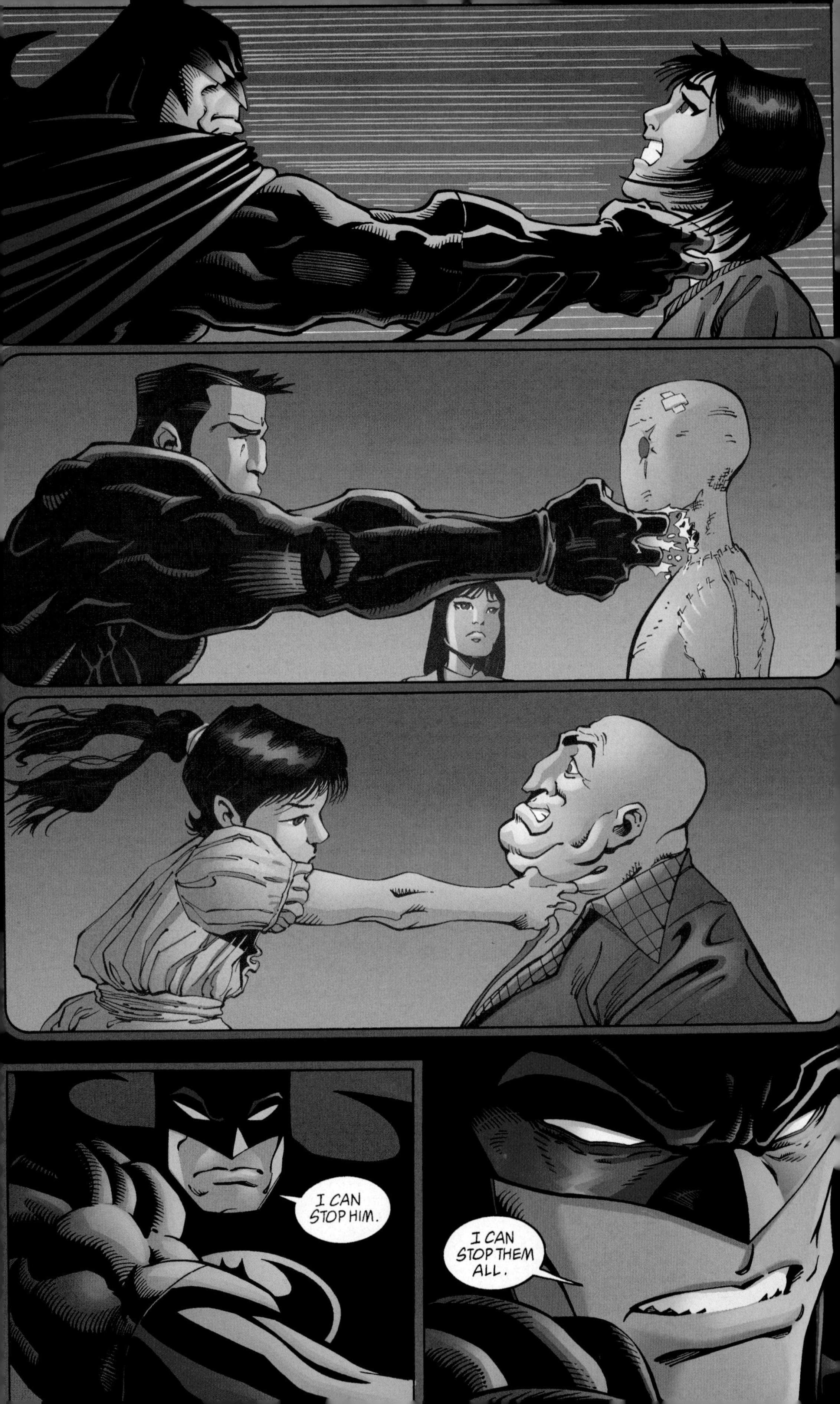

I CAN STOP HIM.
I CAN STOP THEM ALL.

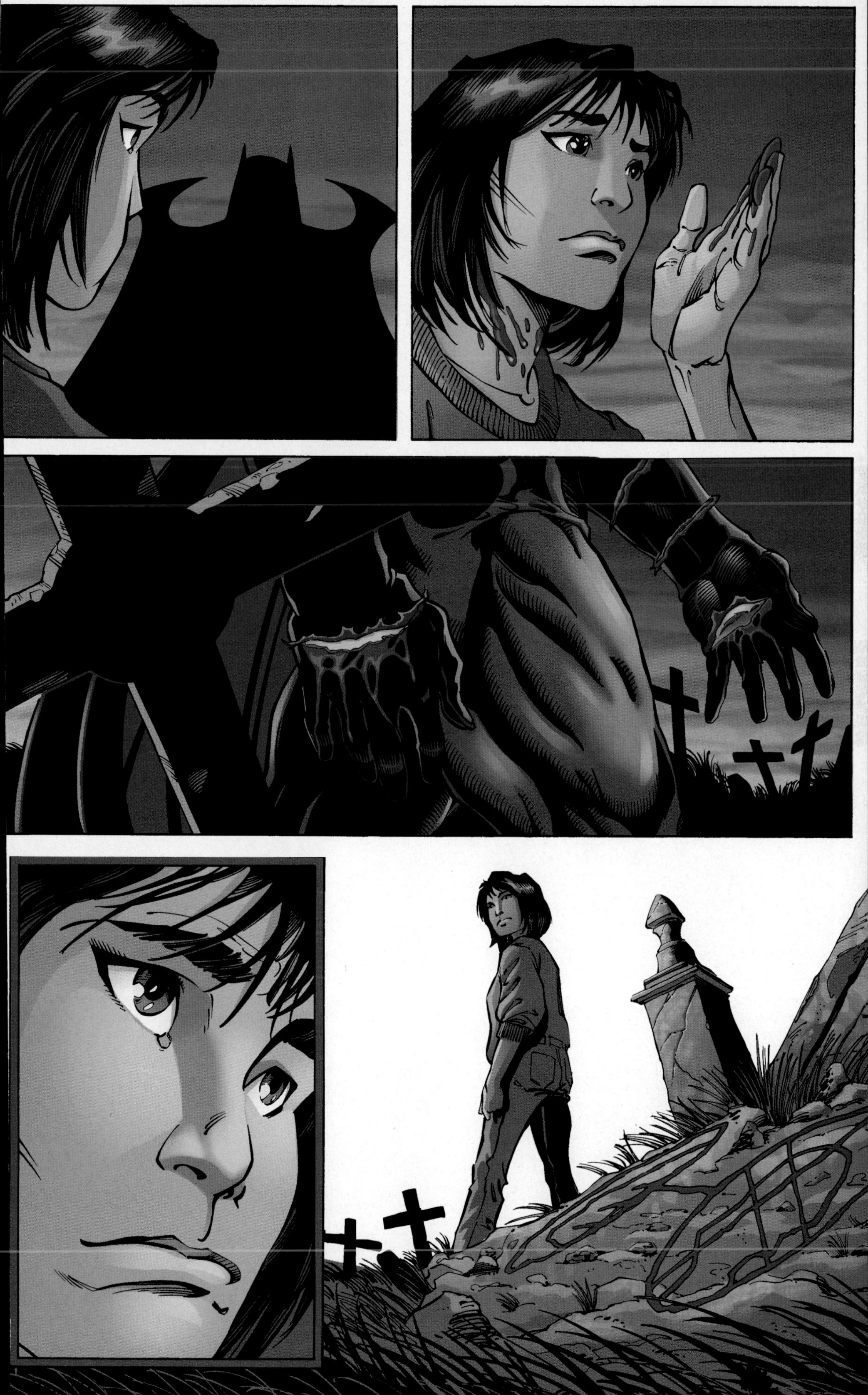

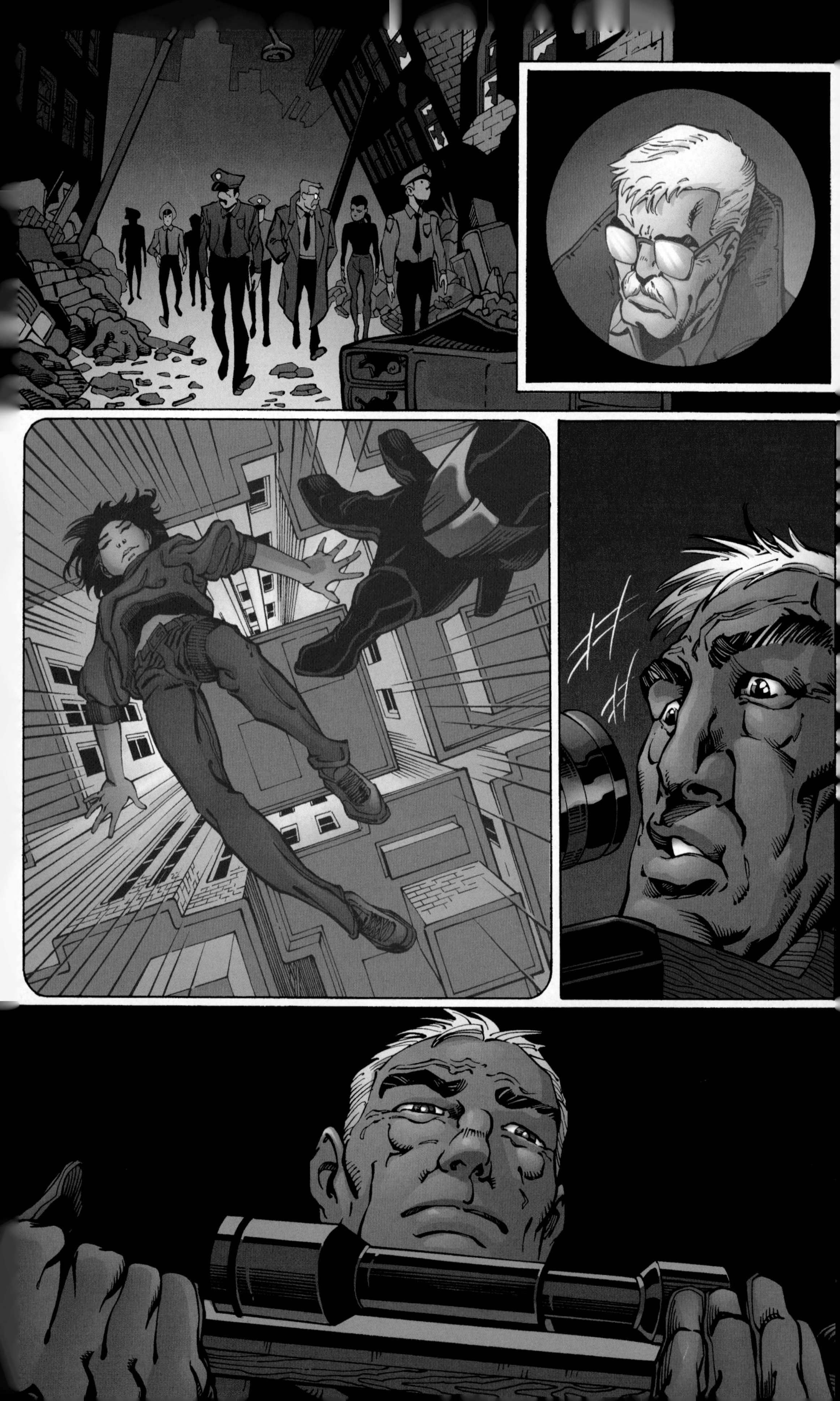

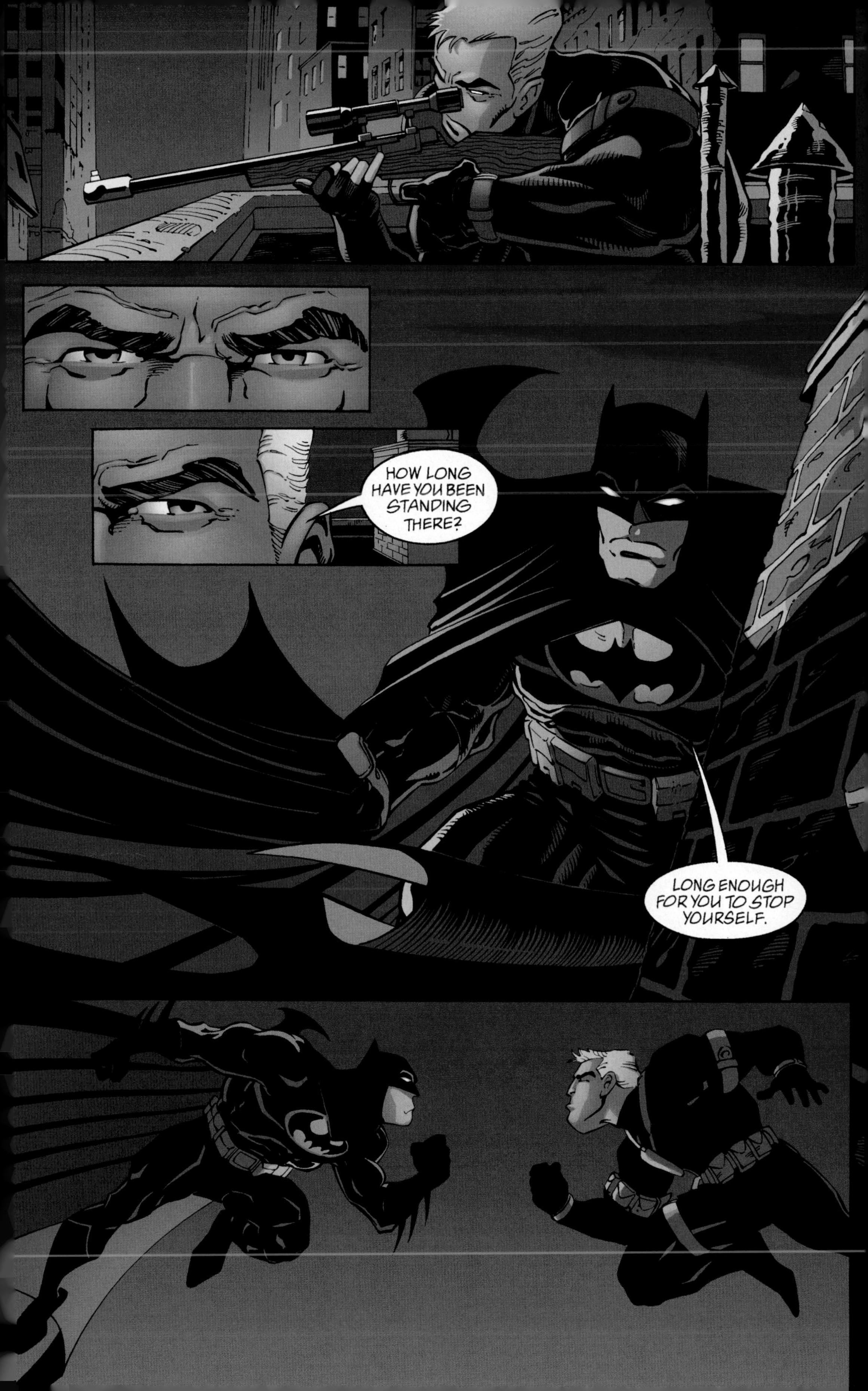
HOW LONG HAVE YOU BEEN STANDING THERE?
LONG ENOUGH FOR YOU TO STOP YOURSELF.

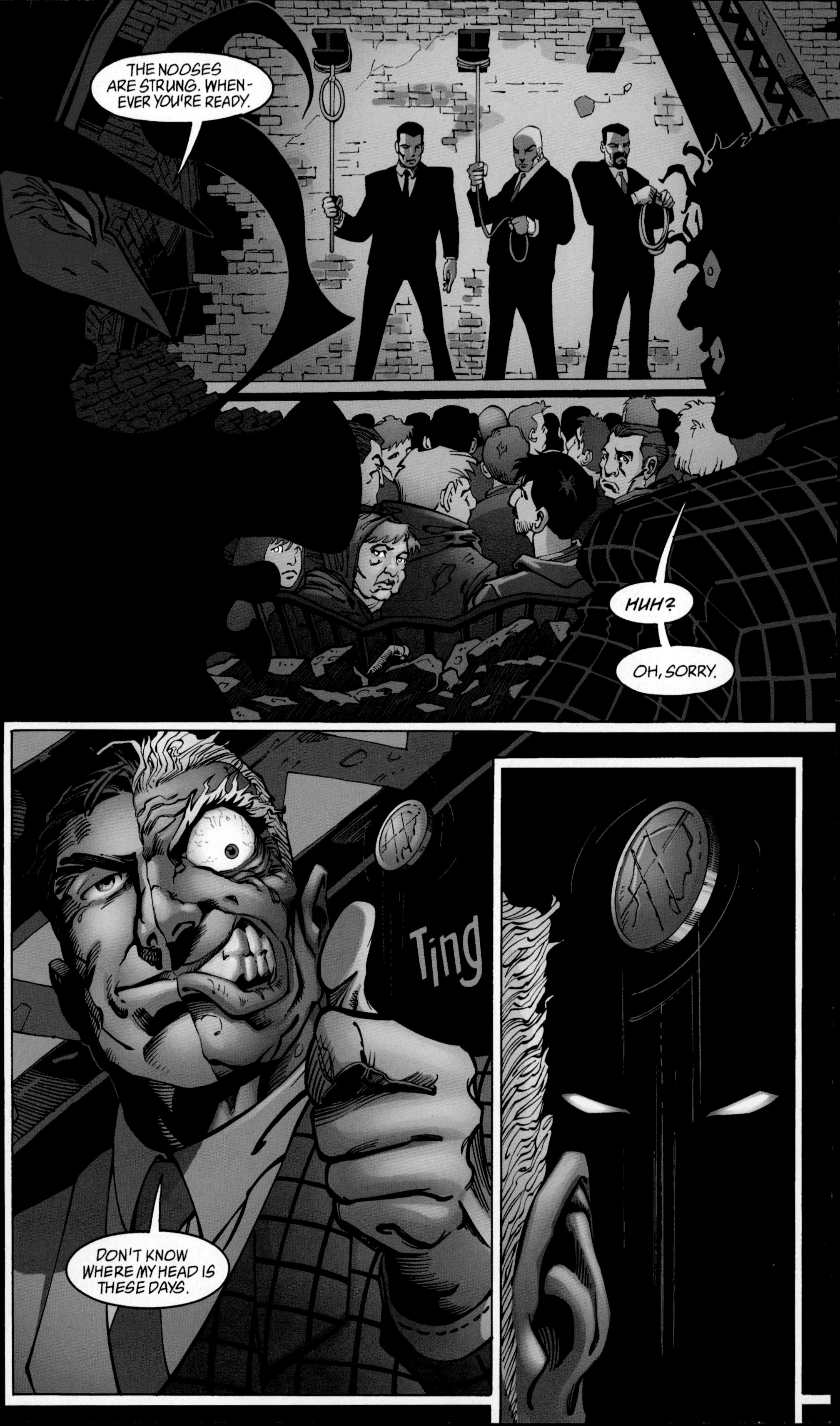
THE NOOSES ARE STRUNG. WHEN-EVER YOU'RE READY.
HUH?
OH, SORRY.
Ting
DON'T KNOW WHERE MY HEAD IS THESE DAYS.

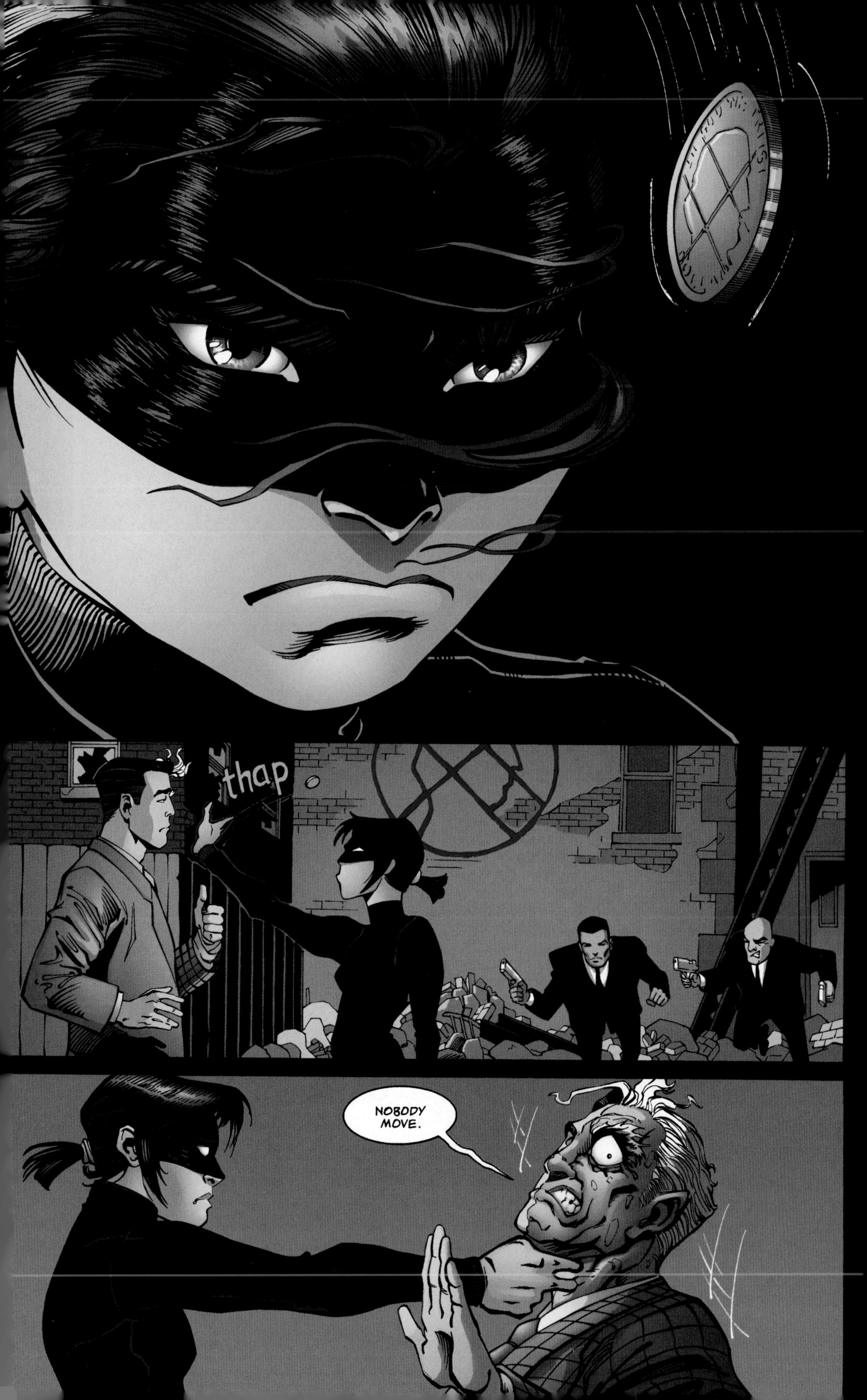
thap
NOBODY MOVE.

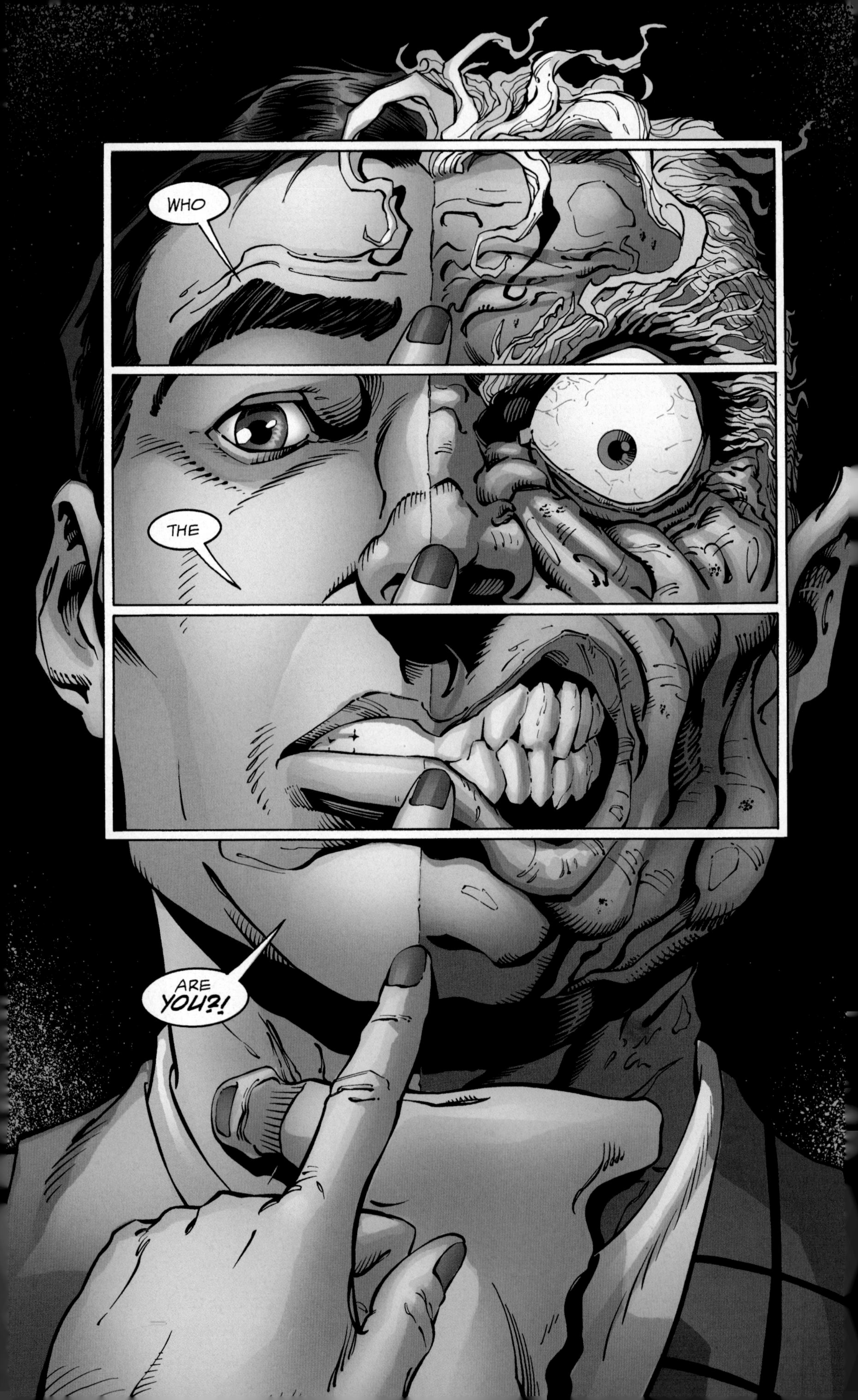
WHO
THE
ARE YOU?!

I KNOW ABOUT YOU.

YOU WON'T KILL ME, SO YOU CAN'T STOP ME.

YOU SURE ABOUT THAT?

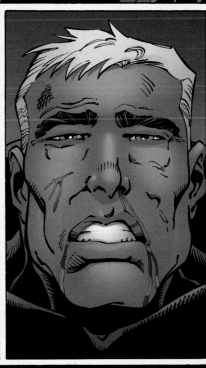

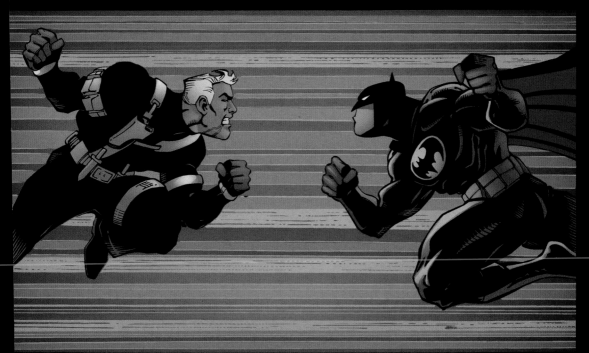

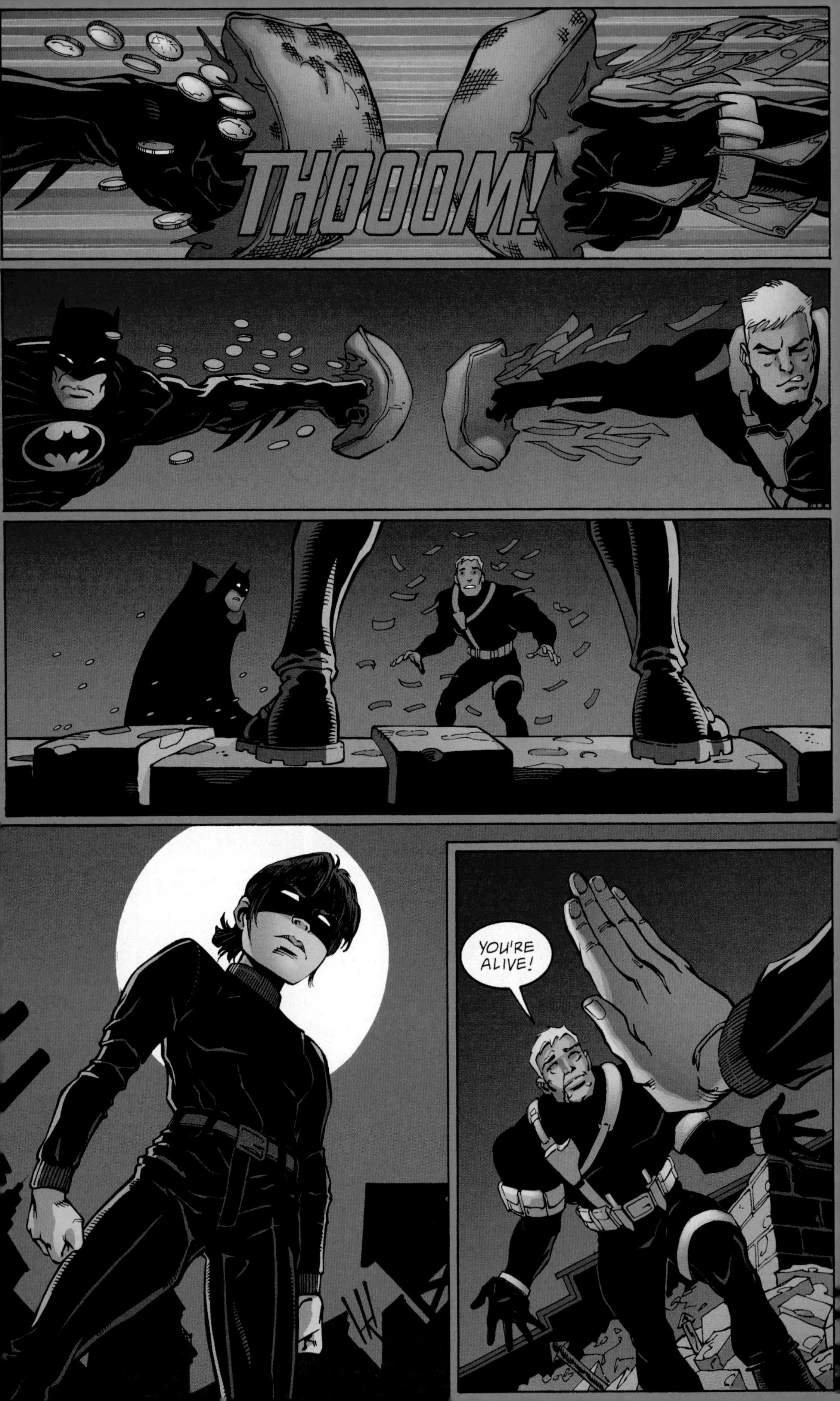
THOOOM!
YOU'RE ALIVE!

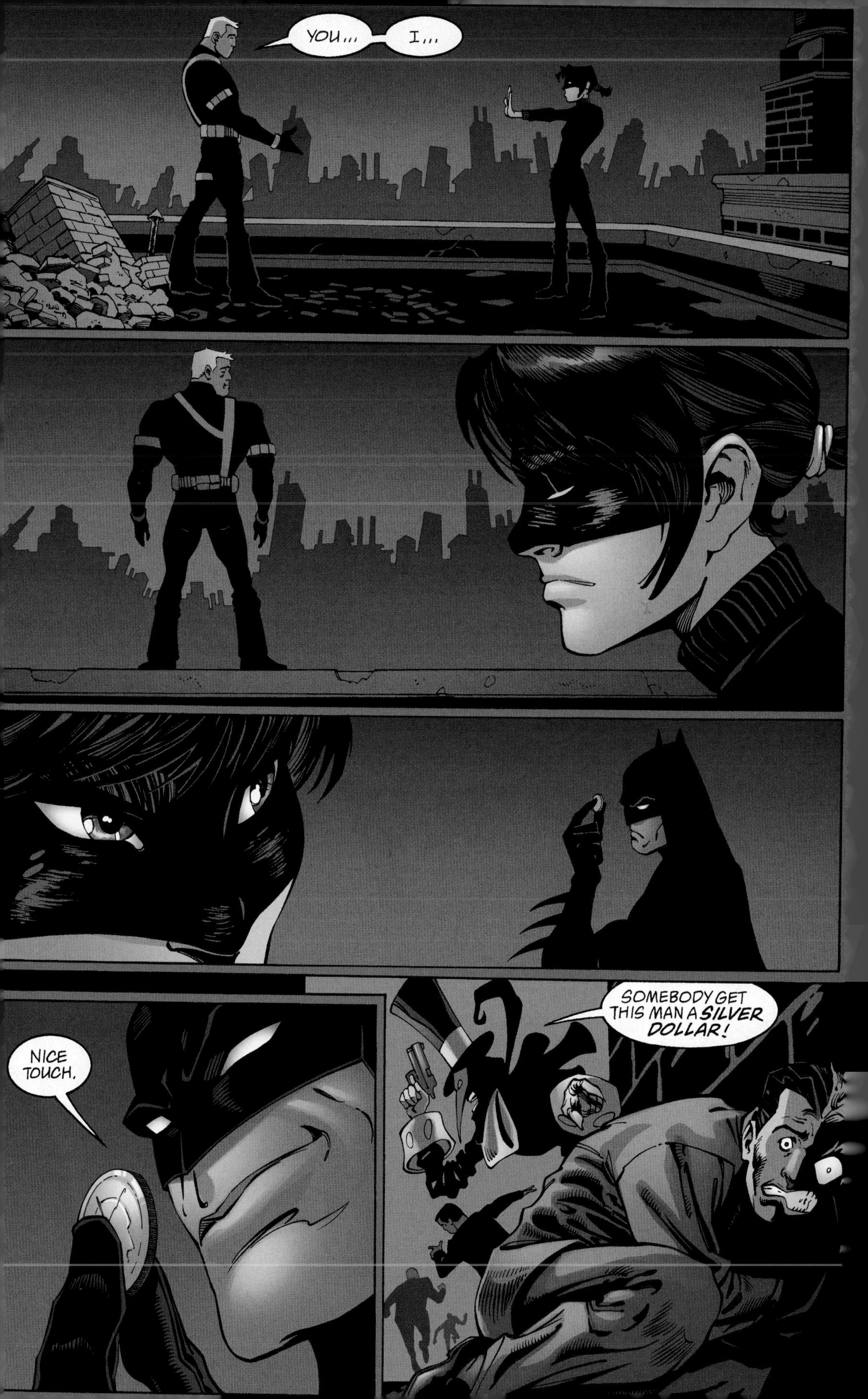
YOU...
I...
NICE TOUCH.
SOMEBODY GET THIS MAN A SILVER DOLLAR!

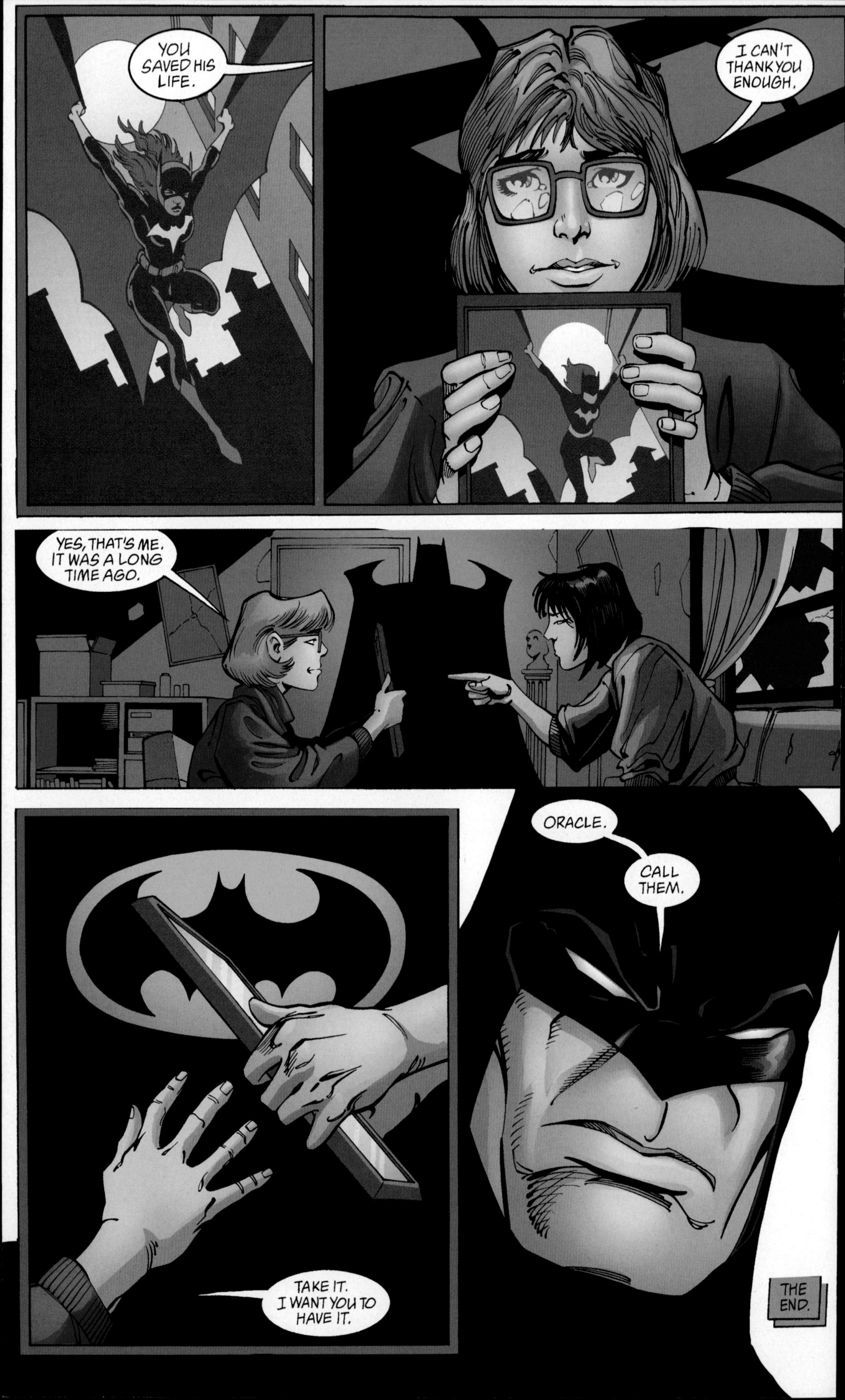
YOU SAVED HIS LIFE.
I CAN'T THANK YOU ENOUGH.
YES, THAT'S ME. IT WAS A LONG TIME AGO.
TAKE IT. I WANT YOU TO HAVE IT.
ORACLE.
CALL THEM.
THE END.

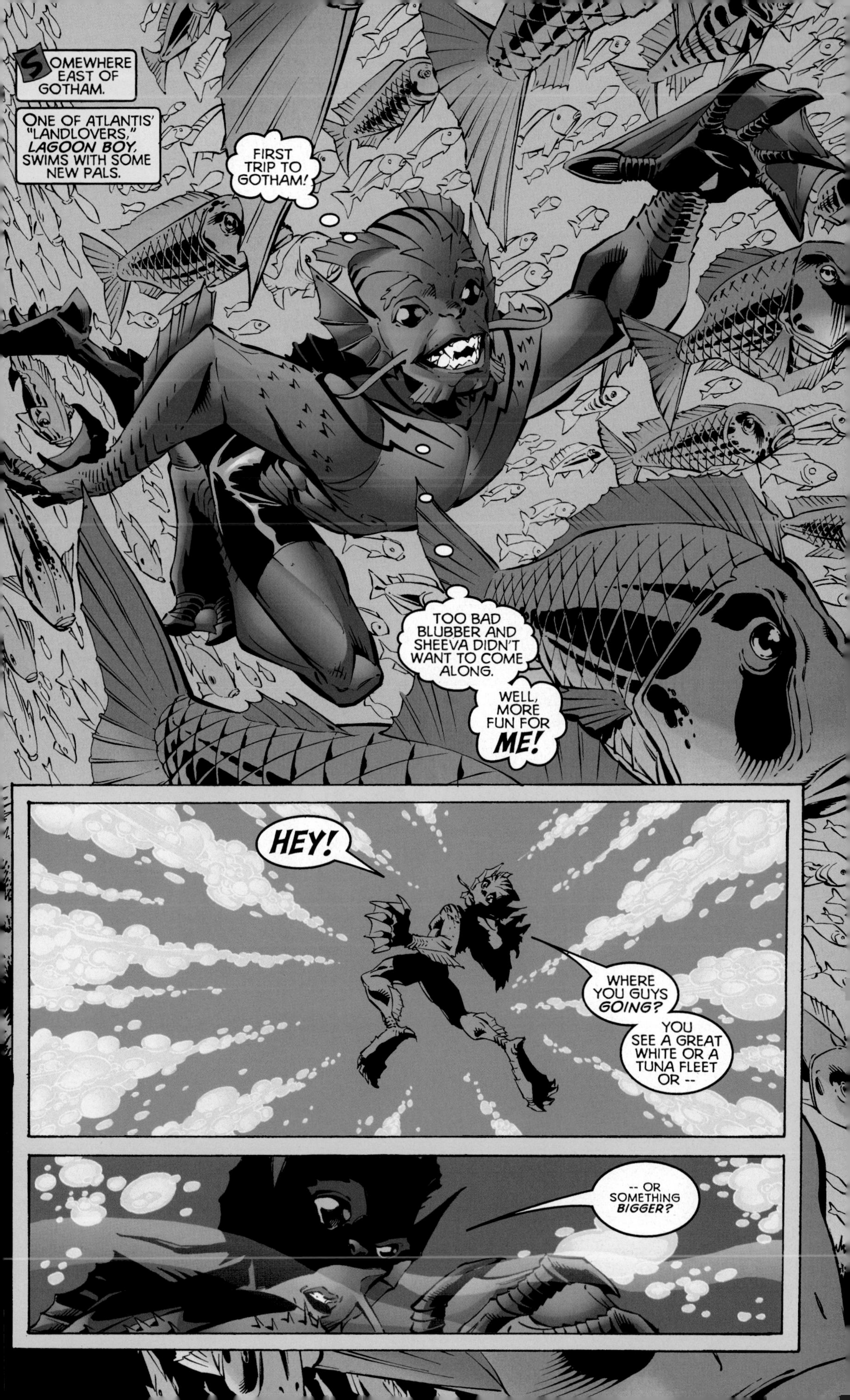
SOMEWHERE EAST OF GOTHAM.
ONE OF ATLANTIS' "LANDLOVERS," LAGOON BOY, SWIMS WITH SOME NEW PALS.
FIRST TRIP TO GOTHAM!
TOO BAD BLUBBER AND SHEEVA DIDN'T WANT TO COME ALONG.
WELL, MORE FUN FOR ME!
HEY!
WHERE YOU GUYS GOING?
YOU SEE A GREAT WHITE OR A TUNA FLEET OR --
-- OR SOMETHING BIGGER?

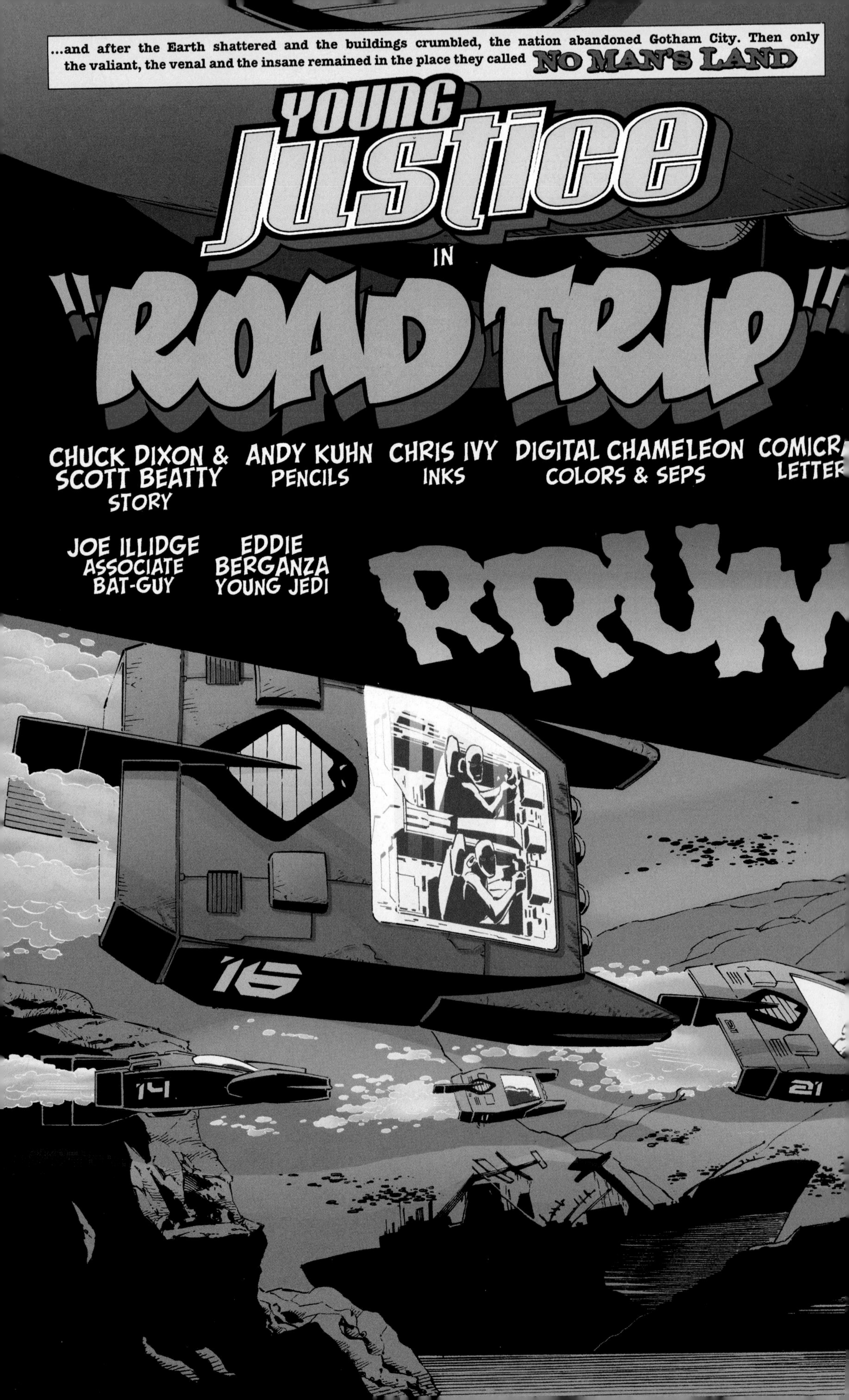

...and after the Earth shattered and the buildings crumbled, the nation abandoned Gotham City. Then only the valiant, the venal and the insane remained in the place they called NO MAN'S LAND
YOUNG JUSTICE
IN
"ROAD TRIP"
CHUCK DIXON & SCOTT BEATTY STORY
ANDY KUHN PENCILS
CHRIS IVY INKS
DIGITAL CHAMELEON COLORS & SEPS
COMICR LETTER
JOE ILLIDGE ASSOCIATE BAT-GUY
EDDIE BERGANZA YOUNG JEDI
RRUM

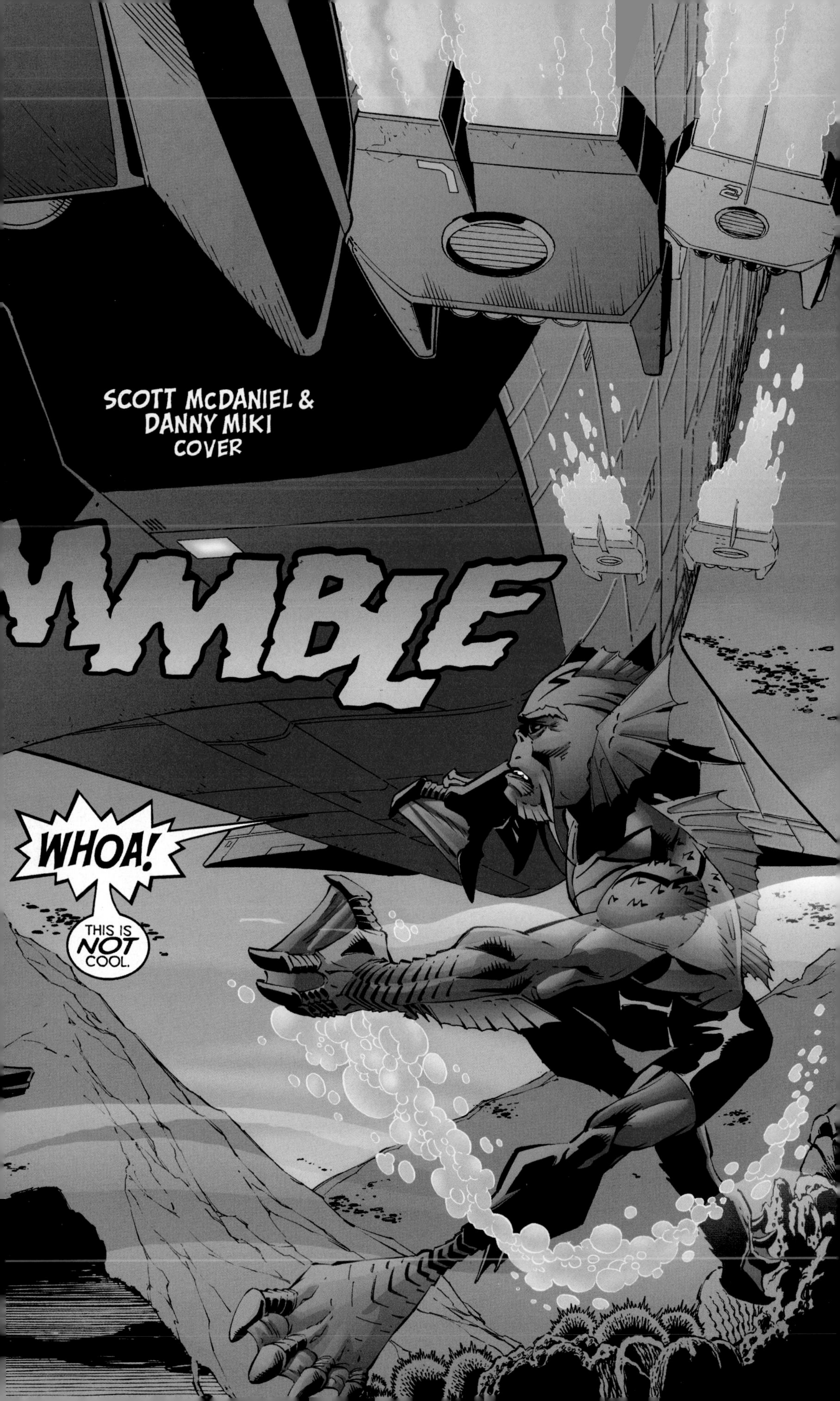
SCOTT McDANIEL &
DANNY MIKI
COVER
MBLE
WHOA!
THIS IS NOT COOL.

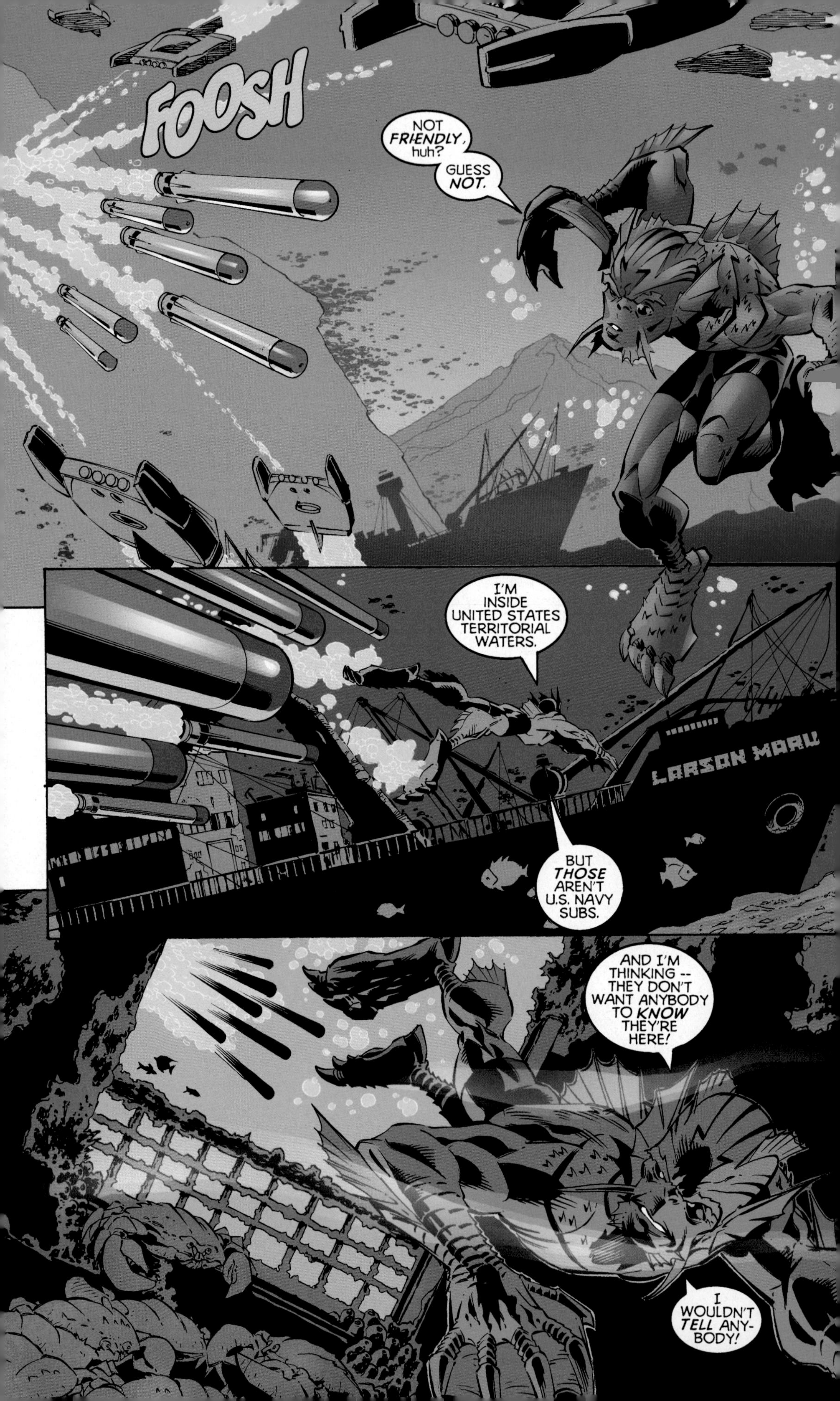
FOOSH
NOT FRIENDLY, huh?
GUESS NOT.
I'M INSIDE UNITED STATES TERRITORIAL WATERS.
LARSON MARU
BUT THOSE AREN'T U.S. NAVY SUBS.
AND I'M THINKING -- THEY DON'T WANT ANYBODY TO KNOW THEY'RE HERE!
I WOULDN'T TELL ANY-BODY!

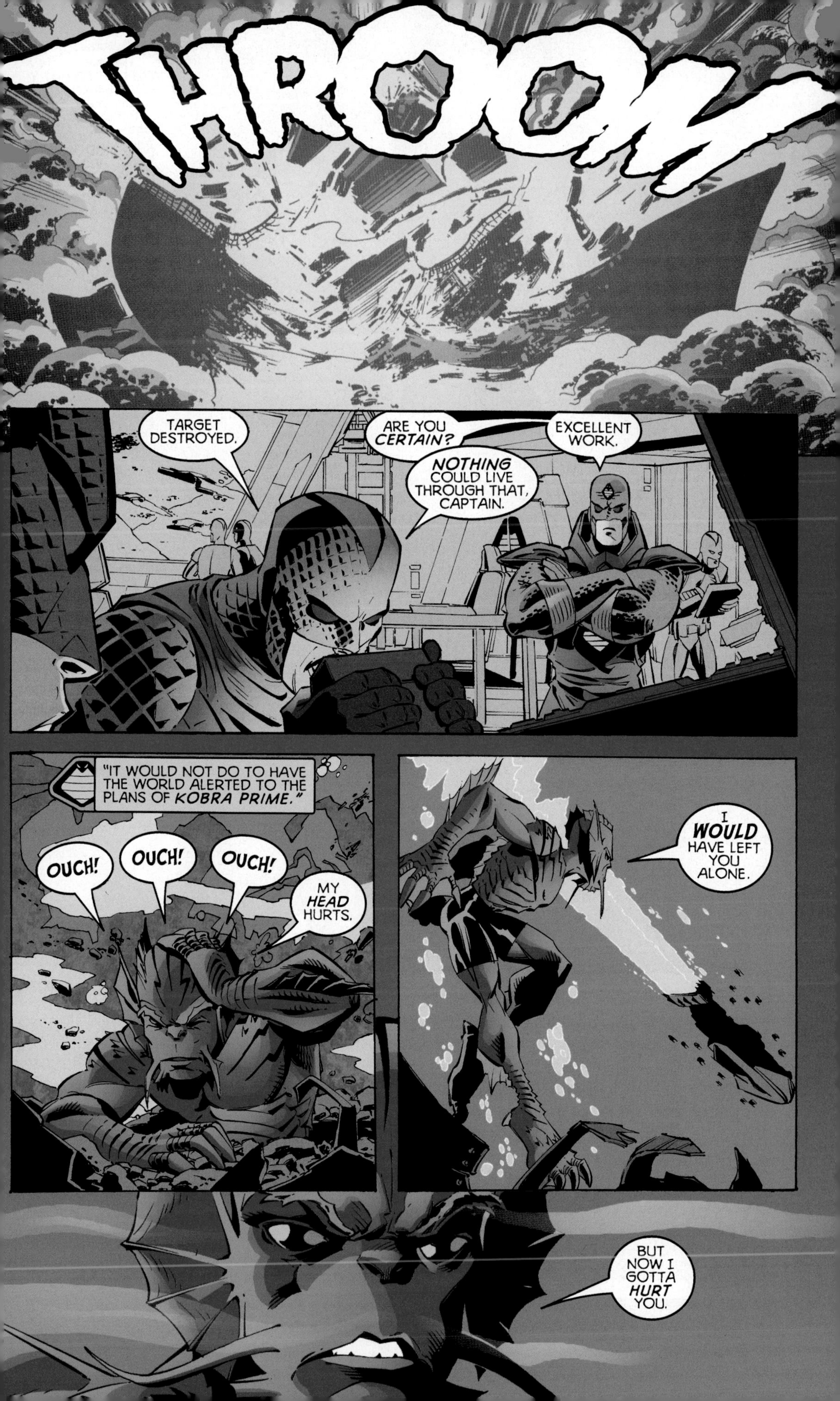
THROOM
TARGET DESTROYED.
ARE YOU CERTAIN?
NOTHING COULD LIVE THROUGH THAT, CAPTAIN.
EXCELLENT WORK.
"IT WOULD NOT DO TO HAVE THE WORLD ALERTED TO THE PLANS OF KOBRA PRIME."
OUCH!
OUCH!
OUCH!
MY HEAD HURTS.
I WOULD HAVE LEFT YOU ALONE.
BUT NOW I GOTTA HURT YOU.

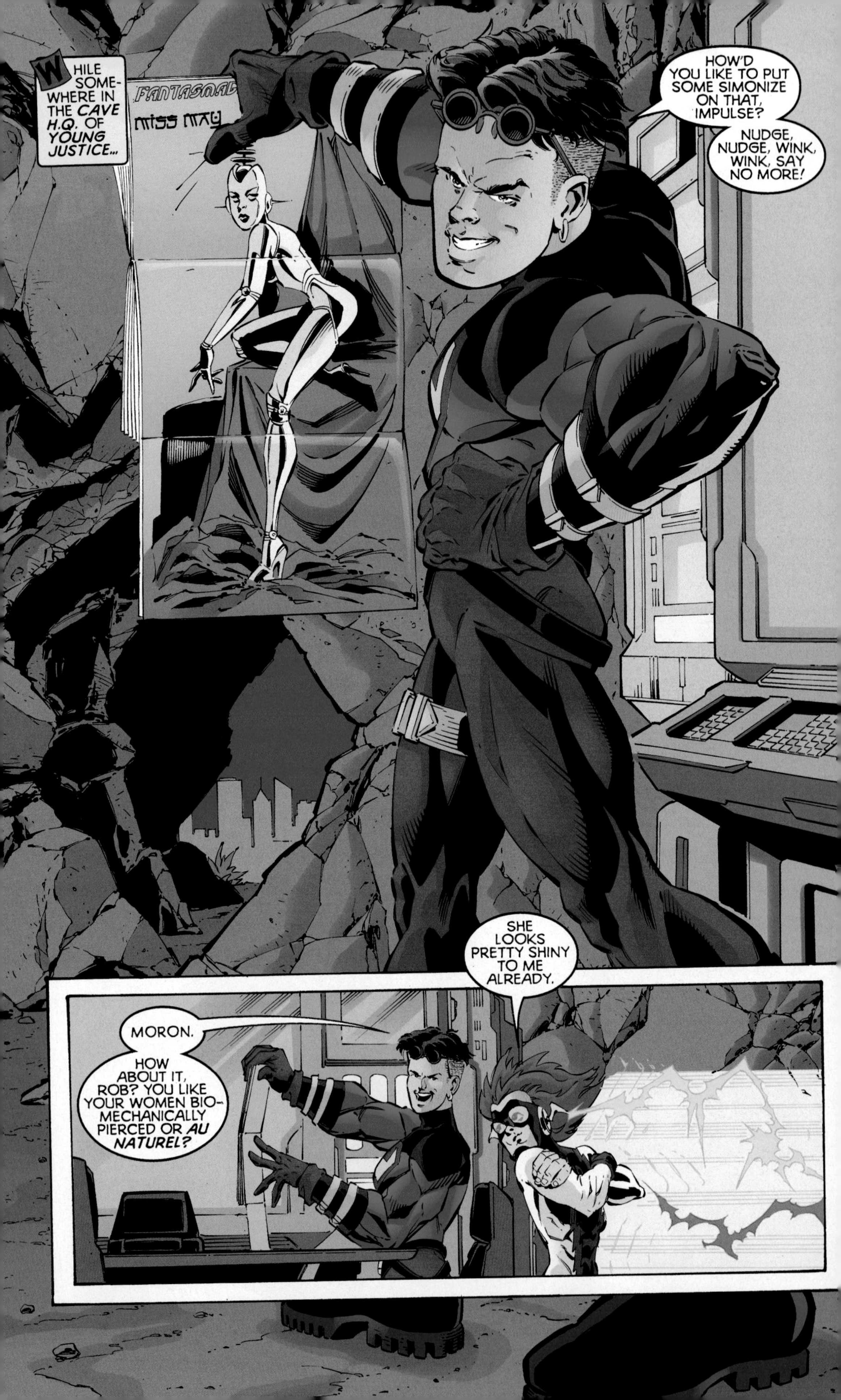
WHILE SOMEWHERE IN THE CAVE H.Q. OF YOUNG JUSTICE...
FANTASMAG
MISS MAY
HOW'D YOU LIKE TO PUT SOME SIMONIZE ON THAT, IMPULSE?
NUDGE, NUDGE, WINK, WINK, SAY NO MORE!
SHE LOOKS PRETTY SHINY TO ME ALREADY.
MORON.
HOW ABOUT IT, ROB? YOU LIKE YOUR WOMEN BIO-MECHANICALLY PIERCED OR AU NATUREL?

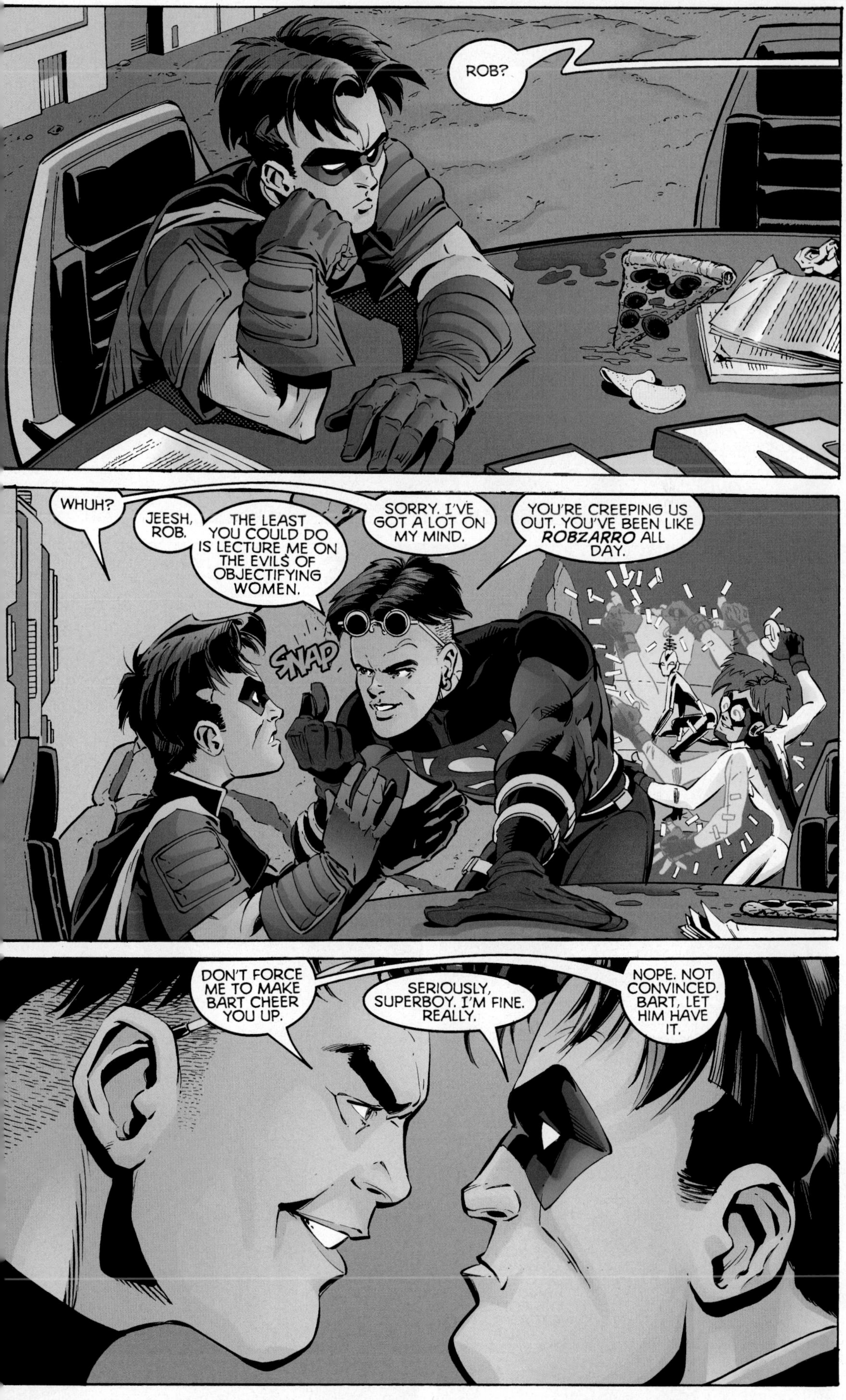
ROB?
WHUH?
JEESH, ROB.
THE LEAST YOU COULD DO IS LECTURE ME ON THE EVILS OF OBJECTIFYING WOMEN.
SORRY. I'VE GOT A LOT ON MY MIND.
YOU'RE CREEPING US OUT. YOU'VE BEEN LIKE ROBZARRO ALL DAY.
SNAP
DON'T FORCE ME TO MAKE BART CHEER YOU UP.
SERIOUSLY, SUPERBOY. I'M FINE. REALLY.
NOPE. NOT CONVINCED. BART, LET HIM HAVE IT.

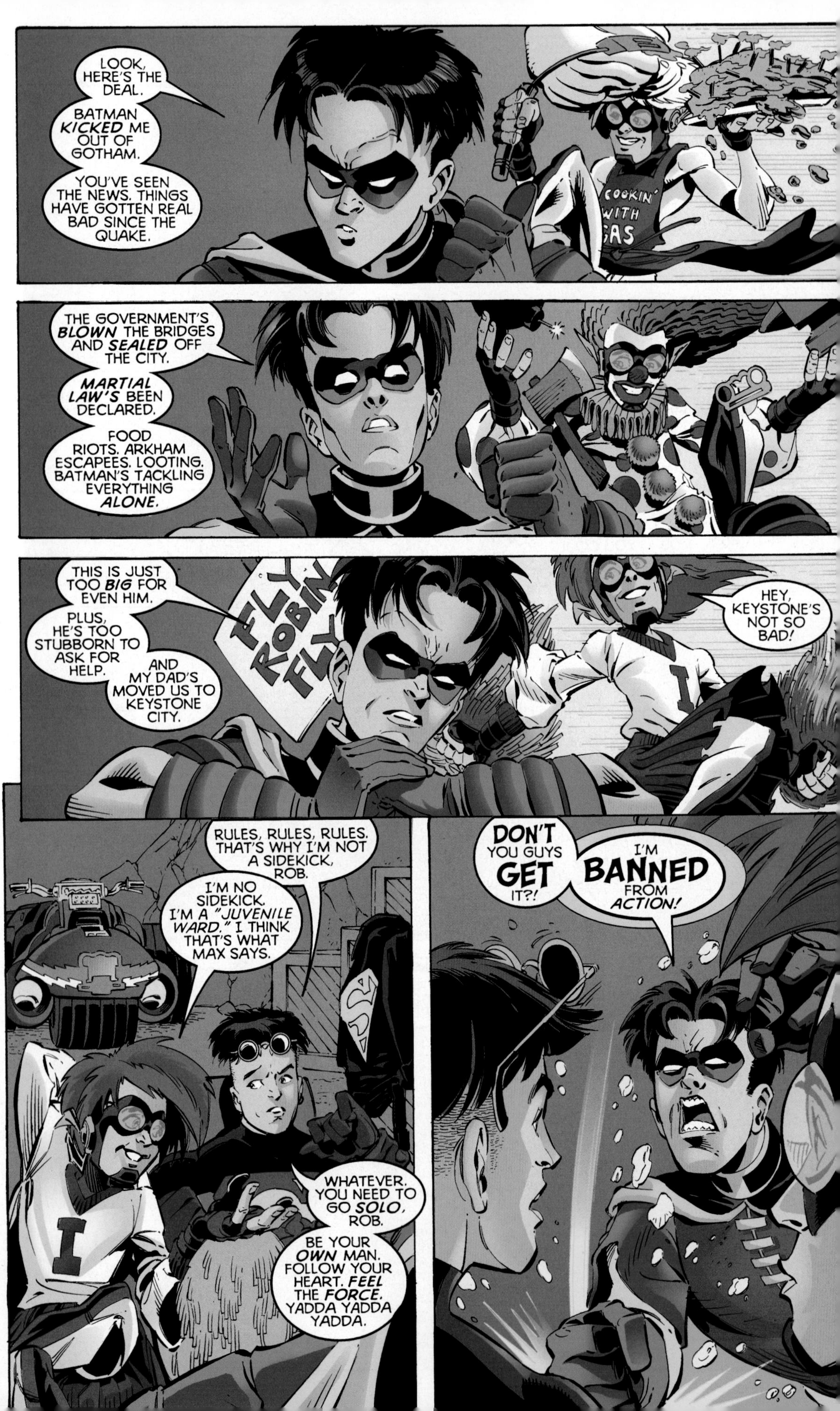

LOOK, HERE'S THE DEAL.
BATMAN KICKED ME OUT OF GOTHAM.
YOU'VE SEEN THE NEWS. THINGS HAVE GOTTEN REAL BAD SINCE THE QUAKE.
COOKIN' WITH GAS
THE GOVERNMENT'S BLOWN THE BRIDGES AND SEALED OFF THE CITY.
MARTIAL LAW'S BEEN DECLARED.
FOOD RIOTS. ARKHAM ESCAPEES. LOOTING. BATMAN'S TACKLING EVERYTHING ALONE.
THIS IS JUST TOO BIG FOR EVEN HIM.
PLUS, HE'S TOO STUBBORN TO ASK FOR HELP.
AND MY DAD'S MOVED US TO KEYSTONE CITY.
FLY ROBIN FLY
HEY, KEYSTONE'S NOT SO BAD!
RULES, RULES, RULES. THAT'S WHY I'M NOT A SIDEKICK, ROB.
I'M NO SIDEKICK. I'M A "JUVENILE WARD." I THINK THAT'S WHAT MAX SAYS.
WHATEVER. YOU NEED TO GO SOLO, ROB.
BE YOUR OWN MAN. FOLLOW YOUR HEART. FEEL THE FORCE. YADDA YADDA YADDA.
DON'T YOU GUYS GET IT?!
I'M BANNED FROM ACTION!

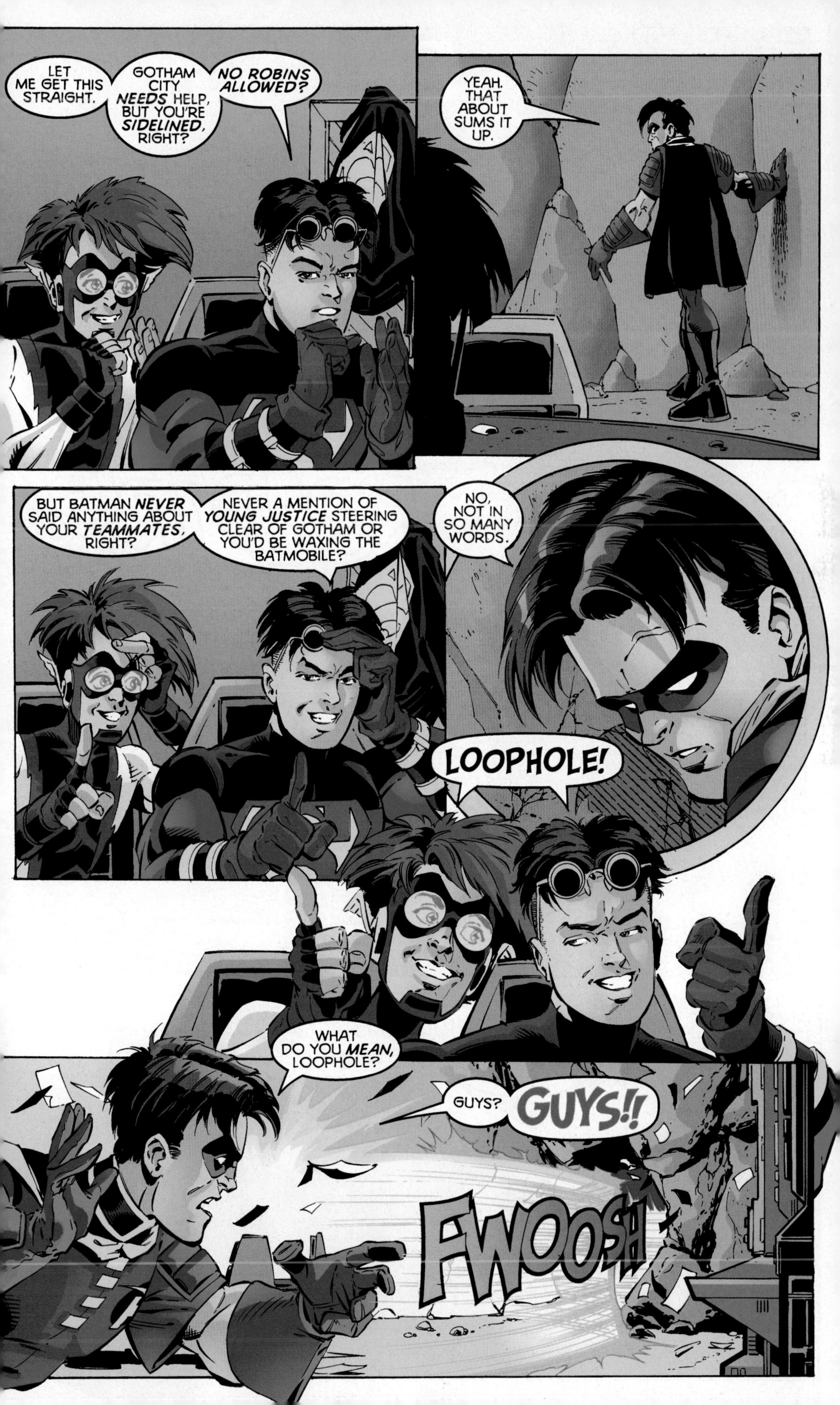

LET ME GET THIS STRAIGHT.
GOTHAM CITY *NEEDS* HELP, BUT YOU'RE *SIDELINED*, RIGHT?
NO ROBINS ALLOWED?
YEAH. THAT ABOUT SUMS IT UP.
BUT BATMAN *NEVER* SAID ANYTHING ABOUT YOUR *TEAMMATES*, RIGHT?
NEVER A MENTION OF *YOUNG JUSTICE* STEERING CLEAR OF GOTHAM OR YOU'D BE WAXING THE BATMOBILE?
NO, NOT IN SO MANY WORDS.
LOOPHOLE!
WHAT DO YOU *MEAN*, LOOPHOLE?
GUYS?
GUYS!!
FWOOSH

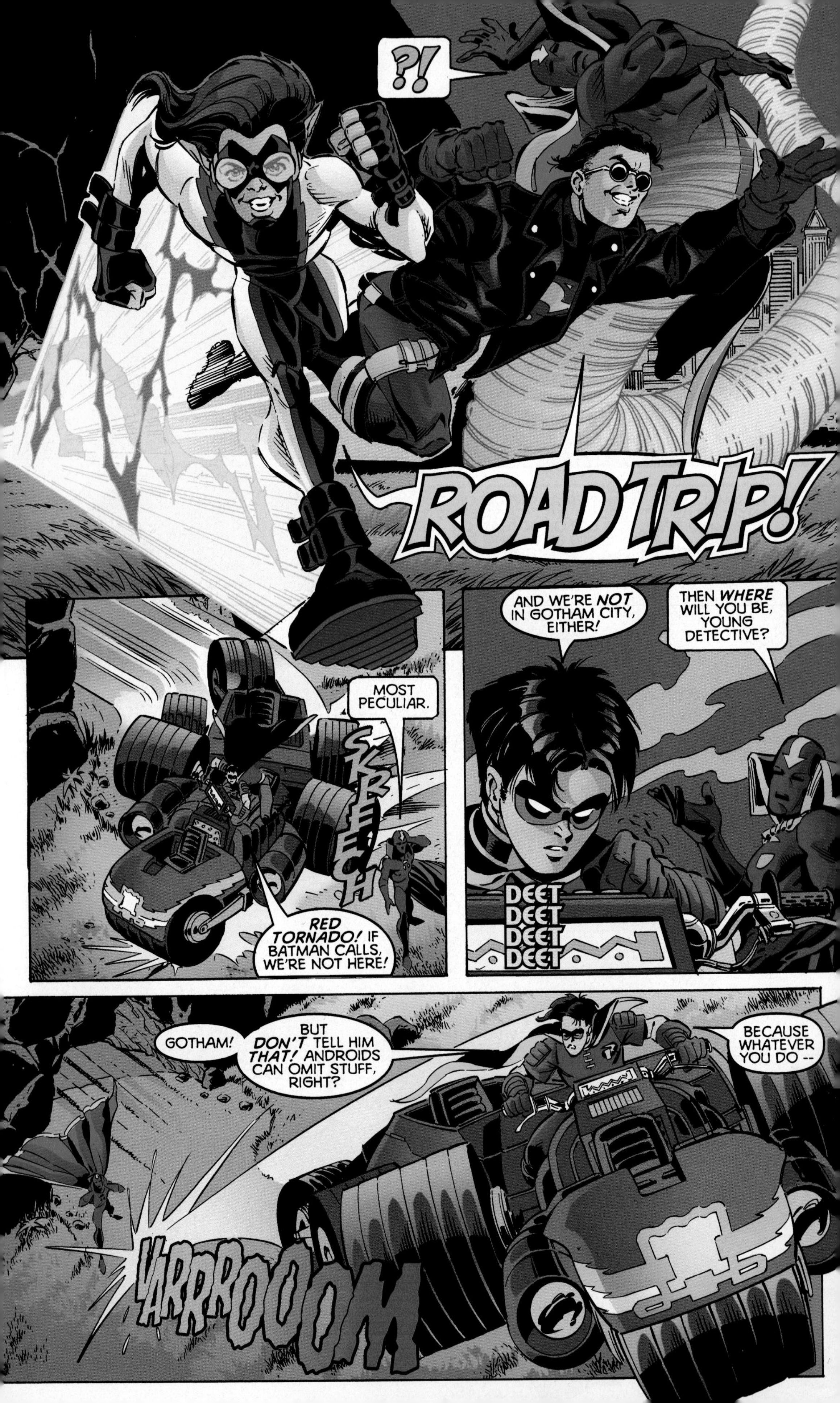

?!
ROAD TRIP!
MOST PECULIAR.
SKREECH
RED TORNADO! IF BATMAN CALLS, WE'RE NOT HERE!
AND WE'RE NOT IN GOTHAM CITY, EITHER!
THEN WHERE WILL YOU BE, YOUNG DETECTIVE?
DEET DEET DEET DEET
GOTHAM!
BUT DON'T TELL HIM THAT! ANDROIDS CAN OMIT STUFF, RIGHT?
BECAUSE WHATEVER YOU DO --
VARRROOOM

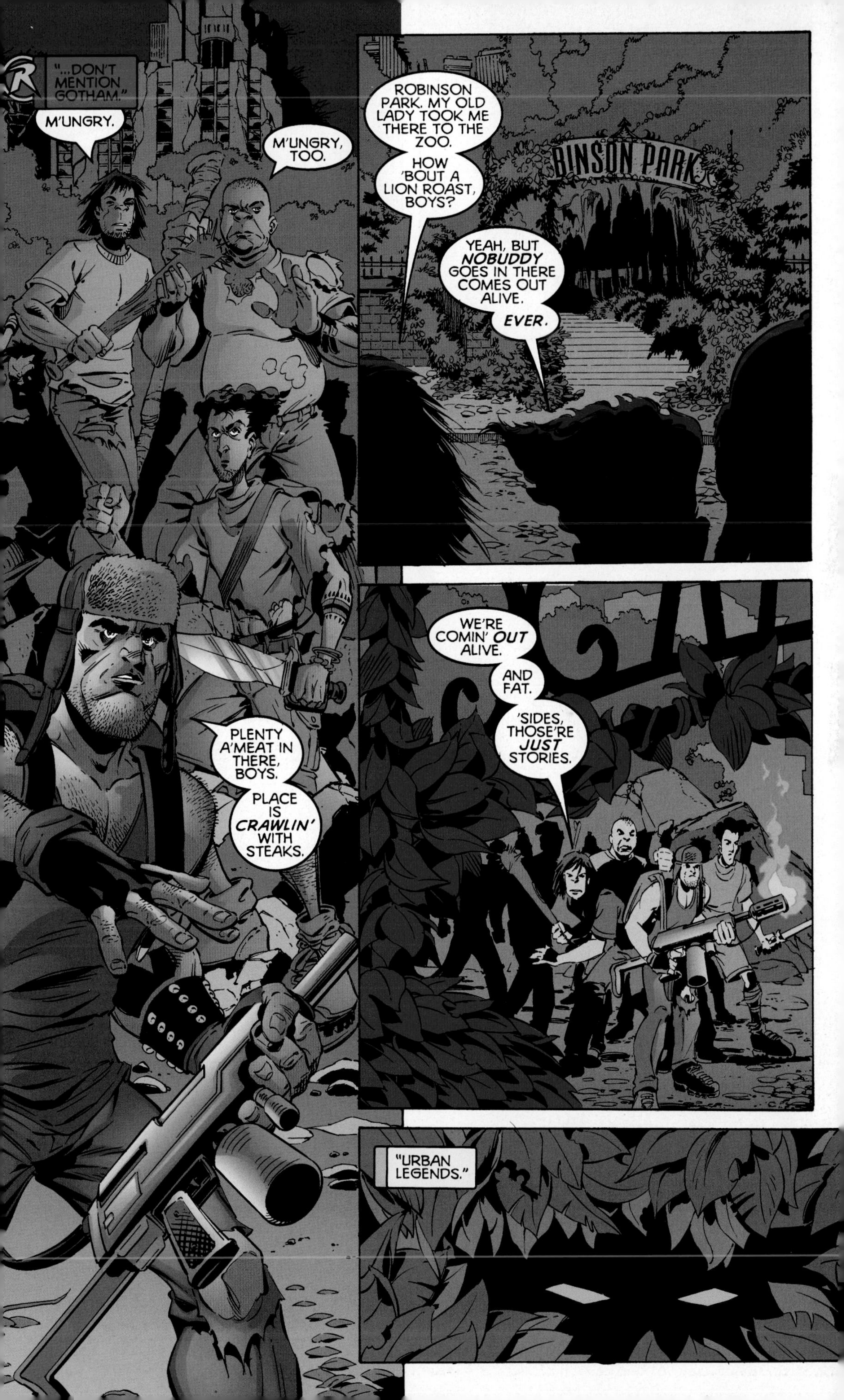
"...DON'T MENTION GOTHAM."
M'UNGRY.
M'UNGRY, TOO.
ROBINSON PARK. MY OLD LADY TOOK ME THERE TO THE ZOO.
HOW 'BOUT A LION ROAST, BOYS?
BINSON PARK
YEAH, BUT NOBUDDY GOES IN THERE COMES OUT ALIVE.
EVER.
PLENTY A'MEAT IN THERE, BOYS.
PLACE IS CRAWLIN' WITH STEAKS.
WE'RE COMIN' OUT ALIVE.
AND FAT.
'SIDES, THOSE'RE JUST STORIES.
"URBAN LEGENDS."

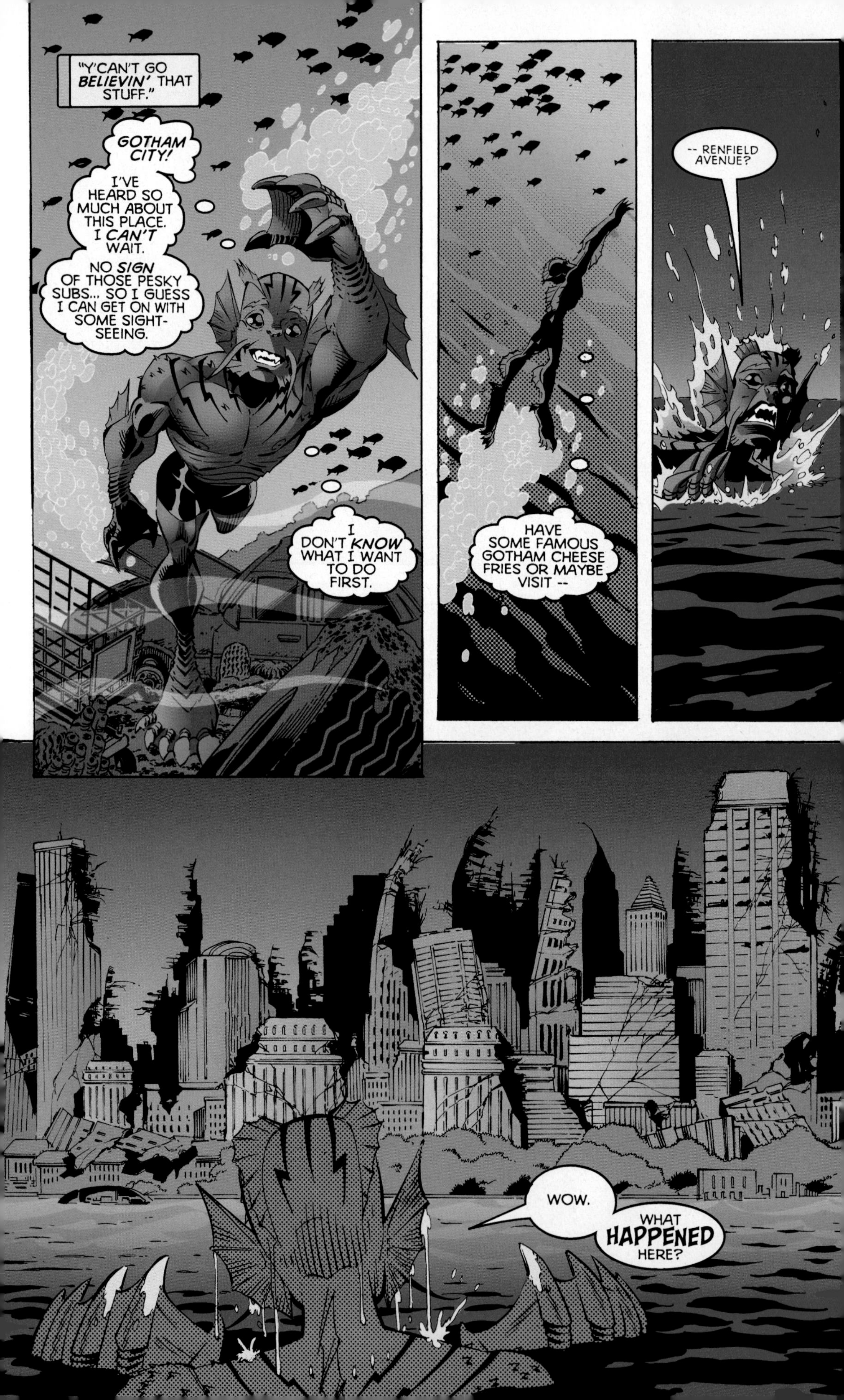
"Y'CAN'T GO *BELIEVIN'* THAT STUFF."
GOTHAM CITY!
I'VE HEARD SO MUCH ABOUT THIS PLACE. I *CAN'T* WAIT.
NO *SIGN* OF THOSE PESKY SUBS... SO I GUESS I CAN GET ON WITH SOME SIGHT-SEEING.
I DON'T *KNOW* WHAT I WANT TO DO FIRST.
HAVE SOME FAMOUS GOTHAM CHEESE FRIES OR MAYBE VISIT --
-- RENFIELD AVENUE?
WOW.
WHAT **HAPPENED** HERE?

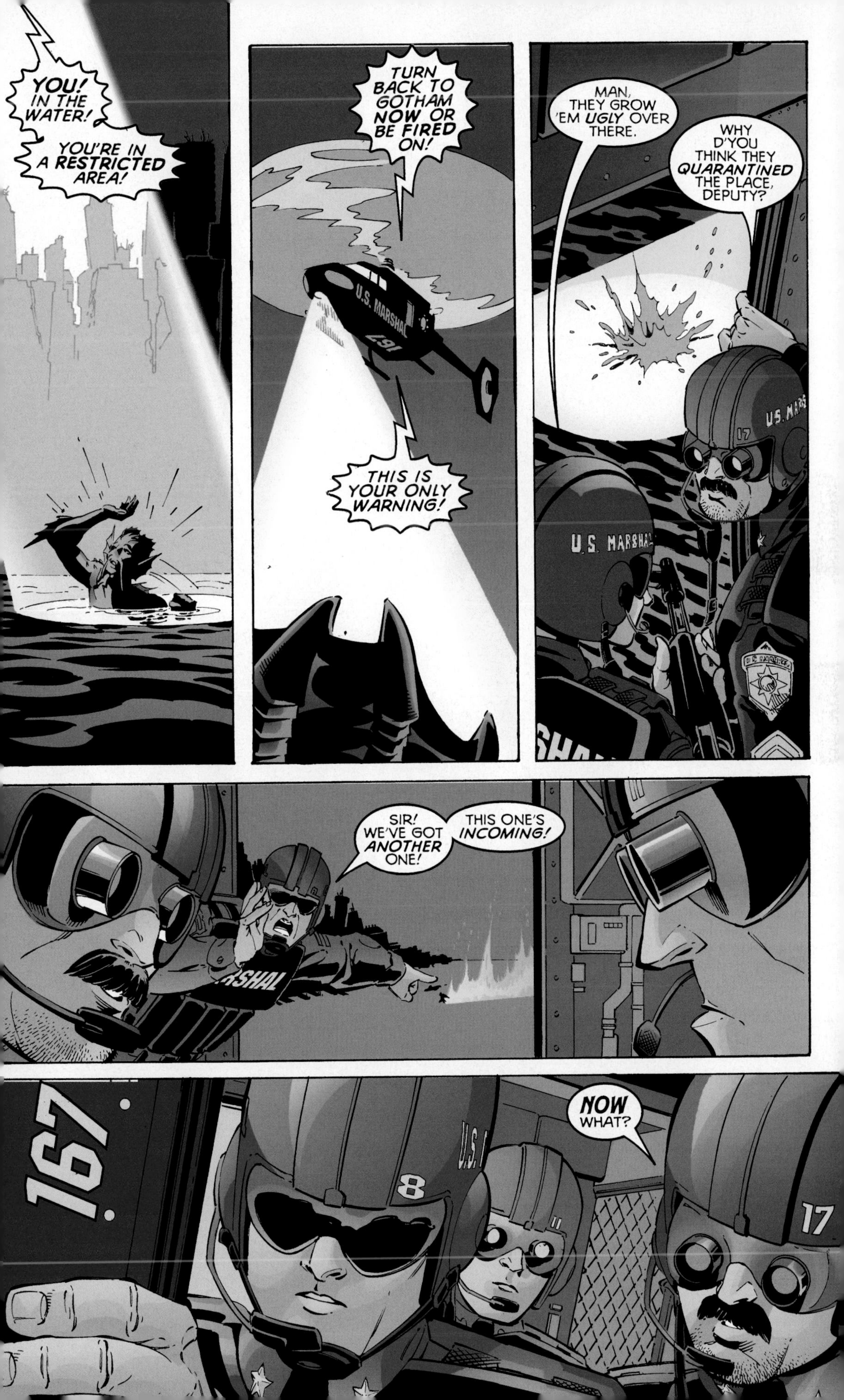

YOU! IN THE WATER!
YOU'RE IN A RESTRICTED AREA!
TURN BACK TO GOTHAM NOW OR BE FIRED ON!
U.S. MARSHAL
167
THIS IS YOUR ONLY WARNING!
MAN, THEY GROW 'EM UGLY OVER THERE.
WHY D'YOU THINK THEY QUARANTINED THE PLACE, DEPUTY?
U.S. MARSHAL
SIR! WE'VE GOT ANOTHER ONE!
THIS ONE'S INCOMING!
MARSHAL
167
NOW WHAT?

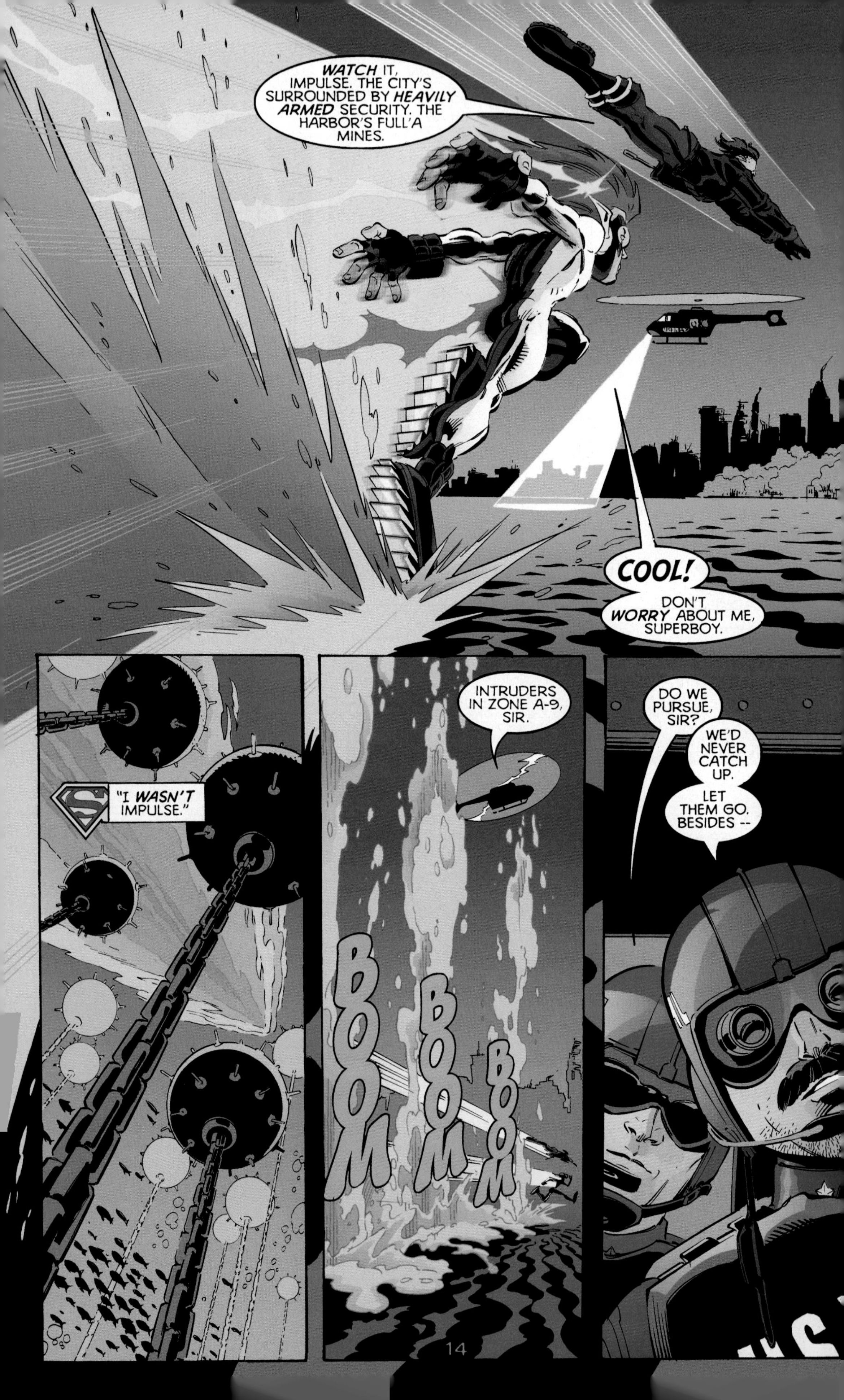
WATCH IT, IMPULSE. THE CITY'S SURROUNDED BY HEAVILY ARMED SECURITY. THE HARBOR'S FULL'A MINES.
COOL!
DON'T WORRY ABOUT ME, SUPERBOY.
"I WASN'T IMPULSE."
INTRUDERS IN ZONE A-9, SIR.
BOOM
BOOM
BOOM
DO WE PURSUE, SIR?
WE'D NEVER CATCH UP.
LET THEM GO. BESIDES --

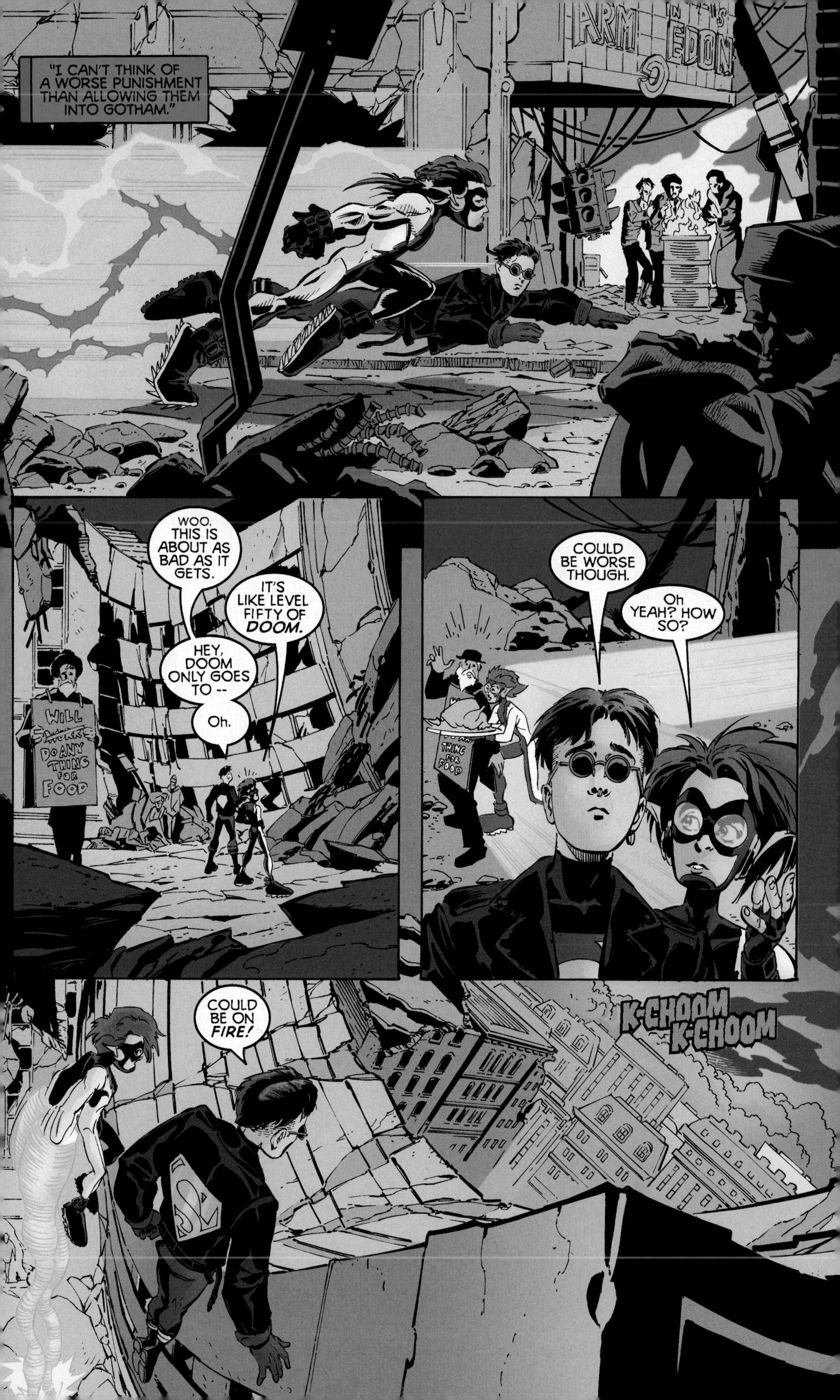
"I CAN'T THINK OF A WORSE PUNISHMENT THAN ALLOWING THEM INTO GOTHAM."
WOO. THIS IS ABOUT AS BAD AS IT GETS.
IT'S LIKE LEVEL FIFTY OF DOOM.
HEY, DOOM ONLY GOES TO --
Oh.
WILL DO ANY THING FOR FOOD
COULD BE WORSE THOUGH.
Oh YEAH? HOW SO?
COULD BE ON FIRE!
K-CHOOM K-CHOOM

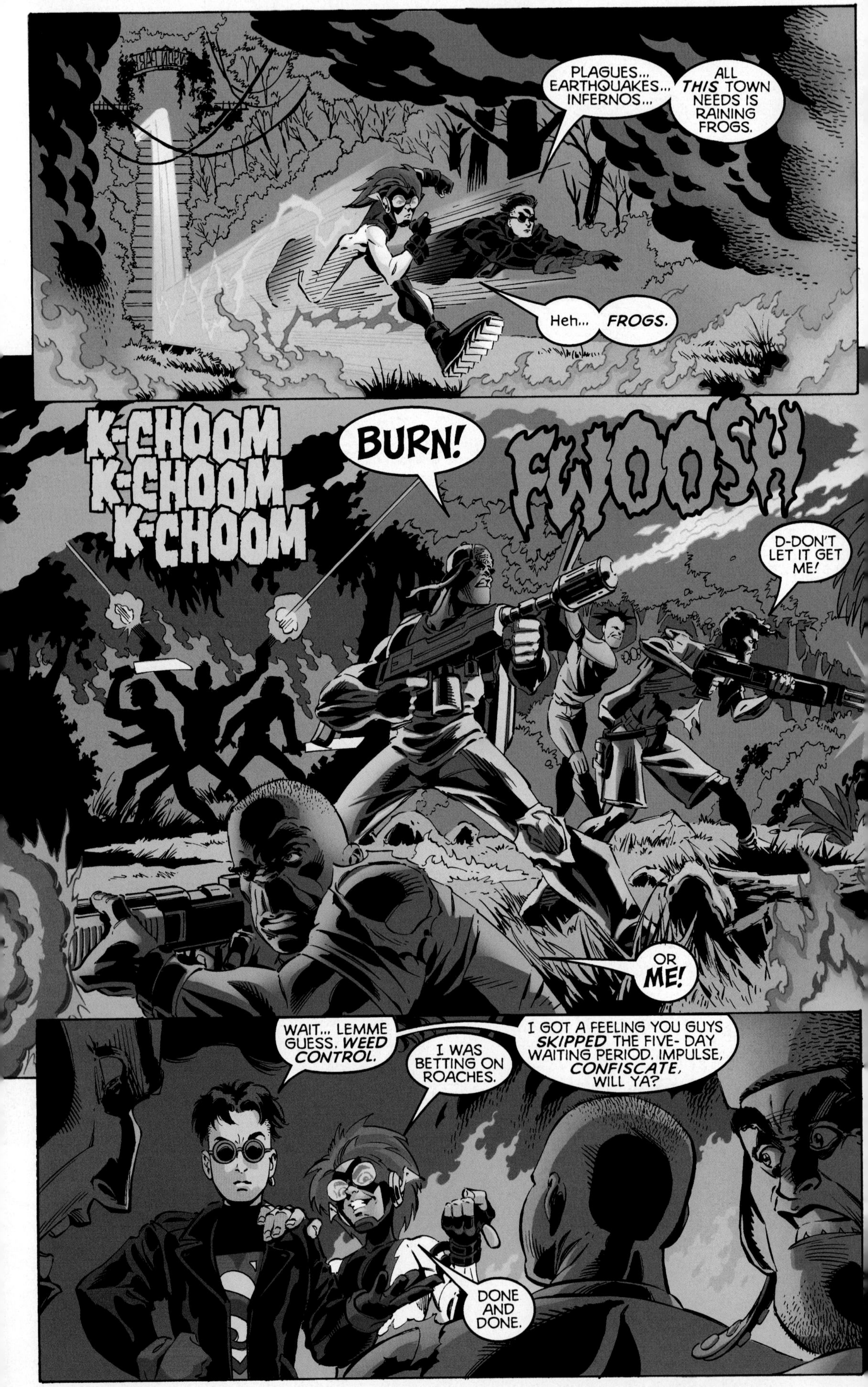

PLAGUES... EARTHQUAKES... INFERNOS...
ALL THIS TOWN NEEDS IS RAINING FROGS.
Heh... FROGS.
K-CHOOM K-CHOOM K-CHOOM
BURN!
FWOOSH
D-DON'T LET IT GET ME!
OR ME!
WAIT... LEMME GUESS. WEED CONTROL.
I WAS BETTING ON ROACHES.
I GOT A FEELING YOU GUYS SKIPPED THE FIVE- DAY WAITING PERIOD. IMPULSE, CONFISCATE, WILL YA?
DONE AND DONE.

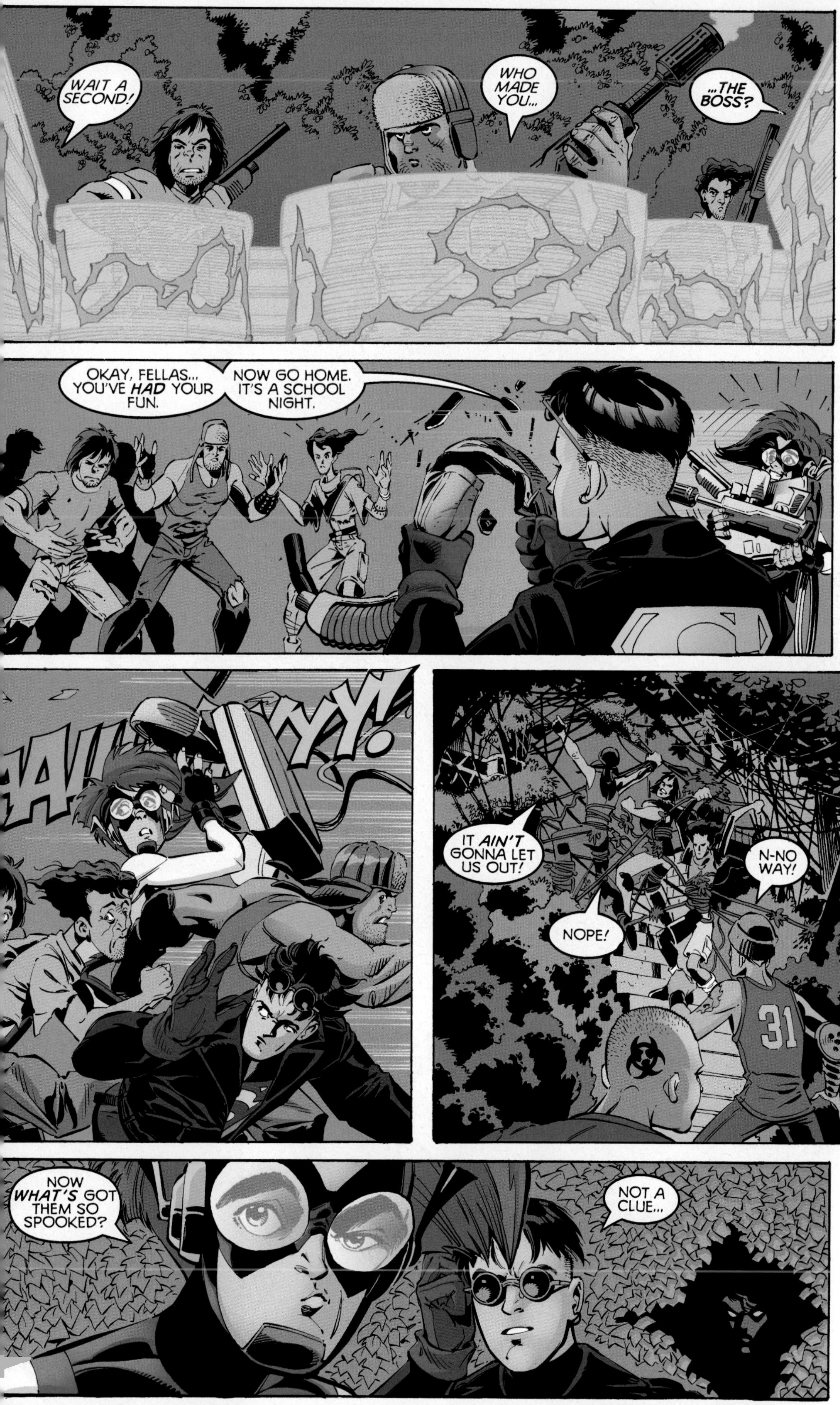
WAIT A SECOND!
WHO MADE YOU...
...THE BOSS?
OKAY, FELLAS... YOU'VE *HAD* YOUR FUN.
NOW GO HOME. IT'S A SCHOOL NIGHT.
IT *AIN'T* GONNA LET US OUT!
N-NO WAY!
NOPE!
NOW *WHAT'S* GOT THEM SO SPOOKED?
NOT A CLUE...

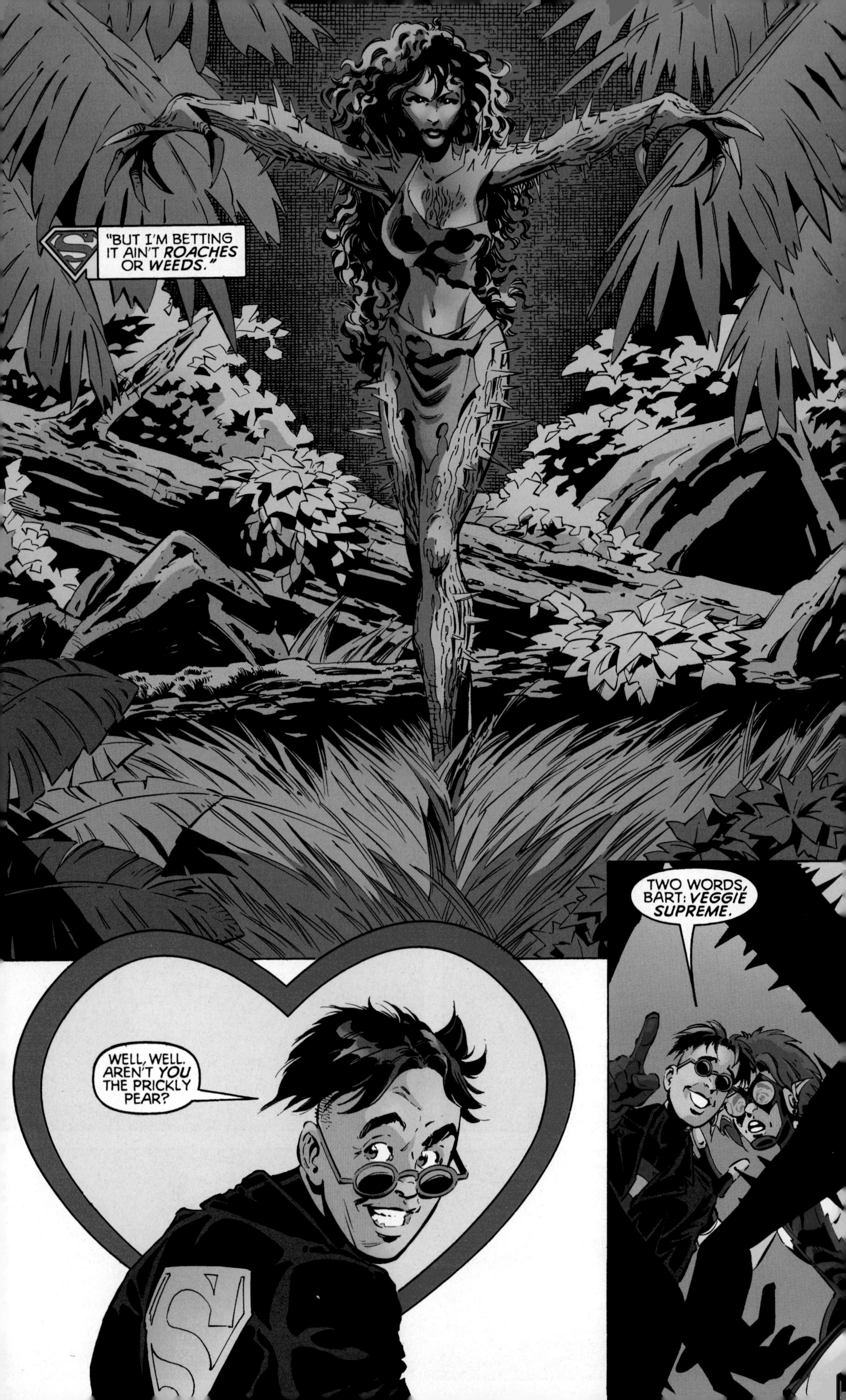
"BUT I'M BETTING IT AIN'T ROACHES OR WEEDS."
WELL, WELL. AREN'T YOU THE PRICKLY PEAR?
TWO WORDS, BART: VEGGIE SUPREME.

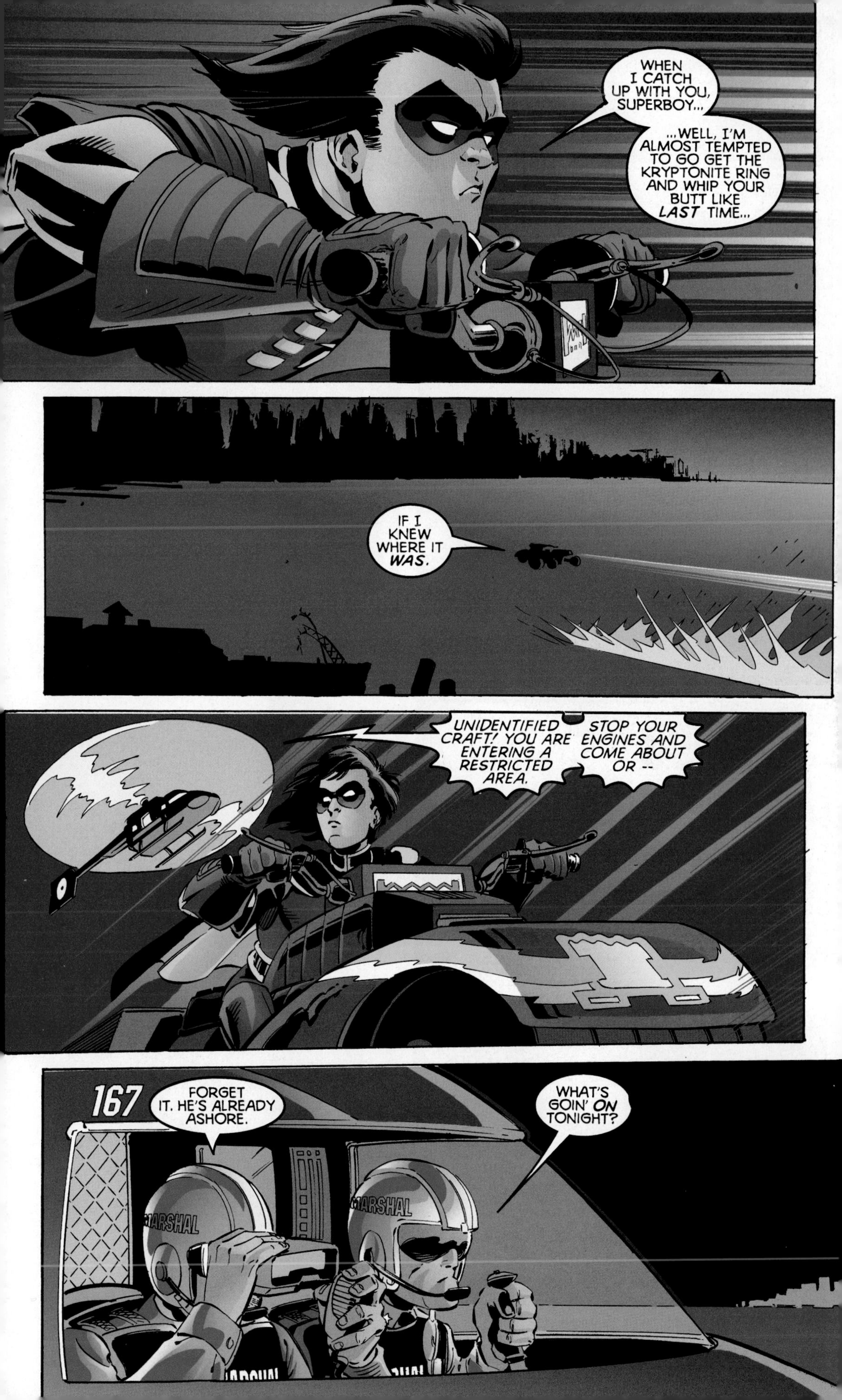
WHEN I CATCH UP WITH YOU, SUPERBOY...
...WELL, I'M ALMOST TEMPTED TO GO GET THE KRYPTONITE RING AND WHIP YOUR BUTT LIKE *LAST* TIME...
IF I KNEW WHERE IT *WAS*.
UNIDENTIFIED CRAFT! YOU ARE ENTERING A RESTRICTED AREA.
STOP YOUR ENGINES AND COME ABOUT OR --
167
FORGET IT. HE'S ALREADY ASHORE.
WHAT'S GOIN' *ON* TONIGHT?
MARSHAL
MARSHAL

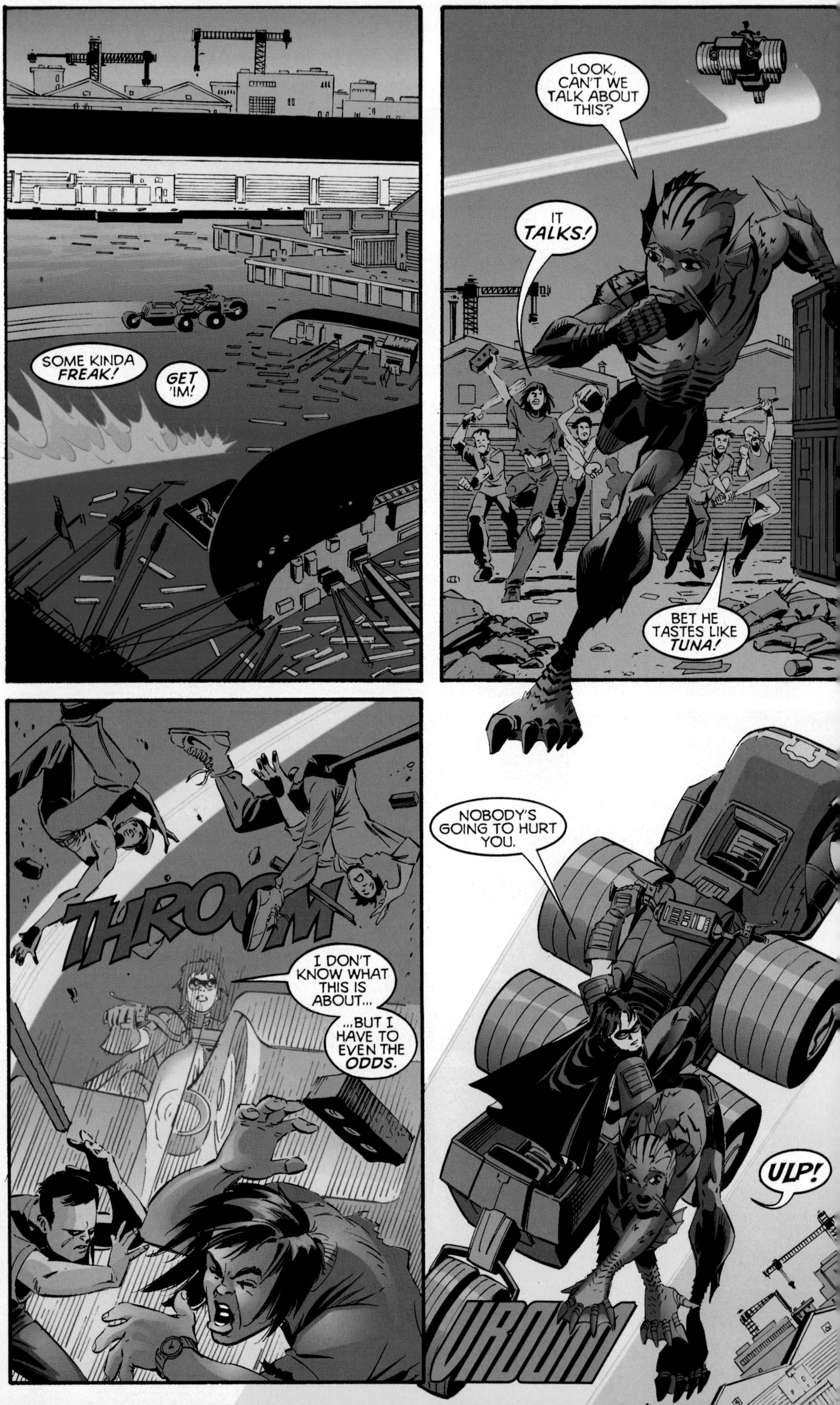
SOME KINDA FREAK!
GET 'IM!
LOOK, CAN'T WE TALK ABOUT THIS?
IT TALKS!
BET HE TASTES LIKE TUNA!
THROOM
I DON'T KNOW WHAT THIS IS ABOUT...
...BUT I HAVE TO EVEN THE ODDS.
NOBODY'S GOING TO HURT YOU.
ULP!
VROOM

THIS IS ONE COOL RIDE.

I'M *LAGOON BOY*.

I'M *ROBIN*. TAKE A *SEAT*, OKAY?

ROBIN? LIKE *BATMAN* AND ROBIN?

YEAH. BUT I'D RATHER NOT RUN INTO BATMAN RIGHT NOW.

WHAT WAS THAT *ABOUT* BACK THERE?

BEATS THE KELP OUTTA ME.

GUESS THOSE GUYS DON'T LIKE OUT-OF-TOWNERS.

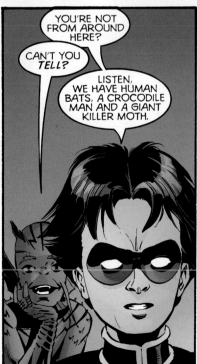

YOU'RE NOT FROM AROUND HERE?

CAN'T YOU *TELL*?

LISTEN, WE HAVE HUMAN BATS, A CROCODILE MAN AND A GIANT KILLER MOTH.

IN GOTHAM *YOU* BLEND.

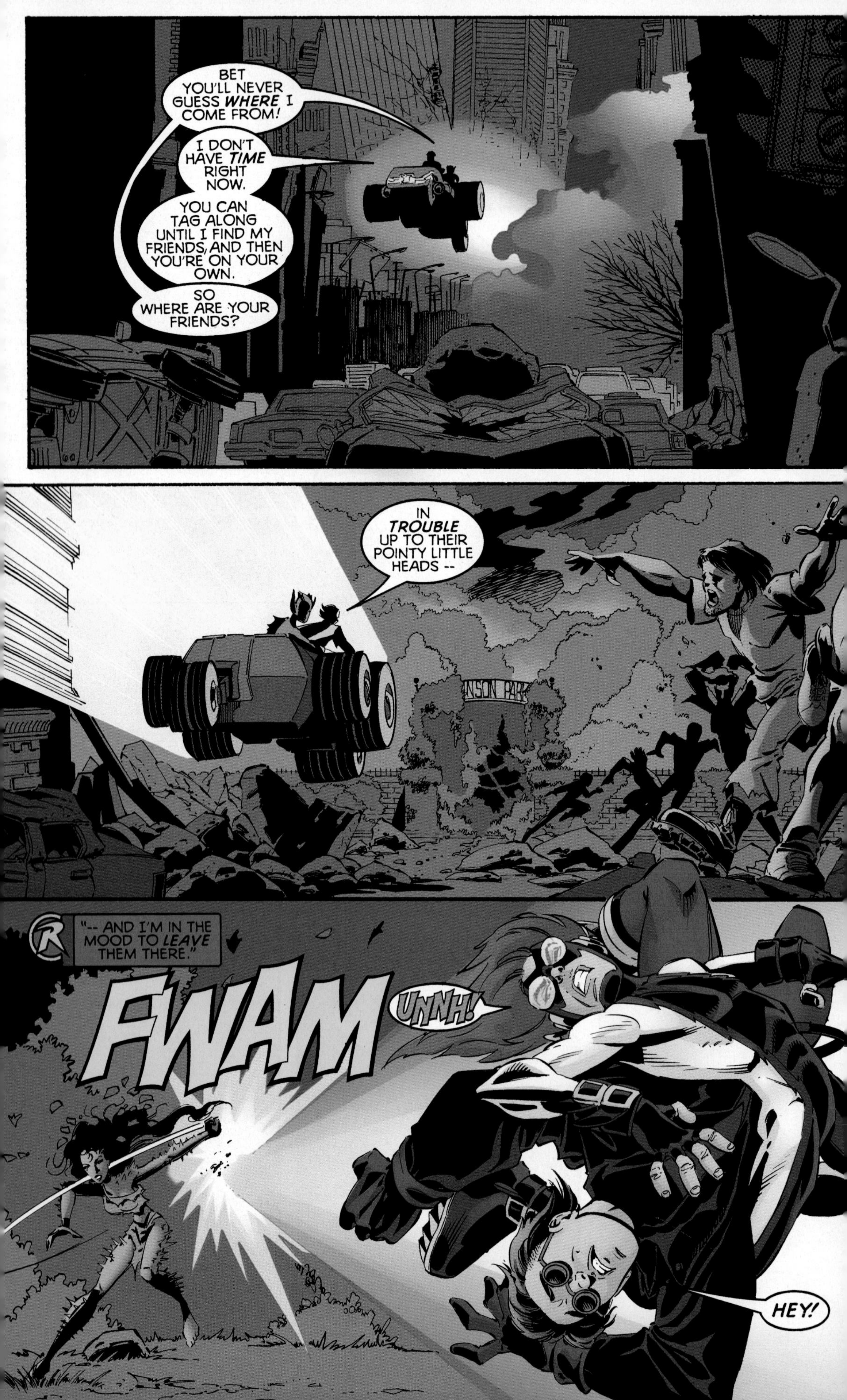

BET YOU'LL NEVER GUESS *WHERE* I COME FROM!
I DON'T HAVE *TIME* RIGHT NOW.
YOU CAN TAG ALONG UNTIL I FIND MY FRIENDS, AND THEN YOU'RE ON YOUR OWN.
SO WHERE ARE YOUR FRIENDS?
IN *TROUBLE* UP TO THEIR POINTY LITTLE HEADS --
"-- AND I'M IN THE MOOD TO *LEAVE* THEM THERE."
FWAM
UNNH!
HEY!

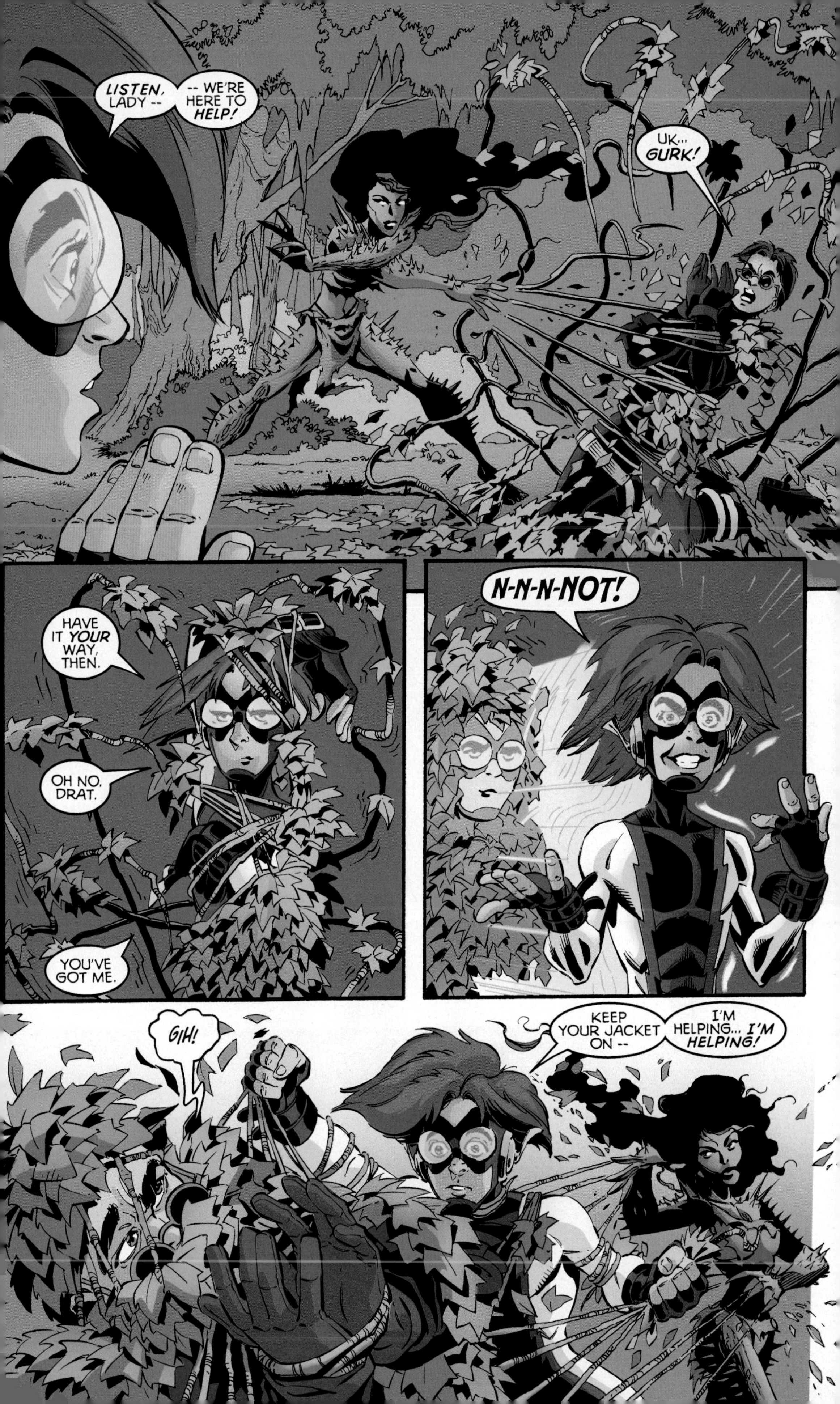

LISTEN, LADY --
-- WE'RE HERE TO HELP!
UK... GURK!
HAVE IT YOUR WAY, THEN.
OH NO. DRAT.
YOU'VE GOT ME.
N-N-N-NOT!
GIH!
KEEP YOUR JACKET ON --
I'M HELPING... I'M HELPING!

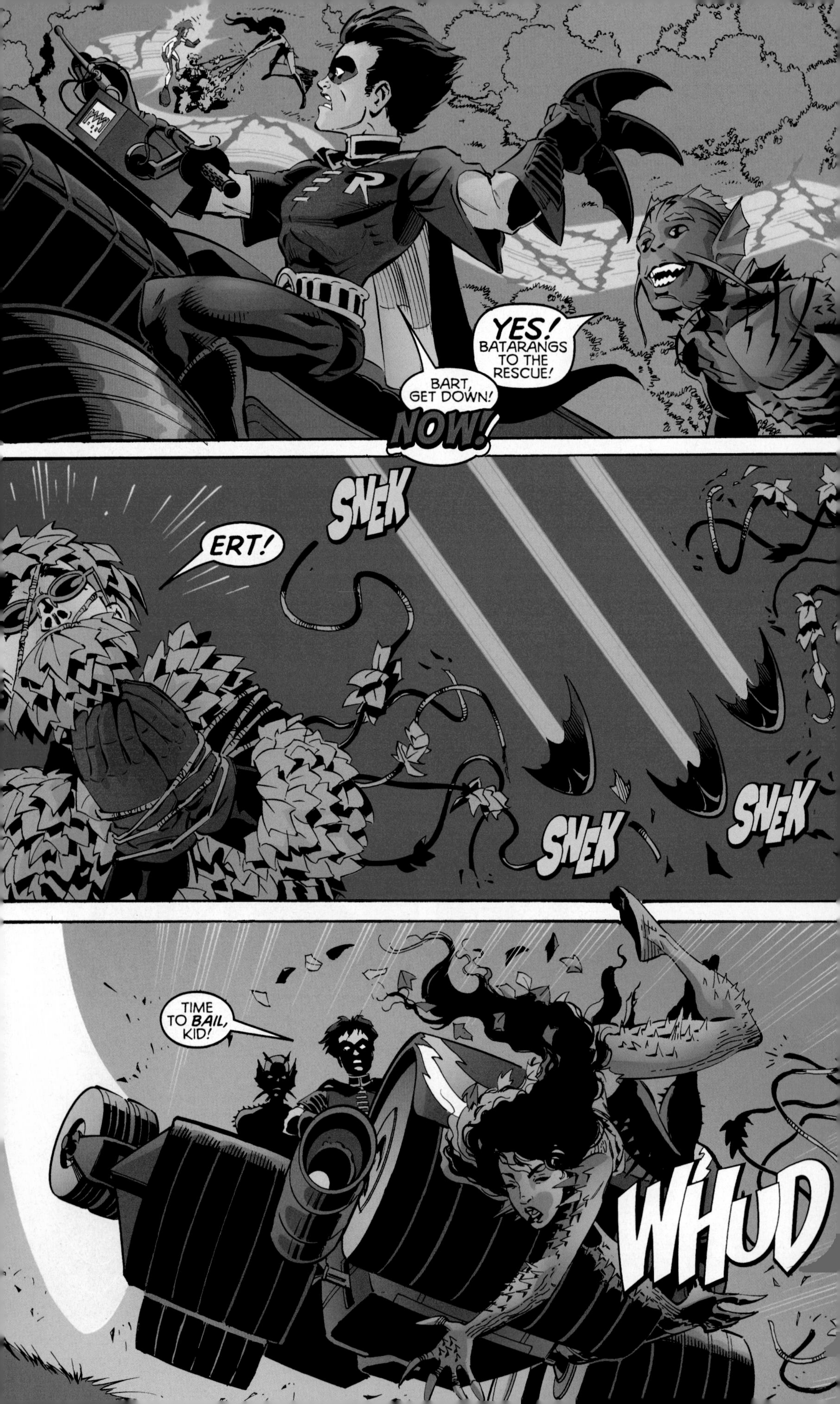
YES! BATARANGS TO THE RESCUE!
BART, GET DOWN! NOW!
ERT!
SNEK
SNEK
SNEK
TIME TO BAIL, KID!
WHUD

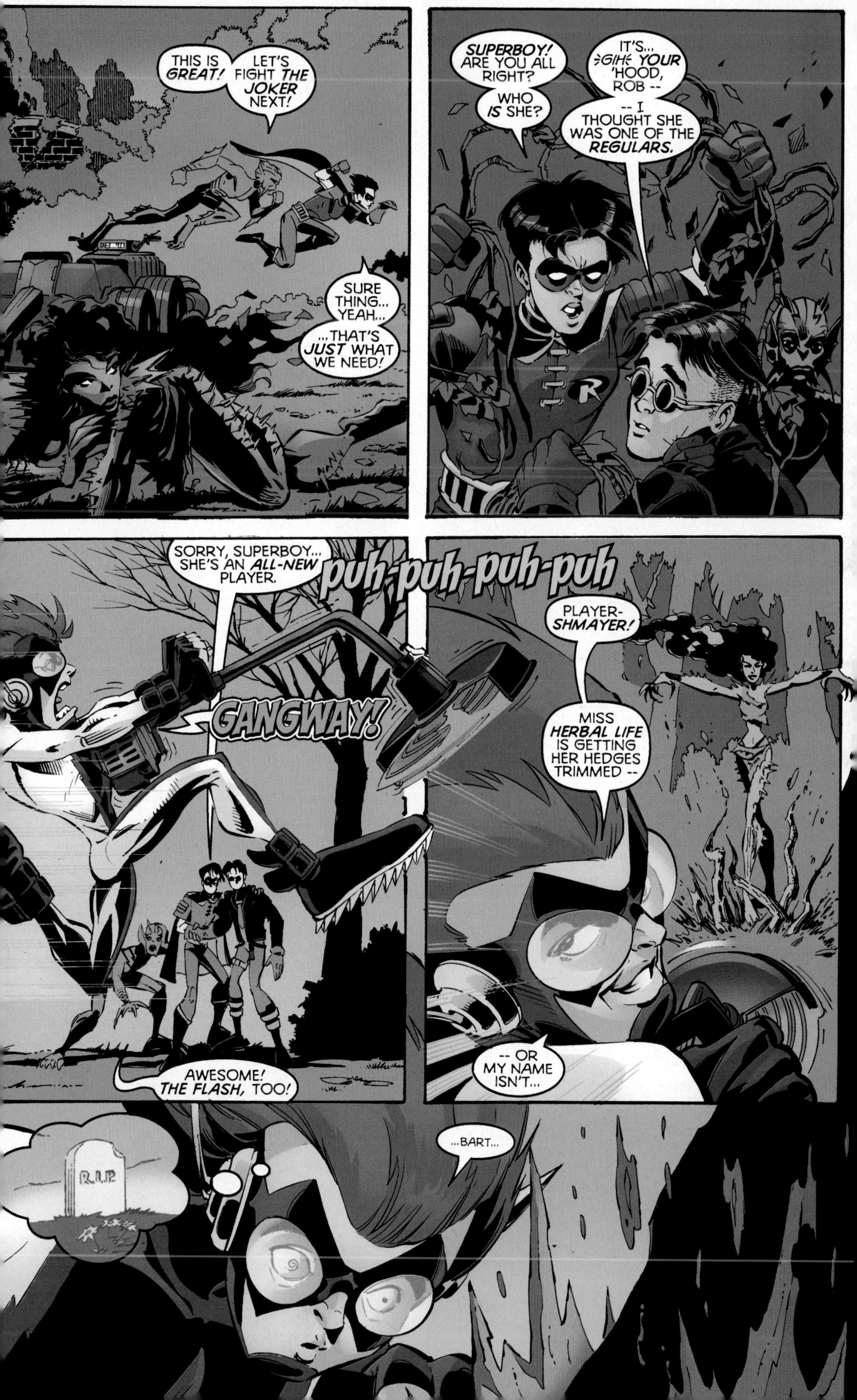

THIS IS GREAT!
LET'S FIGHT THE JOKER NEXT!
SURE THING... YEAH...
...THAT'S JUST WHAT WE NEED!
SUPERBOY! ARE YOU ALL RIGHT?
WHO IS SHE?
IT'S... GIH YOUR 'HOOD, ROB --
-- I THOUGHT SHE WAS ONE OF THE REGULARS.
SORRY, SUPERBOY... SHE'S AN ALL-NEW PLAYER.
puh-puh-puh-puh
GANGWAY!
AWESOME! THE FLASH, TOO!
PLAYER-SHMAYER!
MISS HERBAL LIFE IS GETTING HER HEDGES TRIMMED --
-- OR MY NAME ISN'T...
R.I.P.
...BART...

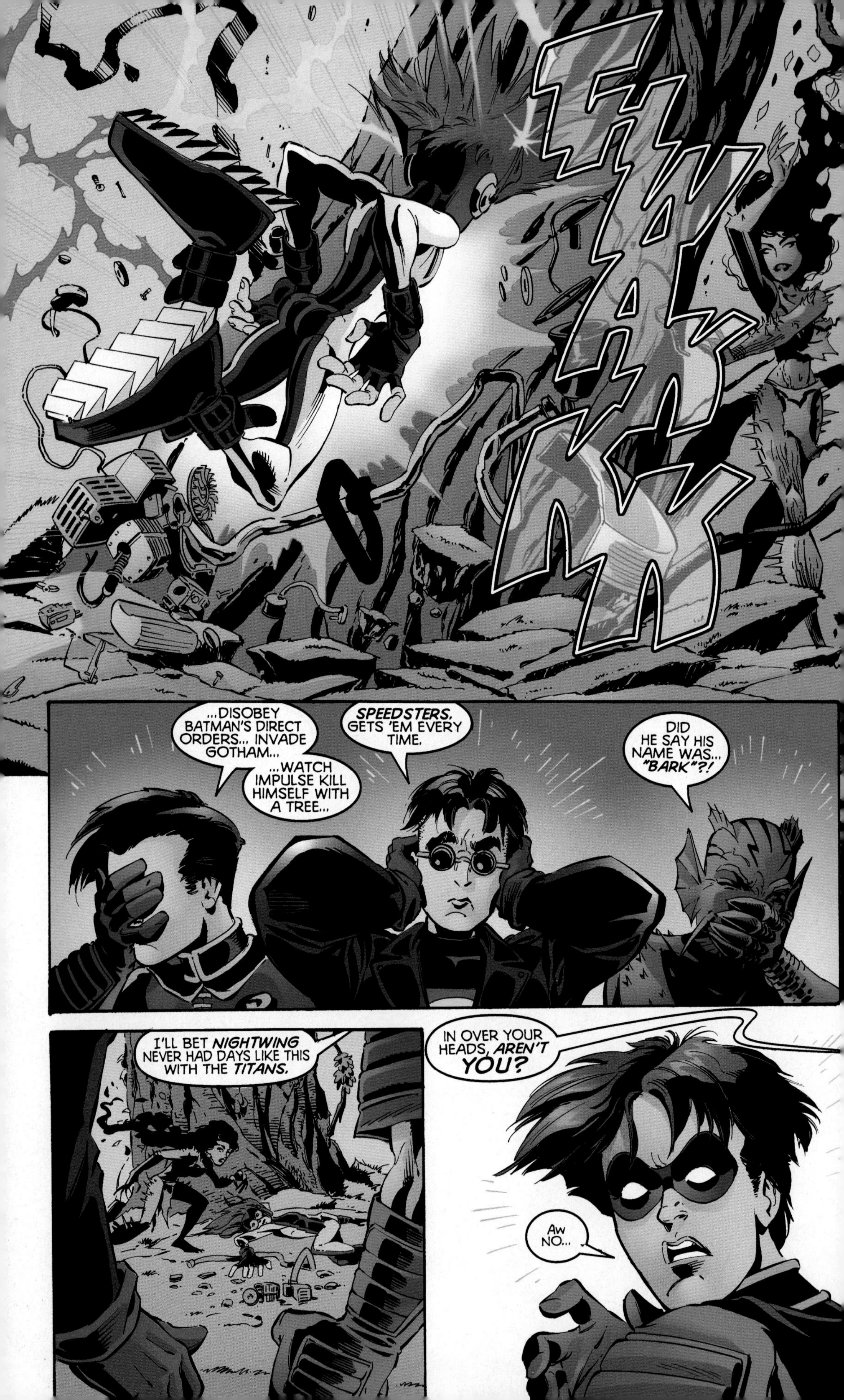
FZZAKK
...DISOBEY BATMAN'S DIRECT ORDERS... INVADE GOTHAM...
...WATCH IMPULSE KILL HIMSELF WITH A TREE...
SPEEDSTERS. GETS 'EM EVERY TIME.
DID HE SAY HIS NAME WAS... "BARK"?!
I'LL BET NIGHTWING NEVER HAD DAYS LIKE THIS WITH THE TITANS.
IN OVER YOUR HEADS, AREN'T YOU?
AW NO...

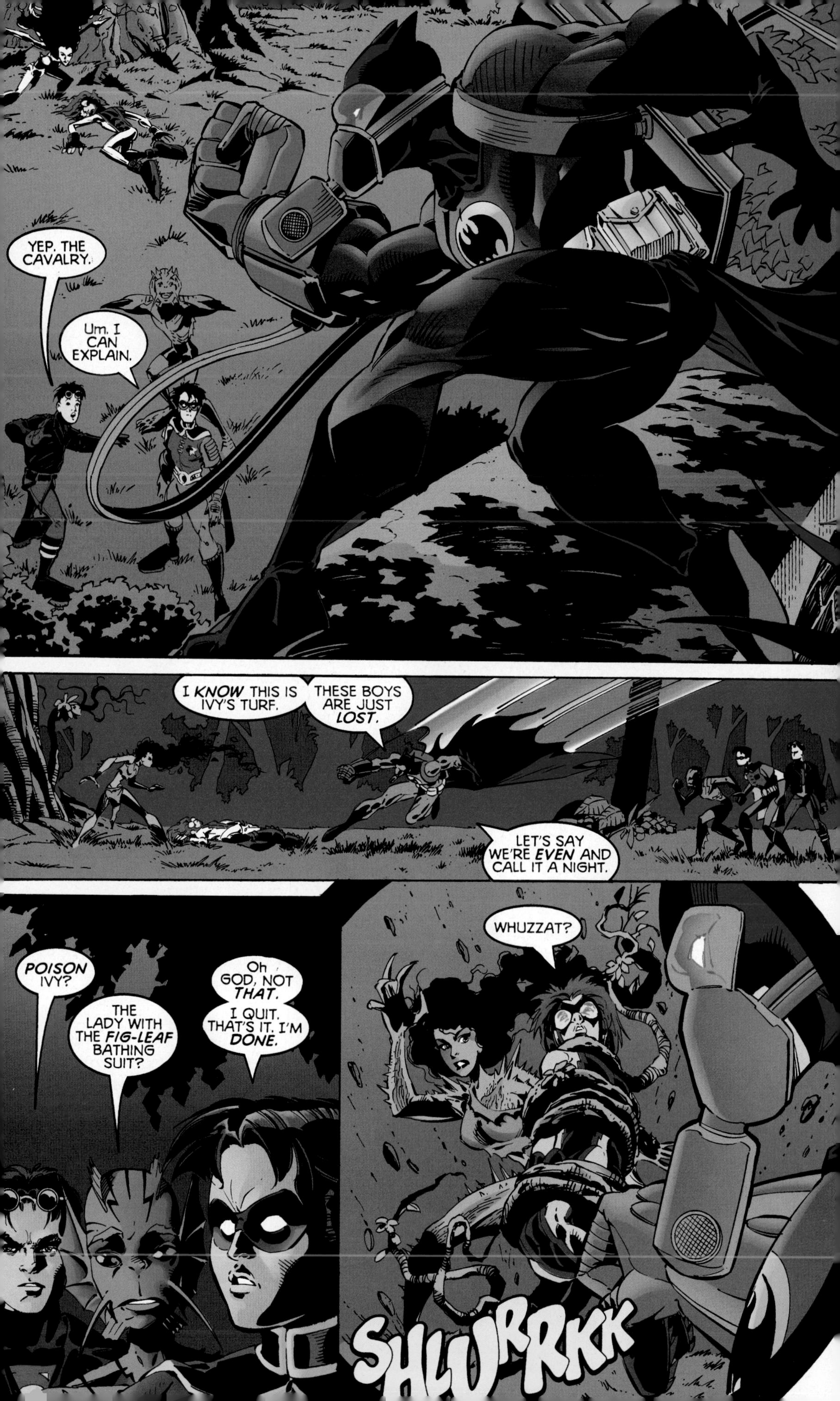
YEP. THE CAVALRY.
Um. I CAN EXPLAIN.
I KNOW THIS IS IVY'S TURF.
THESE BOYS ARE JUST LOST.
LET'S SAY WE'RE EVEN AND CALL IT A NIGHT.
POISON IVY?
THE LADY WITH THE FIG-LEAF BATHING SUIT?
Oh GOD, NOT THAT. I QUIT. THAT'S IT. I'M DONE.
WHUZZAT?
SHLURRKK

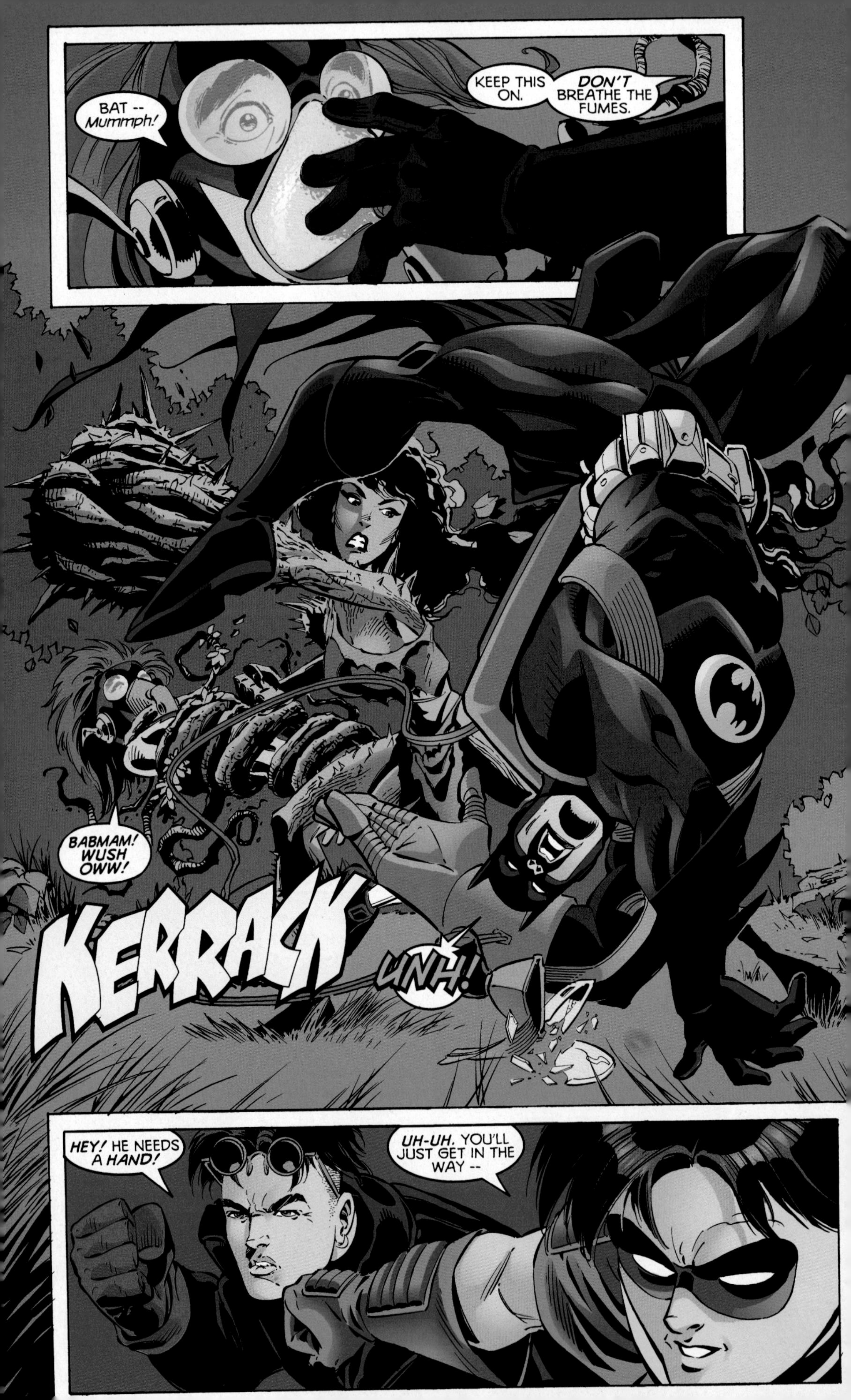
BAT -- Mummph!
KEEP THIS ON.
DON'T BREATHE THE FUMES.
BABMAM! WUSH OWW!
KERRACK
UNH!
HEY! HE NEEDS A HAND!
UH-UH. YOU'LL JUST GET IN THE WAY --

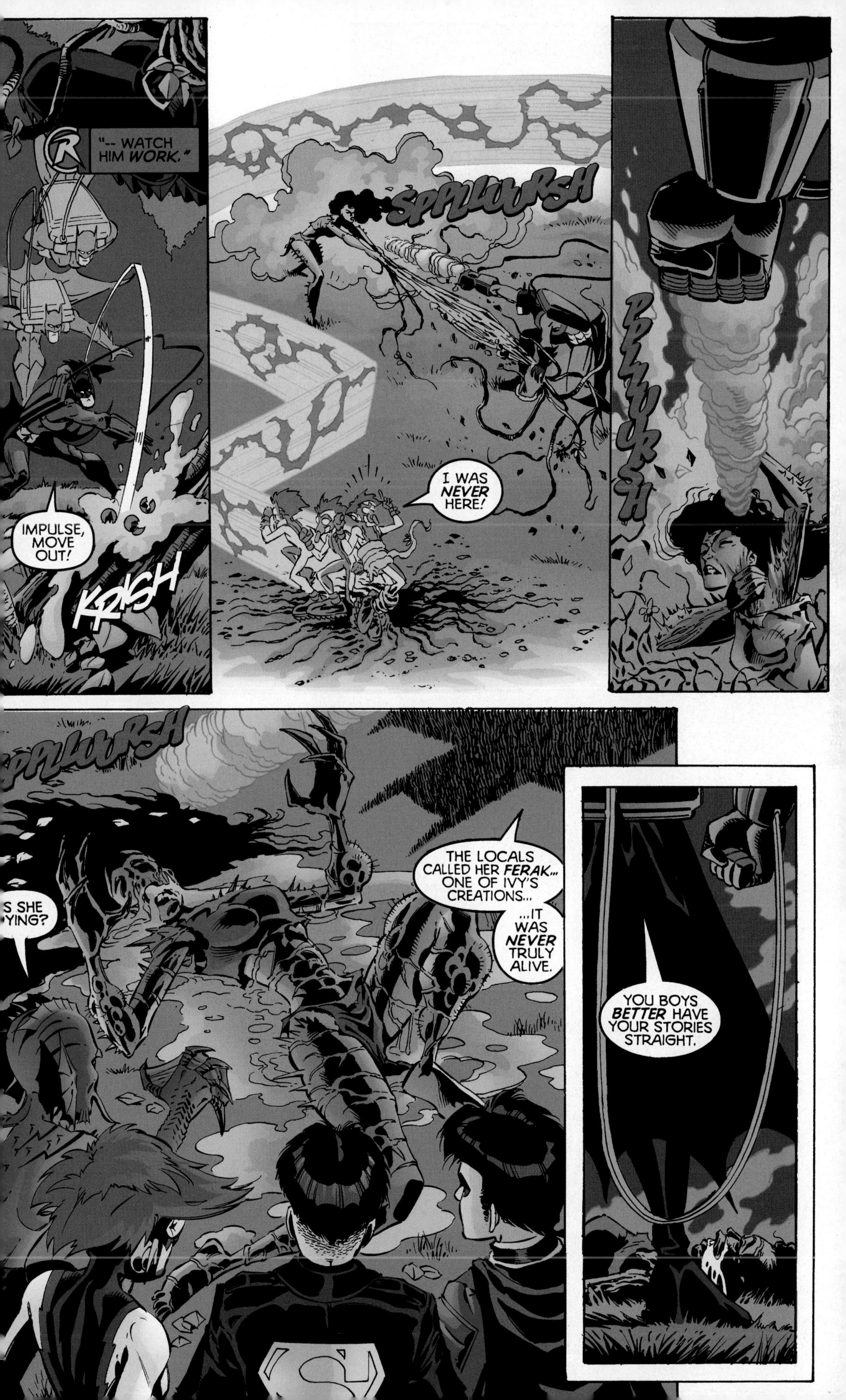
"-- WATCH HIM WORK."
IMPULSE, MOVE OUT!
KRISH
SPPLUUURSH
I WAS NEVER HERE!
PPLUUURSH
SPPLUUURSH
S SHE YING?
THE LOCALS CALLED HER FERAK... ONE OF IVY'S CREATIONS...
...IT WAS NEVER TRULY ALIVE.
YOU BOYS BETTER HAVE YOUR STORIES STRAIGHT.

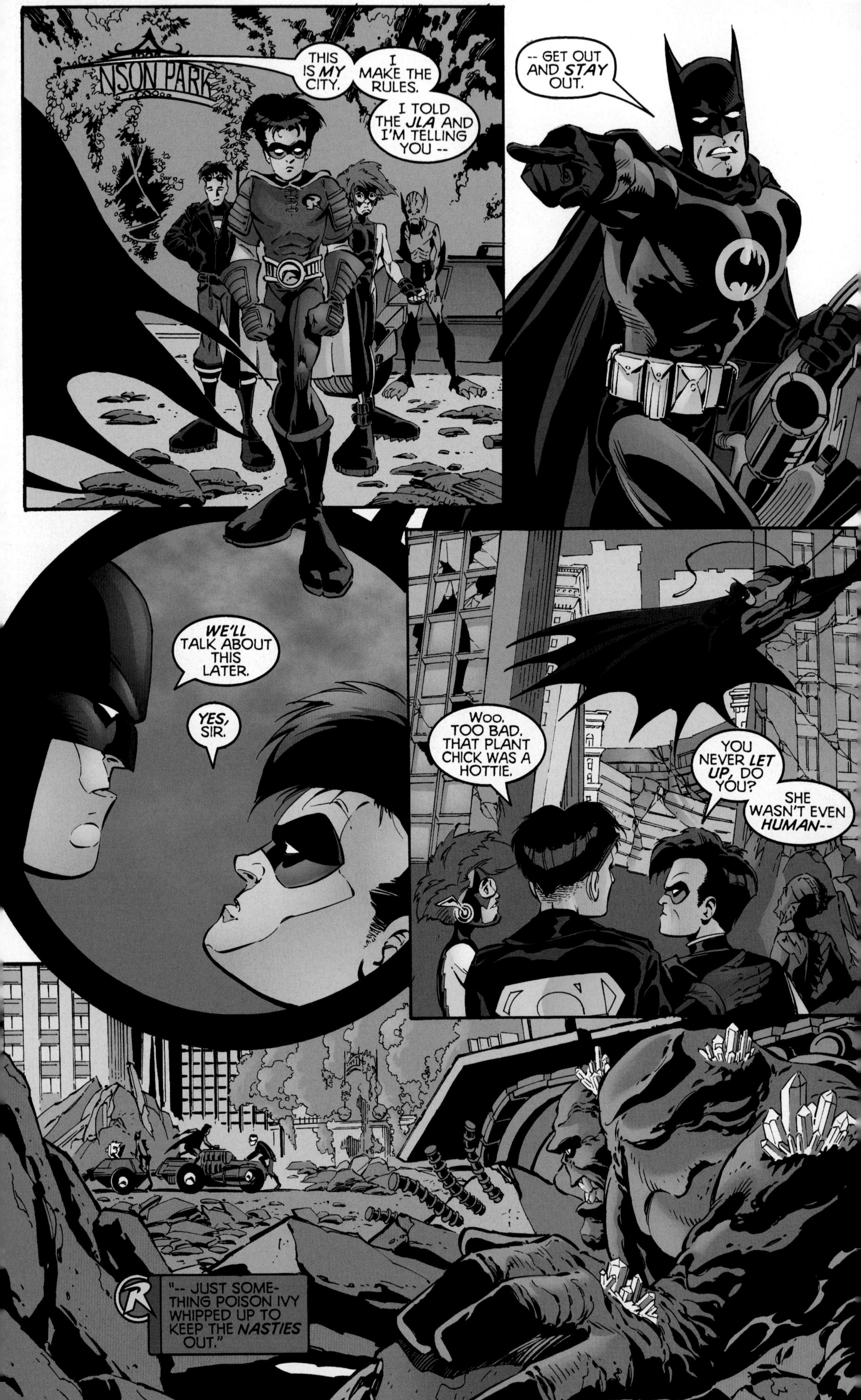
NSON PARK
THIS IS MY CITY.
I MAKE THE RULES.
I TOLD THE JLA AND I'M TELLING YOU --
-- GET OUT AND STAY OUT.
WE'LL TALK ABOUT THIS LATER.
YES, SIR.
Woo. TOO BAD. THAT PLANT CHICK WAS A HOTTIE.
YOU NEVER LET UP, DO YOU?
SHE WASN'T EVEN HUMAN--
"-- JUST SOME-THING POISON IVY WHIPPED UP TO KEEP THE NASTIES OUT."

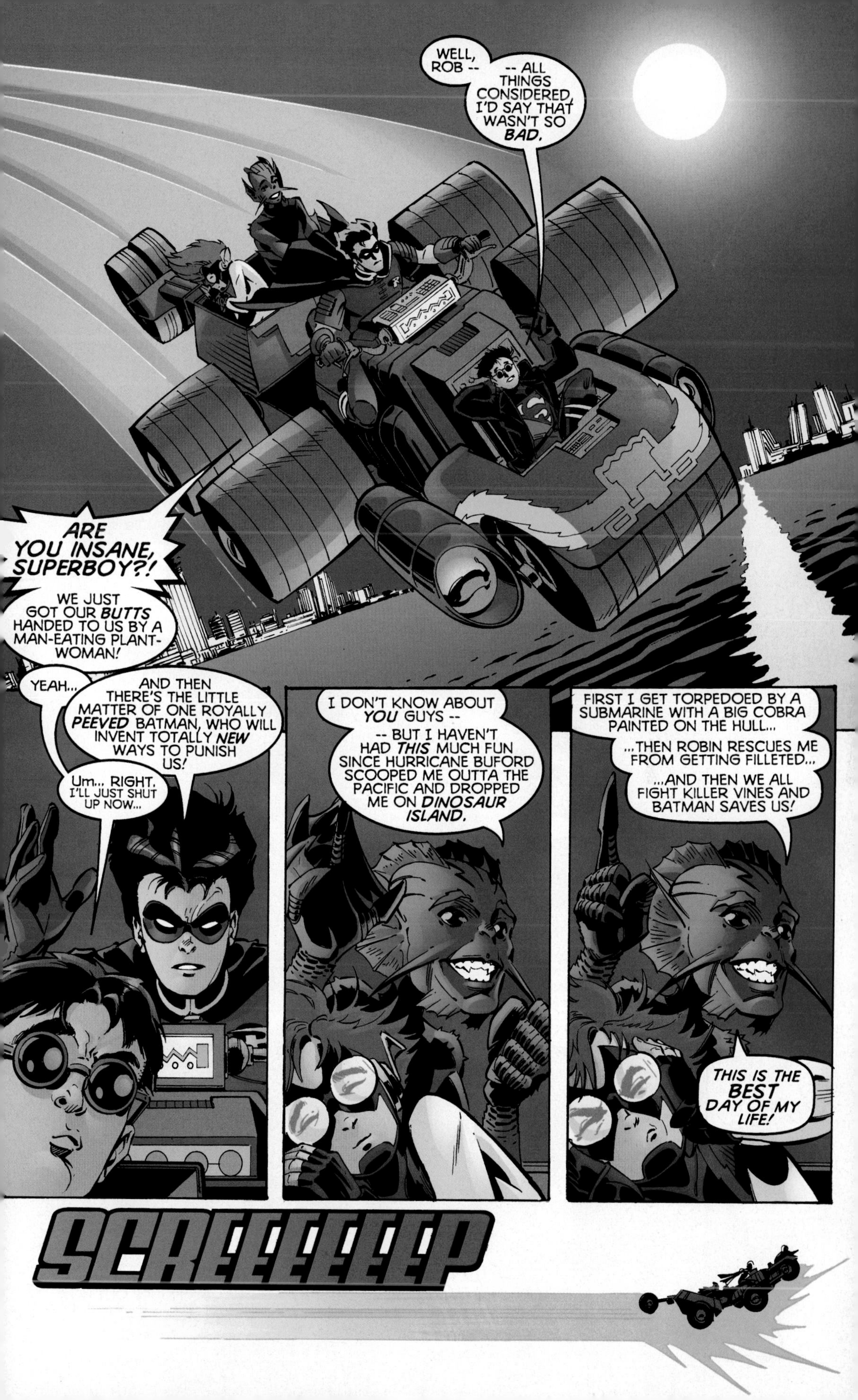

WELL, ROB --
-- ALL THINGS CONSIDERED, I'D SAY THAT WASN'T SO BAD.
ARE YOU INSANE, SUPERBOY?!
WE JUST GOT OUR BUTTS HANDED TO US BY A MAN-EATING PLANT-WOMAN!
YEAH...
AND THEN THERE'S THE LITTLE MATTER OF ONE ROYALLY PEEVED BATMAN, WHO WILL INVENT TOTALLY NEW WAYS TO PUNISH US!
Um... RIGHT. I'LL JUST SHUT UP NOW...
I DON'T KNOW ABOUT YOU GUYS --
-- BUT I HAVEN'T HAD THIS MUCH FUN SINCE HURRICANE BUFORD SCOOPED ME OUTTA THE PACIFIC AND DROPPED ME ON DINOSAUR ISLAND.
FIRST I GET TORPEDOED BY A SUBMARINE WITH A BIG COBRA PAINTED ON THE HULL...
...THEN ROBIN RESCUES ME FROM GETTING FILLETED...
...AND THEN WE ALL FIGHT KILLER VINES AND BATMAN SAVES US!
THIS IS THE BEST DAY OF MY LIFE!
SCREEEEEEP

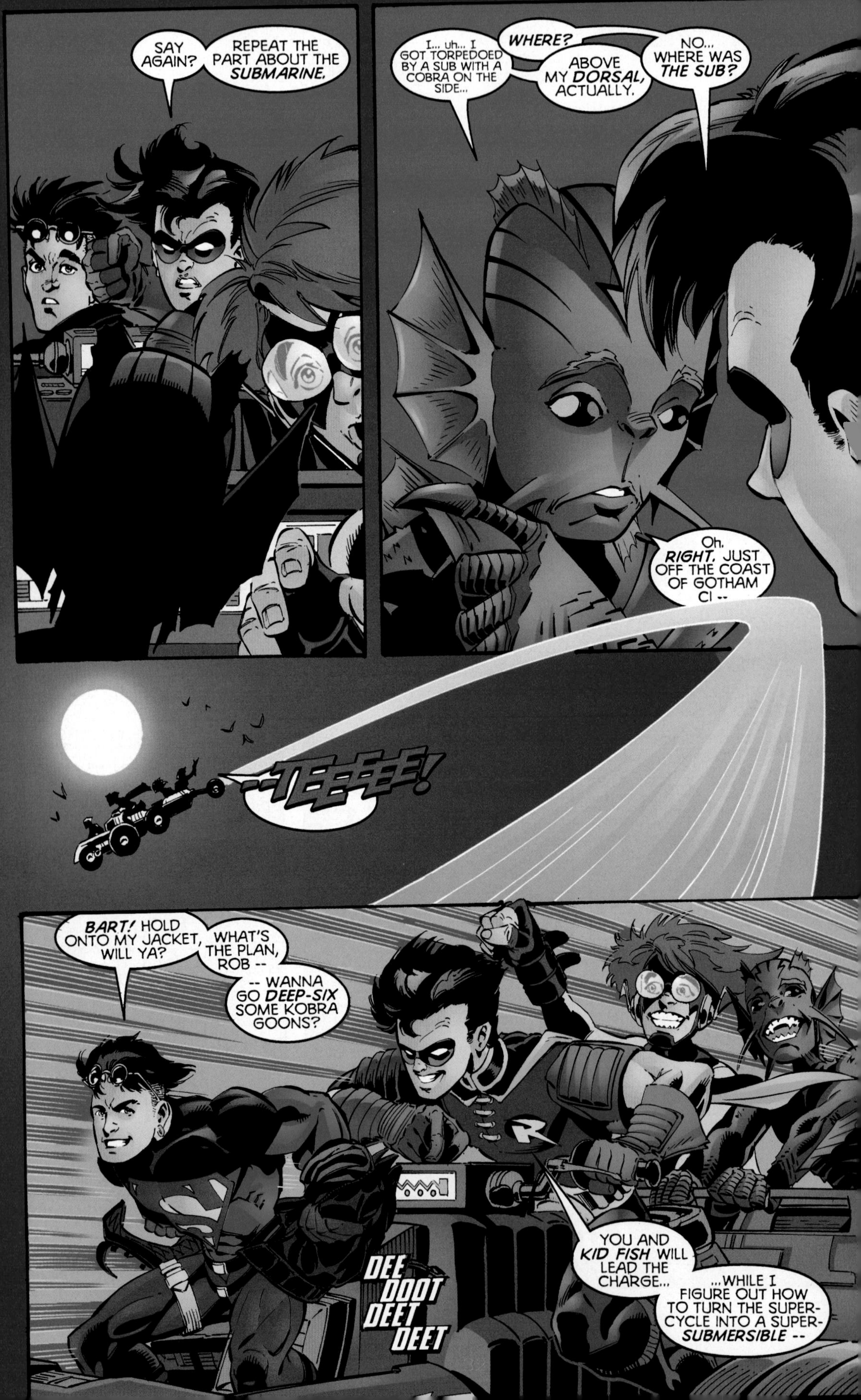
SAY AGAIN?
REPEAT THE PART ABOUT THE SUBMARINE.
I... uh... I GOT TORPEDOED BY A SUB WITH A COBRA ON THE SIDE...
WHERE?
ABOVE MY DORSAL, ACTUALLY.
NO... WHERE WAS THE SUB?
Oh, RIGHT. JUST OFF THE COAST OF GOTHAM CI --
--TEEEEEE!
BART! HOLD ONTO MY JACKET, WILL YA?
WHAT'S THE PLAN, ROB --
-- WANNA GO DEEP-SIX SOME KOBRA GOONS?
YOU AND KID FISH WILL LEAD THE CHARGE...
...WHILE I FIGURE OUT HOW TO TURN THE SUPER-CYCLE INTO A SUPER-SUBMERSIBLE --
DEE DOOT DEET DEET

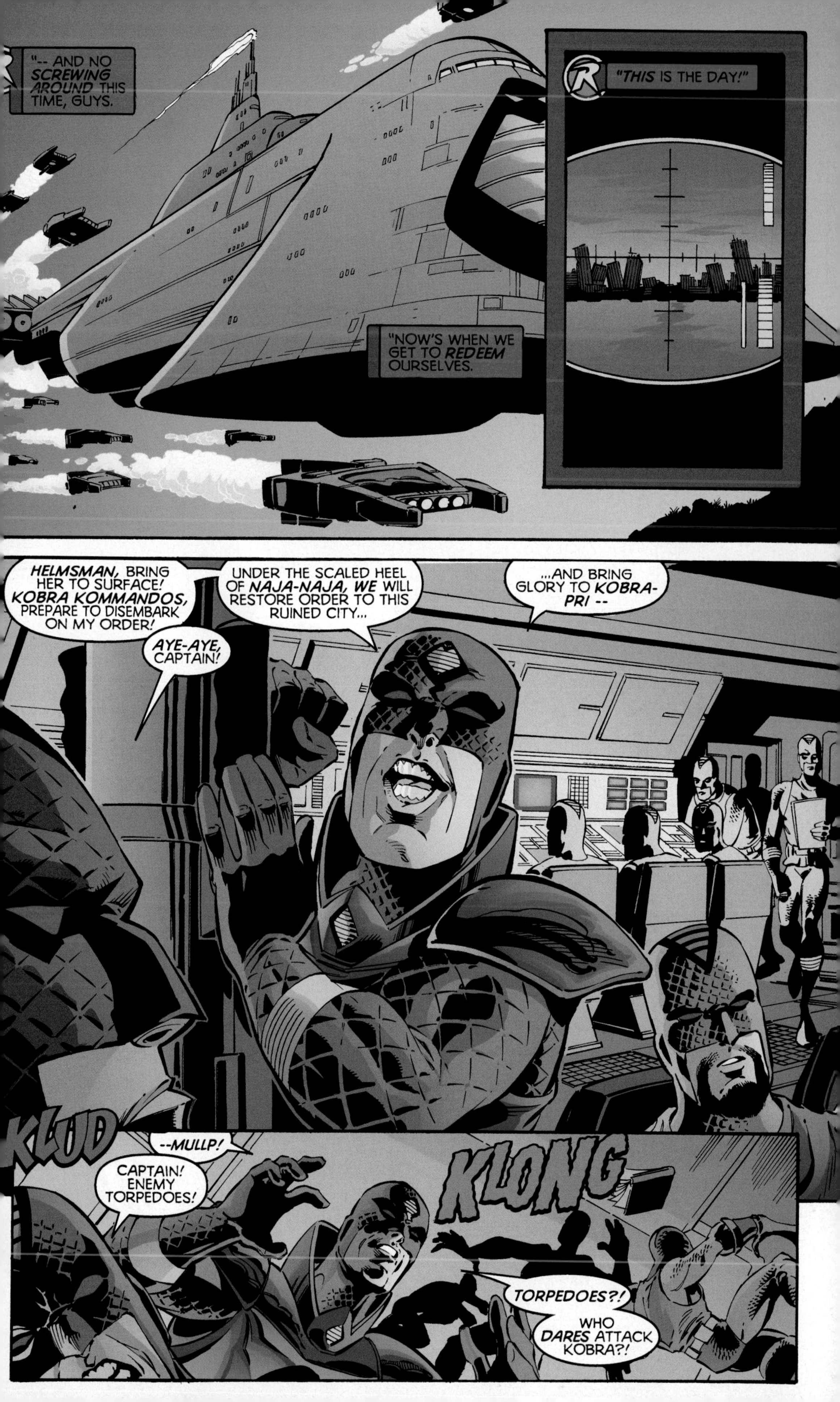
"-- AND NO *SCREWING AROUND* THIS TIME, GUYS.
"*THIS* IS THE DAY!"
"NOW'S WHEN WE GET TO *REDEEM* OURSELVES.
HELMSMAN, BRING HER TO SURFACE! *KOBRA KOMMANDOS,* PREPARE TO DISEMBARK ON MY ORDER!
AYE-AYE, CAPTAIN!
UNDER THE SCALED HEEL OF *NAJA-NAJA, WE* WILL RESTORE ORDER TO THIS RUINED CITY...
...AND BRING GLORY TO *KOBRA-PRI* --
KLUD
--*MULLP!*
CAPTAIN! ENEMY TORPEDOES!
KLONG
TORPEDOES?!
WHO *DARES* ATTACK KOBRA?!

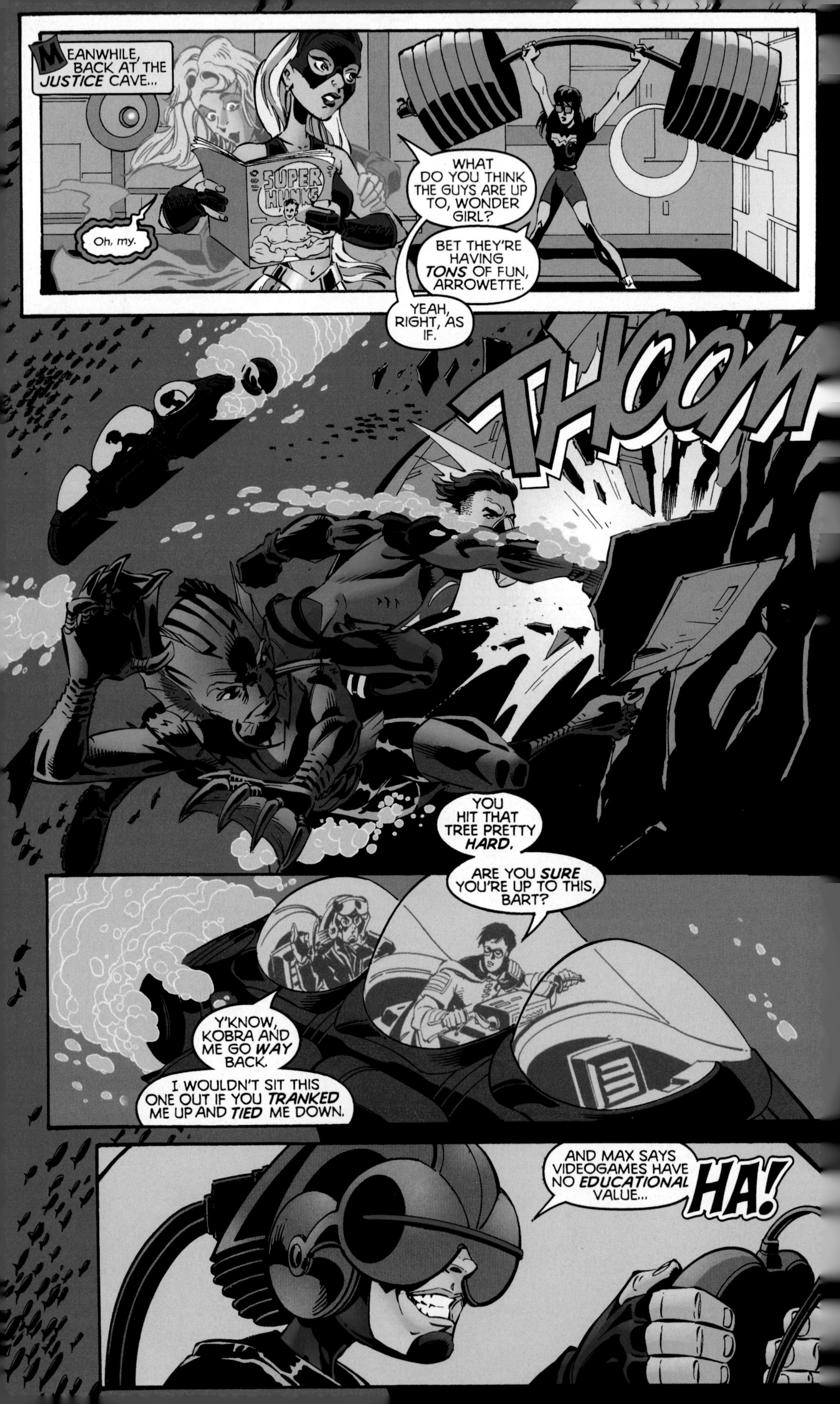

MEANWHILE, BACK AT THE JUSTICE CAVE...
SUPER HUNKS
Oh, my.
WHAT DO YOU THINK THE GUYS ARE UP TO, WONDER GIRL?
BET THEY'RE HAVING TONS OF FUN, ARROWETTE.
YEAH, RIGHT, AS IF.
THOOM
YOU HIT THAT TREE PRETTY HARD.
ARE YOU SURE YOU'RE UP TO THIS, BART?
Y'KNOW, KOBRA AND ME GO WAY BACK.
I WOULDN'T SIT THIS ONE OUT IF YOU TRANKED ME UP AND TIED ME DOWN.
AND MAX SAYS VIDEOGAMES HAVE NO EDUCATIONAL VALUE...
HA!

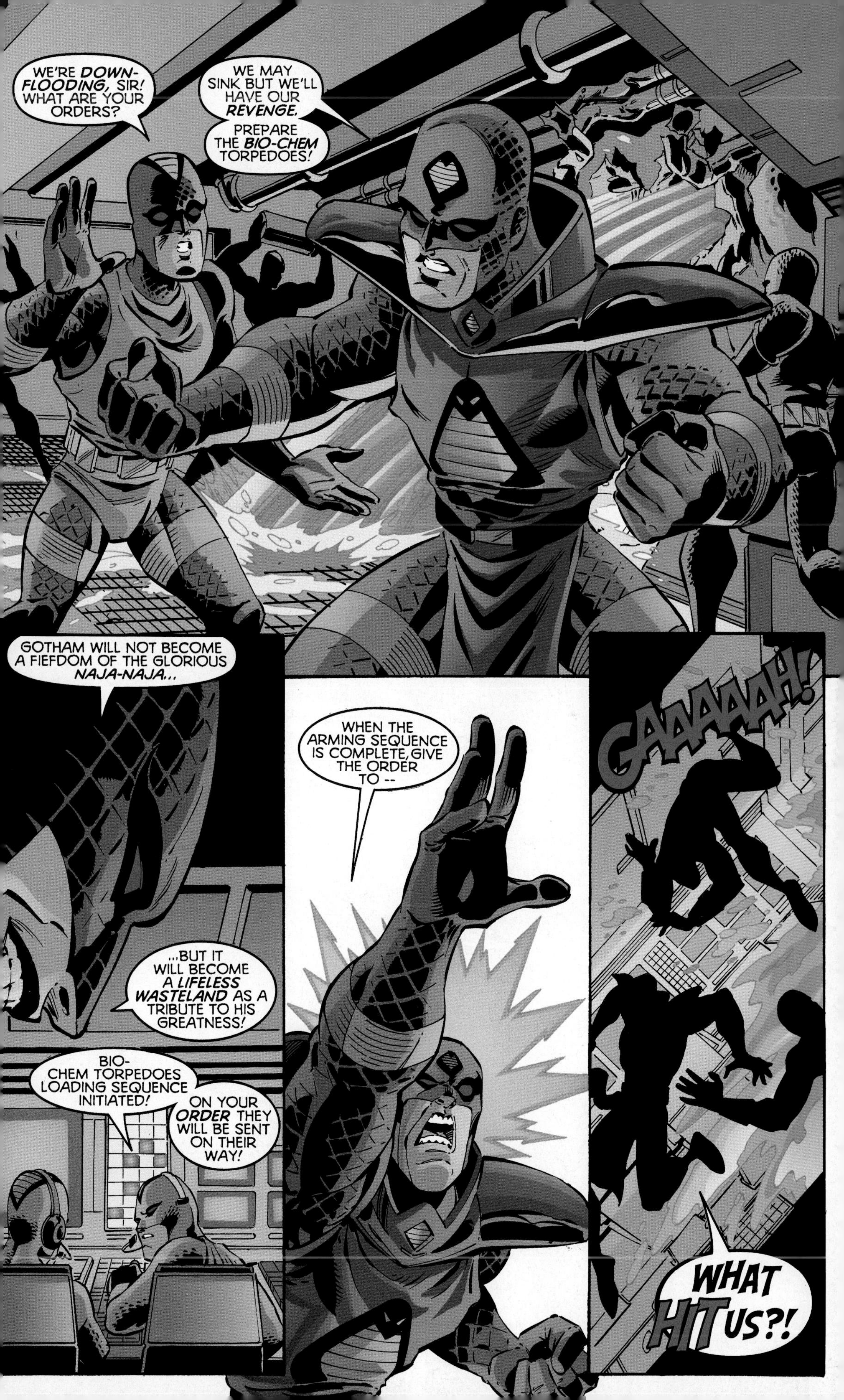
WE'RE DOWN-FLOODING, SIR! WHAT ARE YOUR ORDERS?
WE MAY SINK BUT WE'LL HAVE OUR REVENGE.
PREPARE THE BIO-CHEM TORPEDOES!
GOTHAM WILL NOT BECOME A FIEFDOM OF THE GLORIOUS NAJA-NAJA...
...BUT IT WILL BECOME A LIFELESS WASTELAND AS A TRIBUTE TO HIS GREATNESS!
BIO-CHEM TORPEDOES LOADING SEQUENCE INITIATED!
ON YOUR ORDER THEY WILL BE SENT ON THEIR WAY!
WHEN THE ARMING SEQUENCE IS COMPLETE, GIVE THE ORDER TO --
GAAAAAH!
WHAT HIT US?!

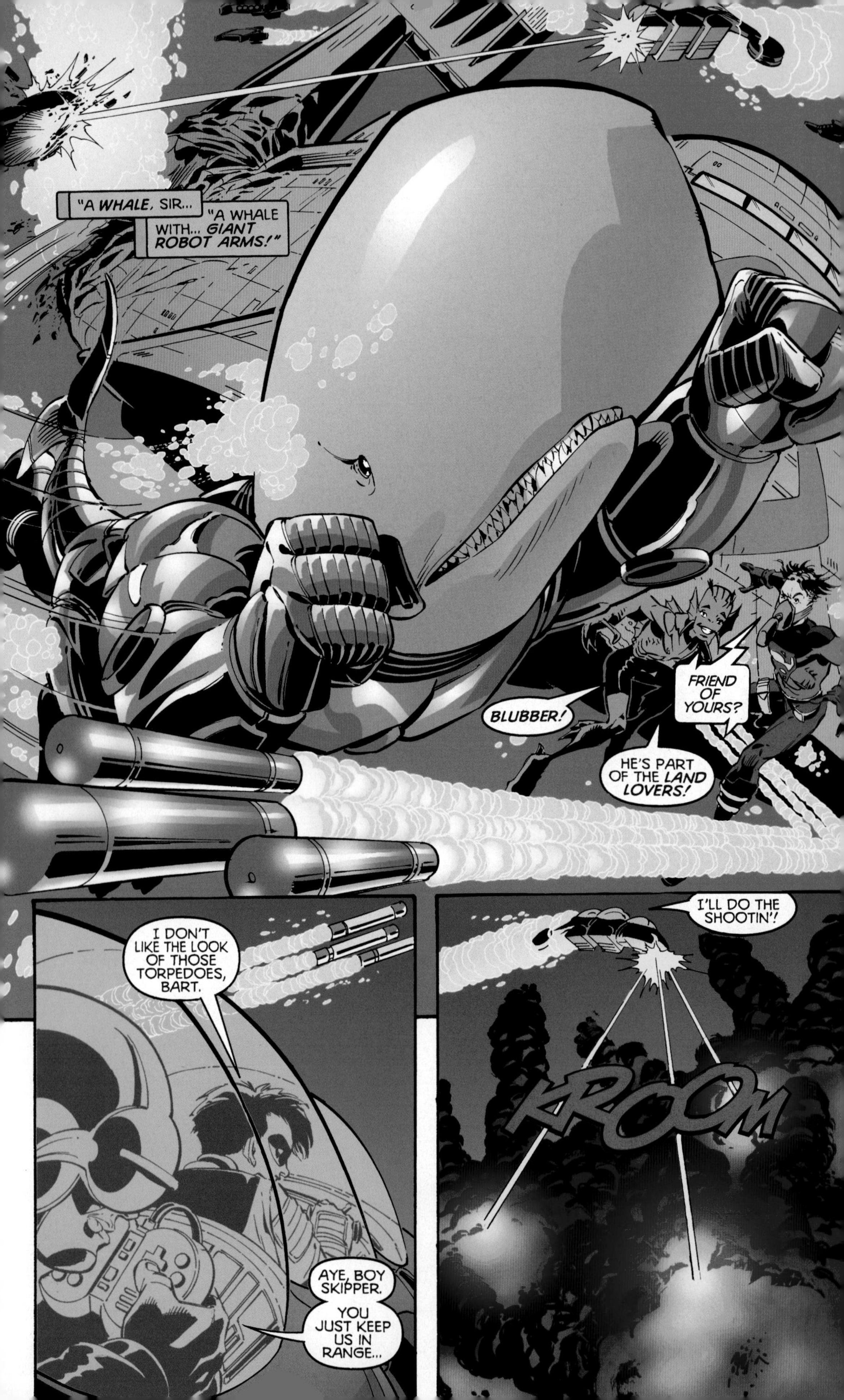
"A WHALE, SIR...
"A WHALE WITH... GIANT ROBOT ARMS!"
BLUBBER!
FRIEND OF YOURS?
HE'S PART OF THE LAND LOVERS!
I DON'T LIKE THE LOOK OF THOSE TORPEDOES, BART.
AYE, BOY SKIPPER.
YOU JUST KEEP US IN RANGE...
I'LL DO THE SHOOTIN'!
KROOOM

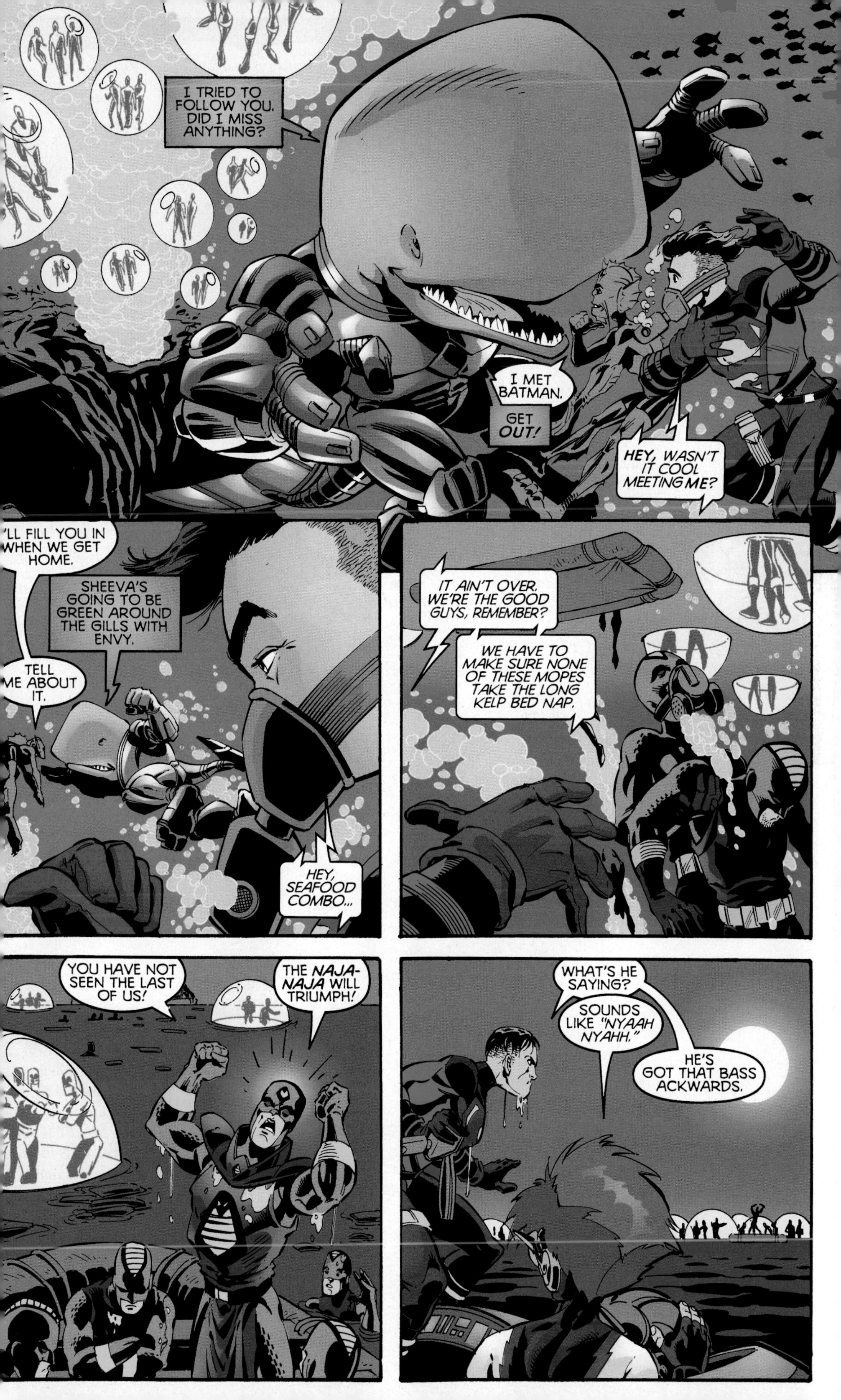

I TRIED TO FOLLOW YOU. DID I MISS ANYTHING?
I MET BATMAN.
GET OUT!
HEY, WASN'T IT COOL MEETING ME?
I'LL FILL YOU IN WHEN WE GET HOME.
SHEEVA'S GOING TO BE GREEN AROUND THE GILLS WITH ENVY.
TELL ME ABOUT IT.
HEY, SEAFOOD COMBO...
IT AIN'T OVER. WE'RE THE GOOD GUYS, REMEMBER?
WE HAVE TO MAKE SURE NONE OF THESE MOPES TAKE THE LONG KELP BED NAP.
YOU HAVE NOT SEEN THE LAST OF US!
THE NAJA-NAJA WILL TRIUMPH!
WHAT'S HE SAYING?
SOUNDS LIKE "NYAAH NYAHH."
HE'S GOT THAT BASS ACKWARDS.

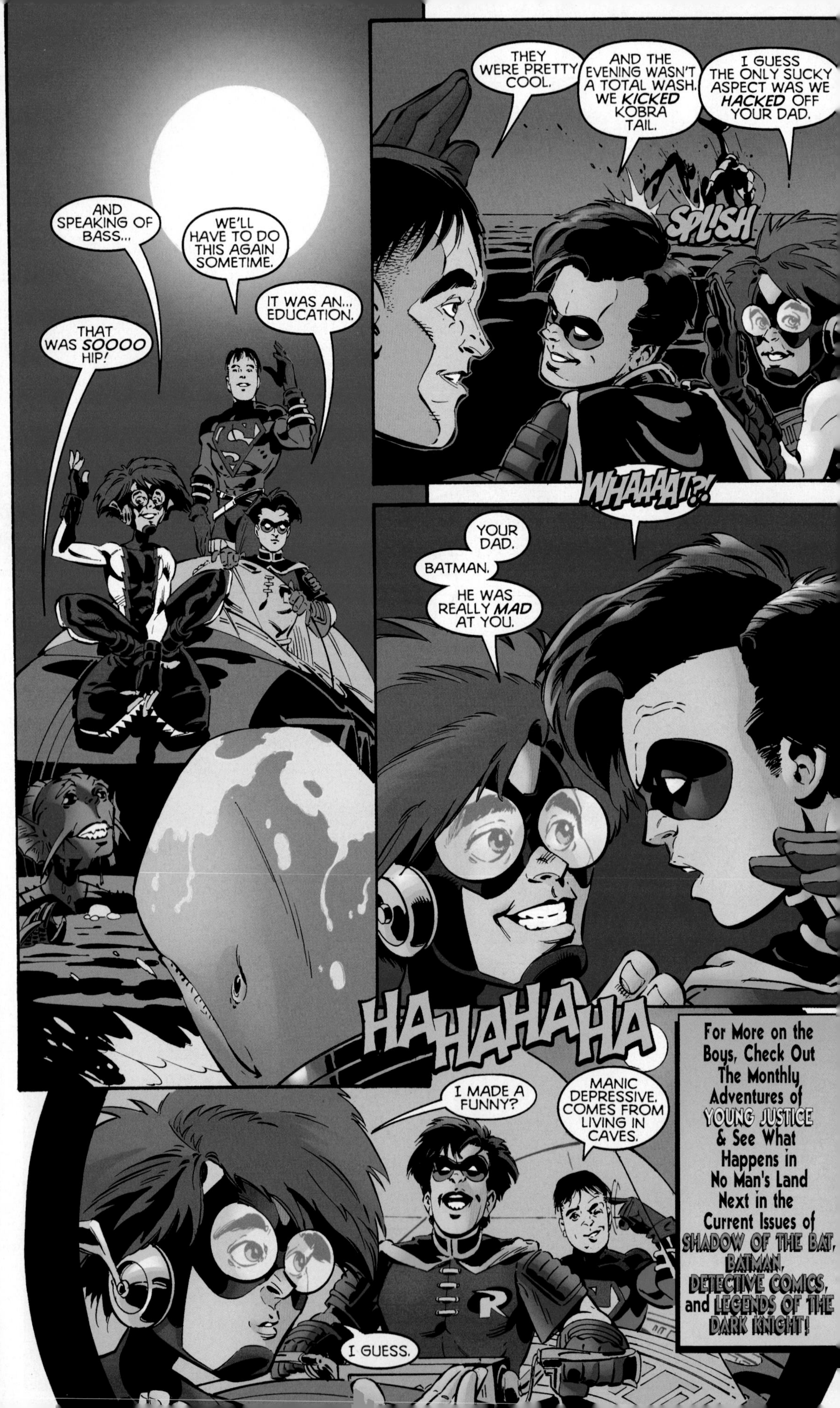
THEY WERE PRETTY COOL.
AND THE EVENING WASN'T A TOTAL WASH. WE KICKED KOBRA TAIL.
I GUESS THE ONLY SUCKY ASPECT WAS WE HACKED OFF YOUR DAD.
SPLISH
AND SPEAKING OF BASS...
WE'LL HAVE TO DO THIS AGAIN SOMETIME.
IT WAS AN... EDUCATION.
THAT WAS SOOOO HIP!
WHAAAAT?!
YOUR DAD.
BATMAN.
HE WAS REALLY MAD AT YOU.
HAHAHAHAHA
I MADE A FUNNY?
MANIC DEPRESSIVE. COMES FROM LIVING IN CAVES.
I GUESS.
For More on the Boys, Check Out The Monthly Adventures of YOUNG JUSTICE & See What Happens in No Man's Land Next in the Current Issues of SHADOW OF THE BAT, BATMAN, DETECTIVE COMICS, and LEGENDS OF THE DARK KNIGHT!

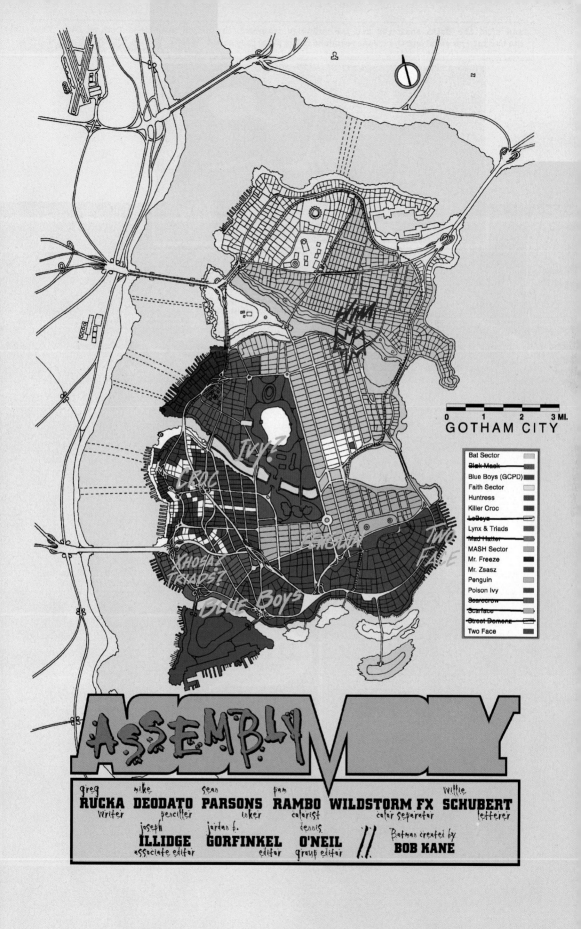

GOTHAM CITY

0 1 2 3 MI.

Bat Sector
Black Mask
Blue Boys (GCPD)
Faith Sector
Huntress
Killer Croc
LeBoys
Lynx & Triads
Mad Hatter
MASH Sector
Mr. Freeze
Mr. Zsasz
Penguin
Poison Ivy
Scarecrow
Scarface
Street Demonz
Two Face

IVY?
CROC
XHOSA? TRIADS?
Blue Boys
TWO FACE

ASSEMBLY

greg
RUCKA
Writer

mike
DEODATO
penciller

sean
PARSONS
inker

pam
RAMBO
colorist

WILDSTORM FX
color separator

willie
SCHUBERT
letterer

joseph
ILLIDGE
associate editor

jordan b.
GORFINKEL
editor

dennis
O'NEIL
group editor

Batman created by
BOB KANE

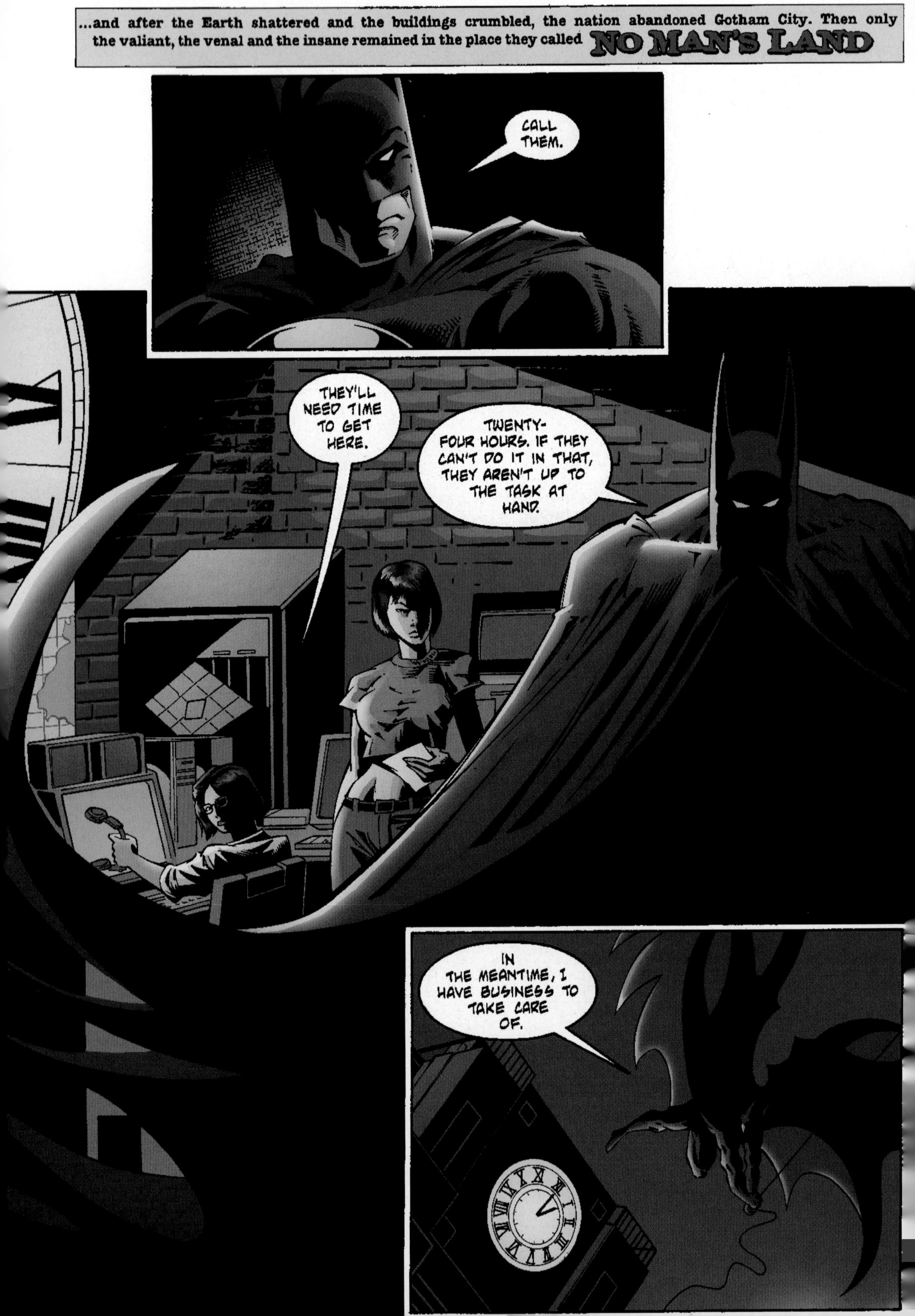
...and after the Earth shattered and the buildings crumbled, the nation abandoned Gotham City. Then only the valiant, the venal and the insane remained in the place they called NO MAN'S LAND
CALL THEM.
THEY'LL NEED TIME TO GET HERE.
TWENTY-FOUR HOURS. IF THEY CAN'T DO IT IN THAT, THEY AREN'T UP TO THE TASK AT HAND.
IN THE MEANTIME, I HAVE BUSINESS TO TAKE CARE OF.

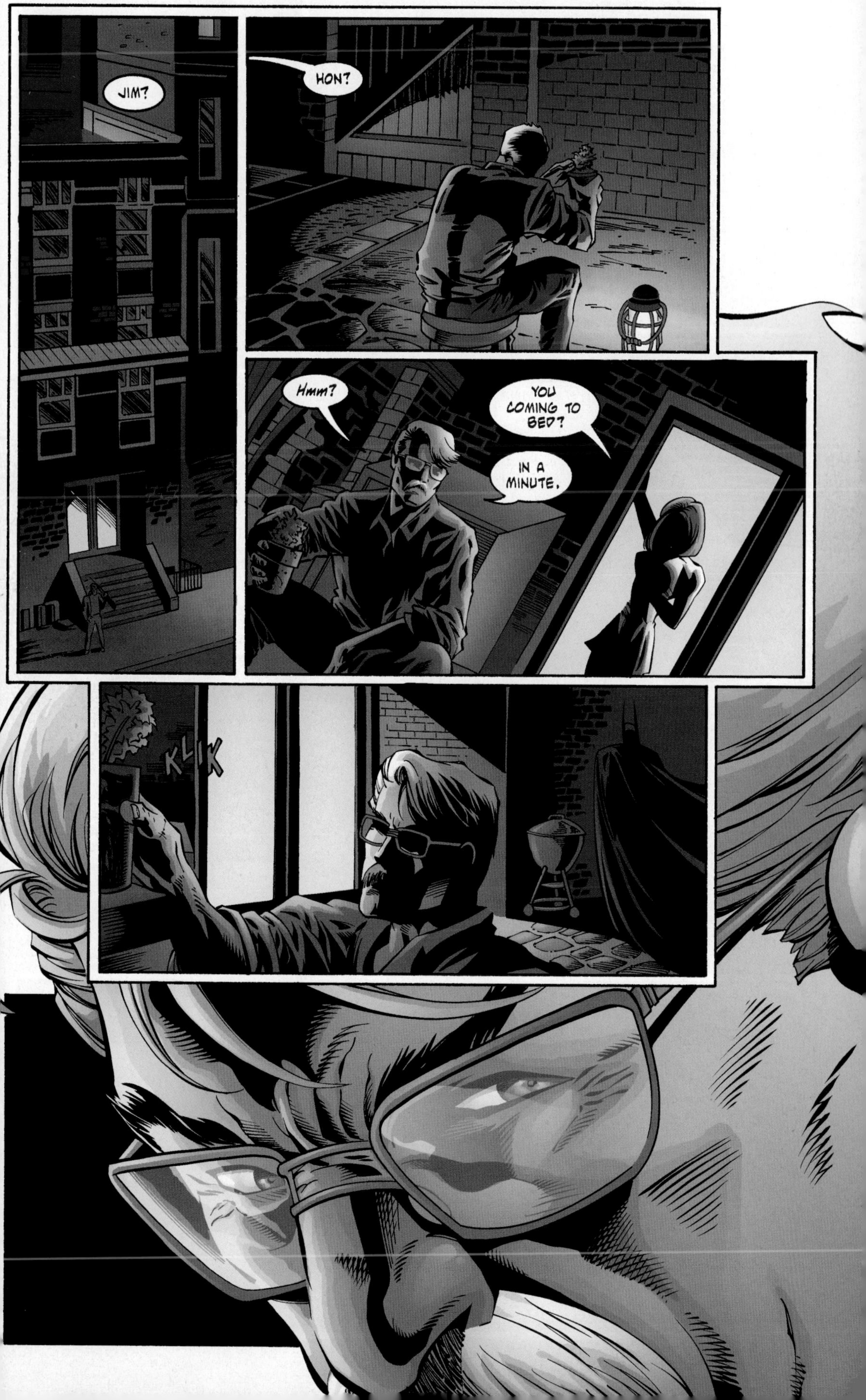
JIM?
HON?
Hmm?
YOU COMING TO BED?
IN A MINUTE.
KLIK

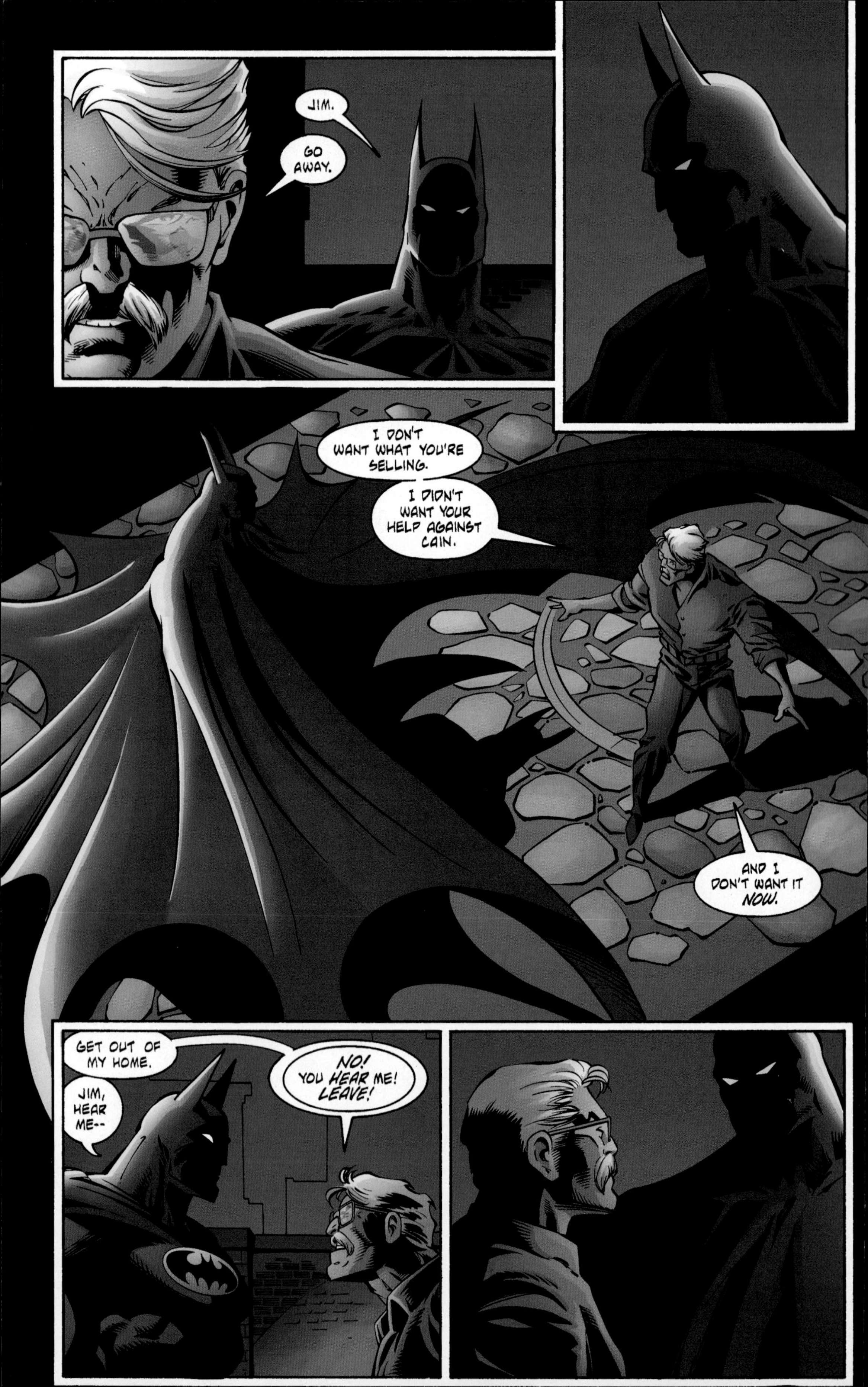
JIM.
GO AWAY.
I DON'T WANT WHAT YOU'RE SELLING.
I DIDN'T WANT YOUR HELP AGAINST CAIN.
AND I DON'T WANT IT NOW.
GET OUT OF MY HOME.
JIM, HEAR ME--
NO! YOU HEAR ME! LEAVE!

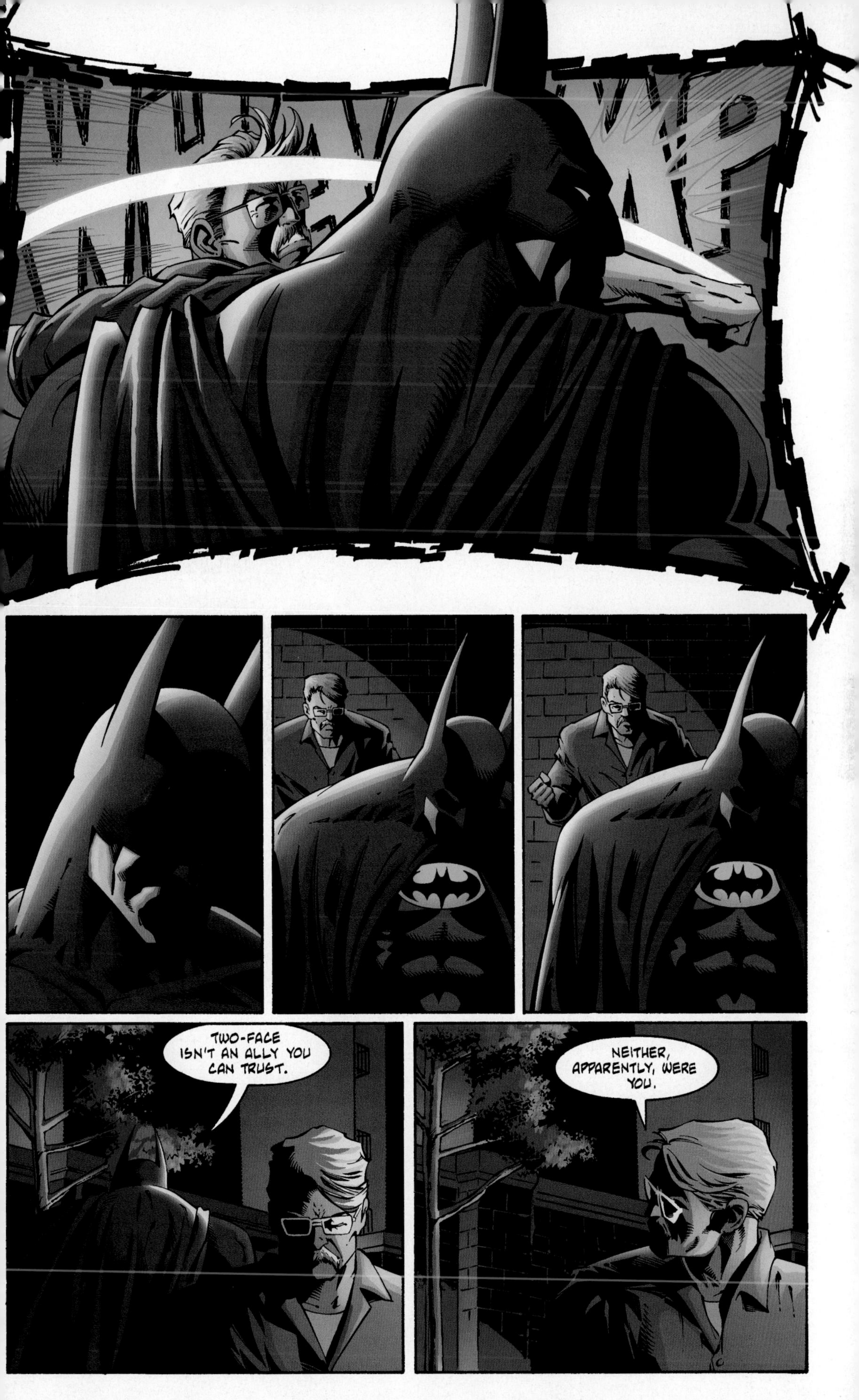
TWO-FACE ISN'T AN ALLY YOU CAN TRUST.
NEITHER, APPARENTLY, WERE YOU.

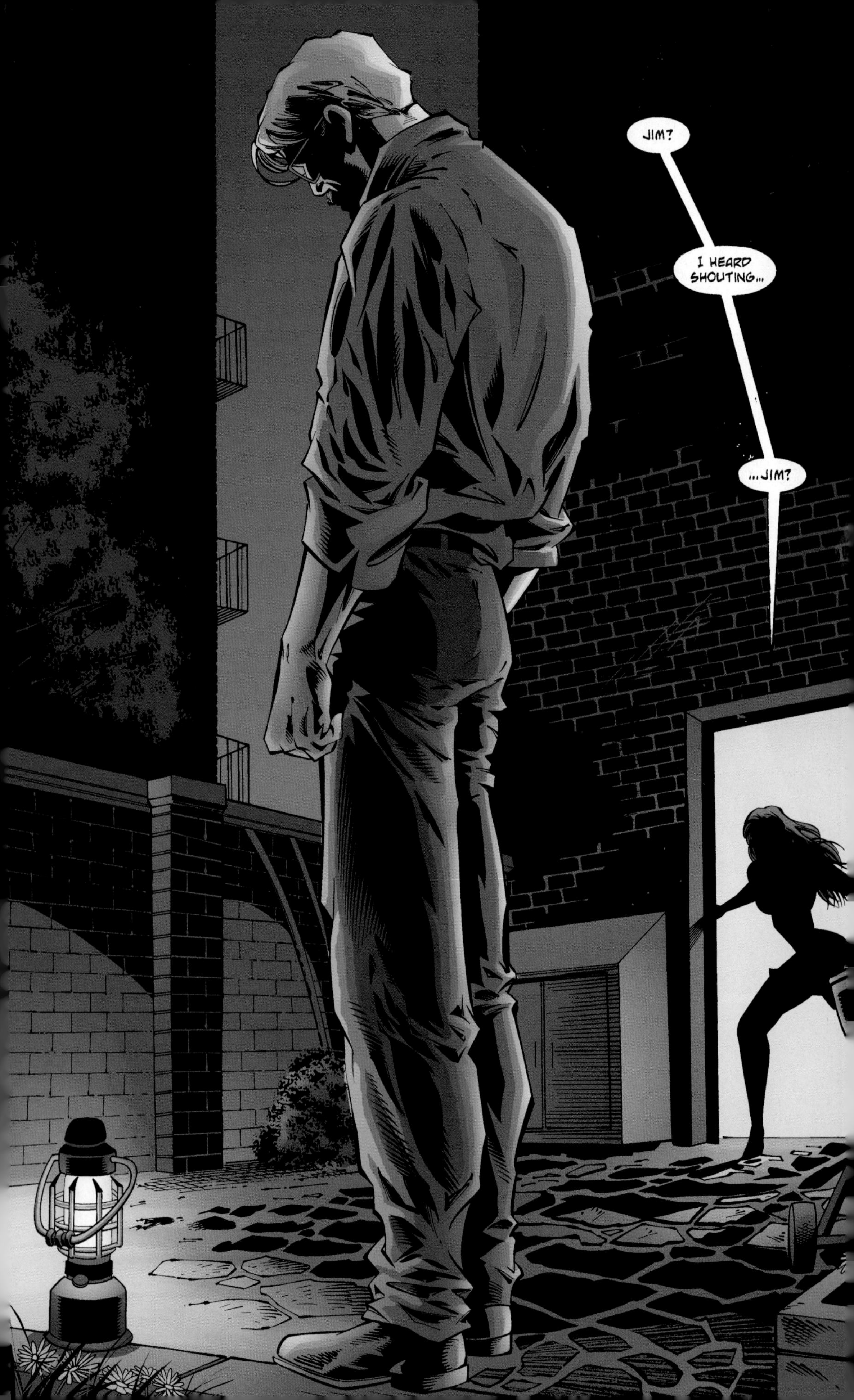
JIM?
I HEARD SHOUTING...
...JIM?

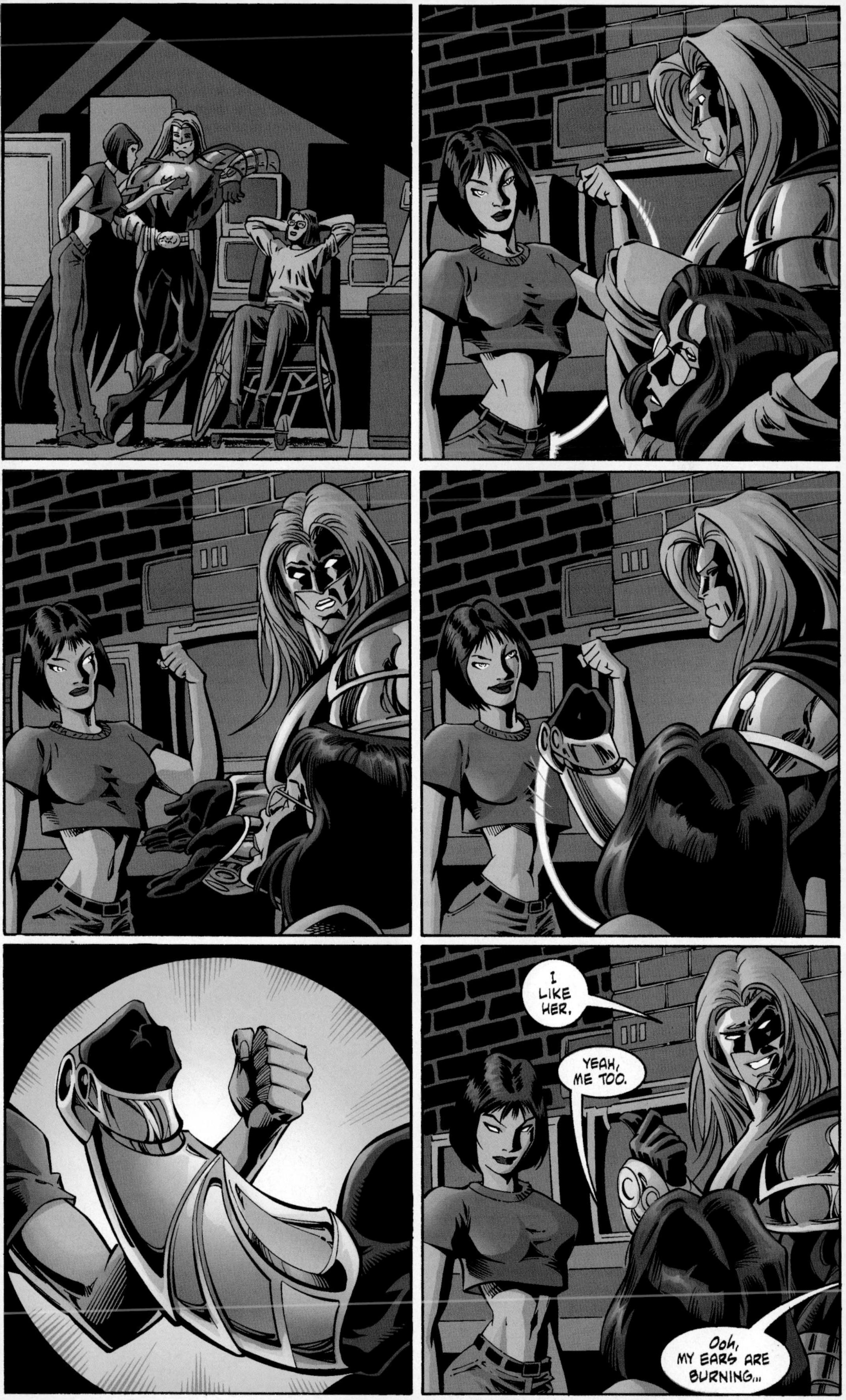
I LIKE HER.
YEAH, ME TOO.
Ooh, MY EARS ARE BURNING...

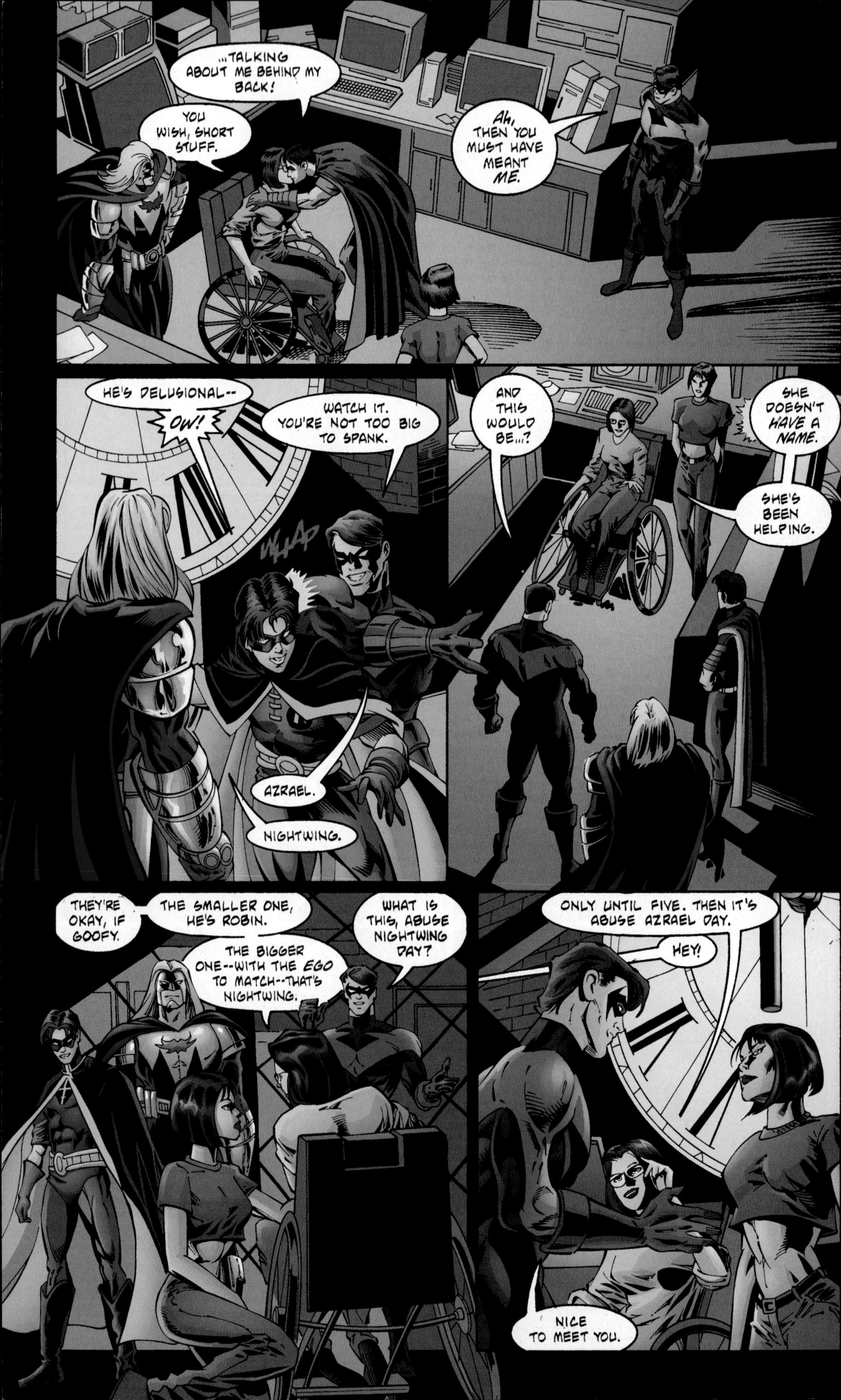
...TALKING ABOUT ME BEHIND MY BACK!
YOU WISH, SHORT STUFF.
AH, THEN YOU MUST HAVE MEANT ME.
HE'S DELUSIONAL-- OW!
WATCH IT. YOU'RE NOT TOO BIG TO SPANK.
WHAP
AZRAEL.
NIGHTWING.
AND THIS WOULD BE...?
SHE DOESN'T HAVE A NAME.
SHE'S BEEN HELPING.
THEY'RE OKAY, IF GOOFY.
THE SMALLER ONE, HE'S ROBIN.
THE BIGGER ONE--WITH THE EGO TO MATCH--THAT'S NIGHTWING.
WHAT IS THIS, ABUSE NIGHTWING DAY?
ONLY UNTIL FIVE. THEN IT'S ABUSE AZRAEL DAY.
HEY!
NICE TO MEET YOU.

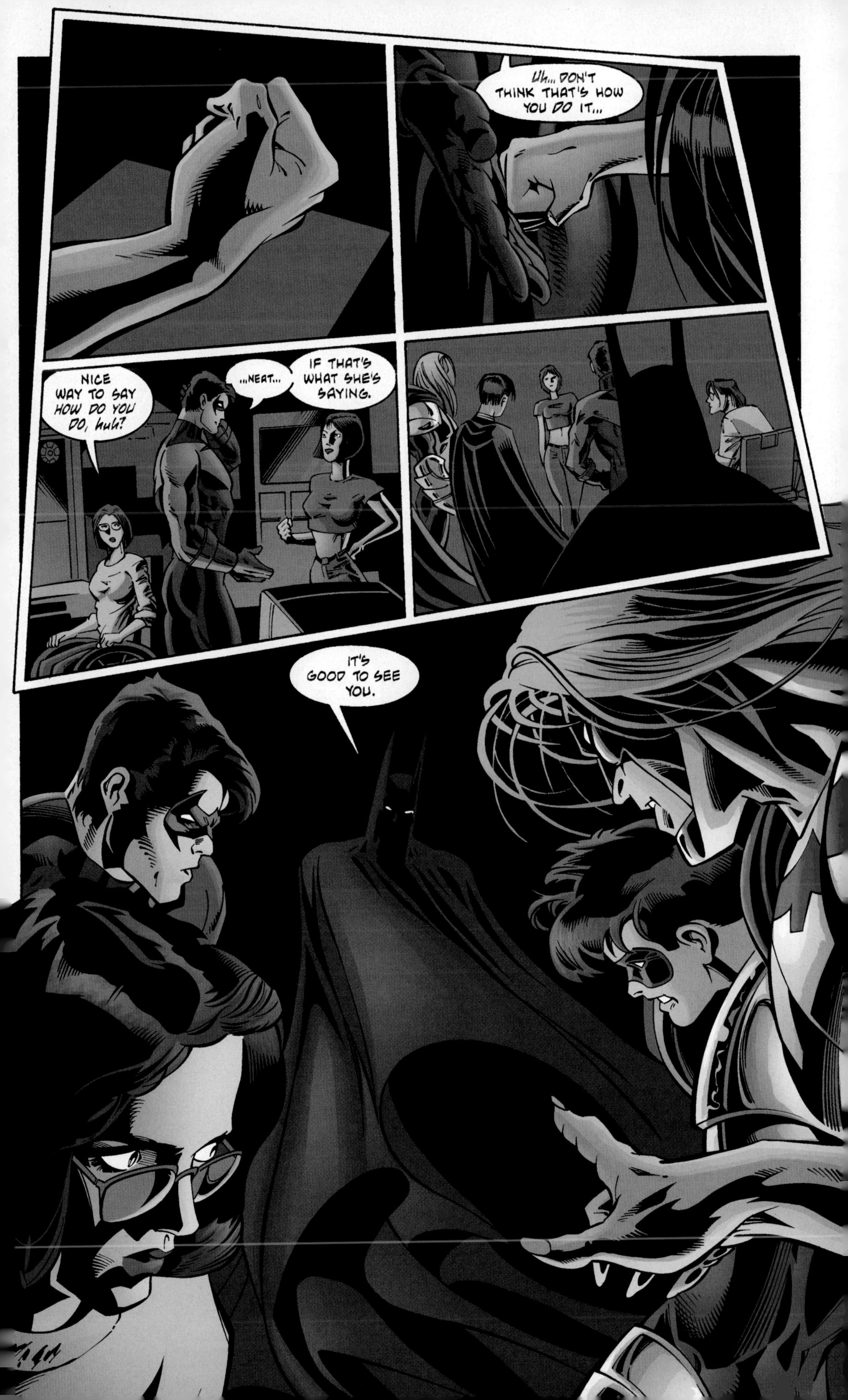
UH... DON'T THINK THAT'S HOW YOU DO IT...
NICE WAY TO SAY HOW DO YOU DO, HUH?
...NEAT...
IF THAT'S WHAT SHE'S SAYING.
IT'S GOOD TO SEE YOU.

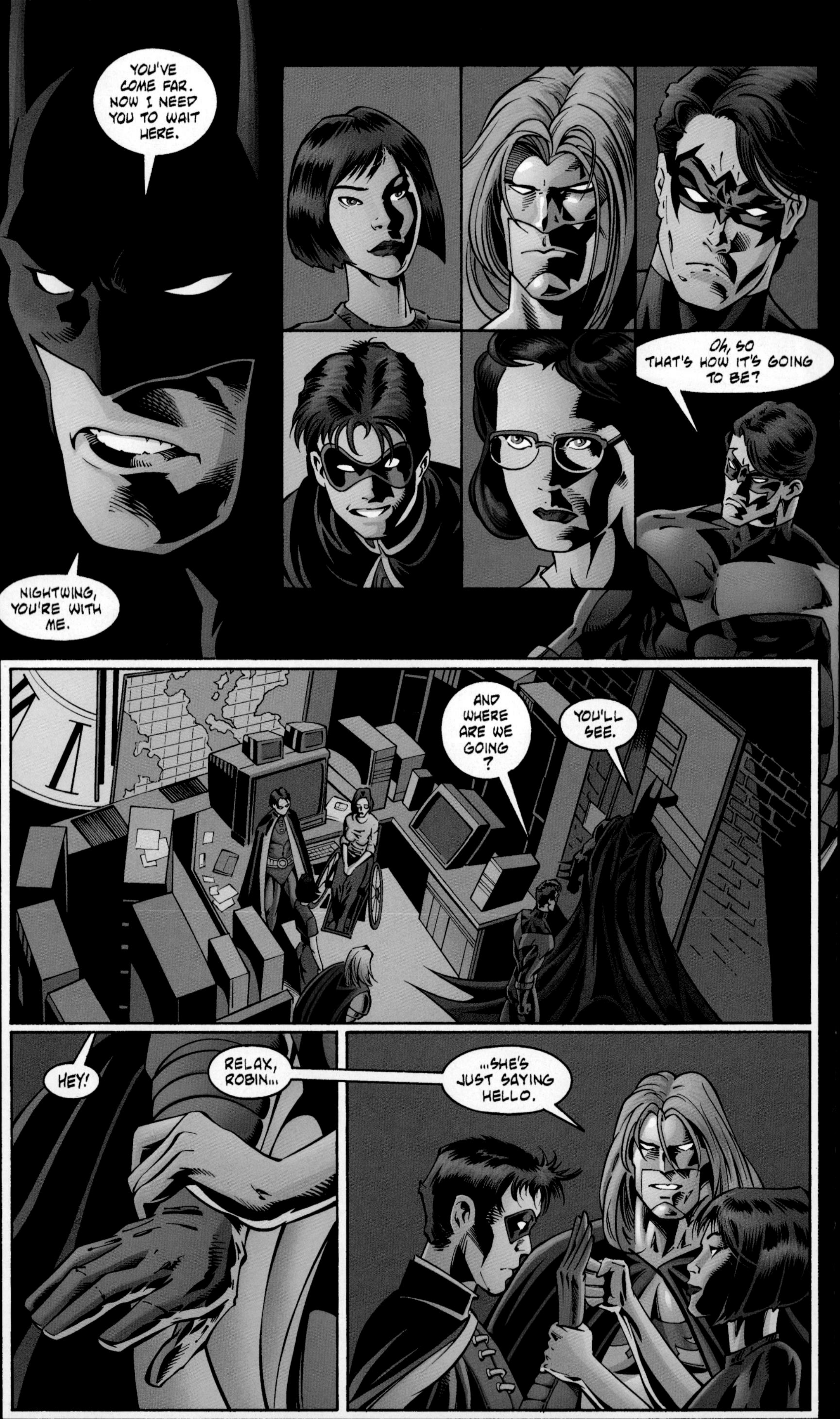
YOU'VE COME FAR. NOW I NEED YOU TO WAIT HERE.
NIGHTWING, YOU'RE WITH ME.
Oh, SO THAT'S HOW IT'S GOING TO BE?
AND WHERE ARE WE GOING ?
YOU'LL SEE.
HEY!
RELAX, ROBIN...
...SHE'S JUST SAYING HELLO.

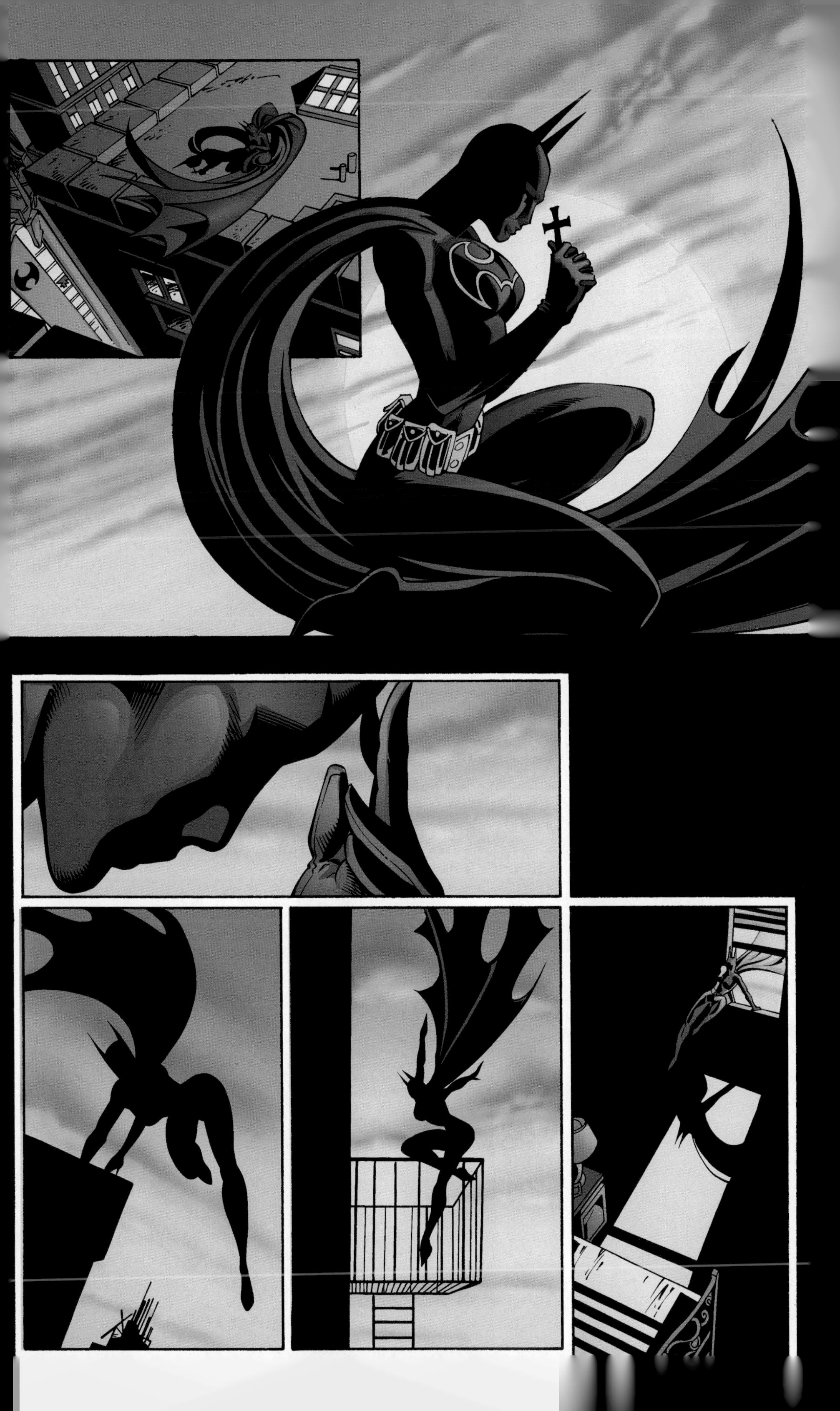

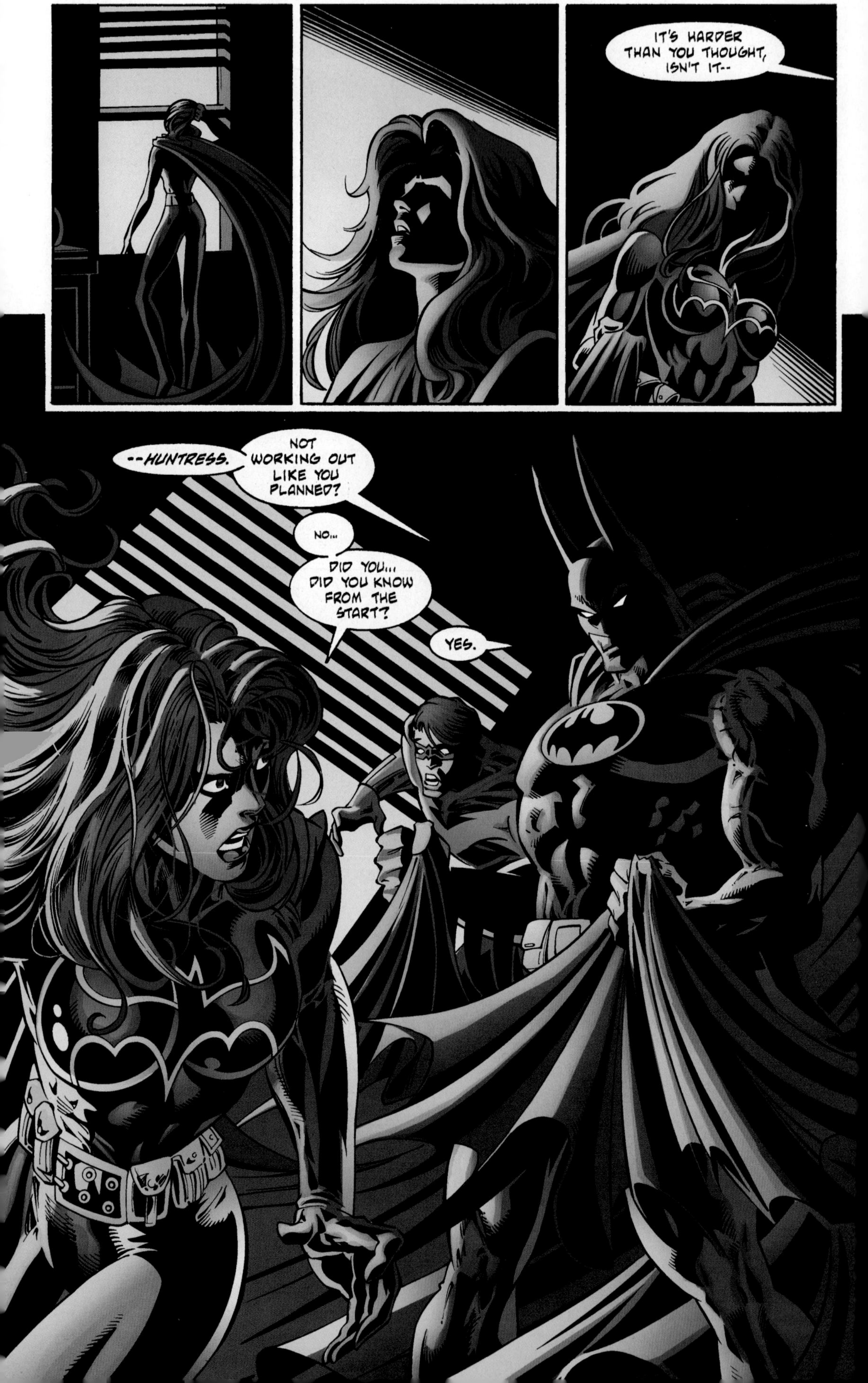
IT'S HARDER THAN YOU THOUGHT, ISN'T IT--
--HUNTRESS.
NOT WORKING OUT LIKE YOU PLANNED?
NO...
DID YOU... DID YOU KNOW FROM THE START?
YES.

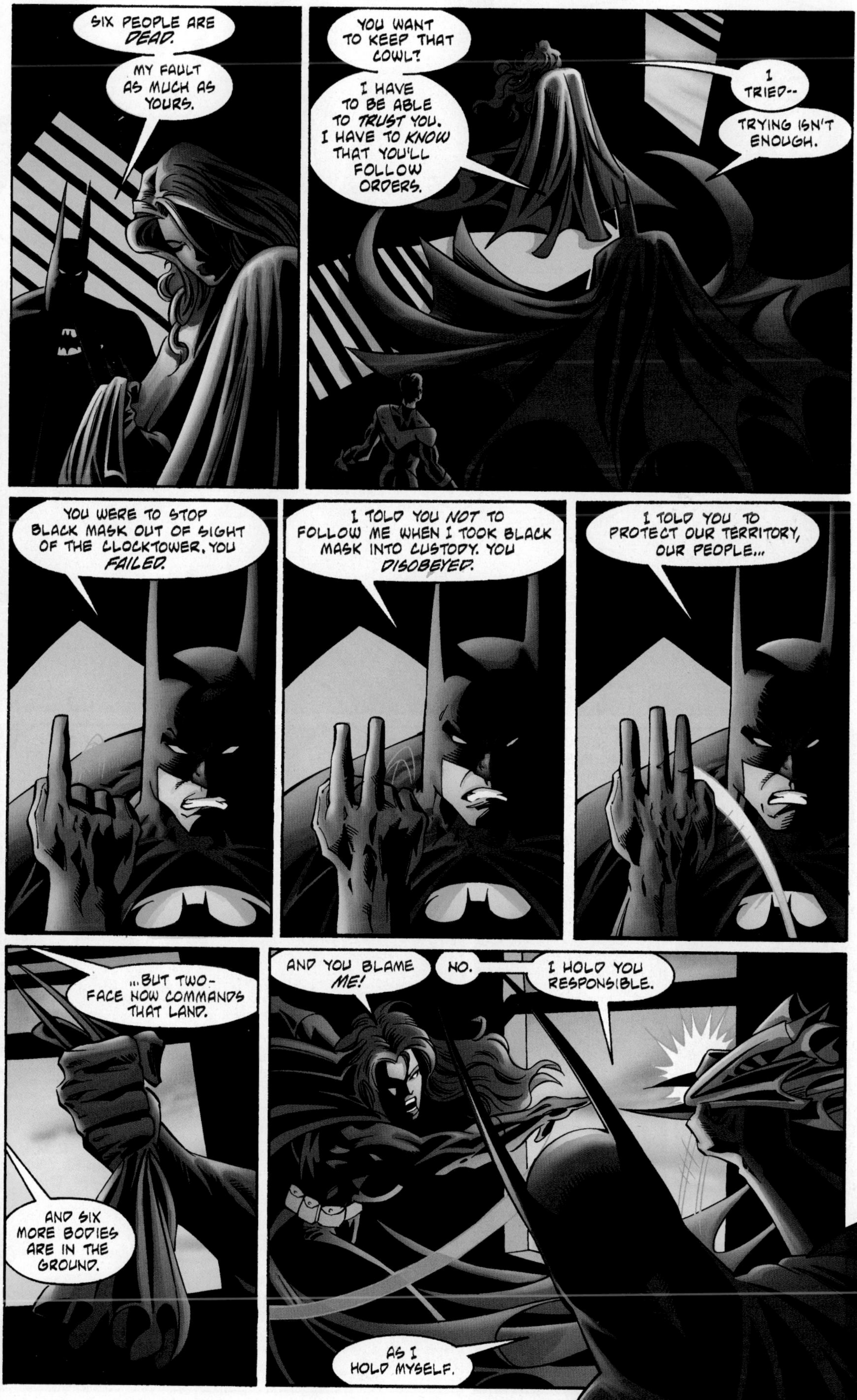
SIX PEOPLE ARE DEAD.
MY FAULT AS MUCH AS YOURS.
YOU WANT TO KEEP THAT COWL?
I HAVE TO BE ABLE TO TRUST YOU. I HAVE TO KNOW THAT YOU'LL FOLLOW ORDERS.
I TRIED--
TRYING ISN'T ENOUGH.
YOU WERE TO STOP BLACK MASK OUT OF SIGHT OF THE CLOCKTOWER. YOU FAILED.
I TOLD YOU NOT TO FOLLOW ME WHEN I TOOK BLACK MASK INTO CUSTODY. YOU DISOBEYED.
I TOLD YOU TO PROTECT OUR TERRITORY, OUR PEOPLE...
...BUT TWO-FACE NOW COMMANDS THAT LAND.
AND SIX MORE BODIES ARE IN THE GROUND.
AND YOU BLAME ME!
NO.
I HOLD YOU RESPONSIBLE.
AS I HOLD MYSELF.

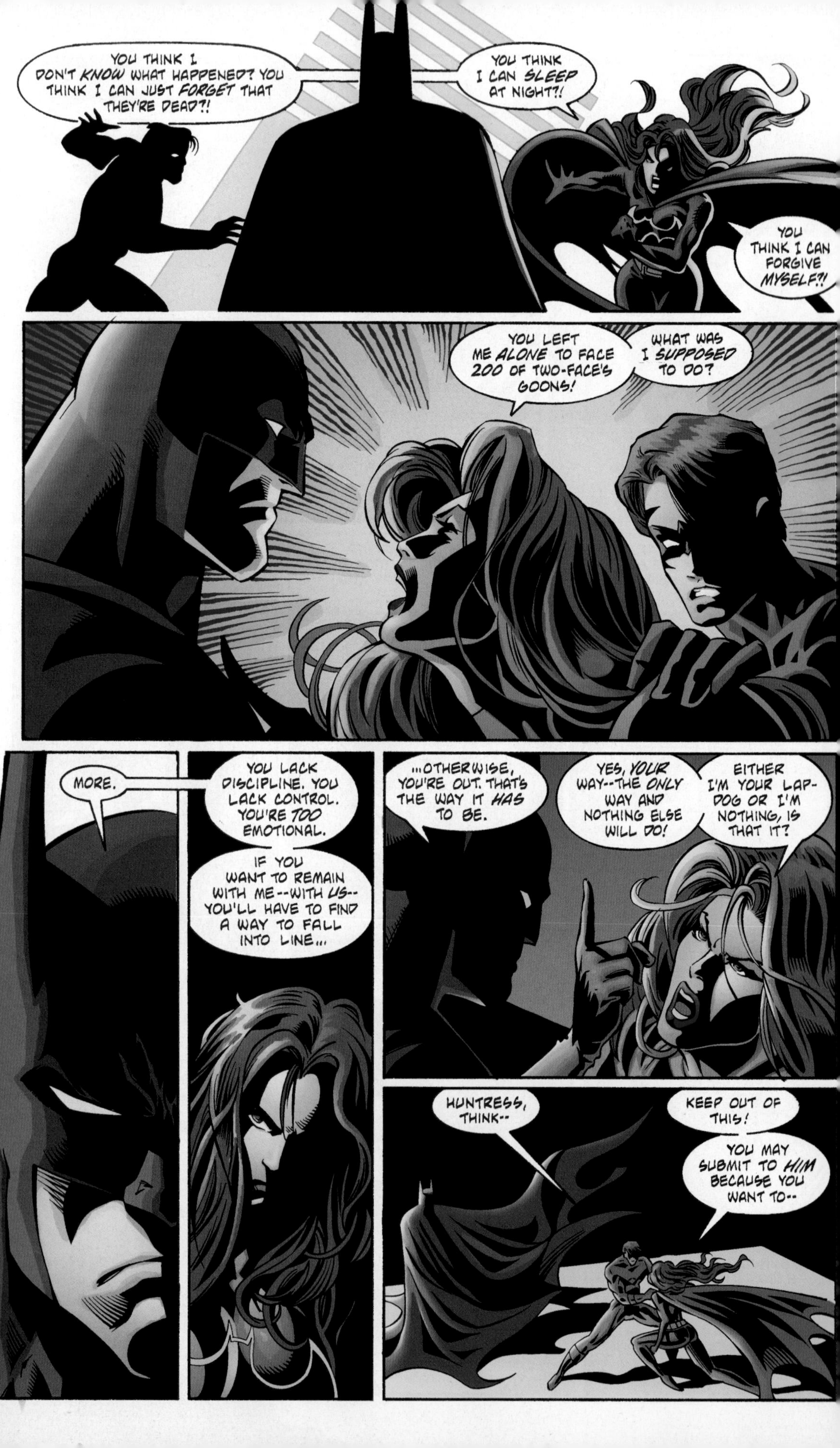

YOU THINK I DON'T KNOW WHAT HAPPENED? YOU THINK I CAN JUST FORGET THAT THEY'RE DEAD?!
YOU THINK I CAN SLEEP AT NIGHT?!
YOU THINK I CAN FORGIVE MYSELF?!
YOU LEFT ME ALONE TO FACE 200 OF TWO-FACE'S GOONS!
WHAT WAS I SUPPOSED TO DO?
MORE.
YOU LACK DISCIPLINE. YOU LACK CONTROL. YOU'RE TOO EMOTIONAL.
IF YOU WANT TO REMAIN WITH ME--WITH US--YOU'LL HAVE TO FIND A WAY TO FALL INTO LINE...
...OTHERWISE, YOU'RE OUT. THAT'S THE WAY IT HAS TO BE.
YES, YOUR WAY--THE ONLY WAY AND NOTHING ELSE WILL DO!
EITHER I'M YOUR LAP-DOG OR I'M NOTHING, IS THAT IT?
HUNTRESS, THINK--
KEEP OUT OF THIS!
YOU MAY SUBMIT TO HIM BECAUSE YOU WANT TO--

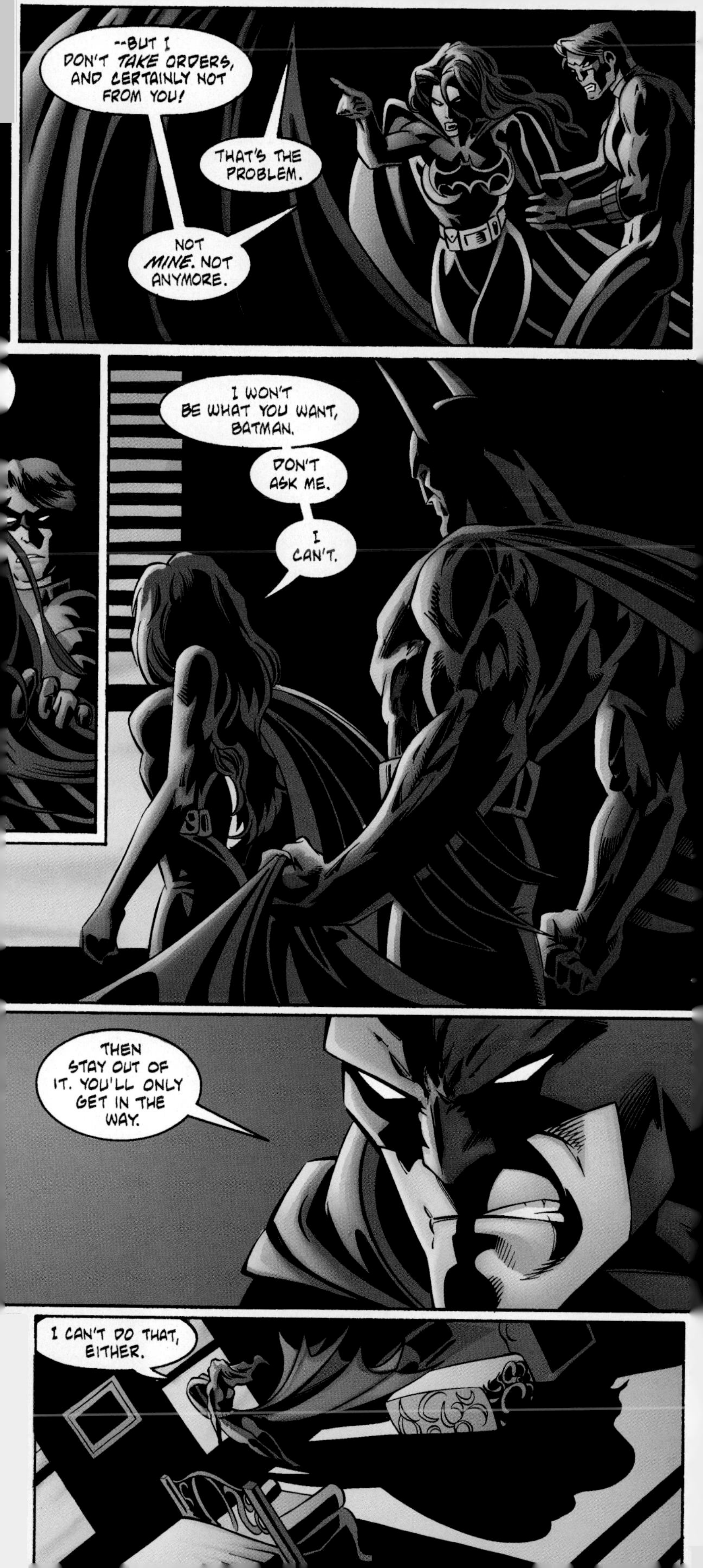
--BUT I DON'T *TAKE* ORDERS, AND CERTAINLY NOT FROM YOU!
THAT'S THE PROBLEM.
NOT *MINE*. NOT ANYMORE.
I WON'T BE WHAT YOU WANT, BATMAN.
DON'T ASK ME.
I CAN'T.
THEN STAY OUT OF IT. YOU'LL ONLY GET IN THE WAY.
I CAN'T DO THAT, EITHER.

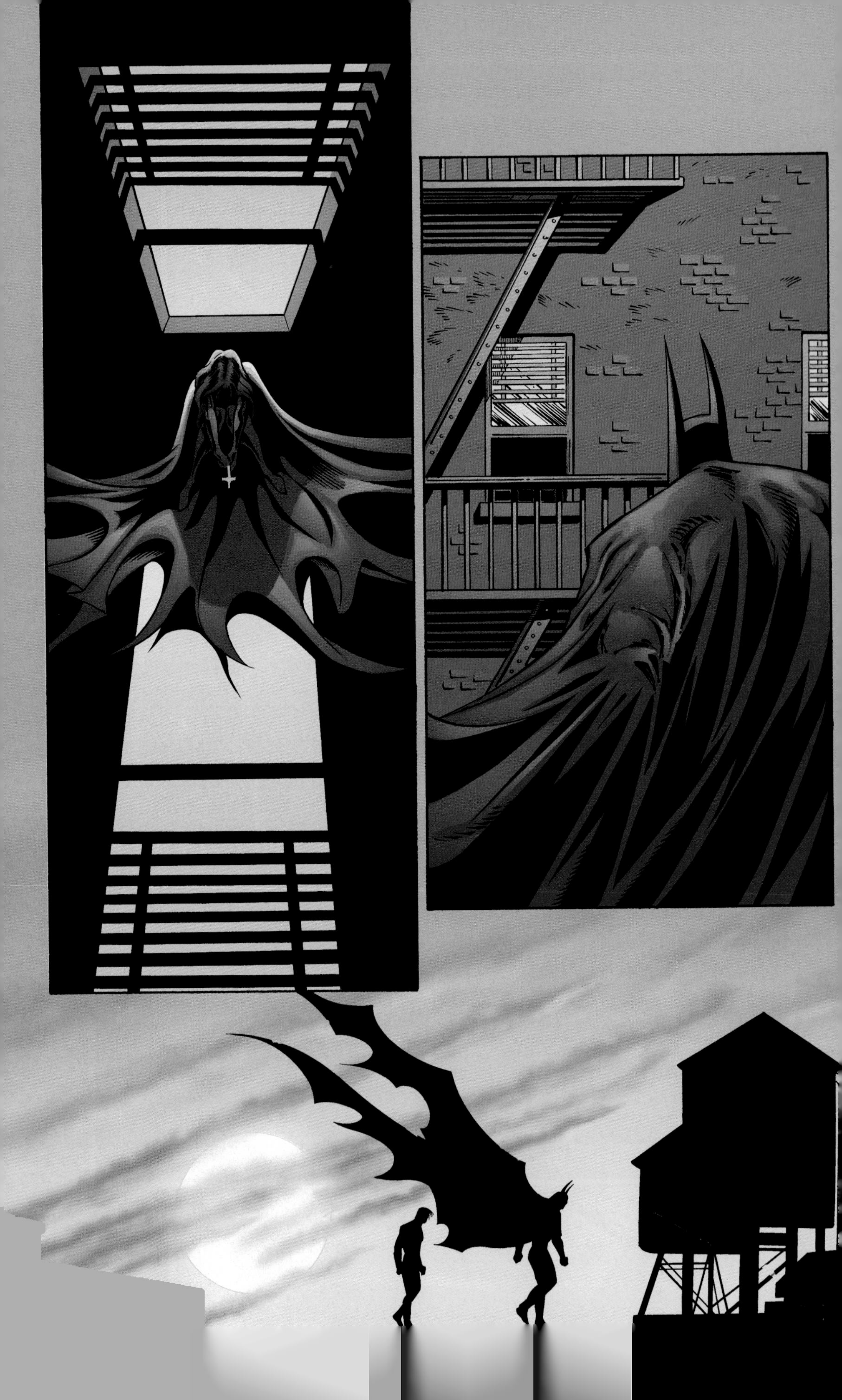

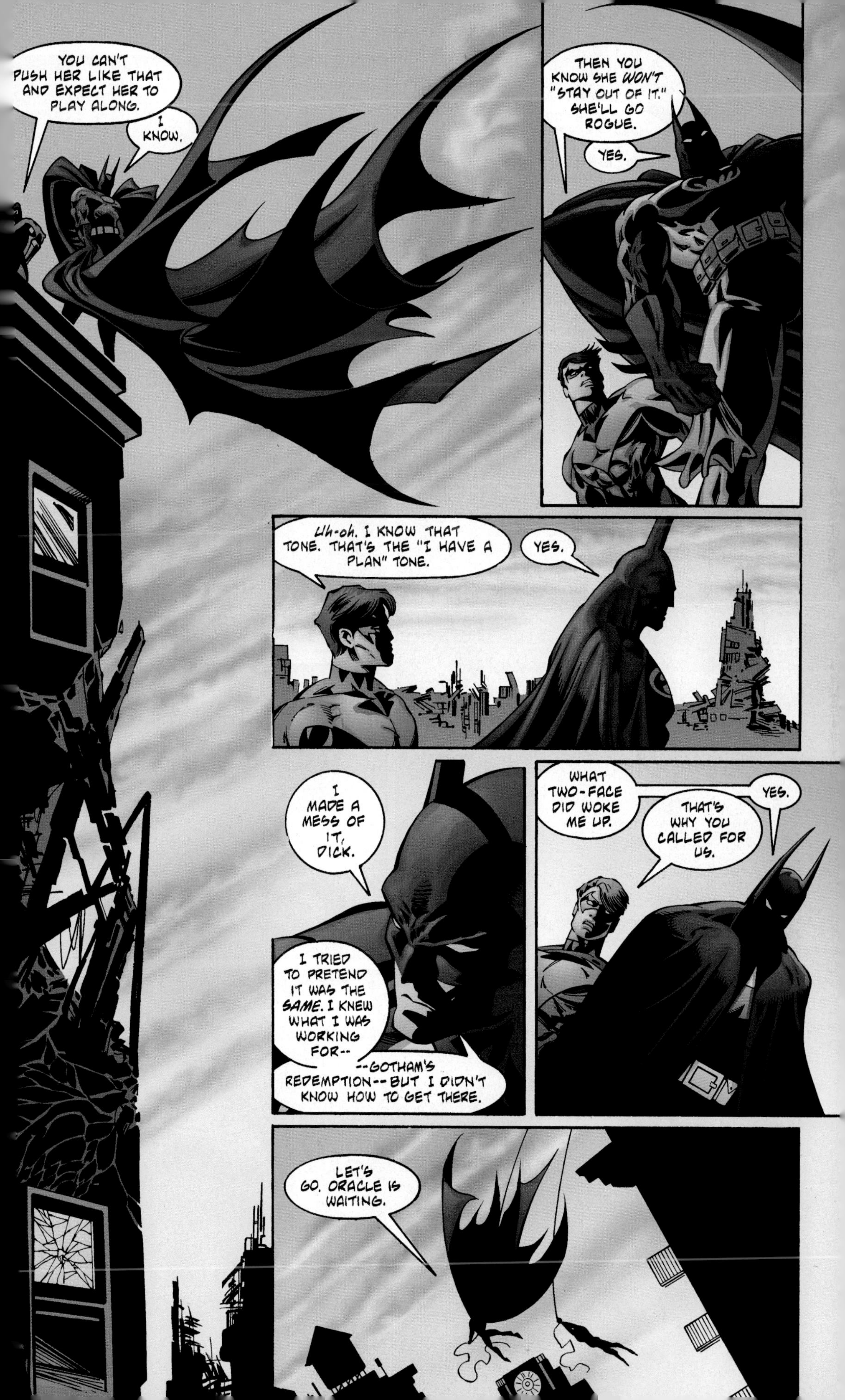
YOU CAN'T PUSH HER LIKE THAT AND EXPECT HER TO PLAY ALONG.
I KNOW.
THEN YOU KNOW SHE *WON'T* "STAY OUT OF IT." SHE'LL GO ROGUE.
YES.
Uh-oh. I KNOW THAT TONE. THAT'S THE "I HAVE A PLAN" TONE.
YES.
I MADE A MESS OF IT, DICK.
I TRIED TO PRETEND IT WAS THE *SAME.* I KNEW WHAT I WAS WORKING FOR--
--GOTHAM'S REDEMPTION--BUT I DIDN'T KNOW HOW TO GET THERE.
WHAT TWO-FACE DID WOKE ME UP.
YES.
THAT'S WHY YOU CALLED FOR US.
LET'S GO. ORACLE IS WAITING.

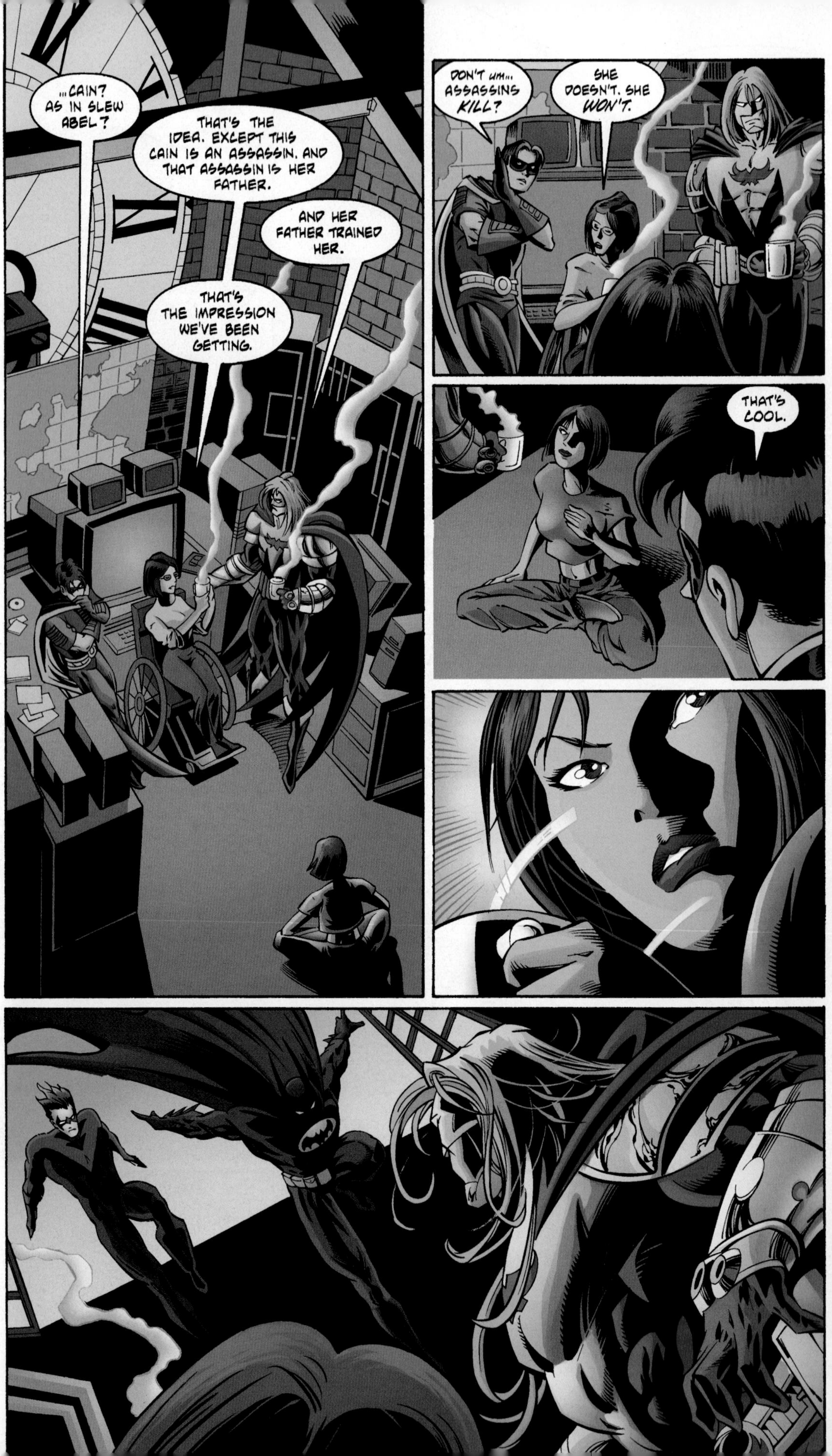
...CAIN? AS IN SLEW ABEL?
THAT'S THE IDEA. EXCEPT THIS CAIN IS AN ASSASSIN. AND THAT ASSASSIN IS HER FATHER.
AND HER FATHER TRAINED HER.
THAT'S THE IMPRESSION WE'VE BEEN GETTING.
DON'T UM... ASSASSINS KILL?
SHE DOESN'T. SHE WON'T.
THAT'S COOL.

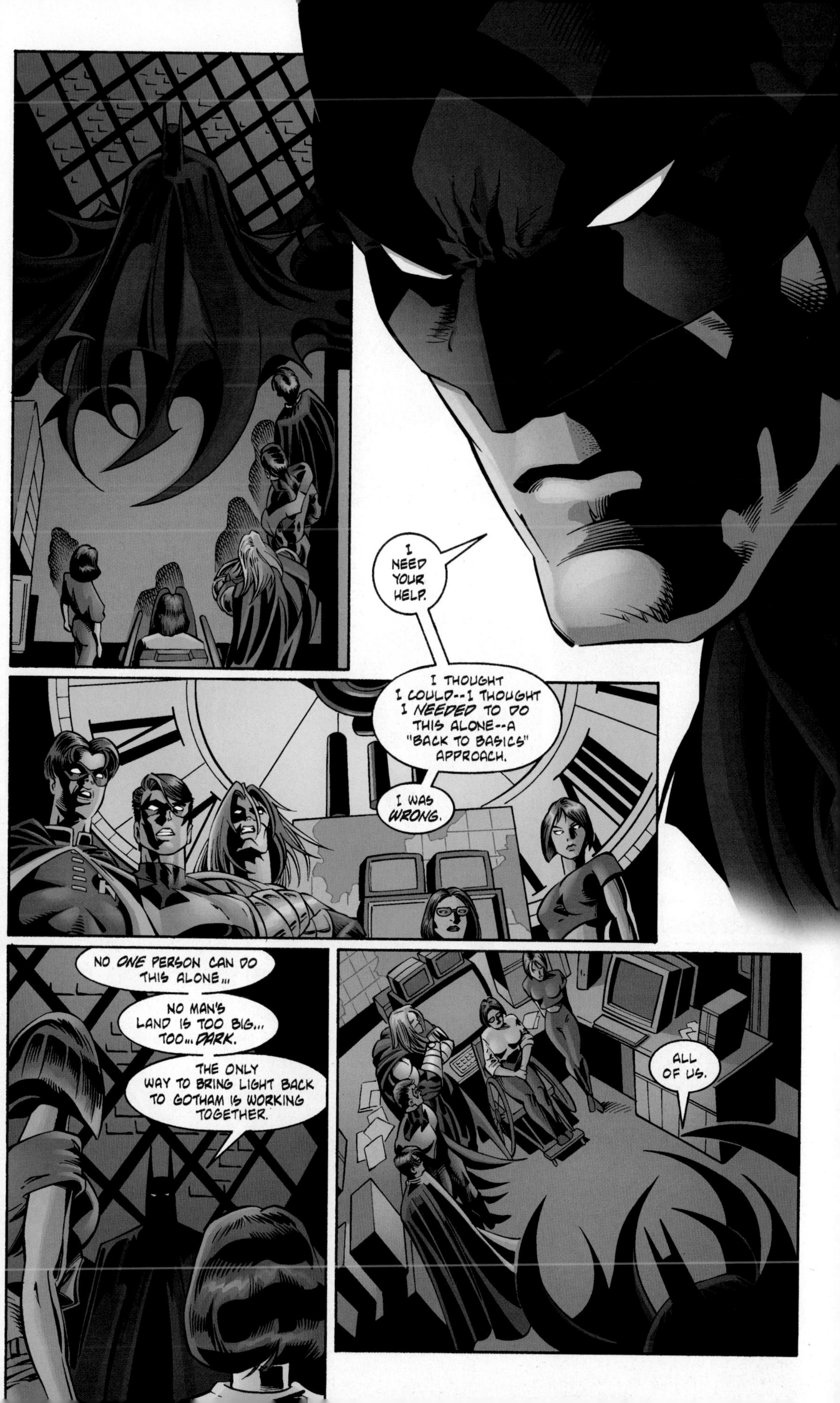
I NEED YOUR HELP.
I THOUGHT I COULD--I THOUGHT I NEEDED TO DO THIS ALONE--A "BACK TO BASICS" APPROACH.
I WAS WRONG.
NO ONE PERSON CAN DO THIS ALONE...
NO MAN'S LAND IS TOO BIG... TOO...DARK.
THE ONLY WAY TO BRING LIGHT BACK TO GOTHAM IS WORKING TOGETHER.
ALL OF US.

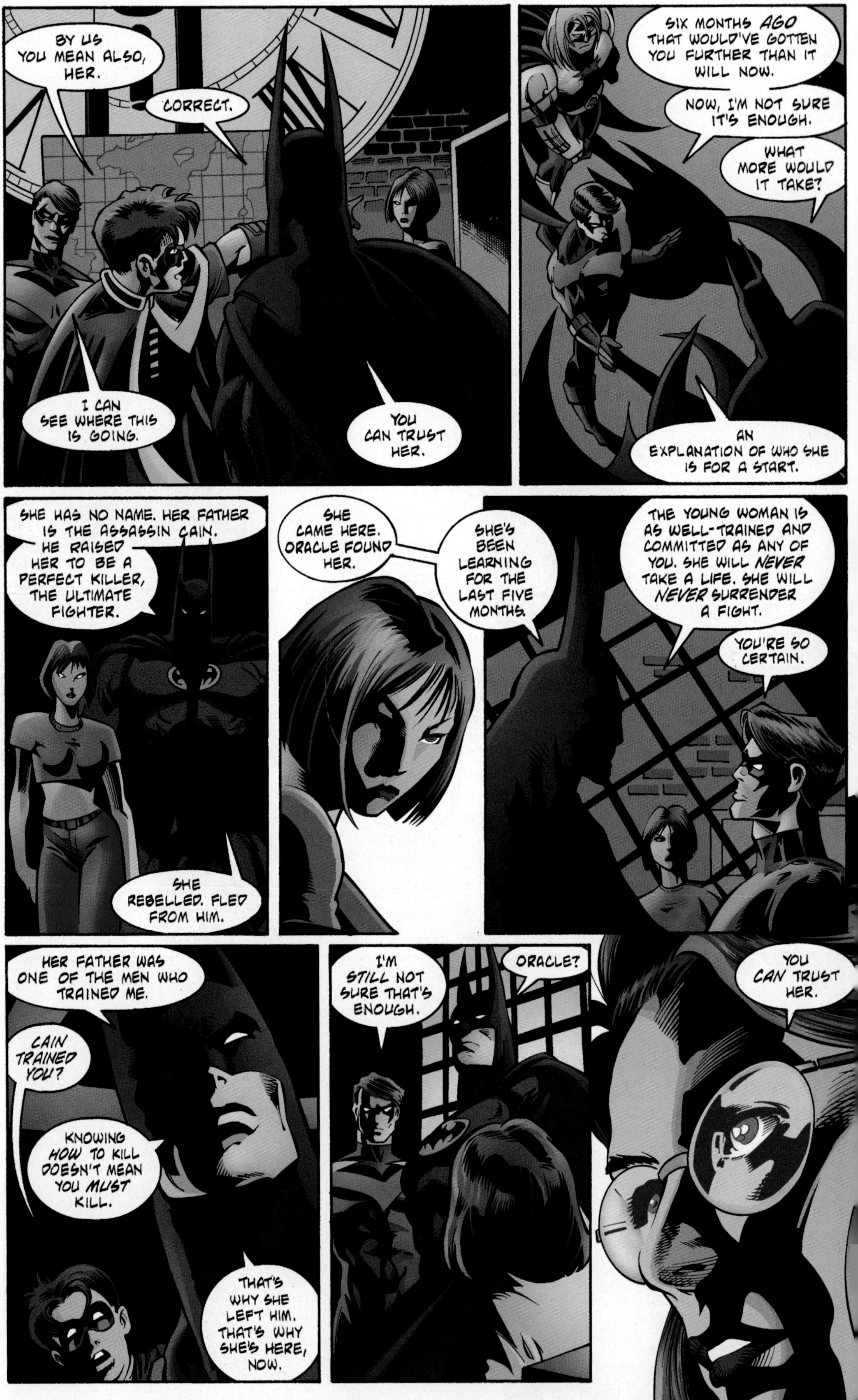
BY US YOU MEAN ALSO, HER.
CORRECT.
I CAN SEE WHERE THIS IS GOING.
YOU CAN TRUST HER.
SIX MONTHS AGO THAT WOULD'VE GOTTEN YOU FURTHER THAN IT WILL NOW.
NOW, I'M NOT SURE IT'S ENOUGH.
WHAT MORE WOULD IT TAKE?
AN EXPLANATION OF WHO SHE IS FOR A START.
SHE HAS NO NAME. HER FATHER IS THE ASSASSIN CAIN.
HE RAISED HER TO BE A PERFECT KILLER, THE ULTIMATE FIGHTER.
SHE REBELLED. FLED FROM HIM.
SHE CAME HERE. ORACLE FOUND HER.
SHE'S BEEN LEARNING FOR THE LAST FIVE MONTHS.
THE YOUNG WOMAN IS AS WELL-TRAINED AND COMMITTED AS ANY OF YOU. SHE WILL NEVER TAKE A LIFE. SHE WILL NEVER SURRENDER A FIGHT.
YOU'RE SO CERTAIN.
HER FATHER WAS ONE OF THE MEN WHO TRAINED ME.
CAIN TRAINED YOU?
KNOWING HOW TO KILL DOESN'T MEAN YOU MUST KILL.
THAT'S WHY SHE LEFT HIM. THAT'S WHY SHE'S HERE, NOW.
I'M STILL NOT SURE THAT'S ENOUGH.
ORACLE?
YOU CAN TRUST HER.

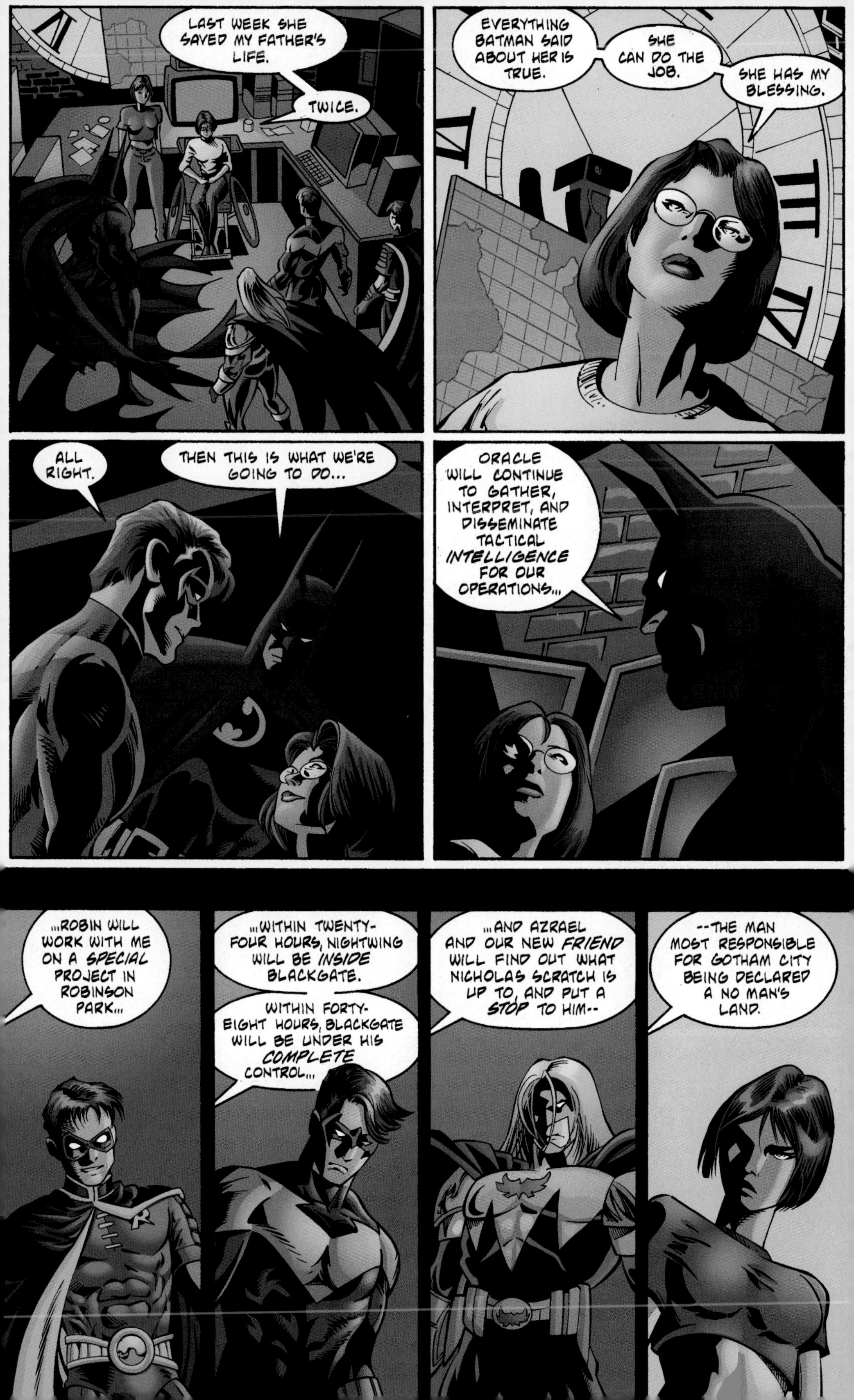
LAST WEEK SHE SAVED MY FATHER'S LIFE.
TWICE.
EVERYTHING BATMAN SAID ABOUT HER IS TRUE.
SHE CAN DO THE JOB.
SHE HAS MY BLESSING.
ALL RIGHT.
THEN THIS IS WHAT WE'RE GOING TO DO...
ORACLE WILL CONTINUE TO GATHER, INTERPRET, AND DISSEMINATE TACTICAL INTELLIGENCE FOR OUR OPERATIONS...
...ROBIN WILL WORK WITH ME ON A SPECIAL PROJECT IN ROBINSON PARK...
...WITHIN TWENTY-FOUR HOURS, NIGHTWING WILL BE INSIDE BLACKGATE.
WITHIN FORTY-EIGHT HOURS, BLACKGATE WILL BE UNDER HIS COMPLETE CONTROL...
...AND AZRAEL AND OUR NEW FRIEND WILL FIND OUT WHAT NICHOLAS SCRATCH IS UP TO, AND PUT A STOP TO HIM--
--THE MAN MOST RESPONSIBLE FOR GOTHAM CITY BEING DECLARED A NO MAN'S LAND.

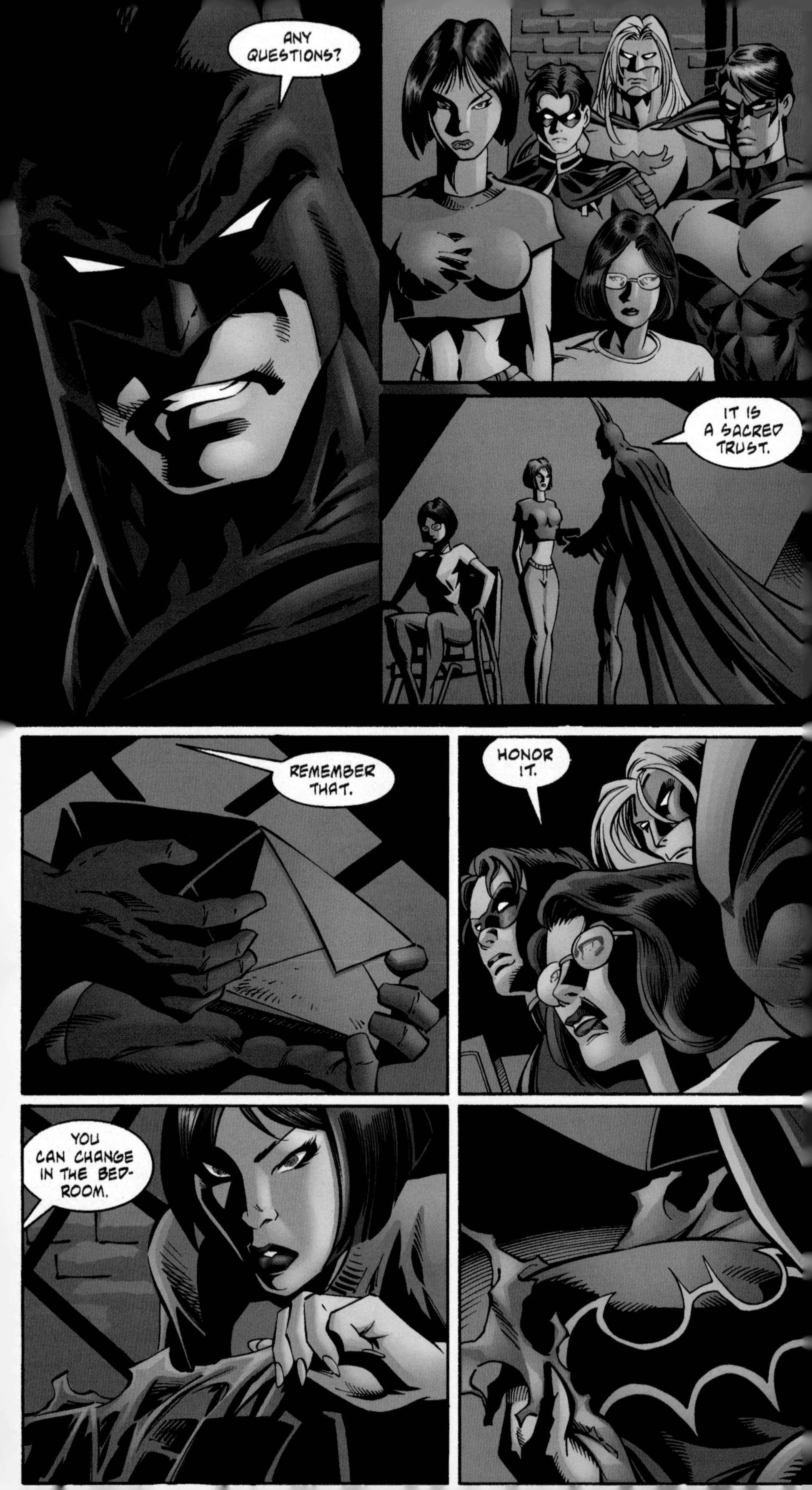
ANY QUESTIONS?
IT IS A SACRED TRUST.
REMEMBER THAT.
HONOR IT.
YOU CAN CHANGE IN THE BED-ROOM.

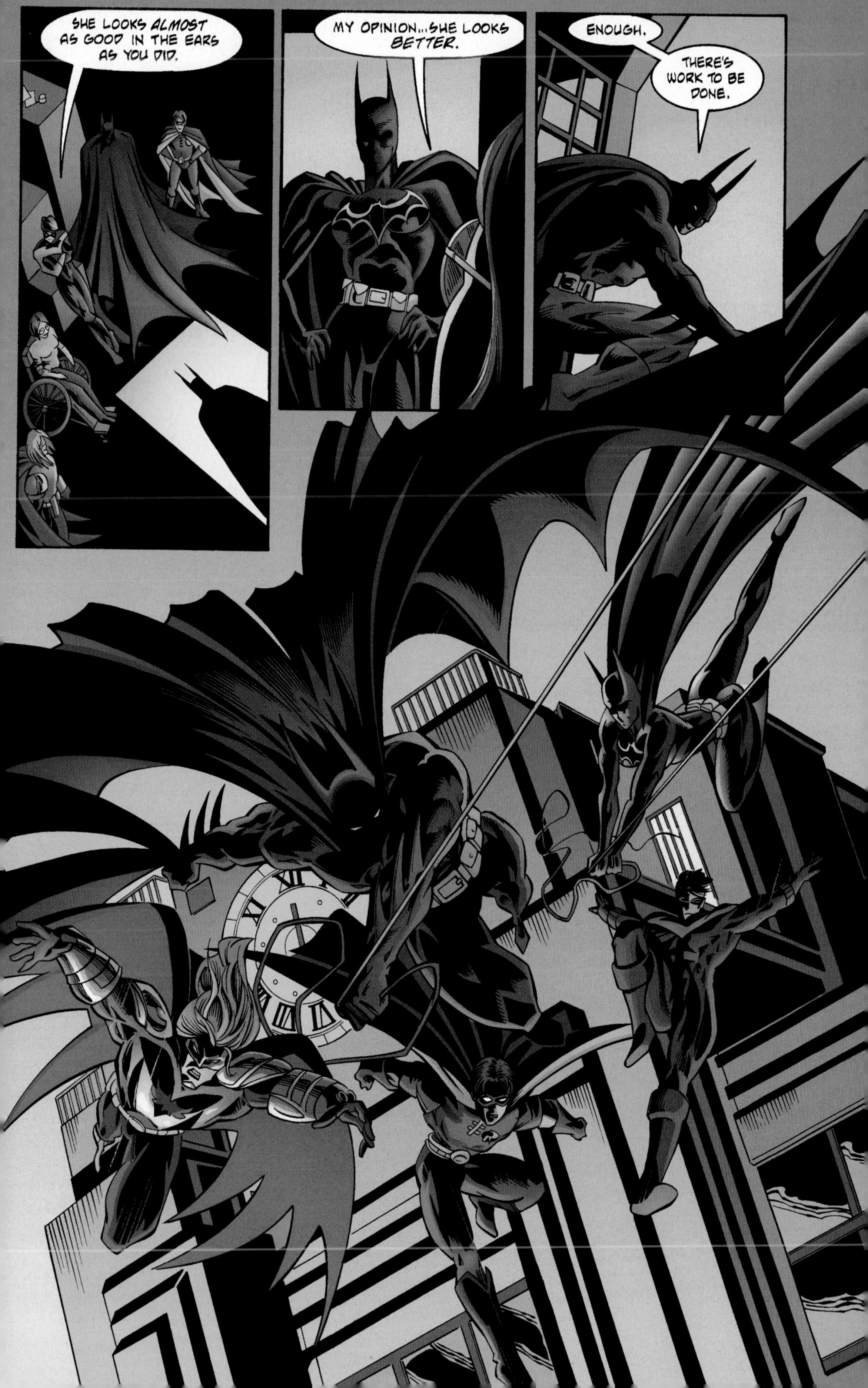
SHE LOOKS ALMOST AS GOOD IN THE EARS AS YOU DID.
MY OPINION... SHE LOOKS BETTER.
ENOUGH.
THERE'S WORK TO BE DONE.

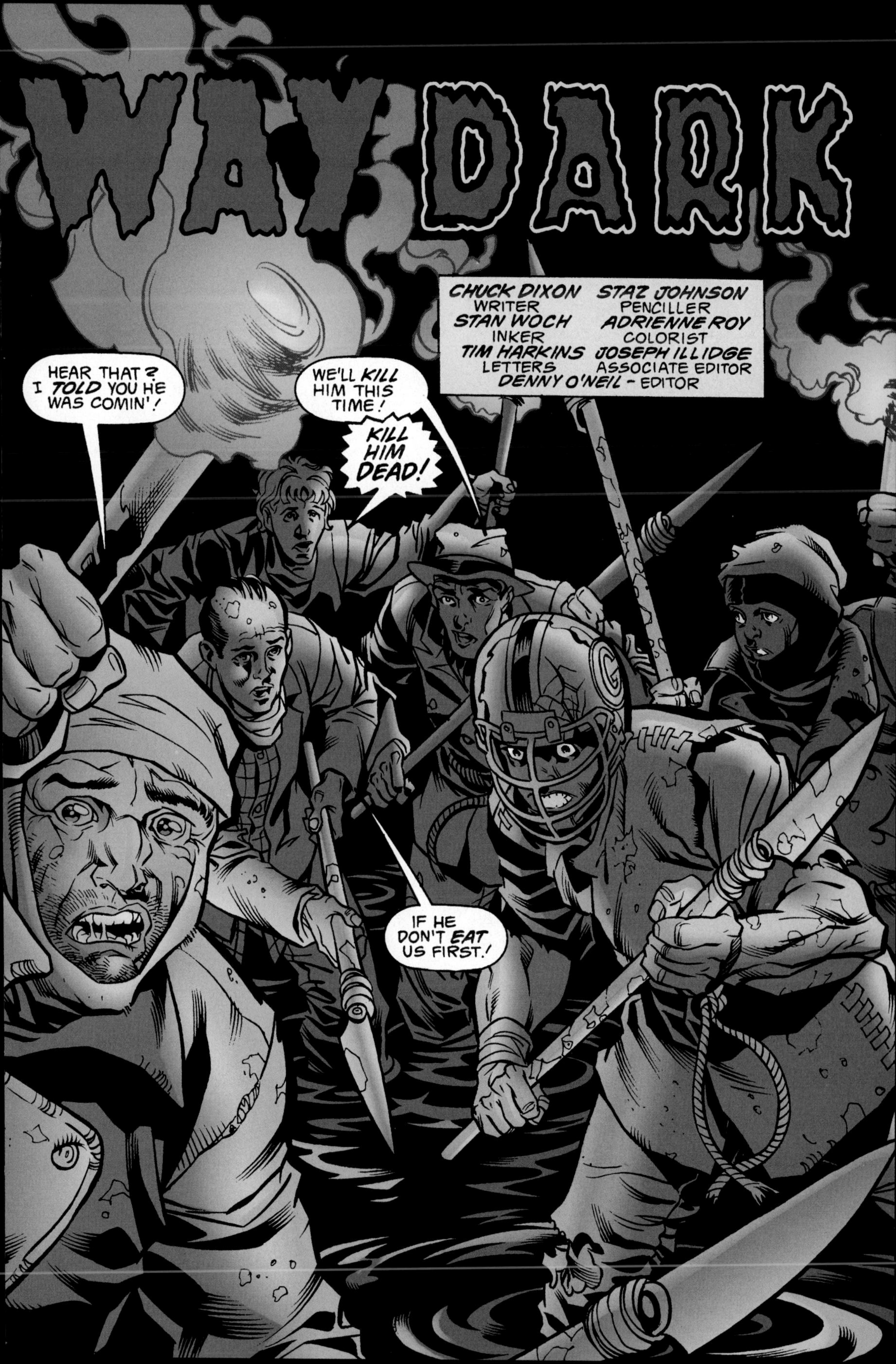
WAY DARK
CHUCK DIXON WRITER
STAZ JOHNSON PENCILLER
STAN WOCH INKER
ADRIENNE ROY COLORIST
TIM HARKINS LETTERS
JOSEPH ILLIDGE ASSOCIATE EDITOR
DENNY O'NEIL - EDITOR
HEAR THAT? I TOLD YOU HE WAS COMIN'!
WE'LL KILL HIM THIS TIME!
KILL HIM DEAD!
IF HE DON'T EAT US FIRST!

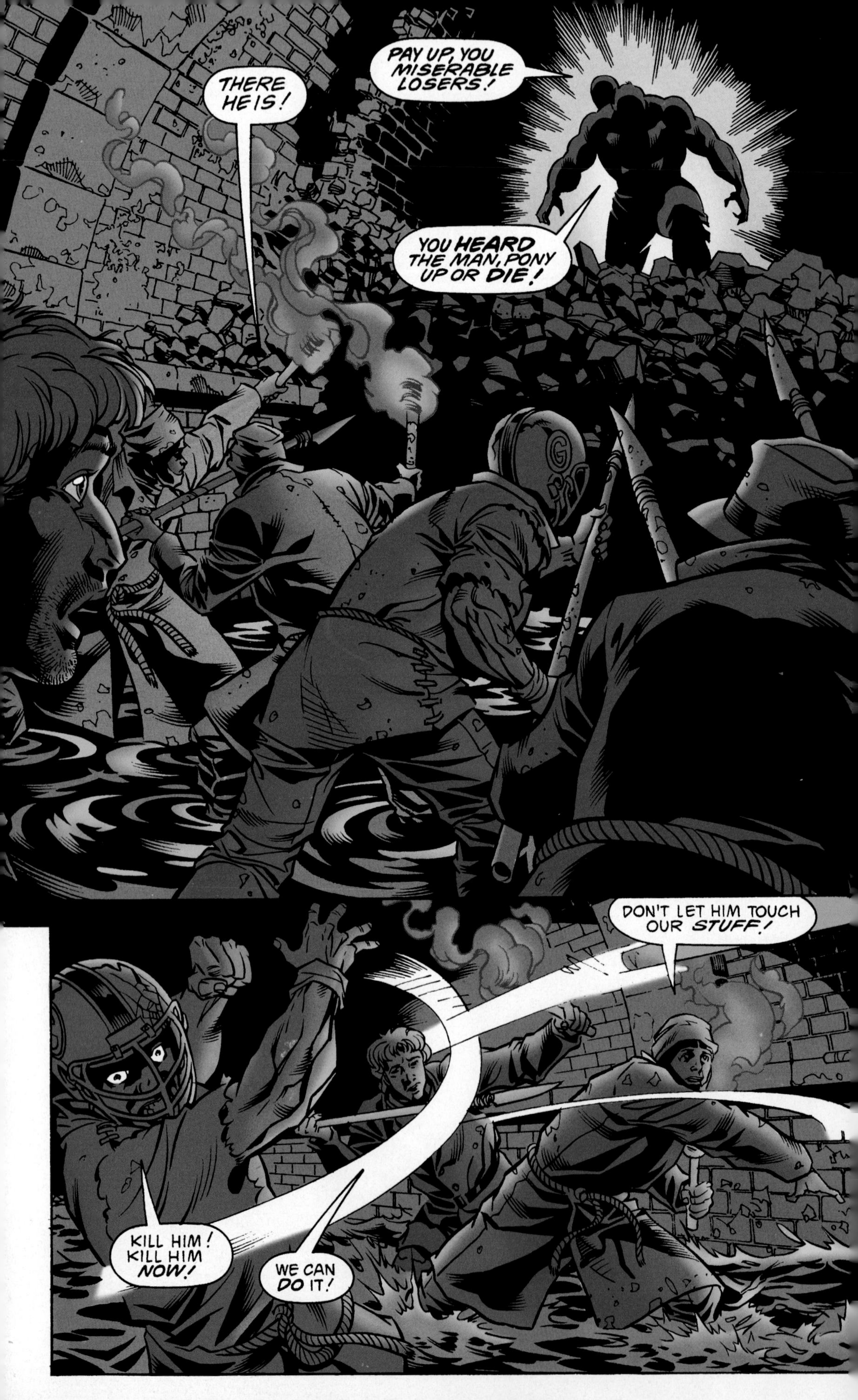
THERE HE IS!
PAY UP, YOU MISERABLE LOSERS!
YOU HEARD THE MAN, PONY UP OR DIE!
DON'T LET HIM TOUCH OUR STUFF!
KILL HIM! KILL HIM NOW!
WE CAN DO IT!

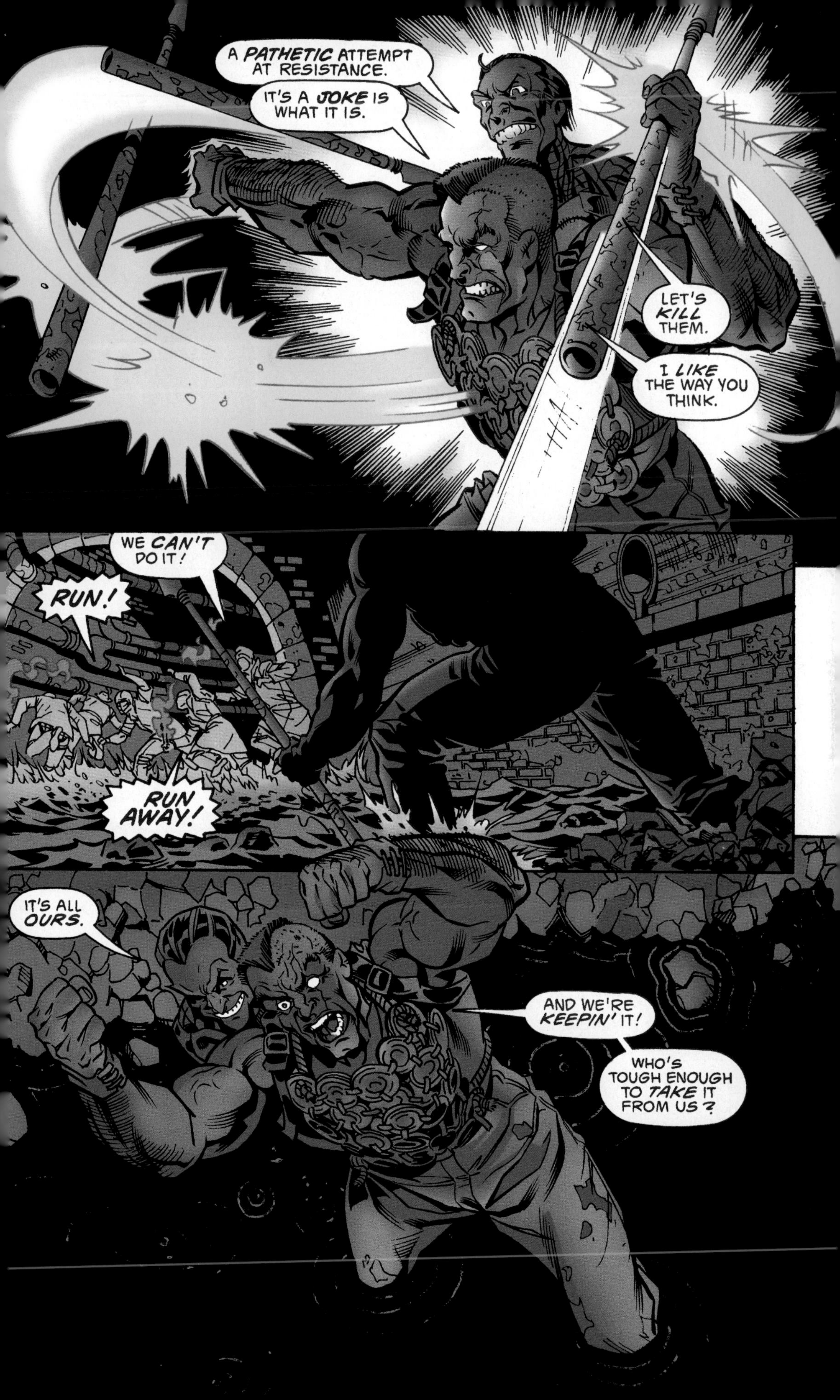
A PATHETIC ATTEMPT AT RESISTANCE.
IT'S A JOKE IS WHAT IT IS.
LET'S KILL THEM.
I LIKE THE WAY YOU THINK.
WE CAN'T DO IT!
RUN!
RUN AWAY!
IT'S ALL OURS.
AND WE'RE KEEPIN' IT!
WHO'S TOUGH ENOUGH TO TAKE IT FROM US?

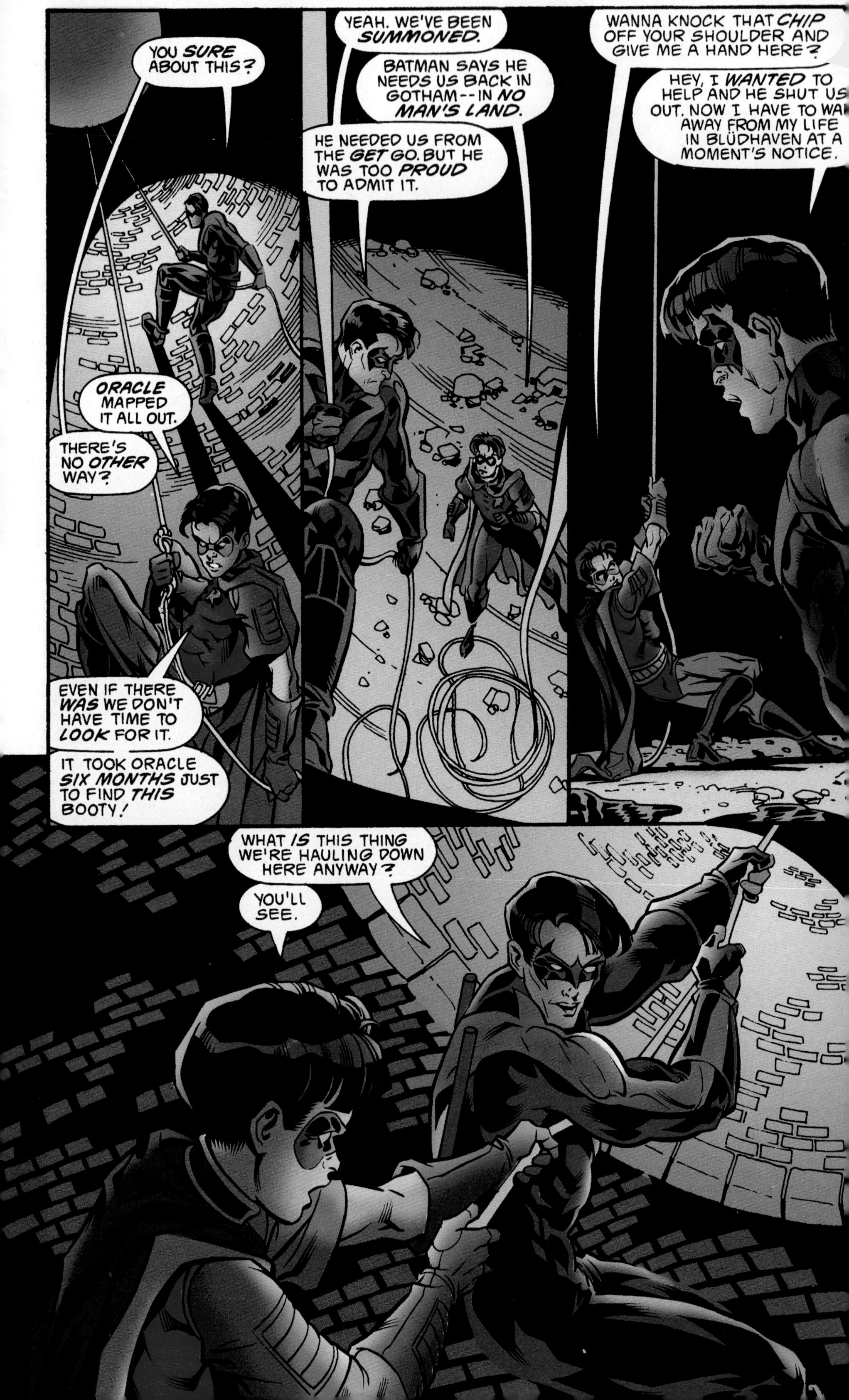
YOU SURE ABOUT THIS?
ORACLE MAPPED IT ALL OUT.
THERE'S NO OTHER WAY?
EVEN IF THERE WAS WE DON'T HAVE TIME TO LOOK FOR IT.
IT TOOK ORACLE SIX MONTHS JUST TO FIND THIS BOOTY!
YEAH. WE'VE BEEN SUMMONED.
BATMAN SAYS HE NEEDS US BACK IN GOTHAM--IN NO MAN'S LAND.
HE NEEDED US FROM THE GET GO. BUT HE WAS TOO PROUD TO ADMIT IT.
WANNA KNOCK THAT CHIP OFF YOUR SHOULDER AND GIVE ME A HAND HERE?
HEY, I WANTED TO HELP AND HE SHUT US OUT. NOW I HAVE TO WA AWAY FROM MY LIFE IN BLÜDHAVEN AT A MOMENT'S NOTICE.
WHAT IS THIS THING WE'RE HAULING DOWN HERE ANYWAY?
YOU'LL SEE.

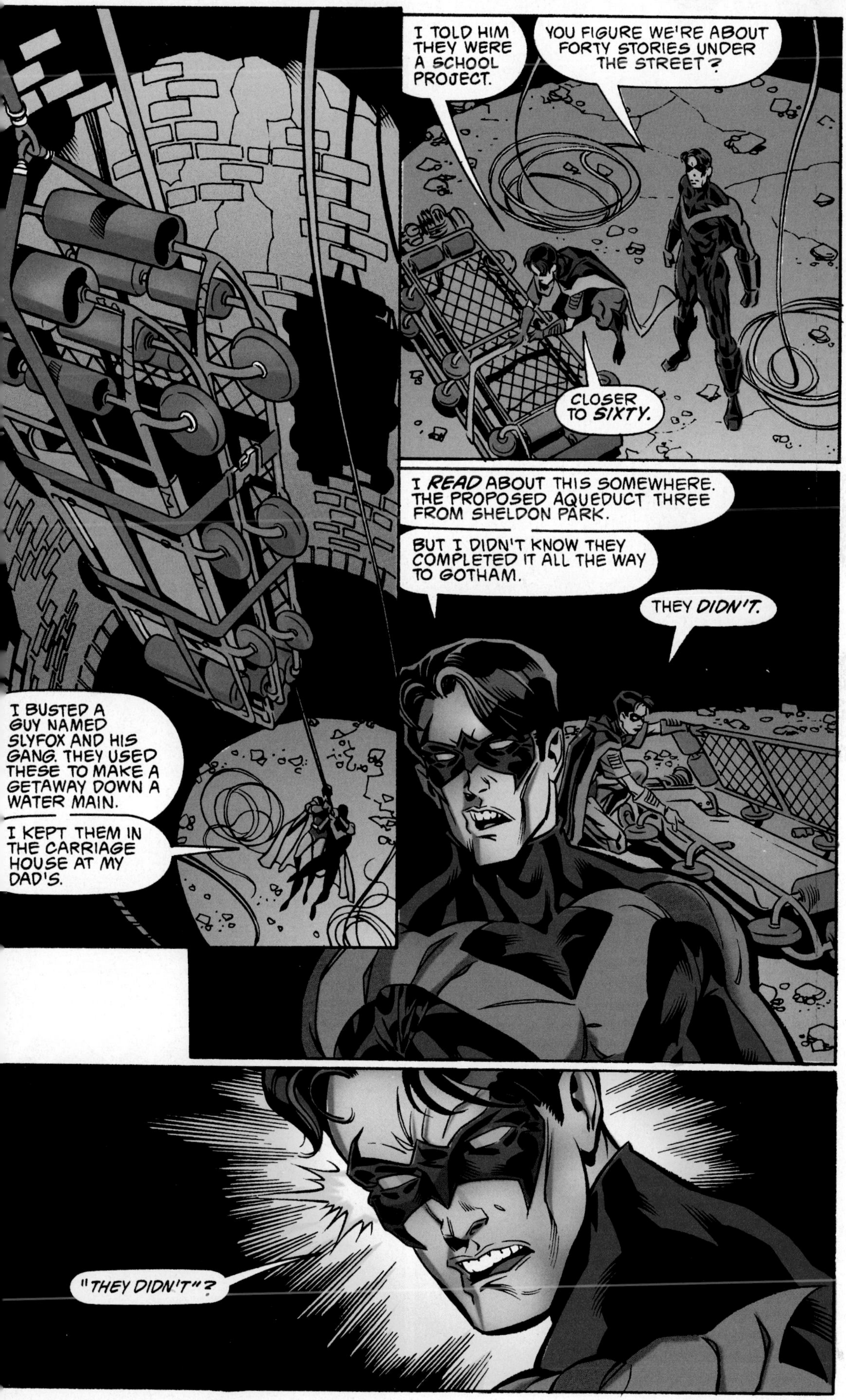
I TOLD HIM THEY WERE A SCHOOL PROJECT.
YOU FIGURE WE'RE ABOUT FORTY STORIES UNDER THE STREET?
CLOSER TO SIXTY.
I BUSTED A GUY NAMED SLYFOX AND HIS GANG. THEY USED THESE TO MAKE A GETAWAY DOWN A WATER MAIN.
I KEPT THEM IN THE CARRIAGE HOUSE AT MY DAD'S.
I READ ABOUT THIS SOMEWHERE. THE PROPOSED AQUEDUCT THREE FROM SHELDON PARK.
BUT I DIDN'T KNOW THEY COMPLETED IT ALL THE WAY TO GOTHAM.
THEY DIDN'T.
"THEY DIDN'T"?

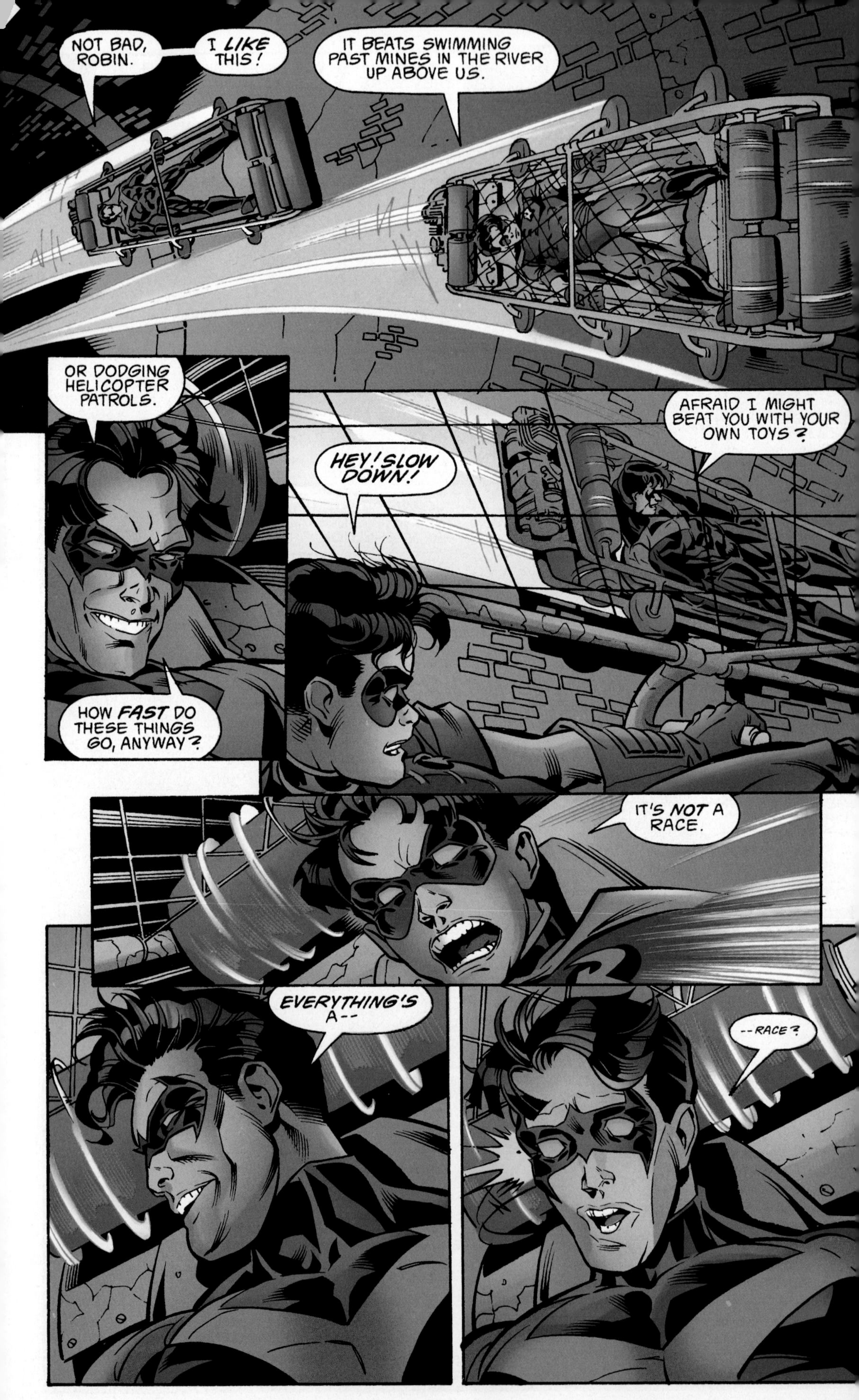
NOT BAD, ROBIN.
I LIKE THIS!
IT BEATS SWIMMING PAST MINES IN THE RIVER UP ABOVE US.
OR DODGING HELICOPTER PATROLS.
HOW FAST DO THESE THINGS GO, ANYWAY?
HEY! SLOW DOWN!
AFRAID I MIGHT BEAT YOU WITH YOUR OWN TOYS?
IT'S NOT A RACE.
EVERYTHING'S A--
--RACE?

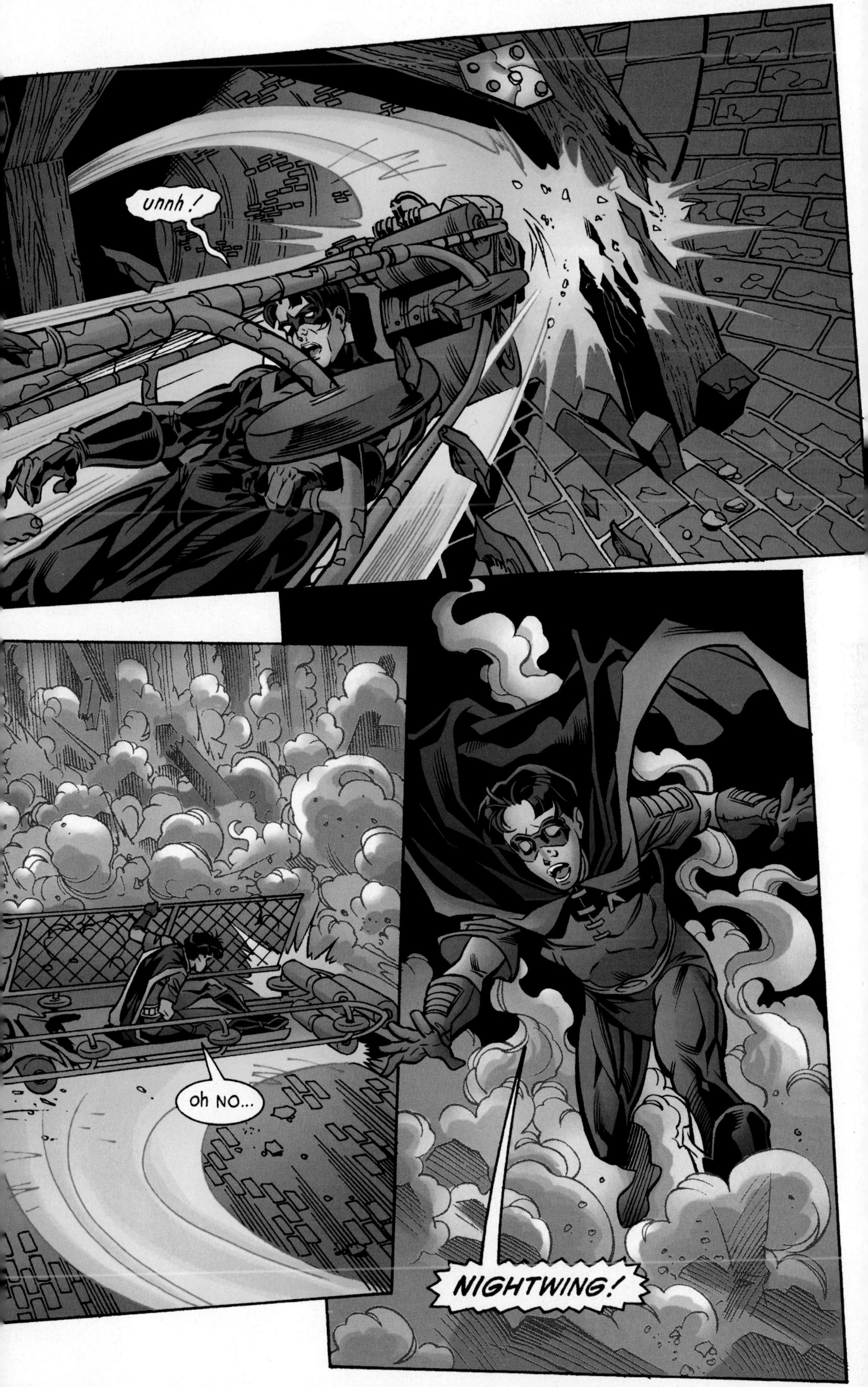

unnh!
oh NO...
NIGHTWING!

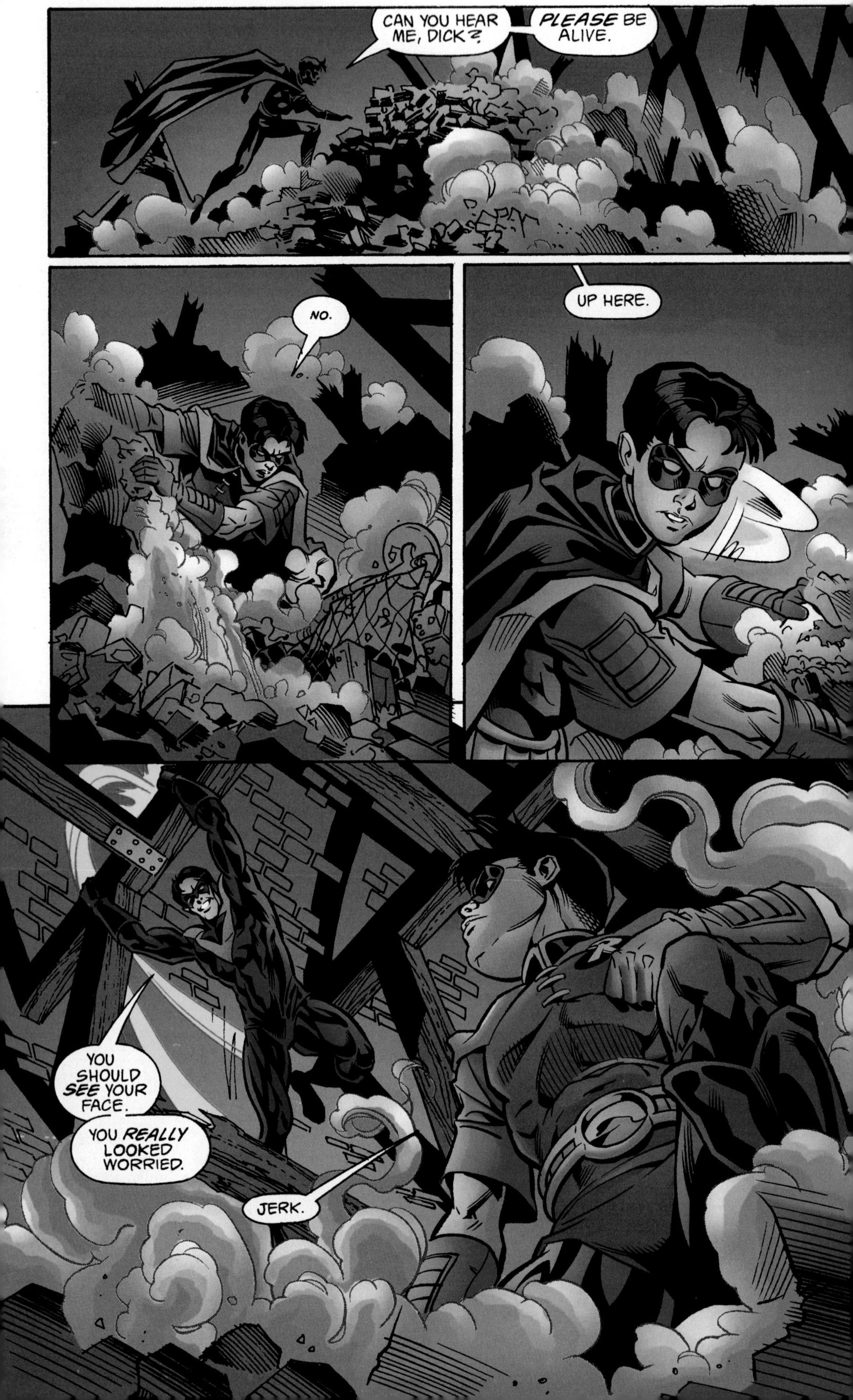
CAN YOU HEAR ME, DICK?
PLEASE BE ALIVE.
NO.
UP HERE.
YOU SHOULD SEE YOUR FACE.
YOU REALLY LOOKED WORRIED.
JERK.

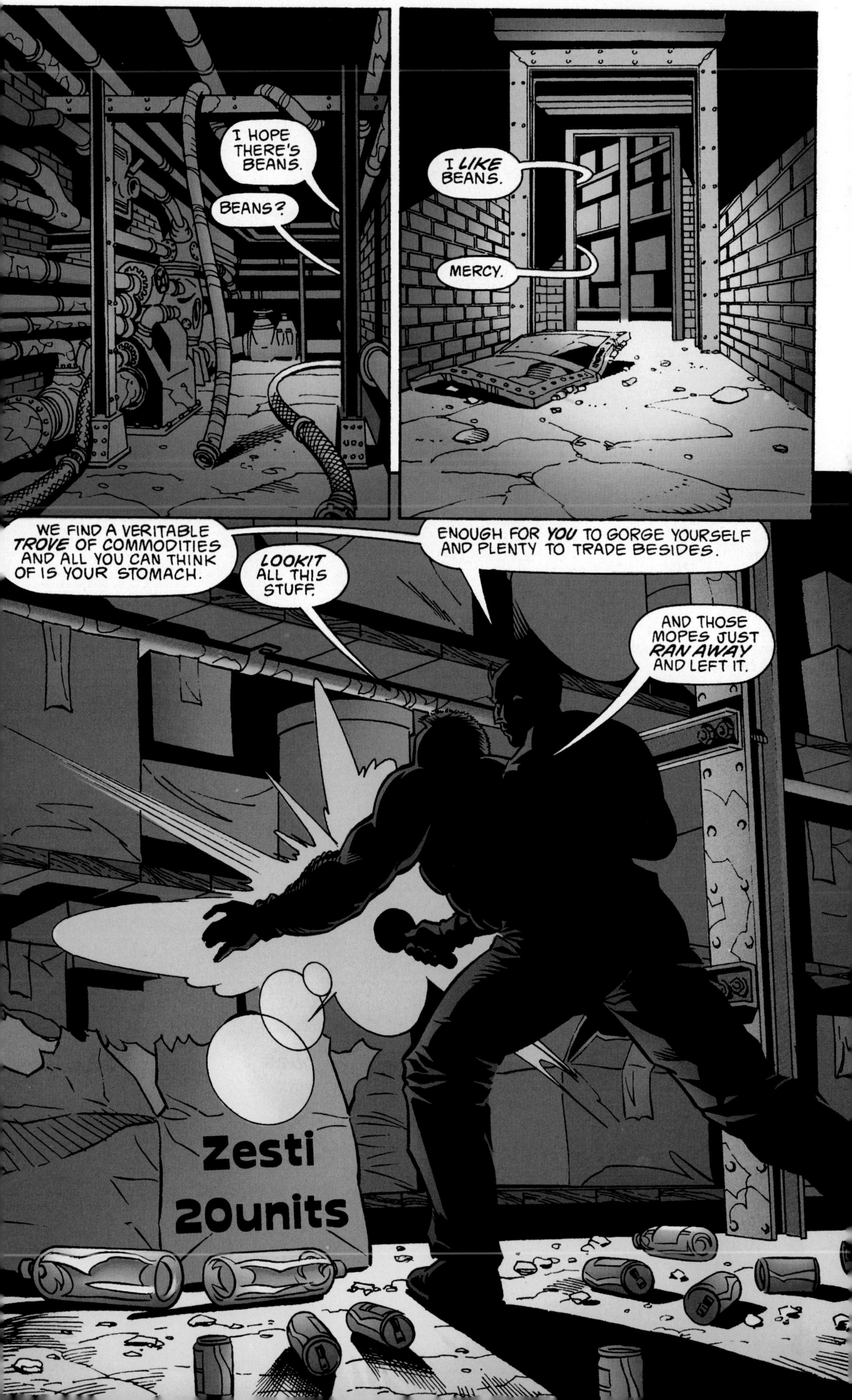
I HOPE THERE'S BEANS.
BEANS?
I LIKE BEANS.
MERCY.
WE FIND A VERITABLE TROVE OF COMMODITIES AND ALL YOU CAN THINK OF IS YOUR STOMACH.
LOOKIT ALL THIS STUFF.
ENOUGH FOR YOU TO GORGE YOURSELF AND PLENTY TO TRADE BESIDES.
AND THOSE MOPES JUST RAN AWAY AND LEFT IT.
Zesti
20units

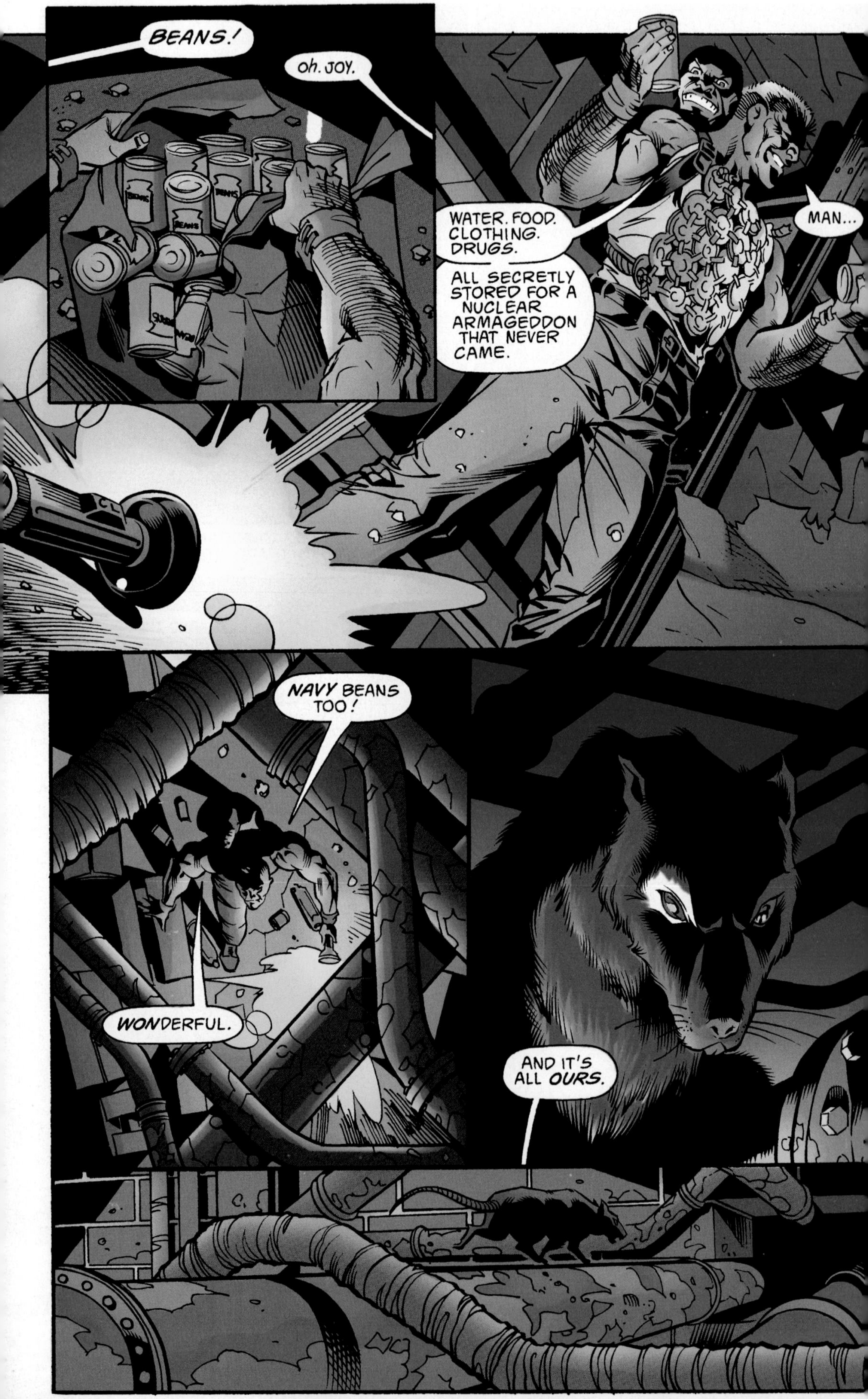

BEANS!
oh. JOY.
WATER. FOOD. CLOTHING. DRUGS.
ALL SECRETLY STORED FOR A NUCLEAR ARMAGEDDON THAT NEVER CAME.
MAN...
NAVY BEANS TOO!
WONDERFUL.
AND IT'S ALL OURS.

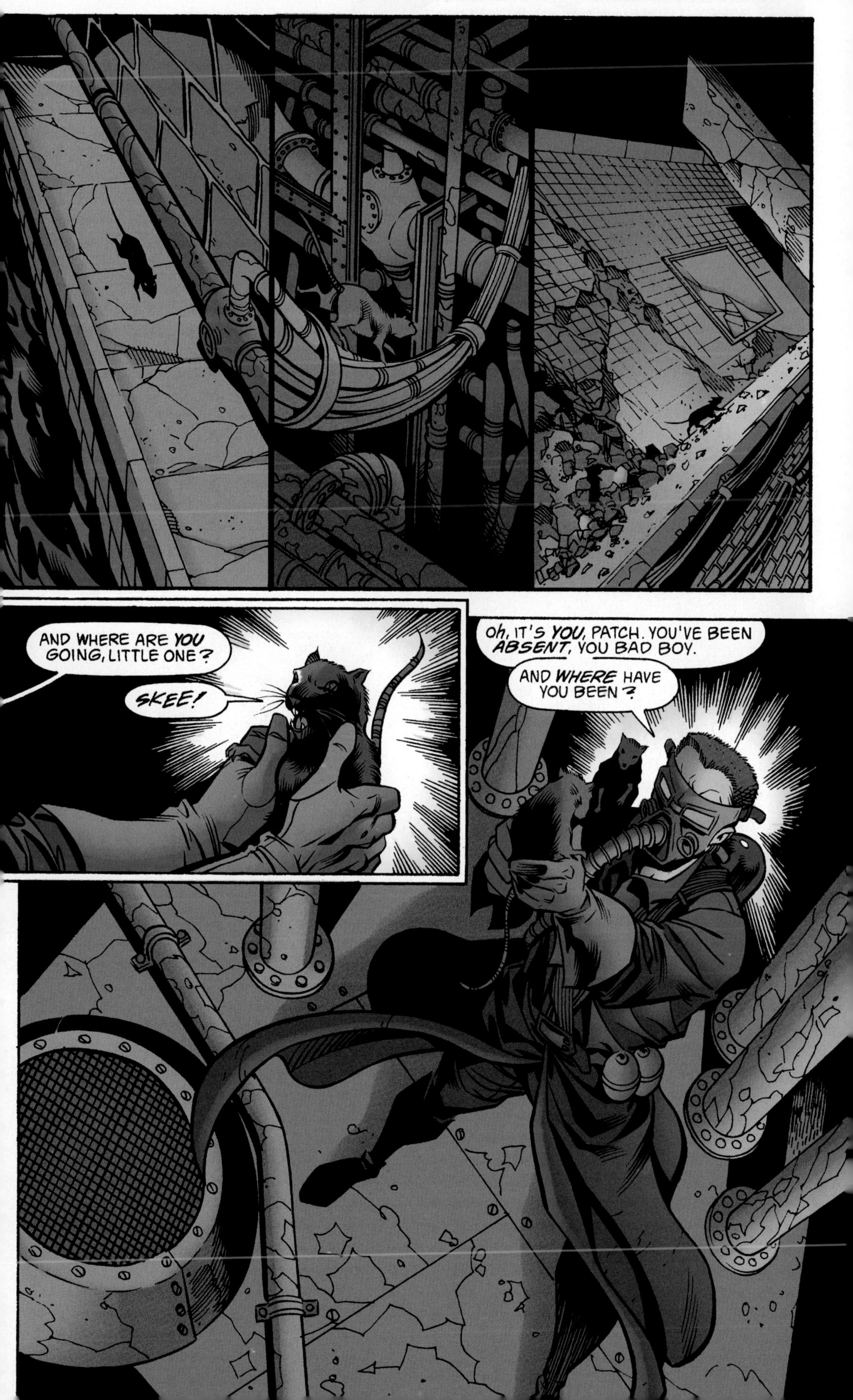
AND WHERE ARE YOU GOING, LITTLE ONE?
SKEE!
Oh, IT'S YOU, PATCH. YOU'VE BEEN ABSENT, YOU BAD BOY.
AND WHERE HAVE YOU BEEN?

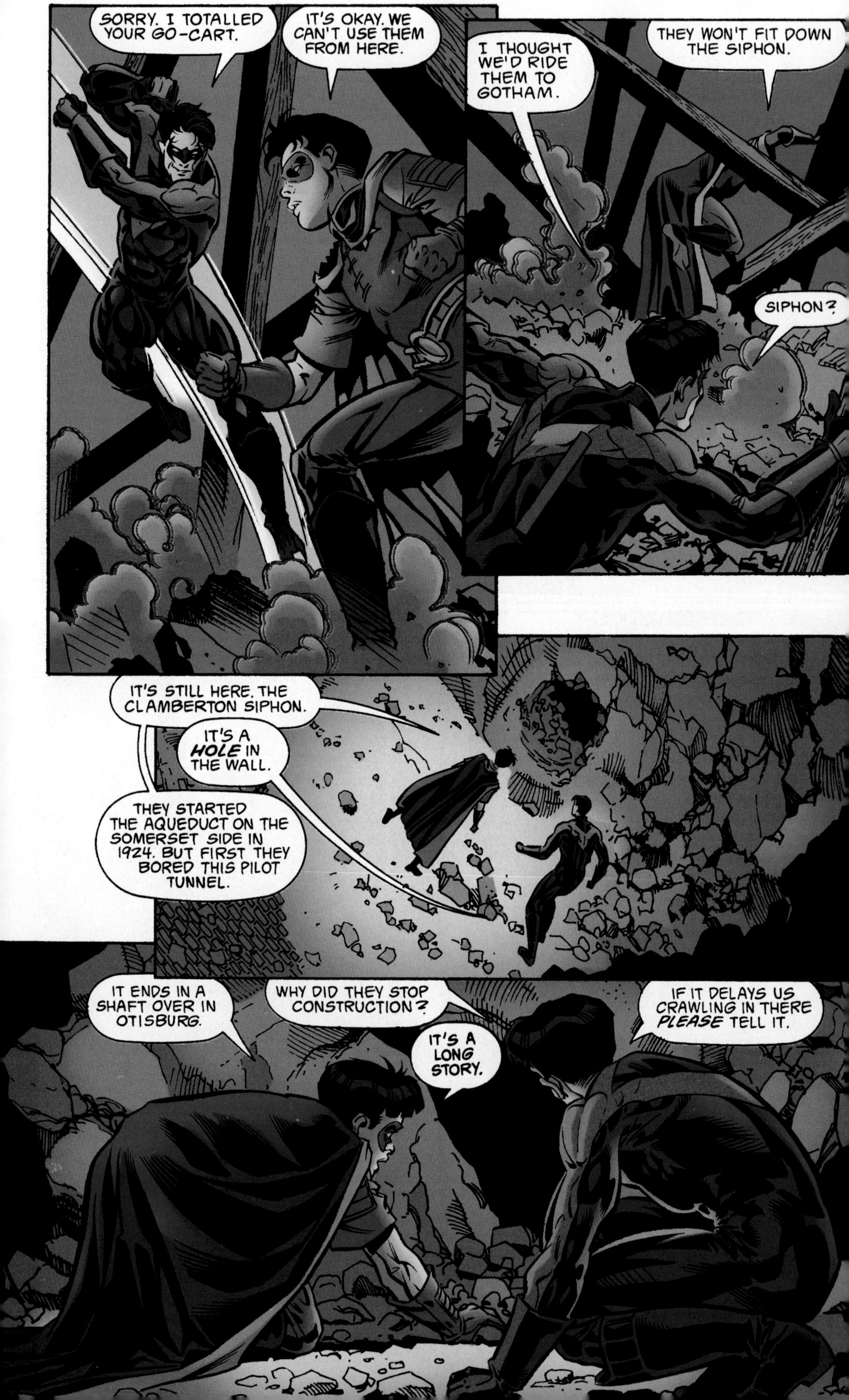
SORRY. I TOTALLED YOUR GO-CART.
IT'S OKAY. WE CAN'T USE THEM FROM HERE.
I THOUGHT WE'D RIDE THEM TO GOTHAM.
THEY WON'T FIT DOWN THE SIPHON.
SIPHON?
IT'S STILL HERE. THE CLAMBERTON SIPHON.
IT'S A HOLE IN THE WALL.
THEY STARTED THE AQUEDUCT ON THE SOMERSET SIDE IN 1924. BUT FIRST THEY BORED THIS PILOT TUNNEL.
IT ENDS IN A SHAFT OVER IN OTISBURG.
WHY DID THEY STOP CONSTRUCTION?
IT'S A LONG STORY.
IF IT DELAYS US CRAWLING IN THERE PLEASE TELL IT.

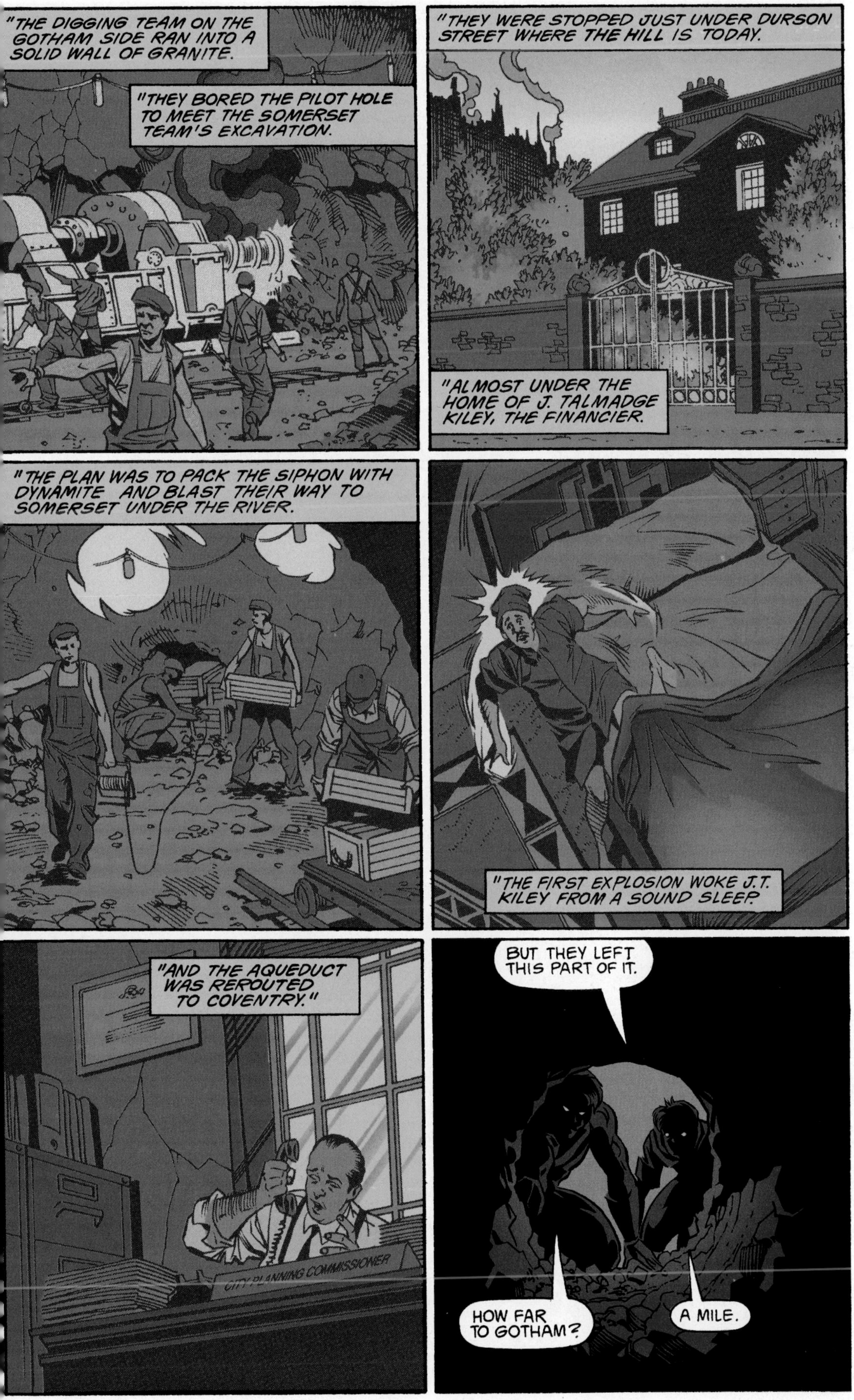
"THE DIGGING TEAM ON THE GOTHAM SIDE RAN INTO A SOLID WALL OF GRANITE.
"THEY BORED THE PILOT HOLE TO MEET THE SOMERSET TEAM'S EXCAVATION.
"THEY WERE STOPPED JUST UNDER DURSON STREET WHERE THE HILL IS TODAY.
"ALMOST UNDER THE HOME OF J. TALMADGE KILEY, THE FINANCIER.
"THE PLAN WAS TO PACK THE SIPHON WITH DYNAMITE AND BLAST THEIR WAY TO SOMERSET UNDER THE RIVER.
"THE FIRST EXPLOSION WOKE J.T. KILEY FROM A SOUND SLEEP.
"AND THE AQUEDUCT WAS REROUTED TO COVENTRY."
CITY PLANNING COMMISSIONER
BUT THEY LEFT THIS PART OF IT.
HOW FAR TO GOTHAM?
A MILE.

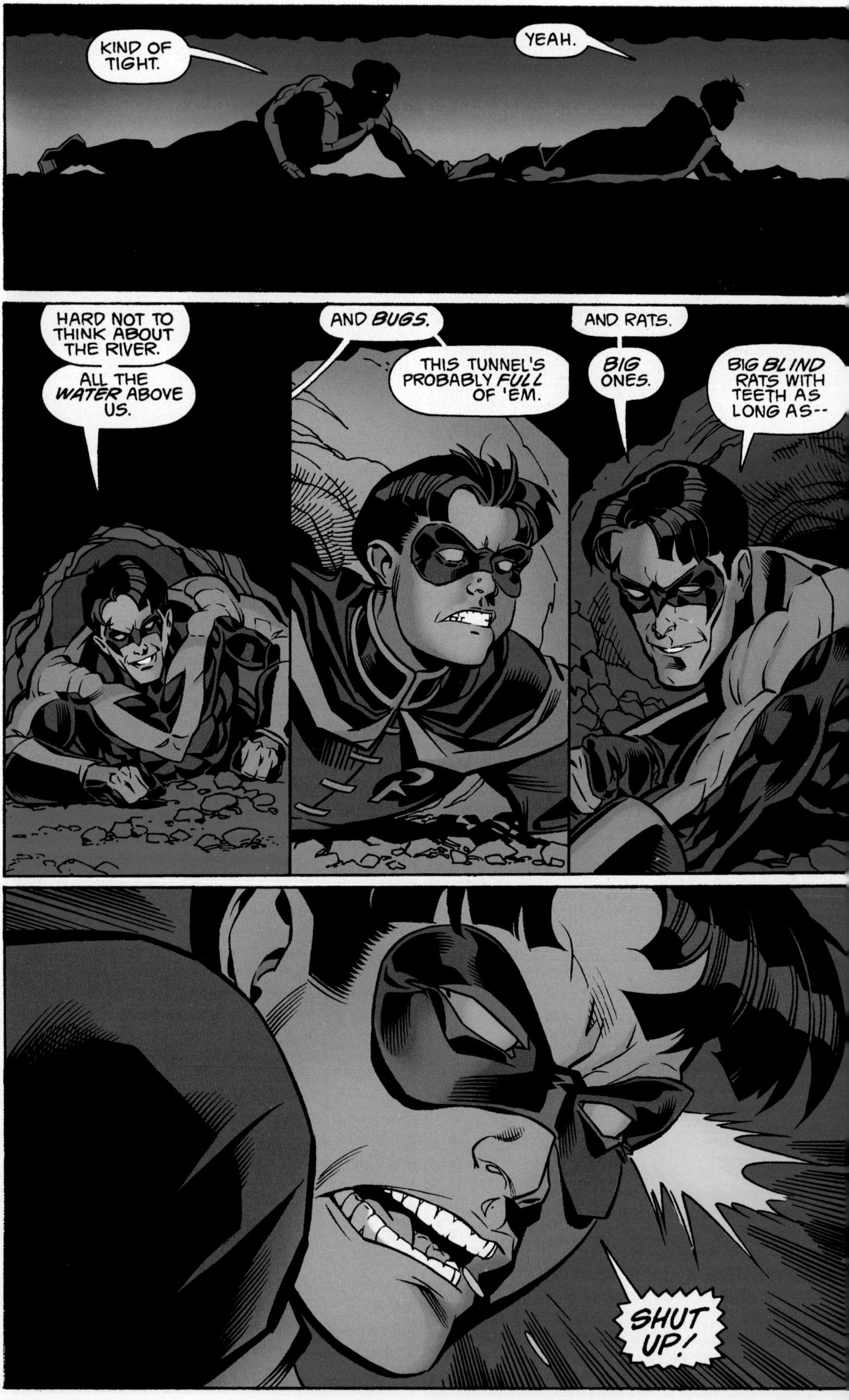
KIND OF TIGHT.
YEAH.
HARD NOT TO THINK ABOUT THE RIVER.
ALL THE WATER ABOVE US.
AND BUGS.
THIS TUNNEL'S PROBABLY FULL OF 'EM.
AND RATS.
BIG ONES.
BIG BLIND RATS WITH TEETH AS LONG AS--
SHUT UP!

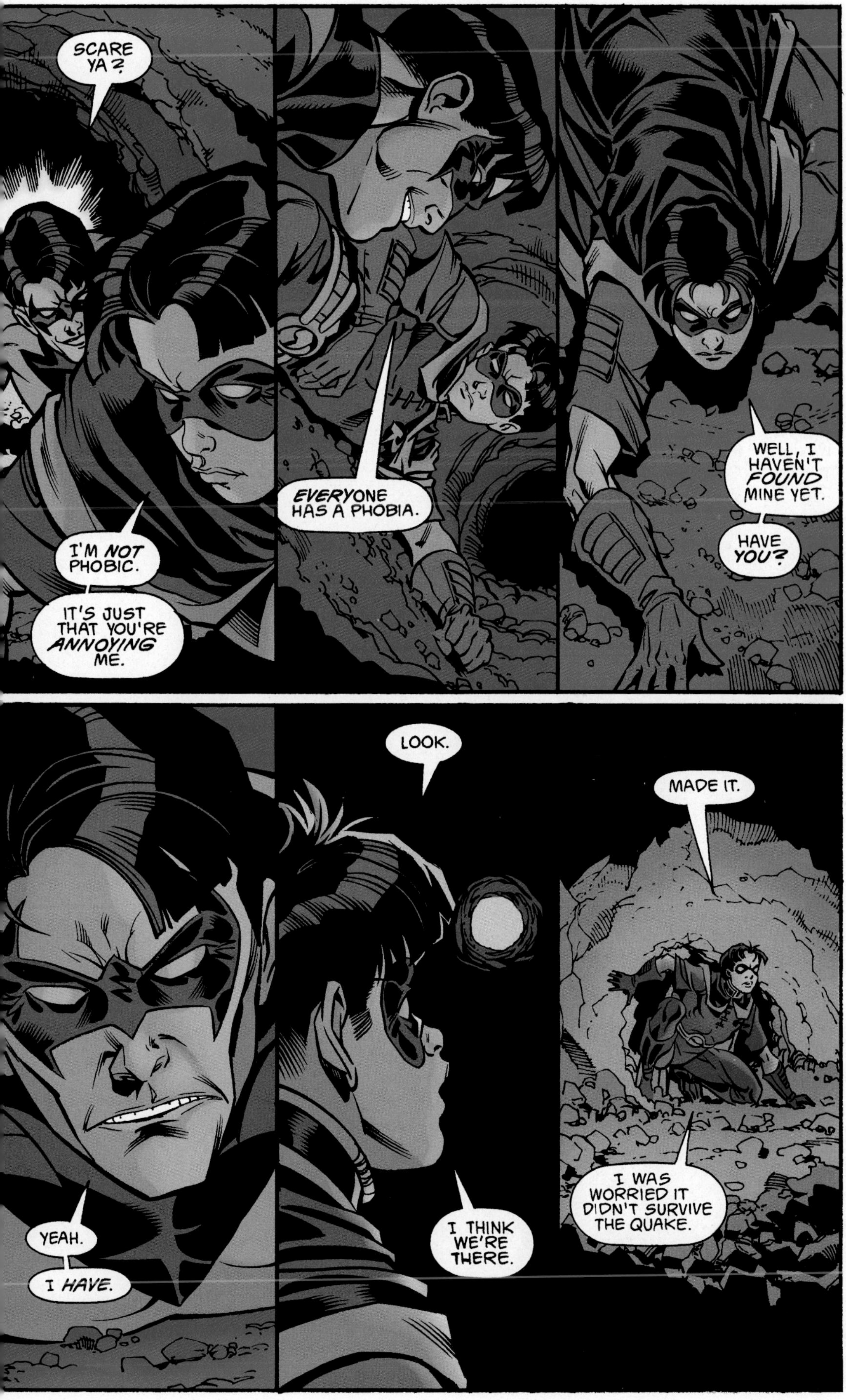
SCARE YA?
I'M *NOT* PHOBIC.
IT'S JUST THAT YOU'RE *ANNOYING* ME.
*EVERY*ONE HAS A PHOBIA.
WELL, I HAVEN'T *FOUND* MINE YET.
HAVE *YOU*?
YEAH.
I *HAVE*.
LOOK.
I THINK WE'RE THERE.
MADE IT.
I WAS WORRIED IT DIDN'T SURVIVE THE QUAKE.

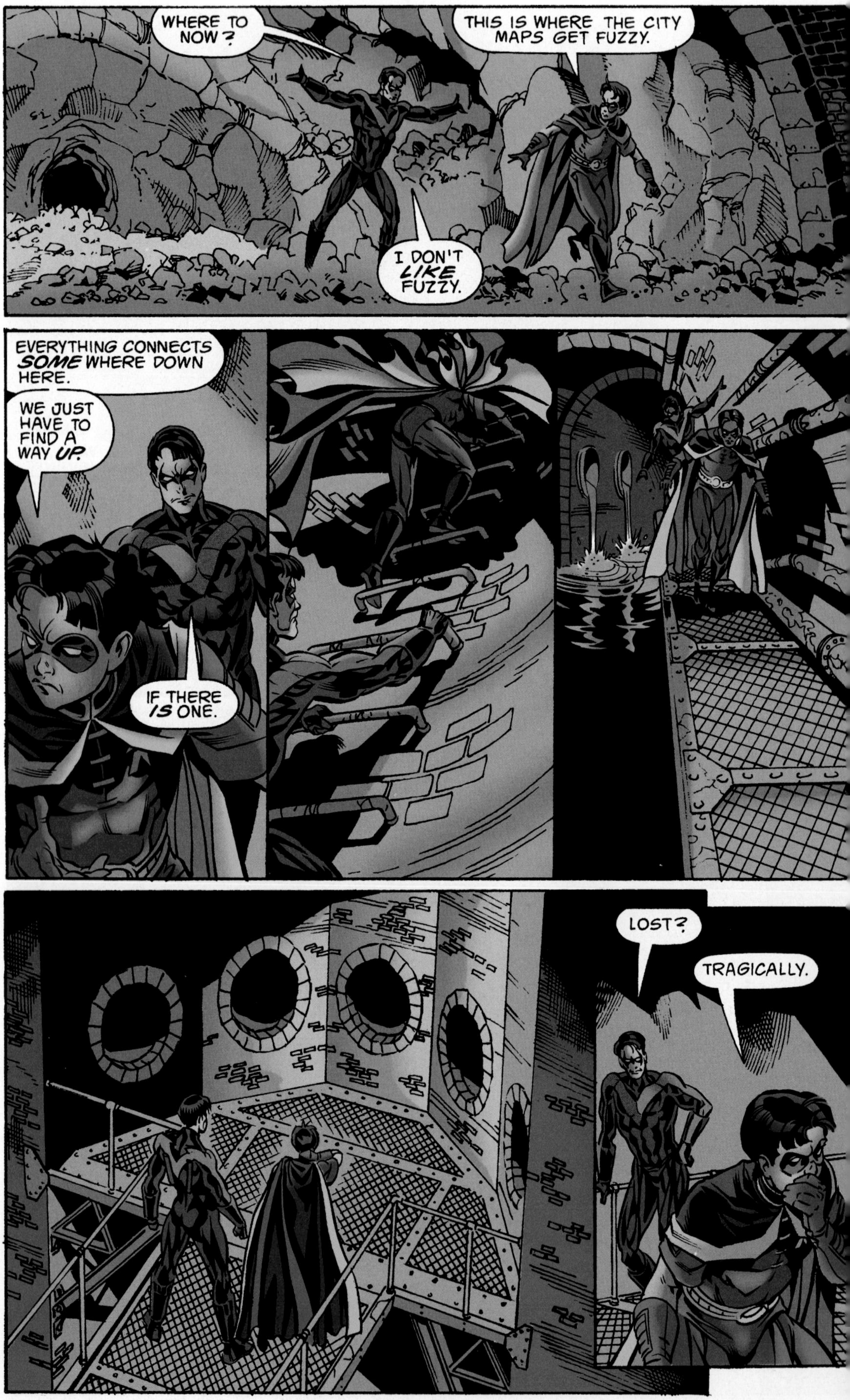
WHERE TO NOW?
THIS IS WHERE THE CITY MAPS GET FUZZY.
I DON'T *LIKE* FUZZY.
EVERYTHING CONNECTS *SOME* WHERE DOWN HERE.
WE JUST HAVE TO FIND A WAY *UP*.
IF THERE *IS* ONE.
LOST?
TRAGICALLY.

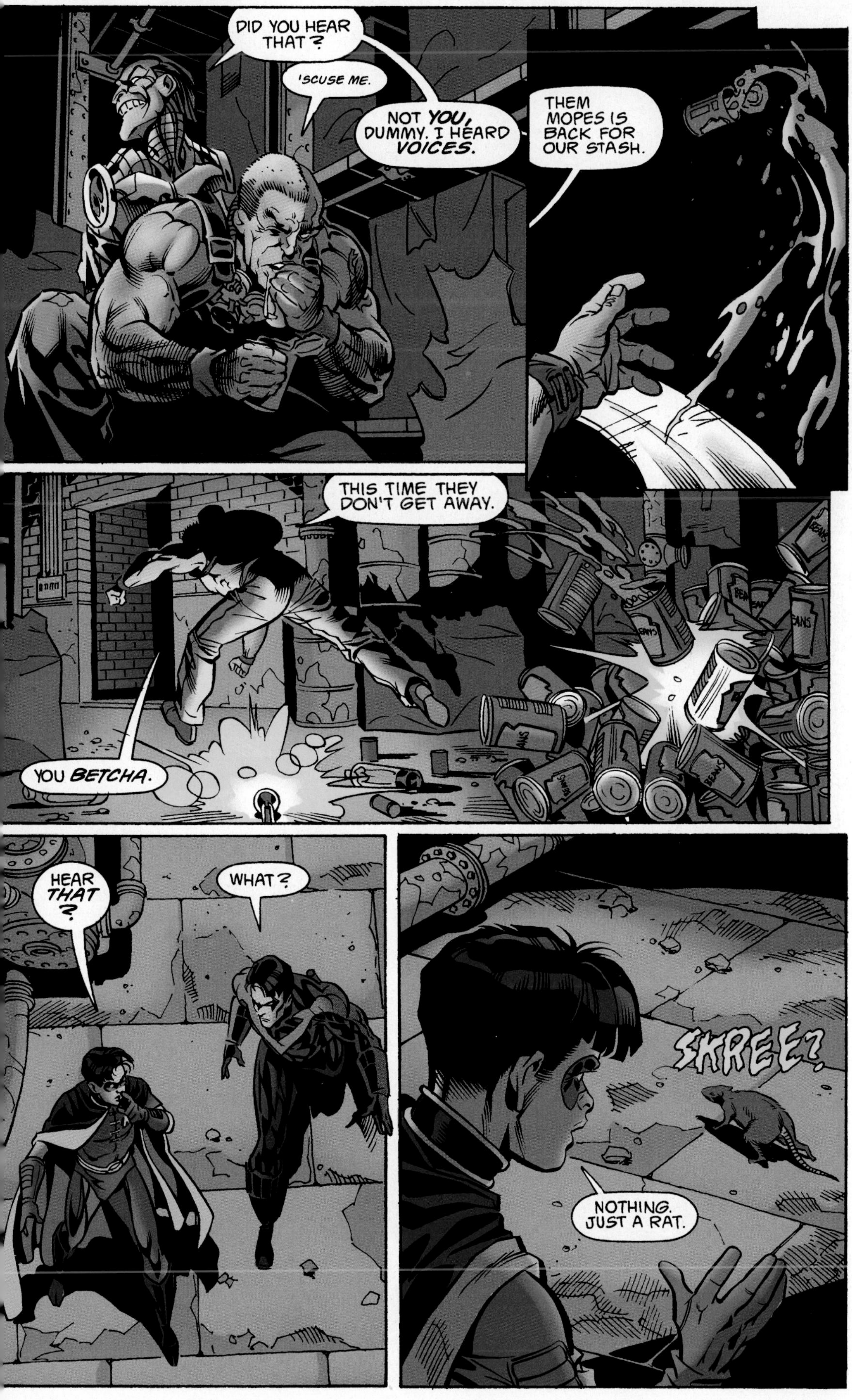
DID YOU HEAR THAT?
'SCUSE ME.
NOT YOU, DUMMY. I HEARD VOICES.
THEM MOPES IS BACK FOR OUR STASH.
THIS TIME THEY DON'T GET AWAY.
YOU BETCHA.
HEAR THAT?
WHAT?
SKREE?
NOTHING. JUST A RAT.

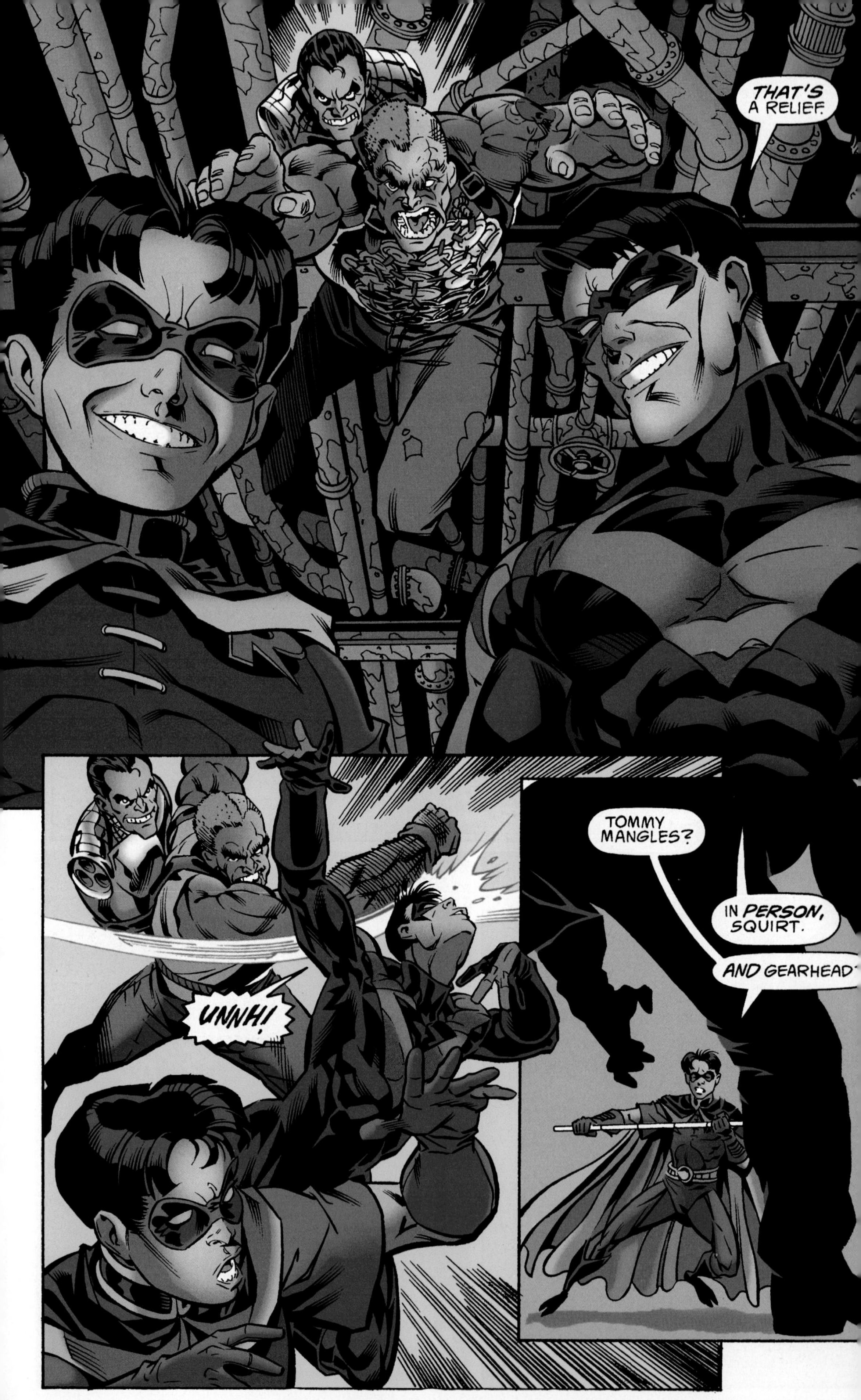
THAT'S A RELIEF.
UNNH!
TOMMY MANGLES?
IN PERSON, SQUIRT.
AND GEARHEAD

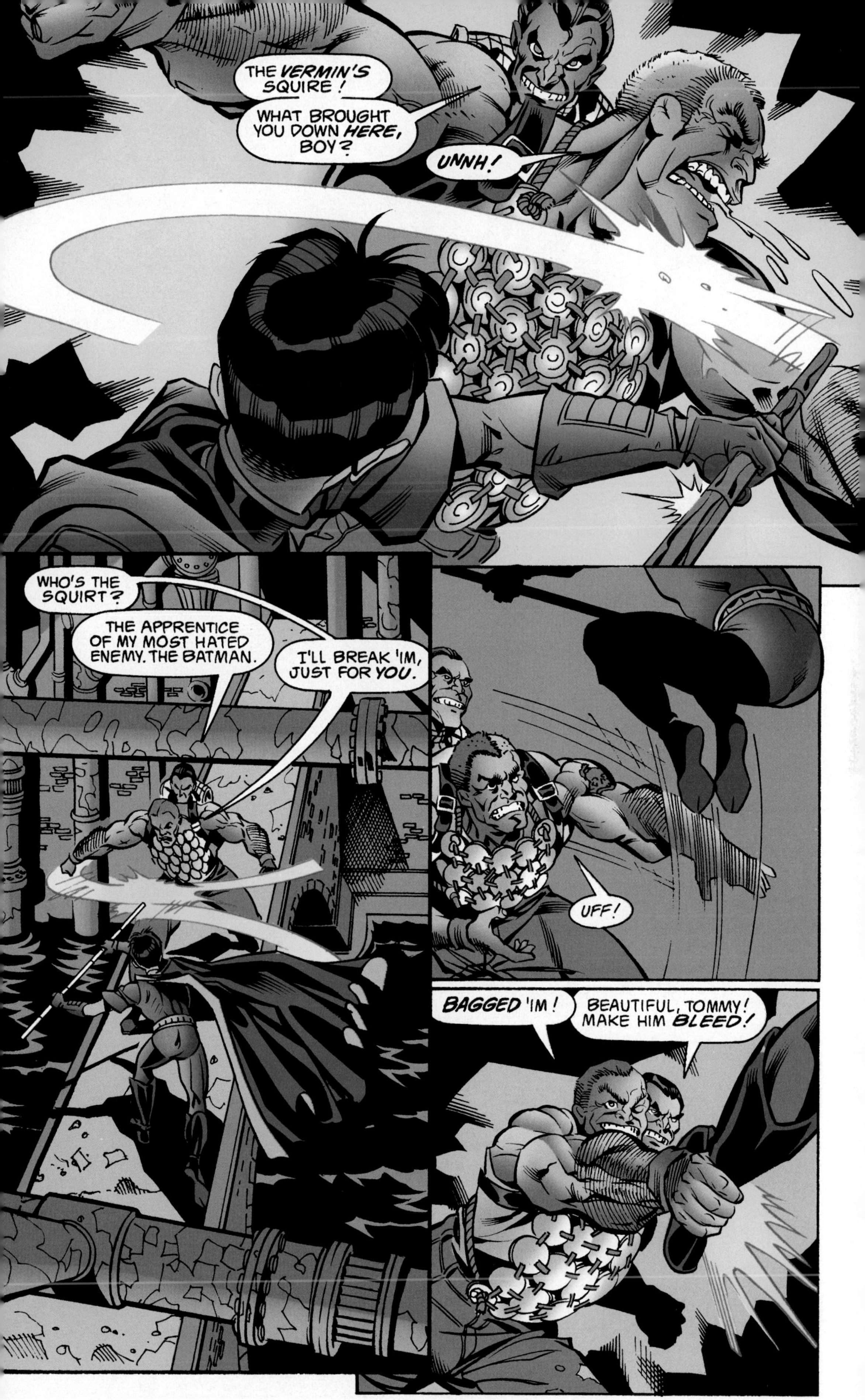
THE VERMIN'S SQUIRE!
WHAT BROUGHT YOU DOWN HERE, BOY?
UNNH!
WHO'S THE SQUIRT?
THE APPRENTICE OF MY MOST HATED ENEMY. THE BATMAN.
I'LL BREAK 'IM, JUST FOR YOU.
UFF!
BAGGED 'IM!
BEAUTIFUL, TOMMY! MAKE HIM BLEED!

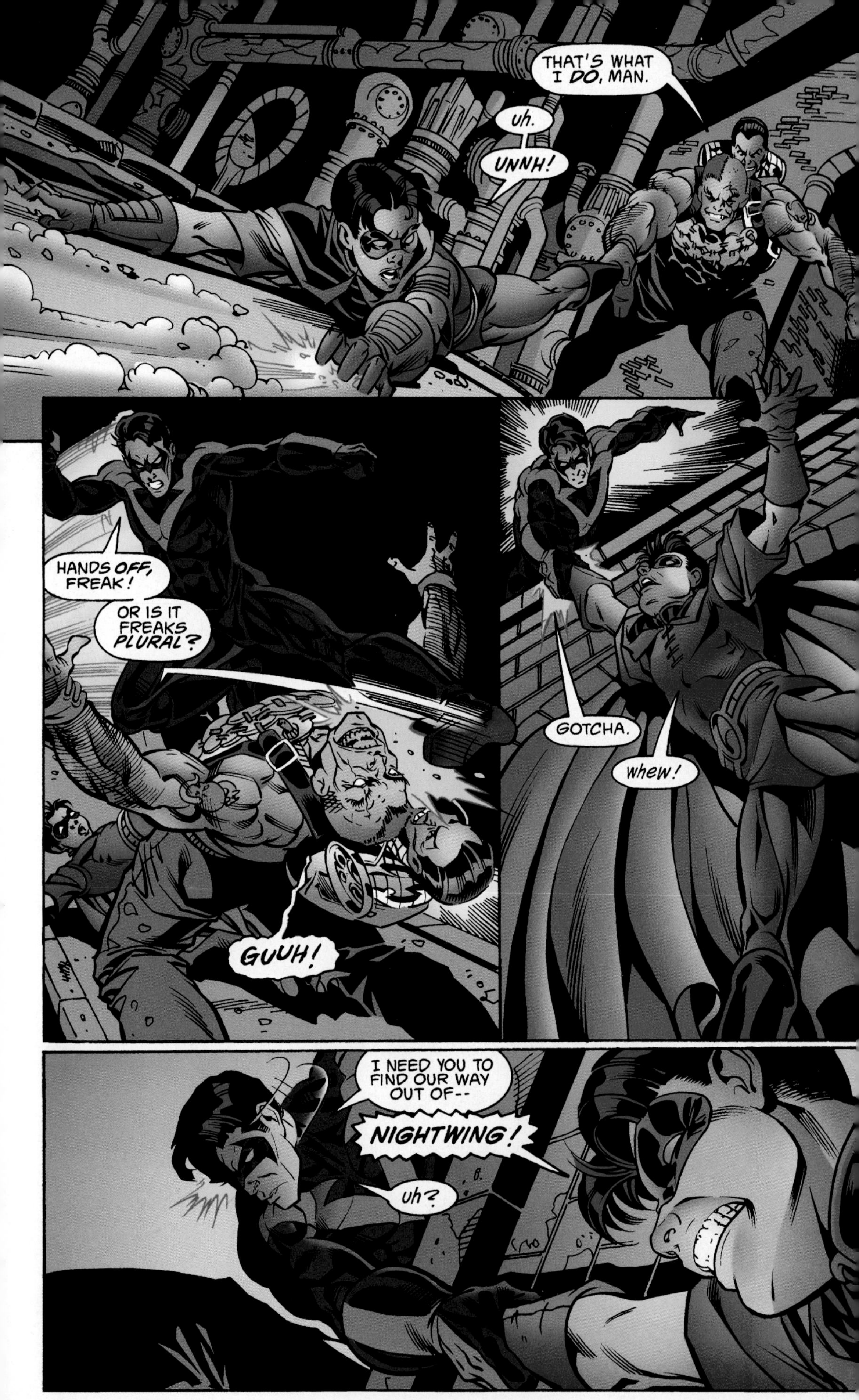
THAT'S WHAT I DO, MAN.
uh.
UNNH!
HANDS OFF, FREAK!
OR IS IT FREAKS PLURAL?
GUUH!
GOTCHA.
whew!
I NEED YOU TO FIND OUR WAY OUT OF--
NIGHTWING!
uh?

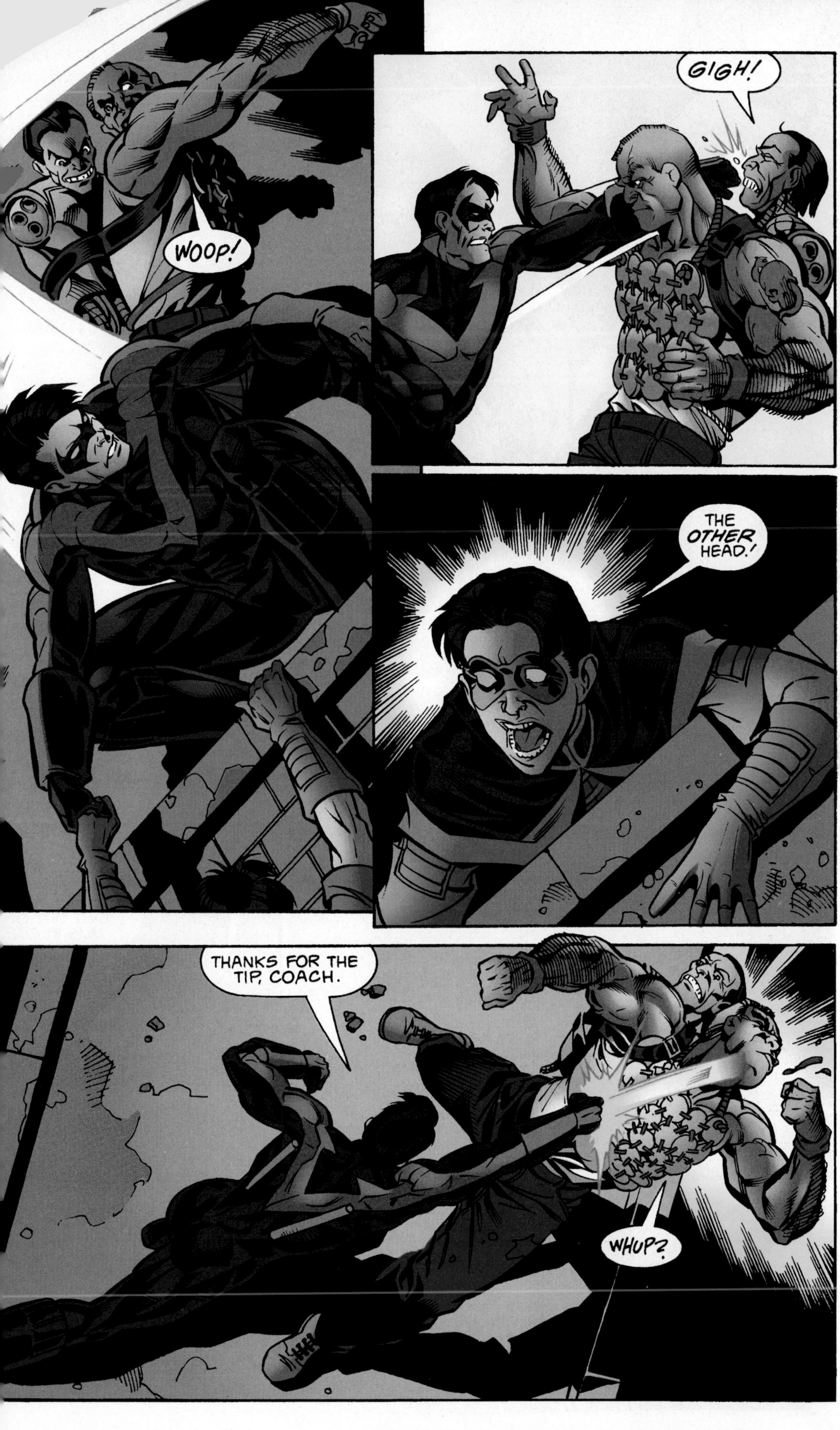
WOOP!
GIGH!
THE OTHER HEAD.!
THANKS FOR THE TIP, COACH.
WHUP?

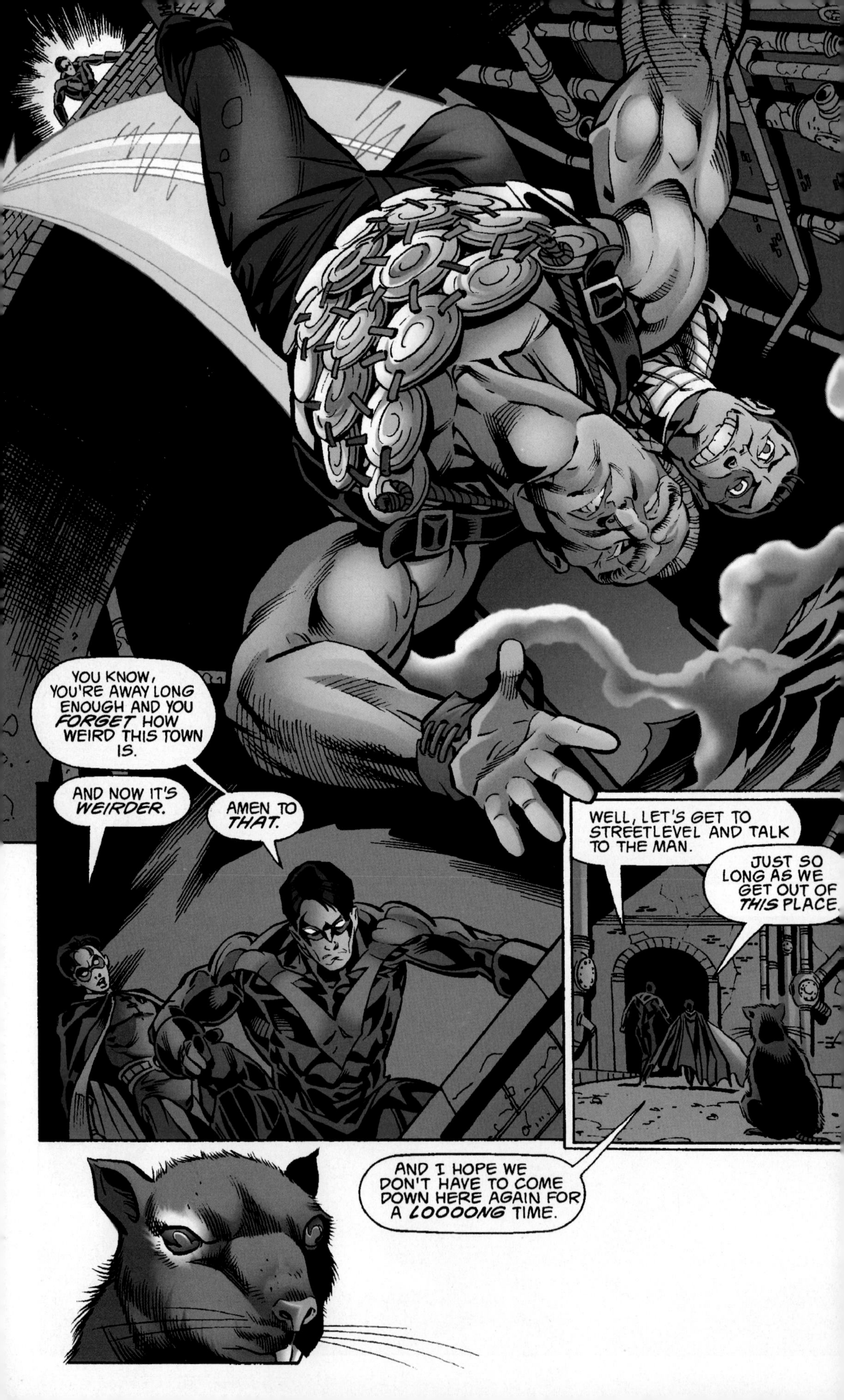
YOU KNOW, YOU'RE AWAY LONG ENOUGH AND YOU *FORGET* HOW WEIRD THIS TOWN IS.
AND NOW IT'S *WEIRDER.*
AMEN TO *THAT.*
WELL, LET'S GET TO STREETLEVEL AND TALK TO THE MAN.
JUST SO LONG AS WE GET OUT OF *THIS* PLACE.
AND I HOPE WE DON'T HAVE TO COME DOWN HERE AGAIN FOR A *LOOOONG* TIME.

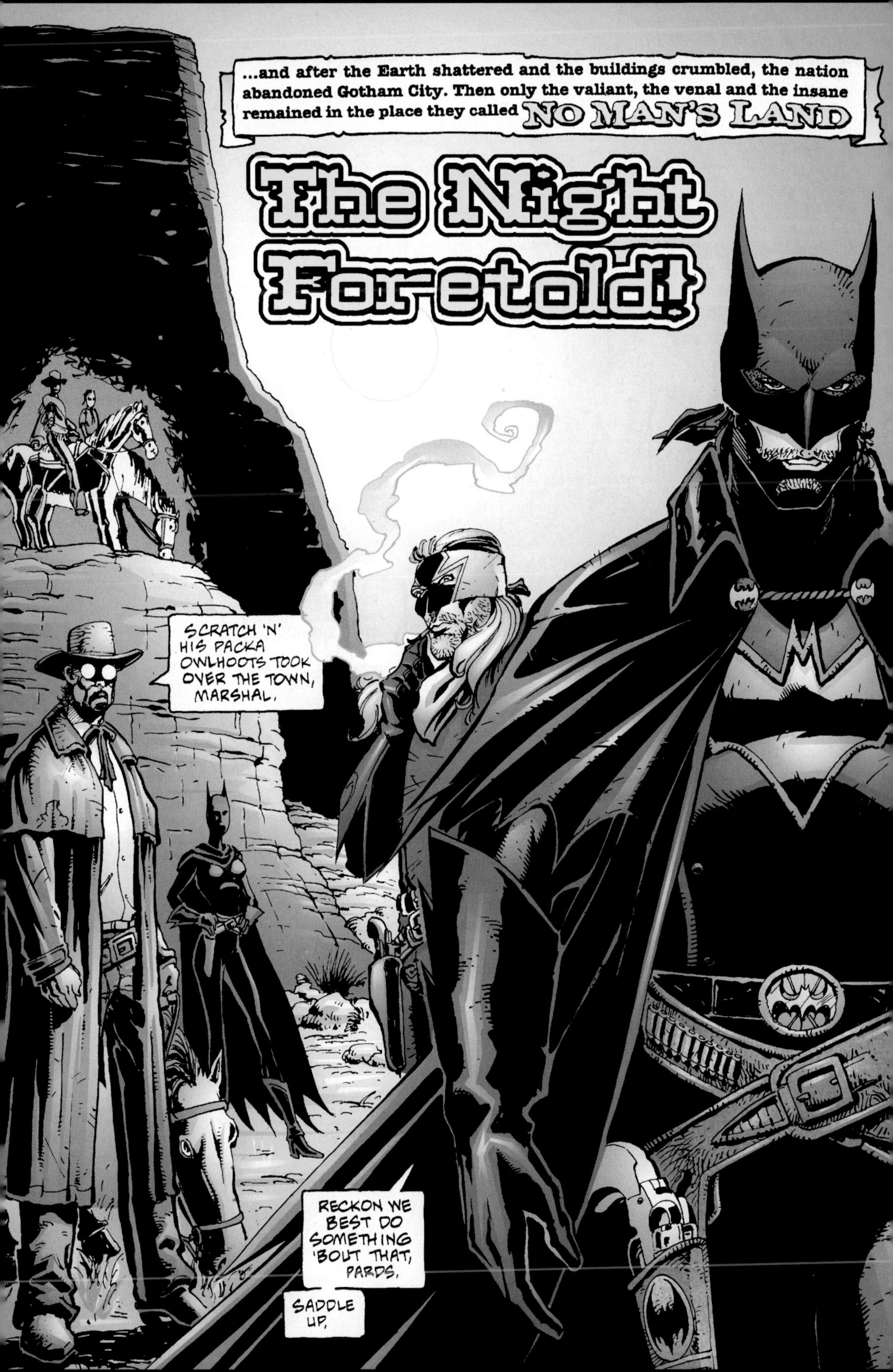

...and after the Earth shattered and the buildings crumbled, the nation abandoned Gotham City. Then only the valiant, the venal and the insane remained in the place they called NO MAN'S LAND
The Night Foretold!
SCRATCH 'N' HIS PACKA OWLHOOTS TOOK OVER THE TOWN, MARSHAL.
RECKON WE BEST DO SOMETHING 'BOUT THAT, PARDS.
SADDLE UP.

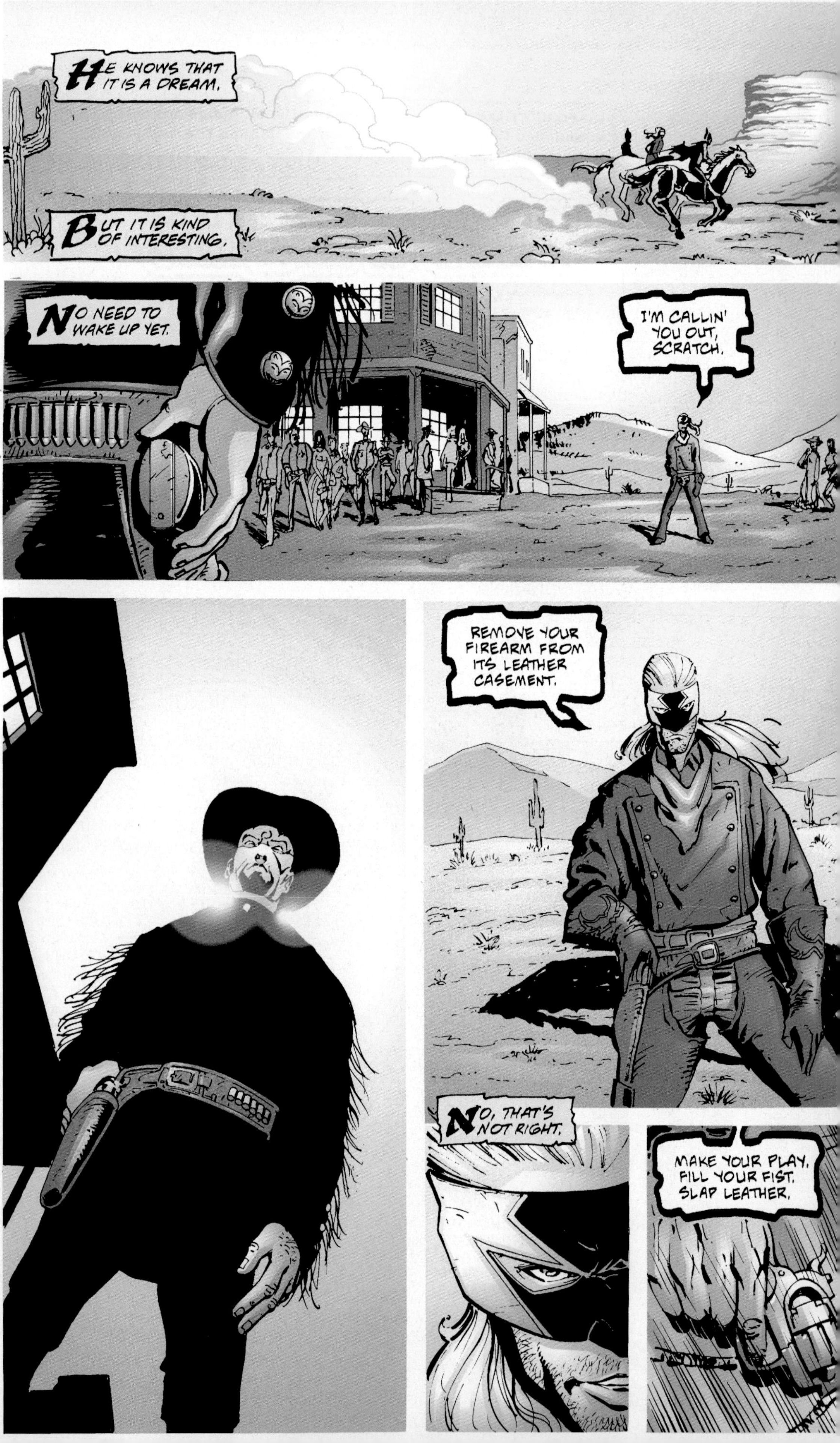
HE KNOWS THAT IT IS A DREAM.
BUT IT IS KIND OF INTERESTING.
NO NEED TO WAKE UP YET.
I'M CALLIN' YOU OUT, SCRATCH.
REMOVE YOUR FIREARM FROM ITS LEATHER CASEMENT.
NO, THAT'S NOT RIGHT.
MAKE YOUR PLAY. FILL YOUR FIST. SLAP LEATHER.

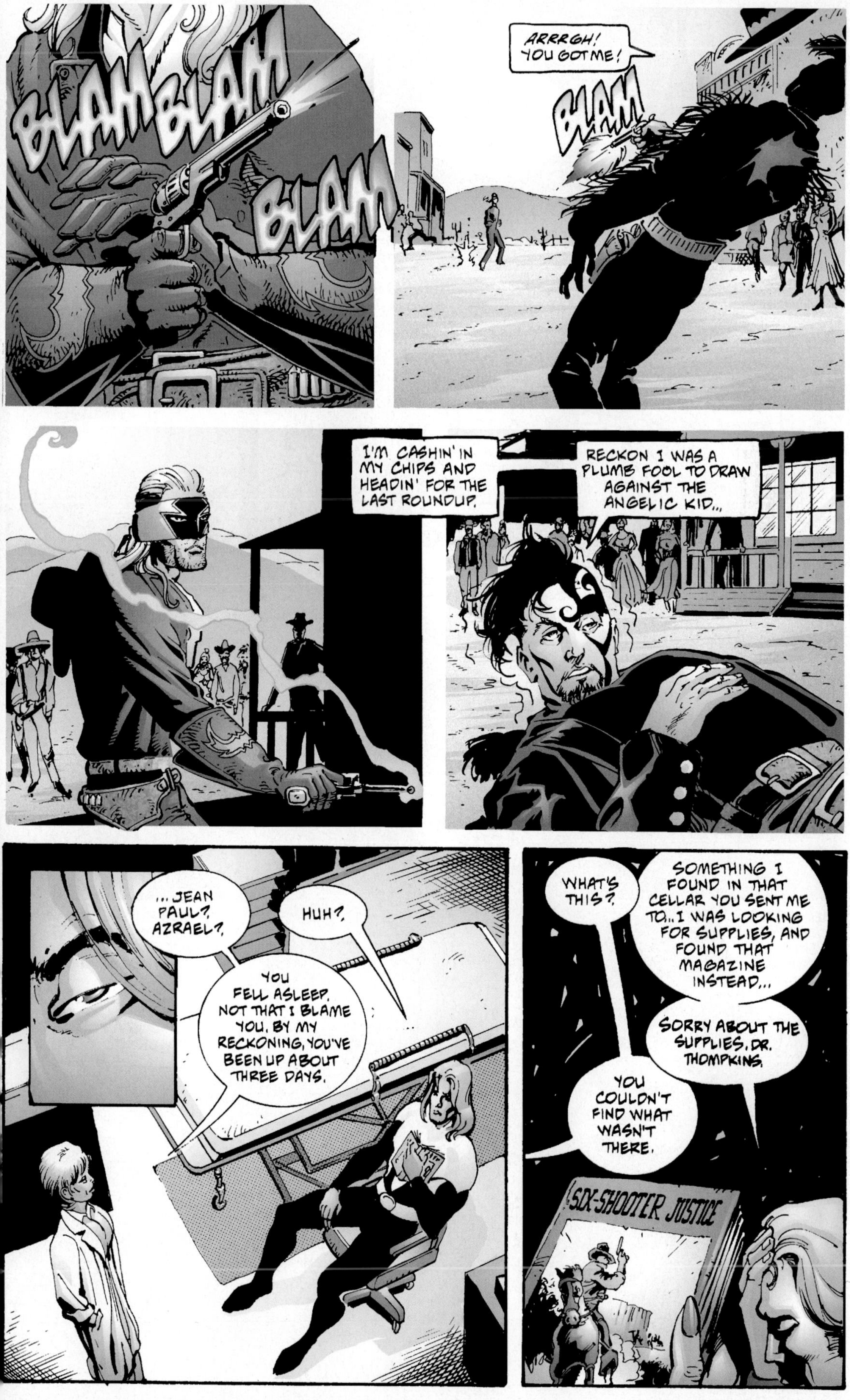
BLAM BLAM
BLAM
ARRRGH! YOU GOT ME!
BLAM
I'M CASHIN' IN MY CHIPS AND HEADIN' FOR THE LAST ROUNDUP.
RECKON I WAS A PLUMB FOOL TO DRAW AGAINST THE ANGELIC KID...
...JEAN PAUL? AZRAEL?
HUH?
YOU FELL ASLEEP. NOT THAT I BLAME YOU. BY MY RECKONING, YOU'VE BEEN UP ABOUT THREE DAYS.
WHAT'S THIS?
SOMETHING I FOUND IN THAT CELLAR YOU SENT ME TO... I WAS LOOKING FOR SUPPLIES, AND FOUND THAT MAGAZINE INSTEAD...
SORRY ABOUT THE SUPPLIES, DR. THOMPKINS.
YOU COULDN'T FIND WHAT WASN'T THERE.
SIX-SHOOTER JUSTICE

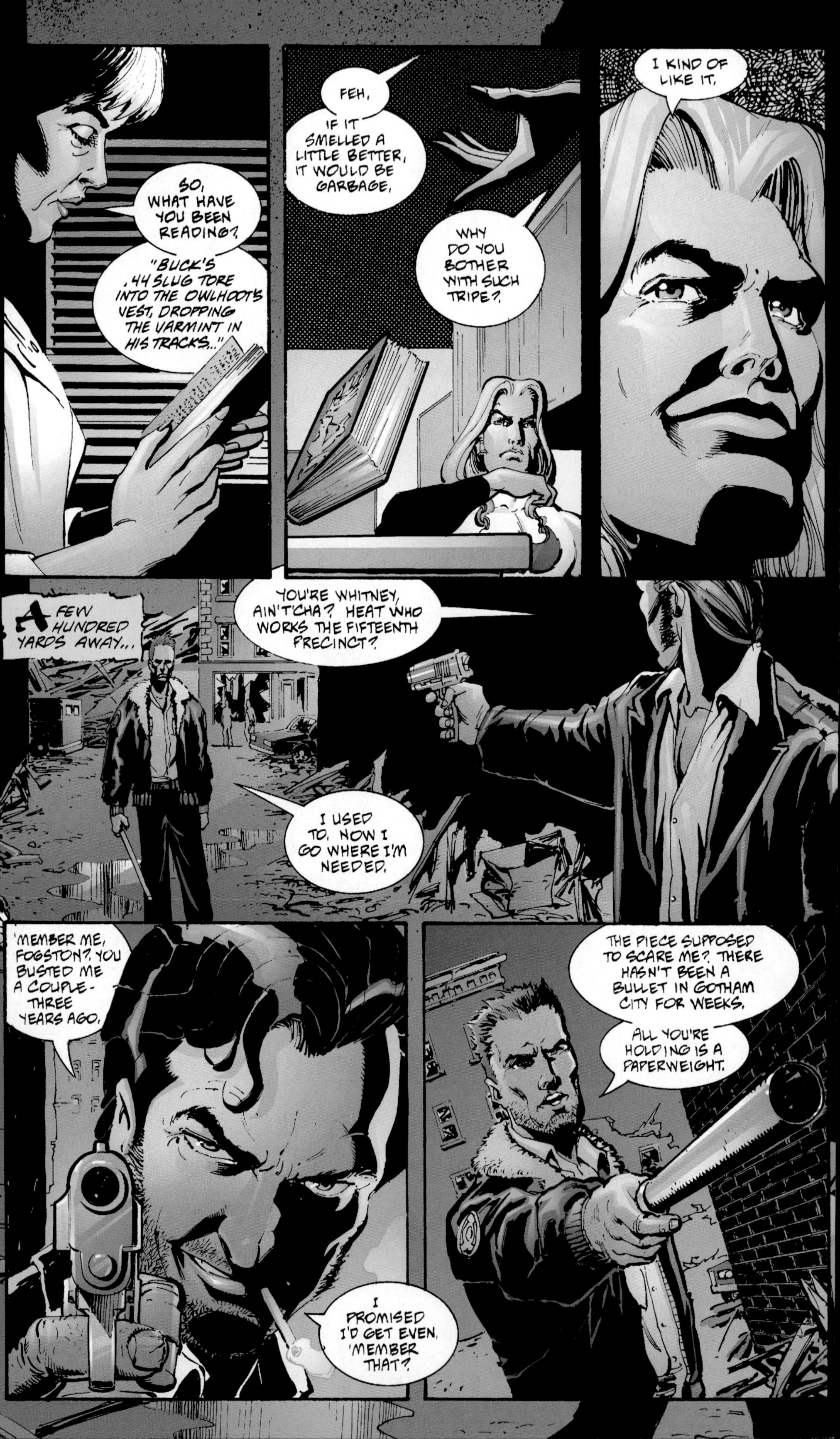
SO, WHAT HAVE YOU BEEN READING?
"BUCK'S .44 SLUG TORE INTO THE OWLHOOT'S VEST, DROPPING THE VARMINT IN HIS TRACKS..."
FEH,
IF IT SMELLED A LITTLE BETTER, IT WOULD BE GARBAGE.
WHY DO YOU BOTHER WITH SUCH TRIPE?
I KIND OF LIKE IT.
A FEW HUNDRED YARDS AWAY...
YOU'RE WHITNEY, AIN'T'CHA? HEAT WHO WORKS THE FIFTEENTH PRECINCT?
I USED TO. NOW I GO WHERE I'M NEEDED.
'MEMBER ME, FOGSTON? YOU BUSTED ME A COUPLE-THREE YEARS AGO.
I PROMISED I'D GET EVEN. 'MEMBER THAT?
THE PIECE SUPPOSED TO SCARE ME? THERE HASN'T BEEN A BULLET IN GOTHAM CITY FOR WEEKS.
ALL YOU'RE HOLDING IS A PAPERWEIGHT.

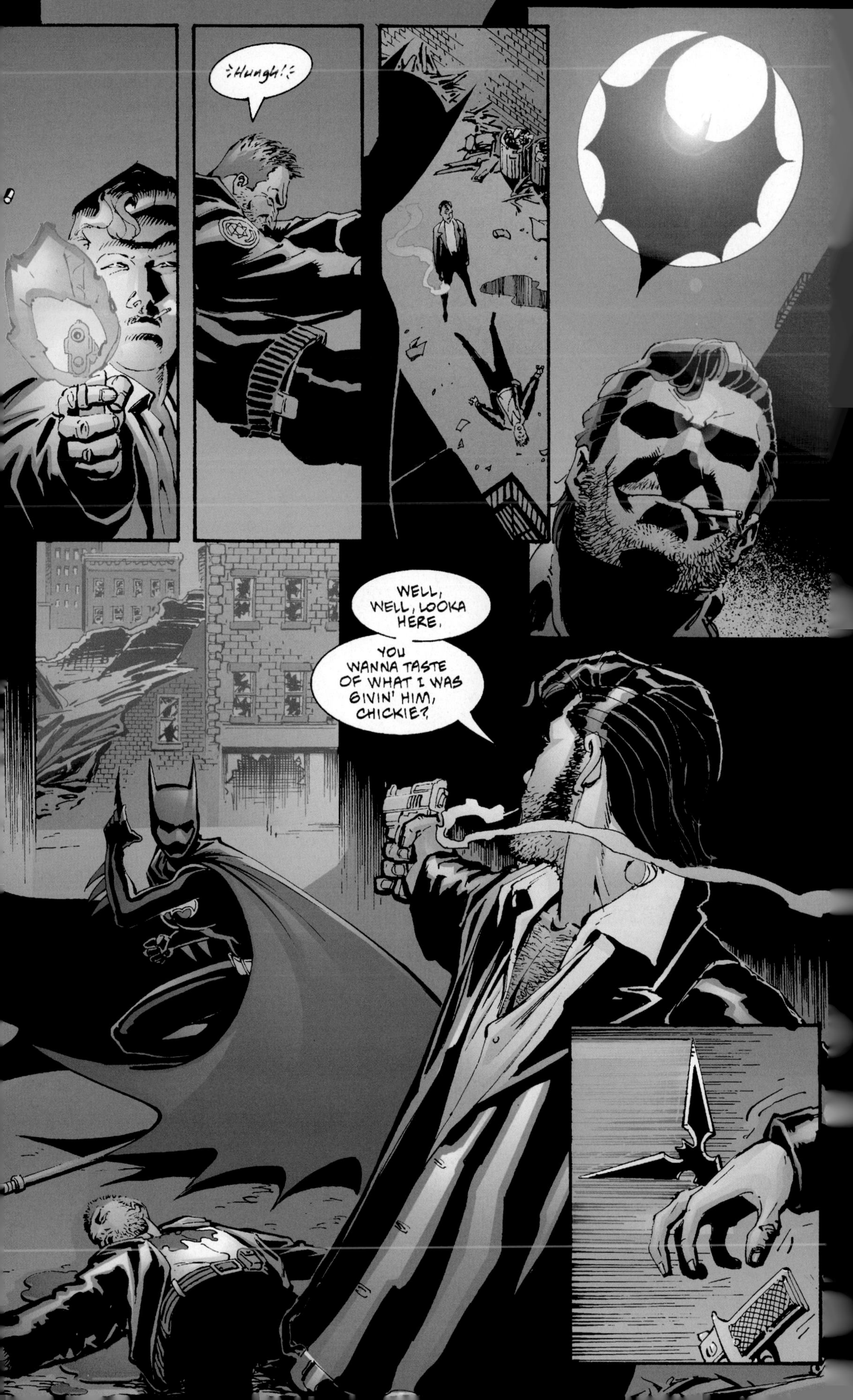
Hungh!
WELL, WELL, LOOKA HERE.
YOU WANNA TASTE OF WHAT I WAS GIVIN' HIM, CHICKIE?

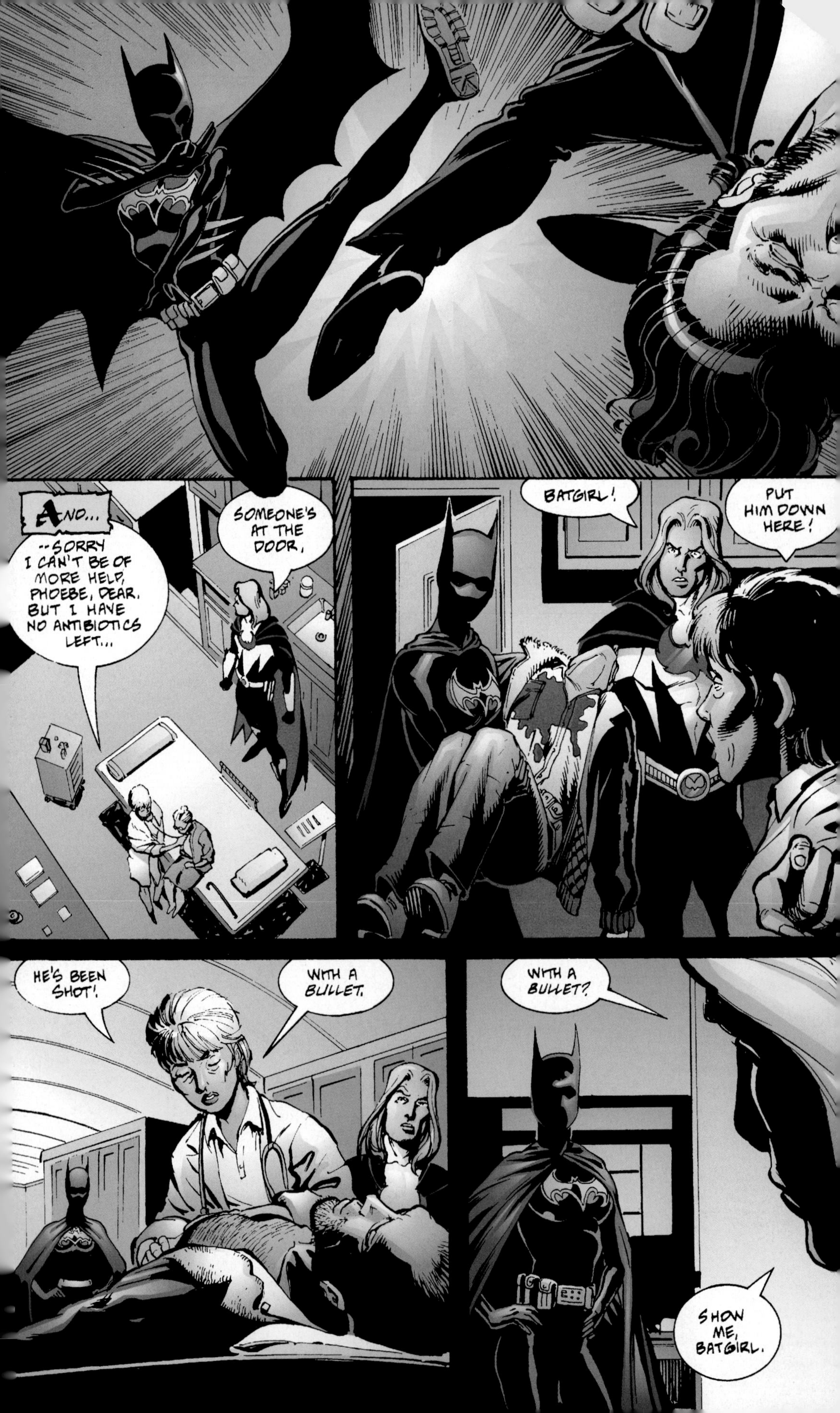
AND...
--SORRY I CAN'T BE OF MORE HELP, PHOEBE, DEAR. BUT I HAVE NO ANTIBIOTICS LEFT...
SOMEONE'S AT THE DOOR.
BATGIRL!
PUT HIM DOWN HERE!
HE'S BEEN SHOT!
WITH A BULLET.
WITH A BULLET?
SHOW ME, BATGIRL.

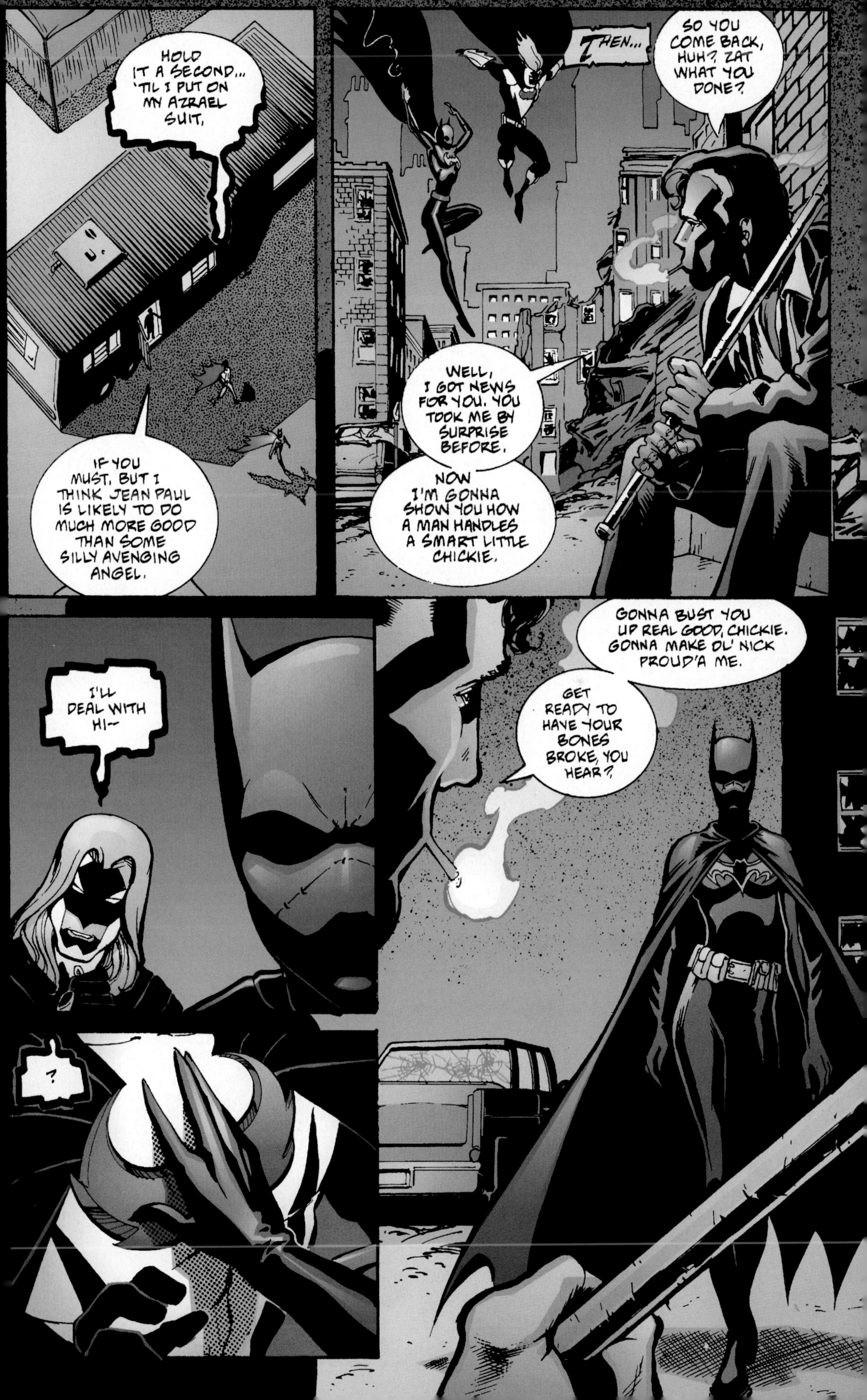
HOLD IT A SECOND... 'TIL I PUT ON MY AZRAEL SUIT.
IF YOU MUST. BUT I THINK JEAN PAUL IS LIKELY TO DO MUCH MORE GOOD THAN SOME SILLY AVENGING ANGEL.
THEN...
SO YOU COME BACK, HUH? ZAT WHAT YOU DONE?
WELL, I GOT NEWS FOR YOU. YOU TOOK ME BY SURPRISE BEFORE.
NOW I'M GONNA SHOW YOU HOW A MAN HANDLES A SMART LITTLE CHICKIE.
I'LL DEAL WITH HI--
GONNA BUST YOU UP REAL GOOD, CHICKIE. GONNA MAKE OL' NICK PROUD'A ME.
GET READY TO HAVE YOUR BONES BROKE, YOU HEAR?
?

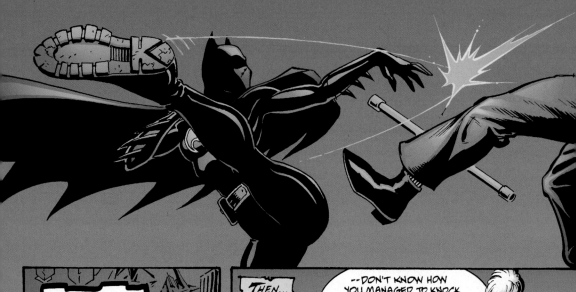

YEAH, WELL, AT LEAST LET ME CARRY HIM TO THE CLINIC.

THEN...

--DON'T KNOW HOW YOU MANAGED TO KNOCK HIM OUT WITHOUT LEAVING A BRUISE. OR GIVING HIM A CONCUSSION. BUT YOU DID.

A CUT, ABOUT A DAY OLD TREATED WITH IODINE.

THERE HASN'T BEEN ANY IODINE AROUND HERE IN MORE THAN A WEEK.

BULLETS...IODINE...HE'S OBVIOUSLY GOT A SUPPLY SOURCE.

AND I JUST REMEMBERED SOMETHING. HE MENTIONED "NICK" -- AS IN NICHOLAS SCRATCH?

I GAVE YOU A JOB.

DON'T YOU THINK IT'S ABOUT TIME YOU DID IT?

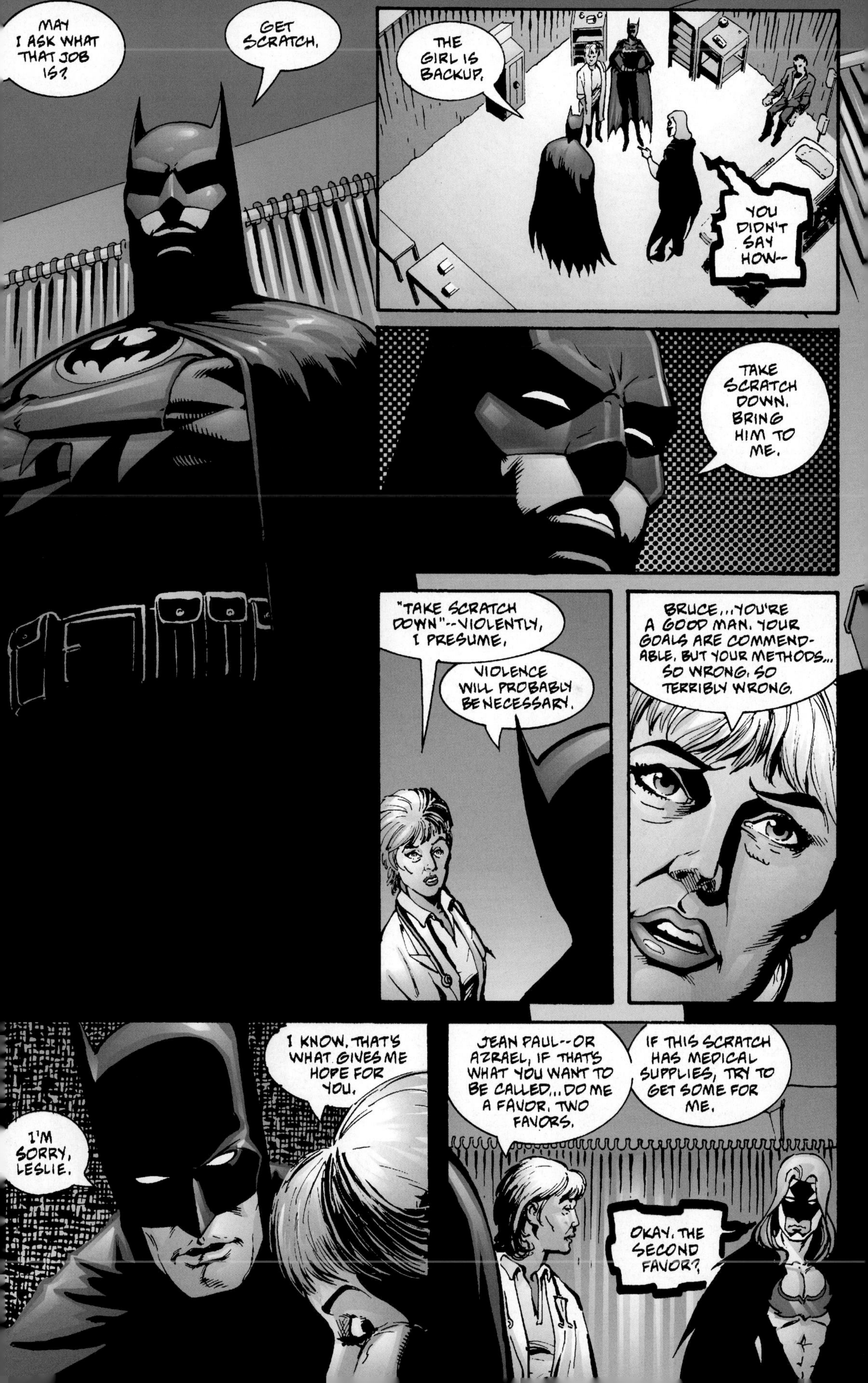

MAY I ASK WHAT THAT JOB IS?
GET SCRATCH.
THE GIRL IS BACKUP.
YOU DIDN'T SAY HOW--
TAKE SCRATCH DOWN. BRING HIM TO ME.
"TAKE SCRATCH DOWN"--VIOLENTLY, I PRESUME.
VIOLENCE WILL PROBABLY BE NECESSARY.
BRUCE...YOU'RE A GOOD MAN. YOUR GOALS ARE COMMENDABLE. BUT YOUR METHODS... SO WRONG. SO TERRIBLY WRONG.
I'M SORRY, LESLIE.
I KNOW. THAT'S WHAT GIVES ME HOPE FOR YOU.
JEAN PAUL--OR AZRAEL, IF THAT'S WHAT YOU WANT TO BE CALLED...DO ME A FAVOR. TWO FAVORS.
IF THIS SCRATCH HAS MEDICAL SUPPLIES, TRY TO GET SOME FOR ME.
OKAY. THE SECOND FAVOR?

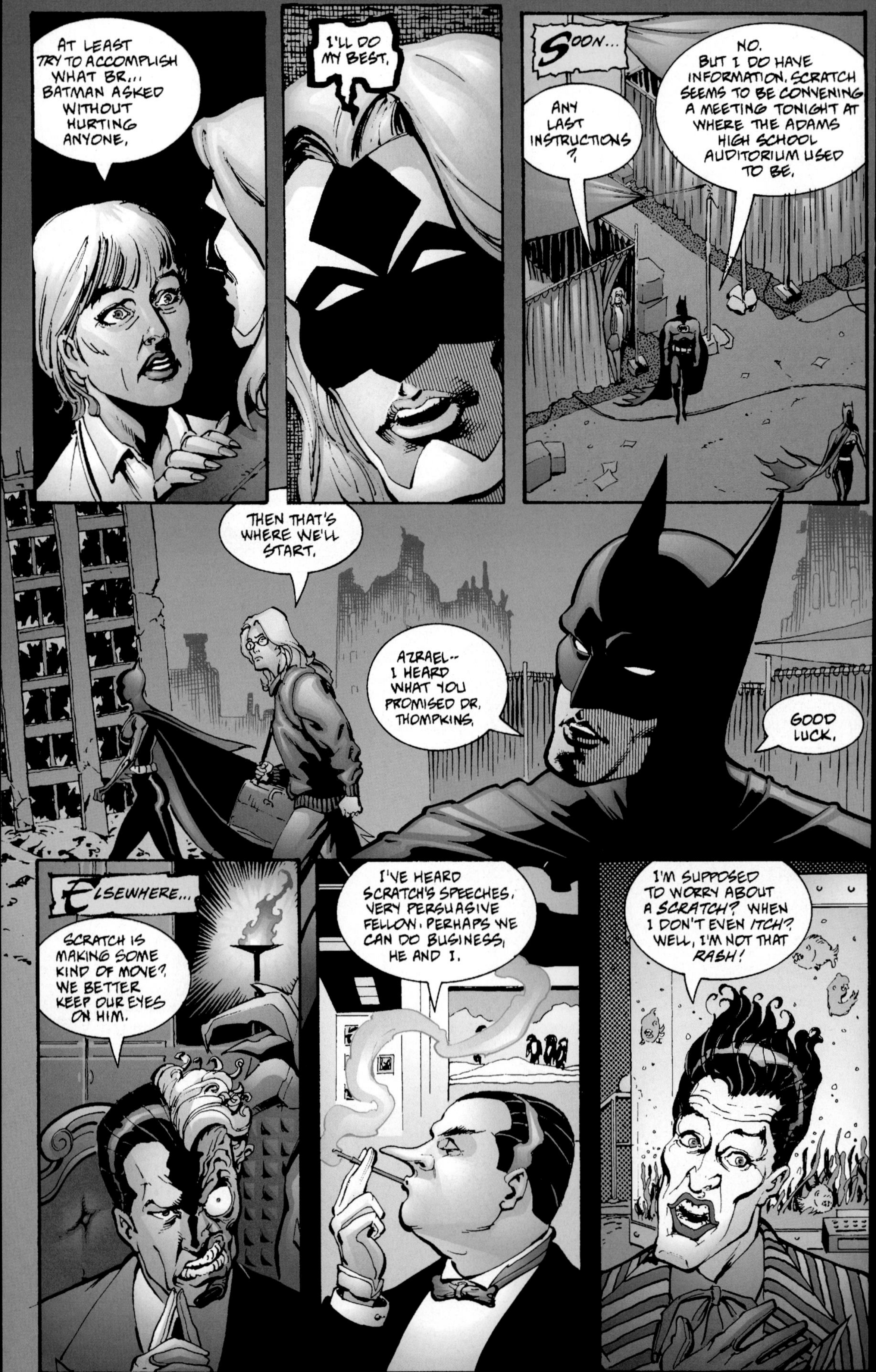
AT LEAST TRY TO ACCOMPLISH WHAT BR... BATMAN ASKED WITHOUT HURTING ANYONE.
I'LL DO MY BEST.
SOON...
ANY LAST INSTRUCTIONS?
NO. BUT I DO HAVE INFORMATION. SCRATCH SEEMS TO BE CONVENING A MEETING TONIGHT AT WHERE THE ADAMS HIGH SCHOOL AUDITORIUM USED TO BE.
THEN THAT'S WHERE WE'LL START.
AZRAEL-- I HEARD WHAT YOU PROMISED DR. THOMPKINS.
GOOD LUCK.
ELSEWHERE...
SCRATCH IS MAKING SOME KIND OF MOVE? WE BETTER KEEP OUR EYES ON HIM.
I'VE HEARD SCRATCH'S SPEECHES. VERY PERSUASIVE FELLOW. PERHAPS WE CAN DO BUSINESS, HE AND I.
I'M SUPPOSED TO WORRY ABOUT A SCRATCH? WHEN I DON'T EVEN ITCH? WELL, I'M NOT THAT RASH!

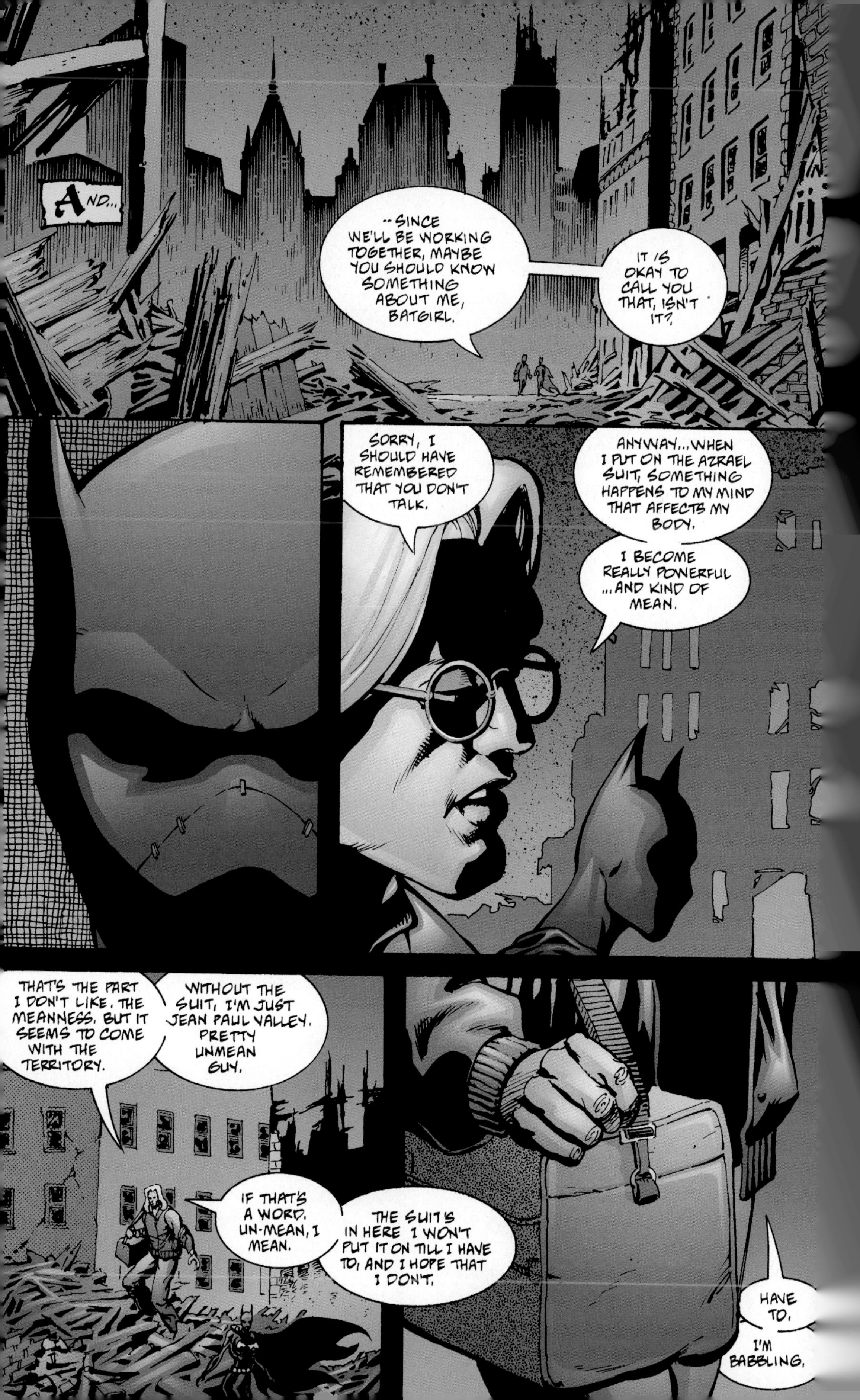
AND...
--SINCE WE'LL BE WORKING TOGETHER, MAYBE YOU SHOULD KNOW SOMETHING ABOUT ME, BATGIRL.
IT IS OKAY TO CALL YOU THAT, ISN'T IT?
SORRY, I SHOULD HAVE REMEMBERED THAT YOU DON'T TALK.
ANYWAY... WHEN I PUT ON THE AZRAEL SUIT, SOMETHING HAPPENS TO MY MIND THAT AFFECTS MY BODY.
I BECOME REALLY POWERFUL ...AND KIND OF MEAN.
THAT'S THE PART I DON'T LIKE. THE MEANNESS. BUT IT SEEMS TO COME WITH THE TERRITORY.
WITHOUT THE SUIT, I'M JUST JEAN PAUL VALLEY. PRETTY UNMEAN GUY.
IF THAT'S A WORD. UN-MEAN, I MEAN.
THE SUIT'S IN HERE. I WON'T PUT IT ON TILL I HAVE TO, AND I HOPE THAT I DON'T.
HAVE TO.
I'M BABBLING.

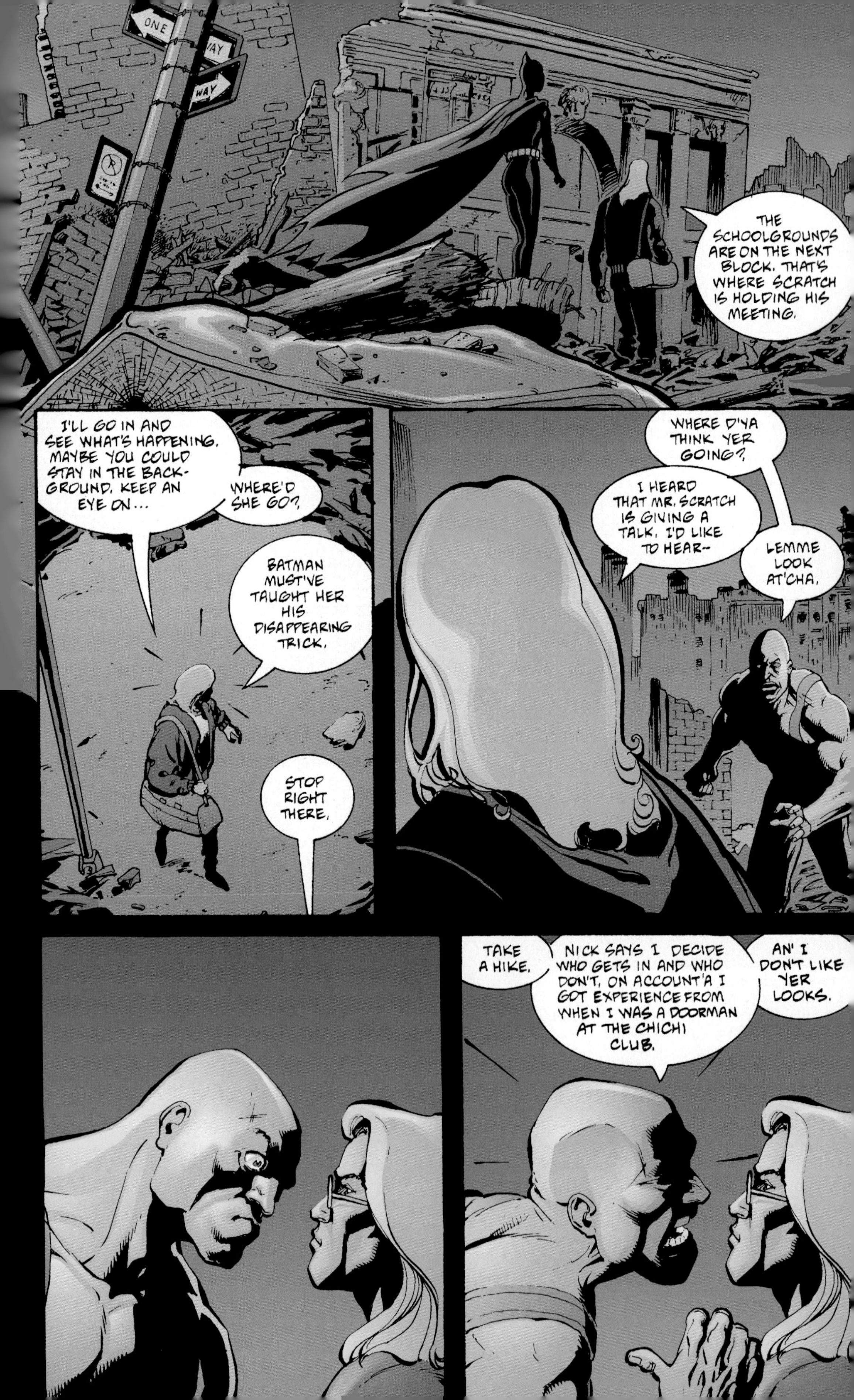

THE SCHOOLGROUNDS ARE ON THE NEXT BLOCK. THAT'S WHERE SCRATCH IS HOLDING HIS MEETING.
I'LL GO IN AND SEE WHAT'S HAPPENING. MAYBE YOU COULD STAY IN THE BACK-GROUND, KEEP AN EYE ON...
WHERE'D SHE GO?
BATMAN MUST'VE TAUGHT HER HIS DISAPPEARING TRICK.
STOP RIGHT THERE.
WHERE D'YA THINK YER GOING?
I HEARD THAT MR. SCRATCH IS GIVING A TALK. I'D LIKE TO HEAR--
LEMME LOOK AT'CHA.
TAKE A HIKE.
NICK SAYS I DECIDE WHO GETS IN AND WHO DON'T, ON ACCOUNT'A I GOT EXPERIENCE FROM WHEN I WAS A DOORMAN AT THE CHICHI CLUB.
AN' I DON'T LIKE YER LOOKS.

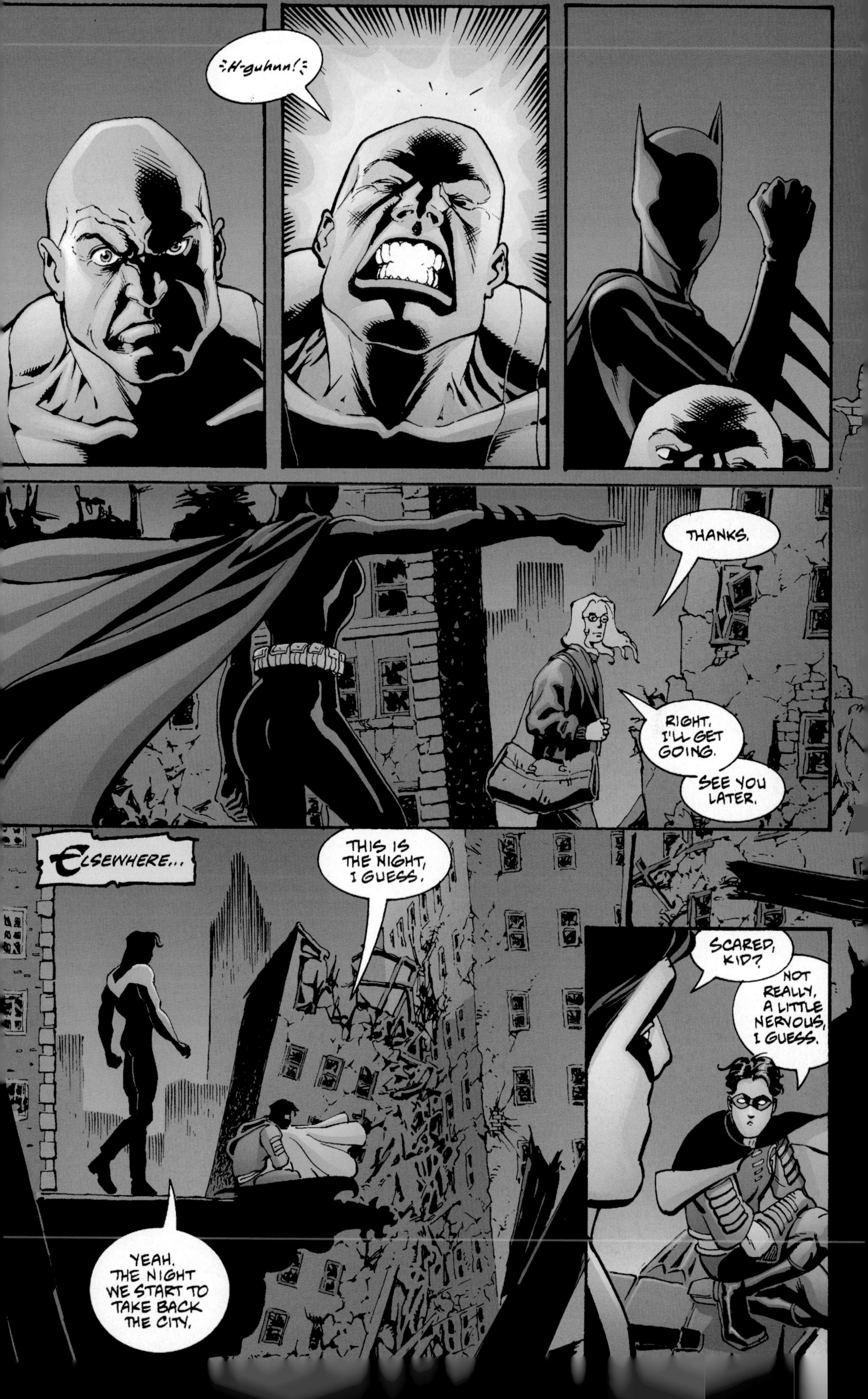
H-guhnn!
THANKS.
RIGHT, I'LL GET GOING.
SEE YOU LATER.
ELSEWHERE...
THIS IS THE NIGHT, I GUESS.
YEAH. THE NIGHT WE START TO TAKE BACK THE CITY.
SCARED, KID?
NOT REALLY, A LITTLE NERVOUS, I GUESS.

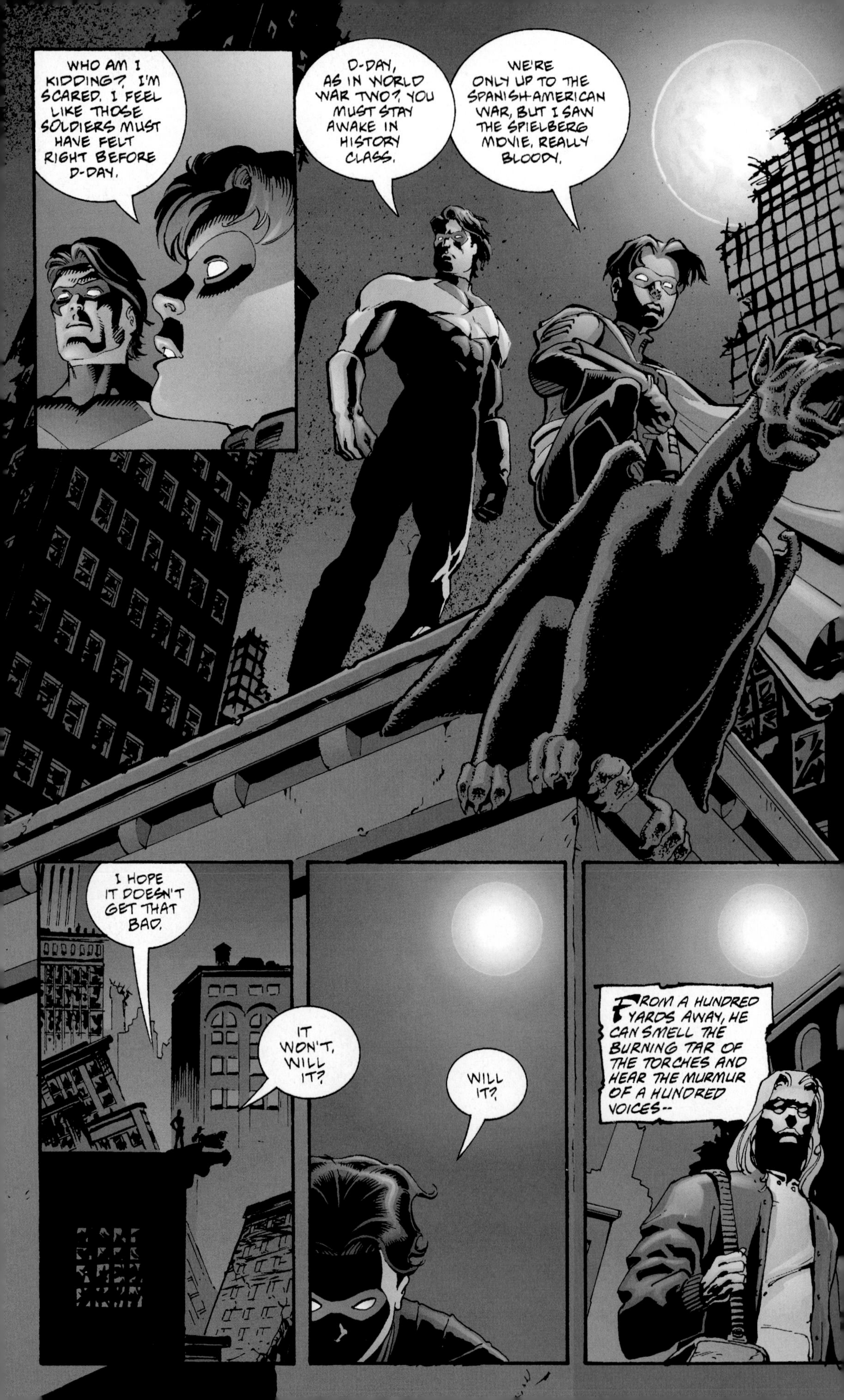
WHO AM I KIDDING? I'M SCARED. I FEEL LIKE THOSE SOLDIERS MUST HAVE FELT RIGHT BEFORE D-DAY.
D-DAY, AS IN WORLD WAR TWO? YOU MUST STAY AWAKE IN HISTORY CLASS.
WE'RE ONLY UP TO THE SPANISH-AMERICAN WAR, BUT I SAW THE SPIELBERG MOVIE. REALLY BLOODY.
I HOPE IT DOESN'T GET THAT BAD.
IT WON'T, WILL IT?
WILL IT?
FROM A HUNDRED YARDS AWAY, HE CAN SMELL THE BURNING TAR OF THE TORCHES AND HEAR THE MURMUR OF A HUNDRED VOICES--

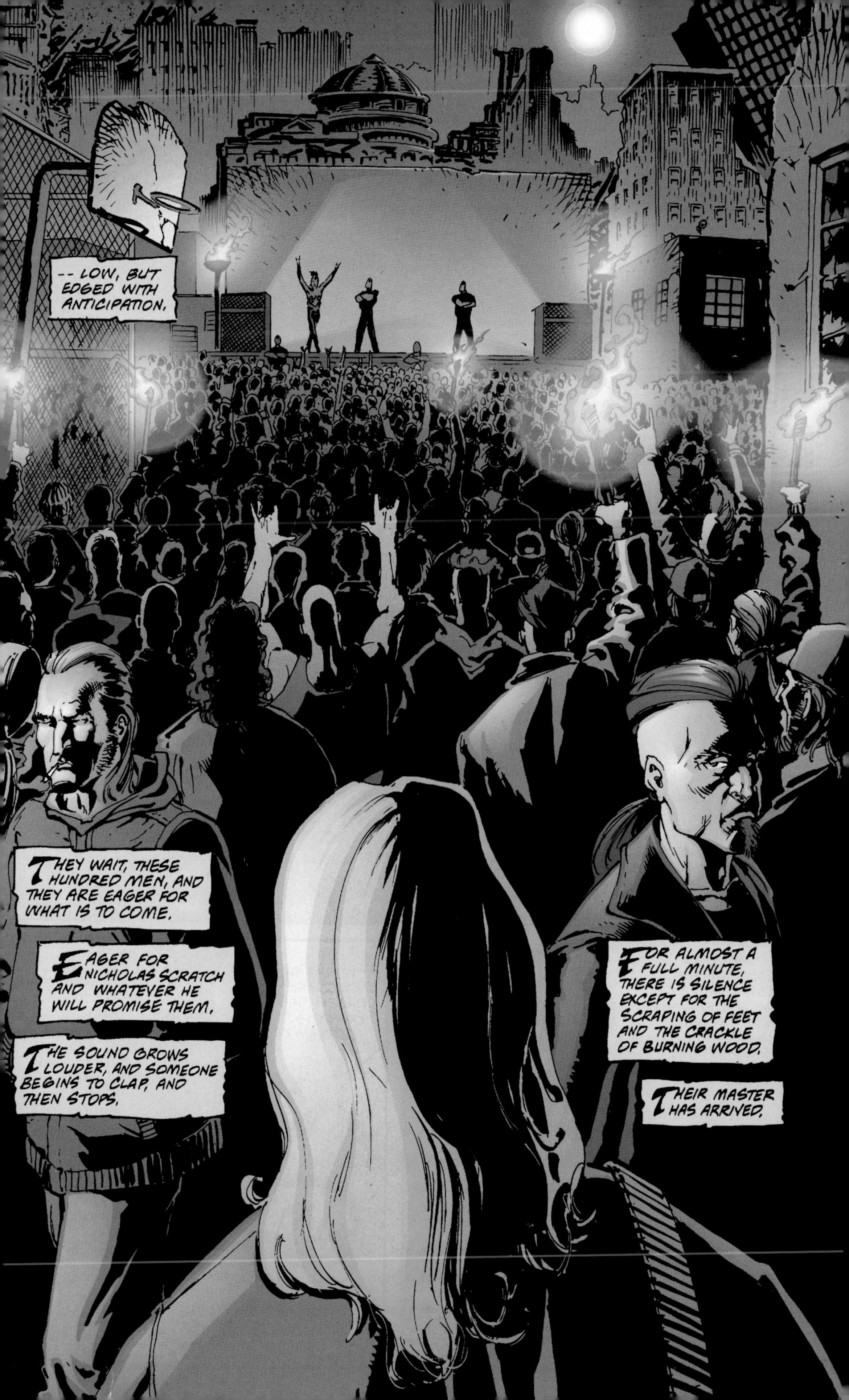
-- LOW, BUT EDGED WITH ANTICIPATION.
THEY WAIT, THESE HUNDRED MEN, AND THEY ARE EAGER FOR WHAT IS TO COME.
EAGER FOR NICHOLAS SCRATCH AND WHATEVER HE WILL PROMISE THEM.
THE SOUND GROWS LOUDER, AND SOMEONE BEGINS TO CLAP, AND THEN STOPS.
FOR ALMOST A FULL MINUTE, THERE IS SILENCE EXCEPT FOR THE SCRAPING OF FEET AND THE CRACKLE OF BURNING WOOD.
THEIR MASTER HAS ARRIVED.

THEY CALL YOU THE DREGS. THE LOST, THE STUPID, THE CRIMINAL AND THE INSANE.

I CALL YOU THE FAVORED, THE SPECIAL, THE SPLENDID.

I CALL YOU THE CHOSEN.

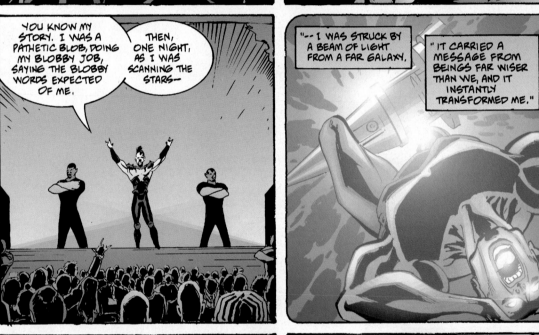

YOU KNOW MY STORY. I WAS A PATHETIC BLOB, DOING MY BLOBBY JOB, SAYING THE BLOBBY WORDS EXPECTED OF ME.

THEN, ONE NIGHT, AS I WAS SCANNING THE STARS--

"-- I WAS STRUCK BY A BEAM OF LIGHT FROM A FAR GALAXY,

" IT CARRIED A MESSAGE FROM BEINGS FAR WISER THAN WE, AND IT INSTANTLY TRANSFORMED ME."

NO MORE BLOB. WITHIN A YEAR I WAS RICH, FAMOUS, BELOVED. BUT ALL THAT WAS ONLY A PREPARATION.

FOR I KNEW SOMETHING MOMENTOUS WAS SOON TO HAPPEN, SOME MOMENTOUS EVENT THAT WOULD POINT THE WAY FOR ME.

IT WAS THE EARTHQUAKE WHICH LEVELED THIS PLACE OF FOOLS, THIS GOTHAM CITY.

INSTANTLY, I RECOGNIZED IT FOR WHAT IT WAS--A CALL TO ACTION.

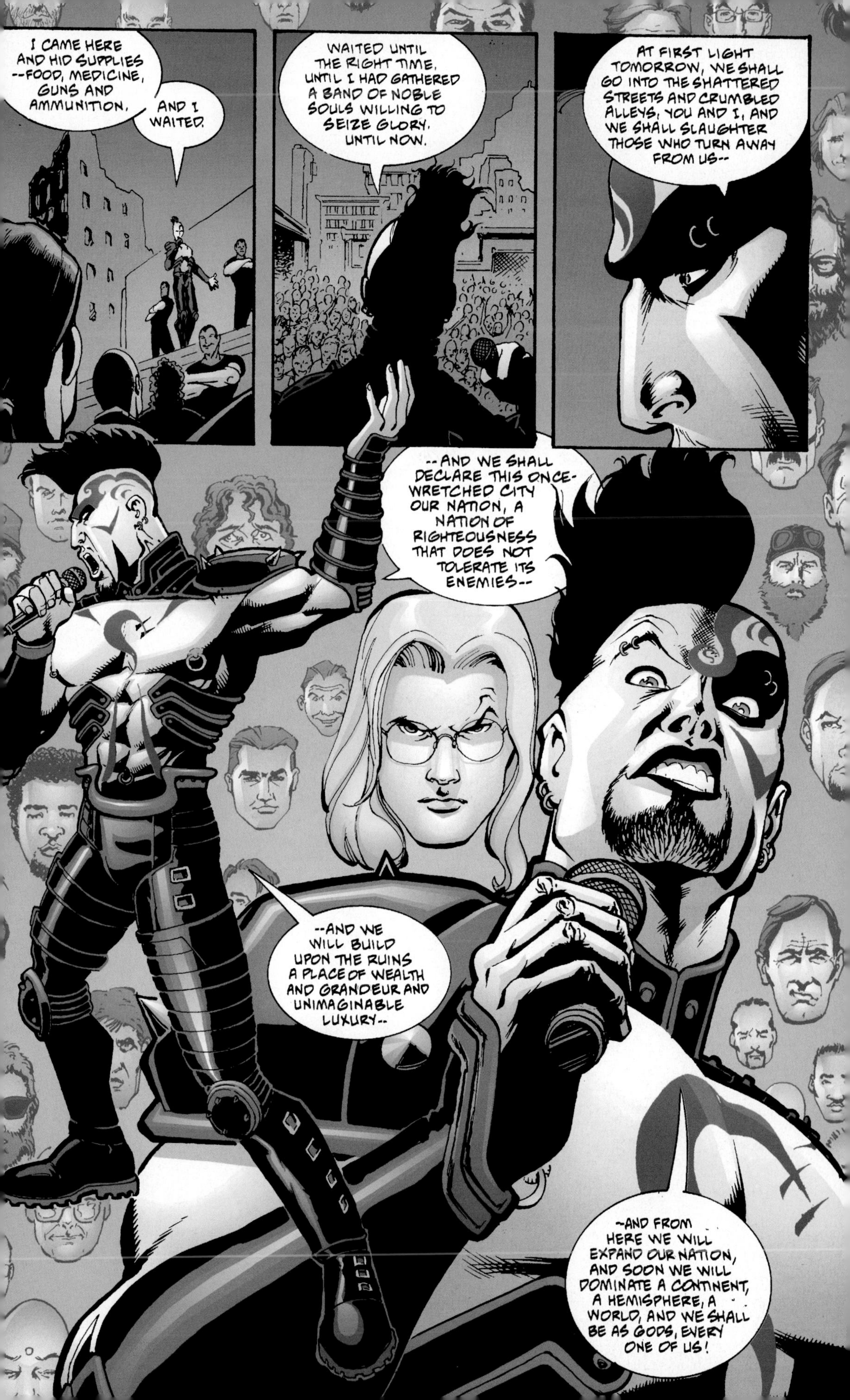
I CAME HERE AND HID SUPPLIES --FOOD, MEDICINE, GUNS AND AMMUNITION.
AND I WAITED.
WAITED UNTIL THE RIGHT TIME, UNTIL I HAD GATHERED A BAND OF NOBLE SOULS WILLING TO SEIZE GLORY. UNTIL NOW.
AT FIRST LIGHT TOMORROW, WE SHALL GO INTO THE SHATTERED STREETS AND CRUMBLED ALLEYS, YOU AND I, AND WE SHALL SLAUGHTER THOSE WHO TURN AWAY FROM US--
--AND WE SHALL DECLARE THIS ONCE-WRETCHED CITY OUR NATION, A NATION OF RIGHTEOUSNESS THAT DOES NOT TOLERATE ITS ENEMIES--
--AND WE WILL BUILD UPON THE RUINS A PLACE OF WEALTH AND GRANDEUR AND UNIMAGINABLE LUXURY--
--AND FROM HERE WE WILL EXPAND OUR NATION, AND SOON WE WILL DOMINATE A CONTINENT, A HEMISPHERE, A WORLD, AND WE SHALL BE AS GODS, EVERY ONE OF US!

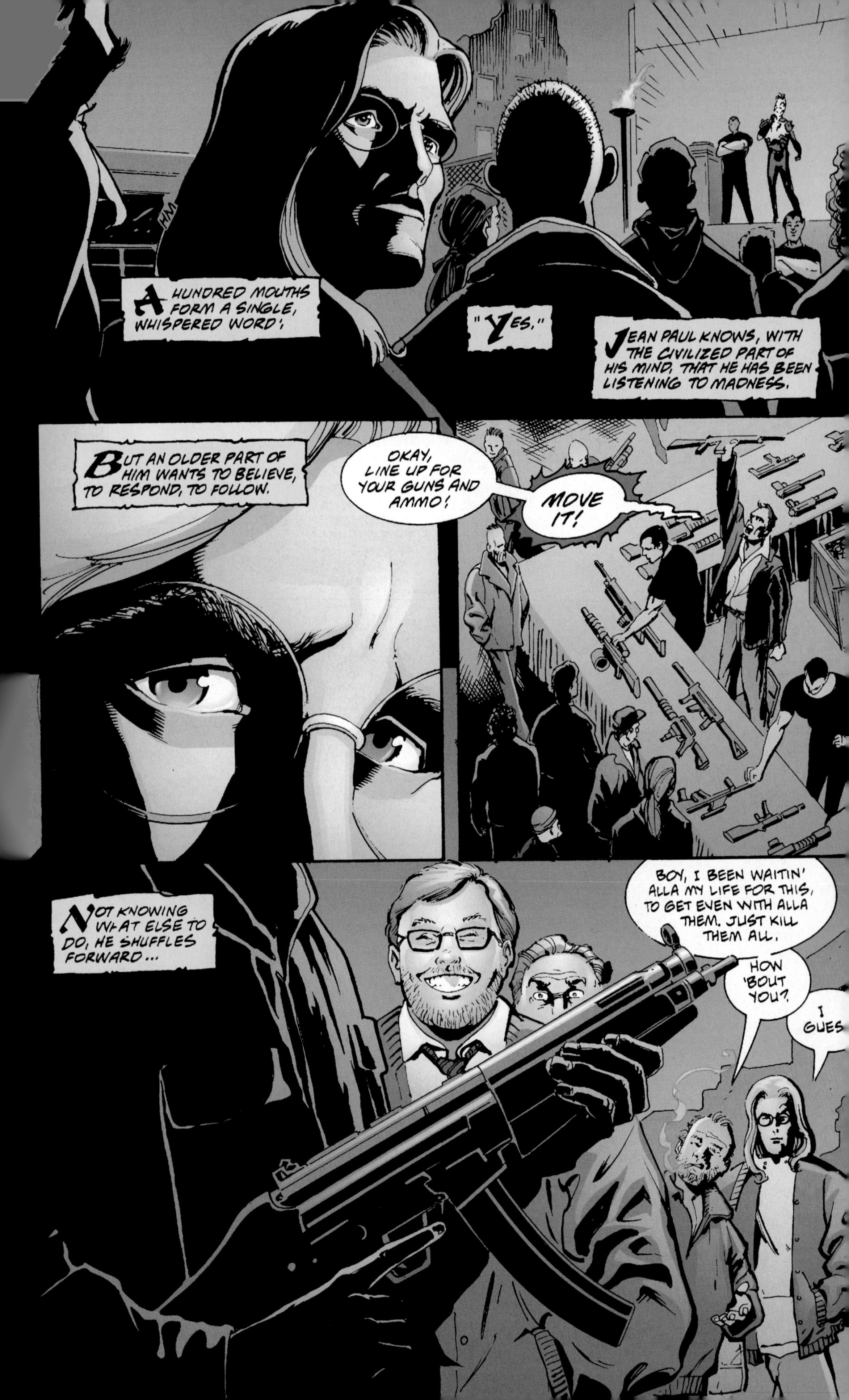
A HUNDRED MOUTHS FORM A SINGLE, WHISPERED WORD:
"YES."
JEAN PAUL KNOWS, WITH THE CIVILIZED PART OF HIS MIND, THAT HE HAS BEEN LISTENING TO MADNESS.
BUT AN OLDER PART OF HIM WANTS TO BELIEVE, TO RESPOND, TO FOLLOW.
OKAY, LINE UP FOR YOUR GUNS AND AMMO!
MOVE IT!
NOT KNOWING WHAT ELSE TO DO, HE SHUFFLES FORWARD...
BOY, I BEEN WAITIN' ALLA MY LIFE FOR THIS, TO GET EVEN WITH ALLA THEM. JUST KILL THEM ALL.
HOW 'BOUT YOU?
I GUES

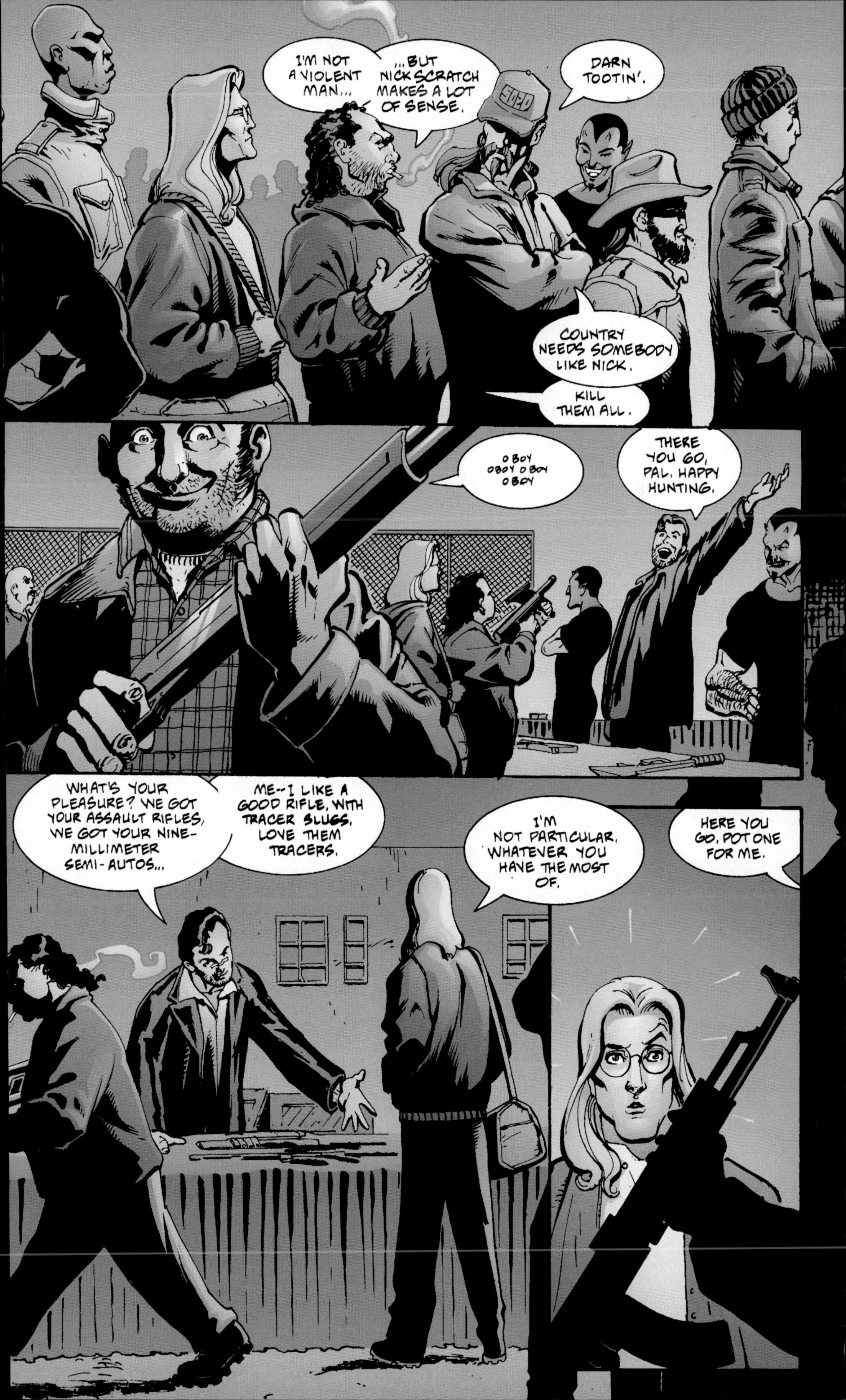
I'M NOT A VIOLENT MAN...
...BUT NICK SCRATCH MAKES A LOT OF SENSE.
DARN TOOTIN'.
COUNTRY NEEDS SOMEBODY LIKE NICK.
KILL THEM ALL.
O BOY OBOY O BOY O BOY
THERE YOU GO, PAL. HAPPY HUNTING.
WHAT'S YOUR PLEASURE? WE GOT YOUR ASSAULT RIFLES, WE GOT YOUR NINE-MILLIMETER SEMI-AUTOS...
ME--I LIKE A GOOD RIFLE, WITH TRACER SLUGS. LOVE THEM TRACERS.
I'M NOT PARTICULAR. WHATEVER YOU HAVE THE MOST OF.
HERE YOU GO. POT ONE FOR ME.

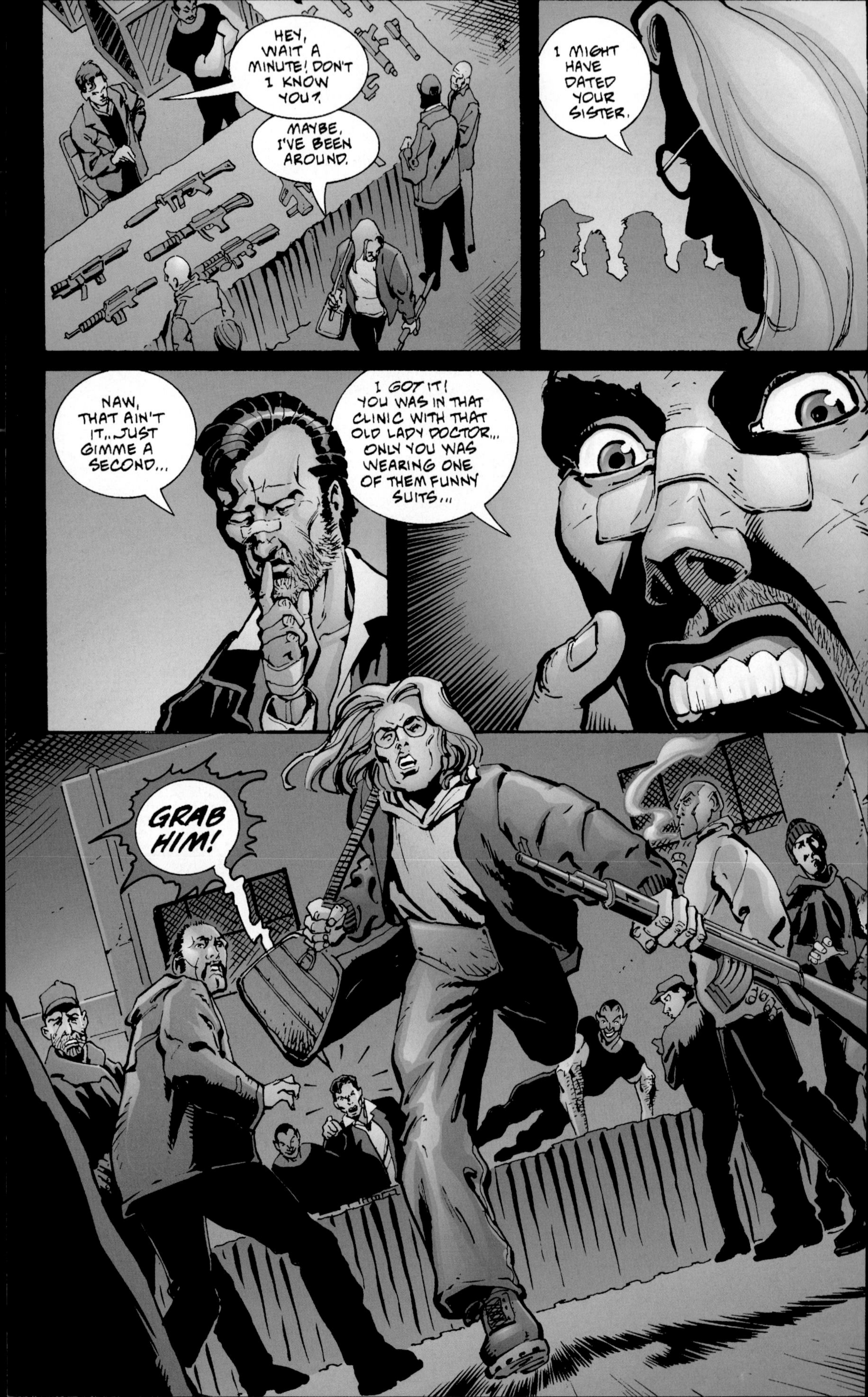
HEY, WAIT A MINUTE! DON'T I KNOW YOU?
MAYBE, I'VE BEEN AROUND.
I MIGHT HAVE DATED YOUR SISTER.
NAW, THAT AIN'T IT.. JUST GIMME A SECOND...
I GOT IT! YOU WAS IN THAT CLINIC WITH THAT OLD LADY DOCTOR... ONLY YOU WAS WEARING ONE OF THEM FUNNY SUITS...
GRAB HIM!

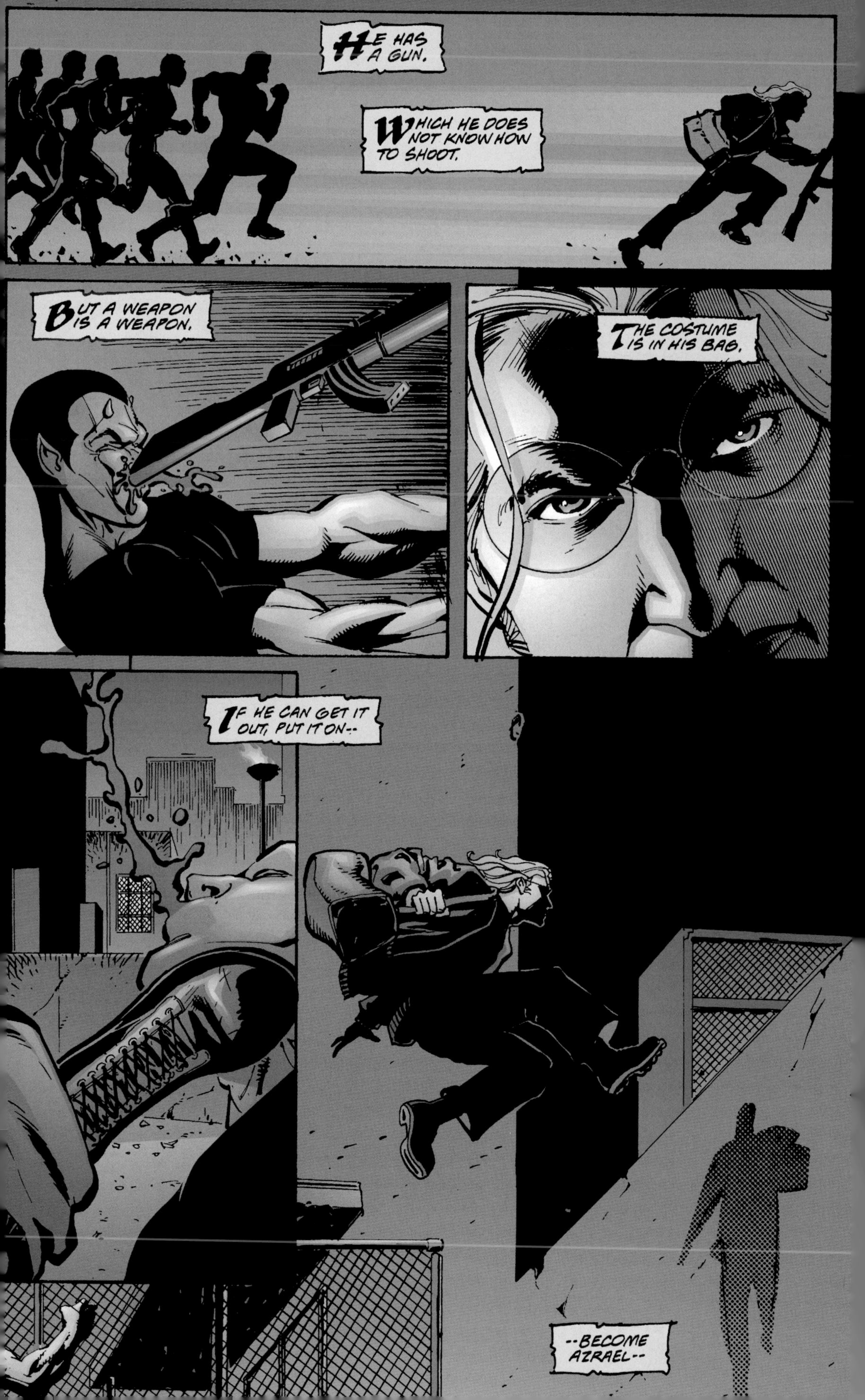
HE HAS A GUN.
WHICH HE DOES NOT KNOW HOW TO SHOOT.
BUT A WEAPON IS A WEAPON.
THE COSTUME IS IN HIS BAG.
IF HE CAN GET IT OUT, PUT IT ON--
--BECOME AZRAEL--

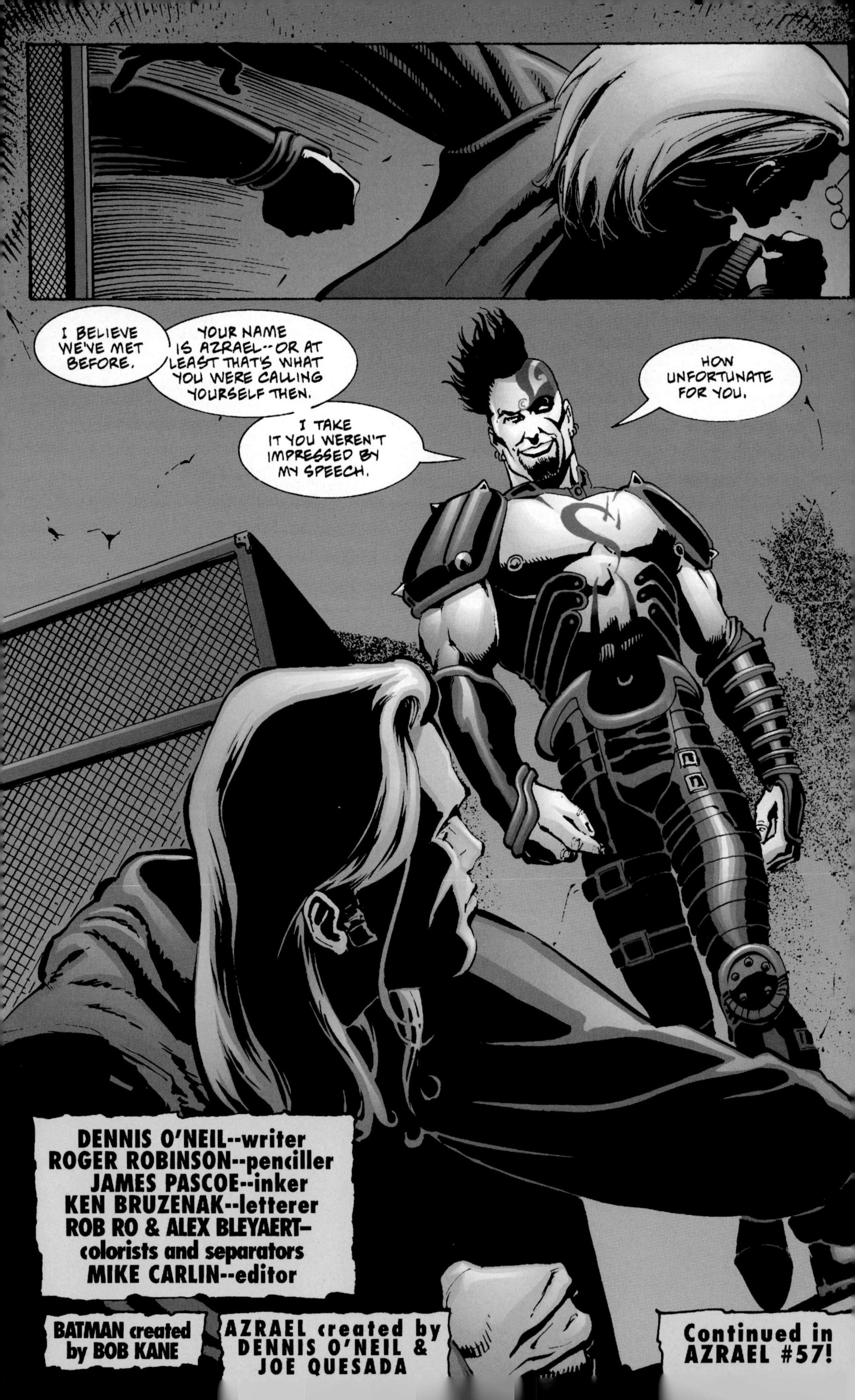
I BELIEVE WE'VE MET BEFORE.
YOUR NAME IS AZRAEL--OR AT LEAST THAT'S WHAT YOU WERE CALLING YOURSELF THEN.
I TAKE IT YOU WEREN'T IMPRESSED BY MY SPEECH.
HOW UNFORTUNATE FOR YOU.
DENNIS O'NEIL--writer
ROGER ROBINSON--penciller
JAMES PASCOE--inker
KEN BRUZENAK--letterer
ROB RO & ALEX BLEYAERT--colorists and separators
MIKE CARLIN--editor
BATMAN created by BOB KANE
AZRAEL created by DENNIS O'NEIL & JOE QUESADA
Continued in AZRAEL #57!

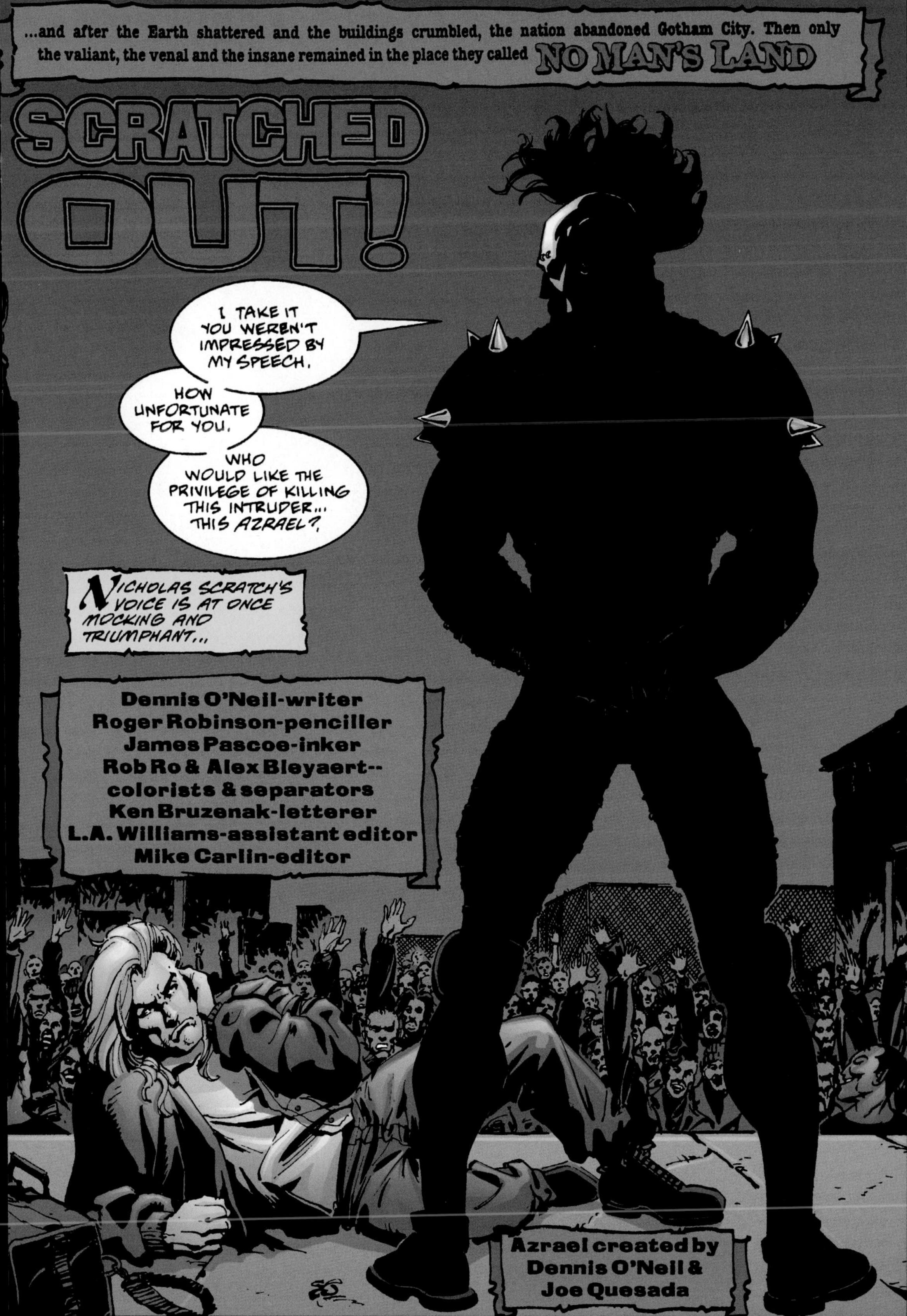
...and after the Earth shattered and the buildings crumbled, the nation abandoned Gotham City. Then only the valiant, the venal and the insane remained in the place they called NO MAN'S LAND
SCRATCHED OUT!
I TAKE IT YOU WEREN'T IMPRESSED BY MY SPEECH.
HOW UNFORTUNATE FOR YOU.
WHO WOULD LIKE THE PRIVILEGE OF KILLING THIS INTRUDER... THIS AZRAEL?
NICHOLAS SCRATCH'S VOICE IS AT ONCE MOCKING AND TRIUMPHANT...
Dennis O'Neil-writer
Roger Robinson-penciller
James Pascoe-inker
Rob Ro & Alex Bleyaert--colorists & separators
Ken Bruzenak-letterer
L.A. Williams-assistant editor
Mike Carlin-editor
Azrael created by Dennis O'Neil & Joe Quesada

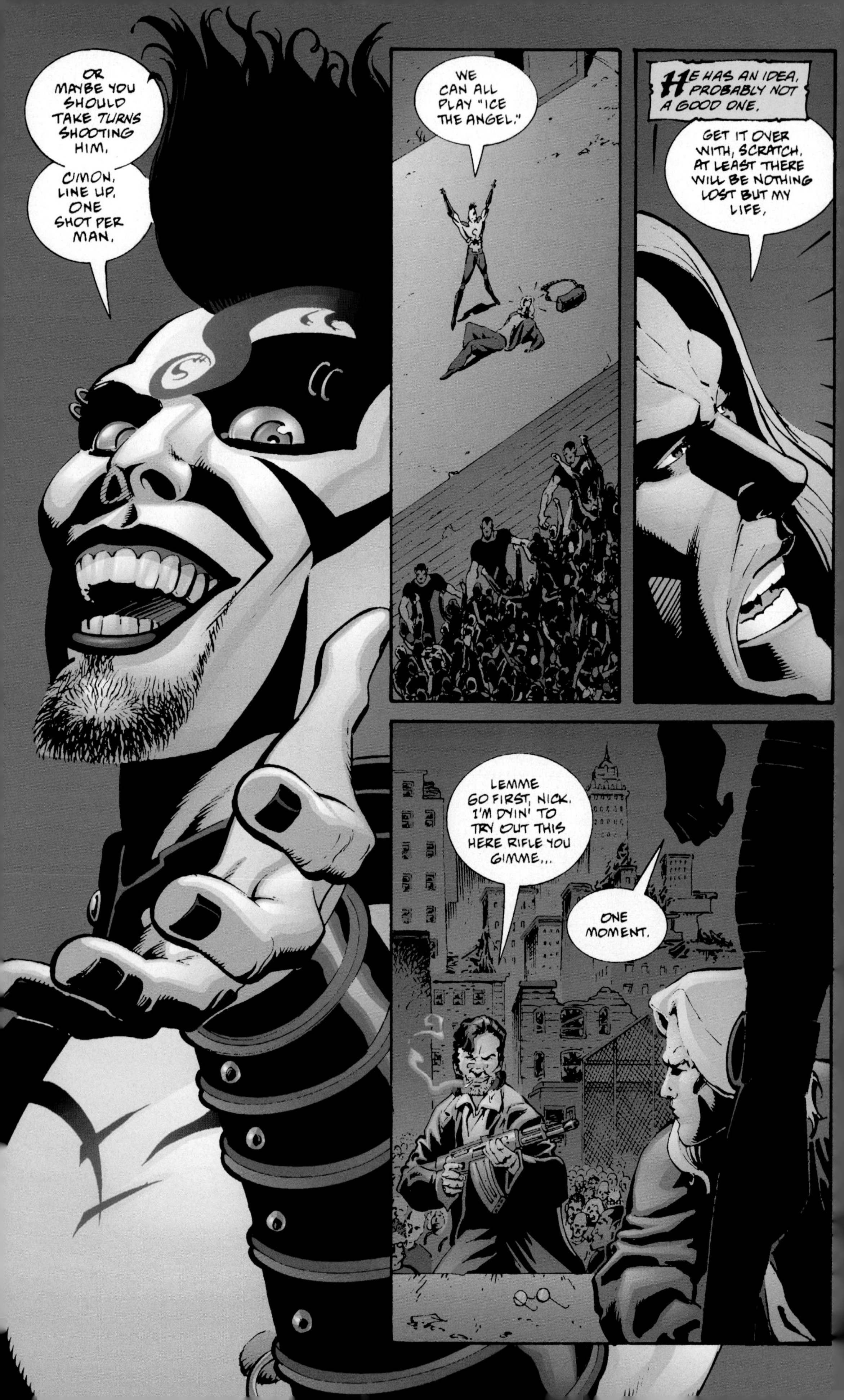
OR MAYBE YOU SHOULD TAKE TURNS SHOOTING HIM.
C'MON. LINE UP. ONE SHOT PER MAN.
WE CAN ALL PLAY "ICE THE ANGEL."
HE HAS AN IDEA, PROBABLY NOT A GOOD ONE.
GET IT OVER WITH, SCRATCH. AT LEAST THERE WILL BE NOTHING LOST BUT MY LIFE.
LEMME GO FIRST, NICK. I'M DYIN' TO TRY OUT THIS HERE RIFLE YOU GIMME...
ONE MOMENT.

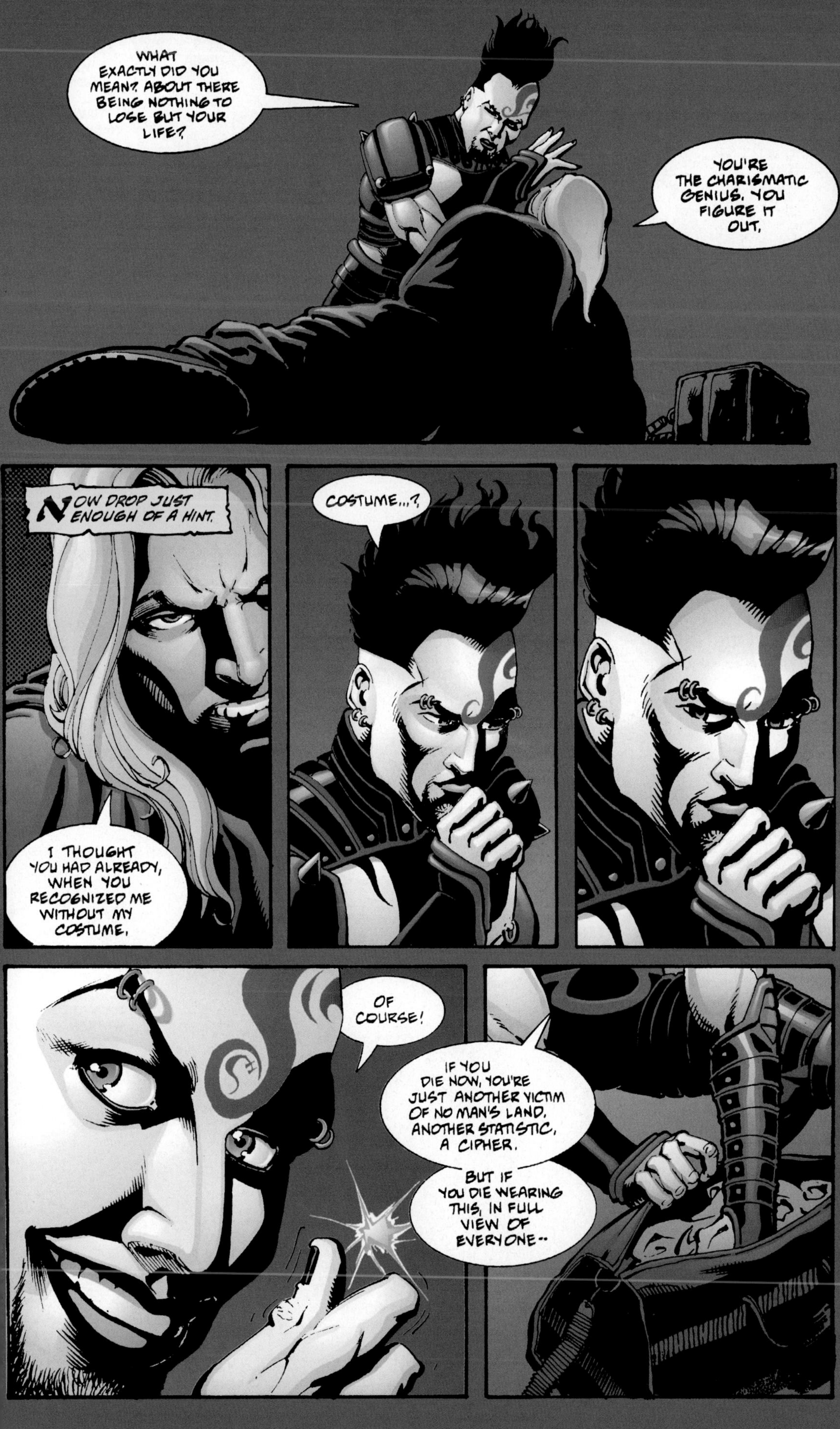
WHAT EXACTLY DID YOU MEAN? ABOUT THERE BEING NOTHING TO LOSE BUT YOUR LIFE?
YOU'RE THE CHARISMATIC GENIUS. YOU FIGURE IT OUT.
NOW DROP JUST ENOUGH OF A HINT.
I THOUGHT YOU HAD ALREADY, WHEN YOU RECOGNIZED ME WITHOUT MY COSTUME.
COSTUME...?
OF COURSE!
IF YOU DIE NOW, YOU'RE JUST ANOTHER VICTIM OF NO MAN'S LAND. ANOTHER STATISTIC. A CIPHER.
BUT IF YOU DIE WEARING THIS, IN FULL VIEW OF EVERYONE--

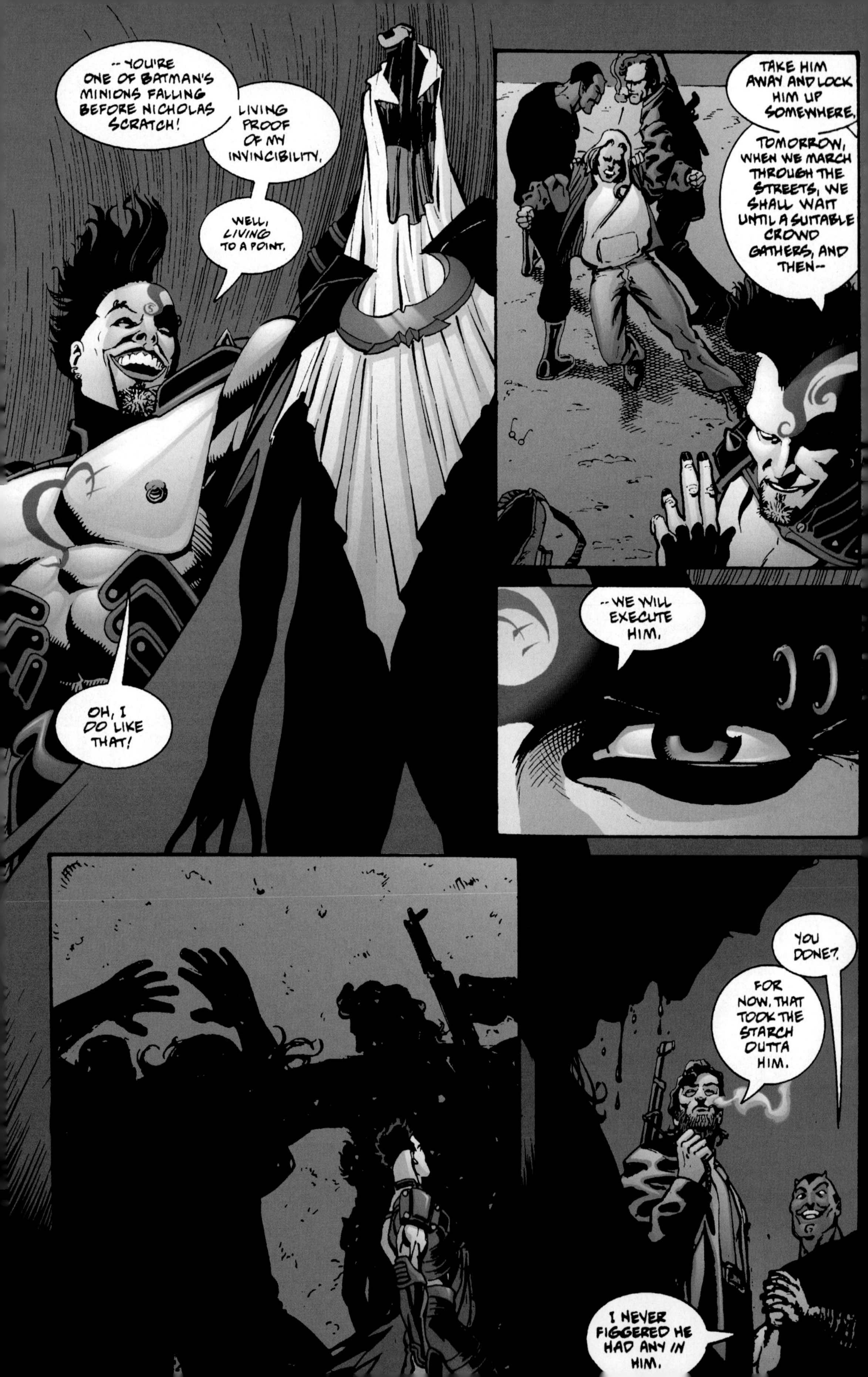
--YOU'RE ONE OF BATMAN'S MINIONS FALLING BEFORE NICHOLAS SCRATCH!
LIVING PROOF OF MY INVINCIBILITY.
WELL, LIVING TO A POINT.
OH, I DO LIKE THAT!
TAKE HIM AWAY AND LOCK HIM UP SOMEWHERE.
TOMORROW, WHEN WE MARCH THROUGH THE STREETS, WE SHALL WAIT UNTIL A SUITABLE CROWD GATHERS, AND THEN--
--WE WILL EXECUTE HIM.
YOU DONE?
FOR NOW. THAT TOOK THE STARCH OUTTA HIM.
I NEVER FIGGERED HE HAD ANY IN HIM.

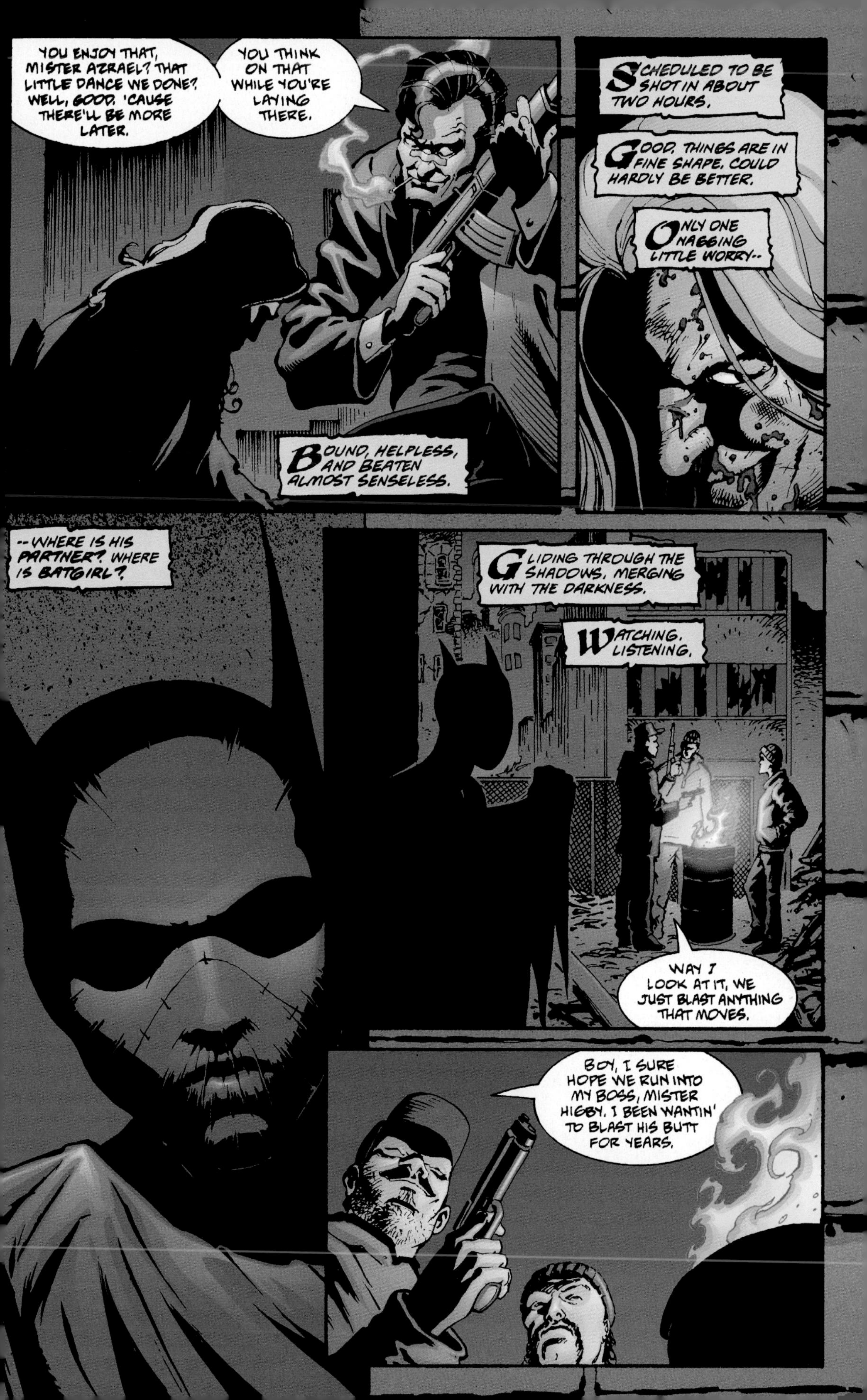
YOU ENJOY THAT, MISTER AZRAEL? THAT LITTLE DANCE WE DONE? WELL, GOOD. 'CAUSE THERE'LL BE MORE LATER.
YOU THINK ON THAT WHILE YOU'RE LAYING THERE.
BOUND, HELPLESS, AND BEATEN ALMOST SENSELESS.
SCHEDULED TO BE SHOT IN ABOUT TWO HOURS.
GOOD. THINGS ARE IN FINE SHAPE. COULD HARDLY BE BETTER.
ONLY ONE NAGGING LITTLE WORRY--
--WHERE IS HIS PARTNER? WHERE IS BATGIRL?
GLIDING THROUGH THE SHADOWS, MERGING WITH THE DARKNESS.
WATCHING, LISTENING.
WAY I LOOK AT IT, WE JUST BLAST ANYTHING THAT MOVES.
BOY, I SURE HOPE WE RUN INTO MY BOSS, MISTER HIGBY. I BEEN WANTIN' TO BLAST HIS BUTT FOR YEARS.

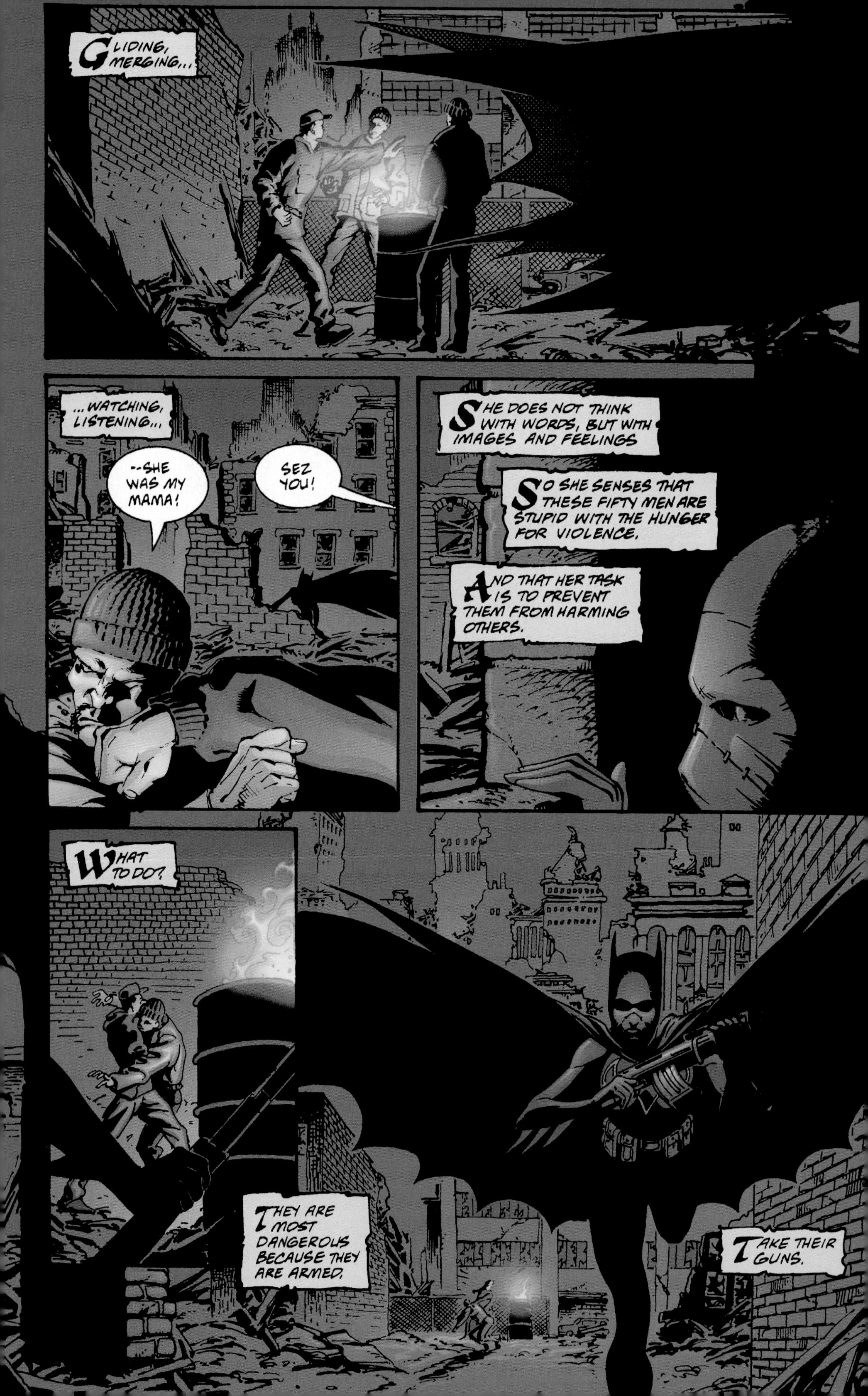
GLIDING, MERGING...
...WATCHING, LISTENING...
--SHE WAS MY MAMA!
SEZ YOU!
SHE DOES NOT THINK WITH WORDS, BUT WITH IMAGES AND FEELINGS
SO SHE SENSES THAT THESE FIFTY MEN ARE STUPID WITH THE HUNGER FOR VIOLENCE.
AND THAT HER TASK IS TO PREVENT THEM FROM HARMING OTHERS.
WHAT TO DO?
THEY ARE MOST DANGEROUS BECAUSE THEY ARE ARMED.
TAKE THEIR GUNS.

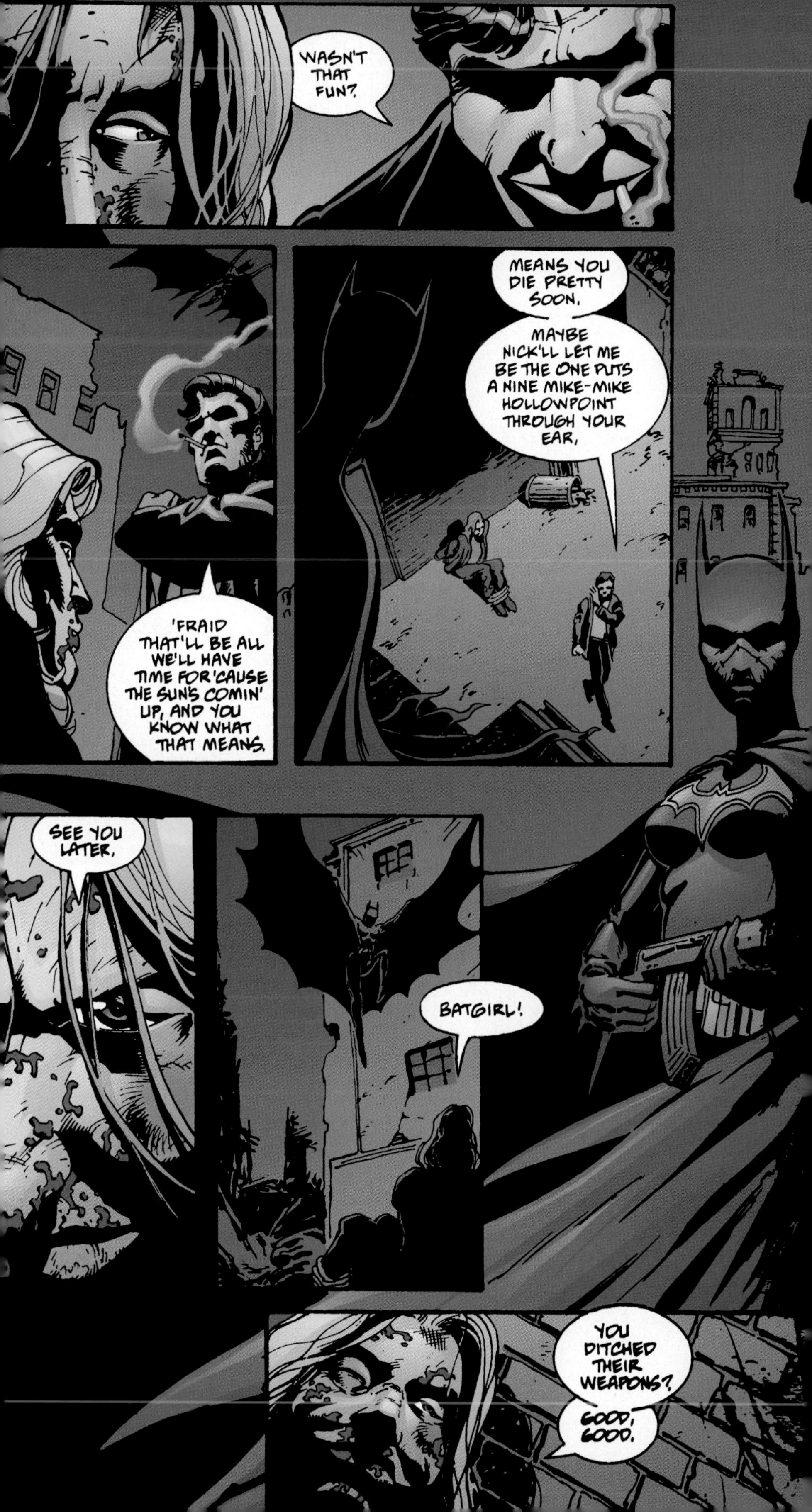
WASN'T THAT FUN?
'FRAID THAT'LL BE ALL WE'LL HAVE TIME FOR 'CAUSE THE SUN'S COMIN' UP, AND YOU KNOW WHAT THAT MEANS.
MEANS YOU DIE PRETTY SOON.
MAYBE NICK'LL LET ME BE THE ONE PUTS A NINE MIKE-MIKE HOLLOWPOINT THROUGH YOUR EAR.
SEE YOU LATER.
BATGIRL!
YOU DITCHED THEIR WEAPONS?
GOOD, GOOD.

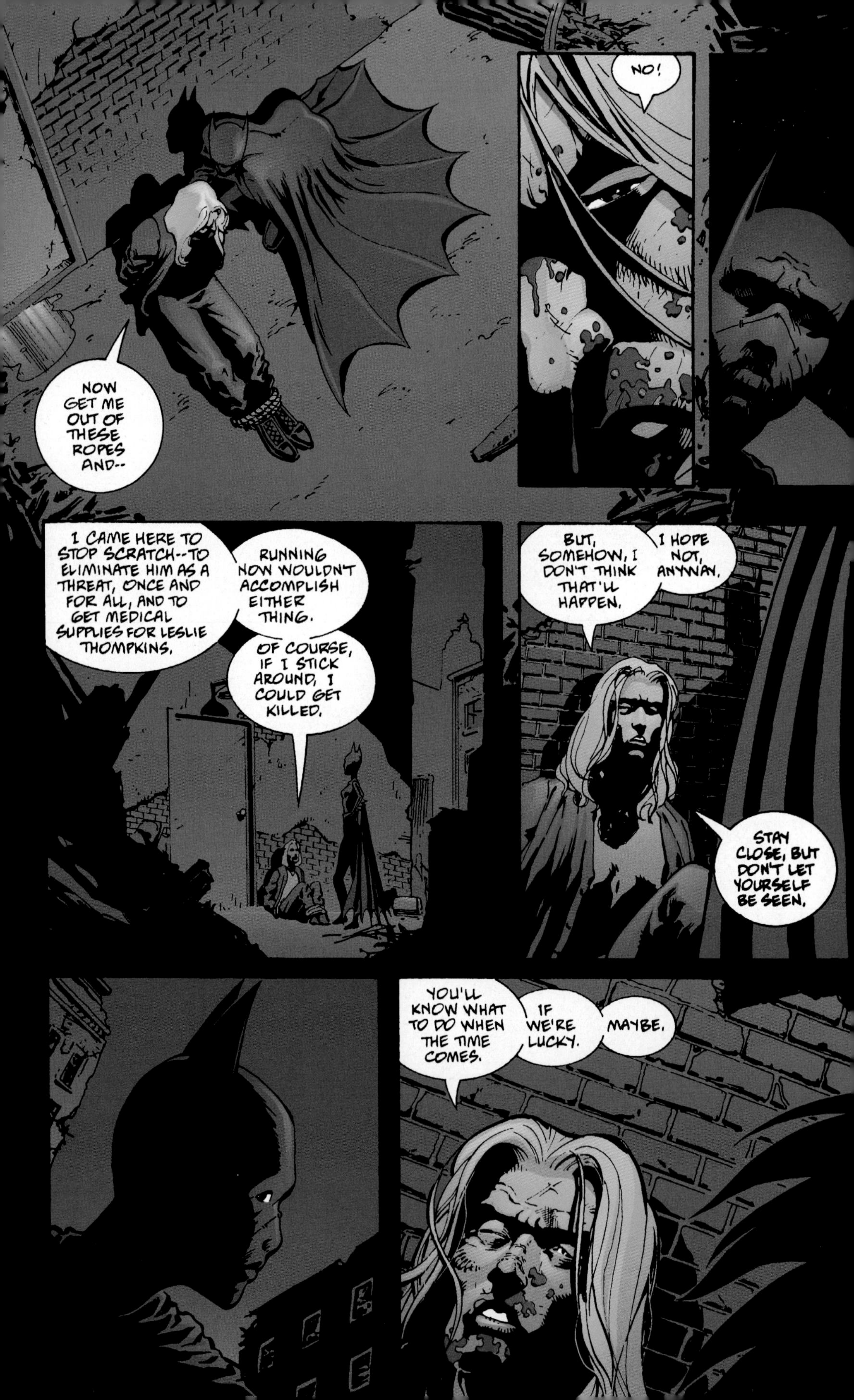
NOW GET ME OUT OF THESE ROPES AND--
NO!
I CAME HERE TO STOP SCRATCH--TO ELIMINATE HIM AS A THREAT, ONCE AND FOR ALL, AND TO GET MEDICAL SUPPLIES FOR LESLIE THOMPKINS.
RUNNING NOW WOULDN'T ACCOMPLISH EITHER THING.
OF COURSE, IF I STICK AROUND, I COULD GET KILLED.
BUT, SOMEHOW, I DON'T THINK THAT'LL HAPPEN.
I HOPE NOT, ANYWAY.
STAY CLOSE, BUT DON'T LET YOURSELF BE SEEN.
YOU'LL KNOW WHAT TO DO WHEN THE TIME COMES.
IF WE'RE LUCKY.
MAYBE.

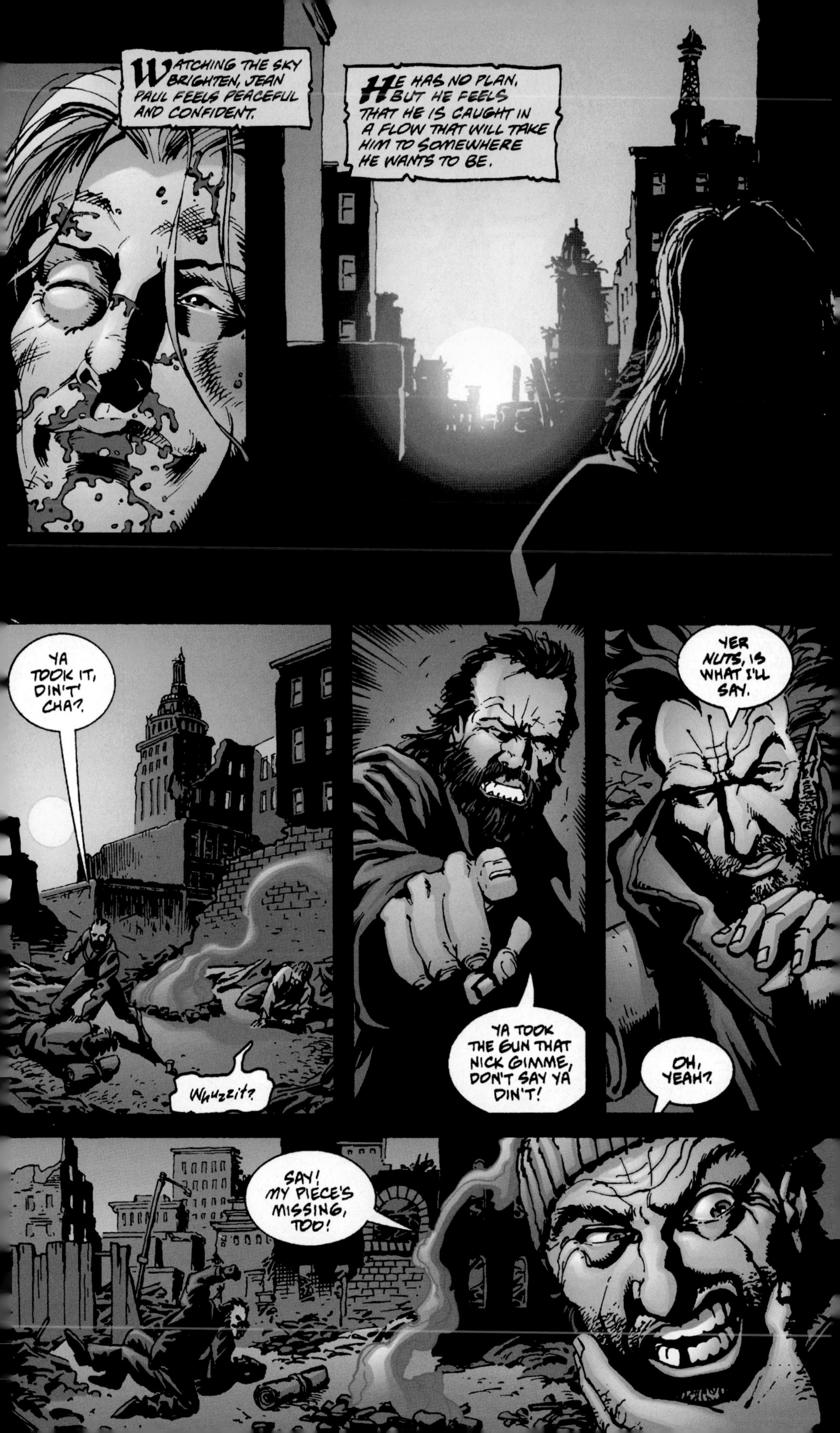
WATCHING THE SKY BRIGHTEN, JEAN PAUL FEELS PEACEFUL AND CONFIDENT.
HE HAS NO PLAN, BUT HE FEELS THAT HE IS CAUGHT IN A FLOW THAT WILL TAKE HIM TO SOMEWHERE HE WANTS TO BE.
YA TOOK IT, DIN'T' CHA?
Whuzzit?
YA TOOK THE GUN THAT NICK GIMME, DON'T SAY YA DIN'T!
YER NUTS, IS WHAT I'LL SAY.
OH, YEAH?
SAY! MY PIECE'S MISSING, TOO!

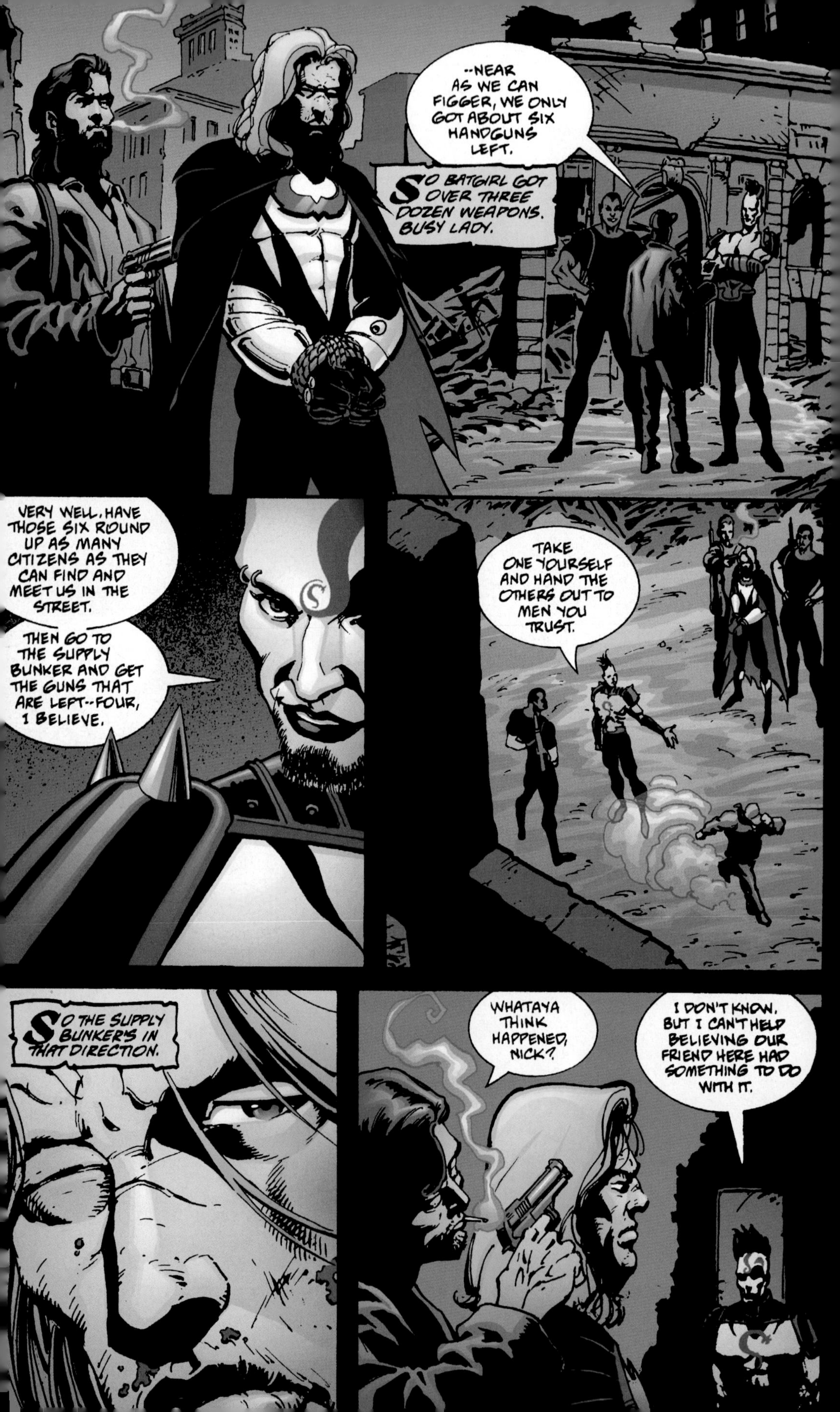
--NEAR AS WE CAN FIGGER, WE ONLY GOT ABOUT SIX HANDGUNS LEFT.
SO BATGIRL GOT OVER THREE DOZEN WEAPONS. BUSY LADY.
VERY WELL. HAVE THOSE SIX ROUND UP AS MANY CITIZENS AS THEY CAN FIND AND MEET US IN THE STREET.
THEN GO TO THE SUPPLY BUNKER AND GET THE GUNS THAT ARE LEFT--FOUR, I BELIEVE.
TAKE ONE YOURSELF AND HAND THE OTHERS OUT TO MEN YOU TRUST.
SO THE SUPPLY BUNKER'S IN THAT DIRECTION.
WHATAYA THINK HAPPENED, NICK?
I DON'T KNOW. BUT I CAN'T HELP BELIEVING OUR FRIEND HERE HAD SOMETHING TO DO WITH IT.

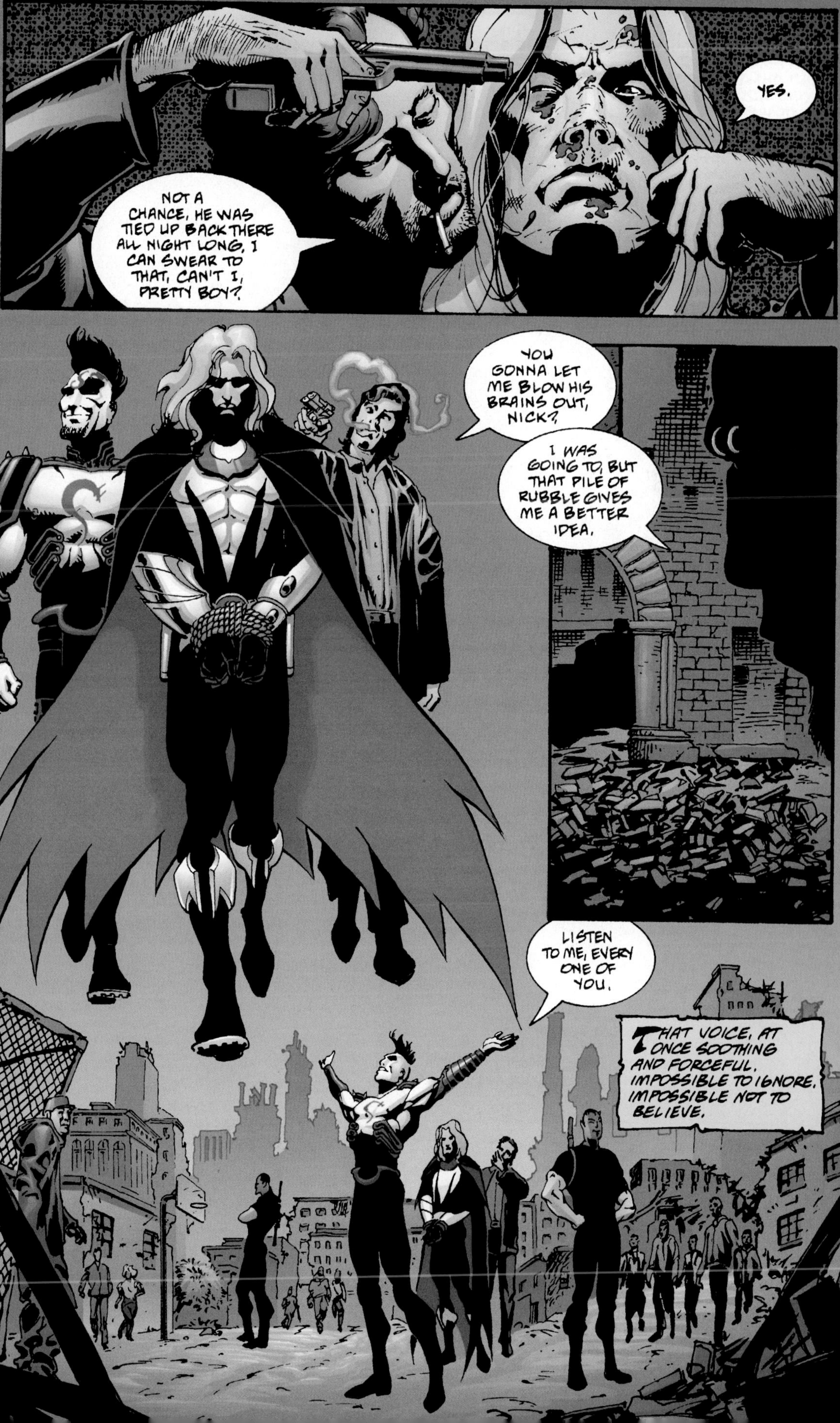
YES.
NOT A CHANCE, HE WAS TIED UP BACK THERE ALL NIGHT LONG, I CAN SWEAR TO THAT, CAN'T I, PRETTY BOY?
YOU GONNA LET ME BLOW HIS BRAINS OUT, NICK?
I WAS GOING TO, BUT THAT PILE OF RUBBLE GIVES ME A BETTER IDEA.
LISTEN TO ME, EVERY ONE OF YOU.
THAT VOICE, AT ONCE SOOTHING AND FORCEFUL. IMPOSSIBLE TO IGNORE. IMPOSSIBLE NOT TO BELIEVE.

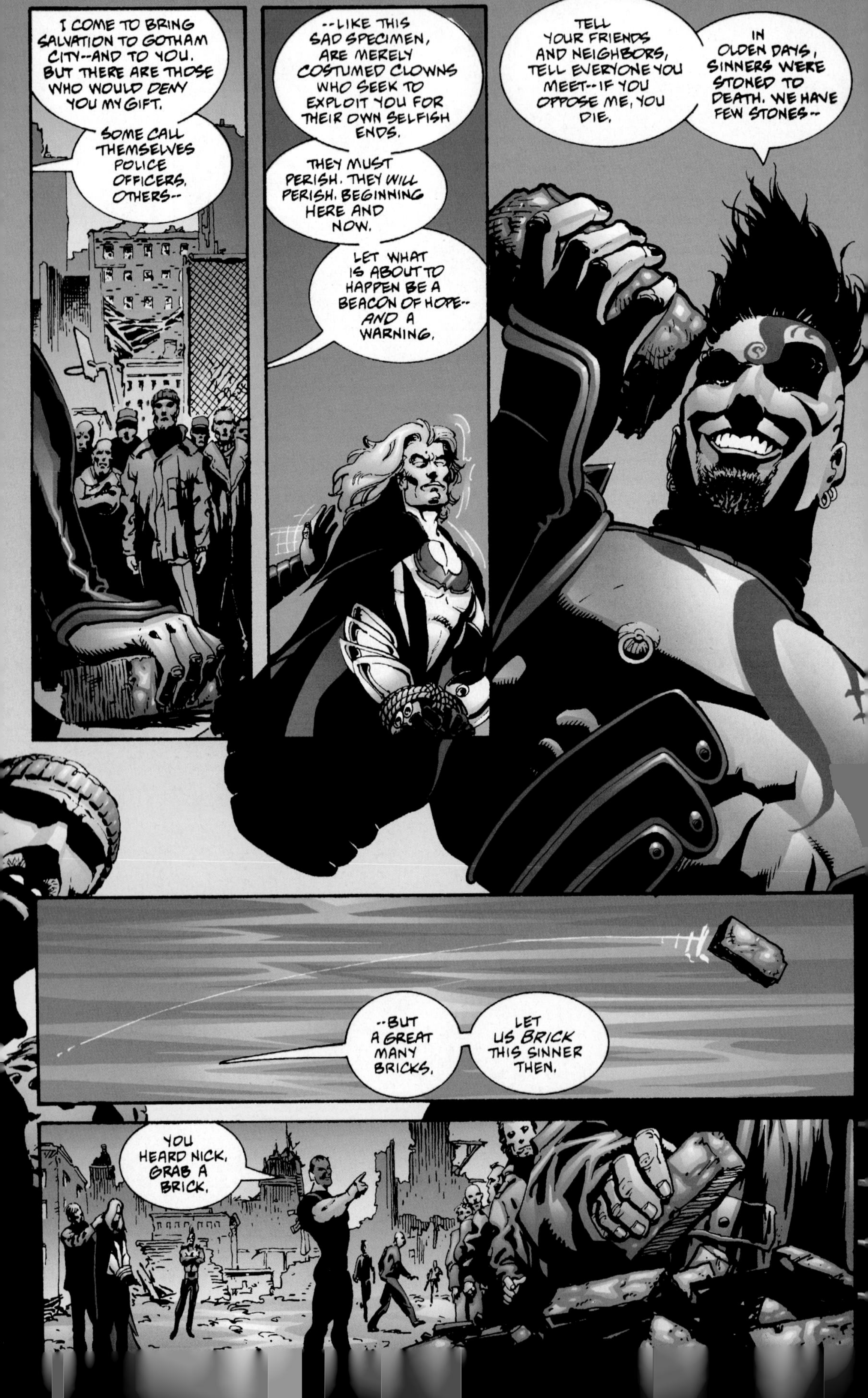

I COME TO BRING SALVATION TO GOTHAM CITY--AND TO YOU. BUT THERE ARE THOSE WHO WOULD *DENY* YOU MY GIFT.
SOME CALL THEMSELVES POLICE OFFICERS. OTHERS--
--LIKE THIS SAD SPECIMEN, ARE MERELY COSTUMED CLOWNS WHO SEEK TO EXPLOIT YOU FOR THEIR OWN SELFISH ENDS.
THEY MUST PERISH. THEY *WILL* PERISH, BEGINNING HERE AND NOW.
LET WHAT IS ABOUT TO HAPPEN BE A BEACON OF HOPE-- *AND* A WARNING.
TELL YOUR FRIENDS AND NEIGHBORS, TELL EVERYONE YOU MEET--IF YOU OPPOSE ME, YOU DIE.
IN OLDEN DAYS, SINNERS WERE STONED TO DEATH. WE HAVE FEW STONES--
--BUT A GREAT MANY BRICKS.
LET US *BRICK* THIS SINNER THEN.
YOU HEARD NICK. GRAB A BRICK.

ME, TOO.

YEAH, THIS'LL BE WAY MORE FUN THAN JUST SHOOTIN' 'IM.

MR. SCRATCH, WITHOUT MY MASK, I'M NOT A COMPLETE SINNER. NOT THAT IT MAKES ANY DIFFERENCE...

YOU'RE RIGHT. A WHOLE SINNER WOULD BE BETTER THAN A PARTIAL ONE.

THANKS FOR YOUR KIND SUGGESTION.

THE COSTUME IS COMPLETE, AND THE PROCESS IT TRIGGERS BEGINS.

FOR A MOMENT, IT IS AS THOUGH HE WERE STANDING APART, WATCHING JEAN PAUL VALLEY BE ABSORBED BY AZRAEL.

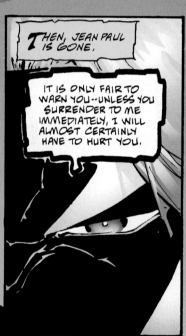

THEN, JEAN PAUL IS GONE.

IT IS ONLY FAIR TO WARN YOU--UNLESS YOU SURRENDER TO ME IMMEDIATELY, I WILL ALMOST CERTAINLY HAVE TO HURT YOU.

I'LL HAVE TO TAKE THAT CHANCE.

YOUR CHOICE.

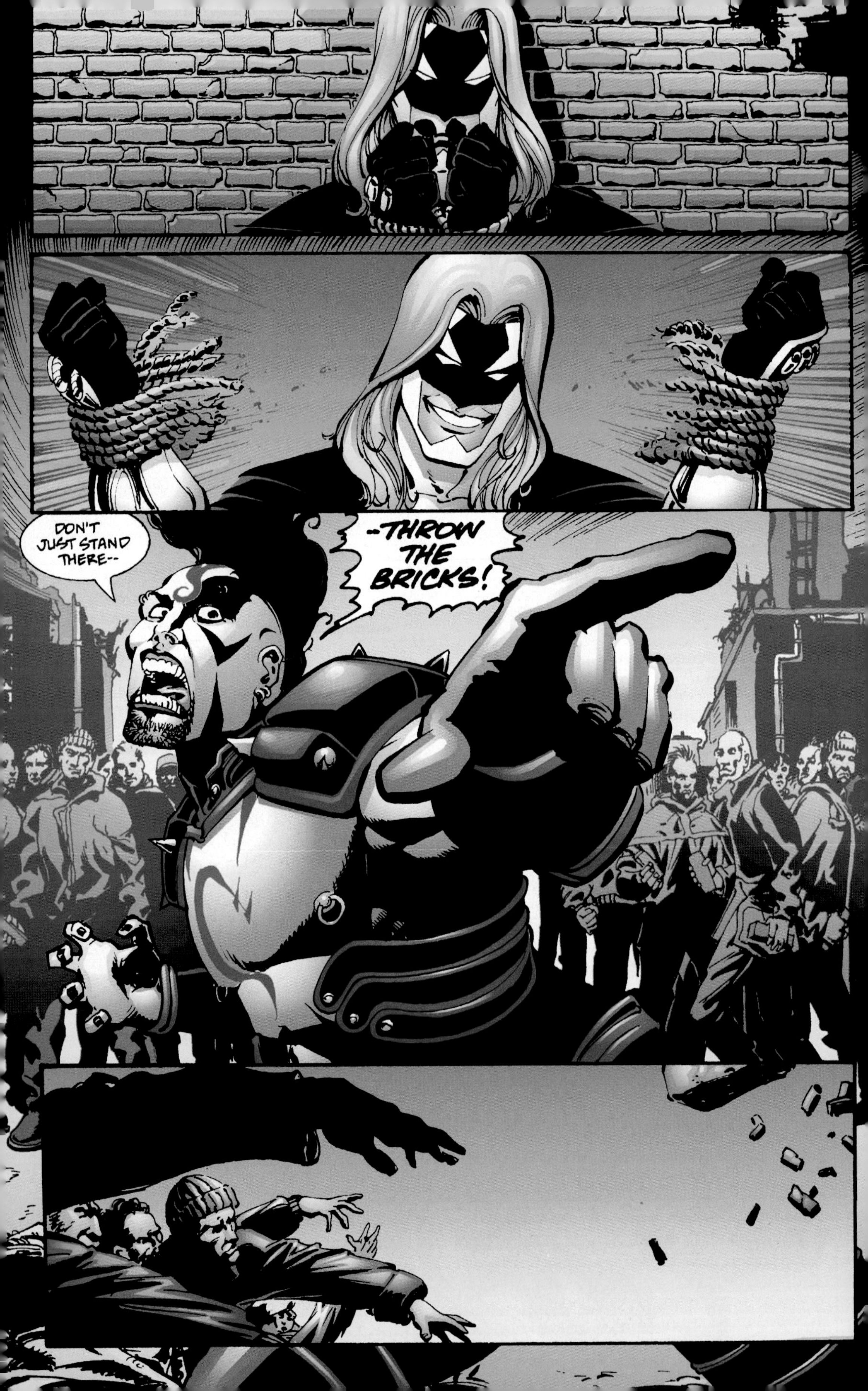
DON'T JUST STAND THERE--
--THROW THE BRICKS!

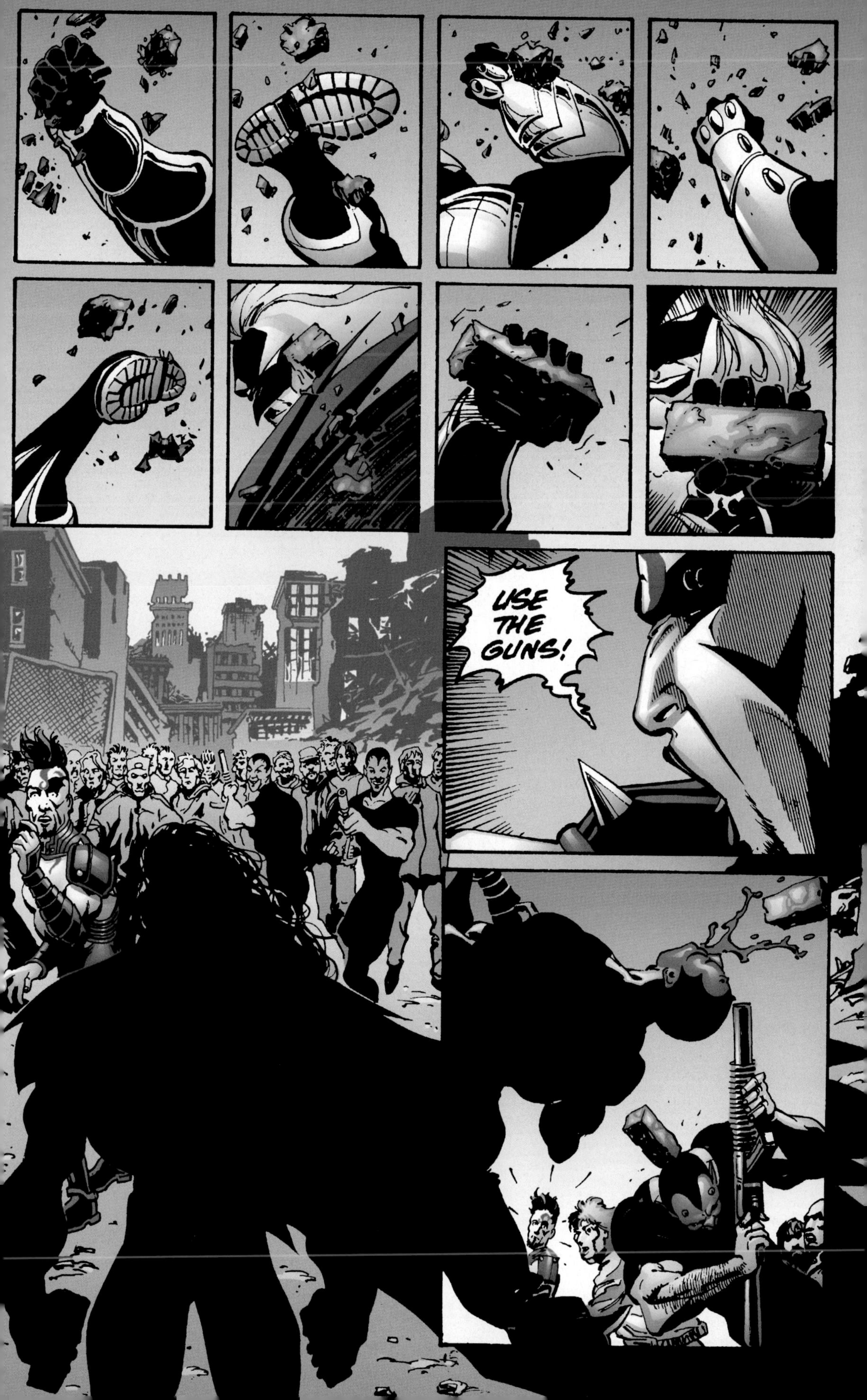
USE THE GUNS!

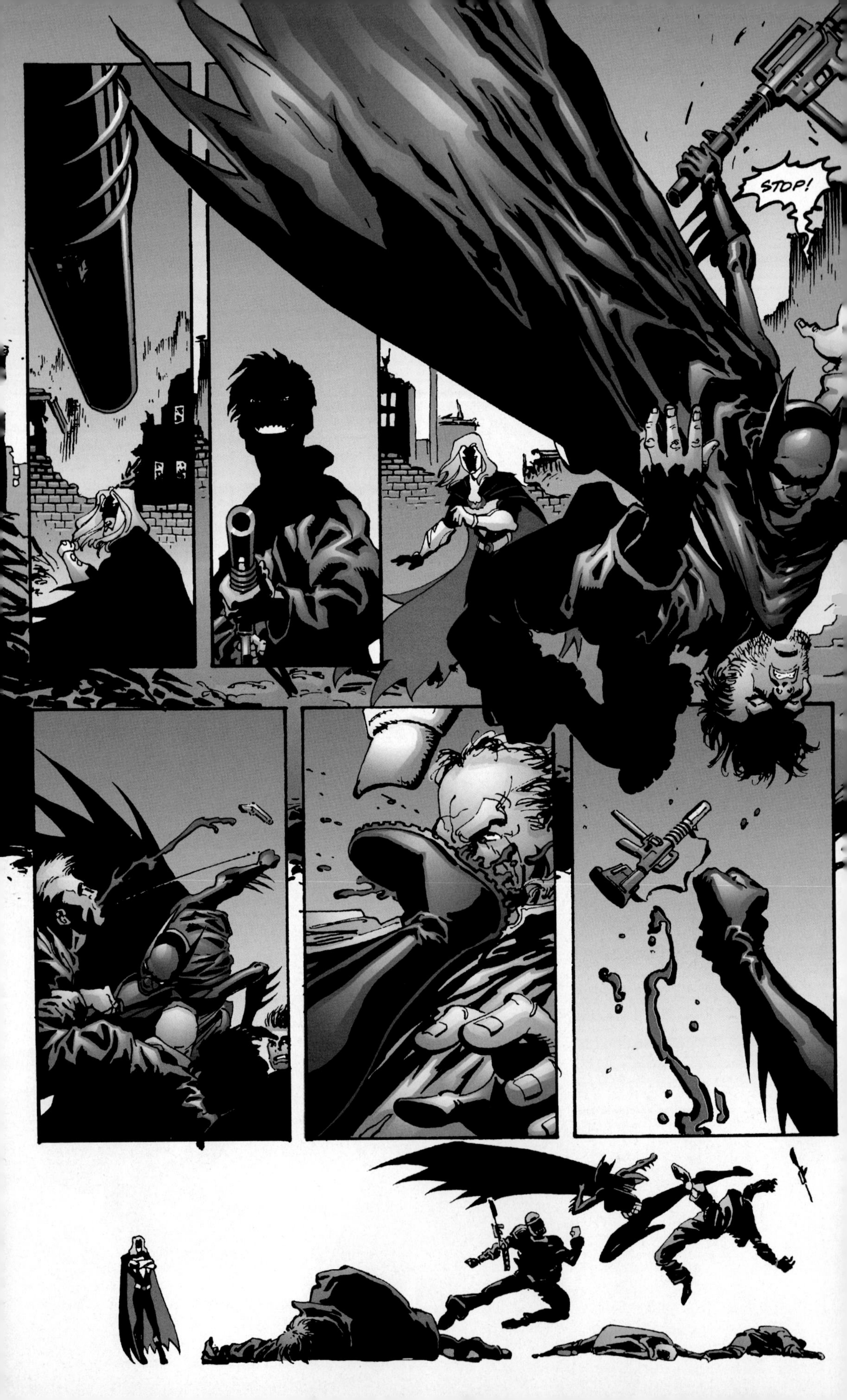
STOP!

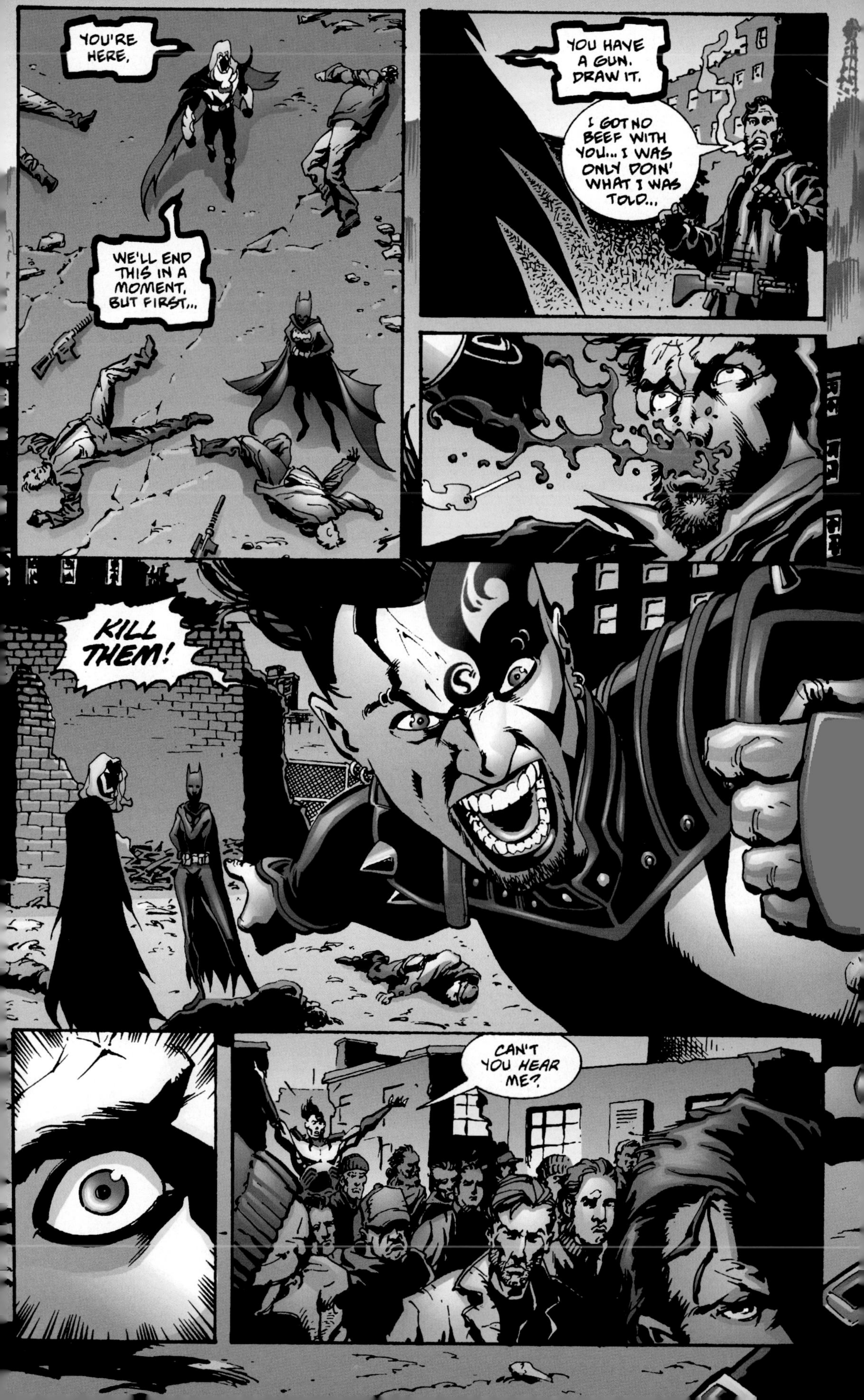
YOU'RE HERE.
WE'LL END THIS IN A MOMENT, BUT FIRST...
YOU HAVE A GUN. DRAW IT.
I GOT NO BEEF WITH YOU... I WAS ONLY DOIN' WHAT I WAS TOLD...
KILL THEM!
CAN'T YOU HEAR ME?

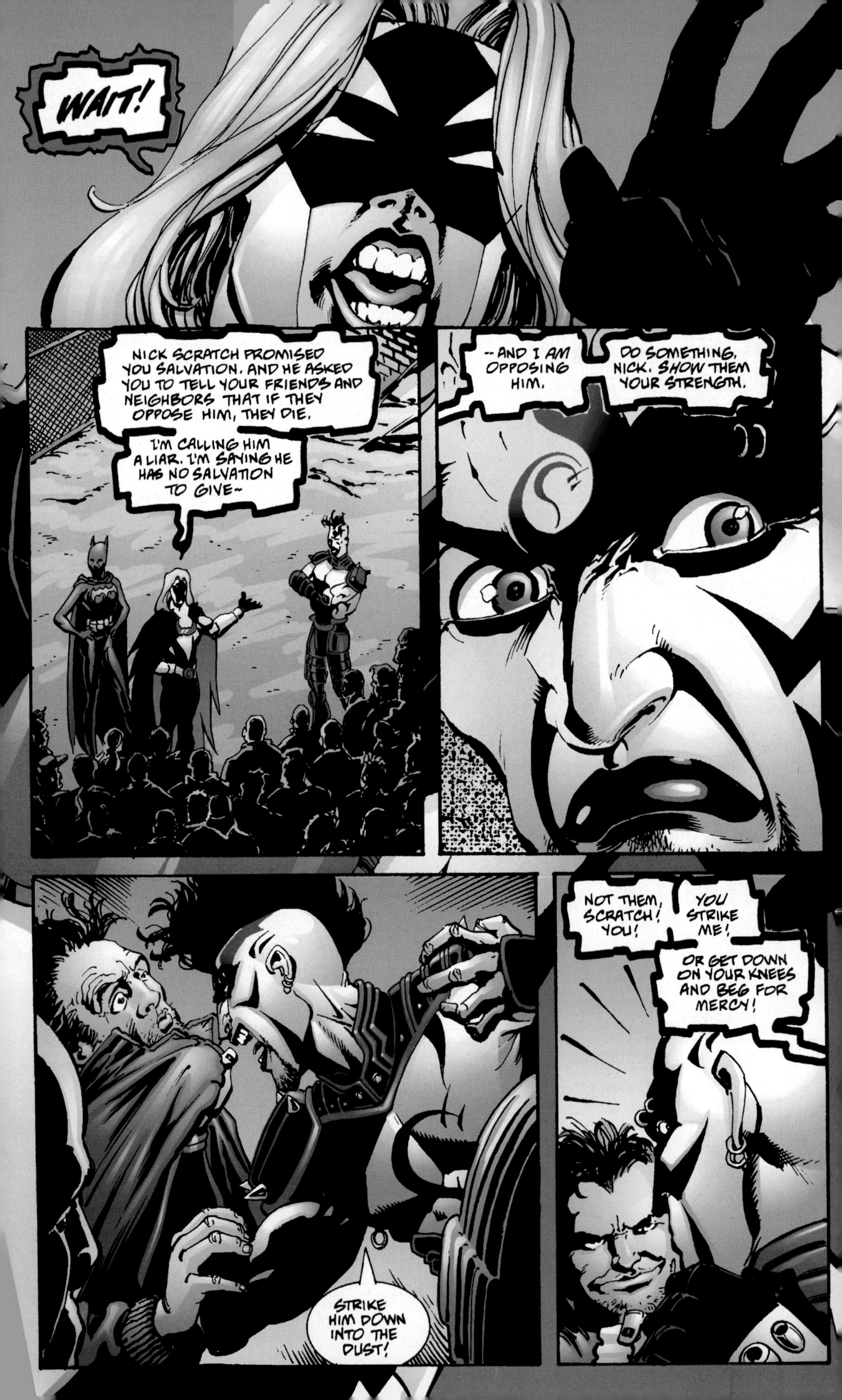
WAIT!
NICK SCRATCH PROMISED YOU SALVATION, AND HE ASKED YOU TO TELL YOUR FRIENDS AND NEIGHBORS THAT IF THEY OPPOSE HIM, THEY DIE.
I'M CALLING HIM A LIAR. I'M SAYING HE HAS NO SALVATION TO GIVE--
--AND I AM OPPOSING HIM.
DO SOMETHING, NICK. SHOW THEM YOUR STRENGTH.
STRIKE HIM DOWN INTO THE DUST!
NOT THEM, SCRATCH! YOU!
YOU STRIKE ME!
OR GET DOWN ON YOUR KNEES AND BEG FOR MERCY!

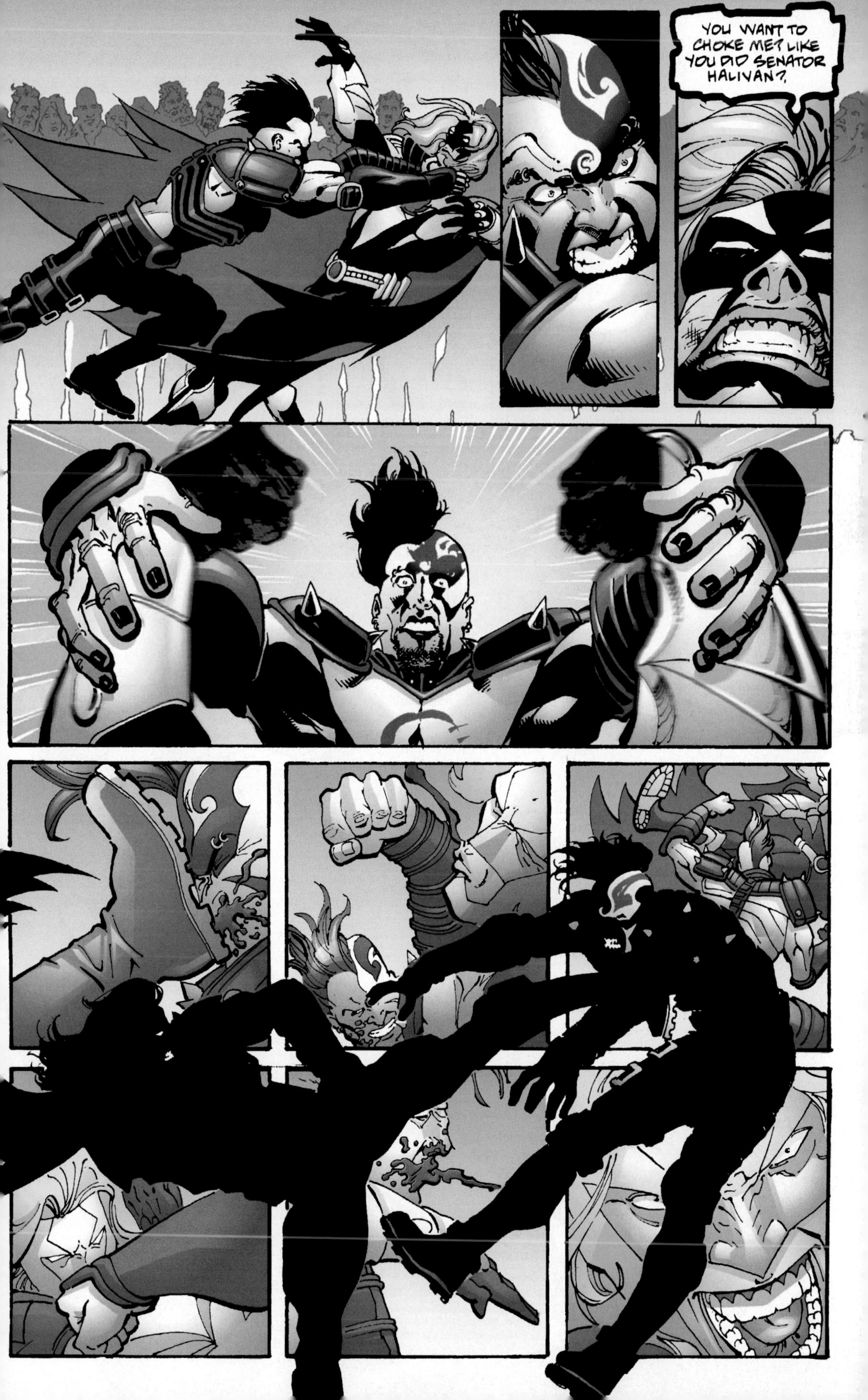
YOU WANT TO CHOKE ME? LIKE YOU DID SENATOR HALIVAN?

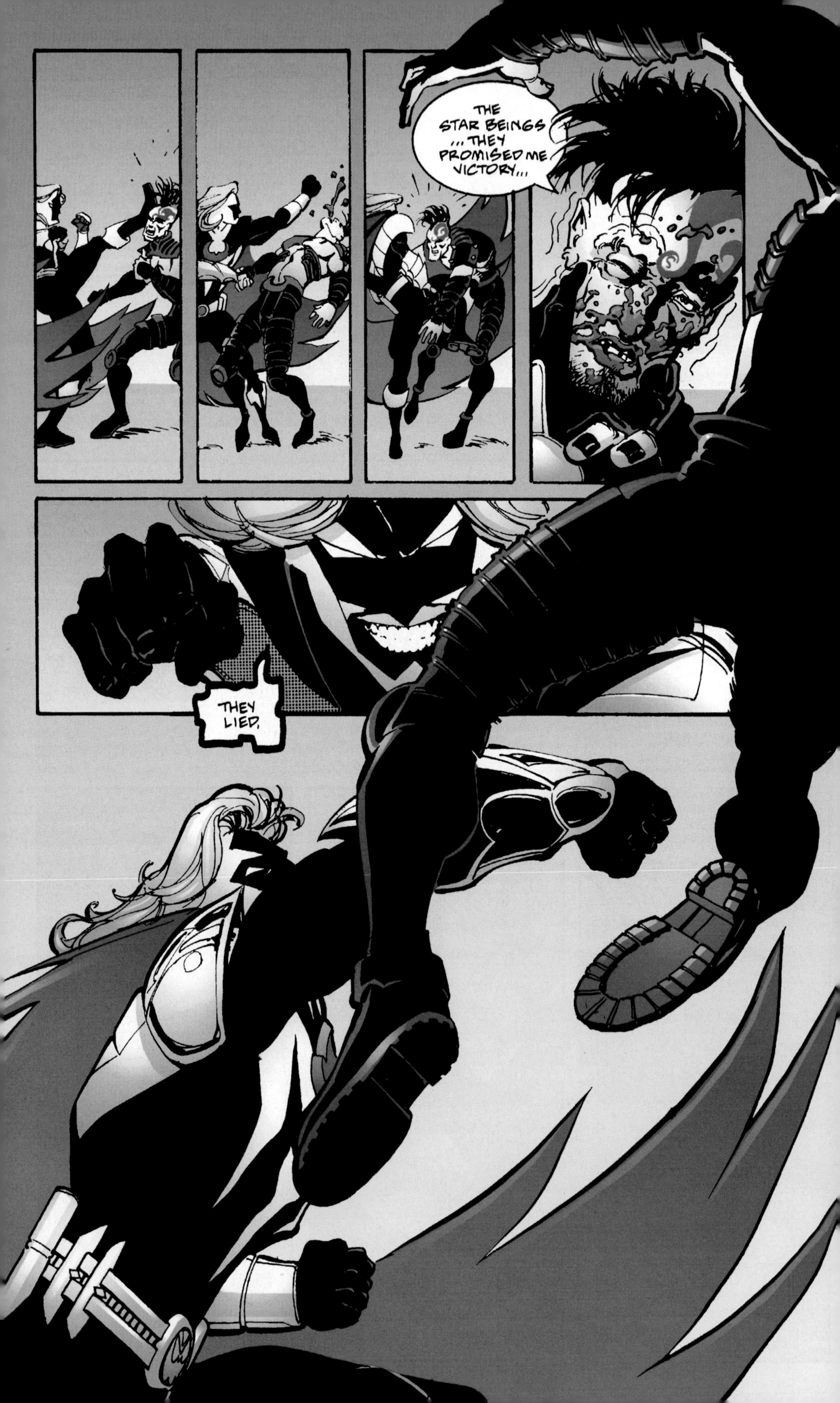
THE STAR BEINGS ...THEY PROMISED ME VICTORY...
THEY LIED.

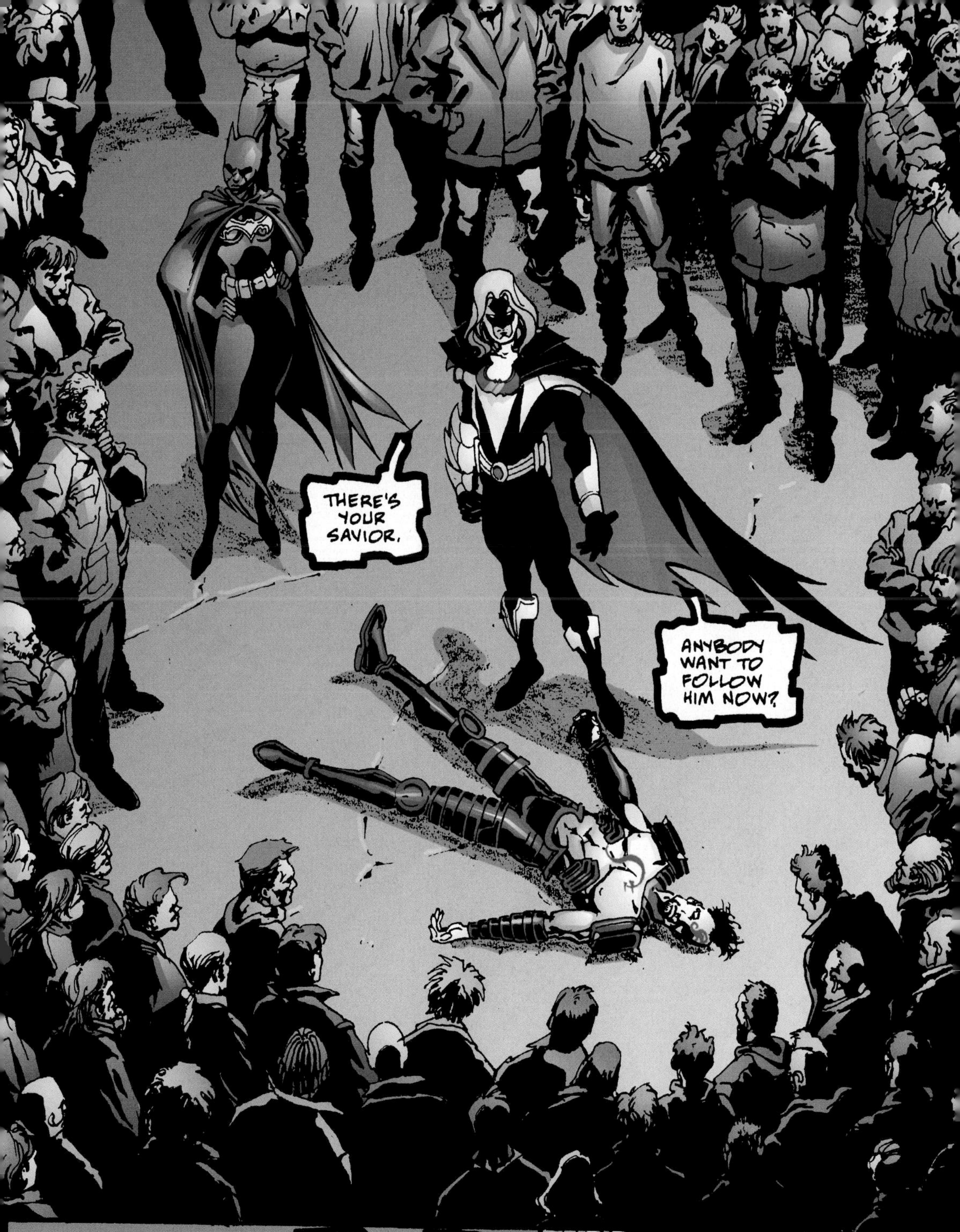
THERE'S YOUR SAVIOR.
ANYBODY WANT TO FOLLOW HIM NOW?

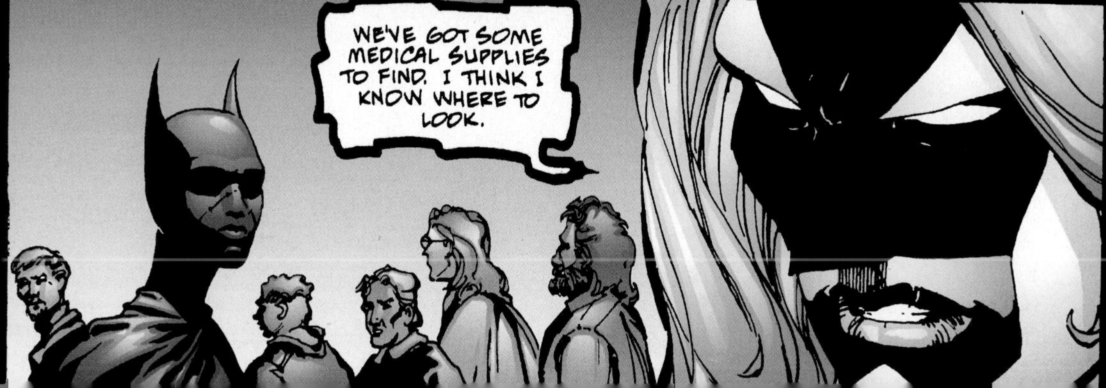
WE'VE GOT SOME MEDICAL SUPPLIES TO FIND. I THINK I KNOW WHERE TO LOOK.

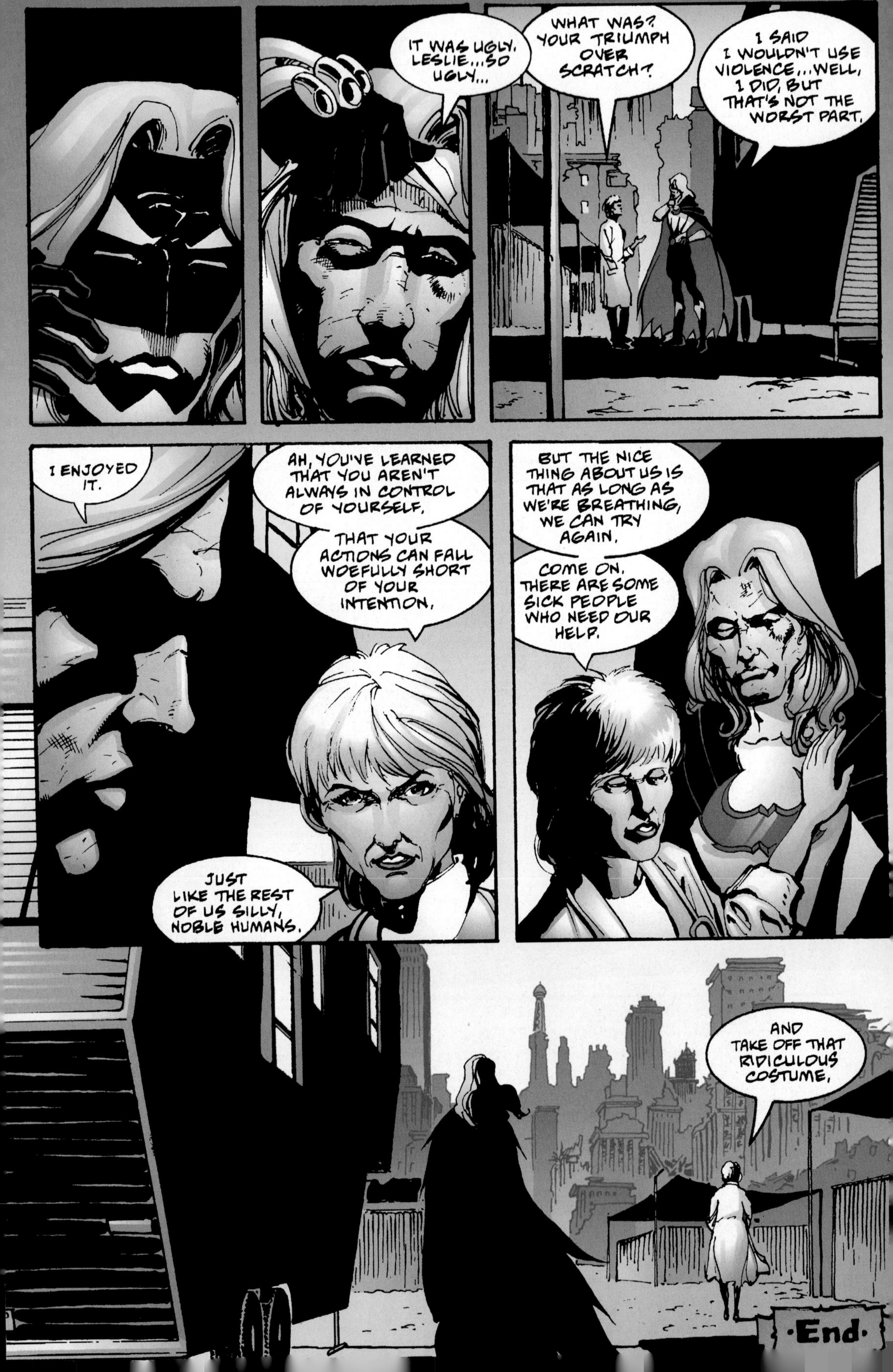
IT WAS UGLY, LESLIE...SO UGLY...
WHAT WAS? YOUR TRIUMPH OVER SCRATCH?
I SAID I WOULDN'T USE VIOLENCE...WELL, I DID, BUT THAT'S NOT THE WORST PART.
I ENJOYED IT.
AH, YOU'VE LEARNED THAT YOU AREN'T ALWAYS IN CONTROL OF YOURSELF.
THAT YOUR ACTIONS CAN FALL WOEFULLY SHORT OF YOUR INTENTION.
JUST LIKE THE REST OF US SILLY, NOBLE HUMANS.
BUT THE NICE THING ABOUT US IS THAT AS LONG AS WE'RE BREATHING, WE CAN TRY AGAIN.
COME ON. THERE ARE SOME SICK PEOPLE WHO NEED OUR HELP.
AND TAKE OFF THAT RIDICULOUS COSTUME.
·End·

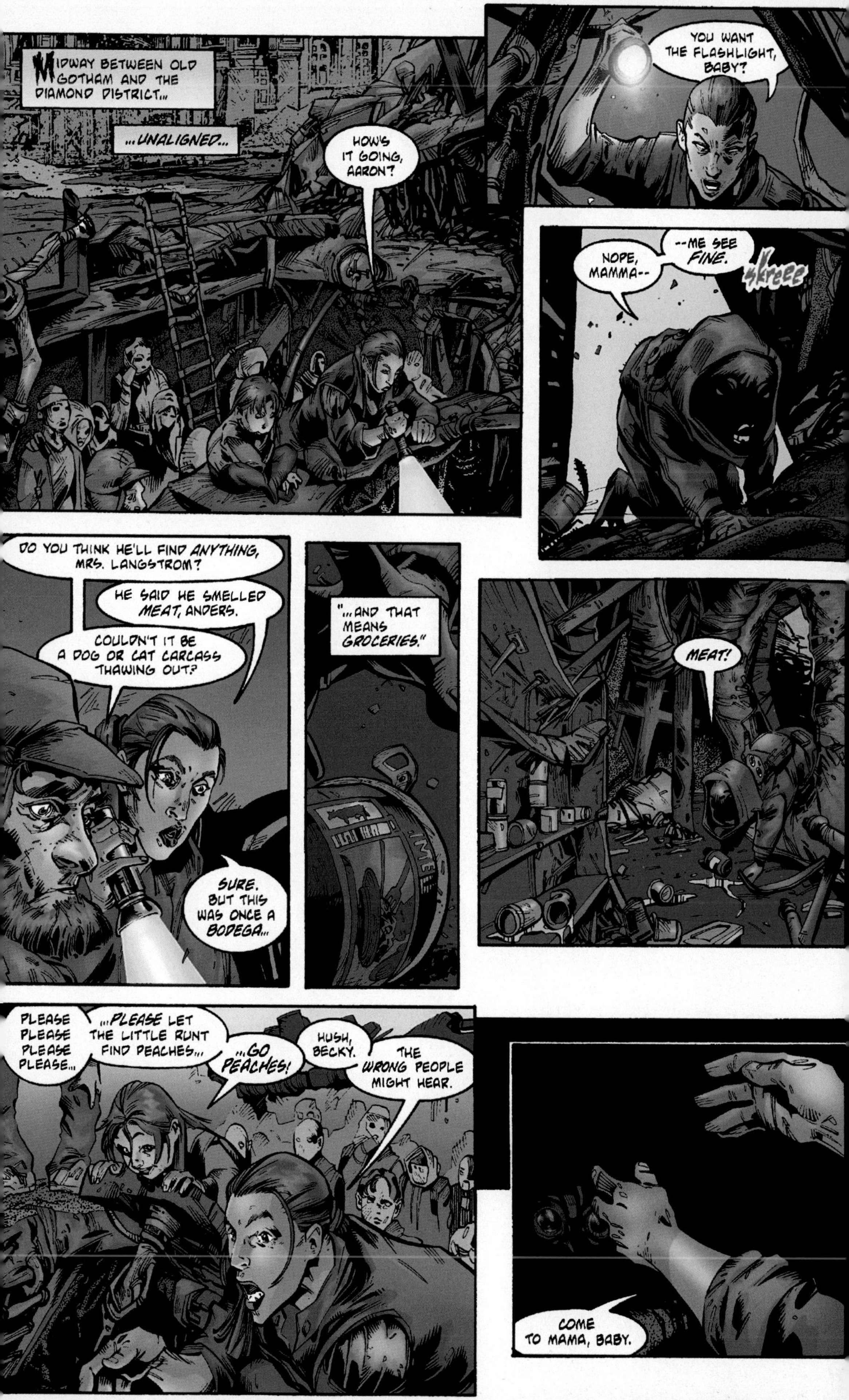
MIDWAY BETWEEN OLD GOTHAM AND THE DIAMOND DISTRICT...
...UNALIGNED...
HOW'S IT GOING, AARON?
YOU WANT THE FLASHLIGHT, BABY?
NOPE, MAMMA--
--ME SEE FINE.
SKREEE
DO YOU THINK HE'LL FIND ANYTHING, MRS. LANGSTROM?
HE SAID HE SMELLED MEAT, ANDERS.
COULDN'T IT BE A DOG OR CAT CARCASS THAWING OUT?
SURE. BUT THIS WAS ONCE A BODEGA...
"...AND THAT MEANS GROCERIES."
MEAT!
PLEASE PLEASE PLEASE PLEASE...
...PLEASE LET THE LITTLE RUNT FIND PEACHES...
...GO PEACHES!
HUSH, BECKY.
THE WRONG PEOPLE MIGHT HEAR.
COME TO MAMA, BABY.

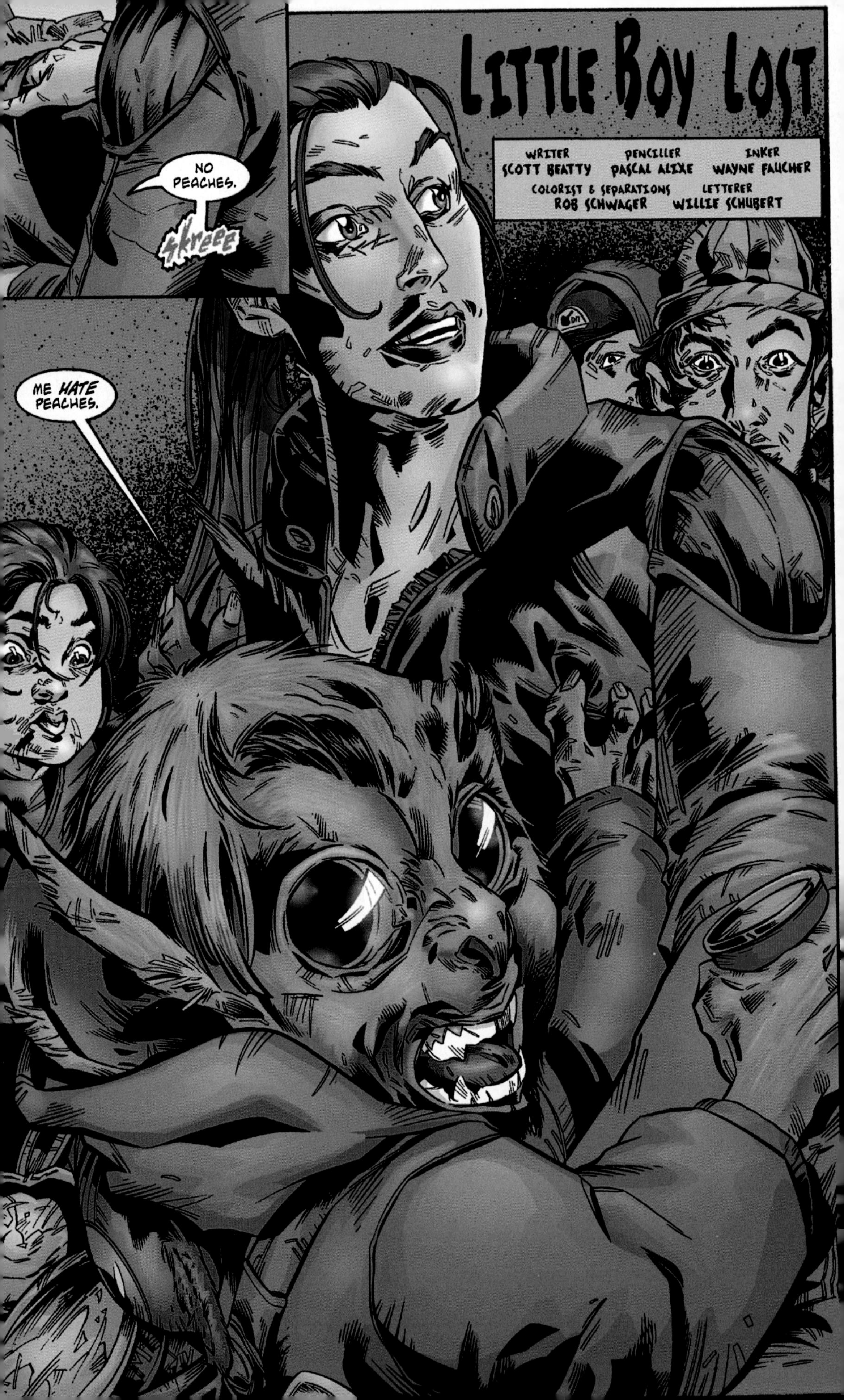
NO PEACHES.
SKREEE
LITTLE BOY LOST
WRITER SCOTT BEATTY
PENCILLER PASCAL ALIXE
INKER WAYNE FAUCHER
COLORIST & SEPARATIONS ROB SCHWAGER
LETTERER WILLIE SCHUBERT
ME HATE PEACHES.

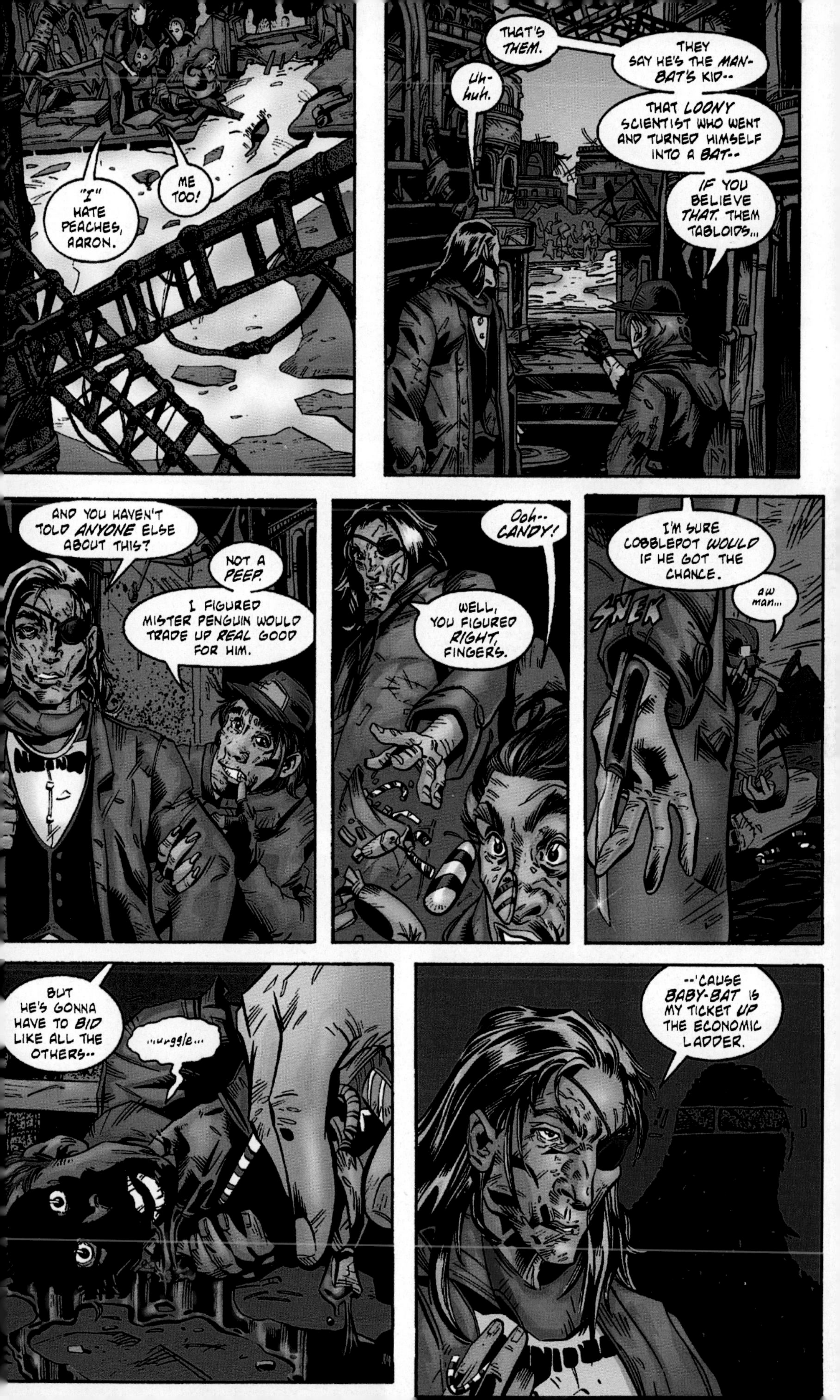
"I" HATE PEACHES, AARON.
ME TOO!
THAT'S THEM.
Uh-huh.
THEY SAY HE'S THE MAN-BAT'S KID--
THAT LOONY SCIENTIST WHO WENT AND TURNED HIMSELF INTO A BAT--
IF YOU BELIEVE THAT. THEM TABLOIDS...
AND YOU HAVEN'T TOLD ANYONE ELSE ABOUT THIS?
NOT A PEEP.
I FIGURED MISTER PENGUIN WOULD TRADE UP REAL GOOD FOR HIM.
Ooh-- CANDY!
WELL, YOU FIGURED RIGHT, FINGERS.
I'M SURE COBBLEPOT WOULD IF HE GOT THE CHANCE.
SNEK
aw man...
BUT HE'S GONNA HAVE TO BID LIKE ALL THE OTHERS--
...urggle...
--'CAUSE BABY-BAT IS MY TICKET UP THE ECONOMIC LADDER.

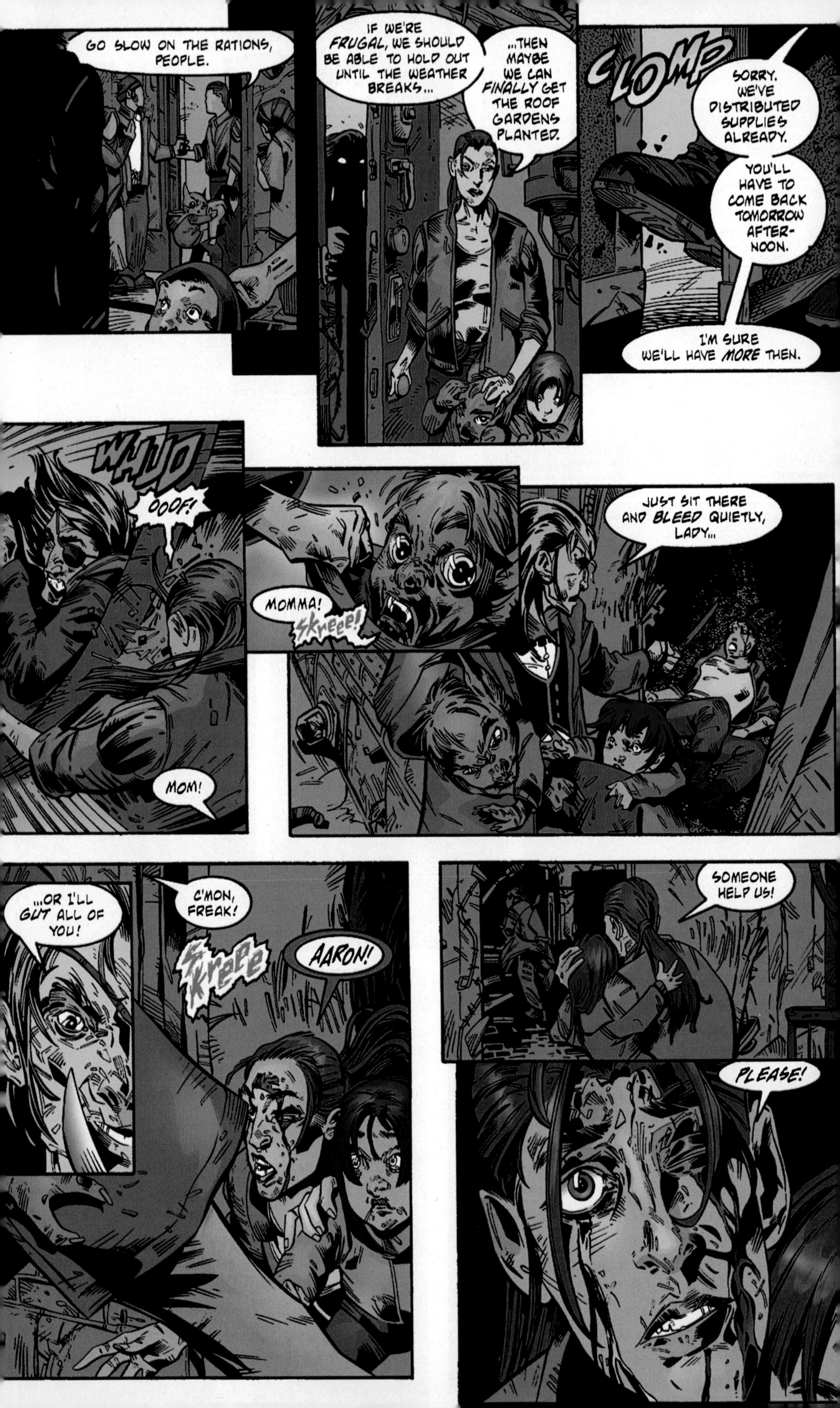

GO SLOW ON THE RATIONS, PEOPLE.
IF WE'RE FRUGAL, WE SHOULD BE ABLE TO HOLD OUT UNTIL THE WEATHER BREAKS...
...THEN MAYBE WE CAN FINALLY GET THE ROOF GARDENS PLANTED.
CLOMP
SORRY. WE'VE DISTRIBUTED SUPPLIES ALREADY.
YOU'LL HAVE TO COME BACK TOMORROW AFTER-NOON.
I'M SURE WE'LL HAVE MORE THEN.
WHUD
OOOF!
MOM!
MOMMA!
SKREEE!
JUST SIT THERE AND BLEED QUIETLY, LADY...
...OR I'LL GUT ALL OF YOU!
C'MON, FREAK!
SKREEE
AARON!
SOMEONE HELP US!
PLEASE!

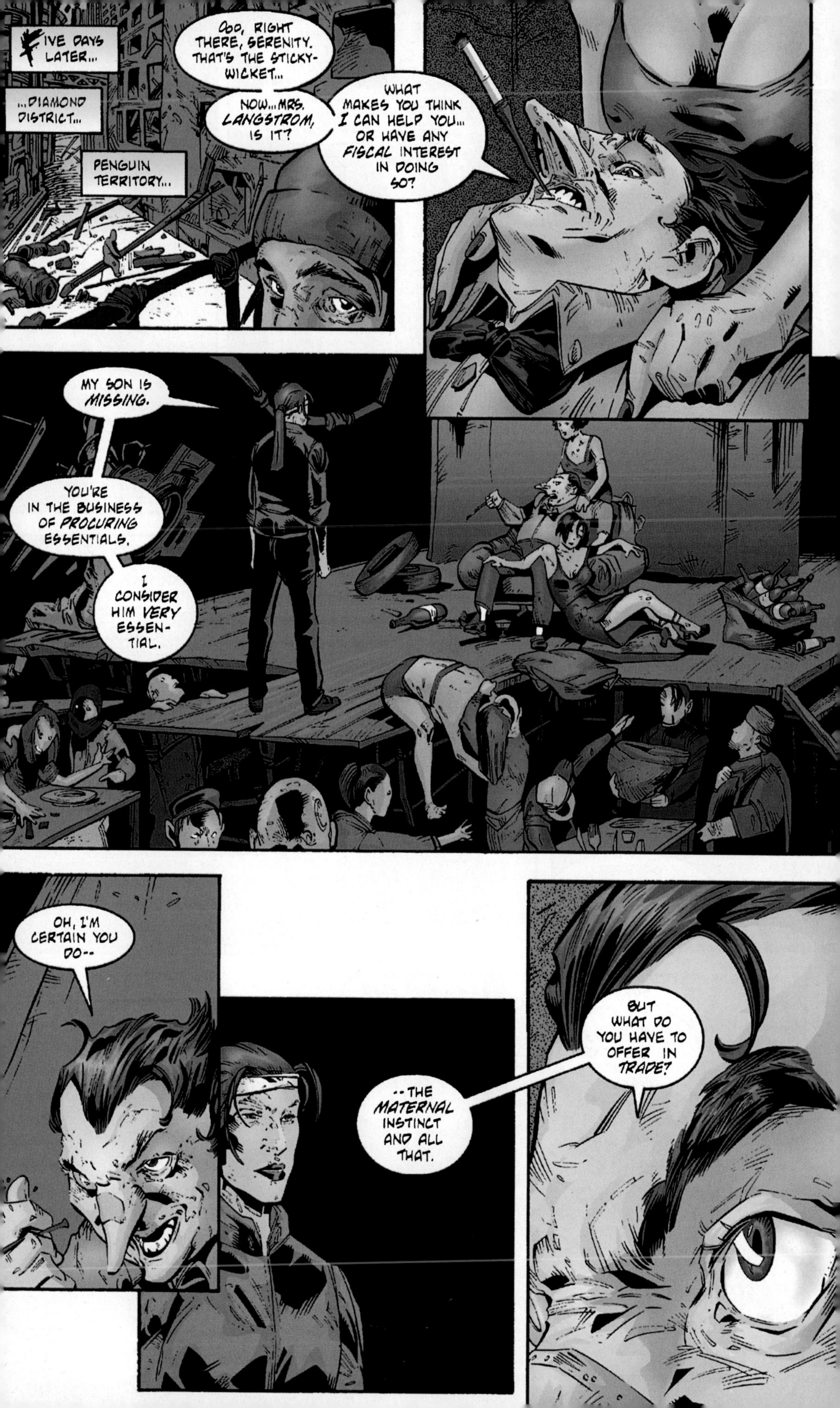
FIVE DAYS LATER...
...DIAMOND DISTRICT...
PENGUIN TERRITORY...
OOO, RIGHT THERE, SERENITY. THAT'S THE STICKY-WICKET...
NOW...MRS. LANGSTROM, IS IT?
WHAT MAKES YOU THINK I CAN HELP YOU... OR HAVE ANY FISCAL INTEREST IN DOING SO?
MY SON IS MISSING.
YOU'RE IN THE BUSINESS OF PROCURING ESSENTIALS.
I CONSIDER HIM VERY ESSEN-TIAL.
OH, I'M CERTAIN YOU DO--
--THE MATERNAL INSTINCT AND ALL THAT.
BUT WHAT DO YOU HAVE TO OFFER IN TRADE?

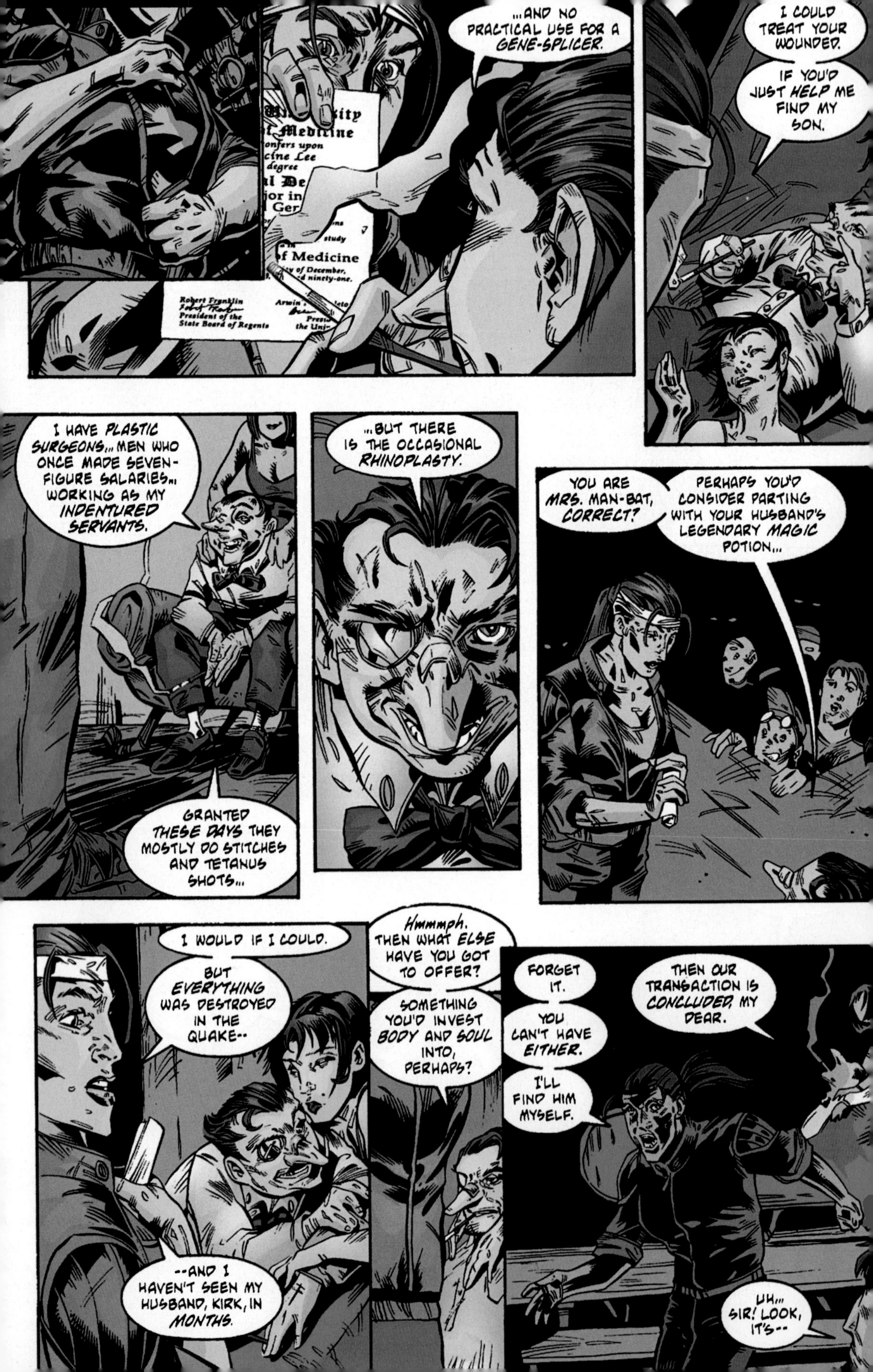
...AND NO PRACTICAL USE FOR A GENE-SPLICER.
Robert Franklin
President of the
State Board of Regents
I COULD TREAT YOUR WOUNDED.
IF YOU'D JUST HELP ME FIND MY SON.
I HAVE PLASTIC SURGEONS... MEN WHO ONCE MADE SEVEN-FIGURE SALARIES... WORKING AS MY INDENTURED SERVANTS.
GRANTED THESE DAYS THEY MOSTLY DO STITCHES AND TETANUS SHOTS...
...BUT THERE IS THE OCCASIONAL RHINOPLASTY.
YOU ARE MRS. MAN-BAT, CORRECT?
PERHAPS YOU'D CONSIDER PARTING WITH YOUR HUSBAND'S LEGENDARY MAGIC POTION...
I WOULD IF I COULD.
BUT EVERYTHING WAS DESTROYED IN THE QUAKE--
--AND I HAVEN'T SEEN MY HUSBAND, KIRK, IN MONTHS.
Hmmmph. THEN WHAT ELSE HAVE YOU GOT TO OFFER?
SOMETHING YOU'D INVEST BODY AND SOUL INTO, PERHAPS?
FORGET IT.
YOU CAN'T HAVE EITHER.
I'LL FIND HIM MYSELF.
THEN OUR TRANSACTION IS CONCLUDED, MY DEAR.
UH... SIR! LOOK, IT'S--

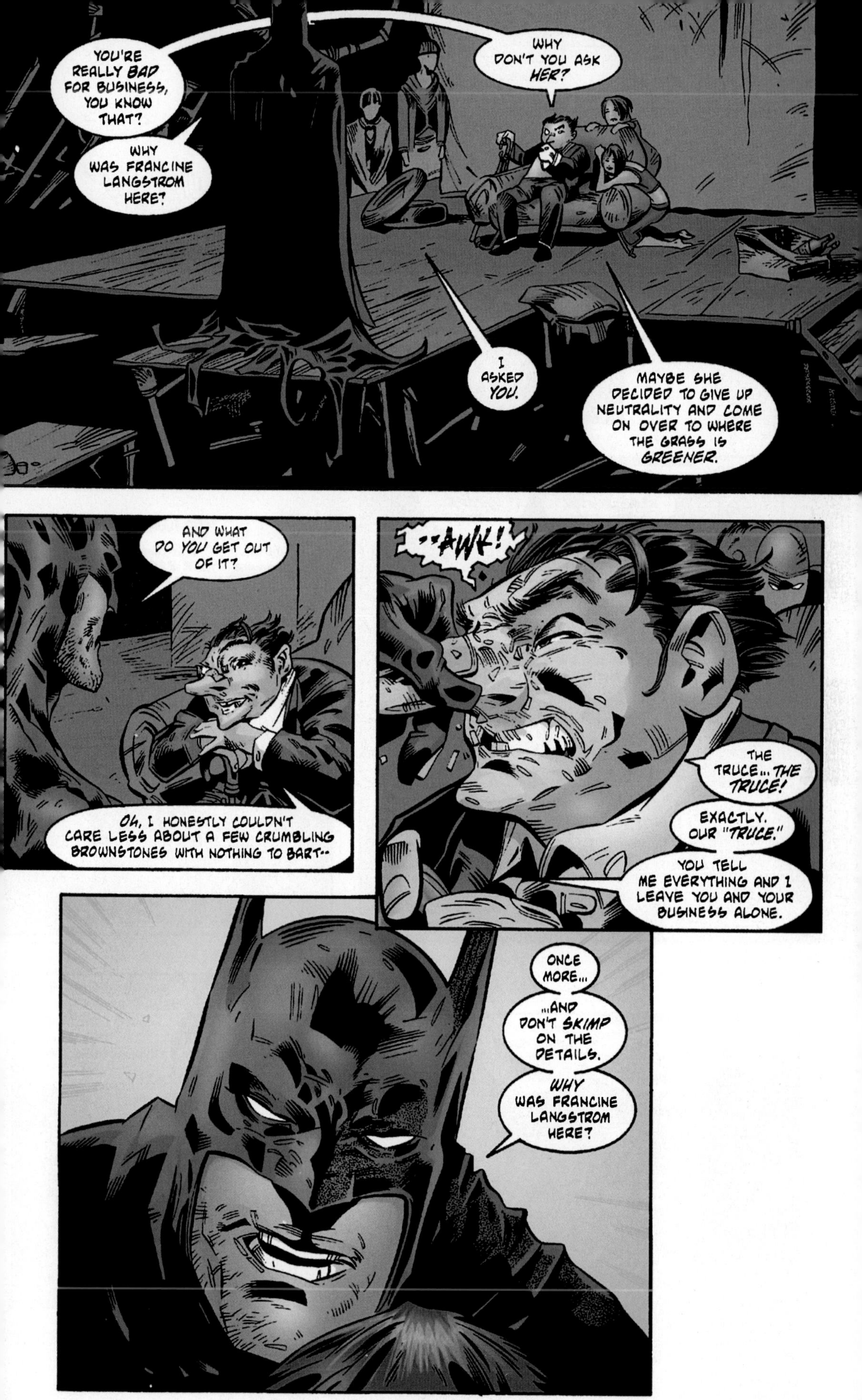
YOU'RE REALLY BAD FOR BUSINESS, YOU KNOW THAT?
WHY WAS FRANCINE LANGSTROM HERE?
WHY DON'T YOU ASK HER?
I ASKED YOU.
MAYBE SHE DECIDED TO GIVE UP NEUTRALITY AND COME ON OVER TO WHERE THE GRASS IS GREENER.
AND WHAT DO YOU GET OUT OF IT?
OH, I HONESTLY COULDN'T CARE LESS ABOUT A FEW CRUMBLING BROWNSTONES WITH NOTHING TO BART--
--AWK!
THE TRUCE... THE TRUCE!
EXACTLY. OUR "TRUCE."
YOU TELL ME EVERYTHING AND I LEAVE YOU AND YOUR BUSINESS ALONE.
ONCE MORE...
...AND DON'T SKIMP ON THE DETAILS.
WHY WAS FRANCINE LANGSTROM HERE?

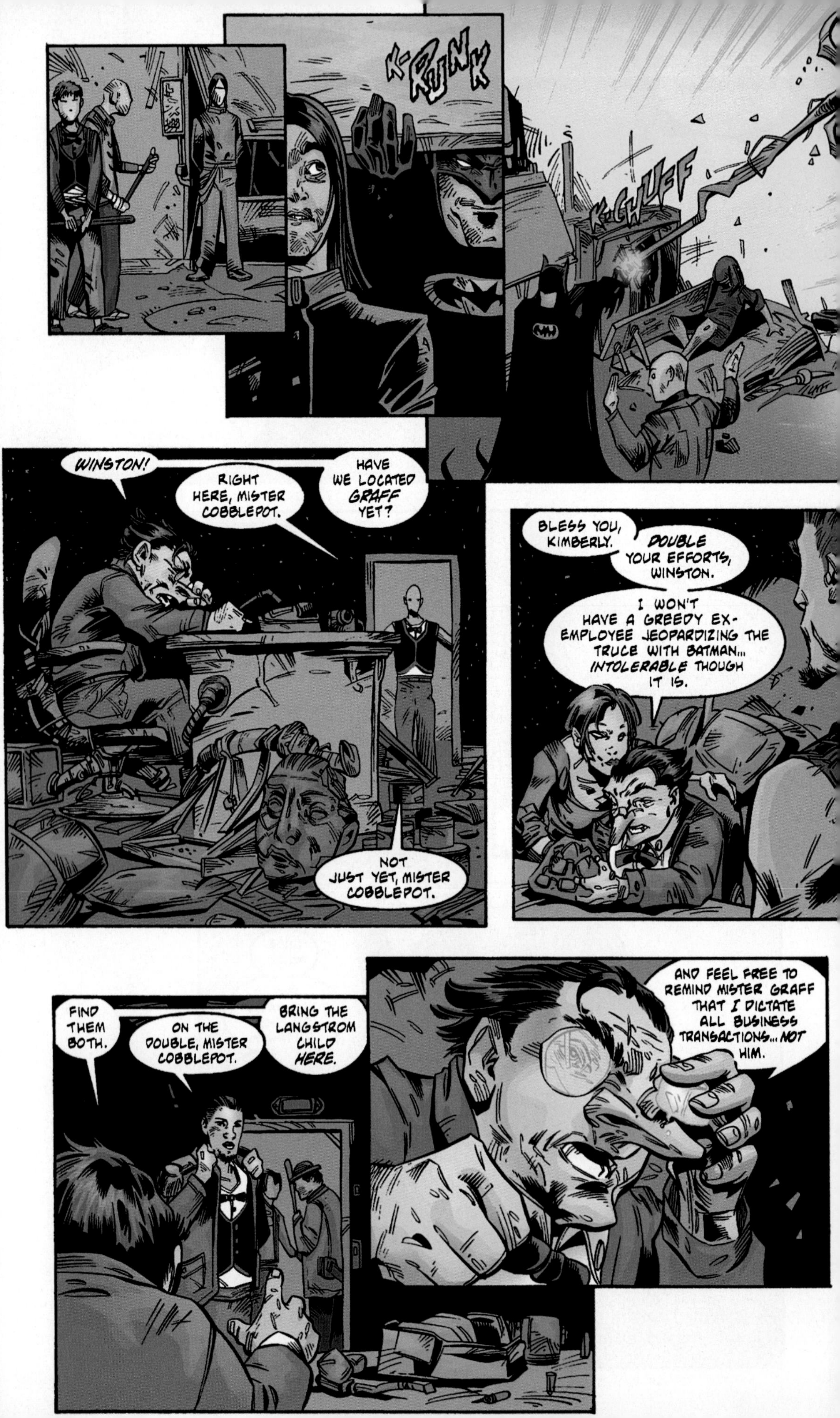
K-RUNK
K-CHUFF
WINSTON!
RIGHT HERE, MISTER COBBLEPOT.
HAVE WE LOCATED GRAFF YET?
NOT JUST YET, MISTER COBBLEPOT.
BLESS YOU, KIMBERLY.
DOUBLE YOUR EFFORTS, WINSTON.
I WON'T HAVE A GREEDY EX-EMPLOYEE JEOPARDIZING THE TRUCE WITH BATMAN... INTOLERABLE THOUGH IT IS.
FIND THEM BOTH.
ON THE DOUBLE, MISTER COBBLEPOT.
BRING THE LANGSTROM CHILD HERE.
AND FEEL FREE TO REMIND MISTER GRAFF THAT I DICTATE ALL BUSINESS TRANSACTIONS... NOT HIM.

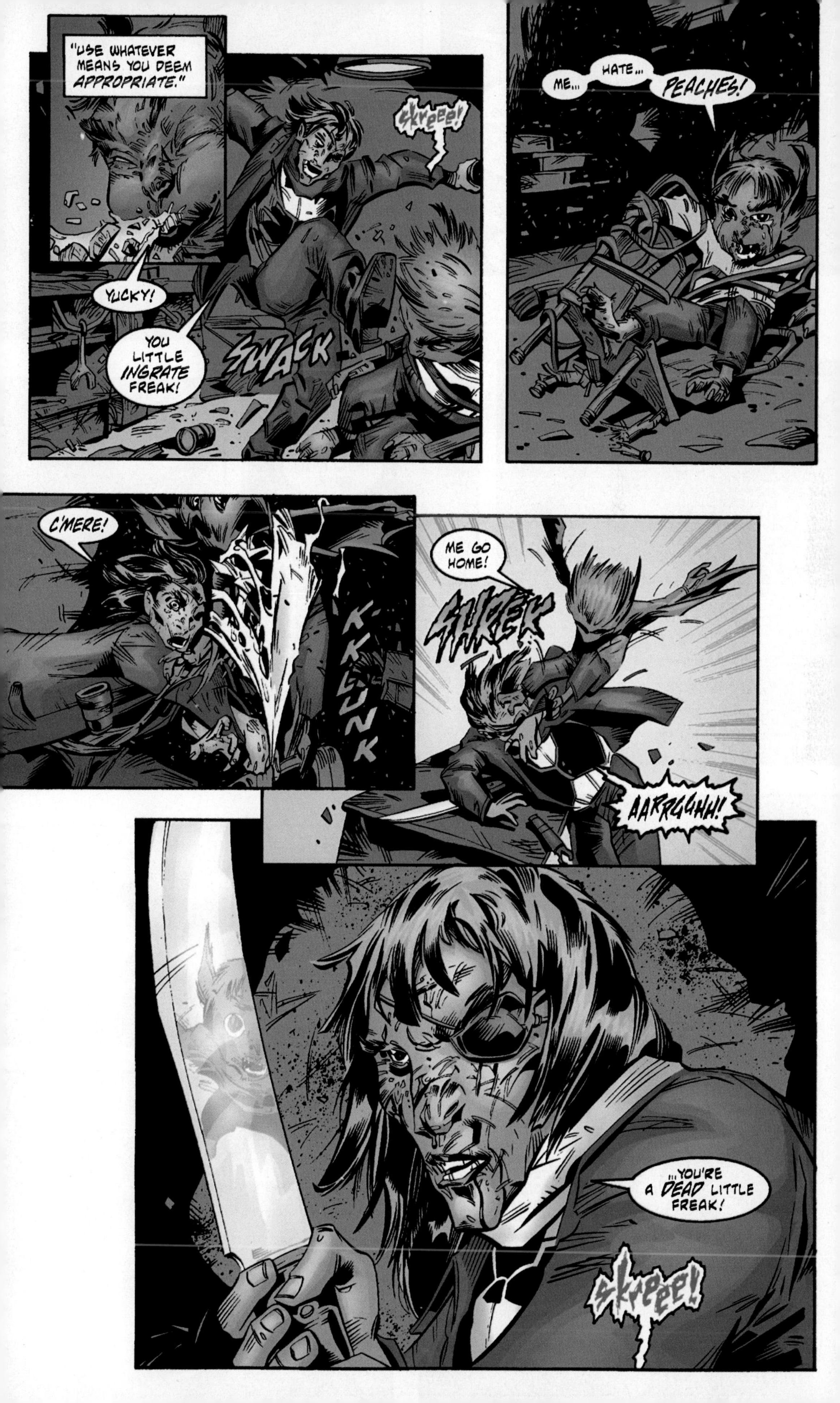
"USE WHATEVER MEANS YOU DEEM APPROPRIATE."
SKREEE!
YUCKY!
YOU LITTLE INGRATE FREAK!
SWACK
ME... HATE... PEACHES!
C'MERE!
K-KLUNK
ME GO HOME!
SHREEK
AARRGGHH!
...YOU'RE A DEAD LITTLE FREAK!
SKREEE!

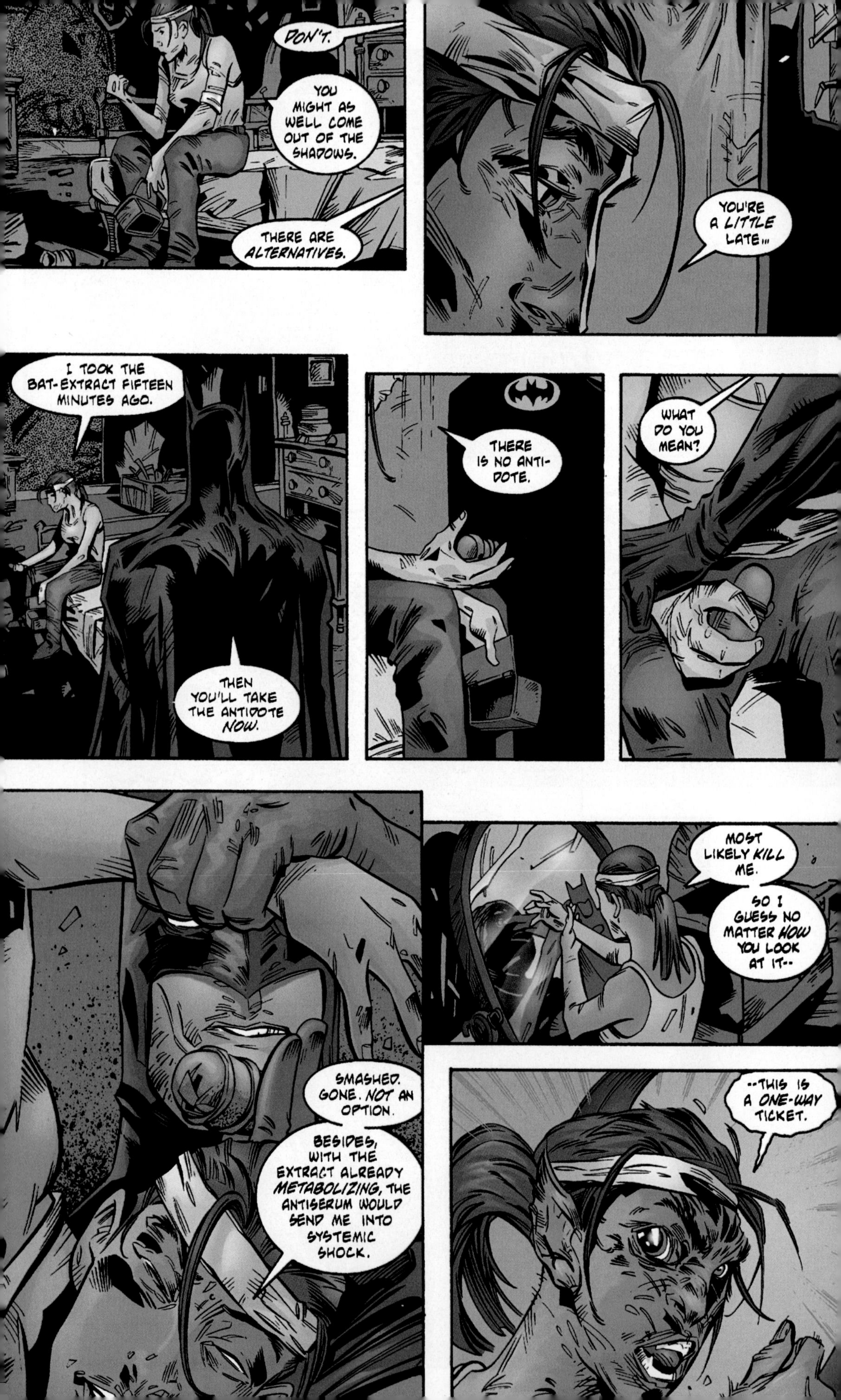
DON'T.
YOU MIGHT AS WELL COME OUT OF THE SHADOWS.
THERE ARE ALTERNATIVES.
YOU'RE A LITTLE LATE...
I TOOK THE BAT-EXTRACT FIFTEEN MINUTES AGO.
THEN YOU'LL TAKE THE ANTIDOTE NOW.
THERE IS NO ANTI-DOTE.
WHAT DO YOU MEAN?
SMASHED. GONE. NOT AN OPTION.
BESIDES, WITH THE EXTRACT ALREADY METABOLIZING, THE ANTISERUM WOULD SEND ME INTO SYSTEMIC SHOCK.
MOST LIKELY KILL ME.
SO I GUESS NO MATTER HOW YOU LOOK AT IT--
--THIS IS A ONE-WAY TICKET.

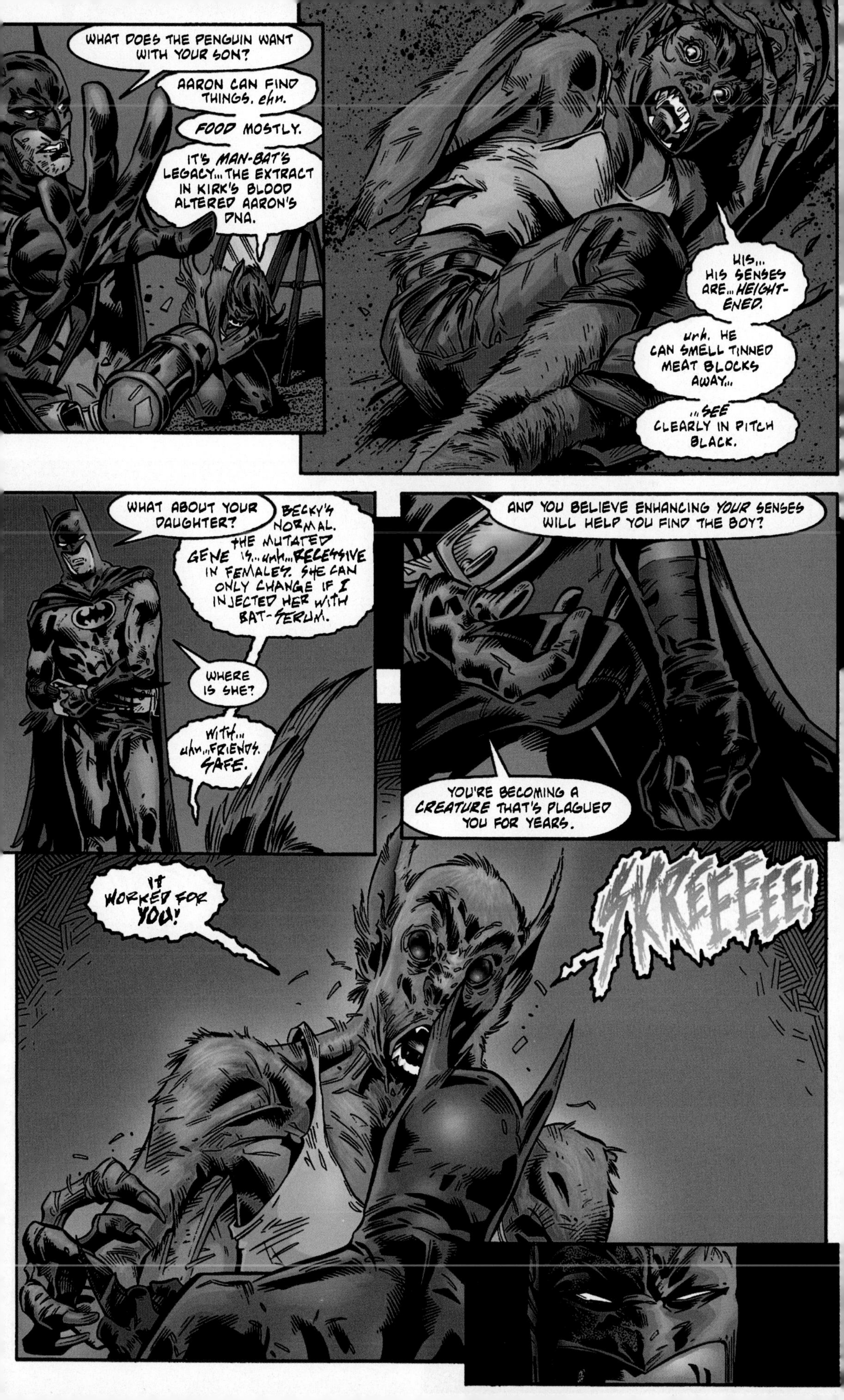
WHAT DOES THE PENGUIN WANT WITH YOUR SON?
AARON CAN FIND THINGS. ehn.
FOOD MOSTLY.
IT'S MAN-BAT'S LEGACY... THE EXTRACT IN KIRK'S BLOOD ALTERED AARON'S DNA.
HIS... HIS SENSES ARE... HEIGHT-ENED.
urh. HE CAN SMELL TINNED MEAT BLOCKS AWAY...
...SEE CLEARLY IN PITCH BLACK.
WHAT ABOUT YOUR DAUGHTER?
BECKY'S NORMAL. THE MUTATED GENE IS... unh... RECESSIVE IN FEMALES. SHE CAN ONLY CHANGE IF I INJECTED HER WITH BAT-SERUM.
WHERE IS SHE?
WITH... uhn... FRIENDS. SAFE.
AND YOU BELIEVE ENHANCING YOUR SENSES WILL HELP YOU FIND THE BOY?
YOU'RE BECOMING A CREATURE THAT'S PLAGUED YOU FOR YEARS.
IT WORKED FOR YOU!
SKREEEEE!

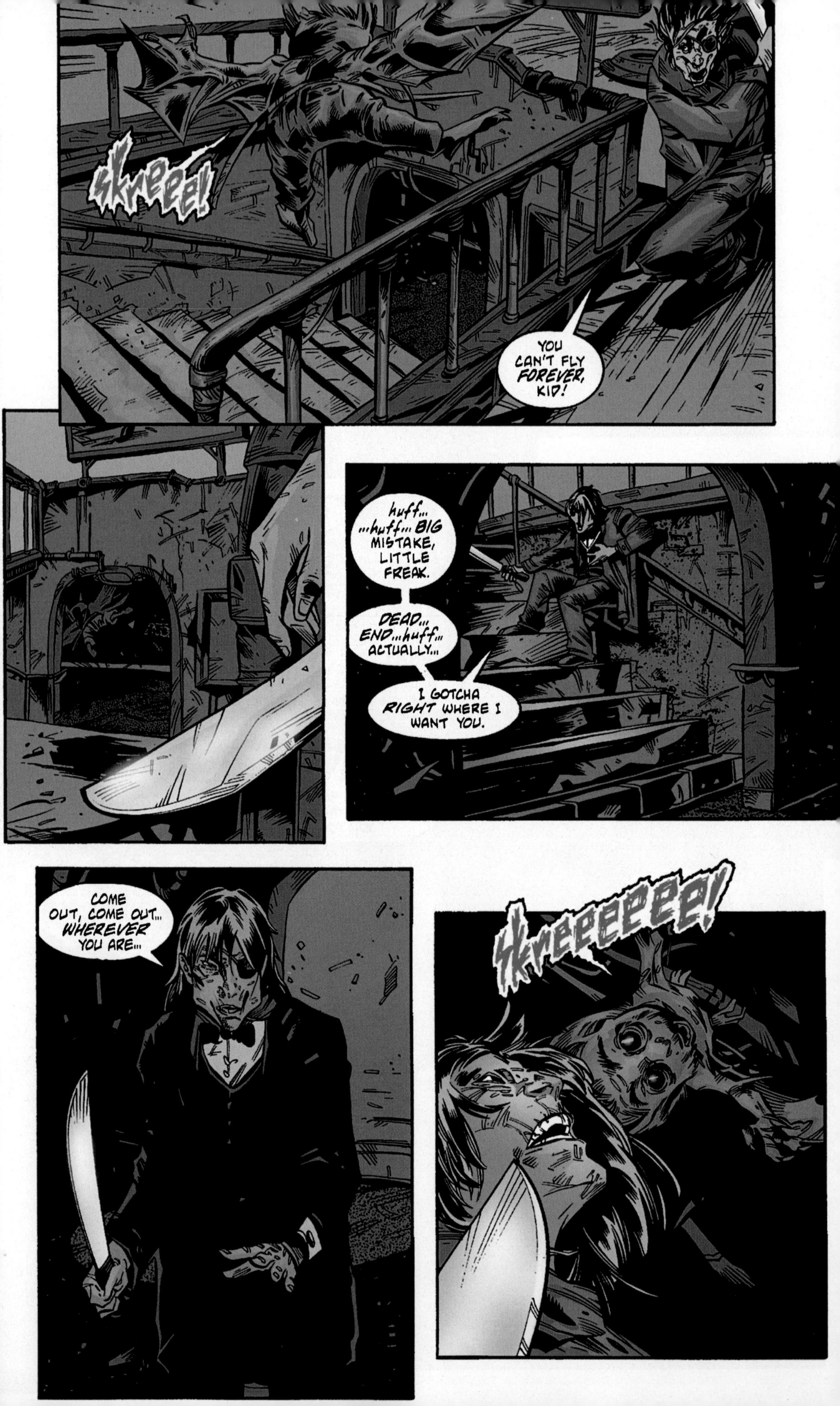
skreee!
YOU CAN'T FLY FOREVER, KID!
huff... ...huff... BIG MISTAKE, LITTLE FREAK.
DEAD... END... huff... ACTUALLY...
I GOTCHA RIGHT WHERE I WANT YOU.
COME OUT, COME OUT... WHEREVER YOU ARE...
skreeeeee!

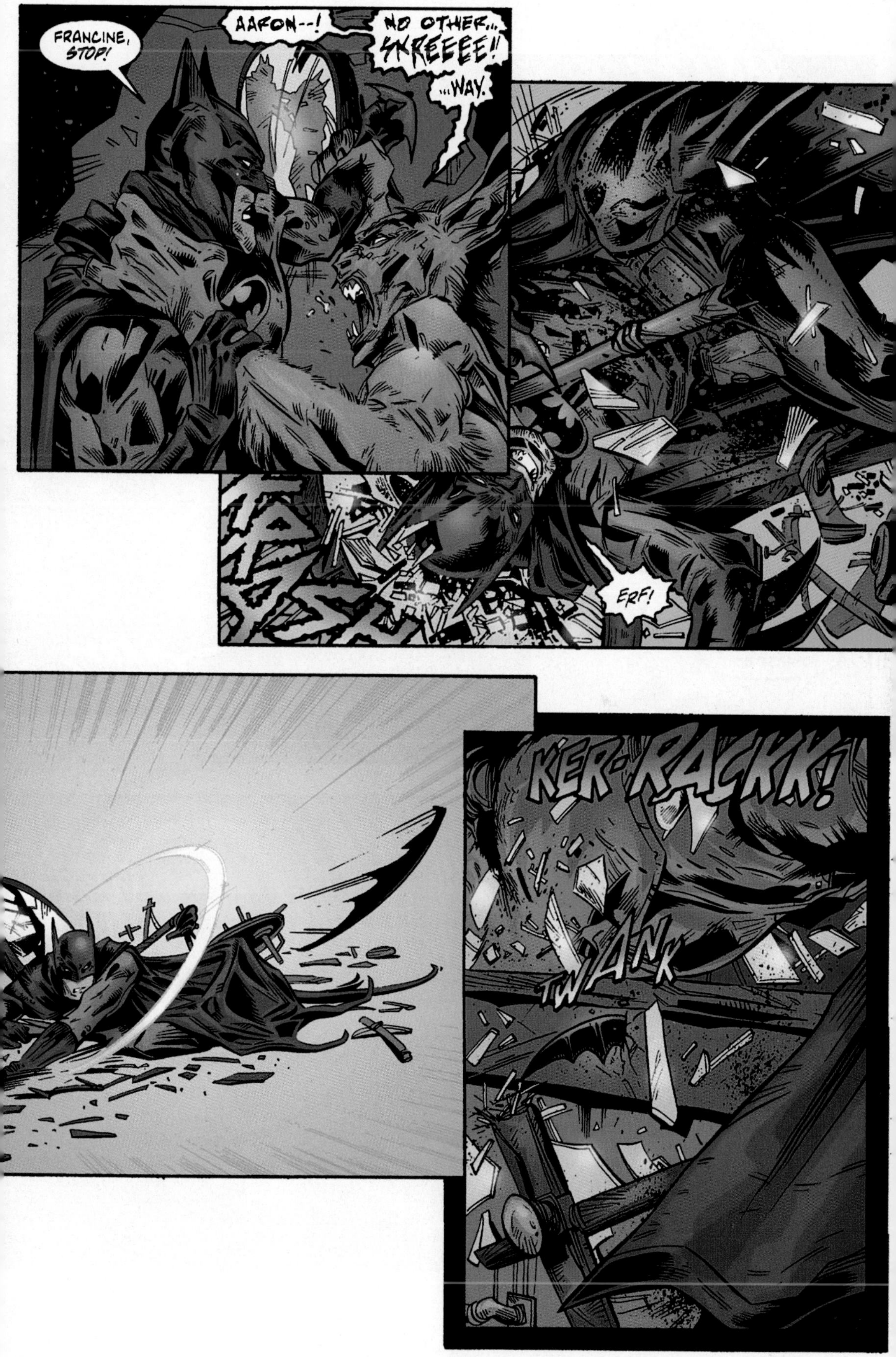
FRANCINE, STOP!
AARON--!
NO OTHER... SKREEEEE!! ...WAY.
ERF!
KER-RACKK!
TWANK

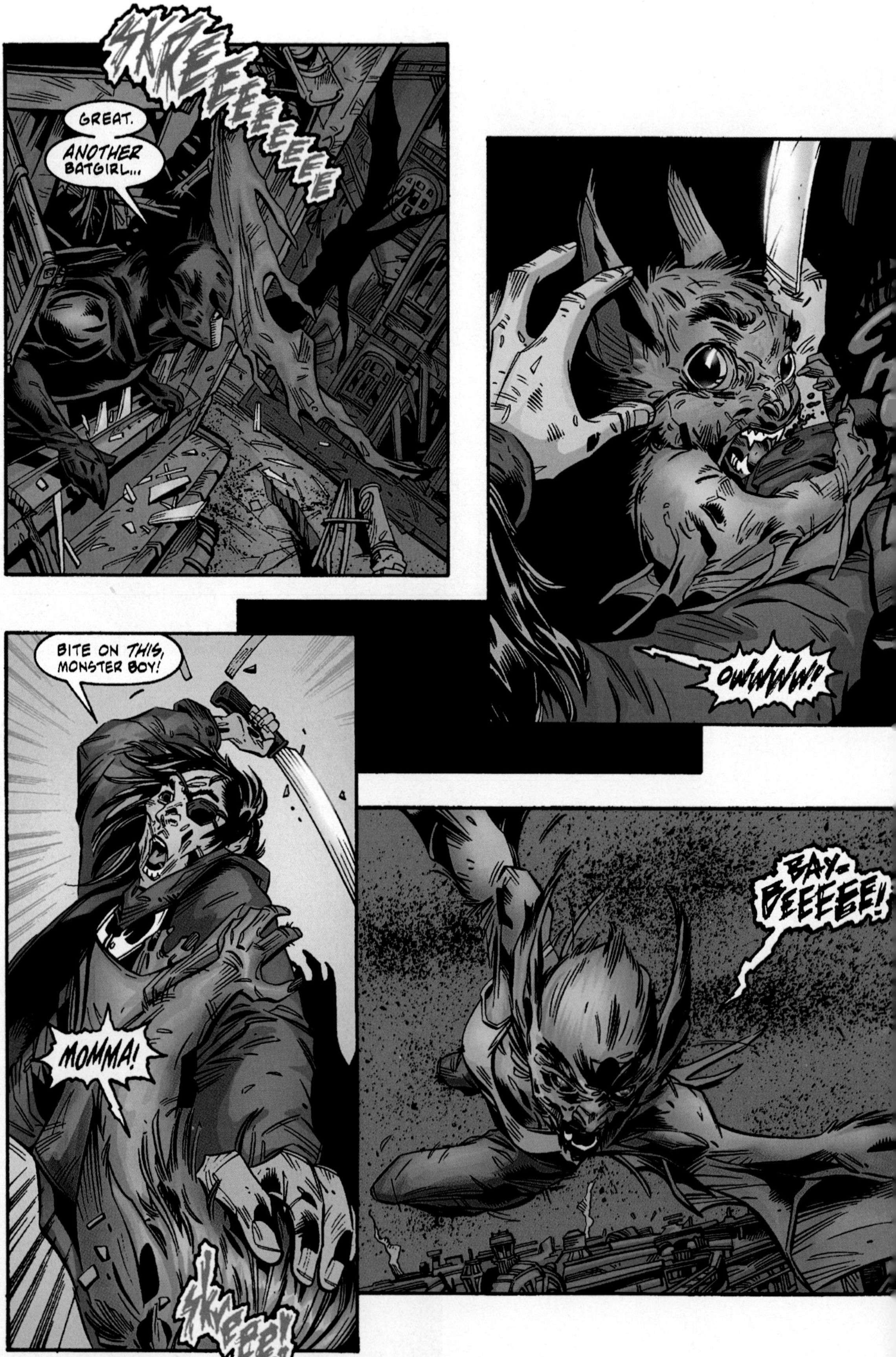
SKREEEEEEEEE
GREAT.
ANOTHER BATGIRL...
OWWWW!
BITE ON THIS, MONSTER BOY!
MOMMA!
SKREEE!
BAY-BEEEEEE!

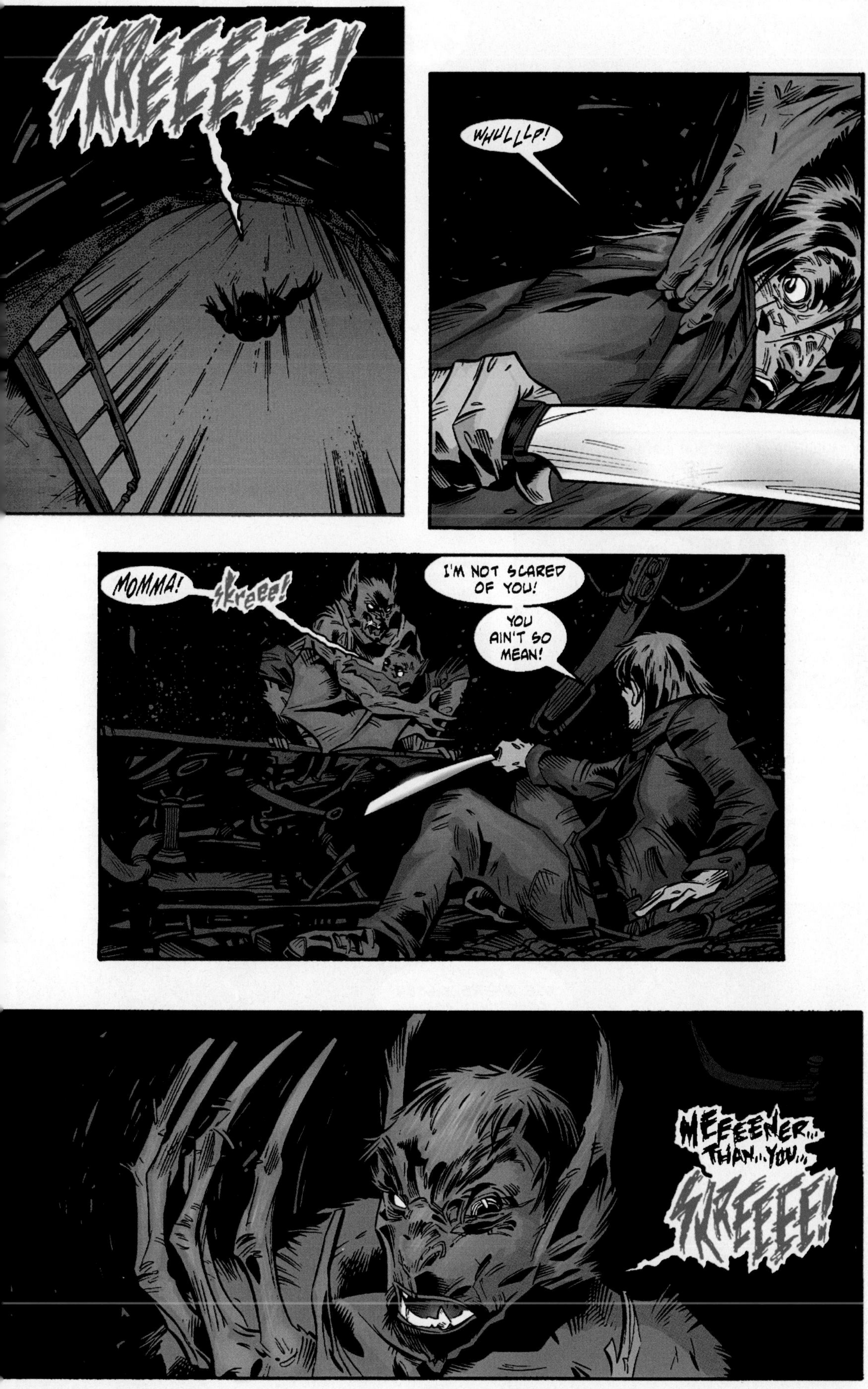
SKREEEEEE!
WHULLLP!
MOMMA!
skreee!
I'M NOT SCARED OF YOU!
YOU AIN'T SO MEAN!
MEEEENER... THAN... YOU...
SKREEEE!

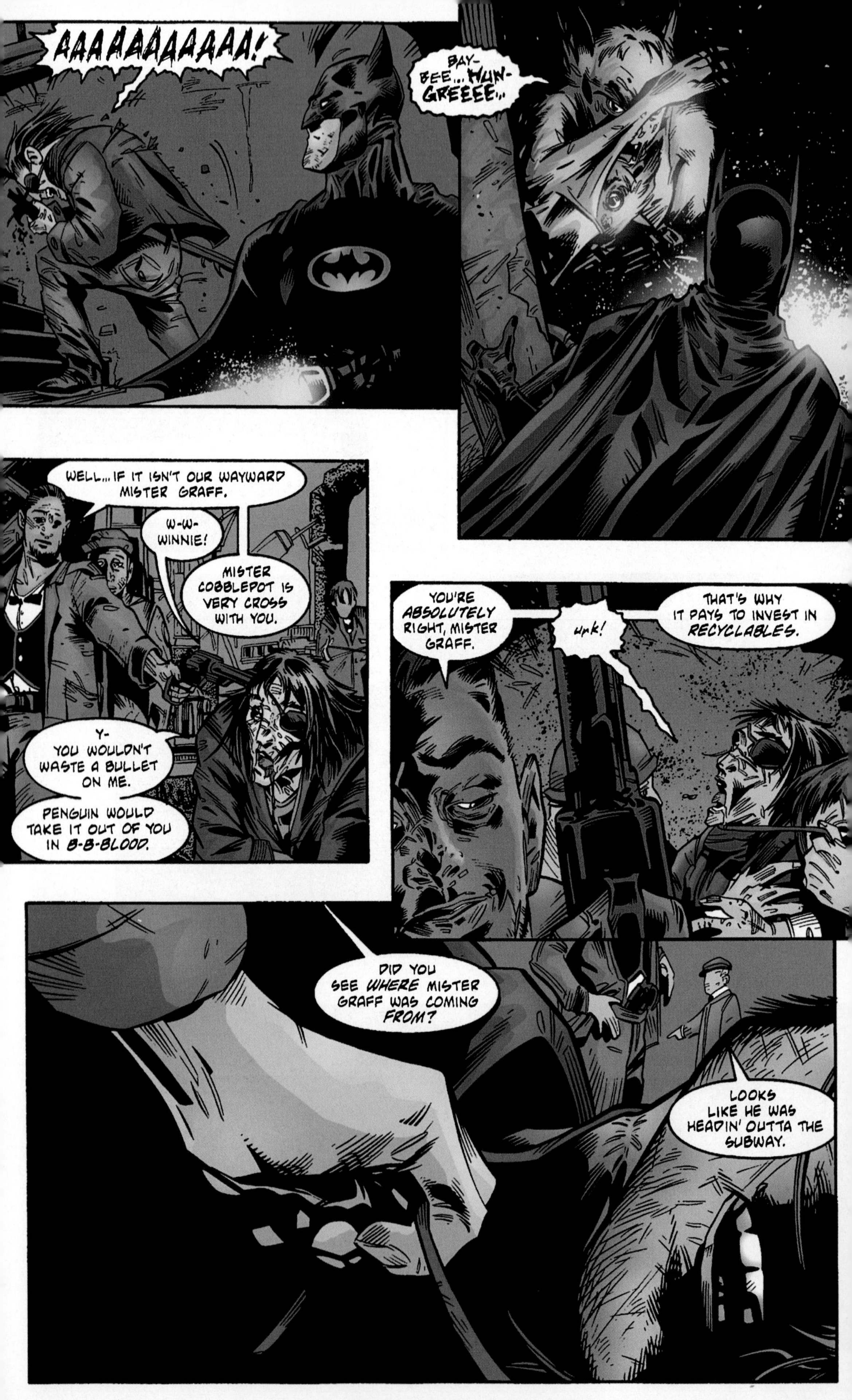
AAAAAAAAAAA!
BAY-BEE... HUN-GREEEE...
WELL... IF IT ISN'T OUR WAYWARD MISTER GRAFF.
W-W-WINNIE!
MISTER COBBLEPOT IS VERY CROSS WITH YOU.
Y-YOU WOULDN'T WASTE A BULLET ON ME.
PENGUIN WOULD TAKE IT OUT OF YOU IN B-B-BLOOD.
YOU'RE ABSOLUTELY RIGHT, MISTER GRAFF.
unk!
THAT'S WHY IT PAYS TO INVEST IN RECYCLABLES.
DID YOU SEE WHERE MISTER GRAFF WAS COMING FROM?
LOOKS LIKE HE WAS HEADIN' OUTTA THE SUBWAY.

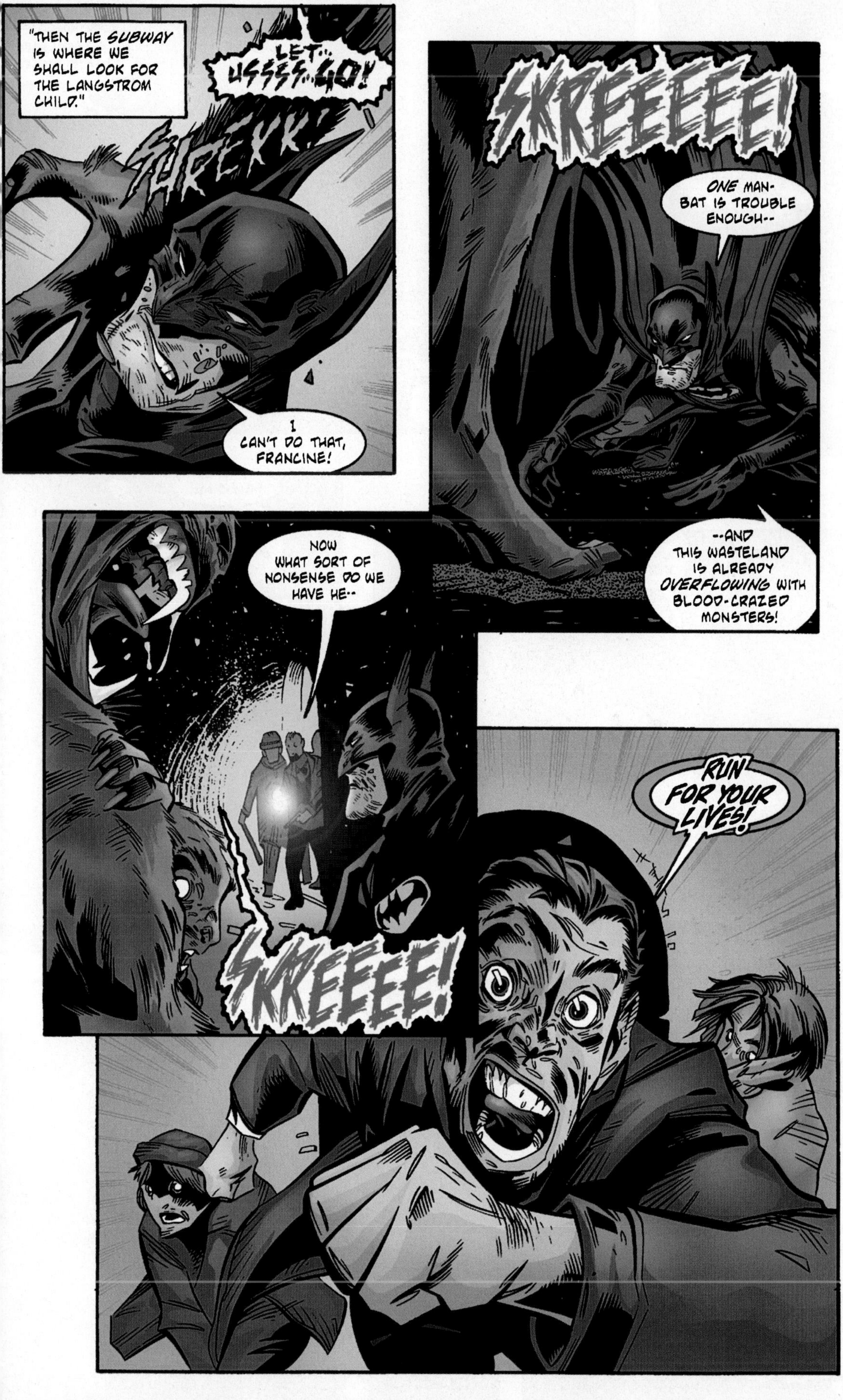
"THEN THE *SUBWAY* IS WHERE WE SHALL LOOK FOR THE LANGSTROM CHILD."
LET... USSSS... GO!
I CAN'T DO THAT, FRANCINE!
SKREEEEEE!
ONE MAN-BAT IS TROUBLE ENOUGH--
--AND THIS WASTELAND IS ALREADY *OVERFLOWING* WITH BLOOD-CRAZED MONSTERS!
NOW WHAT SORT OF NONSENSE DO WE HAVE HE--
SKREEEEE!
RUN FOR YOUR LIVES!

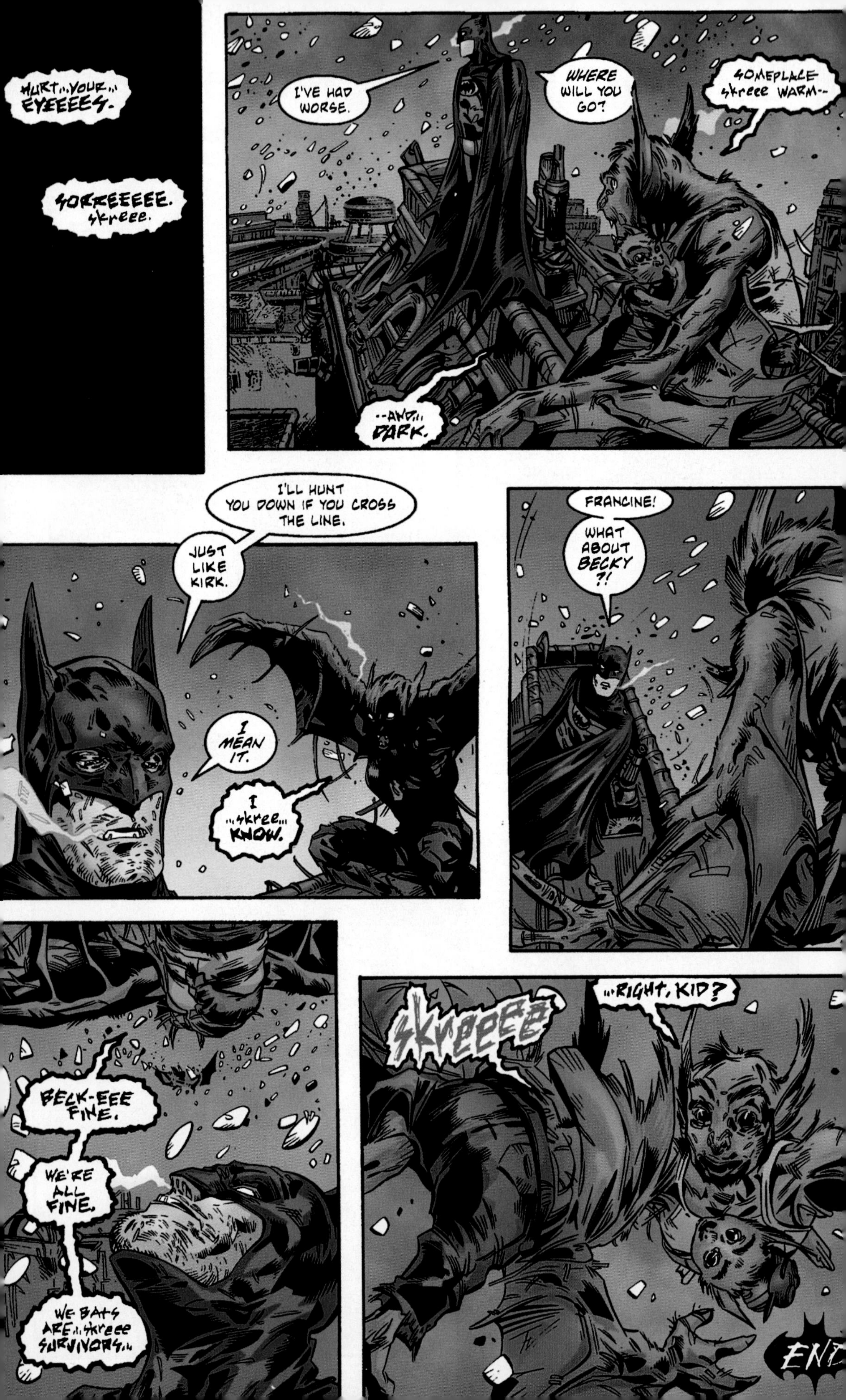
HURT...YOUR... EYEEEES.
SORREEEEE. skreee.
I'VE HAD WORSE.
WHERE WILL YOU GO?
SOMEPLACE skreee WARM--
--AND... DARK.
I'LL HUNT YOU DOWN IF YOU CROSS THE LINE.
JUST LIKE KIRK.
I MEAN IT.
I ...skree... KNOW.
FRANCINE!
WHAT ABOUT BECKY ?!
BECK-EEE FINE.
WE'RE ALL FINE.
WE BATS ARE...skree SURVIVORS...
SKREEEE
...RIGHT, KID?
END

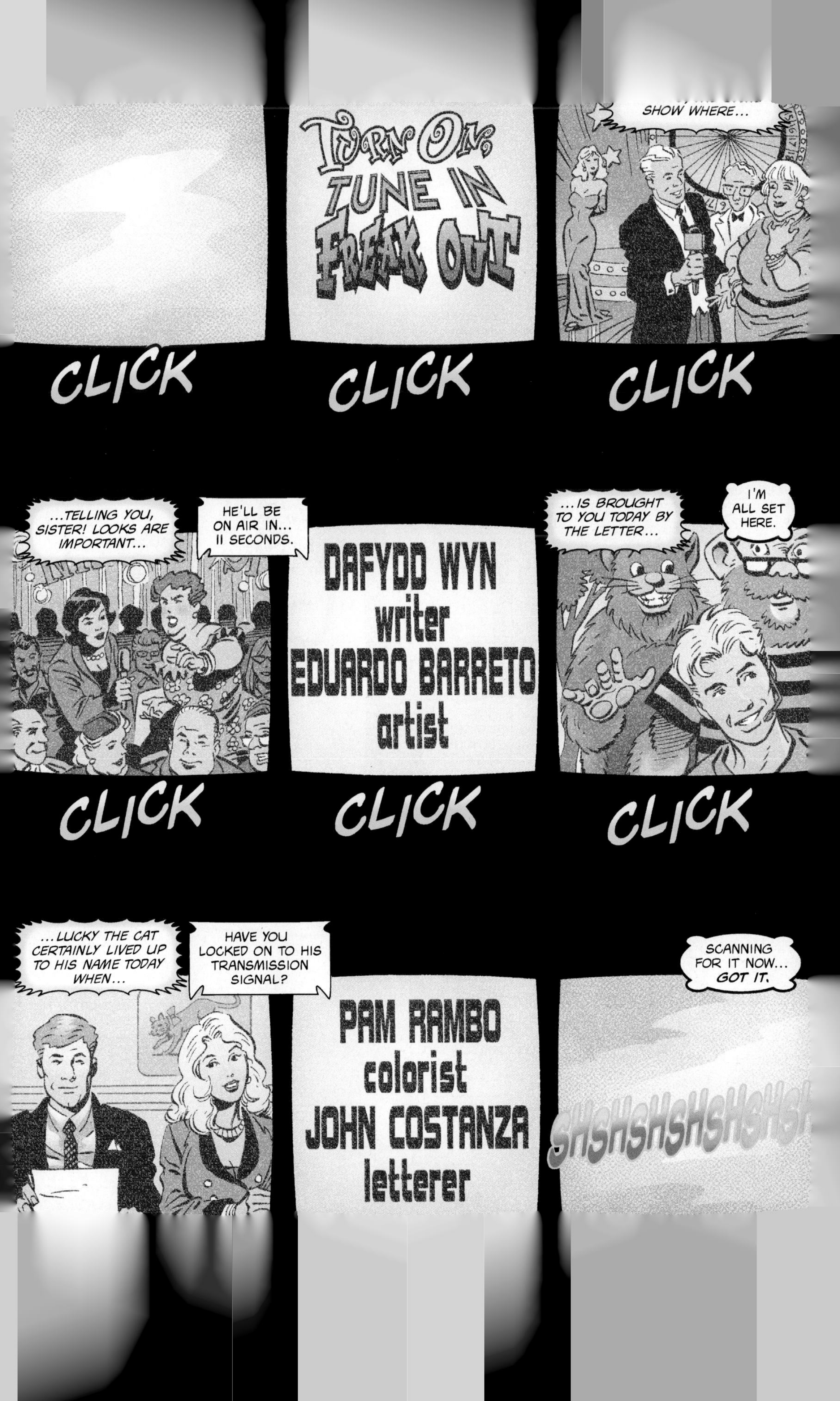

TURN ON, TUNE IN FREAK OUT
SHOW WHERE...
CLICK
CLICK
CLICK
...TELLING YOU, SISTER! LOOKS ARE IMPORTANT...
HE'LL BE ON AIR IN... 11 SECONDS.
DAFYDD WYN writer EDUARDO BARRETO artist
...IS BROUGHT TO YOU TODAY BY THE LETTER...
I'M ALL SET HERE.
CLICK
CLICK
CLICK
...LUCKY THE CAT CERTAINLY LIVED UP TO HIS NAME TODAY WHEN...
HAVE YOU LOCKED ON TO HIS TRANSMISSION SIGNAL?
PAM RAMBO colorist JOHN COSTANZA letterer
SCANNING FOR IT NOW... GOT IT.
SHSHSHSHSHSHSH

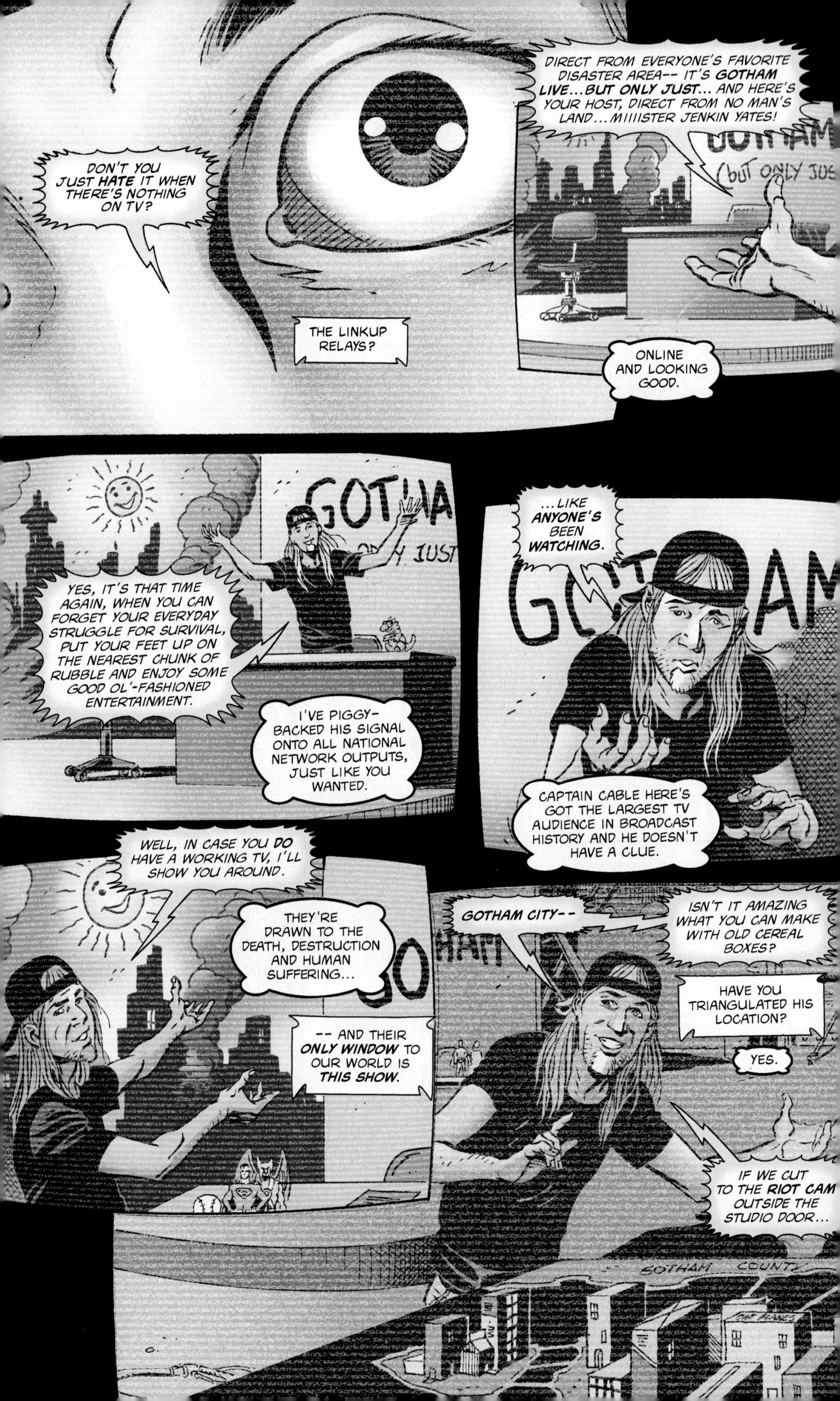

DON'T YOU JUST HATE IT WHEN THERE'S NOTHING ON TV?
DIRECT FROM EVERYONE'S FAVORITE DISASTER AREA-- IT'S GOTHAM LIVE...BUT ONLY JUST... AND HERE'S YOUR HOST, DIRECT FROM NO MAN'S LAND... MIIIISTER JENKIN YATES!
THE LINKUP RELAYS?
ONLINE AND LOOKING GOOD.
YES, IT'S THAT TIME AGAIN, WHEN YOU CAN FORGET YOUR EVERYDAY STRUGGLE FOR SURVIVAL, PUT YOUR FEET UP ON THE NEAREST CHUNK OF RUBBLE AND ENJOY SOME GOOD OL'-FASHIONED ENTERTAINMENT.
I'VE PIGGY-BACKED HIS SIGNAL ONTO ALL NATIONAL NETWORK OUTPUTS, JUST LIKE YOU WANTED.
...LIKE ANYONE'S BEEN WATCHING.
CAPTAIN CABLE HERE'S GOT THE LARGEST TV AUDIENCE IN BROADCAST HISTORY AND HE DOESN'T HAVE A CLUE.
WELL, IN CASE YOU DO HAVE A WORKING TV, I'LL SHOW YOU AROUND.
THEY'RE DRAWN TO THE DEATH, DESTRUCTION AND HUMAN SUFFERING...
-- AND THEIR ONLY WINDOW TO OUR WORLD IS THIS SHOW.
GOTHAM CITY--
ISN'T IT AMAZING WHAT YOU CAN MAKE WITH OLD CEREAL BOXES?
HAVE YOU TRIANGULATED HIS LOCATION?
YES.
IF WE CUT TO THE RIOT CAM OUTSIDE THE STUDIO DOOR...

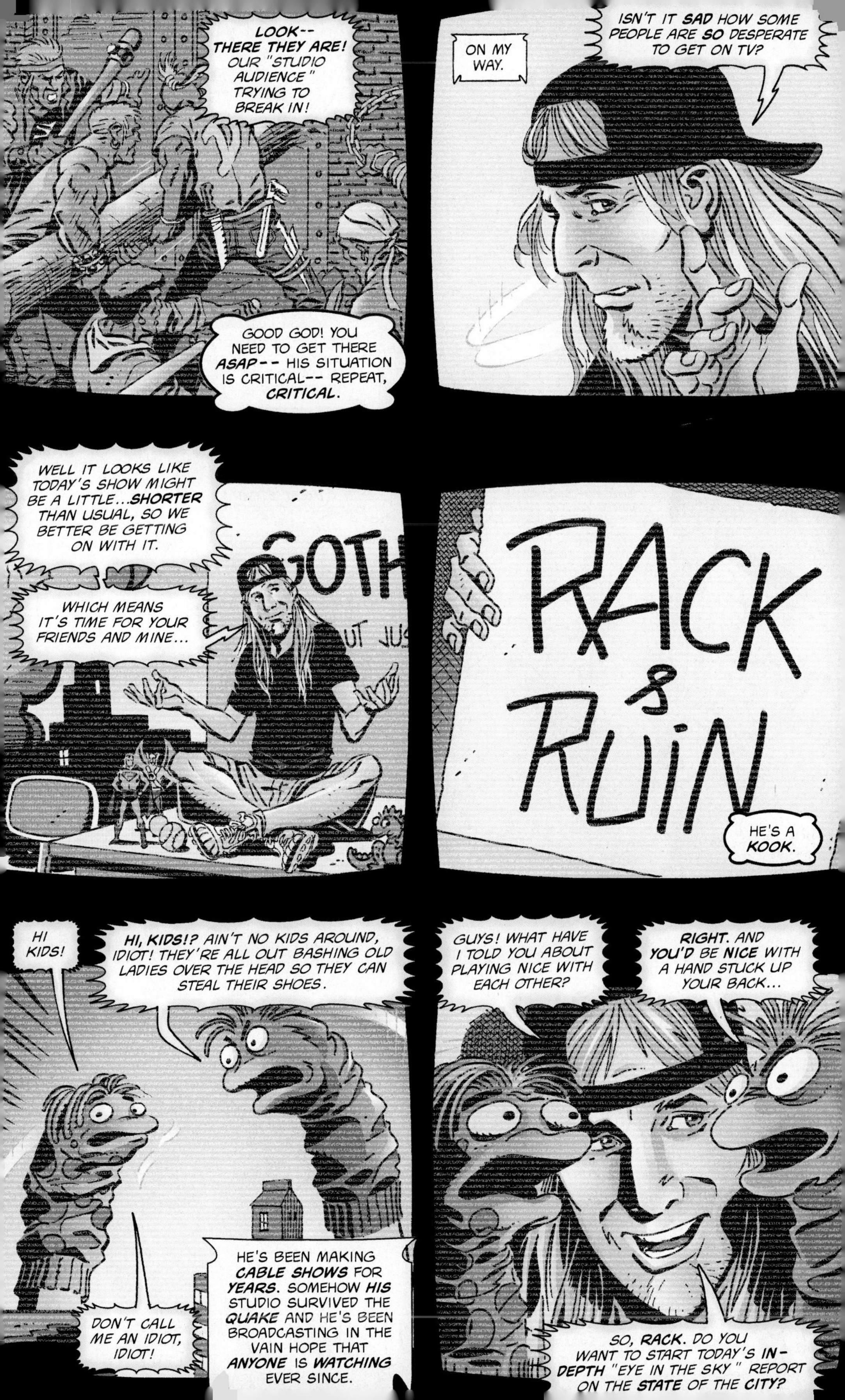
LOOK-- THERE THEY ARE! OUR "STUDIO AUDIENCE" TRYING TO BREAK IN!
GOOD GOD! YOU NEED TO GET THERE ASAP-- HIS SITUATION IS CRITICAL-- REPEAT, CRITICAL.
ON MY WAY.
ISN'T IT SAD HOW SOME PEOPLE ARE SO DESPERATE TO GET ON TV?
WELL IT LOOKS LIKE TODAY'S SHOW MIGHT BE A LITTLE...SHORTER THAN USUAL, SO WE BETTER BE GETTING ON WITH IT.
WHICH MEANS IT'S TIME FOR YOUR FRIENDS AND MINE...
RACK & RUIN
HE'S A KOOK.
HI KIDS!
HI, KIDS!? AIN'T NO KIDS AROUND, IDIOT! THEY'RE ALL OUT BASHING OLD LADIES OVER THE HEAD SO THEY CAN STEAL THEIR SHOES.
DON'T CALL ME AN IDIOT, IDIOT!
HE'S BEEN MAKING CABLE SHOWS FOR YEARS. SOMEHOW HIS STUDIO SURVIVED THE QUAKE AND HE'S BEEN BROADCASTING IN THE VAIN HOPE THAT ANYONE IS WATCHING EVER SINCE.
GUYS! WHAT HAVE I TOLD YOU ABOUT PLAYING NICE WITH EACH OTHER?
RIGHT. AND YOU'D BE NICE WITH A HAND STUCK UP YOUR BACK...
SO, RACK. DO YOU WANT TO START TODAY'S IN-DEPTH "EYE IN THE SKY" REPORT ON THE STATE OF THE CITY?

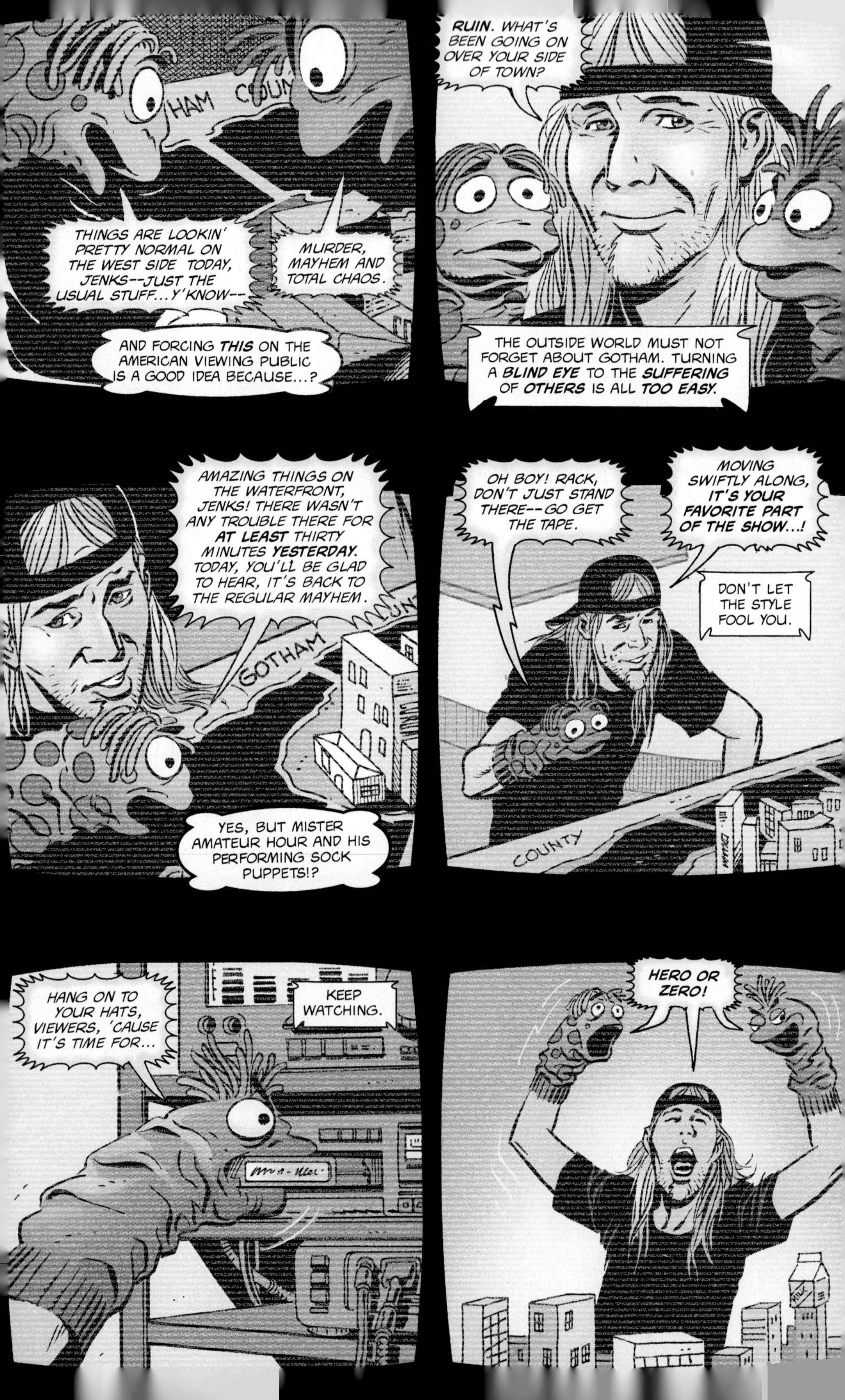
THINGS ARE LOOKIN' PRETTY NORMAL ON THE WEST SIDE TODAY, JENKS--JUST THE USUAL STUFF...Y'KNOW--
MURDER, MAYHEM AND TOTAL CHAOS.
AND FORCING **THIS** ON THE AMERICAN VIEWING PUBLIC IS A GOOD IDEA BECAUSE...?
RUIN. WHAT'S BEEN GOING ON OVER YOUR SIDE OF TOWN?
THE OUTSIDE WORLD MUST NOT FORGET ABOUT GOTHAM. TURNING A **BLIND EYE** TO THE **SUFFERING** OF **OTHERS** IS ALL **TOO EASY.**
AMAZING THINGS ON THE WATERFRONT, JENKS! THERE WASN'T ANY TROUBLE THERE FOR **AT LEAST** THIRTY MINUTES **YESTERDAY**. TODAY, YOU'LL BE GLAD TO HEAR, IT'S BACK TO THE REGULAR MAYHEM.
GOTHAM
YES, BUT MISTER AMATEUR HOUR AND HIS PERFORMING SOCK PUPPETS!?
OH BOY! RACK, DON'T JUST STAND THERE--GO GET THE TAPE.
MOVING SWIFTLY ALONG, **IT'S YOUR FAVORITE PART OF THE SHOW...!**
DON'T LET THE STYLE FOOL YOU.
COUNTY
HANG ON TO YOUR HATS, VIEWERS, 'CAUSE IT'S TIME FOR...
KEEP WATCHING.
HERO OR ZERO!

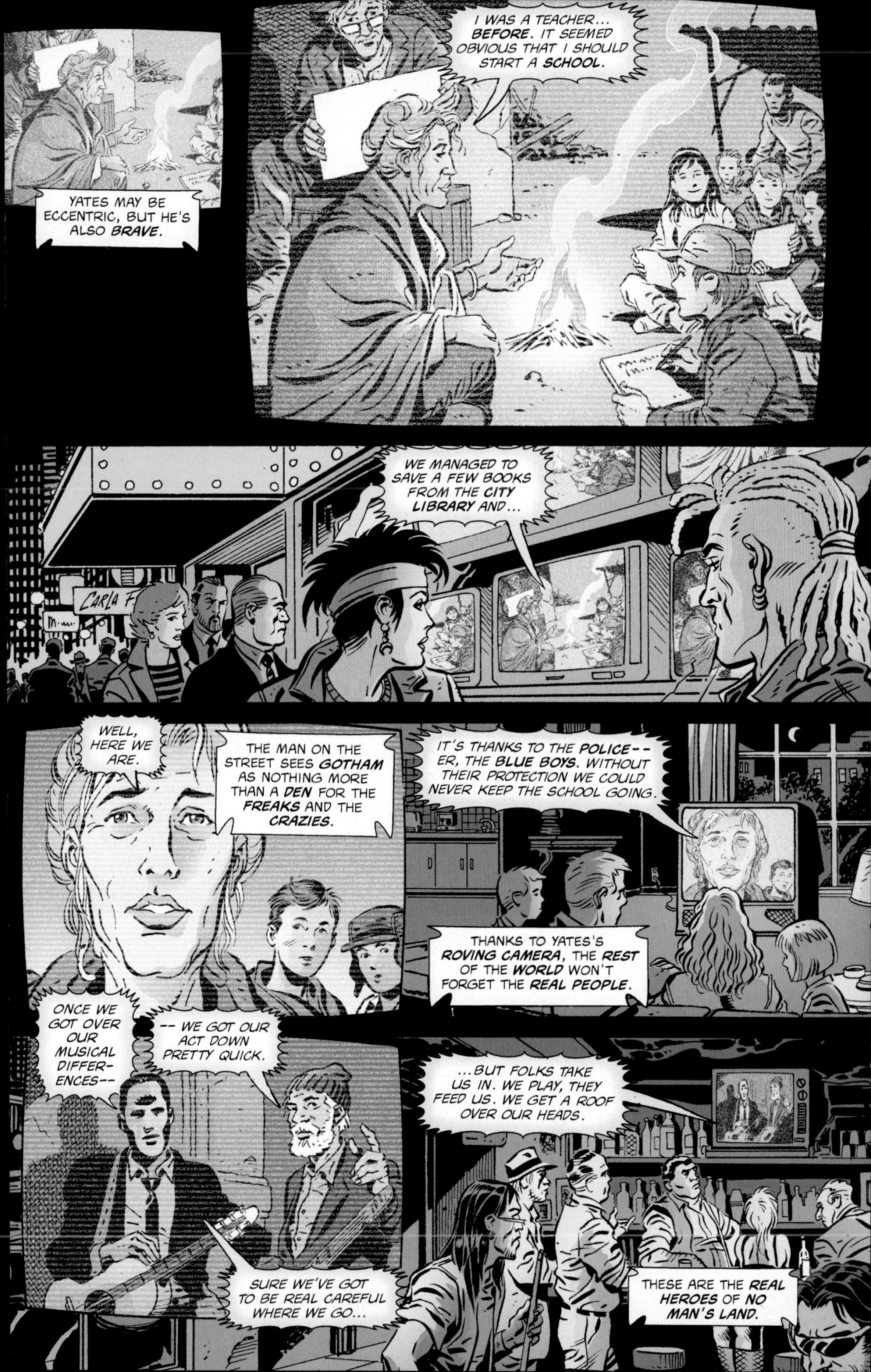

YATES MAY BE ECCENTRIC, BUT HE'S ALSO BRAVE.
I WAS A TEACHER... BEFORE. IT SEEMED OBVIOUS THAT I SHOULD START A SCHOOL.
WE MANAGED TO SAVE A FEW BOOKS FROM THE CITY LIBRARY AND...
CARLA F
WELL, HERE WE ARE.
THE MAN ON THE STREET SEES GOTHAM AS NOTHING MORE THAN A DEN FOR THE FREAKS AND THE CRAZIES.
IT'S THANKS TO THE POLICE-- ER, THE BLUE BOYS. WITHOUT THEIR PROTECTION WE COULD NEVER KEEP THE SCHOOL GOING.
THANKS TO YATES'S ROVING CAMERA, THE REST OF THE WORLD WON'T FORGET THE REAL PEOPLE.
ONCE WE GOT OVER OUR MUSICAL DIFFER-ENCES--
-- WE GOT OUR ACT DOWN PRETTY QUICK.
SURE WE'VE GOT TO BE REAL CAREFUL WHERE WE GO...
...BUT FOLKS TAKE US IN. WE PLAY, THEY FEED US. WE GET A ROOF OVER OUR HEADS.
THESE ARE THE REAL HEROES OF NO MAN'S LAND.

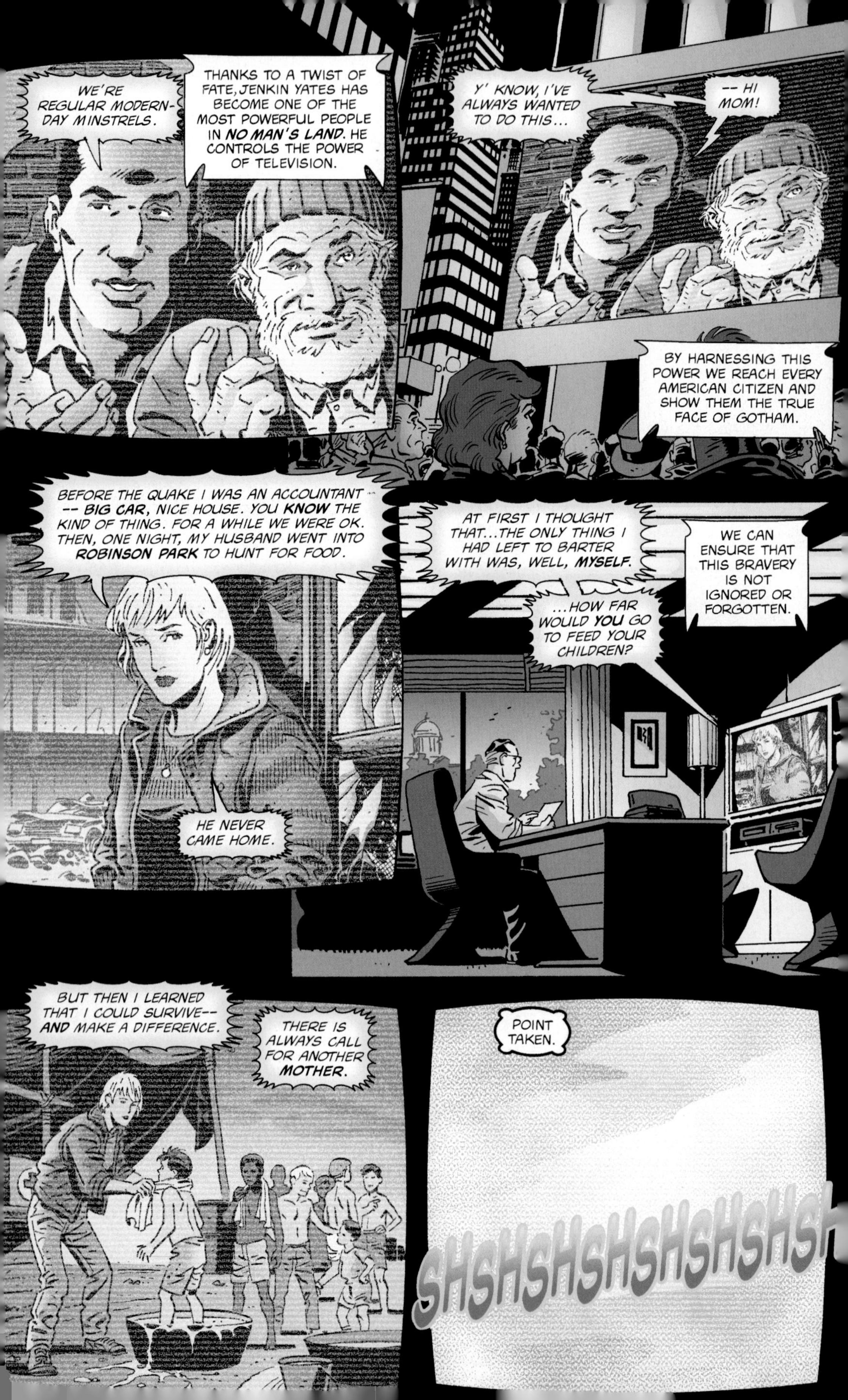
WE'RE REGULAR MODERN-DAY MINSTRELS.
THANKS TO A TWIST OF FATE, JENKIN YATES HAS BECOME ONE OF THE MOST POWERFUL PEOPLE IN NO MAN'S LAND. HE CONTROLS THE POWER OF TELEVISION.
Y' KNOW, I'VE ALWAYS WANTED TO DO THIS...
-- HI MOM!
BY HARNESSING THIS POWER WE REACH EVERY AMERICAN CITIZEN AND SHOW THEM THE TRUE FACE OF GOTHAM.
BEFORE THE QUAKE I WAS AN ACCOUNTANT -- BIG CAR, NICE HOUSE. YOU KNOW THE KIND OF THING. FOR A WHILE WE WERE OK. THEN, ONE NIGHT, MY HUSBAND WENT INTO ROBINSON PARK TO HUNT FOR FOOD.
HE NEVER CAME HOME.
AT FIRST I THOUGHT THAT...THE ONLY THING I HAD LEFT TO BARTER WITH WAS, WELL, MYSELF.
...HOW FAR WOULD YOU GO TO FEED YOUR CHILDREN?
WE CAN ENSURE THAT THIS BRAVERY IS NOT IGNORED OR FORGOTTEN.
BUT THEN I LEARNED THAT I COULD SURVIVE-- AND MAKE A DIFFERENCE.
THERE IS ALWAYS CALL FOR ANOTHER MOTHER.
POINT TAKEN.
SHSHSHSHSHSHSHSHSH

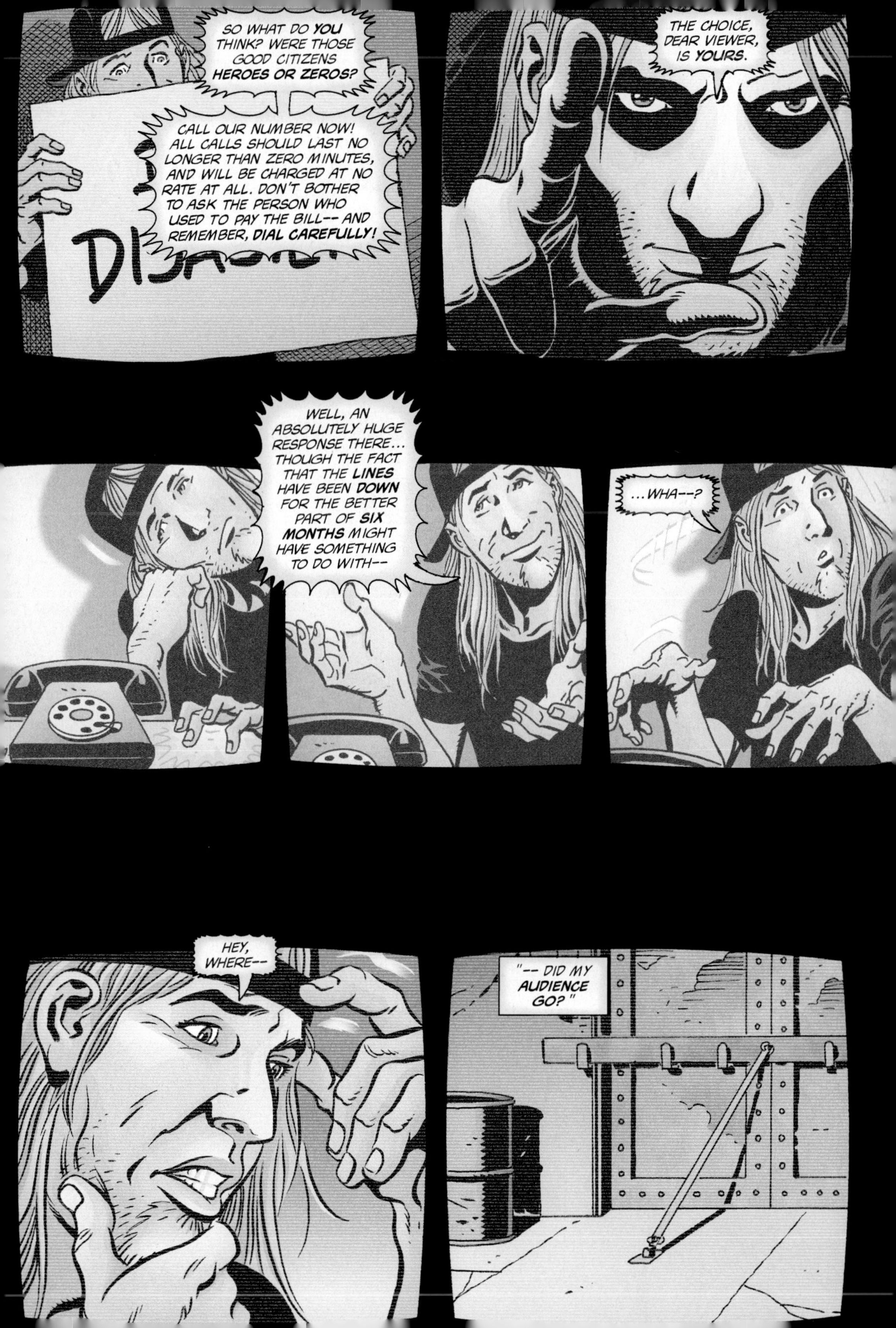
SO WHAT DO YOU THINK? WERE THOSE GOOD CITIZENS HEROES OR ZEROS?
CALL OUR NUMBER NOW! ALL CALLS SHOULD LAST NO LONGER THAN ZERO MINUTES, AND WILL BE CHARGED AT NO RATE AT ALL. DON'T BOTHER TO ASK THE PERSON WHO USED TO PAY THE BILL-- AND REMEMBER, DIAL CAREFULLY!
THE CHOICE, DEAR VIEWER, IS YOURS.
WELL, AN ABSOLUTELY HUGE RESPONSE THERE... THOUGH THE FACT THAT THE LINES HAVE BEEN DOWN FOR THE BETTER PART OF SIX MONTHS MIGHT HAVE SOMETHING TO DO WITH--
...WHA--?
HEY, WHERE--
"-- DID MY AUDIENCE GO?"

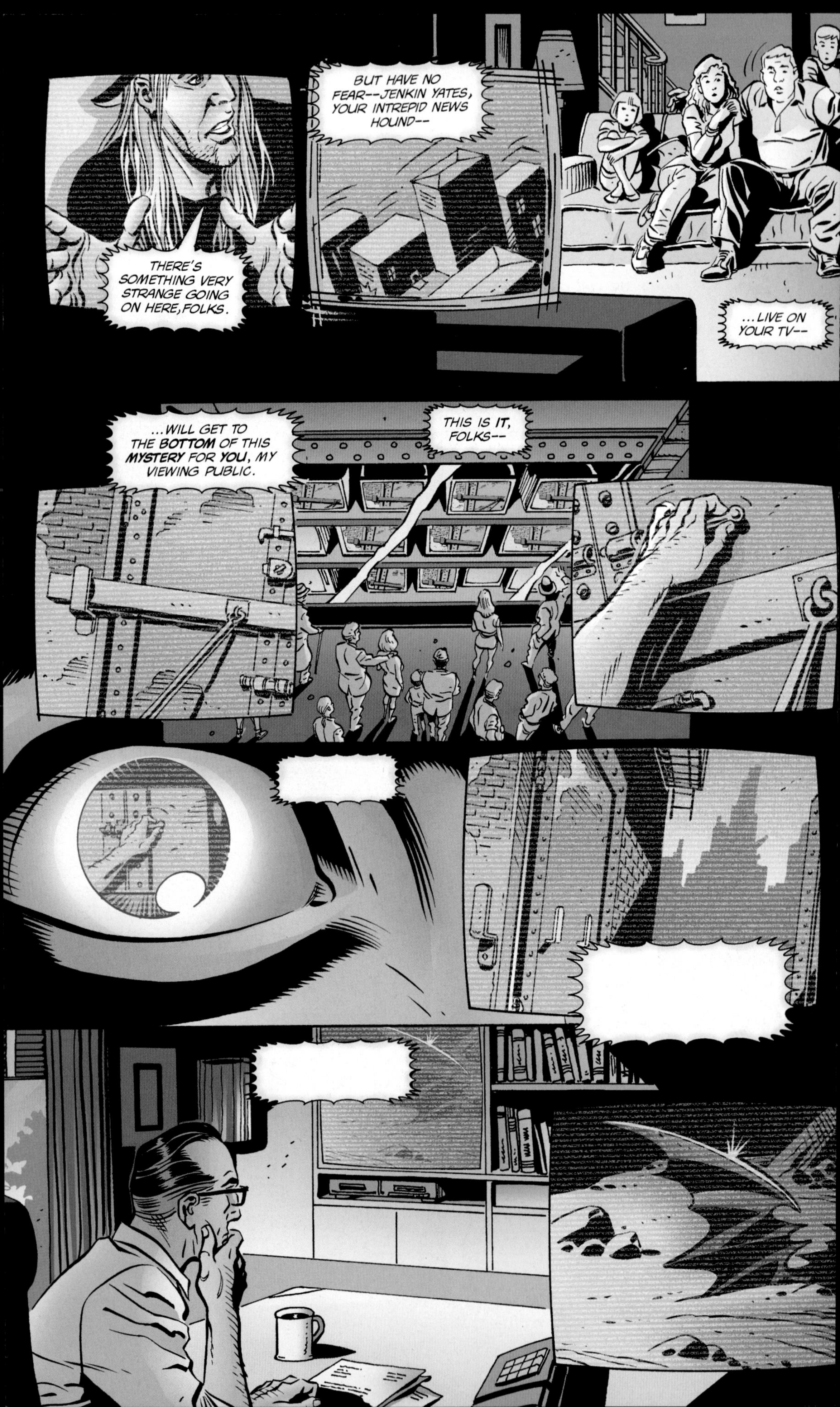
THERE'S SOMETHING VERY STRANGE GOING ON HERE, FOLKS.
BUT HAVE NO FEAR--JENKIN YATES, YOUR INTREPID NEWS HOUND--
...LIVE ON YOUR TV--
...WILL GET TO THE **BOTTOM** OF THIS **MYSTERY** FOR **YOU**, MY VIEWING PUBLIC.
THIS IS **IT**, FOLKS--

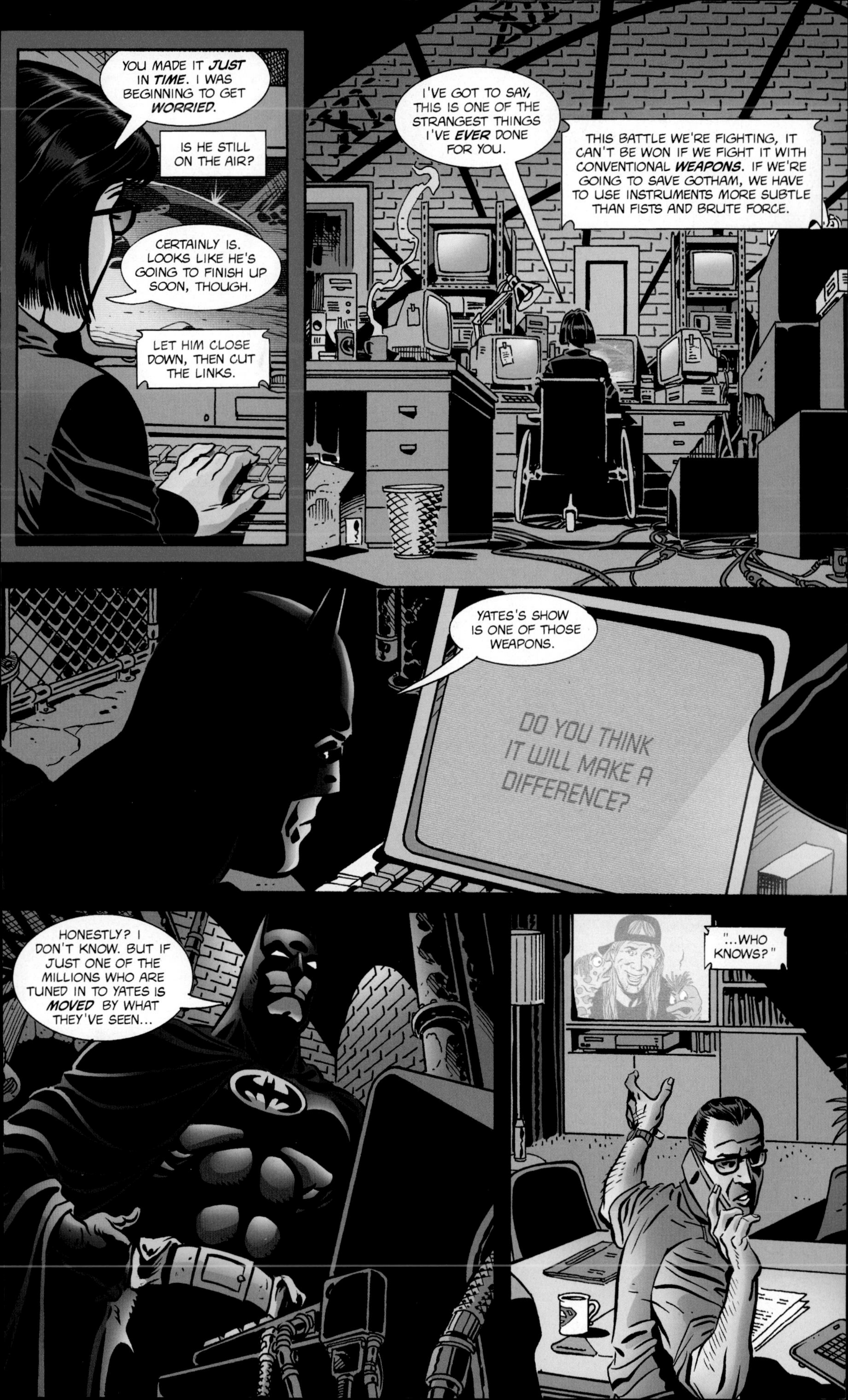

YOU MADE IT JUST IN TIME. I WAS BEGINNING TO GET WORRIED.
IS HE STILL ON THE AIR?
CERTAINLY IS. LOOKS LIKE HE'S GOING TO FINISH UP SOON, THOUGH.
LET HIM CLOSE DOWN, THEN CUT THE LINKS.
I'VE GOT TO SAY, THIS IS ONE OF THE STRANGEST THINGS I'VE EVER DONE FOR YOU.
THIS BATTLE WE'RE FIGHTING, IT CAN'T BE WON IF WE FIGHT IT WITH CONVENTIONAL WEAPONS. IF WE'RE GOING TO SAVE GOTHAM, WE HAVE TO USE INSTRUMENTS MORE SUBTLE THAN FISTS AND BRUTE FORCE.
YATES'S SHOW IS ONE OF THOSE WEAPONS.
DO YOU THINK IT WILL MAKE A DIFFERENCE?
HONESTLY? I DON'T KNOW. BUT IF JUST ONE OF THE MILLIONS WHO ARE TUNED IN TO YATES IS MOVED BY WHAT THEY'VE SEEN...
"...WHO KNOWS?"

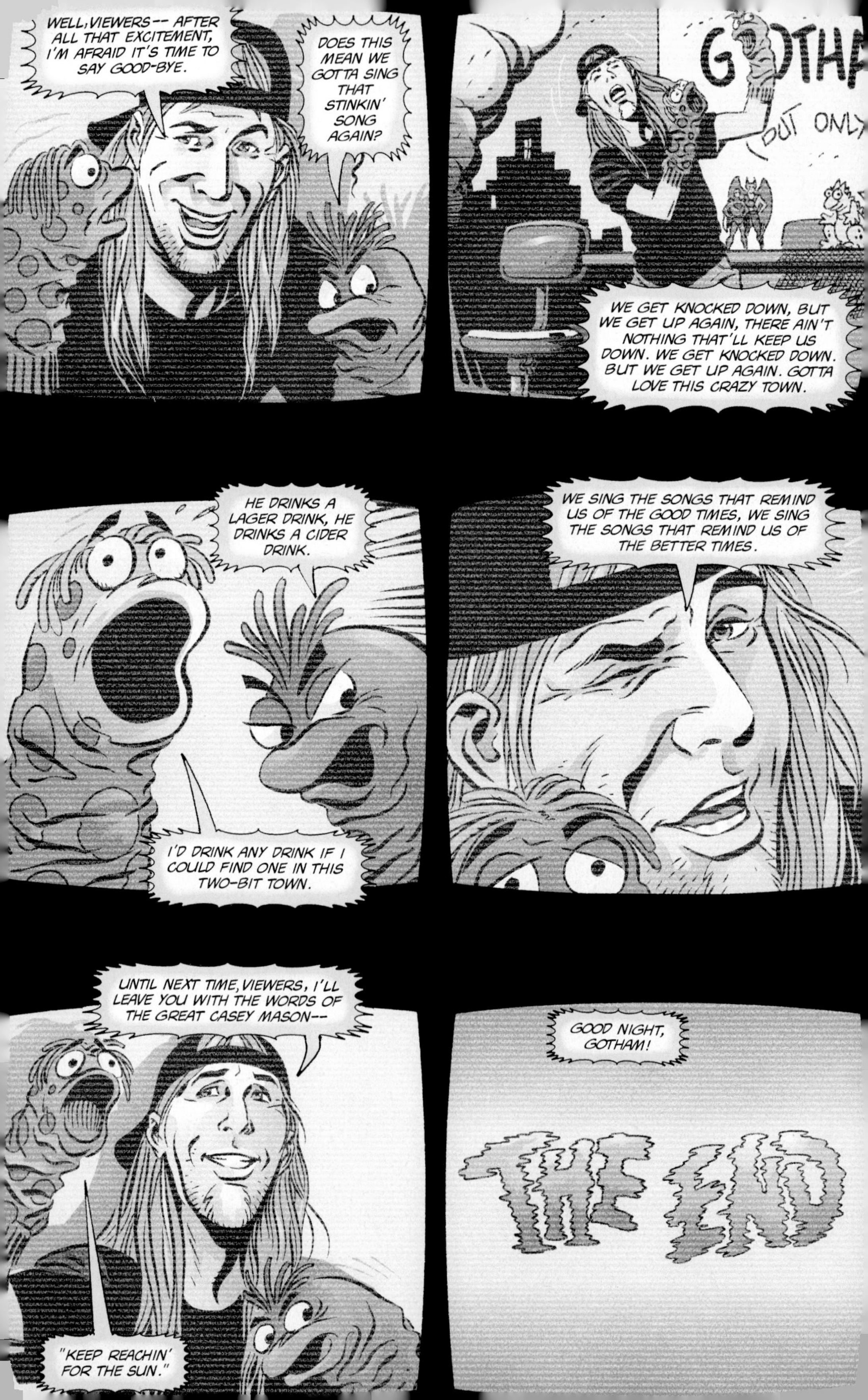
WELL, VIEWERS-- AFTER ALL THAT EXCITEMENT, I'M AFRAID IT'S TIME TO SAY GOOD-BYE.
DOES THIS MEAN WE GOTTA SING THAT STINKIN' SONG AGAIN?
GOTHA
(OUT ONLY
WE GET KNOCKED DOWN, BUT WE GET UP AGAIN, THERE AIN'T NOTHING THAT'LL KEEP US DOWN. WE GET KNOCKED DOWN. BUT WE GET UP AGAIN. GOTTA LOVE THIS CRAZY TOWN.
HE DRINKS A LAGER DRINK, HE DRINKS A CIDER DRINK.
I'D DRINK ANY DRINK IF I COULD FIND ONE IN THIS TWO-BIT TOWN.
WE SING THE SONGS THAT REMIND US OF THE GOOD TIMES, WE SING THE SONGS THAT REMIND US OF THE BETTER TIMES.
UNTIL NEXT TIME, VIEWERS, I'LL LEAVE YOU WITH THE WORDS OF THE GREAT CASEY MASON--
"KEEP REACHIN' FOR THE SUN."
GOOD NIGHT, GOTHAM!
THE END

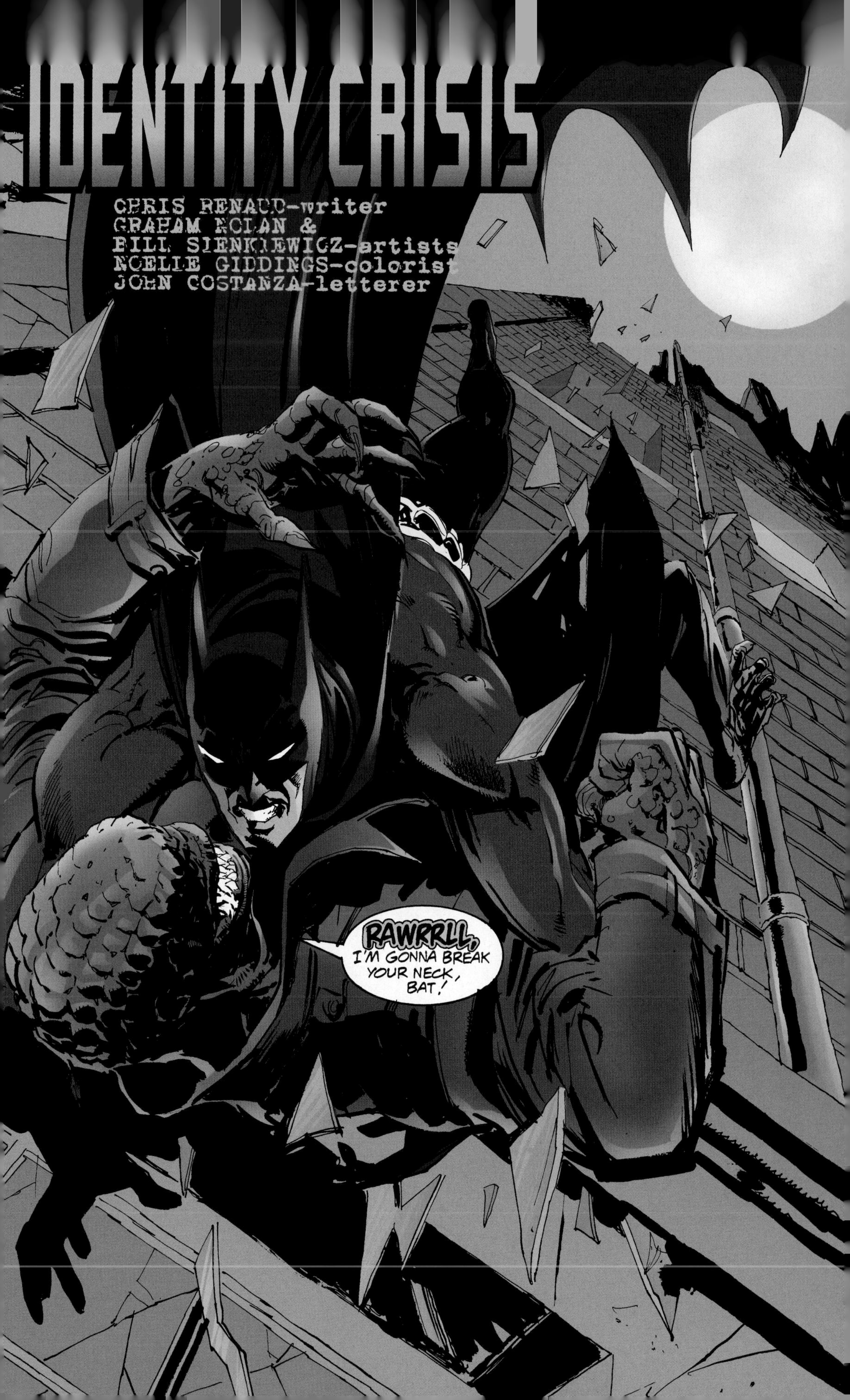
IDENTITY CRISIS
CHRIS RENAUD-writer
GRAHAM NOLAN &
BILL SIENKIEWICZ-artists
NOELLE GIDDINGS-colorist
JOHN COSTANZA-letterer
RAWRRLL, I'M GONNA BREAK YOUR NECK, BAT!

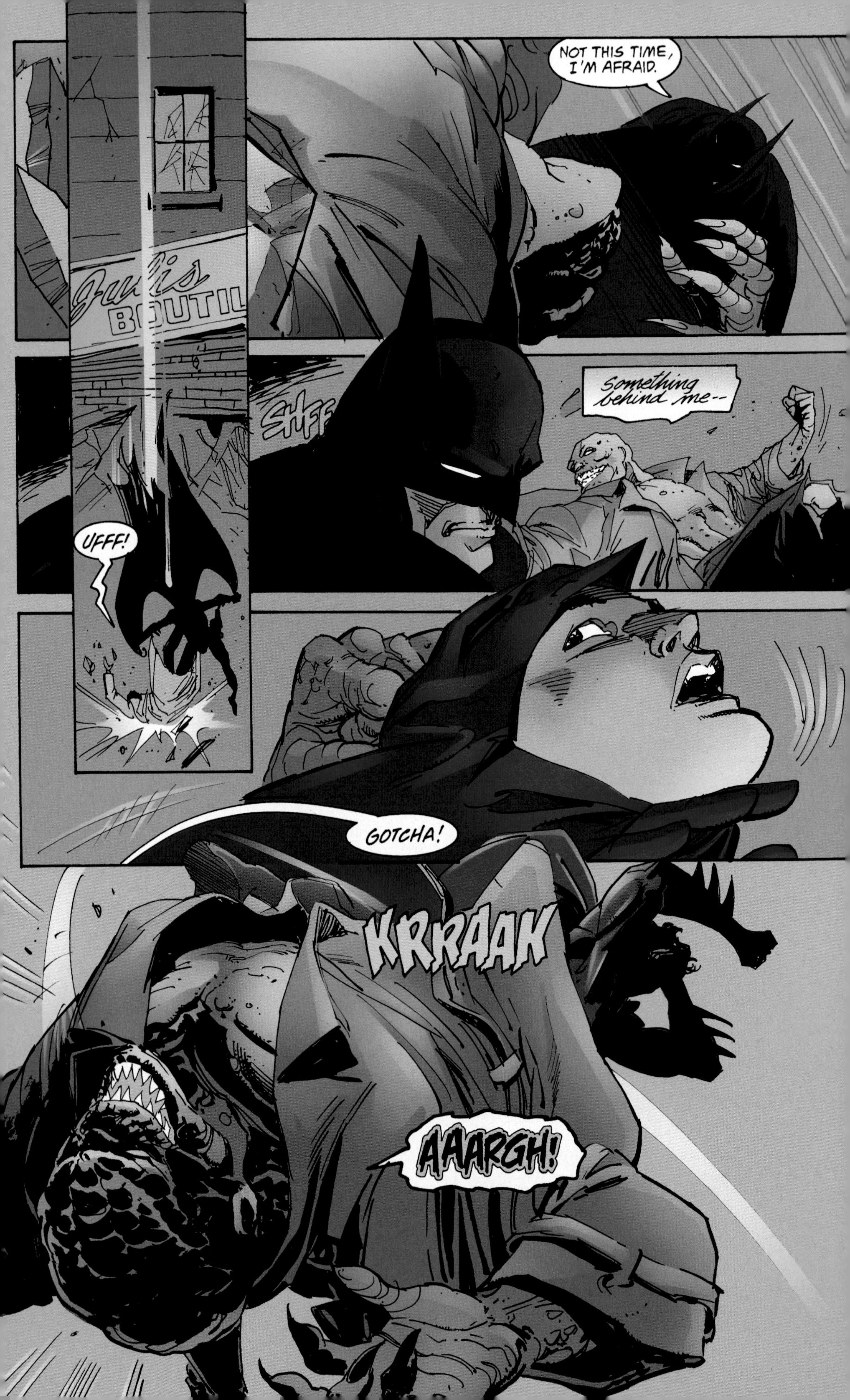
NOT THIS TIME, I'M AFRAID.
Julis
BOUTI
SHFF
something behind me--
UFFF!
GOTCHA!
KRRAAK
AAARGH!

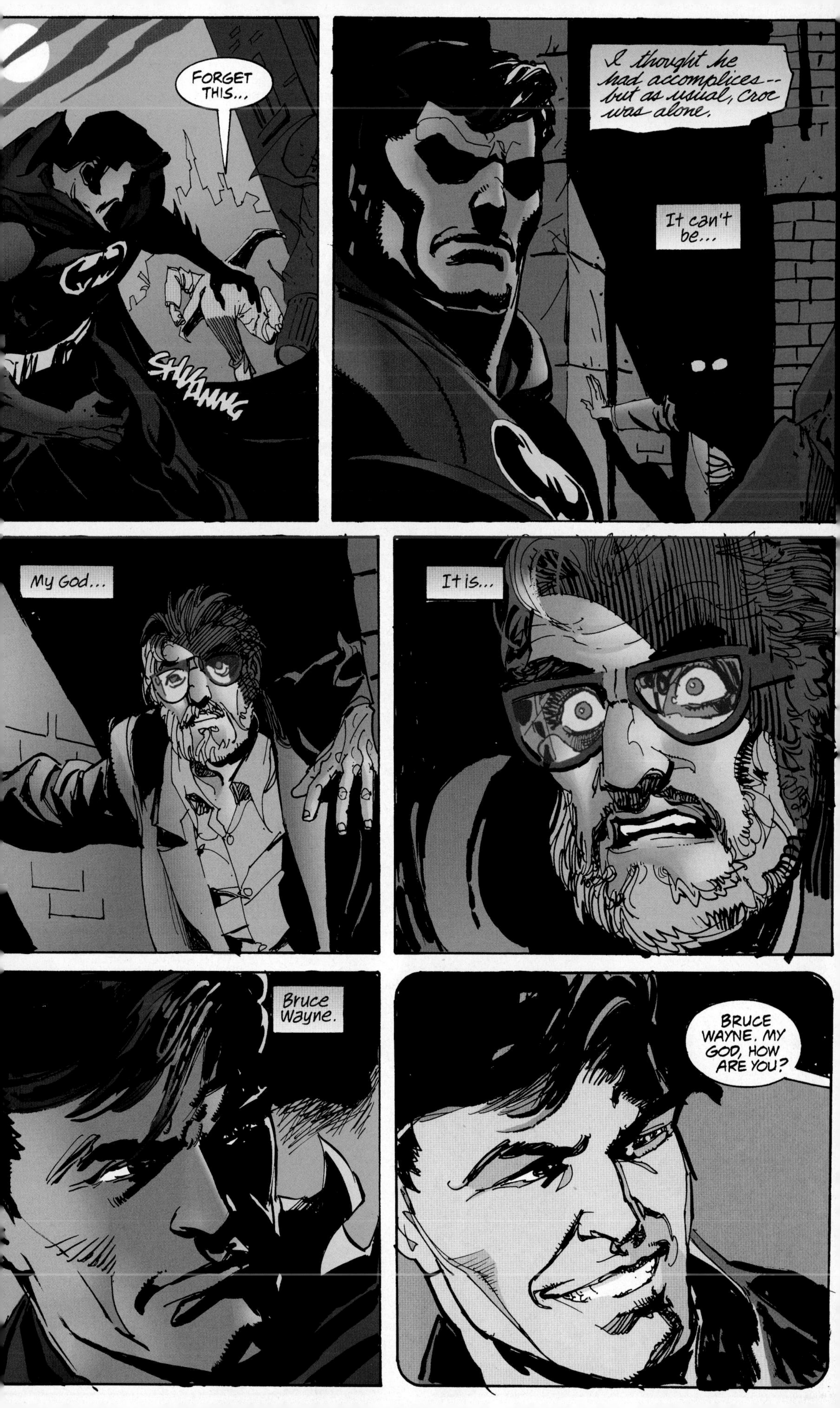
FORGET THIS...
SHVANNG
I thought he had accomplices-- but as usual, Croc was alone.
It can't be...
My God...
It is...
Bruce Wayne.
BRUCE WAYNE. MY GOD, HOW ARE YOU?

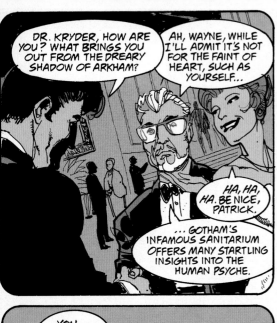

DR. KRYDER, HOW ARE YOU? WHAT BRINGS YOU OUT FROM THE DREARY SHADOW OF ARKHAM?

AH, WAYNE, WHILE I'LL ADMIT IT'S NOT FOR THE FAINT OF HEART, SUCH AS YOURSELF...

HA, HA, HA. BE NICE, PATRICK.

...GOTHAM'S INFAMOUS SANITARIUM OFFERS MANY STARTLING INSIGHTS INTO THE HUMAN PSYCHE.

AS FOR WHY I'M HERE, LAUREN HERE THOUGHT I SHOULD DEVOTE SOME OF MY TIME AND MONEY TO SOMEONE BESIDES THE LOONS IN ARKHAM.

OH, PATRICK...

YOU KNOW, I JUST STARTED WORKING WITH OUR FORMER DISTRICT ATTORNEY. A GOOD FRIEND TO HAVE, ONCE I CURE HIM.

YOU SOUND CONFIDENT.

I'M PUTTING EVERYTHING I HAVE INTO THIS ONE, WAYNE. THERE WOULDN'T BE A PSYCHOLOGY TEXTBOOK IN THE WORLD THAT WON'T TRUMPET MY NAME.

BESIDES, IT'S SIMPLE SCHIZOPHRENIA, ONCE I GET PAST HIS OBSESSIONS, WITH THE NUMBER 2 AND...

"...THE VIGILANTE BATMAN.

"BATMAN...NOW THERE'S A PERSONALITY I WOULDN'T MIND DIGGING INTO. DON'T YOU AGREE, WAYNE?"

I'M SURE IT WOULD BE MOST REVEALING. ANYWAY, GOOD LUCK WITH HARVEY. WHILE I SHARE YOUR ENTHUSIASM FOR MR. DENT'S REDEMPTION, I WOULD BE CAREFUL IF I WERE YOU.

RIGHT, RIGHT... GOOD NIGHT, WAYNE.

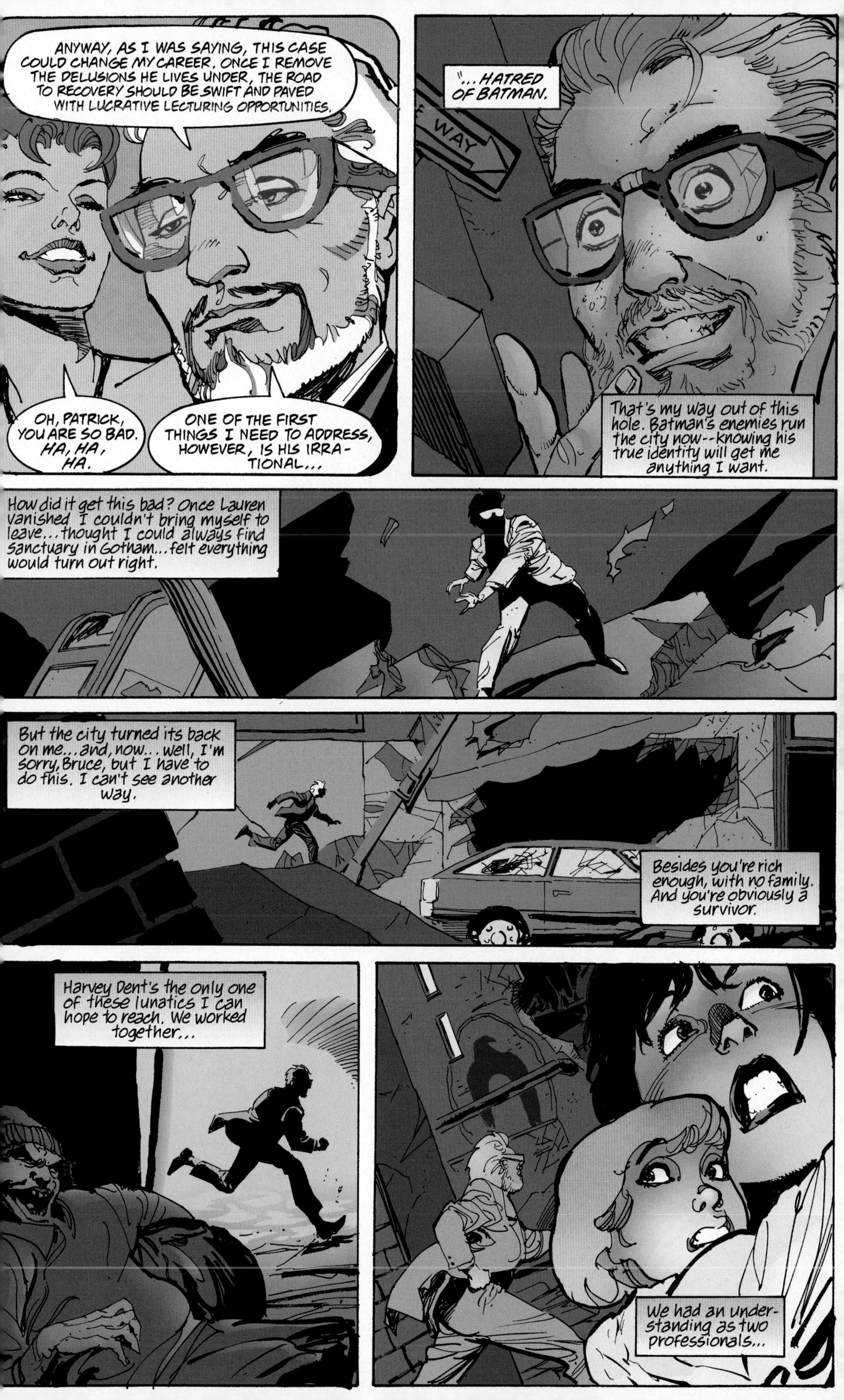
ANYWAY, AS I WAS SAYING, THIS CASE COULD CHANGE MY CAREER. ONCE I REMOVE THE DELUSIONS HE LIVES UNDER, THE ROAD TO RECOVERY SHOULD BE SWIFT AND PAVED WITH LUCRATIVE LECTURING OPPORTUNITIES.
OH, PATRICK, YOU ARE SO BAD. HA, HA, HA.
ONE OF THE FIRST THINGS I NEED TO ADDRESS, HOWEVER, IS HIS IRRA-TIONAL...
"...HATRED OF BATMAN.
WAY
That's my way out of this hole. Batman's enemies run the city now--knowing his true identity will get me anything I want.
How did it get this bad? Once Lauren vanished I couldn't bring myself to leave... thought I could always find sanctuary in Gotham... felt everything would turn out right.
But the city turned its back on me... and, now... well, I'm sorry, Bruce, but I have to do this. I can't see another way.
Besides you're rich enough, with no family. And you're obviously a survivor.
Harvey Dent's the only one of these lunatics I can hope to reach. We worked together...
We had an under-standing as two professionals...

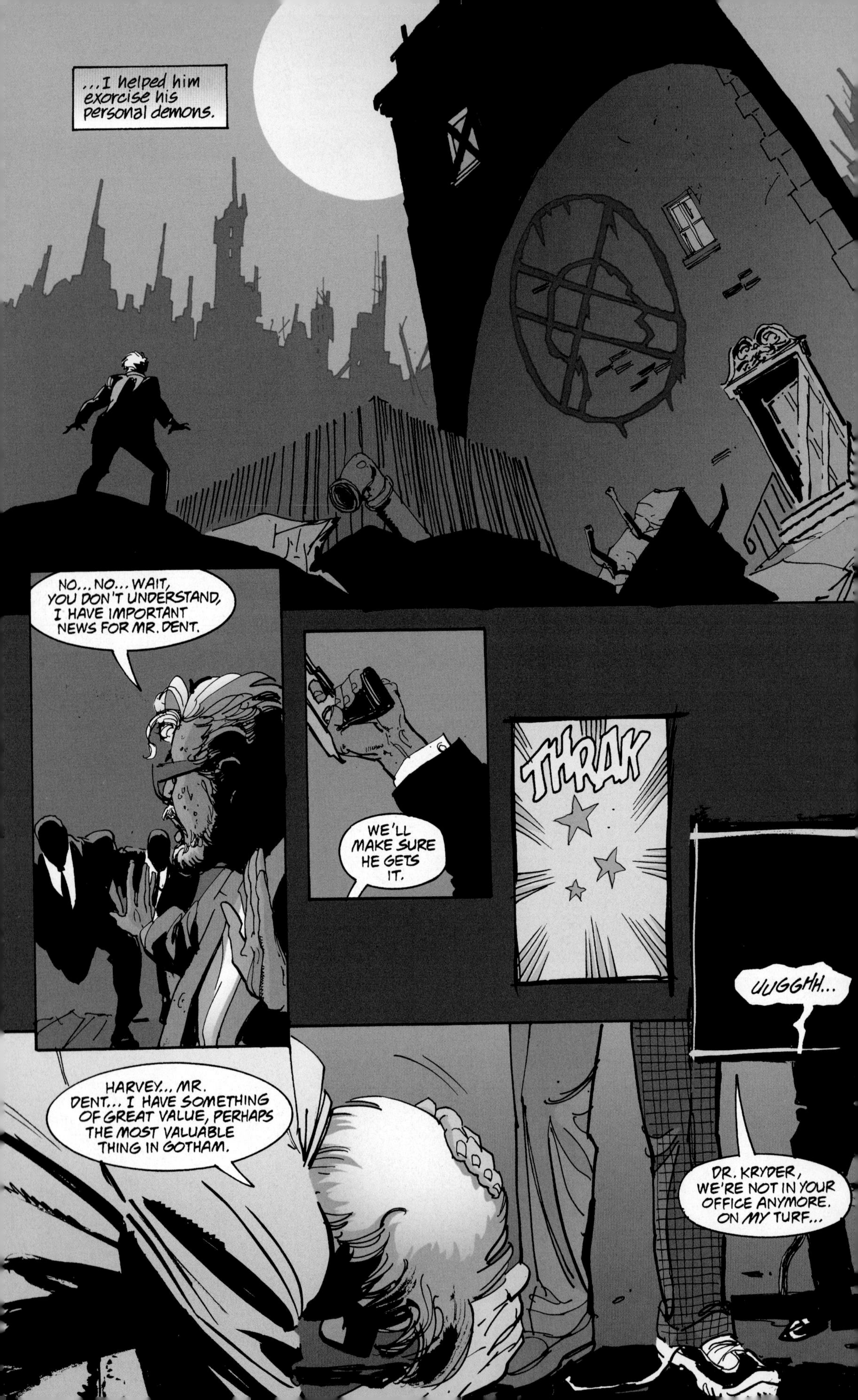
...I helped him exorcise his personal demons.
NO... NO... WAIT, YOU DON'T UNDERSTAND, I HAVE IMPORTANT NEWS FOR MR. DENT.
WE'LL MAKE SURE HE GETS IT.
THRAK
UUGGHH...
HARVEY... MR. DENT... I HAVE SOMETHING OF GREAT VALUE, PERHAPS THE MOST VALUABLE THING IN GOTHAM.
DR. KRYDER, WE'RE NOT IN YOUR OFFICE ANYMORE. ON MY TURF...

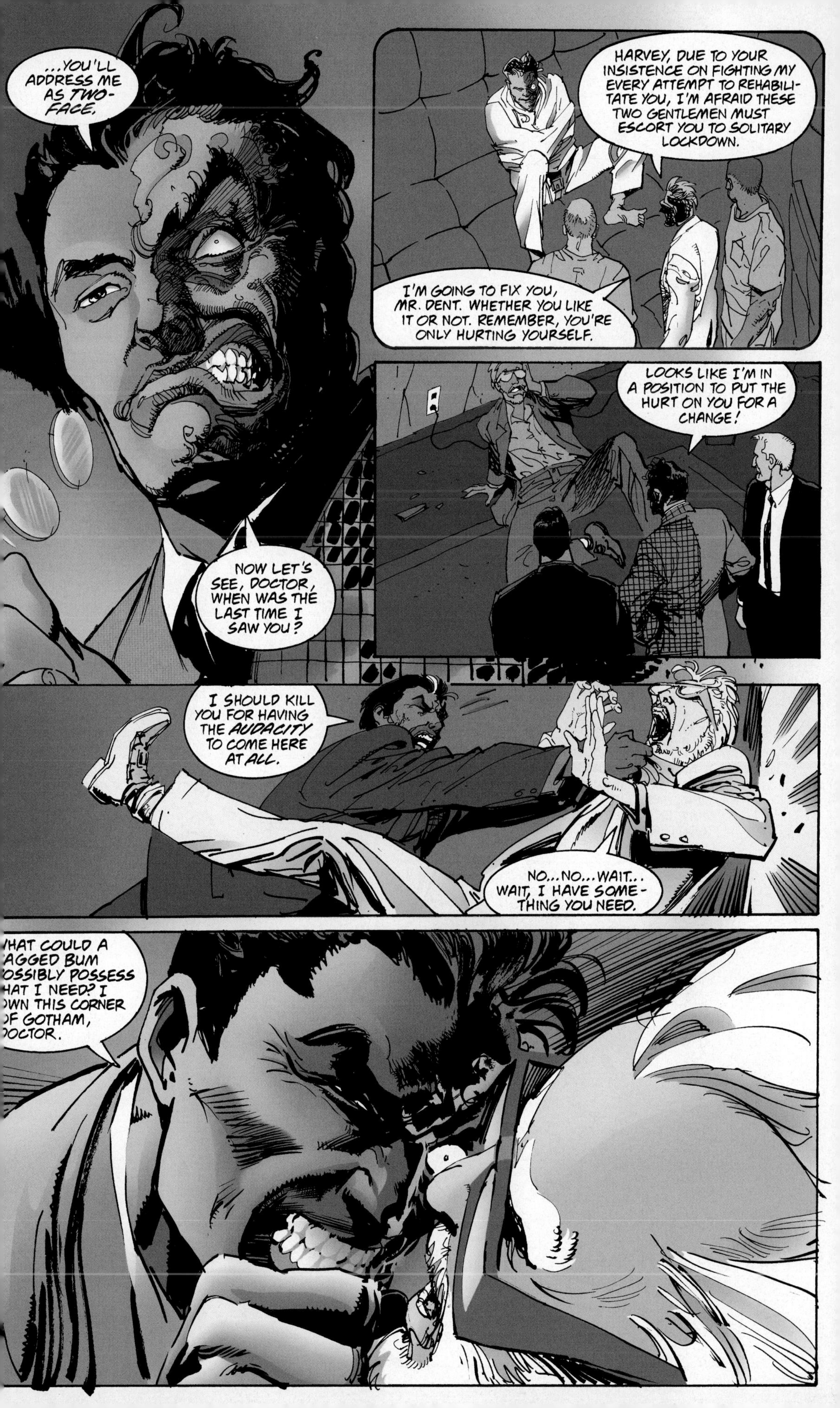
...YOU'LL ADDRESS ME AS TWO-FACE.
HARVEY, DUE TO YOUR INSISTENCE ON FIGHTING MY EVERY ATTEMPT TO REHABILITATE YOU, I'M AFRAID THESE TWO GENTLEMEN MUST ESCORT YOU TO SOLITARY LOCKDOWN.
I'M GOING TO FIX YOU, MR. DENT. WHETHER YOU LIKE IT OR NOT. REMEMBER, YOU'RE ONLY HURTING YOURSELF.
NOW LET'S SEE, DOCTOR, WHEN WAS THE LAST TIME I SAW YOU?
LOOKS LIKE I'M IN A POSITION TO PUT THE HURT ON YOU FOR A CHANGE!
I SHOULD KILL YOU FOR HAVING THE AUDACITY TO COME HERE AT ALL.
NO...NO...WAIT... WAIT, I HAVE SOMETHING YOU NEED.
HAT COULD A AGGED BUM OSSIBLY POSSESS HAT I NEED? I WN THIS CORNER F GOTHAM, OCTOR.

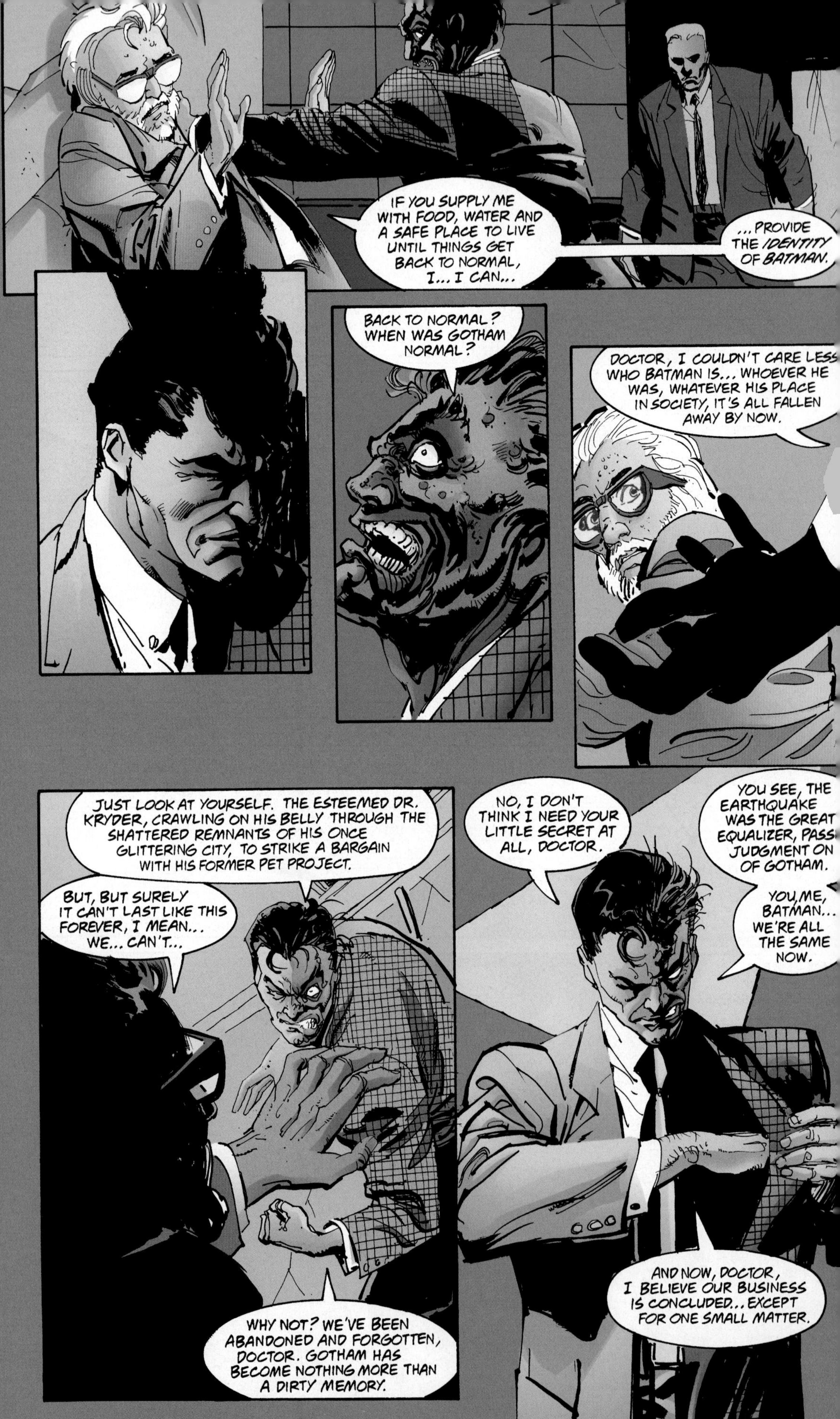
IF YOU SUPPLY ME WITH FOOD, WATER AND A SAFE PLACE TO LIVE UNTIL THINGS GET BACK TO NORMAL, I... I CAN...
...PROVIDE THE IDENTITY OF BATMAN.
BACK TO NORMAL? WHEN WAS GOTHAM NORMAL?
DOCTOR, I COULDN'T CARE LESS WHO BATMAN IS... WHOEVER HE WAS, WHATEVER HIS PLACE IN SOCIETY, IT'S ALL FALLEN AWAY BY NOW.
JUST LOOK AT YOURSELF. THE ESTEEMED DR. KRYDER, CRAWLING ON HIS BELLY THROUGH THE SHATTERED REMNANTS OF HIS ONCE GLITTERING CITY, TO STRIKE A BARGAIN WITH HIS FORMER PET PROJECT.
BUT, BUT SURELY IT CAN'T LAST LIKE THIS FOREVER, I MEAN... WE... CAN'T...
WHY NOT? WE'VE BEEN ABANDONED AND FORGOTTEN, DOCTOR. GOTHAM HAS BECOME NOTHING MORE THAN A DIRTY MEMORY.
NO, I DON'T THINK I NEED YOUR LITTLE SECRET AT ALL, DOCTOR.
YOU SEE, THE EARTHQUAKE WAS THE GREAT EQUALIZER, PASS JUDGMENT ON OF GOTHAM.
YOU, ME, BATMAN... WE'RE ALL THE SAME NOW.
AND NOW, DOCTOR, I BELIEVE OUR BUSINESS IS CONCLUDED... EXCEPT FOR ONE SMALL MATTER.

TING

SLAP

KLI·CHIK

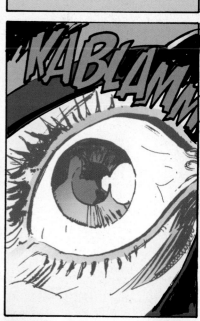
KABLAMMM

KRESHHHH

WUMP!

B...BR...BRUCE WAYNE IS BATMANNNN...

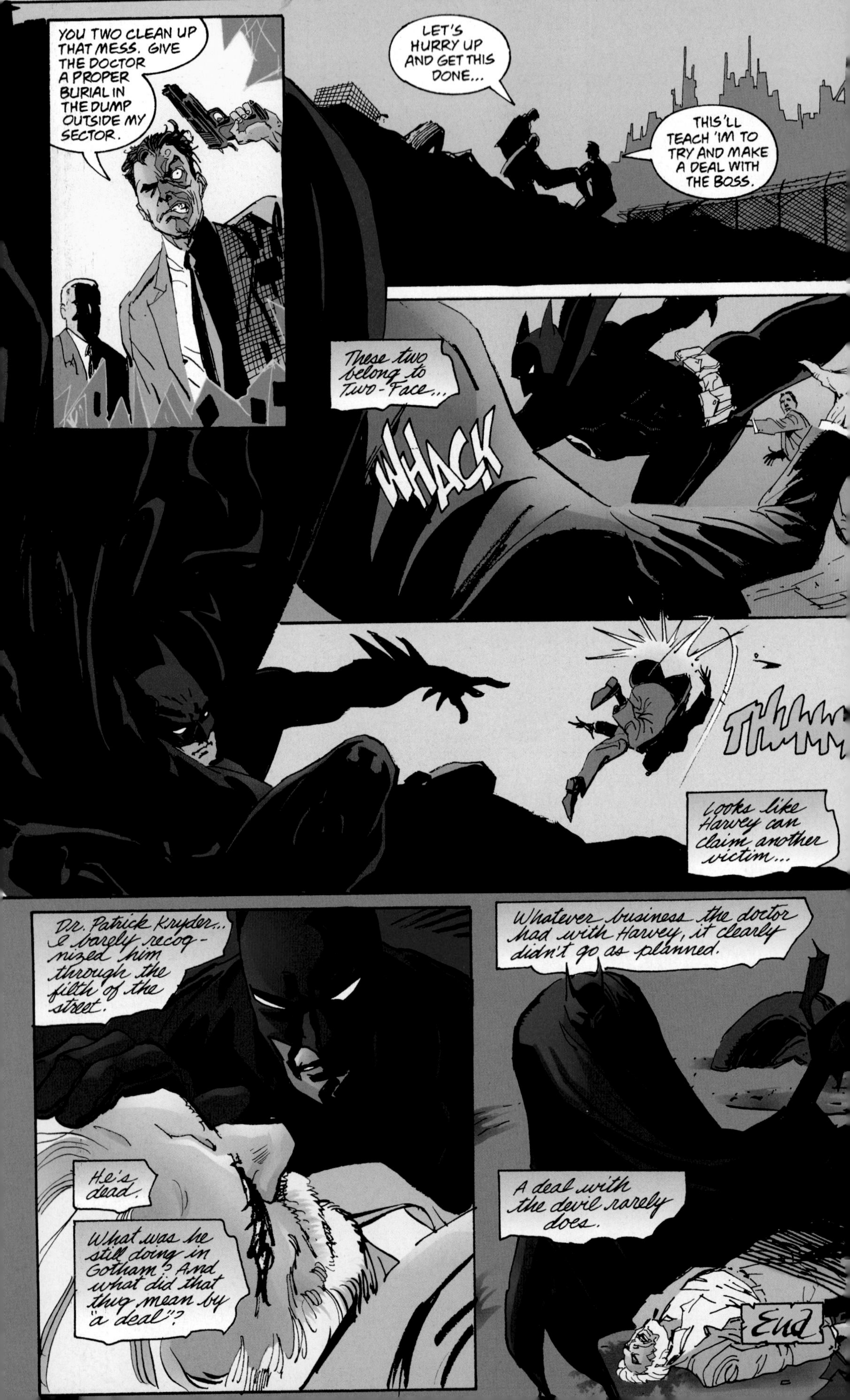

YOU TWO CLEAN UP THAT MESS. GIVE THE DOCTOR A PROPER BURIAL IN THE DUMP OUTSIDE MY SECTOR.
LET'S HURRY UP AND GET THIS DONE...
THIS'LL TEACH 'IM TO TRY AND MAKE A DEAL WITH THE BOSS.
These two belong to Two-Face...
WHACK
THWWW
Looks like Harvey can claim another victim...
Dr. Patrick Kryder... I barely recognized him through the filth of the street.
He's dead.
What was he still doing in Gotham? And what did that thug mean by "a deal"?
Whatever business the doctor had with Harvey, it clearly didn't go as planned.
A deal with the devil rarely does.
End

THE BELLY OF THE BEAST

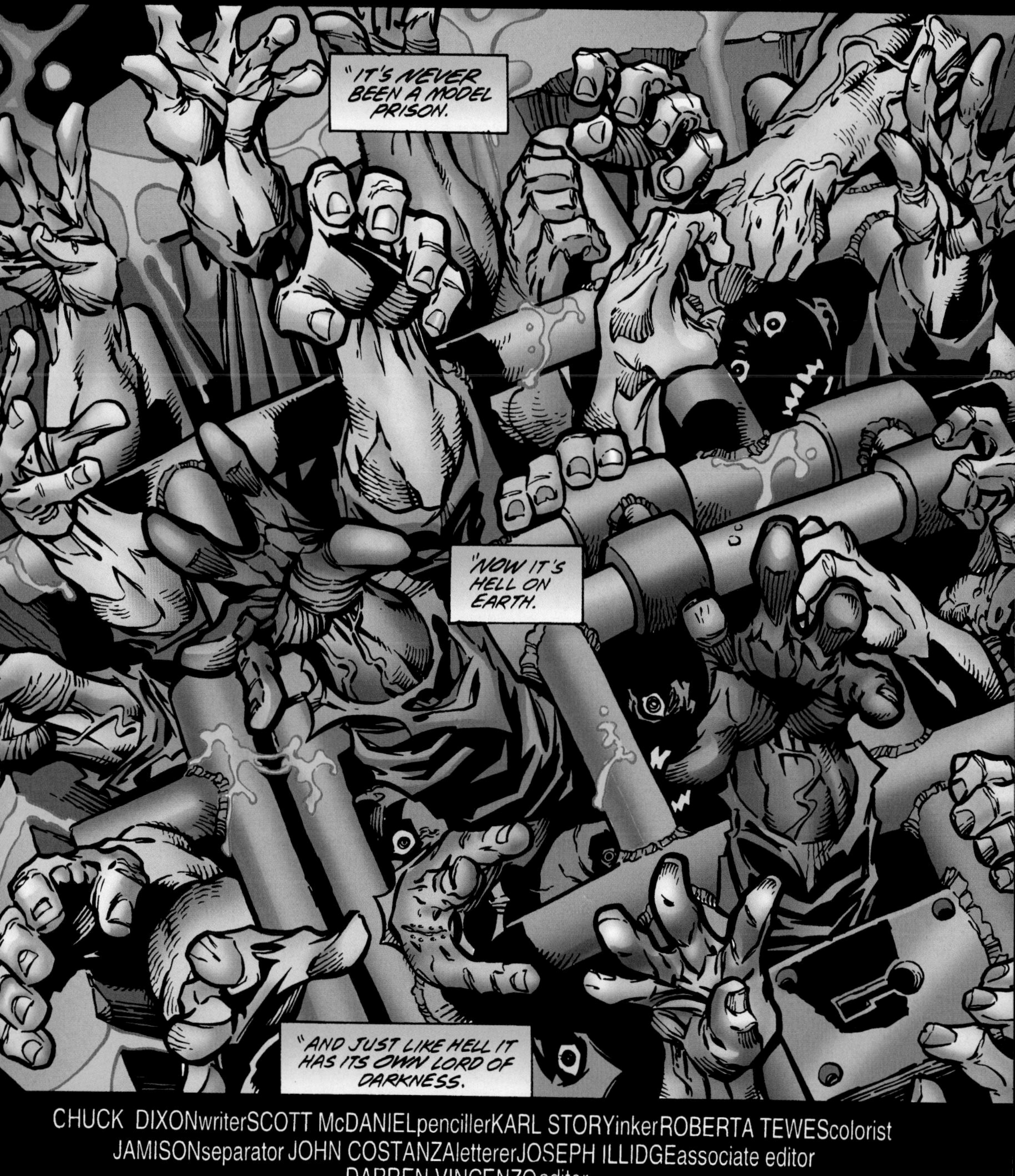
"IT'S NEVER BEEN A MODEL PRISON.
"NOW IT'S HELL ON EARTH.
"AND JUST LIKE HELL IT HAS ITS OWN LORD OF DARKNESS.

CHUCK DIXONwriterSCOTT McDANIELpencillerKARL STORYinkerROBERTA TEWEScolorist JAMISONseparator JOHN COSTANZAlettererJOSEPH ILLIDGEassociate editor DARREN VINCENZOeditor

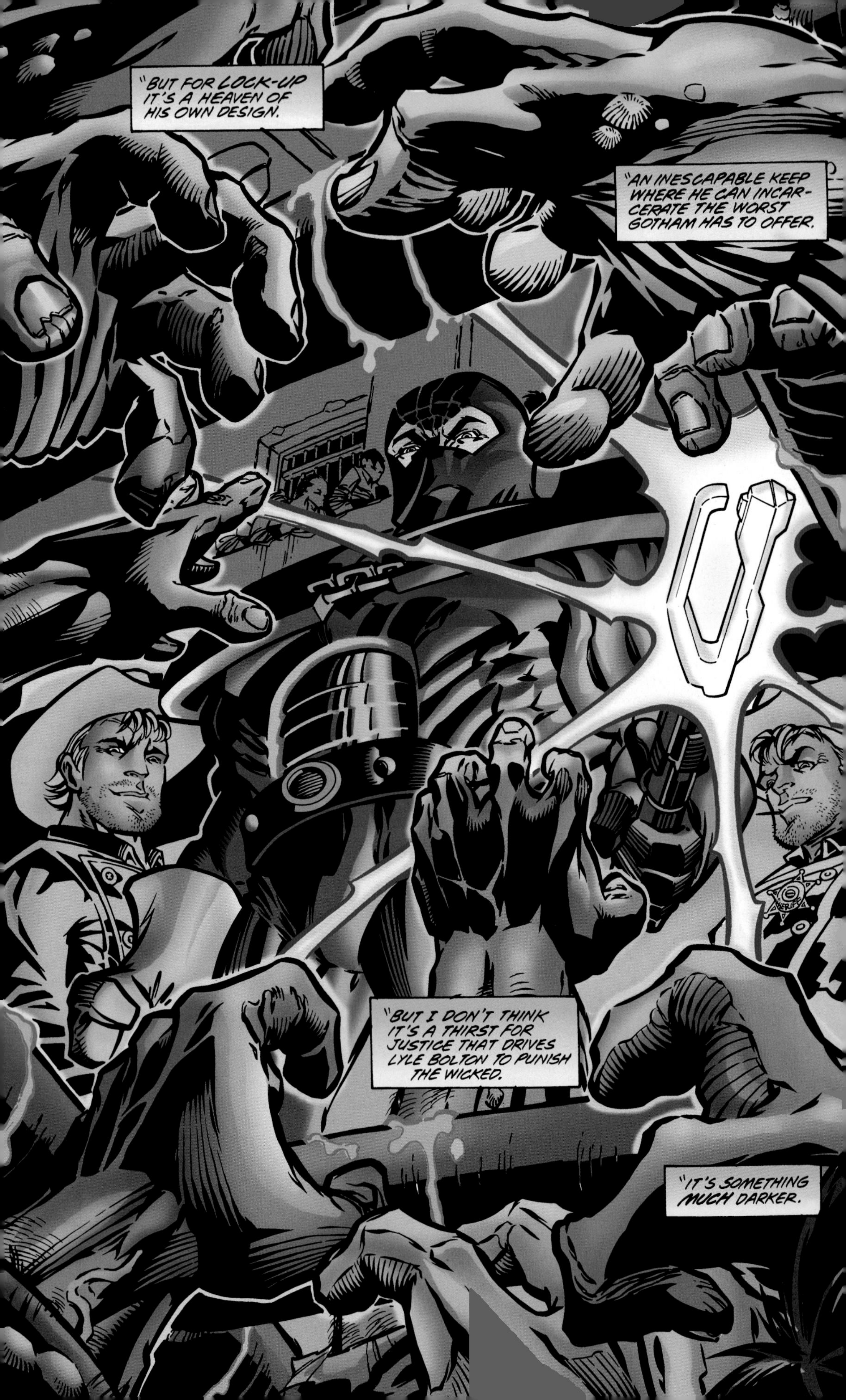
"BUT FOR LOCK-UP IT'S A HEAVEN OF HIS OWN DESIGN.
"AN INESCAPABLE KEEP WHERE HE CAN INCARCERATE THE WORST GOTHAM HAS TO OFFER.
"BUT I DON'T THINK IT'S A THIRST FOR JUSTICE THAT DRIVES LYLE BOLTON TO PUNISH THE WICKED.
"IT'S SOMETHING MUCH DARKER.

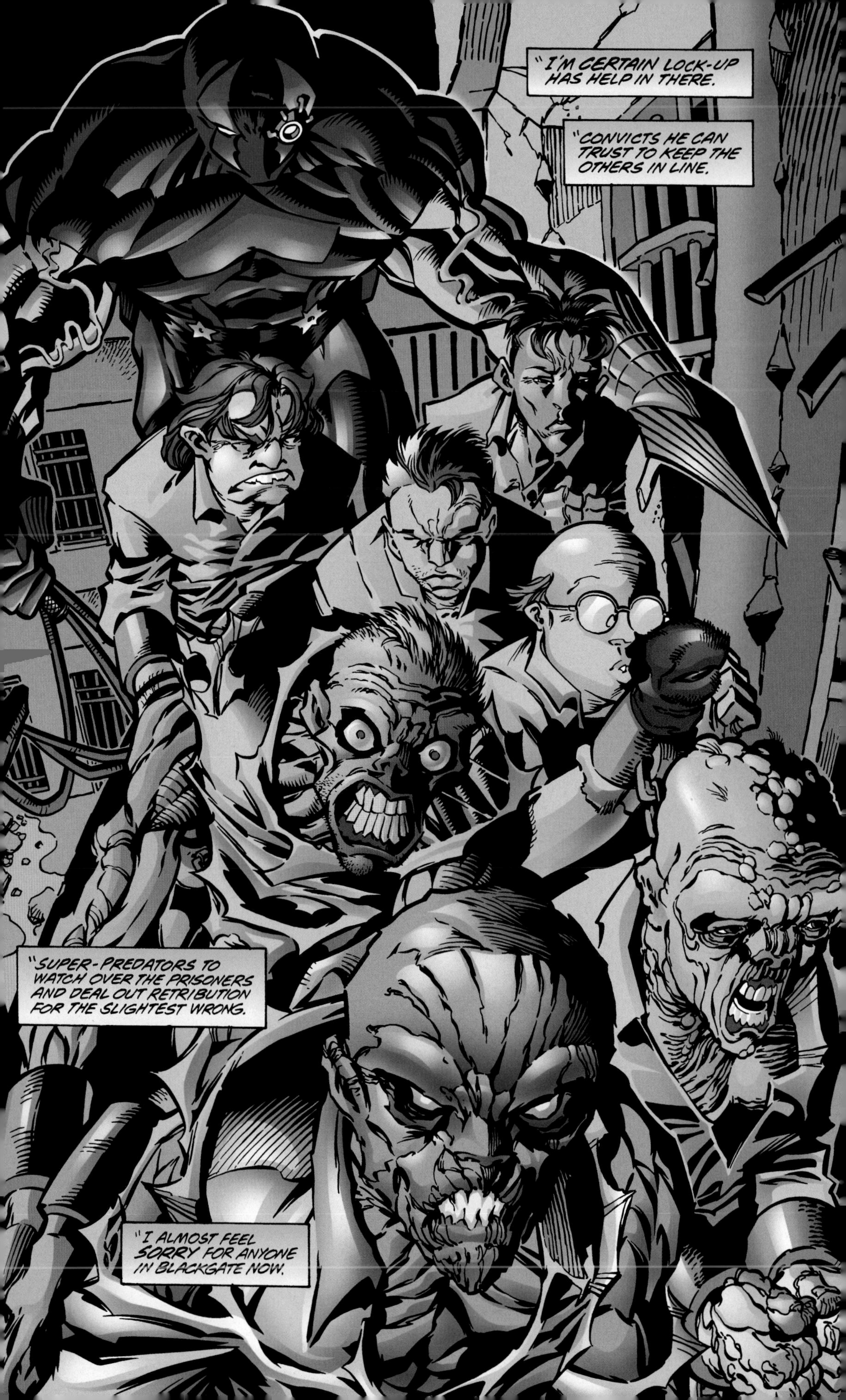
"I'M CERTAIN LOCK-UP HAS HELP IN THERE.
"CONVICTS HE CAN TRUST TO KEEP THE OTHERS IN LINE.
"SUPER-PREDATORS TO WATCH OVER THE PRISONERS AND DEAL OUT RETRIBUTION FOR THE SLIGHTEST WRONG.
"I ALMOST FEEL SORRY FOR ANYONE IN BLACKGATE NOW.

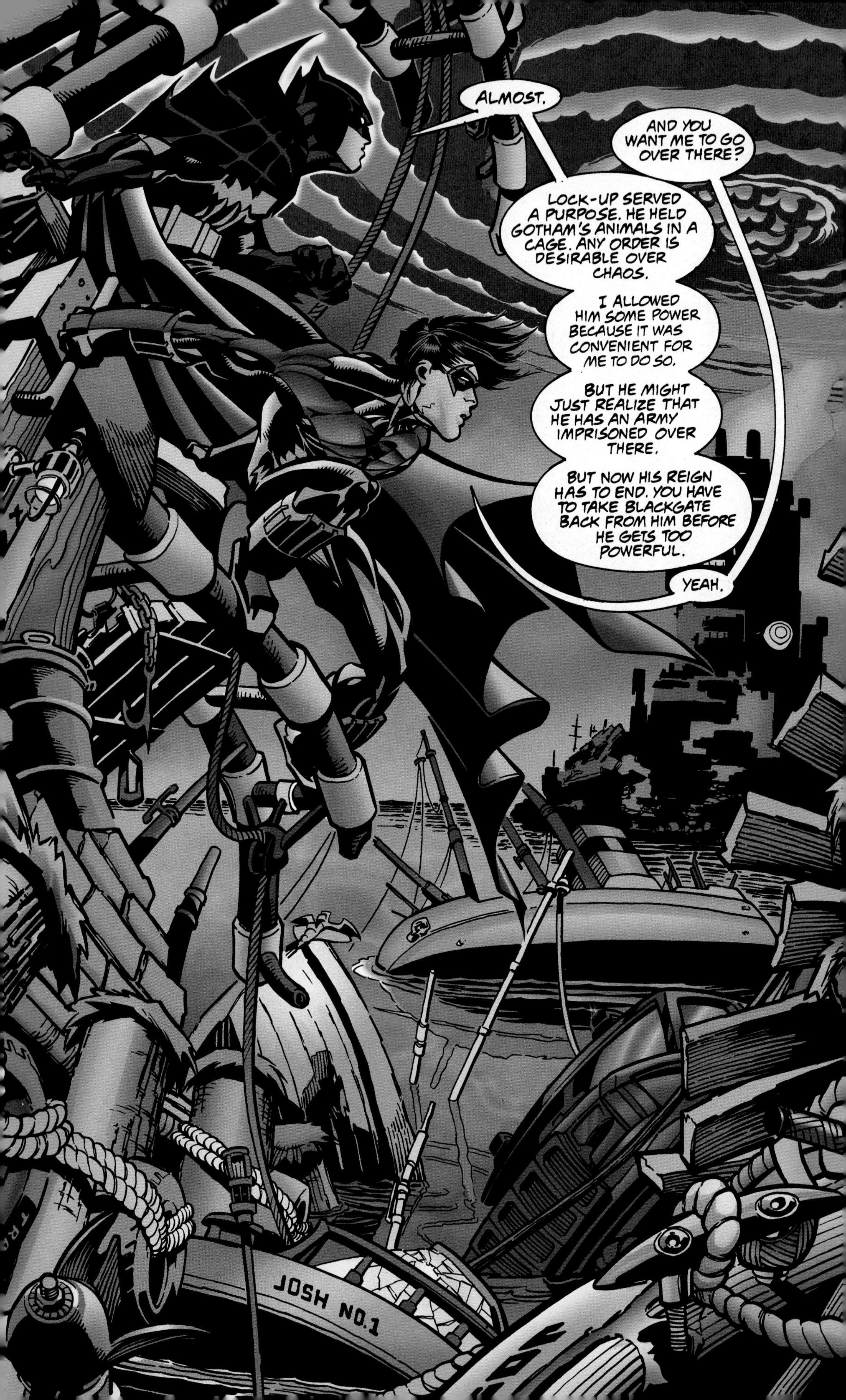
ALMOST.
AND YOU WANT ME TO GO OVER THERE?
LOCK-UP SERVED A PURPOSE. HE HELD GOTHAM'S ANIMALS IN A CAGE. ANY ORDER IS DESIRABLE OVER CHAOS.
I ALLOWED HIM SOME POWER BECAUSE IT WAS CONVENIENT FOR ME TO DO SO.
BUT HE MIGHT JUST REALIZE THAT HE HAS AN ARMY IMPRISONED OVER THERE.
BUT NOW HIS REIGN HAS TO END. YOU HAVE TO TAKE BLACKGATE BACK FROM HIM BEFORE HE GETS TOO POWERFUL.
YEAH.
JOSH NO.1

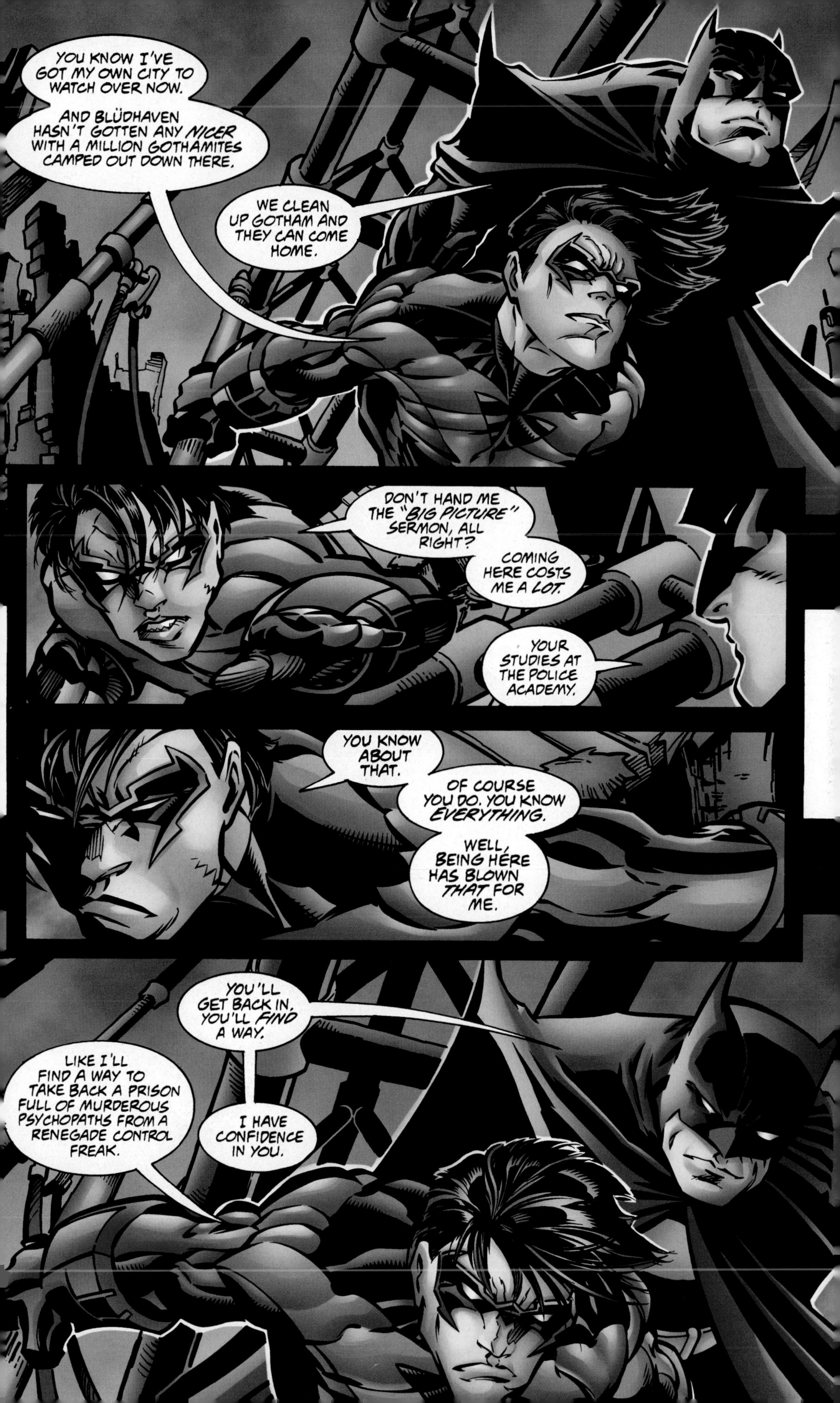
YOU KNOW I'VE GOT MY OWN CITY TO WATCH OVER NOW.
AND BLÜDHAVEN HASN'T GOTTEN ANY *NICER* WITH A MILLION GOTHAMITES CAMPED OUT DOWN THERE.
WE CLEAN UP GOTHAM AND THEY CAN COME HOME.
DON'T HAND ME THE "*BIG PICTURE*" SERMON, ALL RIGHT?
COMING HERE COSTS ME A *LOT.*
YOUR STUDIES AT THE POLICE ACADEMY.
YOU KNOW ABOUT THAT.
OF COURSE YOU DO. YOU KNOW *EVERYTHING.*
WELL, BEING HERE HAS BLOWN *THAT* FOR ME.
YOU'LL GET BACK IN, YOU'LL *FIND* A WAY.
LIKE I'LL FIND A WAY TO TAKE BACK A PRISON FULL OF MURDEROUS PSYCHOPATHS FROM A RENEGADE CONTROL FREAK.
I HAVE CONFIDENCE IN YOU.

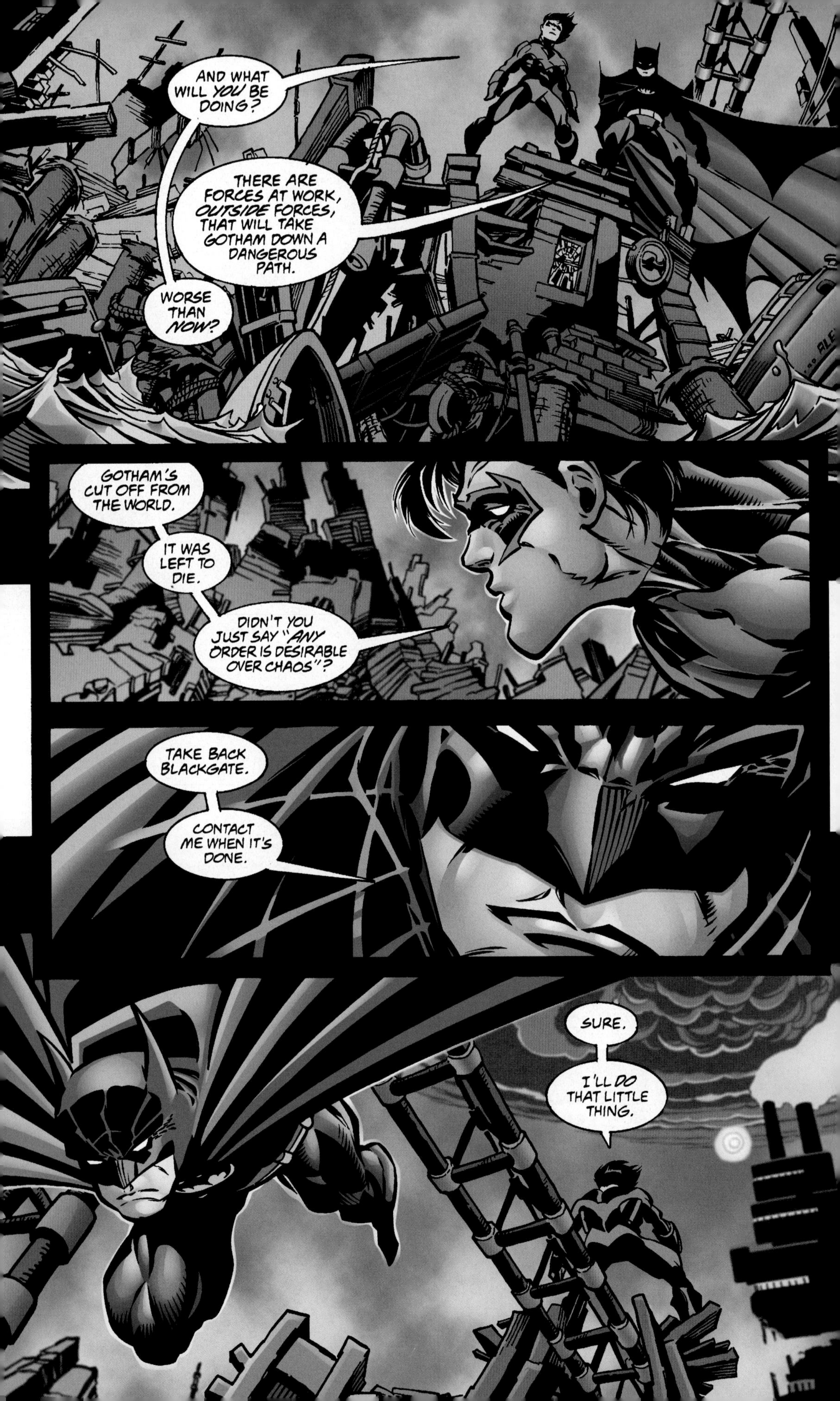
AND WHAT WILL YOU BE DOING?
THERE ARE FORCES AT WORK, OUTSIDE FORCES, THAT WILL TAKE GOTHAM DOWN A DANGEROUS PATH.
WORSE THAN NOW?
GOTHAM'S CUT OFF FROM THE WORLD.
IT WAS LEFT TO DIE.
DIDN'T YOU JUST SAY "ANY ORDER IS DESIRABLE OVER CHAOS"?
TAKE BACK BLACKGATE.
CONTACT ME WHEN IT'S DONE.
SURE.
I'LL DO THAT LITTLE THING.

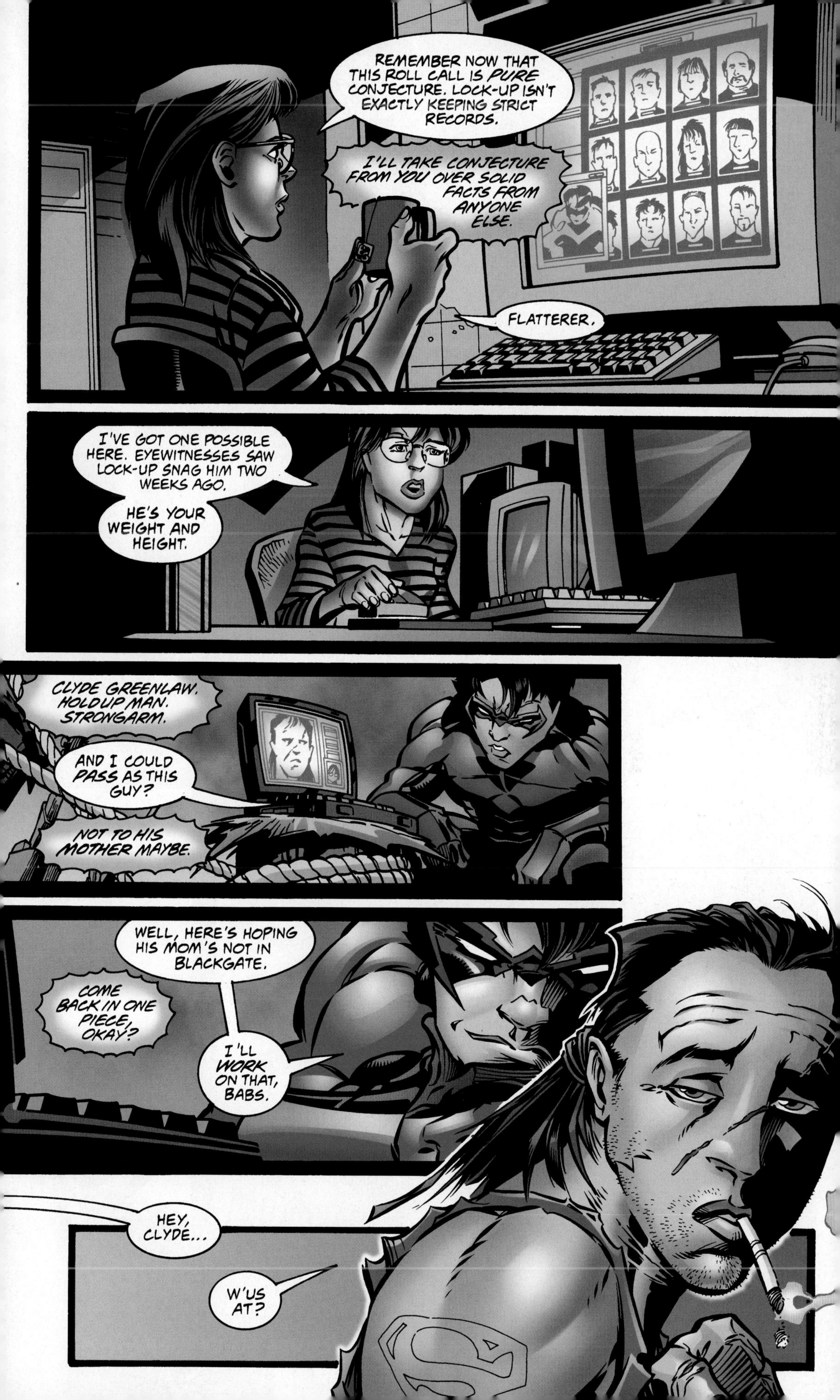
REMEMBER NOW THAT THIS ROLL CALL IS PURE CONJECTURE. LOCK-UP ISN'T EXACTLY KEEPING STRICT RECORDS.
I'LL TAKE CONJECTURE FROM YOU OVER SOLID FACTS FROM ANYONE ELSE.
FLATTERER.
I'VE GOT ONE POSSIBLE HERE. EYEWITNESSES SAW LOCK-UP SNAG HIM TWO WEEKS AGO.
HE'S YOUR WEIGHT AND HEIGHT.
CLYDE GREENLAW. HOLDUP MAN. STRONGARM.
AND I COULD PASS AS THIS GUY?
NOT TO HIS MOTHER MAYBE.
WELL, HERE'S HOPING HIS MOM'S NOT IN BLACKGATE.
COME BACK IN ONE PIECE, OKAY?
I'LL WORK ON THAT, BABS.
HEY, CLYDE...
W'US AT?

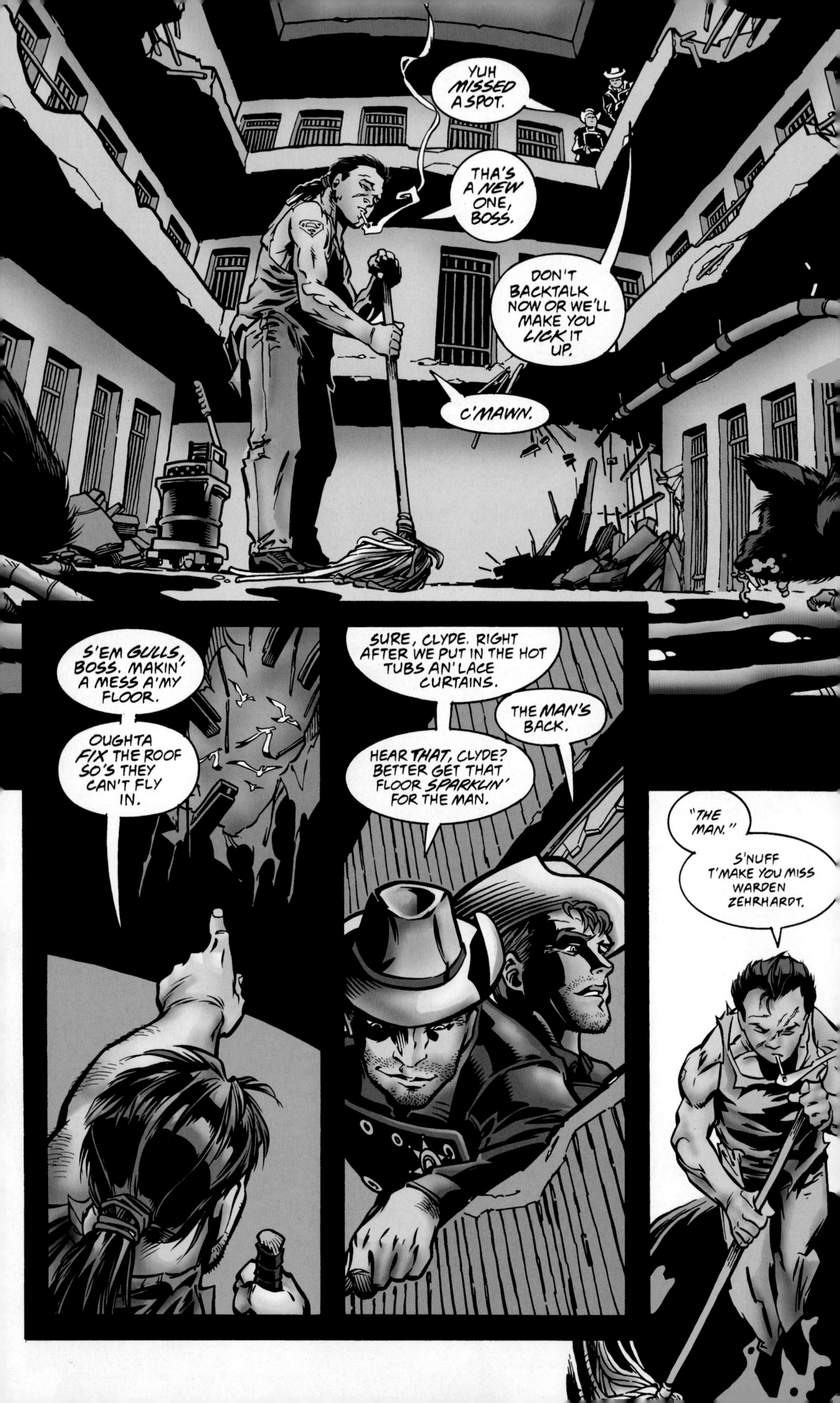
YUH MISSED A SPOT.
THA'S A NEW ONE, BOSS.
DON'T BACKTALK NOW OR WE'LL MAKE YOU LICK IT UP.
C'MAWN.
S'EM GULLS, BOSS. MAKIN' A MESS A'MY FLOOR.
OUGHTA FIX THE ROOF SO'S THEY CAN'T FLY IN.
SURE, CLYDE. RIGHT AFTER WE PUT IN THE HOT TUBS AN' LACE CURTAINS.
THE MAN'S BACK.
HEAR THAT, CLYDE? BETTER GET THAT FLOOR SPARKLIN' FOR THE MAN.
"THE MAN."
S'NUFF T'MAKE YOU MISS WARDEN ZEHRHARDT.

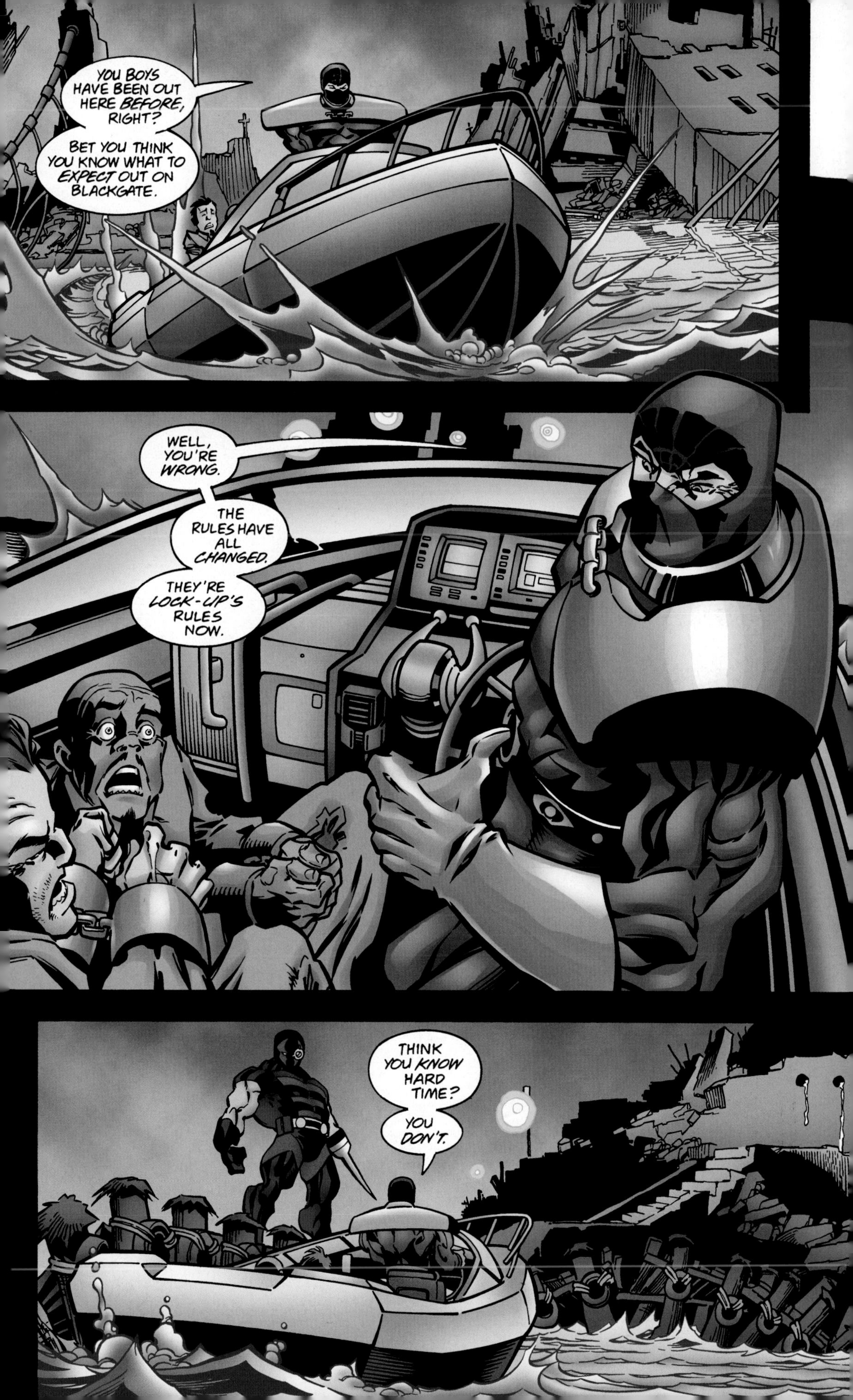
YOU BOYS HAVE BEEN OUT HERE *BEFORE,* RIGHT?
BET YOU THINK YOU KNOW WHAT TO *EXPECT* OUT ON BLACKGATE.
WELL, YOU'RE *WRONG.*
THE RULES HAVE ALL *CHANGED.*
THEY'RE *LOCK-UP'S* RULES NOW.
THINK YOU *KNOW* HARD TIME?
YOU *DON'T.*

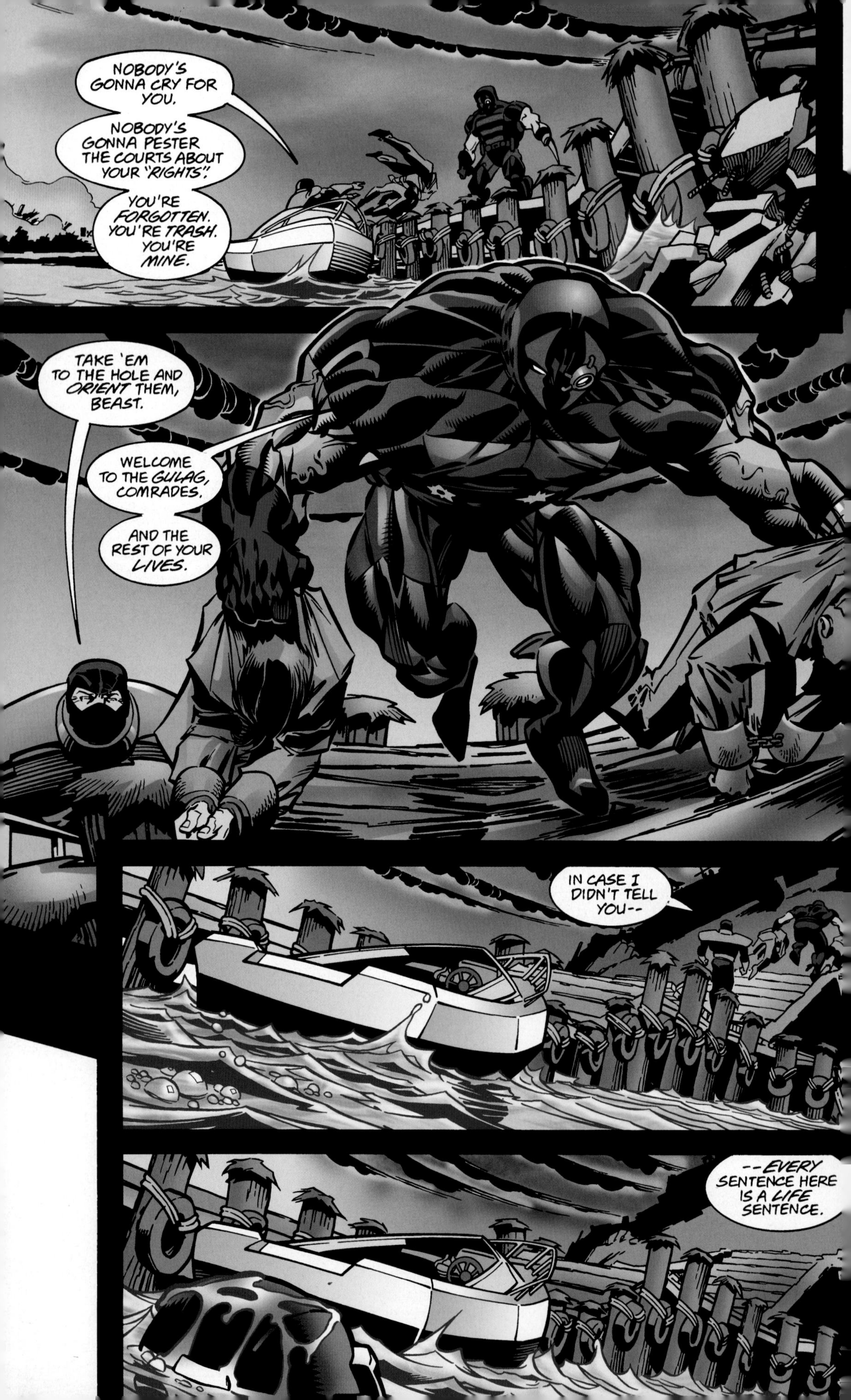
NOBODY'S GONNA CRY FOR YOU.
NOBODY'S GONNA PESTER THE COURTS ABOUT YOUR "RIGHTS."
YOU'RE FORGOTTEN. YOU'RE TRASH. YOU'RE MINE.
TAKE 'EM TO THE HOLE AND ORIENT THEM, BEAST.
WELCOME TO THE GULAG, COMRADES.
AND THE REST OF YOUR LIVES.
IN CASE I DIDN'T TELL YOU--
--EVERY SENTENCE HERE IS A LIFE SENTENCE.

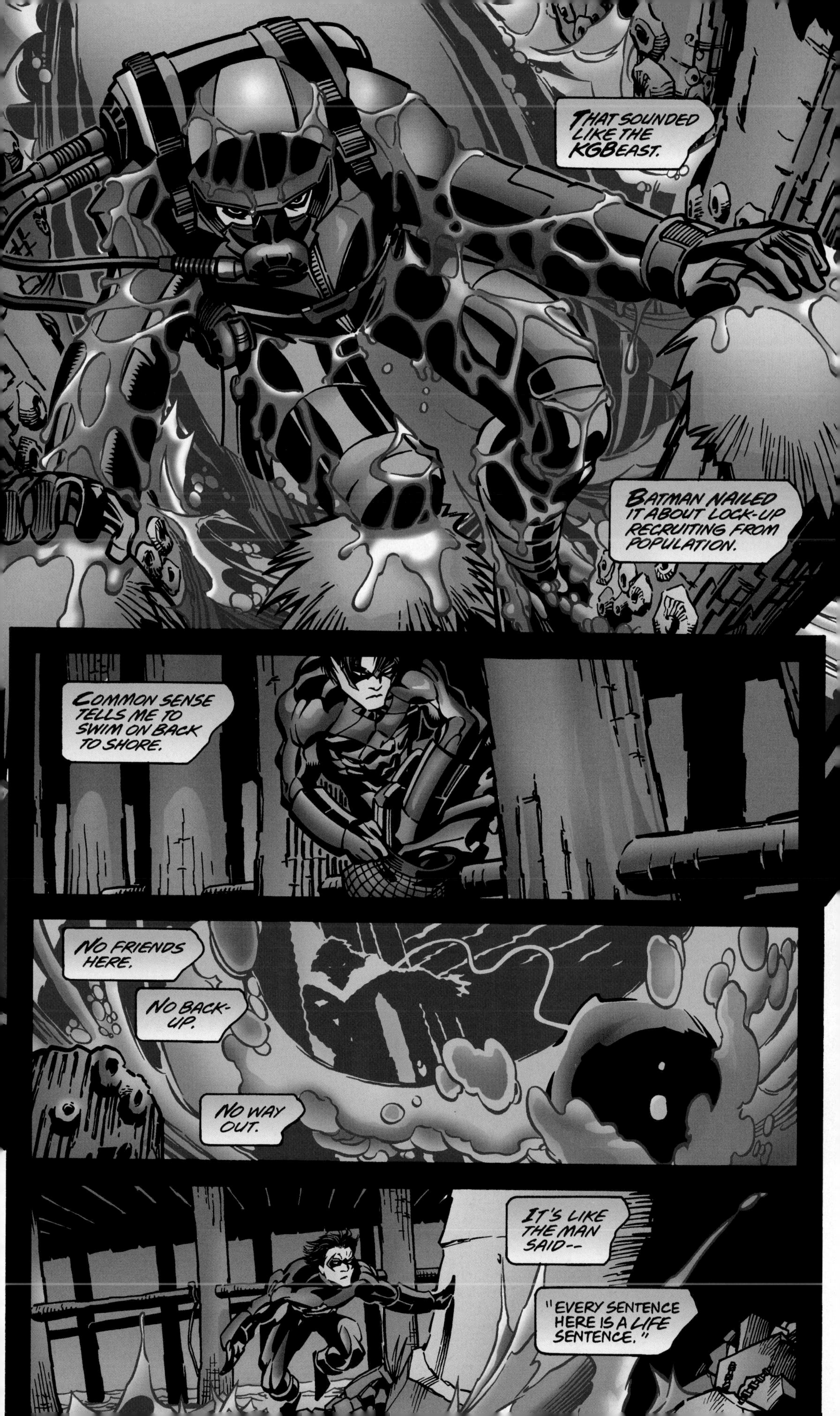
THAT SOUNDED LIKE THE KGBEAST.
BATMAN NAILED IT ABOUT LOCK-UP RECRUITING FROM POPULATION.
COMMON SENSE TELLS ME TO SWIM ON BACK TO SHORE.
NO FRIENDS HERE.
NO BACK-UP.
NO WAY OUT.
IT'S LIKE THE MAN SAID--
"EVERY SENTENCE HERE IS A LIFE SENTENCE."

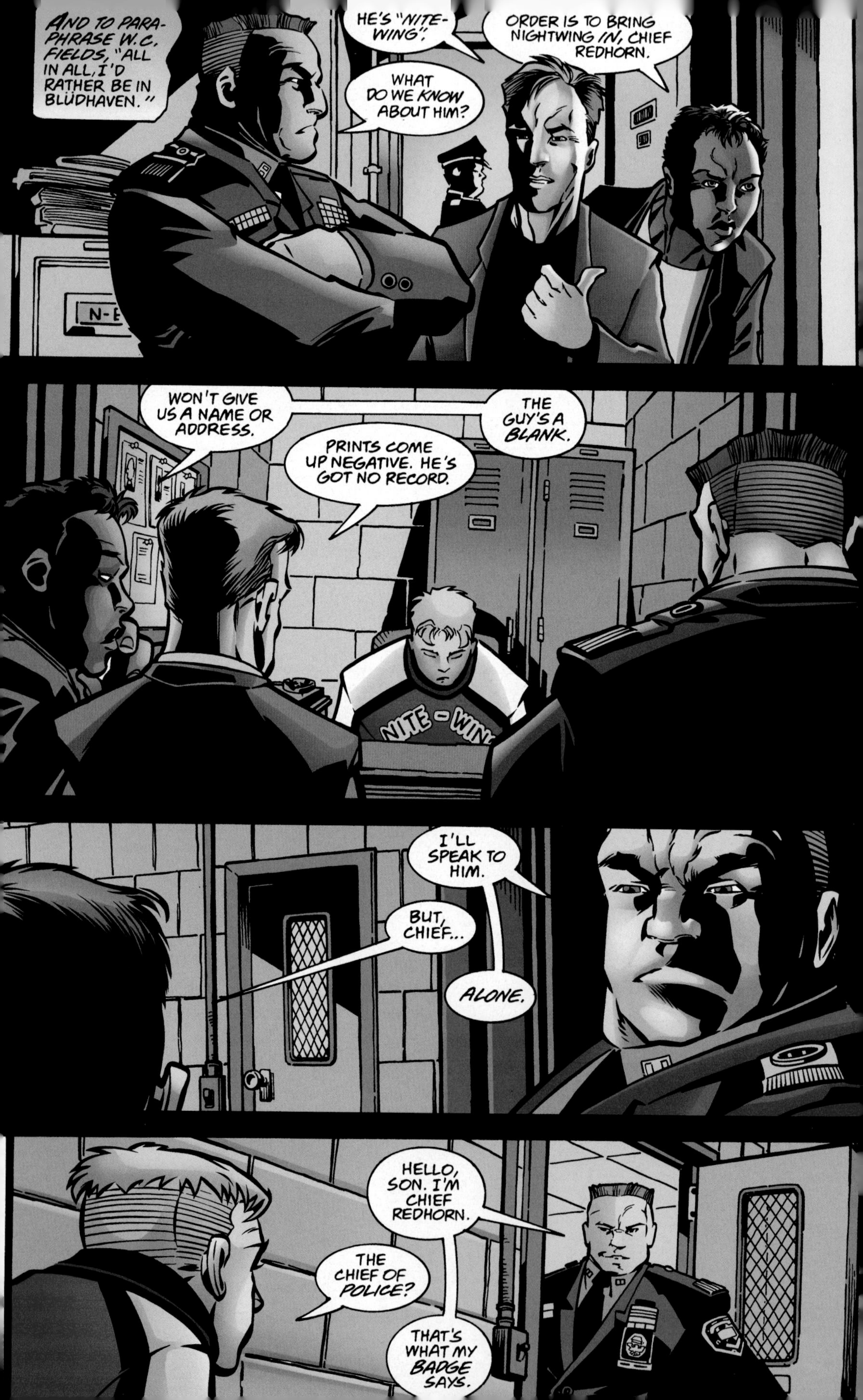
AND TO PARAPHRASE W.C. FIELDS, "ALL IN ALL, I'D RATHER BE IN BLÜDHAVEN."
HE'S "NITE-WING".
WHAT DO WE KNOW ABOUT HIM?
ORDER IS TO BRING NIGHTWING IN, CHIEF REDHORN.
WON'T GIVE US A NAME OR ADDRESS.
THE GUY'S A BLANK.
PRINTS COME UP NEGATIVE. HE'S GOT NO RECORD.
NITE-WIN
I'LL SPEAK TO HIM.
BUT, CHIEF...
ALONE.
HELLO, SON. I'M CHIEF REDHORN.
THE CHIEF OF POLICE?
THAT'S WHAT MY BADGE SAYS.

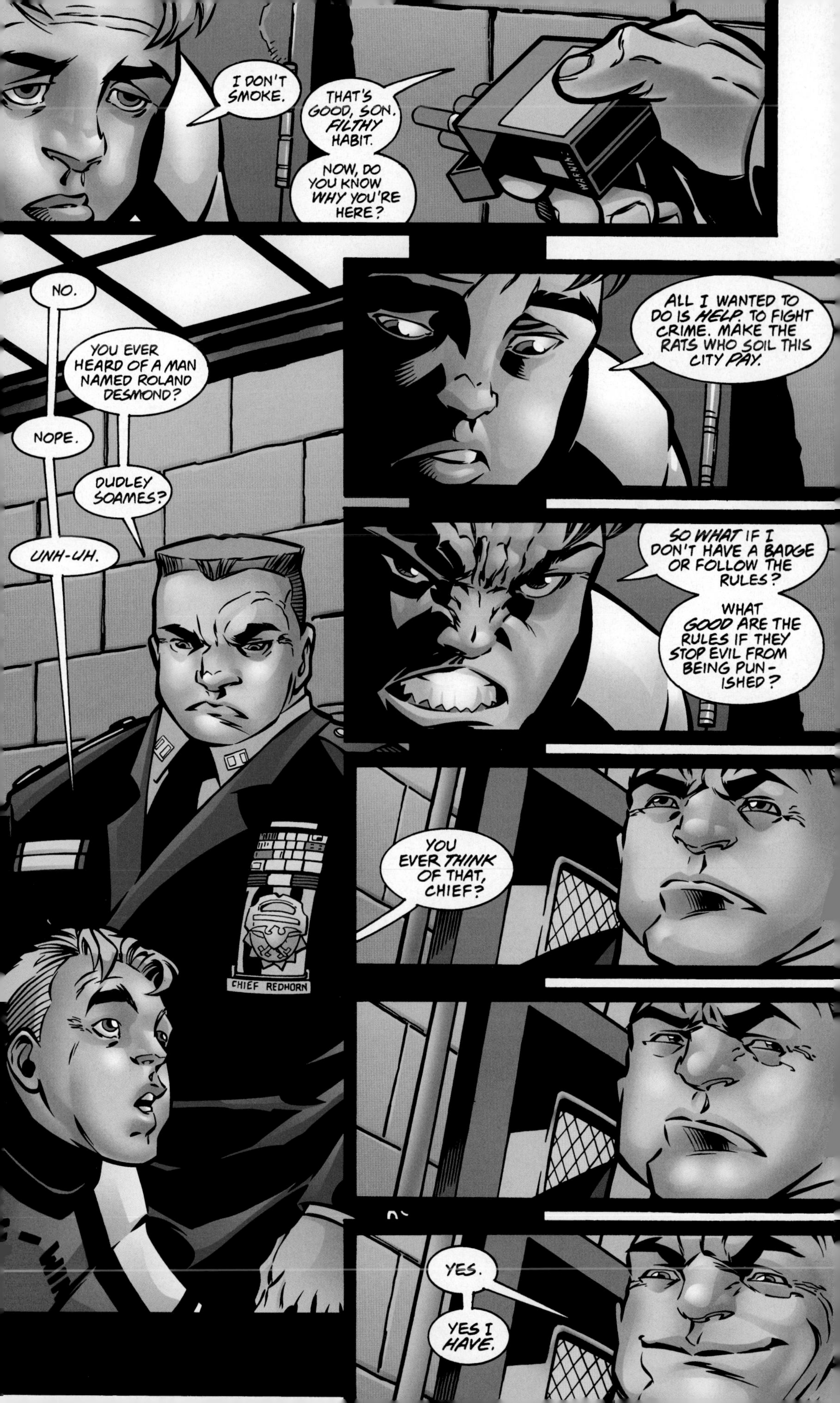
I DON'T SMOKE.
THAT'S GOOD, SON. FILTHY HABIT.
NOW, DO YOU KNOW WHY YOU'RE HERE?
NO.
YOU EVER HEARD OF A MAN NAMED ROLAND DESMOND?
NOPE.
DUDLEY SOAMES?
UNH-UH.
CHIEF REDHORN
ALL I WANTED TO DO IS HELP. TO FIGHT CRIME. MAKE THE RATS WHO SOIL THIS CITY PAY.
SO WHAT IF I DON'T HAVE A BADGE OR FOLLOW THE RULES?
WHAT GOOD ARE THE RULES IF THEY STOP EVIL FROM BEING PUN-ISHED?
YOU EVER THINK OF THAT, CHIEF?
YES.
YES I HAVE.

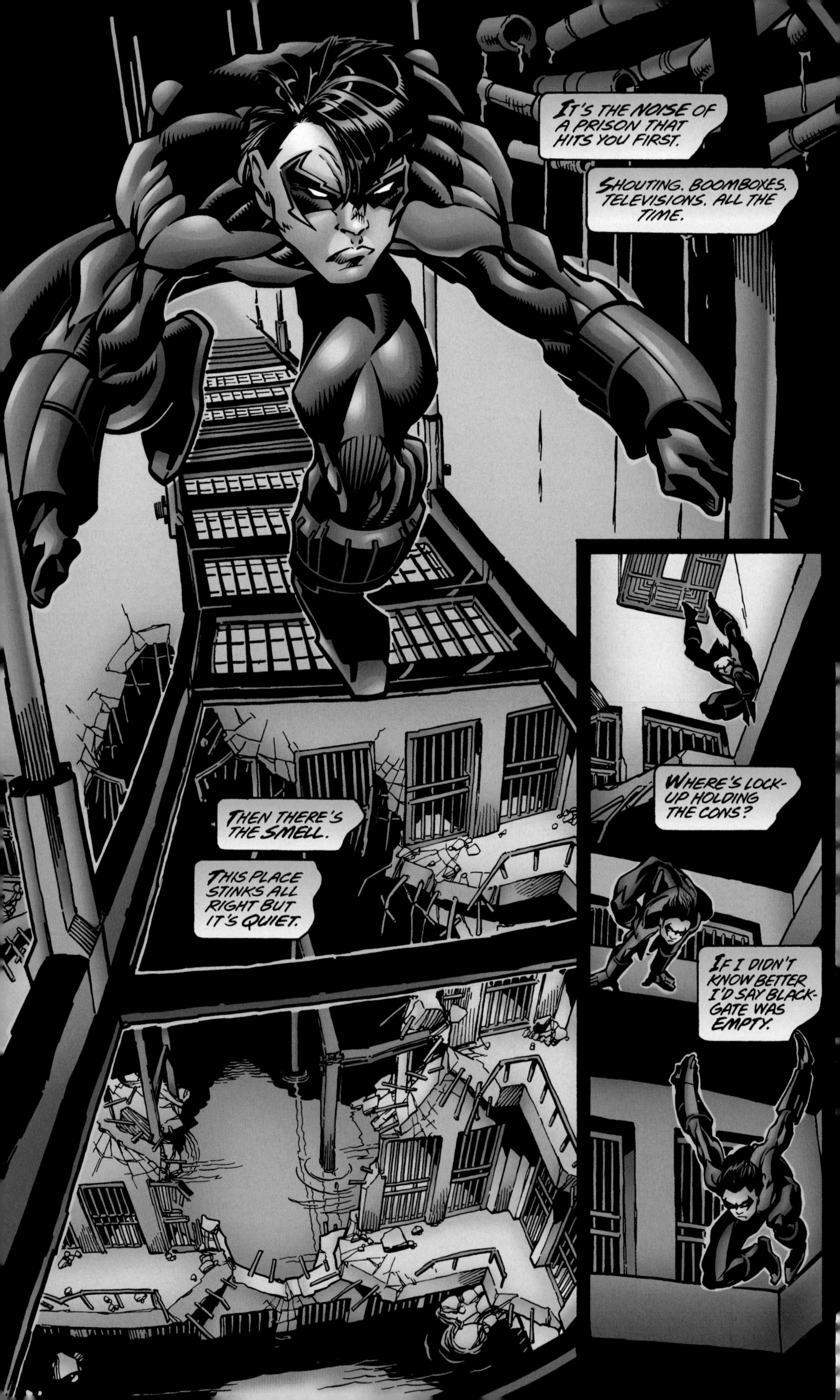
IT'S THE NOISE OF A PRISON THAT HITS YOU FIRST.
SHOUTING. BOOMBOXES. TELEVISIONS. ALL THE TIME.
THEN THERE'S THE SMELL.
THIS PLACE STINKS ALL RIGHT BUT IT'S QUIET.
WHERE'S LOCK-UP HOLDING THE CONS?
IF I DIDN'T KNOW BETTER I'D SAY BLACK-GATE WAS EMPTY.

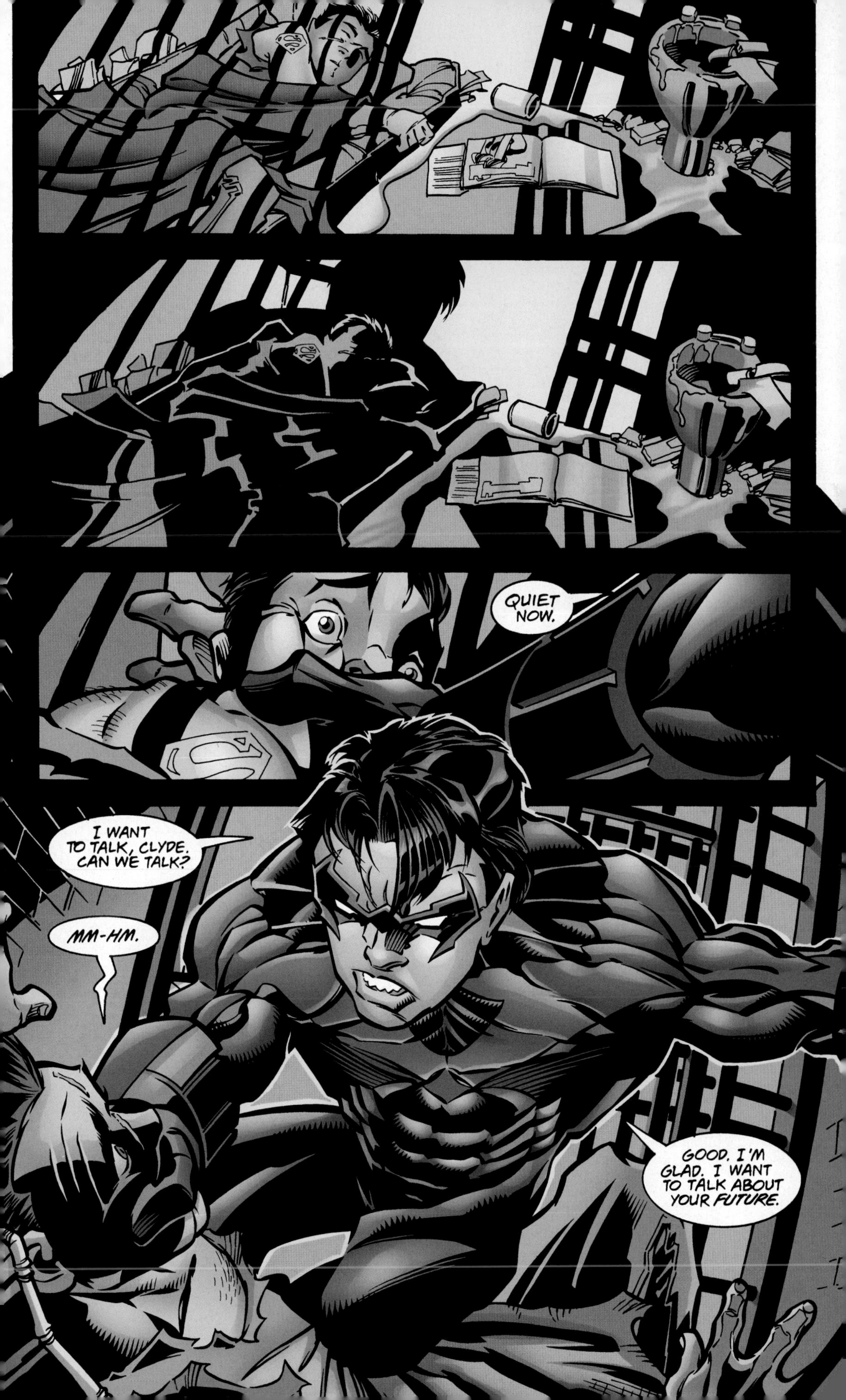
QUIET NOW.
I WANT TO TALK, CLYDE. CAN WE TALK?
MM-HM.
GOOD. I'M GLAD. I WANT TO TALK ABOUT YOUR FUTURE.

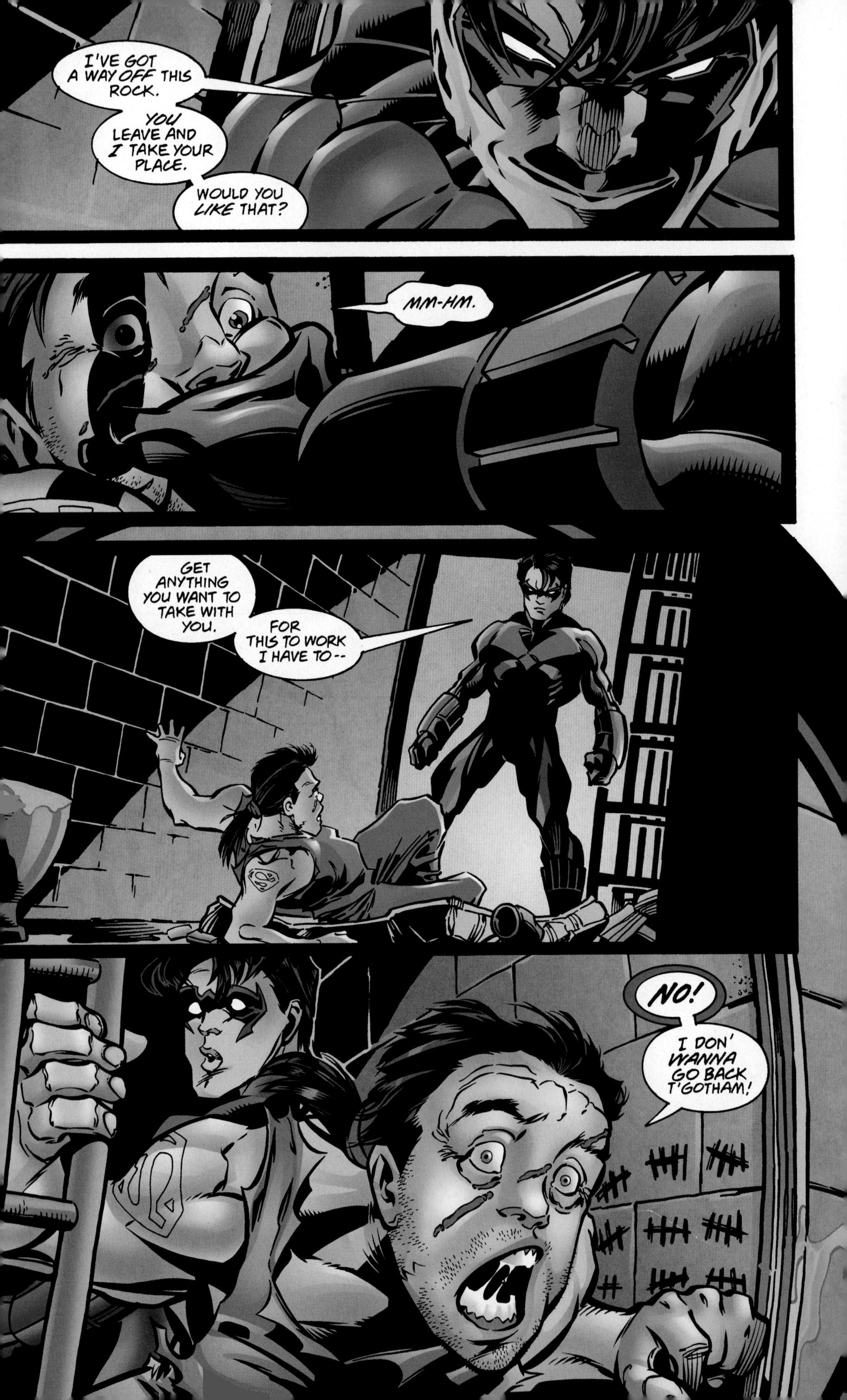
I'VE GOT A WAY OFF THIS ROCK.
YOU LEAVE AND I TAKE YOUR PLACE.
WOULD YOU LIKE THAT?
MM-HM.
GET ANYTHING YOU WANT TO TAKE WITH YOU.
FOR THIS TO WORK I HAVE TO--
NO!
I DON' WANNA GO BACK T'GOTHAM!

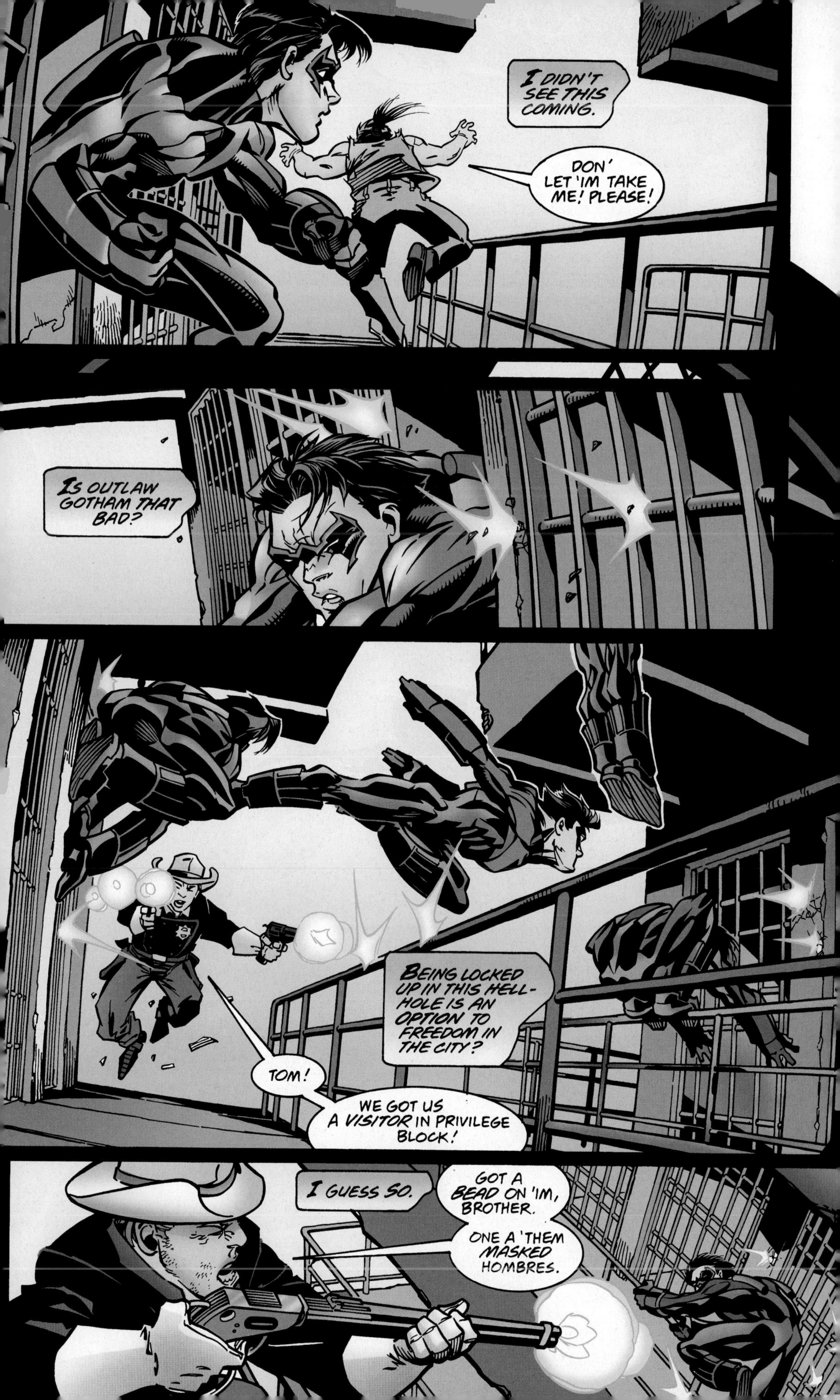

I DIDN'T SEE THIS COMING.
DON' LET 'IM TAKE ME! PLEASE!
IS OUTLAW GOTHAM THAT BAD?
BEING LOCKED UP IN THIS HELL-HOLE IS AN OPTION TO FREEDOM IN THE CITY?
TOM!
WE GOT US A VISITOR IN PRIVILEGE BLOCK!
I GUESS SO.
GOT A BEAD ON 'IM, BROTHER.
ONE A 'THEM MASKED HOMBRES.

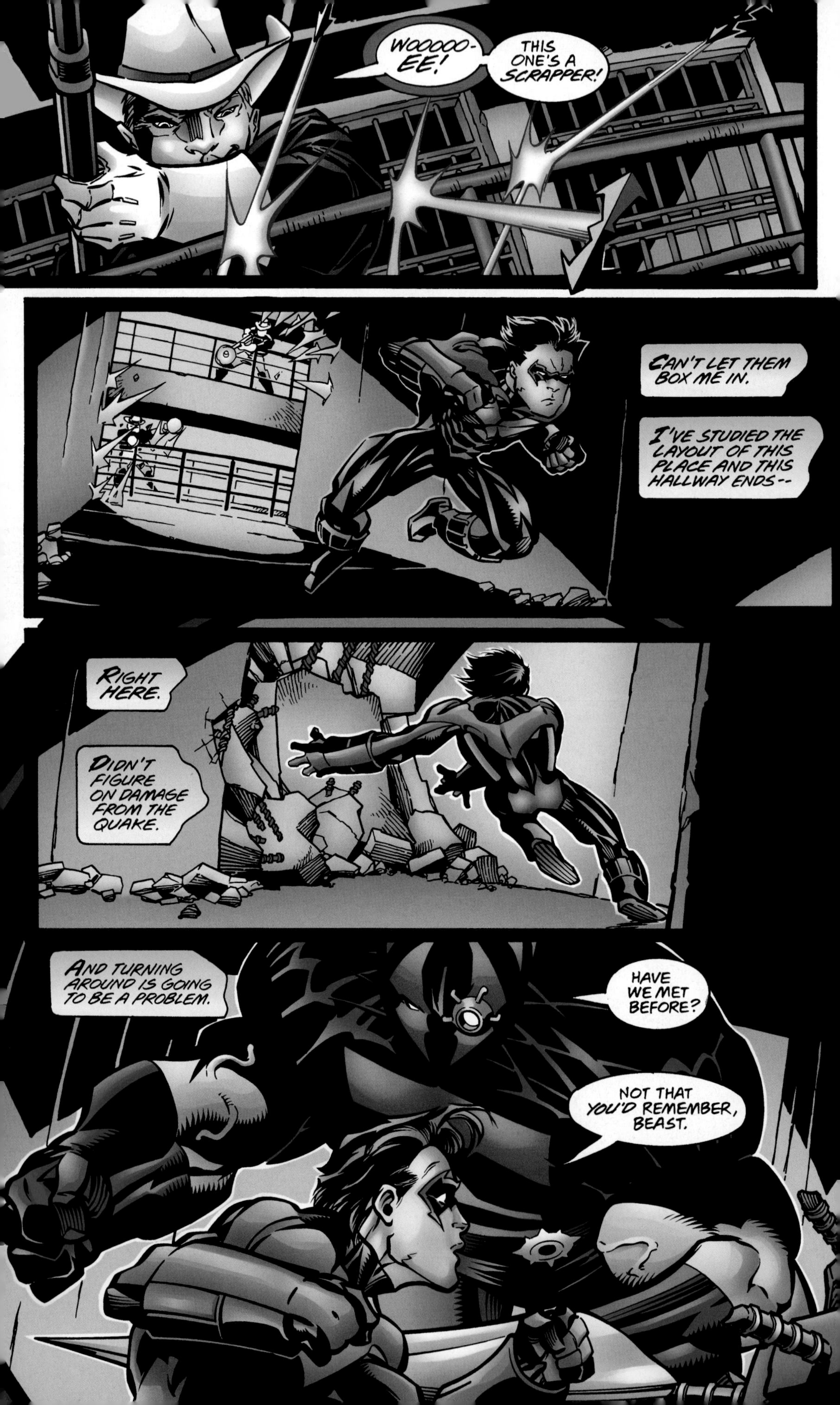
WOOOOO-EE!
THIS ONE'S A SCRAPPER!
CAN'T LET THEM BOX ME IN.
I'VE STUDIED THE LAYOUT OF THIS PLACE AND THIS HALLWAY ENDS--
RIGHT HERE.
DIDN'T FIGURE ON DAMAGE FROM THE QUAKE.
AND TURNING AROUND IS GOING TO BE A PROBLEM.
HAVE WE MET BEFORE?
NOT THAT YOU'D REMEMBER, BEAST.

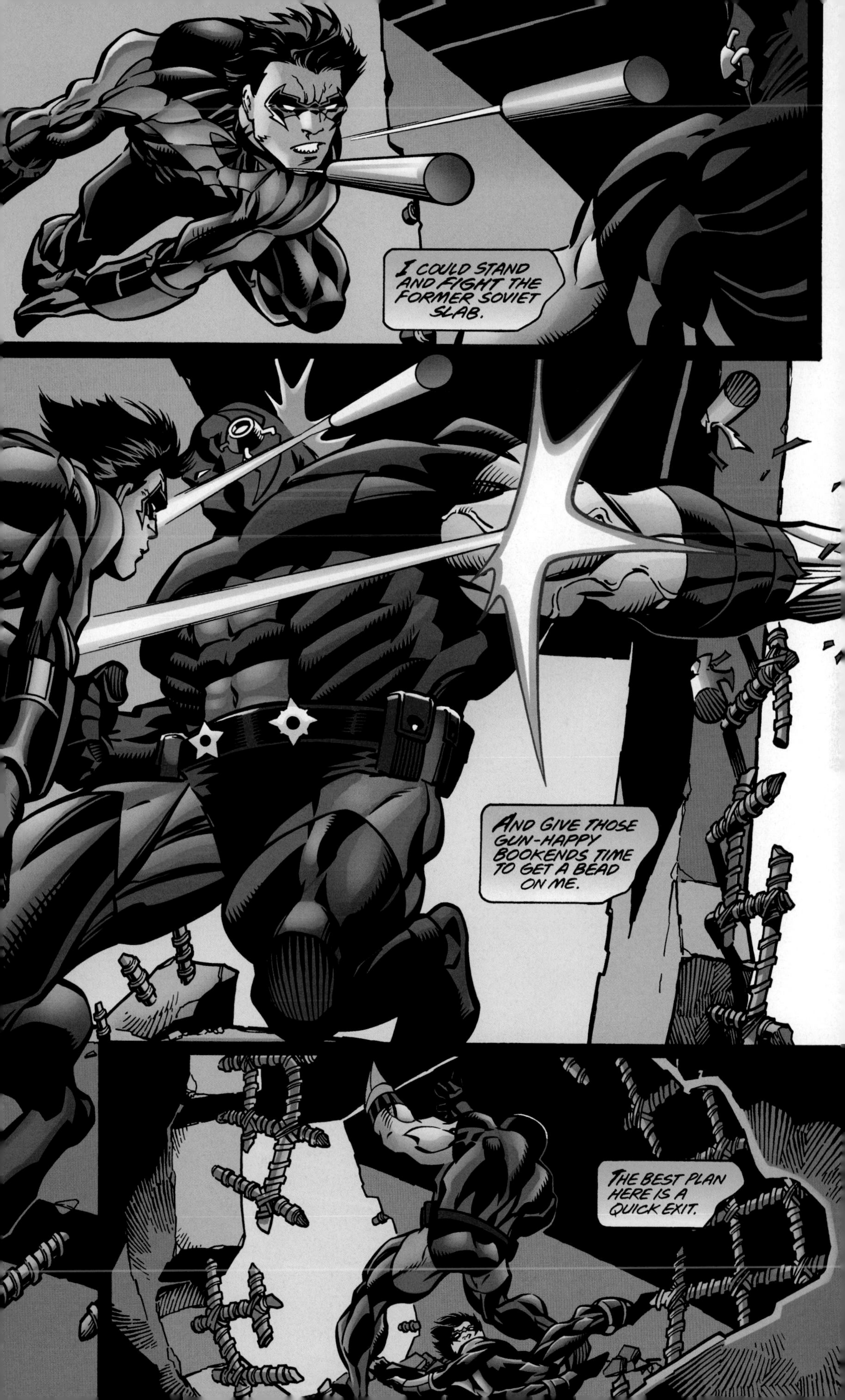
I COULD STAND AND FIGHT THE FORMER SOVIET SLAB.
AND GIVE THOSE GUN-HAPPY BOOKENDS TIME TO GET A BEAD ON ME.
THE BEST PLAN HERE IS A QUICK EXIT.

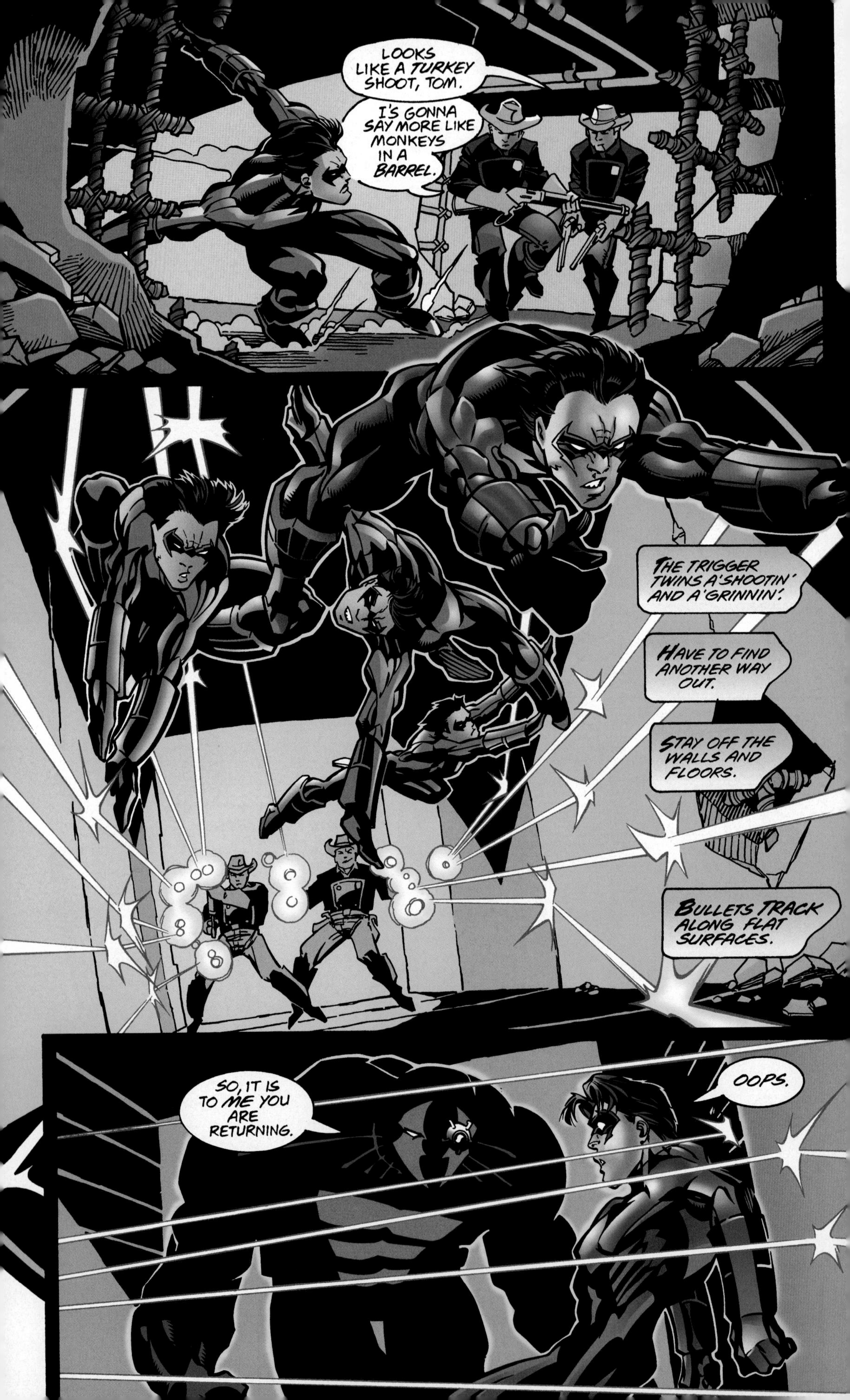

LOOKS LIKE A TURKEY SHOOT, TOM.
I'S GONNA SAY MORE LIKE MONKEYS IN A BARREL.
THE TRIGGER TWINS A'SHOOTIN' AND A'GRINNIN'.
HAVE TO FIND ANOTHER WAY OUT.
STAY OFF THE WALLS AND FLOORS.
BULLETS TRACK ALONG FLAT SURFACES.
SO, IT IS TO ME YOU ARE RETURNING.
OOPS.

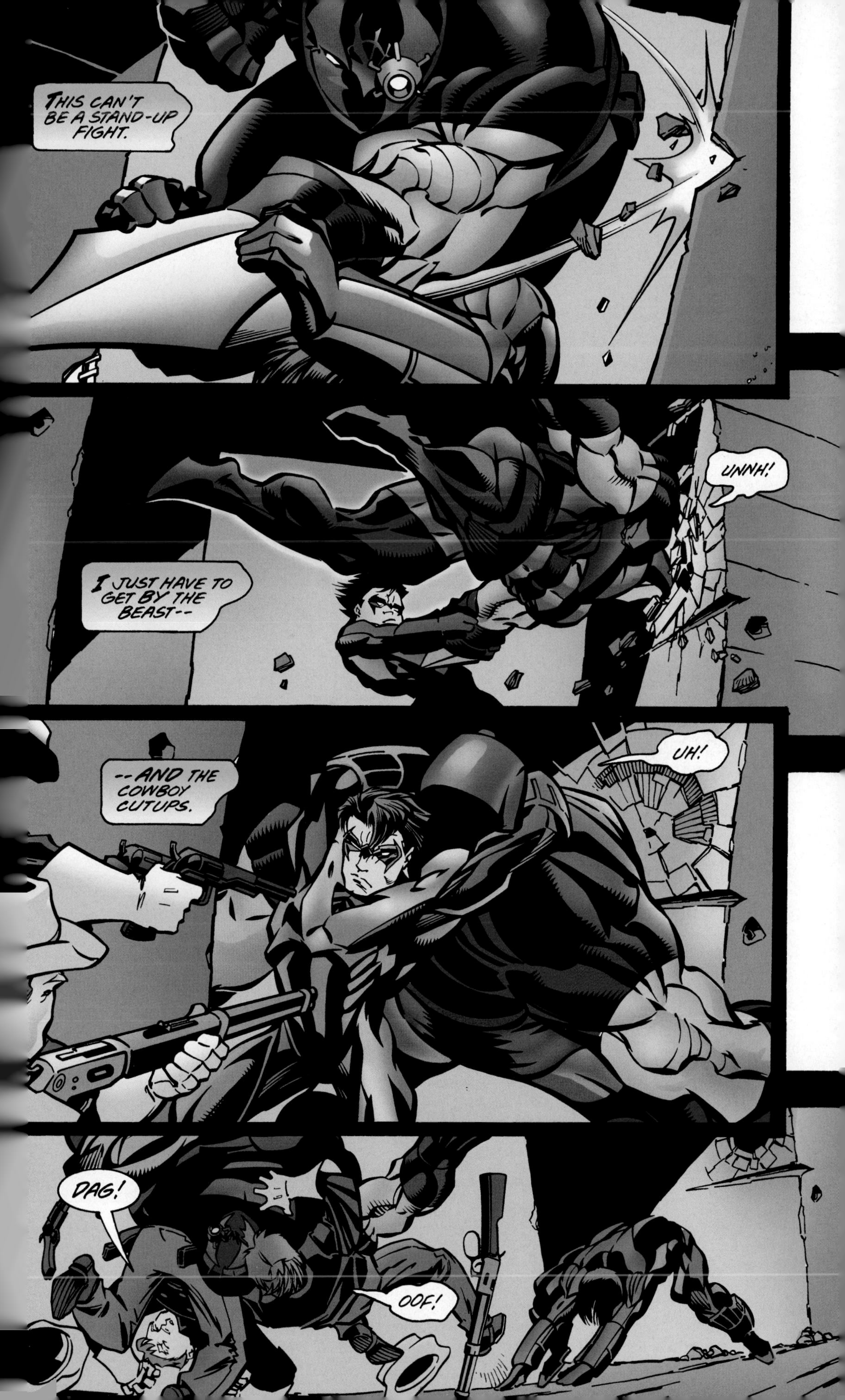
THIS CAN'T BE A STAND-UP FIGHT.
UNNH!
I JUST HAVE TO GET BY THE BEAST--
UH!
--AND THE COWBOY CUTUPS.
DAG!
OOF!

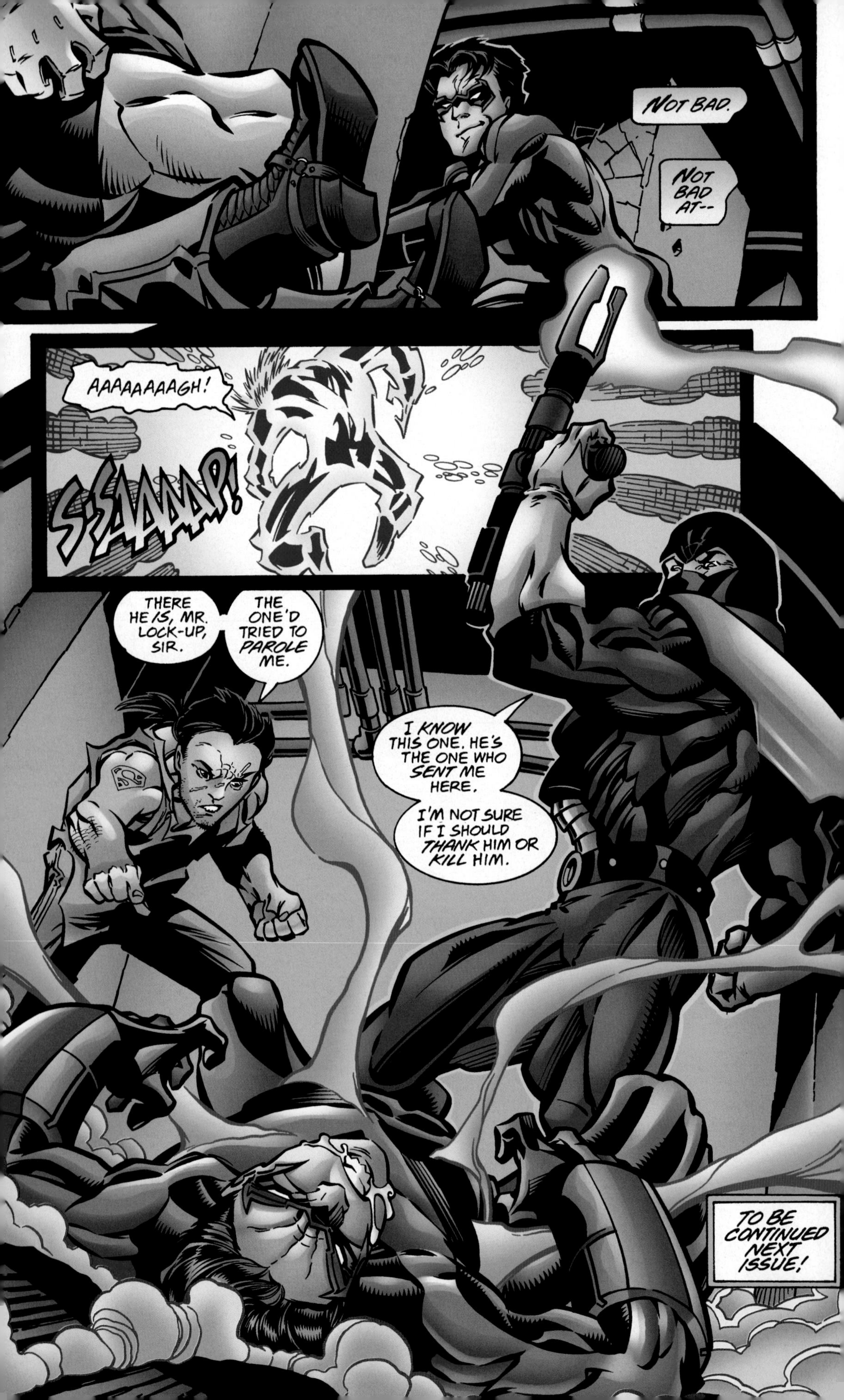
NOT BAD.
NOT BAD AT--
AAAAAAAAGH!
S-SLAAAP!
THERE HE IS, MR. LOCK-UP, SIR.
THE ONE'D TRIED TO PAROLE ME.
I KNOW THIS ONE. HE'S THE ONE WHO SENT ME HERE.
I'M NOT SURE IF I SHOULD THANK HIM OR KILL HIM.
TO BE CONTINUED NEXT ISSUE!

NOTHING BUT TIME

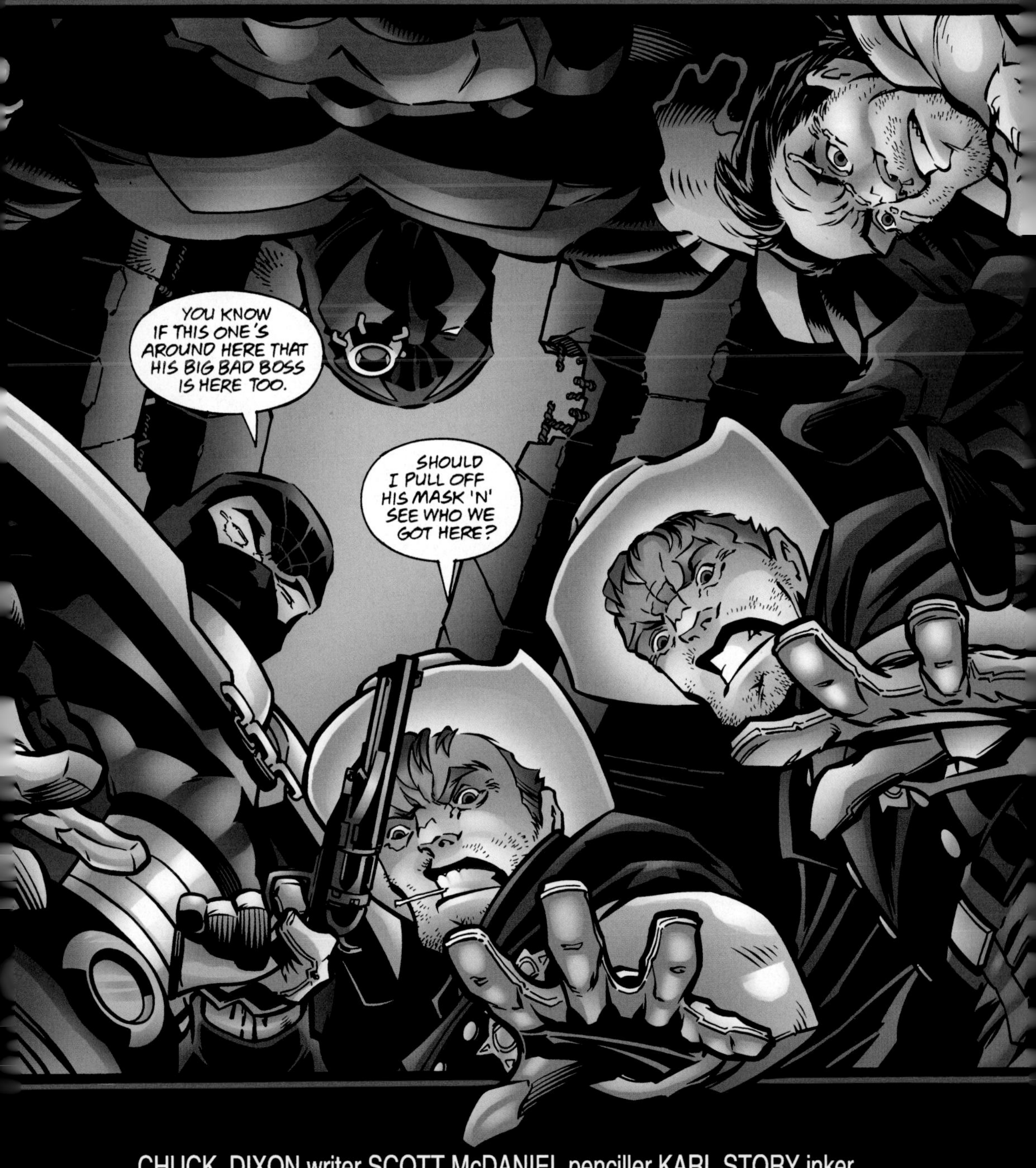

YOU KNOW IF THIS ONE'S AROUND HERE THAT HIS BIG BAD BOSS IS HERE TOO.
SHOULD I PULL OFF HIS MASK 'N' SEE WHO WE GOT HERE?

CHUCK DIXON writer SCOTT McDANIEL penciller KARL STORY inker
ROBERTA TEWES colorist JAMISON separator JOHN COSTANZA letterer
JOSEPH ILLIDGE associate editor DARREN VINCENZO warden

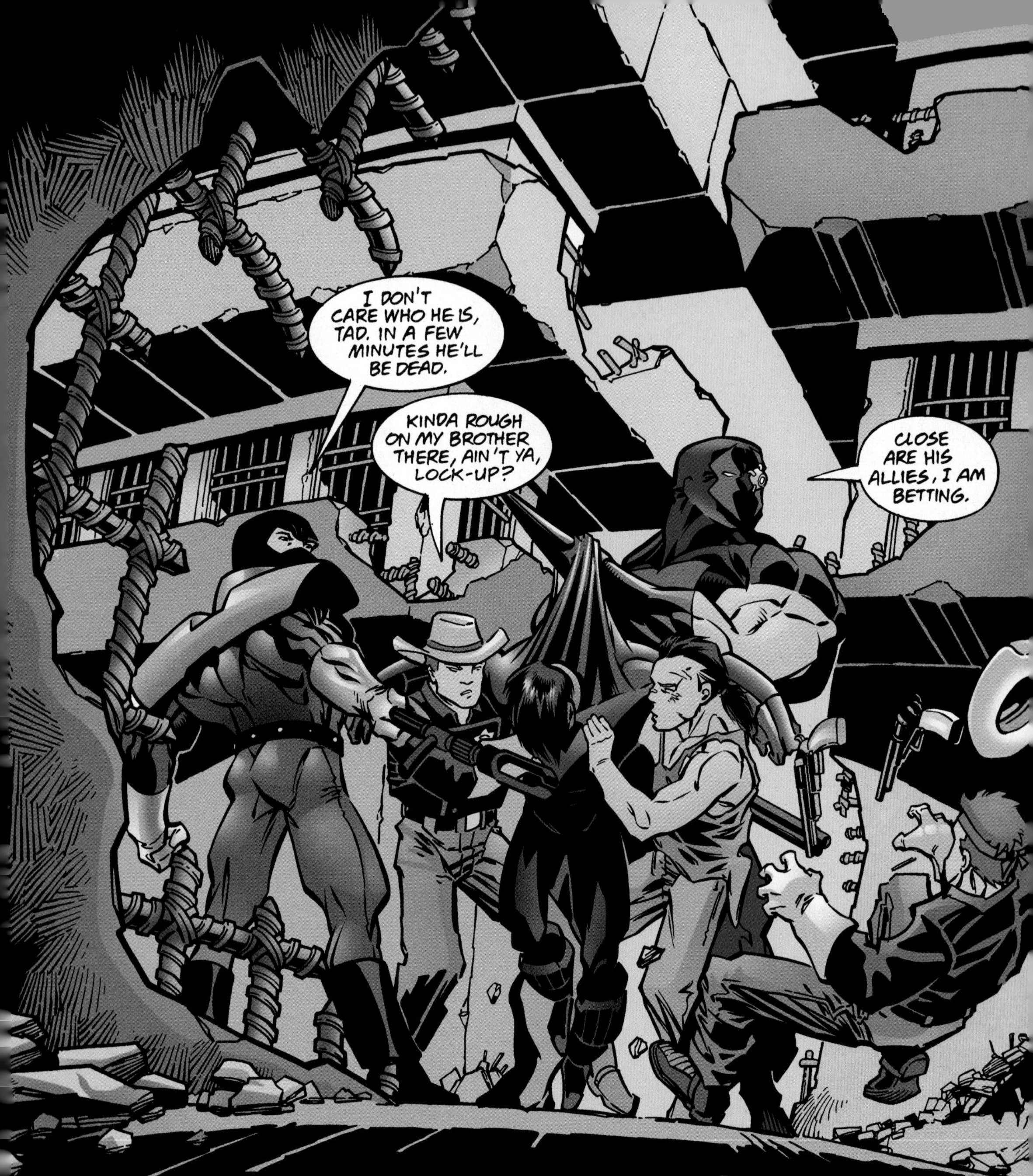
I DON'T CARE WHO HE IS, TAD. IN A FEW MINUTES HE'LL BE DEAD.
KINDA ROUGH ON MY BROTHER THERE, AIN'T YA, LOCK-UP?
CLOSE ARE HIS ALLIES, I AM BETTING.

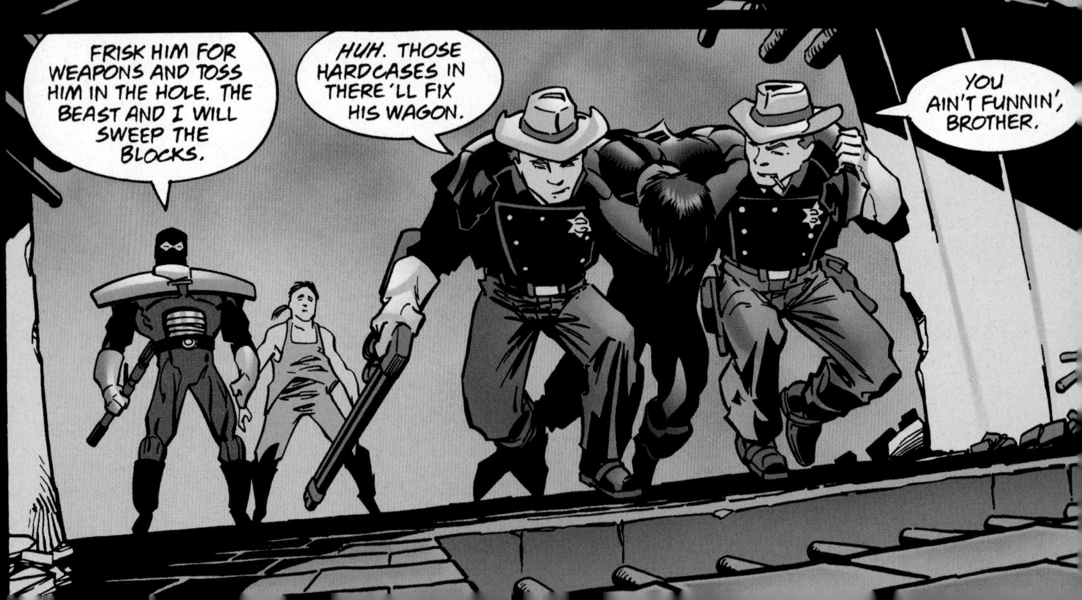
FRISK HIM FOR WEAPONS AND TOSS HIM IN THE HOLE. THE BEAST AND I WILL SWEEP THE BLOCKS.
HUH. THOSE HARDCASES IN THERE'LL FIX HIS WAGON.
YOU AIN'T FUNNIN', BROTHER.

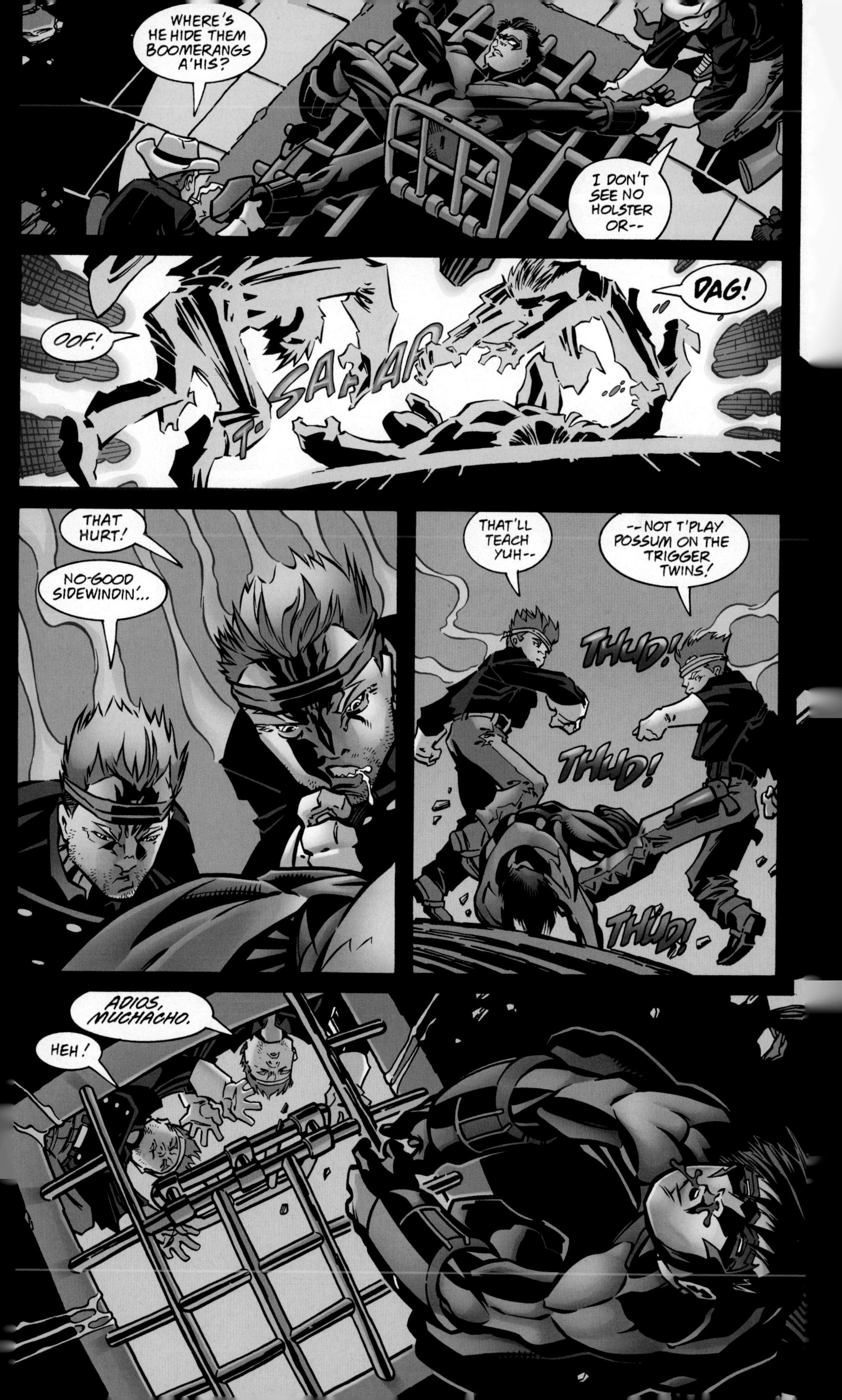
WHERE'S HE HIDE THEM BOOMERANGS A'HIS?
I DON'T SEE NO HOLSTER OR--
DAG!
OOF!
T-SAHAP
THAT HURT!
NO-GOOD SIDEWINDIN'...
THAT'LL TEACH YUH--
--NOT T'PLAY POSSUM ON THE TRIGGER TWINS!
THUD!
THUD!
THUD!
ADIOS, MUCHACHO.
HEH!

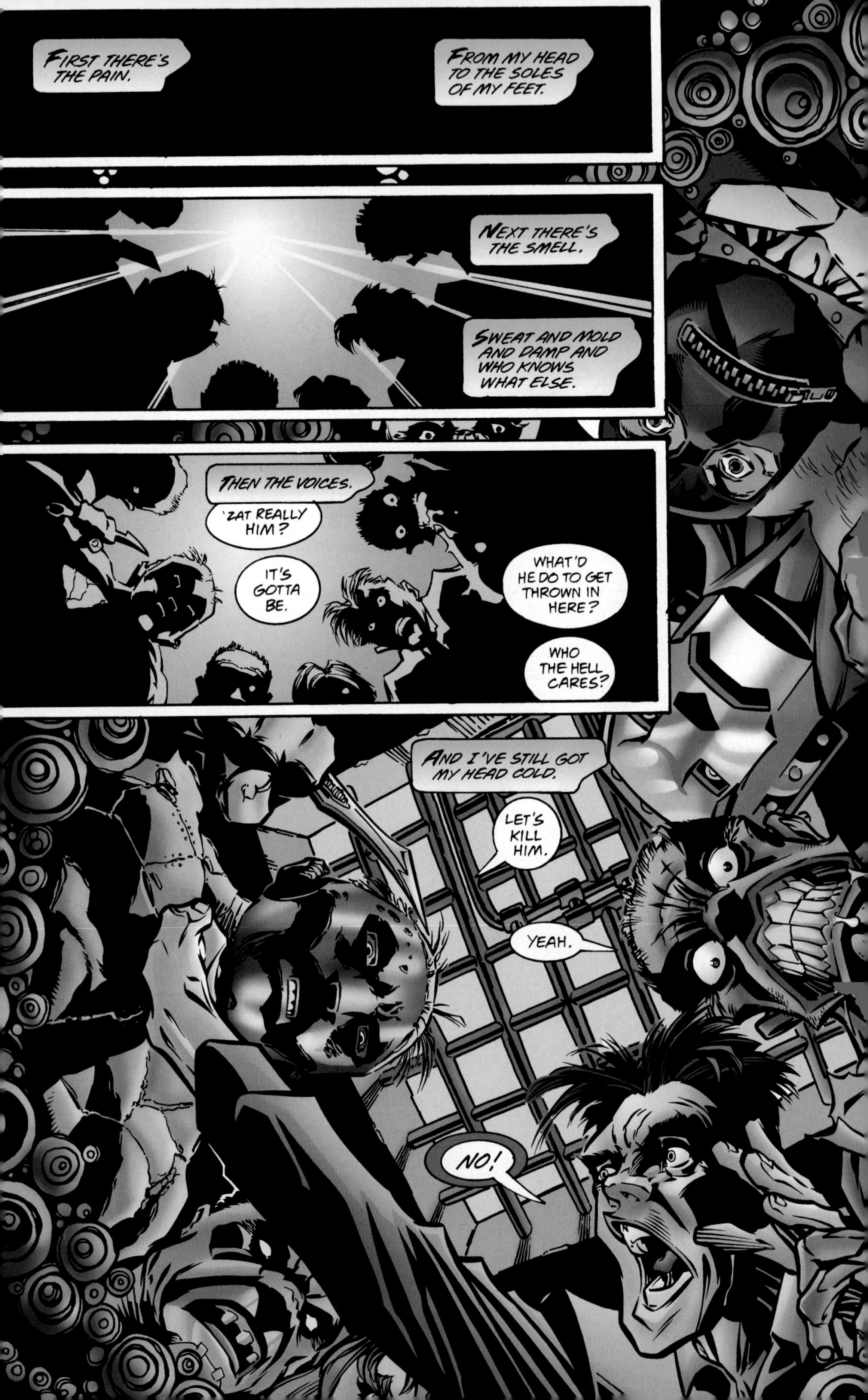
FIRST THERE'S THE PAIN.
FROM MY HEAD TO THE SOLES OF MY FEET.
NEXT THERE'S THE SMELL.
SWEAT AND MOLD AND DAMP AND WHO KNOWS WHAT ELSE.
THEN THE VOICES.
'ZAT REALLY HIM?
IT'S GOTTA BE.
WHAT'D HE DO TO GET THROWN IN HERE?
WHO THE HELL CARES?
AND I'VE STILL GOT MY HEAD COLD.
LET'S KILL HIM.
YEAH.
NO!

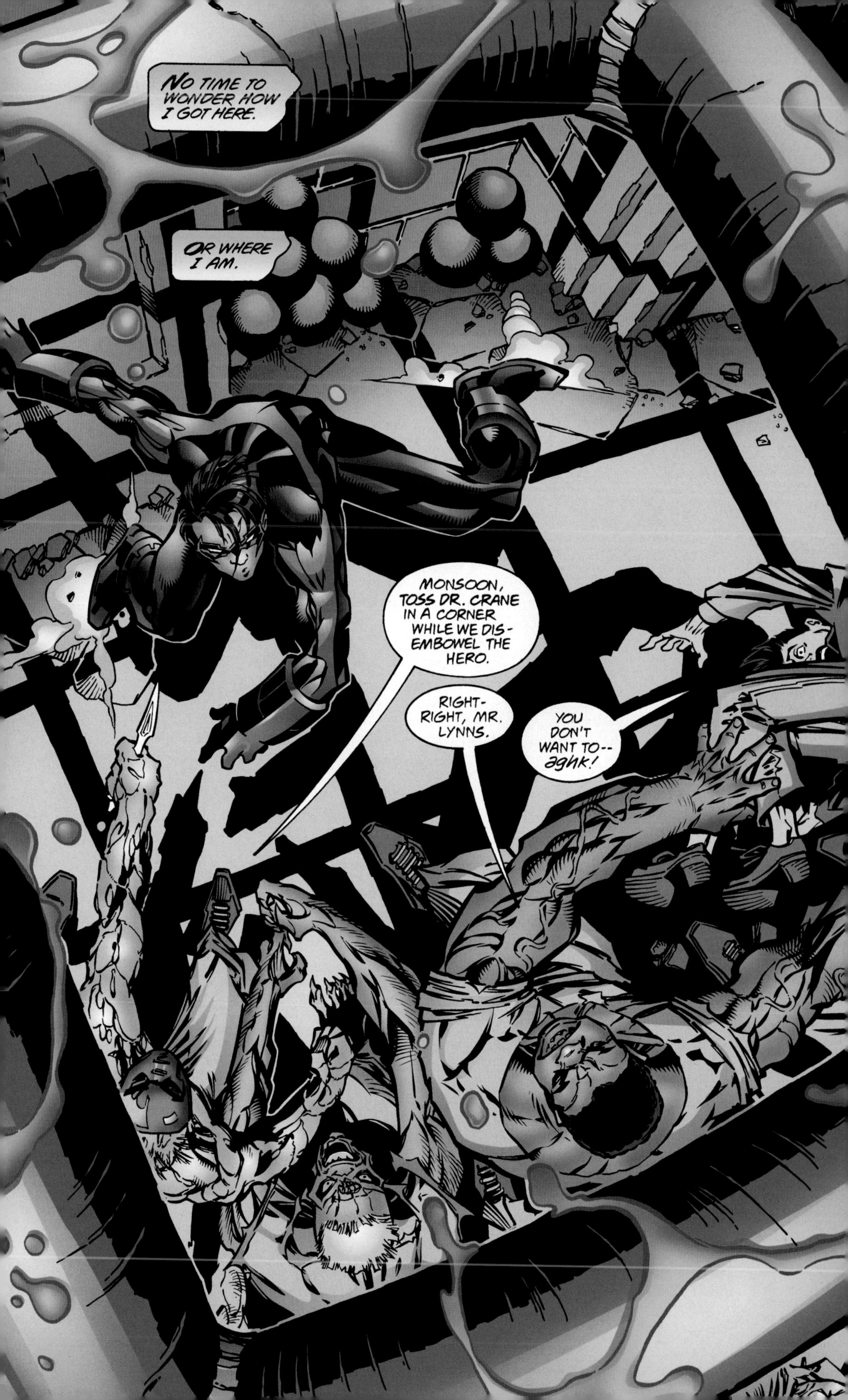
NO TIME TO WONDER HOW I GOT HERE.
OR WHERE I AM.
MONSOON, TOSS DR. CRANE IN A CORNER WHILE WE DIS-EMBOWEL THE HERO.
RIGHT-RIGHT, MR. LYNNS.
YOU DON'T WANT TO-- aghk!

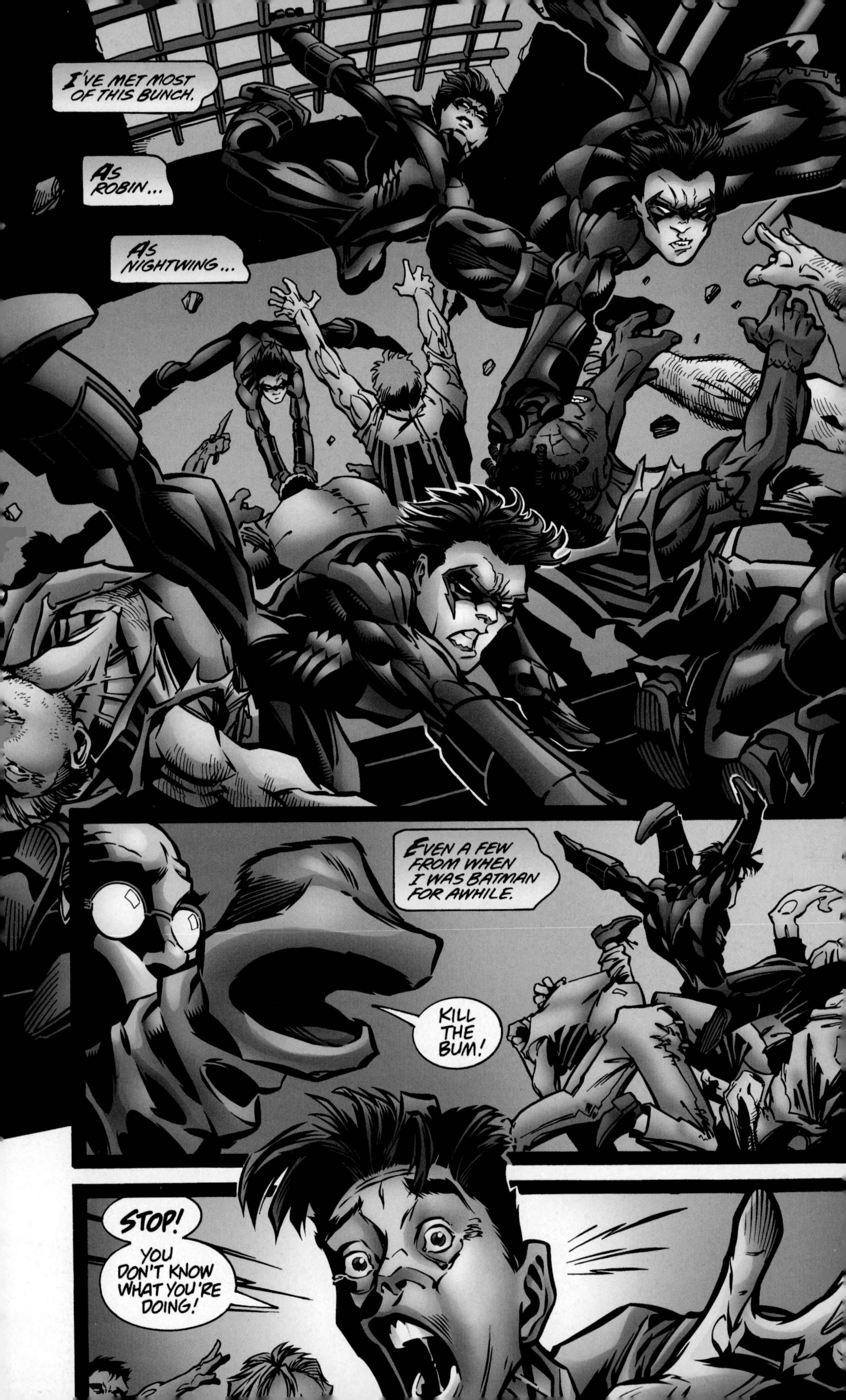
I'VE MET MOST OF THIS BUNCH.
AS ROBIN...
AS NIGHTWING...
EVEN A FEW FROM WHEN I WAS BATMAN FOR AWHILE.
KILL THE BUM!
STOP!
YOU DON'T KNOW WHAT YOU'RE DOING!

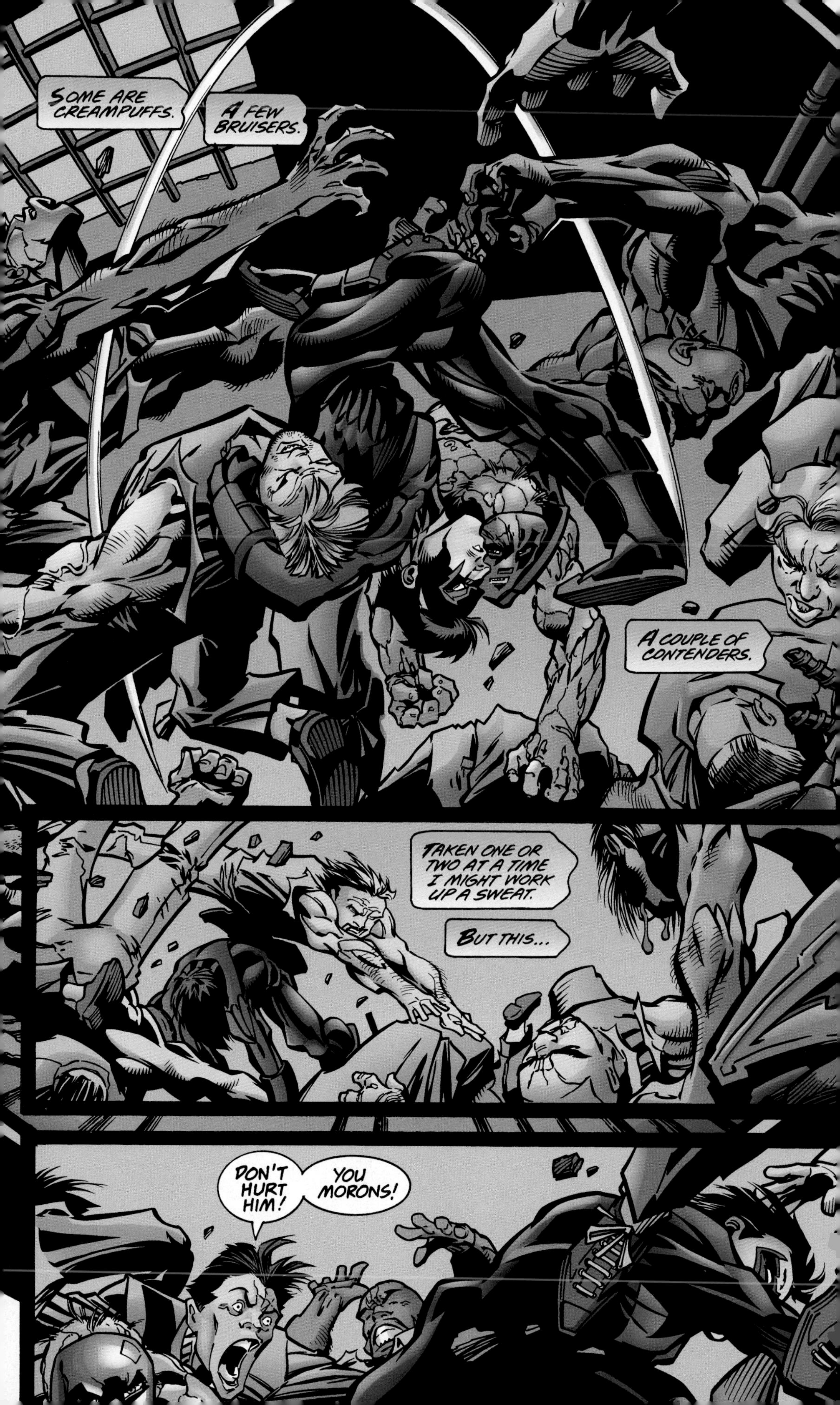
SOME ARE CREAMPUFFS.
A FEW BRUISERS.
A COUPLE OF CONTENDERS.
TAKEN ONE OR TWO AT A TIME I MIGHT WORK UP A SWEAT.
BUT THIS...
DON'T HURT HIM!
YOU MORONS!

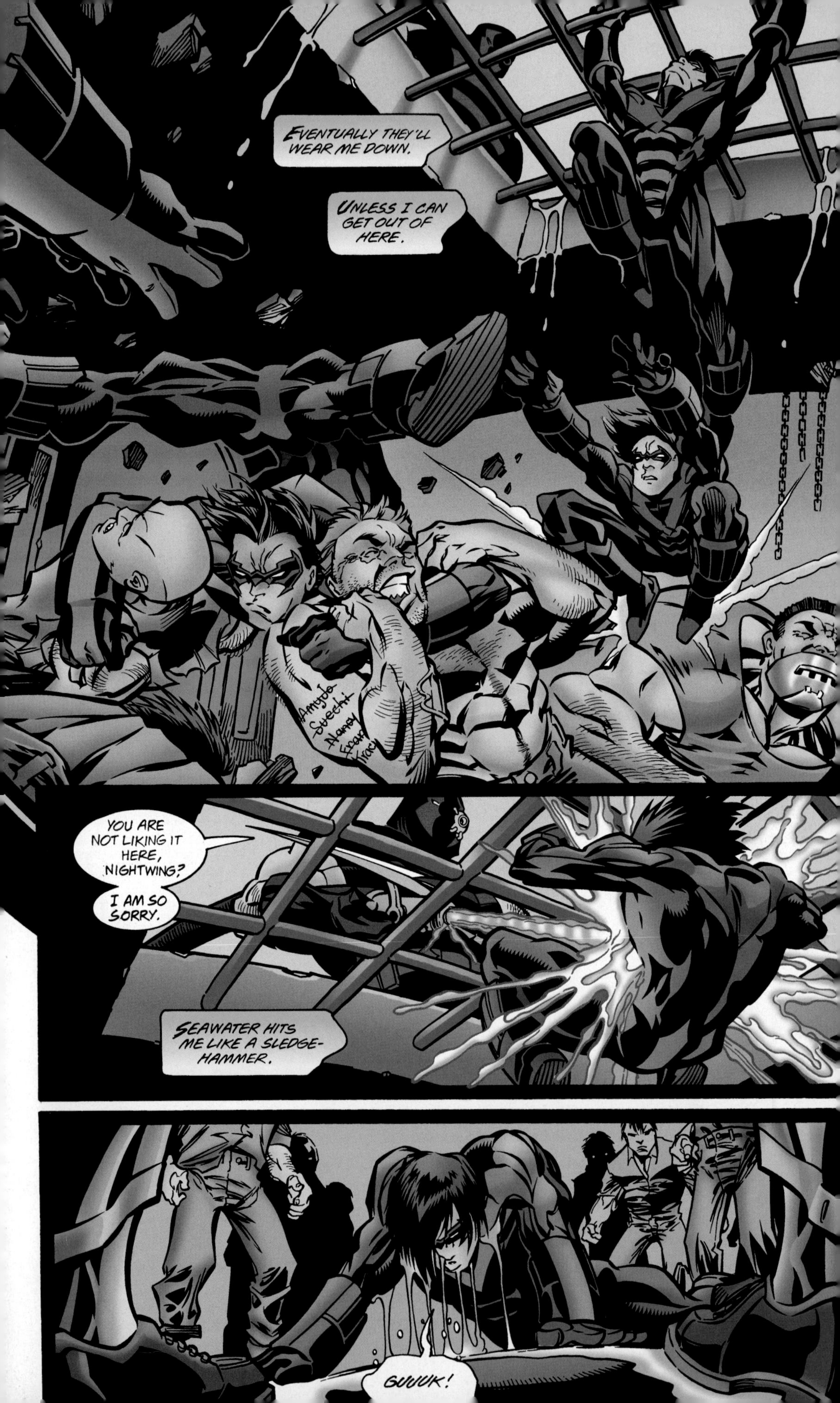
EVENTUALLY THEY'LL WEAR ME DOWN.
UNLESS I CAN GET OUT OF HERE.
YOU ARE NOT LIKING IT HERE, NIGHTWING?
I AM SO SORRY.
SEAWATER HITS ME LIKE A SLEDGE-HAMMER.
GUUUK!

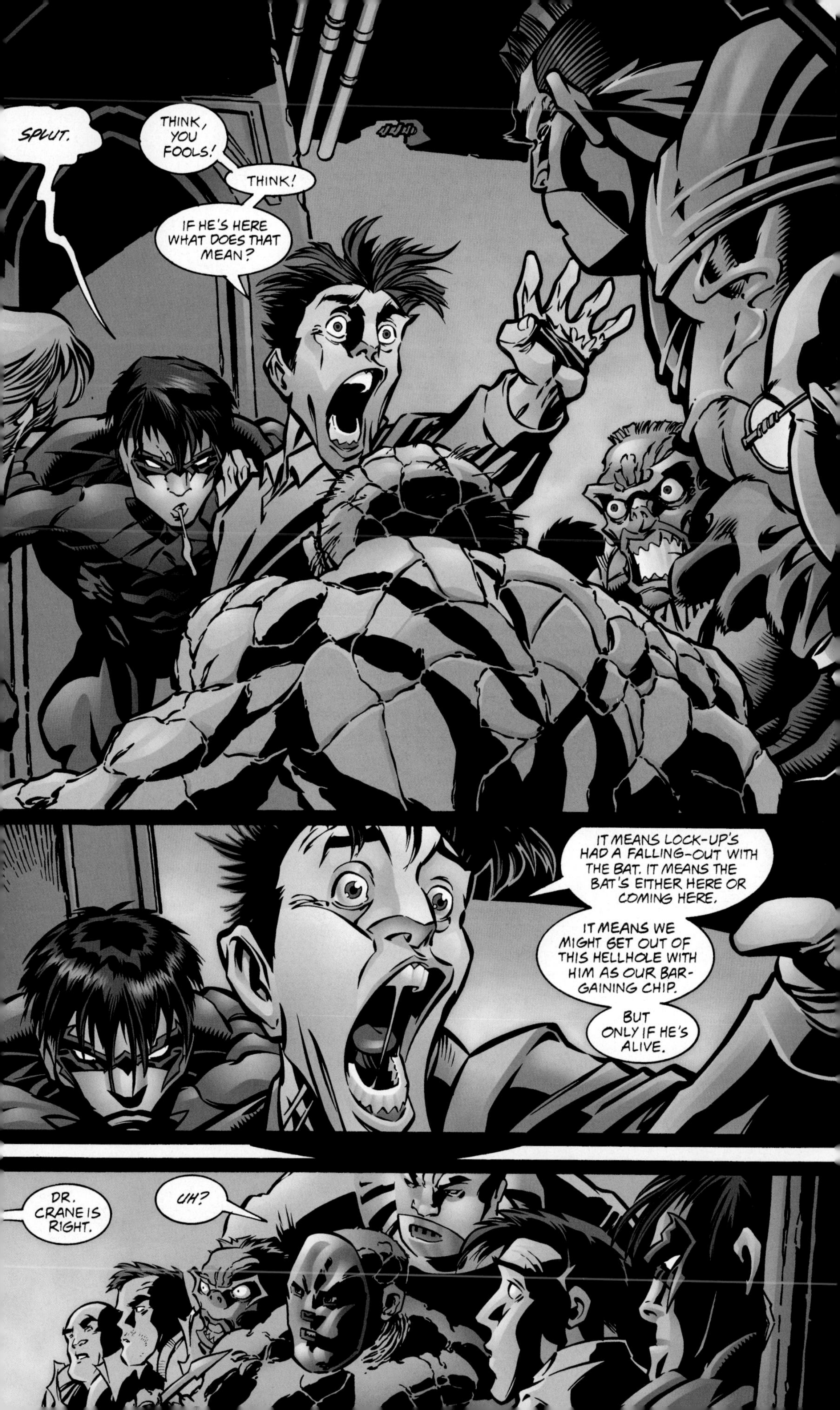
SPLUT.
THINK, YOU FOOLS!
THINK!
IF HE'S HERE WHAT DOES THAT MEAN?
IT MEANS LOCK-UP'S HAD A FALLING-OUT WITH THE BAT. IT MEANS THE BAT'S EITHER HERE OR COMING HERE.
IT MEANS WE MIGHT GET OUT OF THIS HELLHOLE WITH HIM AS OUR BARGAINING CHIP.
BUT ONLY IF HE'S ALIVE.
DR. CRANE IS RIGHT.
UH?

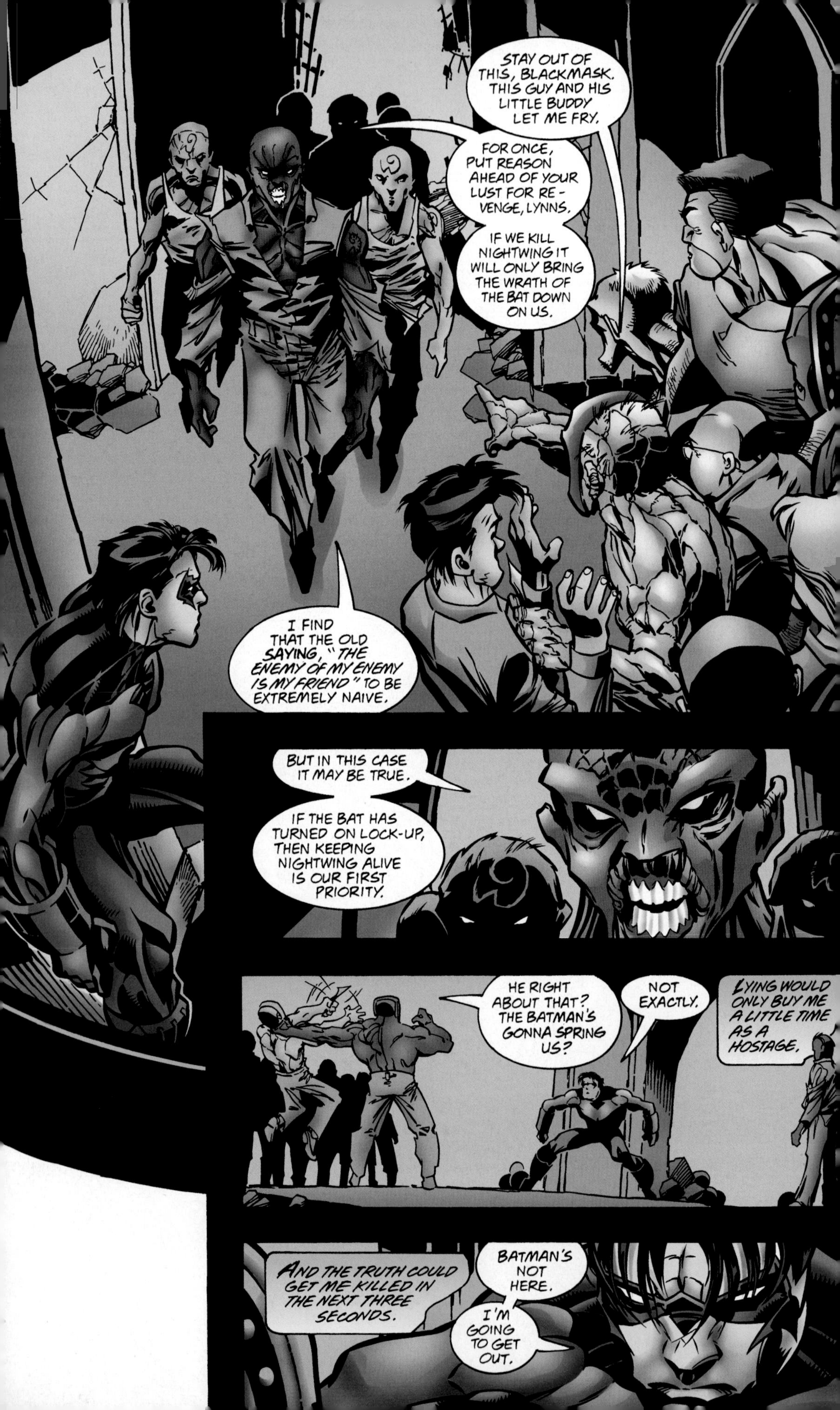
STAY OUT OF THIS, BLACKMASK. THIS GUY AND HIS LITTLE BUDDY LET ME FRY.
FOR ONCE, PUT REASON AHEAD OF YOUR LUST FOR RE-VENGE, LYNNS.
IF WE KILL NIGHTWING IT WILL ONLY BRING THE WRATH OF THE BAT DOWN ON US.
I FIND THAT THE OLD SAYING, "THE ENEMY OF MY ENEMY IS MY FRIEND" TO BE EXTREMELY NAIVE.
BUT IN THIS CASE IT MAY BE TRUE.
IF THE BAT HAS TURNED ON LOCK-UP, THEN KEEPING NIGHTWING ALIVE IS OUR FIRST PRIORITY.
HE RIGHT ABOUT THAT? THE BATMAN'S GONNA SPRING US?
NOT EXACTLY.
LYING WOULD ONLY BUY ME A LITTLE TIME AS A HOSTAGE.
AND THE TRUTH COULD GET ME KILLED IN THE NEXT THREE SECONDS.
BATMAN'S NOT HERE.
I'M GOING TO GET OUT.

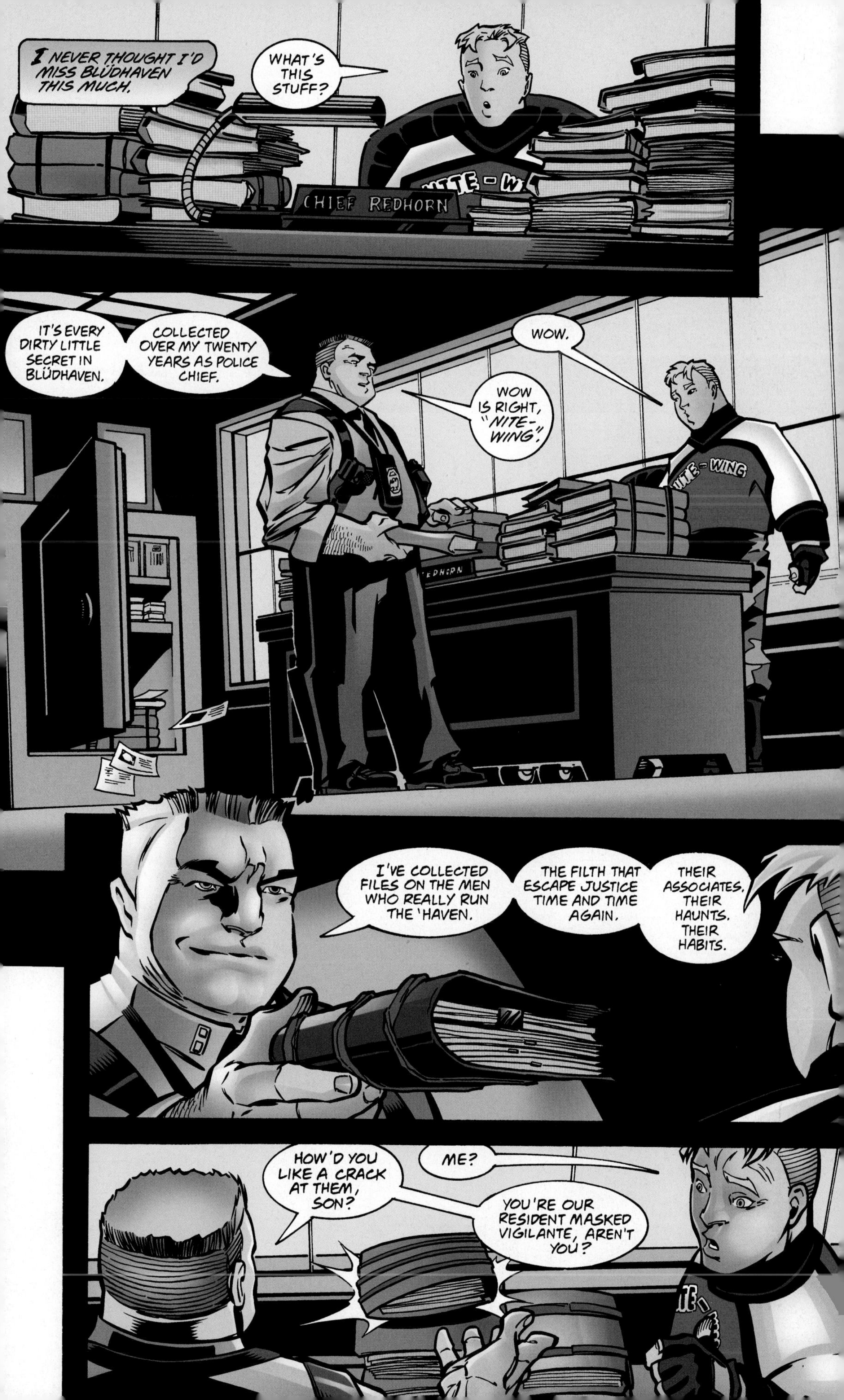
I NEVER THOUGHT I'D MISS BLÜDHAVEN THIS MUCH.
WHAT'S THIS STUFF?
CHIEF REDHORN
IT'S EVERY DIRTY LITTLE SECRET IN BLÜDHAVEN.
COLLECTED OVER MY TWENTY YEARS AS POLICE CHIEF.
WOW.
WOW IS RIGHT, "NITE-WING".
I'VE COLLECTED FILES ON THE MEN WHO REALLY RUN THE 'HAVEN.
THE FILTH THAT ESCAPE JUSTICE TIME AND TIME AGAIN.
THEIR ASSOCIATES. THEIR HAUNTS. THEIR HABITS.
HOW'D YOU LIKE A CRACK AT THEM, SON?
ME?
YOU'RE OUR RESIDENT MASKED VIGILANTE, AREN'T YOU?

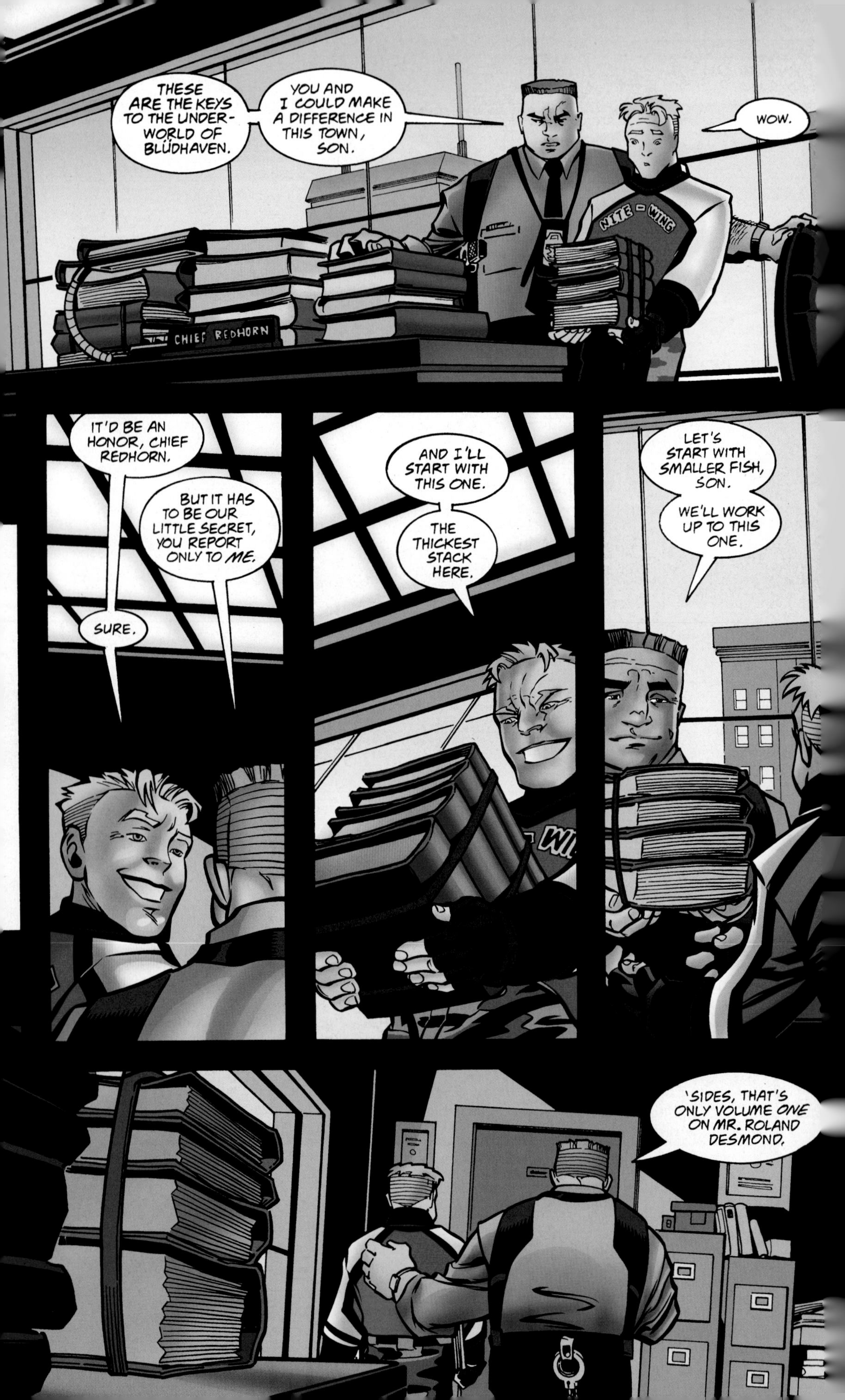
THESE ARE THE KEYS TO THE UNDER-WORLD OF BLÜDHAVEN.
YOU AND I COULD MAKE A DIFFERENCE IN THIS TOWN, SON.
WOW.
CHIEF REDHORN
NITE-WING
IT'D BE AN HONOR, CHIEF REDHORN.
BUT IT HAS TO BE OUR LITTLE SECRET, YOU REPORT ONLY TO *ME*.
SURE.
AND I'LL START WITH THIS ONE.
THE THICKEST STACK HERE.
LET'S START WITH SMALLER FISH, SON.
WE'LL WORK UP TO THIS ONE.
'SIDES, THAT'S ONLY VOLUME *ONE* ON MR. ROLAND DESMOND.

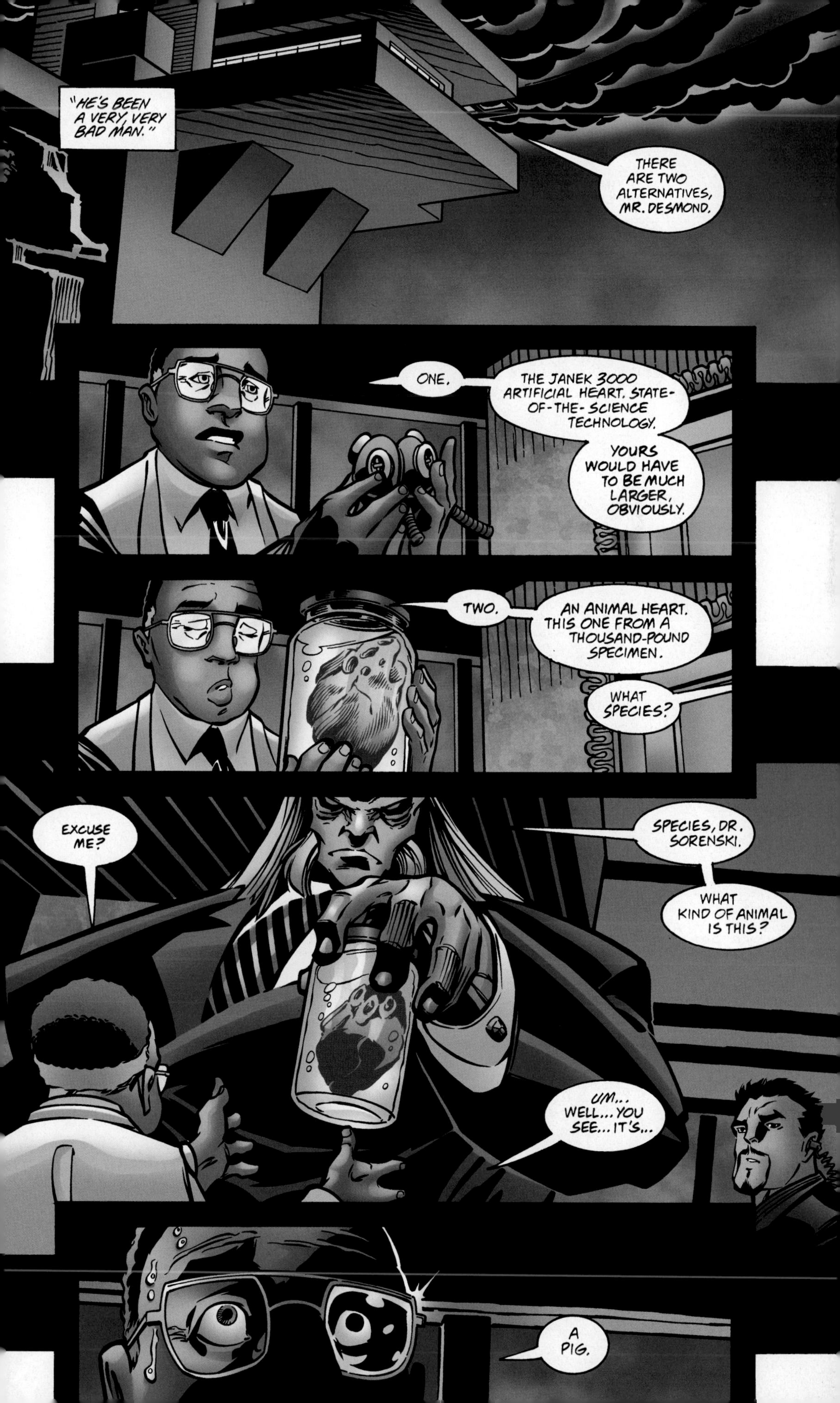
"HE'S BEEN A VERY, VERY BAD MAN."
THERE ARE TWO ALTERNATIVES, MR. DESMOND.
ONE.
THE JANEK 3000 ARTIFICIAL HEART. STATE-OF-THE-SCIENCE TECHNOLOGY.
YOURS WOULD HAVE TO BE MUCH LARGER, OBVIOUSLY.
TWO.
AN ANIMAL HEART. THIS ONE FROM A THOUSAND-POUND SPECIMEN.
WHAT SPECIES?
EXCUSE ME?
SPECIES, DR. SORENSKI.
WHAT KIND OF ANIMAL IS THIS?
UM... WELL... YOU SEE... IT'S...
A PIG.

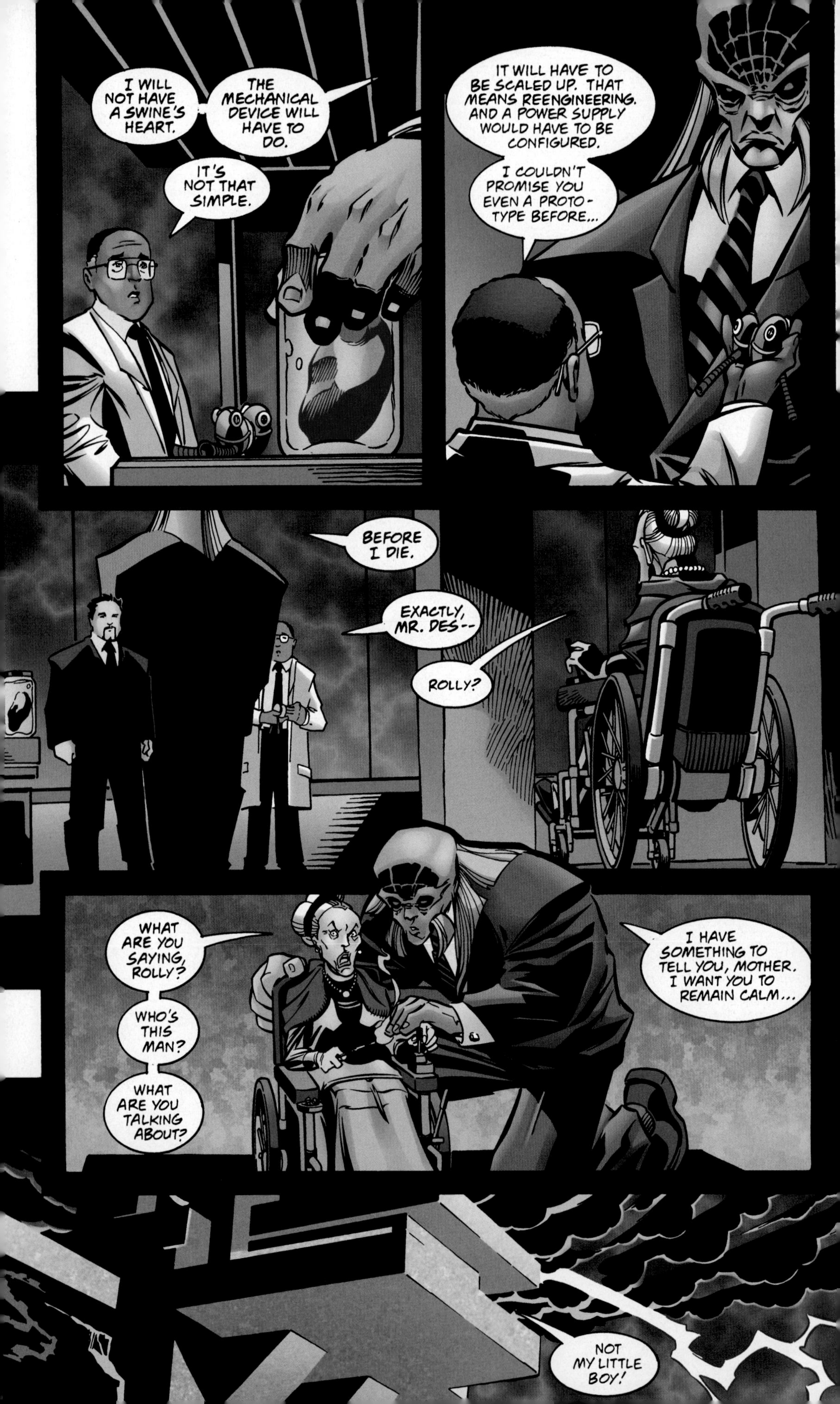
I WILL NOT HAVE A SWINE'S HEART.
THE MECHANICAL DEVICE WILL HAVE TO DO.
IT'S NOT THAT SIMPLE.
IT WILL HAVE TO BE SCALED UP. THAT MEANS REENGINEERING. AND A POWER SUPPLY WOULD HAVE TO BE CONFIGURED.
I COULDN'T PROMISE YOU EVEN A PROTO-TYPE BEFORE...
BEFORE I DIE.
EXACTLY, MR. DES--
ROLLY?
WHAT ARE YOU SAYING, ROLLY?
WHO'S THIS MAN?
WHAT ARE YOU TALKING ABOUT?
I HAVE SOMETHING TO TELL YOU, MOTHER. I WANT YOU TO REMAIN CALM...
NOT MY LITTLE BOY!

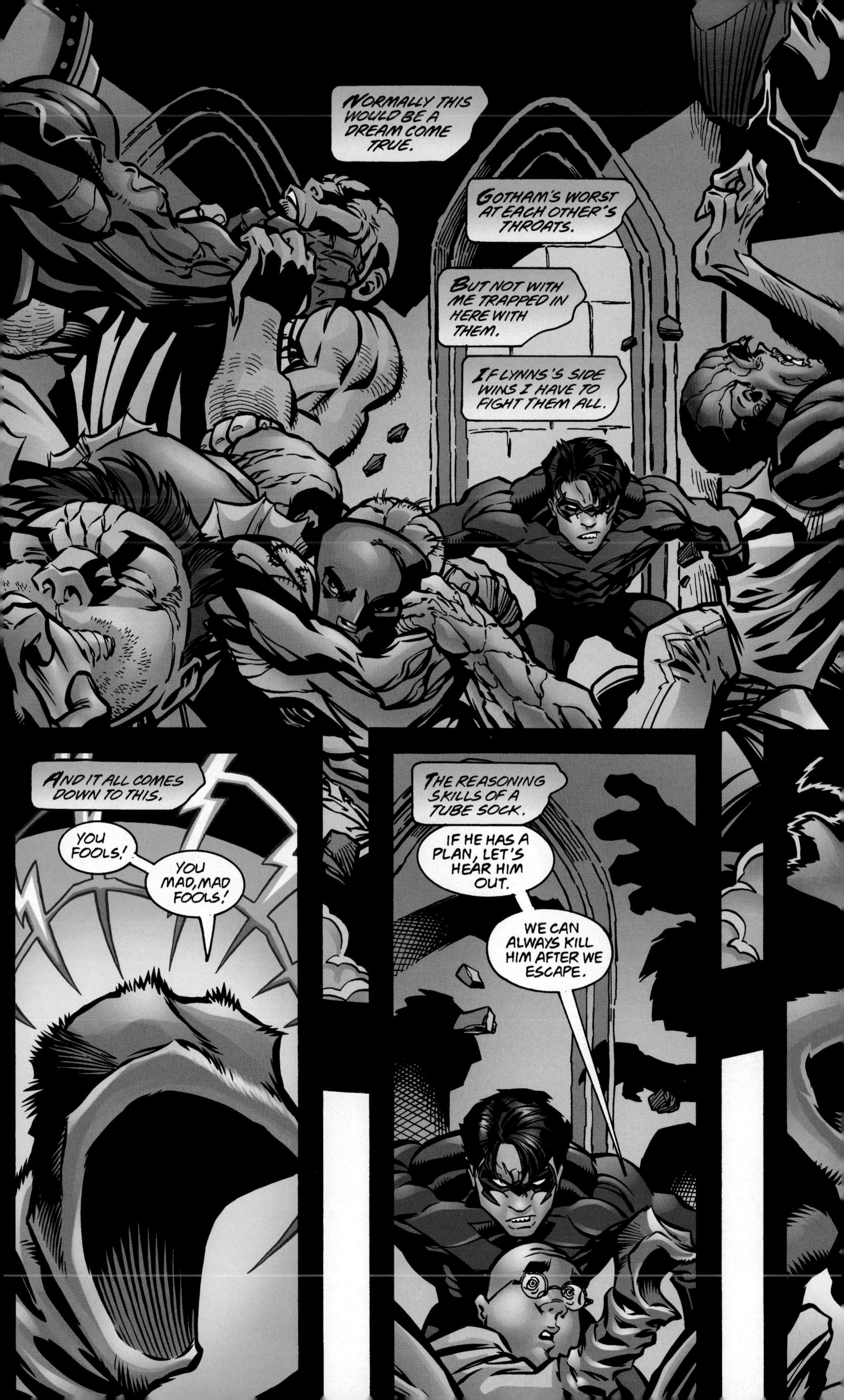
NORMALLY THIS WOULD BE A DREAM COME TRUE.
GOTHAM'S WORST AT EACH OTHER'S THROATS.
BUT NOT WITH ME TRAPPED IN HERE WITH THEM.
IF LYNNS'S SIDE WINS I HAVE TO FIGHT THEM ALL.
AND IT ALL COMES DOWN TO THIS.
YOU FOOLS!
YOU MAD, MAD FOOLS!
THE REASONING SKILLS OF A TUBE SOCK.
IF HE HAS A PLAN, LET'S HEAR HIM OUT.
WE CAN ALWAYS KILL HIM AFTER WE ESCAPE.

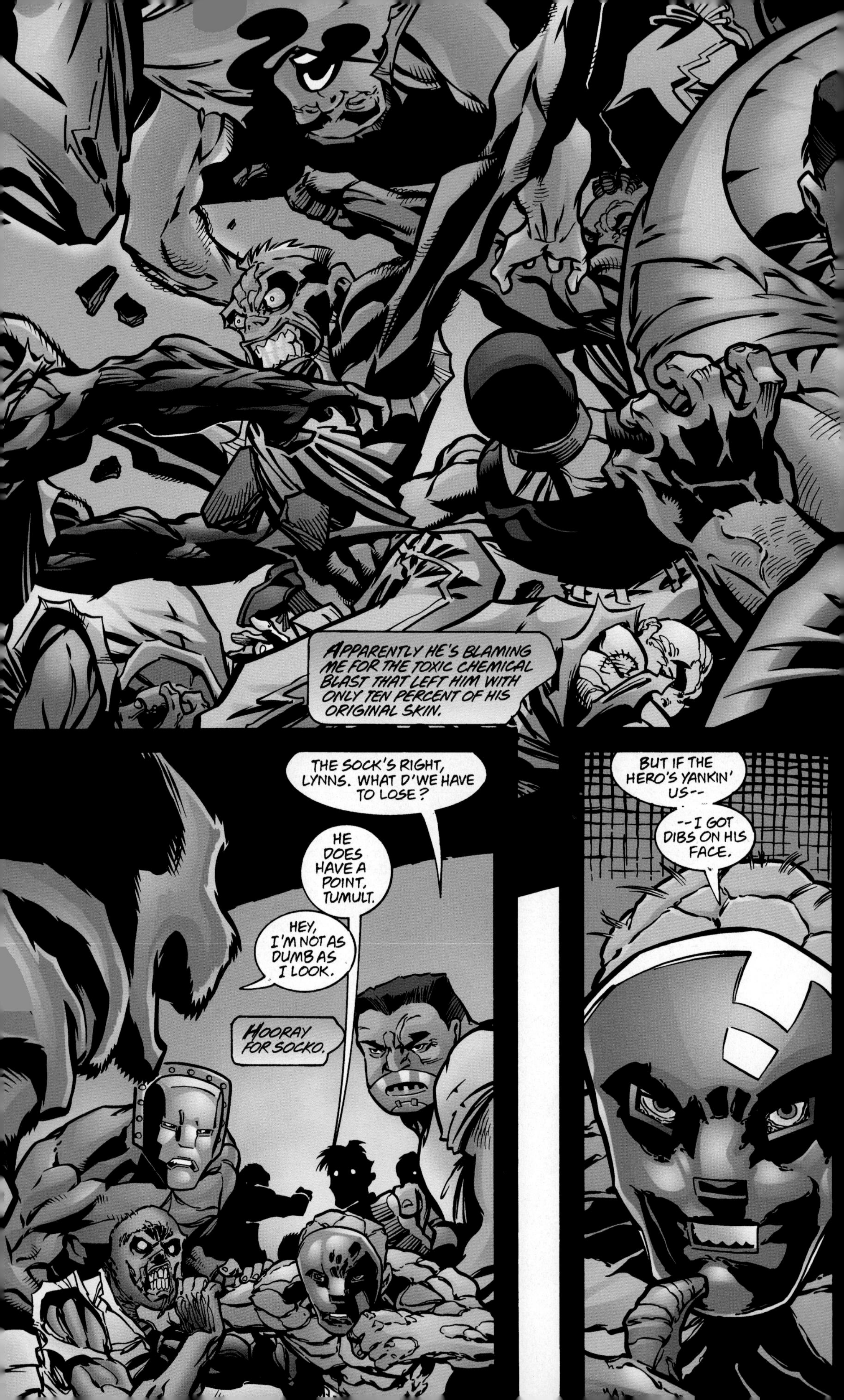
APPARENTLY HE'S BLAMING ME FOR THE TOXIC CHEMICAL BLAST THAT LEFT HIM WITH ONLY TEN PERCENT OF HIS ORIGINAL SKIN.
THE SOCK'S RIGHT, LYNNS. WHAT D'WE HAVE TO LOSE?
HE DOES HAVE A POINT, TUMULT.
HEY, I'M NOT AS DUMB AS I LOOK.
HOORAY FOR SOCKO.
BUT IF THE HERO'S YANKIN' US--
--I GOT DIBS ON HIS FACE.

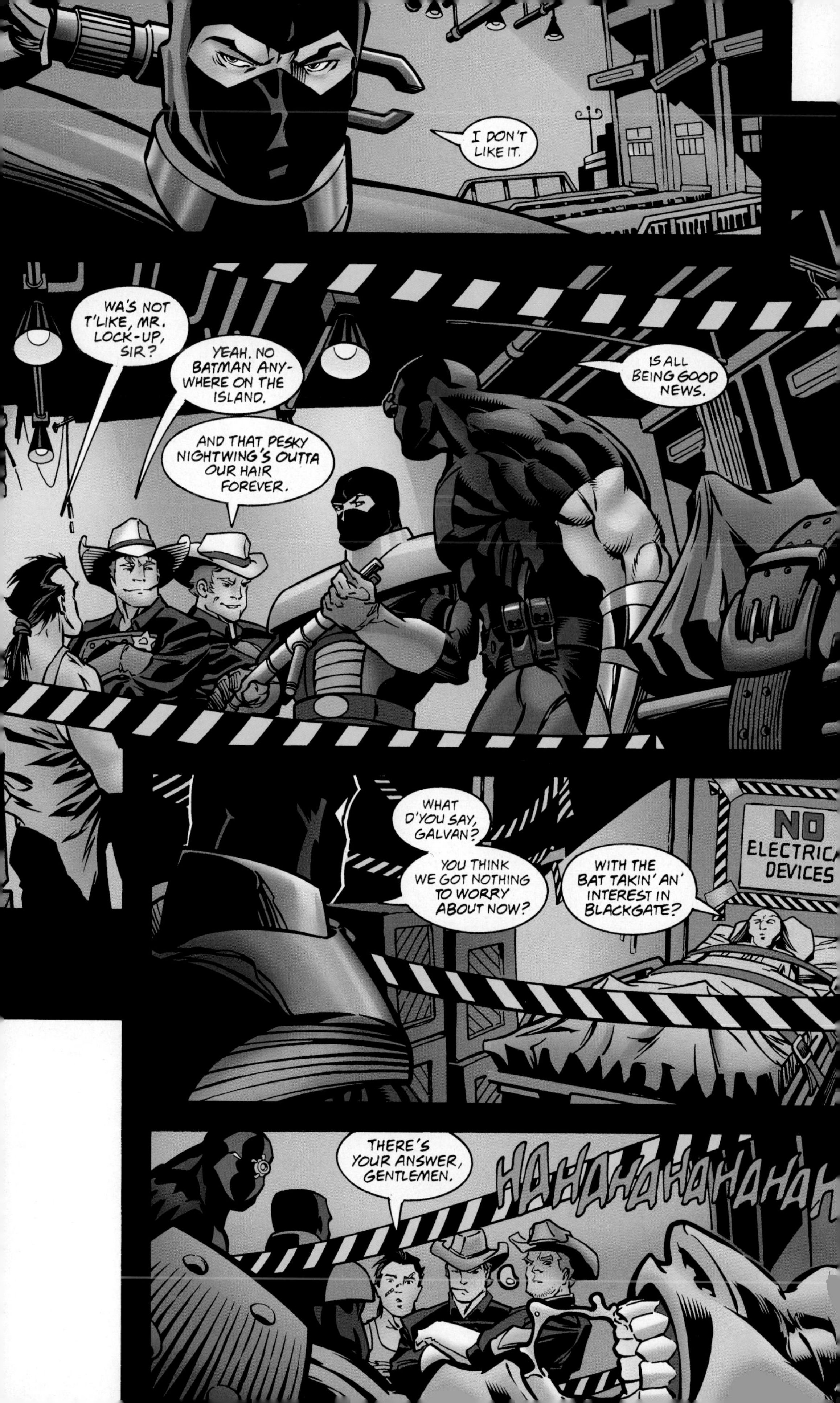

I DON'T LIKE IT.
WA'S NOT T'LIKE, MR. LOCK-UP, SIR?
YEAH. NO BATMAN ANYWHERE ON THE ISLAND.
AND THAT PESKY NIGHTWING'S OUTTA OUR HAIR FOREVER.
IS ALL BEING GOOD NEWS.
WHAT D'YOU SAY, GALVAN?
YOU THINK WE GOT NOTHING TO WORRY ABOUT NOW?
WITH THE BAT TAKIN' AN' INTEREST IN BLACKGATE?
NO ELECTRICAL DEVICES
THERE'S YOUR ANSWER, GENTLEMEN.
HAHAHAHAHAHAHAH

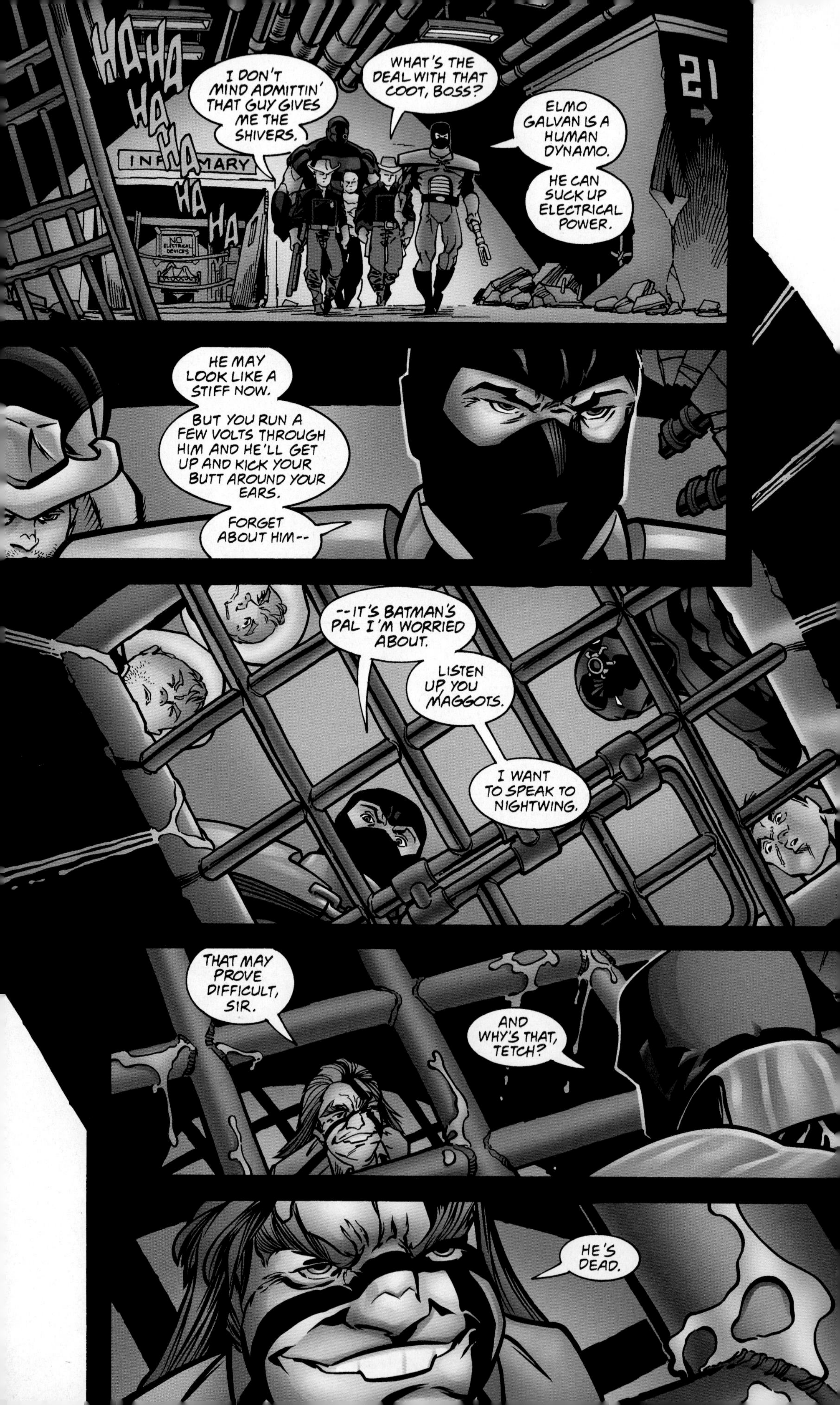
HA HA HA HA HA HA HA
INFIRMARY
NO ELECTRICAL DEVICES
21
I DON'T MIND ADMITTIN' THAT GUY GIVES ME THE SHIVERS.
WHAT'S THE DEAL WITH THAT COOT, BOSS?
ELMO GALVAN IS A HUMAN DYNAMO.
HE CAN SUCK UP ELECTRICAL POWER.
HE MAY LOOK LIKE A STIFF NOW.
BUT YOU RUN A FEW VOLTS THROUGH HIM AND HE'LL GET UP AND KICK YOUR BUTT AROUND YOUR EARS.
FORGET ABOUT HIM--
--IT'S BATMAN'S PAL I'M WORRIED ABOUT.
LISTEN UP YOU MAGGOTS.
I WANT TO SPEAK TO NIGHTWING.
THAT MAY PROVE DIFFICULT, SIR.
AND WHY'S THAT, TETCH?
HE'S DEAD.

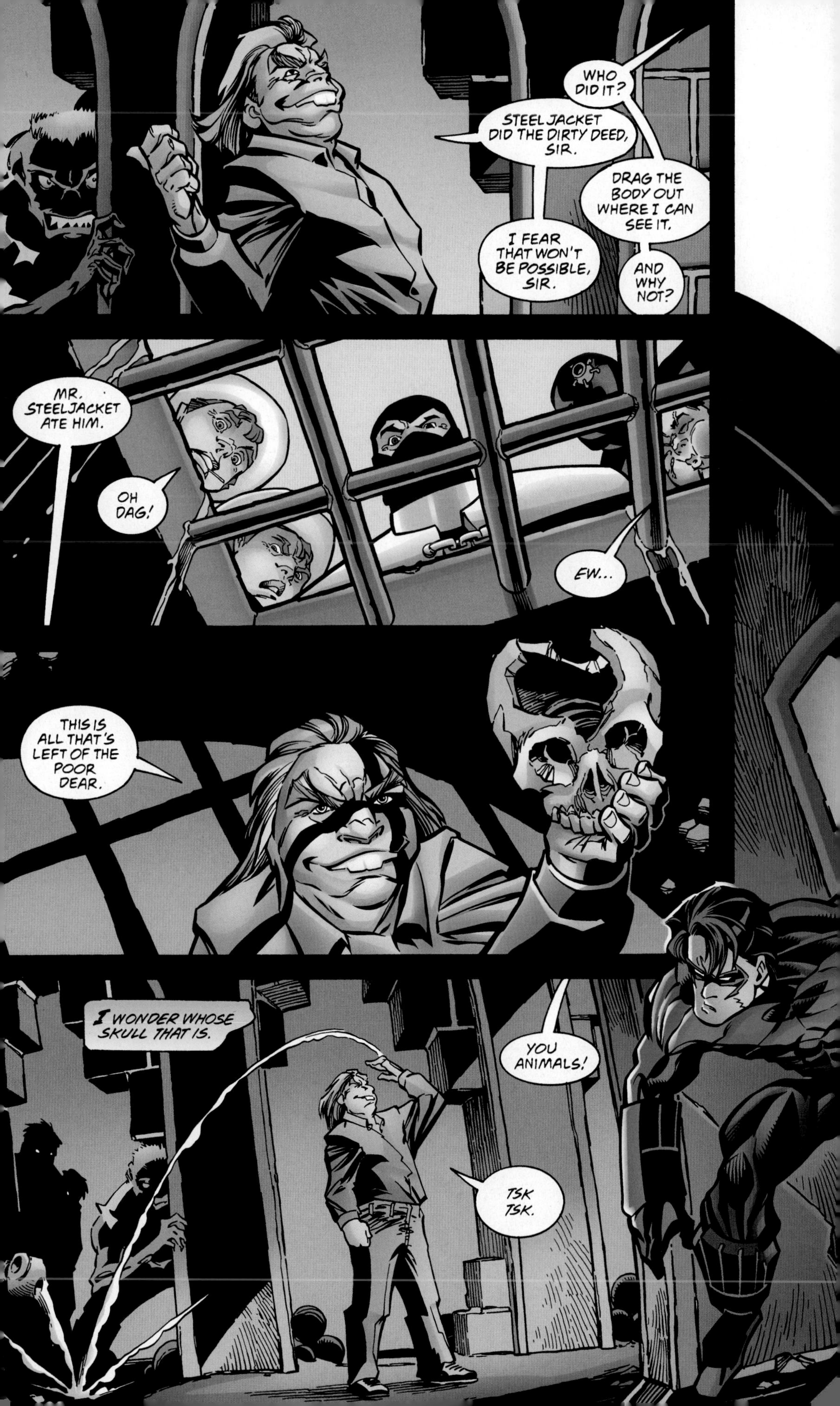
WHO DID IT?
STEEL JACKET DID THE DIRTY DEED, SIR.
DRAG THE BODY OUT WHERE I CAN SEE IT.
I FEAR THAT WON'T BE POSSIBLE, SIR.
AND WHY NOT?
MR. STEELJACKET ATE HIM.
OH DAG!
EW...
THIS IS ALL THAT'S LEFT OF THE POOR DEAR.
I WONDER WHOSE SKULL THAT IS.
YOU ANIMALS!
TSK TSK.

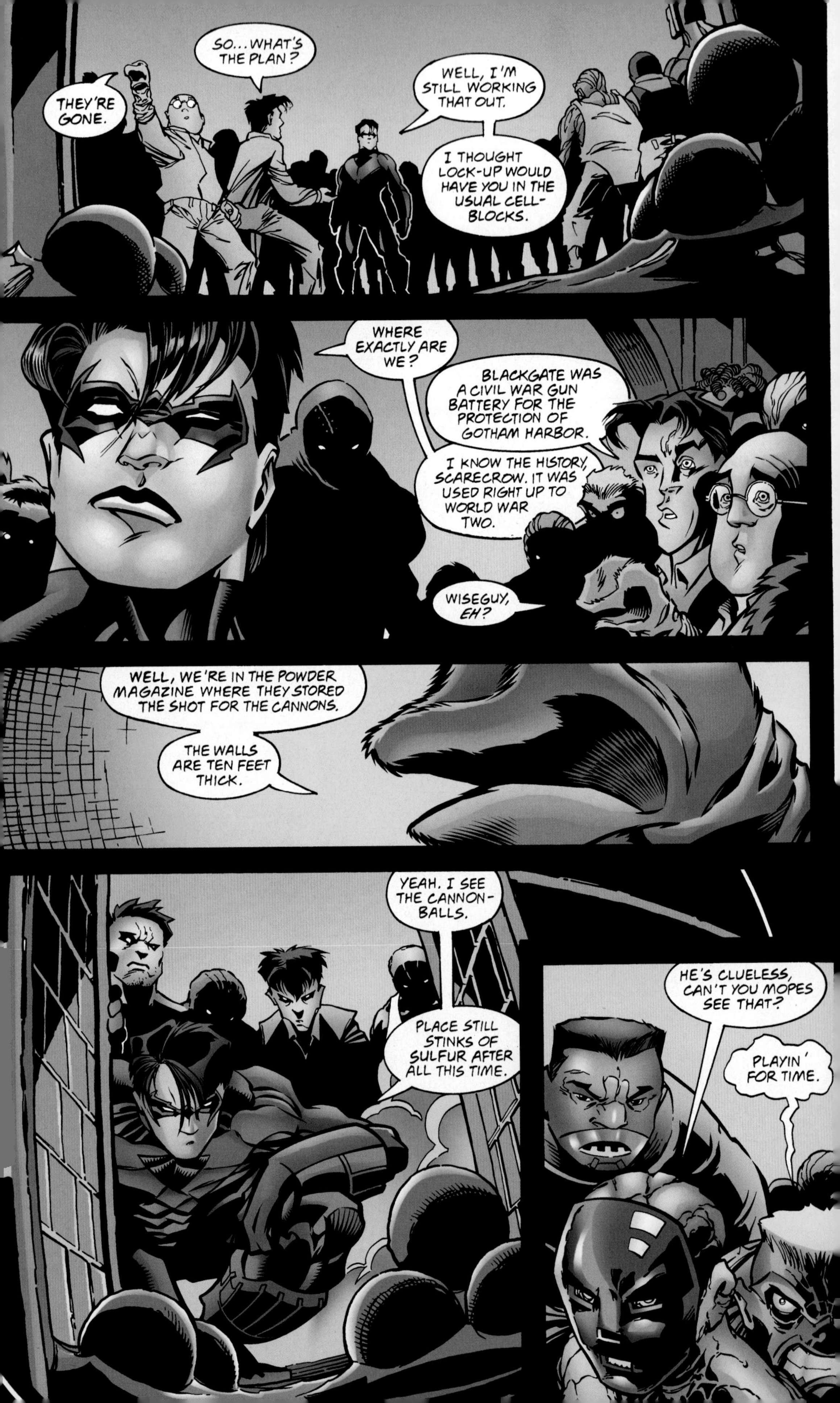
THEY'RE GONE.
SO...WHAT'S THE PLAN?
WELL, I'M STILL WORKING THAT OUT.
I THOUGHT LOCK-UP WOULD HAVE YOU IN THE USUAL CELL-BLOCKS.
WHERE EXACTLY ARE WE?
BLACKGATE WAS A CIVIL WAR GUN BATTERY FOR THE PROTECTION OF GOTHAM HARBOR.
I KNOW THE HISTORY, SCARECROW. IT WAS USED RIGHT UP TO WORLD WAR TWO.
WISEGUY, EH?
WELL, WE'RE IN THE POWDER MAGAZINE WHERE THEY STORED THE SHOT FOR THE CANNONS.
THE WALLS ARE TEN FEET THICK.
YEAH. I SEE THE CANNON-BALLS.
PLACE STILL STINKS OF SULFUR AFTER ALL THIS TIME.
HE'S CLUELESS, CAN'T YOU MOPES SEE THAT?
PLAYIN' FOR TIME.

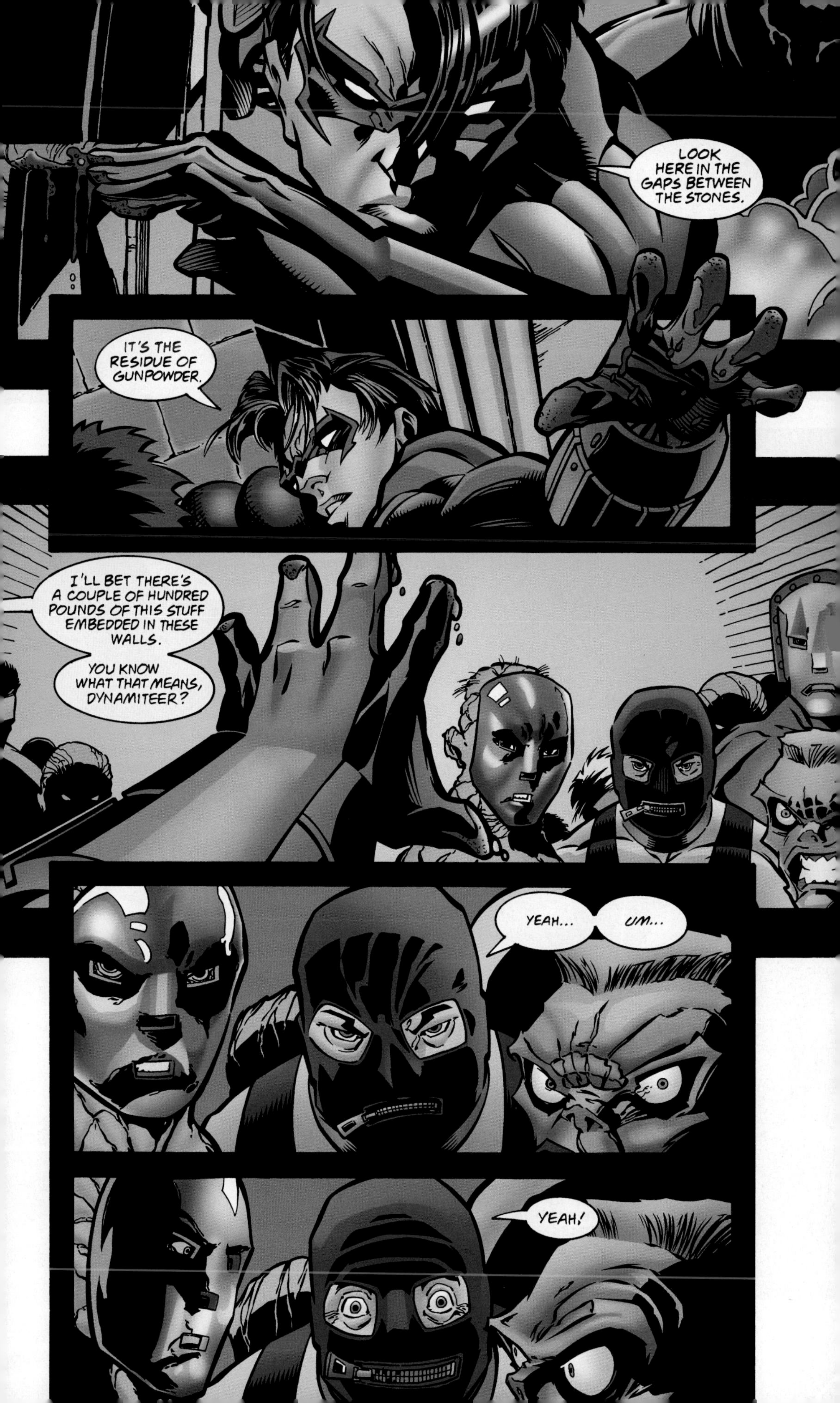
LOOK HERE IN THE GAPS BETWEEN THE STONES.
IT'S THE RESIDUE OF GUNPOWDER.
I'LL BET THERE'S A COUPLE OF HUNDRED POUNDS OF THIS STUFF EMBEDDED IN THESE WALLS.
YOU KNOW WHAT THAT MEANS, DYNAMITEER?
YEAH...
UM...
YEAH!

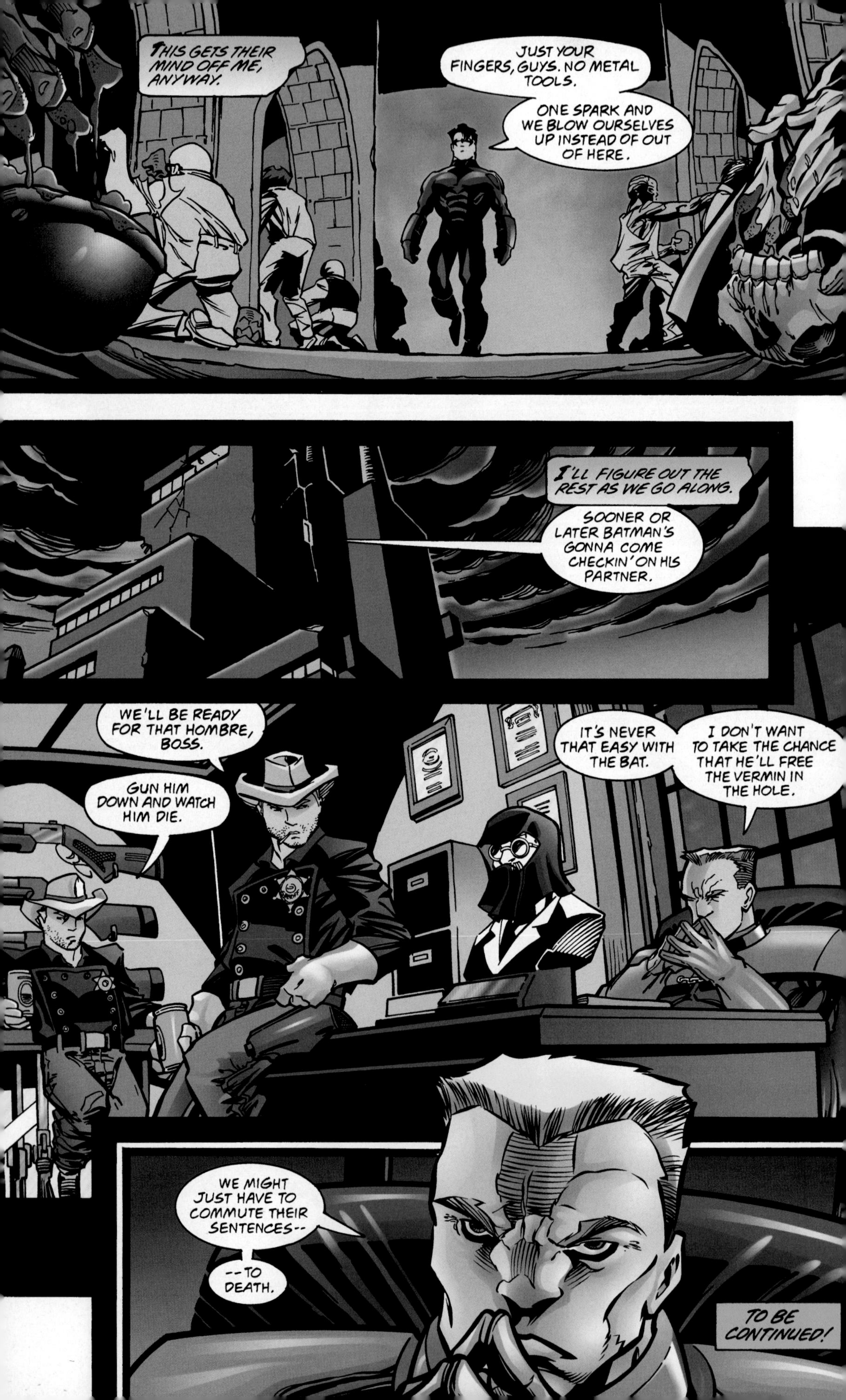
THIS GETS THEIR MIND OFF ME, ANYWAY.
JUST YOUR FINGERS, GUYS. NO METAL TOOLS.
ONE SPARK AND WE BLOW OURSELVES UP INSTEAD OF OUT OF HERE.
I'LL FIGURE OUT THE REST AS WE GO ALONG.
SOONER OR LATER BATMAN'S GONNA COME CHECKIN' ON HIS PARTNER.
WE'LL BE READY FOR THAT HOMBRE, BOSS.
GUN HIM DOWN AND WATCH HIM DIE.
IT'S NEVER THAT EASY WITH THE BAT.
I DON'T WANT TO TAKE THE CHANCE THAT HE'LL FREE THE VERMIN IN THE HOLE.
WE MIGHT JUST HAVE TO COMMUTE THEIR SENTENCES--
--TO DEATH.
TO BE CONTINUED!

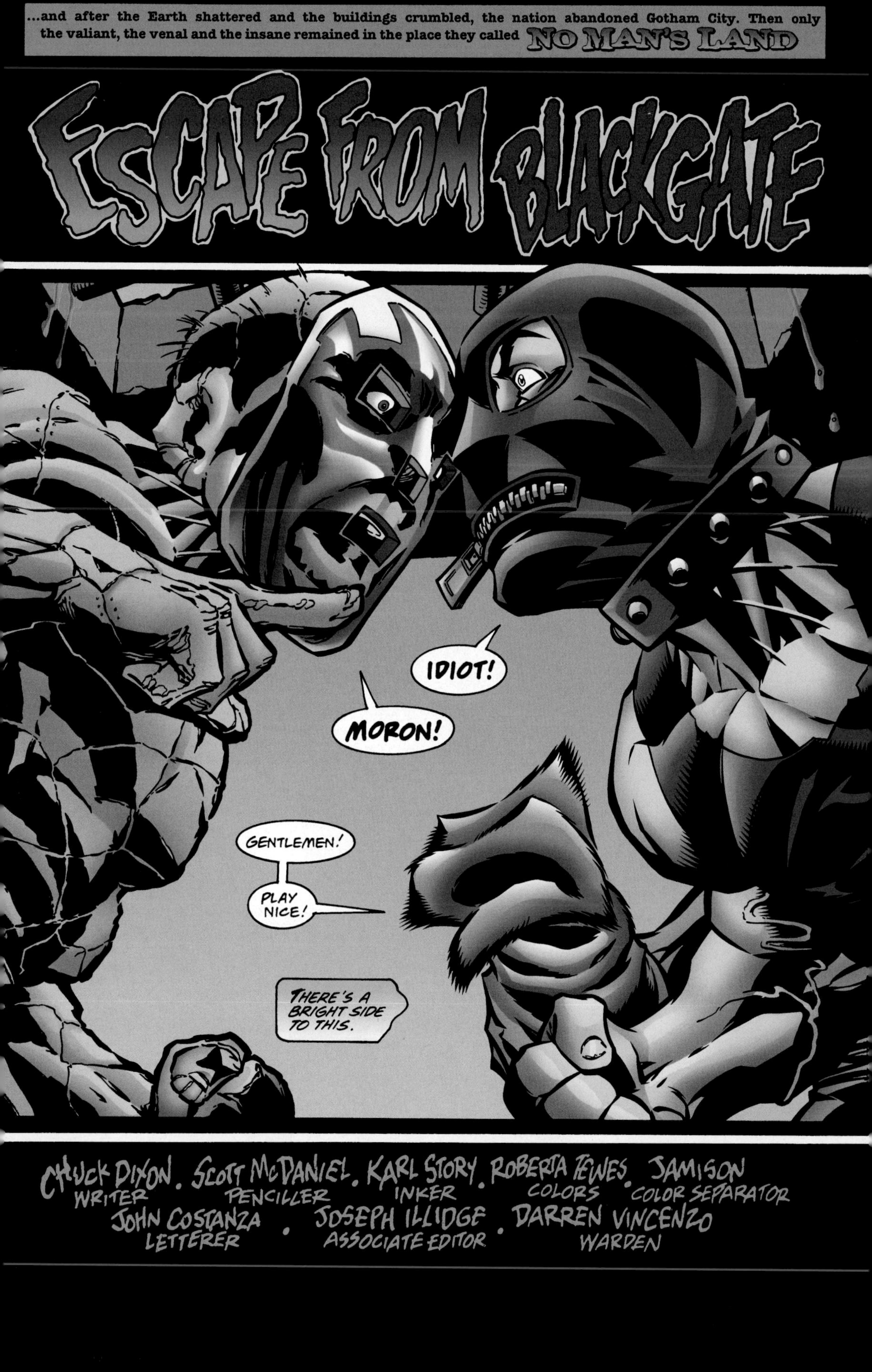
...and after the Earth shattered and the buildings crumbled, the nation abandoned Gotham City. Then only the valiant, the venal and the insane remained in the place they called NO MAN'S LAND
ESCAPE FROM BLACKGATE
IDIOT!
MORON!
GENTLEMEN!
PLAY NICE!
THERE'S A BRIGHT SIDE TO THIS.
CHUCK DIXON WRITER . SCOTT McDANIEL PENCILLER . KARL STORY INKER . ROBERTA TEWES COLORS . JAMISON COLOR SEPARATOR
JOHN COSTANZA LETTERER . JOSEPH ILLIDGE ASSOCIATE EDITOR . DARREN VINCENZO WARDEN

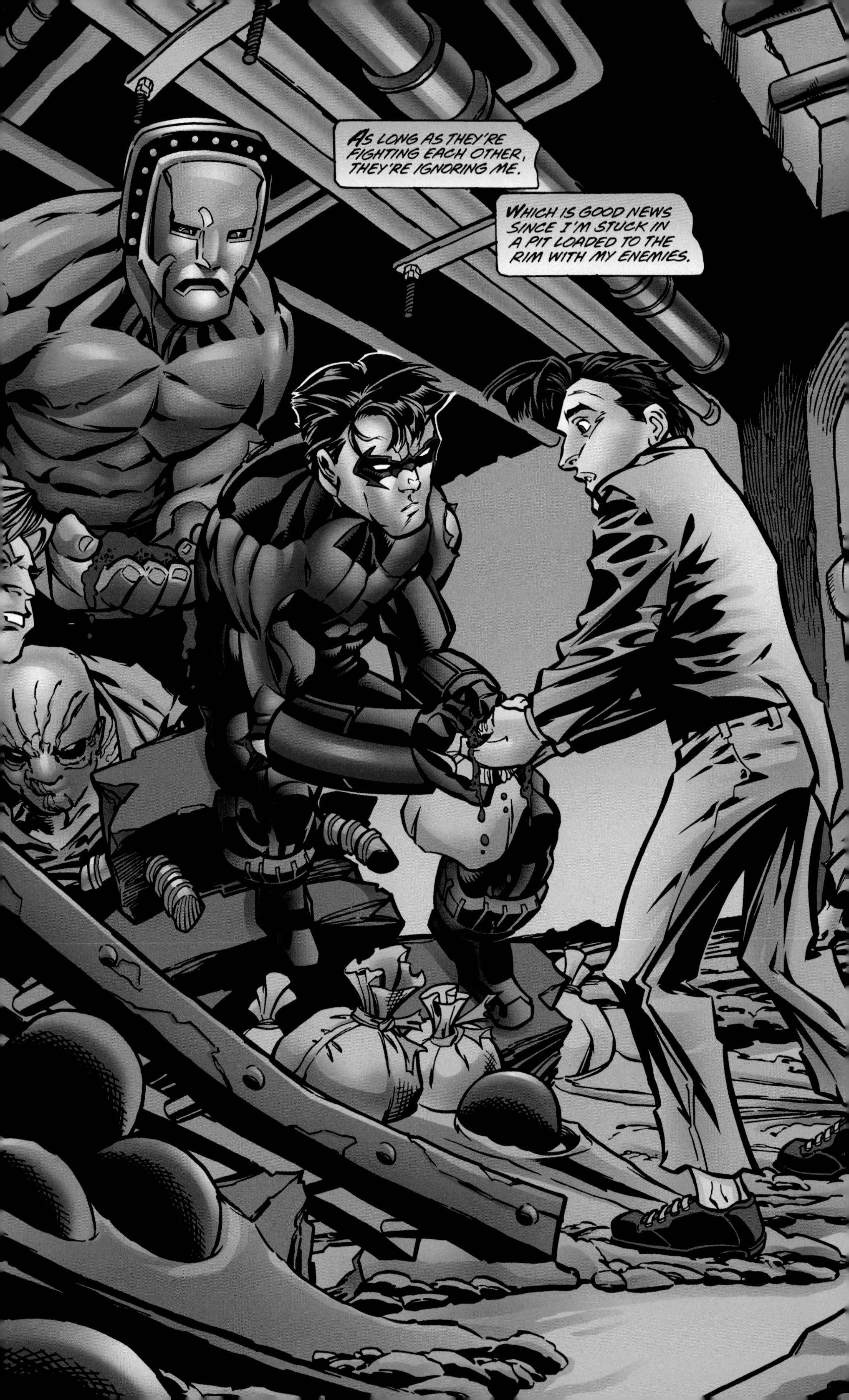
AS LONG AS THEY'RE FIGHTING EACH OTHER, THEY'RE IGNORING ME.
WHICH IS GOOD NEWS SINCE I'M STUCK IN A PIT LOADED TO THE RIM WITH MY ENEMIES.

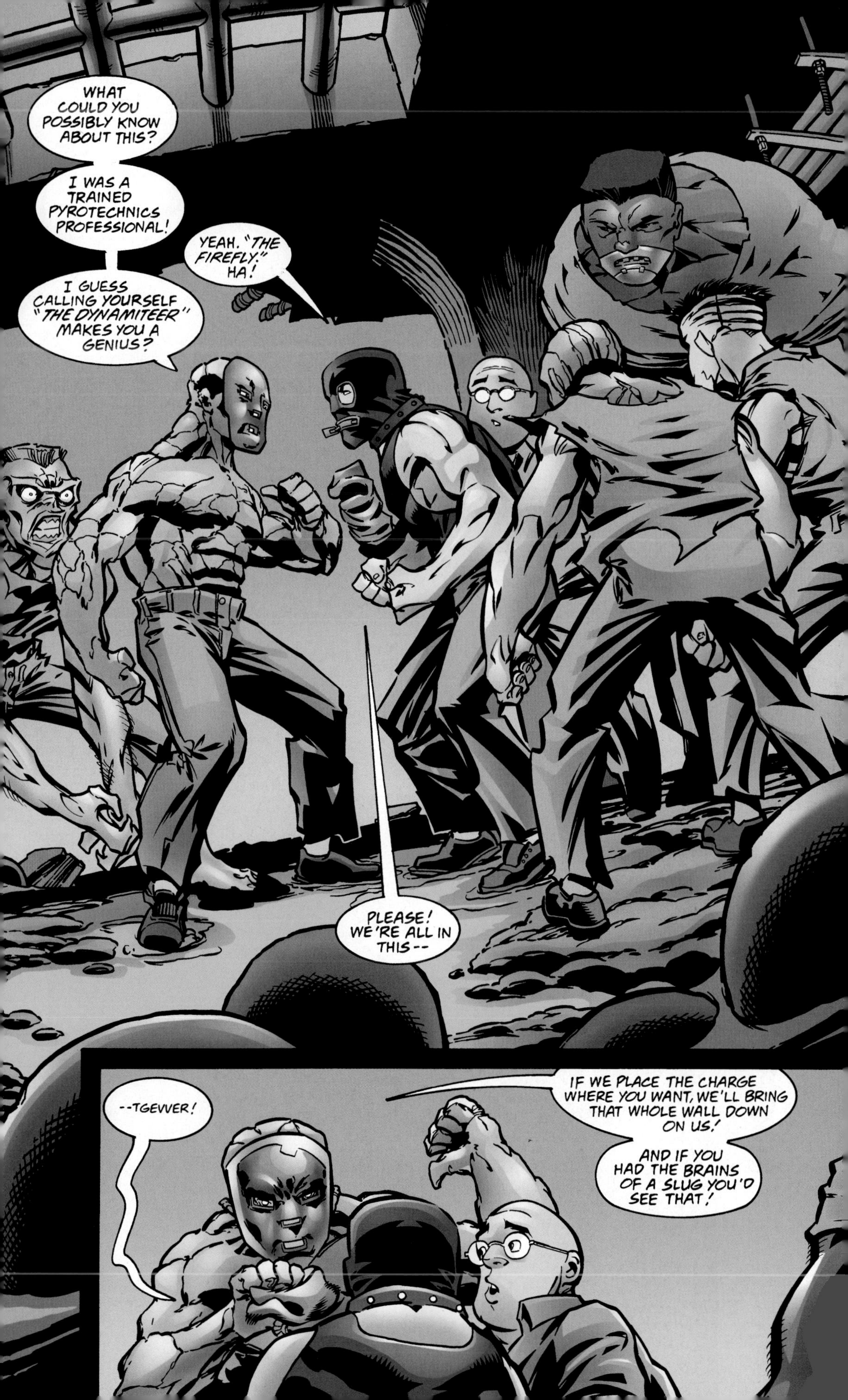
WHAT COULD YOU POSSIBLY KNOW ABOUT THIS?
I WAS A TRAINED PYROTECHNICS PROFESSIONAL!
I GUESS CALLING YOURSELF "THE DYNAMITEER" MAKES YOU A GENIUS?
YEAH. "THE FIREFLY." HA!
PLEASE! WE'RE ALL IN THIS--
--TGEVVER!
IF WE PLACE THE CHARGE WHERE YOU WANT, WE'LL BRING THAT WHOLE WALL DOWN ON US!
AND IF YOU HAD THE BRAINS OF A SLUG YOU'D SEE THAT!

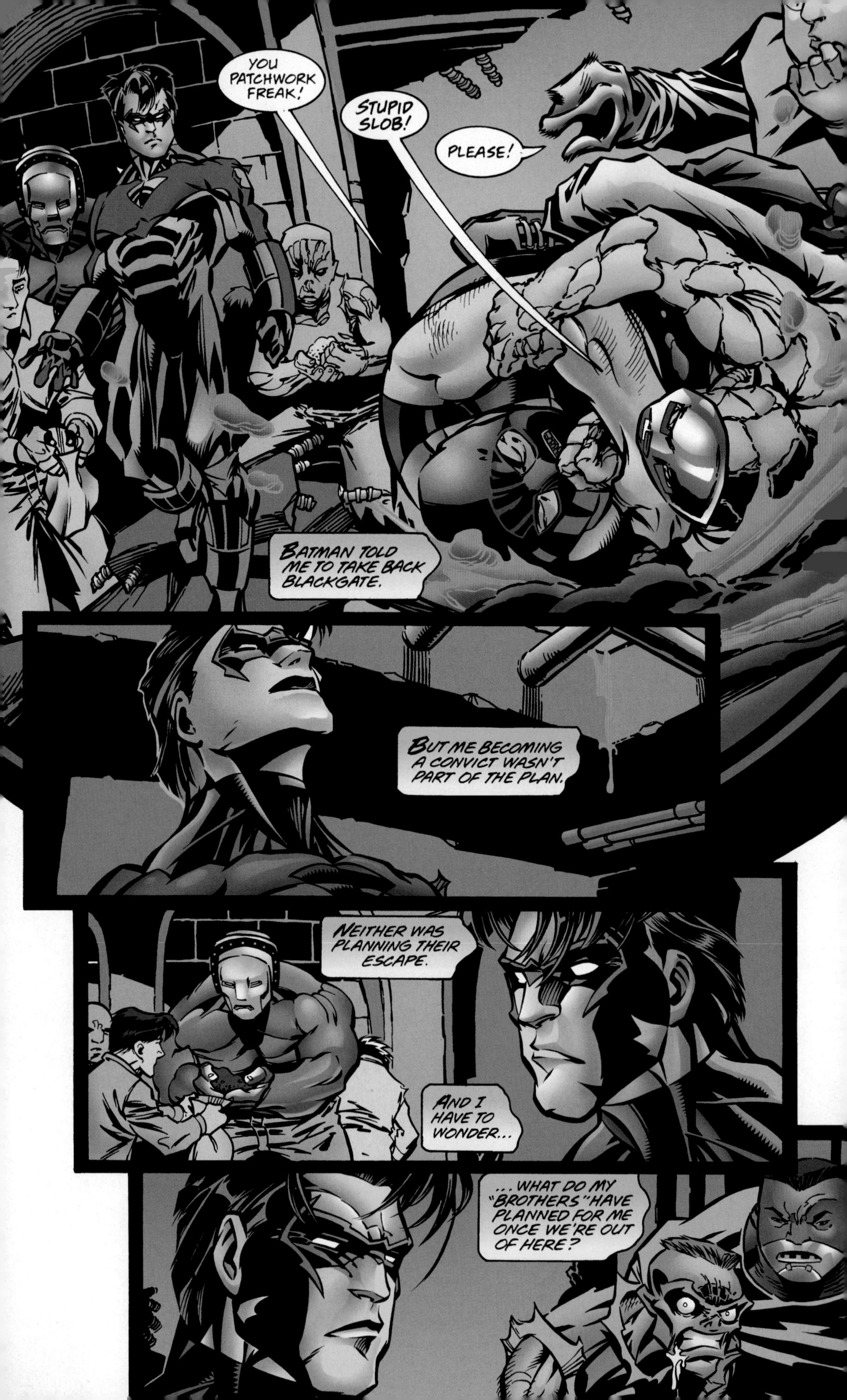
YOU PATCHWORK FREAK!
STUPID SLOB!
PLEASE!
BATMAN TOLD ME TO TAKE BACK BLACKGATE.
BUT ME BECOMING A CONVICT WASN'T PART OF THE PLAN.
NEITHER WAS PLANNING THEIR ESCAPE.
AND I HAVE TO WONDER...
...WHAT DO MY "BROTHERS" HAVE PLANNED FOR ME ONCE WE'RE OUT OF HERE?

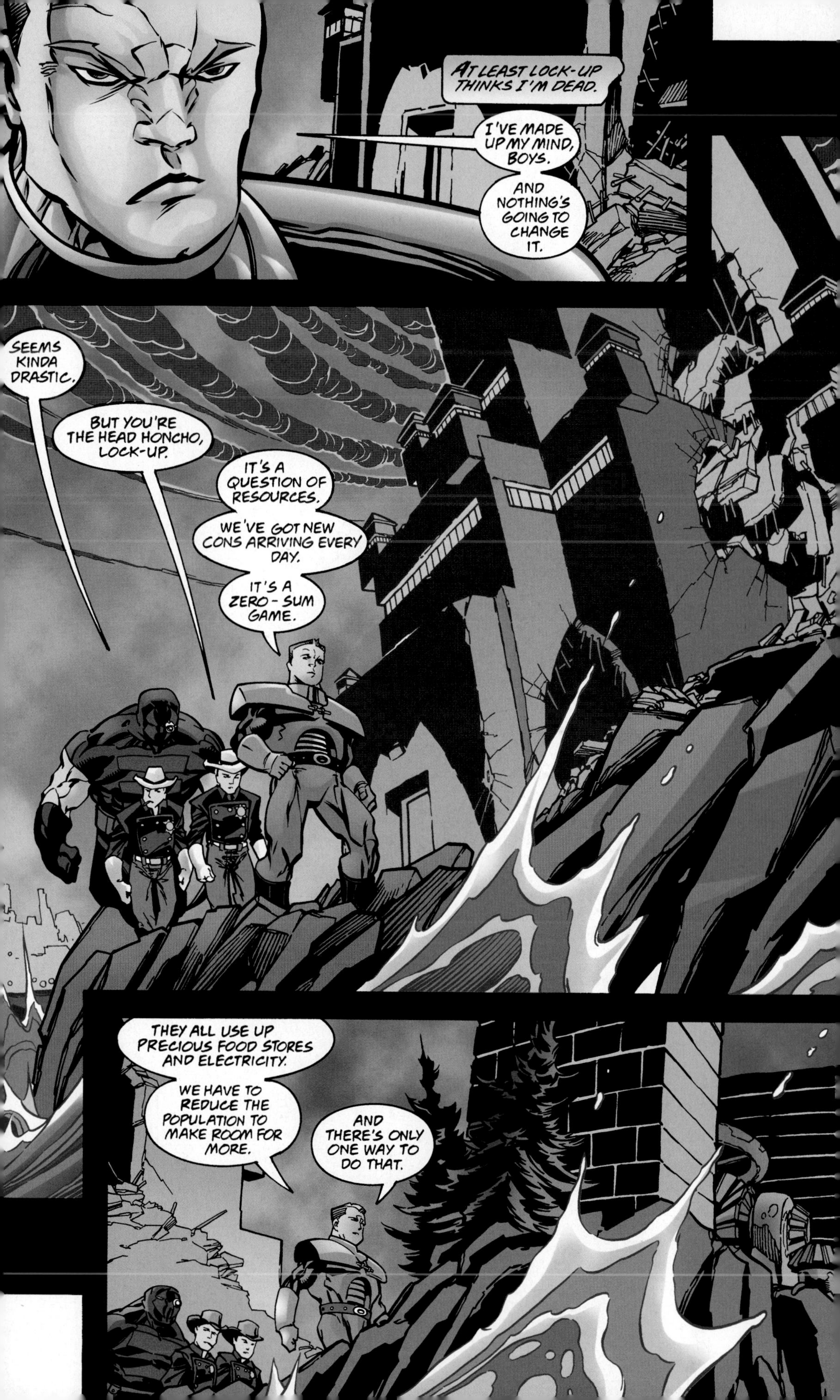
AT LEAST LOCK-UP THINKS I'M DEAD.
I'VE MADE UP MY MIND, BOYS.
AND NOTHING'S GOING TO CHANGE IT.
SEEMS KINDA DRASTIC.
BUT YOU'RE THE HEAD HONCHO, LOCK-UP.
IT'S A QUESTION OF RESOURCES.
WE'VE GOT NEW CONS ARRIVING EVERY DAY.
IT'S A ZERO-SUM GAME.
THEY ALL USE UP PRECIOUS FOOD STORES AND ELECTRICITY.
WE HAVE TO REDUCE THE POPULATION TO MAKE ROOM FOR MORE.
AND THERE'S ONLY ONE WAY TO DO THAT.

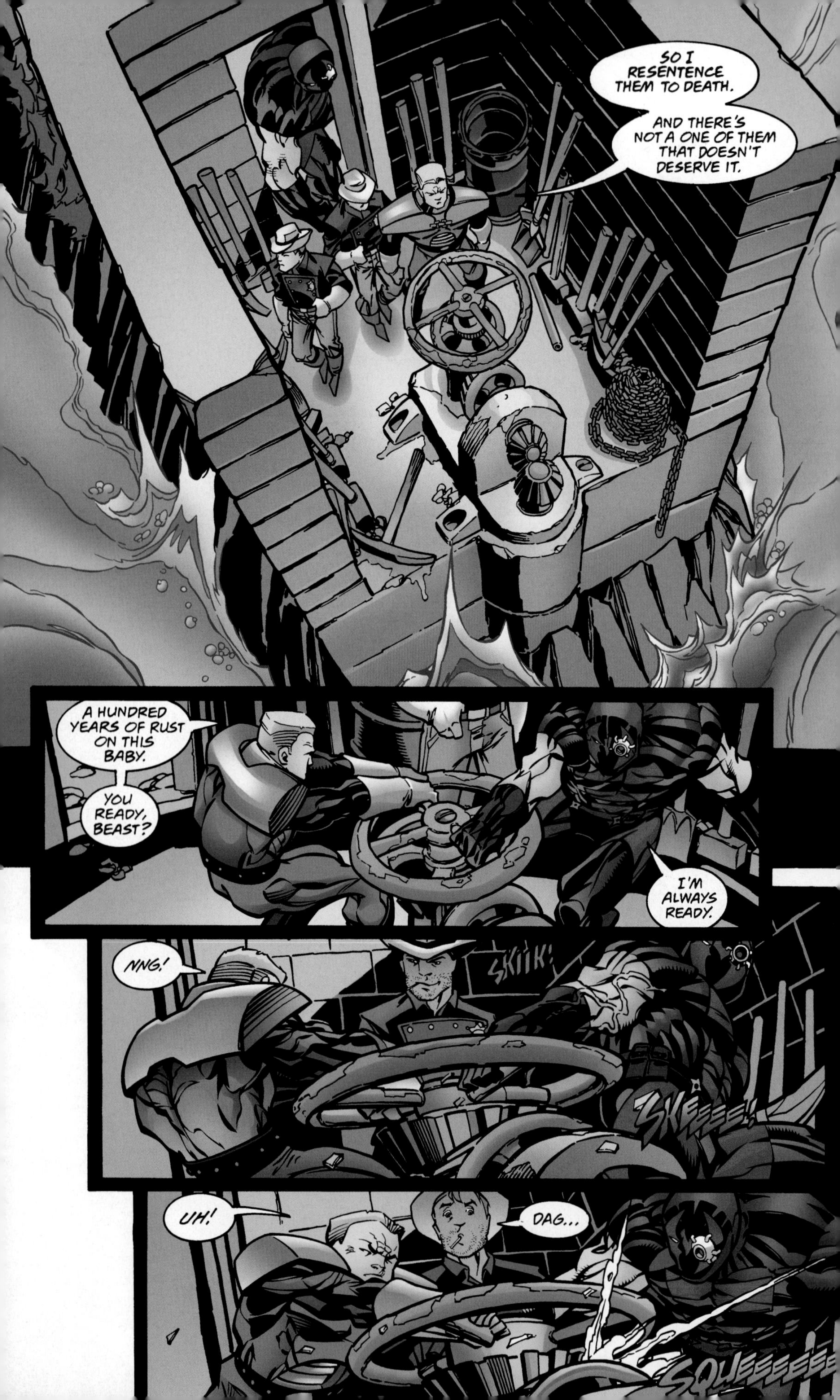
SO I RESENTENCE THEM TO DEATH.
AND THERE'S NOT A ONE OF THEM THAT DOESN'T DESERVE IT.
A HUNDRED YEARS OF RUST ON THIS BABY.
YOU READY, BEAST?
I'M ALWAYS READY.
NNG!
SKIIK!
SKEEEE!
UH!
DAG...
SQUEEEEEE

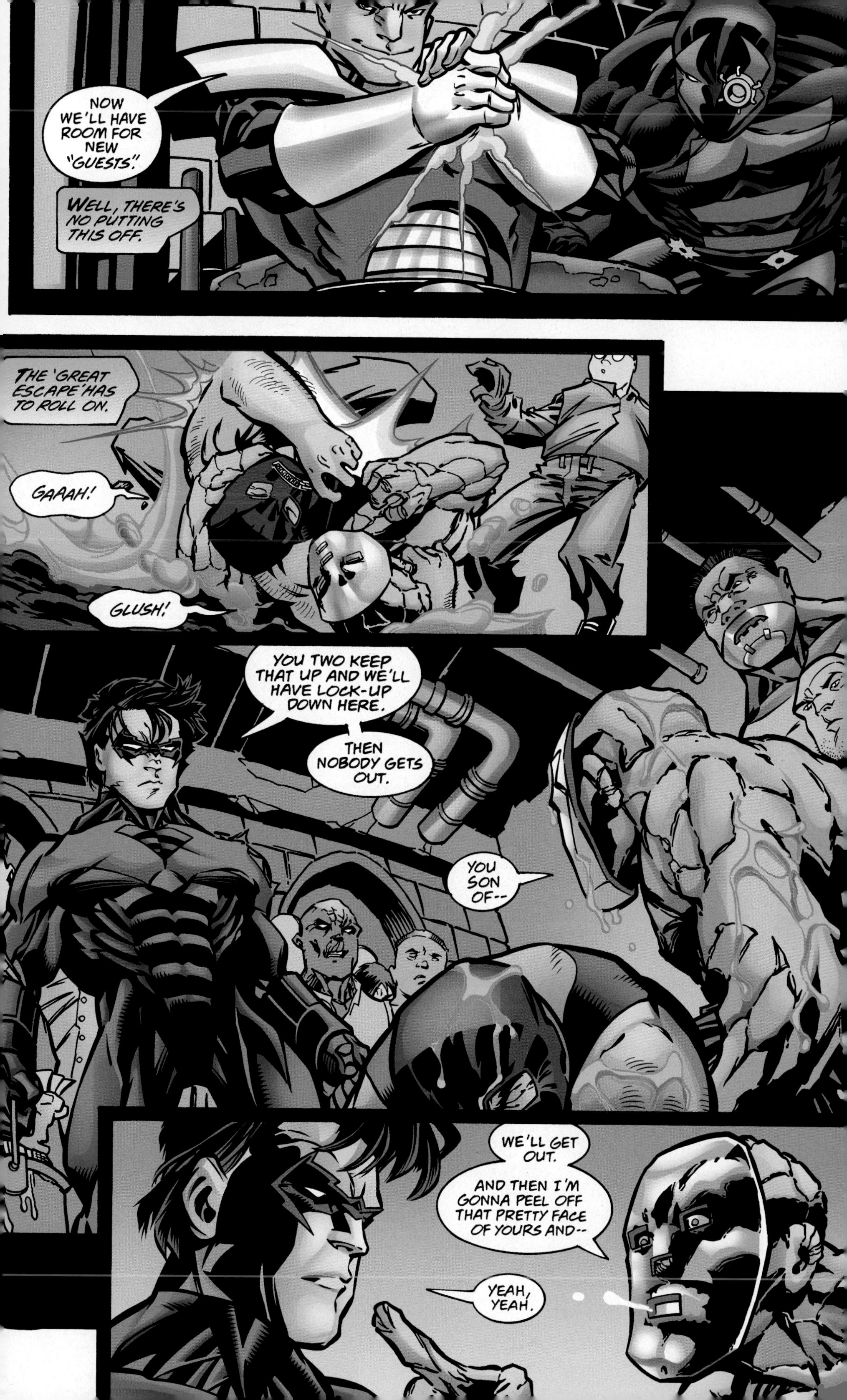
NOW WE'LL HAVE ROOM FOR NEW "GUESTS."
WELL, THERE'S NO PUTTING THIS OFF.
THE 'GREAT ESCAPE' HAS TO ROLL ON.
GAAAH!
GLUSH!
YOU TWO KEEP THAT UP AND WE'LL HAVE LOCK-UP DOWN HERE.
THEN NOBODY GETS OUT.
YOU SON OF--
WE'LL GET OUT.
AND THEN I'M GONNA PEEL OFF THAT PRETTY FACE OF YOURS AND--
YEAH, YEAH.

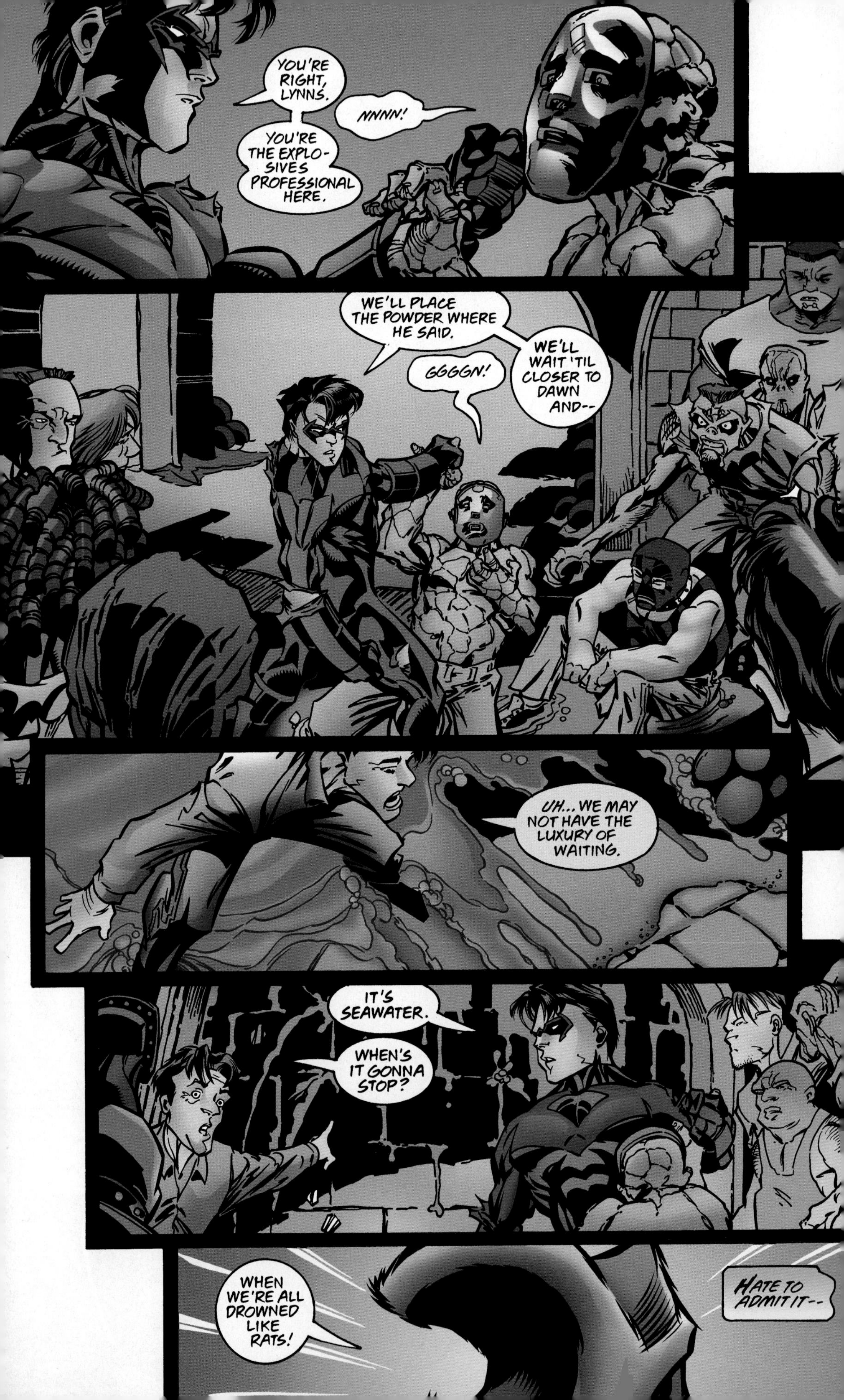
YOU'RE RIGHT, LYNNS.
NNNN!
YOU'RE THE EXPLO-SIVES PROFESSIONAL HERE.
WE'LL PLACE THE POWDER WHERE HE SAID.
GGGGN!
WE'LL WAIT 'TIL CLOSER TO DAWN AND--
UH... WE MAY NOT HAVE THE LUXURY OF WAITING.
IT'S SEAWATER.
WHEN'S IT GONNA STOP?
WHEN WE'RE ALL DROWNED LIKE RATS!
HATE TO ADMIT IT--

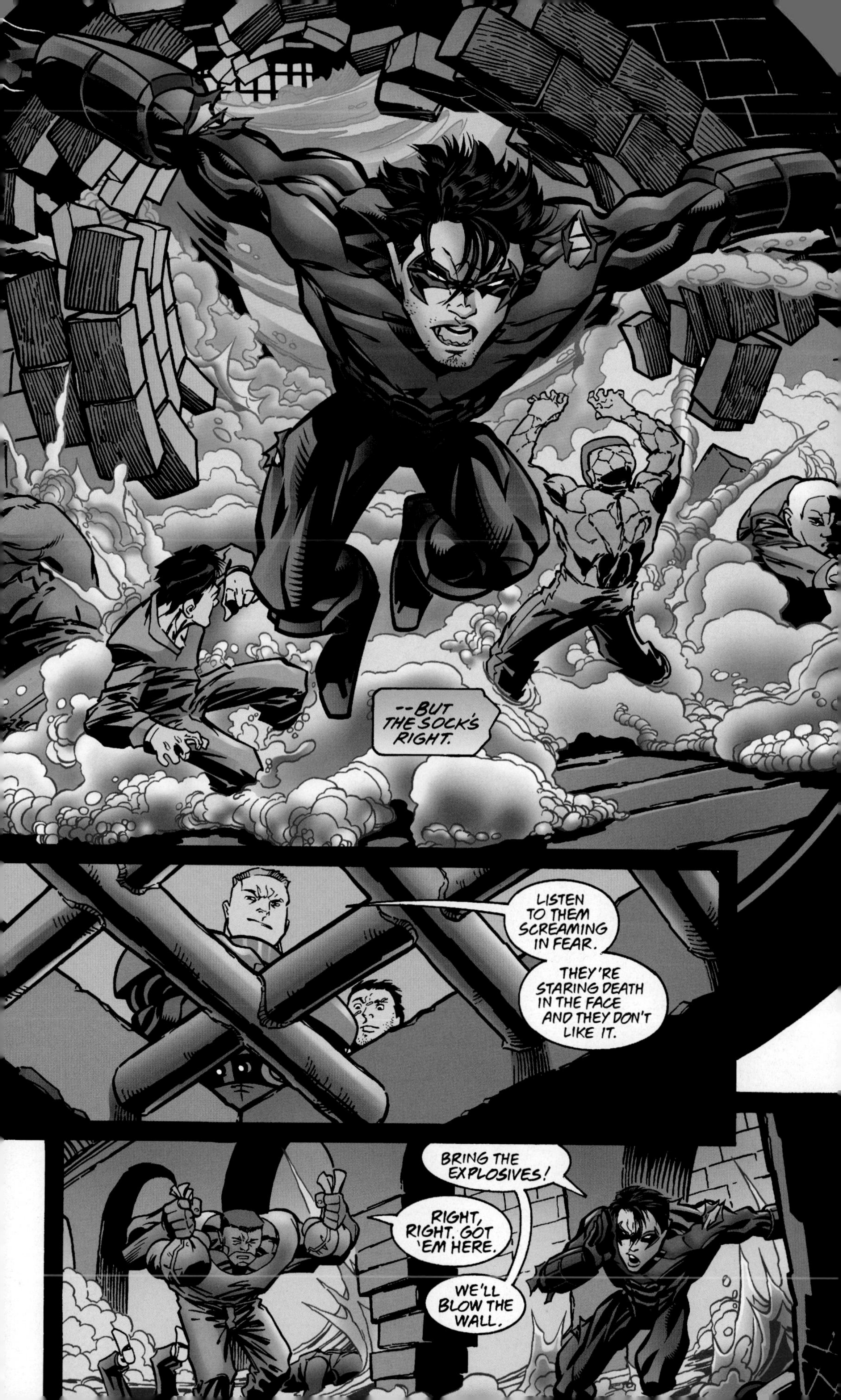
--BUT THE SOCK'S RIGHT.
LISTEN TO THEM SCREAMING IN FEAR.
THEY'RE STARING DEATH IN THE FACE AND THEY DON'T LIKE IT.
BRING THE EXPLOSIVES!
RIGHT, RIGHT. GOT 'EM HERE.
WE'LL BLOW THE WALL.

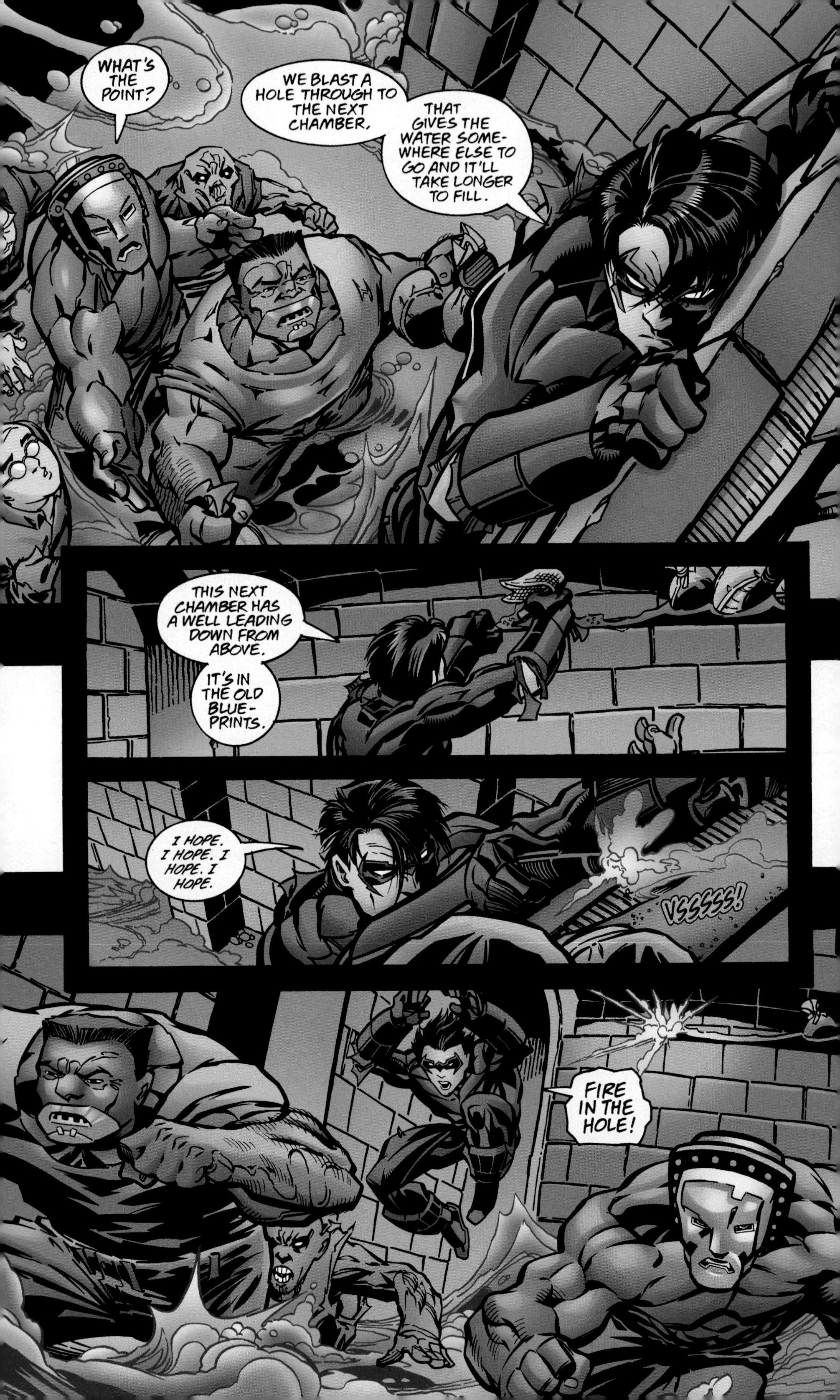
WHAT'S THE POINT?
WE BLAST A HOLE THROUGH TO THE NEXT CHAMBER,
THAT GIVES THE WATER SOME-WHERE ELSE TO GO AND IT'LL TAKE LONGER TO FILL.
THIS NEXT CHAMBER HAS A WELL LEADING DOWN FROM ABOVE.
IT'S IN THE OLD BLUE-PRINTS.
I HOPE. I HOPE. I HOPE. I HOPE.
VSSSSS!
FIRE IN THE HOLE!

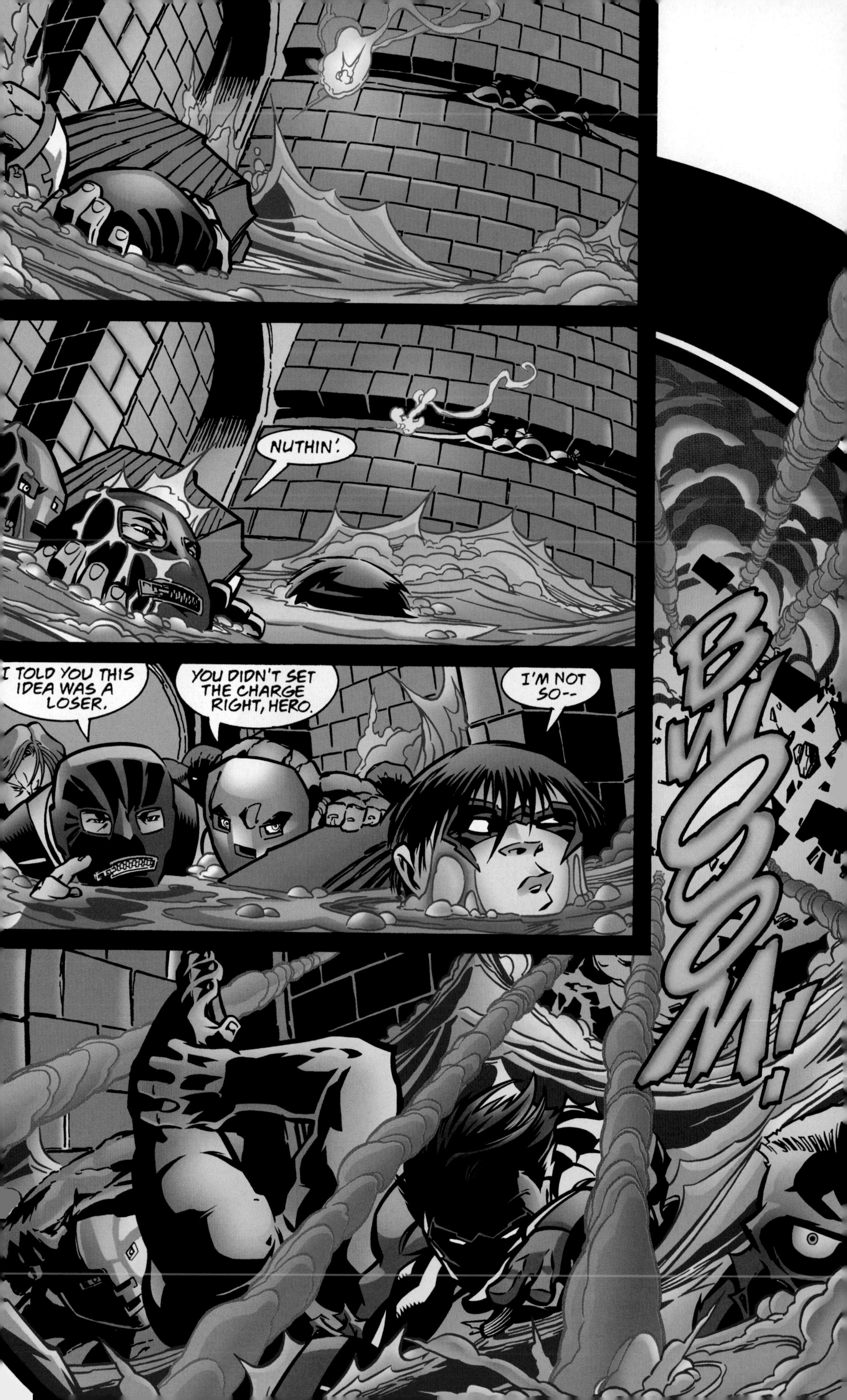
NUTHIN'.
I TOLD YOU THIS IDEA WAS A LOSER.
YOU DIDN'T SET THE CHARGE RIGHT, HERO.
I'M NOT SO--
BWOOOM!

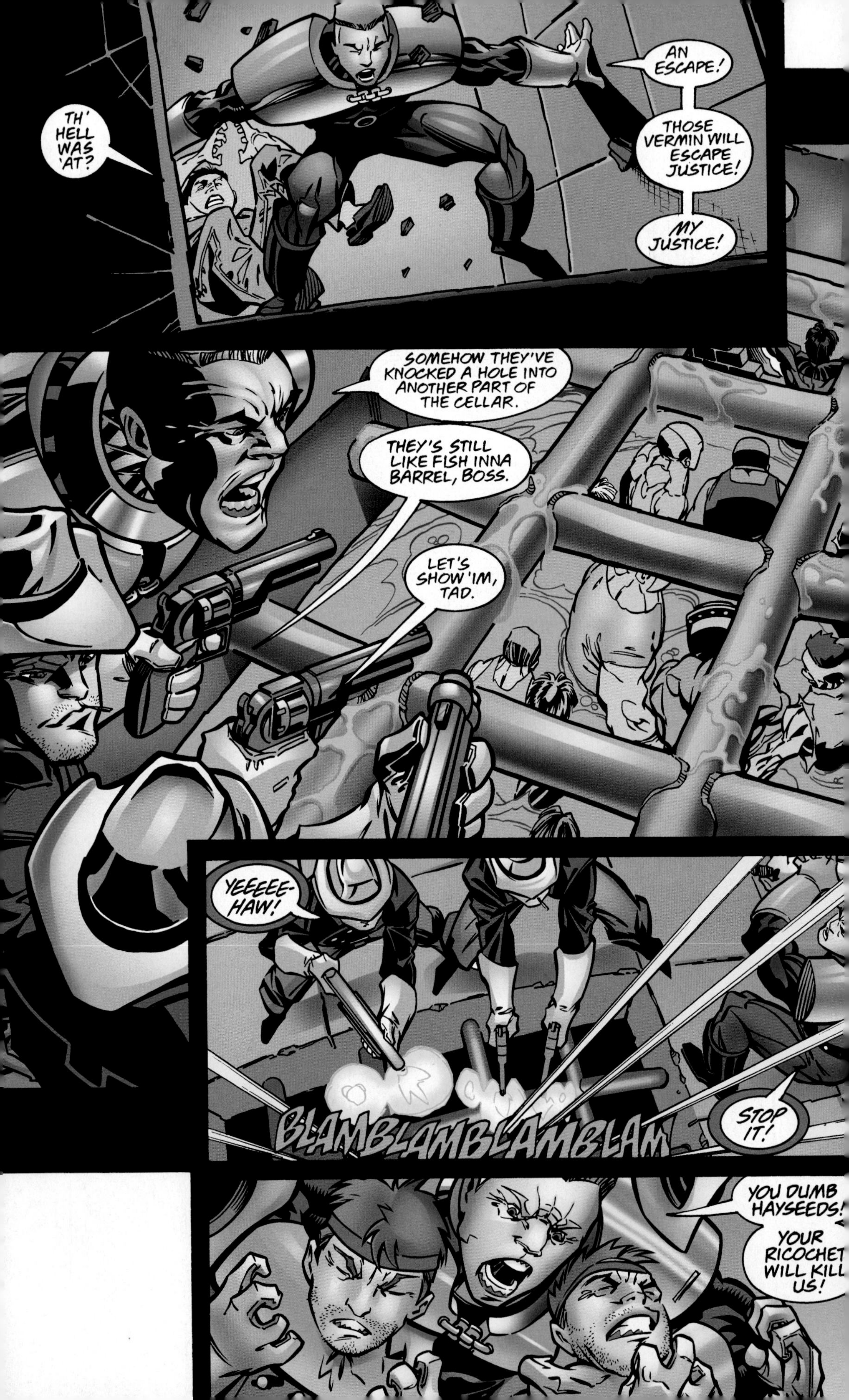
TH' HELL WAS 'AT?
AN ESCAPE!
THOSE VERMIN WILL ESCAPE JUSTICE!
MY JUSTICE!
SOMEHOW THEY'VE KNOCKED A HOLE INTO ANOTHER PART OF THE CELLAR.
THEY'S STILL LIKE FISH INNA BARREL, BOSS.
LET'S SHOW 'IM, TAD.
YEEEEE-HAW!
BLAMBLAMBLAMBLAM
STOP IT!
YOU DUMB HAYSEEDS!
YOUR RICOCHET WILL KILL US!

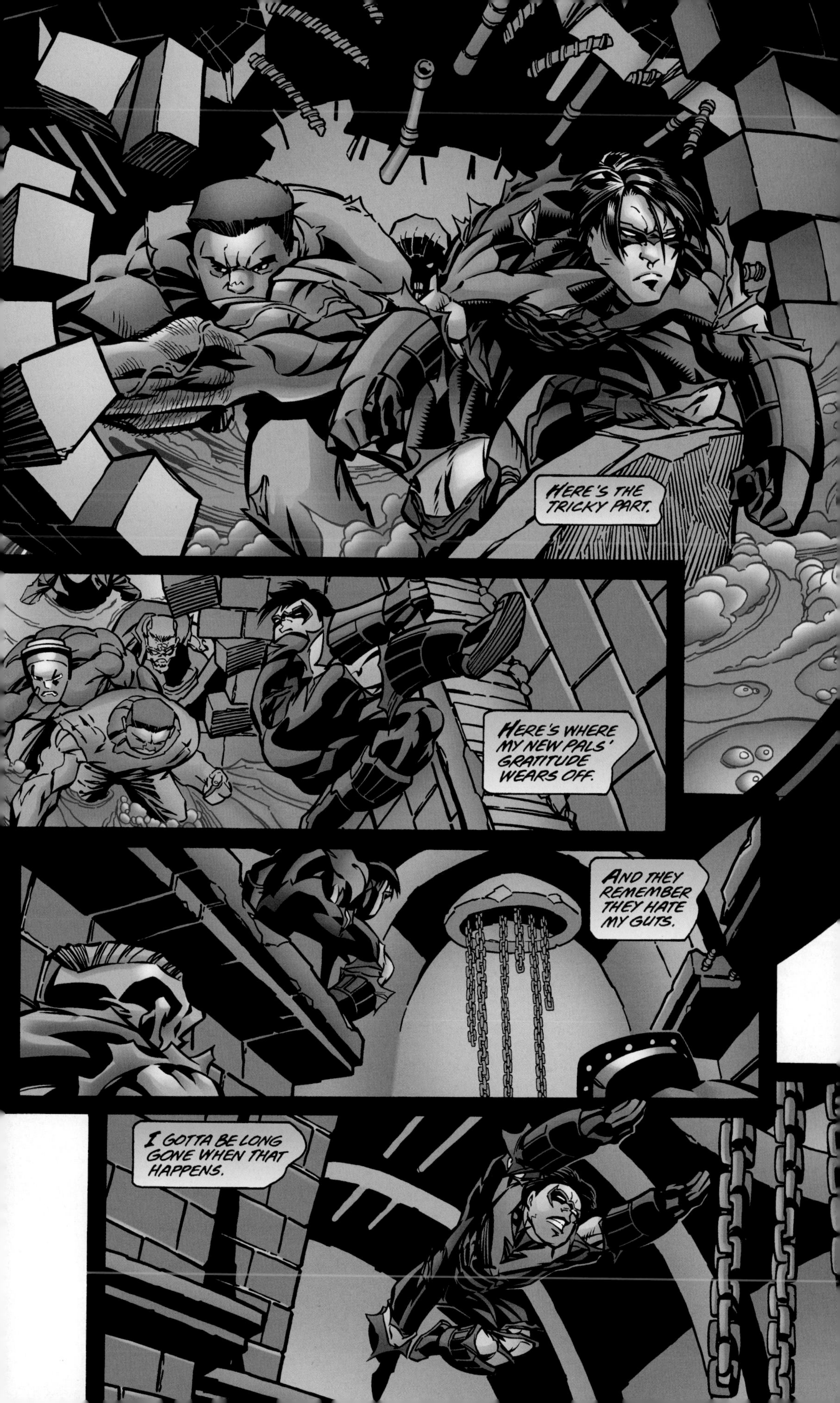
HERE'S THE TRICKY PART.
HERE'S WHERE MY NEW PALS' GRATITUDE WEARS OFF.
AND THEY REMEMBER THEY HATE MY GUTS.
I GOTTA BE LONG GONE WHEN THAT HAPPENS.

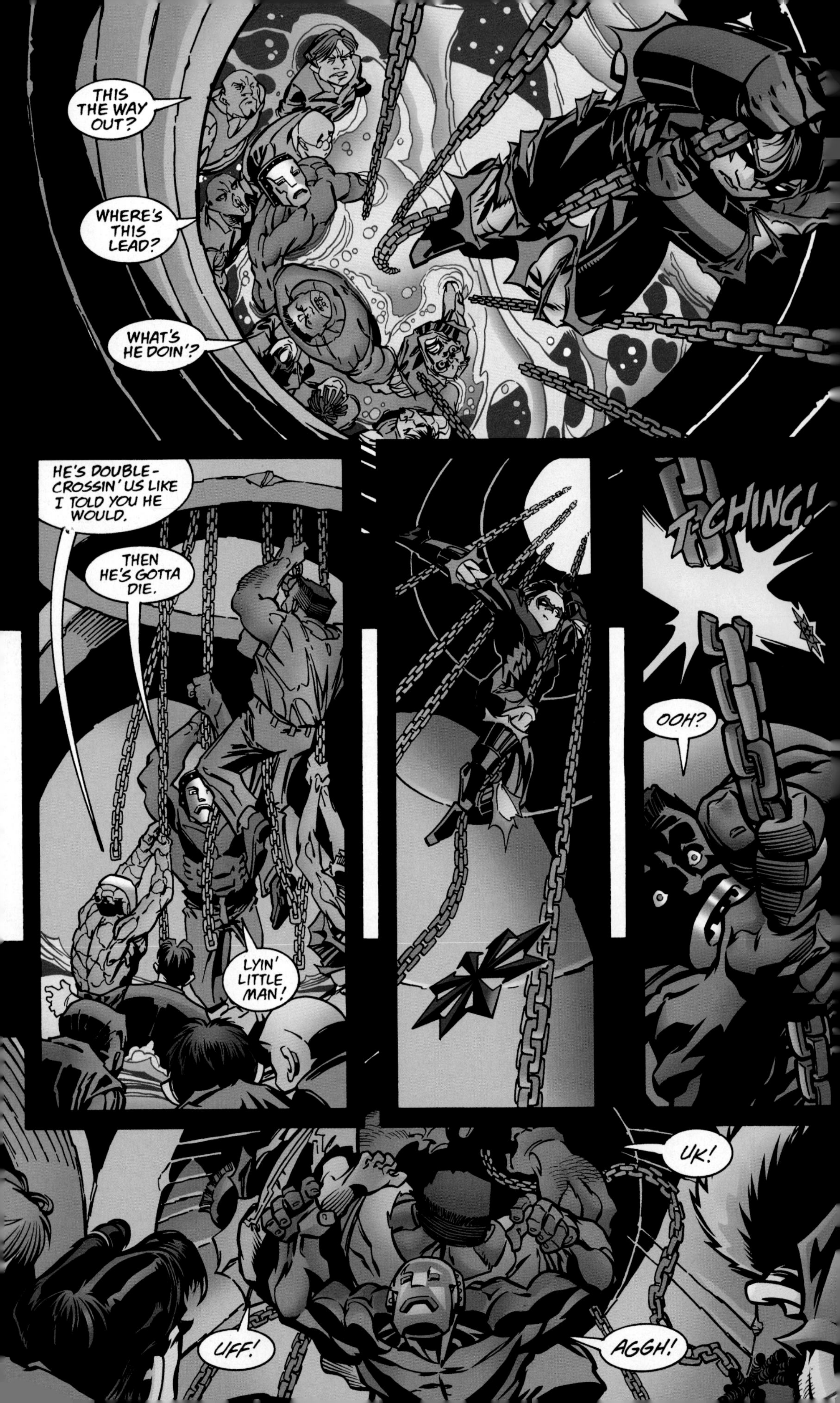
THIS THE WAY OUT?
WHERE'S THIS LEAD?
WHAT'S HE DOIN'?
HE'S DOUBLE-CROSSIN' US LIKE I TOLD YOU HE WOULD.
THEN HE'S GOTTA DIE.
LYIN' LITTLE MAN!
T-CHING!
OOH?
UK!
UFF!
AGGH!

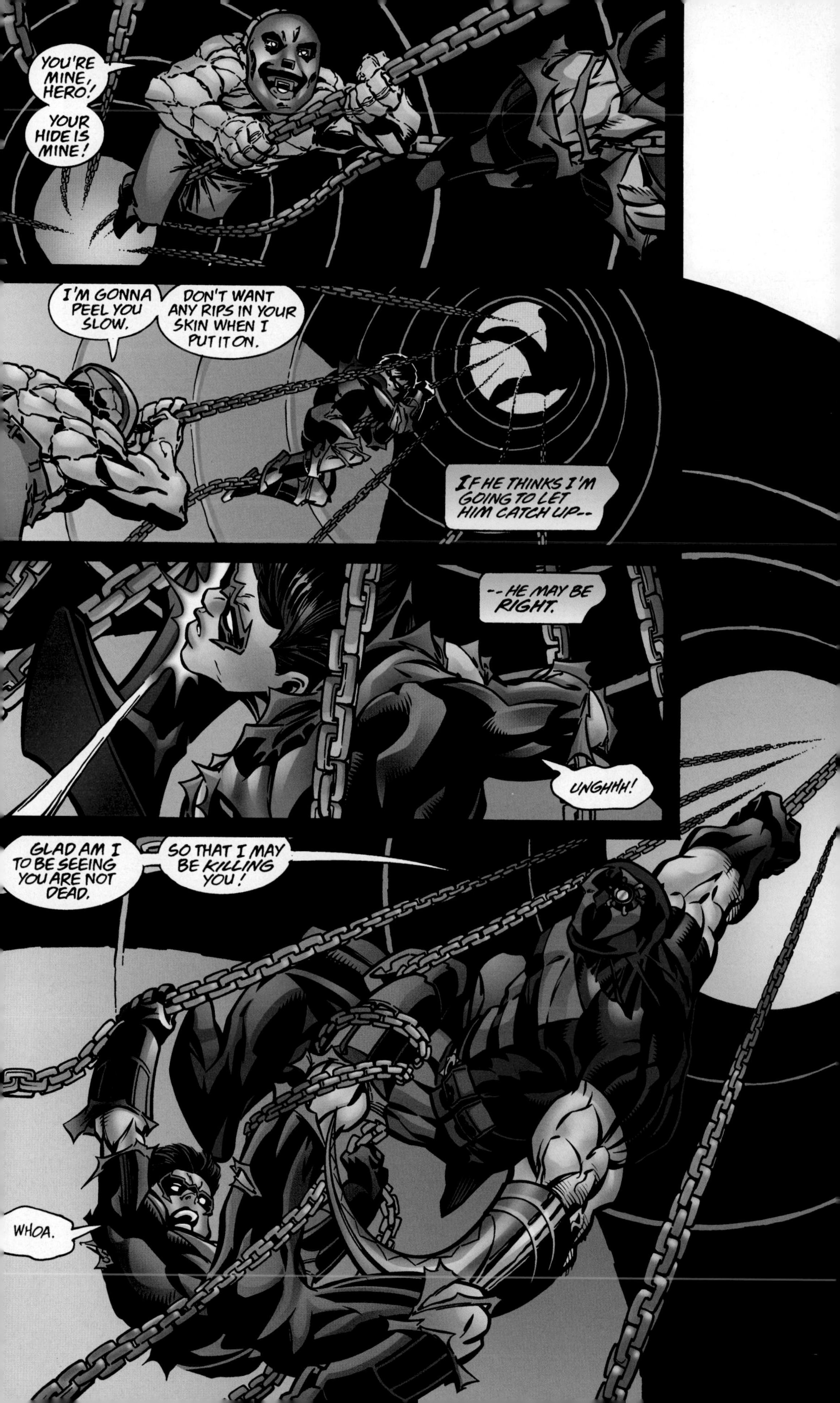
YOU'RE MINE, HERO!
YOUR HIDE IS MINE!
I'M GONNA PEEL YOU SLOW.
DON'T WANT ANY RIPS IN YOUR SKIN WHEN I PUT IT ON.
IF HE THINKS I'M GOING TO LET HIM CATCH UP--
--HE MAY BE RIGHT.
UNGHHH!
GLAD AM I TO BE SEEING YOU ARE NOT DEAD.
SO THAT I MAY BE KILLING YOU!
WHOA.

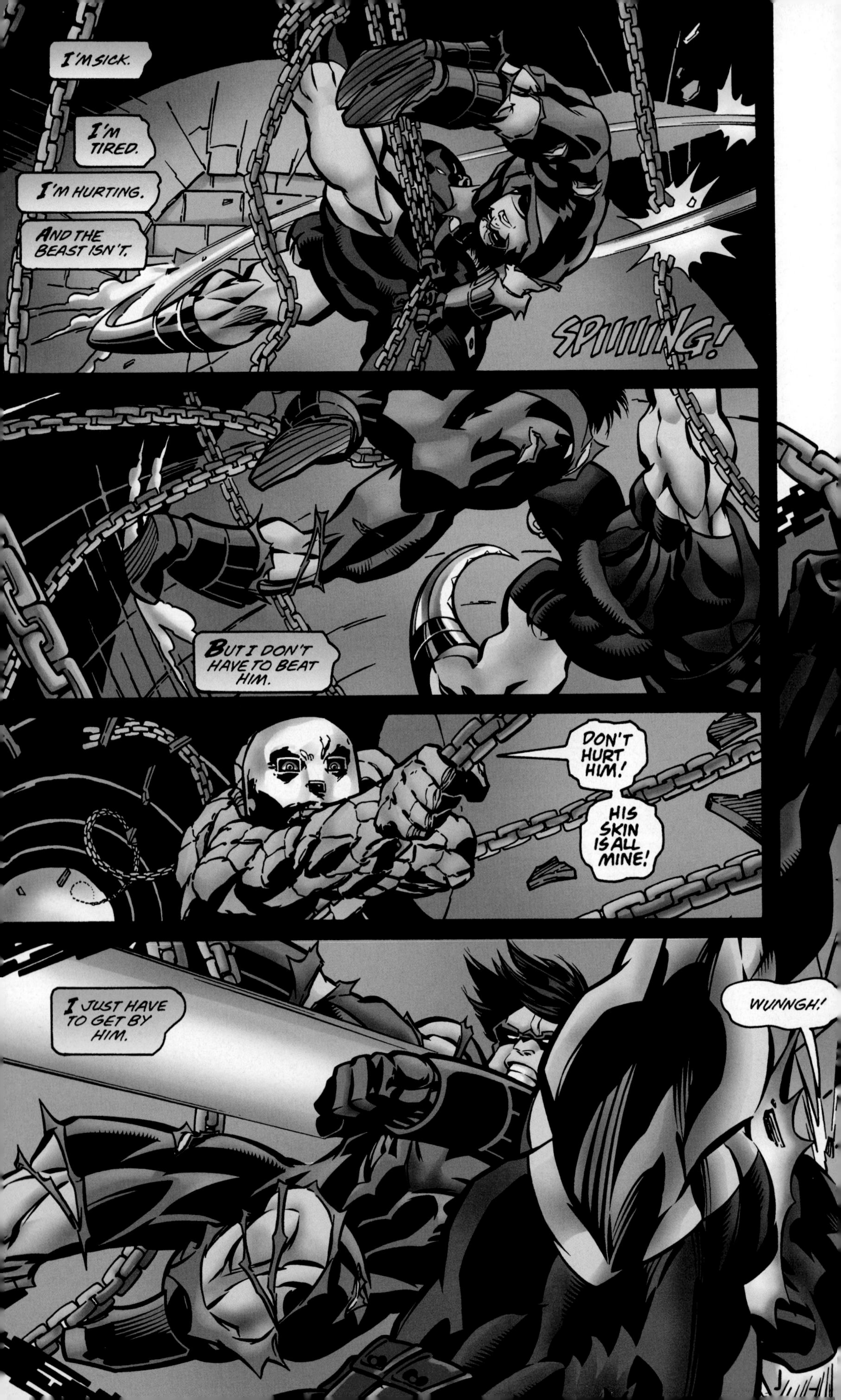
I'M SICK.
I'M TIRED.
I'M HURTING.
AND THE BEAST ISN'T.
SPIIIIING!
BUT I DON'T HAVE TO BEAT HIM.
DON'T HURT HIM!
HIS SKIN IS ALL MINE!
I JUST HAVE TO GET BY HIM.
WUNNGH!

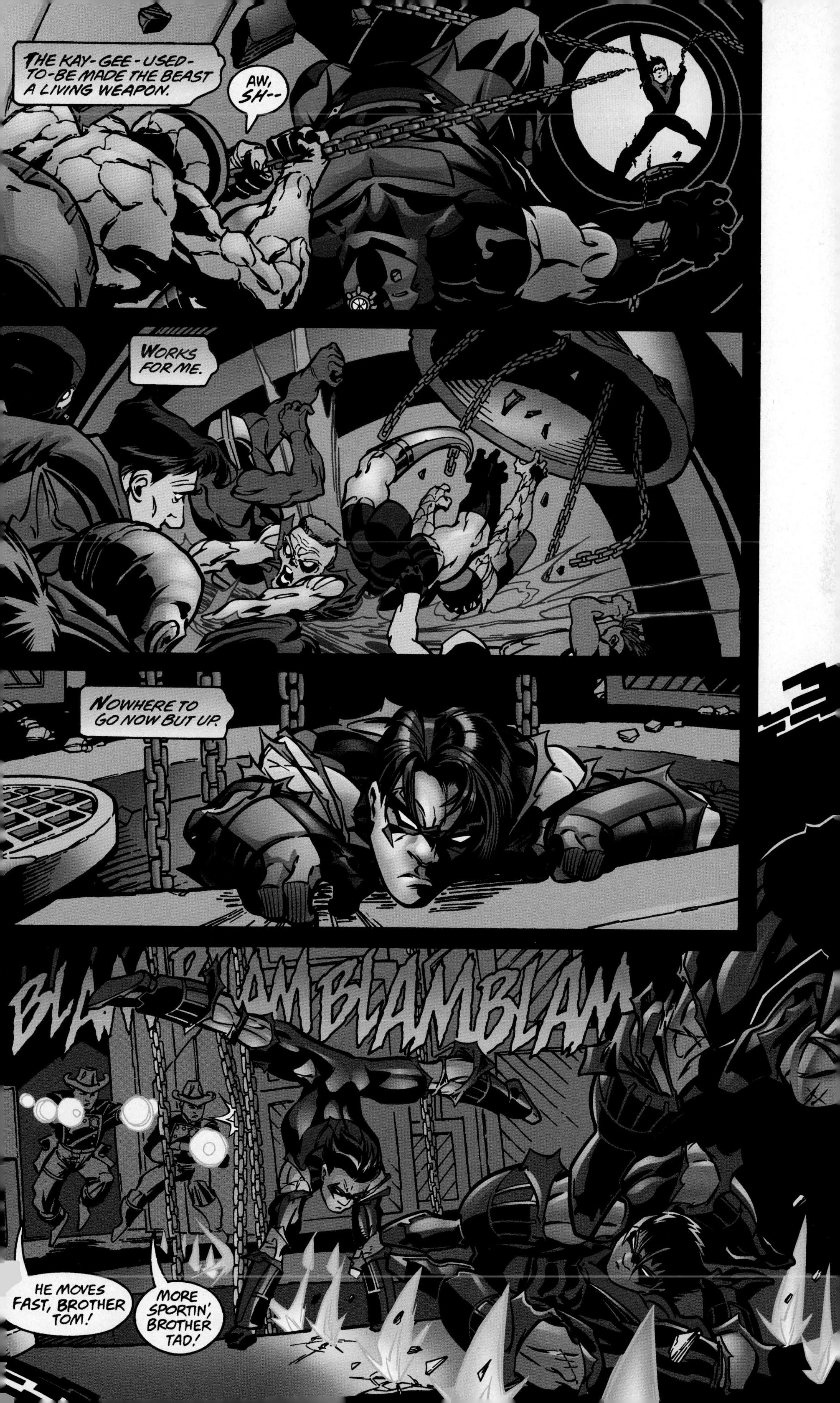
THE KAY-GEE-USED-TO-BE MADE THE BEAST A LIVING WEAPON.
AW, SH--
WORKS FOR ME.
NOWHERE TO GO NOW BUT UP.
BLAMBLAMBLAM
HE MOVES FAST, BROTHER TOM!
MORE SPORTIN', BROTHER TAD!

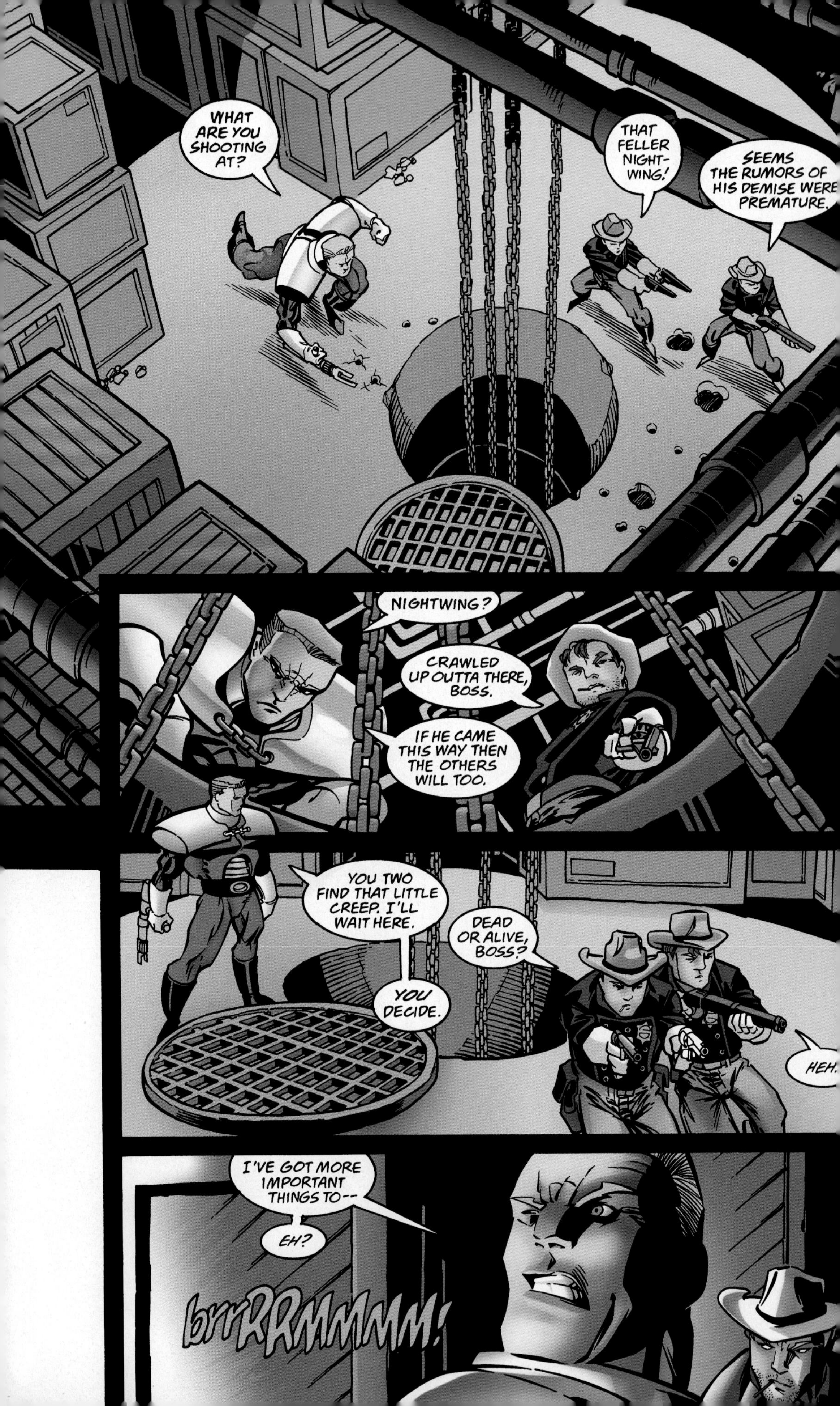
WHAT ARE YOU SHOOTING AT?
THAT FELLER NIGHT-WING!
SEEMS THE RUMORS OF HIS DEMISE WERE PREMATURE.
NIGHTWING?
CRAWLED UP OUTTA THERE, BOSS.
IF HE CAME THIS WAY THEN THE OTHERS WILL TOO.
YOU TWO FIND THAT LITTLE CREEP. I'LL WAIT HERE.
DEAD OR ALIVE, BOSS?
YOU DECIDE.
HEH.
I'VE GOT MORE IMPORTANT THINGS TO--
EH?
brrRRMMMM!

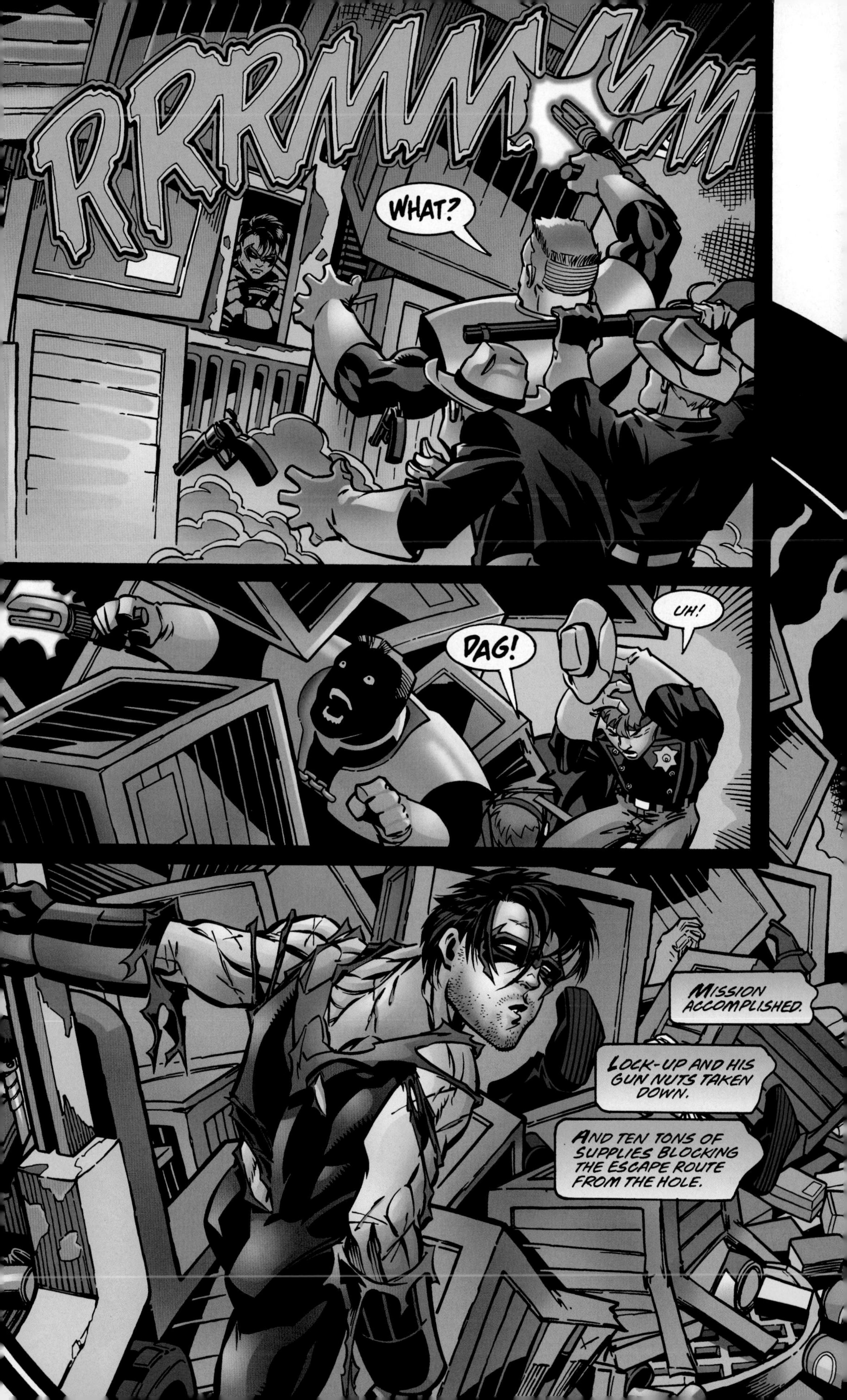
RRRMMMMMM
WHAT?
DAG!
UH!
MISSION ACCOMPLISHED.
LOCK-UP AND HIS GUN NUTS TAKEN DOWN.
AND TEN TONS OF SUPPLIES BLOCKING THE ESCAPE ROUTE FROM THE HOLE.

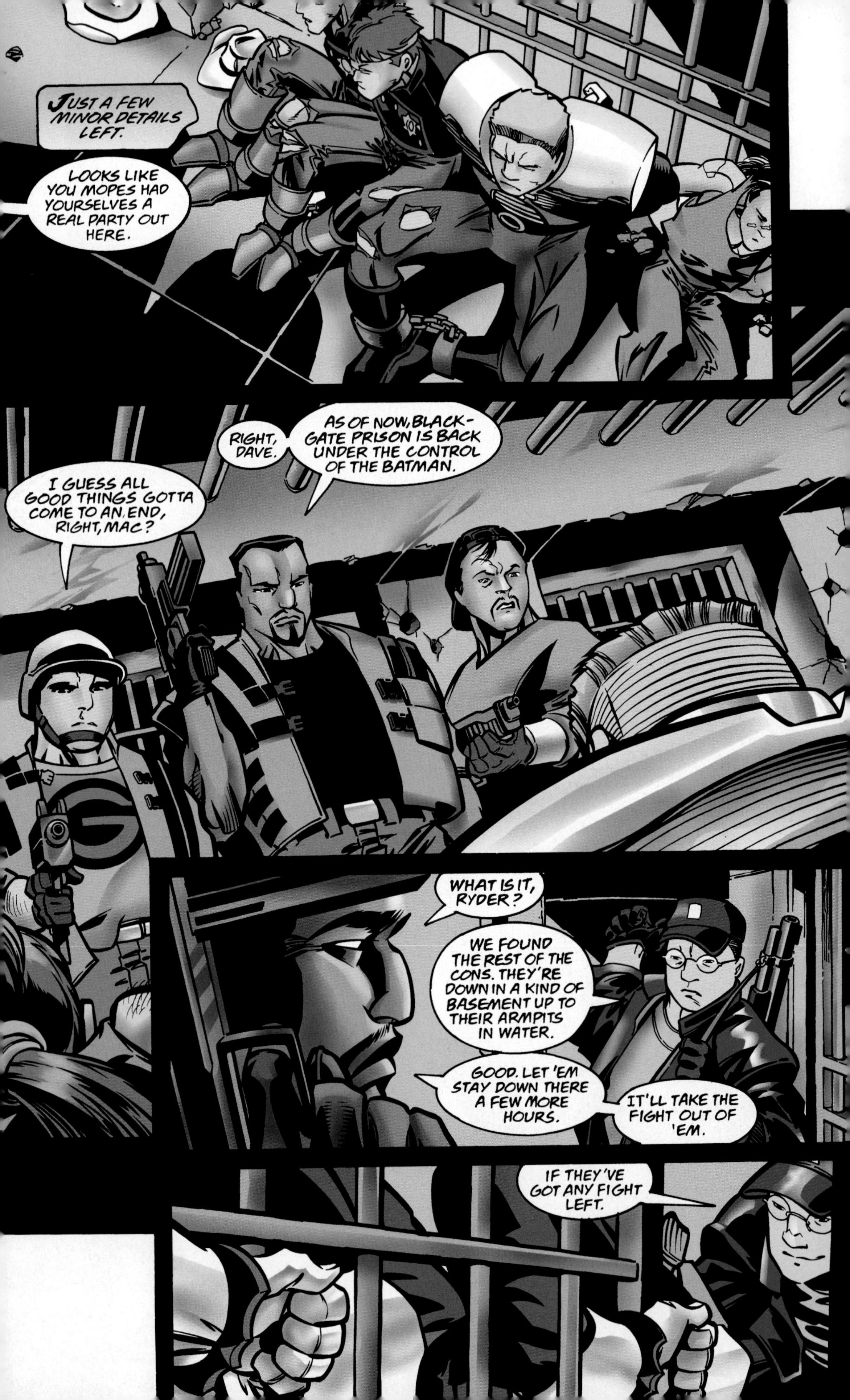
JUST A FEW MINOR DETAILS LEFT.
LOOKS LIKE YOU MOPES HAD YOURSELVES A REAL PARTY OUT HERE.
I GUESS ALL GOOD THINGS GOTTA COME TO AN END, RIGHT, MAC?
RIGHT, DAVE.
AS OF NOW, BLACKGATE PRISON IS BACK UNDER THE CONTROL OF THE BATMAN.
WHAT IS IT, RYDER?
WE FOUND THE REST OF THE CONS. THEY'RE DOWN IN A KIND OF BASEMENT UP TO THEIR ARMPITS IN WATER.
GOOD. LET 'EM STAY DOWN THERE A FEW MORE HOURS.
IT'LL TAKE THE FIGHT OUT OF 'EM.
IF THEY'VE GOT ANY FIGHT LEFT.

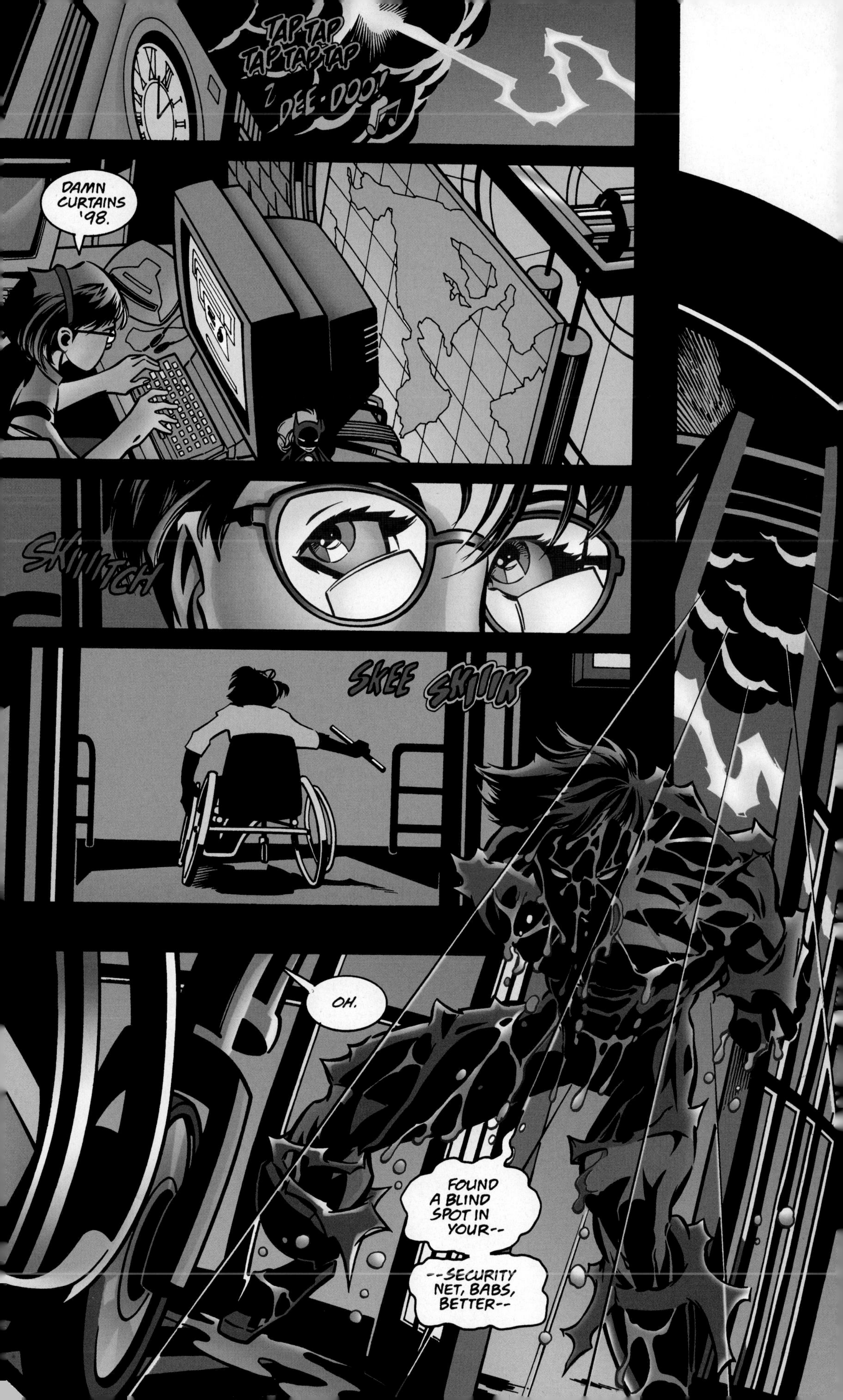
TAP TAP
TAP TAP TAP
DEE-DOO!
DAMN CURTAINS '98.
SKIIITCH
SKEE
SKIIIK
OH.
FOUND A BLIND SPOT IN YOUR--
--SECURITY NET, BABS, BETTER--

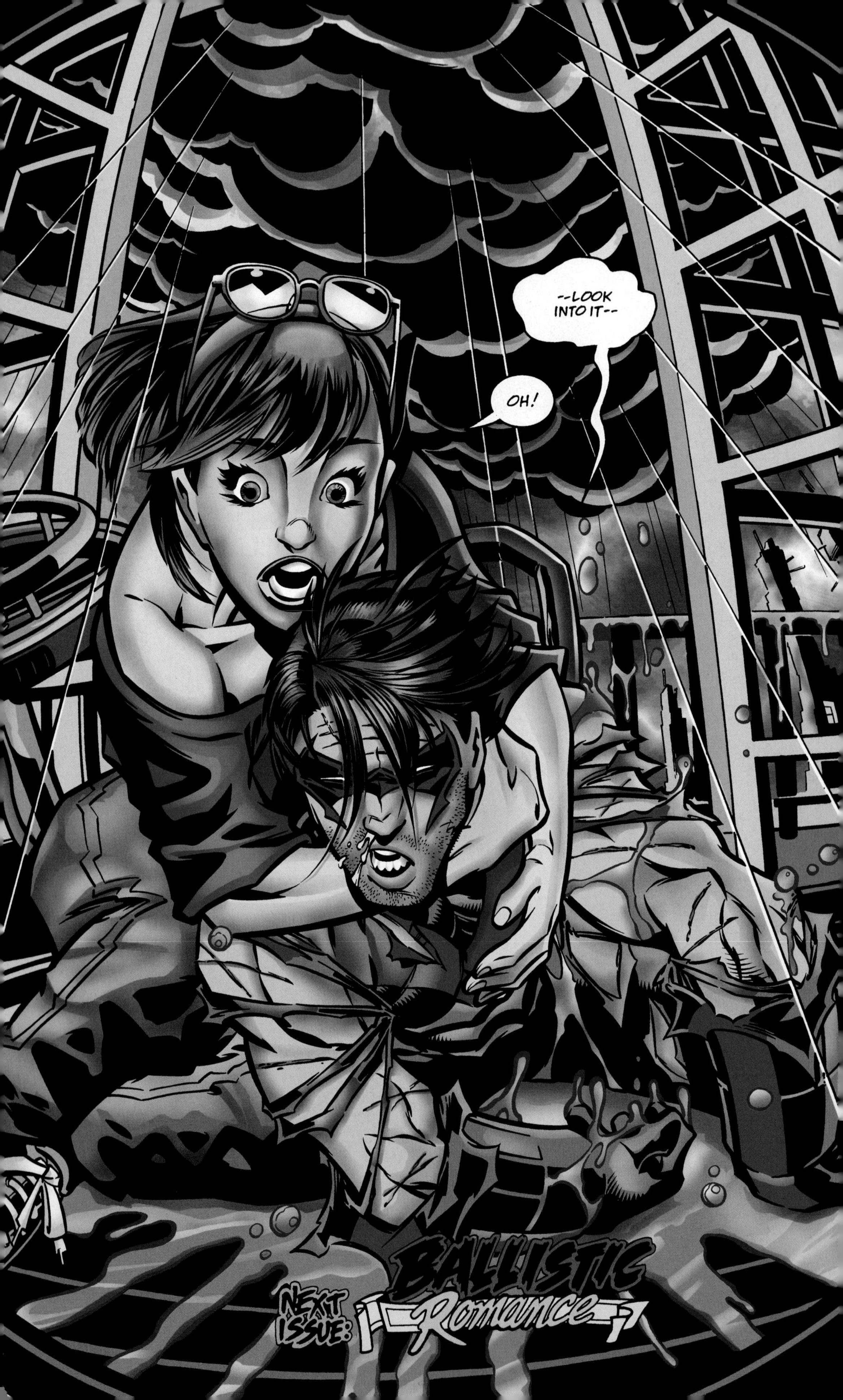
--LOOK INTO IT--
OH!
NEXT ISSUE: BALLISTIC Romance

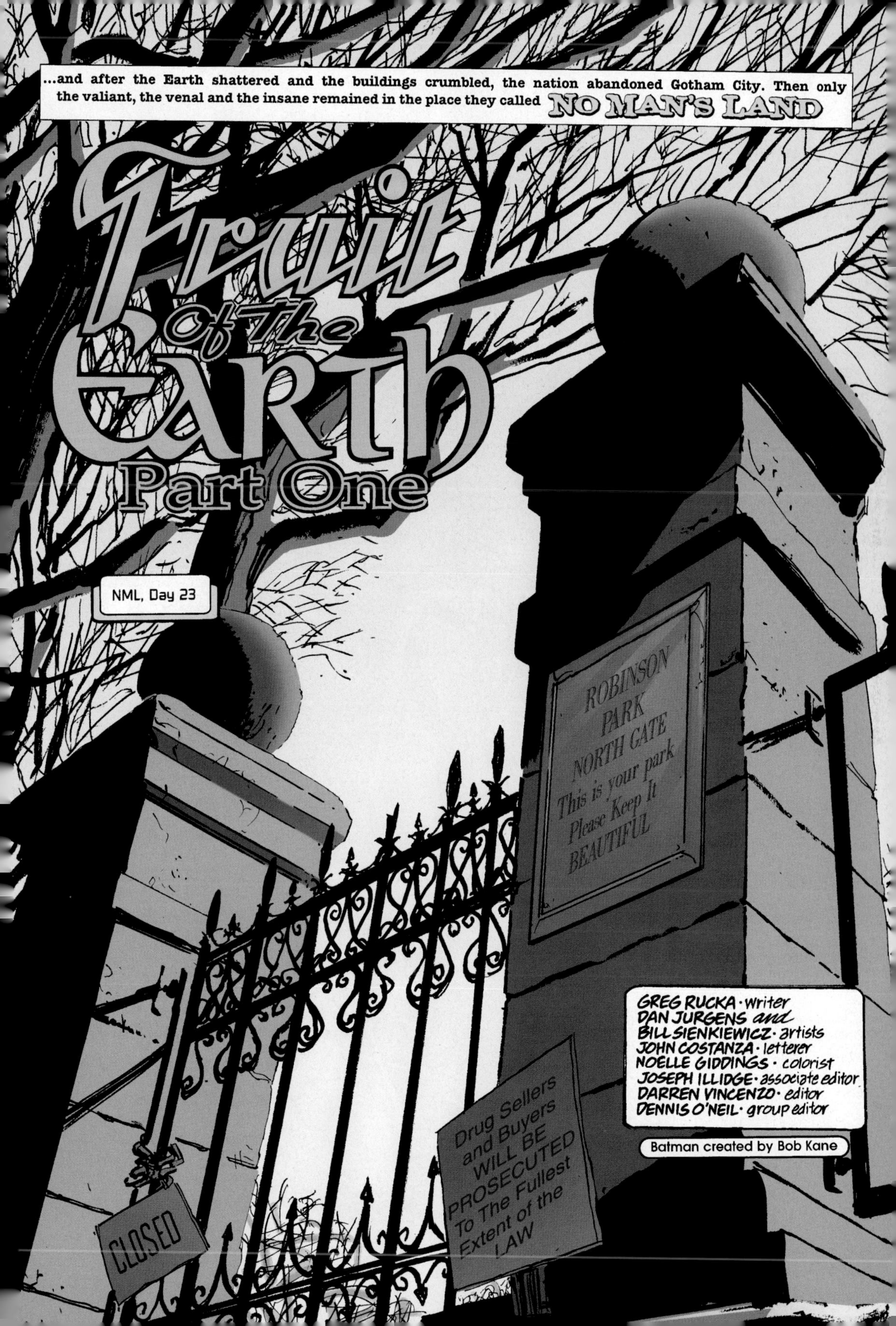
...and after the Earth shattered and the buildings crumbled, the nation abandoned Gotham City. Then only the valiant, the venal and the insane remained in the place they called NO MAN'S LAND
Fruit Of The Earth
Part One
NML, Day 23
ROBINSON PARK NORTH GATE This is your park Please Keep It BEAUTIFUL
GREG RUCKA · writer
DAN JURGENS and
BILL SIENKIEWICZ · artists
JOHN COSTANZA · letterer
NOELLE GIDDINGS · colorist
JOSEPH ILLIDGE · associate editor
DARREN VINCENZO · editor
DENNIS O'NEIL · group editor
Batman created by Bob Kane
Drug Sellers and Buyers WILL BE PROSECUTED To The Fullest Extent of the LAW
CLOSED

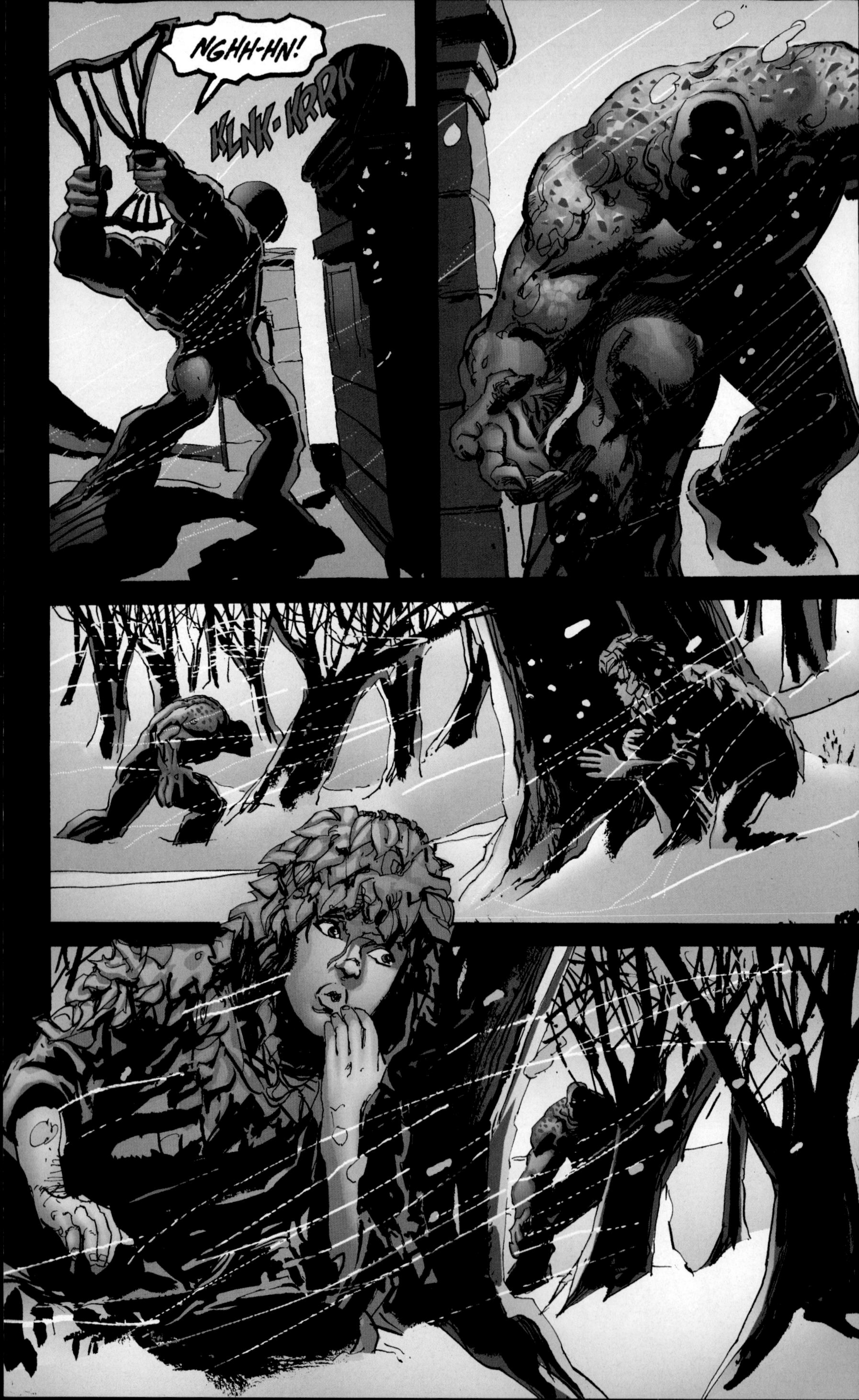
NGHH-HN!
KLNK-KRRK

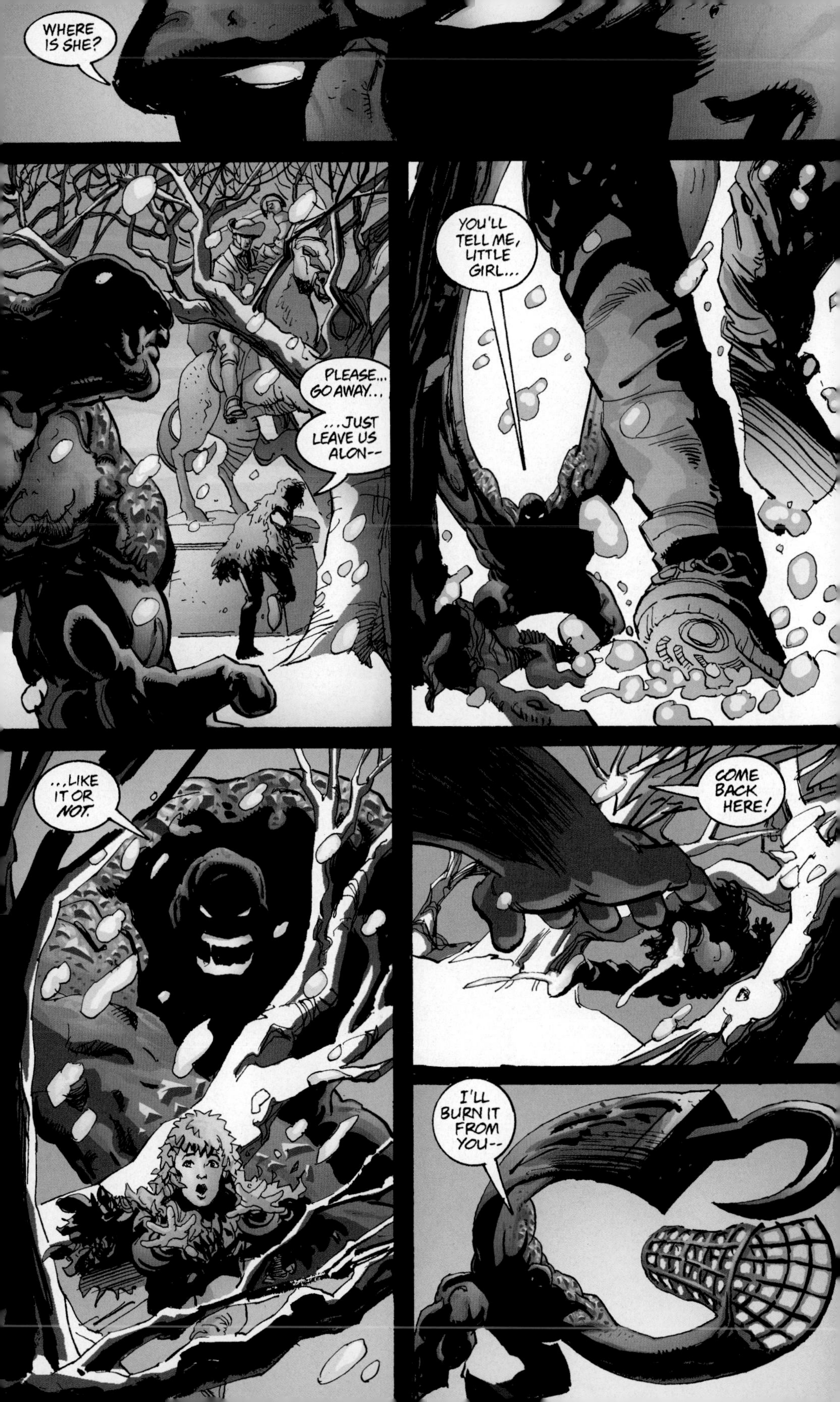
WHERE IS SHE?
PLEASE... GO AWAY...
...JUST LEAVE US ALON--
YOU'LL TELL ME, LITTLE GIRL...
...LIKE IT OR NOT.
COME BACK HERE!
I'LL BURN IT FROM YOU--

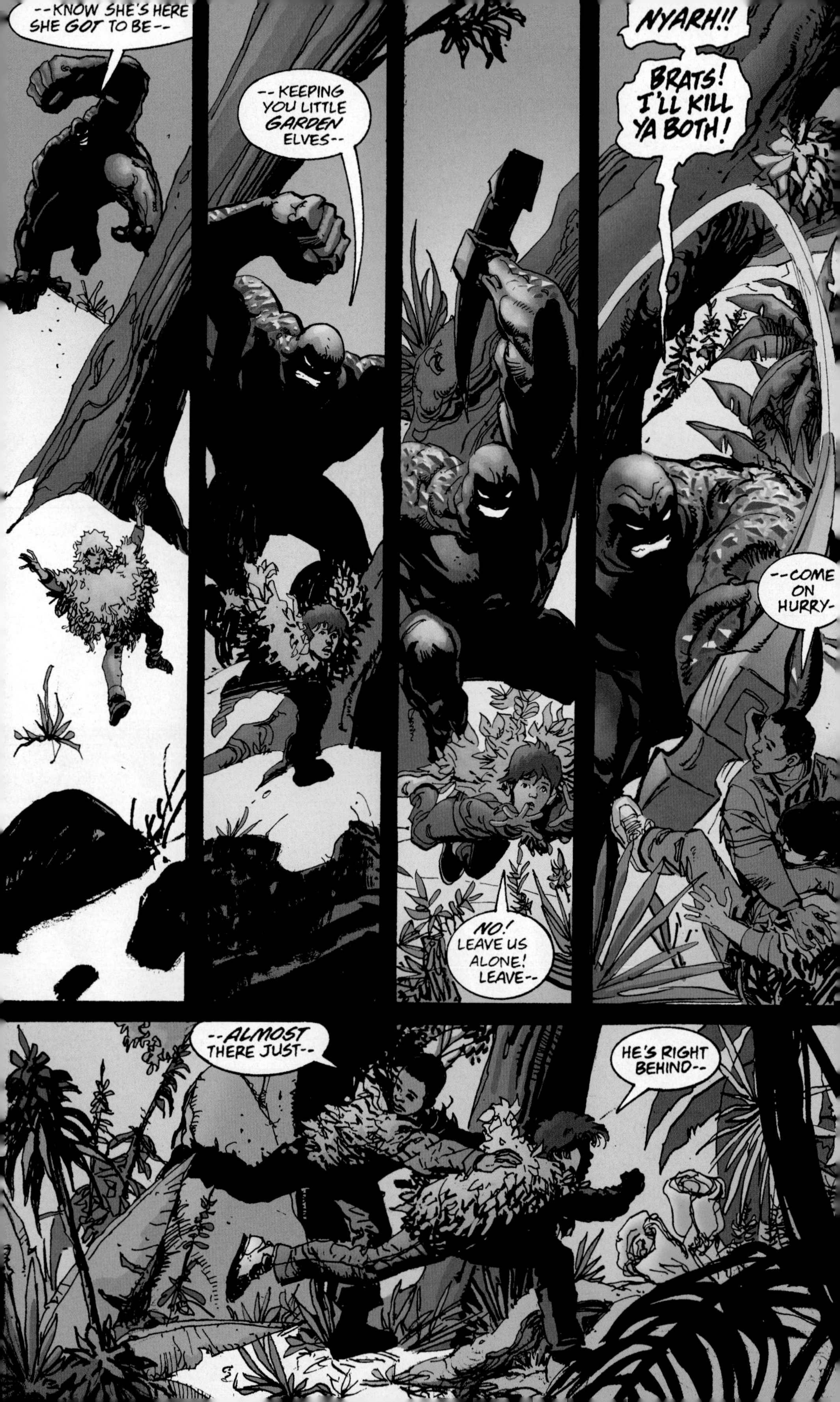
--KNOW SHE'S HERE SHE GOT TO BE--
--KEEPING YOU LITTLE GARDEN ELVES--
NYARH!!
BRATS! I'LL KILL YA BOTH!
--COME ON HURRY-
NO! LEAVE US ALONE! LEAVE--
--ALMOST THERE JUST--
HE'S RIGHT BEHIND--

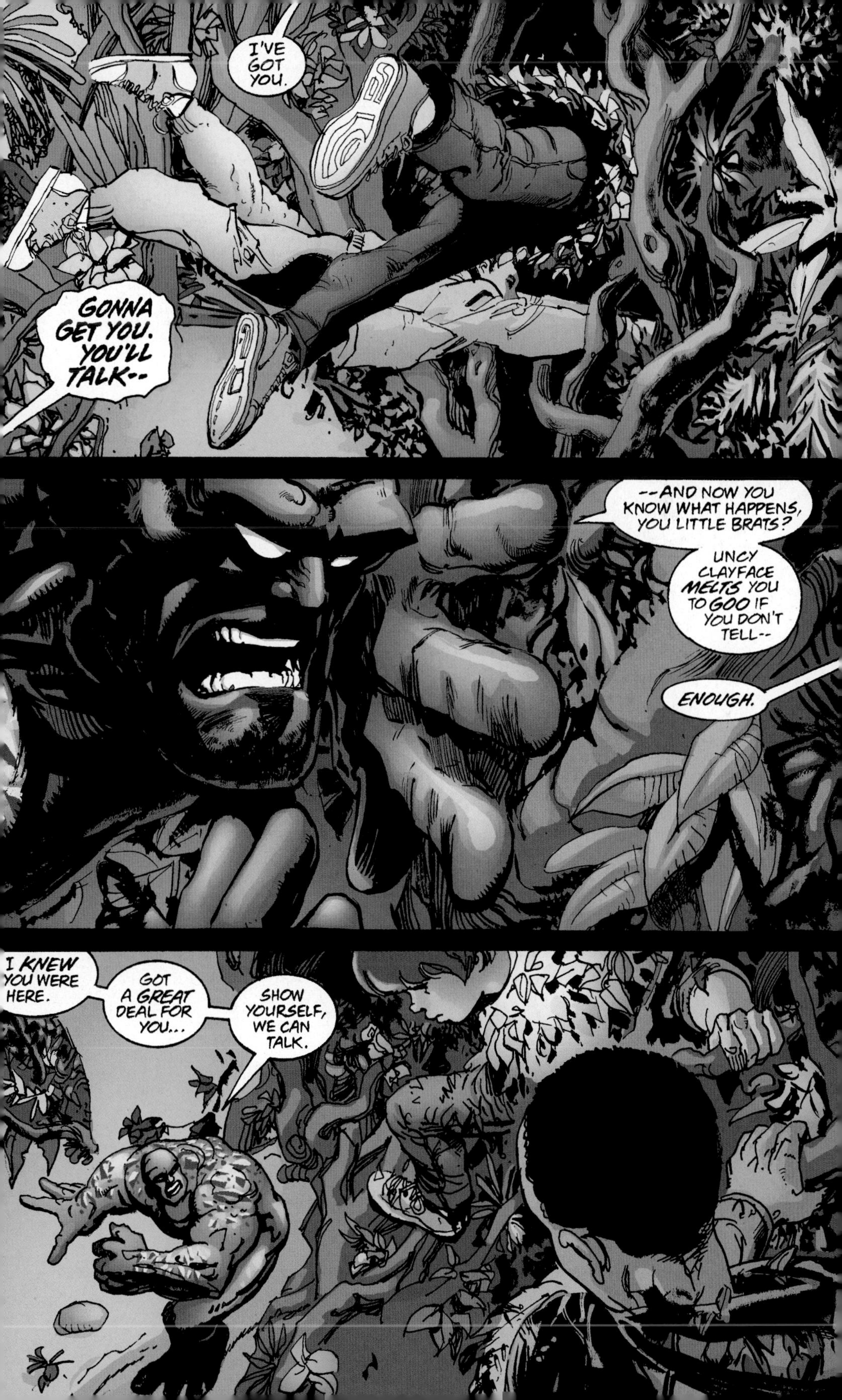
I'VE GOT YOU.
GONNA GET YOU. YOU'LL TALK--
--AND NOW YOU KNOW WHAT HAPPENS, YOU LITTLE BRATS?
UNCY CLAYFACE MELTS YOU TO GOO IF YOU DON'T TELL--
ENOUGH.
I KNEW YOU WERE HERE.
GOT A GREAT DEAL FOR YOU...
SHOW YOURSELF, WE CAN TALK.

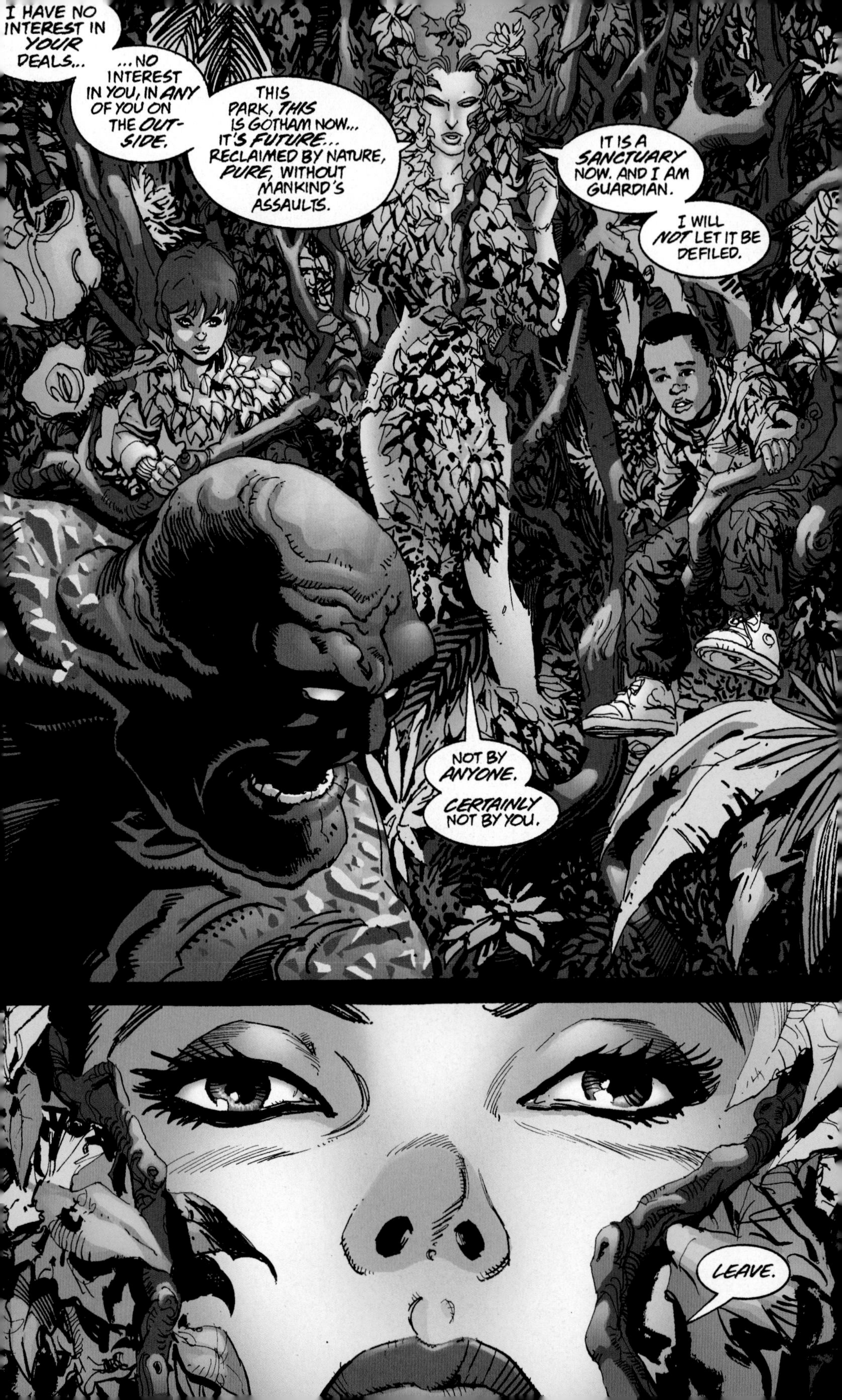

I HAVE NO INTEREST IN YOUR DEALS...
...NO INTEREST IN YOU, IN ANY OF YOU ON THE OUT-SIDE.
THIS PARK, THIS IS GOTHAM NOW... IT'S FUTURE... RECLAIMED BY NATURE, PURE, WITHOUT MANKIND'S ASSAULTS.
IT IS A SANCTUARY NOW. AND I AM GUARDIAN.
I WILL NOT LET IT BE DEFILED.
NOT BY ANYONE.
CERTAINLY NOT BY YOU.
LEAVE.

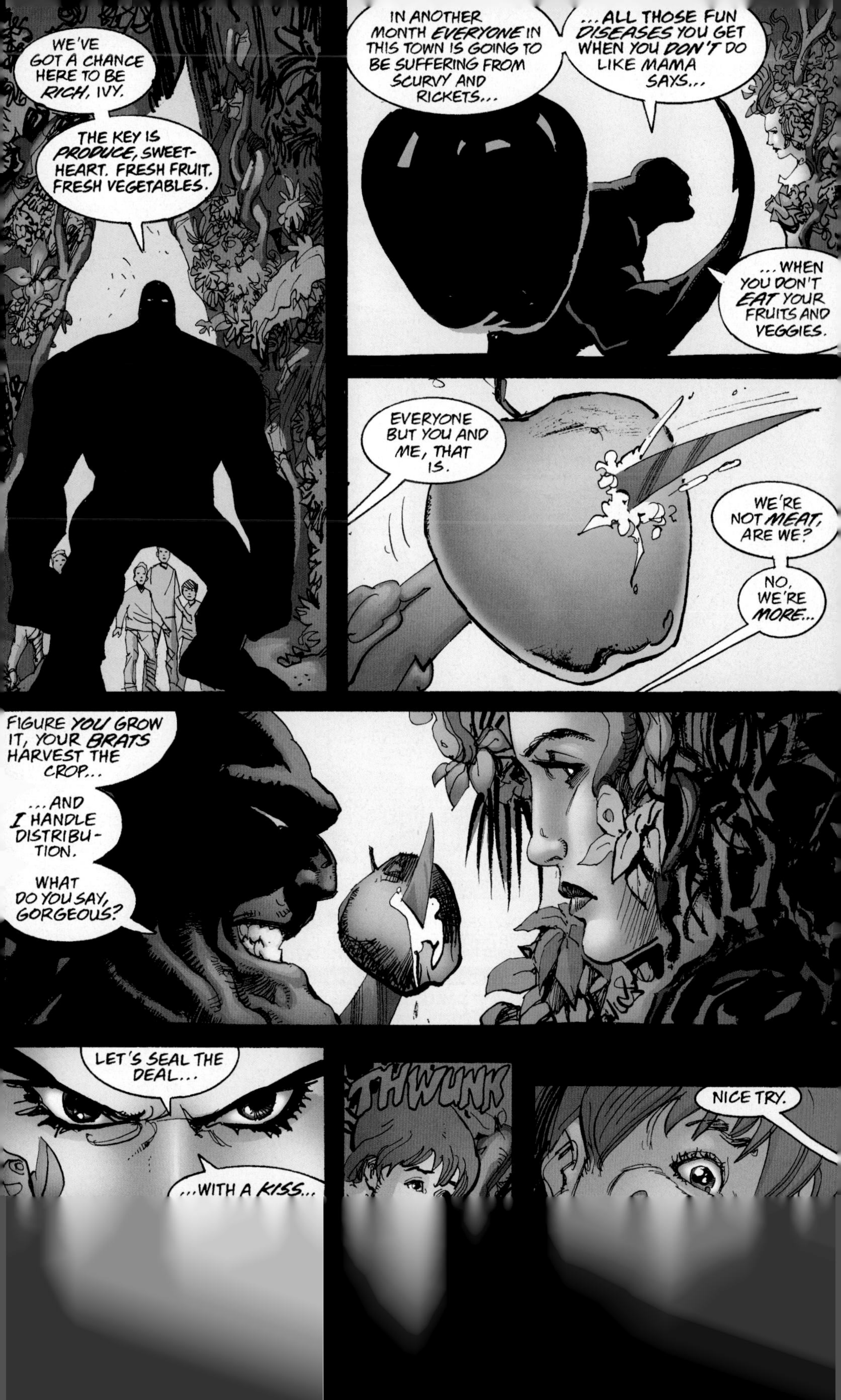
WE'VE GOT A CHANCE HERE TO BE RICH, IVY.
THE KEY IS PRODUCE, SWEET-HEART. FRESH FRUIT. FRESH VEGETABLES.
IN ANOTHER MONTH EVERYONE IN THIS TOWN IS GOING TO BE SUFFERING FROM SCURVY AND RICKETS...
...ALL THOSE FUN DISEASES YOU GET WHEN YOU DON'T DO LIKE MAMA SAYS...
...WHEN YOU DON'T EAT YOUR FRUITS AND VEGGIES.
EVERYONE BUT YOU AND ME, THAT IS.
WE'RE NOT MEAT, ARE WE?
NO, WE'RE MORE...
FIGURE YOU GROW IT, YOUR BRATS HARVEST THE CROP...
...AND I HANDLE DISTRIBU-TION.
WHAT DO YOU SAY, GORGEOUS?
LET'S SEAL THE DEAL...
...WITH A KISS...
THWUNK
NICE TRY.

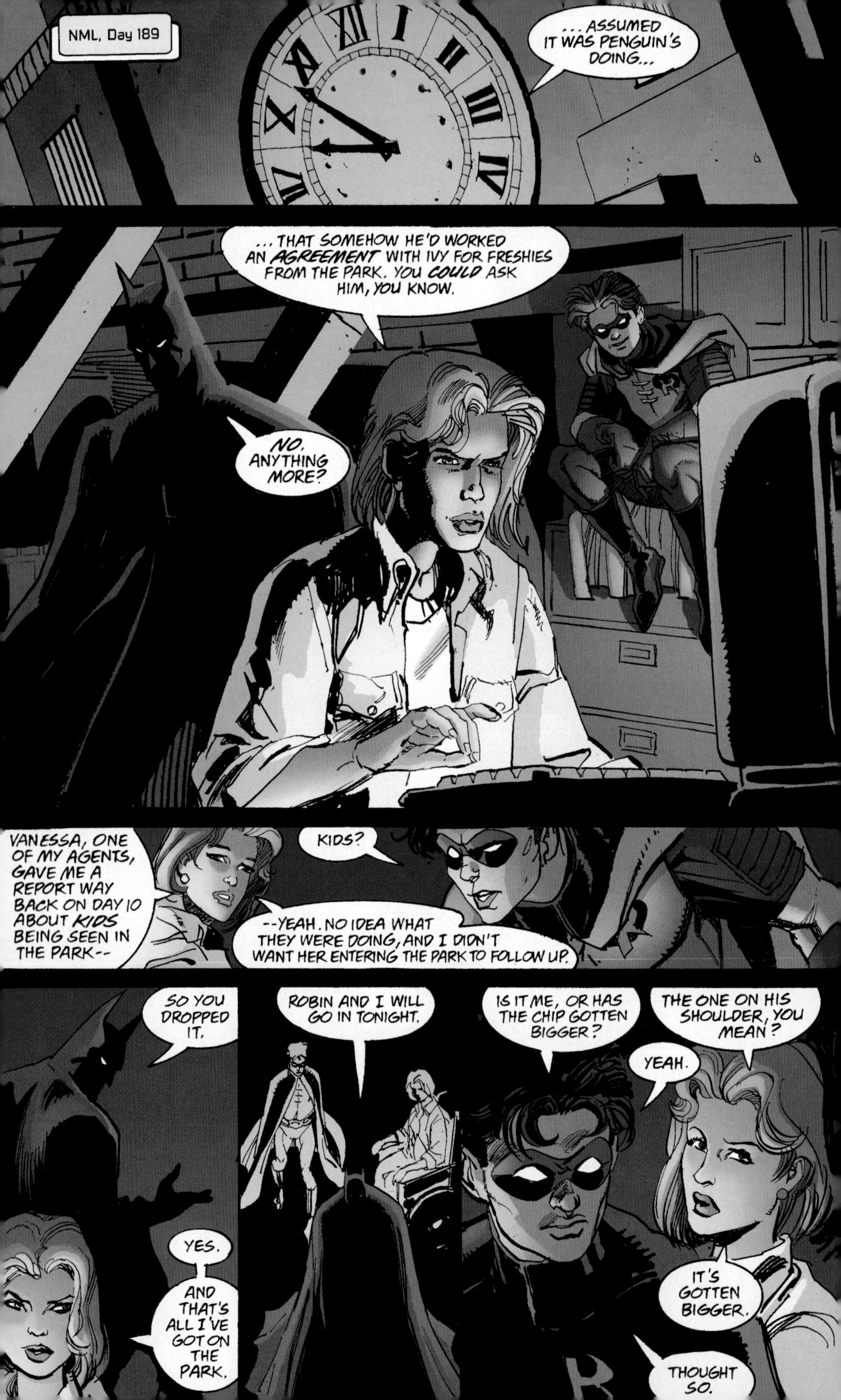
NML, Day 189
...ASSUMED IT WAS PENGUIN'S DOING...
...THAT SOMEHOW HE'D WORKED AN AGREEMENT WITH IVY FOR FRESHIES FROM THE PARK. YOU COULD ASK HIM, YOU KNOW.
NO. ANYTHING MORE?
VANESSA, ONE OF MY AGENTS, GAVE ME A REPORT WAY BACK ON DAY 10 ABOUT KIDS BEING SEEN IN THE PARK--
KIDS?
--YEAH. NO IDEA WHAT THEY WERE DOING, AND I DIDN'T WANT HER ENTERING THE PARK TO FOLLOW UP.
SO YOU DROPPED IT.
YES.
AND THAT'S ALL I'VE GOT ON THE PARK.
ROBIN AND I WILL GO IN TONIGHT.
IS IT ME, OR HAS THE CHIP GOTTEN BIGGER?
THE ONE ON HIS SHOULDER, YOU MEAN?
YEAH.
IT'S GOTTEN BIGGER.
THOUGHT SO.

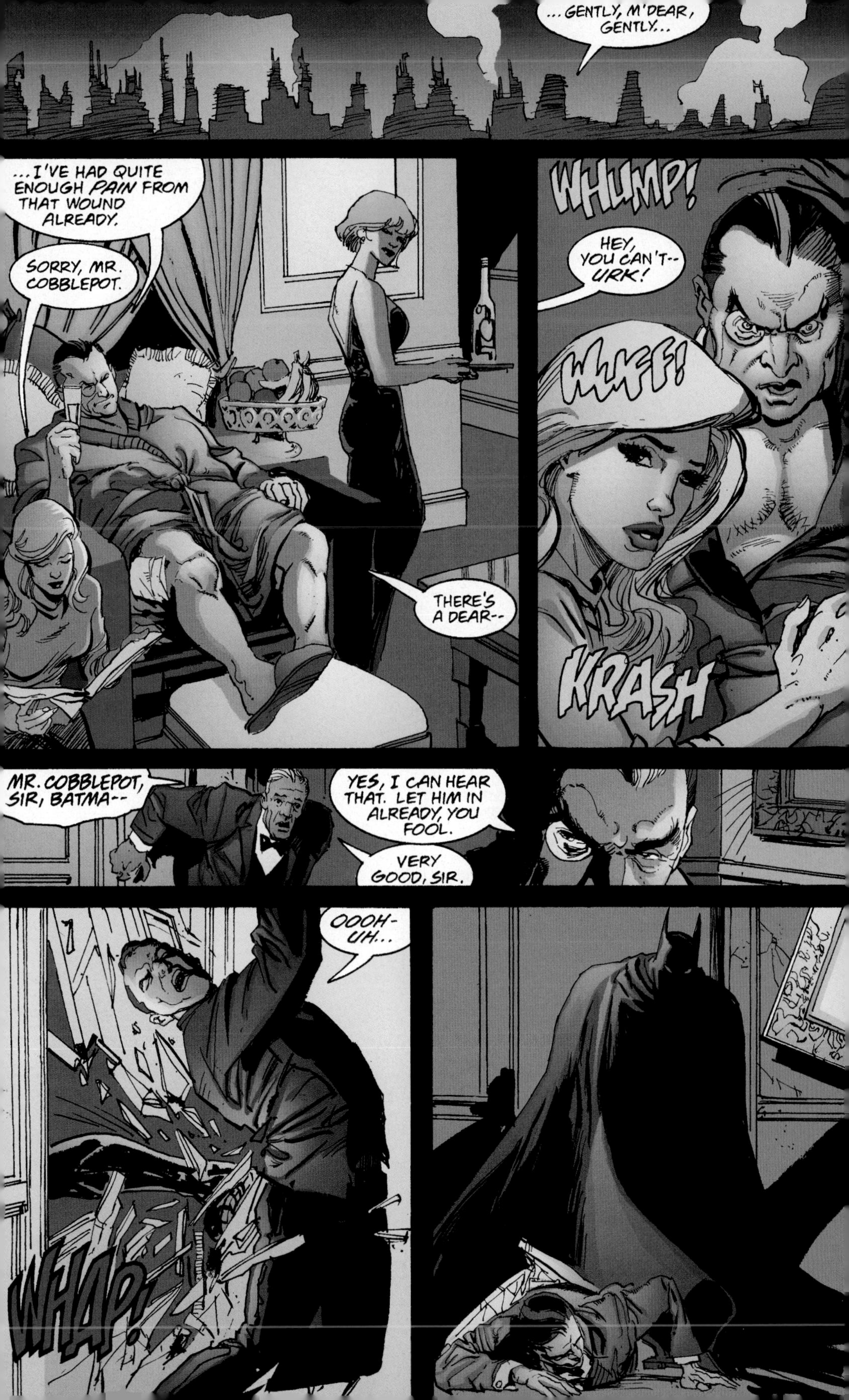
...GENTLY, M'DEAR, GENTLY...
...I'VE HAD QUITE ENOUGH PAIN FROM THAT WOUND ALREADY.
SORRY, MR. COBBLEPOT.
THERE'S A DEAR--
WHUMP!
HEY, YOU CAN'T-- URK!
WUFF!
KRASH
MR. COBBLEPOT, SIR, BATMA--
YES, I CAN HEAR THAT. LET HIM IN ALREADY, YOU FOOL.
VERY GOOD, SIR.
OOOH-UH...
WHAP!

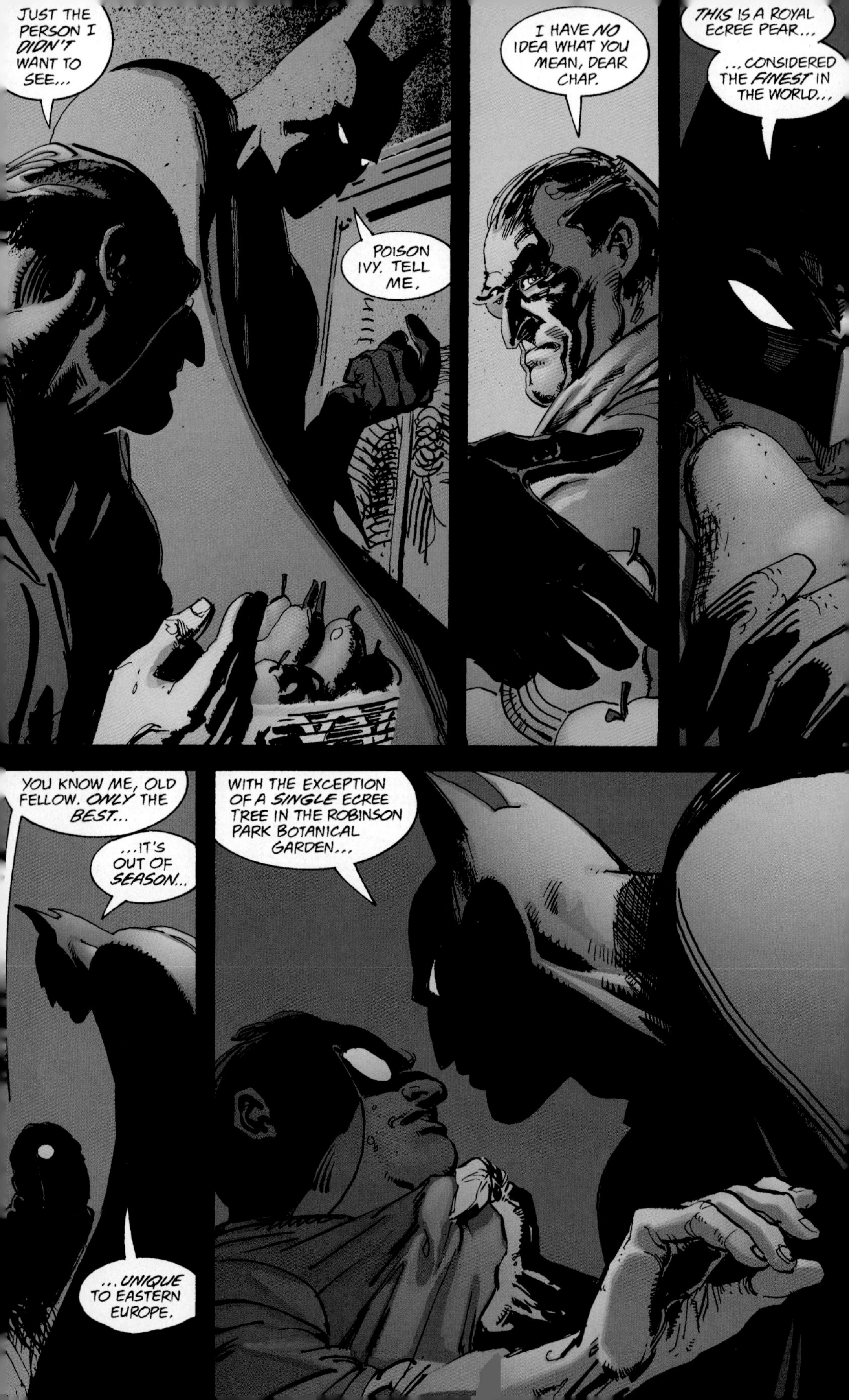

JUST THE PERSON I DIDN'T WANT TO SEE...
POISON IVY. TELL ME.
I HAVE NO IDEA WHAT YOU MEAN, DEAR CHAP.
THIS IS A ROYAL ECREE PEAR...
...CONSIDERED THE FINEST IN THE WORLD...
YOU KNOW ME, OLD FELLOW. ONLY THE BEST...
...IT'S OUT OF SEASON...
...UNIQUE TO EASTERN EUROPE.
WITH THE EXCEPTION OF A SINGLE ECREE TREE IN THE ROBINSON PARK BOTANICAL GARDEN...

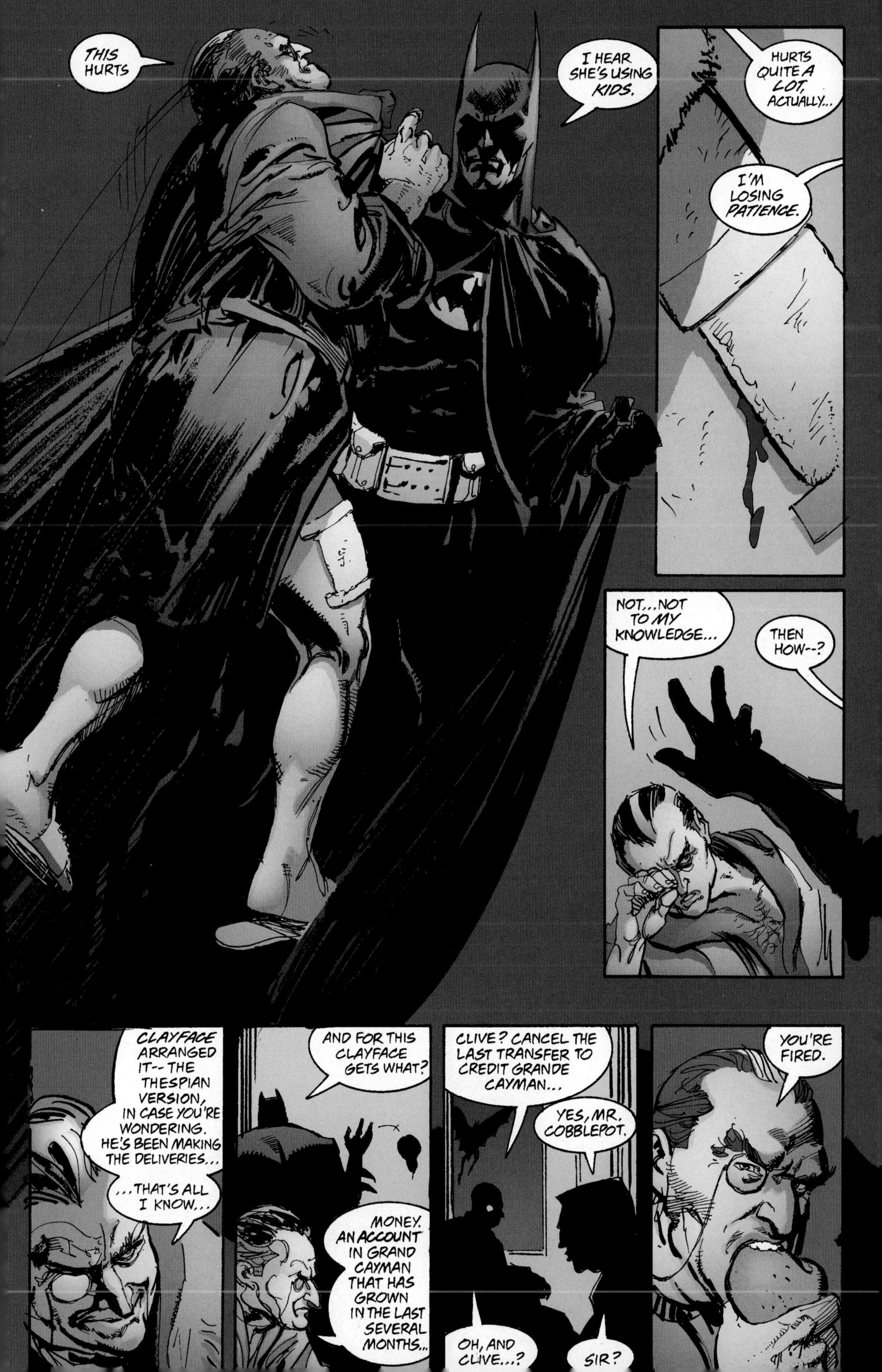
THIS HURTS
I HEAR SHE'S USING KIDS.
HURTS QUITE A LOT, ACTUALLY...
I'M LOSING PATIENCE.
NOT...NOT TO MY KNOWLEDGE...
THEN HOW--?
CLAYFACE ARRANGED IT-- THE THESPIAN VERSION, IN CASE YOU'RE WONDERING. HE'S BEEN MAKING THE DELIVERIES...
...THAT'S ALL I KNOW...
AND FOR THIS CLAYFACE GETS WHAT?
MONEY. AN ACCOUNT IN GRAND CAYMAN THAT HAS GROWN IN THE LAST SEVERAL MONTHS...
CLIVE? CANCEL THE LAST TRANSFER TO CREDIT GRANDE CAYMAN...
YES, MR. COBBLEPOT.
OH, AND CLIVE...?
SIR?
YOU'RE FIRED.

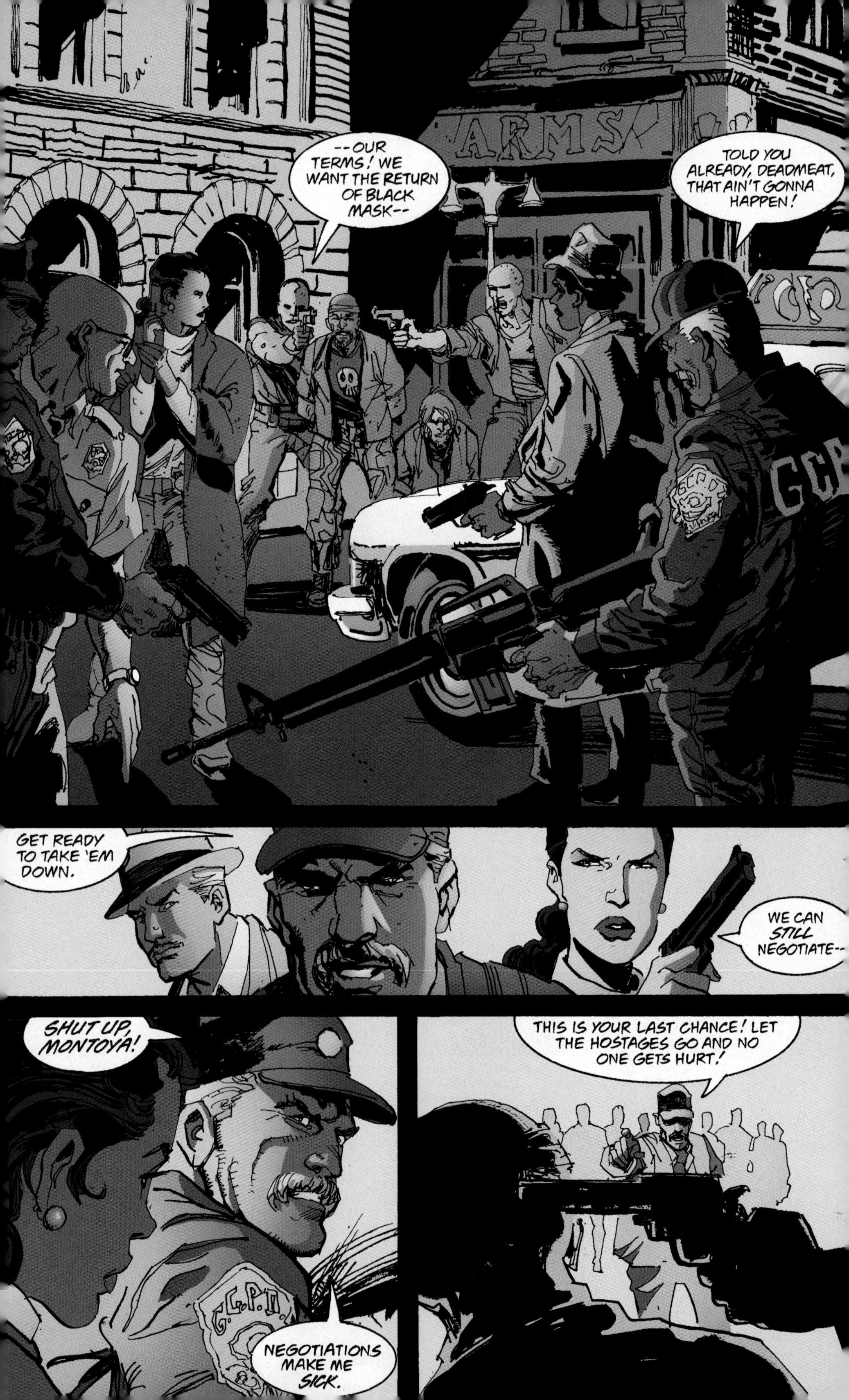
ARMS
--OUR TERMS! WE WANT THE RETURN OF BLACK MASK--
TOLD YOU ALREADY, DEADMEAT, THAT AIN'T GONNA HAPPEN!
GCPD
GET READY TO TAKE 'EM DOWN.
WE CAN STILL NEGOTIATE--
SHUT UP, MONTOYA!
NEGOTIATIONS MAKE ME SICK.
THIS IS YOUR LAST CHANCE! LET THE HOSTAGES GO AND NO ONE GETS HURT!

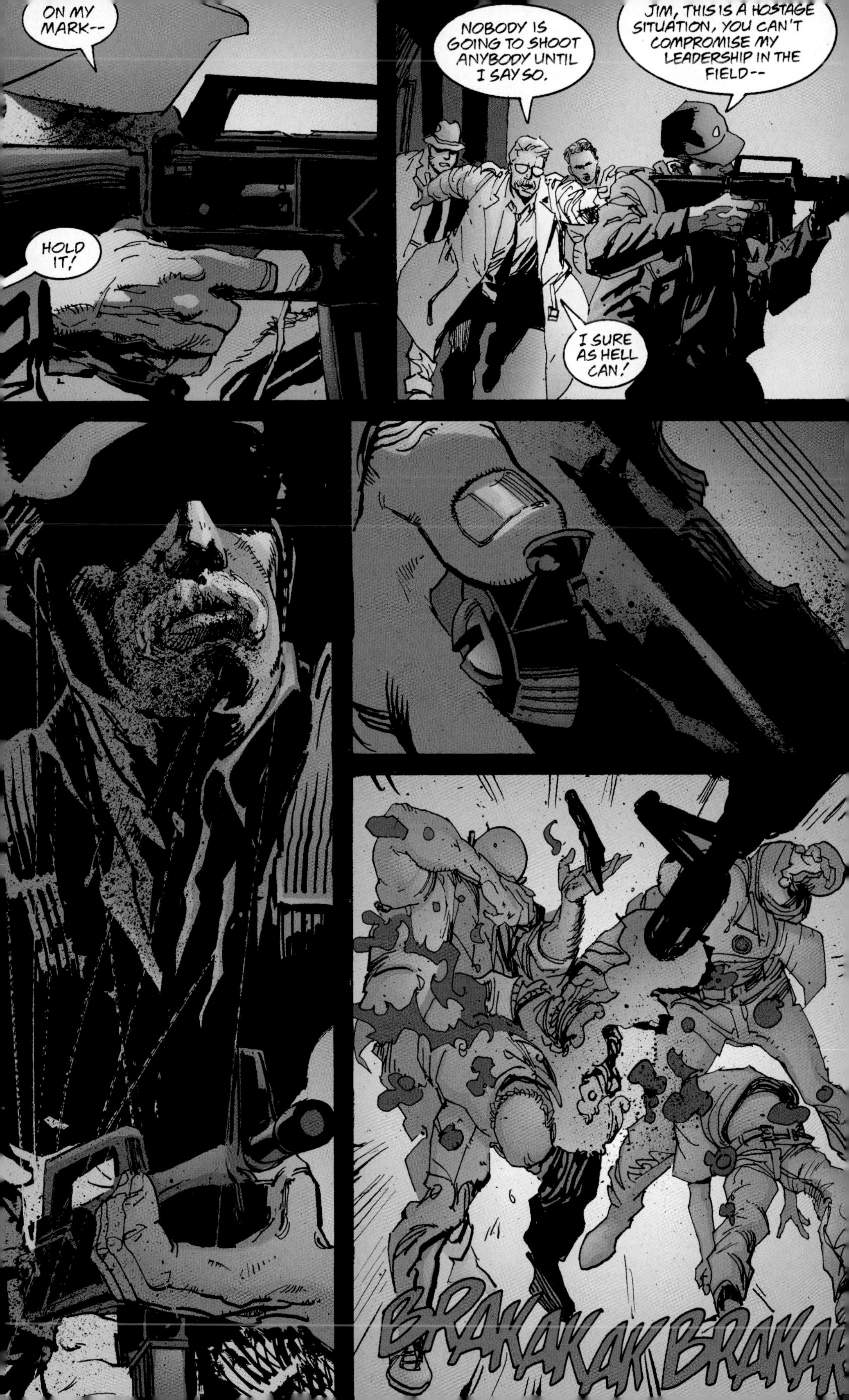

ON MY MARK--
HOLD IT!
NOBODY IS GOING TO SHOOT ANYBODY UNTIL I SAY SO.
JIM, THIS IS A HOSTAGE SITUATION, YOU CAN'T COMPROMISE MY LEADERSHIP IN THE FIELD--
I SURE AS HELL CAN!
BRAKAKAK BRAKAK

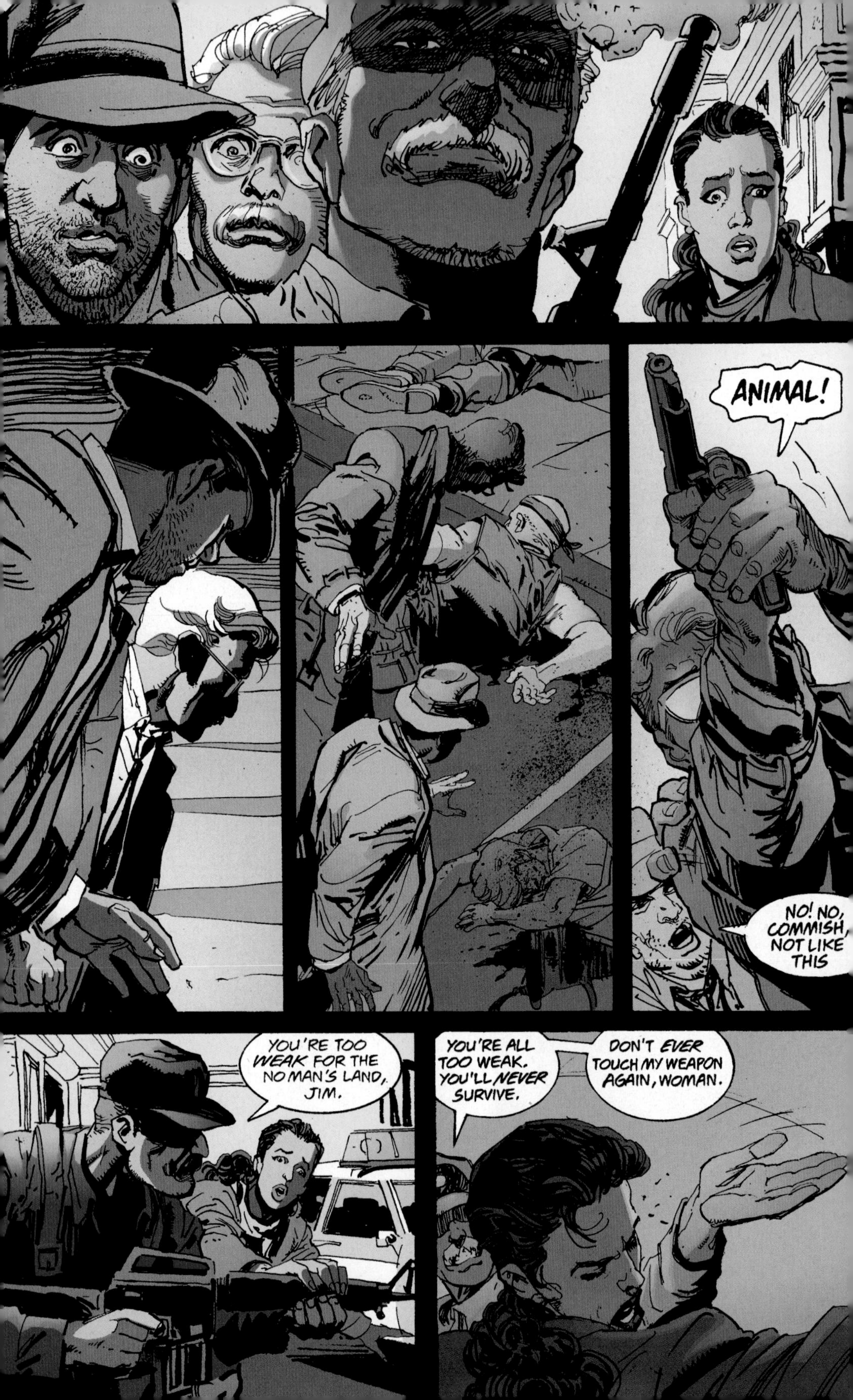
ANIMAL!
NO! NO, COMMISH, NOT LIKE THIS
YOU'RE TOO WEAK FOR THE NO MAN'S LAND, JIM.
YOU'RE ALL TOO WEAK. YOU'LL NEVER SURVIVE.
DON'T EVER TOUCH MY WEAPON AGAIN, WOMAN.

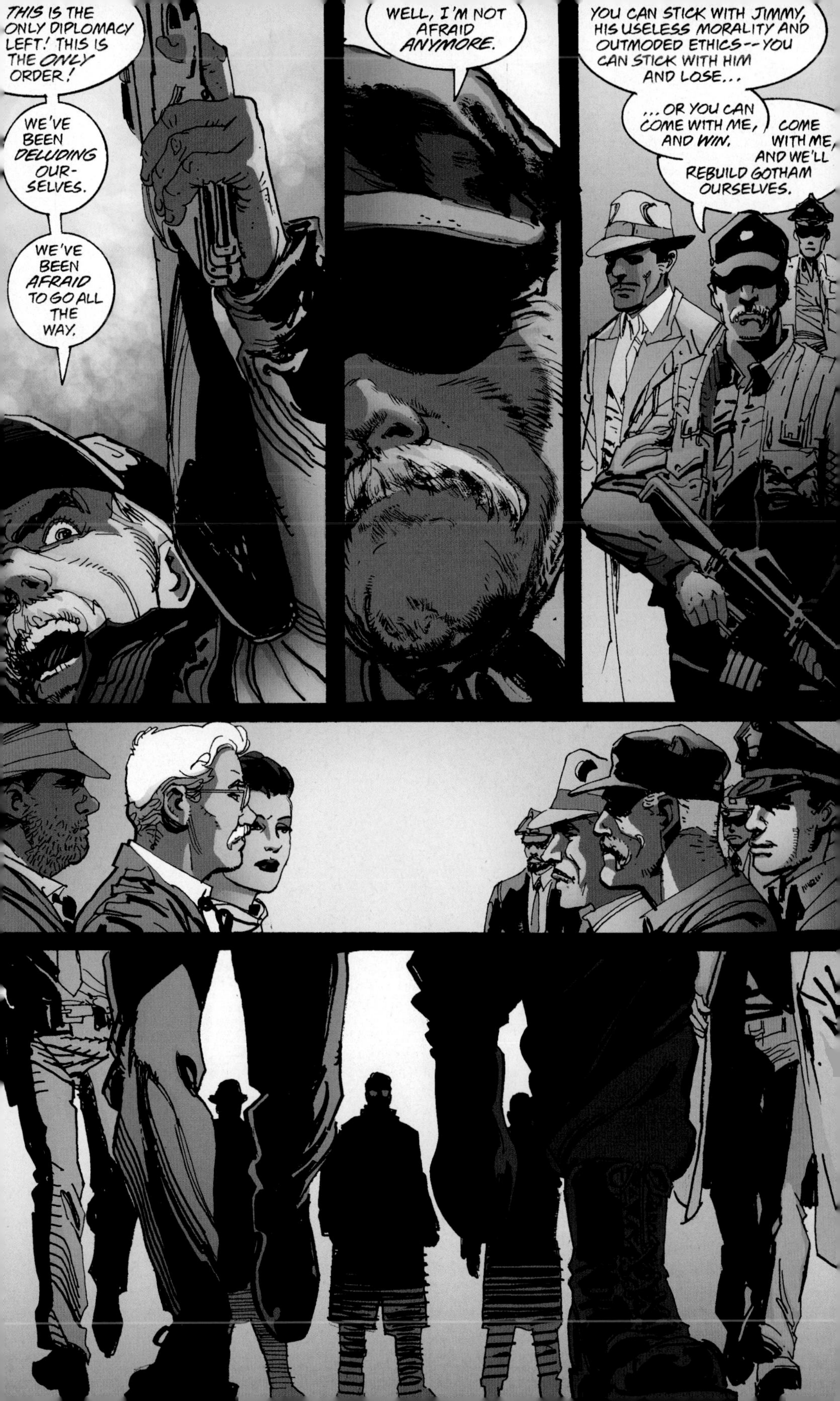
THIS IS THE ONLY DIPLOMACY LEFT! THIS IS THE ONLY ORDER!
WE'VE BEEN DELUDING OURSELVES.
WE'VE BEEN AFRAID TO GO ALL THE WAY.
WELL, I'M NOT AFRAID ANYMORE.
YOU CAN STICK WITH JIMMY, HIS USELESS MORALITY AND OUTMODED ETHICS--YOU CAN STICK WITH HIM AND LOSE...
...OR YOU CAN COME WITH ME, AND WIN.
COME WITH ME, AND WE'LL REBUILD GOTHAM OURSELVES.

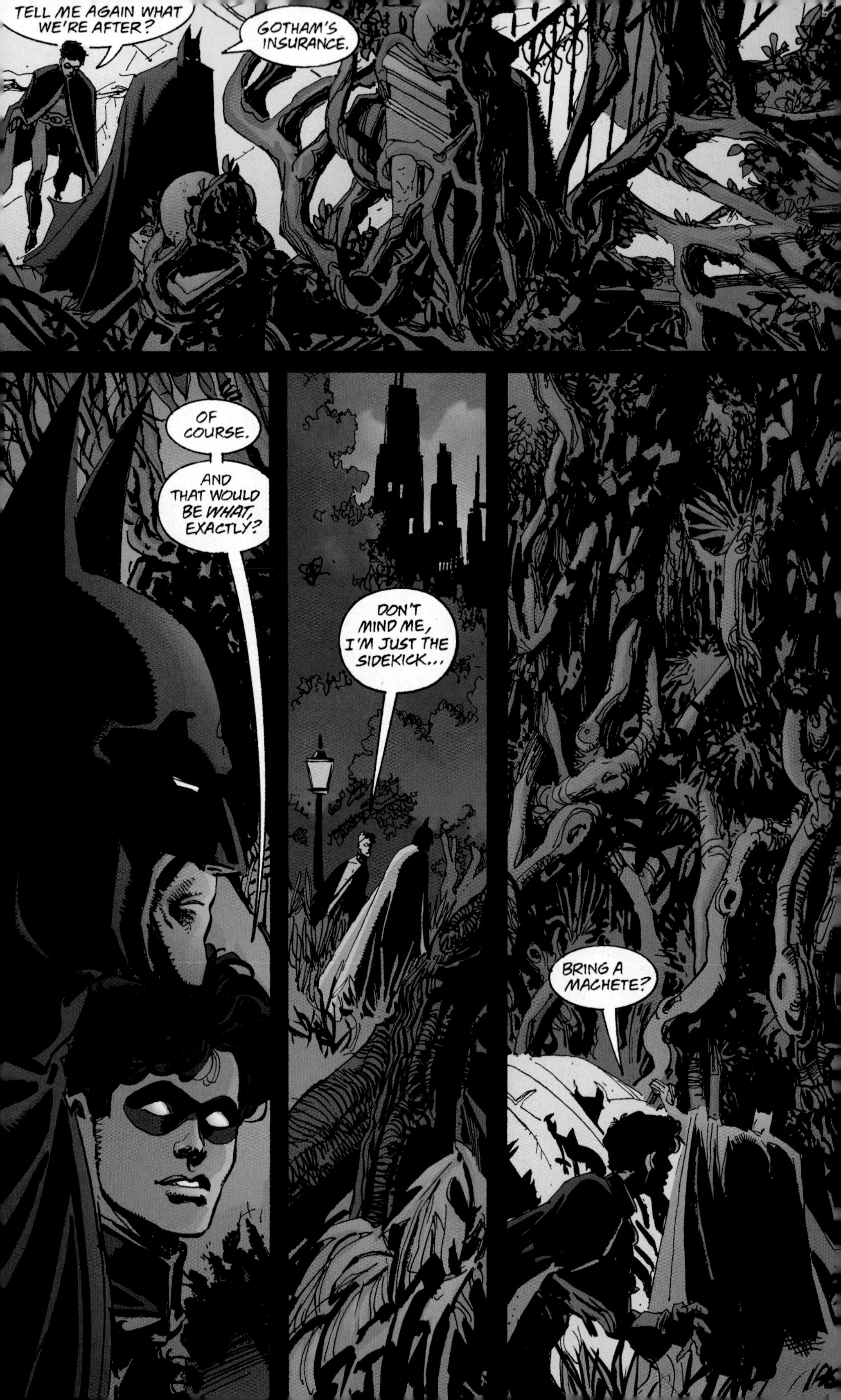

TELL ME AGAIN WHAT WE'RE AFTER?
GOTHAM'S INSURANCE.
OF COURSE.
AND THAT WOULD BE WHAT, EXACTLY?
DON'T MIND ME, I'M JUST THE SIDEKICK...
BRING A MACHETE?

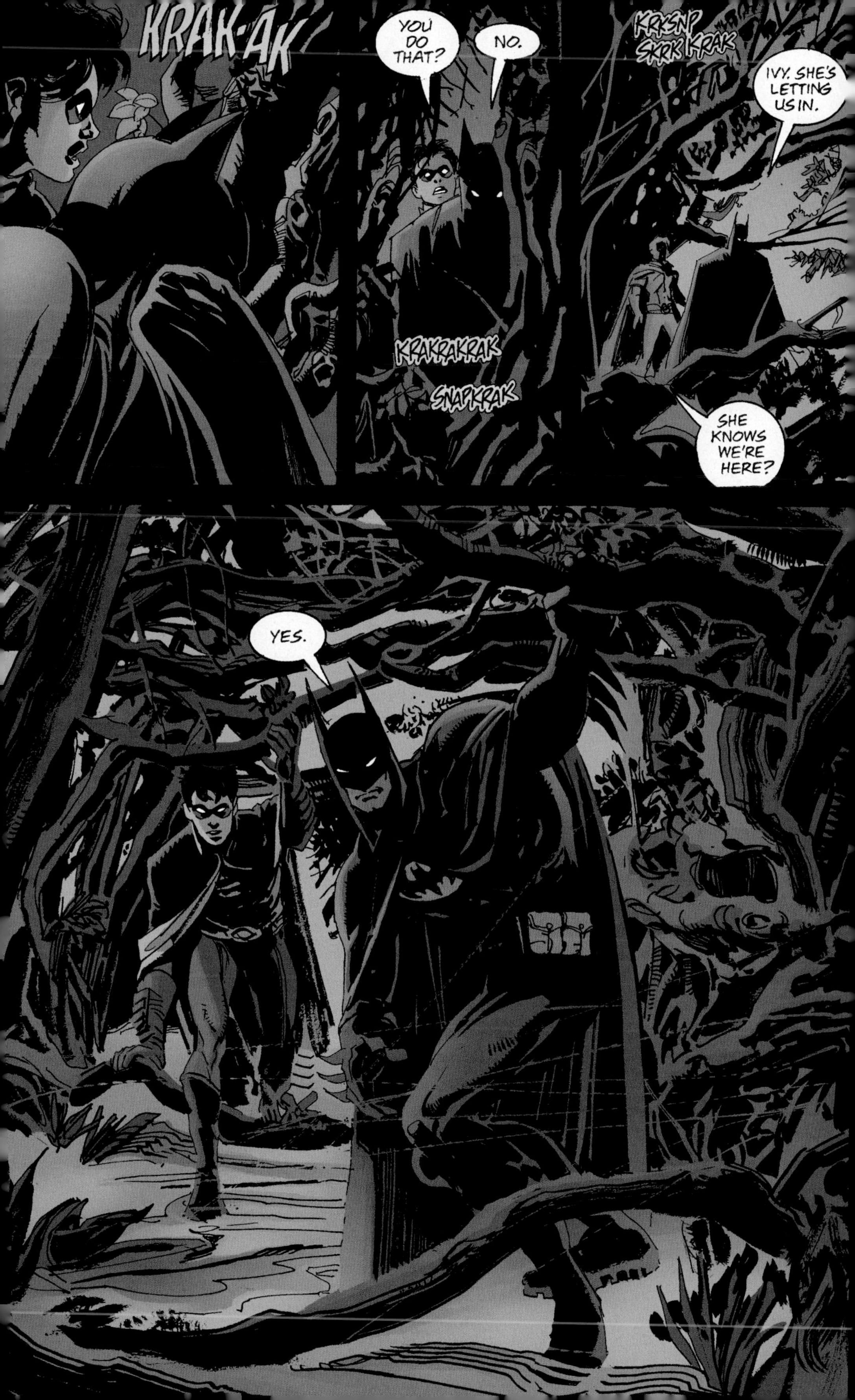
KRAK-AK
YOU DO THAT?
NO.
KRAKRAKRAK
SNAPKRAK
KRKSNP SKRK KRAK
IVY. SHE'S LETTING US IN.
SHE KNOWS WE'RE HERE?
YES.

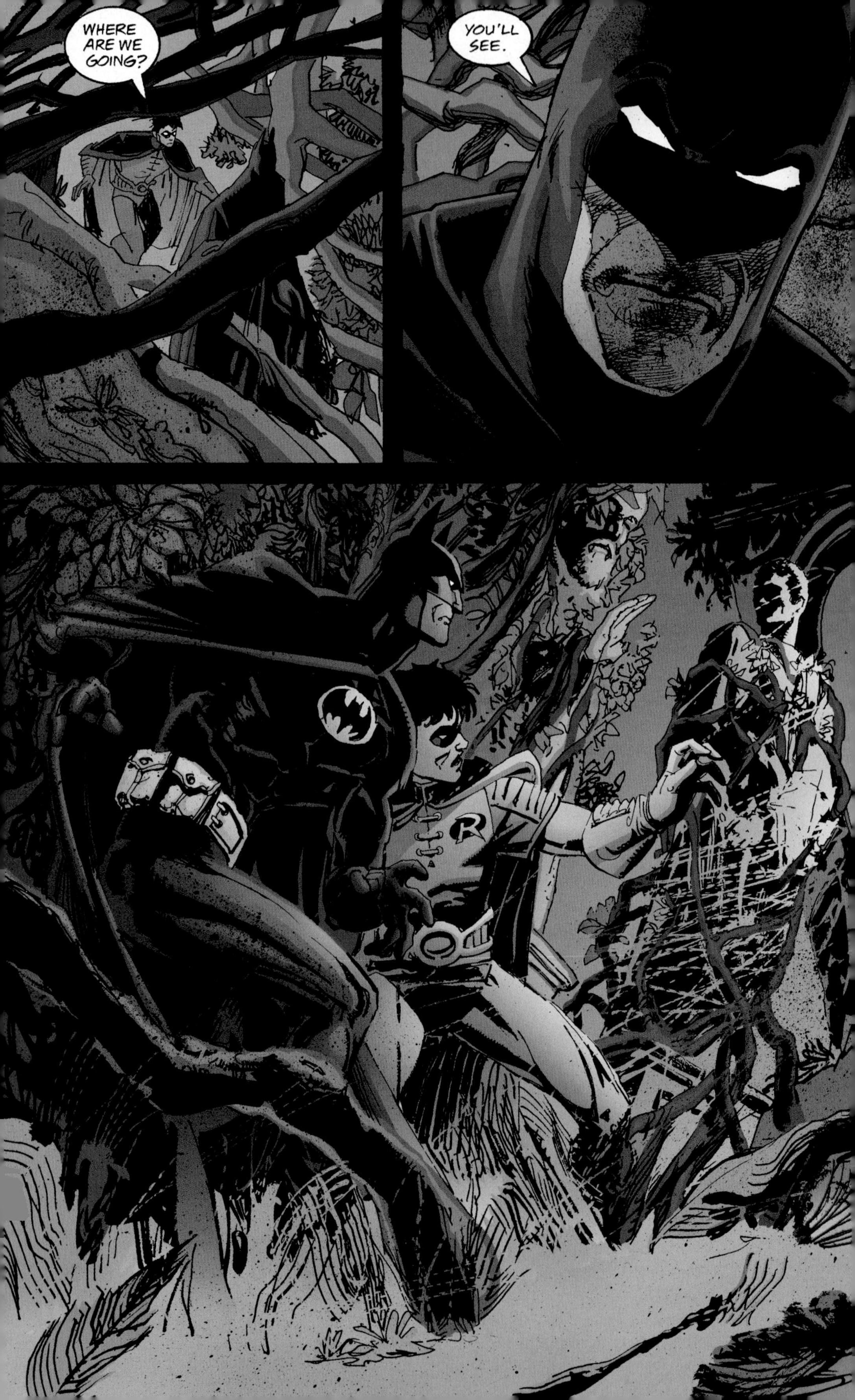
WHERE ARE WE GOING?
YOU'LL SEE.

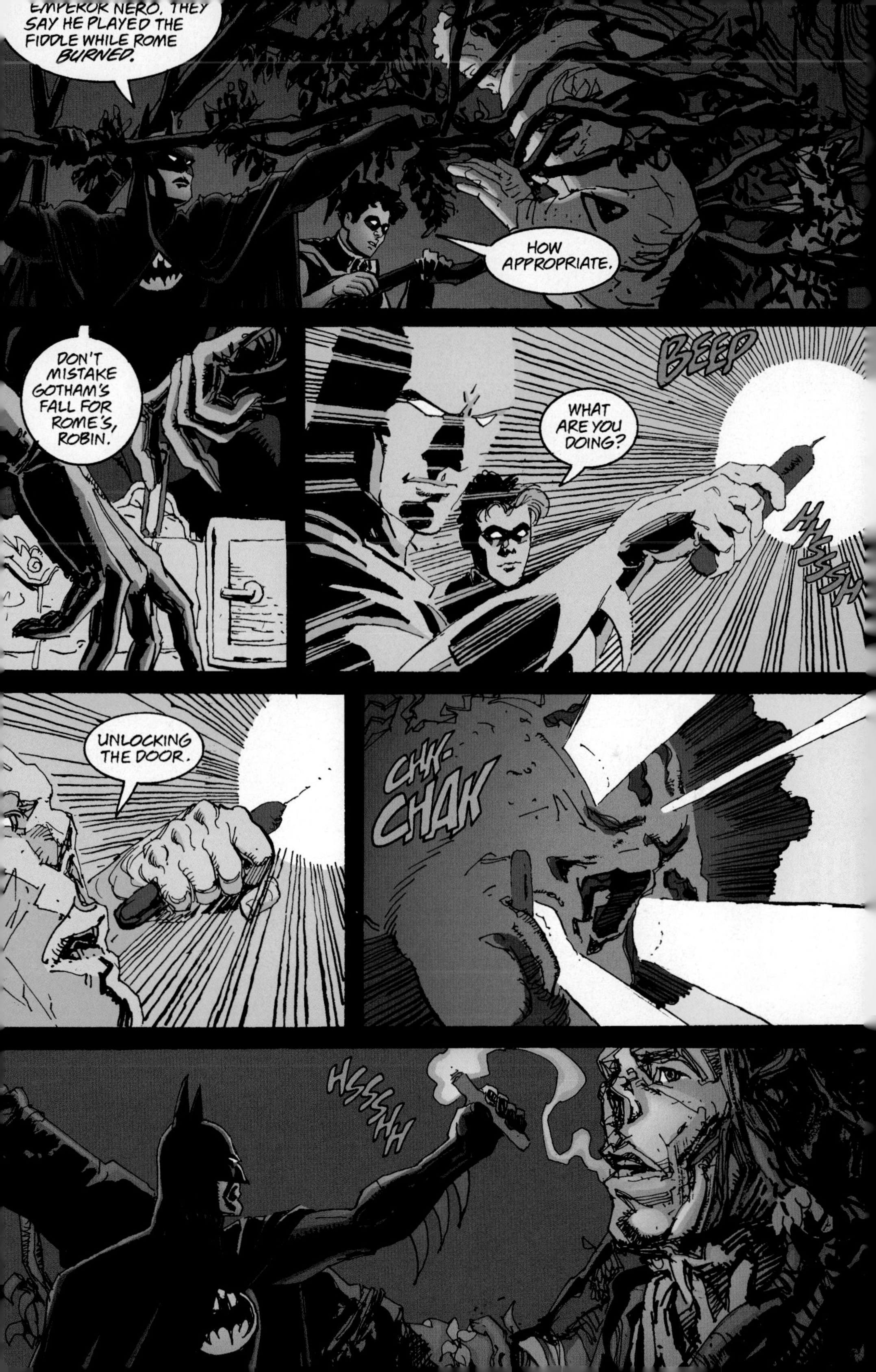
EMPEROR NERO, THEY SAY HE PLAYED THE FIDDLE WHILE ROME BURNED.
HOW APPROPRIATE.
DON'T MISTAKE GOTHAM'S FALL FOR ROME'S, ROBIN.
BEEP
WHAT ARE YOU DOING?
HHSSSH
UNLOCKING THE DOOR.
CHK-CHAK
HSSSHH

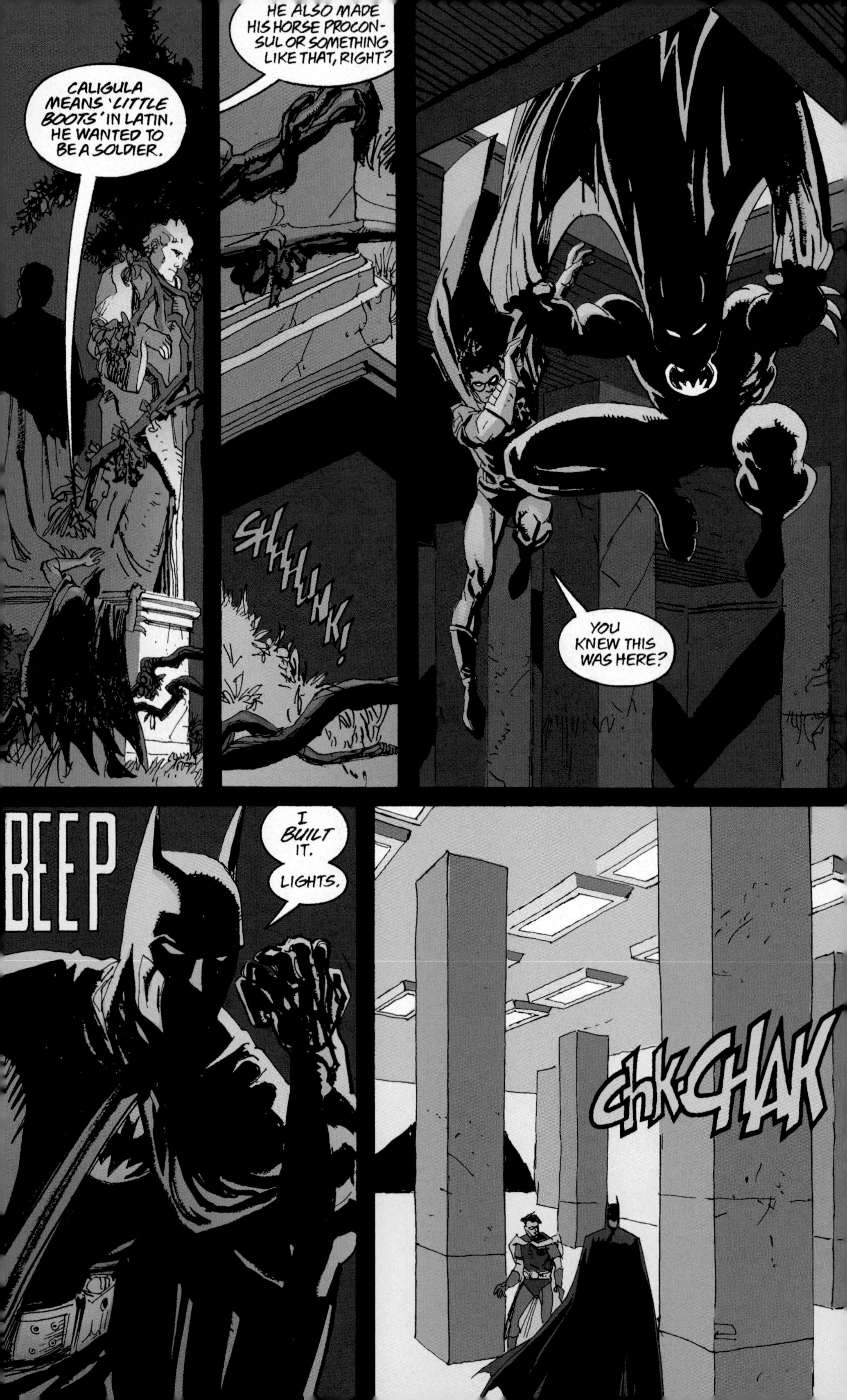
CALIGULA MEANS 'LITTLE BOOTS' IN LATIN. HE WANTED TO BE A SOLDIER.
HE ALSO MADE HIS HORSE PROCON-SUL OR SOMETHING LIKE THAT, RIGHT?
SHHHUNK!
YOU KNEW THIS WAS HERE?
BEEP
I BUILT IT.
LIGHTS.
ChK-CHAK

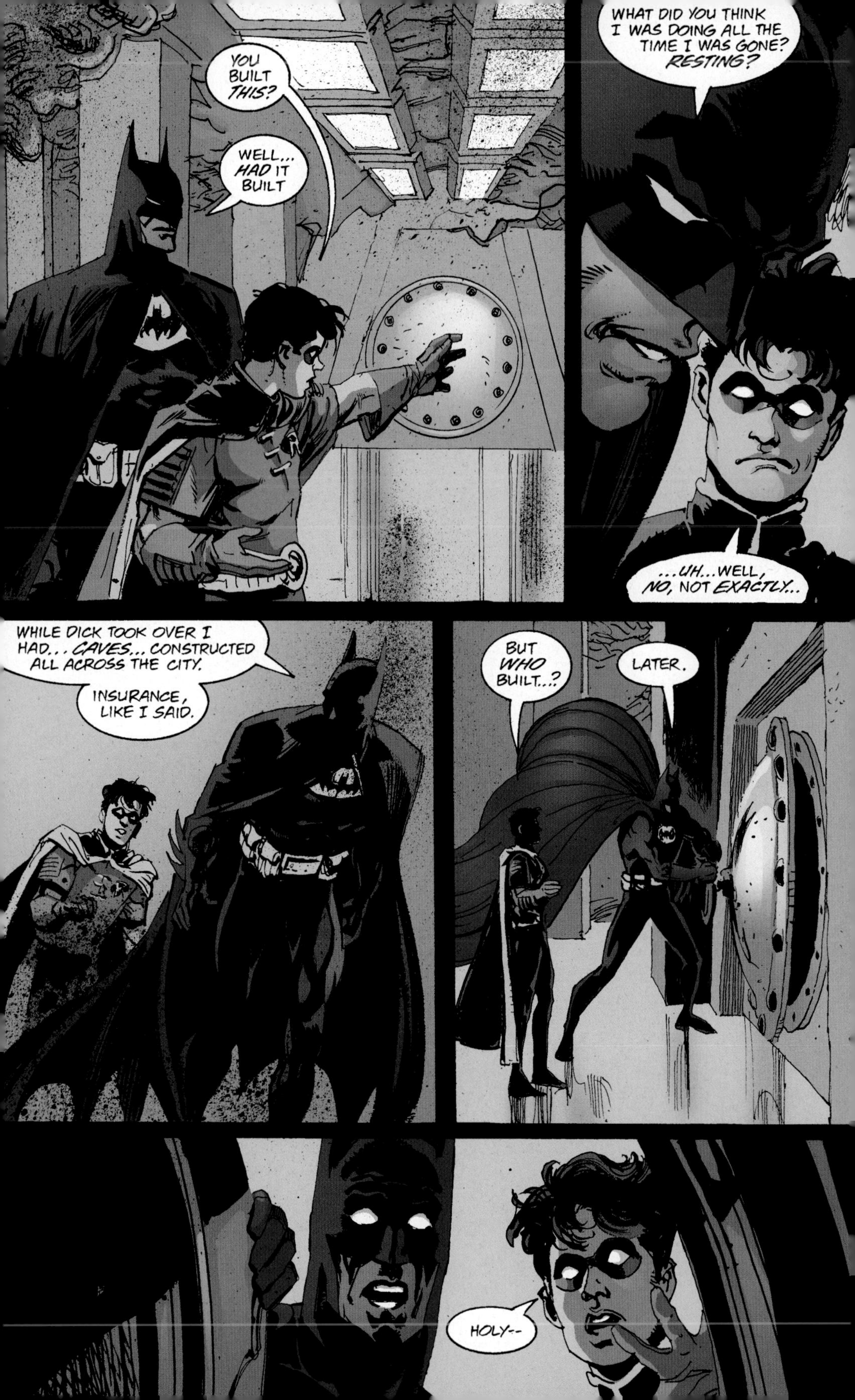
YOU BUILT THIS?
WELL... HAD IT BUILT
WHAT DID YOU THINK I WAS DOING ALL THE TIME I WAS GONE? RESTING?
...UH...WELL, NO, NOT EXACTLY...
WHILE DICK TOOK OVER I HAD... CAVES... CONSTRUCTED ALL ACROSS THE CITY.
INSURANCE, LIKE I SAID.
BUT WHO BUILT...?
LATER.
HOLY--

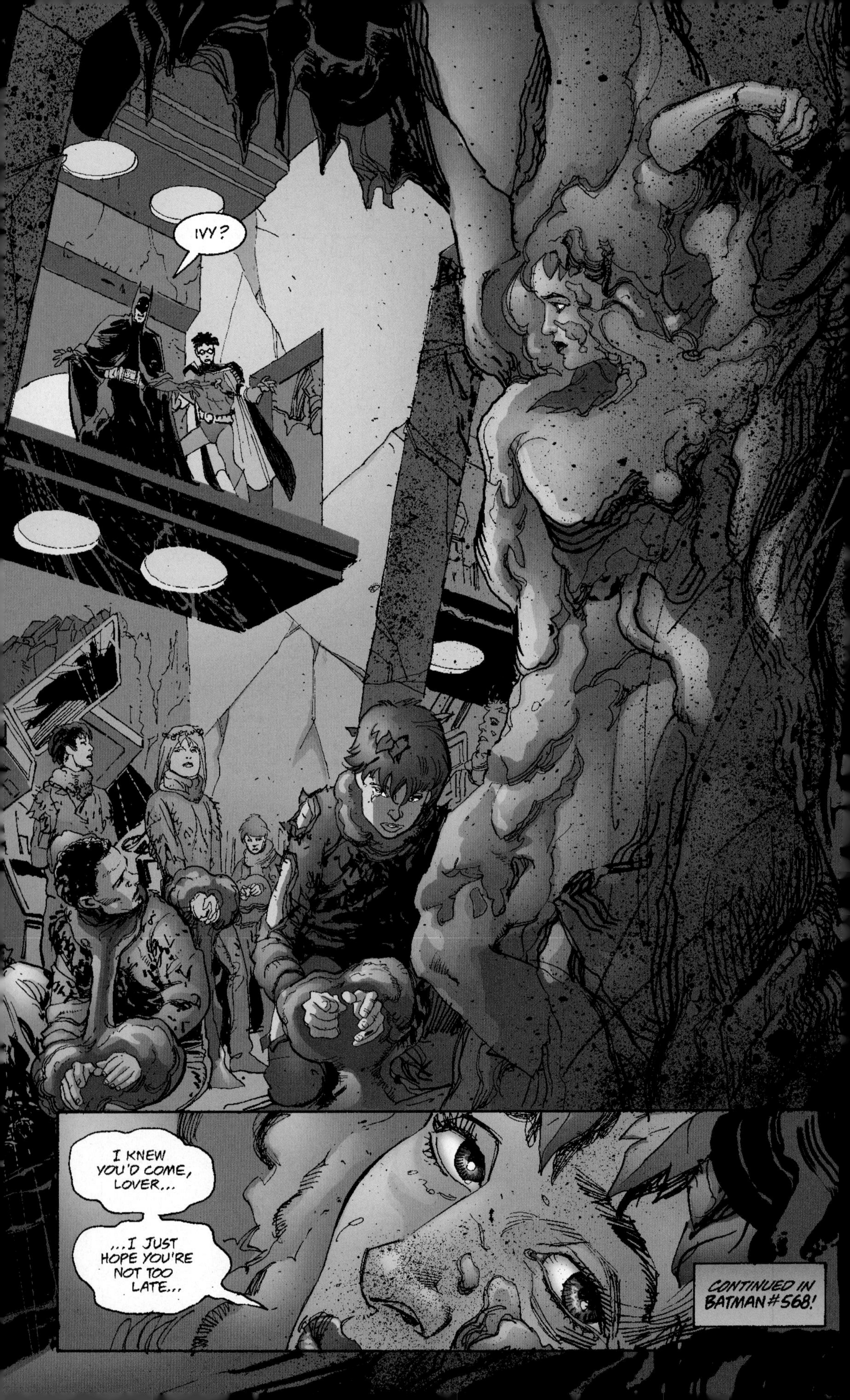
IVY?
I KNEW YOU'D COME, LOVER...
...I JUST HOPE YOU'RE NOT TOO LATE...
CONTINUED IN BATMAN #568!

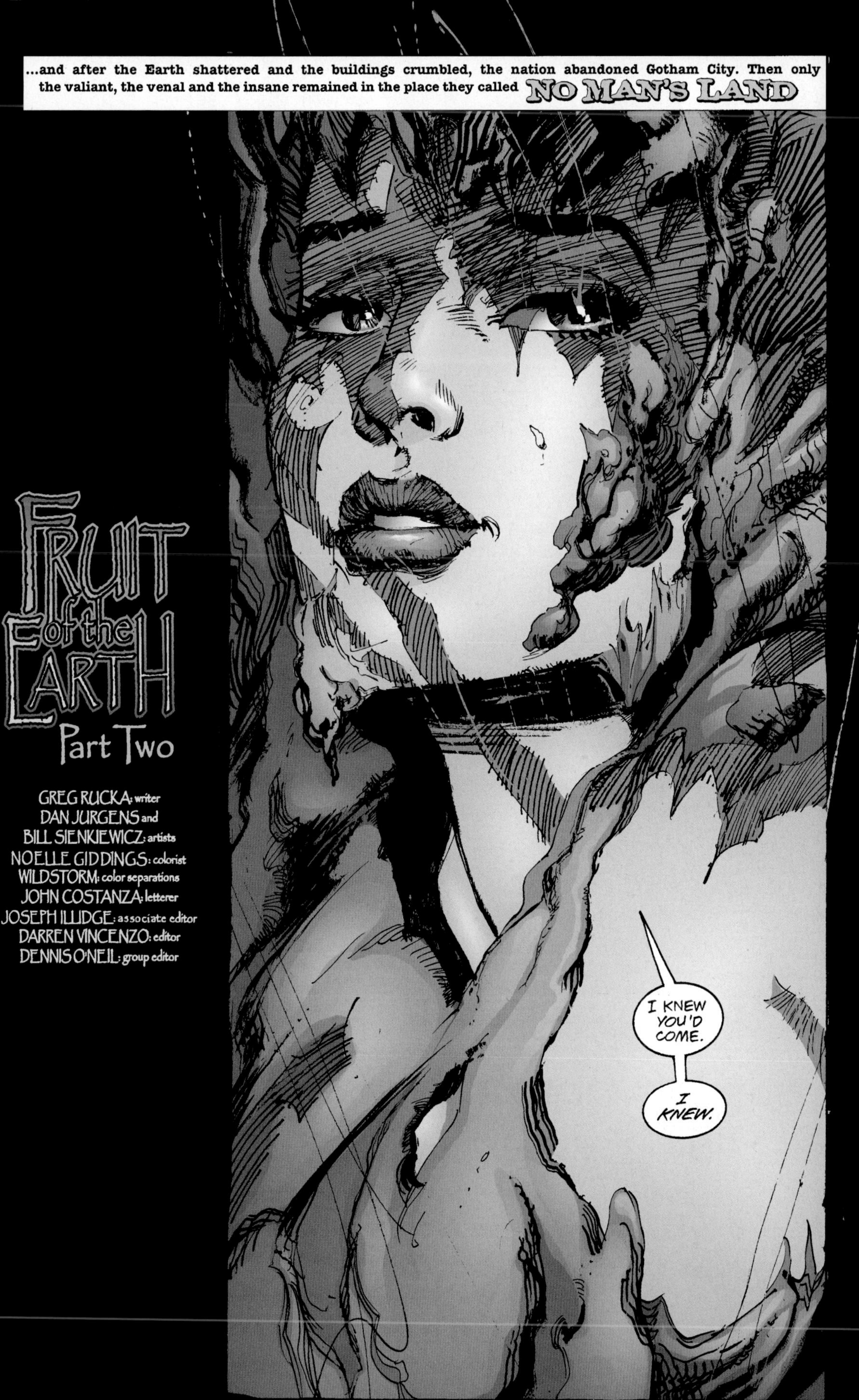
...and after the Earth shattered and the buildings crumbled, the nation abandoned Gotham City. Then only the valiant, the venal and the insane remained in the place they called NO MAN'S LAND
FRUIT of the EARTH
Part Two
GREG RUCKA: writer
DAN JURGENS and
BILL SIENKIEWICZ: artists
NOELLE GIDDINGS: colorist
WILDSTORM: color separations
JOHN COSTANZA: letterer
JOSEPH ILLIDGE: associate editor
DARREN VINCENZO: editor
DENNIS O'NEIL: group editor
I KNEW YOU'D COME.
I KNEW.

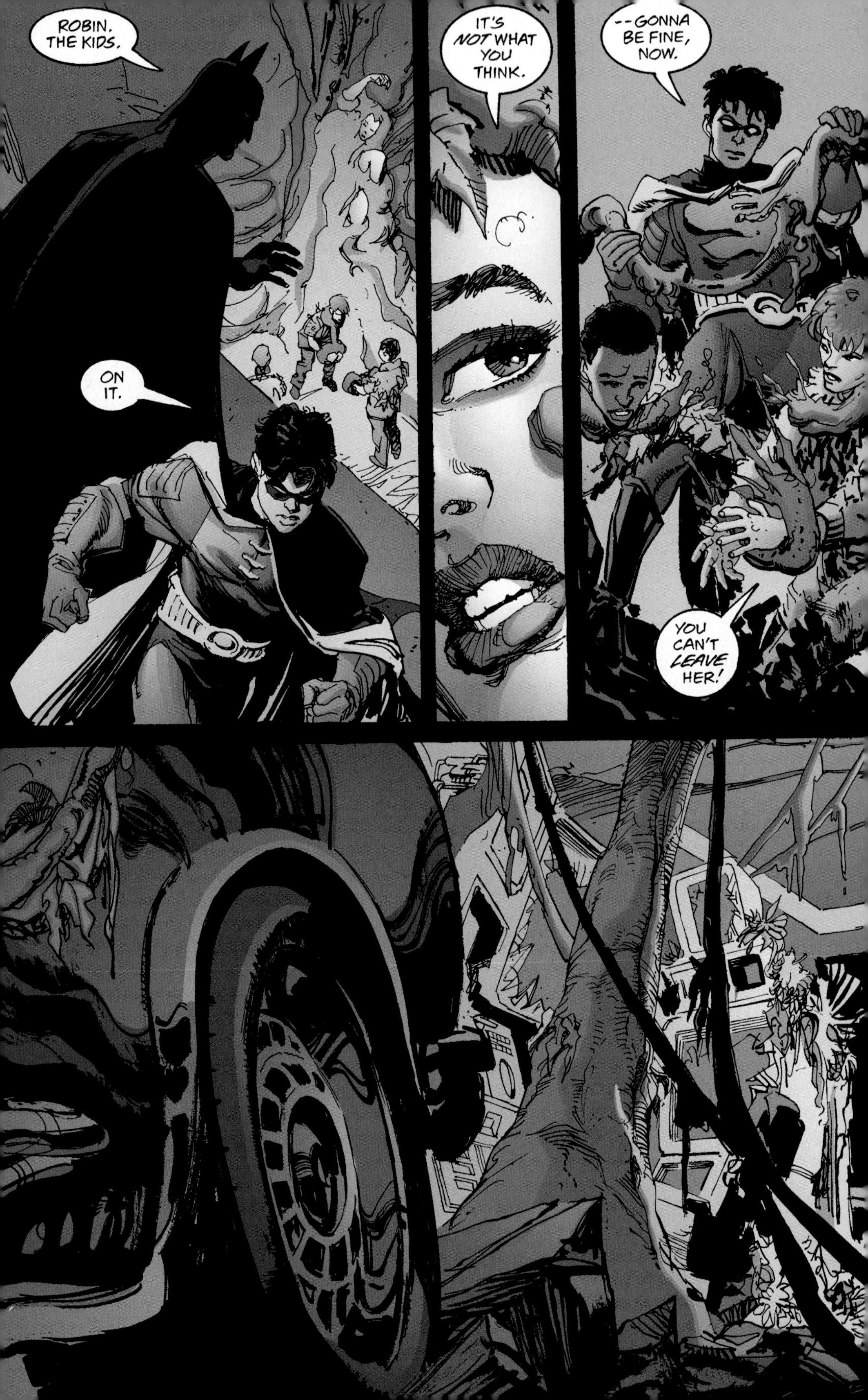
ROBIN. THE KIDS.
ON IT.
IT'S *NOT* WHAT YOU THINK.
--GONNA BE FINE, NOW.
YOU CAN'T *LEAVE* HER!

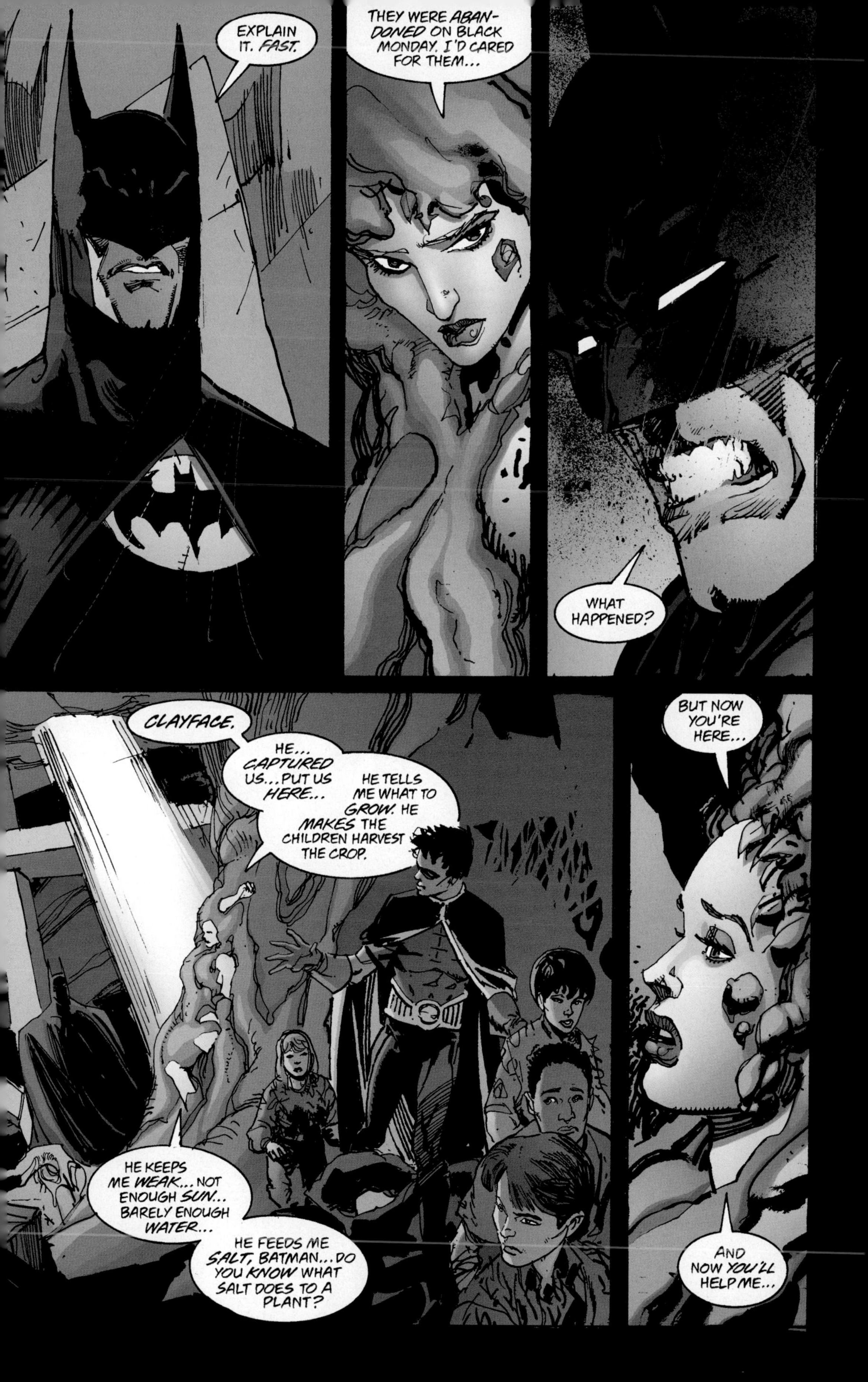
EXPLAIN IT. FAST.
THEY WERE ABAN-DONED ON BLACK MONDAY. I'D CARED FOR THEM...
WHAT HAPPENED?
CLAYFACE.
HE... CAPTURED US... PUT US HERE...
HE TELLS ME WHAT TO GROW. HE MAKES THE CHILDREN HARVEST THE CROP.
HE KEEPS ME WEAK... NOT ENOUGH SUN... BARELY ENOUGH WATER...
HE FEEDS ME SALT, BATMAN... DO YOU KNOW WHAT SALT DOES TO A PLANT?
BUT NOW YOU'RE HERE...
AND NOW YOU'LL HELP ME...

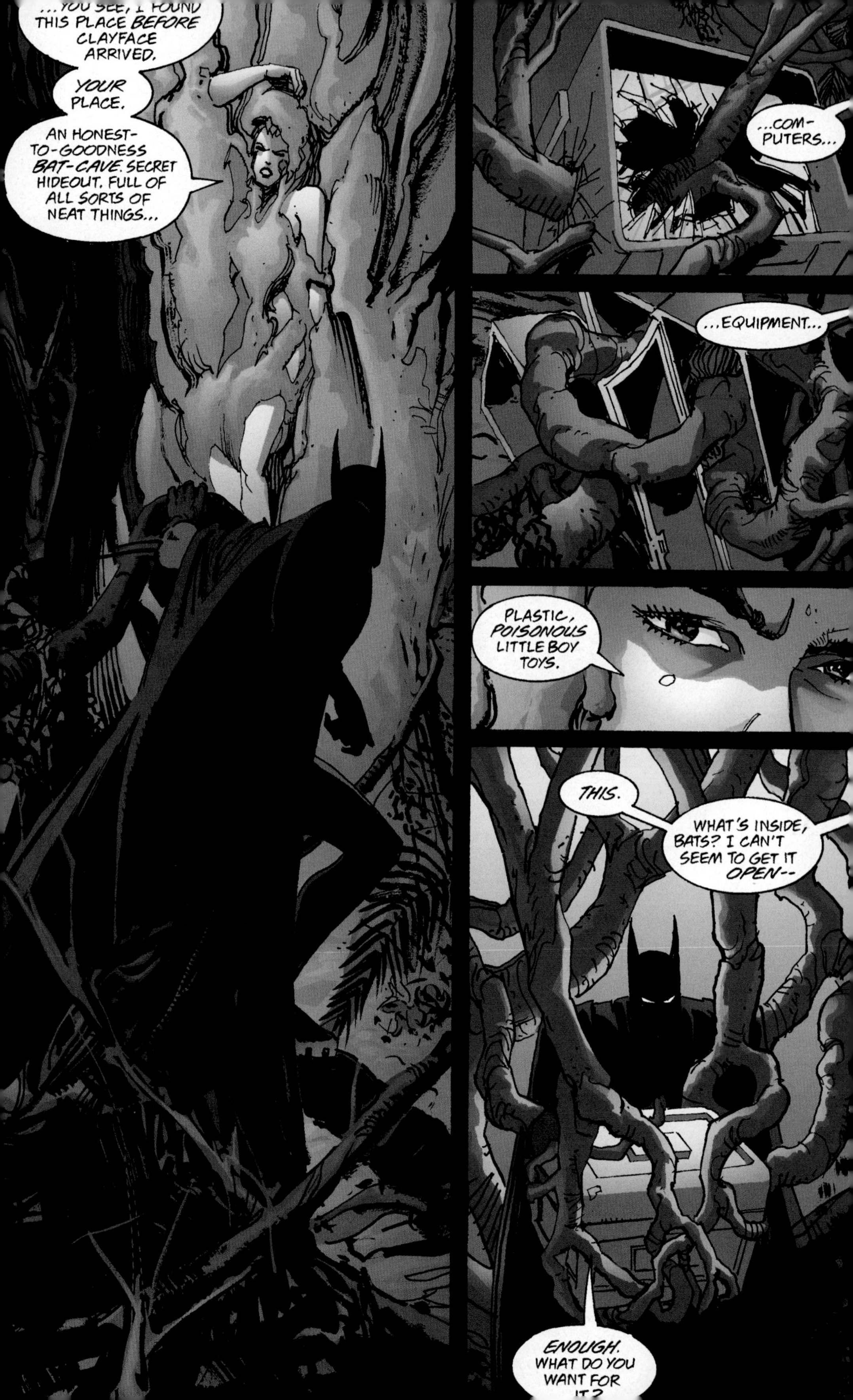
...YOU SEE, I FOUND THIS PLACE *BEFORE* CLAYFACE ARRIVED.
YOUR PLACE.
AN HONEST-TO-GOODNESS *BAT-CAVE*. SECRET HIDEOUT. FULL OF ALL SORTS OF NEAT THINGS...
...COM-PUTERS...
...EQUIPMENT...
PLASTIC, *POISONOUS* LITTLE BOY TOYS.
THIS.
WHAT'S INSIDE, BATS? I CAN'T SEEM TO GET IT *OPEN*--
ENOUGH. WHAT DO YOU WANT FOR

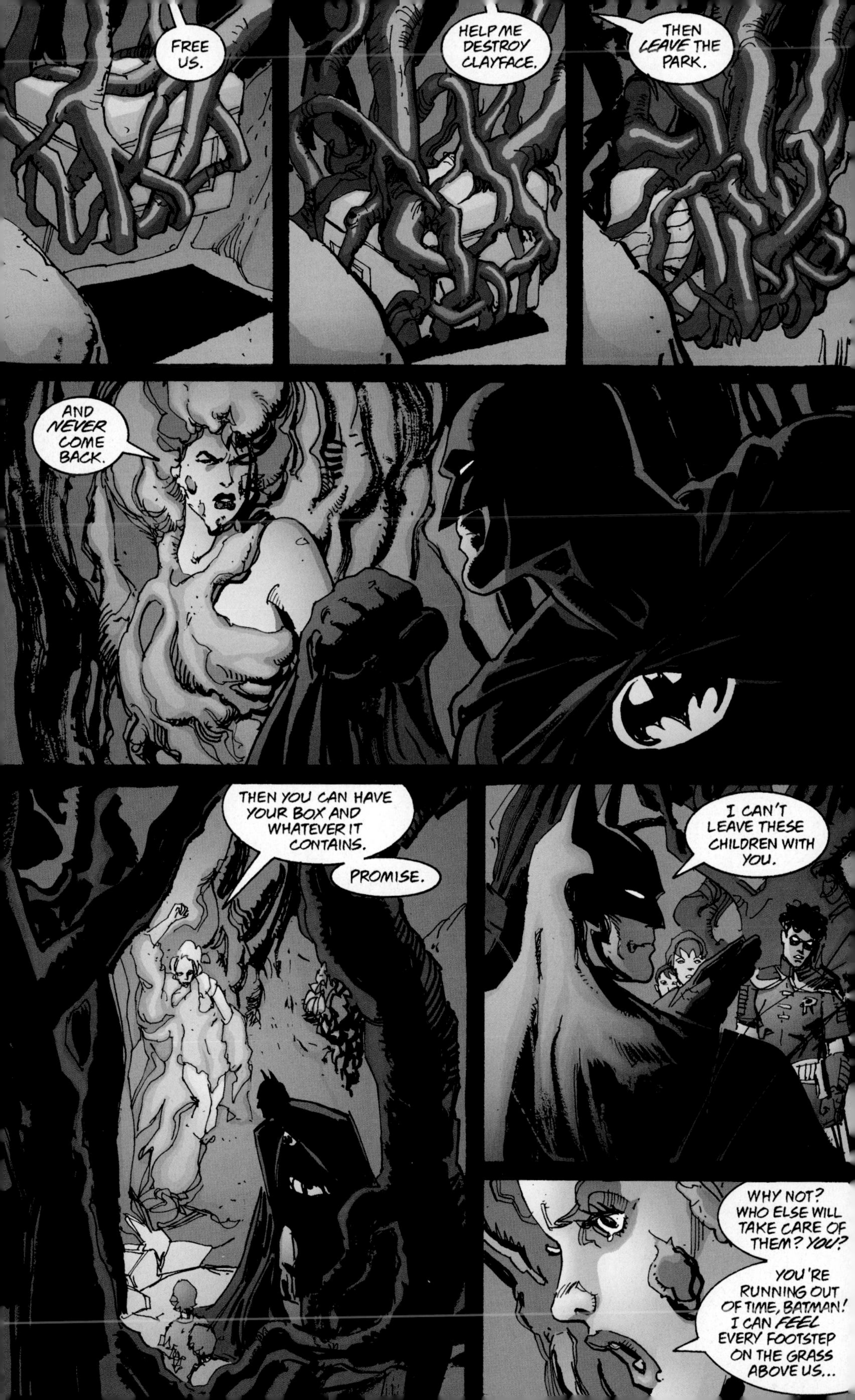
FREE US.
HELP ME DESTROY CLAYFACE.
THEN LEAVE THE PARK.
AND NEVER COME BACK.
THEN YOU CAN HAVE YOUR BOX AND WHATEVER IT CONTAINS.
PROMISE.
I CAN'T LEAVE THESE CHILDREN WITH YOU.
WHY NOT? WHO ELSE WILL TAKE CARE OF THEM? YOU?
YOU'RE RUNNING OUT OF TIME, BATMAN! I CAN FEEL EVERY FOOTSTEP ON THE GRASS ABOVE US...

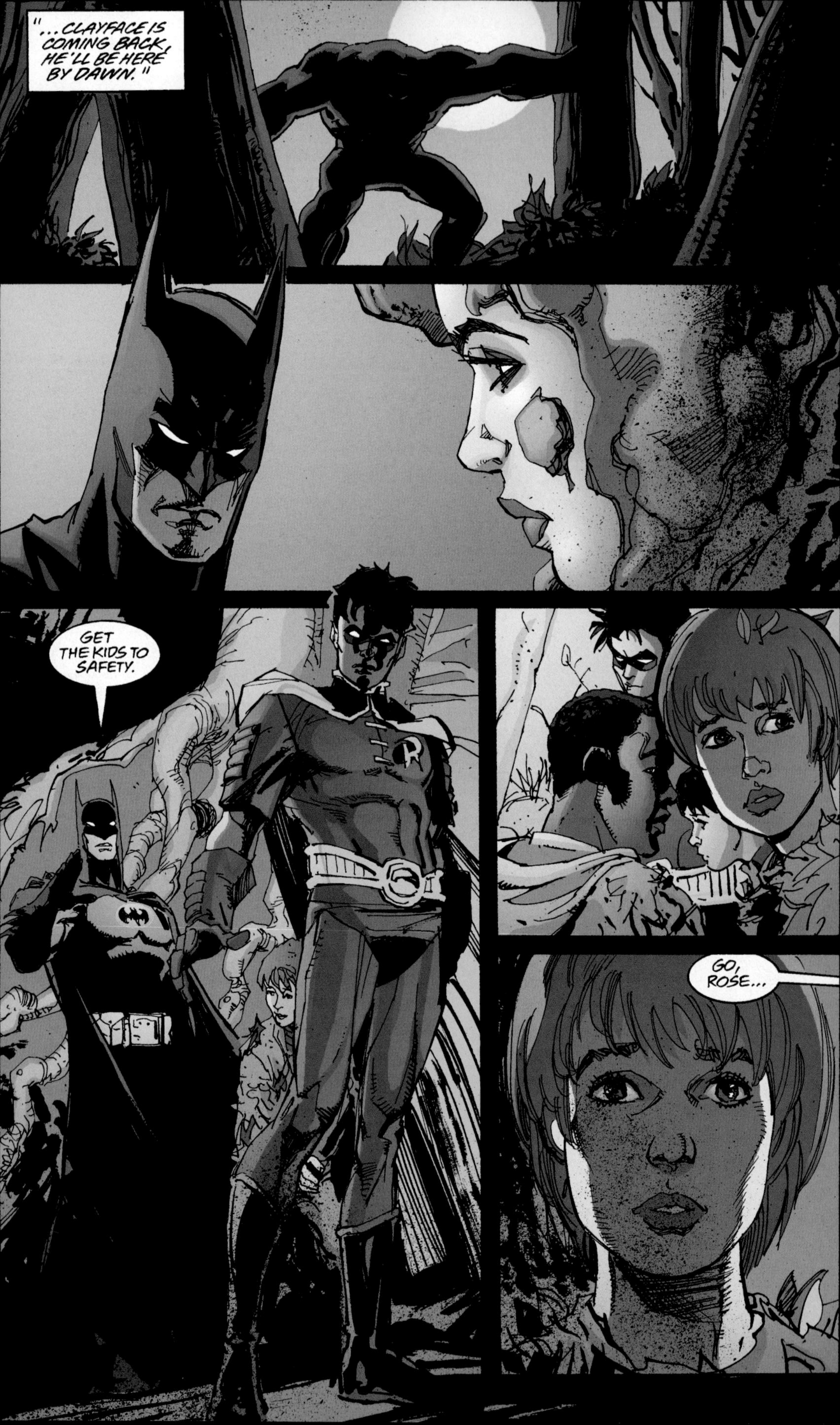
"...CLAYFACE IS COMING BACK, HE'LL BE HERE BY DAWN."
GET THE KIDS TO SAFETY.
GO, ROSE...

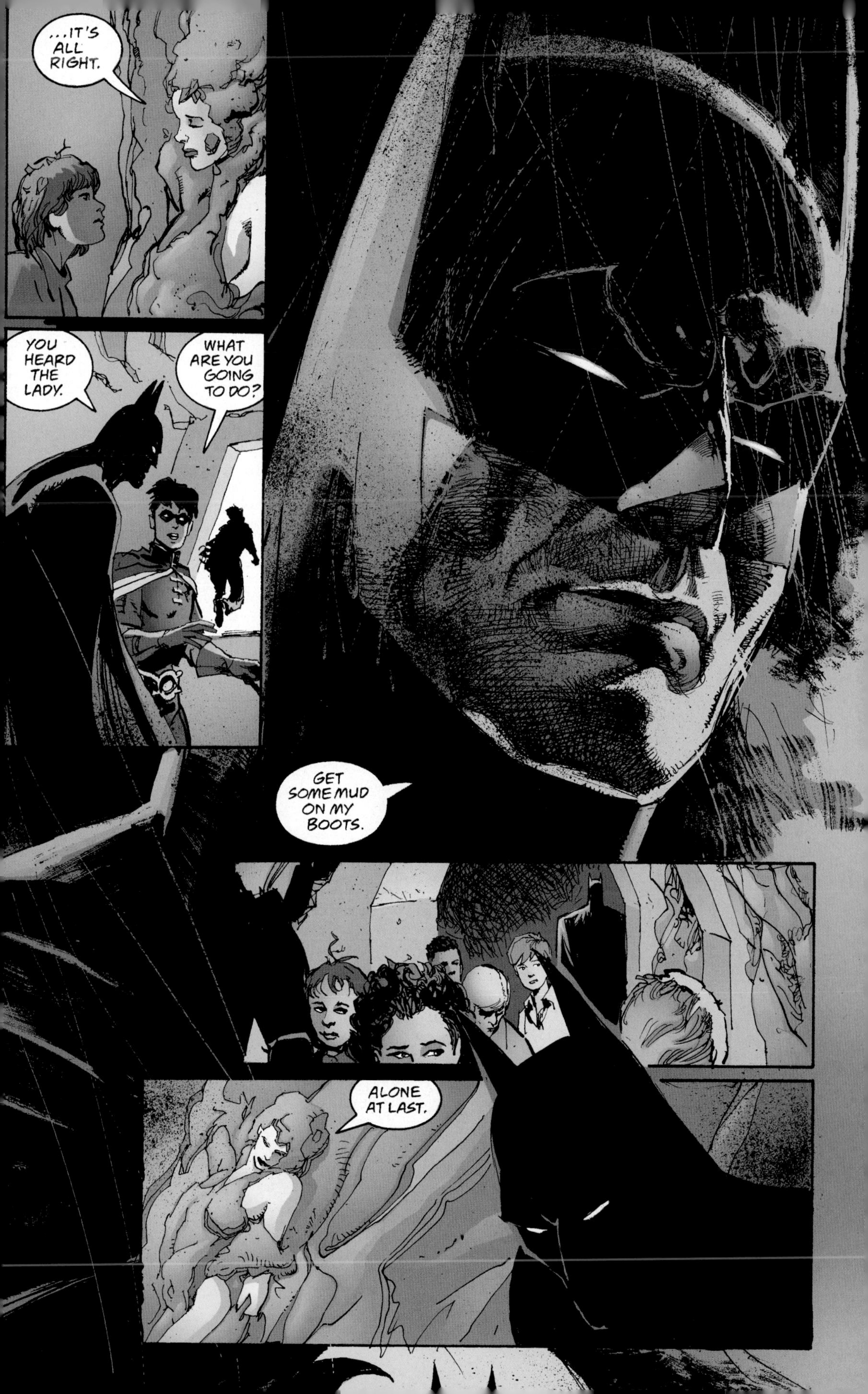
...IT'S ALL RIGHT.
YOU HEARD THE LADY.
WHAT ARE YOU GOING TO DO?
GET SOME MUD ON MY BOOTS.
ALONE AT LAST.

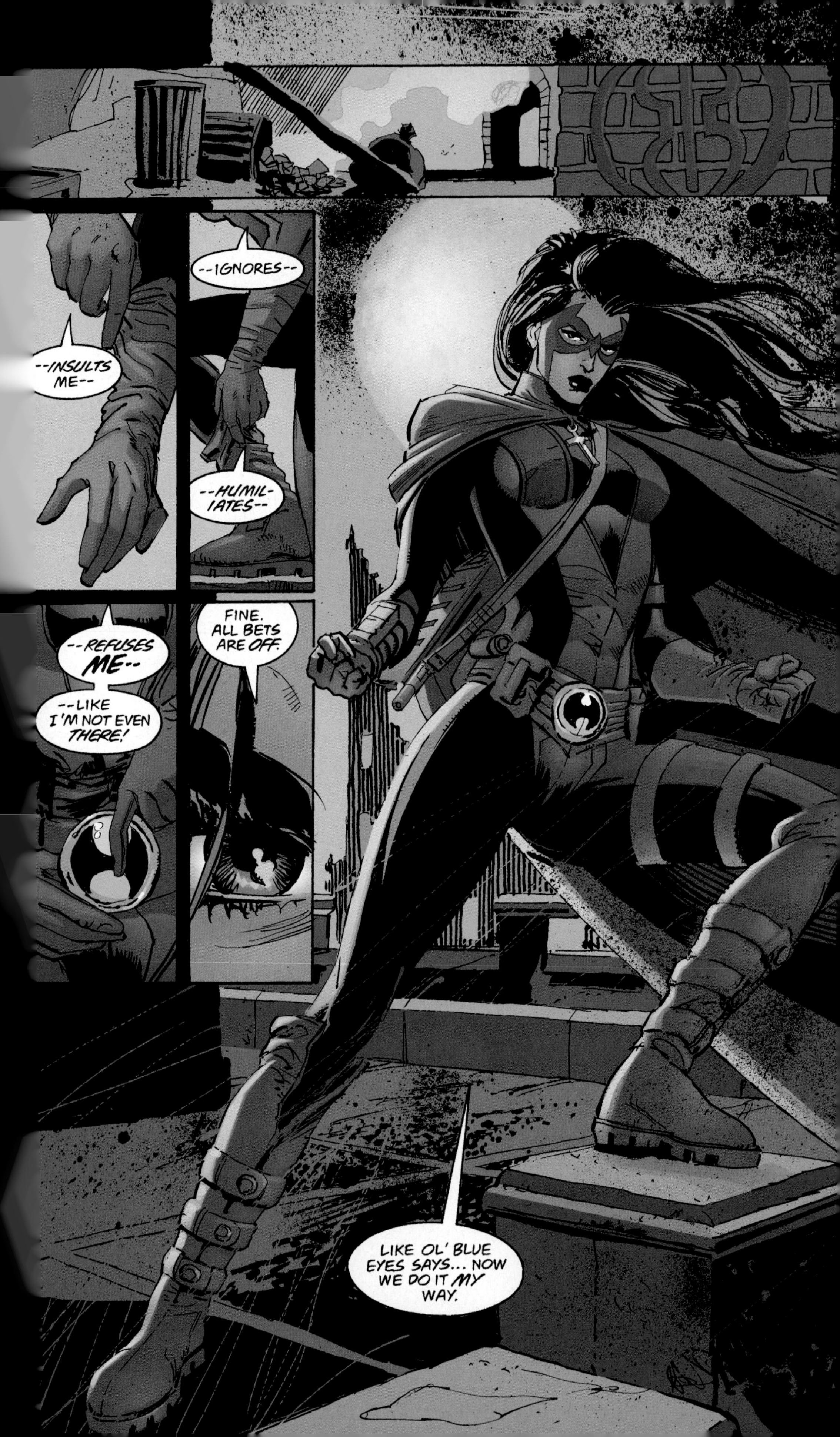

--INSULTS ME--
--IGNORES--
--HUMIL-IATES--
--REFUSES ME--
--LIKE I'M NOT EVEN THERE!
FINE. ALL BETS ARE OFF.
LIKE OL' BLUE EYES SAYS... NOW WE DO IT MY WAY.

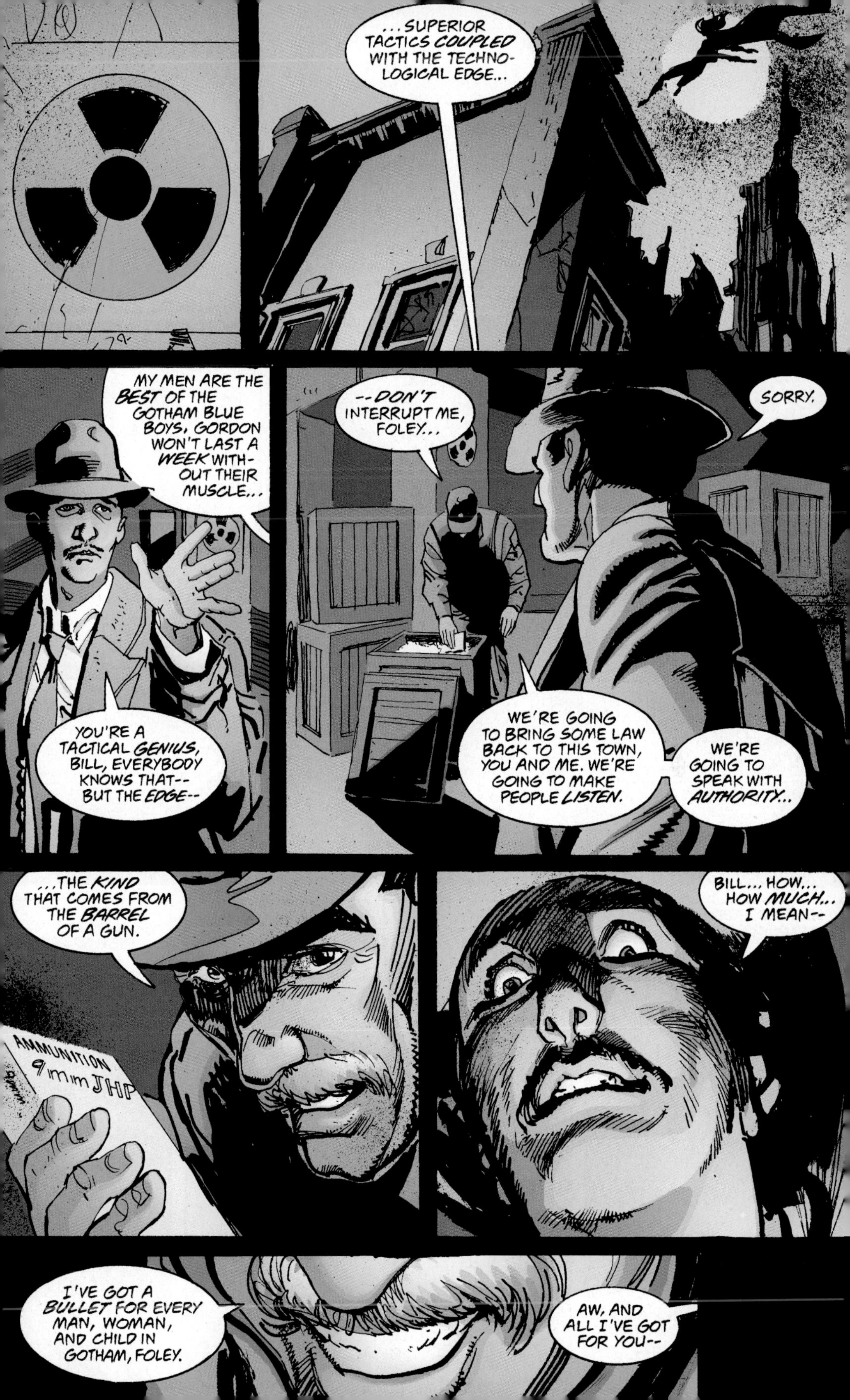
...SUPERIOR TACTICS COUPLED WITH THE TECHNOLOGICAL EDGE...
MY MEN ARE THE BEST OF THE GOTHAM BLUE BOYS, GORDON WON'T LAST A WEEK WITHOUT THEIR MUSCLE...
YOU'RE A TACTICAL GENIUS, BILL, EVERYBODY KNOWS THAT--BUT THE EDGE--
--DON'T INTERRUPT ME, FOLEY...
SORRY.
WE'RE GOING TO BRING SOME LAW BACK TO THIS TOWN, YOU AND ME. WE'RE GOING TO MAKE PEOPLE LISTEN.
WE'RE GOING TO SPEAK WITH AUTHORITY...
...THE KIND THAT COMES FROM THE BARREL OF A GUN.
AMMUNITION 9mm JHP
BILL... HOW... HOW MUCH... I MEAN--
I'VE GOT A BULLET FOR EVERY MAN, WOMAN, AND CHILD IN GOTHAM, FOLEY.
AW, AND ALL I'VE GOT FOR YOU--

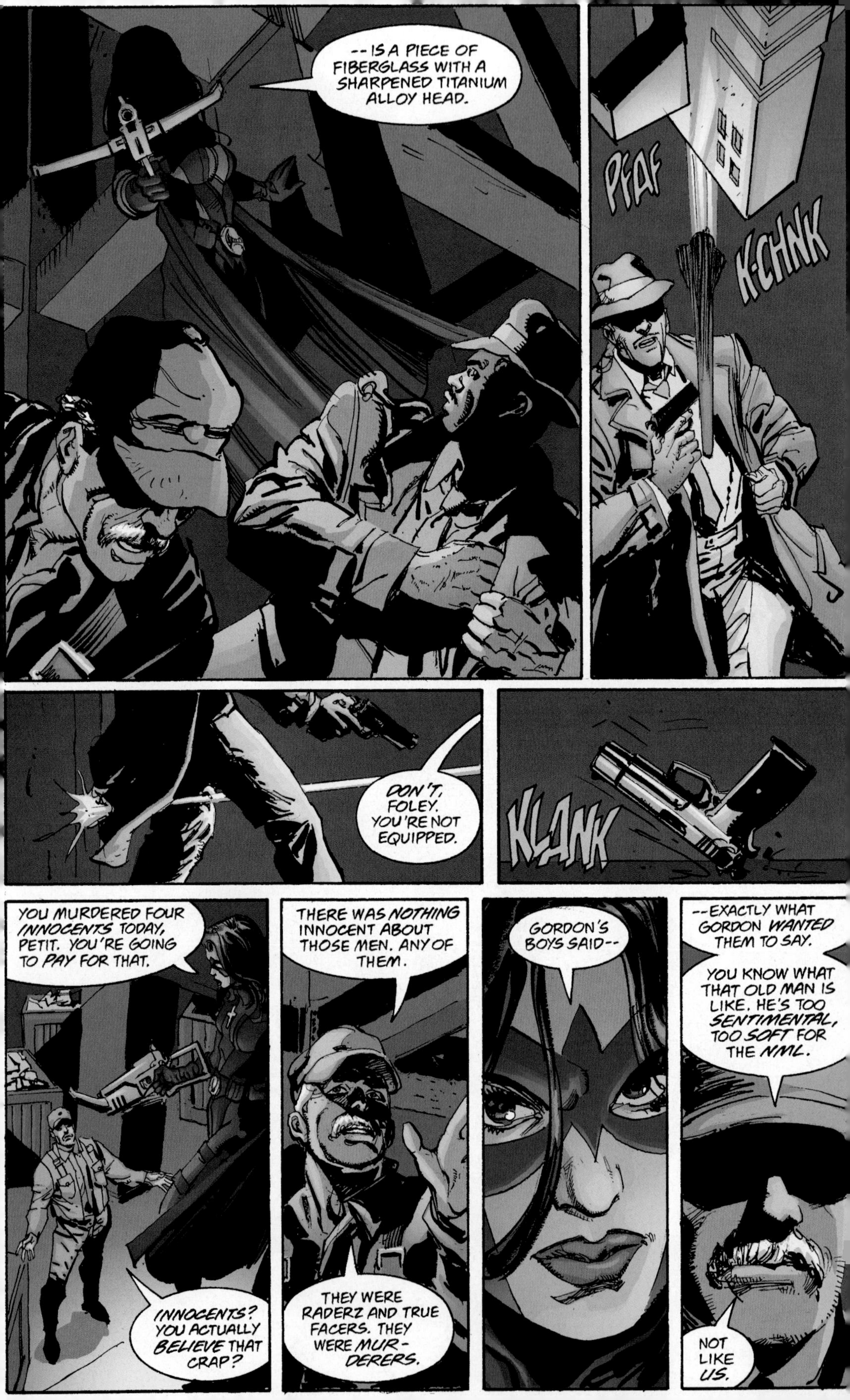
--IS A PIECE OF FIBERGLASS WITH A SHARPENED TITANIUM ALLOY HEAD.
PFAF
K-CHNK
DON'T, FOLEY. YOU'RE NOT EQUIPPED.
KLANK
YOU MURDERED FOUR INNOCENTS TODAY, PETIT. YOU'RE GOING TO PAY FOR THAT.
INNOCENTS? YOU ACTUALLY BELIEVE THAT CRAP?
THERE WAS NOTHING INNOCENT ABOUT THOSE MEN. ANY OF THEM.
THEY WERE RADERZ AND TRUE FACERS. THEY WERE MUR-DERERS.
GORDON'S BOYS SAID--
--EXACTLY WHAT GORDON WANTED THEM TO SAY.
YOU KNOW WHAT THAT OLD MAN IS LIKE. HE'S TOO SENTIMENTAL, TOO SOFT FOR THE NML.
NOT LIKE US.

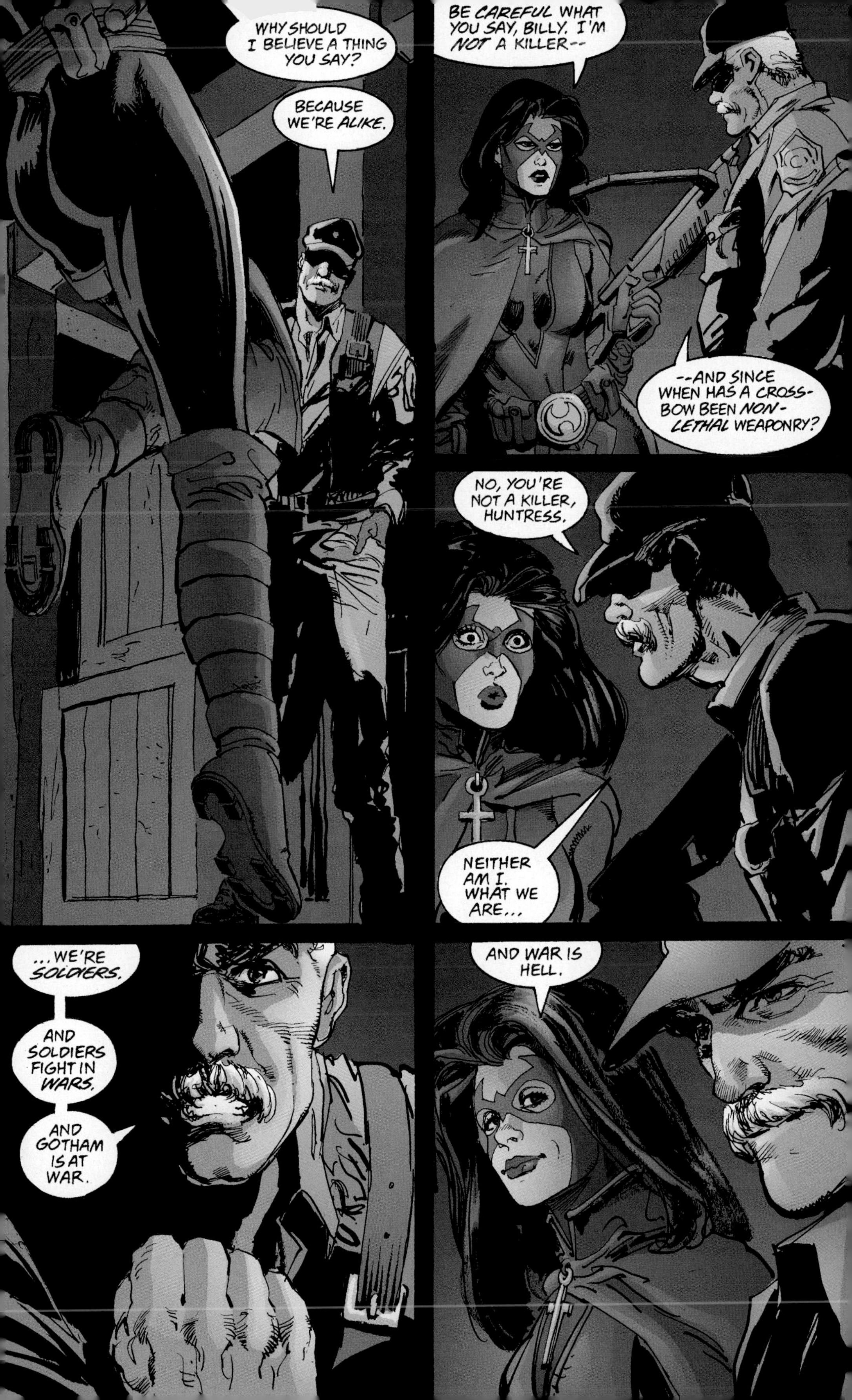
WHY SHOULD I BELIEVE A THING YOU SAY?
BECAUSE WE'RE ALIKE.
BE CAREFUL WHAT YOU SAY, BILLY. I'M NOT A KILLER--
--AND SINCE WHEN HAS A CROSS-BOW BEEN NON-LETHAL WEAPONRY?
NO, YOU'RE NOT A KILLER, HUNTRESS.
NEITHER AM I. WHAT WE ARE...
...WE'RE SOLDIERS.
AND SOLDIERS FIGHT IN WARS.
AND GOTHAM IS AT WAR.
AND WAR IS HELL.

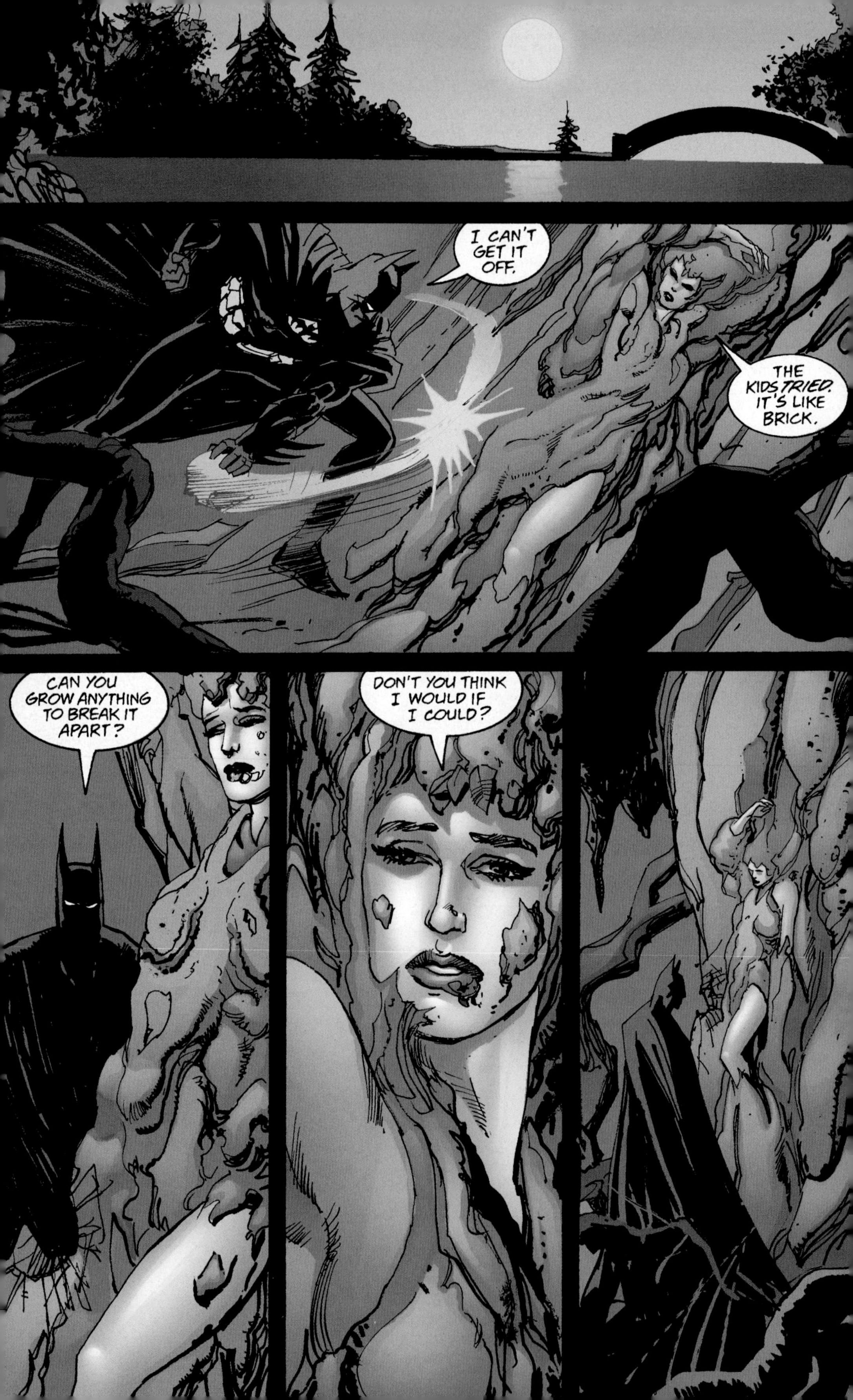

I CAN'T GET IT OFF.
THE KIDS TRIED. IT'S LIKE BRICK.
CAN YOU GROW ANYTHING TO BREAK IT APART?
DON'T YOU THINK I WOULD IF I COULD?

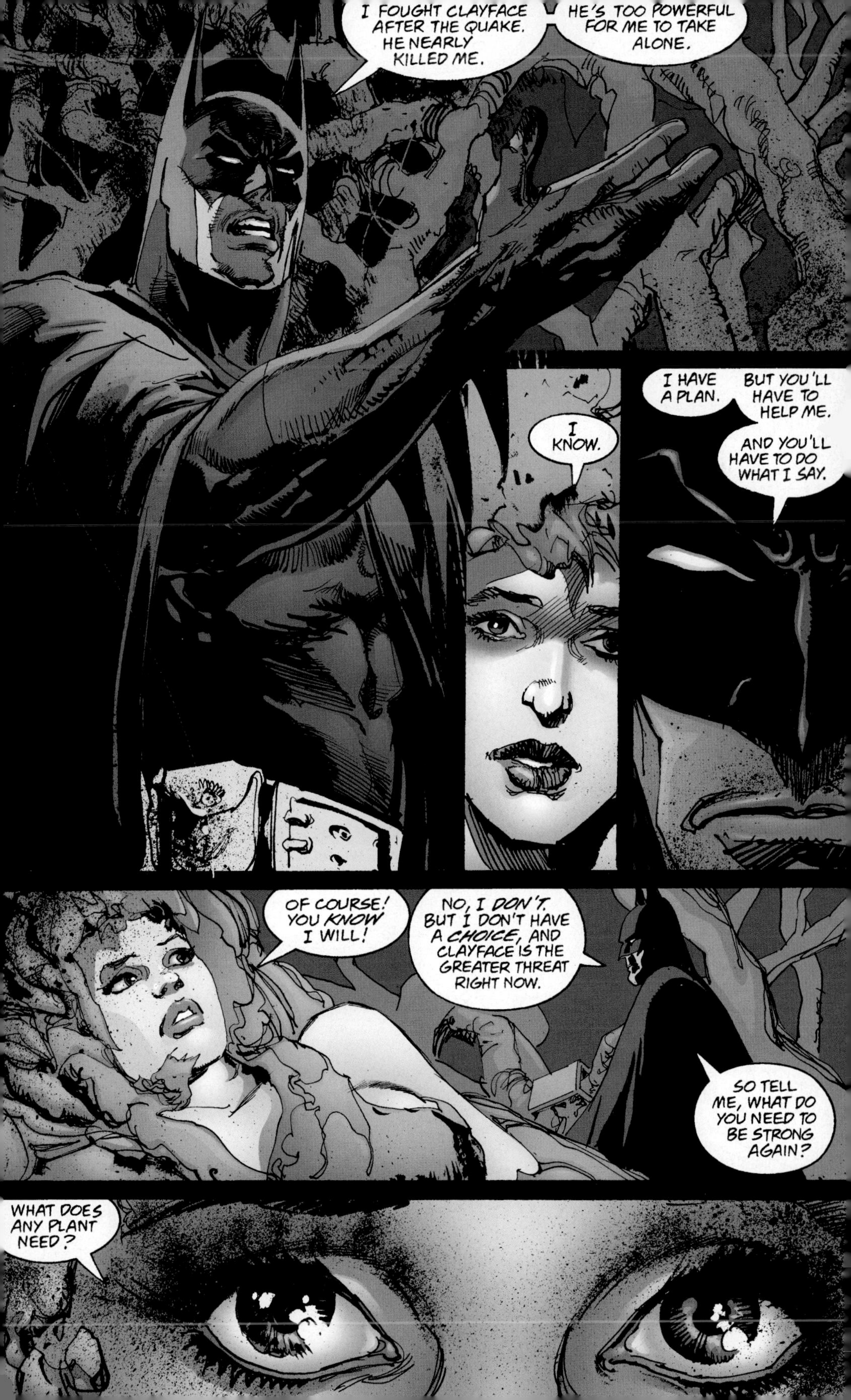
I FOUGHT CLAYFACE AFTER THE QUAKE. HE NEARLY KILLED ME.
HE'S TOO POWERFUL FOR ME TO TAKE ALONE.
I KNOW.
I HAVE A PLAN.
BUT YOU'LL HAVE TO HELP ME.
AND YOU'LL HAVE TO DO WHAT I SAY.
OF COURSE! YOU *KNOW* I WILL!
NO, I *DON'T*. BUT I DON'T HAVE A *CHOICE*, AND CLAYFACE IS THE GREATER THREAT RIGHT NOW.
SO TELL ME, WHAT DO YOU NEED TO BE STRONG AGAIN?
WHAT DOES ANY PLANT NEED?

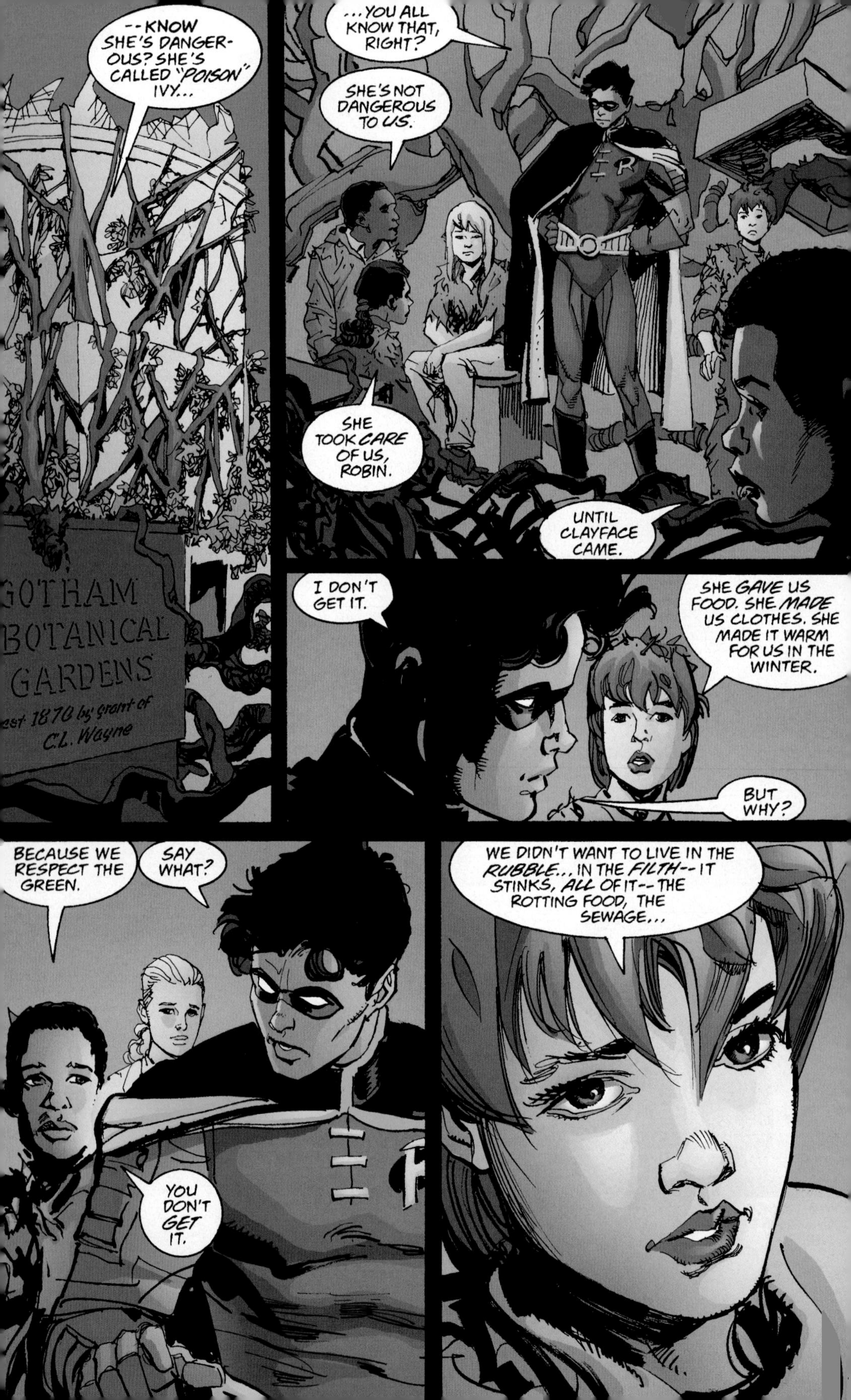
--KNOW SHE'S DANGEROUS? SHE'S CALLED "POISON" IVY...
GOTHAM BOTANICAL GARDENS est. 1870 by grant of C.L. Wayne
...YOU ALL KNOW THAT, RIGHT?
SHE'S NOT DANGEROUS TO US.
SHE TOOK CARE OF US, ROBIN.
UNTIL CLAYFACE CAME.
I DON'T GET IT.
SHE GAVE US FOOD. SHE MADE US CLOTHES. SHE MADE IT WARM FOR US IN THE WINTER.
BUT WHY?
BECAUSE WE RESPECT THE GREEN.
SAY WHAT?
YOU DON'T GET IT.
WE DIDN'T WANT TO LIVE IN THE RUBBLE... IN THE FILTH--IT STINKS, ALL OF IT--THE ROTTING FOOD, THE SEWAGE...

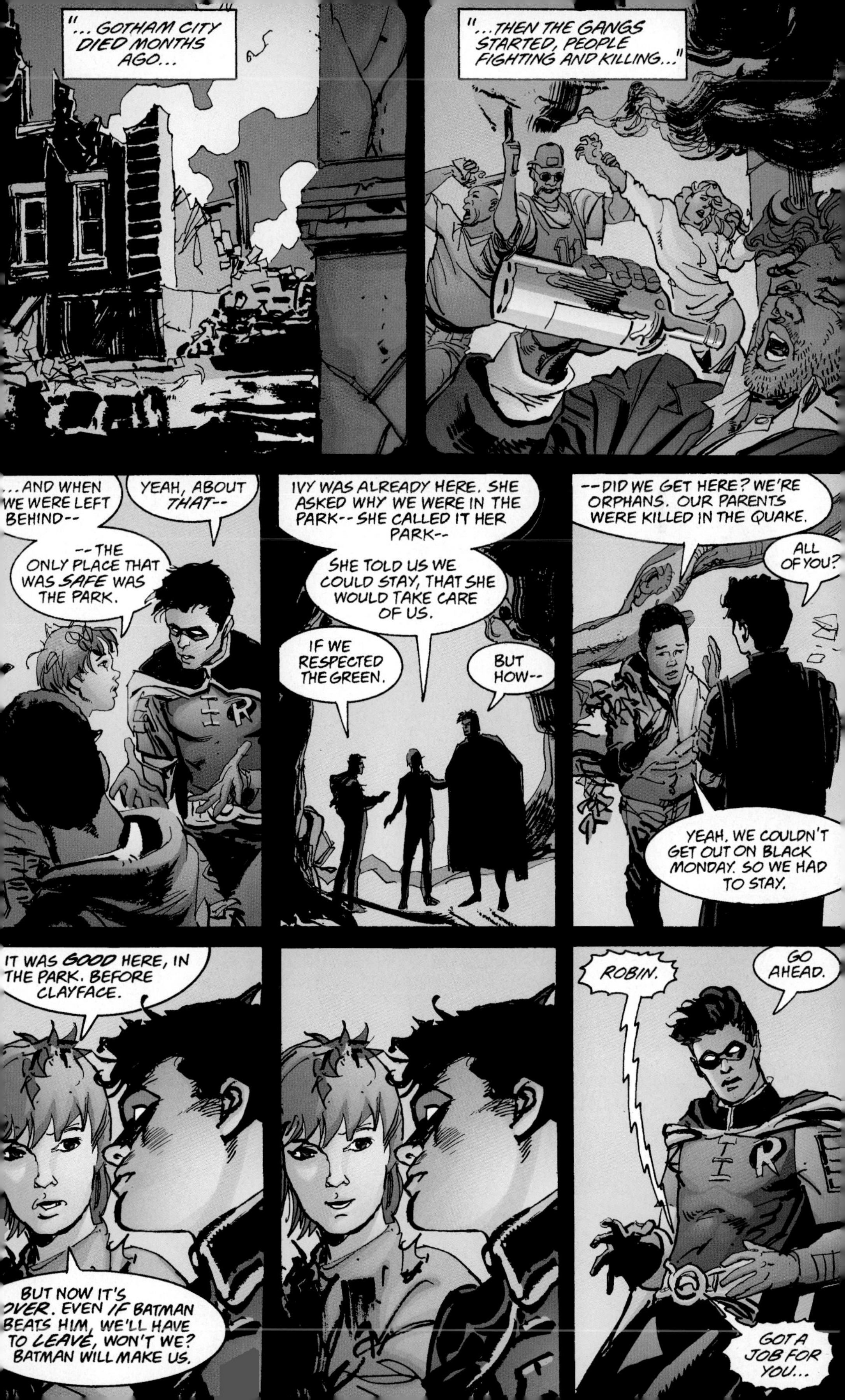
"...GOTHAM CITY DIED MONTHS AGO...
"...THEN THE GANGS STARTED, PEOPLE FIGHTING AND KILLING..."
...AND WHEN WE WERE LEFT BEHIND--
YEAH, ABOUT THAT--
--THE ONLY PLACE THAT WAS SAFE WAS THE PARK.
IVY WAS ALREADY HERE. SHE ASKED WHY WE WERE IN THE PARK--SHE CALLED IT HER PARK--
SHE TOLD US WE COULD STAY, THAT SHE WOULD TAKE CARE OF US.
IF WE RESPECTED THE GREEN.
BUT HOW--
--DID WE GET HERE? WE'RE ORPHANS. OUR PARENTS WERE KILLED IN THE QUAKE.
ALL OF YOU?
YEAH, WE COULDN'T GET OUT ON BLACK MONDAY. SO WE HAD TO STAY.
IT WAS GOOD HERE, IN THE PARK. BEFORE CLAYFACE.
BUT NOW IT'S OVER. EVEN IF BATMAN BEATS HIM, WE'LL HAVE TO LEAVE, WON'T WE? BATMAN WILL MAKE US.
ROBIN.
GO AHEAD.
GOT A JOB FOR YOU...

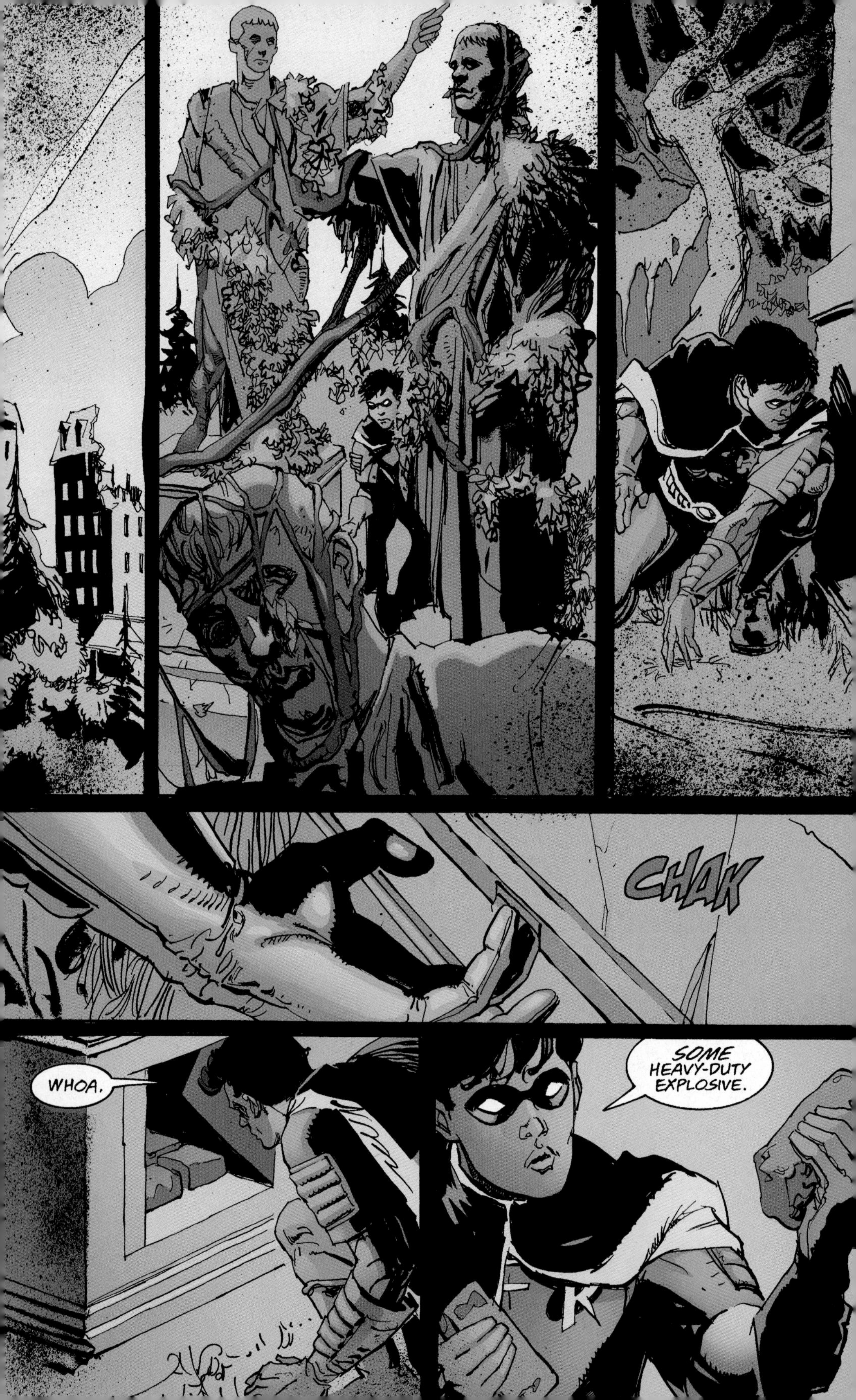
CHAK
WHOA.
SOME HEAVY-DUTY EXPLOSIVE.

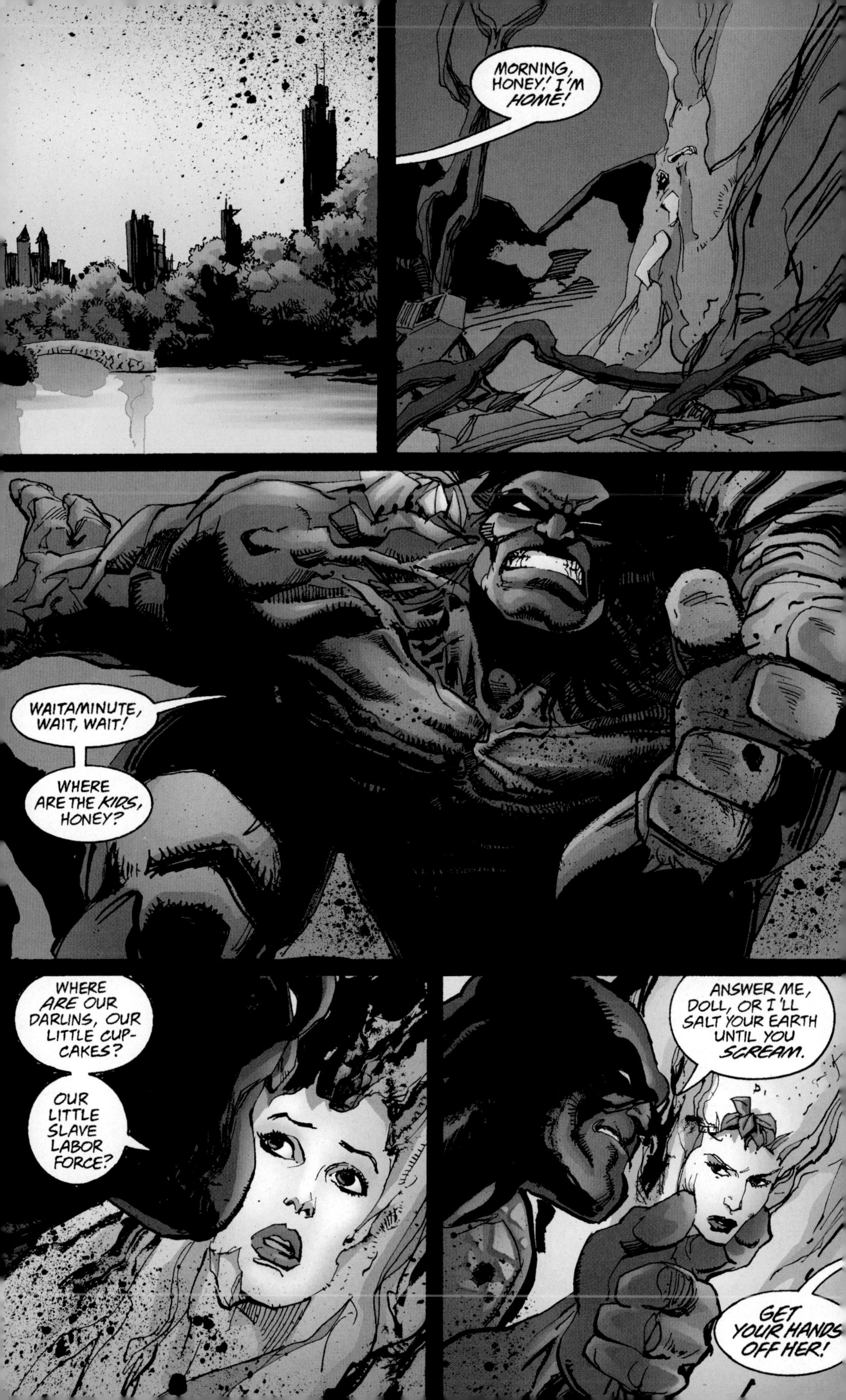
MORNING, HONEY! I'M HOME!
WAITAMINUTE, WAIT, WAIT!
WHERE ARE THE KIDS, HONEY?
WHERE ARE OUR DARLINS, OUR LITTLE CUP-CAKES?
OUR LITTLE SLAVE LABOR FORCE?
ANSWER ME, DOLL, OR I'LL SALT YOUR EARTH UNTIL YOU SCREAM.
GET YOUR HANDS OFF HER!

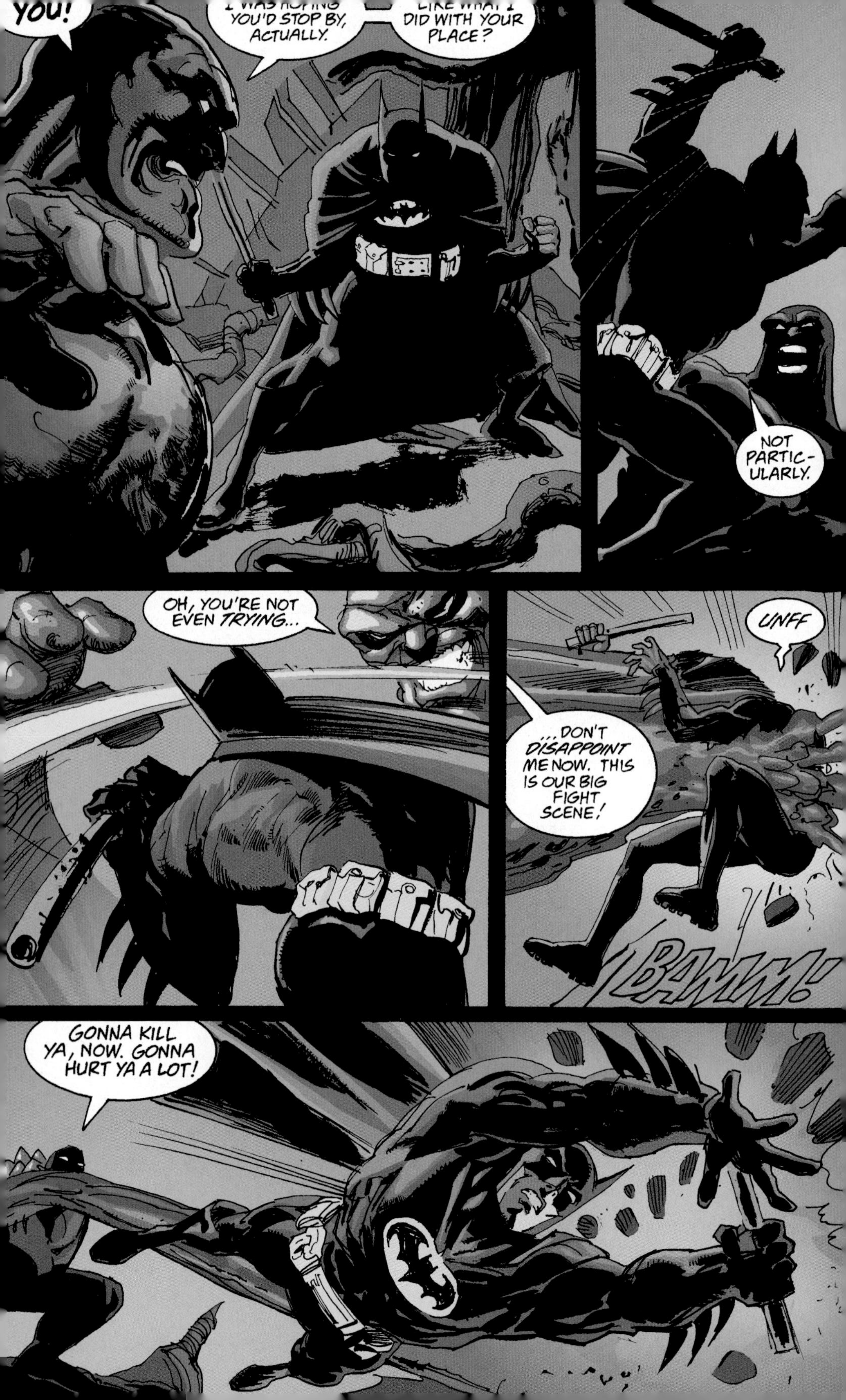
YOU!
YOU'D STOP BY, ACTUALLY.
DID WITH YOUR PLACE?
NOT PARTIC-ULARLY.
OH, YOU'RE NOT EVEN TRYING...
UNFF
...DON'T DISAPPOINT ME NOW. THIS IS OUR BIG FIGHT SCENE!
BAMM!
GONNA KILL YA, NOW. GONNA HURT YA A LOT!

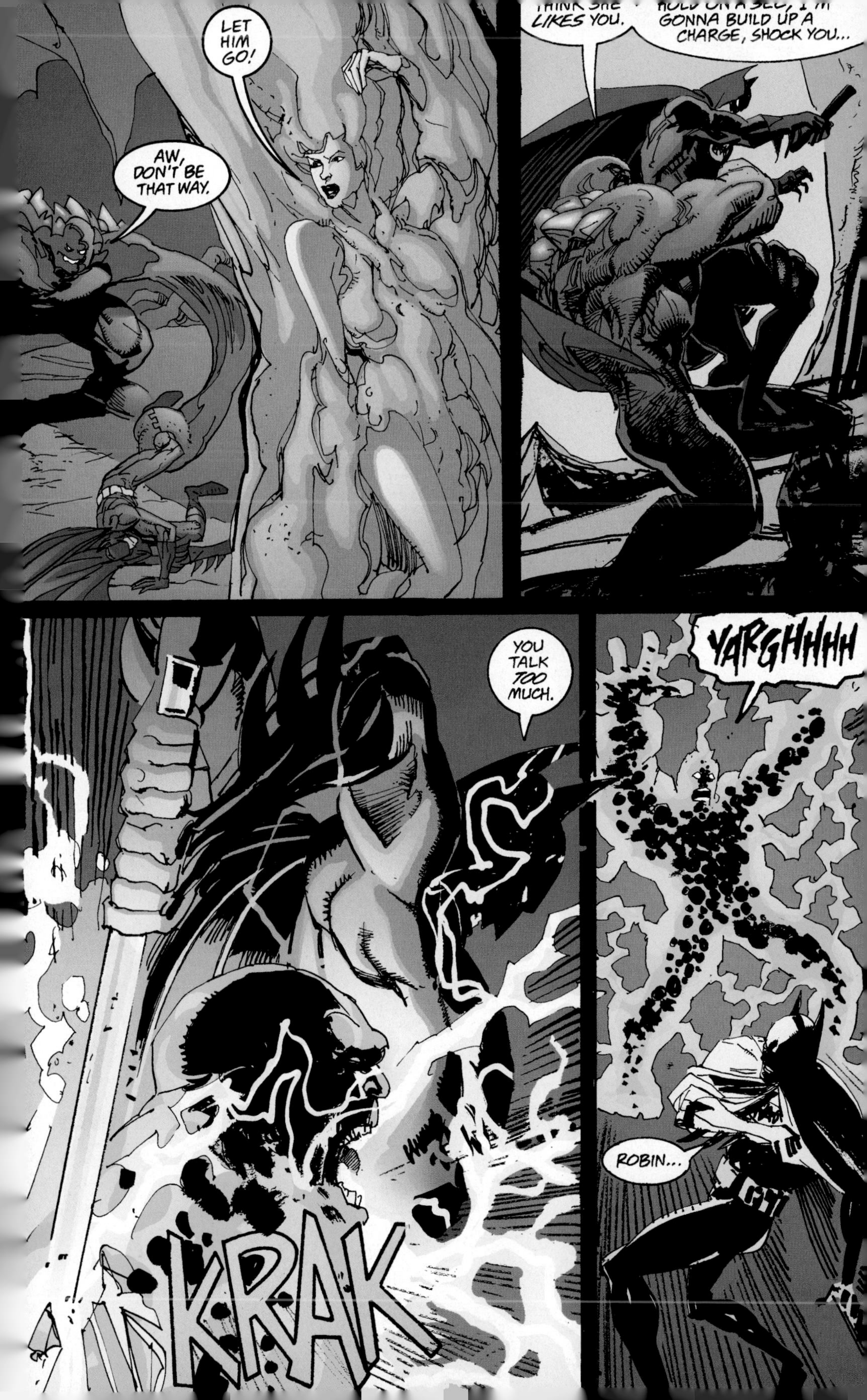
LET HIM GO!
AW, DON'T BE THAT WAY.
LIKES YOU.
GONNA BUILD UP A CHARGE, SHOCK YOU...
YOU TALK TOO MUCH.
KRAK
YARGHHHH
ROBIN...

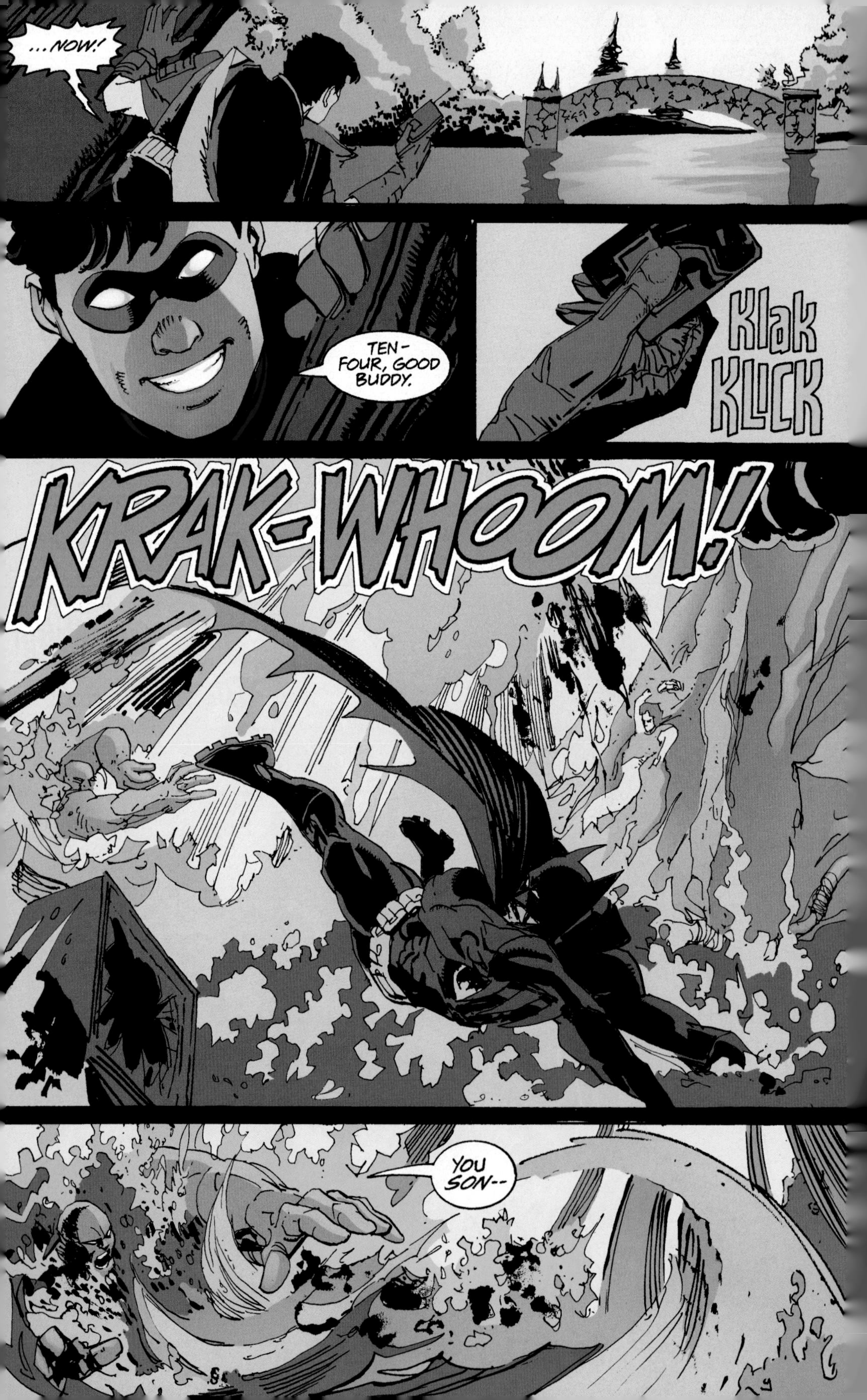
...NOW!
TEN-FOUR, GOOD BUDDY.
Klak
KLICK
KRAK-WHOOM!
YOU SON--

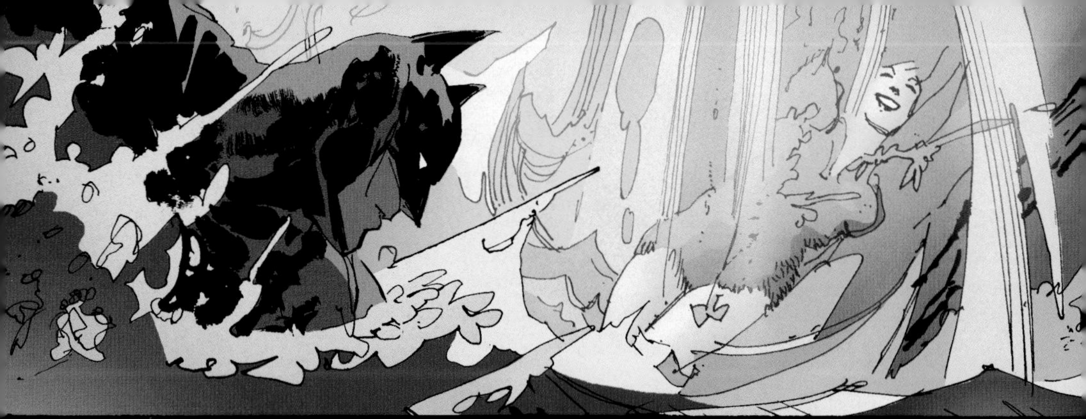
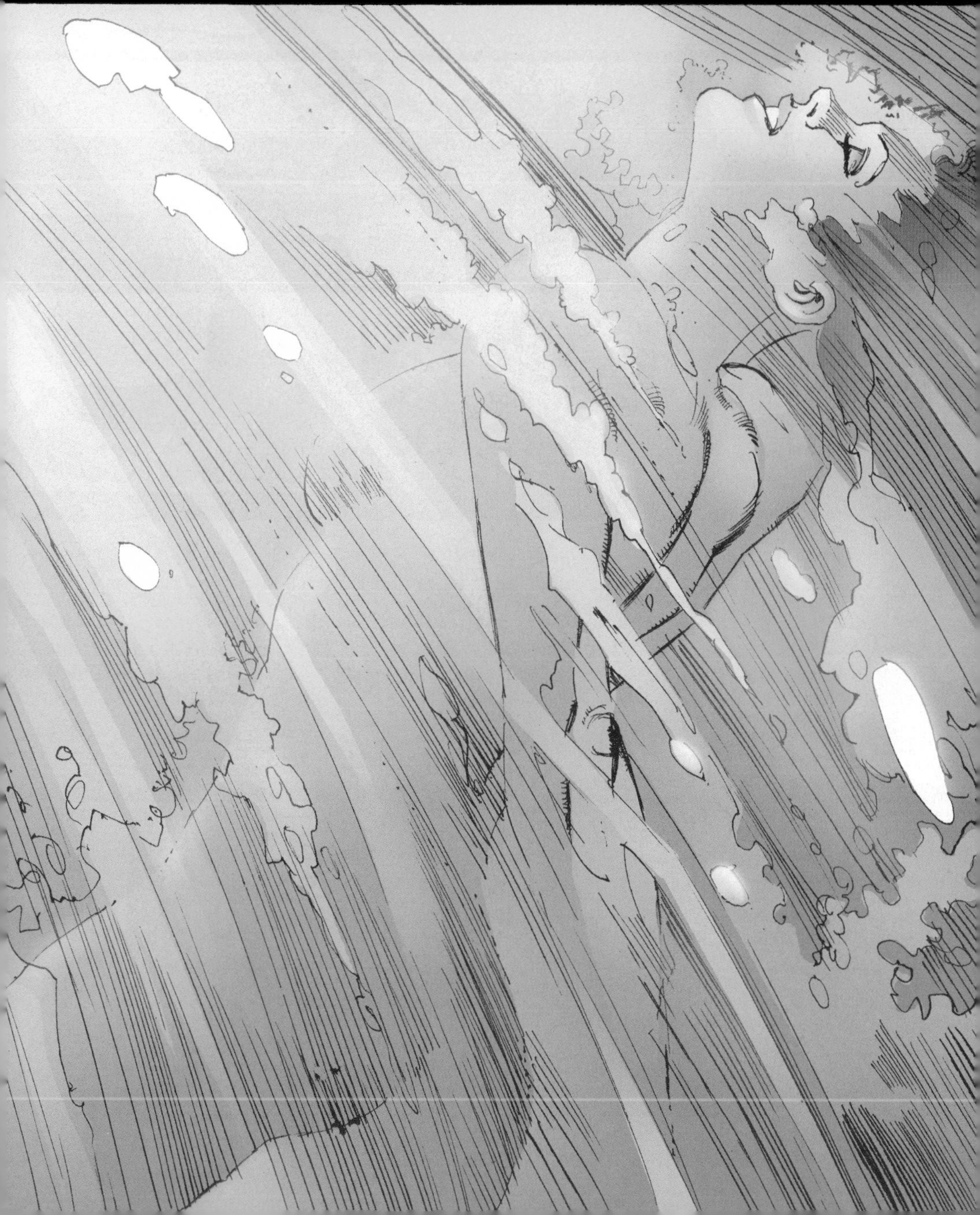

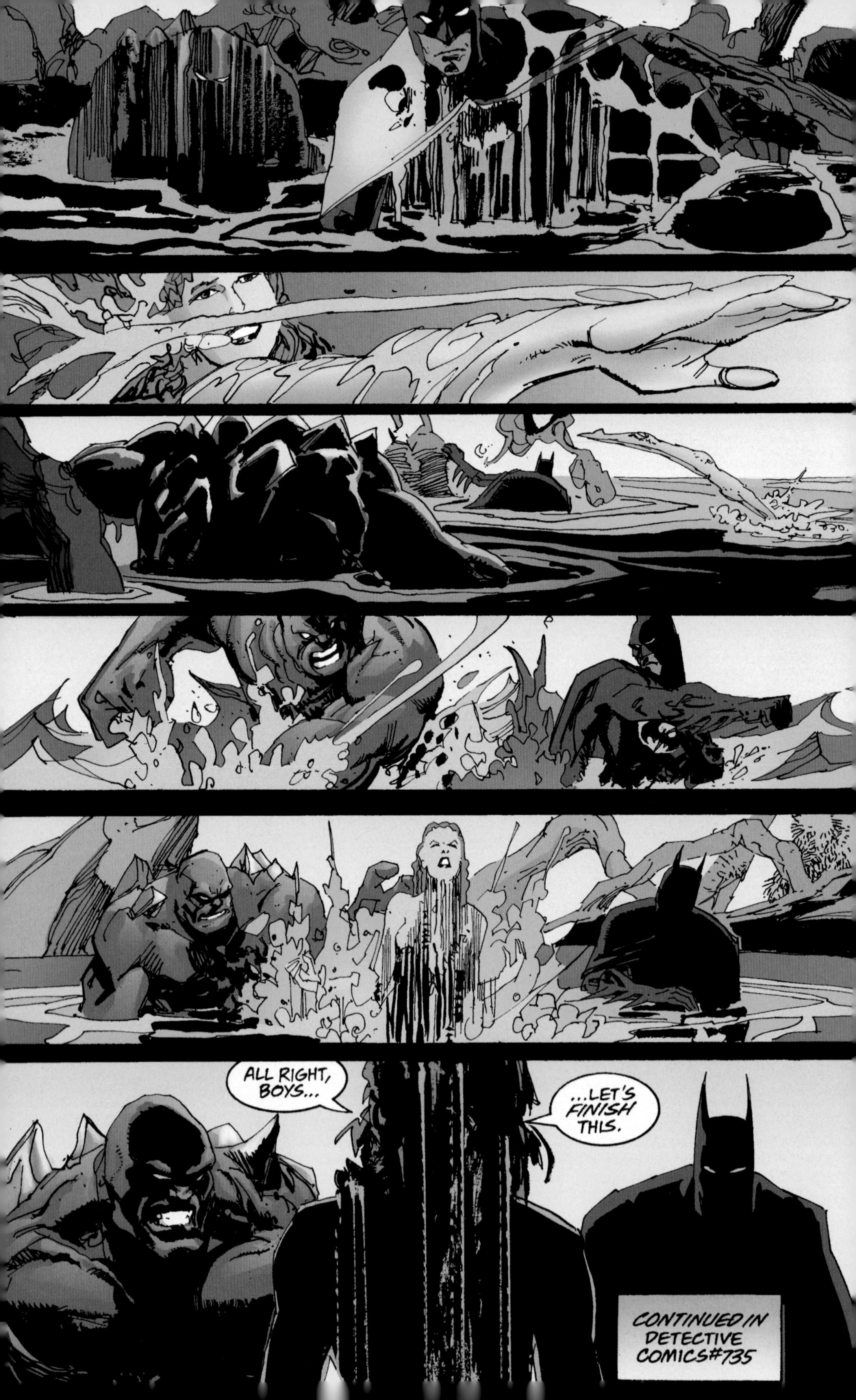
ALL RIGHT, BOYS...
...LET'S FINISH THIS.
CONTINUED IN DETECTIVE COMICS #735

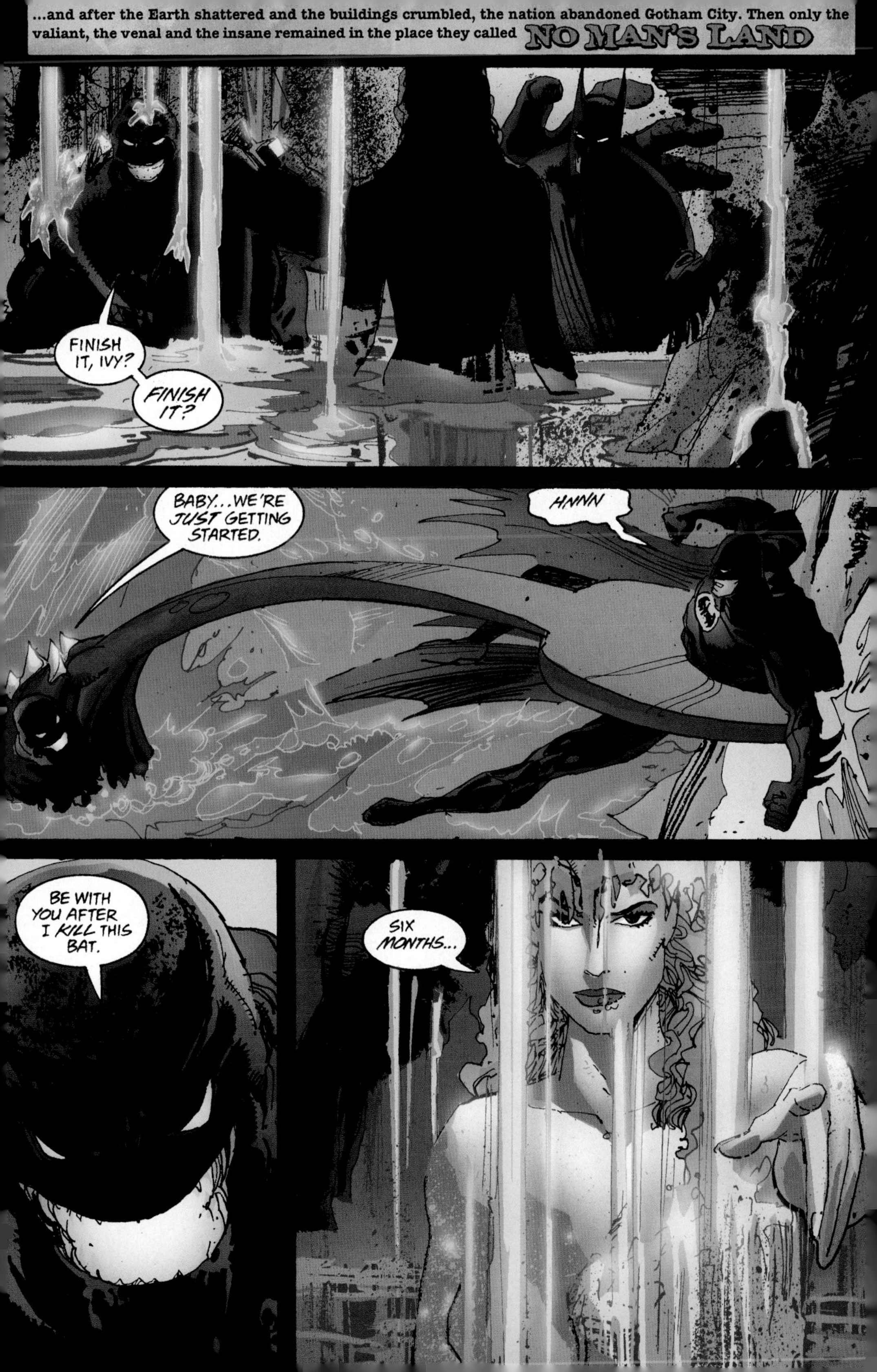
...and after the Earth shattered and the buildings crumbled, the nation abandoned Gotham City. Then only the valiant, the venal and the insane remained in the place they called NO MAN'S LAND
FINISH IT, IVY?
FINISH IT?
BABY...WE'RE JUST GETTING STARTED.
HNNN
BE WITH YOU AFTER I KILL THIS BAT.
SIX MONTHS...

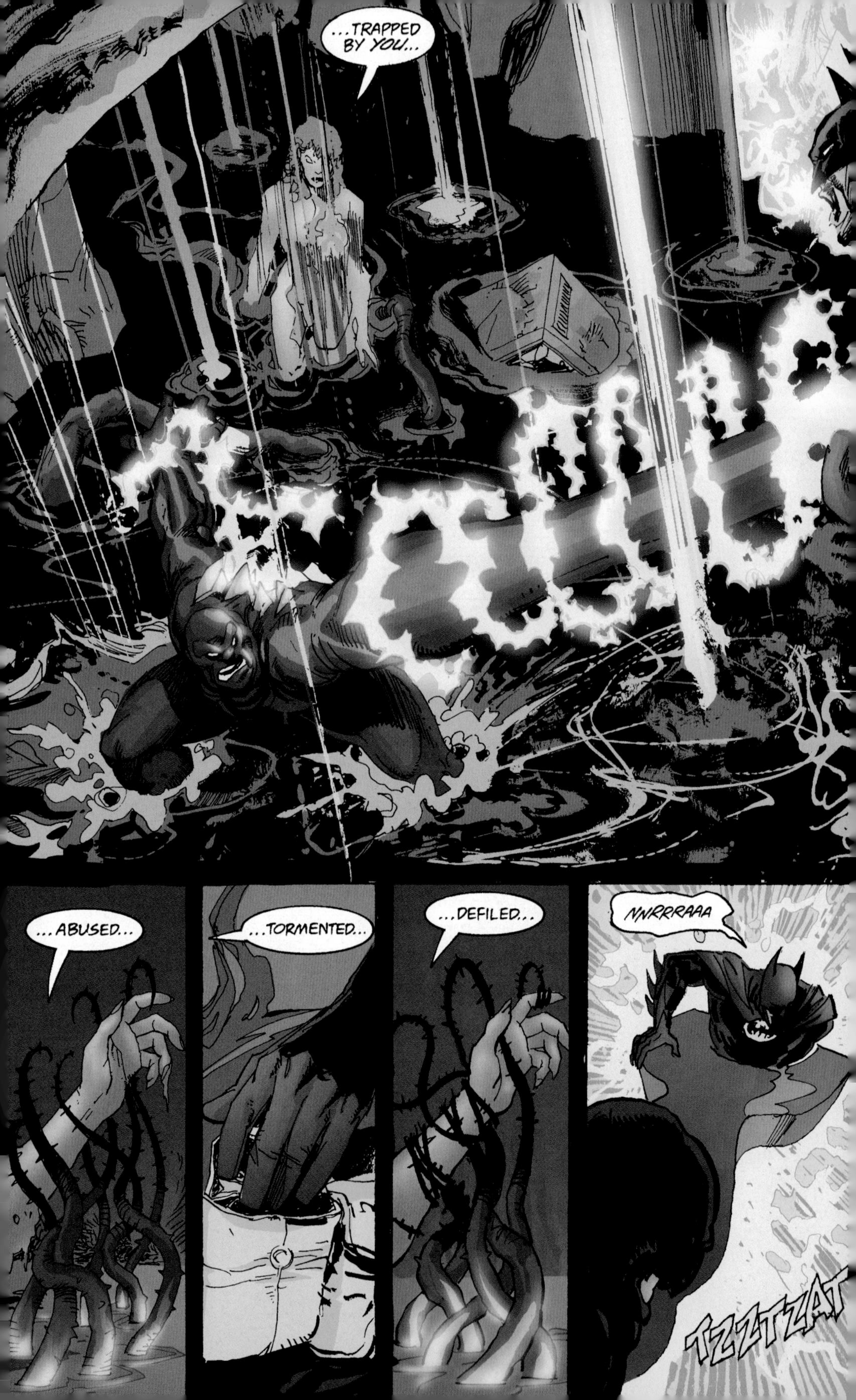
...TRAPPED BY YOU...
...ABUSED...
...TORMENTED...
...DEFILED...
NNRRRAAA
TZZTZAT

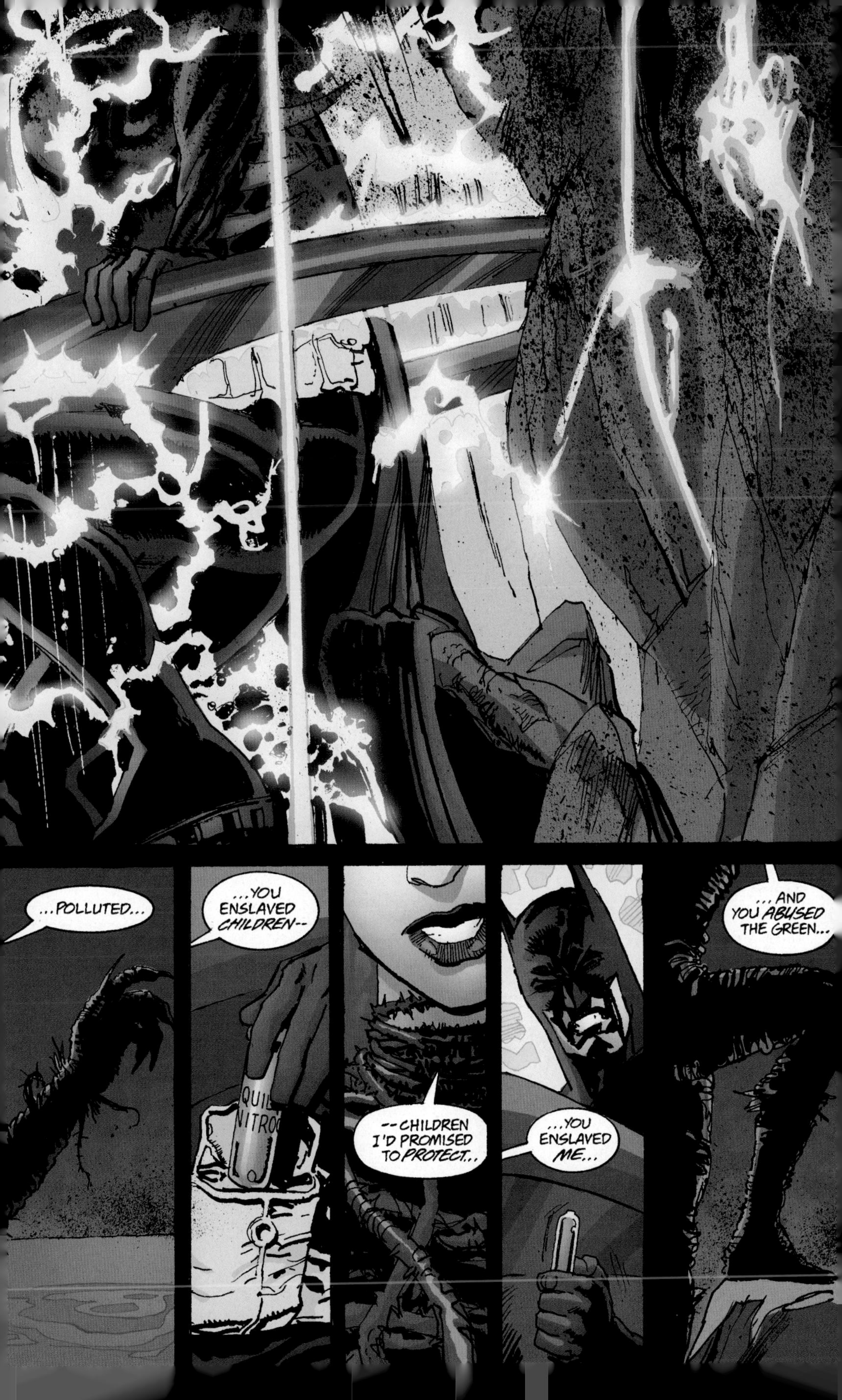
...POLLUTED...
...YOU ENSLAVED CHILDREN--
QUIL NITRO
--CHILDREN I'D PROMISED TO PROTECT...
...YOU ENSLAVED ME...
...AND YOU ABUSED THE GREEN...

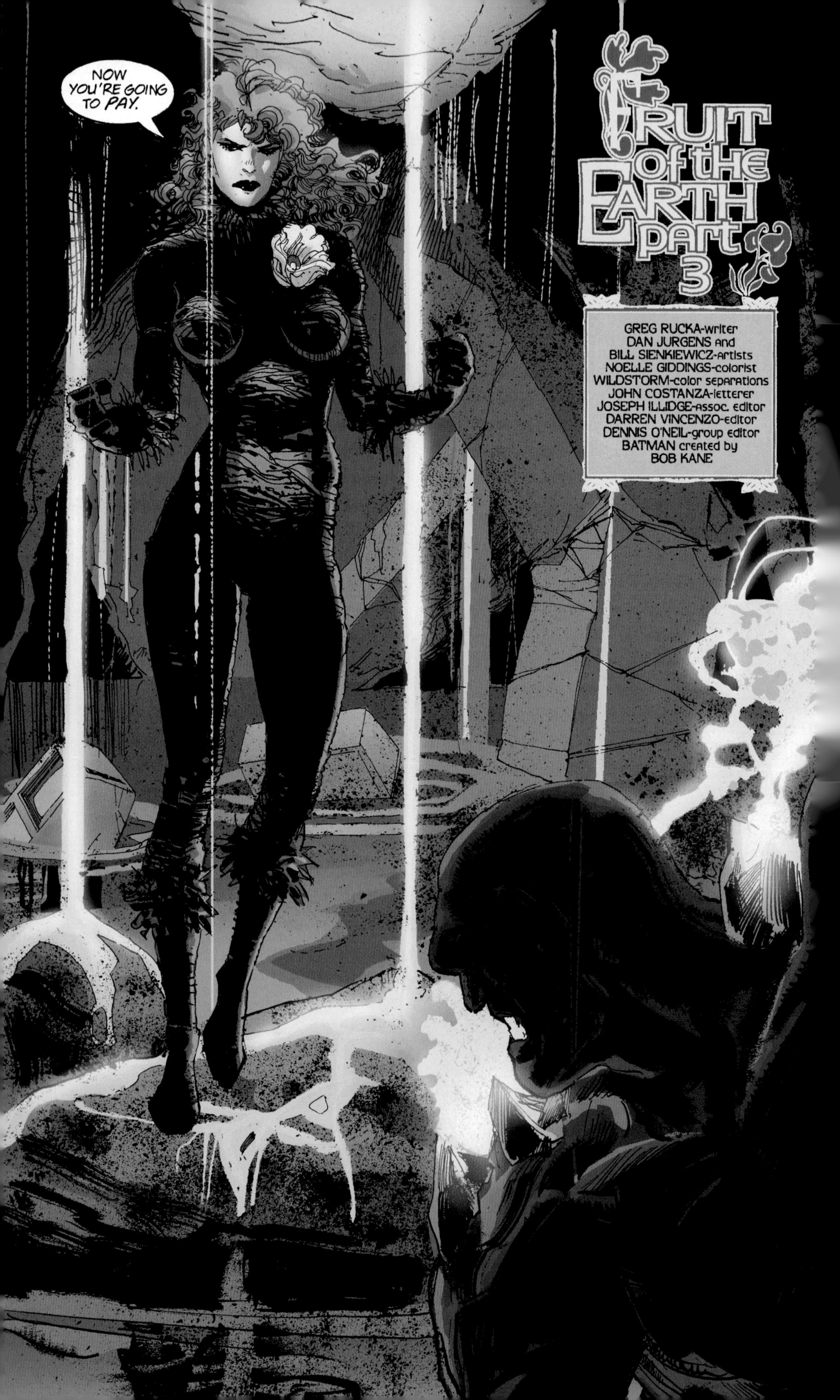
NOW YOU'RE GOING TO PAY.
FRUIT of the EARTH part 3
GREG RUCKA-writer
DAN JURGENS and
BILL SIENKIEWICZ-artists
NOELLE GIDDINGS-colorist
WILDSTORM-color separations
JOHN COSTANZA-letterer
JOSEPH ILLIDGE-assoc. editor
DARREN VINCENZO-editor
DENNIS O'NEIL-group editor
BATMAN created by
BOB KANE

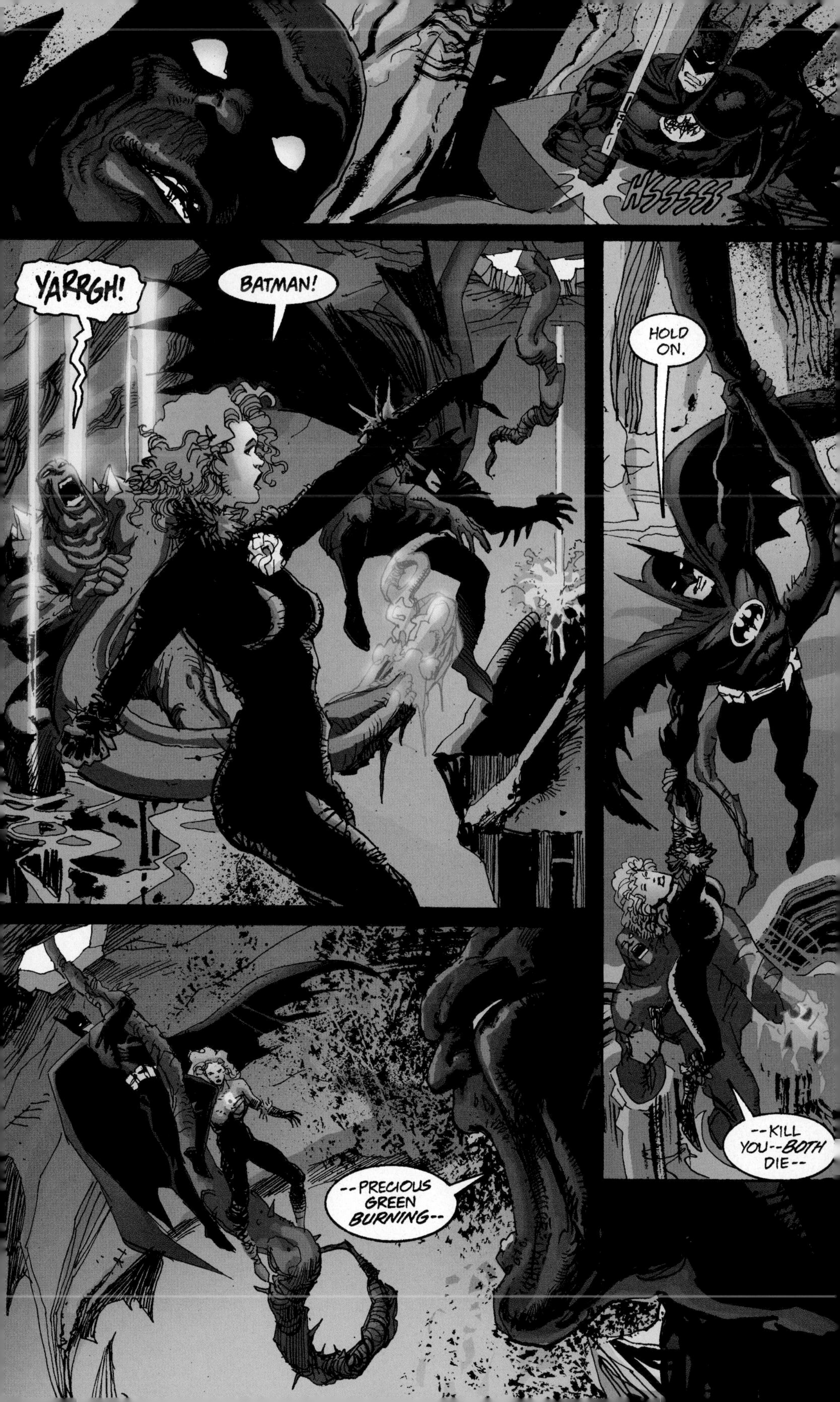
HSSSSS
YARRGH!
BATMAN!
HOLD ON.
--KILL YOU--BOTH DIE--
--PRECIOUS GREEN BURNING--

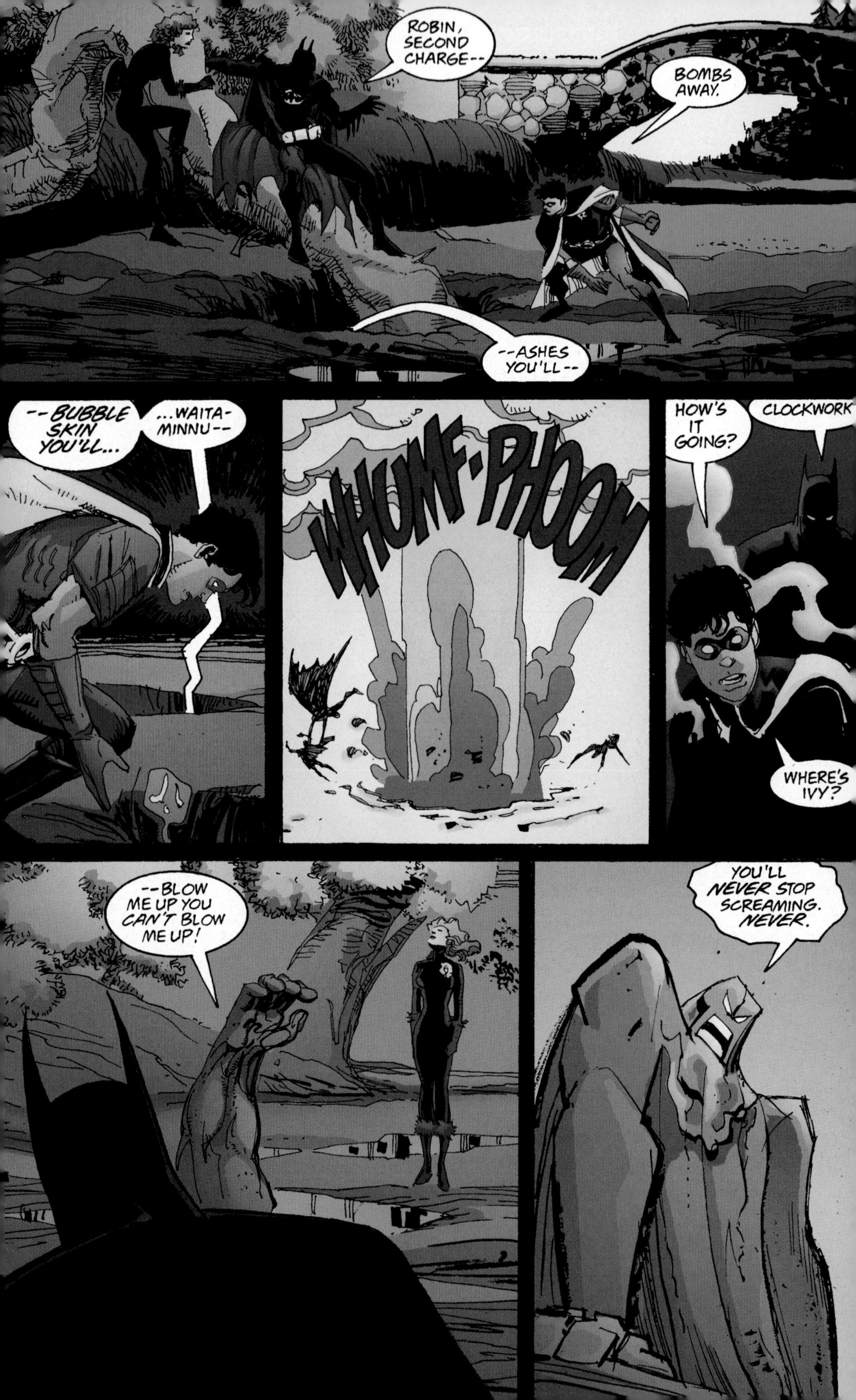
ROBIN, SECOND CHARGE--
BOMBS AWAY.
--ASHES YOU'LL--
--BUBBLE SKIN YOU'LL...
...WAITA-MINNU--
WHUMF-PHOOM
HOW'S IT GOING?
CLOCKWORK
WHERE'S IVY?
--BLOW ME UP YOU CAN'T BLOW ME UP!
YOU'LL NEVER STOP SCREAMING. NEVER.

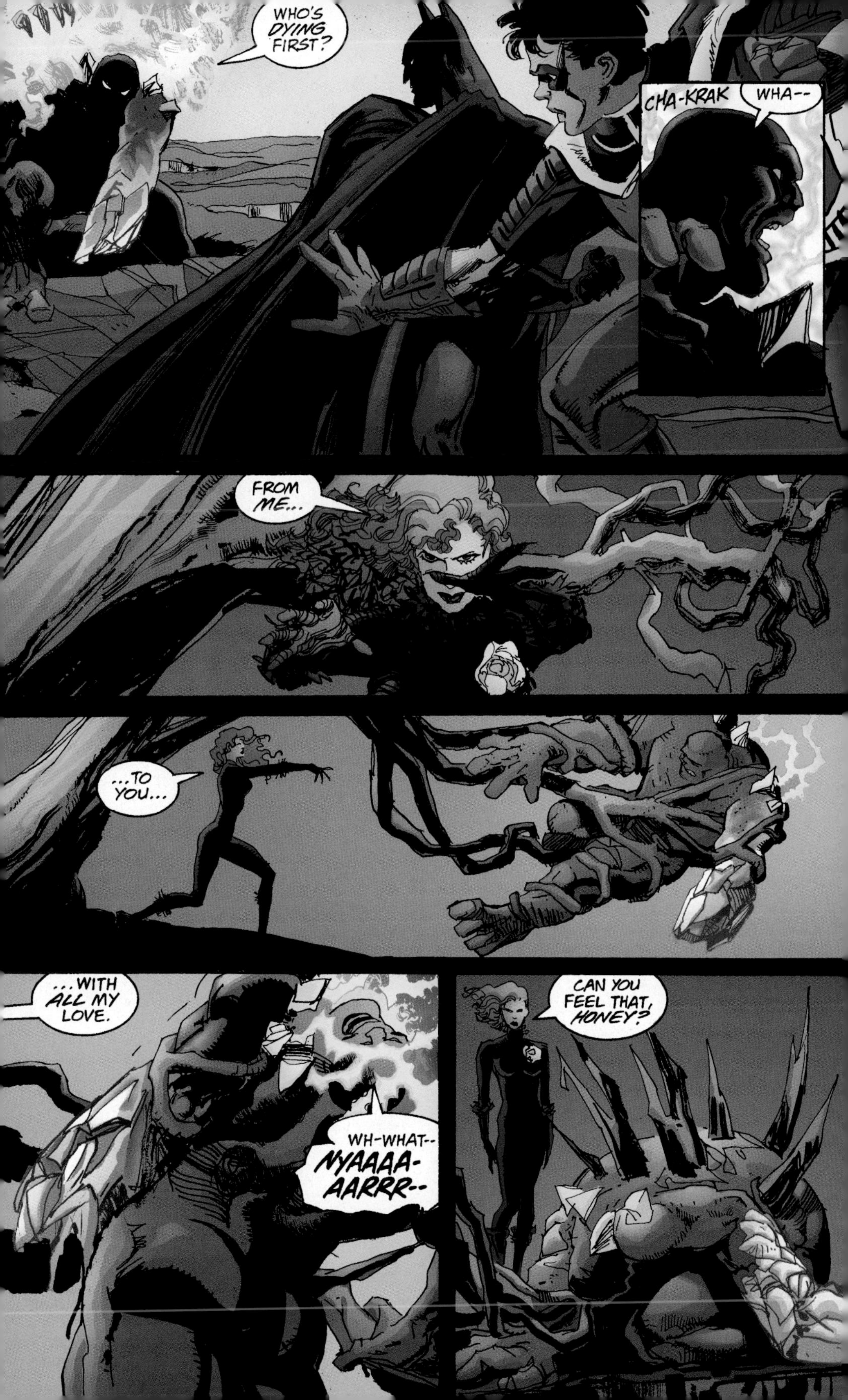
WHO'S DYING FIRST?
CHA-KRAK
WHA--
FROM ME...
...TO YOU...
...WITH ALL MY LOVE.
WH-WHAT--
NYAAAA-AARRR--
CAN YOU FEEL THAT, HONEY?

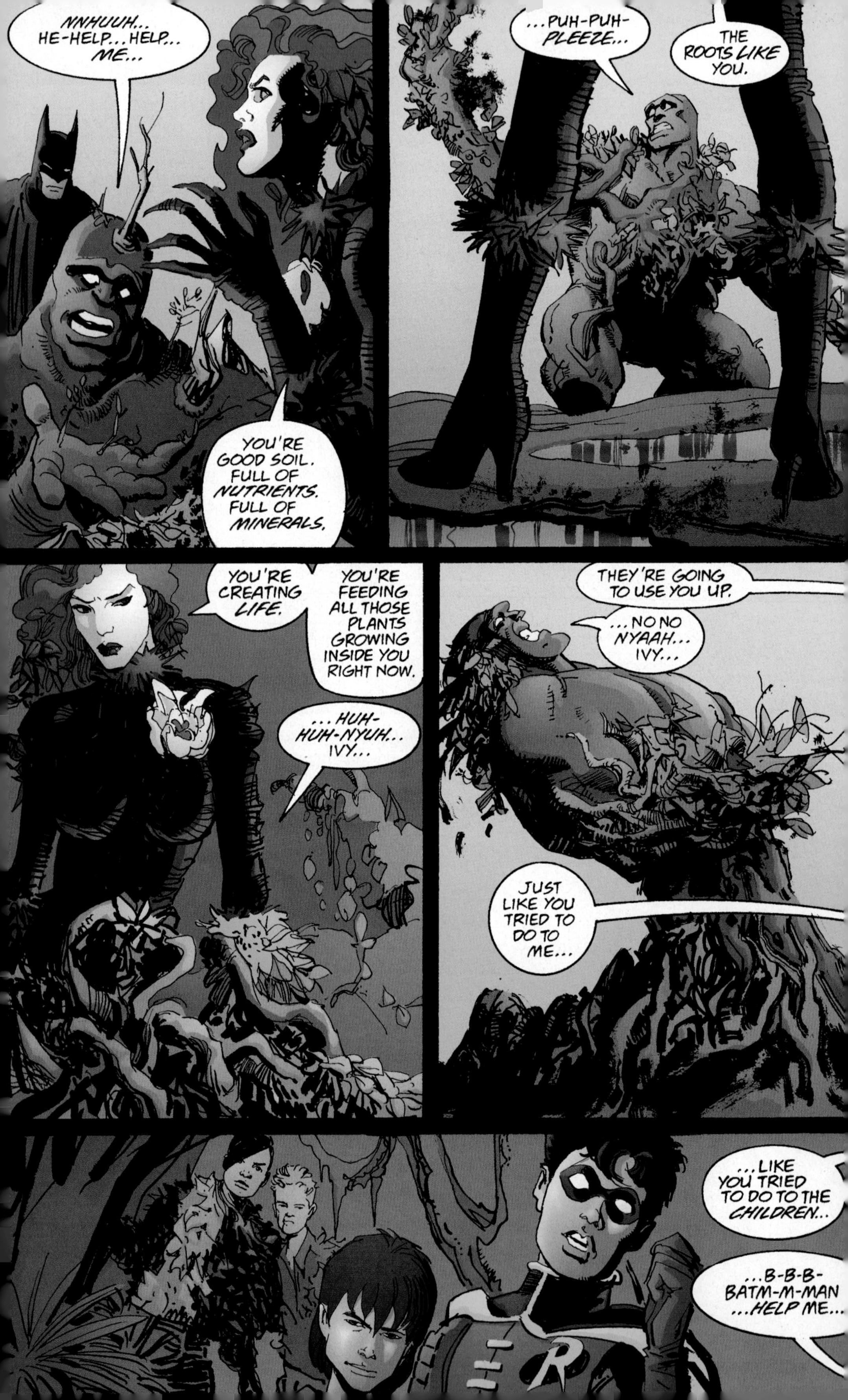
NNHUUH... HE-HELP...HELP... ME...
YOU'RE GOOD SOIL. FULL OF NUTRIENTS. FULL OF MINERALS.
...PUH-PUH-PLEEZE...
THE ROOTS LIKE YOU.
YOU'RE CREATING LIFE.
YOU'RE FEEDING ALL THOSE PLANTS GROWING INSIDE YOU RIGHT NOW.
...HUH-HUH-NYUH... IVY...
THEY'RE GOING TO USE YOU UP.
...NO NO NYAAH... IVY...
JUST LIKE YOU TRIED TO DO TO ME...
...LIKE YOU TRIED TO DO TO THE CHILDREN...
...B-B-B-BATM-M-MAN ...HELP ME...

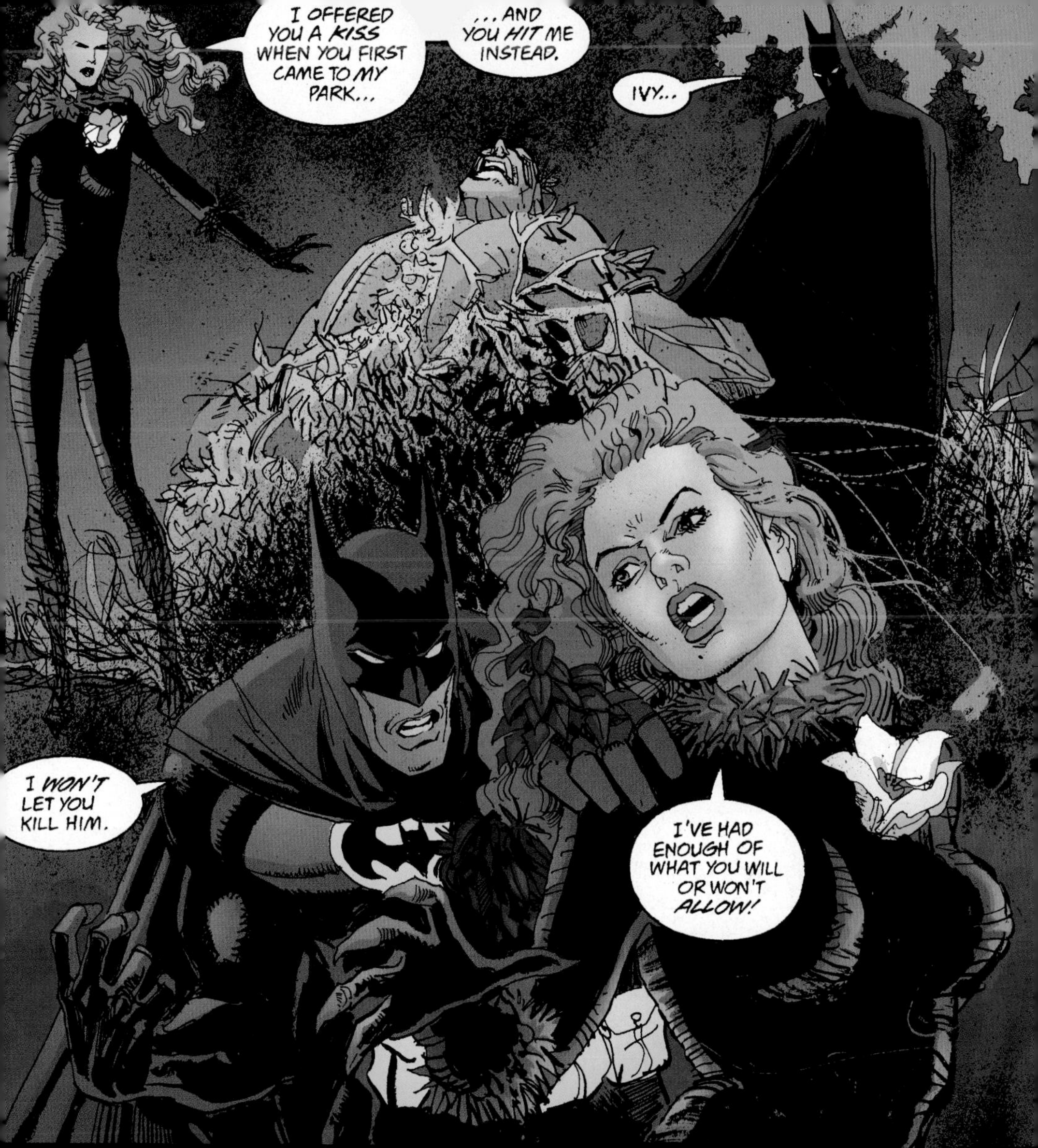
I OFFERED YOU A KISS WHEN YOU FIRST CAME TO MY PARK...
...AND YOU HIT ME INSTEAD.
IVY...
I WON'T LET YOU KILL HIM.
I'VE HAD ENOUGH OF WHAT YOU WILL OR WON'T ALLOW!

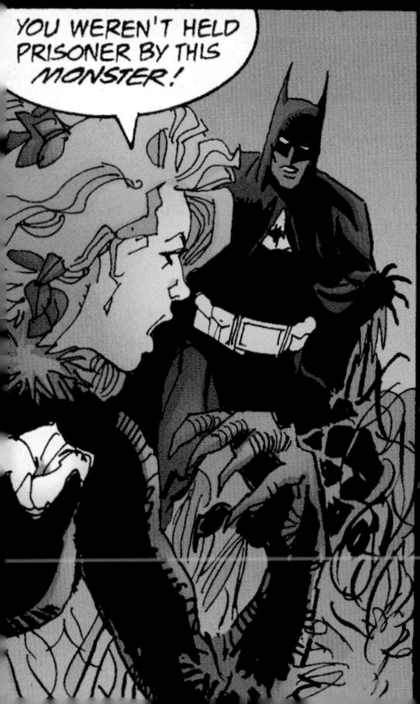
YOU WEREN'T HELD PRISONER BY THIS MONSTER!

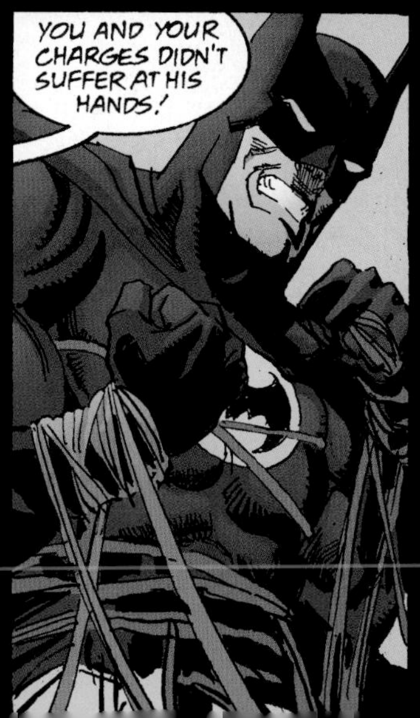
YOU AND YOUR CHARGES DIDN'T SUFFER AT HIS HANDS!

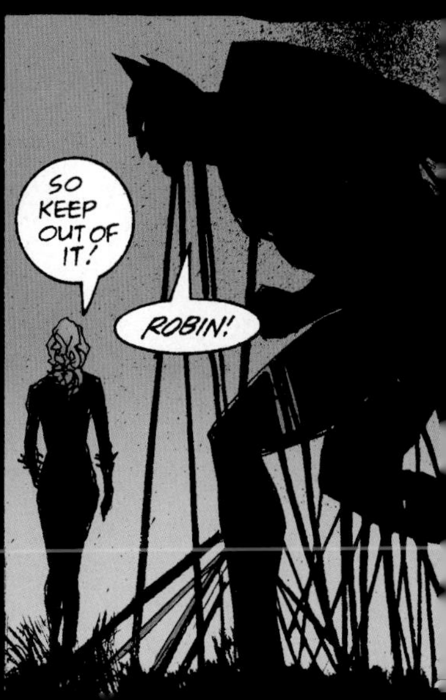
SO KEEP OUT OF IT!
ROBIN!

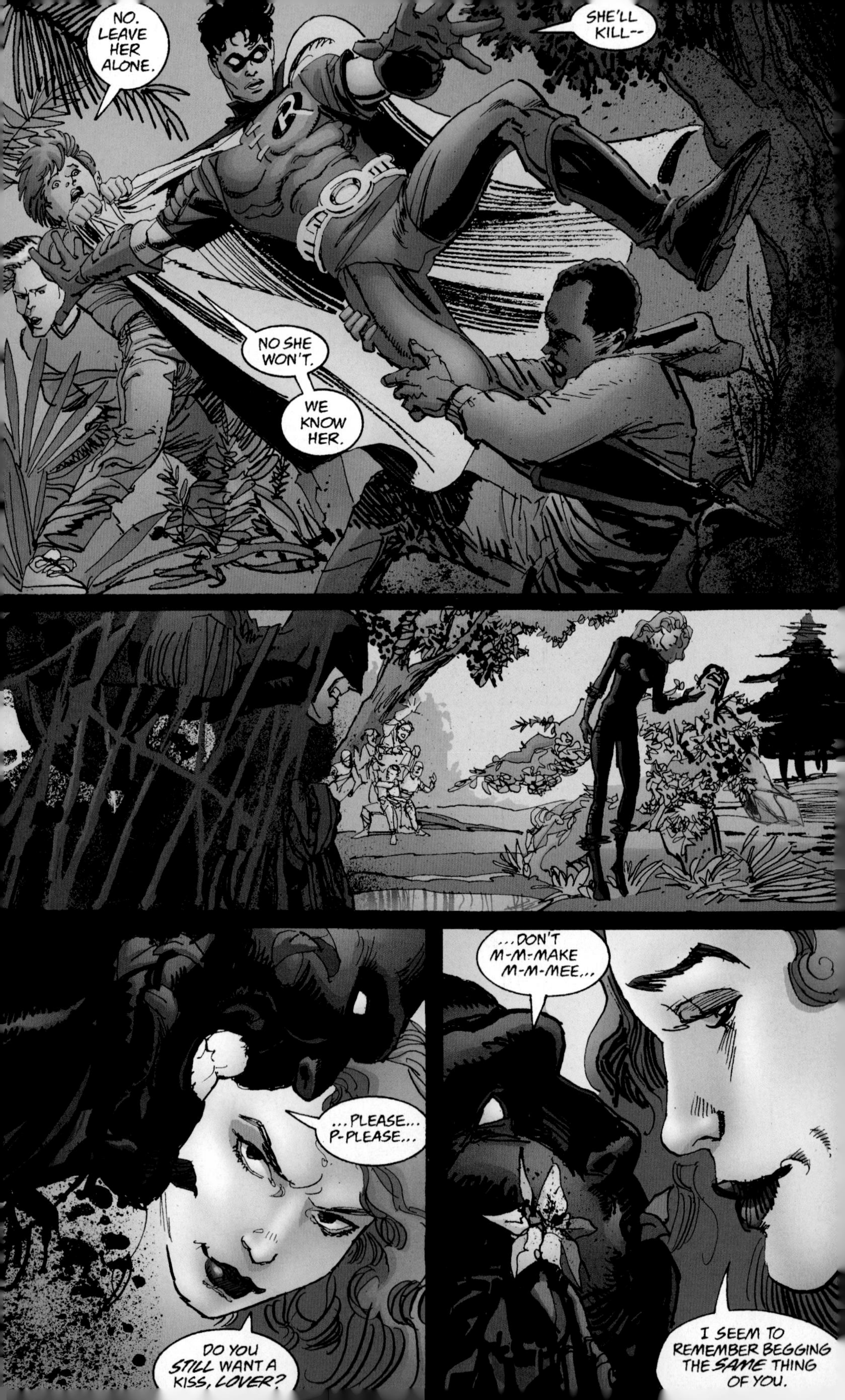
NO. LEAVE HER ALONE.
SHE'LL KILL--
NO SHE WON'T.
WE KNOW HER.
...PLEASE... P-PLEASE...
DO YOU STILL WANT A KISS, LOVER?
...DON'T M-M-MAKE M-M-MEE...
I SEEM TO REMEMBER BEGGING THE SAME THING OF YOU.

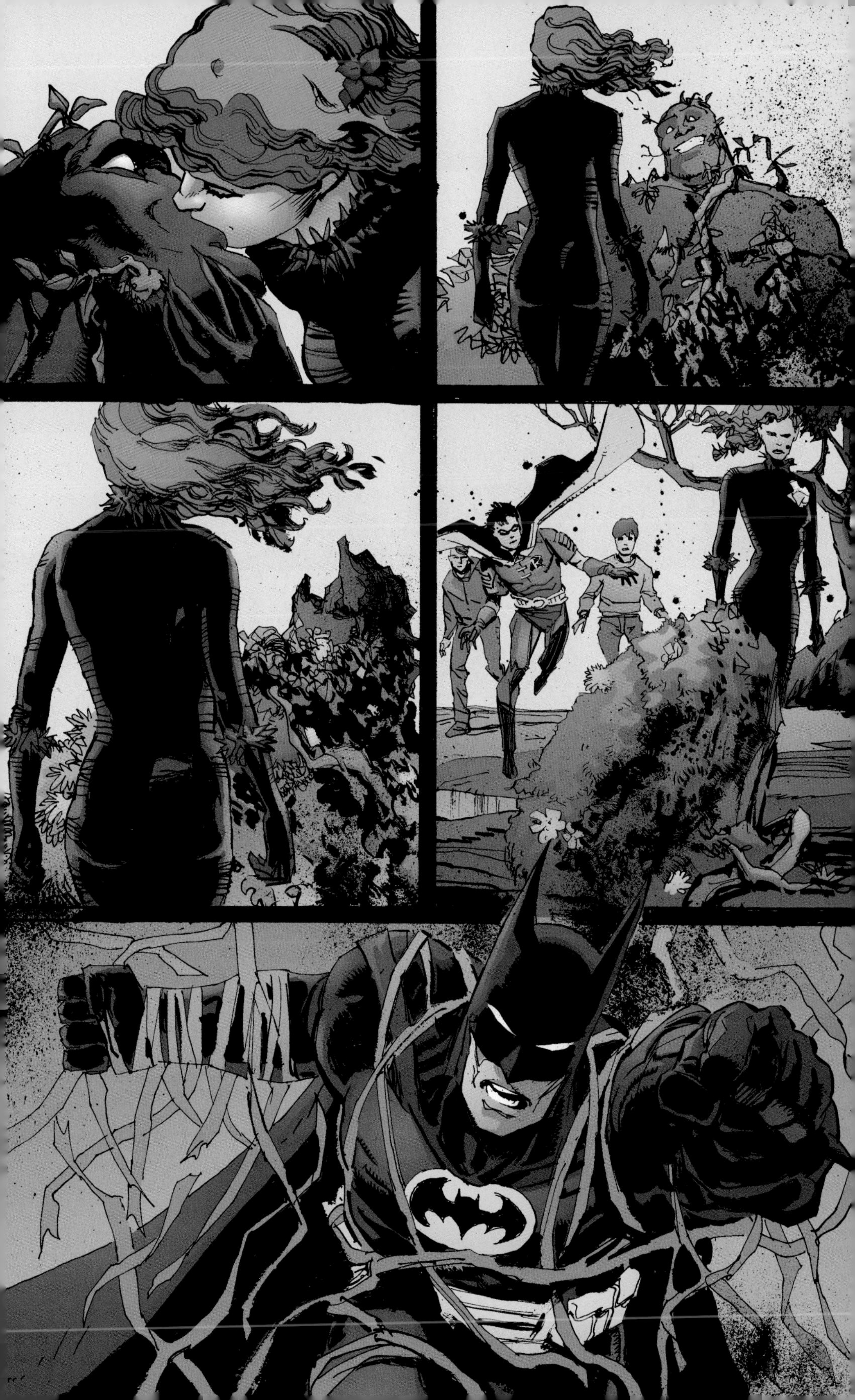

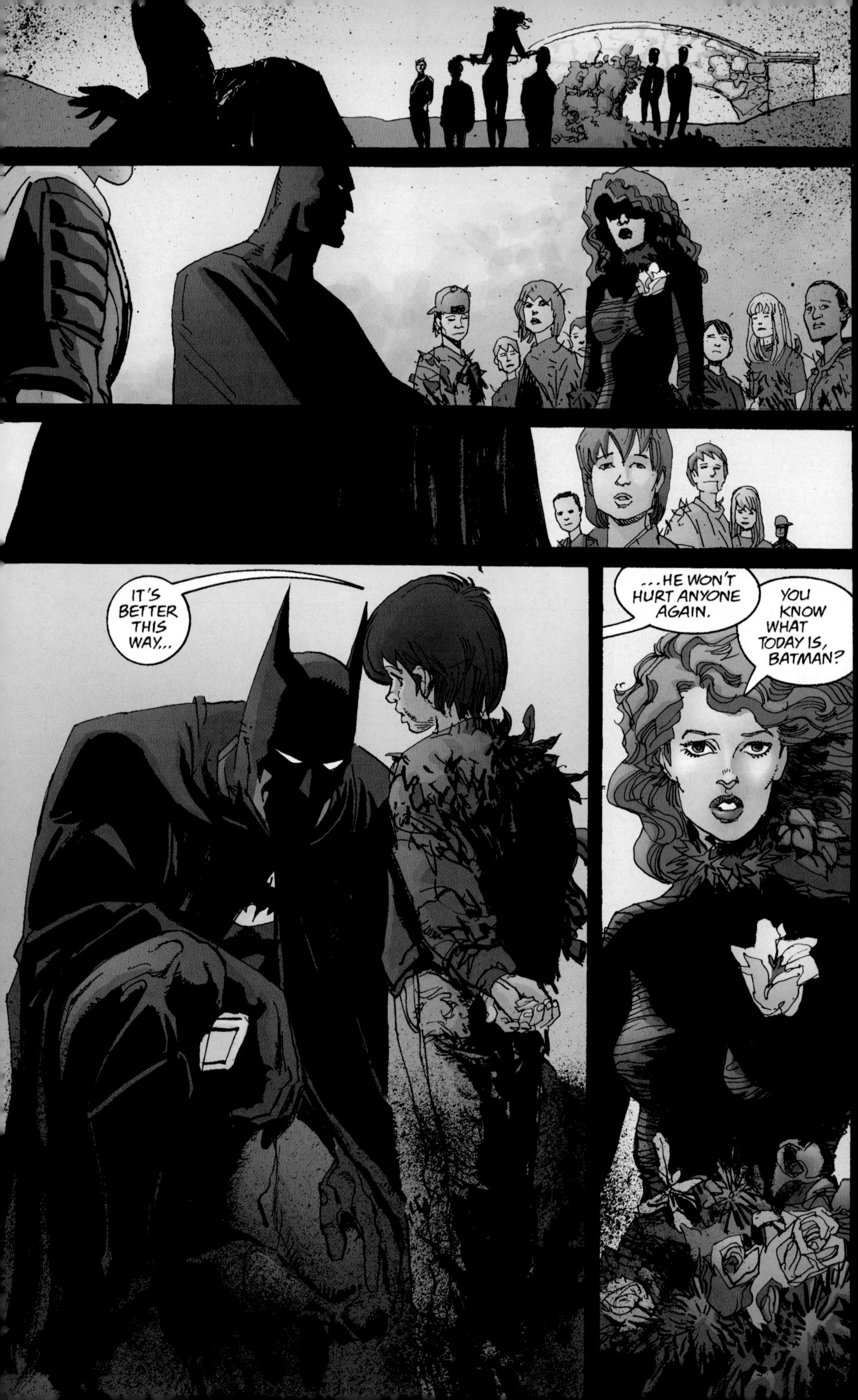
IT'S BETTER THIS WAY...
...HE WON'T HURT ANYONE AGAIN.
YOU KNOW WHAT TODAY IS, BATMAN?

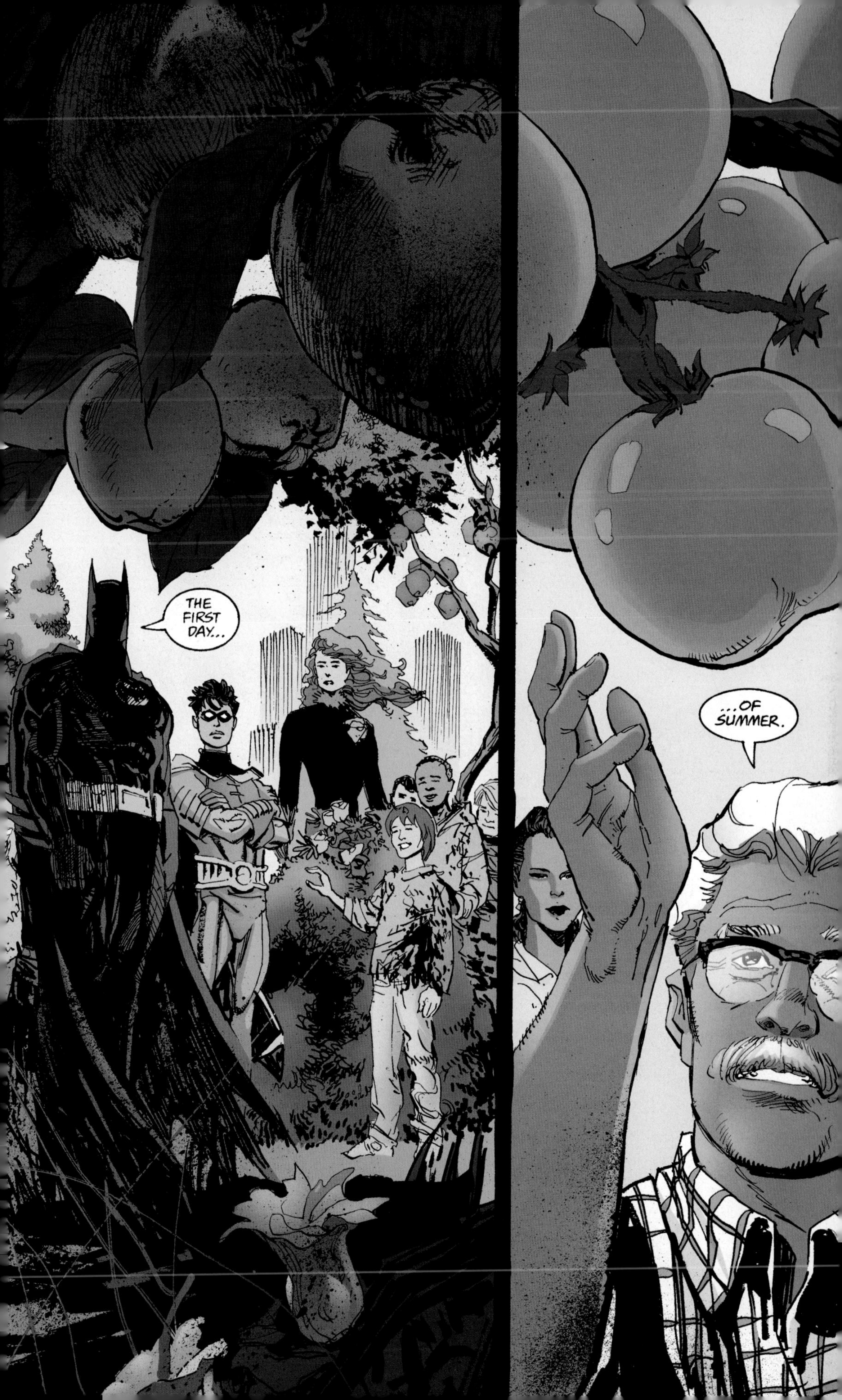
THE FIRST DAY...
...OF SUMMER.

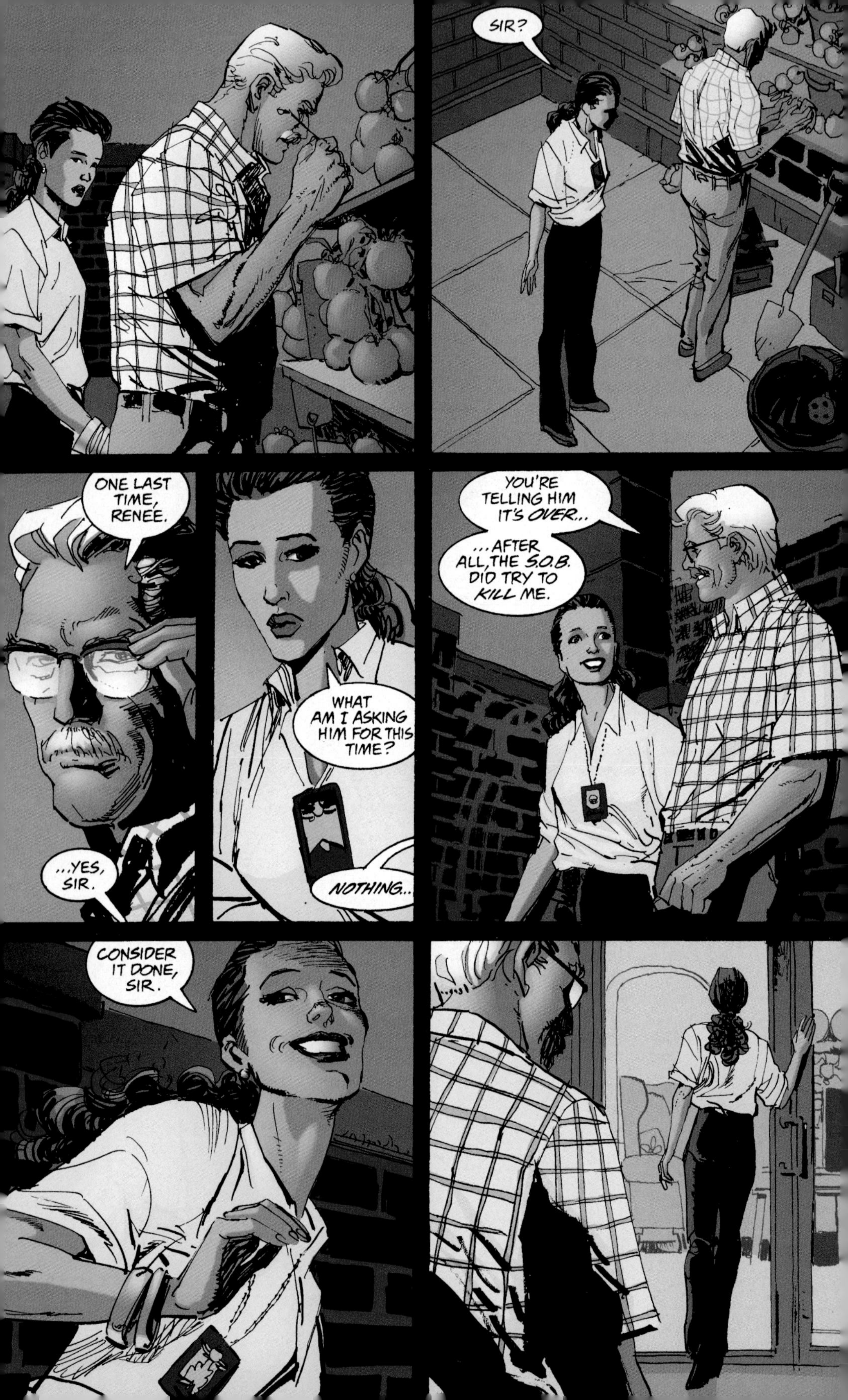
SIR?
ONE LAST TIME, RENEE.
WHAT AM I ASKING HIM FOR THIS TIME?
...YES, SIR.
NOTHING...
YOU'RE TELLING HIM IT'S OVER...
...AFTER ALL, THE S.O.B. DID TRY TO KILL ME.
CONSIDER IT DONE, SIR.

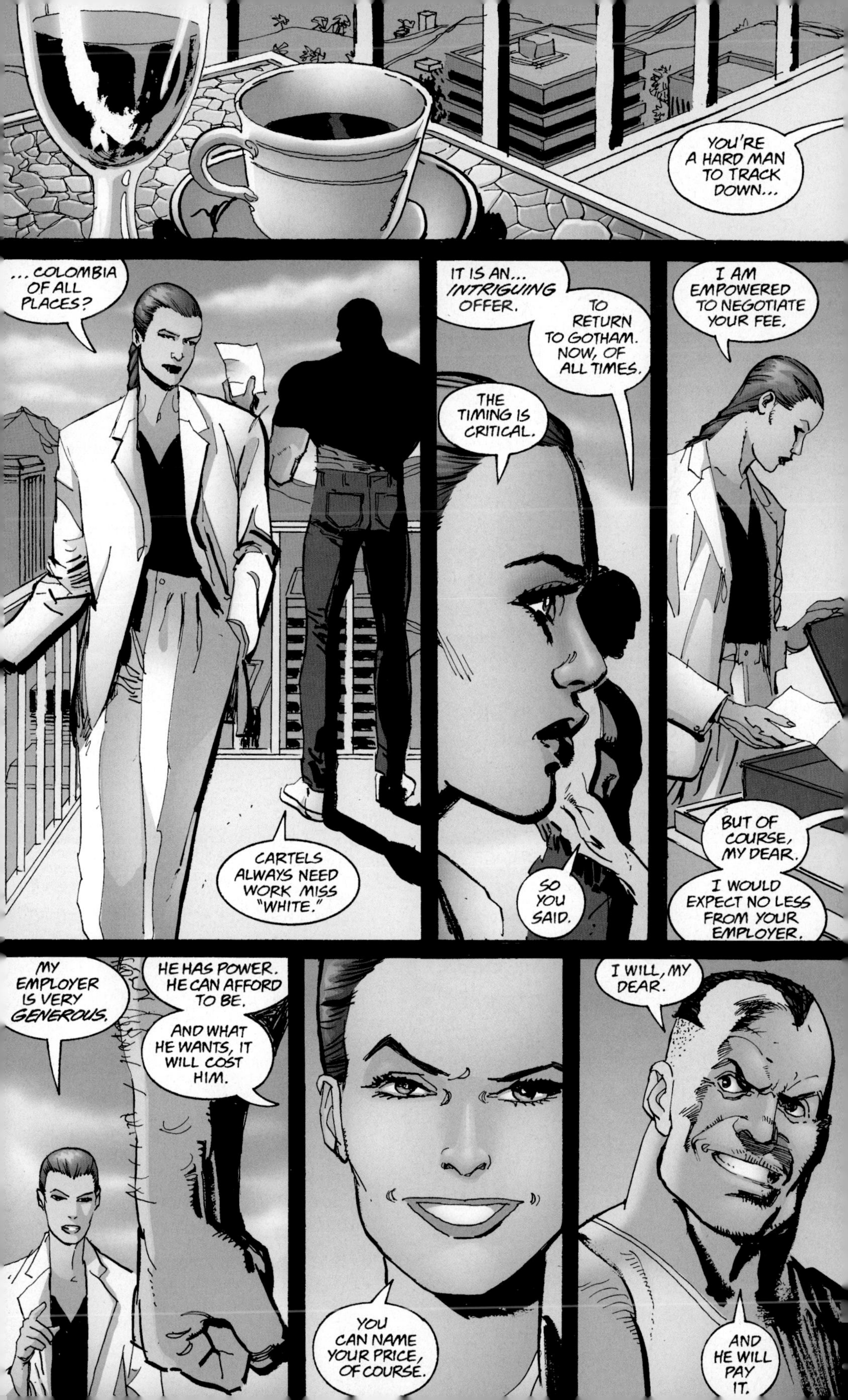

YOU'RE A HARD MAN TO TRACK DOWN...
...COLOMBIA OF ALL PLACES?
CARTELS ALWAYS NEED WORK MISS "WHITE."
IT IS AN... INTRIGUING OFFER.
TO RETURN TO GOTHAM. NOW, OF ALL TIMES.
THE TIMING IS CRITICAL.
SO YOU SAID.
I AM EMPOWERED TO NEGOTIATE YOUR FEE.
BUT OF COURSE, MY DEAR.
I WOULD EXPECT NO LESS FROM YOUR EMPLOYER.
MY EMPLOYER IS VERY GENEROUS.
HE HAS POWER. HE CAN AFFORD TO BE.
AND WHAT HE WANTS, IT WILL COST HIM.
YOU CAN NAME YOUR PRICE, OF COURSE.
I WILL, MY DEAR.
AND HE WILL PAY IT.

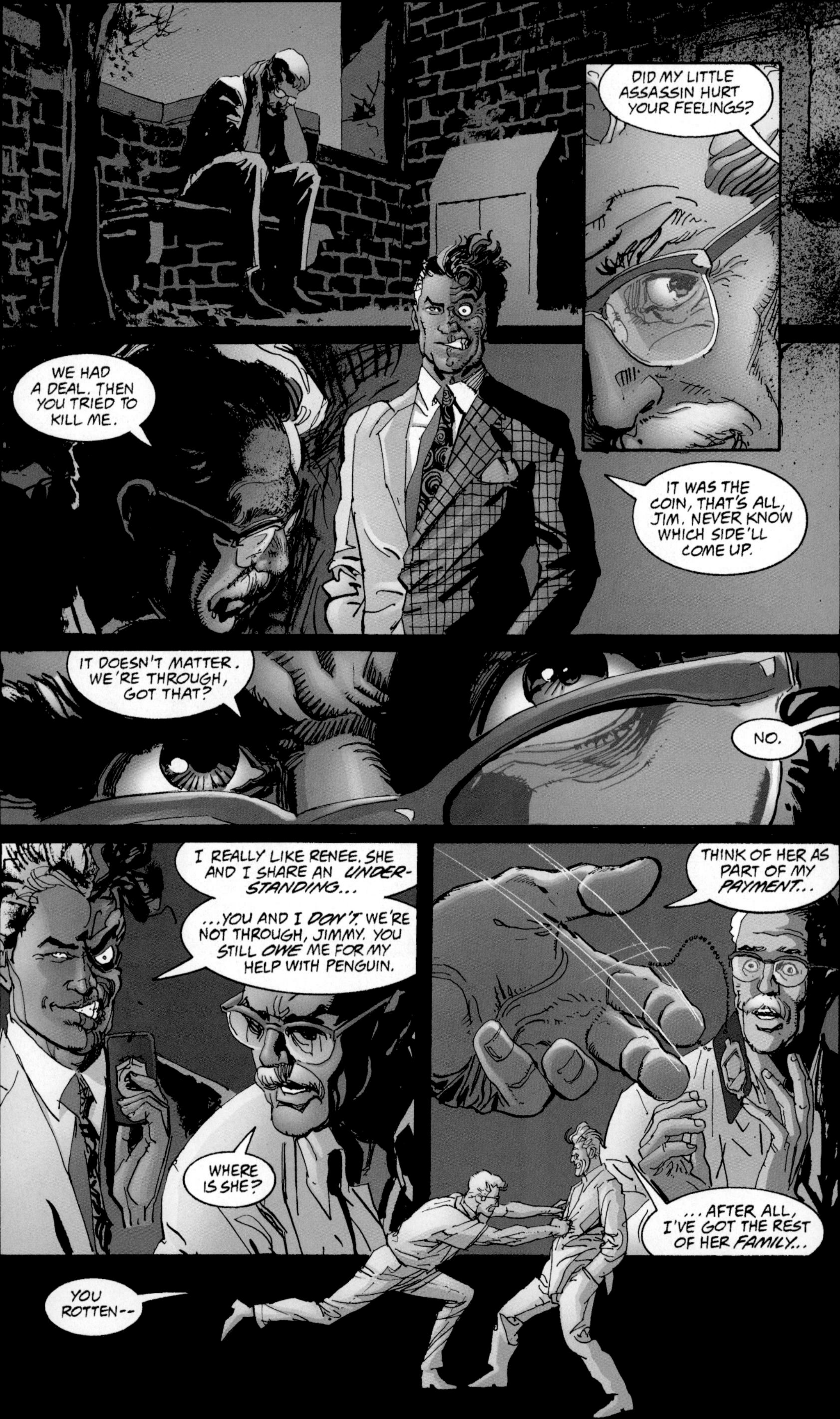
DID MY LITTLE ASSASSIN HURT YOUR FEELINGS?
WE HAD A DEAL. THEN YOU TRIED TO KILL ME.
IT WAS THE COIN, THAT'S ALL, JIM. NEVER KNOW WHICH SIDE'LL COME UP.
IT DOESN'T MATTER. WE'RE THROUGH, GOT THAT?
NO.
I REALLY LIKE RENEE. SHE AND I SHARE AN *UNDER-STANDING*...
...YOU AND I *DON'T*. WE'RE NOT THROUGH, JIMMY. YOU STILL *OWE* ME FOR MY HELP WITH PENGUIN.
WHERE IS SHE?
THINK OF HER AS PART OF MY *PAYMENT*...
...AFTER ALL, I'VE GOT THE REST OF HER *FAMILY*...
YOU ROTTEN--

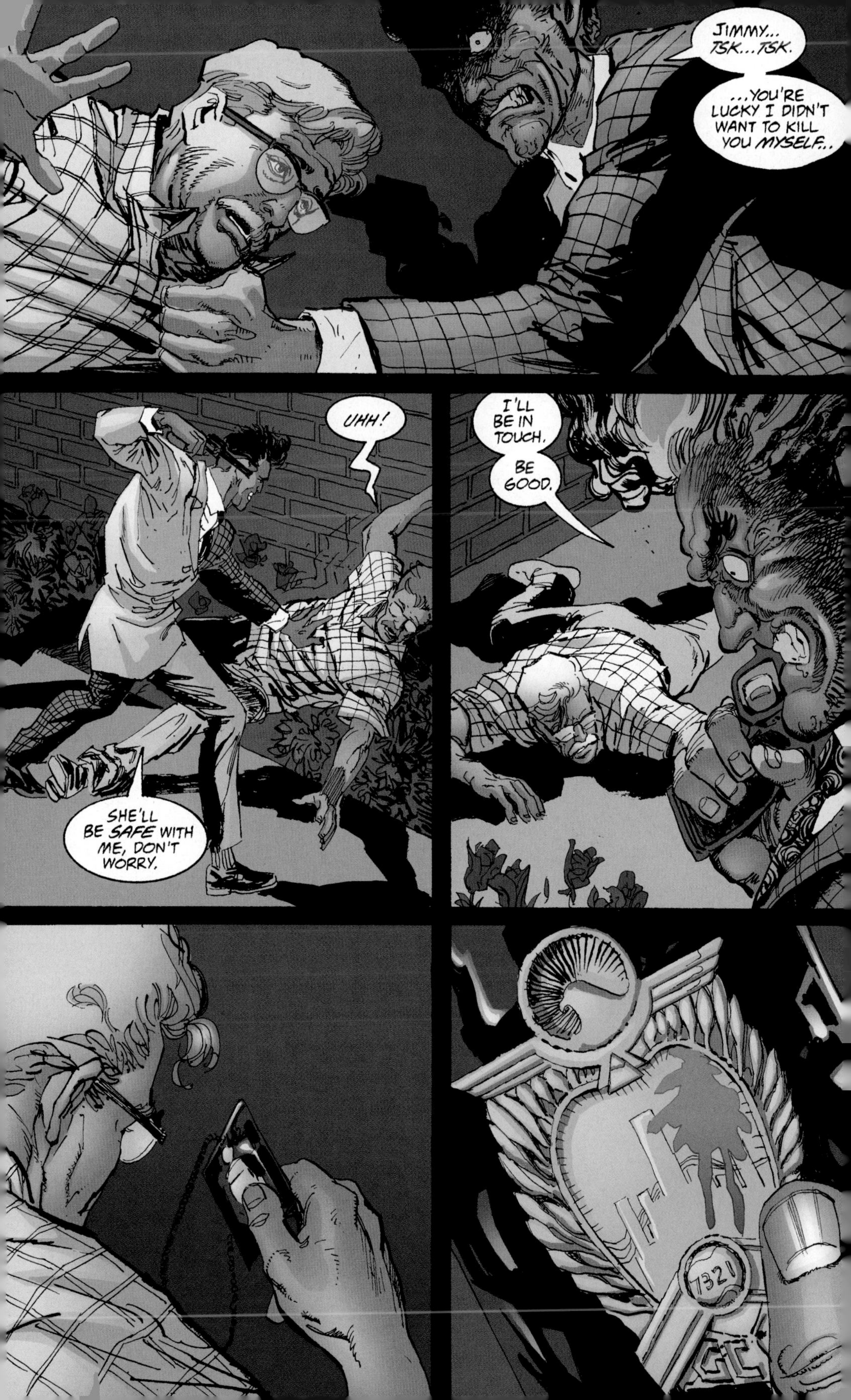
JIMMY... TSK...TSK.
...YOU'RE LUCKY I DIDN'T WANT TO KILL YOU MYSELF...
UHH!
SHE'LL BE SAFE WITH ME, DON'T WORRY.
I'LL BE IN TOUCH.
BE GOOD.
7321
GC

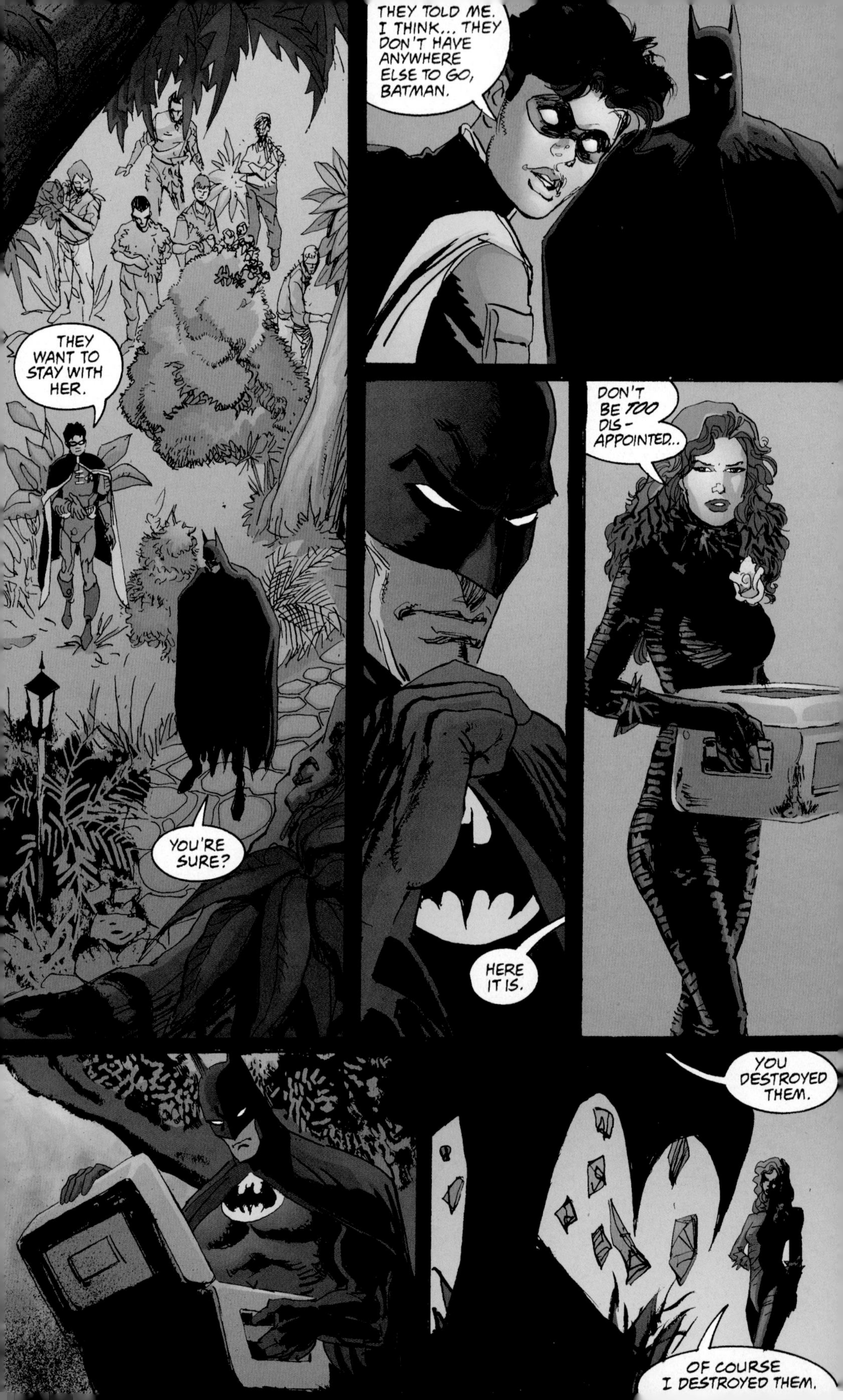
THEY WANT TO STAY WITH HER.
YOU'RE SURE?
THEY TOLD ME. I THINK... THEY DON'T HAVE ANYWHERE ELSE TO GO, BATMAN.
HERE IT IS.
DON'T BE TOO DIS-APPOINTED...
YOU DESTROYED THEM.
OF COURSE I DESTROYED THEM.

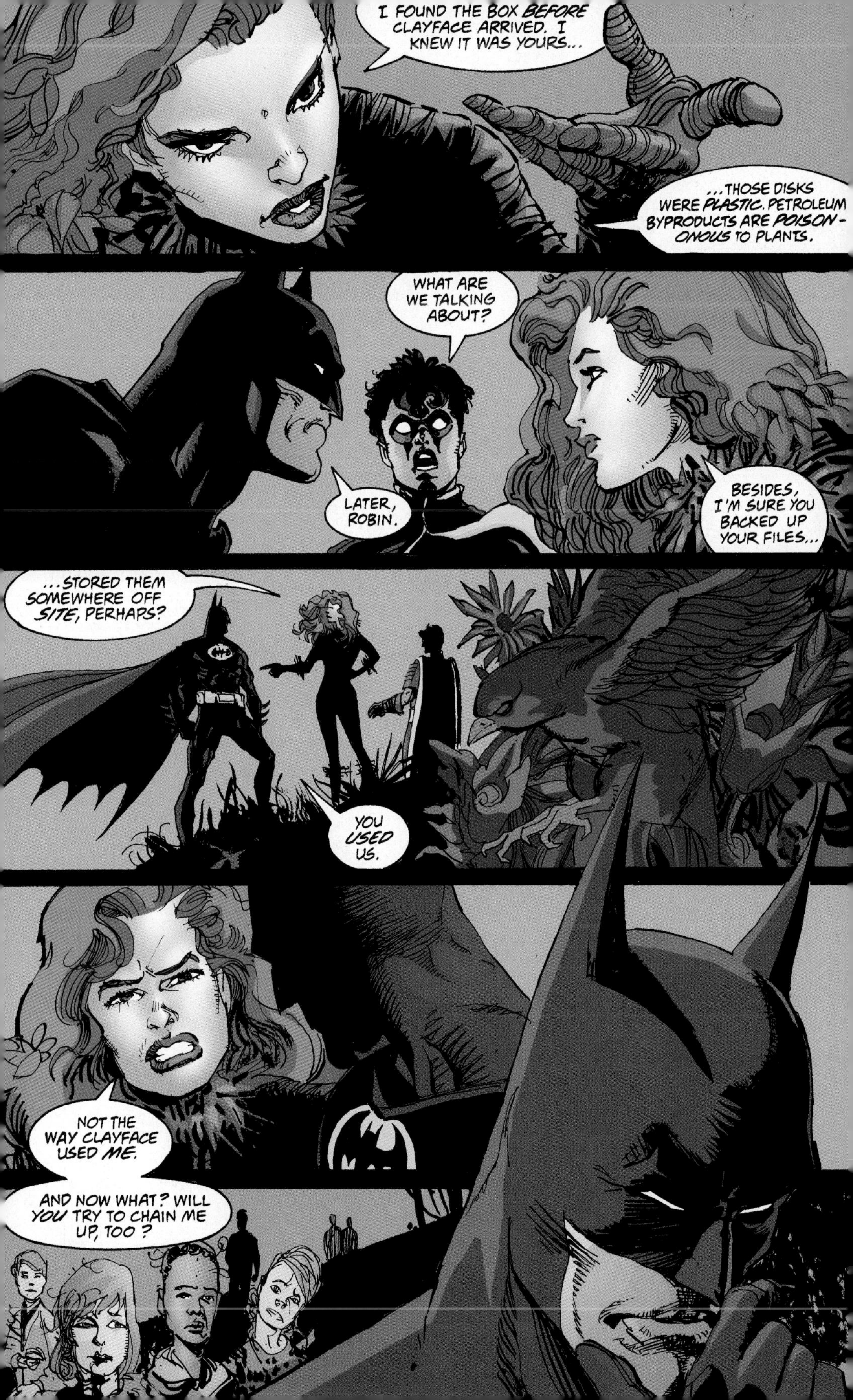
I FOUND THE BOX BEFORE CLAYFACE ARRIVED. I KNEW IT WAS YOURS...
...THOSE DISKS WERE PLASTIC. PETROLEUM BYPRODUCTS ARE POISON-ONOUS TO PLANTS.
WHAT ARE WE TALKING ABOUT?
LATER, ROBIN.
BESIDES, I'M SURE YOU BACKED UP YOUR FILES...
...STORED THEM SOMEWHERE OFF SITE, PERHAPS?
YOU USED US.
NOT THE WAY CLAYFACE USED ME.
AND NOW WHAT? WILL YOU TRY TO CHAIN ME UP, TOO?

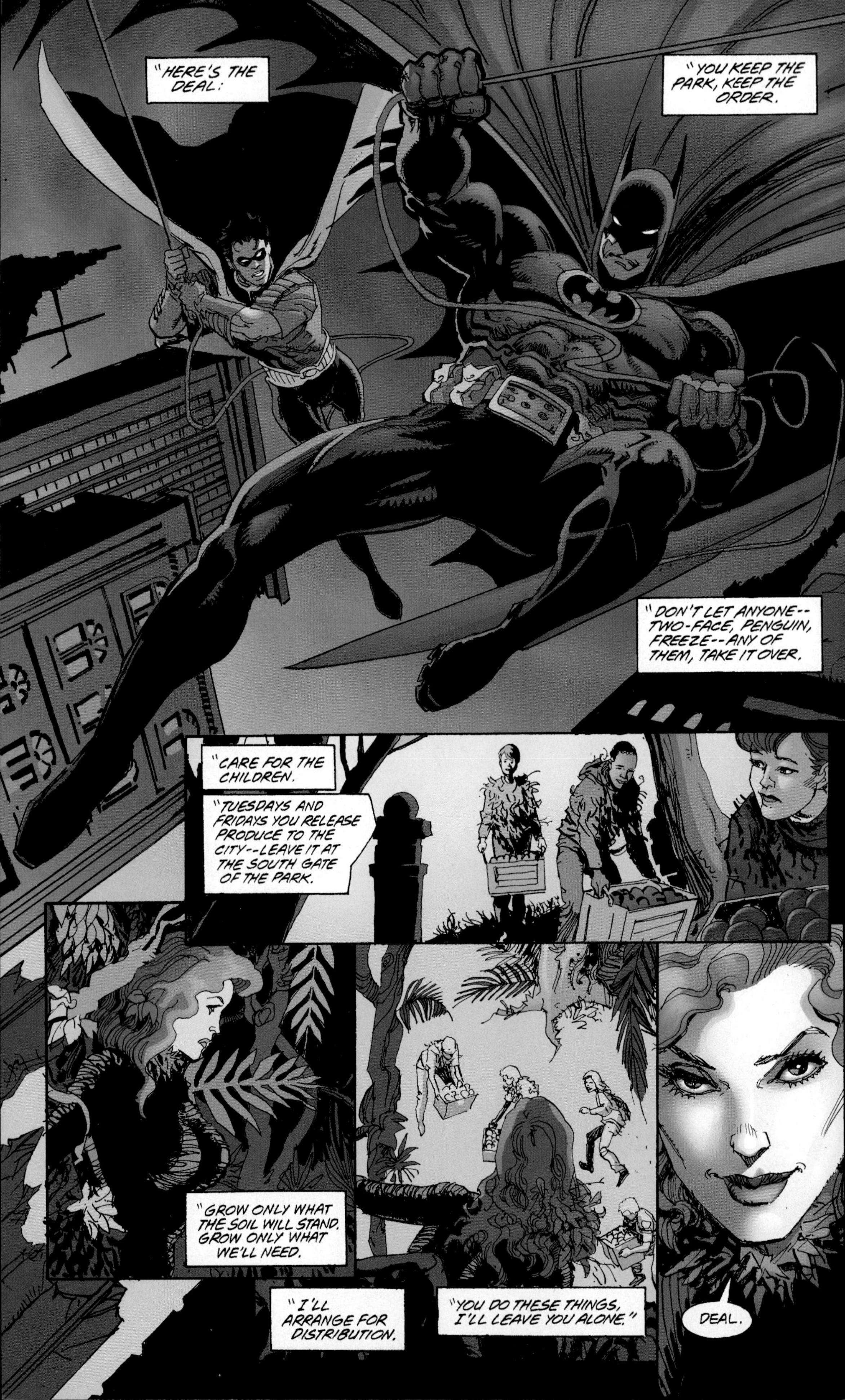
"HERE'S THE DEAL:
"YOU KEEP THE PARK, KEEP THE ORDER.
"DON'T LET ANYONE-- TWO-FACE, PENGUIN, FREEZE--ANY OF THEM, TAKE IT OVER.
"CARE FOR THE CHILDREN.
"TUESDAYS AND FRIDAYS YOU RELEASE PRODUCE TO THE CITY--LEAVE IT AT THE SOUTH GATE OF THE PARK.
"GROW ONLY WHAT THE SOIL WILL STAND. GROW ONLY WHAT WE'LL NEED.
"I'LL ARRANGE FOR DISTRIBUTION.
"YOU DO THESE THINGS, I'LL LEAVE YOU ALONE."
DEAL.

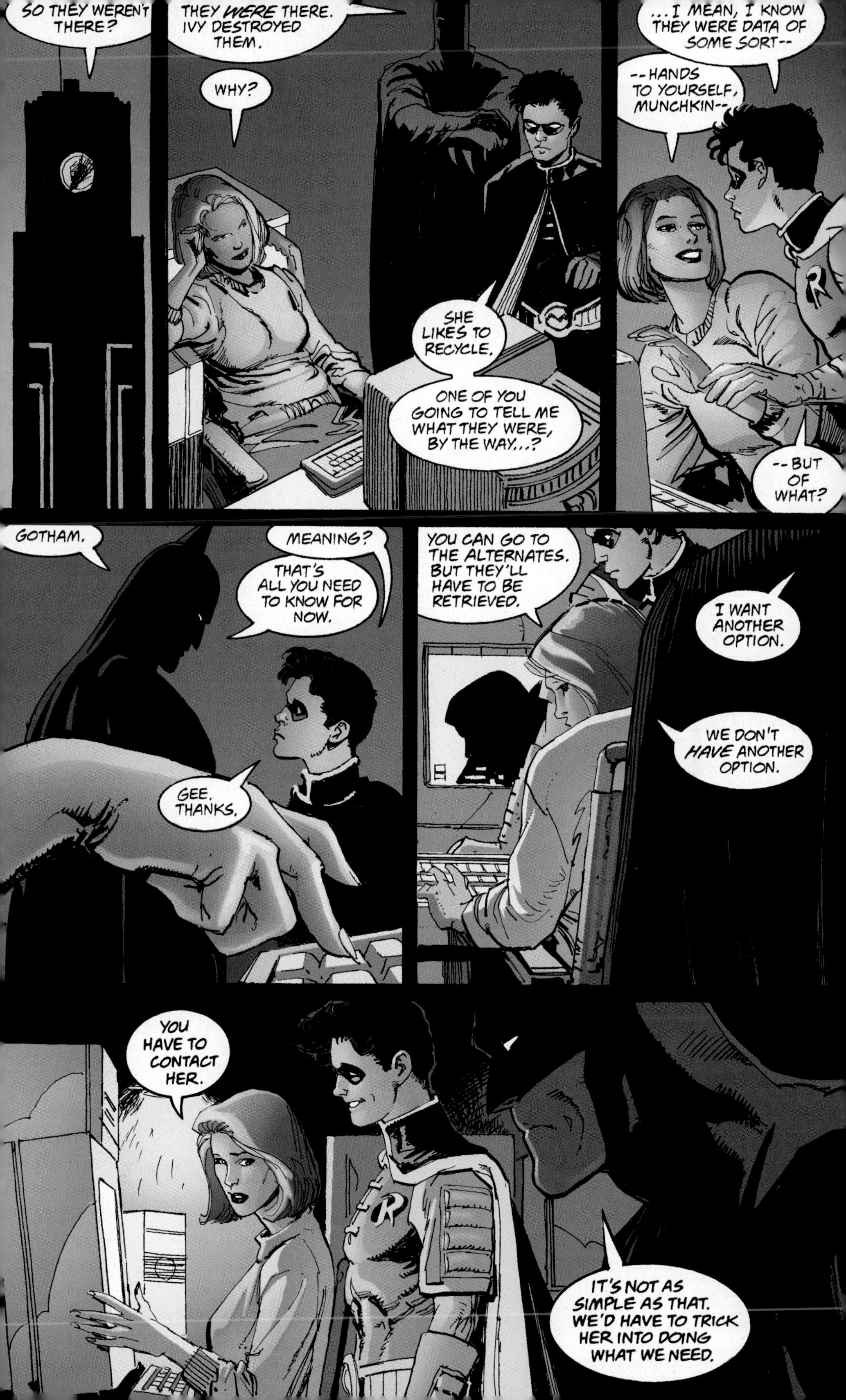
SO THEY WEREN'T THERE?
THEY WERE THERE. IVY DESTROYED THEM.
WHY?
SHE LIKES TO RECYCLE.
ONE OF YOU GOING TO TELL ME WHAT THEY WERE, BY THE WAY...?
...I MEAN, I KNOW THEY WERE DATA OF SOME SORT--
--HANDS TO YOURSELF, MUNCHKIN--
--BUT OF WHAT?
GOTHAM.
MEANING?
THAT'S ALL YOU NEED TO KNOW FOR NOW.
GEE. THANKS.
YOU CAN GO TO THE ALTERNATES. BUT THEY'LL HAVE TO BE RETRIEVED.
I WANT ANOTHER OPTION.
WE DON'T HAVE ANOTHER OPTION.
YOU HAVE TO CONTACT HER.
IT'S NOT AS SIMPLE AS THAT. WE'D HAVE TO TRICK HER INTO DOING WHAT WE NEED.

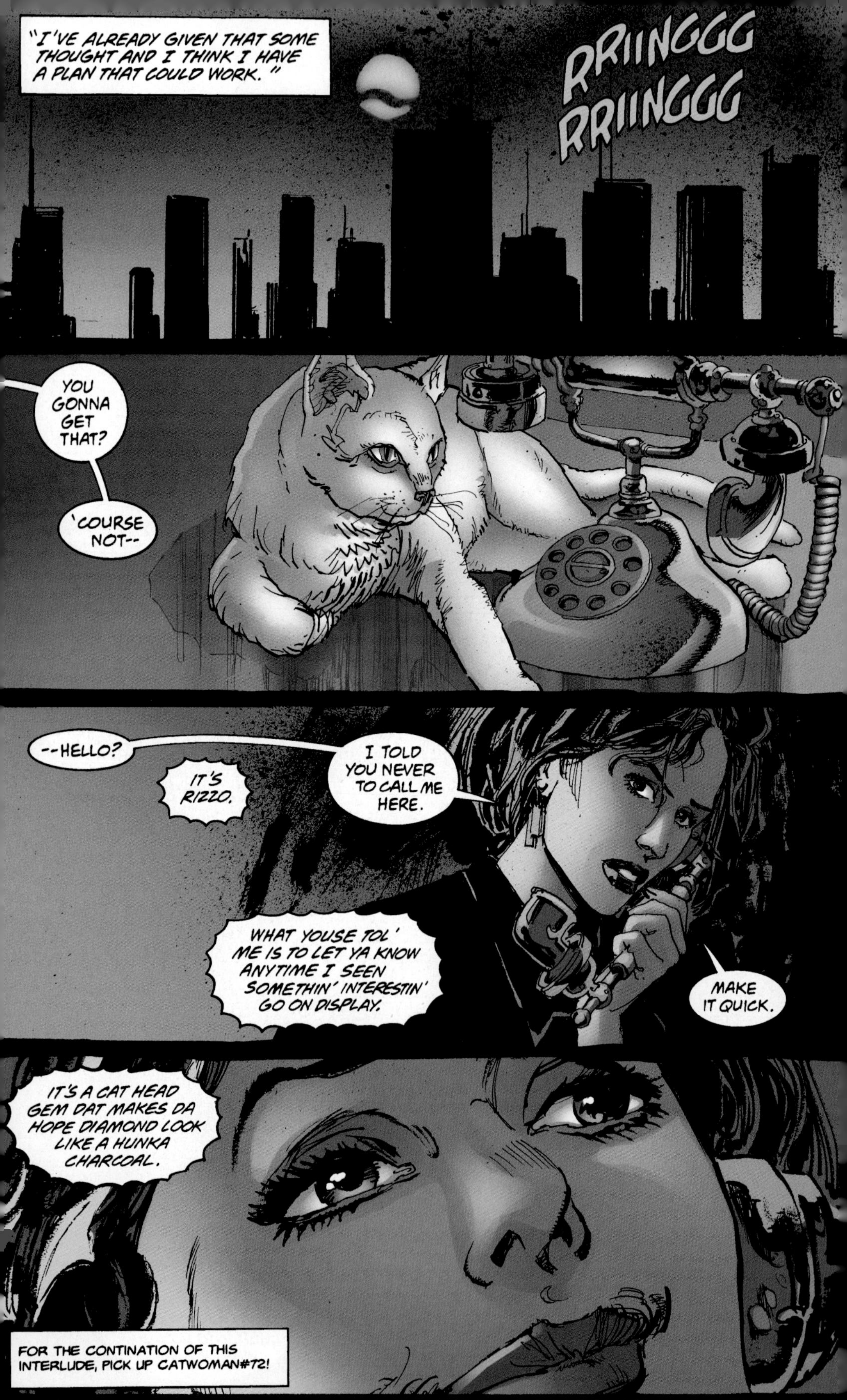
"I'VE ALREADY GIVEN THAT SOME THOUGHT AND I THINK I HAVE A PLAN THAT COULD WORK."
RRIINGGG RRIINGGG
YOU GONNA GET THAT?
'COURSE NOT--
--HELLO?
IT'S RIZZO.
I TOLD YOU NEVER TO CALL ME HERE.
WHAT YOUSE TOL' ME IS TO LET YA KNOW ANYTIME I SEEN SOMETHIN' INTERESTIN' GO ON DISPLAY.
MAKE IT QUICK.
IT'S A CAT HEAD GEM DAT MAKES DA HOPE DIAMOND LOOK LIKE A HUNKA CHARCOAL.
FOR THE CONTINATION OF THIS INTERLUDE, PICK UP CATWOMAN#72!

" NO MAN'S LAND" CONTINUES IN LEGENDS OF THE DARK KNIGHT#121

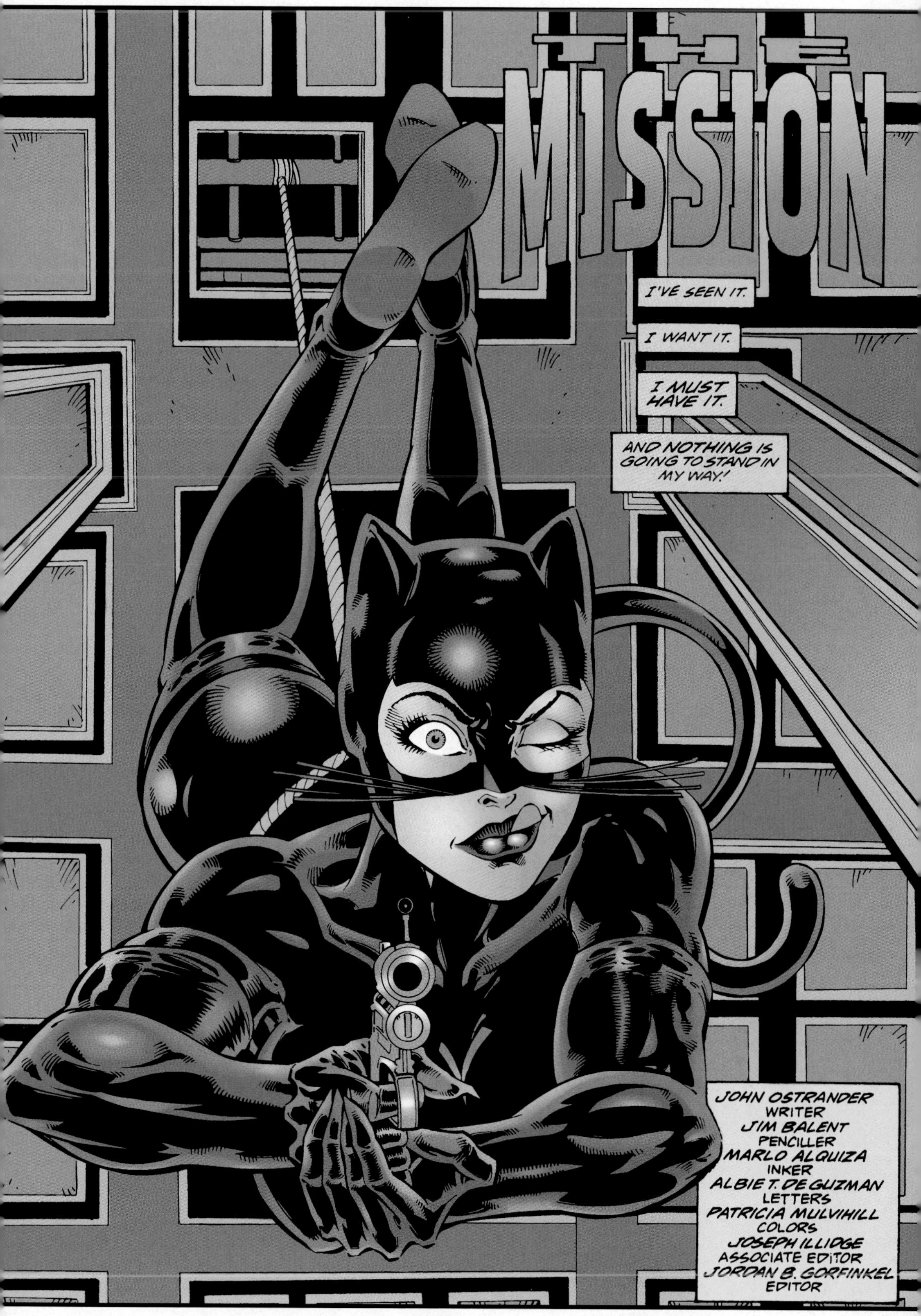

THE MISSION
I'VE SEEN IT.
I WANT IT.
I MUST HAVE IT.
AND NOTHING IS GOING TO STAND IN MY WAY!
JOHN OSTRANDER WRITER
JIM BALENT PENCILLER
MARLO ALQUIZA INKER
ALBIE T. DE GUZMAN LETTERS
PATRICIA MULVIHILL COLORS
JOSEPH ILLIDGE ASSOCIATE EDITOR
JORDAN B. GORFINKEL EDITOR

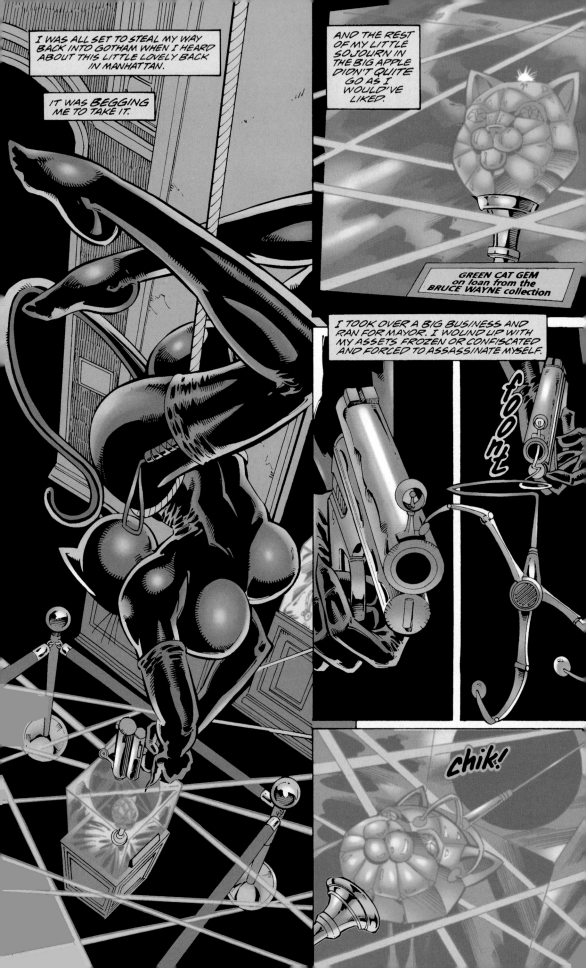

I WAS ALL SET TO STEAL MY WAY BACK INTO GOTHAM WHEN I HEARD ABOUT THIS LITTLE LOVELY BACK IN MANHATTAN.

IT WAS *BEGGING* ME TO TAKE IT.

AND THE REST OF MY LITTLE SOJOURN IN THE BIG APPLE DIDN'T QUITE GO AS I WOULD'VE LIKED.

GREEN CAT GEM
on loan from the
BRUCE WAYNE collection

I TOOK OVER A BIG BUSINESS AND RAN FOR MAYOR. I WOUND UP WITH MY ASSETS FROZEN OR CONFISCATED AND FORCED TO ASSASSINATE MYSELF.

foomf!

chik!

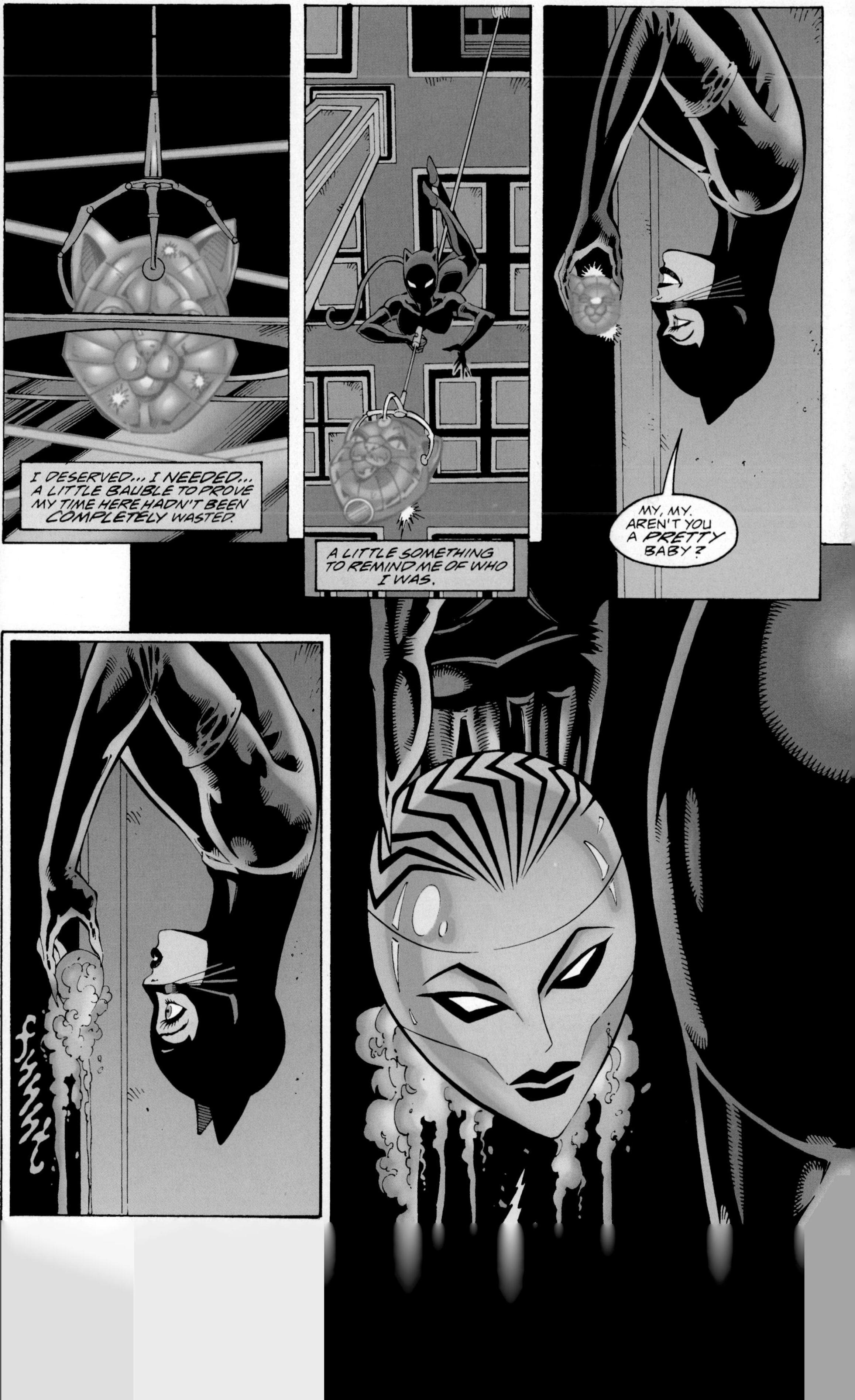
I DESERVED... I NEEDED... A LITTLE BAUBLE TO PROVE MY TIME HERE HADN'T BEEN COMPLETELY WASTED.
A LITTLE SOMETHING TO REMIND ME OF WHO I WAS.
MY, MY. AREN'T YOU A PRETTY BABY?
FSSSHT

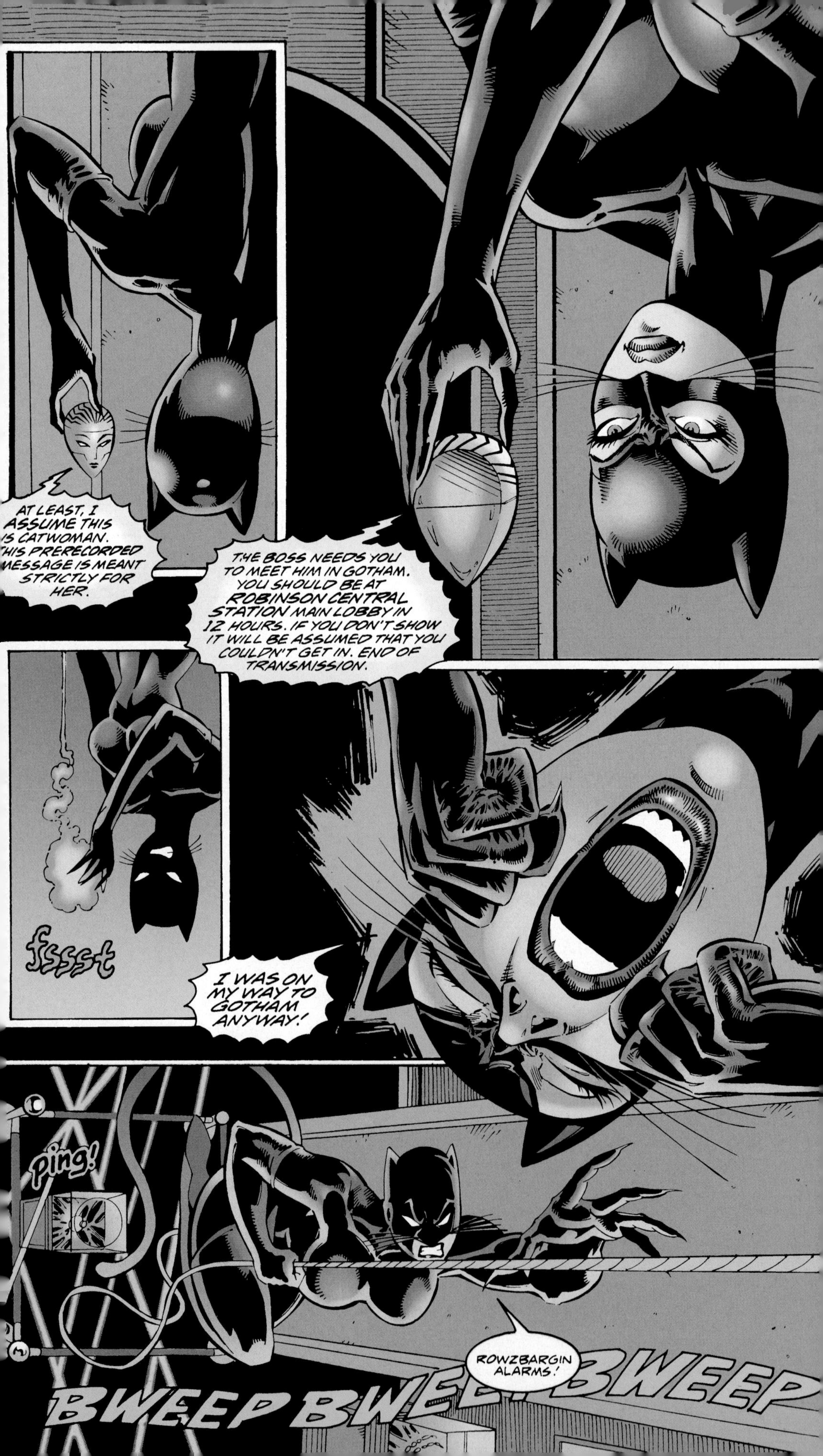
AT LEAST, I ASSUME THIS IS CATWOMAN. THIS PRERECORDED MESSAGE IS MEANT STRICTLY FOR HER.
THE BOSS NEEDS YOU TO MEET HIM IN GOTHAM. YOU SHOULD BE AT ROBINSON CENTRAL STATION MAIN LOBBY IN 12 HOURS. IF YOU DON'T SHOW IT WILL BE ASSUMED THAT YOU COULDN'T GET IN. END OF TRANSMISSION.
fssst
I WAS ON MY WAY TO GOTHAM ANYWAY!
ping!
ROWZBARGIN ALARMS!
BWEEP BWEEP BWEEP

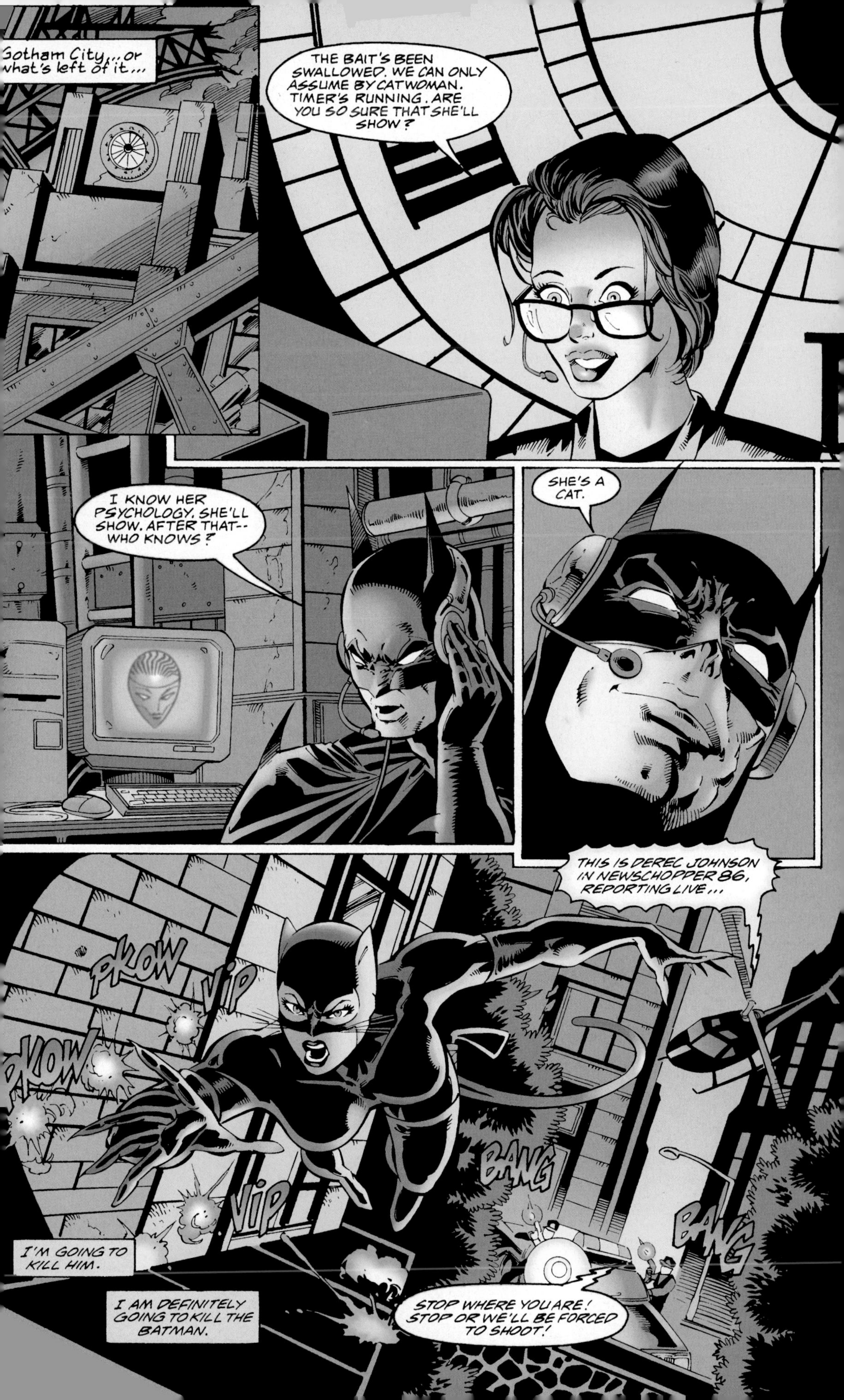

Gotham City... or what's left of it...
THE BAIT'S BEEN SWALLOWED. WE CAN ONLY ASSUME BY CATWOMAN. TIMER'S RUNNING. ARE YOU SO SURE THAT SHE'LL SHOW?
I KNOW HER PSYCHOLOGY. SHE'LL SHOW. AFTER THAT-- WHO KNOWS?
SHE'S A CAT.
THIS IS DEREC JOHNSON IN NEWSCHOPPER 86, REPORTING LIVE...
PKOW
VIP
KOW
BANG
VIP
BANG
I'M GOING TO KILL HIM.
I AM DEFINITELY GOING TO KILL THE BATMAN.
STOP WHERE YOU ARE! STOP OR WE'LL BE FORCED TO SHOOT!

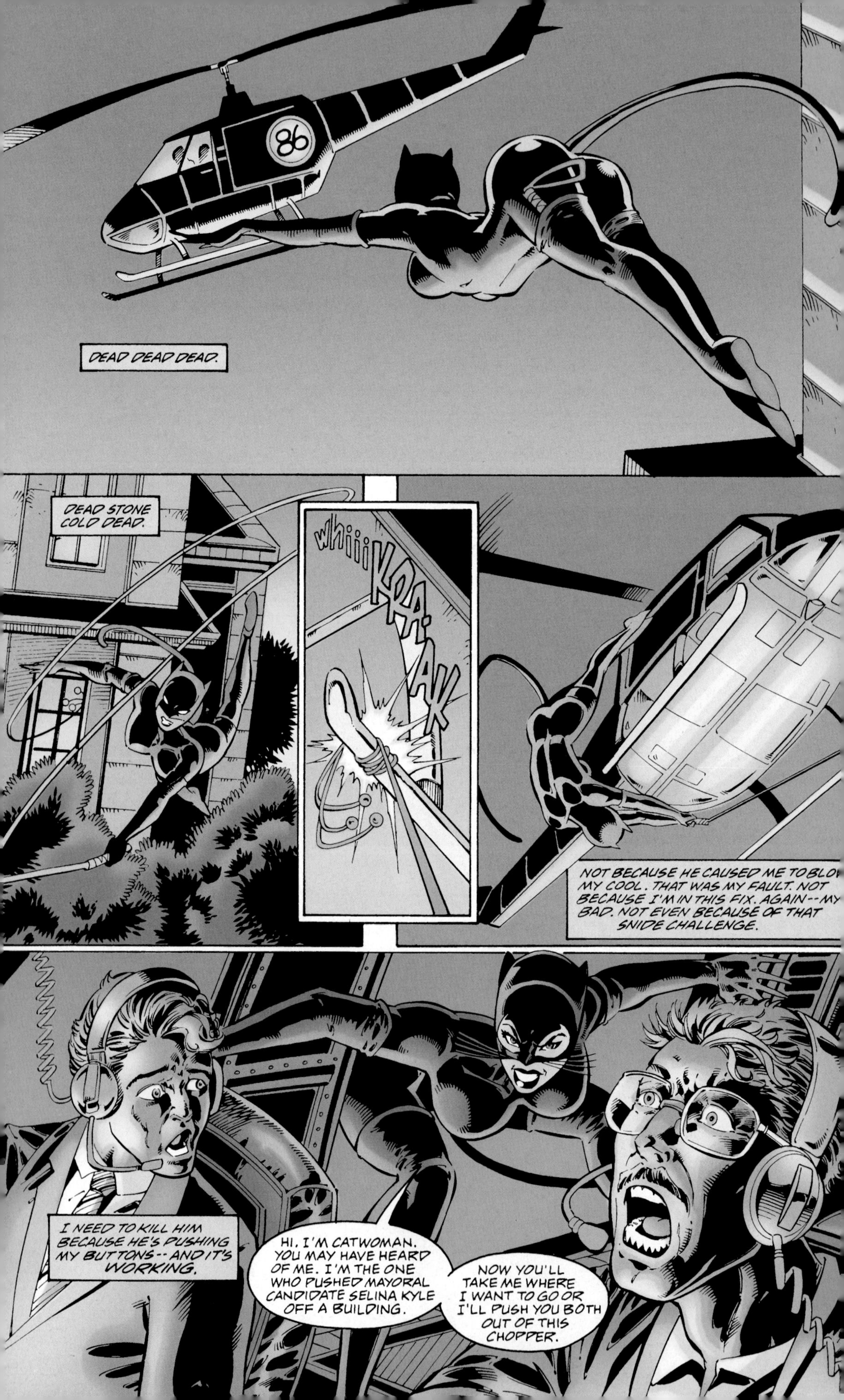
DEAD DEAD DEAD.
DEAD STONE COLD DEAD.
whiiiKRA-AK
NOT BECAUSE HE CAUSED ME TO BLOW MY COOL. THAT WAS MY FAULT. NOT BECAUSE I'M IN THIS FIX. AGAIN--MY BAD. NOT EVEN BECAUSE OF THAT SNIDE CHALLENGE.
I NEED TO KILL HIM BECAUSE HE'S PUSHING MY BUTTONS--AND IT'S WORKING.
HI. I'M CATWOMAN. YOU MAY HAVE HEARD OF ME. I'M THE ONE WHO PUSHED MAYORAL CANDIDATE SELINA KYLE OFF A BUILDING.
NOW YOU'LL TAKE ME WHERE I WANT TO GO OR I'LL PUSH YOU BOTH OUT OF THIS CHOPPER.

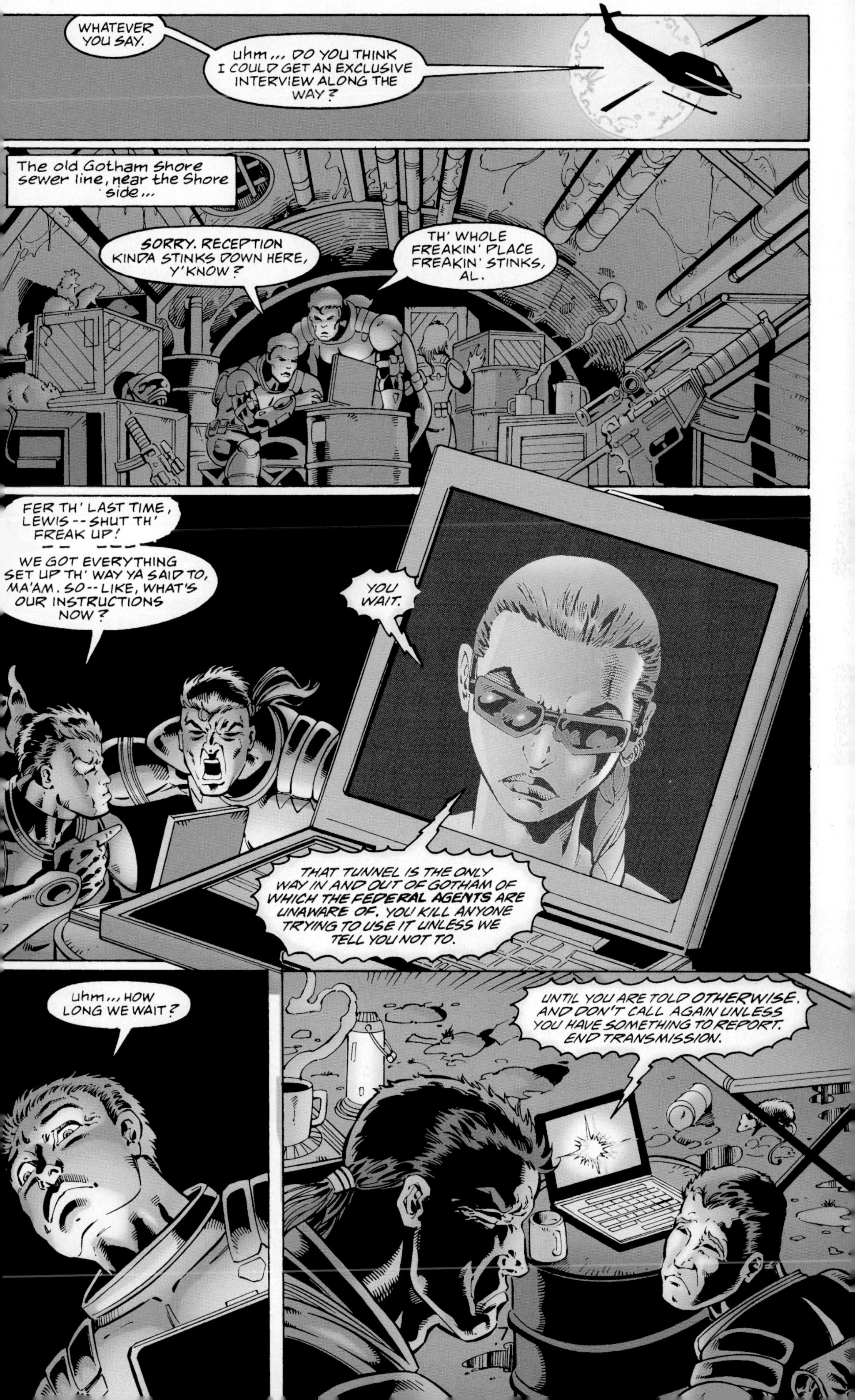
WHATEVER YOU SAY.
uhm... DO YOU THINK I COULD GET AN EXCLUSIVE INTERVIEW ALONG THE WAY?
The old Gotham Shore sewer line, near the Shore side...
SORRY. RECEPTION KINDA STINKS DOWN HERE, Y'KNOW?
TH' WHOLE FREAKIN' PLACE FREAKIN' STINKS, AL.
FER TH' LAST TIME, LEWIS--SHUT TH' FREAK UP!
WE GOT EVERYTHING SET UP TH' WAY YA SAID TO, MA'AM. SO--LIKE, WHAT'S OUR INSTRUCTIONS NOW?
YOU WAIT.
THAT TUNNEL IS THE ONLY WAY IN AND OUT OF GOTHAM OF WHICH THE FEDERAL AGENTS ARE UNAWARE OF. YOU KILL ANYONE TRYING TO USE IT UNLESS WE TELL YOU NOT TO.
uhm... HOW LONG WE WAIT?
UNTIL YOU ARE TOLD OTHERWISE. AND DON'T CALL AGAIN UNLESS YOU HAVE SOMETHING TO REPORT. END TRANSMISSION.

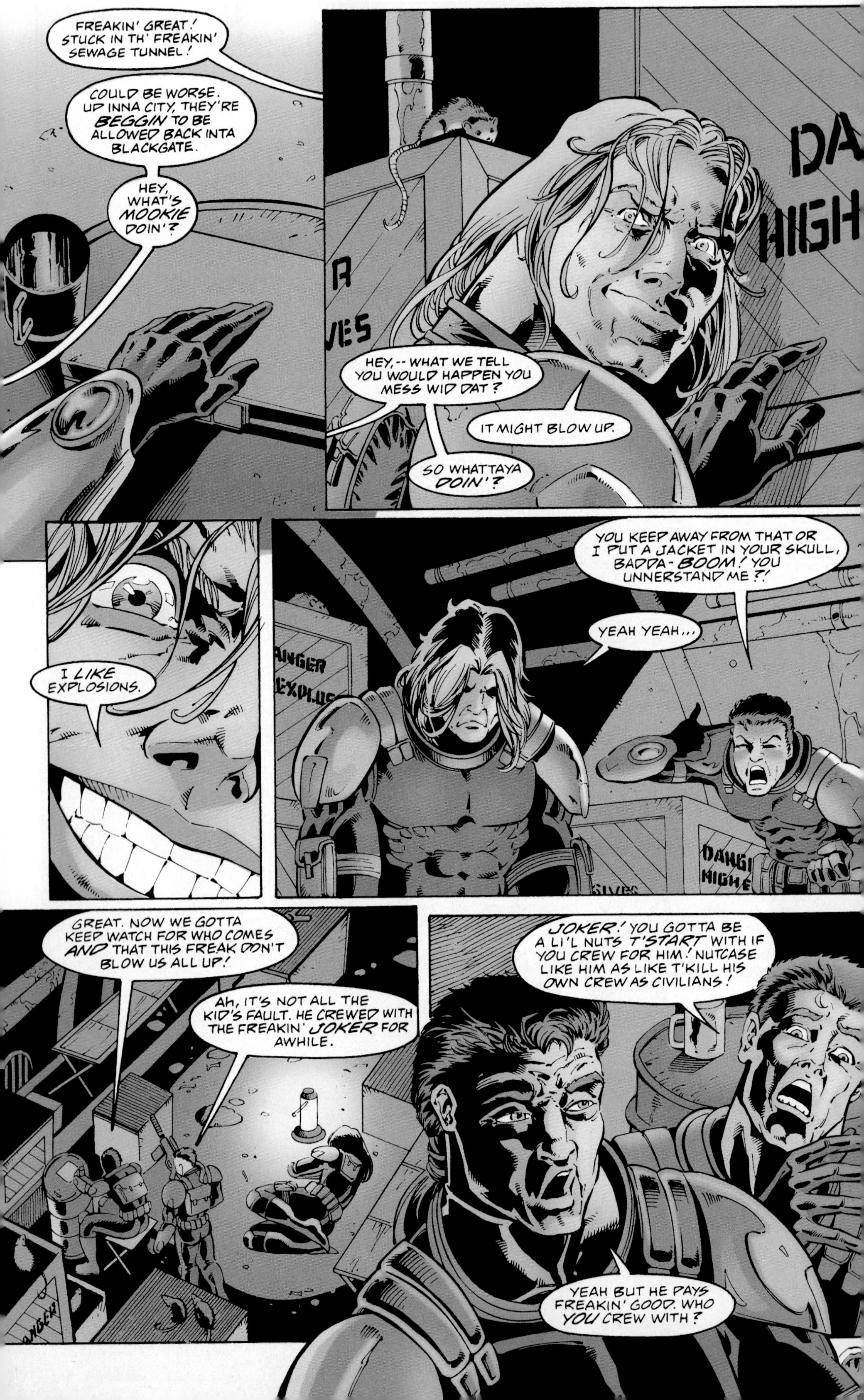
FREAKIN' GREAT! STUCK IN TH' FREAKIN' SEWAGE TUNNEL!
COULD BE WORSE. UP INNA CITY, THEY'RE BEGGIN TO BE ALLOWED BACK INTA BLACKGATE.
HEY, WHAT'S MOOKIE DOIN'?
DA
HIGH
R
VES
HEY,-- WHAT WE TELL YOU WOULD HAPPEN YOU MESS WID DAT?
IT MIGHT BLOW UP.
SO WHATTAYA DOIN'?
I LIKE EXPLOSIONS.
YOU KEEP AWAY FROM THAT OR I PUT A JACKET IN YOUR SKULL, BADDA-BOOM! YOU UNNERSTAND ME?!
YEAH YEAH...
ANGER
EXPLOS
DANG
HIGH E
SIVES
GREAT. NOW WE GOTTA KEEP WATCH FOR WHO COMES AND THAT THIS FREAK DON'T BLOW US ALL UP!
Ah, IT'S NOT ALL THE KID'S FAULT. HE CREWED WITH THE FREAKIN' JOKER FOR AWHILE.
JOKER! YOU GOTTA BE A LI'L NUTS T'START WITH IF YOU CREW FOR HIM! NUTCASE LIKE HIM AS LIKE T'KILL HIS OWN CREW AS CIVILIANS!
YEAH BUT HE PAYS FREAKIN' GOOD. WHO YOU CREW WITH?
ANGER

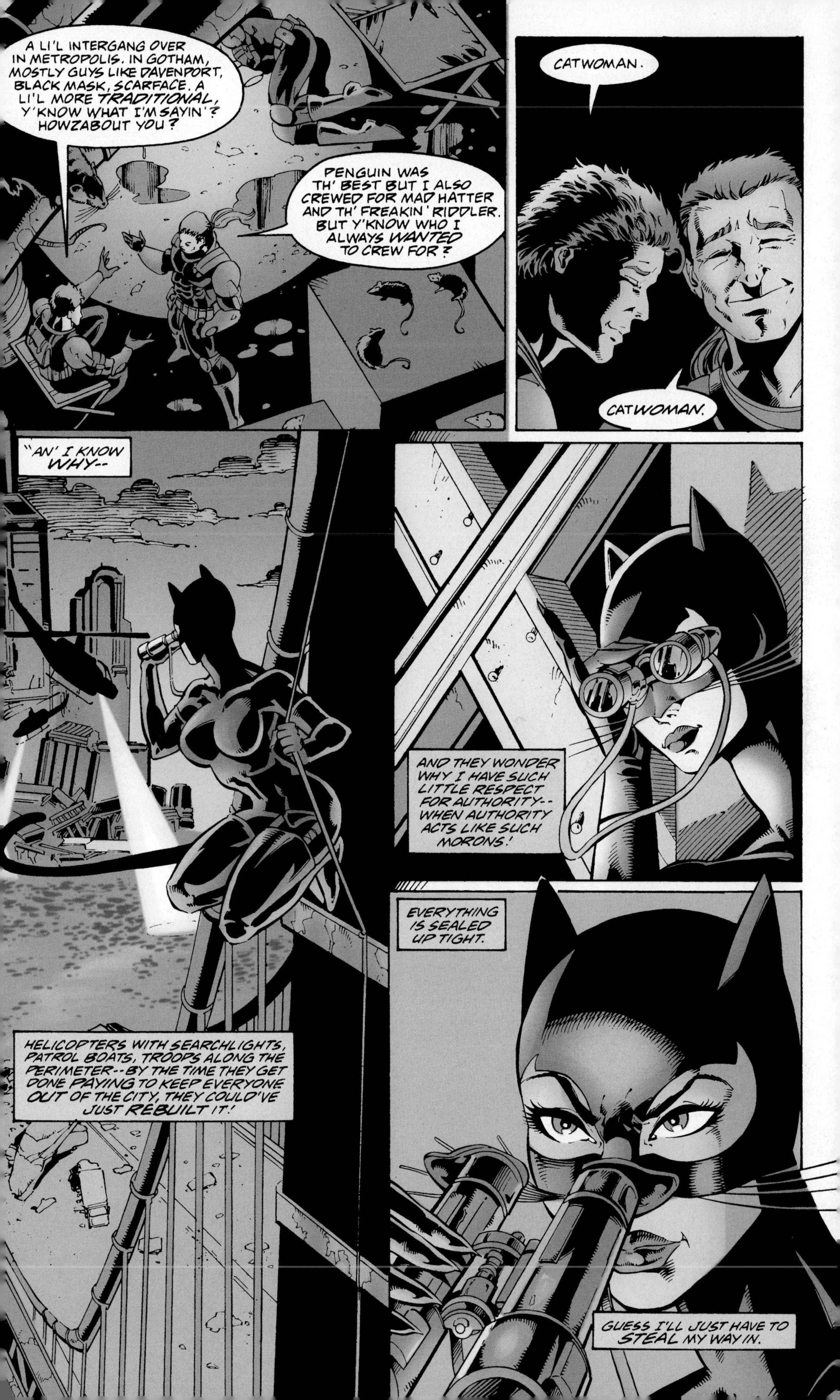
A LI'L INTERGANG OVER IN METROPOLIS. IN GOTHAM, MOSTLY GUYS LIKE DAVENPORT, BLACK MASK, SCARFACE. A LI'L MORE TRADITIONAL, Y'KNOW WHAT I'M SAYIN'? HOWZABOUT YOU?
PENGUIN WAS TH' BEST BUT I ALSO CREWED FOR MAD HATTER AND TH' FREAKIN' RIDDLER. BUT Y'KNOW WHO I ALWAYS WANTED TO CREW FOR?
CATWOMAN.
CATWOMAN.
"AN' I KNOW WHY--
HELICOPTERS WITH SEARCHLIGHTS, PATROL BOATS, TROOPS ALONG THE PERIMETER--BY THE TIME THEY GET DONE PAYING TO KEEP EVERYONE OUT OF THE CITY, THEY COULD'VE JUST REBUILT IT!
AND THEY WONDER WHY I HAVE SUCH LITTLE RESPECT FOR AUTHORITY--WHEN AUTHORITY ACTS LIKE SUCH MORONS!
EVERYTHING IS SEALED UP TIGHT.
GUESS I'LL JUST HAVE TO STEAL MY WAY IN.

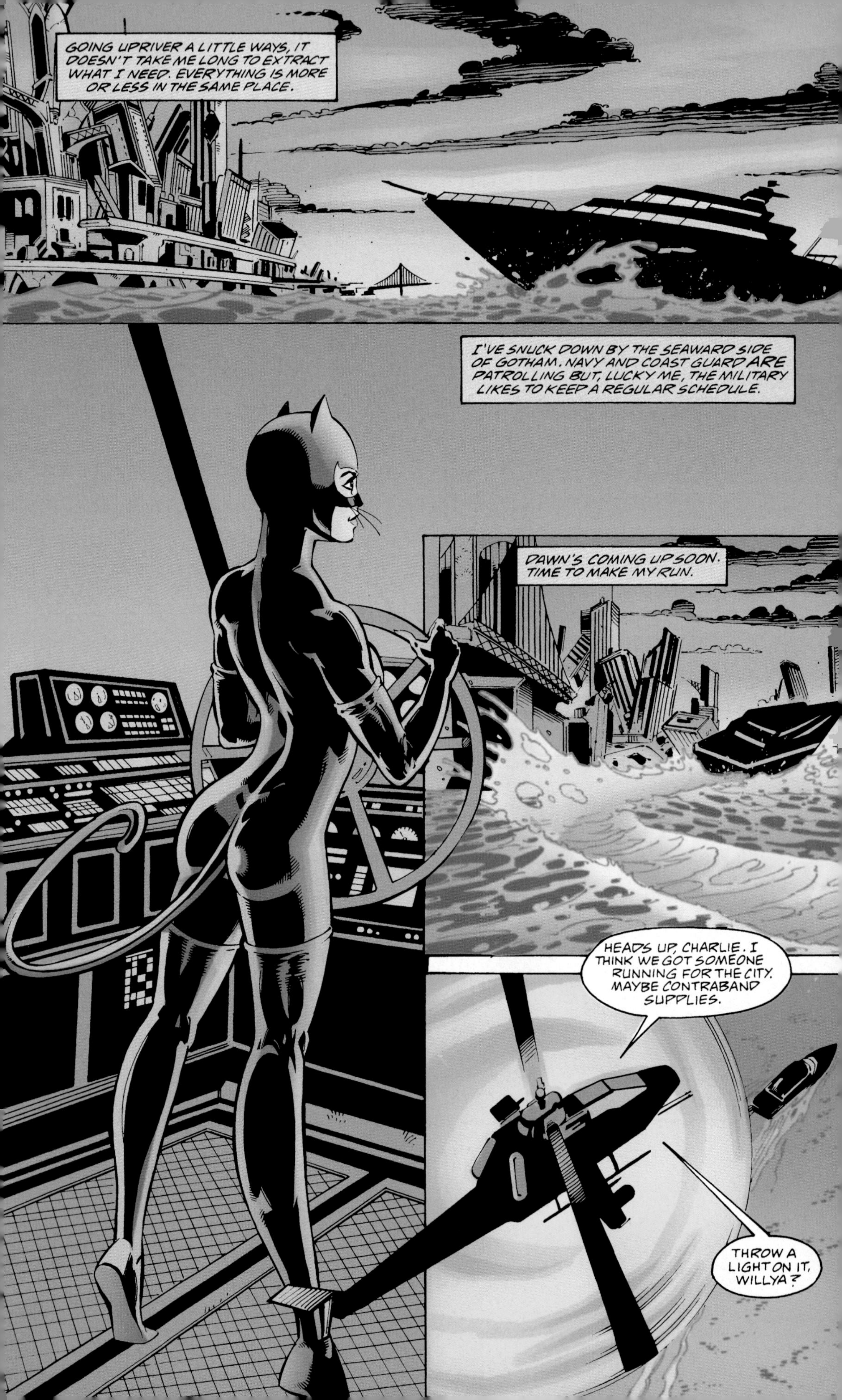
GOING UPRIVER A LITTLE WAYS, IT DOESN'T TAKE ME LONG TO EXTRACT WHAT I NEED. EVERYTHING IS MORE OR LESS IN THE SAME PLACE.
I'VE SNUCK DOWN BY THE SEAWARD SIDE OF GOTHAM. NAVY AND COAST GUARD ARE PATROLLING BUT, LUCKY ME, THE MILITARY LIKES TO KEEP A REGULAR SCHEDULE.
DAWN'S COMING UP SOON. TIME TO MAKE MY RUN.
HEADS UP, CHARLIE. I THINK WE GOT SOMEONE RUNNING FOR THE CITY. MAYBE CONTRABAND SUPPLIES.
THROW A LIGHT ON IT, WILLYA?

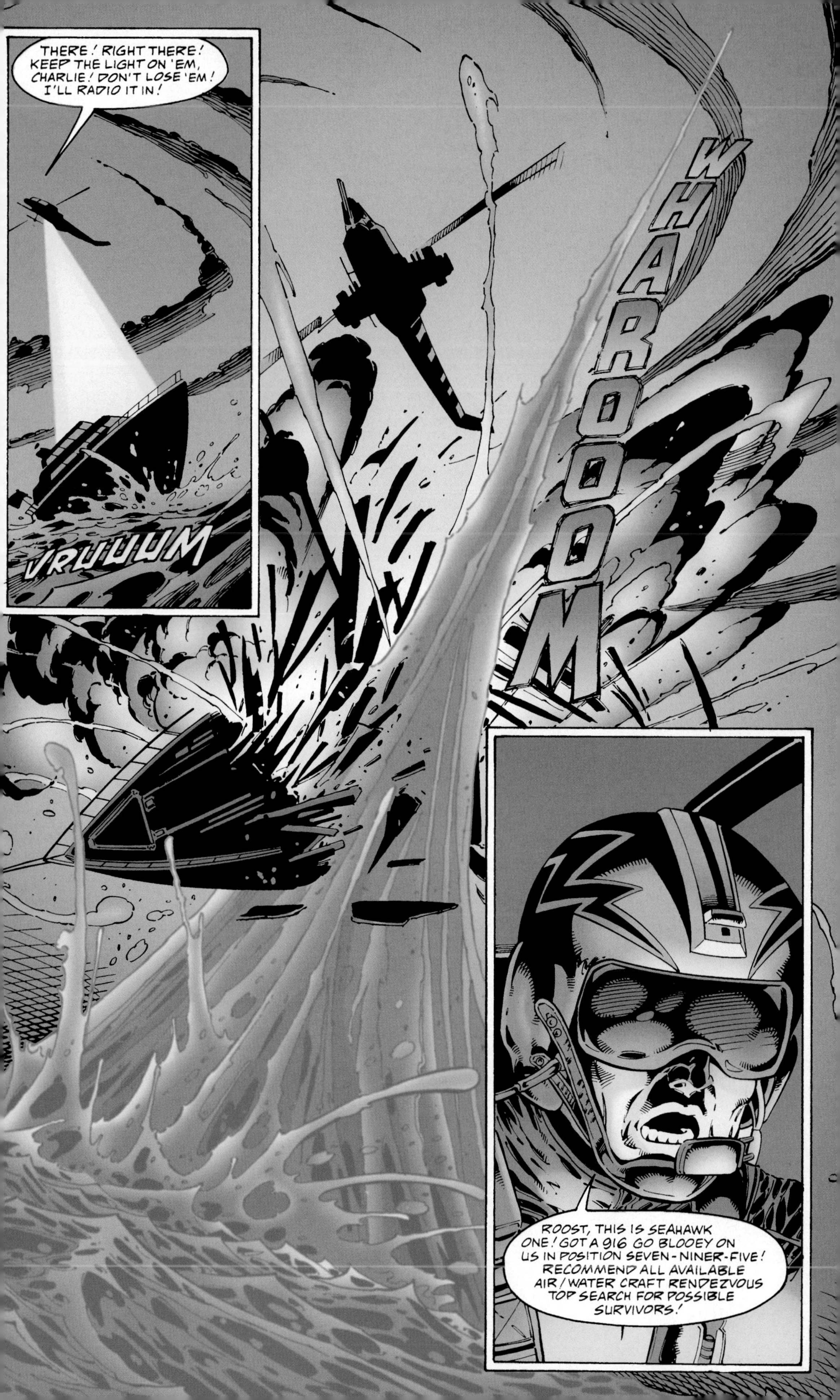
THERE! RIGHT THERE! KEEP THE LIGHT ON 'EM, CHARLIE! DON'T LOSE 'EM! I'LL RADIO IT IN!
VRUUUM
WHAROOOOM
ROOST, THIS IS SEAHAWK ONE! GOT A 916 GO BLOOEY ON US IN POSITION SEVEN-NINER-FIVE! RECOMMEND ALL AVAILABLE AIR/WATER CRAFT RENDEZVOUS TOP SEARCH FOR POSSIBLE SURVIVORS!

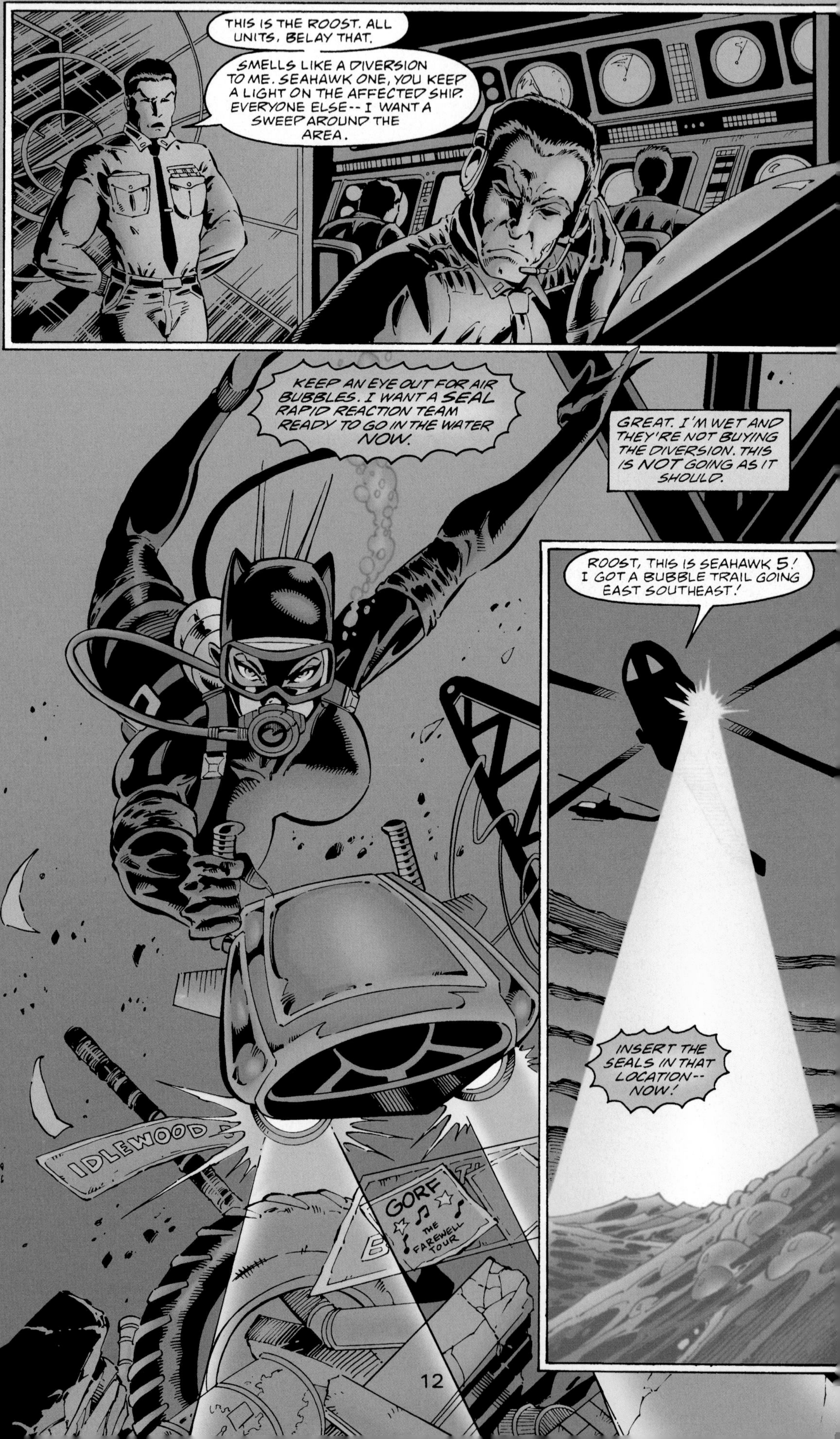

THIS IS THE ROOST. ALL UNITS, BELAY THAT.
SMELLS LIKE A DIVERSION TO ME. SEAHAWK ONE, YOU KEEP A LIGHT ON THE AFFECTED SHIP. EVERYONE ELSE-- I WANT A SWEEP AROUND THE AREA.
KEEP AN EYE OUT FOR AIR BUBBLES. I WANT A SEAL RAPID REACTION TEAM READY TO GO IN THE WATER NOW.
GREAT. I'M WET AND THEY'RE NOT BUYING THE DIVERSION. THIS IS NOT GOING AS IT SHOULD.
ROOST, THIS IS SEAHAWK 5! I GOT A BUBBLE TRAIL GOING EAST SOUTHEAST!
INSERT THE SEALS IN THAT LOCATION-- NOW!
IDLEWOOD
GORF THE FAREWELL TOUR

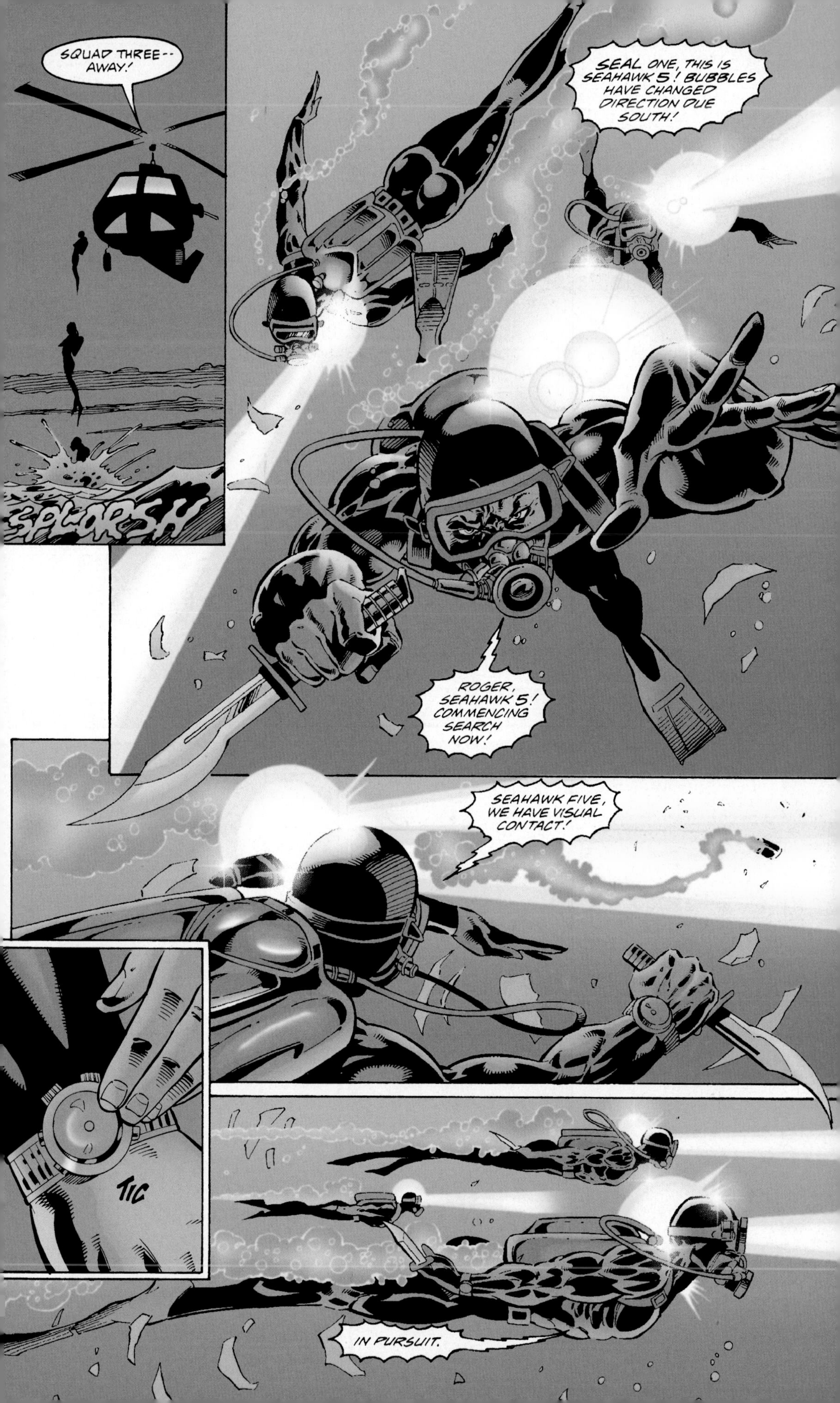
SQUAD THREE-- AWAY!
SPLOOSH
SEAL ONE, THIS IS SEAHAWK 5! BUBBLES HAVE CHANGED DIRECTION DUE SOUTH!
ROGER, SEAHAWK 5! COMMENCING SEARCH NOW!
SEAHAWK FIVE, WE HAVE VISUAL CONTACT!
TIC
IN PURSUIT.

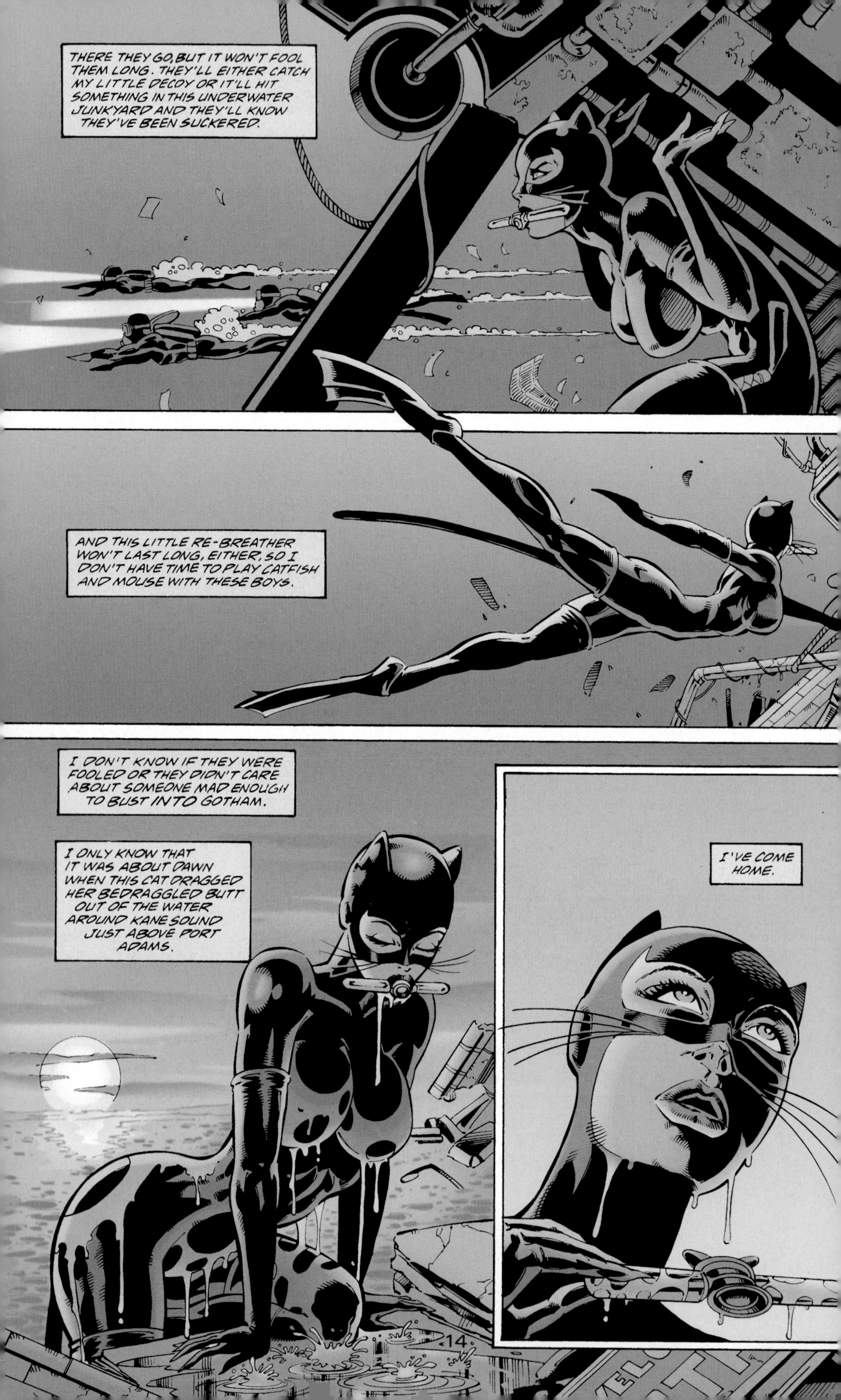
THERE THEY GO, BUT IT WON'T FOOL THEM LONG. THEY'LL EITHER CATCH MY LITTLE DECOY OR IT'LL HIT SOMETHING IN THIS UNDERWATER JUNKYARD AND THEY'LL KNOW THEY'VE BEEN SUCKERED.
AND THIS LITTLE RE-BREATHER WON'T LAST LONG, EITHER, SO I DON'T HAVE TIME TO PLAY CATFISH AND MOUSE WITH THESE BOYS.
I DON'T KNOW IF THEY WERE FOOLED OR THEY DIDN'T CARE ABOUT SOMEONE MAD ENOUGH TO BUST INTO GOTHAM.
I ONLY KNOW THAT IT WAS ABOUT DAWN WHEN THIS CAT DRAGGED HER BEDRAGGLED BUTT OUT OF THE WATER AROUND KANE SOUND JUST ABOVE PORT ADAMS.
I'VE COME HOME.

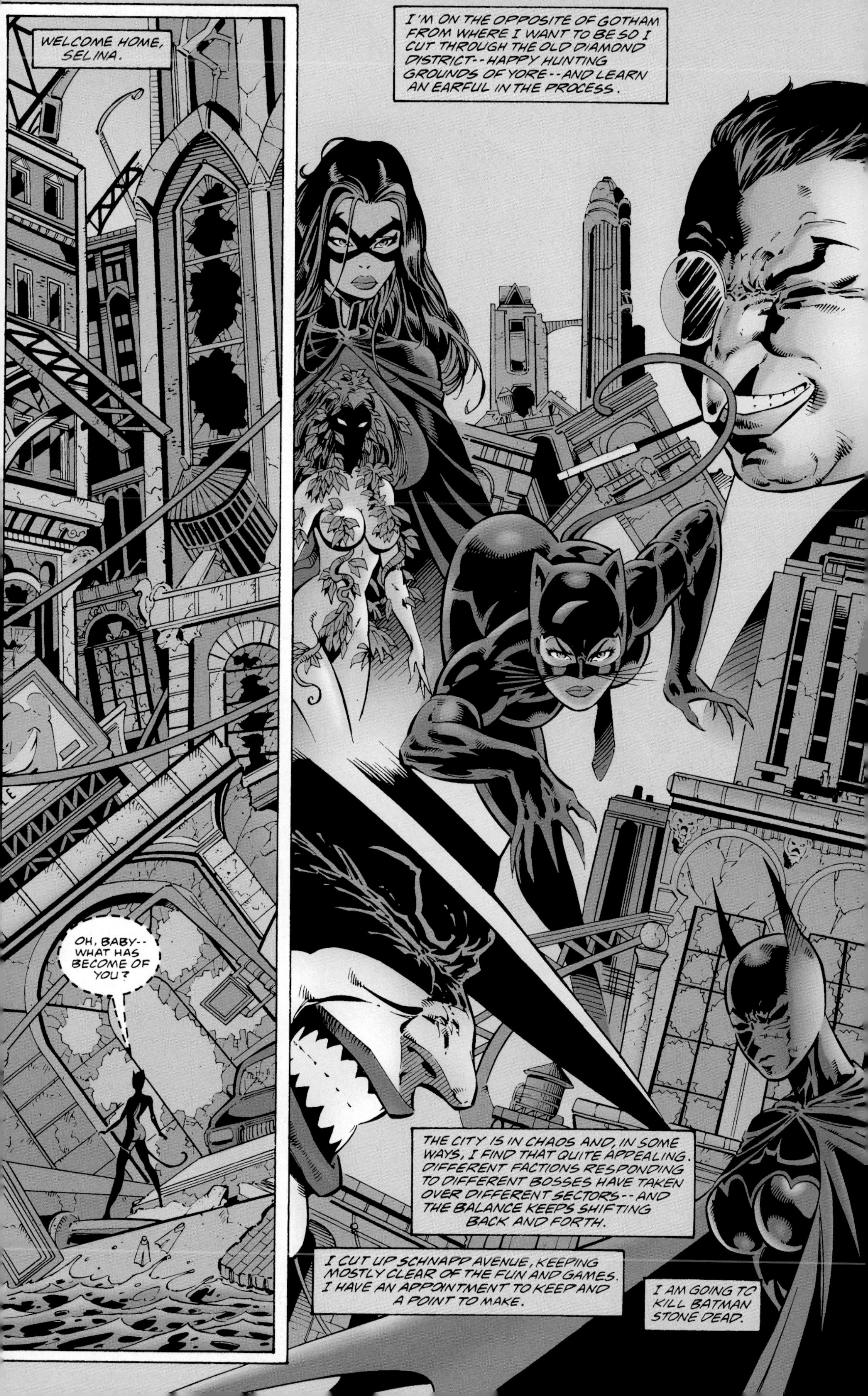
WELCOME HOME, SELINA.
OH, BABY-- WHAT HAS BECOME OF YOU?
I'M ON THE OPPOSITE OF GOTHAM FROM WHERE I WANT TO BE SO I CUT THROUGH THE OLD DIAMOND DISTRICT--HAPPY HUNTING GROUNDS OF YORE--AND LEARN AN EARFUL IN THE PROCESS.
THE CITY IS IN CHAOS AND, IN SOME WAYS, I FIND THAT QUITE APPEALING. DIFFERENT FACTIONS RESPONDING TO DIFFERENT BOSSES HAVE TAKEN OVER DIFFERENT SECTORS--AND THE BALANCE KEEPS SHIFTING BACK AND FORTH.
I CUT UP SCHNAPP AVENUE, KEEPING MOSTLY CLEAR OF THE FUN AND GAMES. I HAVE AN APPOINTMENT TO KEEP AND A POINT TO MAKE.
I AM GOING TO KILL BATMAN STONE DEAD.

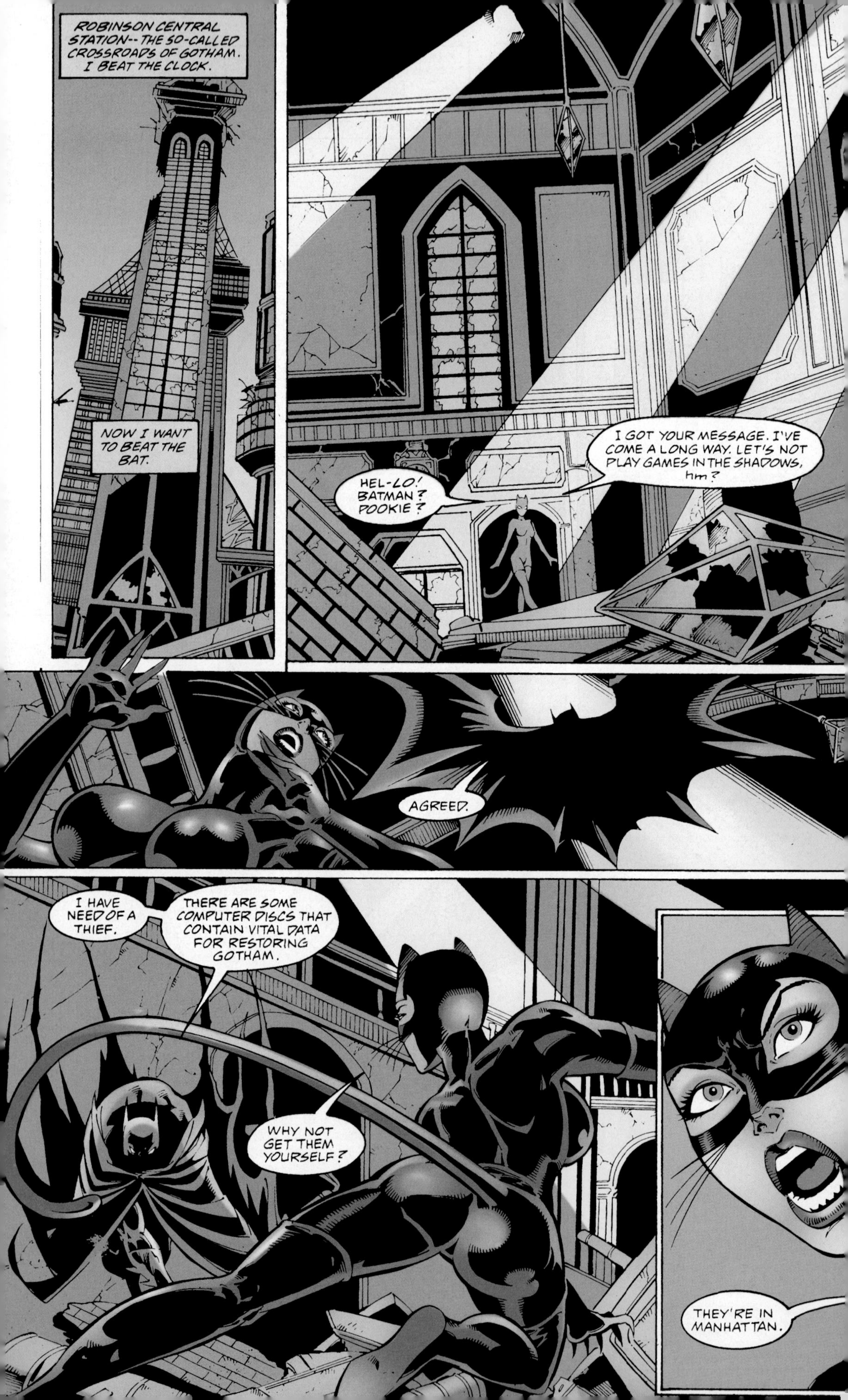
ROBINSON CENTRAL STATION-- THE SO-CALLED CROSSROADS OF GOTHAM. I BEAT THE CLOCK.
NOW I WANT TO BEAT THE BAT.
HEL-LO! BATMAN? POOKIE?
I GOT YOUR MESSAGE. I'VE COME A LONG WAY. LET'S NOT PLAY GAMES IN THE SHADOWS, hm?
AGREED.
I HAVE NEED OF A THIEF.
THERE ARE SOME COMPUTER DISCS THAT CONTAIN VITAL DATA FOR RESTORING GOTHAM.
WHY NOT GET THEM YOURSELF?
THEY'RE IN MANHATTAN.

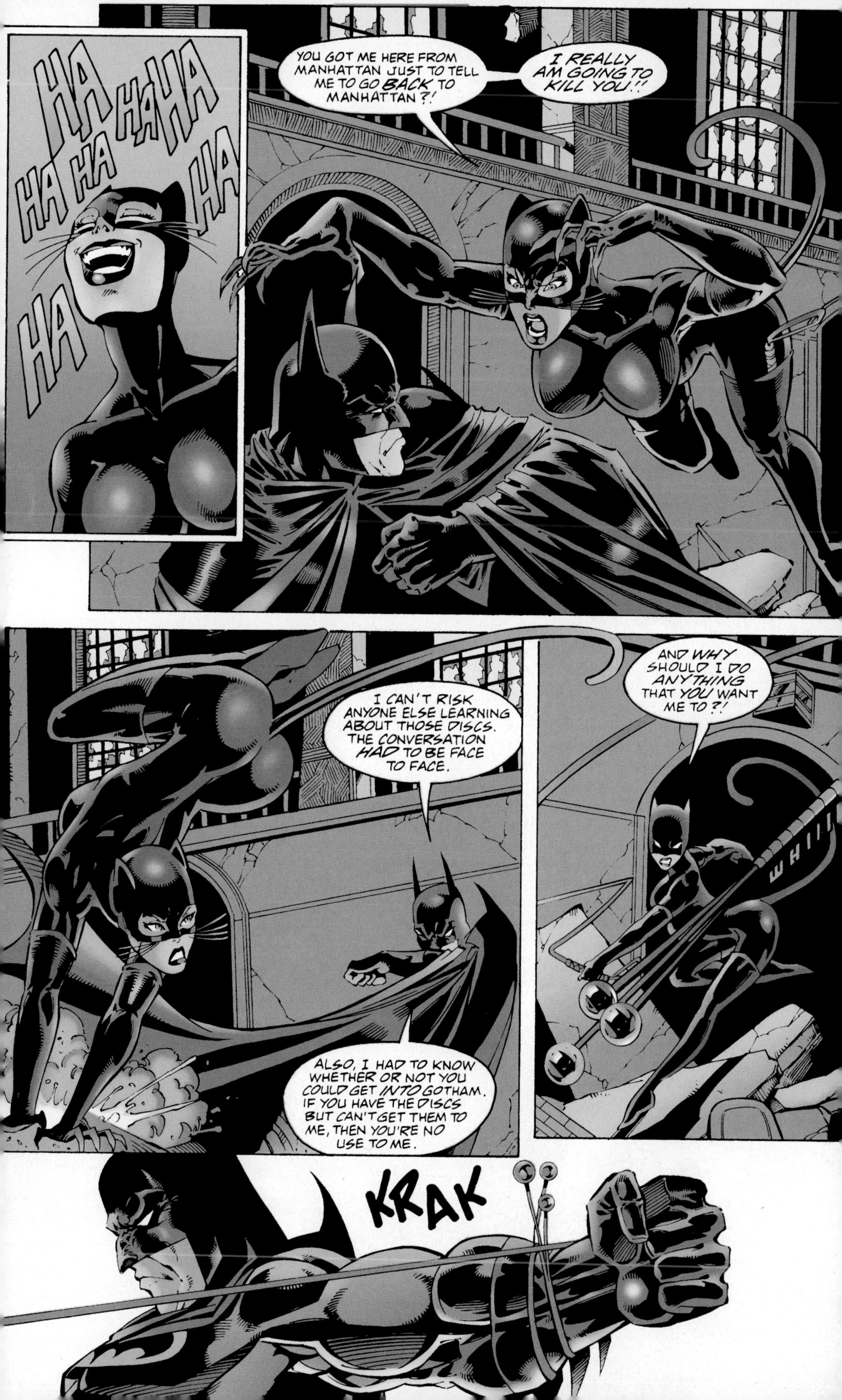
HA HA HA HA HA HA HA HA
YOU GOT ME HERE FROM MANHATTAN JUST TO TELL ME TO GO BACK TO MANHATTAN ?!
I REALLY AM GOING TO KILL YOU!!
I CAN'T RISK ANYONE ELSE LEARNING ABOUT THOSE DISCS. THE CONVERSATION HAD TO BE FACE TO FACE.
ALSO, I HAD TO KNOW WHETHER OR NOT YOU COULD GET INTO GOTHAM. IF YOU HAVE THE DISCS BUT CAN'T GET THEM TO ME, THEN YOU'RE NO USE TO ME.
AND WHY SHOULD I DO ANYTHING THAT YOU WANT ME TO ?!
WHIII
KRAK

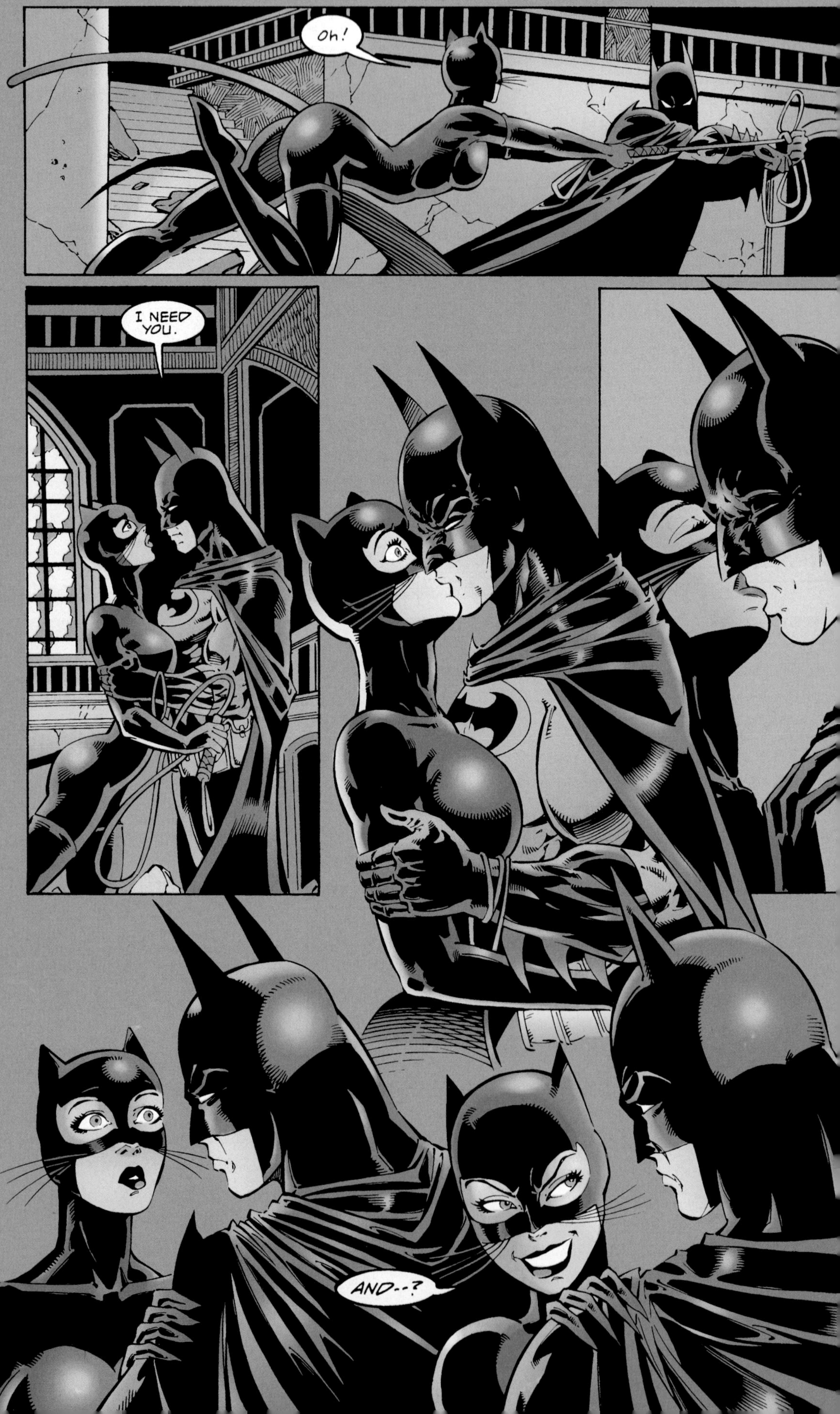
Oh!
I NEED YOU.
AND--?

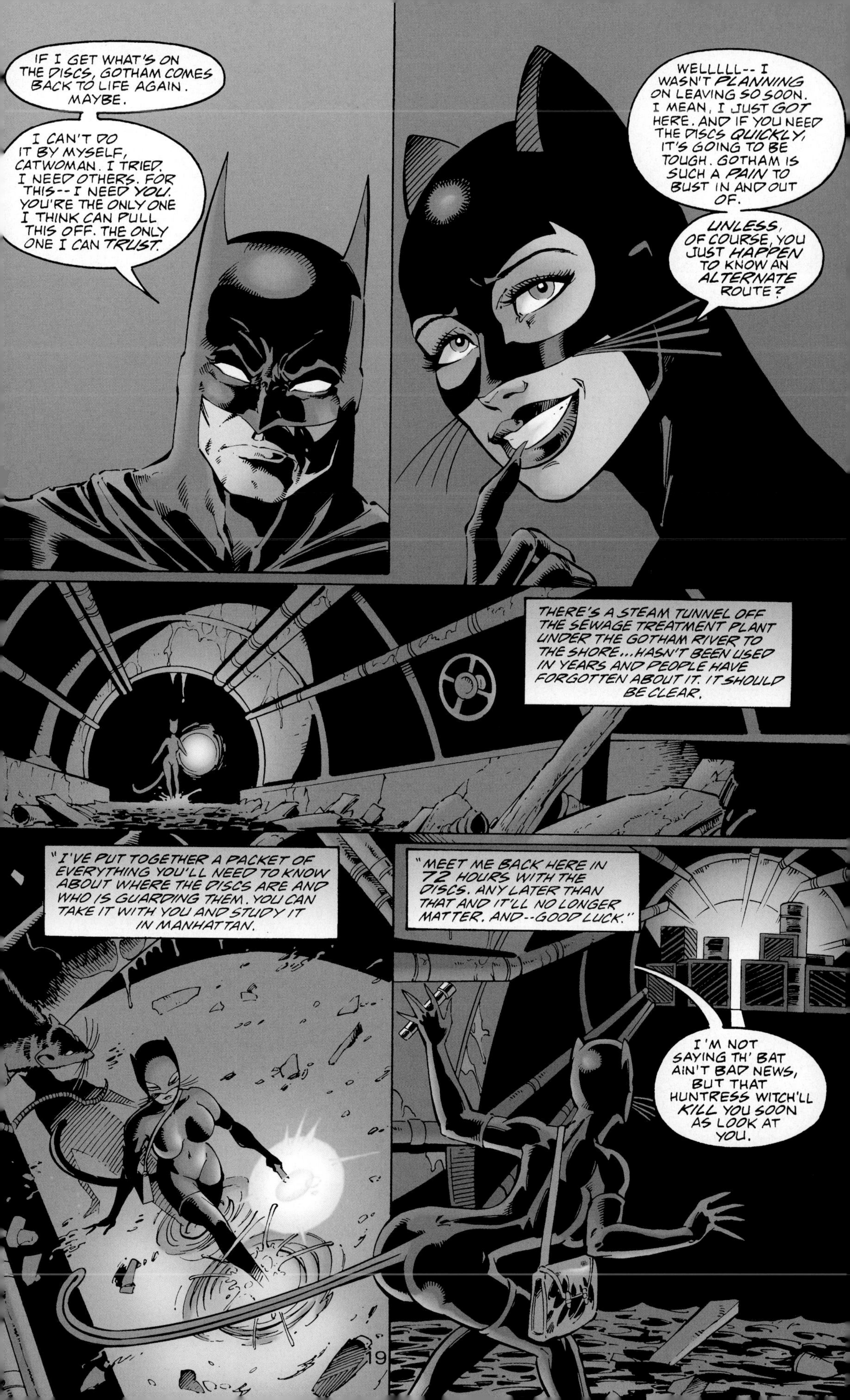
IF I GET WHAT'S ON THE DISCS, GOTHAM COMES BACK TO LIFE AGAIN. MAYBE.
I CAN'T DO IT BY MYSELF, CATWOMAN. I TRIED. I NEED OTHERS. FOR THIS-- I NEED YOU. YOU'RE THE ONLY ONE I THINK CAN PULL THIS OFF. THE ONLY ONE I CAN TRUST.
WELLLLLL-- I WASN'T PLANNING ON LEAVING SO SOON. I MEAN, I JUST GOT HERE. AND IF YOU NEED THE DISCS QUICKLY, IT'S GOING TO BE TOUGH. GOTHAM IS SUCH A PAIN TO BUST IN AND OUT OF.
UNLESS, OF COURSE, YOU JUST HAPPEN TO KNOW AN ALTERNATE ROUTE?
THERE'S A STEAM TUNNEL OFF THE SEWAGE TREATMENT PLANT UNDER THE GOTHAM RIVER TO THE SHORE...HASN'T BEEN USED IN YEARS AND PEOPLE HAVE FORGOTTEN ABOUT IT. IT SHOULD BE CLEAR.
"I'VE PUT TOGETHER A PACKET OF EVERYTHING YOU'LL NEED TO KNOW ABOUT WHERE THE DISCS ARE AND WHO IS GUARDING THEM. YOU CAN TAKE IT WITH YOU AND STUDY IT IN MANHATTAN.
"MEET ME BACK HERE IN 72 HOURS WITH THE DISCS. ANY LATER THAN THAT AND IT'LL NO LONGER MATTER. AND--GOOD LUCK."
I'M NOT SAYING TH' BAT AIN'T BAD NEWS, BUT THAT HUNTRESS WITCH'LL KILL YOU SOON AS LOOK AT YOU.

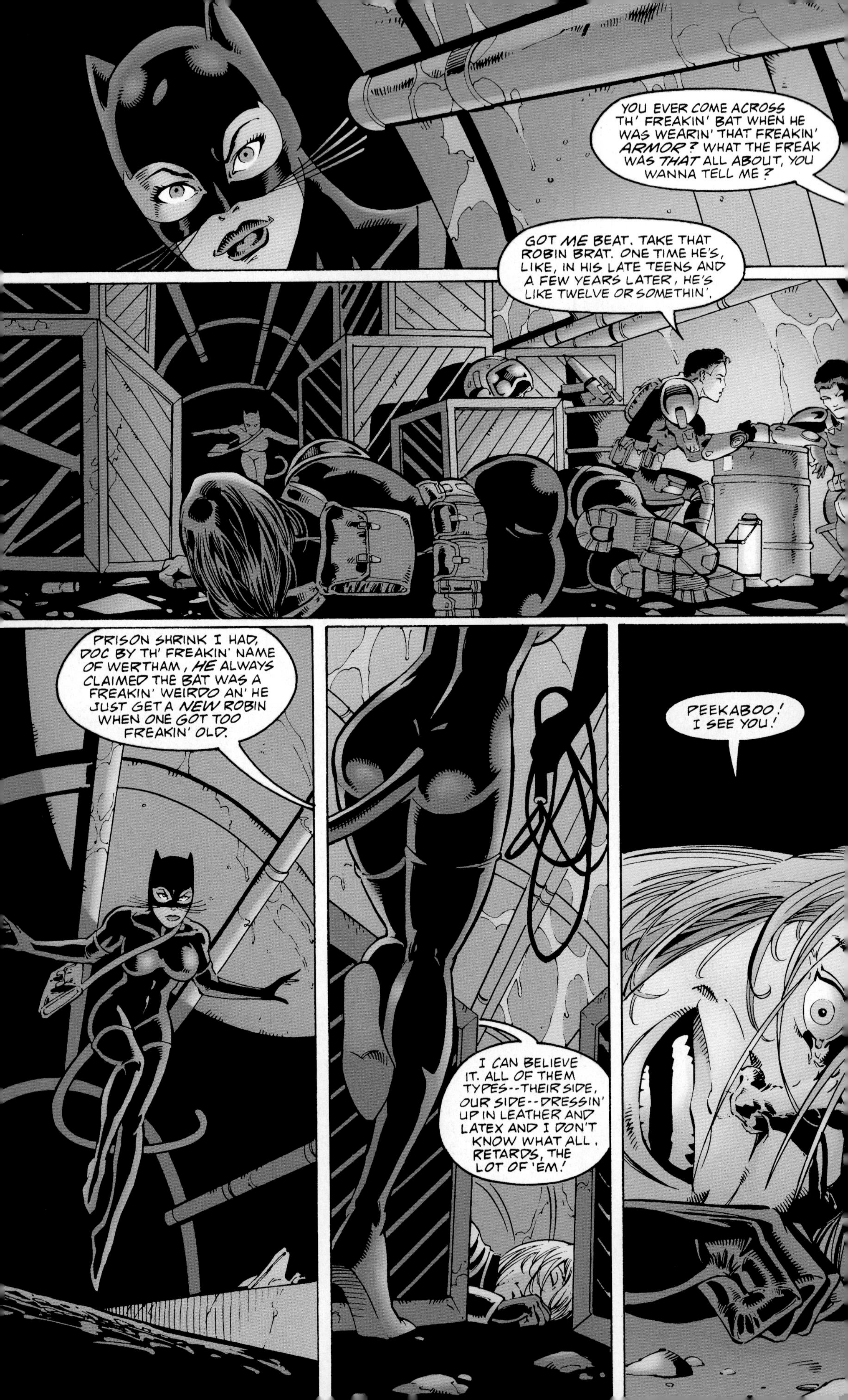
YOU EVER COME ACROSS TH' FREAKIN' BAT WHEN HE WAS WEARIN' THAT FREAKIN' ARMOR? WHAT THE FREAK WAS THAT ALL ABOUT, YOU WANNA TELL ME?
GOT ME BEAT. TAKE THAT ROBIN BRAT. ONE TIME HE'S, LIKE, IN HIS LATE TEENS AND A FEW YEARS LATER, HE'S LIKE TWELVE OR SOMETHIN'.
PRISON SHRINK I HAD, DOC BY TH' FREAKIN' NAME OF WERTHAM, HE ALWAYS CLAIMED THE BAT WAS A FREAKIN' WEIRDO AN' HE JUST GET A NEW ROBIN WHEN ONE GOT TOO FREAKIN' OLD.
I CAN BELIEVE IT. ALL OF THEM TYPES--THEIR SIDE, OUR SIDE--DRESSIN' UP IN LEATHER AND LATEX AND I DON'T KNOW WHAT ALL. RETARDS, THE LOT OF 'EM!
PEEKABOO! I SEE YOU!

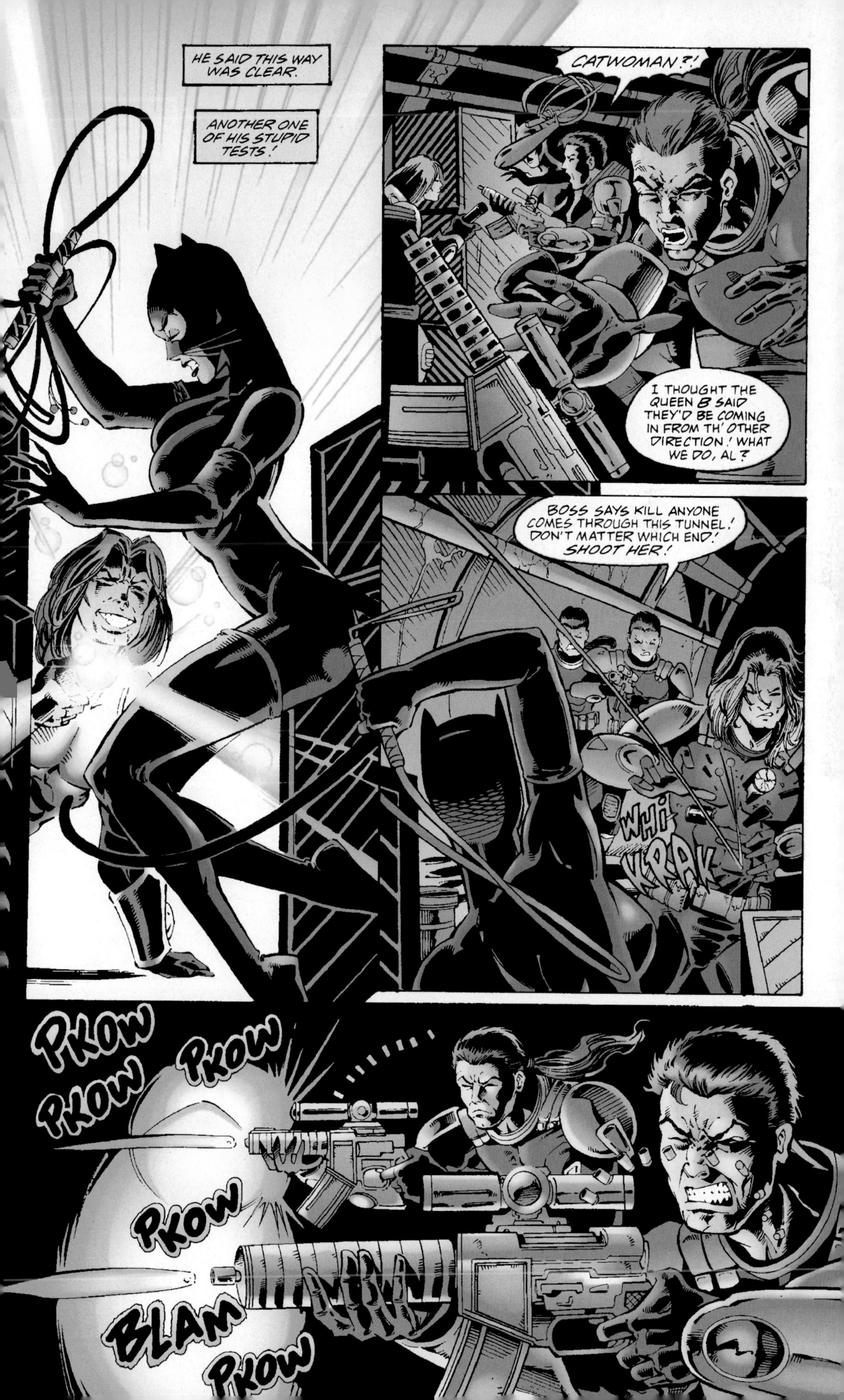
HE SAID THIS WAY WAS CLEAR.
ANOTHER ONE OF HIS STUPID TESTS!
CATWOMAN?!
I THOUGHT THE QUEEN B SAID THEY'D BE COMING IN FROM TH' OTHER DIRECTION! WHAT WE DO, AL?
BOSS SAYS KILL ANYONE COMES THROUGH THIS TUNNEL! DON'T MATTER WHICH END! SHOOT HER!
WHI
VRAK
PKOW
PKOW
PKOW
PKOW
BLAM
PKOW

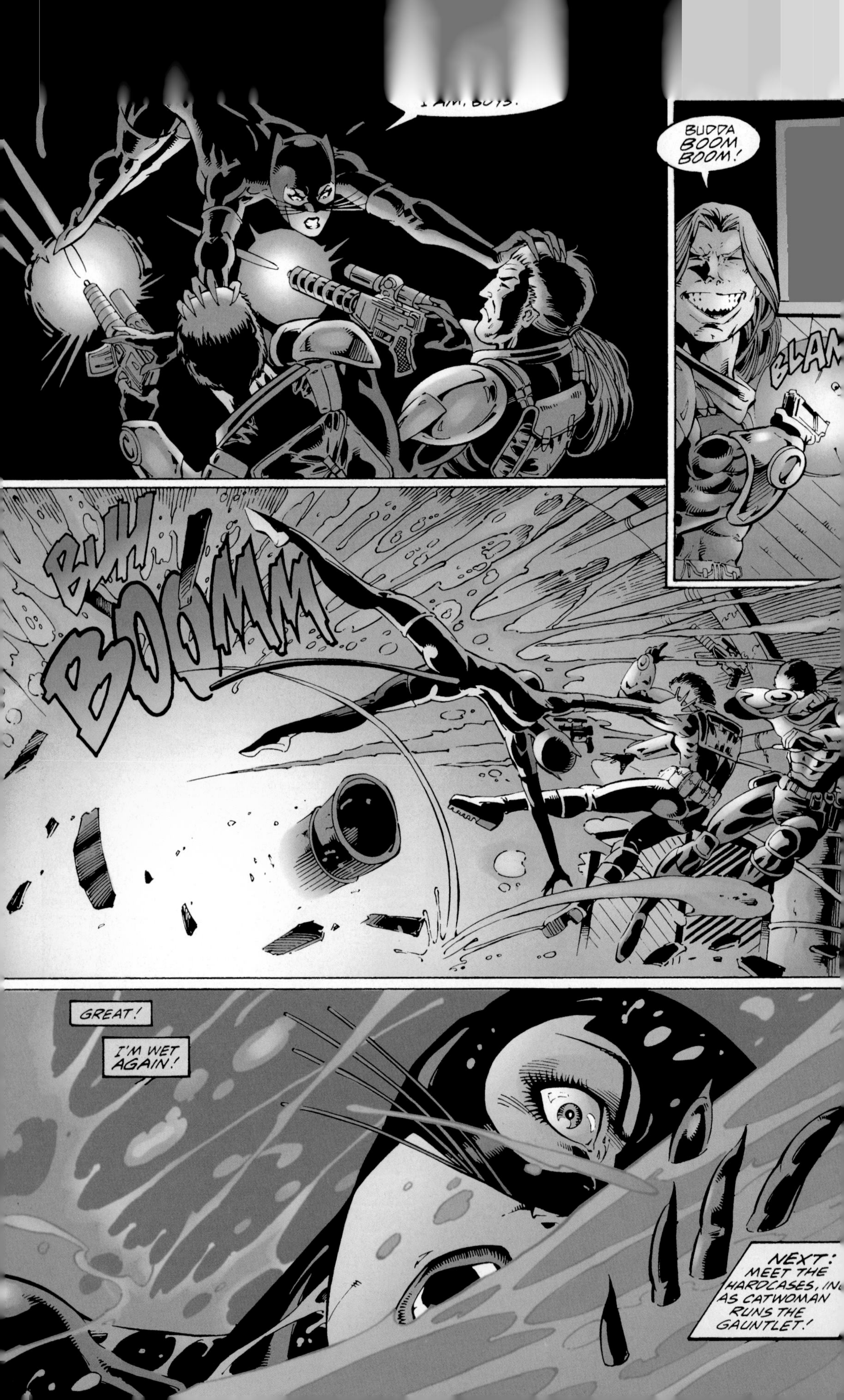
I AM, BOYS.
BUDDA BOOM BOOM!
BUH BOOMM
GREAT!
I'M WET AGAIN!
NEXT: MEET THE HARDCASES, INC AS CATWOMAN RUNS THE GAUNTLET!

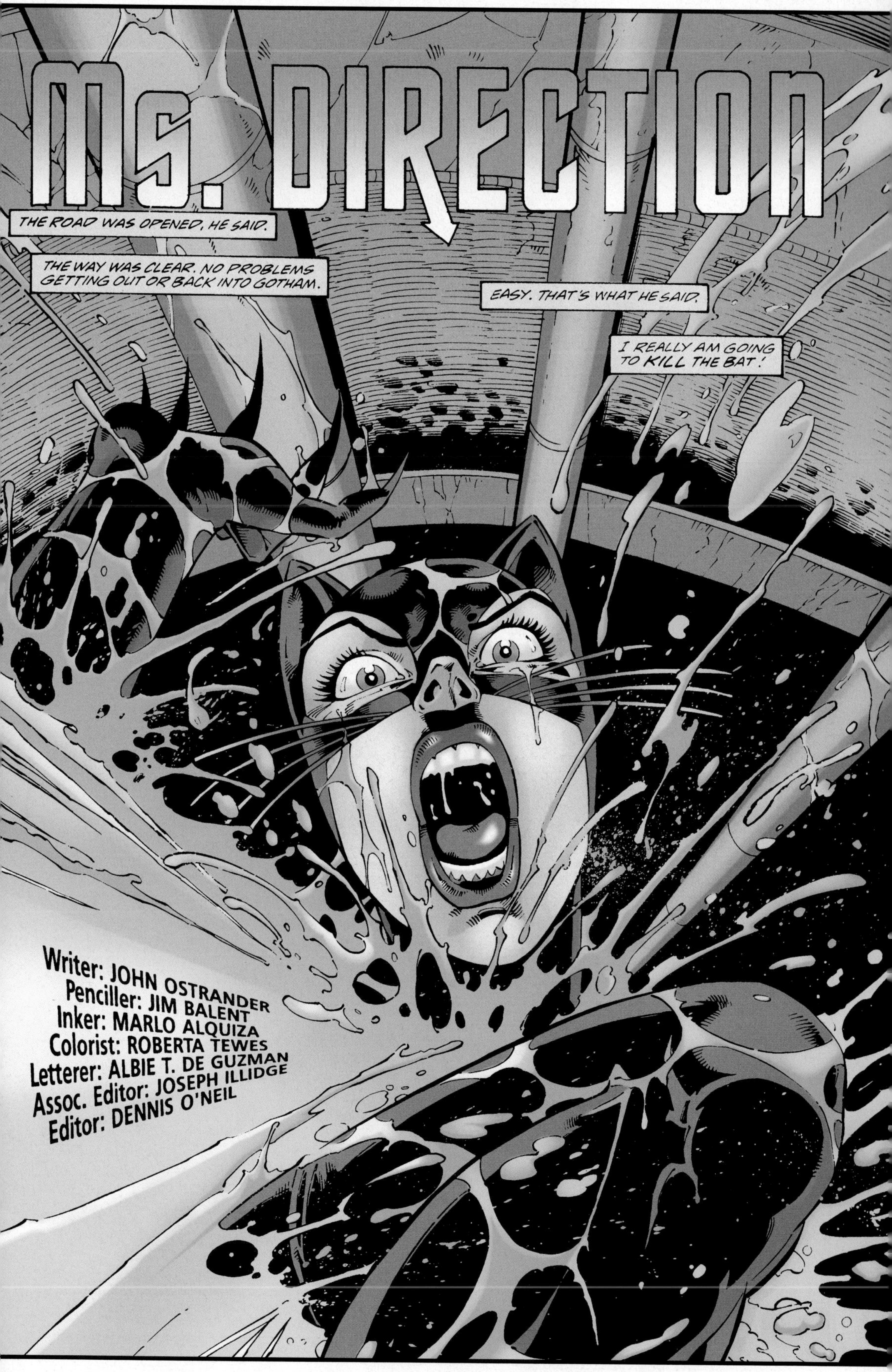
MS. DIRECTION
THE ROAD WAS OPENED, HE SAID.
THE WAY WAS CLEAR. NO PROBLEMS GETTING OUT OR BACK INTO GOTHAM.
EASY. THAT'S WHAT HE SAID.
I REALLY AM GOING TO KILL THE BAT!
Writer: JOHN OSTRANDER
Penciller: JIM BALENT
Inker: MARLO ALQUIZA
Colorist: ROBERTA TEWES
Letterer: ALBIE T. DE GUZMAN
Assoc. Editor: JOSEPH ILLIDGE
Editor: DENNIS O'NEIL

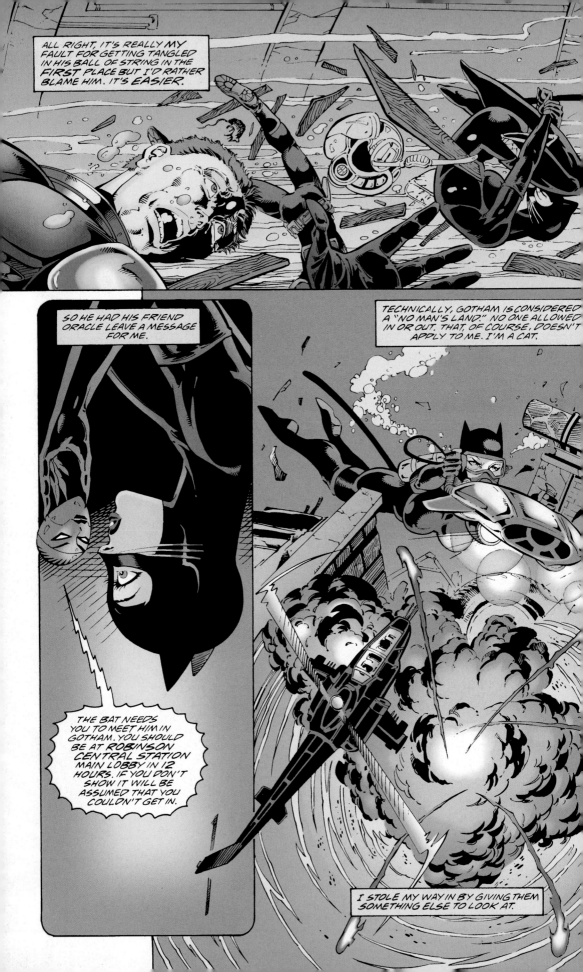

ALL RIGHT, IT'S REALLY MY FAULT FOR GETTING TANGLED IN HIS BALL OF STRING IN THE FIRST PLACE BUT I'D RATHER BLAME HIM. IT'S EASIER.

SO HE HAD HIS FRIEND ORACLE LEAVE A MESSAGE FOR ME.

TECHNICALLY, GOTHAM IS CONSIDERED A "NO MAN'S LAND." NO ONE ALLOWED IN OR OUT. THAT, OF COURSE, DOESN'T APPLY TO ME. I'M A CAT.

THE BAT NEEDS YOU TO MEET HIM IN GOTHAM. YOU SHOULD BE AT ROBINSON CENTRAL STATION MAIN LOBBY IN 12 HOURS. IF YOU DON'T SHOW IT WILL BE ASSUMED THAT YOU COULDN'T GET IN.

I STOLE MY WAY IN BY GIVING THEM SOMETHING ELSE TO LOOK AT.

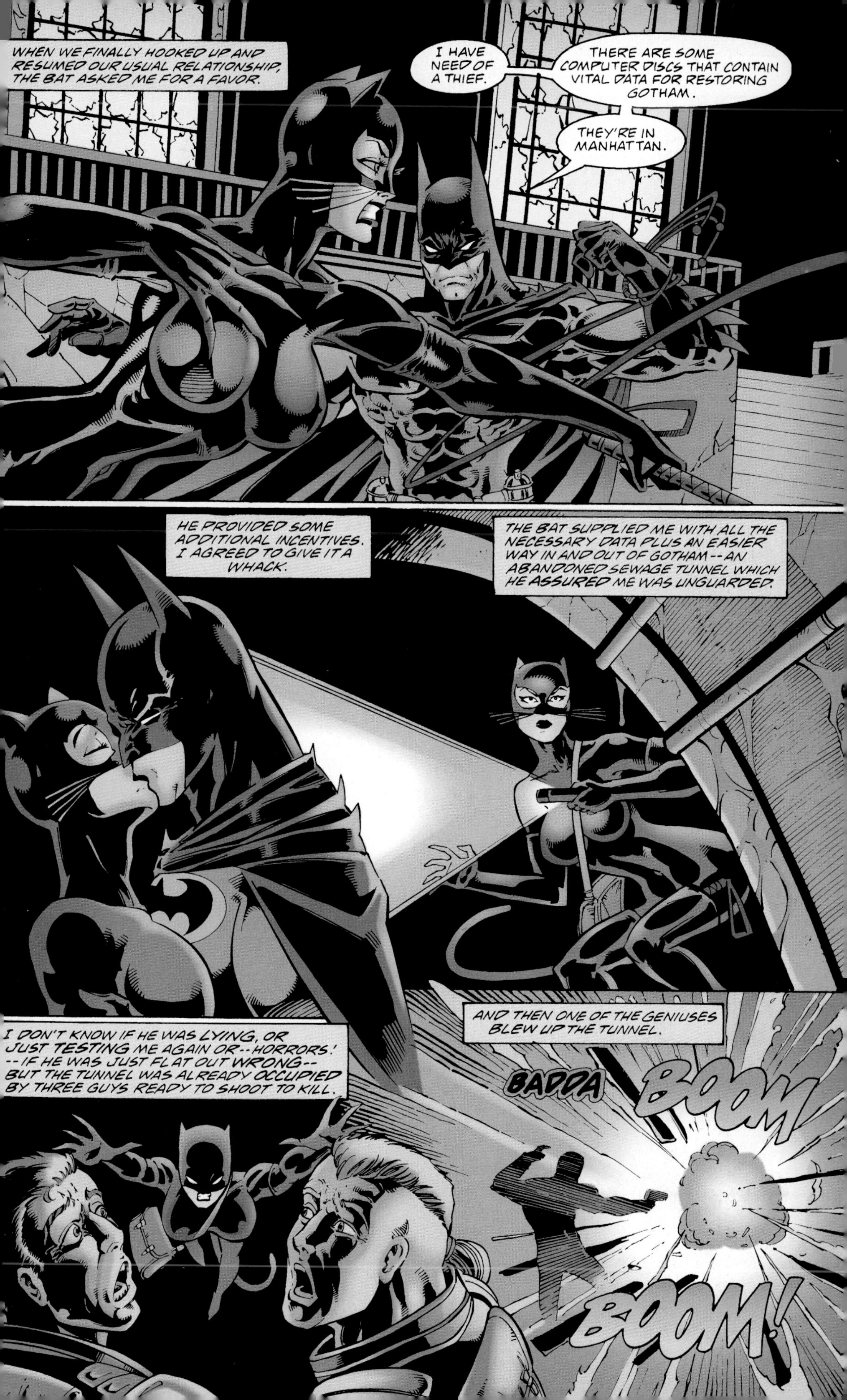
WHEN WE FINALLY HOOKED UP AND RESUMED OUR USUAL RELATIONSHIP, THE BAT ASKED ME FOR A FAVOR.
I HAVE NEED OF A THIEF.
THERE ARE SOME COMPUTER DISCS THAT CONTAIN VITAL DATA FOR RESTORING GOTHAM.
THEY'RE IN MANHATTAN.
HE PROVIDED SOME ADDITIONAL INCENTIVES. I AGREED TO GIVE IT A WHACK.
THE BAT SUPPLIED ME WITH ALL THE NECESSARY DATA PLUS AN EASIER WAY IN AND OUT OF GOTHAM -- AN ABANDONED SEWAGE TUNNEL WHICH HE ASSURED ME WAS UNGUARDED.
I DON'T KNOW IF HE WAS LYING, OR JUST TESTING ME AGAIN OR -- HORRORS! -- IF HE WAS JUST FLAT OUT WRONG -- BUT THE TUNNEL WAS ALREADY OCCUPIED BY THREE GUYS READY TO SHOOT TO KILL.
AND THEN ONE OF THE GENIUSES BLEW UP THE TUNNEL.
BADDA BOOM
BOOM!

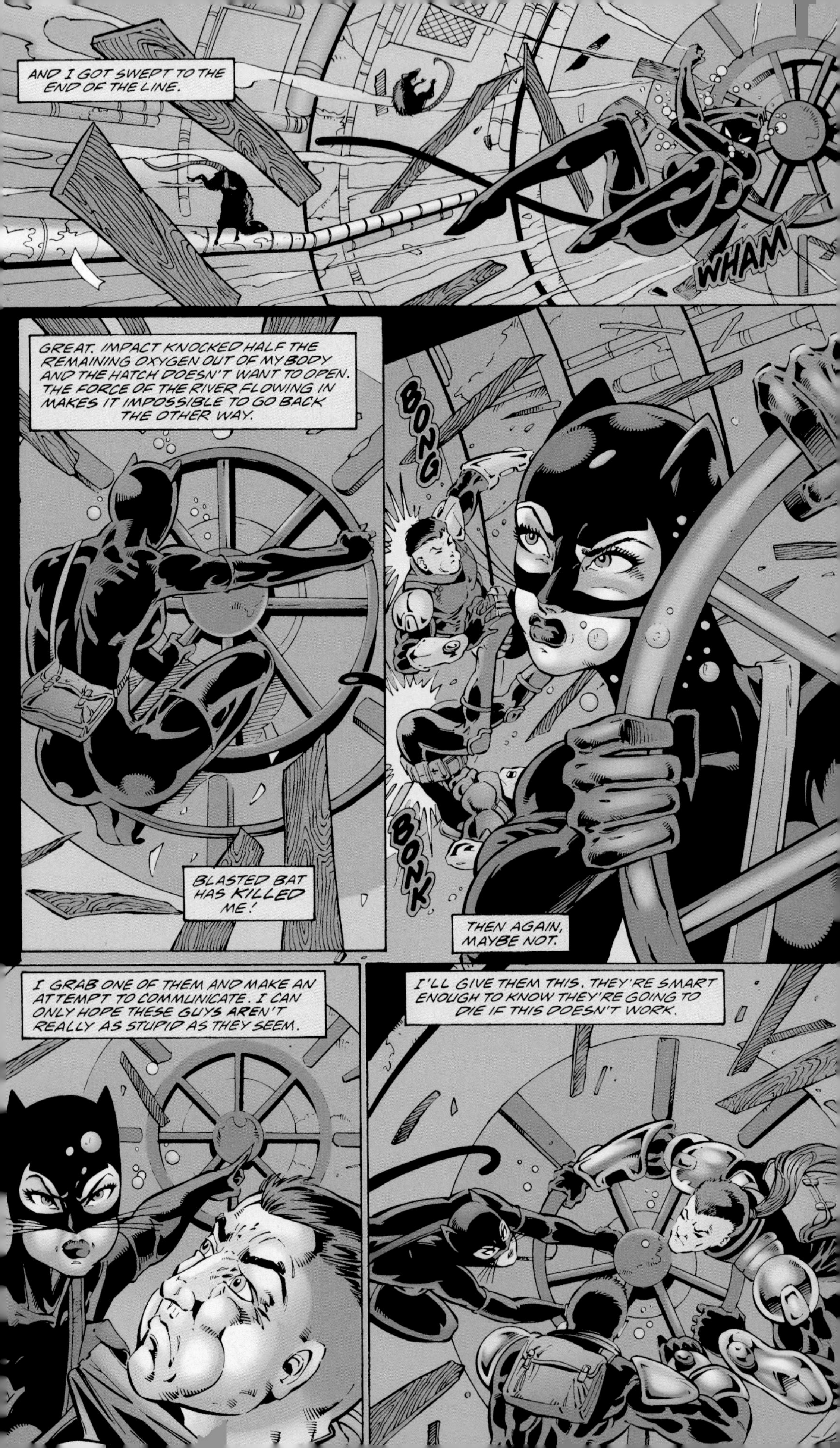
AND I GOT SWEPT TO THE END OF THE LINE.
WHAM
GREAT. IMPACT KNOCKED HALF THE REMAINING OXYGEN OUT OF MY BODY AND THE HATCH DOESN'T WANT TO OPEN. THE FORCE OF THE RIVER FLOWING IN MAKES IT IMPOSSIBLE TO GO BACK THE OTHER WAY.
BLASTED BAT HAS KILLED ME!
BONG
BONK
THEN AGAIN, MAYBE NOT.
I GRAB ONE OF THEM AND MAKE AN ATTEMPT TO COMMUNICATE. I CAN ONLY HOPE THESE GUYS AREN'T REALLY AS STUPID AS THEY SEEM.
I'LL GIVE THEM THIS. THEY'RE SMART ENOUGH TO KNOW THEY'RE GOING TO DIE IF THIS DOESN'T WORK.

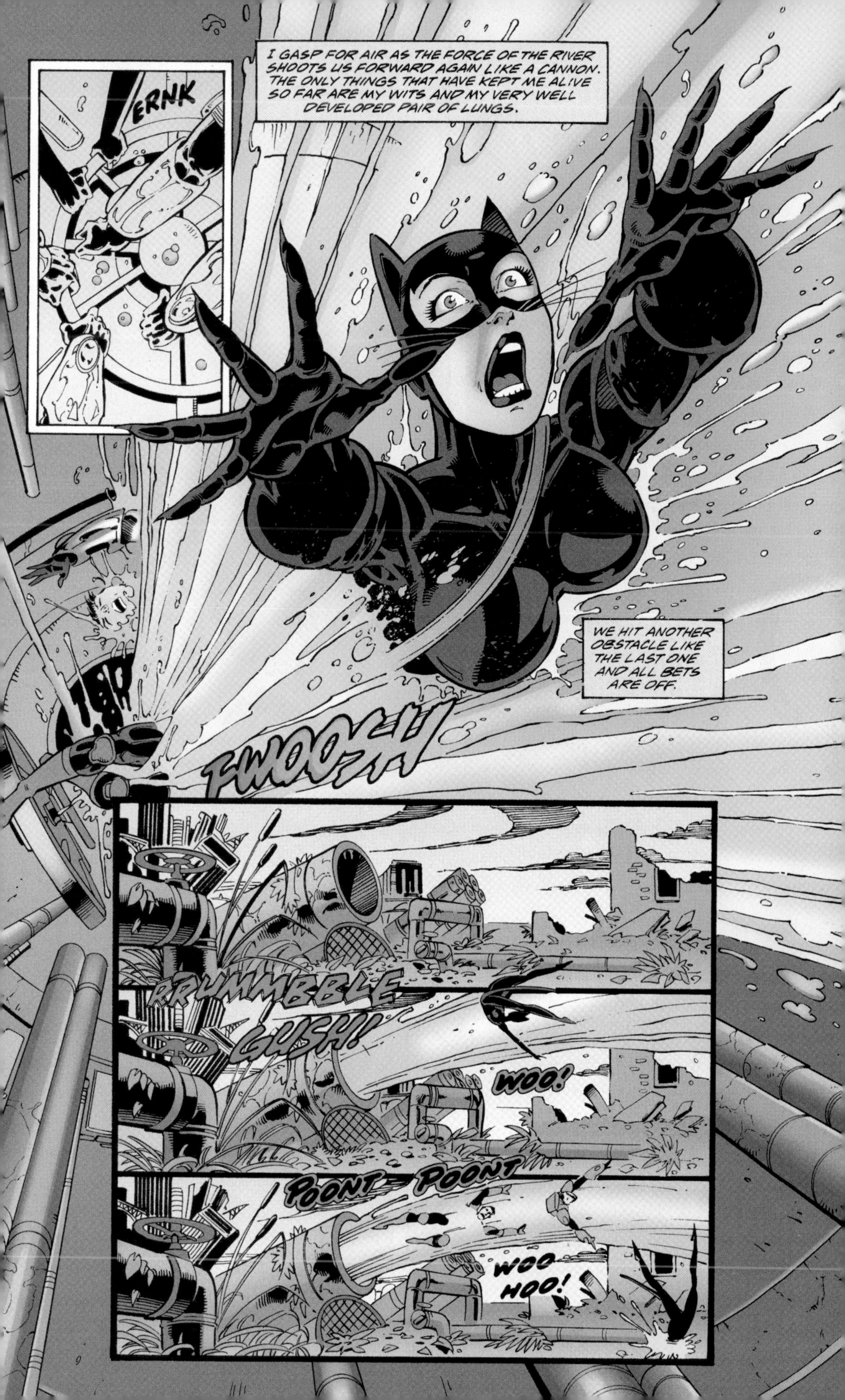
ERNK
I GASP FOR AIR AS THE FORCE OF THE RIVER SHOOTS US FORWARD AGAIN LIKE A CANNON. THE ONLY THINGS THAT HAVE KEPT ME ALIVE SO FAR ARE MY WITS AND MY VERY WELL DEVELOPED PAIR OF LUNGS.
WE HIT ANOTHER OBSTACLE LIKE THE LAST ONE AND ALL BETS ARE OFF.
FWOOSH
KRUMMBBLE
GUSH!
WOO!
POONT POONT
WOO HOO!

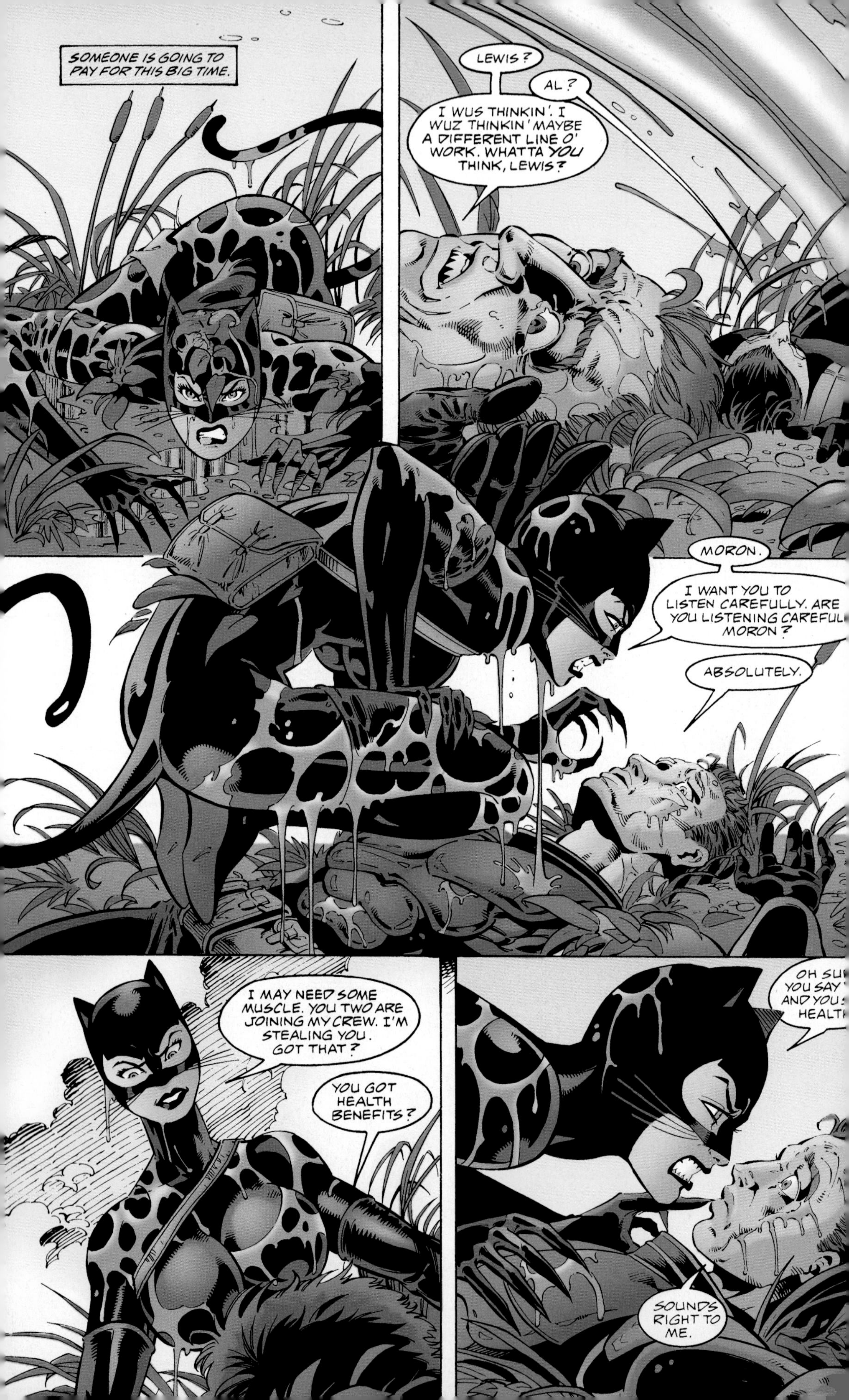
SOMEONE IS GOING TO PAY FOR THIS BIG TIME.
LEWIS?
AL?
I WUS THINKIN'. I WUZ THINKIN' MAYBE A DIFFERENT LINE O' WORK. WHATTA YOU THINK, LEWIS?
MORON.
I WANT YOU TO LISTEN CAREFULLY. ARE YOU LISTENING CAREFUL MORON?
ABSOLUTELY.
I MAY NEED SOME MUSCLE. YOU TWO ARE JOINING MY CREW. I'M STEALING YOU. GOT THAT?
YOU GOT HEALTH BENEFITS?
OH SU
YOU SAY
AND YOU
HEALT
SOUNDS RIGHT TO ME.

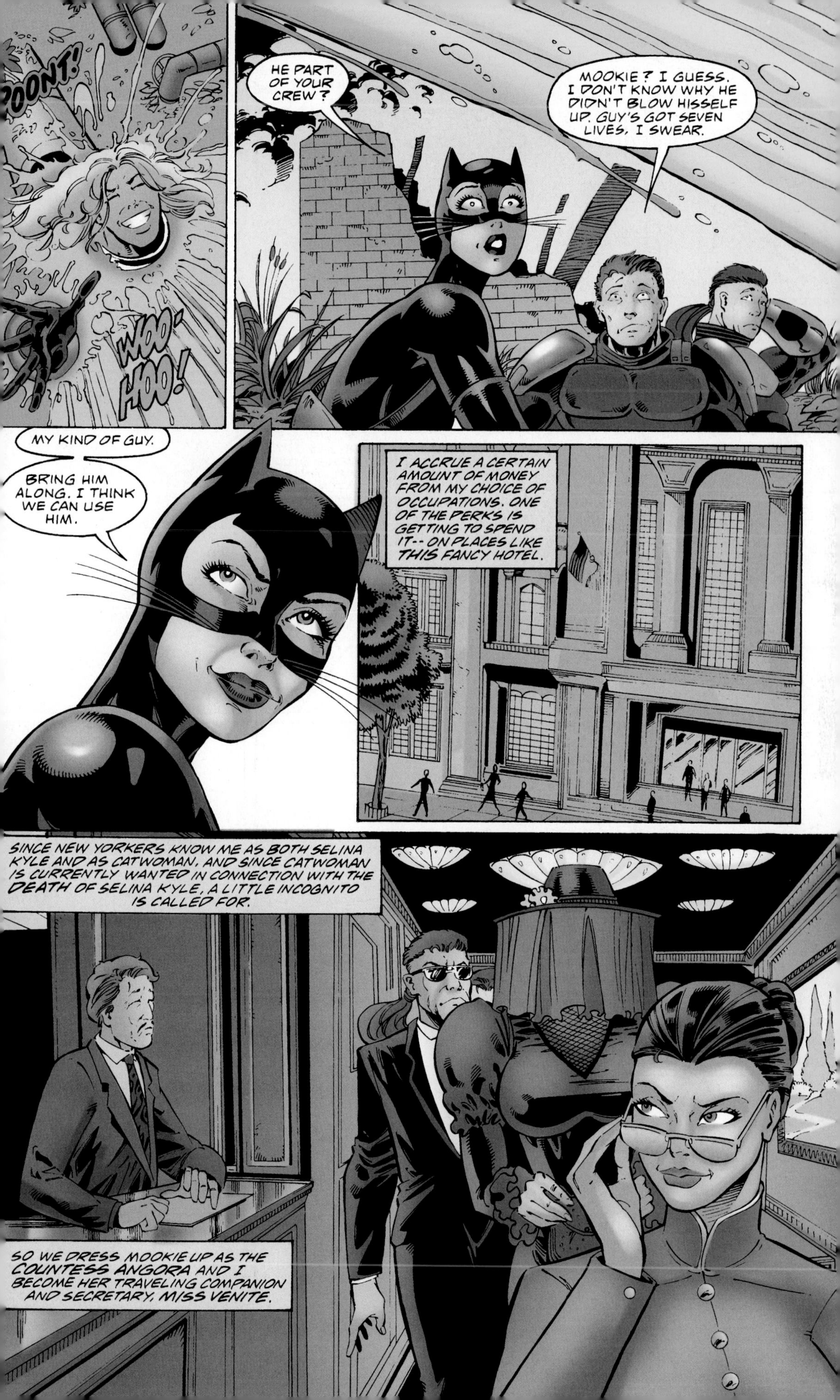
POONT!
WOO-HOO!
HE PART OF YOUR CREW?
MOOKIE? I GUESS. I DON'T KNOW WHY HE DIDN'T BLOW HISSELF UP. GUY'S GOT SEVEN LIVES, I SWEAR.
MY KIND OF GUY.
BRING HIM ALONG. I THINK WE CAN USE HIM.
I ACCRUE A CERTAIN AMOUNT OF MONEY FROM MY CHOICE OF OCCUPATIONS. ONE OF THE PERKS IS GETTING TO SPEND IT-- ON PLACES LIKE THIS FANCY HOTEL.
SINCE NEW YORKERS KNOW ME AS BOTH SELINA KYLE AND AS CATWOMAN, AND SINCE CATWOMAN IS CURRENTLY WANTED IN CONNECTION WITH THE DEATH OF SELINA KYLE, A LITTLE INCOGNITO IS CALLED FOR.
SO WE DRESS MOOKIE UP AS THE COUNTESS ANGORA AND I BECOME HER TRAVELING COMPANION AND SECRETARY, MISS VENITE.

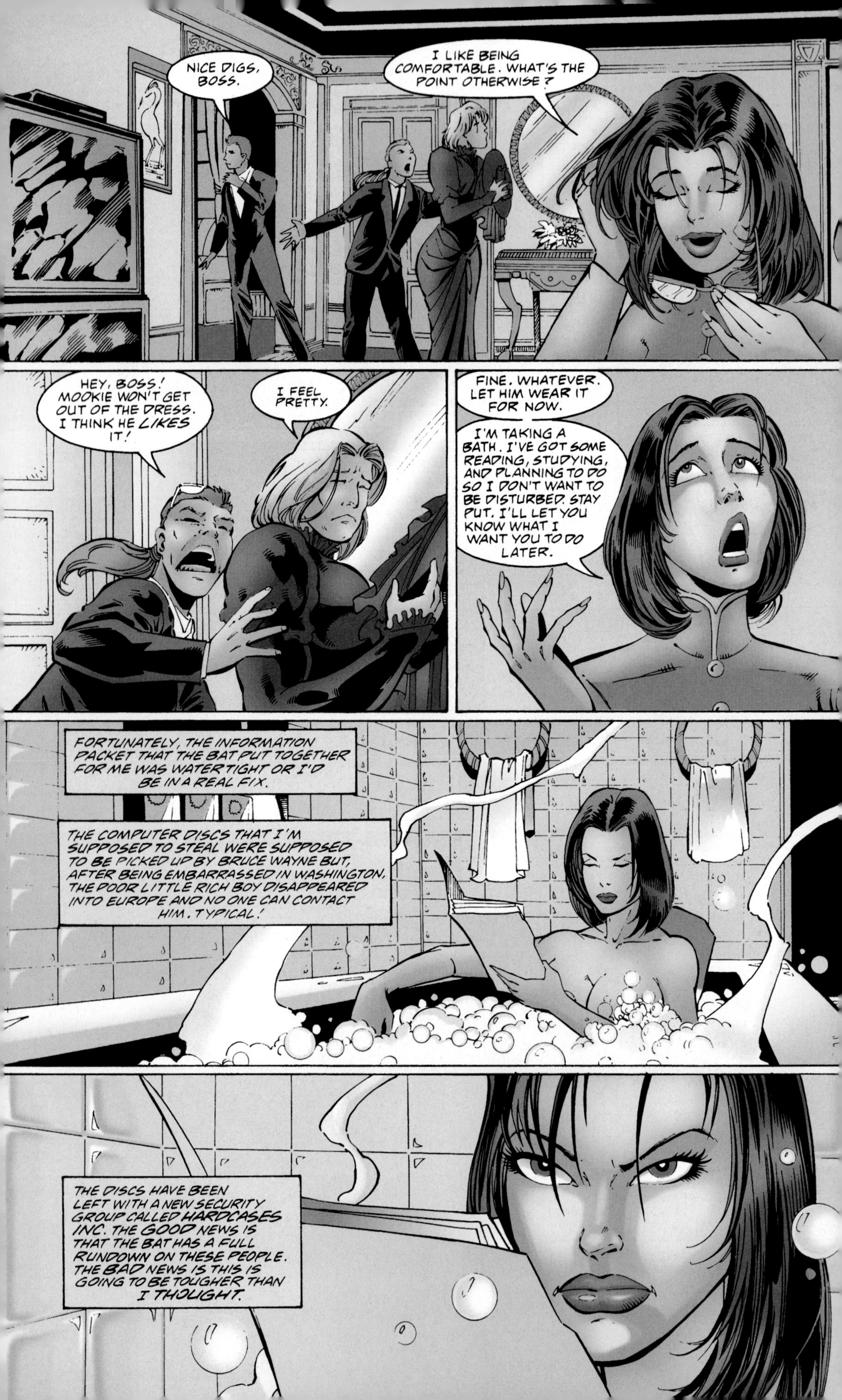
NICE DIGS, BOSS.
I LIKE BEING COMFORTABLE. WHAT'S THE POINT OTHERWISE?
HEY, BOSS! MOOKIE WON'T GET OUT OF THE DRESS. I THINK HE LIKES IT!
I FEEL PRETTY.
FINE. WHATEVER. LET HIM WEAR IT FOR NOW.
I'M TAKING A BATH. I'VE GOT SOME READING, STUDYING, AND PLANNING TO DO SO I DON'T WANT TO BE DISTURBED. STAY PUT. I'LL LET YOU KNOW WHAT I WANT YOU TO DO LATER.
FORTUNATELY, THE INFORMATION PACKET THAT THE BAT PUT TOGETHER FOR ME WAS WATERTIGHT OR I'D BE IN A REAL FIX.
THE COMPUTER DISCS THAT I'M SUPPOSED TO STEAL WERE SUPPOSED TO BE PICKED UP BY BRUCE WAYNE BUT, AFTER BEING EMBARRASSED IN WASHINGTON, THE POOR LITTLE RICH BOY DISAPPEARED INTO EUROPE AND NO ONE CAN CONTACT HIM. TYPICAL!
THE DISCS HAVE BEEN LEFT WITH A NEW SECURITY GROUP CALLED HARDCASES INC. THE GOOD NEWS IS THAT THE BAT HAS A FULL RUNDOWN ON THESE PEOPLE. THE BAD NEWS IS THIS IS GOING TO BE TOUGHER THAN I THOUGHT.

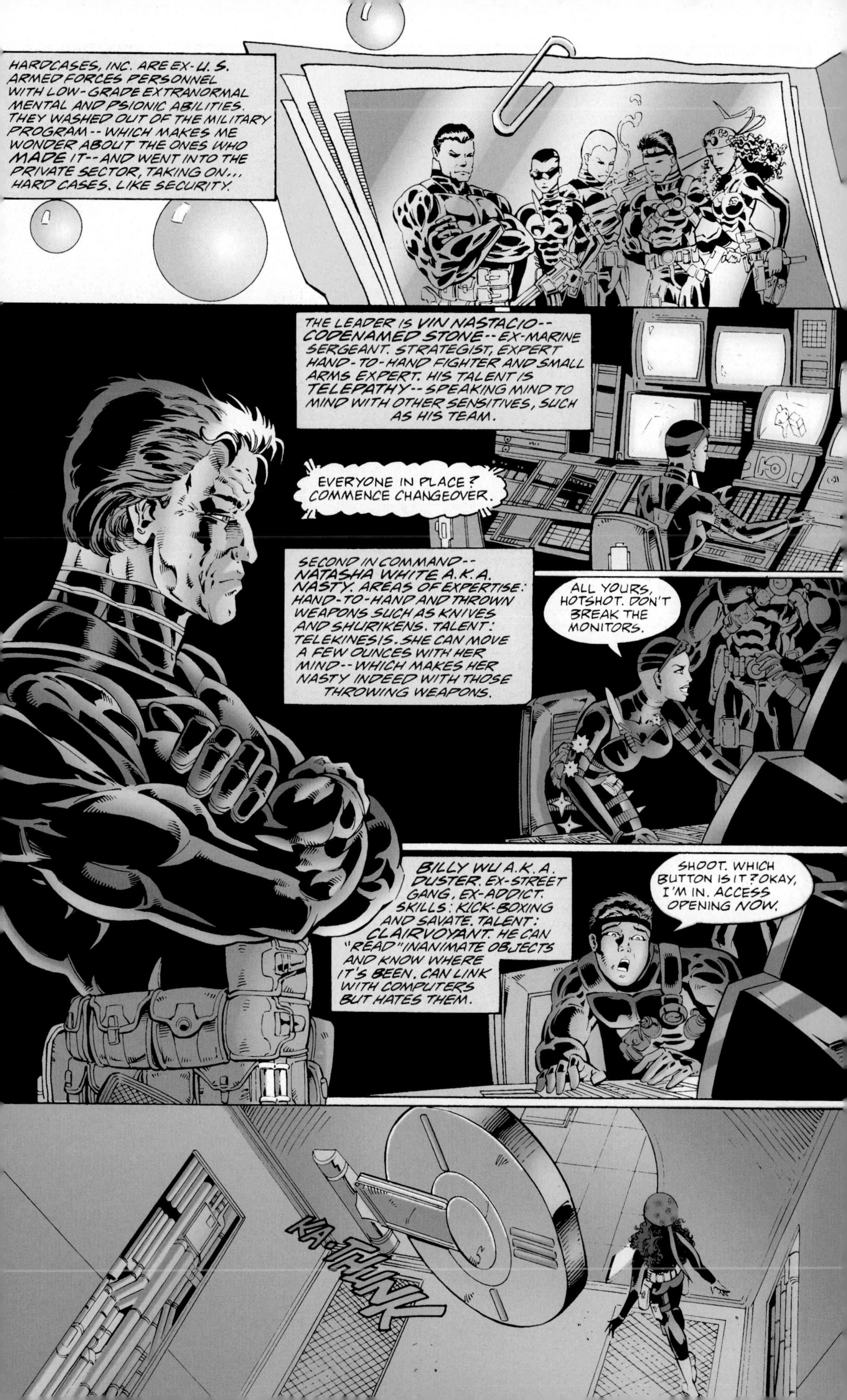
HARDCASES, INC. ARE EX-U.S. ARMED FORCES PERSONNEL WITH LOW-GRADE EXTRANORMAL MENTAL AND PSIONIC ABILITIES. THEY WASHED OUT OF THE MILITARY PROGRAM -- WHICH MAKES ME WONDER ABOUT THE ONES WHO MADE IT -- AND WENT INTO THE PRIVATE SECTOR, TAKING ON... HARD CASES. LIKE SECURITY.
THE LEADER IS VIN NASTACIO -- CODENAMED STONE -- EX-MARINE SERGEANT. STRATEGIST, EXPERT HAND-TO-HAND FIGHTER AND SMALL ARMS EXPERT. HIS TALENT IS TELEPATHY -- SPEAKING MIND TO MIND WITH OTHER SENSITIVES, SUCH AS HIS TEAM.
EVERYONE IN PLACE? COMMENCE CHANGEOVER.
SECOND IN COMMAND -- NATASHA WHITE A.K.A. NASTY. AREAS OF EXPERTISE: HAND-TO-HAND AND THROWN WEAPONS SUCH AS KNIVES AND SHURIKENS. TALENT: TELEKINESIS. SHE CAN MOVE A FEW OUNCES WITH HER MIND -- WHICH MAKES HER NASTY INDEED WITH THOSE THROWING WEAPONS.
ALL YOURS, HOTSHOT. DON'T BREAK THE MONITORS.
BILLY WU A.K.A. DUSTER. EX-STREET GANG, EX-ADDICT. SKILLS: KICK-BOXING AND SAVATE. TALENT: CLAIRVOYANT. HE CAN "READ" INANIMATE OBJECTS AND KNOW WHERE IT'S BEEN. CAN LINK WITH COMPUTERS BUT HATES THEM.
SHOOT. WHICH BUTTON IS IT? OKAY, I'M IN. ACCESS OPENING NOW.
KA-THUNK

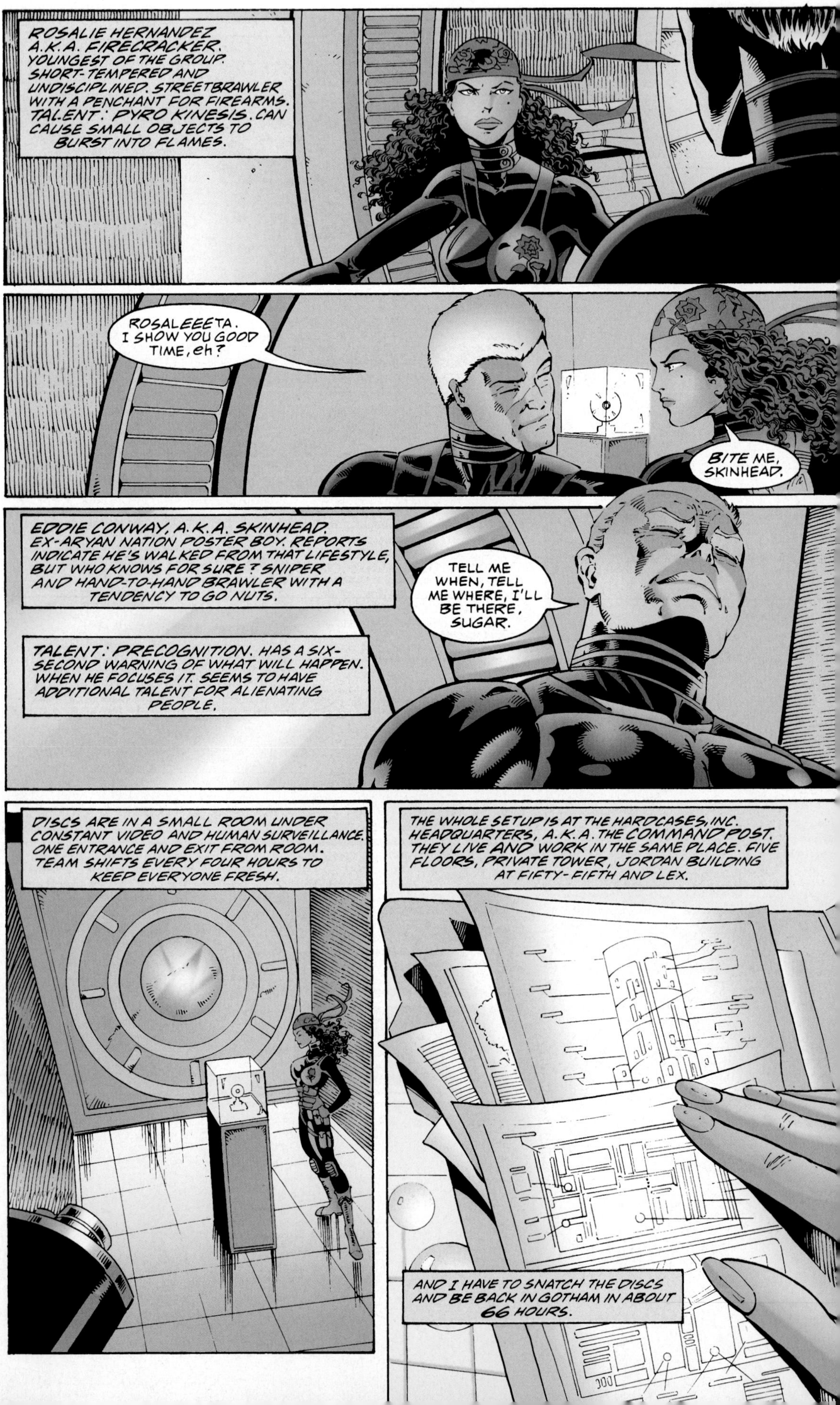
ROSALIE HERNANDEZ A.K.A. FIRECRACKER. YOUNGEST OF THE GROUP. SHORT-TEMPERED AND UNDISCIPLINED. STREETBRAWLER WITH A PENCHANT FOR FIREARMS. TALENT: PYRO KINESIS. CAN CAUSE SMALL OBJECTS TO BURST INTO FLAMES.
ROSALEEETA. I SHOW YOU GOOD TIME, eh?
BITE ME, SKINHEAD.
EDDIE CONWAY, A.K.A. SKINHEAD. EX-ARYAN NATION POSTER BOY. REPORTS INDICATE HE'S WALKED FROM THAT LIFESTYLE, BUT WHO KNOWS FOR SURE? SNIPER AND HAND-TO-HAND BRAWLER WITH A TENDENCY TO GO NUTS.
TELL ME WHEN, TELL ME WHERE, I'LL BE THERE, SUGAR.
TALENT: PRECOGNITION. HAS A SIX-SECOND WARNING OF WHAT WILL HAPPEN. WHEN HE FOCUSES IT. SEEMS TO HAVE ADDITIONAL TALENT FOR ALIENATING PEOPLE.
DISCS ARE IN A SMALL ROOM UNDER CONSTANT VIDEO AND HUMAN SURVEILLANCE. ONE ENTRANCE AND EXIT FROM ROOM. TEAM SHIFTS EVERY FOUR HOURS TO KEEP EVERYONE FRESH.
THE WHOLE SETUP IS AT THE HARDCASES, INC. HEADQUARTERS, A.K.A. THE COMMAND POST. THEY LIVE AND WORK IN THE SAME PLACE. FIVE FLOORS, PRIVATE TOWER, JORDAN BUILDING AT FIFTY-FIFTH AND LEX.
AND I HAVE TO SNATCH THE DISCS AND BE BACK IN GOTHAM IN ABOUT 66 HOURS.

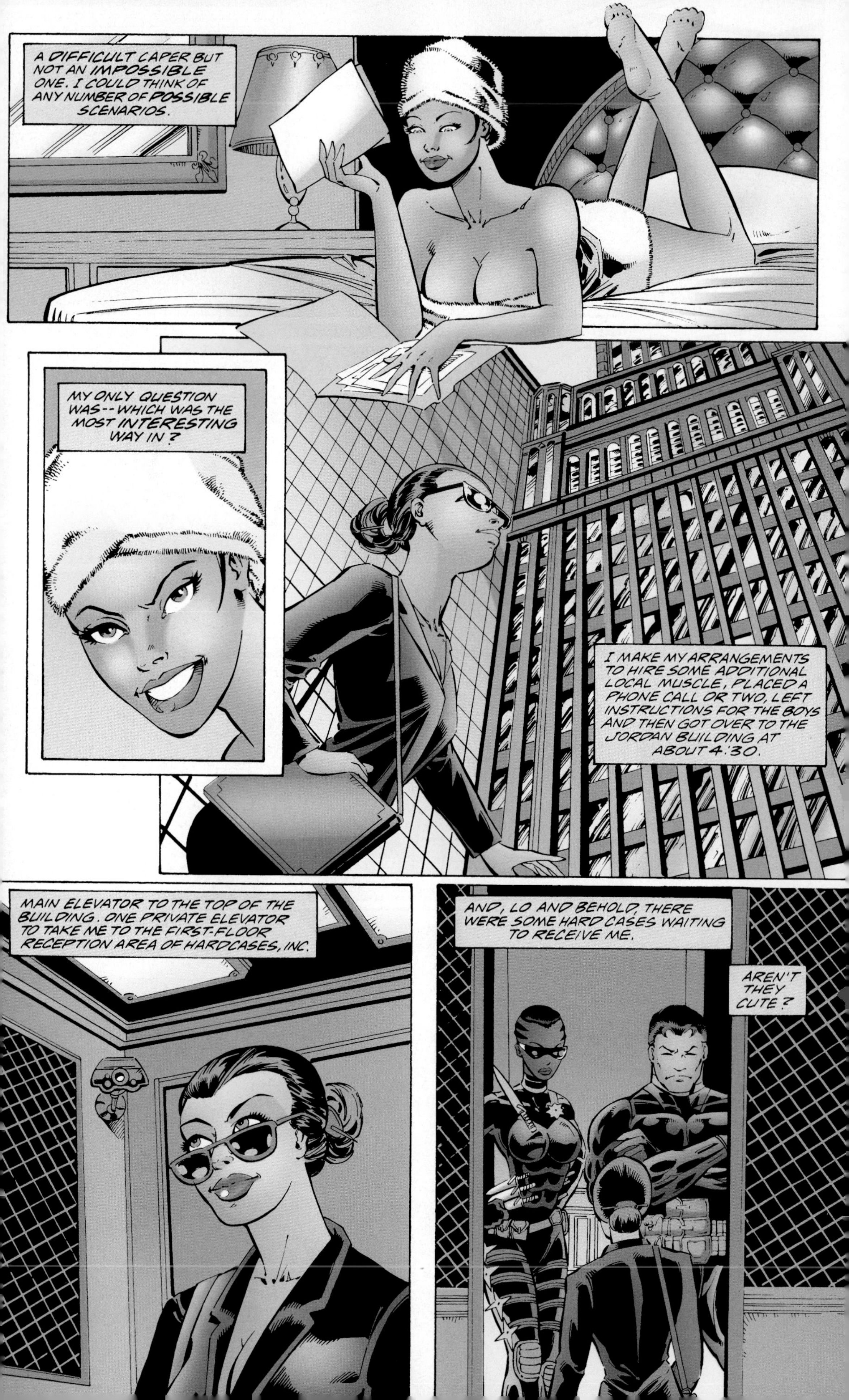
A DIFFICULT CAPER BUT NOT AN IMPOSSIBLE ONE. I COULD THINK OF ANY NUMBER OF POSSIBLE SCENARIOS.
MY ONLY QUESTION WAS--WHICH WAS THE MOST INTERESTING WAY IN?
I MAKE MY ARRANGEMENTS TO HIRE SOME ADDITIONAL LOCAL MUSCLE, PLACED A PHONE CALL OR TWO, LEFT INSTRUCTIONS FOR THE BOYS AND THEN GOT OVER TO THE JORDAN BUILDING AT ABOUT 4:30.
MAIN ELEVATOR TO THE TOP OF THE BUILDING. ONE PRIVATE ELEVATOR TO TAKE ME TO THE FIRST-FLOOR RECEPTION AREA OF HARDCASES, INC.
AND, LO AND BEHOLD, THERE WERE SOME HARD CASES WAITING TO RECEIVE ME.
AREN'T THEY CUTE?

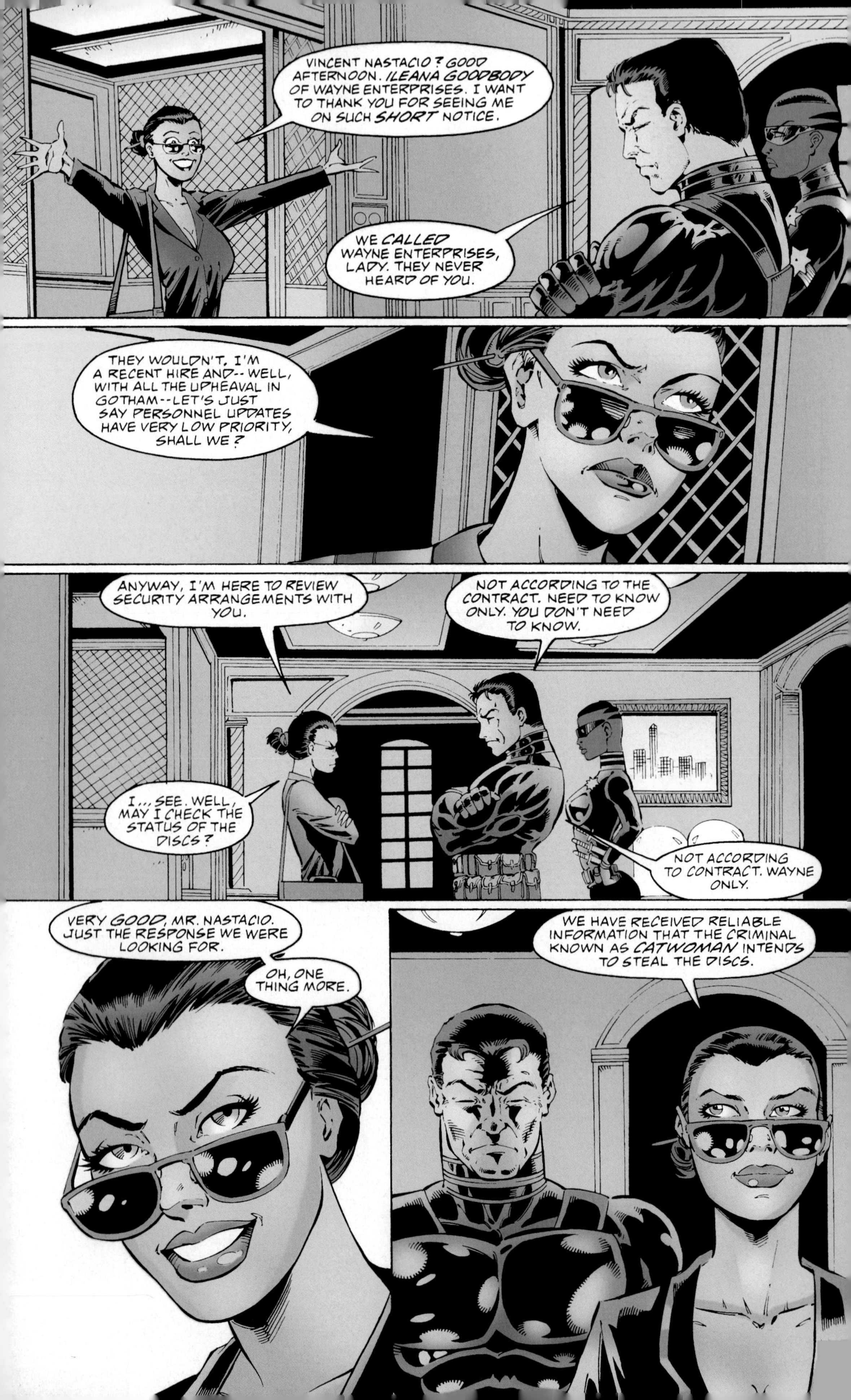
VINCENT NASTACIO? GOOD AFTERNOON. ILEANA GOODBODY OF WAYNE ENTERPRISES. I WANT TO THANK YOU FOR SEEING ME ON SUCH SHORT NOTICE.
WE CALLED WAYNE ENTERPRISES, LADY. THEY NEVER HEARD OF YOU.
THEY WOULDN'T. I'M A RECENT HIRE AND-- WELL, WITH ALL THE UPHEAVAL IN GOTHAM--LET'S JUST SAY PERSONNEL UPDATES HAVE VERY LOW PRIORITY, SHALL WE?
ANYWAY, I'M HERE TO REVIEW SECURITY ARRANGEMENTS WITH YOU.
NOT ACCORDING TO THE CONTRACT. NEED TO KNOW ONLY. YOU DON'T NEED TO KNOW.
I... SEE. WELL, MAY I CHECK THE STATUS OF THE DISCS?
NOT ACCORDING TO CONTRACT. WAYNE ONLY.
VERY GOOD, MR. NASTACIO. JUST THE RESPONSE WE WERE LOOKING FOR.
OH, ONE THING MORE.
WE HAVE RECEIVED RELIABLE INFORMATION THAT THE CRIMINAL KNOWN AS CATWOMAN INTENDS TO STEAL THE DISCS.

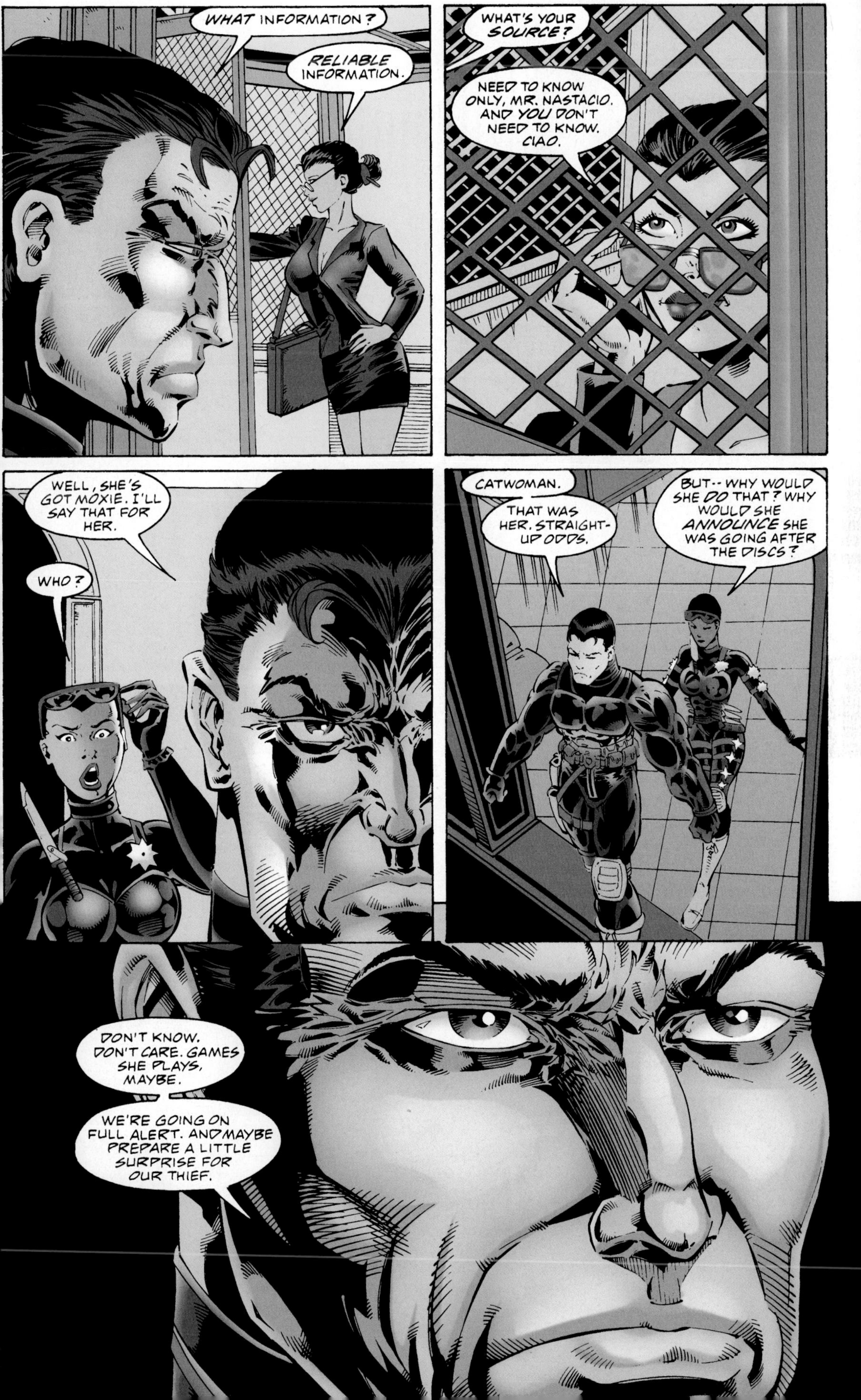
WHAT INFORMATION?
RELIABLE INFORMATION.
WHAT'S YOUR SOURCE?
NEED TO KNOW ONLY, MR. NASTACIO. AND YOU DON'T NEED TO KNOW. CIAO.
WELL, SHE'S GOT MOXIE. I'LL SAY THAT FOR HER.
WHO?
CATWOMAN.
THAT WAS HER. STRAIGHT-UP ODDS.
BUT-- WHY WOULD SHE DO THAT? WHY WOULD SHE ANNOUNCE SHE WAS GOING AFTER THE DISCS?
DON'T KNOW. DON'T CARE. GAMES SHE PLAYS, MAYBE.
WE'RE GOING ON FULL ALERT. AND MAYBE PREPARE A LITTLE SURPRISE FOR OUR THIEF.

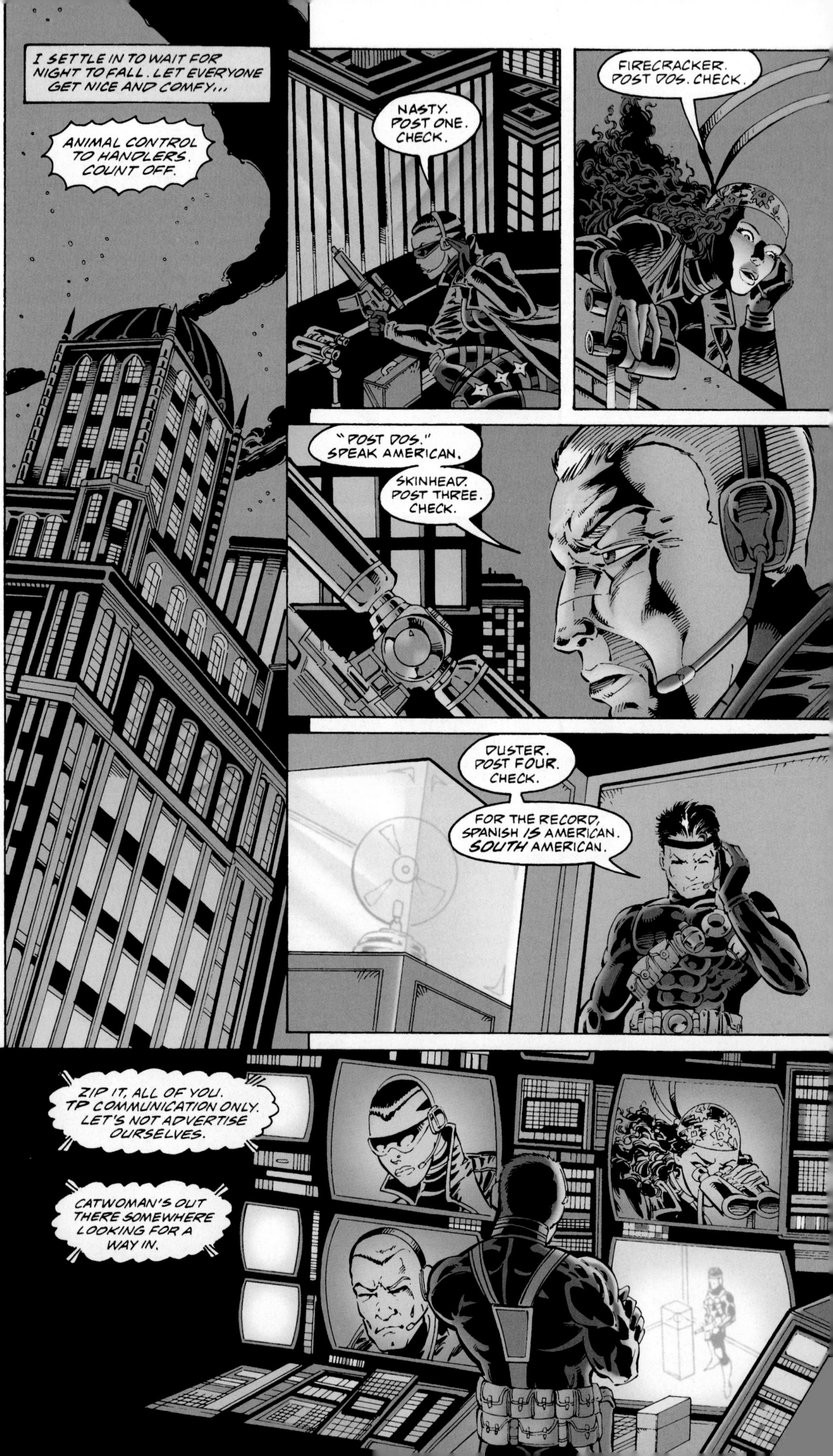
I SETTLE IN TO WAIT FOR NIGHT TO FALL. LET EVERYONE GET NICE AND COMFY...
ANIMAL CONTROL TO HANDLERS. COUNT OFF.
NASTY. POST ONE. CHECK.
FIRECRACKER. POST DOS. CHECK.
"POST DOS." SPEAK AMERICAN.
SKINHEAD. POST THREE. CHECK.
DUSTER. POST FOUR. CHECK.
FOR THE RECORD, SPANISH IS AMERICAN. SOUTH AMERICAN.
ZIP IT, ALL OF YOU. TP COMMUNICATION ONLY. LET'S NOT ADVERTISE OURSELVES.
CATWOMAN'S OUT THERE SOMEWHERE LOOKING FOR A WAY IN.

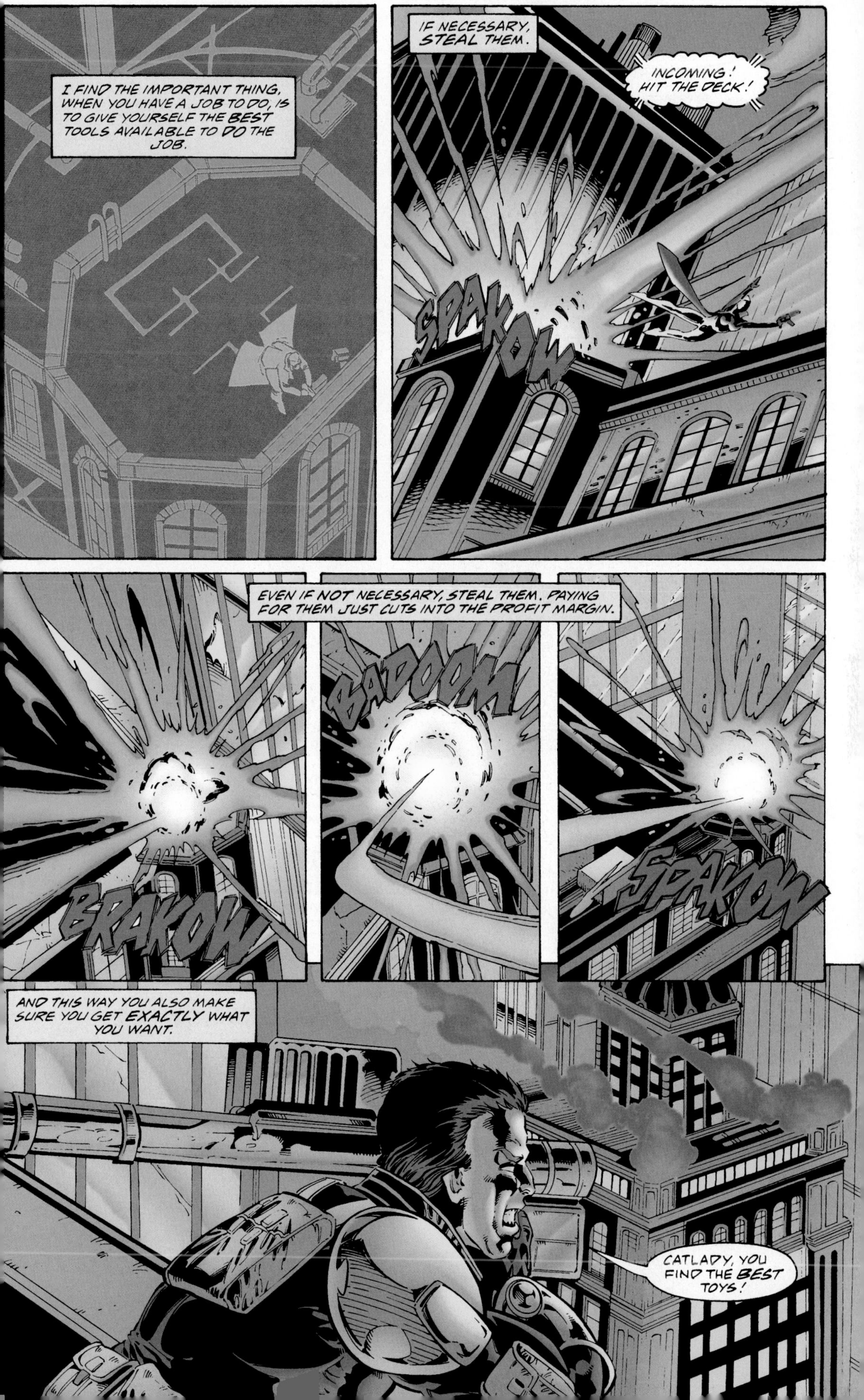
I FIND THE IMPORTANT THING, WHEN YOU HAVE A JOB TO DO, IS TO GIVE YOURSELF THE BEST TOOLS AVAILABLE TO DO THE JOB.
IF NECESSARY, STEAL THEM.
INCOMING! HIT THE DECK!
SPAKOW
EVEN IF NOT NECESSARY, STEAL THEM. PAYING FOR THEM JUST CUTS INTO THE PROFIT MARGIN.
BRAKOW
BADOOM
SPAKOW
AND THIS WAY YOU ALSO MAKE SURE YOU GET EXACTLY WHAT YOU WANT.
CATLADY, YOU FIND THE BEST TOYS!

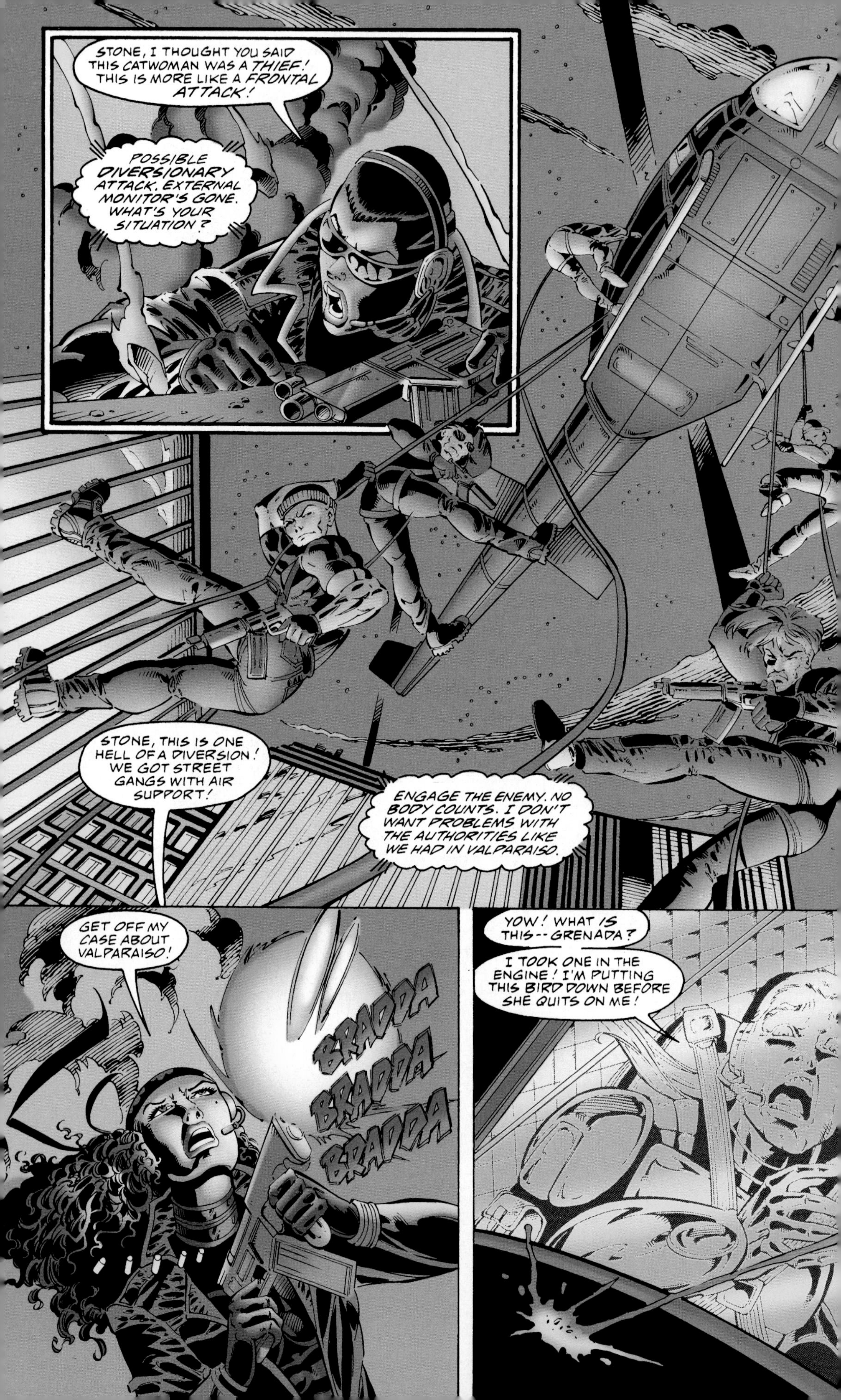
STONE, I THOUGHT YOU SAID THIS CATWOMAN WAS A THIEF! THIS IS MORE LIKE A FRONTAL ATTACK!
POSSIBLE DIVERSIONARY ATTACK. EXTERNAL MONITOR'S GONE. WHAT'S YOUR SITUATION?
STONE, THIS IS ONE HELL OF A DIVERSION! WE GOT STREET GANGS WITH AIR SUPPORT!
ENGAGE THE ENEMY. NO BODY COUNTS. I DON'T WANT PROBLEMS WITH THE AUTHORITIES LIKE WE HAD IN VALPARAISO.
GET OFF MY CASE ABOUT VALPARAISO!
BRADDA BRADDA BRADDA
YOW! WHAT IS THIS--GRENADA?
I TOOK ONE IN THE ENGINE! I'M PUTTING THIS BIRD DOWN BEFORE SHE QUITS ON ME!

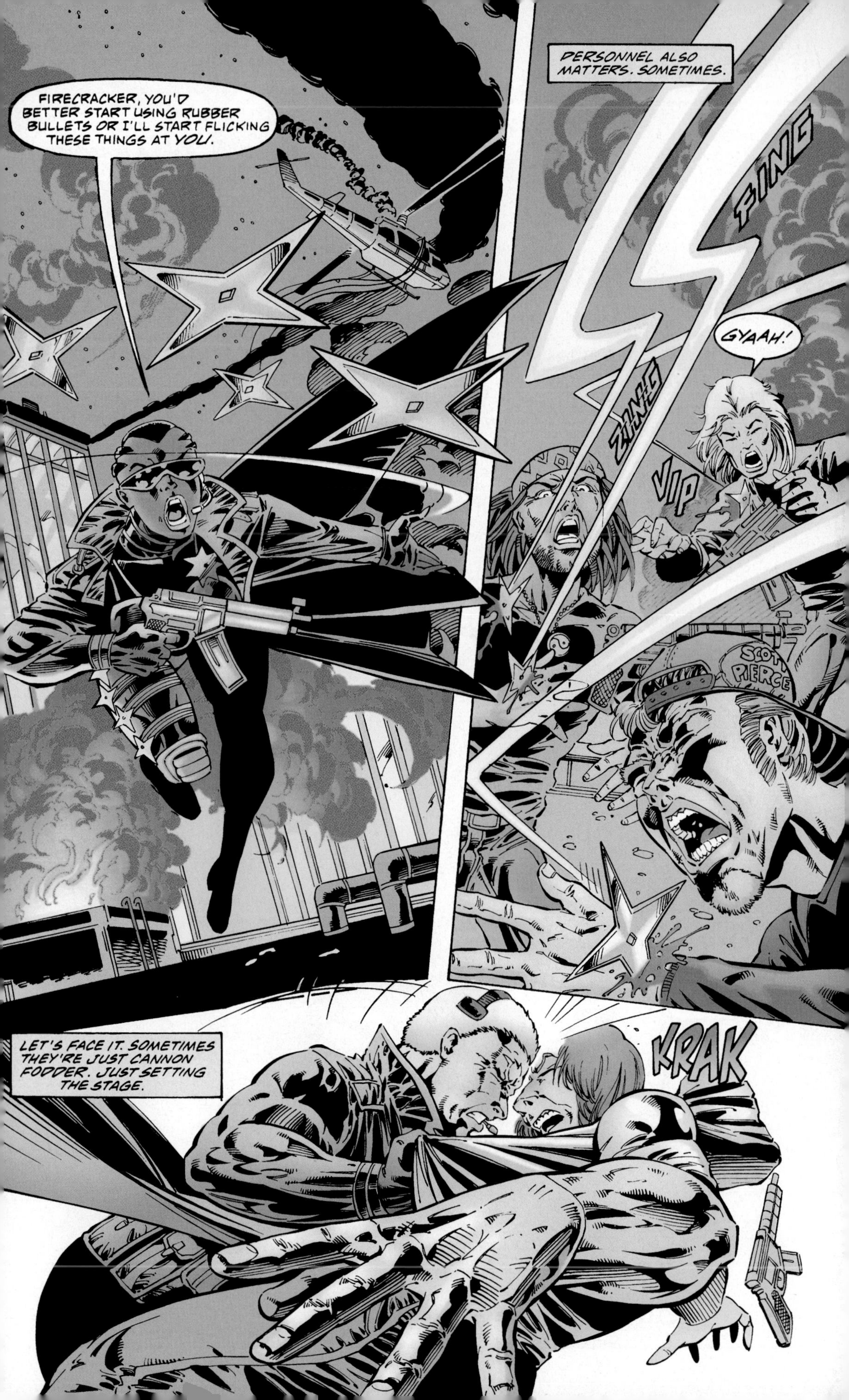
FIRECRACKER, YOU'D BETTER START USING RUBBER BULLETS OR I'LL START FLICKING THESE THINGS AT YOU.
PERSONNEL ALSO MATTERS. SOMETIMES.
FING
GYAAH!
ZING
VIP
SCOTT PIERCE
LET'S FACE IT. SOMETIMES THEY'RE JUST CANNON FODDER. JUST SETTING THE STAGE.
KRAK

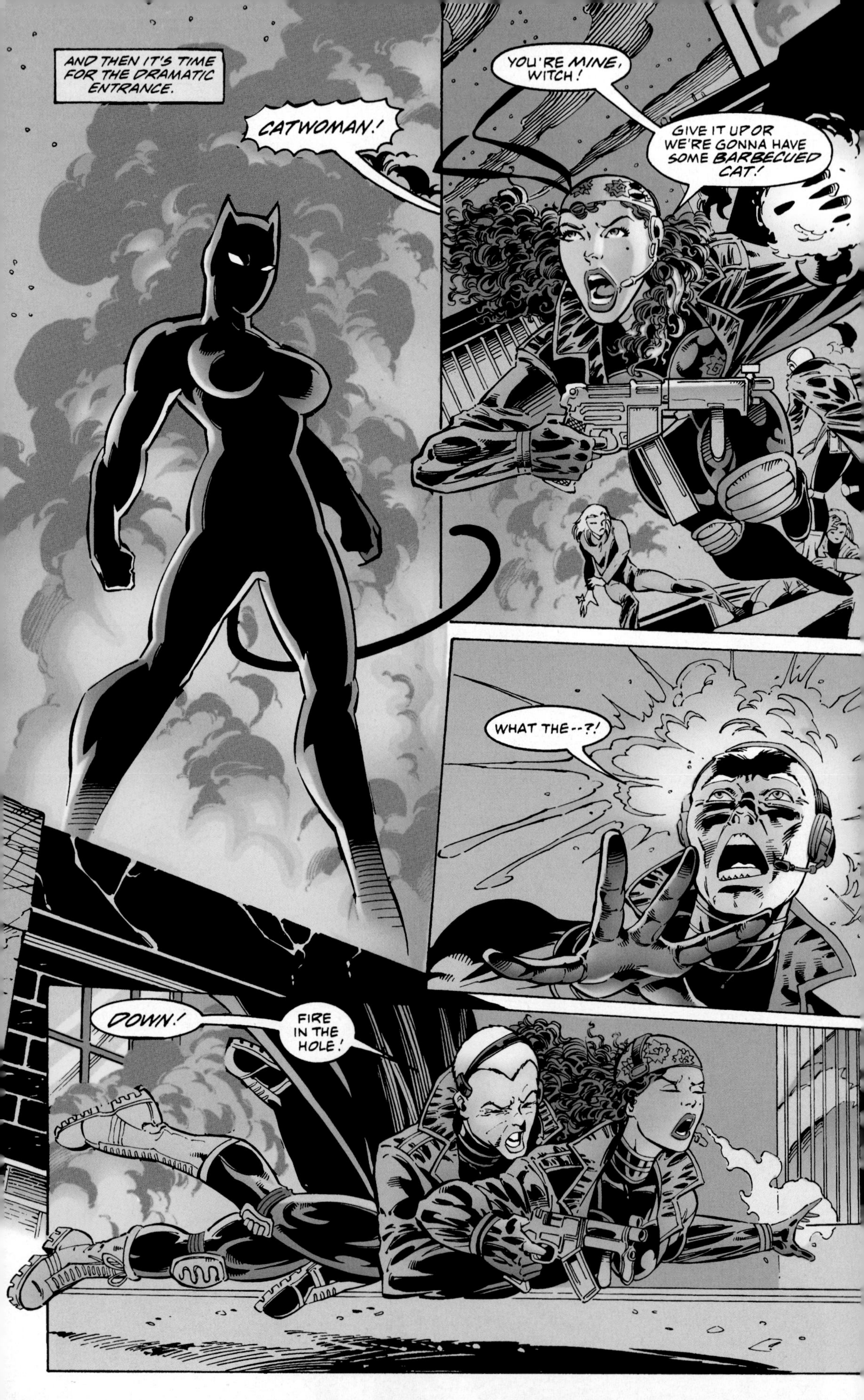

AND THEN IT'S TIME FOR THE DRAMATIC ENTRANCE.
CATWOMAN!
YOU'RE MINE, WITCH!
GIVE IT UP OR WE'RE GONNA HAVE SOME BARBECUED CAT!
WHAT THE--?!
DOWN!
FIRE IN THE HOLE!

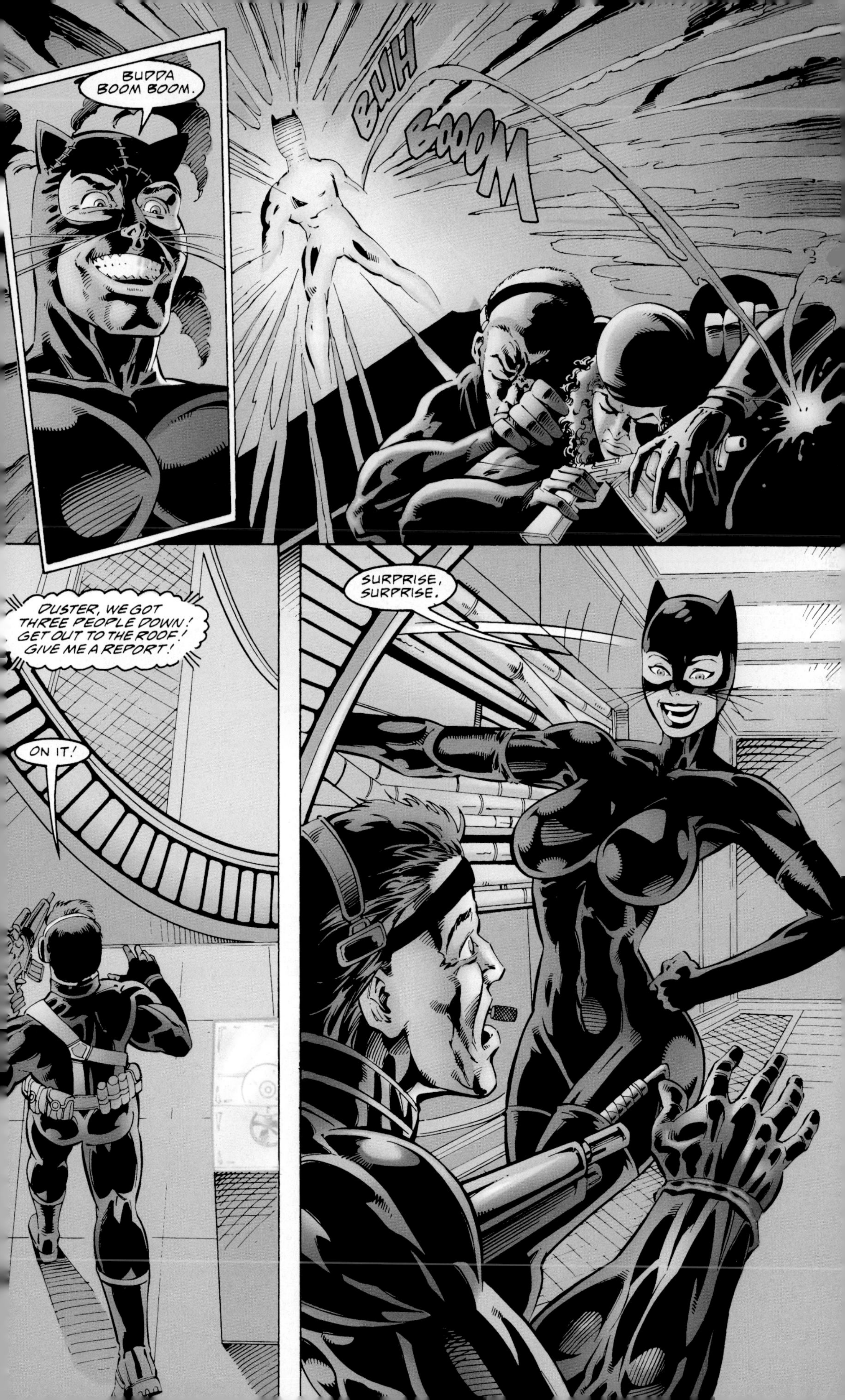
BUDDA BOOM BOOM.
BUH
BOOOM
DUSTER, WE GOT THREE PEOPLE DOWN! GET OUT TO THE ROOF! GIVE ME A REPORT!
ON IT!
SURPRISE, SURPRISE.

SFX: **KLOK**

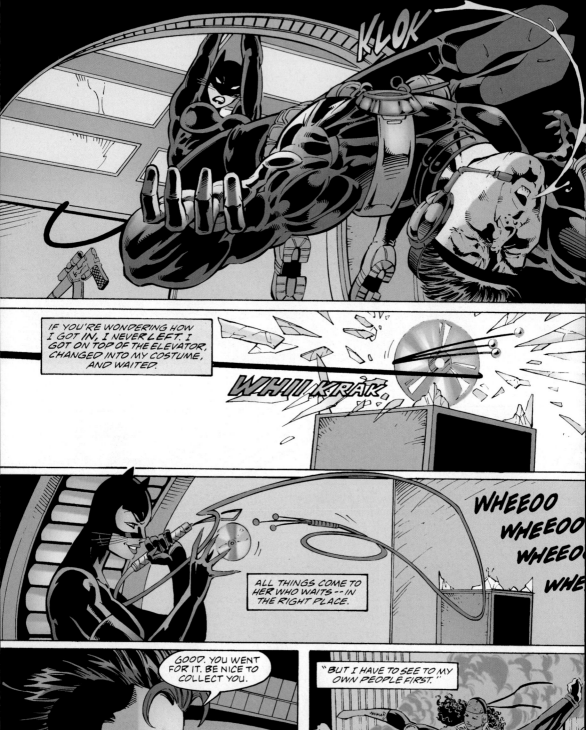

If you're wondering how I got in, I never left. I got on top of the elevator, changed into my costume, and waited.

SFX: **WHII KRAK.**

SFX: WHEEOO WHEEOO WHEEOO WHE

All things come to her who waits -- in the right place.

Good. You went for it. Be nice to collect you.

"But I have to see to my own people first."

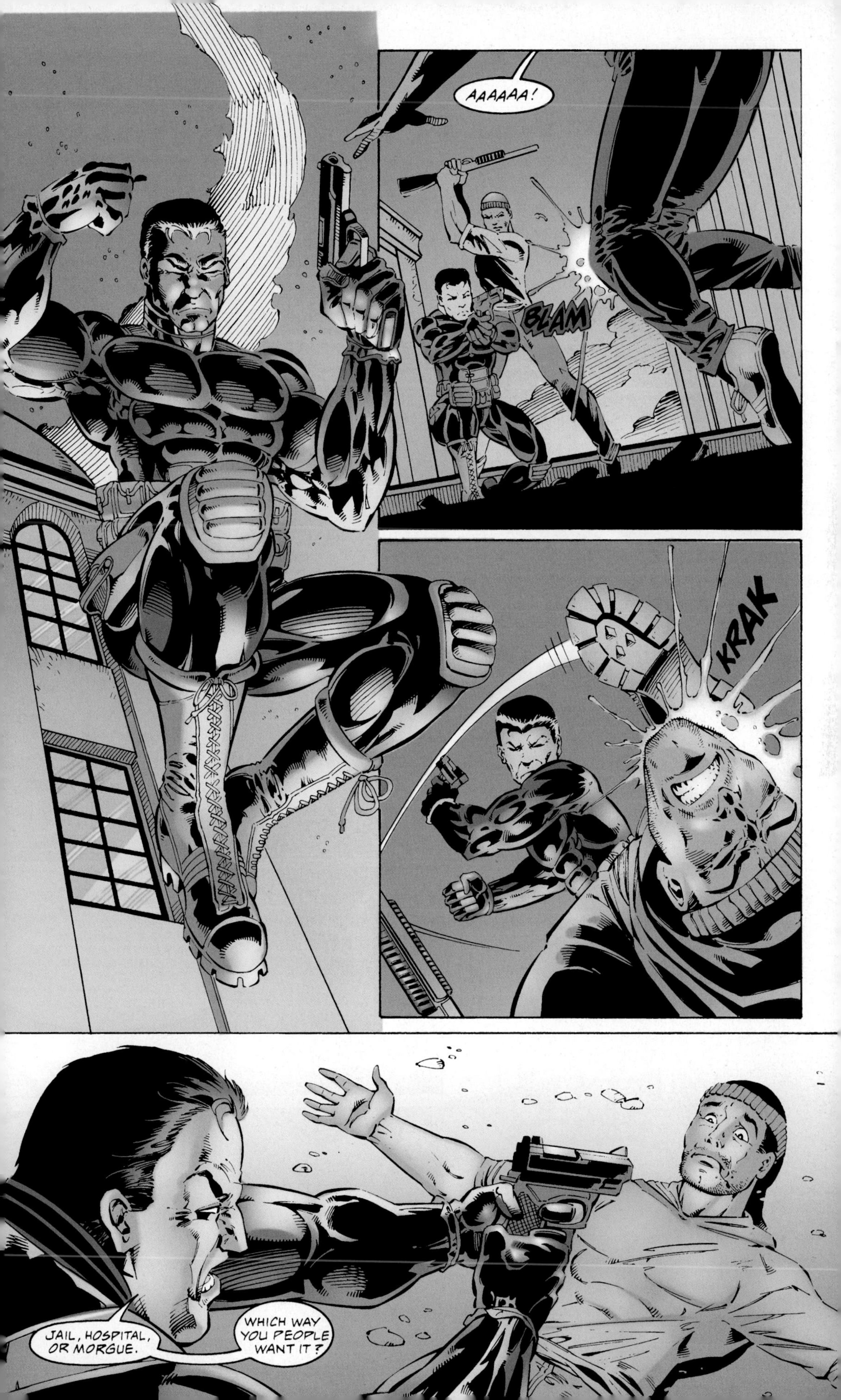
AAAAAA!
BLAM
KRAK
JAIL, HOSPITAL, OR MORGUE.
WHICH WAY YOU PEOPLE WANT IT?

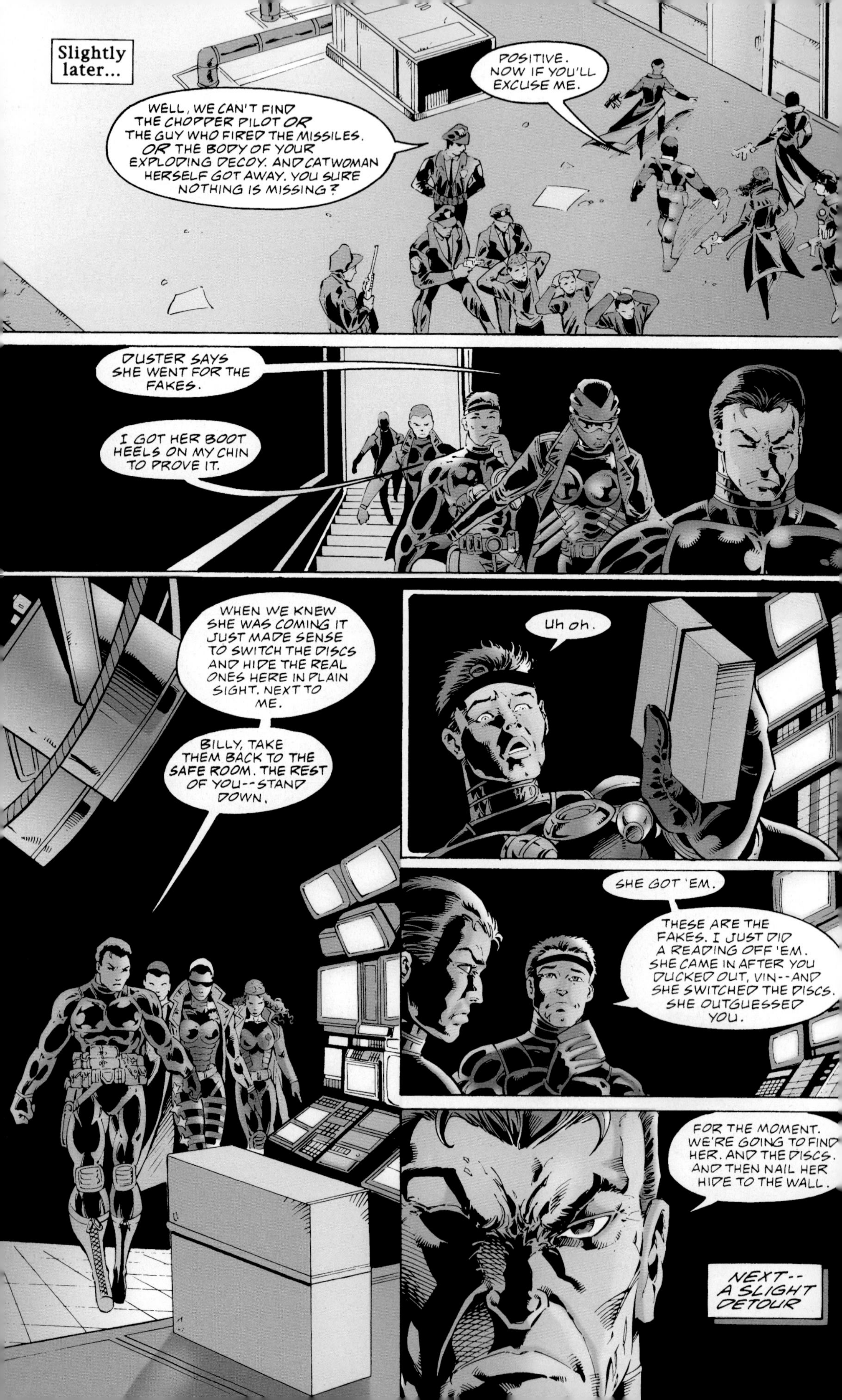
Slightly later...
WELL, WE CAN'T FIND THE CHOPPER PILOT OR THE GUY WHO FIRED THE MISSILES. OR THE BODY OF YOUR EXPLODING DECOY. AND CATWOMAN HERSELF GOT AWAY. YOU SURE NOTHING IS MISSING?
POSITIVE. NOW IF YOU'LL EXCUSE ME.
DUSTER SAYS SHE WENT FOR THE FAKES.
I GOT HER BOOT HEELS ON MY CHIN TO PROVE IT.
WHEN WE KNEW SHE WAS COMING IT JUST MADE SENSE TO SWITCH THE DISCS AND HIDE THE REAL ONES HERE IN PLAIN SIGHT. NEXT TO ME.
BILLY, TAKE THEM BACK TO THE SAFE ROOM. THE REST OF YOU--STAND DOWN.
Uh oh.
SHE GOT 'EM.
THESE ARE THE FAKES. I JUST DID A READING OFF 'EM. SHE CAME IN AFTER YOU DUCKED OUT, VIN--AND SHE SWITCHED THE DISCS. SHE OUTGUESSED YOU.
FOR THE MOMENT. WE'RE GOING TO FIND HER. AND THE DISCS. AND THEN NAIL HER HIDE TO THE WALL.
NEXT-- A SLIGHT DETOUR

...and after the Earth shattered and the buildings crumbled, the nation abandoned Gotham City. Then only the valiant, the venal and the insane remained in the place they called NO MAN'S LAND
SEE WHAT I GOT?
JOHN OSTRANDER WRITER
JIM BALENT PENCILLER
MARLO ALQUIZA INKER
ALBERT DE GUZMAN LETTERS
ROBERTA TEWES COLORS
FRANK BERRIOS ASST. EDITOR
MATT IDELSON EDITOR
A SLIGHT DETOUR

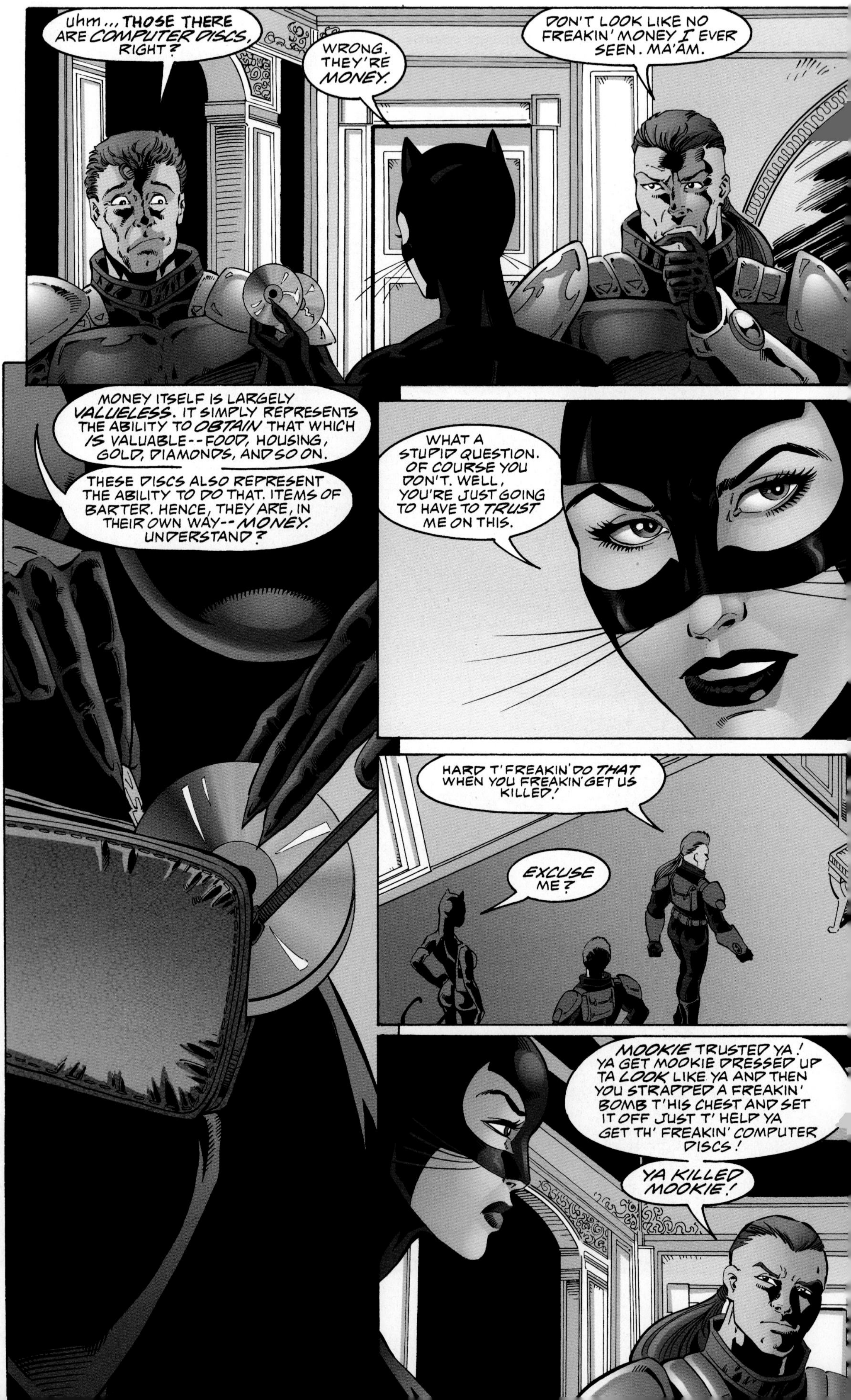
uhm... THOSE THERE ARE COMPUTER DISCS, RIGHT?
WRONG. THEY'RE MONEY.
DON'T LOOK LIKE NO FREAKIN' MONEY I EVER SEEN. MA'AM.
MONEY ITSELF IS LARGELY VALUELESS. IT SIMPLY REPRESENTS THE ABILITY TO OBTAIN THAT WHICH IS VALUABLE--FOOD, HOUSING, GOLD, DIAMONDS, AND SO ON.
THESE DISCS ALSO REPRESENT THE ABILITY TO DO THAT. ITEMS OF BARTER. HENCE, THEY ARE, IN THEIR OWN WAY--MONEY. UNDERSTAND?
WHAT A STUPID QUESTION. OF COURSE YOU DON'T. WELL, YOU'RE JUST GOING TO HAVE TO TRUST ME ON THIS.
HARD T'FREAKIN' DO THAT WHEN YOU FREAKIN' GET US KILLED!
EXCUSE ME?
MOOKIE TRUSTED YA! YA GET MOOKIE DRESSED UP TA LOOK LIKE YA AND THEN YOU STRAPPED A FREAKIN' BOMB T'HIS CHEST AND SET IT OFF JUST T' HELP YA GET TH' FREAKIN' COMPUTER DISCS!
YA KILLED MOOKIE!

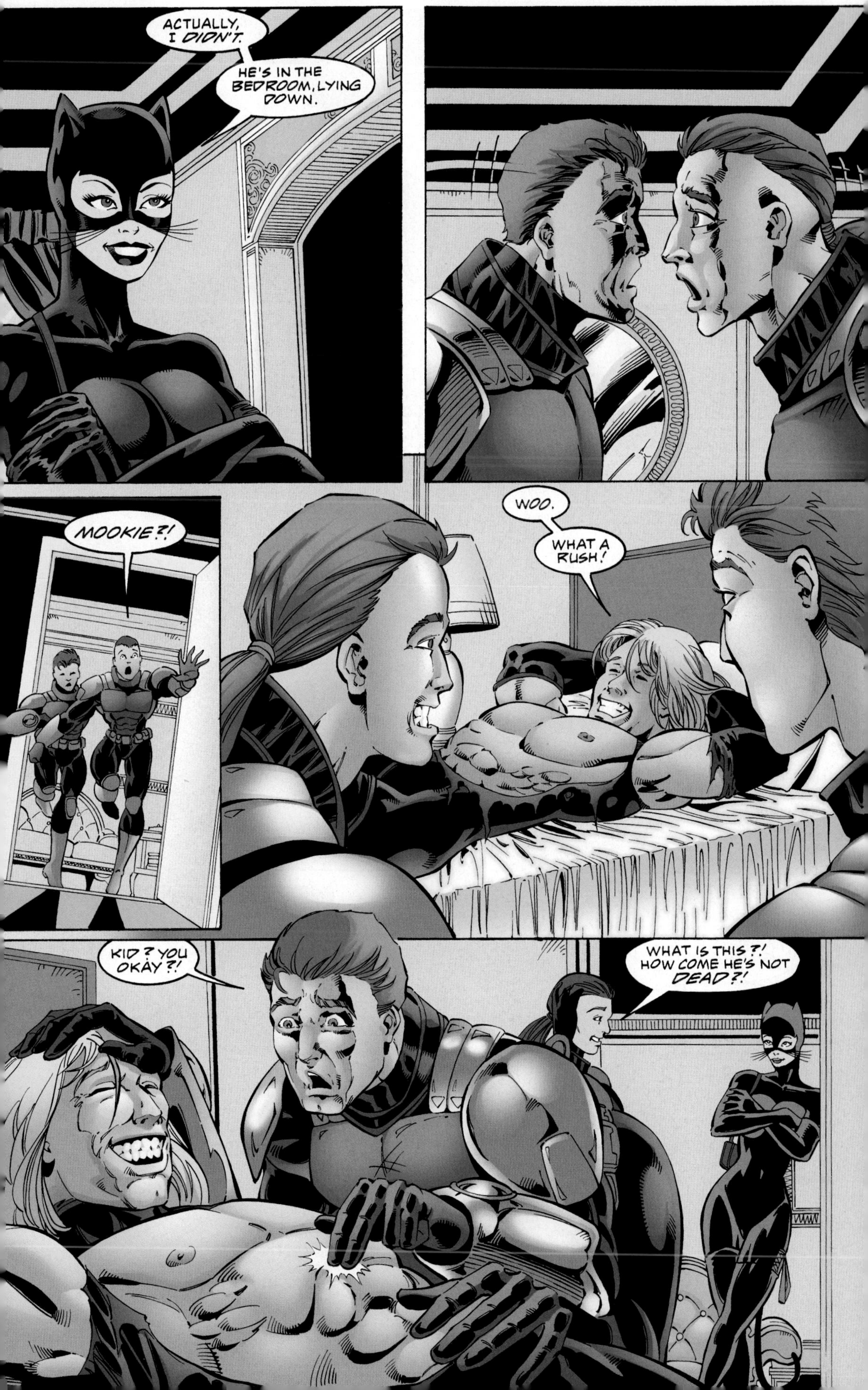
ACTUALLY, I DIDN'T.
HE'S IN THE BEDROOM, LYING DOWN.
MOOKIE?!
WOO.
WHAT A RUSH!
KID? YOU OKAY?!
WHAT IS THIS?! HOW COME HE'S NOT DEAD?!

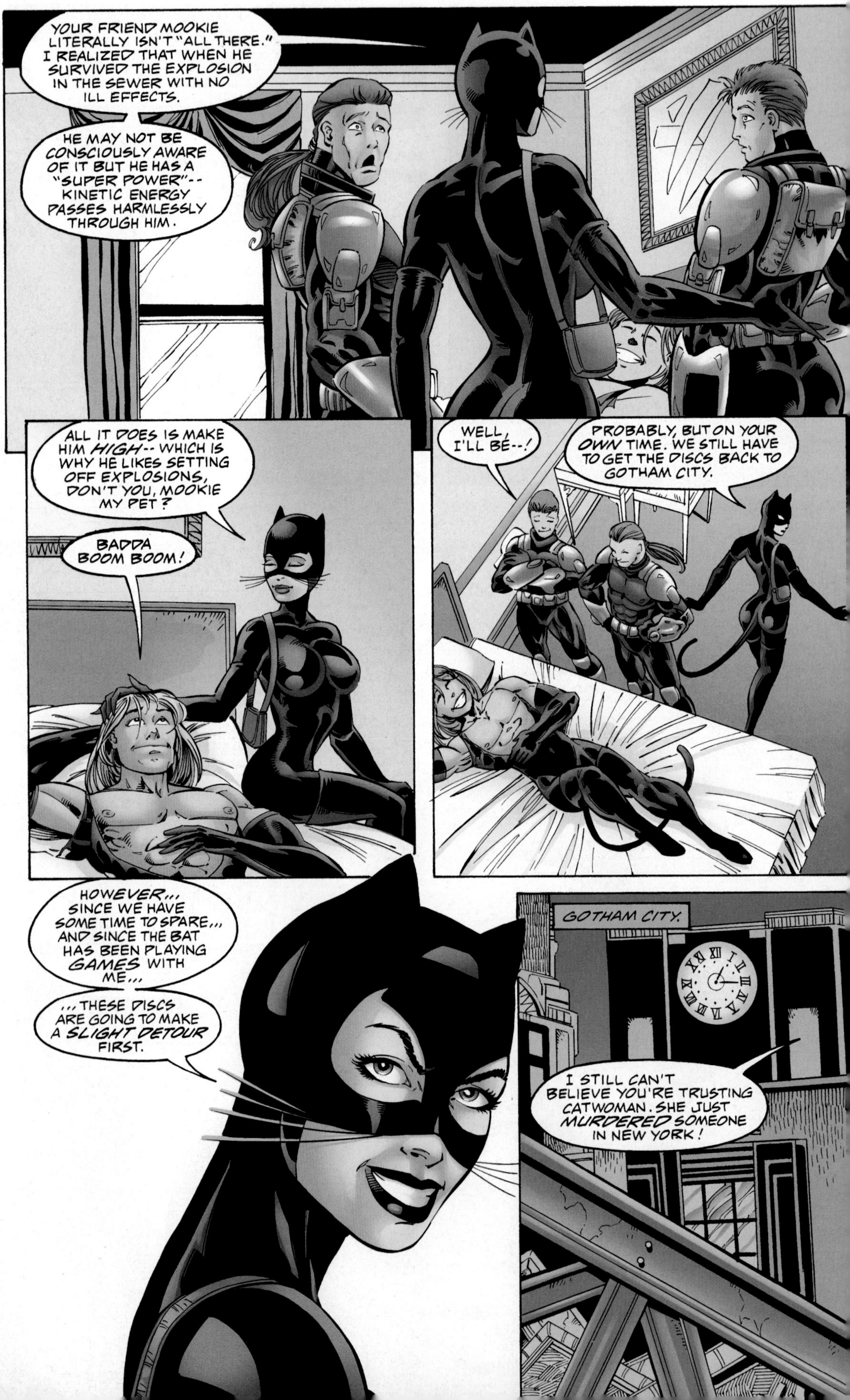
YOUR FRIEND MOOKIE LITERALLY ISN'T "ALL THERE." I REALIZED THAT WHEN HE SURVIVED THE EXPLOSION IN THE SEWER WITH NO ILL EFFECTS.
HE MAY NOT BE CONSCIOUSLY AWARE OF IT BUT HE HAS A "SUPER POWER"-- KINETIC ENERGY PASSES HARMLESSLY THROUGH HIM.
ALL IT DOES IS MAKE HIM HIGH-- WHICH IS WHY HE LIKES SETTING OFF EXPLOSIONS, DON'T YOU, MOOKIE MY PET?
BADDA BOOM BOOM!
WELL, I'LL BE--!
PROBABLY, BUT ON YOUR OWN TIME. WE STILL HAVE TO GET THE DISCS BACK TO GOTHAM CITY.
HOWEVER... SINCE WE HAVE SOME TIME TO SPARE... AND SINCE THE BAT HAS BEEN PLAYING GAMES WITH ME...
...THESE DISCS ARE GOING TO MAKE A SLIGHT DETOUR FIRST.
GOTHAM CITY.
I STILL CAN'T BELIEVE YOU'RE TRUSTING CATWOMAN. SHE JUST MURDERED SOMEONE IN NEW YORK!

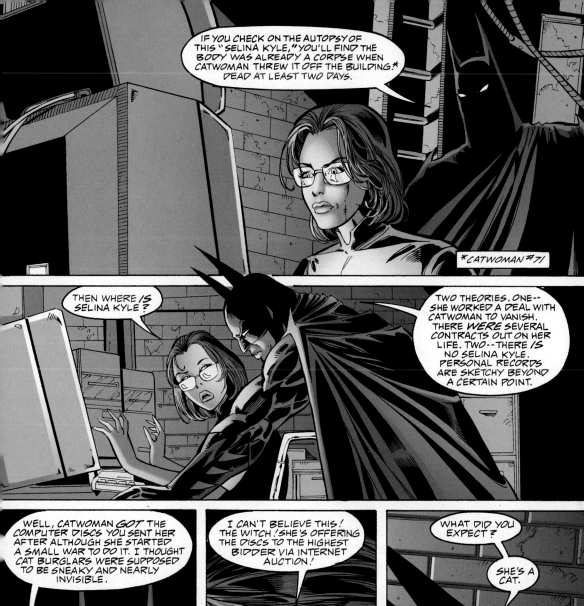

IF YOU CHECK ON THE AUTOPSY OF THIS "SELINA KYLE," YOU'LL FIND THE BODY WAS ALREADY A CORPSE WHEN CATWOMAN THREW IT OFF THE BUILDING.* DEAD AT LEAST TWO DAYS.

*CATWOMAN #71

THEN WHERE *IS* SELINA KYLE?

TWO THEORIES. ONE-- SHE WORKED A DEAL WITH CATWOMAN TO VANISH. THERE *WERE* SEVERAL CONTRACTS OUT ON HER LIFE. TWO--THERE *IS* NO SELINA KYLE. PERSONAL RECORDS ARE SKETCHY BEYOND A CERTAIN POINT.

WELL, CATWOMAN *GOT* THE COMPUTER DISCS YOU SENT HER AFTER ALTHOUGH SHE STARTED A SMALL WAR TO DO IT. I THOUGHT CAT BURGLARS WERE SUPPOSED TO BE SNEAKY AND NEARLY INVISIBLE.

MOST CAT BURGLARS DON'T WEAR SPANDEX OR CARRY A WHIP.

I CAN'T BELIEVE THIS! THE WITCH! SHE'S OFFERING THE DISCS TO THE HIGHEST BIDDER VIA INTERNET AUCTION!

WHAT DID YOU EXPECT?

SHE'S A CAT.

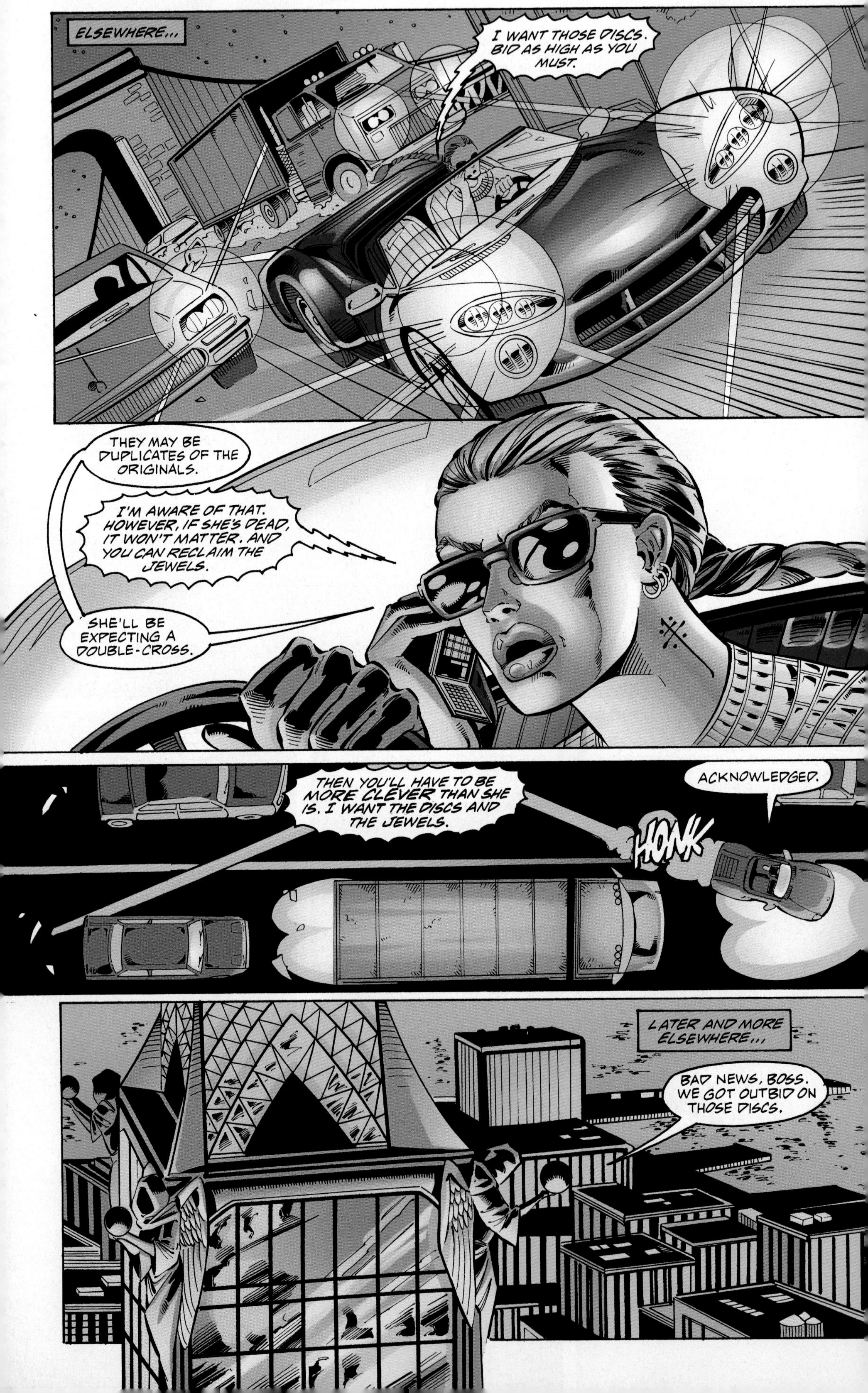
ELSEWHERE...
I WANT THOSE DISCS. BID AS HIGH AS YOU MUST.
THEY MAY BE DUPLICATES OF THE ORIGINALS.
I'M AWARE OF THAT. HOWEVER, IF SHE'S DEAD, IT WON'T MATTER. AND YOU CAN RECLAIM THE JEWELS.
SHE'LL BE EXPECTING A DOUBLE-CROSS.
THEN YOU'LL HAVE TO BE MORE CLEVER THAN SHE IS. I WANT THE DISCS AND THE JEWELS.
ACKNOWLEDGED.
HONK
LATER AND MORE ELSEWHERE...
BAD NEWS, BOSS. WE GOT OUTBID ON THOSE DISCS.

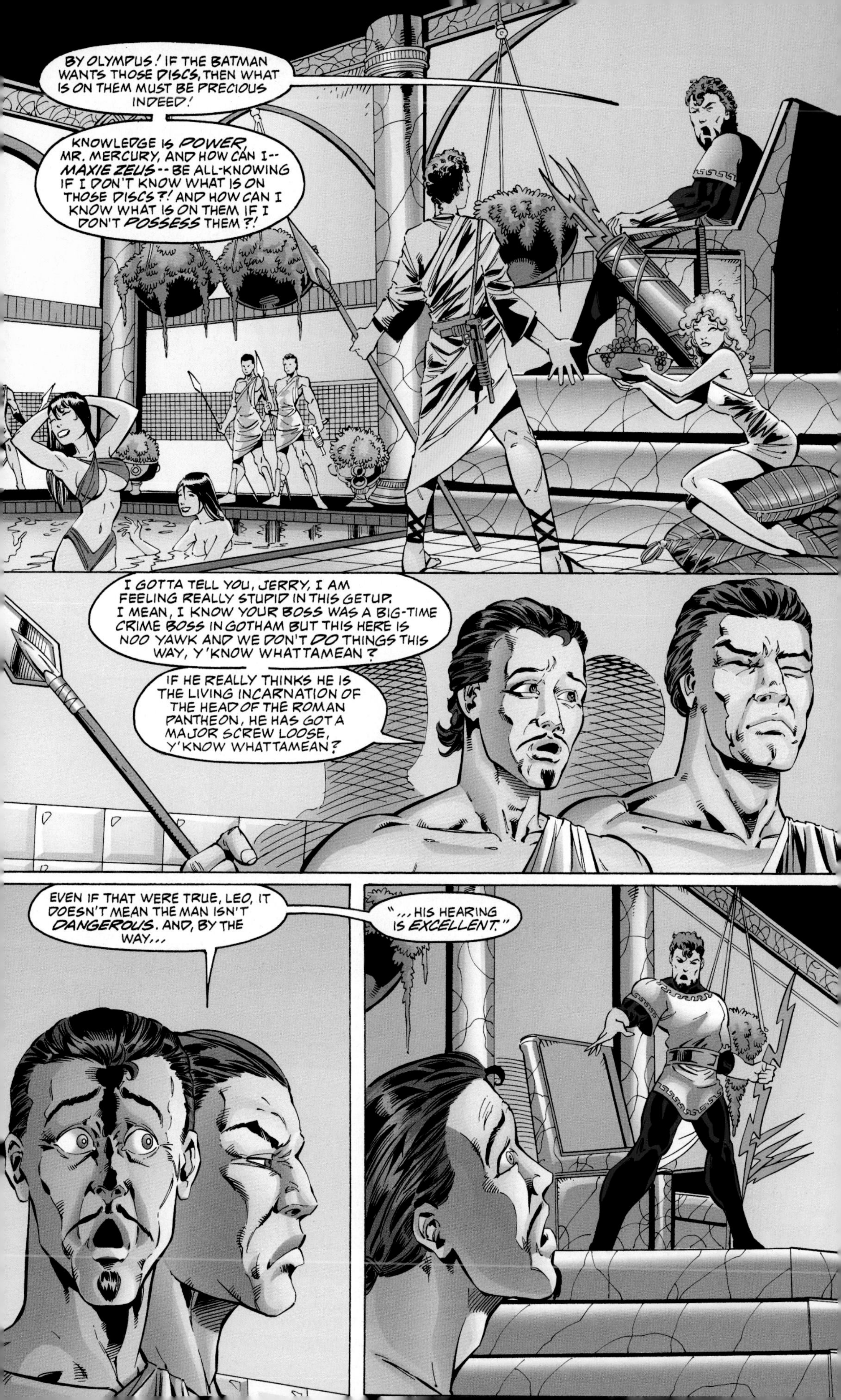
BY OLYMPUS! IF THE BATMAN WANTS THOSE DISCS, THEN WHAT IS ON THEM MUST BE PRECIOUS INDEED!
KNOWLEDGE IS POWER, MR. MERCURY, AND HOW CAN I-- MAXIE ZEUS-- BE ALL-KNOWING IF I DON'T KNOW WHAT IS ON THOSE DISCS?! AND HOW CAN I KNOW WHAT IS ON THEM IF I DON'T POSSESS THEM?!
I GOTTA TELL YOU, JERRY, I AM FEELING REALLY STUPID IN THIS GETUP. I MEAN, I KNOW YOUR BOSS WAS A BIG-TIME CRIME BOSS IN GOTHAM BUT THIS HERE IS NOO YAWK AND WE DON'T DO THINGS THIS WAY, Y'KNOW WHATTAMEAN?
IF HE REALLY THINKS HE IS THE LIVING INCARNATION OF THE HEAD OF THE ROMAN PANTHEON, HE HAS GOT A MAJOR SCREW LOOSE, Y'KNOW WHATTAMEAN?
EVEN IF THAT WERE TRUE, LEO, IT DOESN'T MEAN THE MAN ISN'T DANGEROUS. AND, BY THE WAY...
"...HIS HEARING IS EXCELLENT."

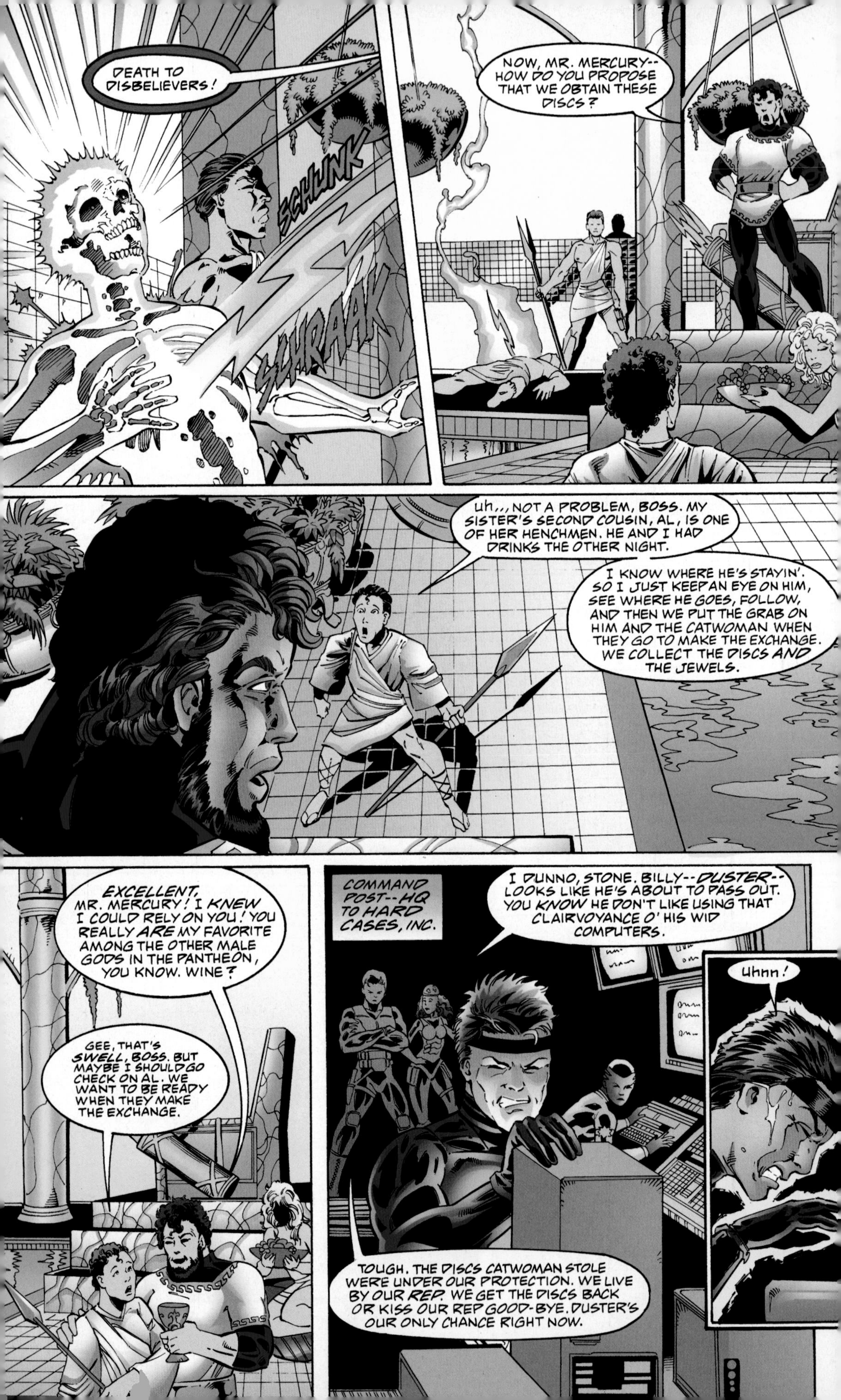
DEATH TO DISBELIEVERS!
SCHLUNK
SHRAAK
NOW, MR. MERCURY-- HOW DO YOU PROPOSE THAT WE OBTAIN THESE DISCS?
UH... NOT A PROBLEM, BOSS. MY SISTER'S SECOND COUSIN, AL, IS ONE OF HER HENCHMEN. HE AND I HAD DRINKS THE OTHER NIGHT.
I KNOW WHERE HE'S STAYIN'. SO I JUST KEEP AN EYE ON HIM, SEE WHERE HE GOES, FOLLOW, AND THEN WE PUT THE GRAB ON HIM AND THE CATWOMAN WHEN THEY GO TO MAKE THE EXCHANGE. WE COLLECT THE DISCS AND THE JEWELS.
EXCELLENT, MR. MERCURY! I KNEW I COULD RELY ON YOU! YOU REALLY ARE MY FAVORITE AMONG THE OTHER MALE GODS IN THE PANTHEON, YOU KNOW. WINE?
GEE, THAT'S SWELL, BOSS. BUT MAYBE I SHOULD GO CHECK ON AL. WE WANT TO BE READY WHEN THEY MAKE THE EXCHANGE.
COMMAND POST--HQ TO HARD CASES, INC.
I DUNNO, STONE. BILLY--DUSTER--LOOKS LIKE HE'S ABOUT TO PASS OUT. YOU KNOW HE DON'T LIKE USING THAT CLAIRVOYANCE O' HIS WID COMPUTERS.
UHNN!
TOUGH. THE DISCS CATWOMAN STOLE WERE UNDER OUR PROTECTION. WE LIVE BY OUR REP. WE GET THE DISCS BACK OR KISS OUR REP GOOD-BYE. DUSTER'S OUR ONLY CHANCE RIGHT NOW.

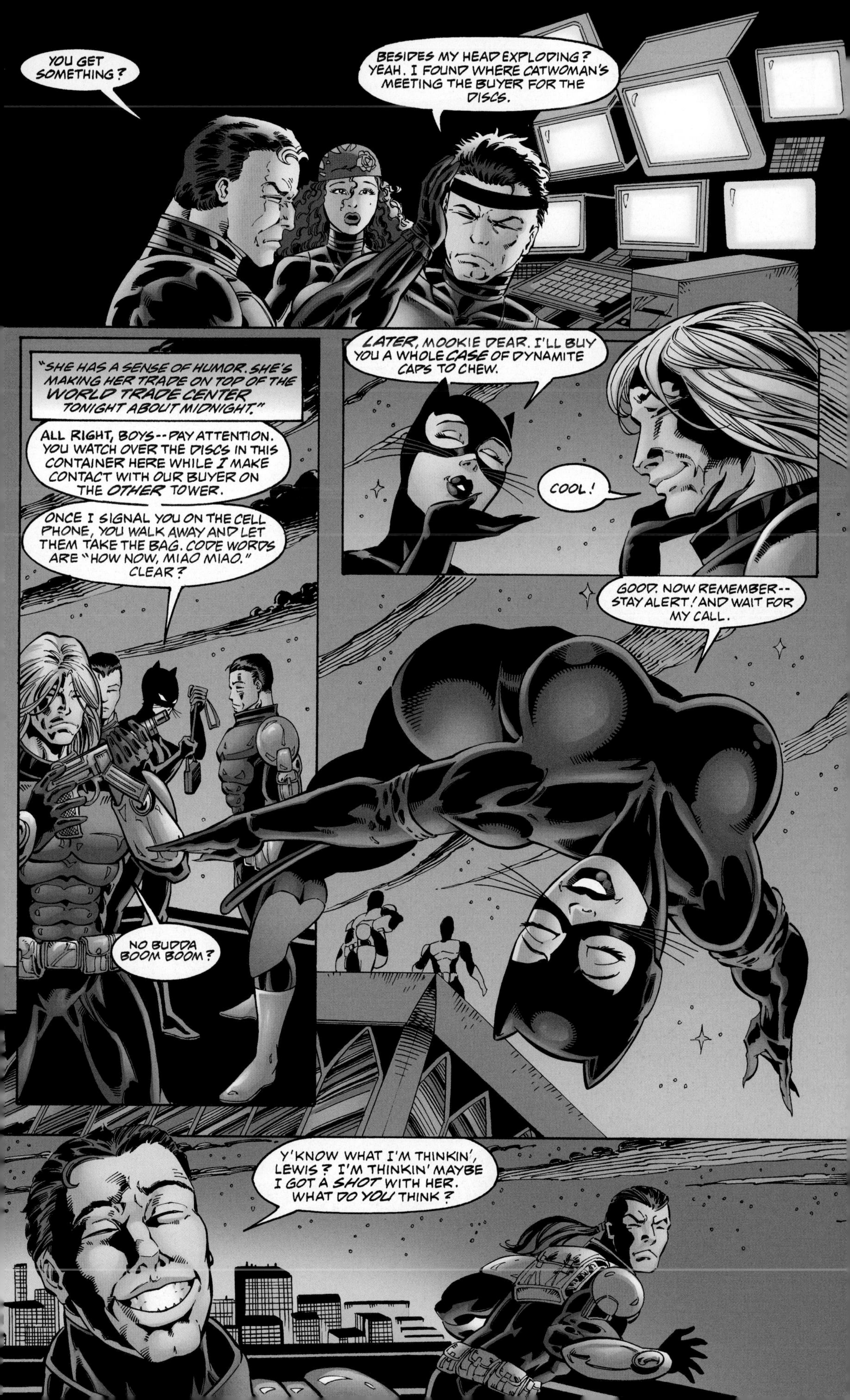
YOU GET SOMETHING?
BESIDES MY HEAD EXPLODING? YEAH. I FOUND WHERE CATWOMAN'S MEETING THE BUYER FOR THE DISCS.
"SHE HAS A SENSE OF HUMOR. SHE'S MAKING HER TRADE ON TOP OF THE WORLD TRADE CENTER TONIGHT ABOUT MIDNIGHT."
ALL RIGHT, BOYS--PAY ATTENTION. YOU WATCH OVER THE DISCS IN THIS CONTAINER HERE WHILE I MAKE CONTACT WITH OUR BUYER ON THE OTHER TOWER.
ONCE I SIGNAL YOU ON THE CELL PHONE, YOU WALK AWAY AND LET THEM TAKE THE BAG. CODE WORDS ARE "HOW NOW, MIAO MIAO." CLEAR?
NO BUDDA BOOM BOOM?
LATER, MOOKIE DEAR. I'LL BUY YOU A WHOLE CASE OF DYNAMITE CAPS TO CHEW.
COOL!
GOOD. NOW REMEMBER--STAY ALERT! AND WAIT FOR MY CALL.
Y'KNOW WHAT I'M THINKIN', LEWIS? I'M THINKIN' MAYBE I GOT A SHOT WITH HER. WHAT DO YOU THINK?

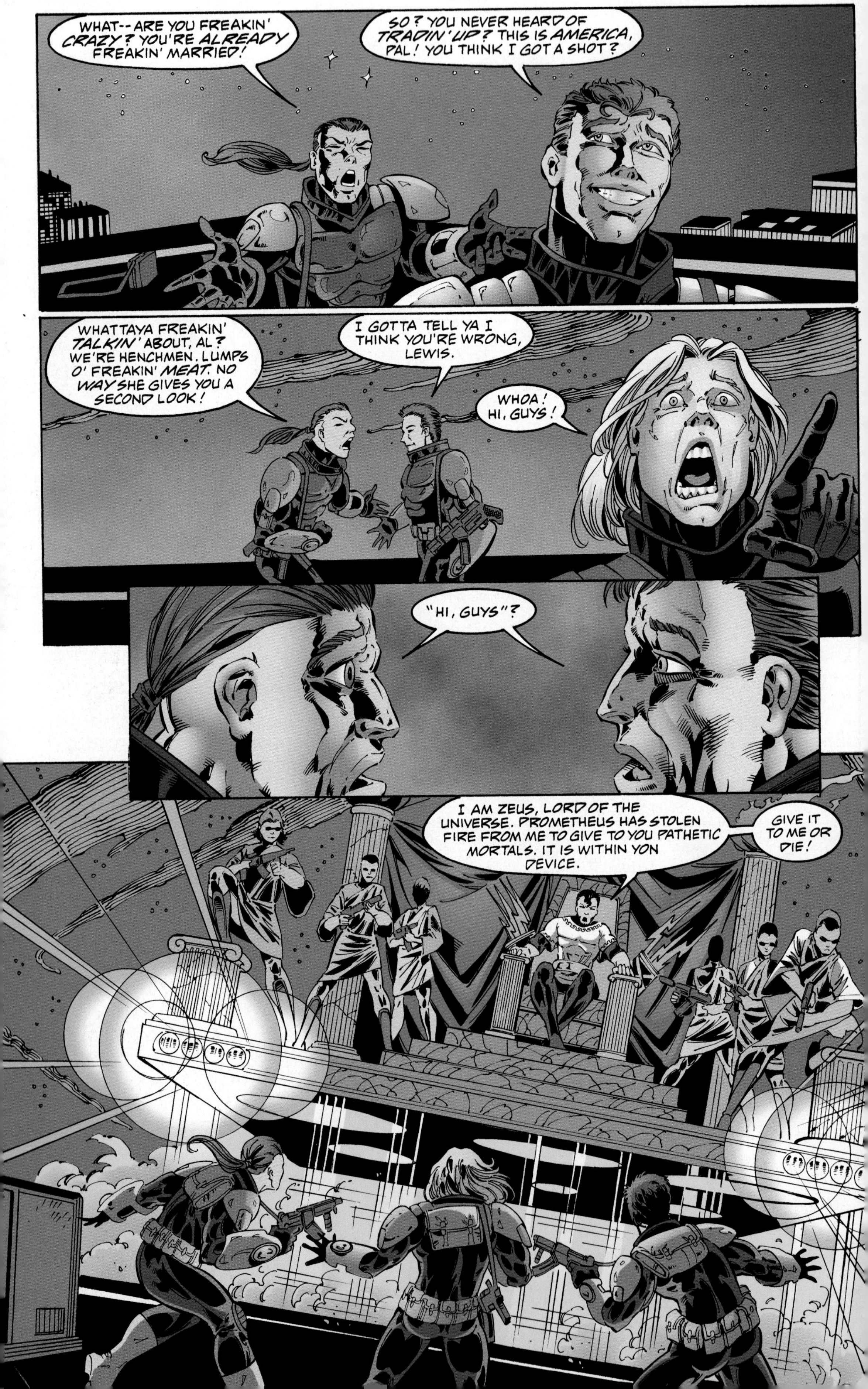
WHAT--ARE YOU FREAKIN' CRAZY? YOU'RE ALREADY FREAKIN' MARRIED!
SO? YOU NEVER HEARD OF TRADIN' UP? THIS IS AMERICA, PAL! YOU THINK I GOT A SHOT?
WHATTAYA FREAKIN' TALKIN' ABOUT, AL? WE'RE HENCHMEN. LUMPS O' FREAKIN' MEAT. NO WAY SHE GIVES YOU A SECOND LOOK!
I GOTTA TELL YA I THINK YOU'RE WRONG, LEWIS.
WHOA! HI, GUYS!
"HI, GUYS"?
I AM ZEUS, LORD OF THE UNIVERSE. PROMETHEUS HAS STOLEN FIRE FROM ME TO GIVE TO YOU PATHETIC MORTALS. IT IS WITHIN YON DEVICE.
GIVE IT TO ME OR DIE!

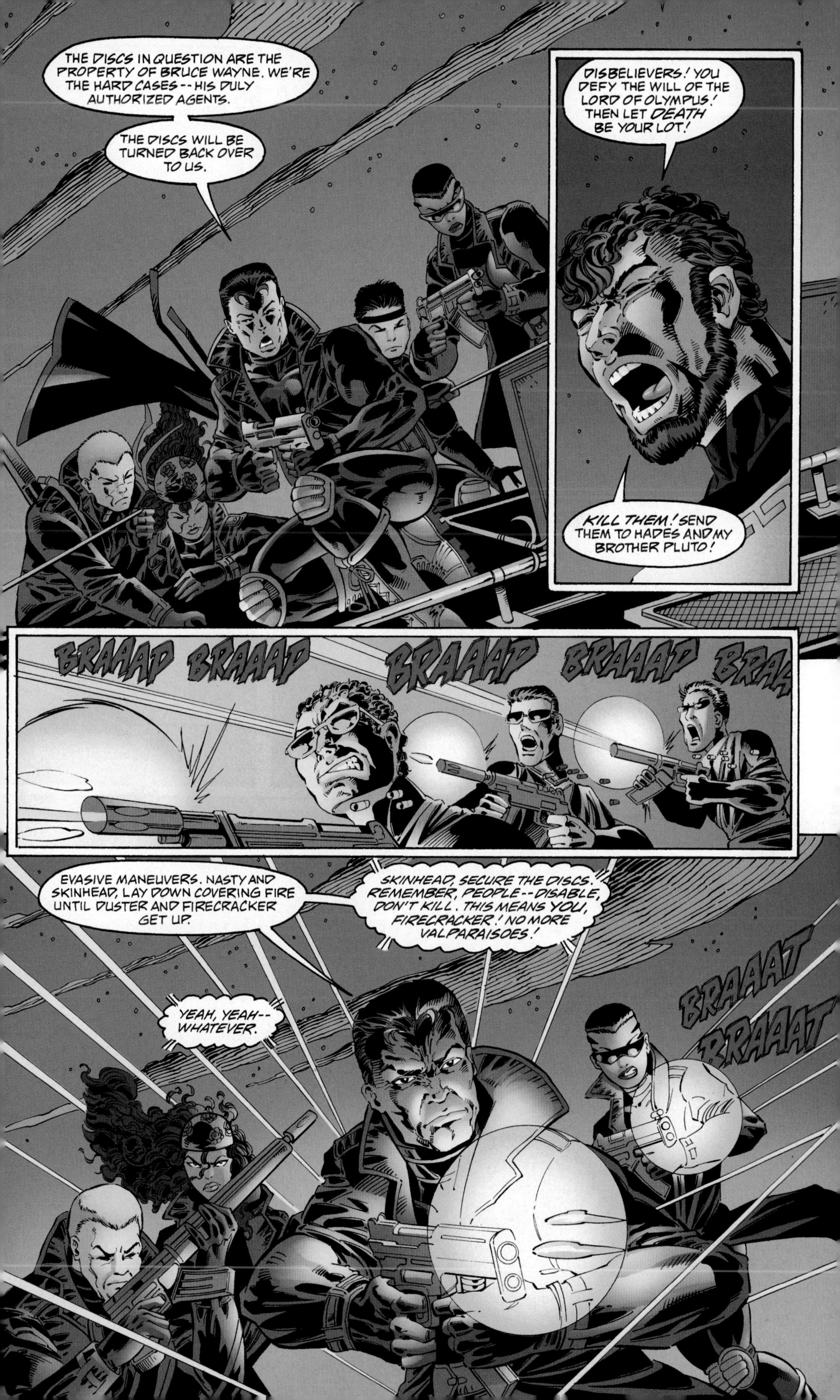

THE DISCS IN QUESTION ARE THE PROPERTY OF BRUCE WAYNE. WE'RE THE HARD CASES -- HIS DULY AUTHORIZED AGENTS.
THE DISCS WILL BE TURNED BACK OVER TO US.
DISBELIEVERS! YOU DEFY THE WILL OF THE LORD OF OLYMPUS! THEN LET DEATH BE YOUR LOT!
KILL THEM! SEND THEM TO HADES AND MY BROTHER PLUTO!
BRAAAP BRAAAP BRAAAP BRAAAP
EVASIVE MANEUVERS. NASTY AND SKINHEAD, LAY DOWN COVERING FIRE UNTIL DUSTER AND FIRECRACKER GET UP.
SKINHEAD, SECURE THE DISCS. REMEMBER, PEOPLE--DISABLE, DON'T KILL. THIS MEANS YOU, FIRECRACKER! NO MORE VALPARAISOES!
YEAH, YEAH-- WHATEVER.
BRAAAT BRAAAT

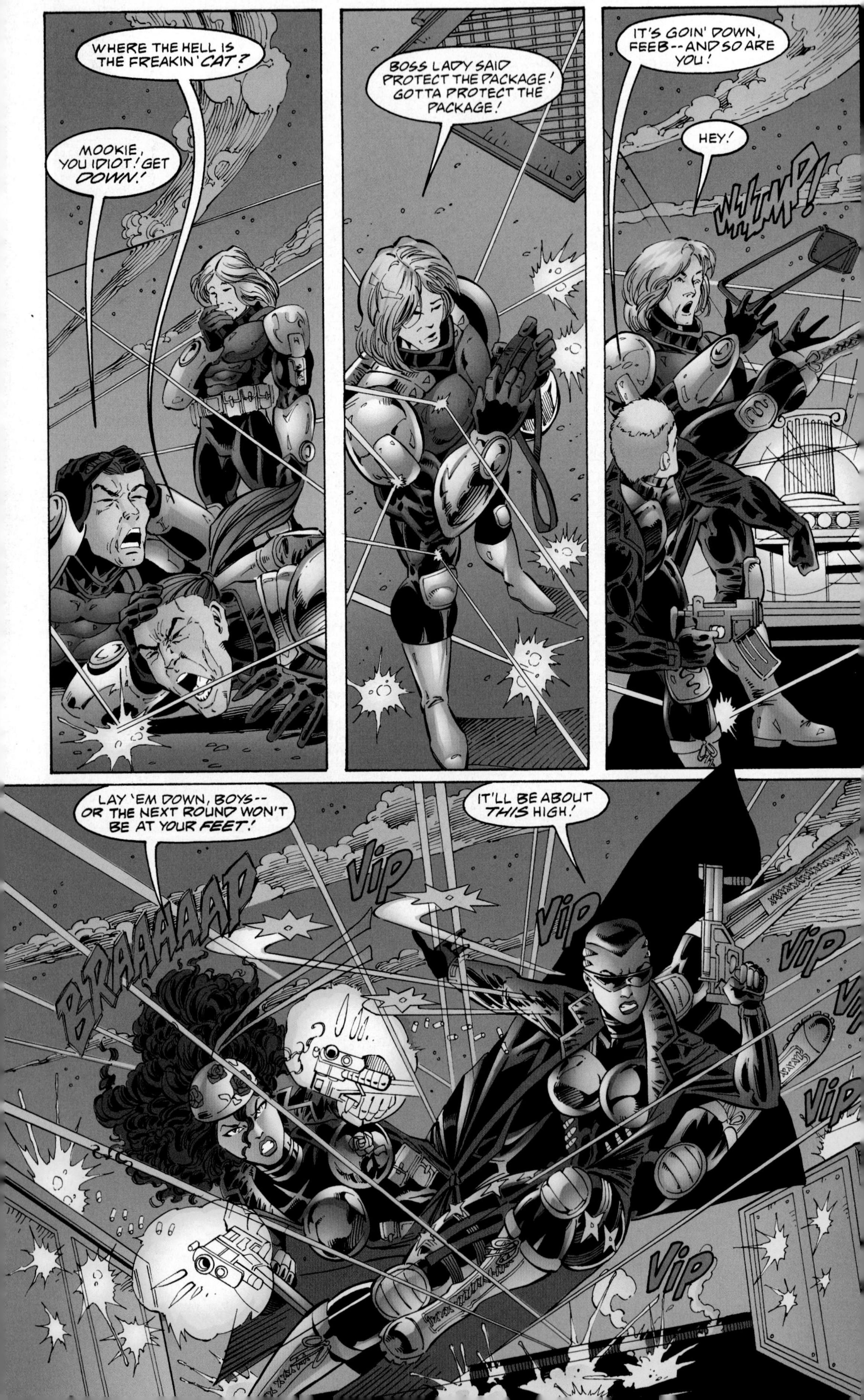

WHERE THE HELL IS THE FREAKIN' CAT?
MOOKIE, YOU IDIOT! GET DOWN!
BOSS LADY SAID PROTECT THE PACKAGE! GOTTA PROTECT THE PACKAGE!
IT'S GOIN' DOWN, FEEB--AND SO ARE YOU!
HEY!
WHUMP!
LAY 'EM DOWN, BOYS-- OR THE NEXT ROUND WON'T BE AT YOUR FEET!
IT'LL BE ABOUT THIS HIGH!
BRAAAAAP
VIP
VIP
VIP
VIP
VIP

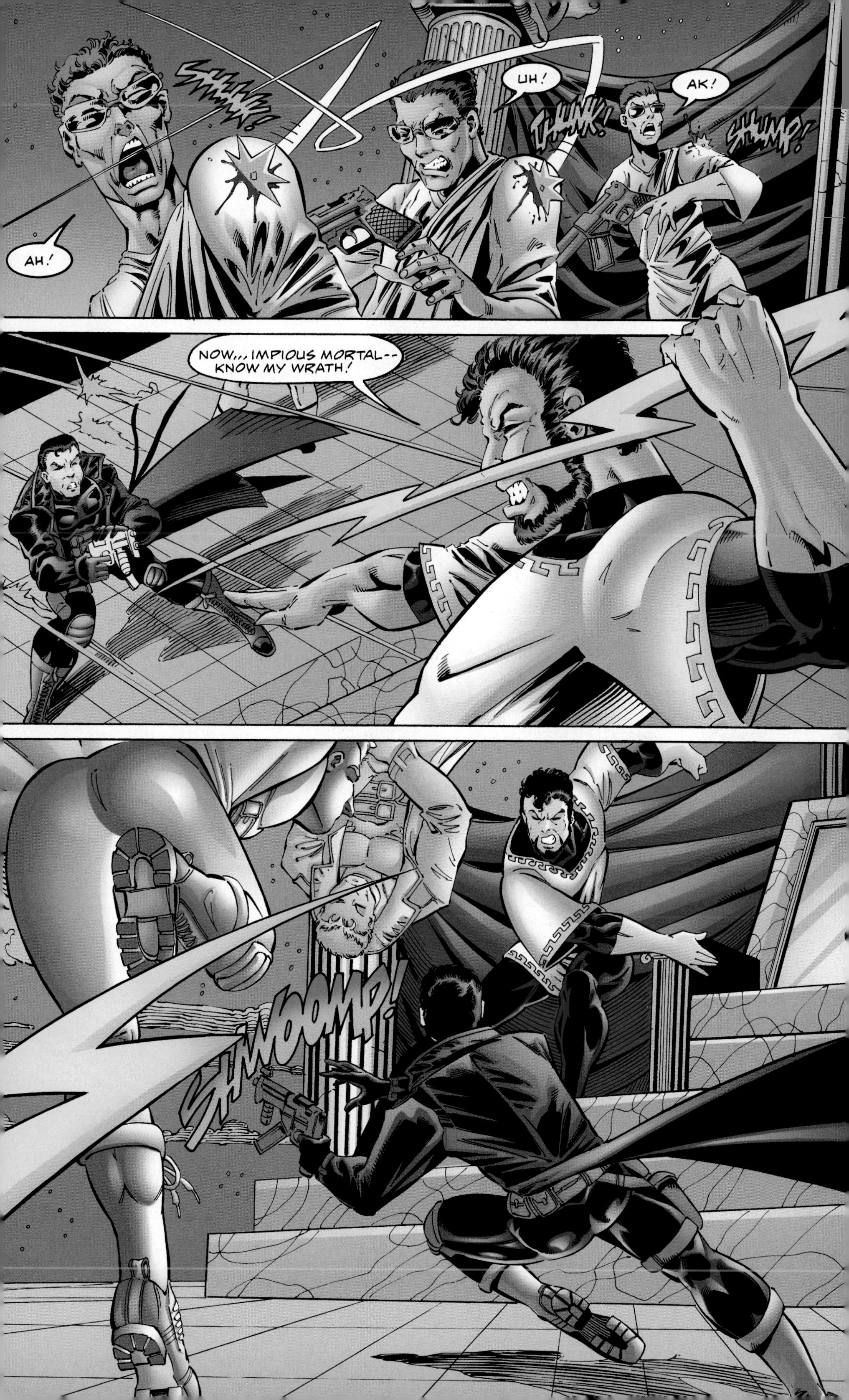
SHHHK!
UH!
AK!
THUNK!
SHUMP!
AH!
NOW... IMPIOUS MORTAL--
KNOW MY WRATH!
SHWOOMP!

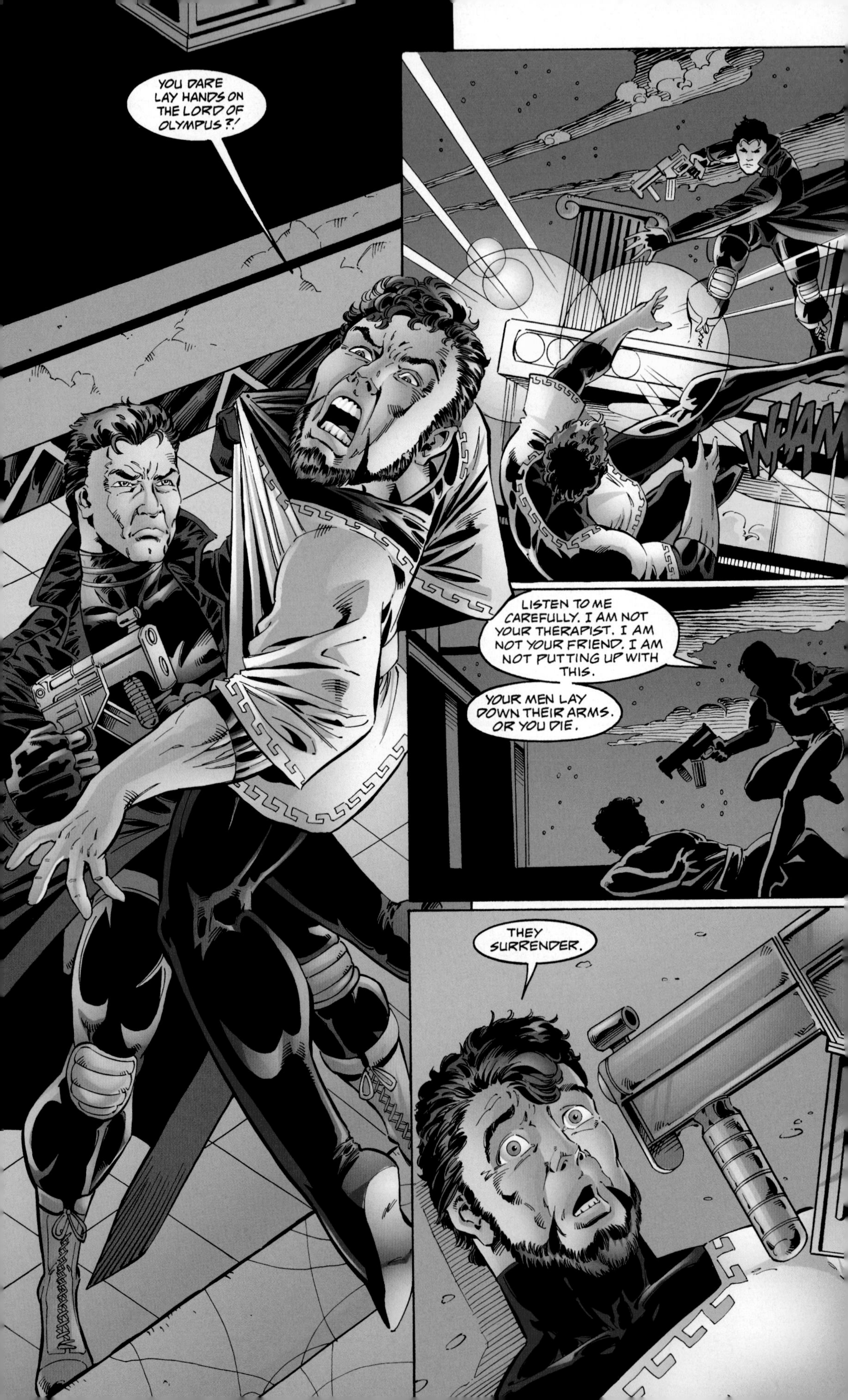
YOU DARE LAY HANDS ON THE LORD OF OLYMPUS?!
WHAM
LISTEN TO ME CAREFULLY. I AM NOT YOUR THERAPIST. I AM NOT YOUR FRIEND. I AM NOT PUTTING UP WITH THIS.
YOUR MEN LAY DOWN THEIR ARMS. OR YOU DIE.
THEY SURRENDER.

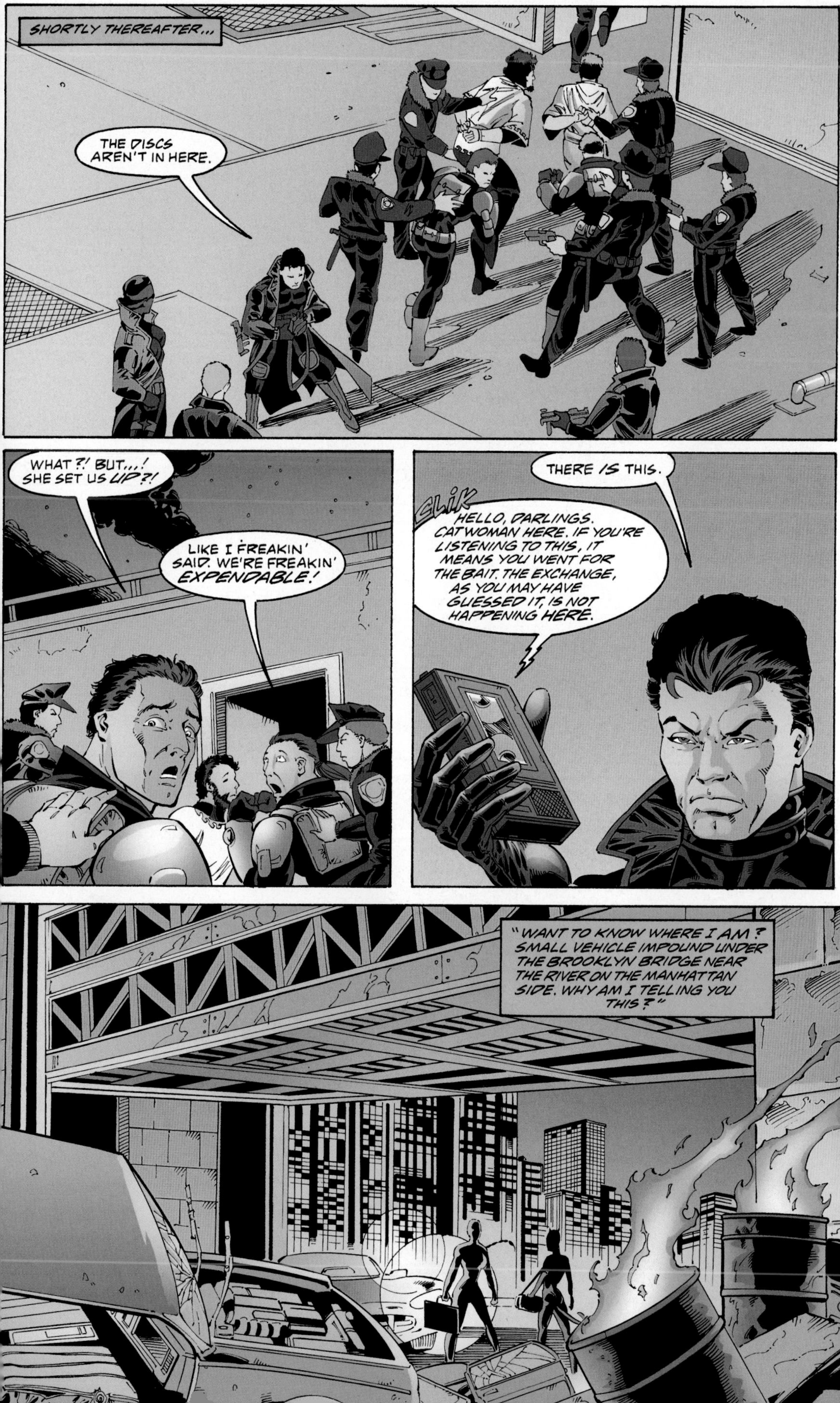
SHORTLY THEREAFTER...
THE DISCS AREN'T IN HERE.
WHAT?! BUT...! SHE SET US UP?!
LIKE I FREAKIN' SAID. WE'RE FREAKIN' EXPENDABLE!
THERE IS THIS.
CLIK
HELLO, DARLINGS. CATWOMAN HERE. IF YOU'RE LISTENING TO THIS, IT MEANS YOU WENT FOR THE BAIT. THE EXCHANGE, AS YOU MAY HAVE GUESSED IT, IS NOT HAPPENING HERE.
"WANT TO KNOW WHERE I AM? SMALL VEHICLE IMPOUND UNDER THE BROOKLYN BRIDGE NEAR THE RIVER ON THE MANHATTAN SIDE. WHY AM I TELLING YOU THIS?"

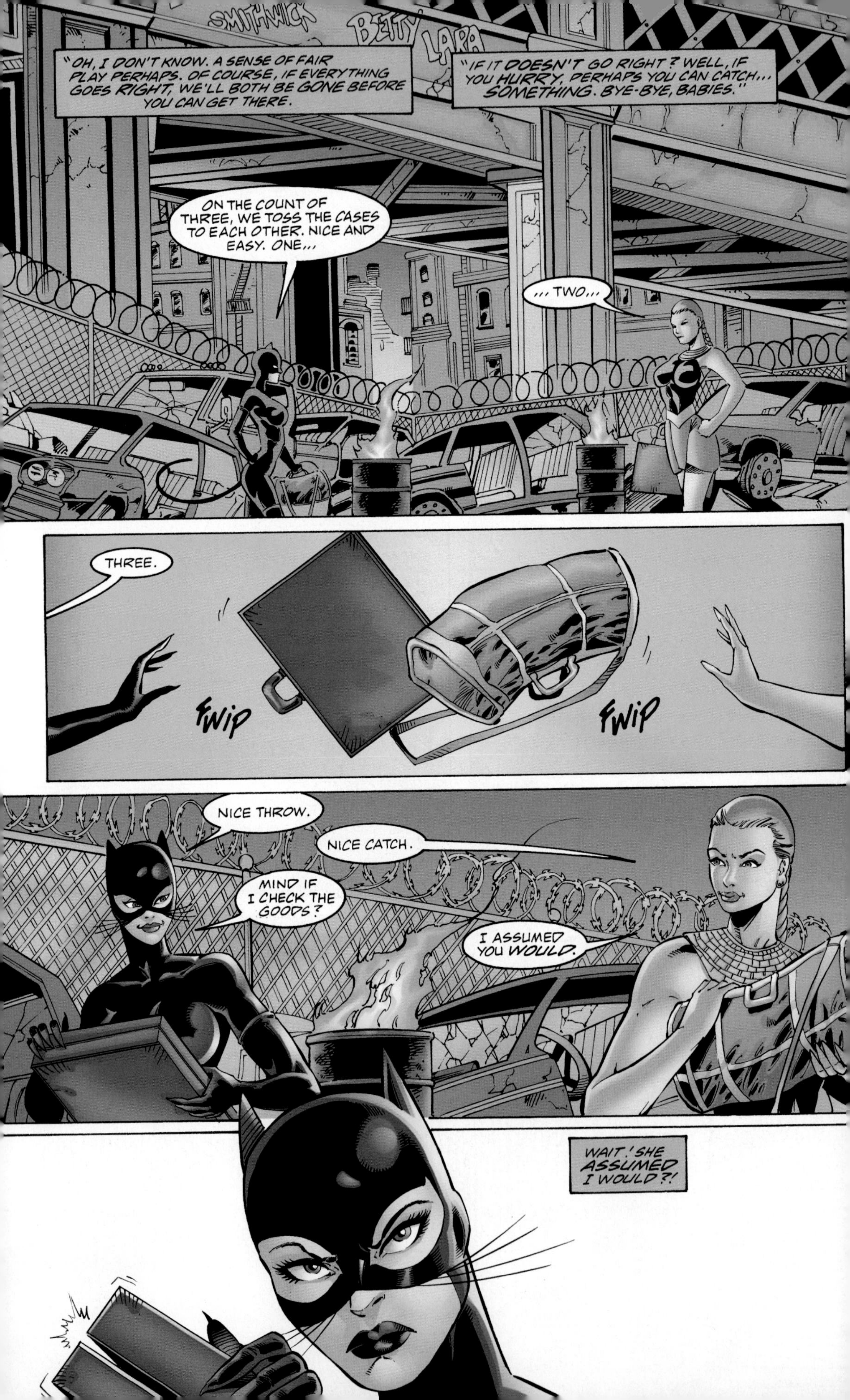
SMITHWICK
BETTY
LARA
"OH, I DON'T KNOW. A SENSE OF FAIR PLAY PERHAPS. OF COURSE, IF EVERYTHING GOES RIGHT, WE'LL BOTH BE GONE BEFORE YOU CAN GET THERE.
"IF IT DOESN'T GO RIGHT? WELL, IF YOU HURRY, PERHAPS YOU CAN CATCH... SOMETHING. BYE-BYE, BABIES."
ON THE COUNT OF THREE, WE TOSS THE CASES TO EACH OTHER. NICE AND EASY. ONE...
...TWO...
THREE.
FWIP
FWIP
NICE THROW.
NICE CATCH.
MIND IF I CHECK THE GOODS?
I ASSUMED YOU WOULD.
WAIT! SHE ASSUMED I WOULD?!

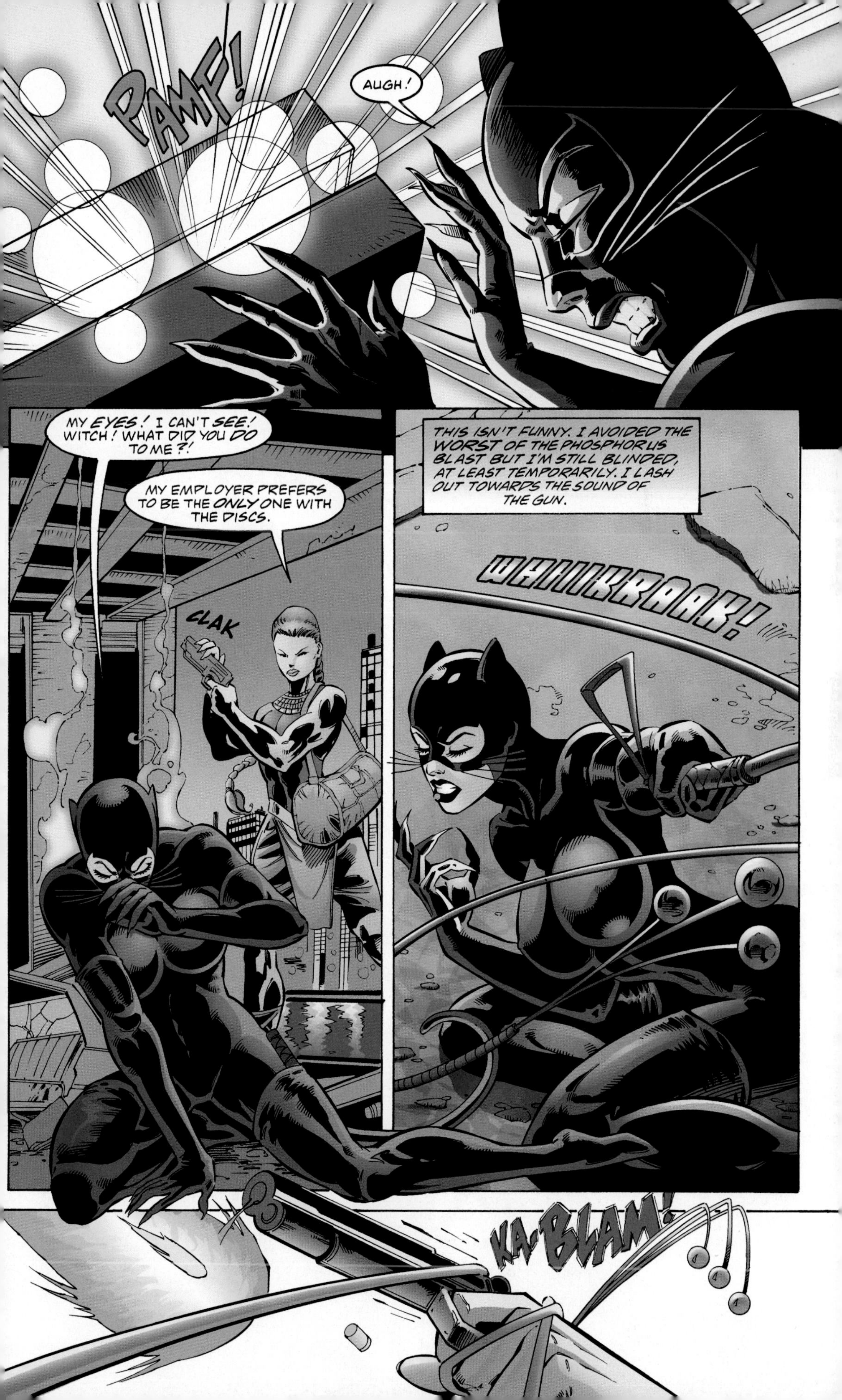
PAMF!
AUGH!
MY EYES! I CAN'T SEE! WITCH! WHAT DID YOU DO TO ME?!
MY EMPLOYER PREFERS TO BE THE ONLY ONE WITH THE DISCS.
CLAK
THIS ISN'T FUNNY. I AVOIDED THE WORST OF THE PHOSPHORUS BLAST BUT I'M STILL BLINDED, AT LEAST TEMPORARILY. I LASH OUT TOWARDS THE SOUND OF THE GUN.
WHIIIKRAAK!
KA-BLAM!

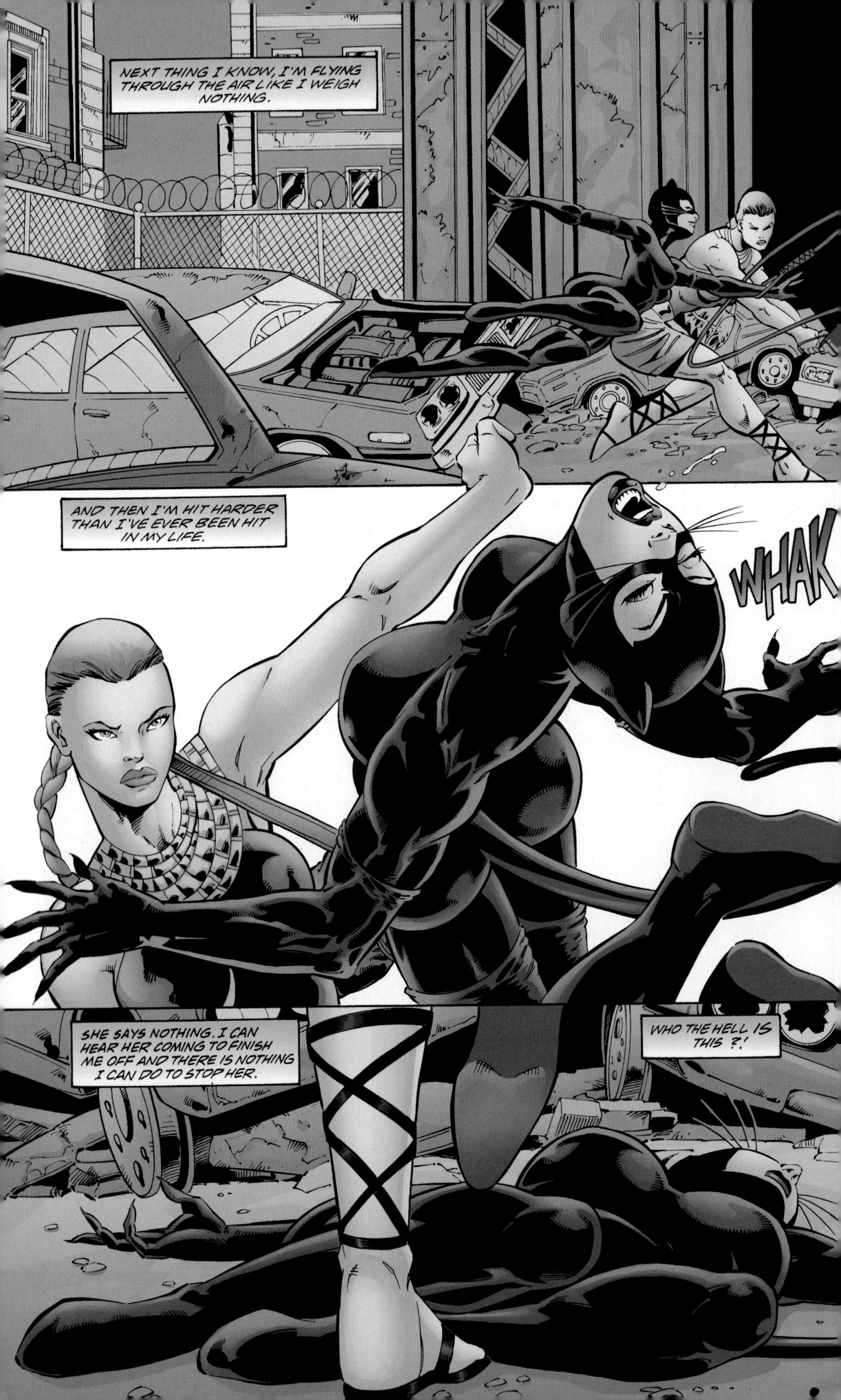
NEXT THING I KNOW, I'M FLYING THROUGH THE AIR LIKE I WEIGH NOTHING.
AND THEN I'M HIT HARDER THAN I'VE EVER BEEN HIT IN MY LIFE.
WHAK
SHE SAYS NOTHING. I CAN HEAR HER COMING TO FINISH ME OFF AND THERE IS NOTHING I CAN DO TO STOP HER.
WHO THE HELL IS THIS ?!

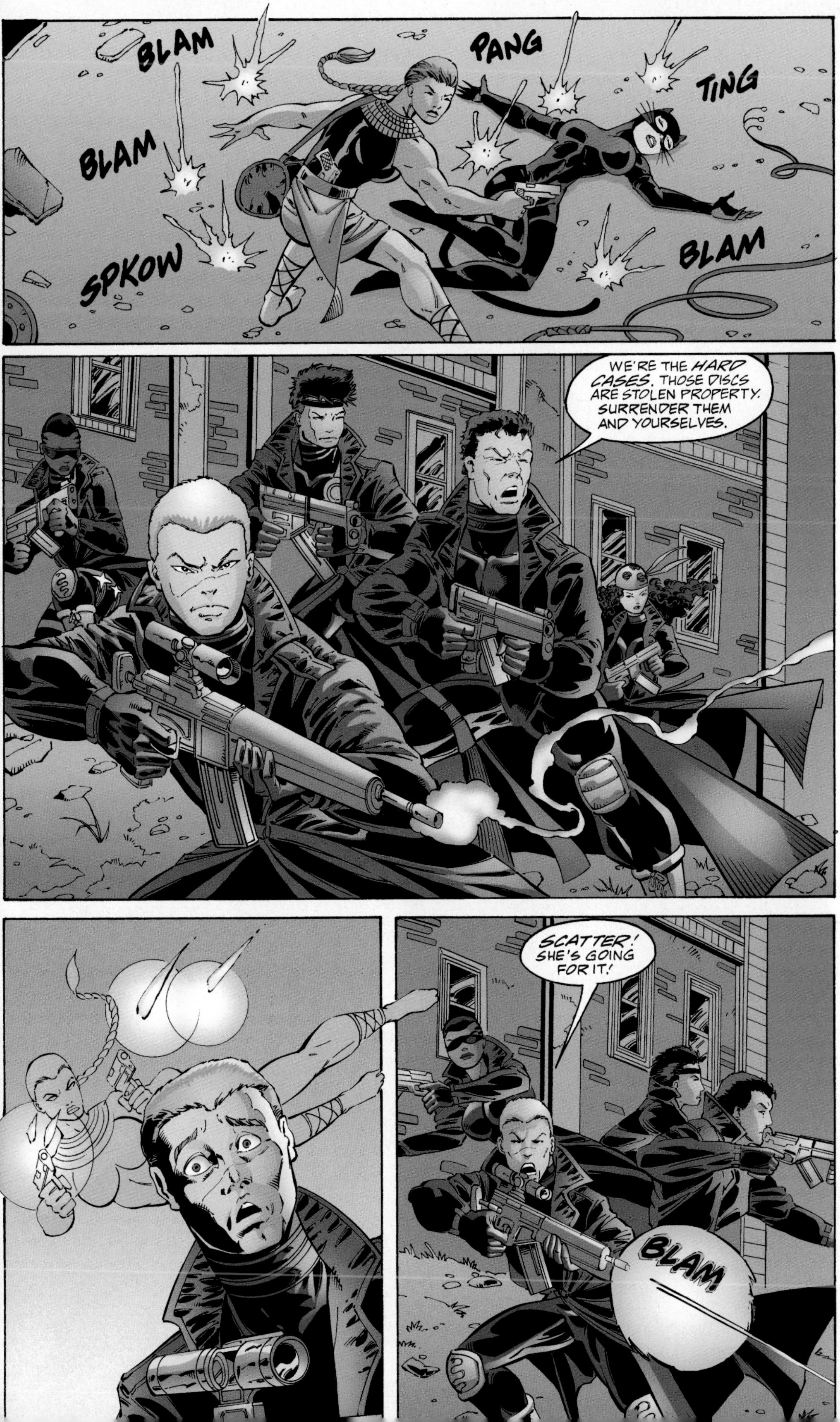
BLAM
PANG
TING
BLAM
SPKOW
BLAM
WE'RE THE HARD CASES. THOSE DISCS ARE STOLEN PROPERTY. SURRENDER THEM AND YOURSELVES.
SCATTER! SHE'S GOING FOR IT!
BLAM

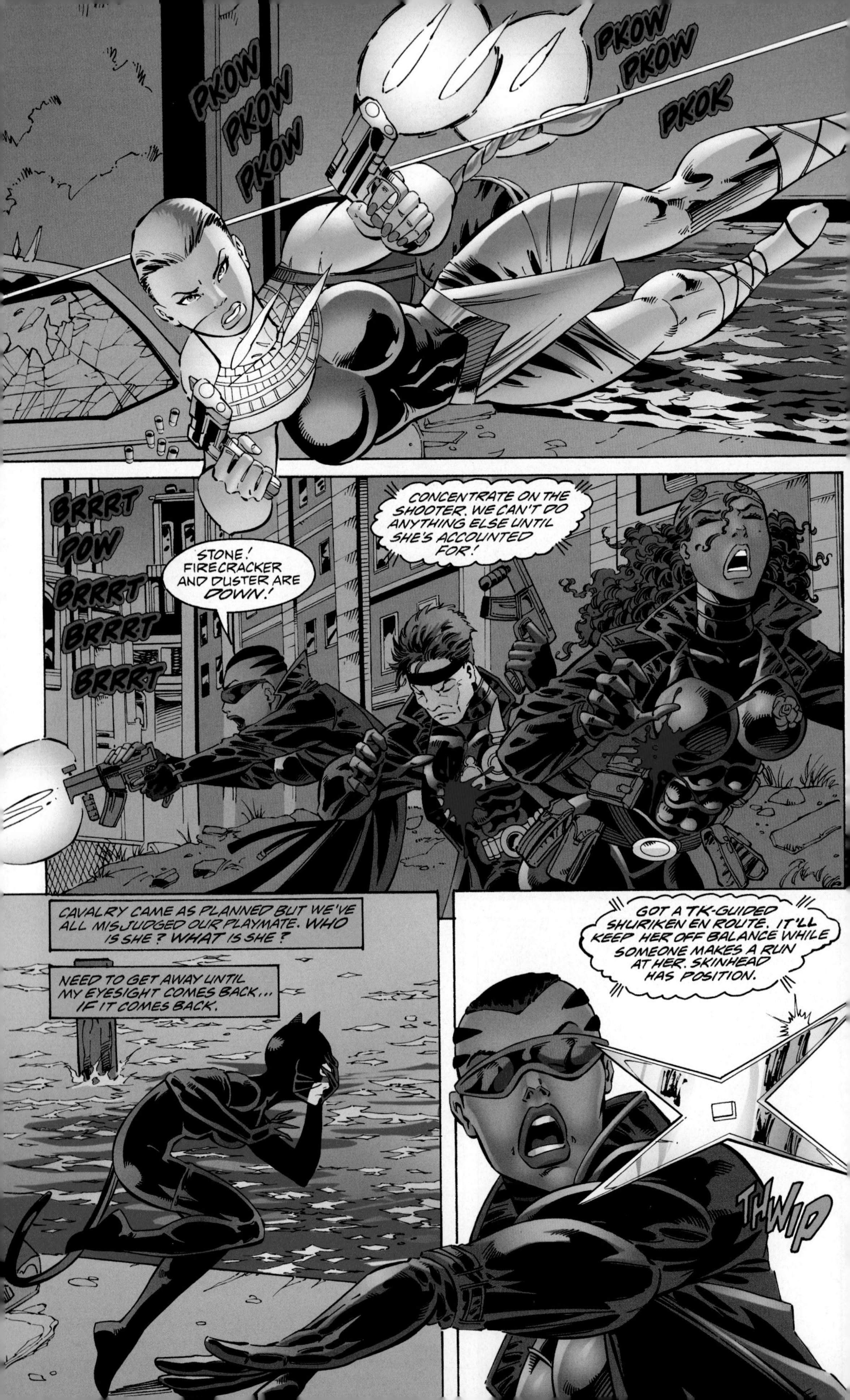
PKOW
PKOW
PKOW
PKOW
PKOW
PKOK
BRRRT
POW
BRRRT
BRRRT
BRRRT
STONE! FIRECRACKER AND DUSTER ARE DOWN!
CONCENTRATE ON THE SHOOTER. WE CAN'T DO ANYTHING ELSE UNTIL SHE'S ACCOUNTED FOR!
CAVALRY CAME AS PLANNED BUT WE'VE ALL MISJUDGED OUR PLAYMATE. WHO IS SHE? WHAT IS SHE?
NEED TO GET AWAY UNTIL MY EYESIGHT COMES BACK... IF IT COMES BACK.
GOT A TK-GUIDED SHURIKEN EN ROUTE. IT'LL KEEP HER OFF BALANCE WHILE SOMEONE MAKES A RUN AT HER. SKINHEAD HAS POSITION.
THWIP

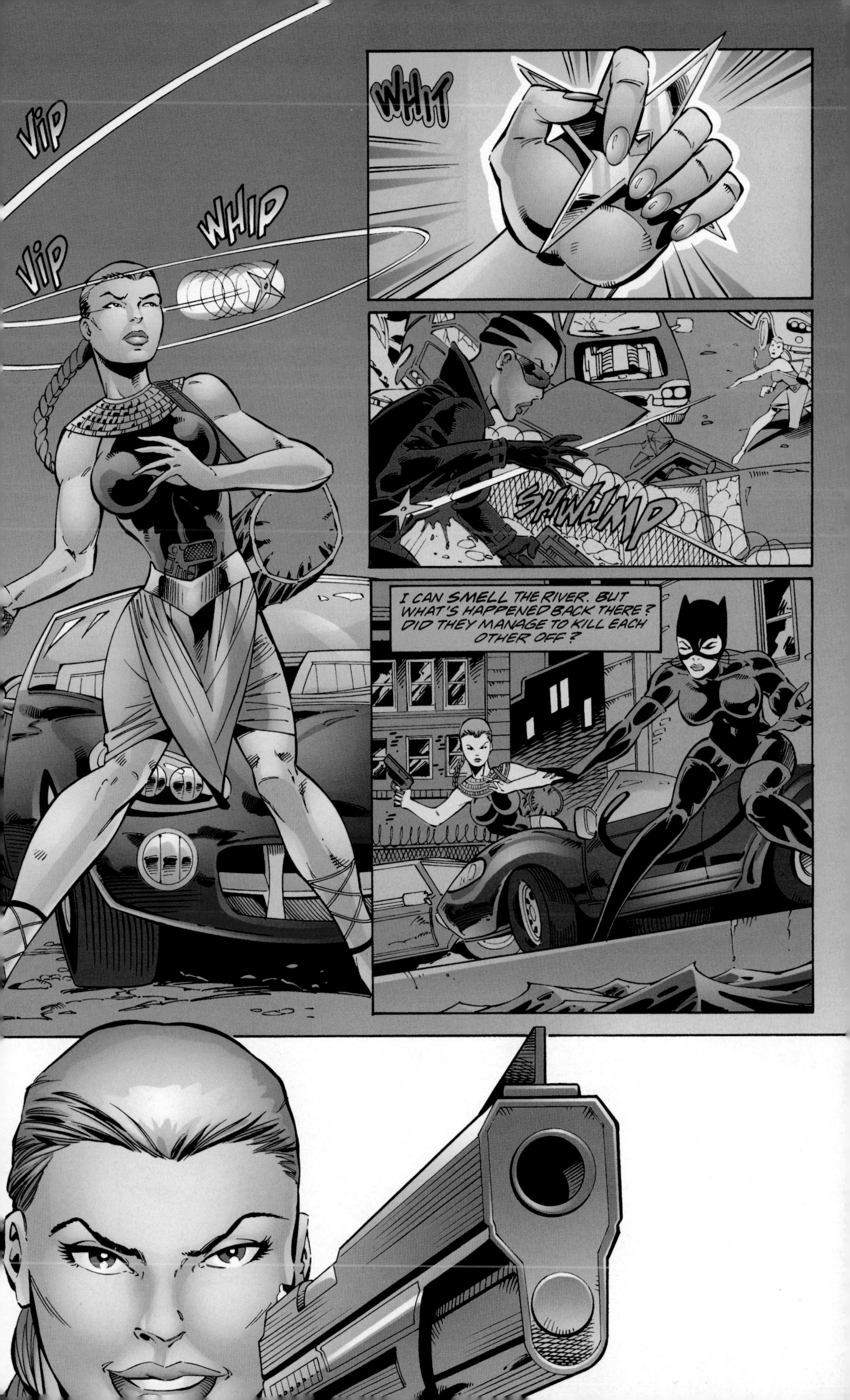
VIP
WHIP
VIP
WHIT
SHWUMP
I CAN SMELL THE RIVER. BUT WHAT'S HAPPENED BACK THERE? DID THEY MANAGE TO KILL EACH OTHER OFF?

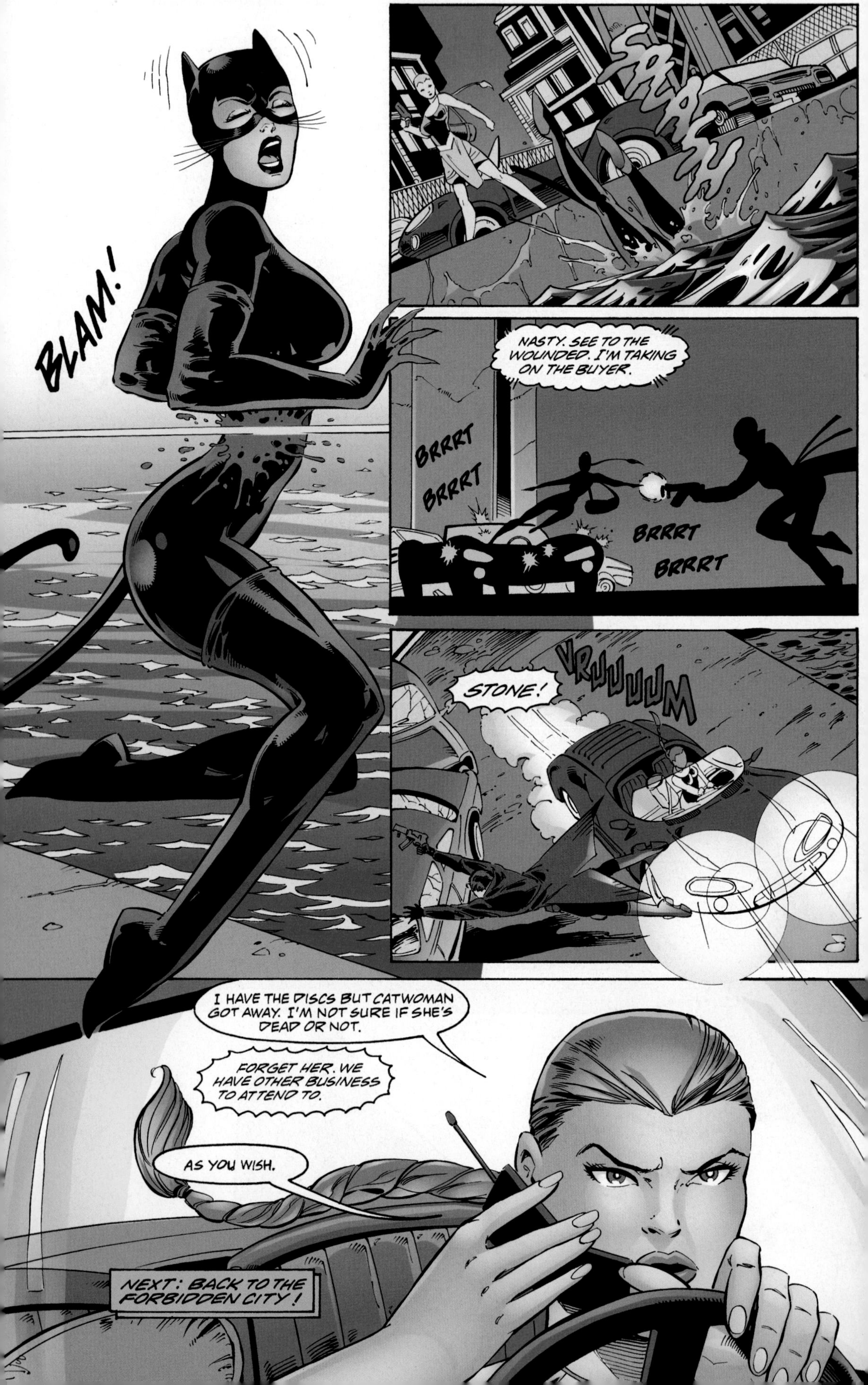
SPLASH
BLAM!
NASTY. SEE TO THE WOUNDED. I'M TAKING ON THE BUYER.
BRRRT
BRRRT
BRRRT
BRRRT
STONE!
VRUUUUM
I HAVE THE DISCS BUT CATWOMAN GOT AWAY. I'M NOT SURE IF SHE'S DEAD OR NOT.
FORGET HER. WE HAVE OTHER BUSINESS TO ATTEND TO.
AS YOU WISH.
NEXT: BACK TO THE FORBIDDEN CITY!

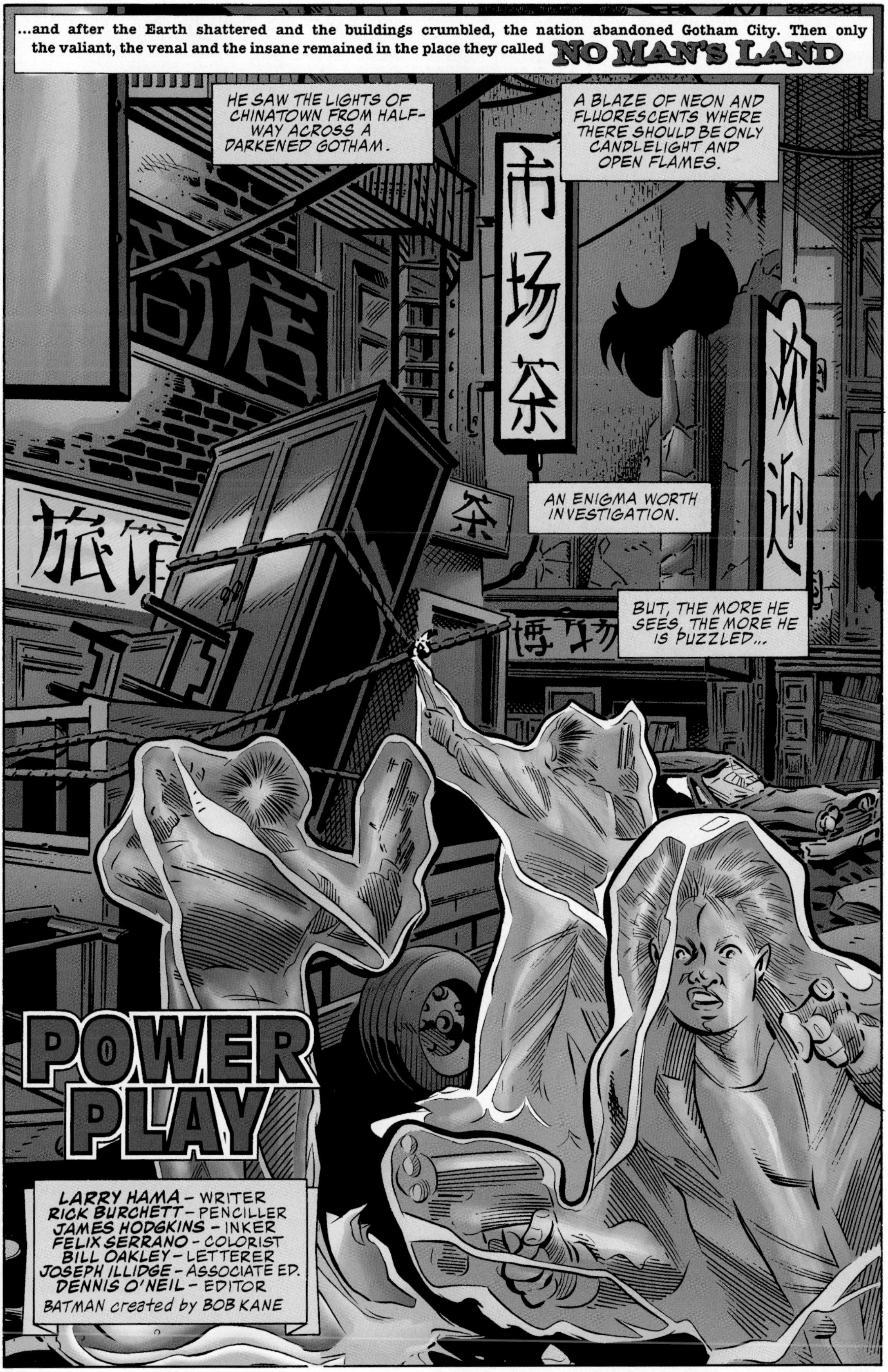

...and after the Earth shattered and the buildings crumbled, the nation abandoned Gotham City. Then only the valiant, the venal and the insane remained in the place they called NO MAN'S LAND
HE SAW THE LIGHTS OF CHINATOWN FROM HALF-WAY ACROSS A DARKENED GOTHAM.
A BLAZE OF NEON AND FLUORESCENTS WHERE THERE SHOULD BE ONLY CANDLELIGHT AND OPEN FLAMES.
AN ENIGMA WORTH INVESTIGATION.
BUT, THE MORE HE SEES, THE MORE HE IS PUZZLED...
POWER PLAY
LARRY HAMA - WRITER
RICK BURCHETT - PENCILLER
JAMES HODGKINS - INKER
FELIX SERRANO - COLORIST
BILL OAKLEY - LETTERER
JOSEPH ILLIDGE - ASSOCIATE ED.
DENNIS O'NEIL - EDITOR
BATMAN created by BOB KANE

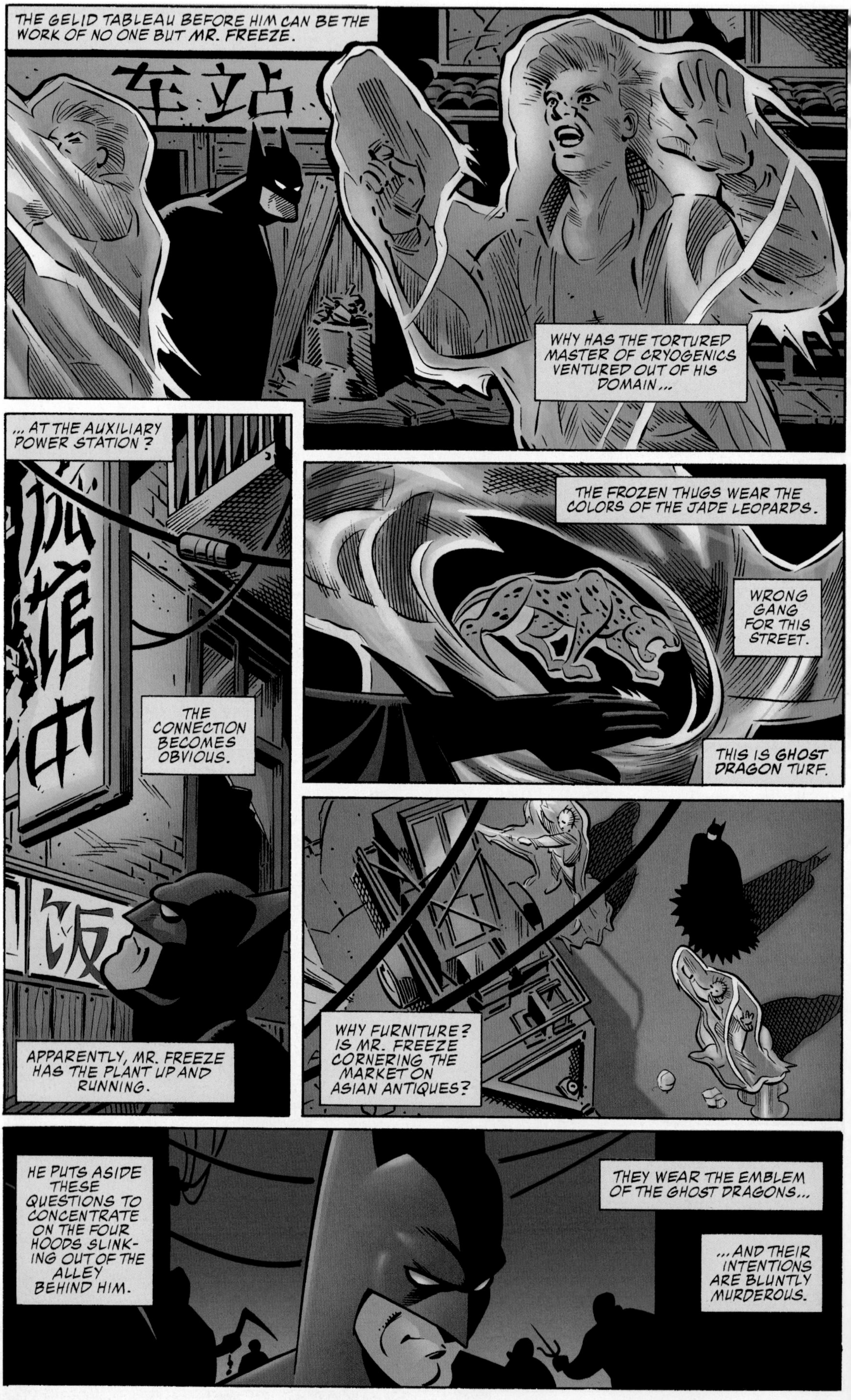
THE GELID TABLEAU BEFORE HIM CAN BE THE WORK OF NO ONE BUT MR. FREEZE.
WHY HAS THE TORTURED MASTER OF CRYOGENICS VENTURED OUT OF HIS DOMAIN...
... AT THE AUXILIARY POWER STATION?
THE CONNECTION BECOMES OBVIOUS.
APPARENTLY, MR. FREEZE HAS THE PLANT UP AND RUNNING.
THE FROZEN THUGS WEAR THE COLORS OF THE JADE LEOPARDS.
WRONG GANG FOR THIS STREET.
THIS IS GHOST DRAGON TURF.
WHY FURNITURE? IS MR. FREEZE CORNERING THE MARKET ON ASIAN ANTIQUES?
HE PUTS ASIDE THESE QUESTIONS TO CONCENTRATE ON THE FOUR HOODS SLINKING OUT OF THE ALLEY BEHIND HIM.
THEY WEAR THE EMBLEM OF THE GHOST DRAGONS...
...AND THEIR INTENTIONS ARE BLUNTLY MURDEROUS.

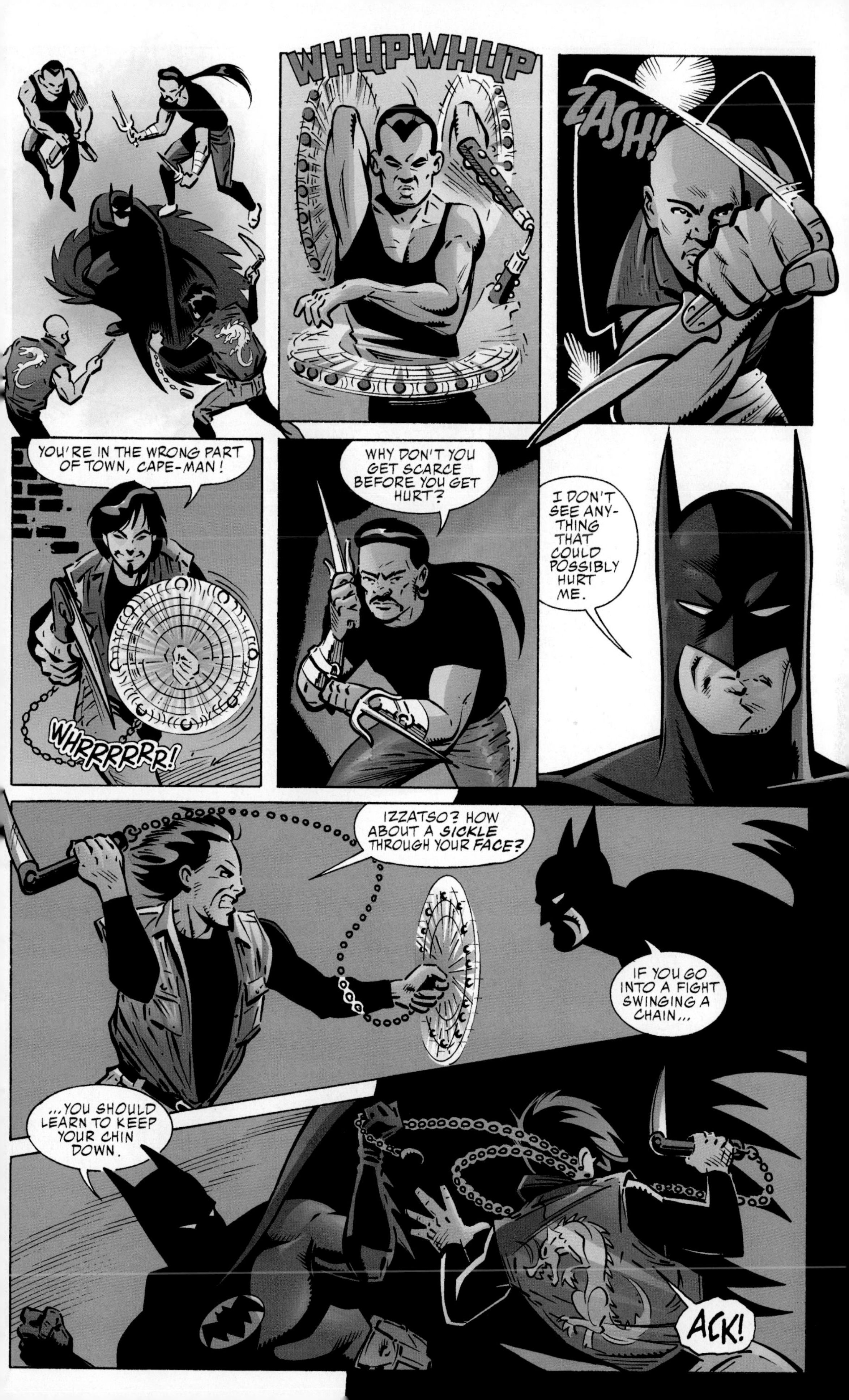
WHUPWHUP
ZASH!
YOU'RE IN THE WRONG PART OF TOWN, CAPE-MAN!
WHRRRRRR!
WHY DON'T YOU GET SCARCE BEFORE YOU GET HURT?
I DON'T SEE ANY-THING THAT COULD POSSIBLY HURT ME.
IZZATSO? HOW ABOUT A SICKLE THROUGH YOUR FACE?
IF YOU GO INTO A FIGHT SWINGING A CHAIN...
...YOU SHOULD LEARN TO KEEP YOUR CHIN DOWN.
ACK!

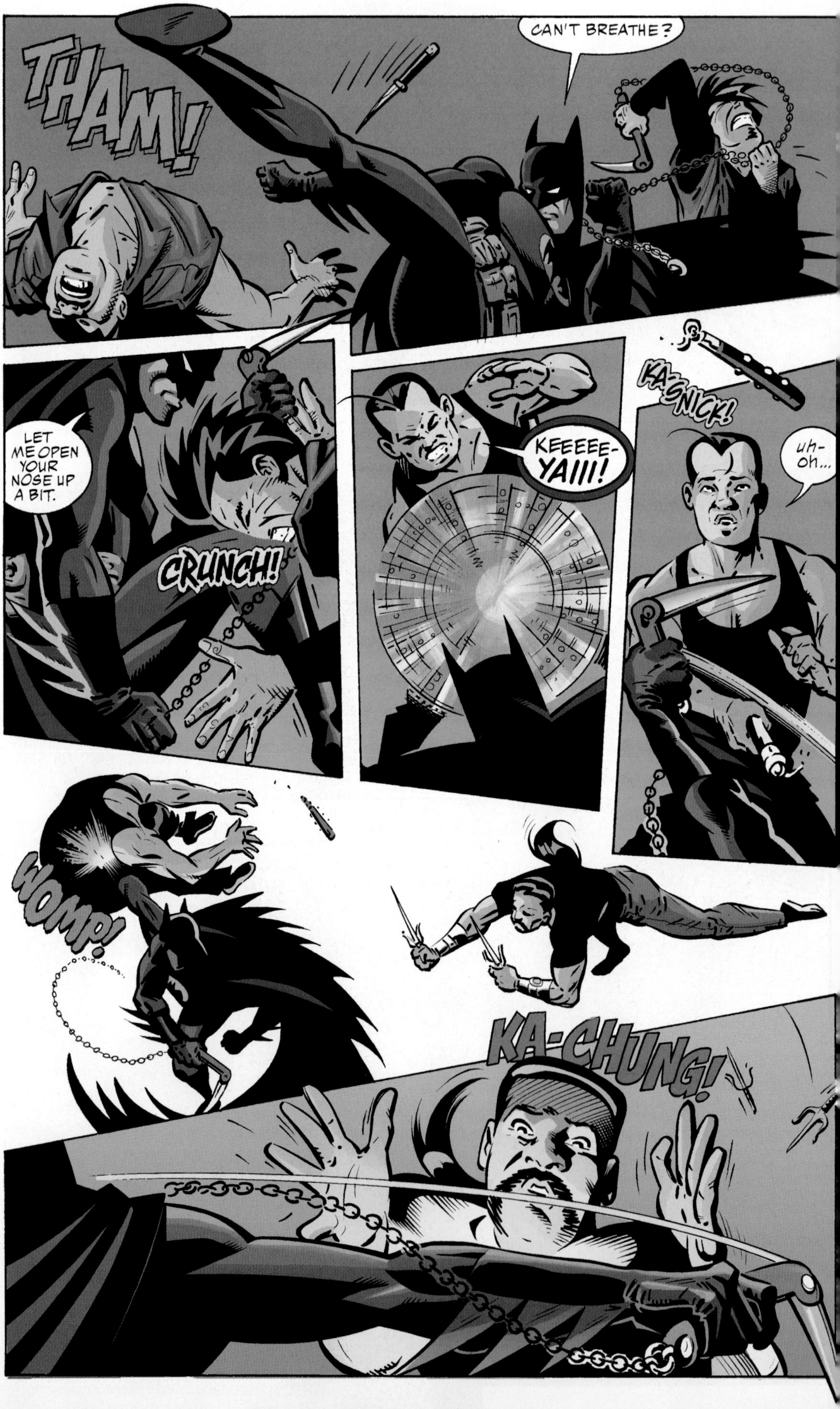
THAM!
CAN'T BREATHE?
LET ME OPEN YOUR NOSE UP A BIT.
CRUNCH!
KEEEEE-YAIII!
KA-SNICK!
uh-oh...
WOMP!
KA-CHUNG!

I GIVE UP! D-DON'T KILL ME!

I DON'T KILL.

BUT I AM NOT AVERSE TO INFLICT-ING *PAIN*...

...UNLESS I GET SOME ANSWERS.

..., SPECIFICALLY, WHY IS MR. FREEZE INVOLVED IN CHINA-TOWN DISPUTES?

IT'S ABOUT POWER. WE WANT IT, HE'S GOT IT.

WE SUPPLY HIM WITH STUFF TO BURN AND HE RUNS US A CABLE.

THE LEOPARDS WERE TRYING TO CUT INTO OUR ACTION. FREEZE BELIEVES IN FREEZING HIS ASSETS-- HA, HA!

I'M NOT LAUGHING.

IS FREEZE STILL IN CHINATOWN?

NO WAY! HE'S BACK UP THE RIVER...

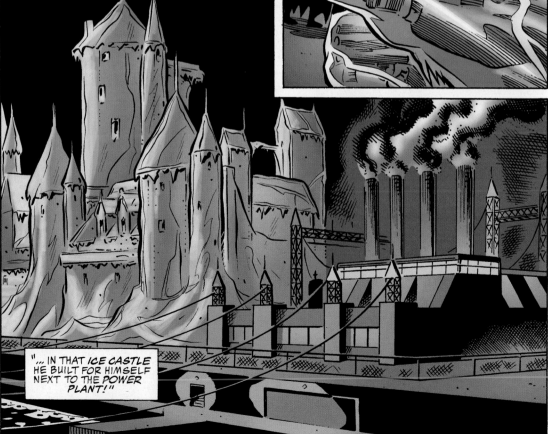

"... IN THAT *ICE CASTLE* HE BUILT FOR HIMSELF NEXT TO THE *POWER PLANT!*"

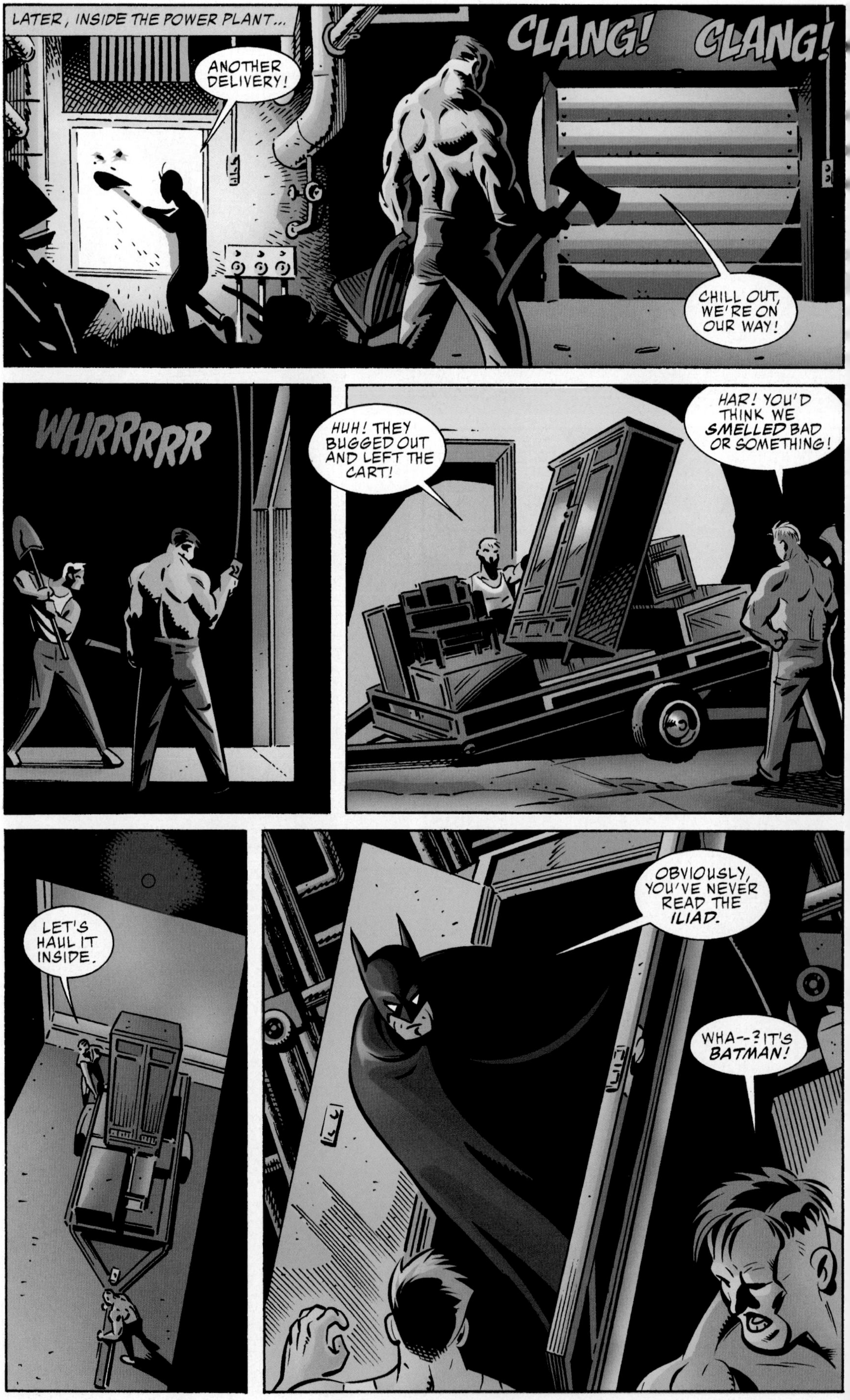

LATER, INSIDE THE POWER PLANT...
ANOTHER DELIVERY!
CLANG! CLANG!
CHILL OUT, WE'RE ON OUR WAY!
WHRRRRR
HUH! THEY BUGGED OUT AND LEFT THE CART!
HAR! YOU'D THINK WE SMELLED BAD OR SOMETHING!
LET'S HAUL IT INSIDE.
OBVIOUSLY, YOU'VE NEVER READ THE ILIAD.
WHA--?IT'S BATMAN!

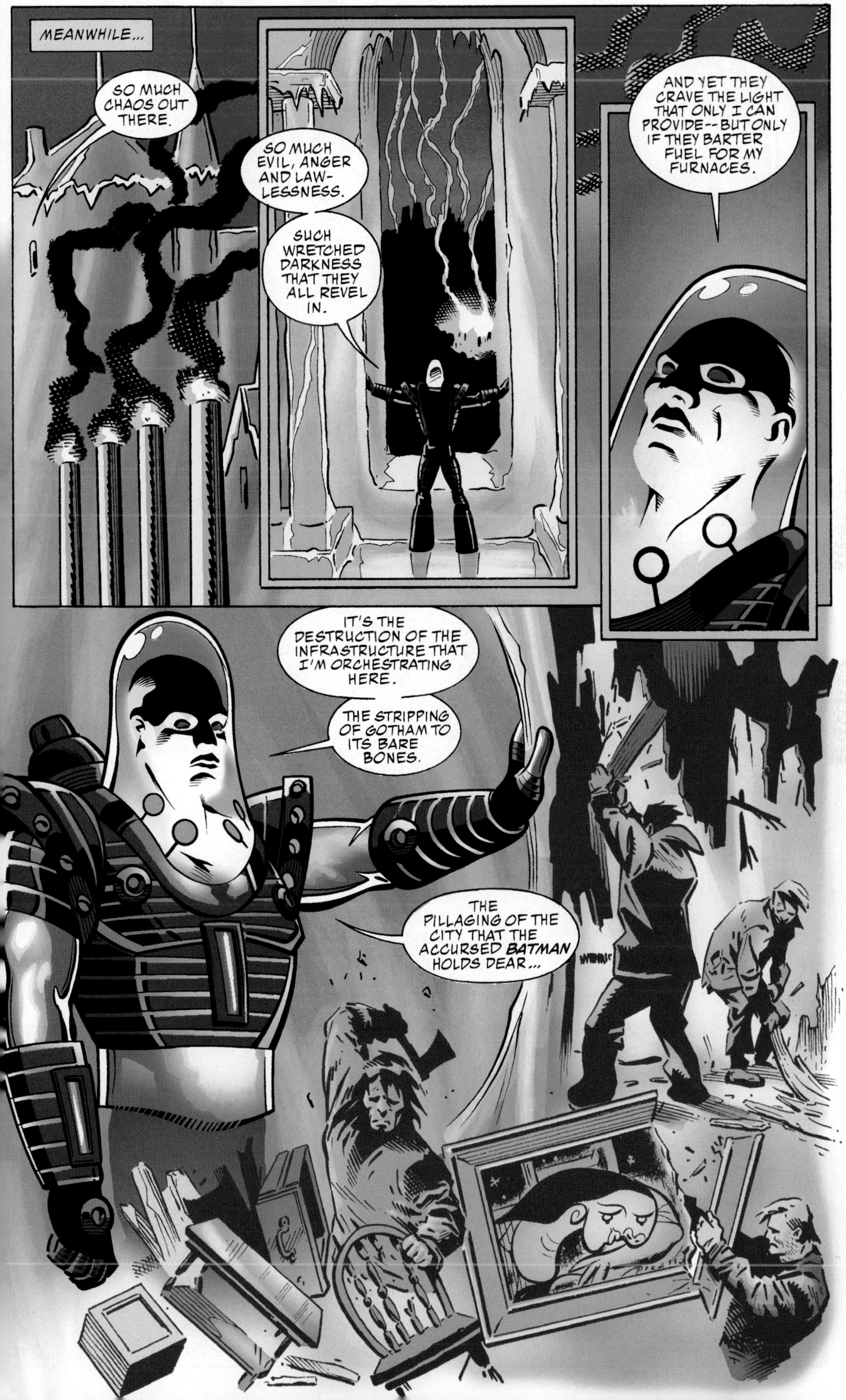
MEANWHILE...
SO MUCH CHAOS OUT THERE.
SO MUCH EVIL, ANGER AND LAWLESSNESS.
SUCH WRETCHED DARKNESS THAT THEY ALL REVEL IN.
AND YET THEY CRAVE THE LIGHT THAT ONLY I CAN PROVIDE-- BUT ONLY IF THEY BARTER FUEL FOR MY FURNACES.
IT'S THE DESTRUCTION OF THE INFRASTRUCTURE THAT I'M ORCHESTRATING HERE.
THE STRIPPING OF GOTHAM TO ITS BARE BONES.
THE PILLAGING OF THE CITY THAT THE ACCURSED BATMAN HOLDS DEAR...

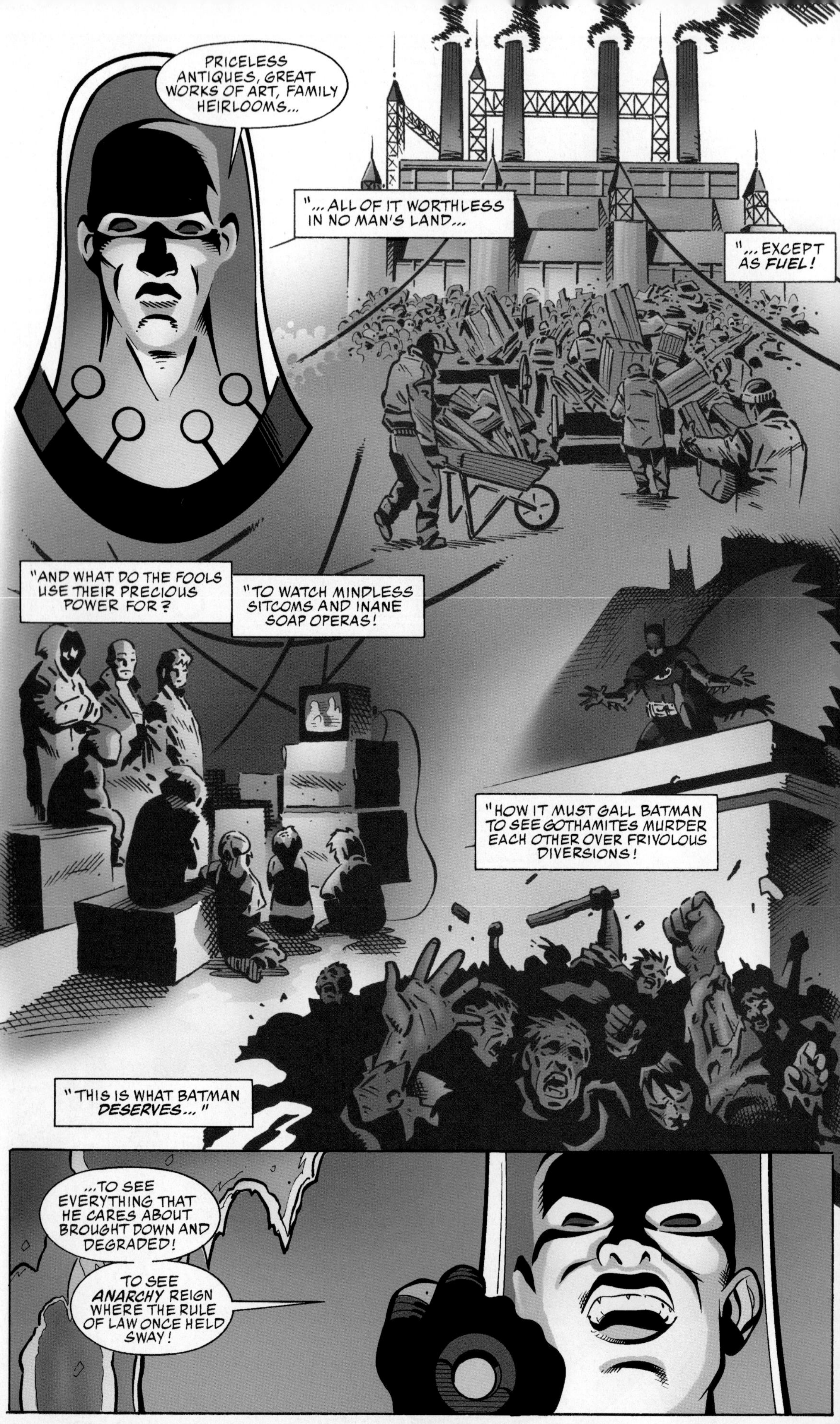
PRICELESS ANTIQUES, GREAT WORKS OF ART, FAMILY HEIRLOOMS...
"... ALL OF IT WORTHLESS IN NO MAN'S LAND...
"... EXCEPT AS FUEL!
"AND WHAT DO THE FOOLS USE THEIR PRECIOUS POWER FOR?
"TO WATCH MINDLESS SITCOMS AND INANE SOAP OPERAS!
"HOW IT MUST GALL BATMAN TO SEE GOTHAMITES MURDER EACH OTHER OVER FRIVOLOUS DIVERSIONS!
"THIS IS WHAT BATMAN DESERVES..."
...TO SEE EVERYTHING THAT HE CARES ABOUT BROUGHT DOWN AND DEGRADED!
TO SEE ANARCHY REIGN WHERE THE RULE OF LAW ONCE HELD SWAY!

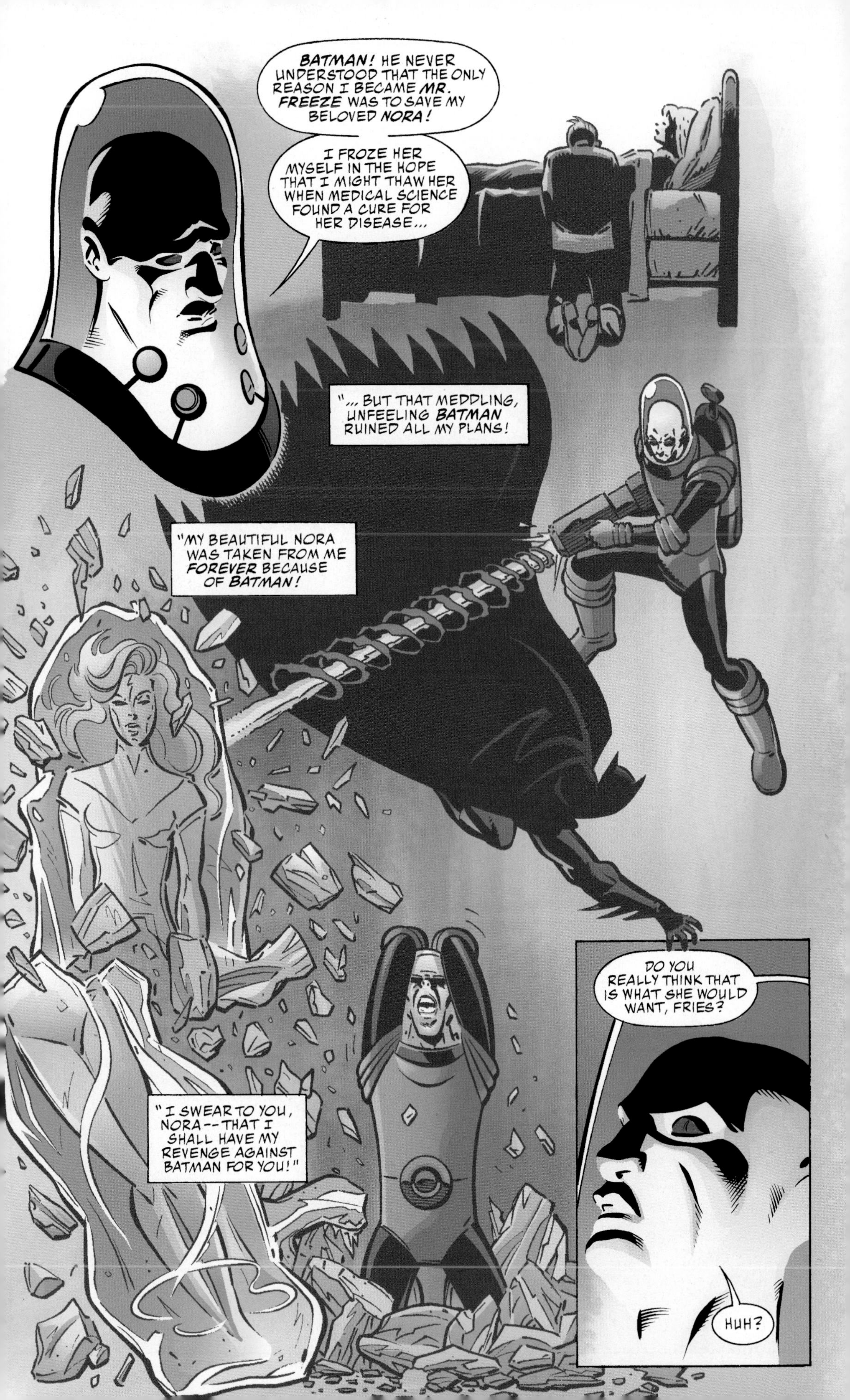
BATMAN! HE NEVER UNDERSTOOD THAT THE ONLY REASON I BECAME MR. FREEZE WAS TO SAVE MY BELOVED NORA!
I FROZE HER MYSELF IN THE HOPE THAT I MIGHT THAW HER WHEN MEDICAL SCIENCE FOUND A CURE FOR HER DISEASE...
"...BUT THAT MEDDLING, UNFEELING BATMAN RUINED ALL MY PLANS!
"MY BEAUTIFUL NORA WAS TAKEN FROM ME FOREVER BECAUSE OF BATMAN!
"I SWEAR TO YOU, NORA--THAT I SHALL HAVE MY REVENGE AGAINST BATMAN FOR YOU!"
DO YOU REALLY THINK THAT IS WHAT SHE WOULD WANT, FRIES?
HUH?

BY ALL ACCOUNTS, YOUR WIFE WAS A KIND, GENTLE, LOVING PERSON.

IS THIS ANY WAY TO MEMORIALIZE A PERSON LIKE THAT?

ALL THIS, ALL THE CHAOS AND SUFFERING YOU'VE CAUSED-- WHAT WOULD YOUR SAINTED NORA THINK ABOUT ALL THAT?

DID YOU EVER STOP TO THINK--?

THERE ARE THINGS IN THIS WORLD THAT ARE *TOO PAINFUL* TO THINK ABOUT!

THERE IS ONLY ONE THING THAT CAN BLOCK OUT THE PAIN--

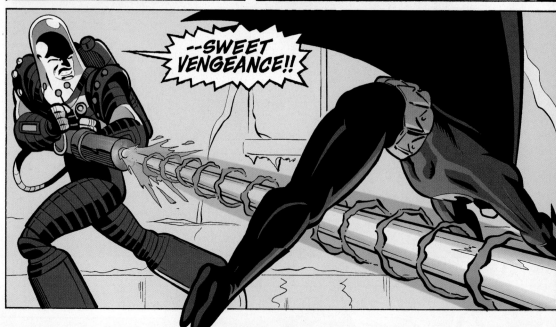

--SWEET VENGEANCE!!

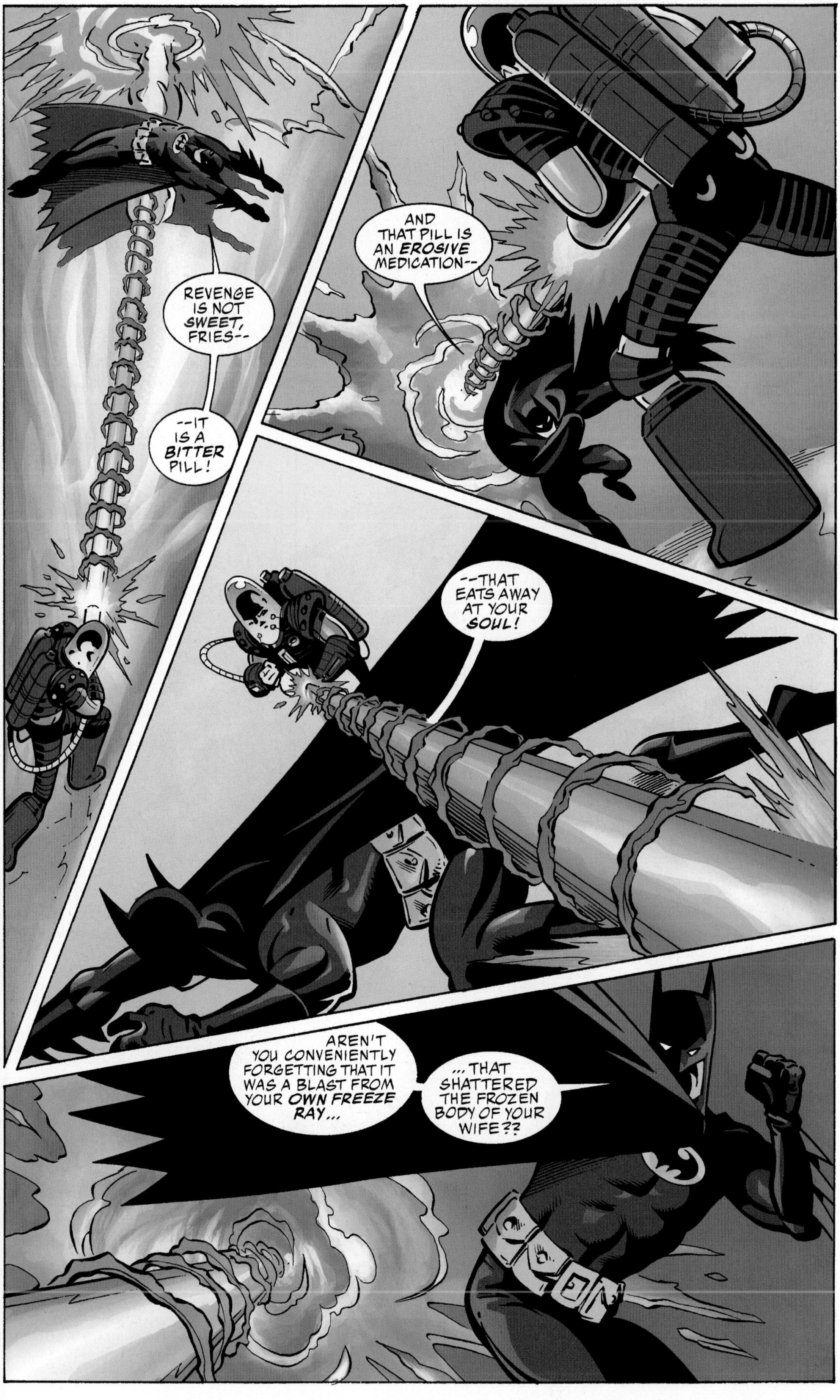
REVENGE IS NOT SWEET, FRIES--
--IT IS A BITTER PILL!
AND THAT PILL IS AN EROSIVE MEDICATION--
--THAT EATS AWAY AT YOUR SOUL!
AREN'T YOU CONVENIENTLY FORGETTING THAT IT WAS A BLAST FROM YOUR OWN FREEZE RAY...
...THAT SHATTERED THE FROZEN BODY OF YOUR WIFE??

HOW *DARE* YOU INSINUATE THAT I WAS RESPONSIBLE FOR THE DEATH OF NORA?!

AFTER MUCH PONDERING, I HAVE COME TO THE INEVITABLE CONCLUSION THAT *YOU* PURPOSELY SET UP THAT SITUATION BY POSITIONING YOURSELF IN FRONT OF NORA AND *BAITING* ME TO SHOOT!

YOU ARE *DOUBLY* CULPABLE!

WHAT ABOUT YOUR *OWN* MOTIVATIONS?

WHY ARE YOU COMING AFTER *ME* WHEN PENGUIN AND OTHER VILLAINS HAVE THEIR OWN BAILIWICKS OF CRIMINAL ENDEAVOR?

COULD IT HAVE SOMETHING TO DO WITH WHAT I DID TO *ROBIN...*?

...OR IS THERE SOME *OLDER, DEEPER* ROOT TO YOUR VIGILANTISM?

JUST *WHY* DO YOU DO WHAT YOU DO? IT DOESN'T SEEM LIKE THE SORT OF LIFELONG DEDICATION THAT ONE MAKES ARBITRARILY!

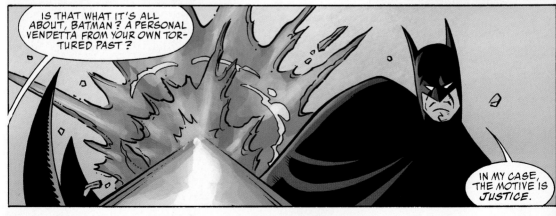

IS THAT WHAT IT'S ALL ABOUT, BATMAN? A PERSONAL VENDETTA FROM YOUR OWN TORTURED PAST?

IN MY CASE, THE MOTIVE IS *JUSTICE.*

JUSTICE? HAH! A RATIONALIZATION IF EVER THERE WAS ONE!

WHAT ARE YOU REACHING FOR BEHIND YOUR BACK?

THROW IT AWAY TO YOUR SIDE, OR--

IT'S A BATARANG, MR. FREEZE...

...THEY HAVE A WAY OF COMING BACK ON YOU!

MY FREEZE RAY!

CLANG!

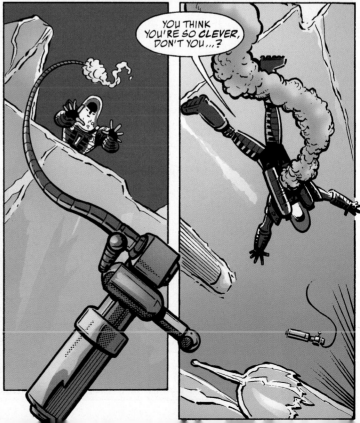

YOU THINK YOU'RE SO CLEVER, DON'T YOU...?

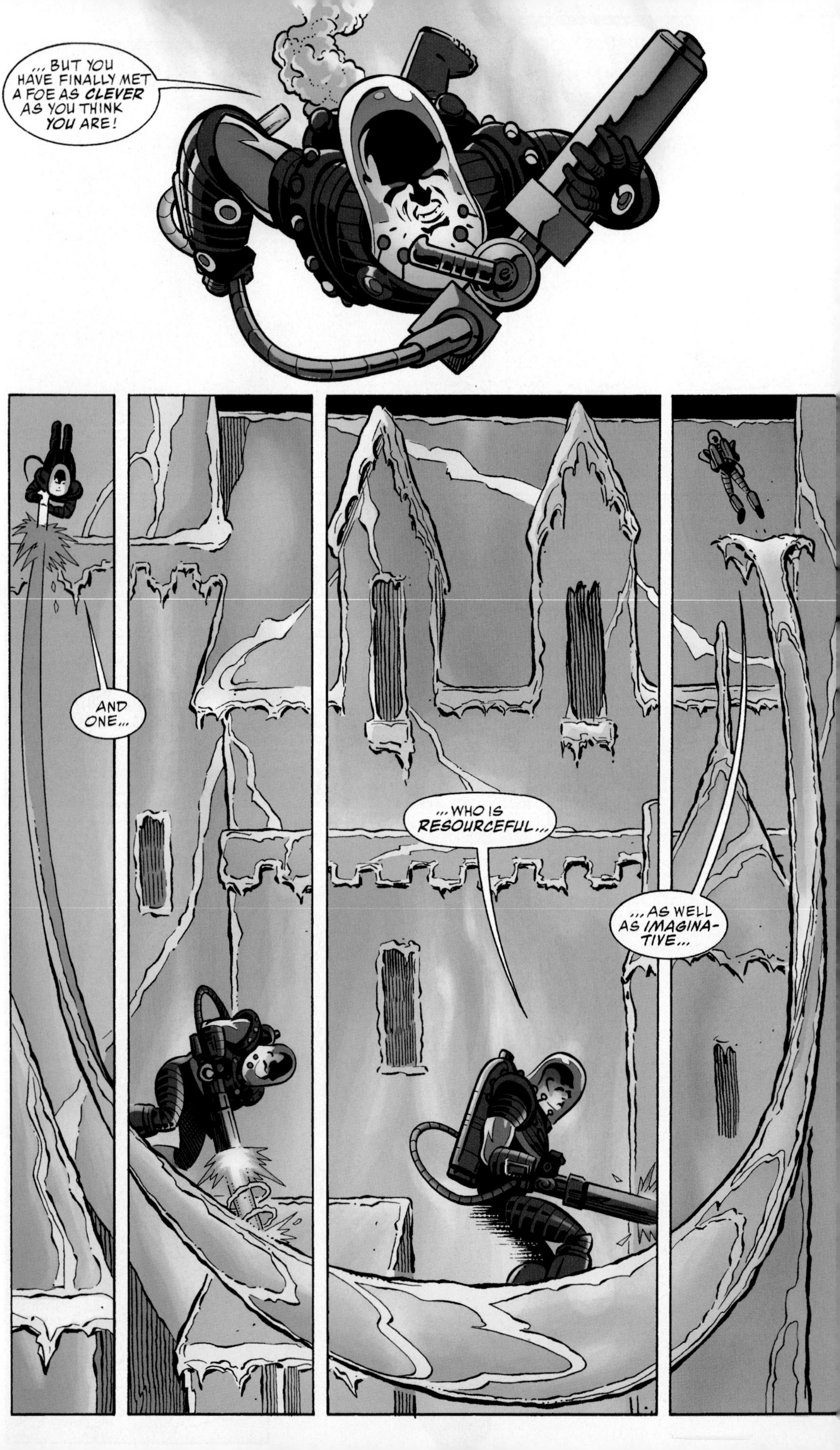
...BUT YOU HAVE FINALLY MET A FOE AS CLEVER AS YOU THINK YOU ARE!
AND ONE...
...WHO IS RESOURCEFUL...
...AS WELL AS IMAGINA-TIVE...

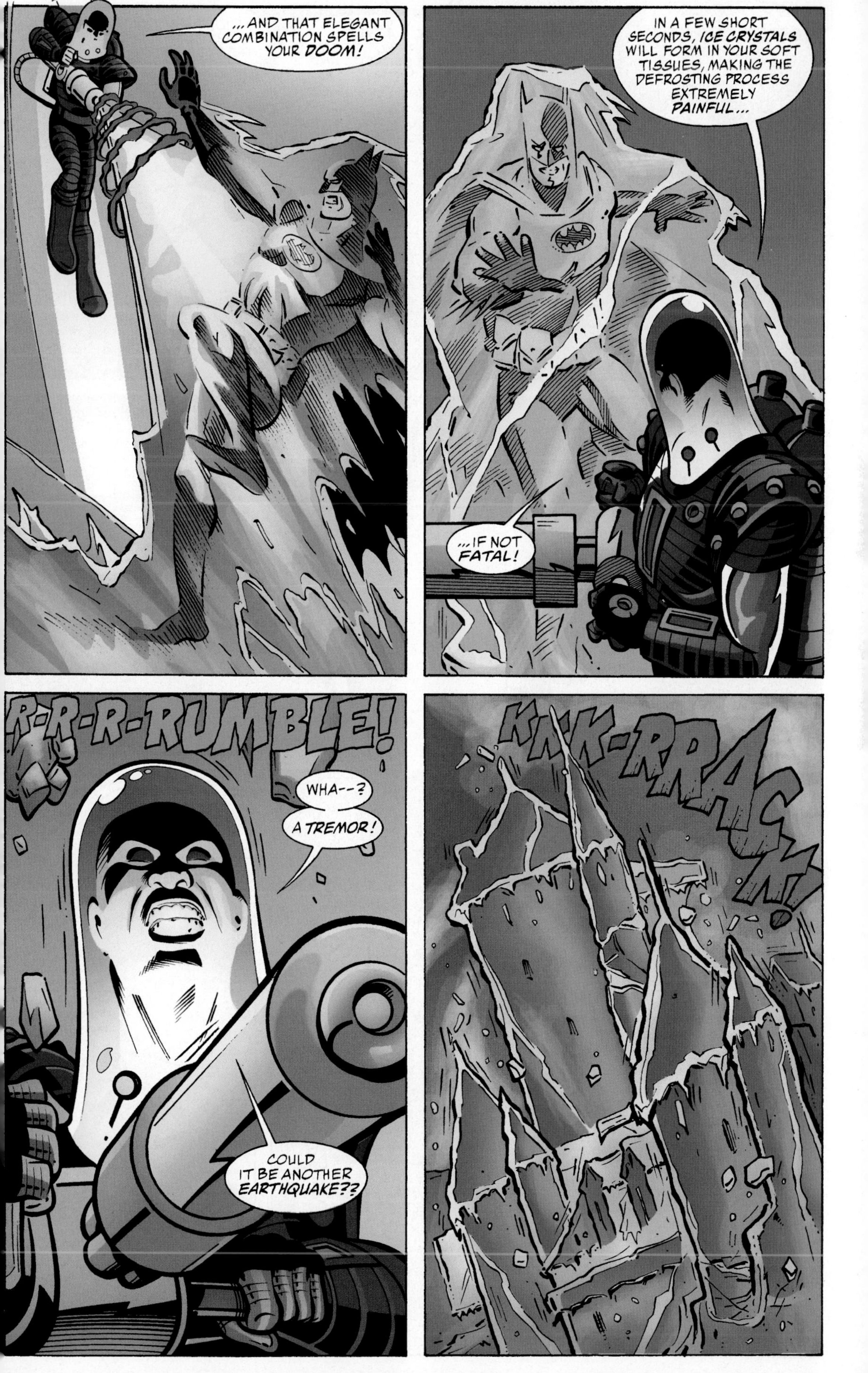
...AND THAT ELEGANT COMBINATION SPELLS YOUR DOOM!
IN A FEW SHORT SECONDS, ICE CRYSTALS WILL FORM IN YOUR SOFT TISSUES, MAKING THE DEFROSTING PROCESS EXTREMELY PAINFUL...
...IF NOT FATAL!
R-R-R-RUMBLE!
WHA--?
A TREMOR!
COULD IT BE ANOTHER EARTHQUAKE??
KNK-RRACK!

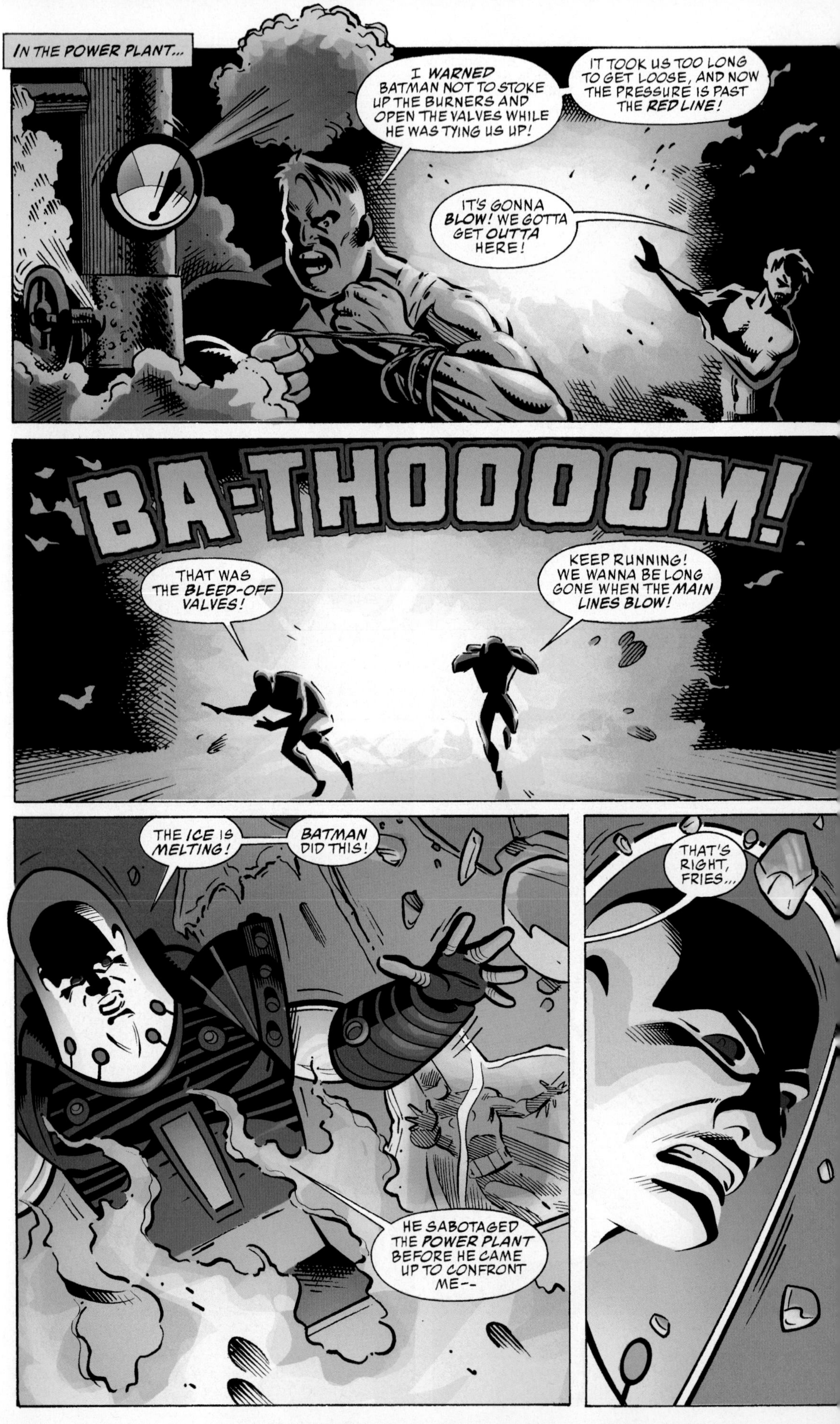

IN THE POWER PLANT...
I WARNED BATMAN NOT TO STOKE UP THE BURNERS AND OPEN THE VALVES WHILE HE WAS TYING US UP!
IT TOOK US TOO LONG TO GET LOOSE, AND NOW THE PRESSURE IS PAST THE RED LINE!
IT'S GONNA BLOW! WE GOTTA GET OUTTA HERE!
BA-THOOOOM!
THAT WAS THE BLEED-OFF VALVES!
KEEP RUNNING! WE WANNA BE LONG GONE WHEN THE MAIN LINES BLOW!
THE ICE IS MELTING!
BATMAN DID THIS!
HE SABOTAGED THE POWER PLANT BEFORE HE CAME UP TO CONFRONT ME--
THAT'S RIGHT, FRIES...

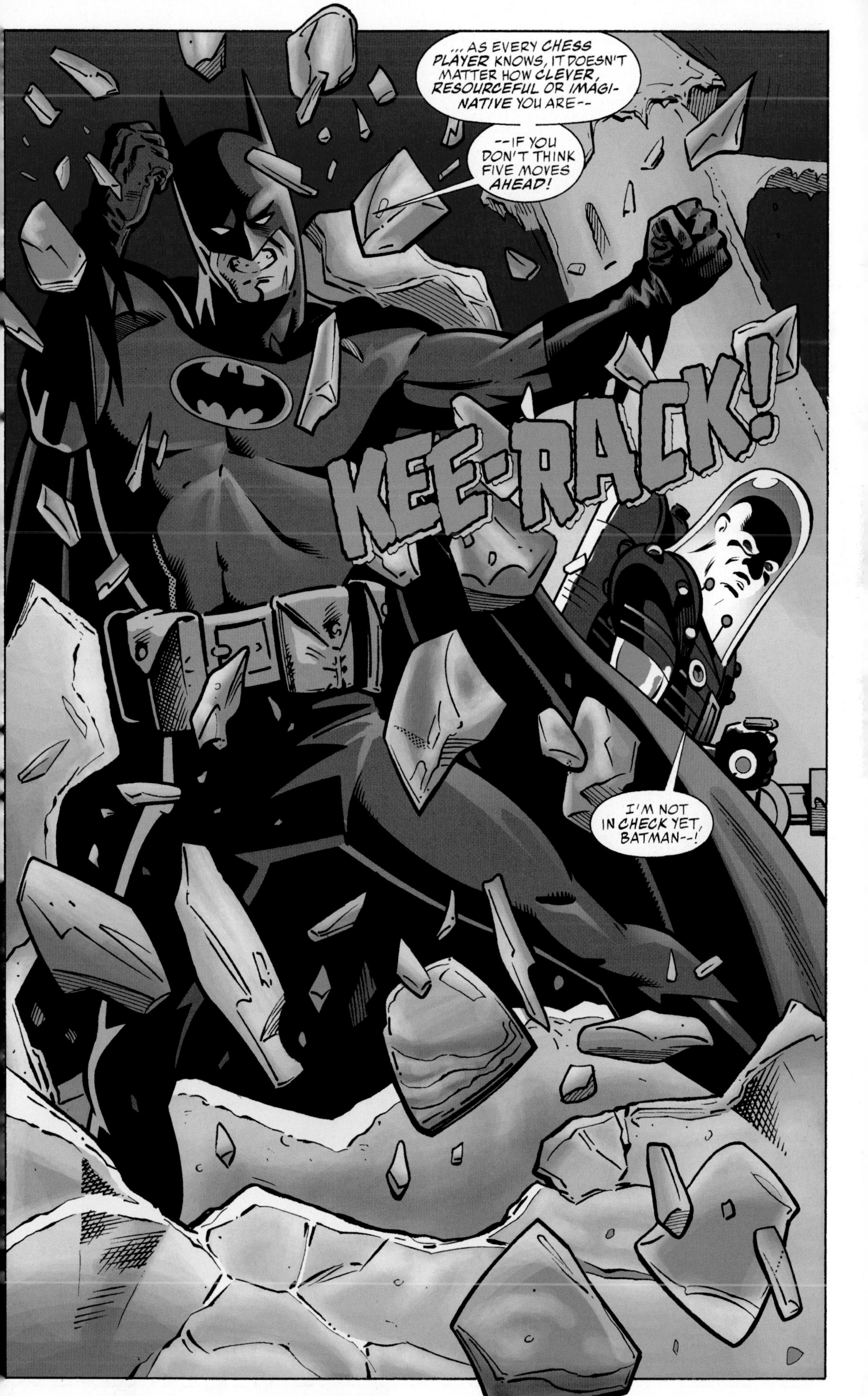
...AS EVERY CHESS PLAYER KNOWS, IT DOESN'T MATTER HOW CLEVER, RESOURCEFUL OR IMAGI-NATIVE YOU ARE--
--IF YOU DON'T THINK FIVE MOVES AHEAD!
KEE-RACK!
I'M NOT IN CHECK YET, BATMAN--!

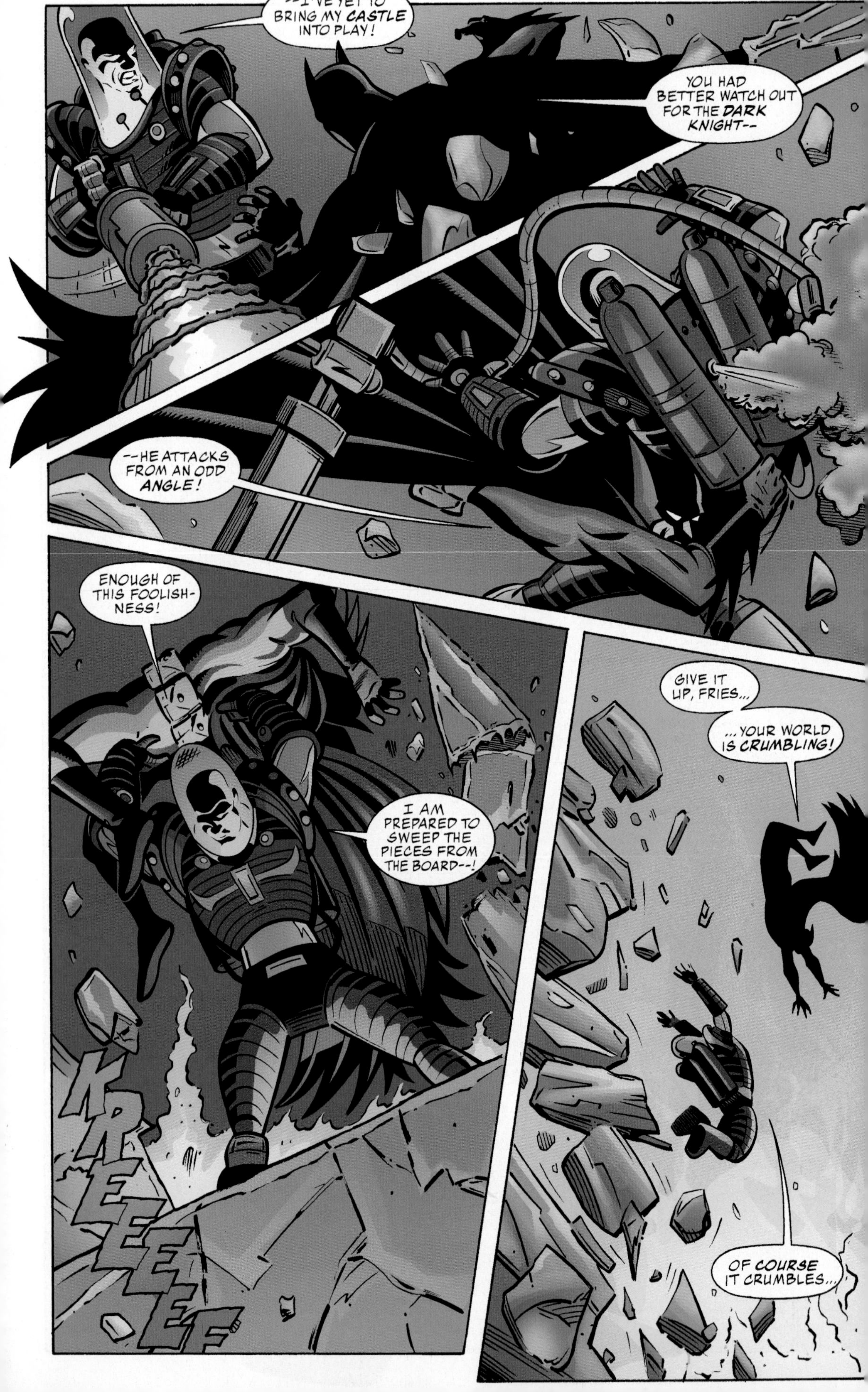
--I'VE YET TO BRING MY CASTLE INTO PLAY!
YOU HAD BETTER WATCH OUT FOR THE DARK KNIGHT--
--HE ATTACKS FROM AN ODD ANGLE!
ENOUGH OF THIS FOOLISHNESS!
I AM PREPARED TO SWEEP THE PIECES FROM THE BOARD--!
KREEEEEF
GIVE IT UP, FRIES...
...YOUR WORLD IS CRUMBLING!
OF COURSE IT CRUMBLES...

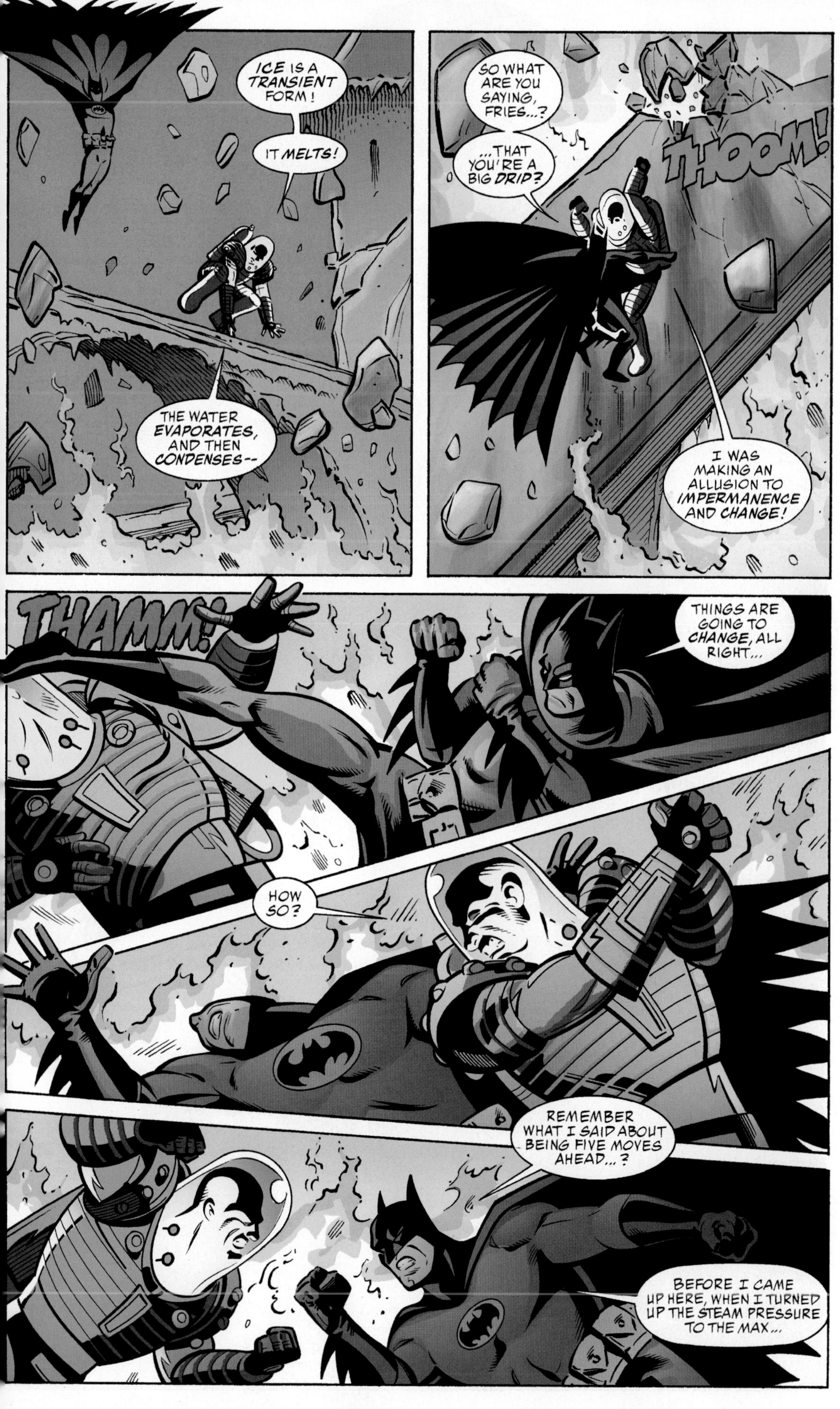
ICE IS A TRANSIENT FORM!
IT MELTS!
THE WATER EVAPORATES, AND THEN CONDENSES--
SO WHAT ARE YOU SAYING, FRIES...?
...THAT YOU'RE A BIG DRIP?
THOOM!
I WAS MAKING AN ALLUSION TO IMPERMANENCE AND CHANGE!
THAMM!
THINGS ARE GOING TO CHANGE, ALL RIGHT...
HOW SO?
REMEMBER WHAT I SAID ABOUT BEING FIVE MOVES AHEAD...?
BEFORE I CAME UP HERE, WHEN I TURNED UP THE STEAM PRESSURE TO THE MAX...

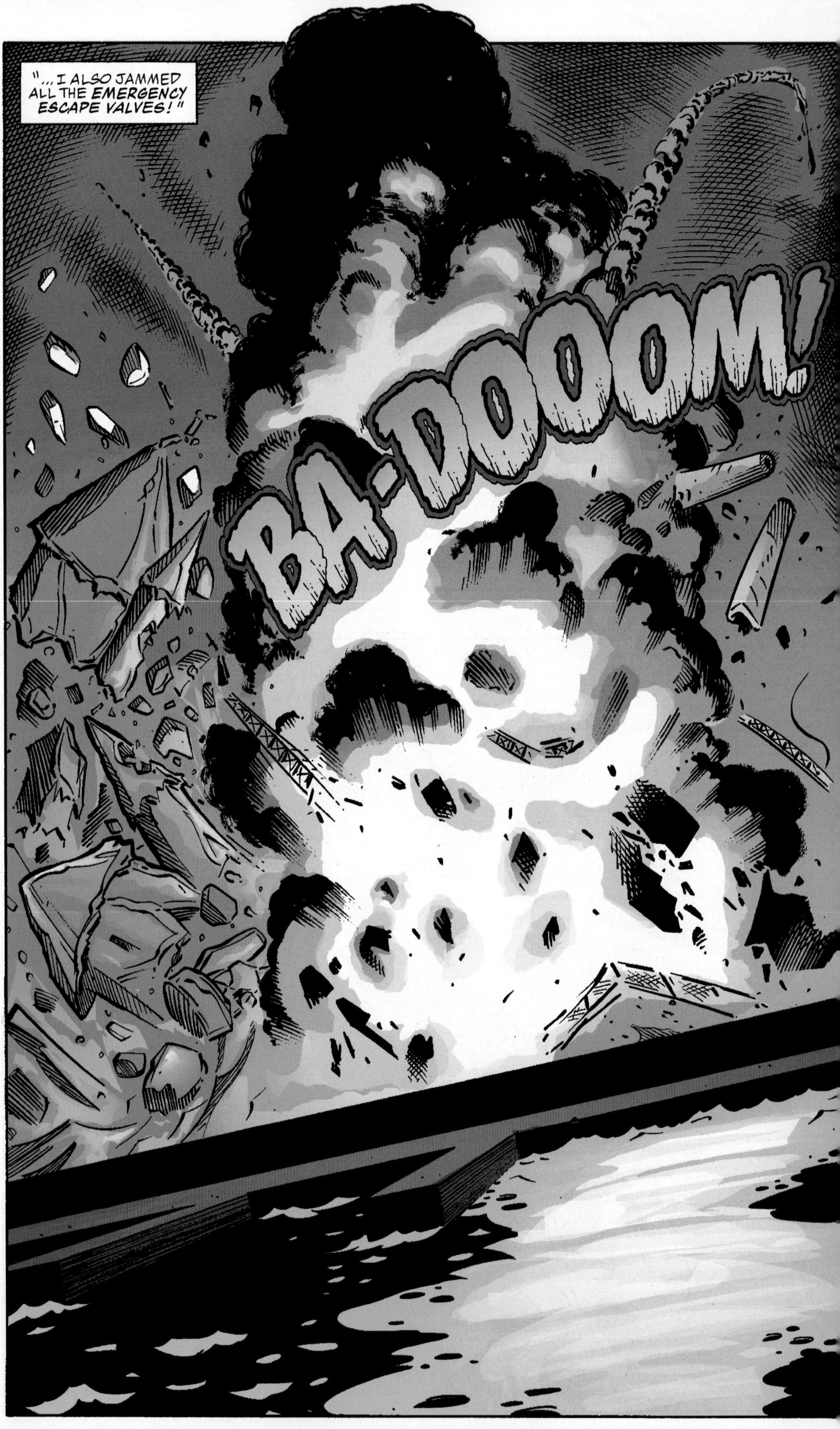
"...I ALSO JAMMED ALL THE EMERGENCY ESCAPE VALVES!"
BA-DOOOOM!

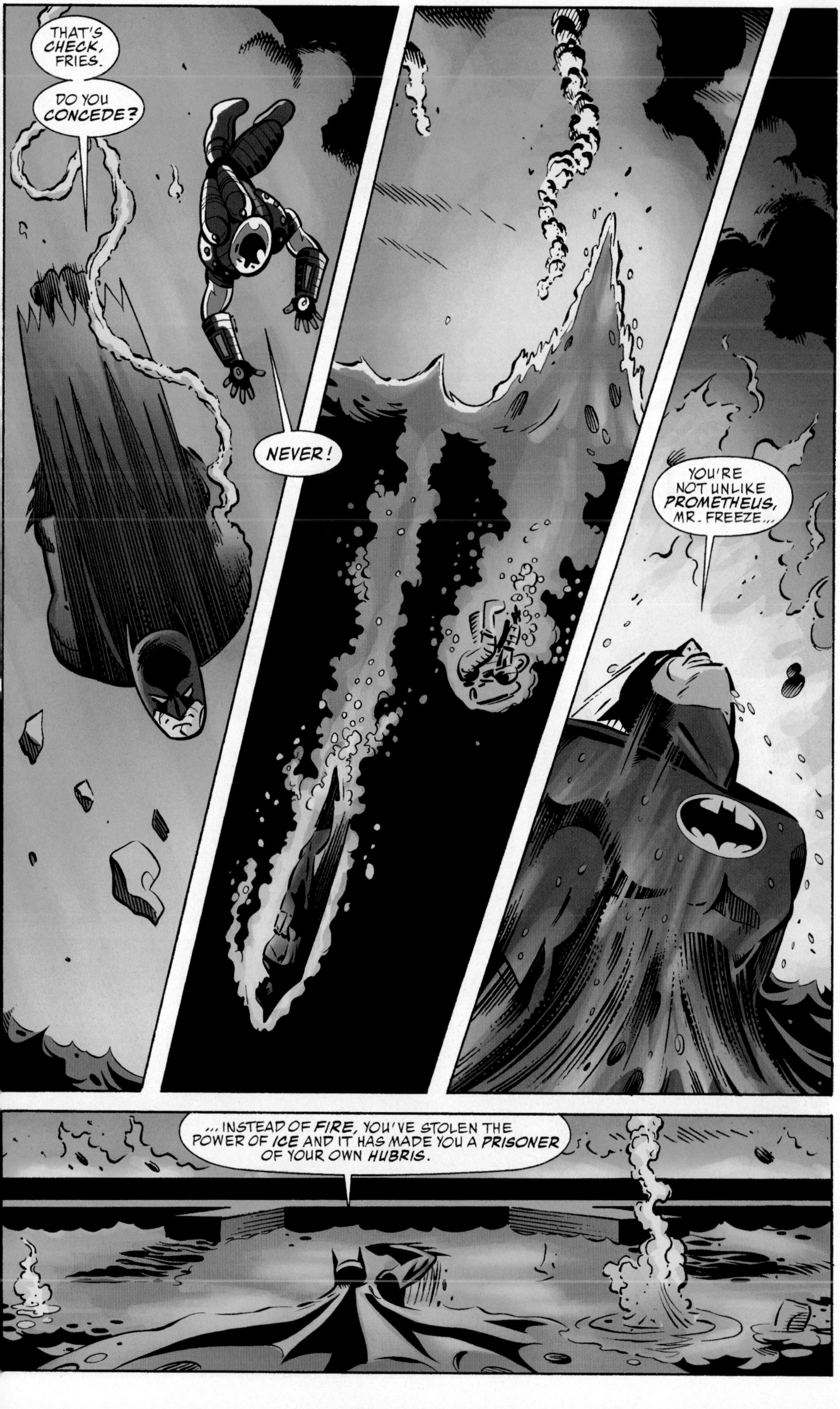
THAT'S CHECK, FRIES.
DO YOU CONCEDE?
NEVER!
YOU'RE NOT UNLIKE PROMETHEUS, MR. FREEZE...
...INSTEAD OF FIRE, YOU'VE STOLEN THE POWER OF ICE AND IT HAS MADE YOU A PRISONER OF YOUR OWN HUBRIS.

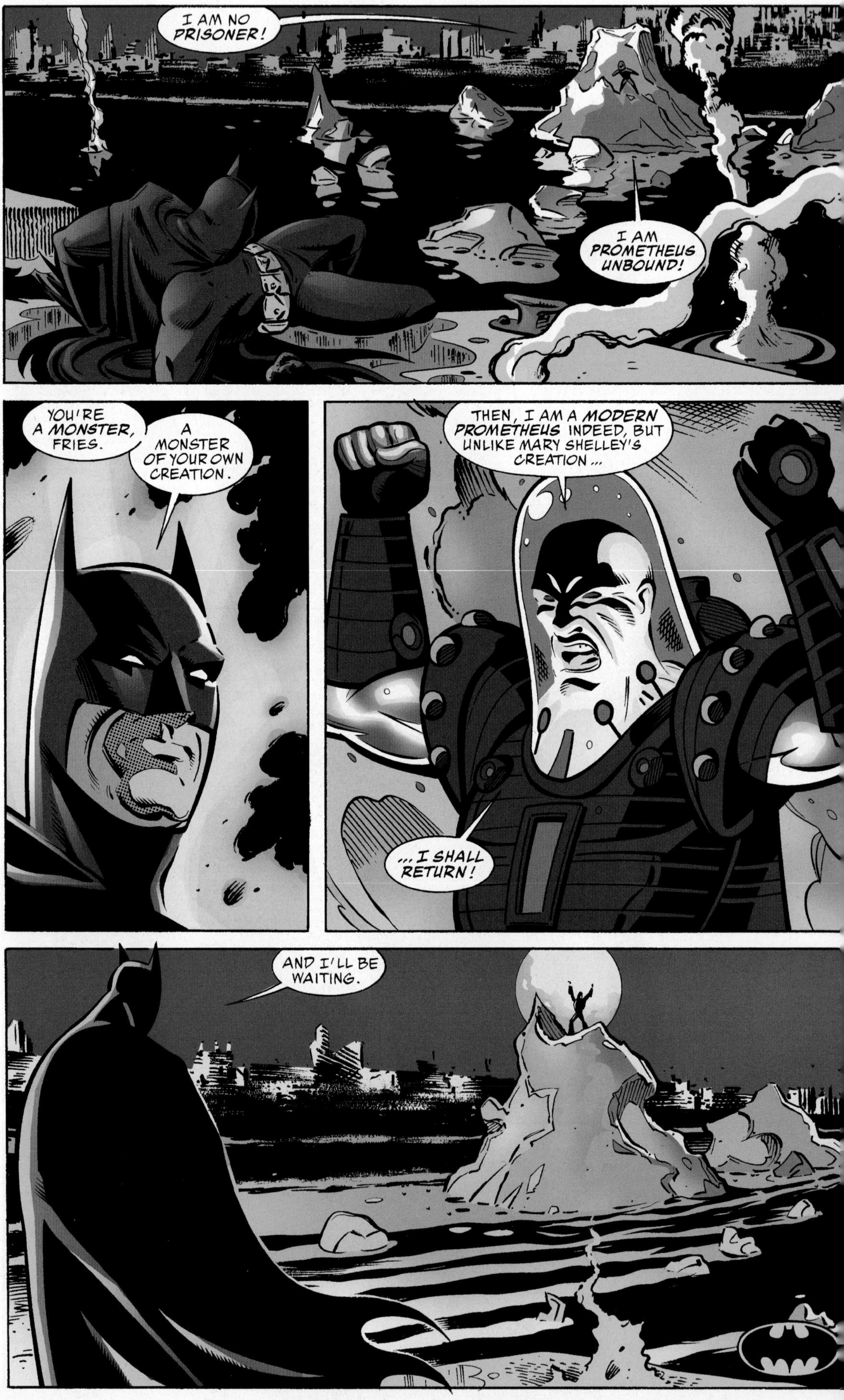
I AM NO PRISONER!
I AM PROMETHEUS UNBOUND!
YOU'RE A MONSTER, FRIES.
A MONSTER OF YOUR OWN CREATION.
THEN, I AM A MODERN PROMETHEUS INDEED, BUT UNLIKE MARY SHELLEY'S CREATION...
...I SHALL RETURN!
AND I'LL BE WAITING.

COVER GALLERY

BATMAN: LEGENDS OF THE DARK KNIGHT #119
Cover artist: Brian Bolland

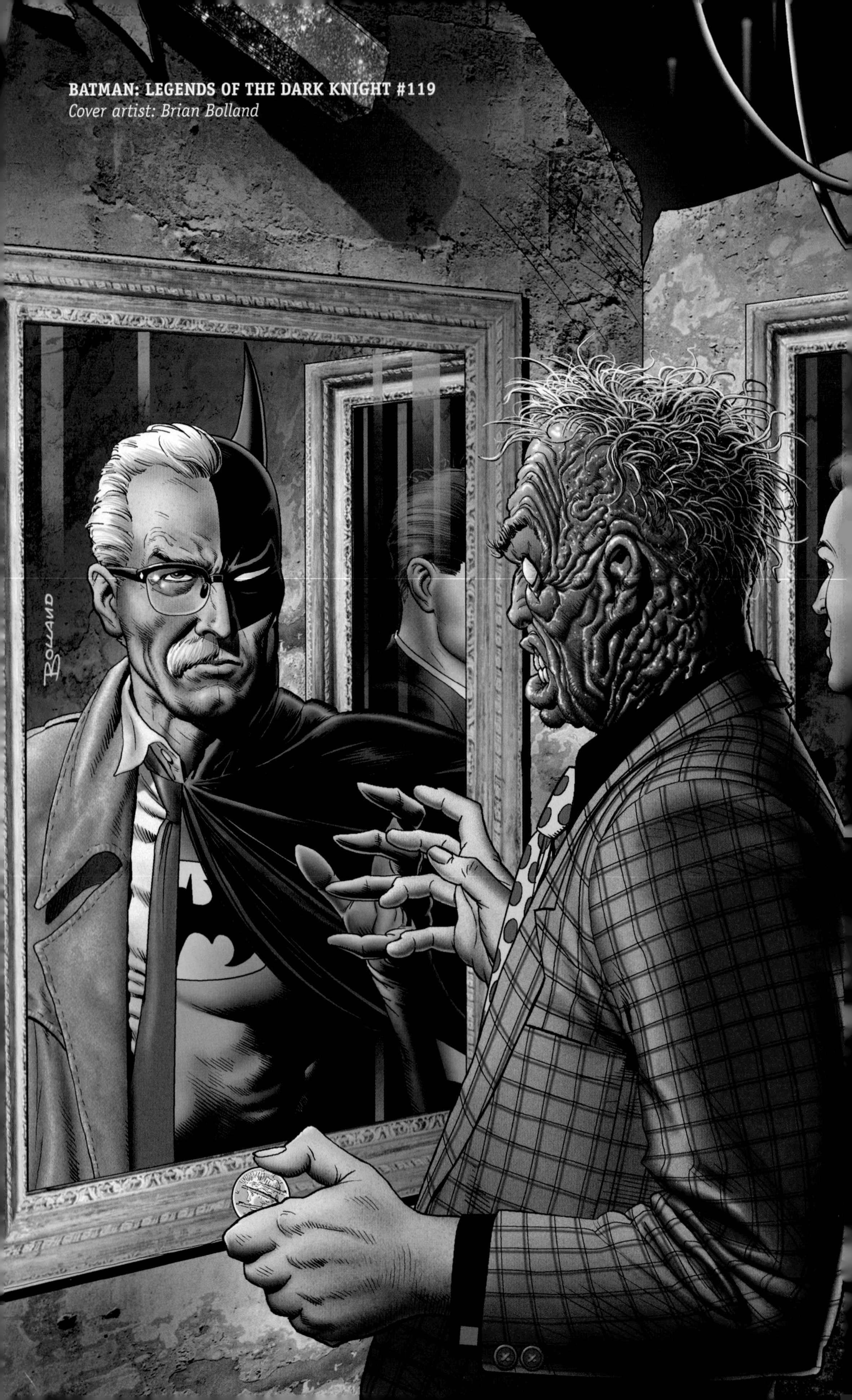
BOLLAND

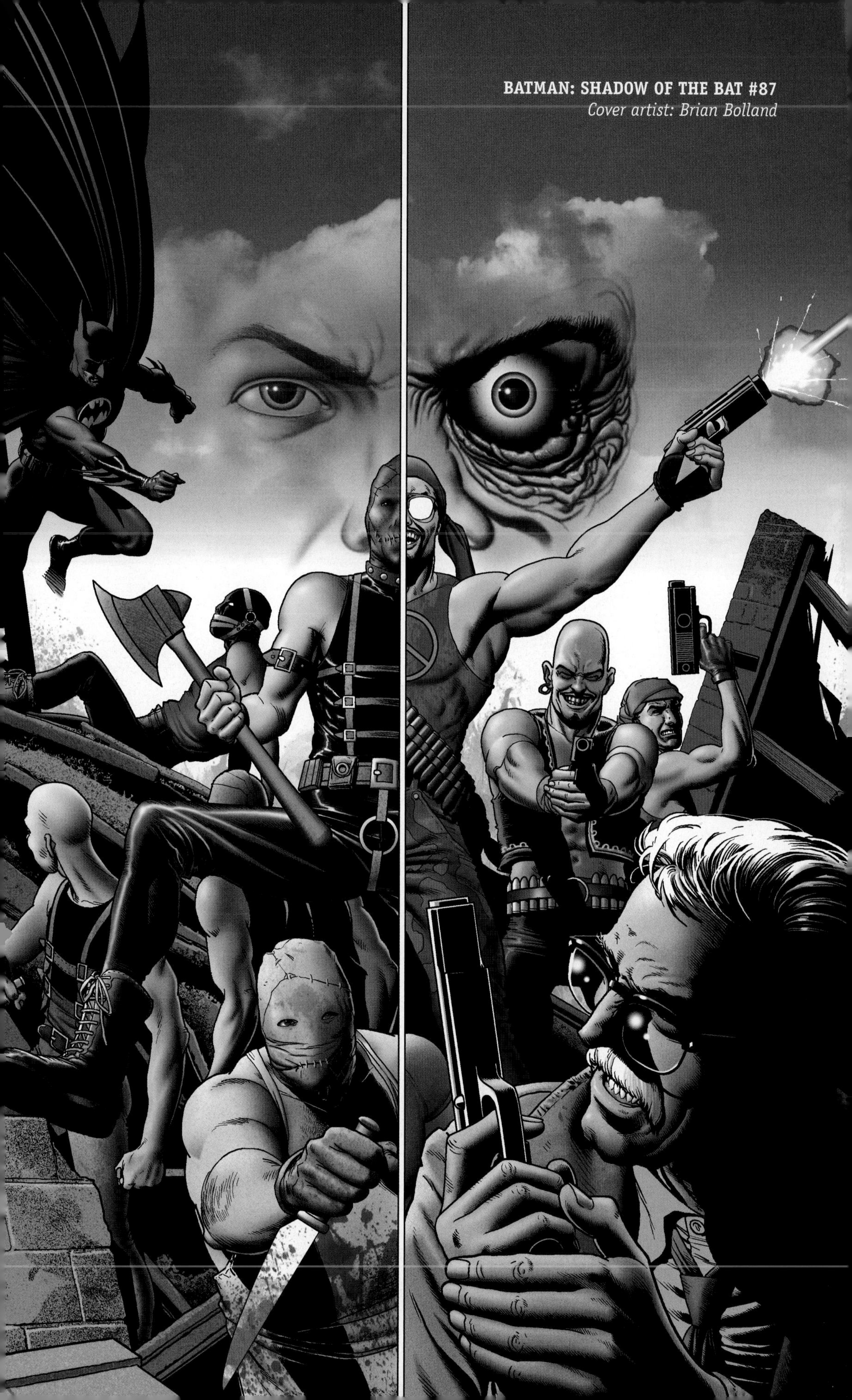

BATMAN: SHADOW OF THE BAT #87
Cover artist: Brian Bolland

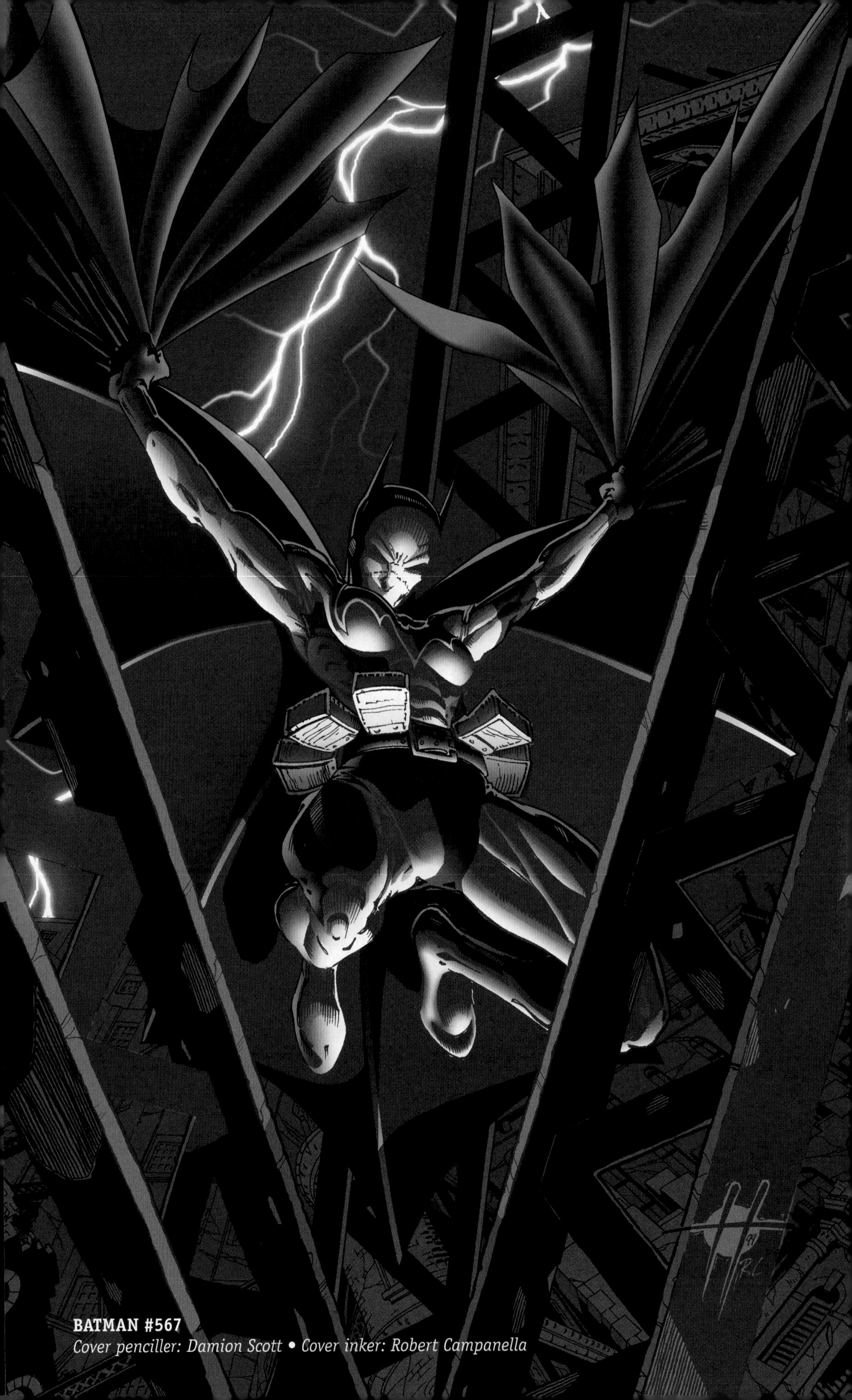

BATMAN #567
Cover penciller: Damion Scott • Cover inker: Robert Campanella

DETECTIVE COMICS #734

Cover penciller: Damion Scott • Cover inker: Robert Campanella

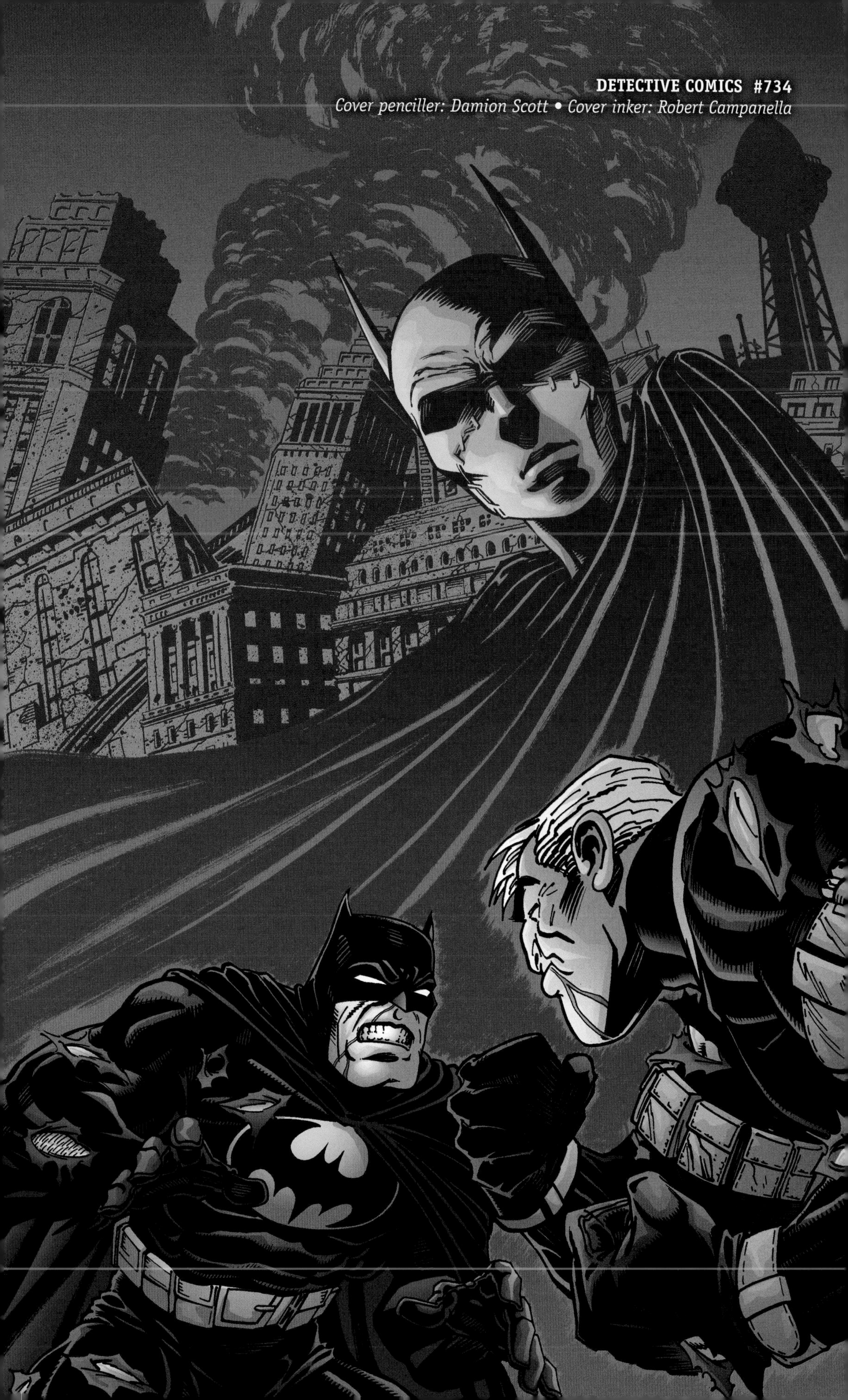

YOUNG JUSTICE: NO MAN'S LAND #1

Cover penciller: Scott McDaniel • Cover inker: Danny Miki

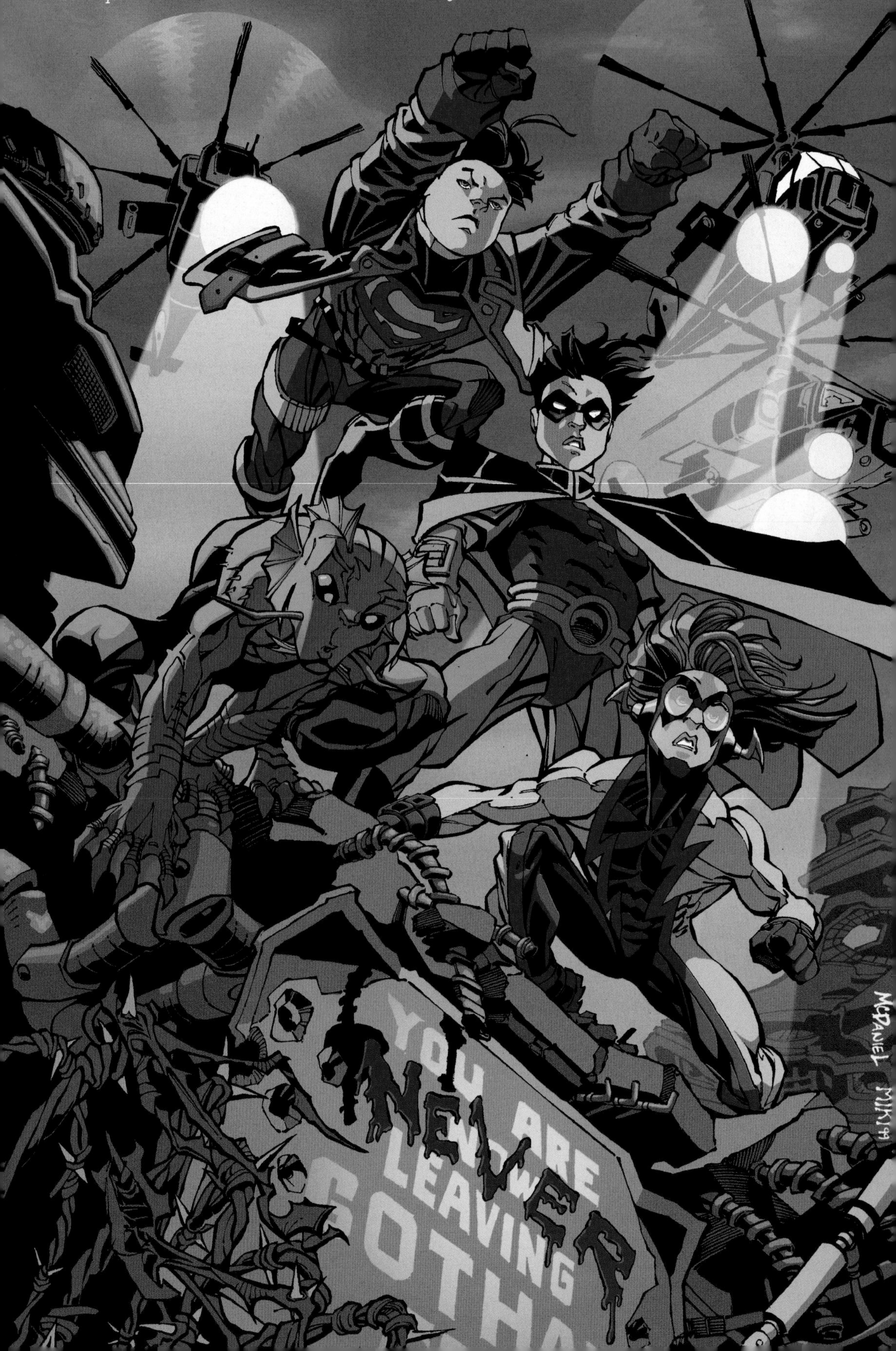

YOU ARE NOW LEAVING
NEVER
McDANIEL
MIKI '99

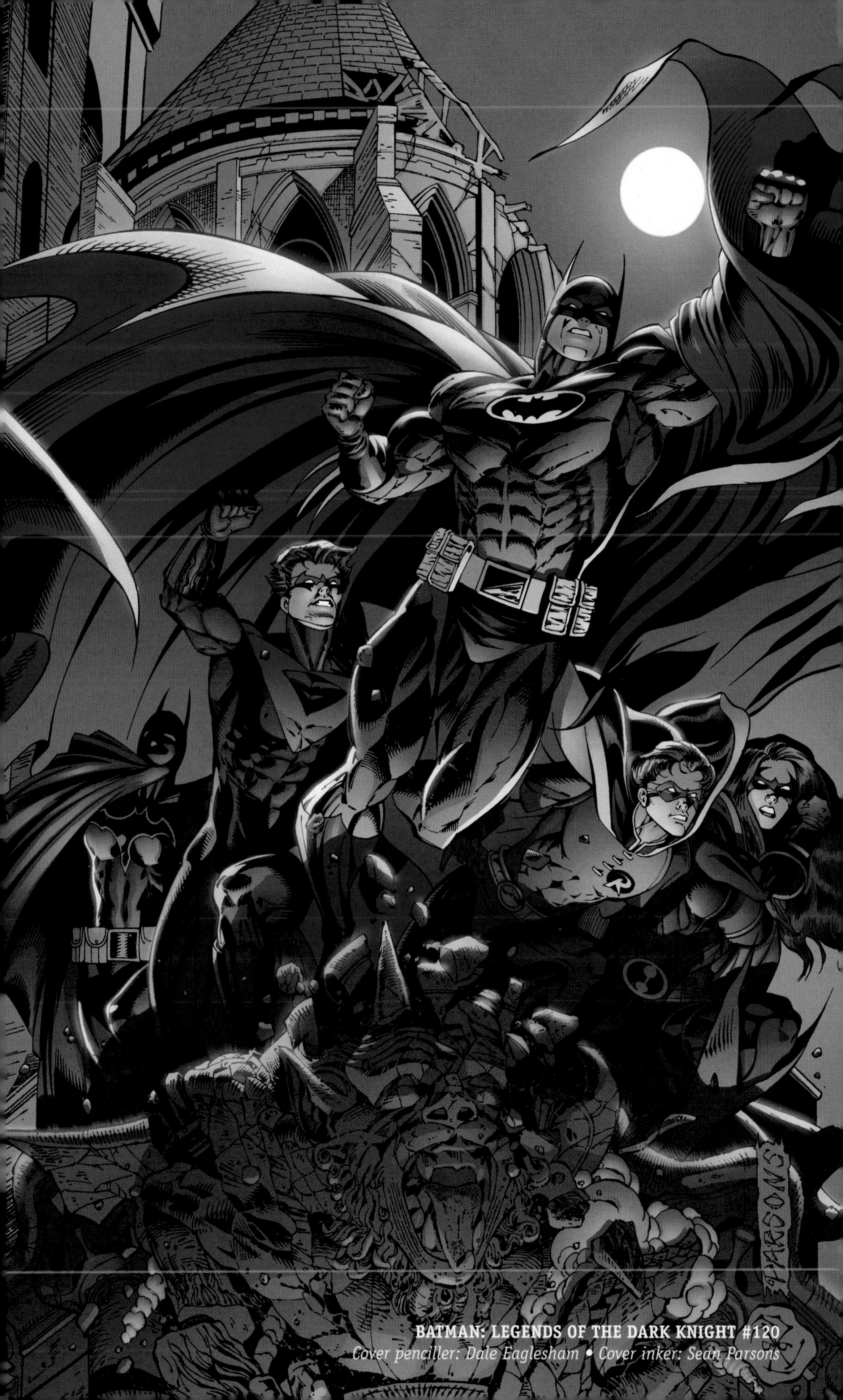

BATMAN: LEGENDS OF THE DARK KNIGHT #120
Cover penciller: Dale Eaglesham • Cover inker: Sean Parsons

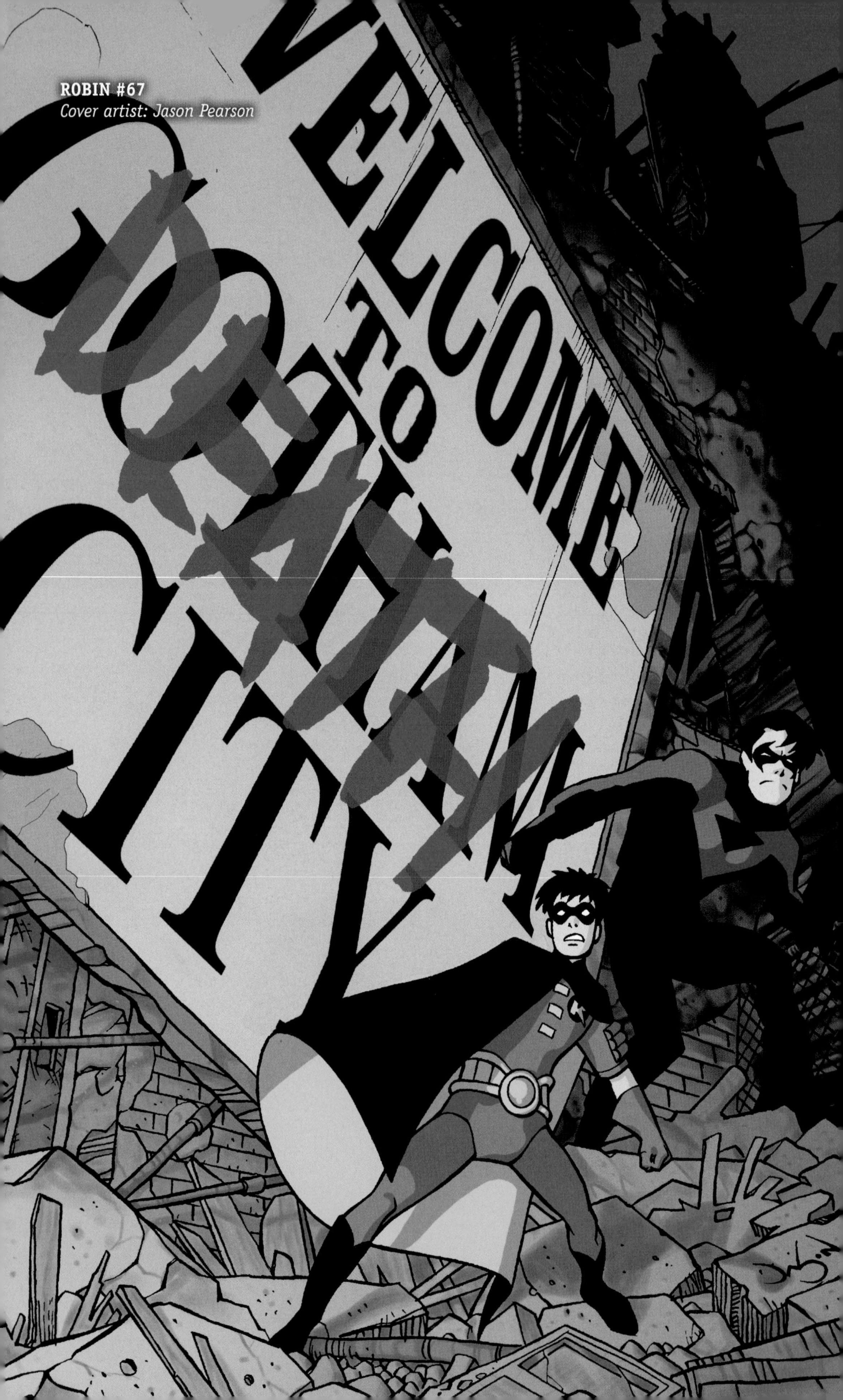
WELCOME
TO
GOTHAM
CITY

ROBIN #67
Cover artist: Jason Pearson

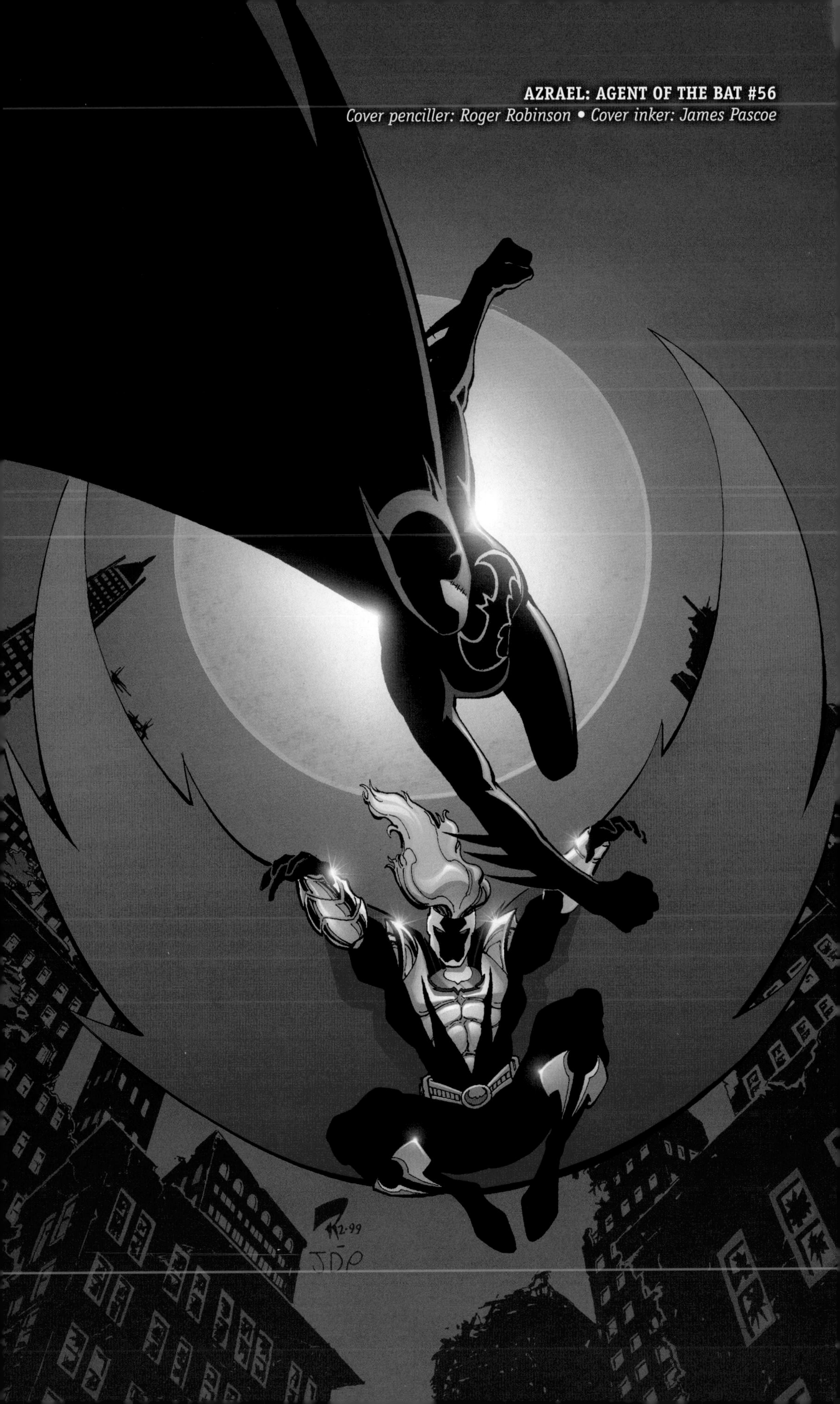

AZRAEL: AGENT OF THE BAT #56

Cover penciller: Roger Robinson • Cover inker: James Pascoe

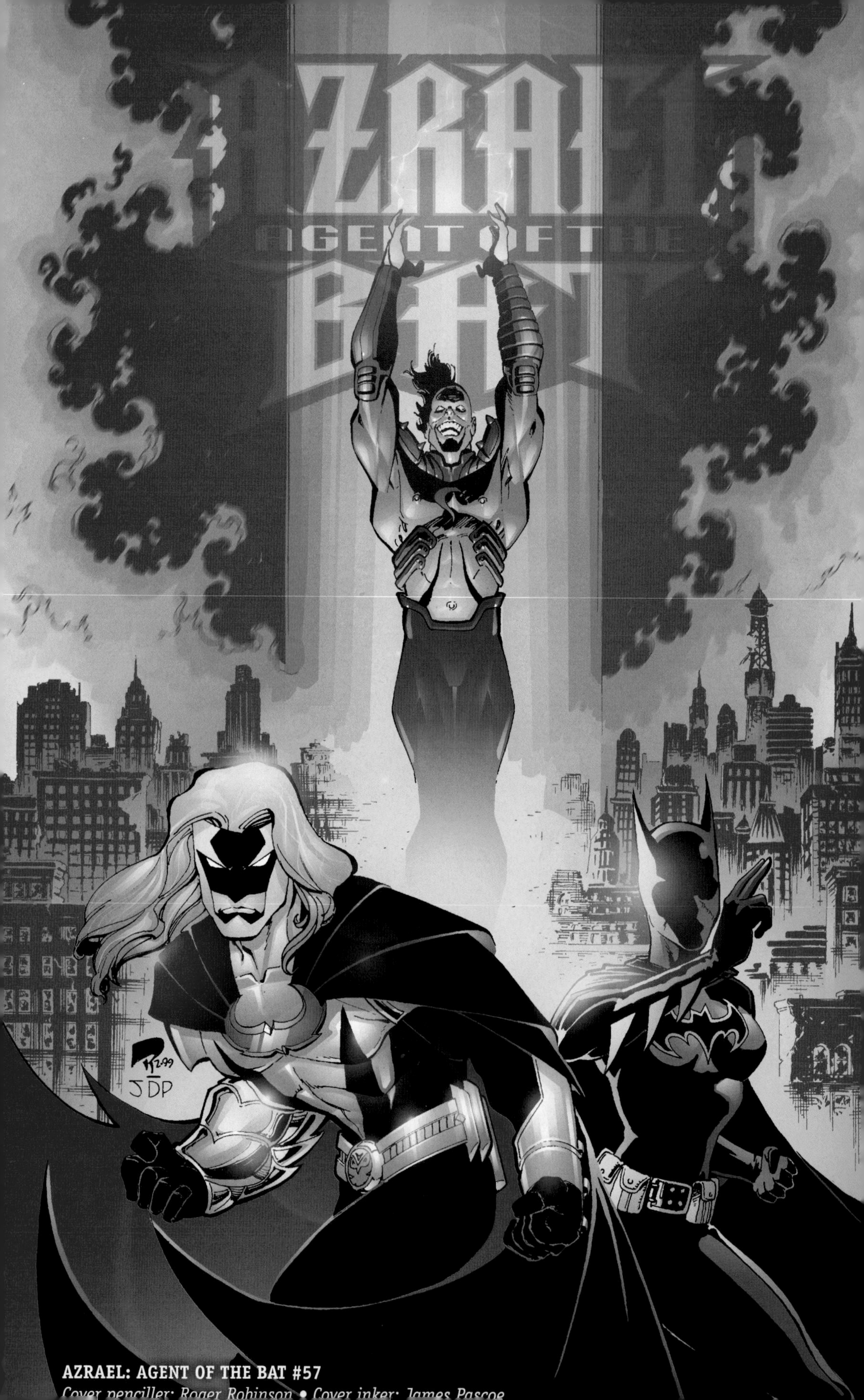
AGENT OF THE

AZRAEL: AGENT OF THE BAT #57

Cover penciller: Roger Robinson • Cover inker: James Pascoe

BATMAN CHRONICLES #17

Cover penciller: Pascal Alixe • Cover inker: Aaron Sowd

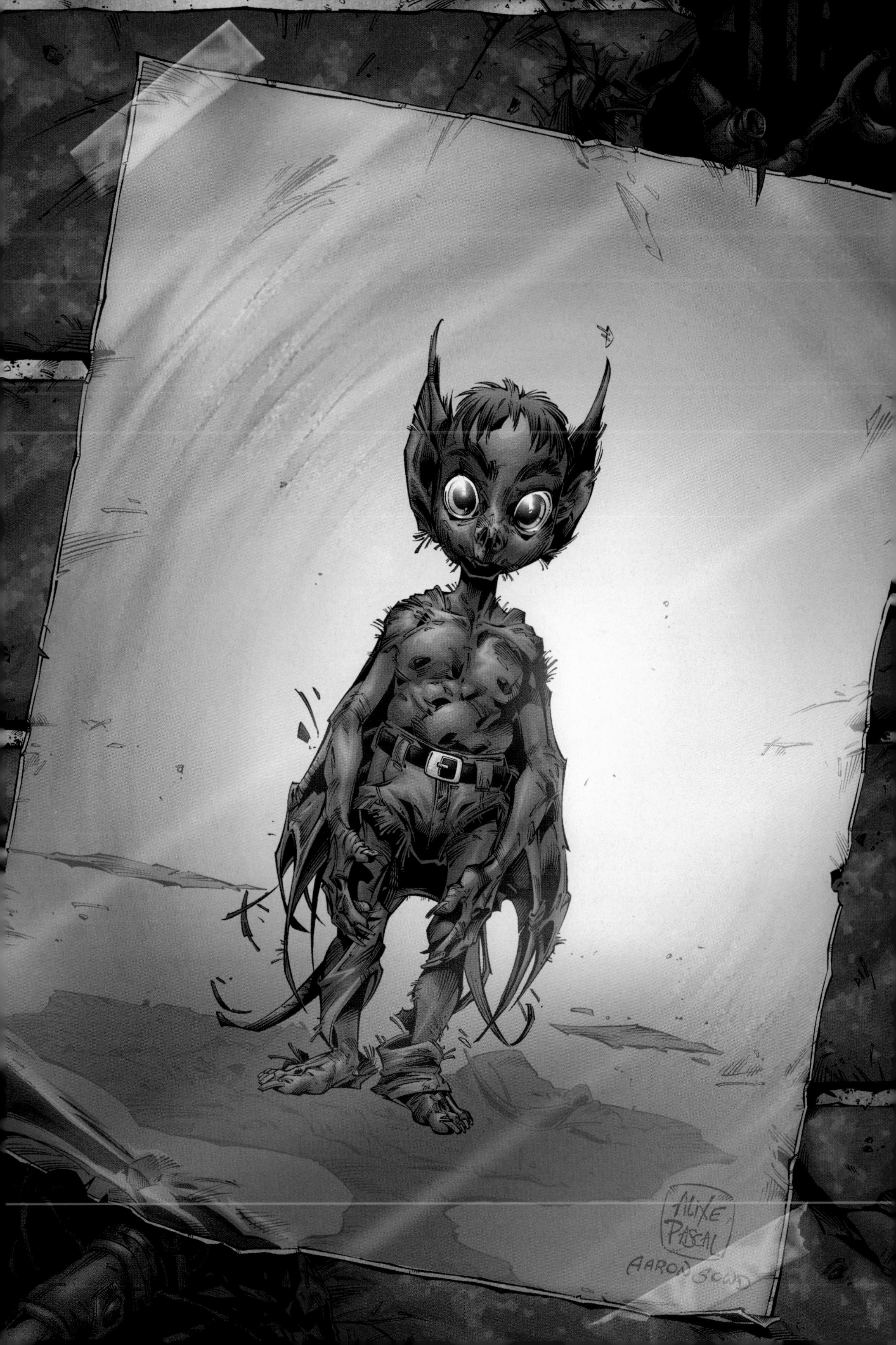
ALIXE PASCAL
AARON SOWD

NIGHTWING #35
Cover penciller: Scott McDaniel • Cover inker: Karl Story

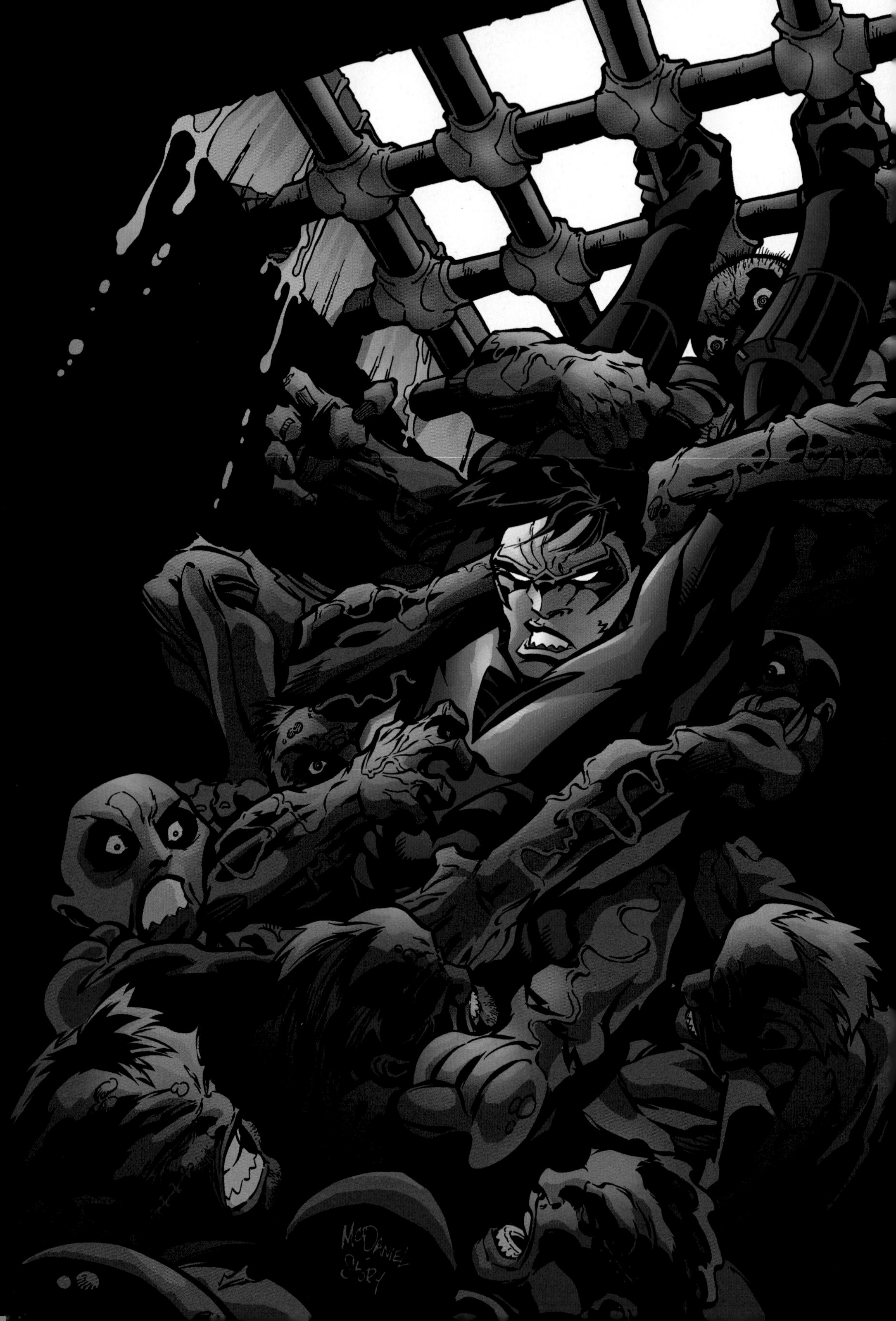

NIGHTWING #36

Cover penciller: Scott McDaniel • Cover inker: Karl Story

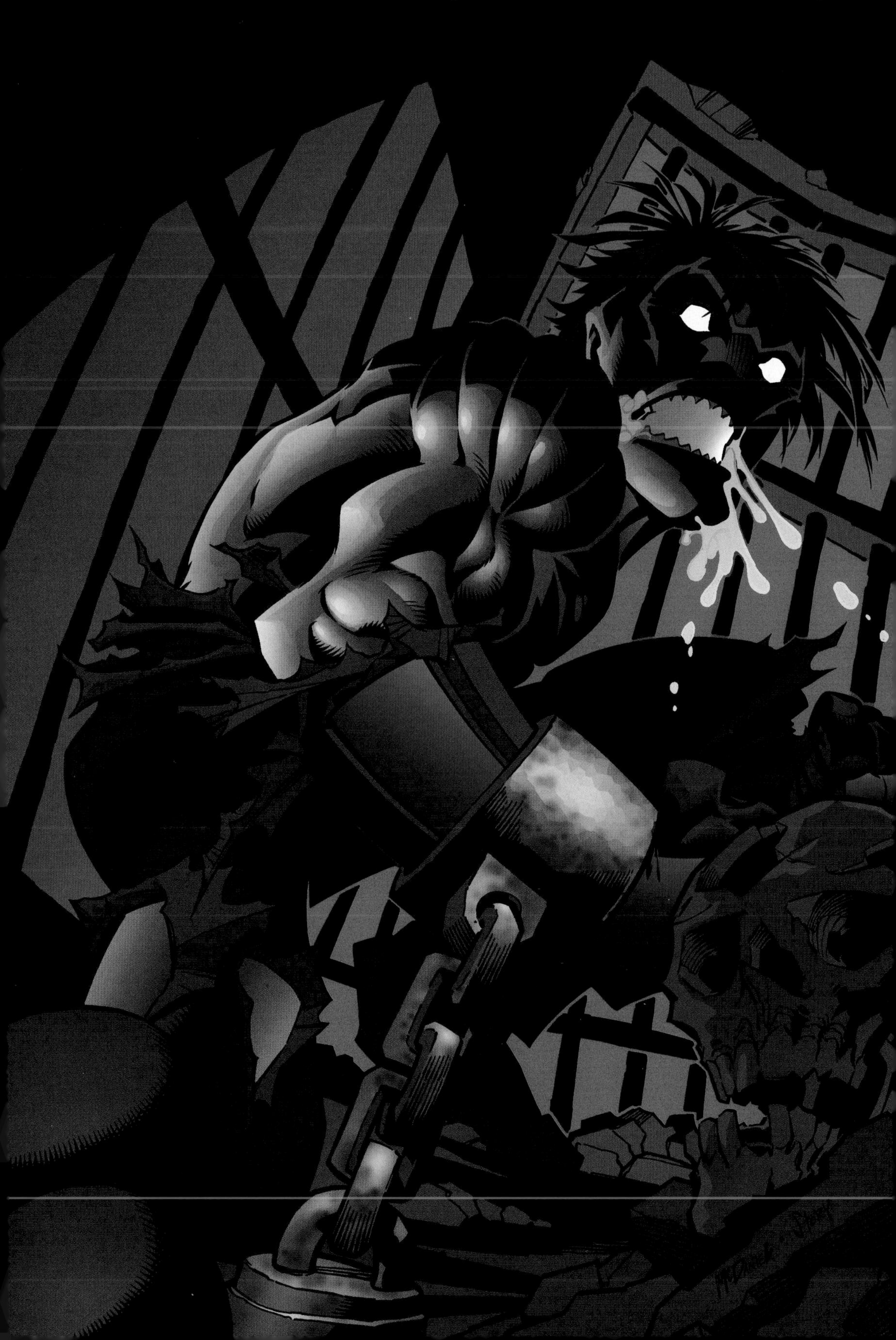

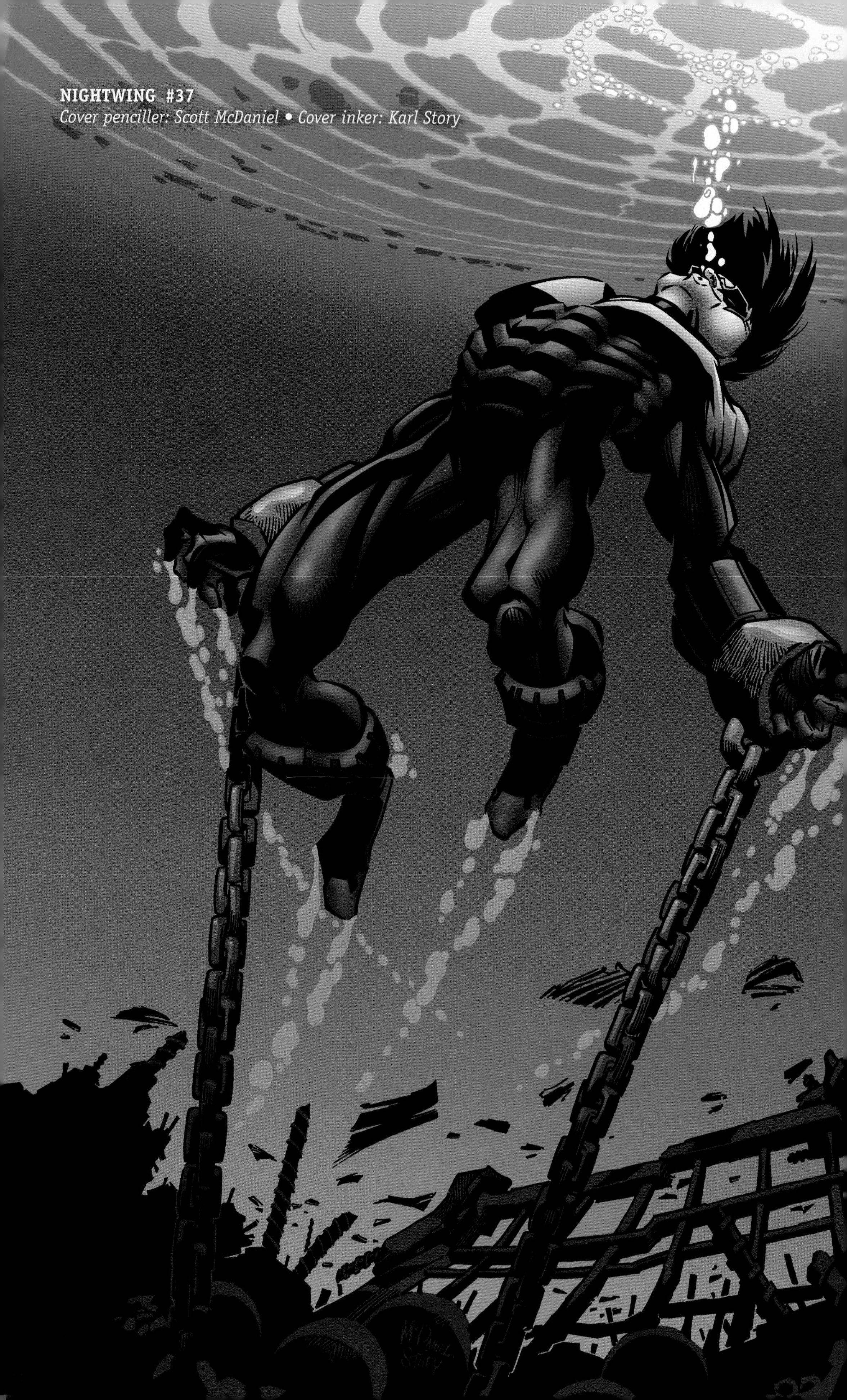

NIGHTWING #37
Cover penciller: Scott McDaniel • Cover inker: Karl Story

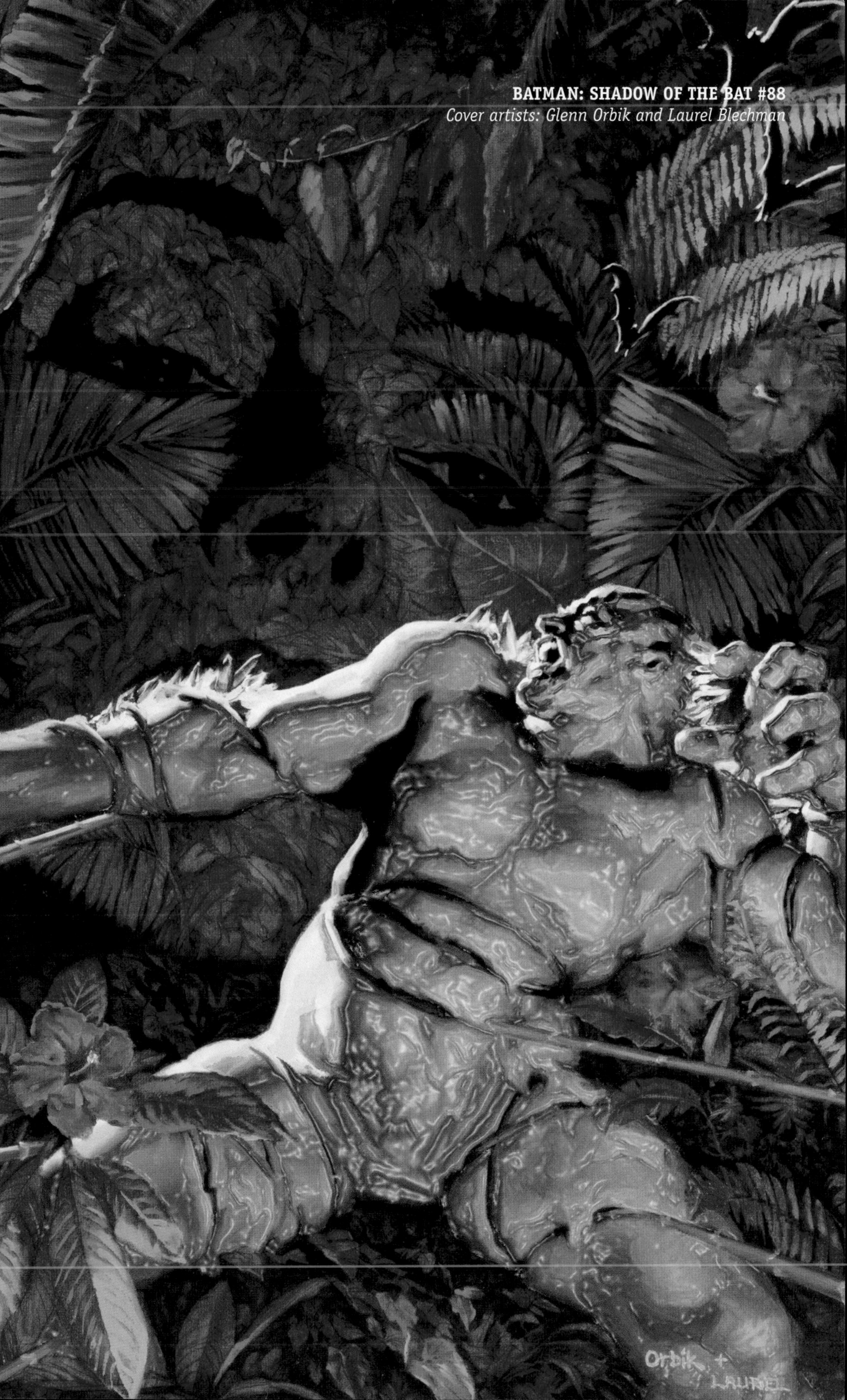
Orbik + LAUREL

BATMAN: SHADOW OF THE BAT #88
Cover artists: Glenn Orbik and Laurel Blechman

BATMAN #568
Cover artists: Glenn Orbik and Laurel Blechman

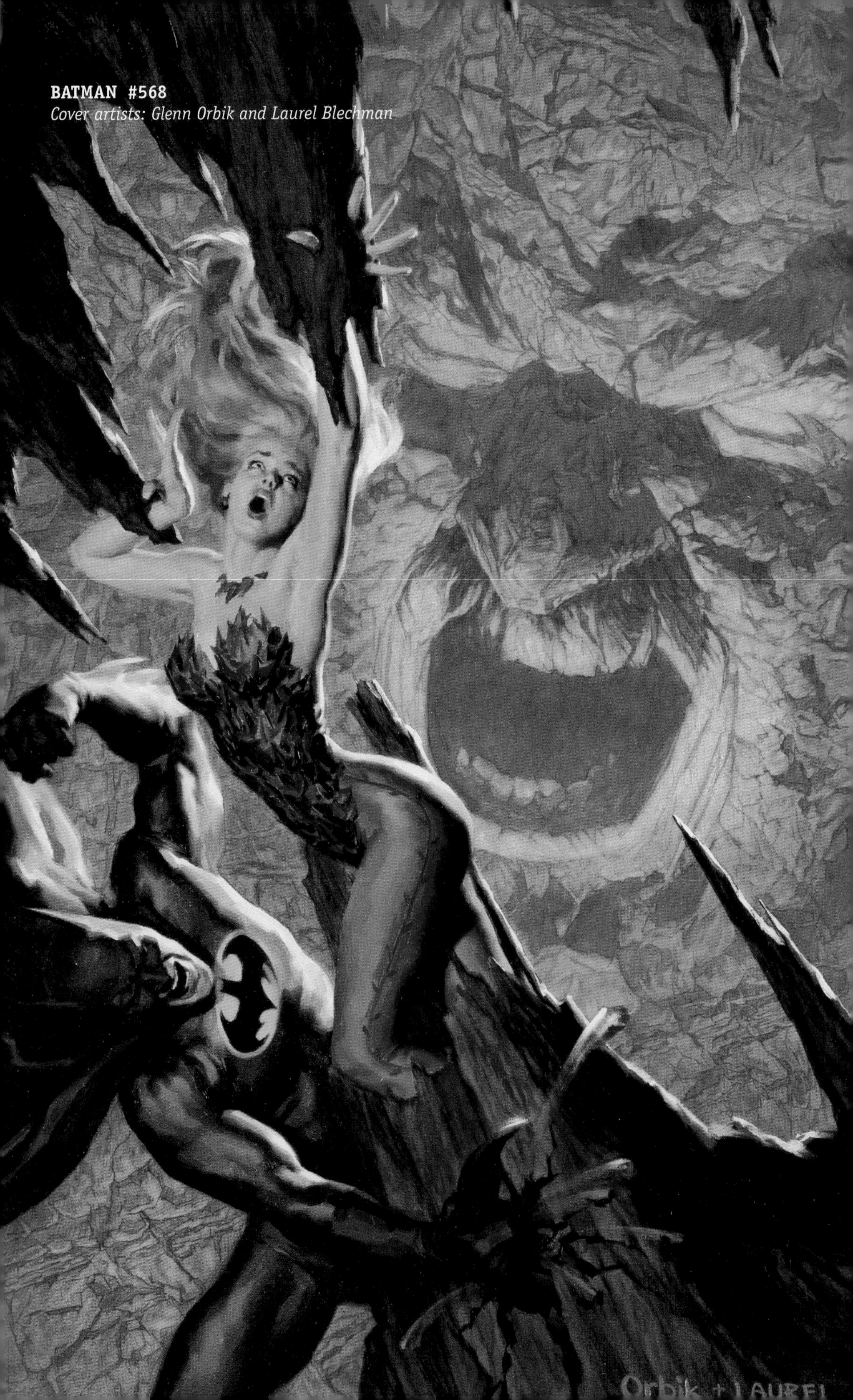
Orbik + LAUREL

DETECTIVE COMICS #735

Cover artists: Glenn Orbik and Laurel Blechman

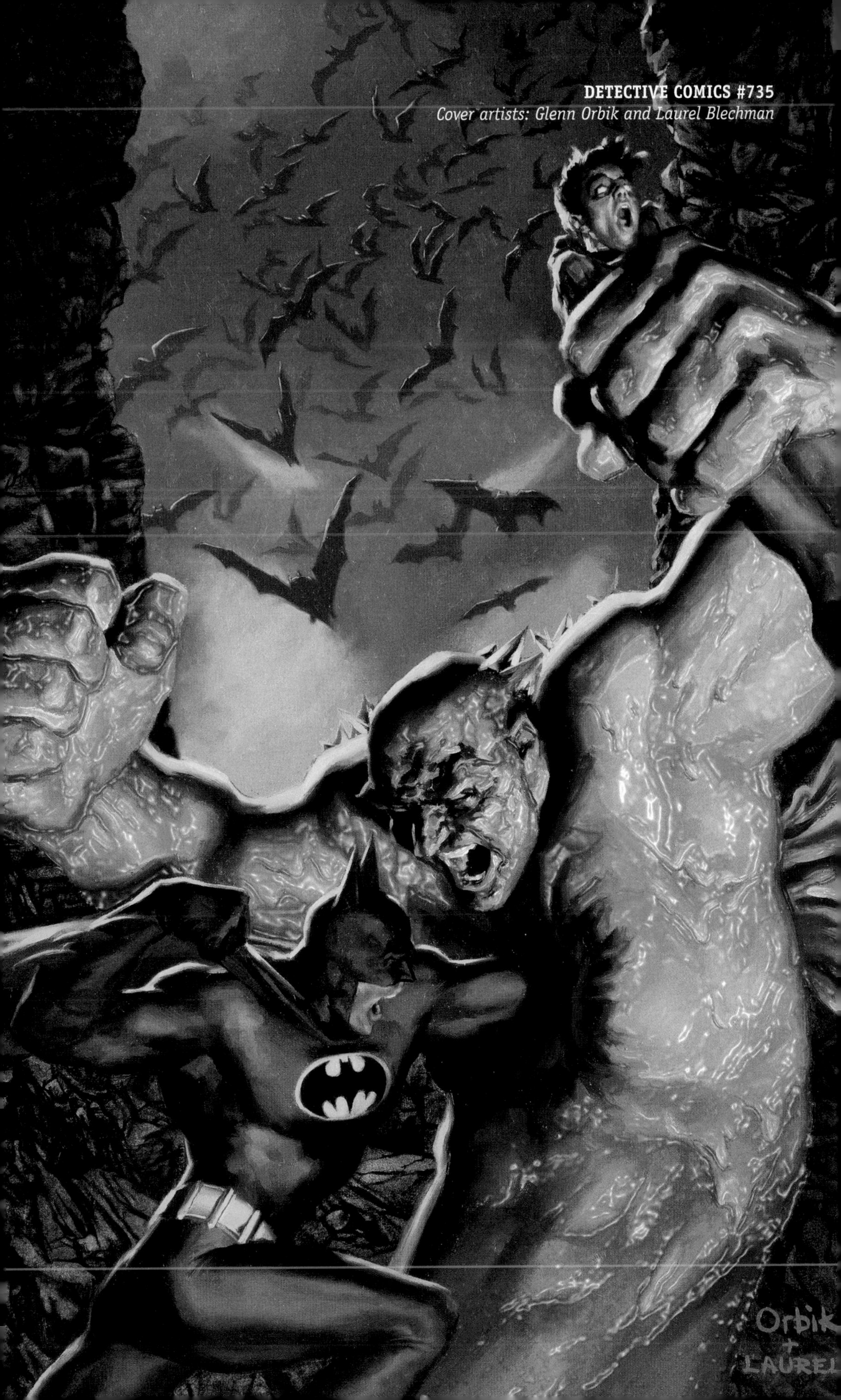
Orbik
+
LAUREL

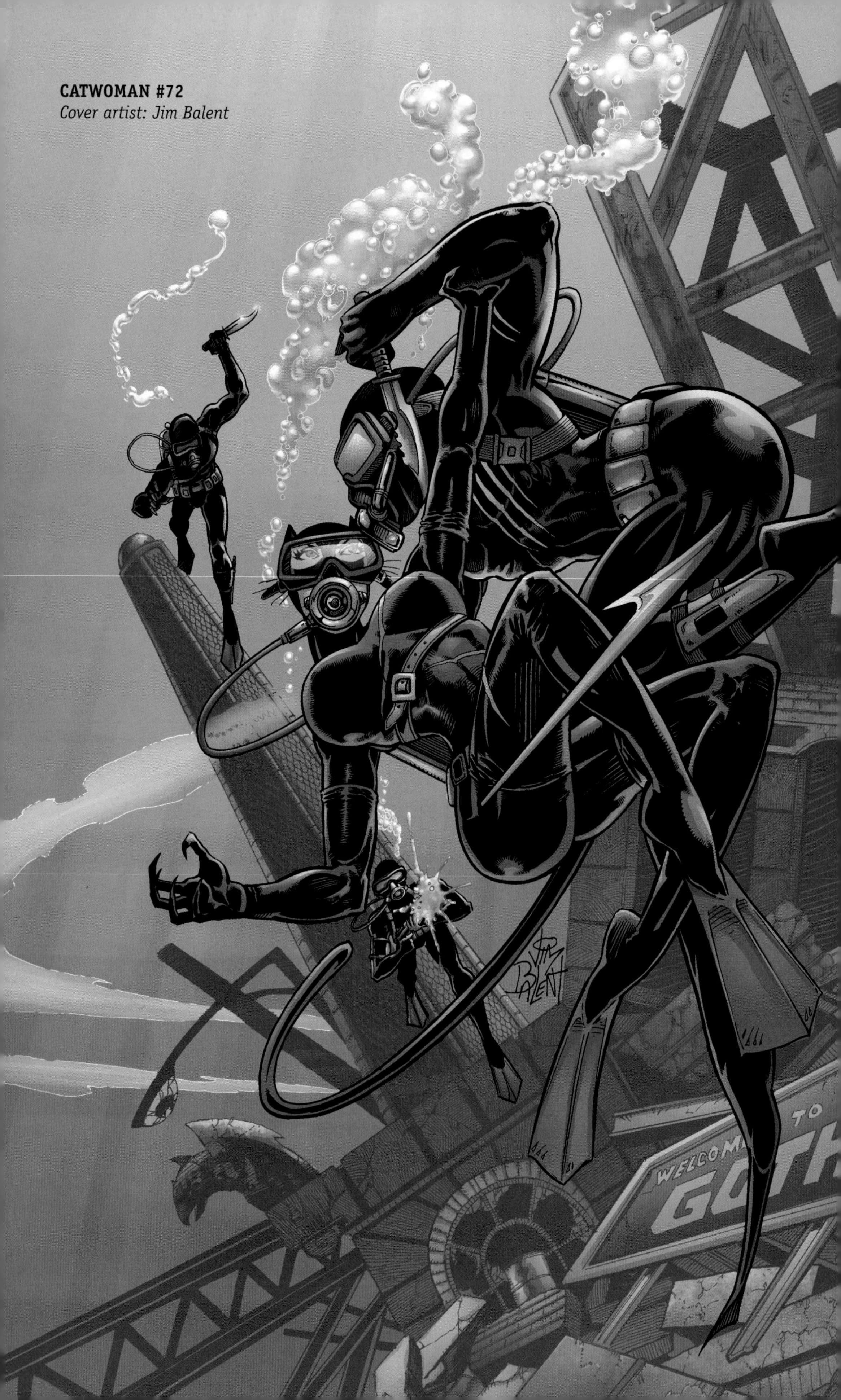
WELCOM
TO
GOT
JIM BALENT

CATWOMAN #72
Cover artist: Jim Balent

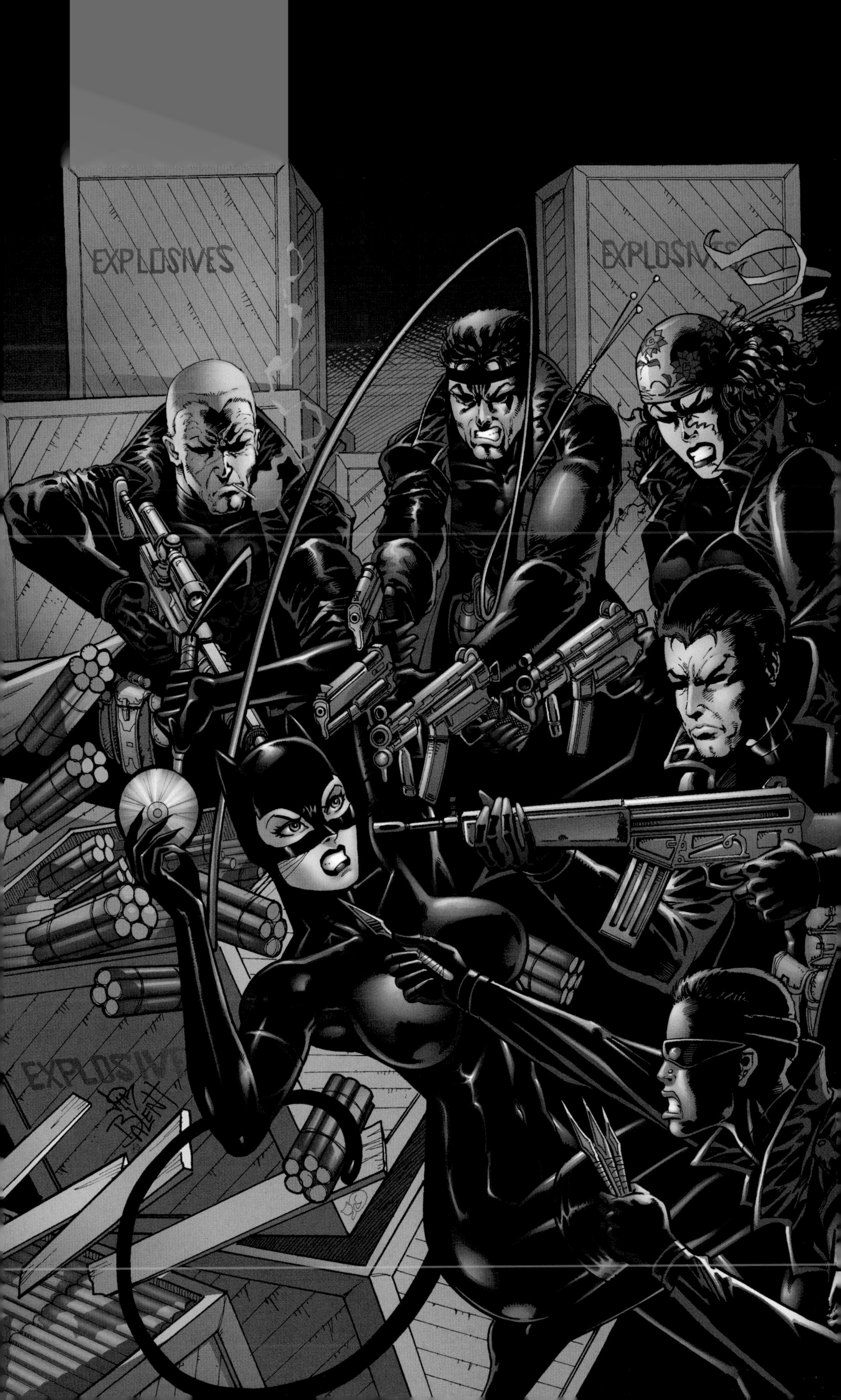
EXPLOSIVES
EXPLOSIVES

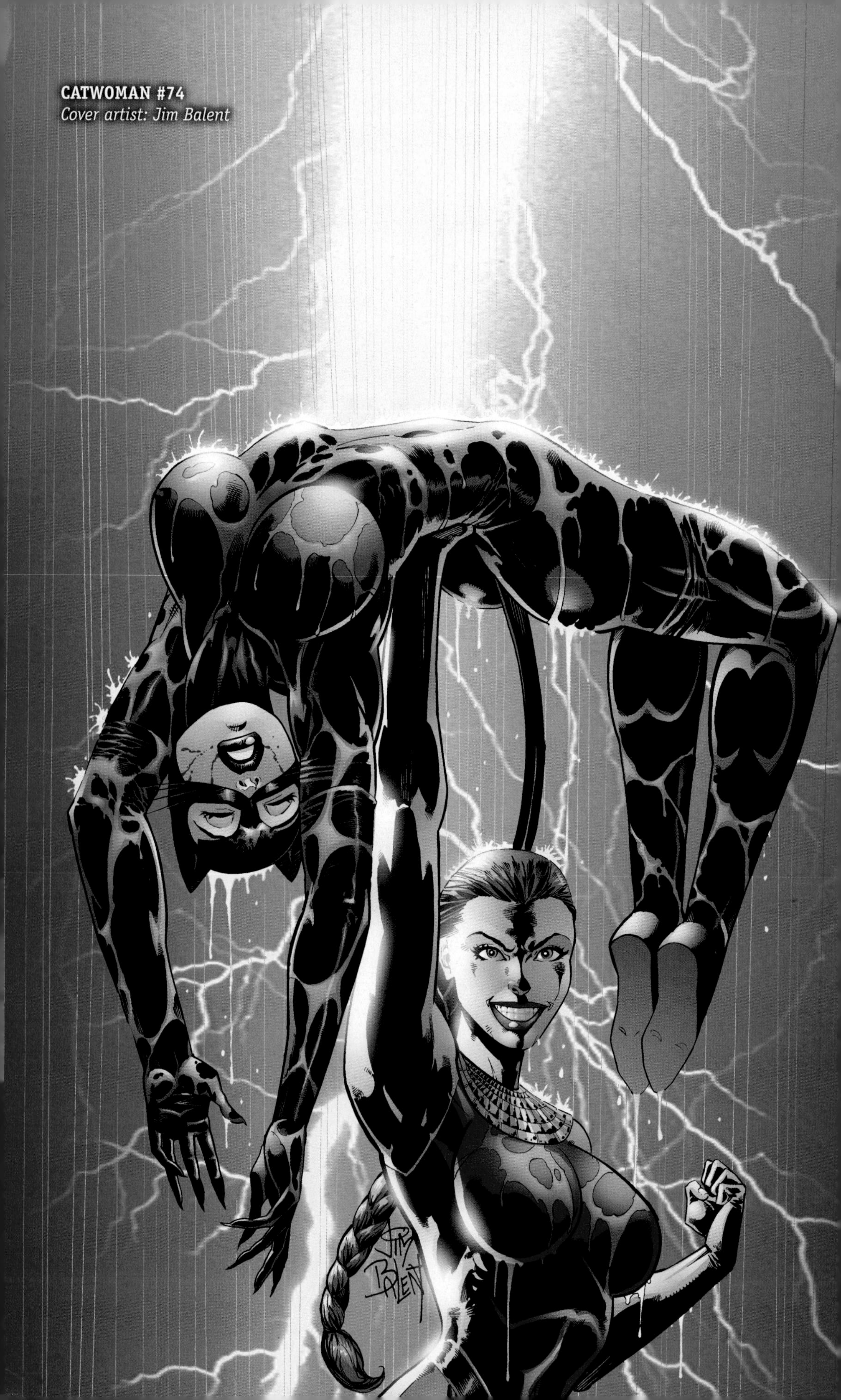

CATWOMAN #74
Cover artist: Jim Balent

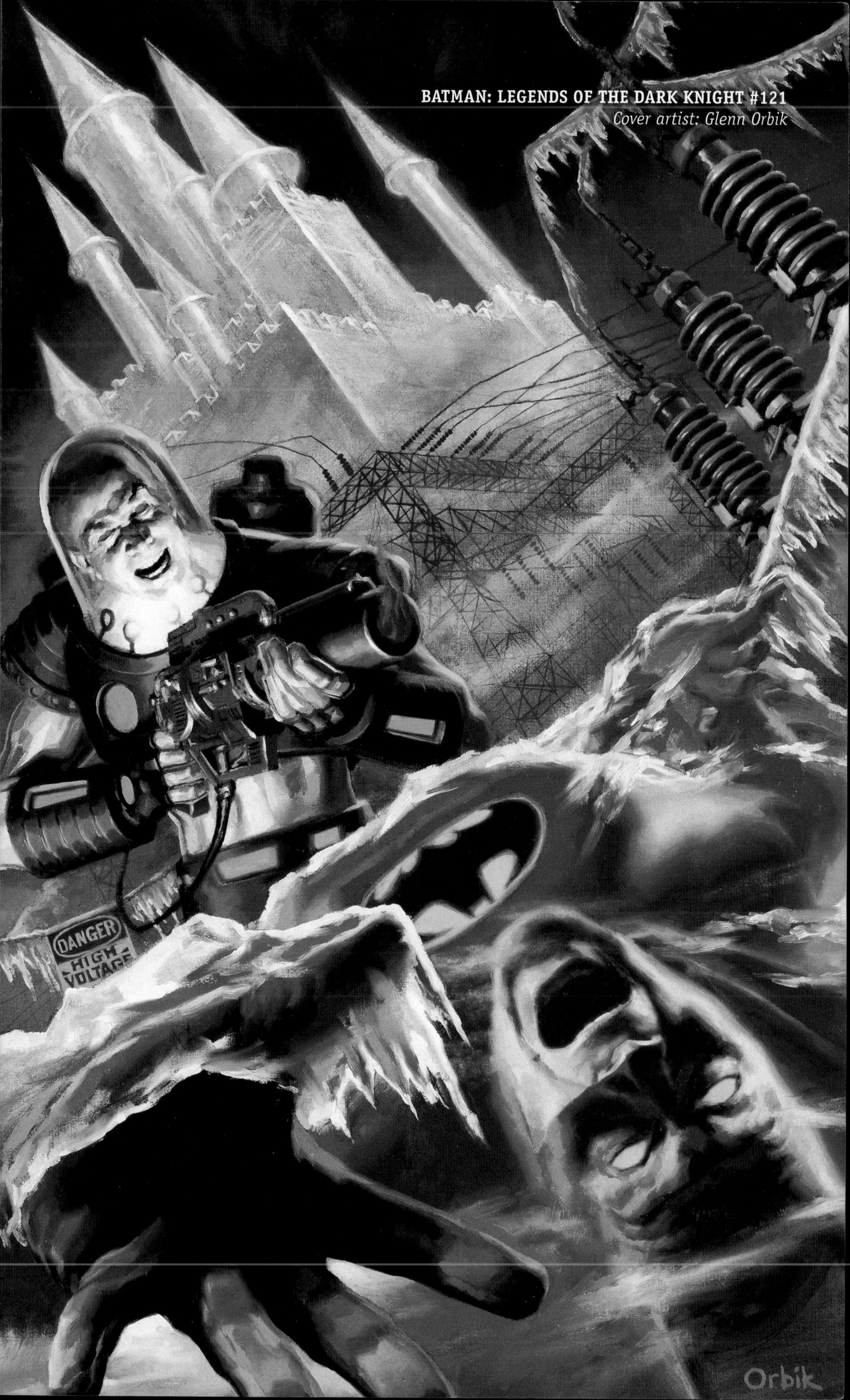
DANGER
HIGH VOLTAGE
Orbik

BATMAN: LEGENDS OF THE DARK KNIGHT #121
Cover artist: Glenn Orbik

BATMAN: NO MAN'S LAND GALLERY

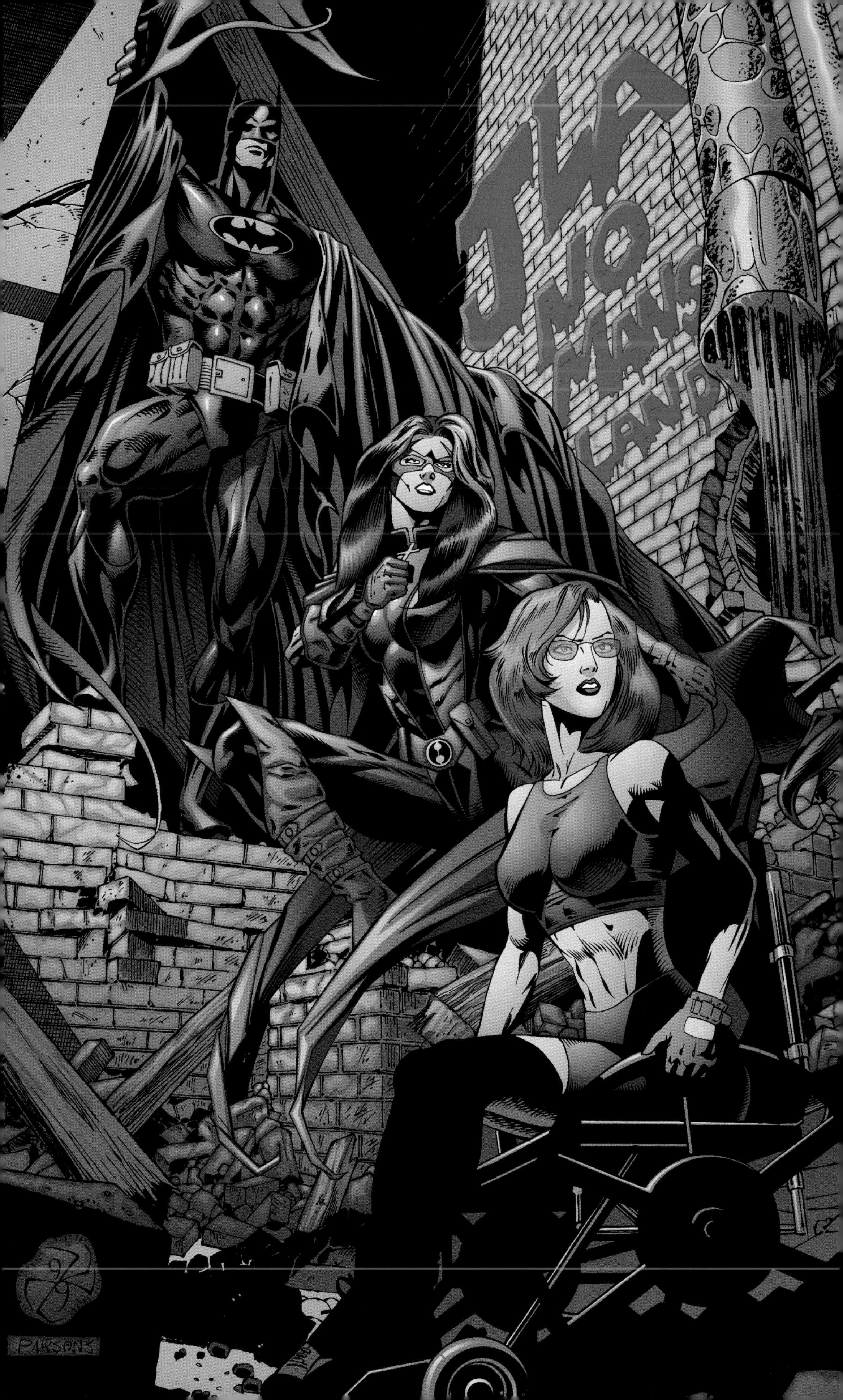
JLA
NO MAN
LAND
PARSONS

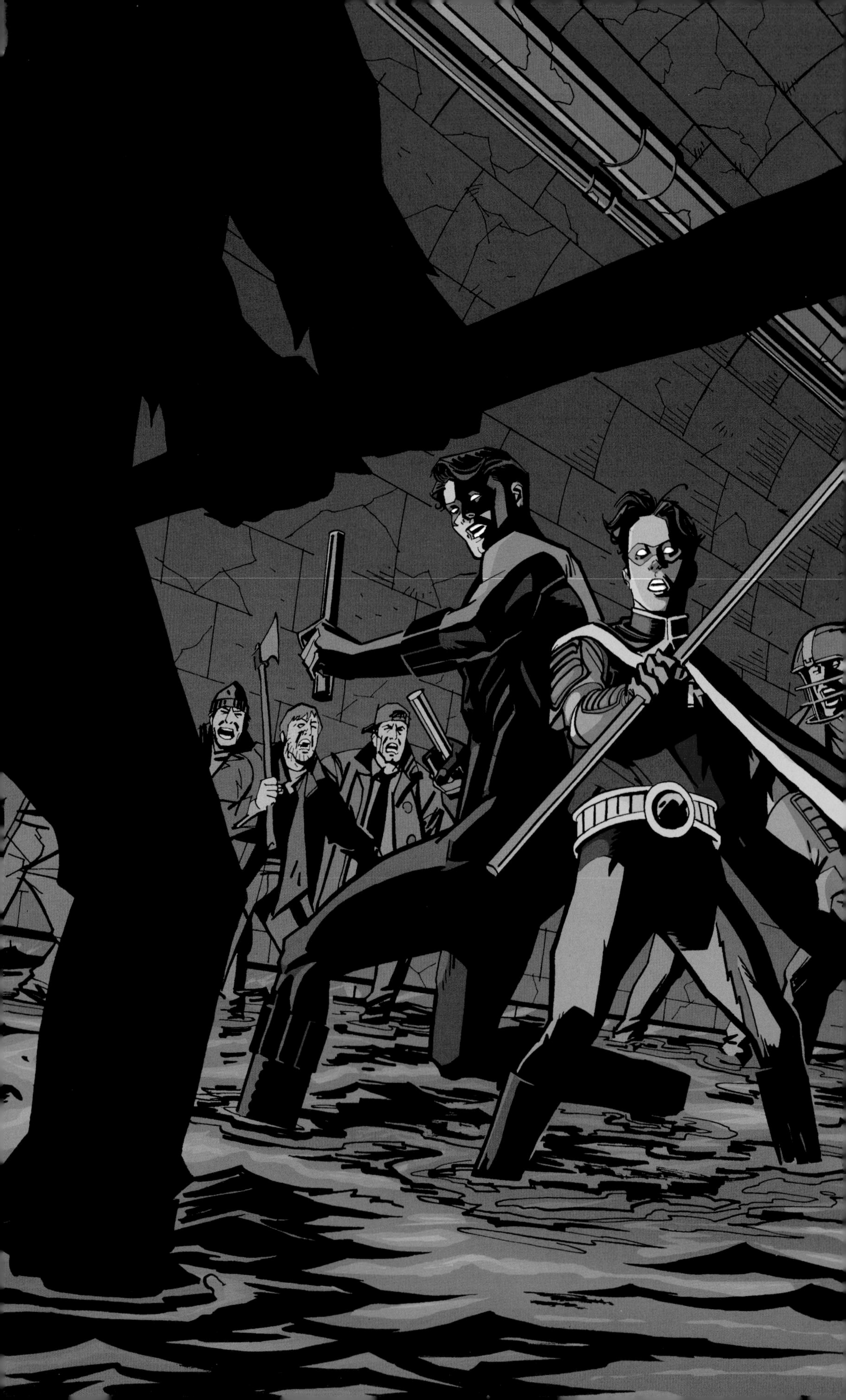

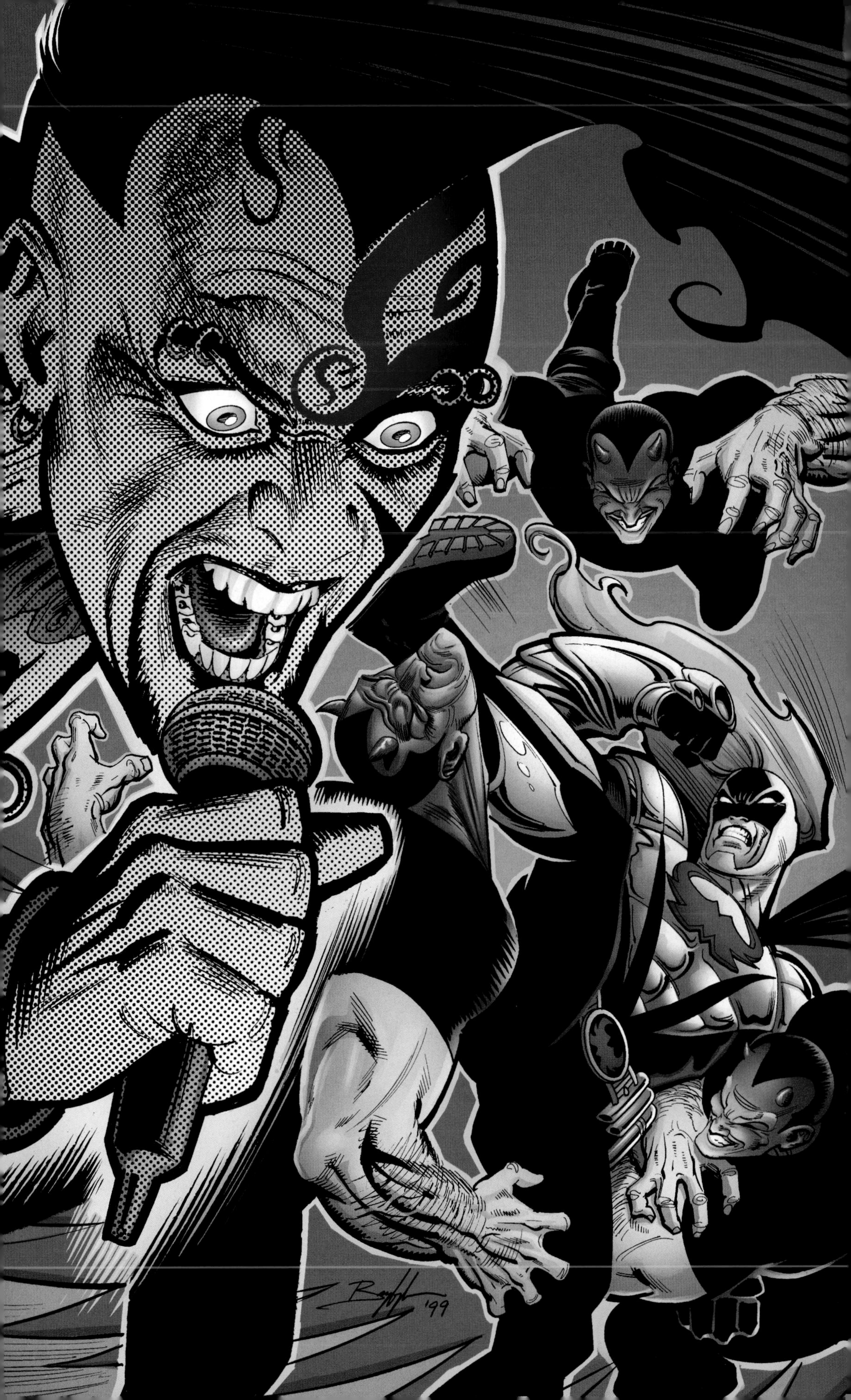

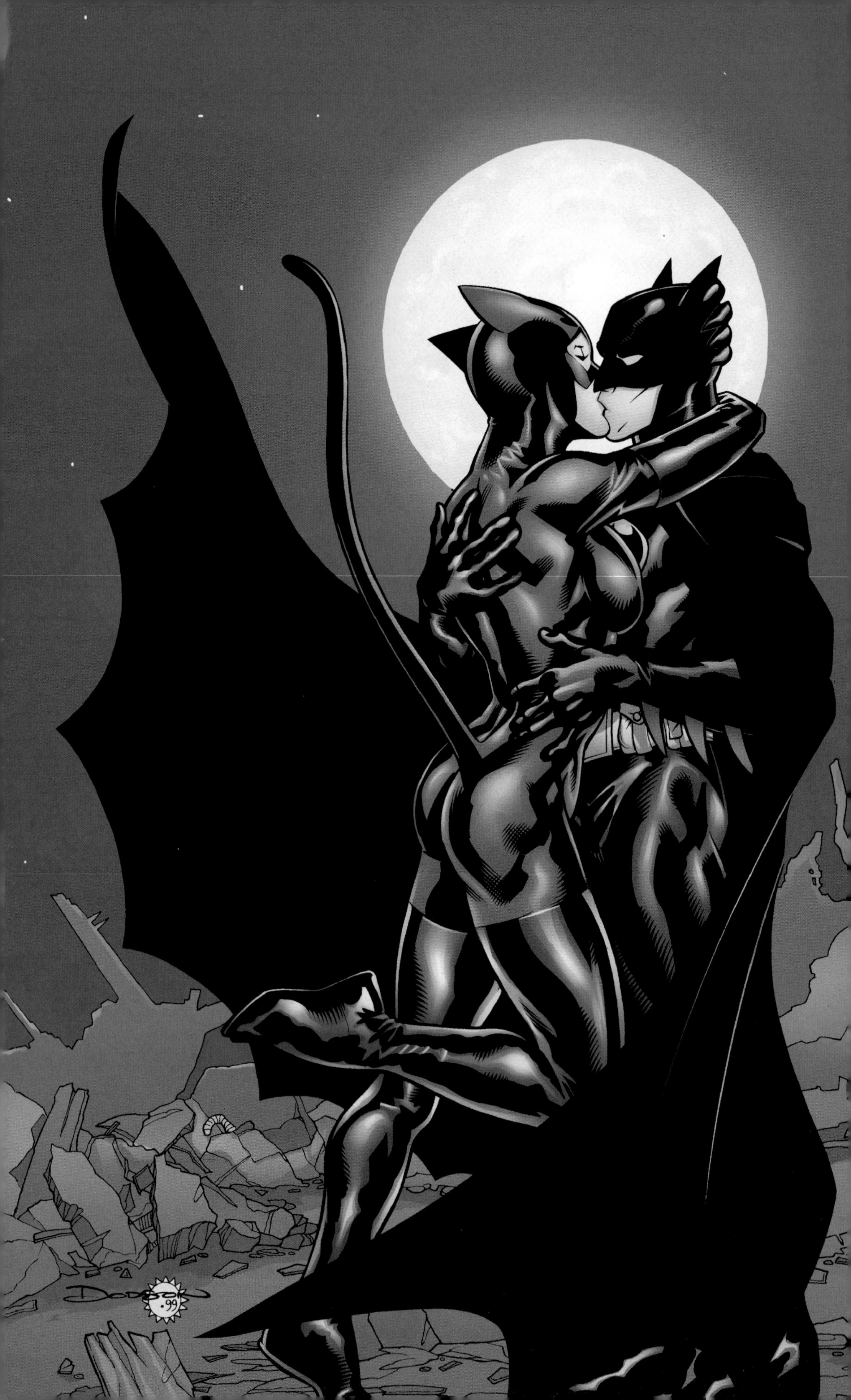

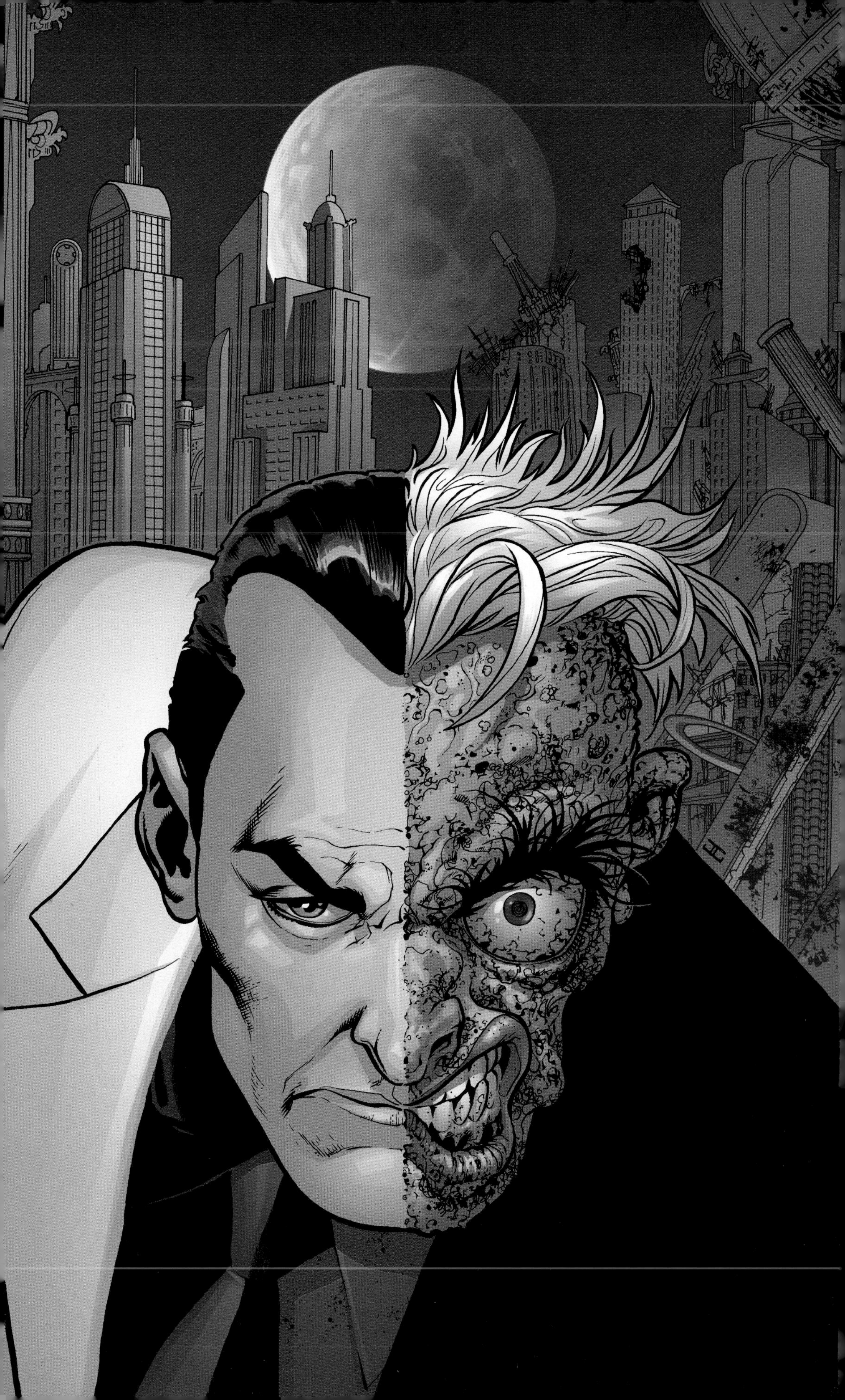

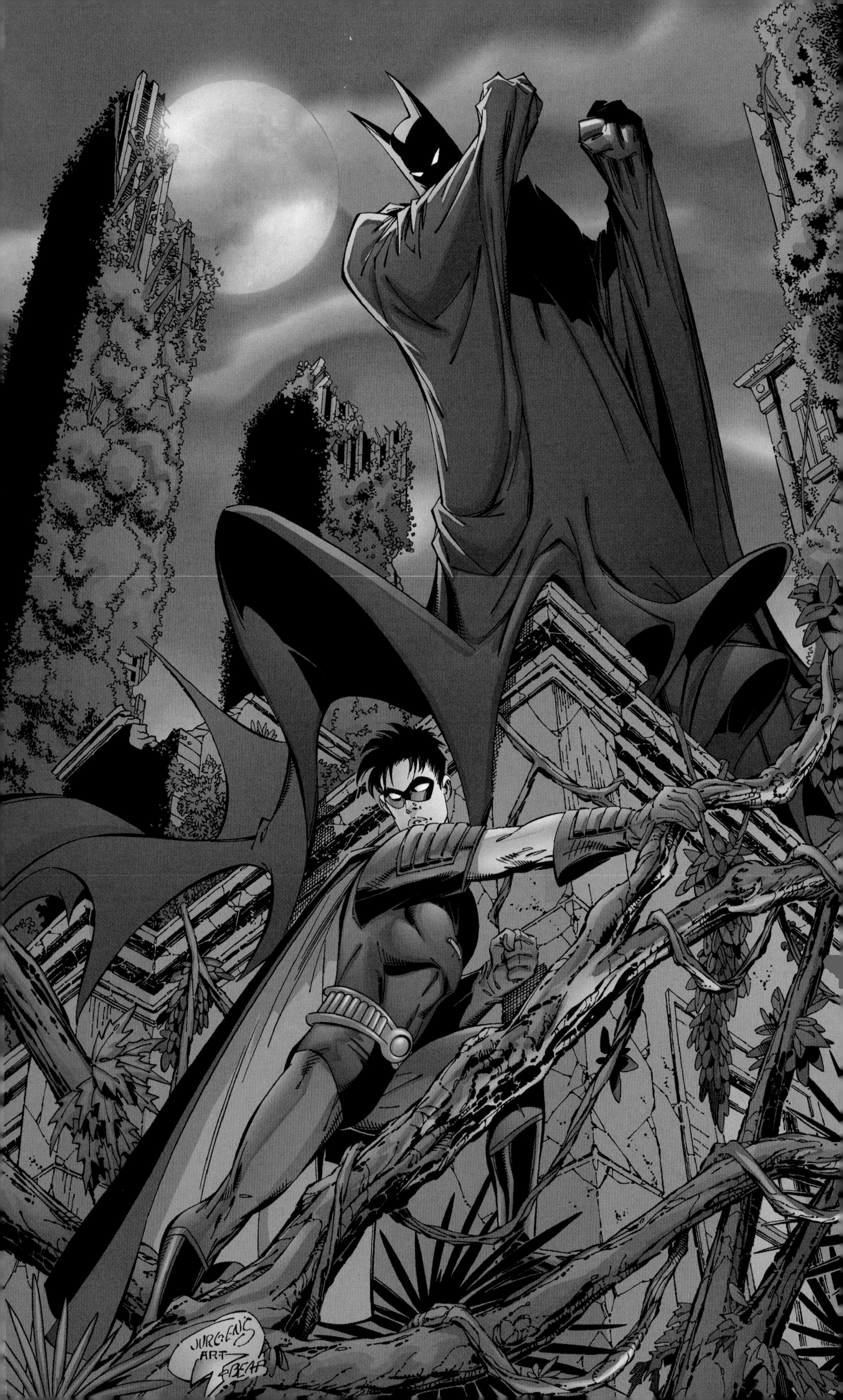
JURGENS
ART
BEAR

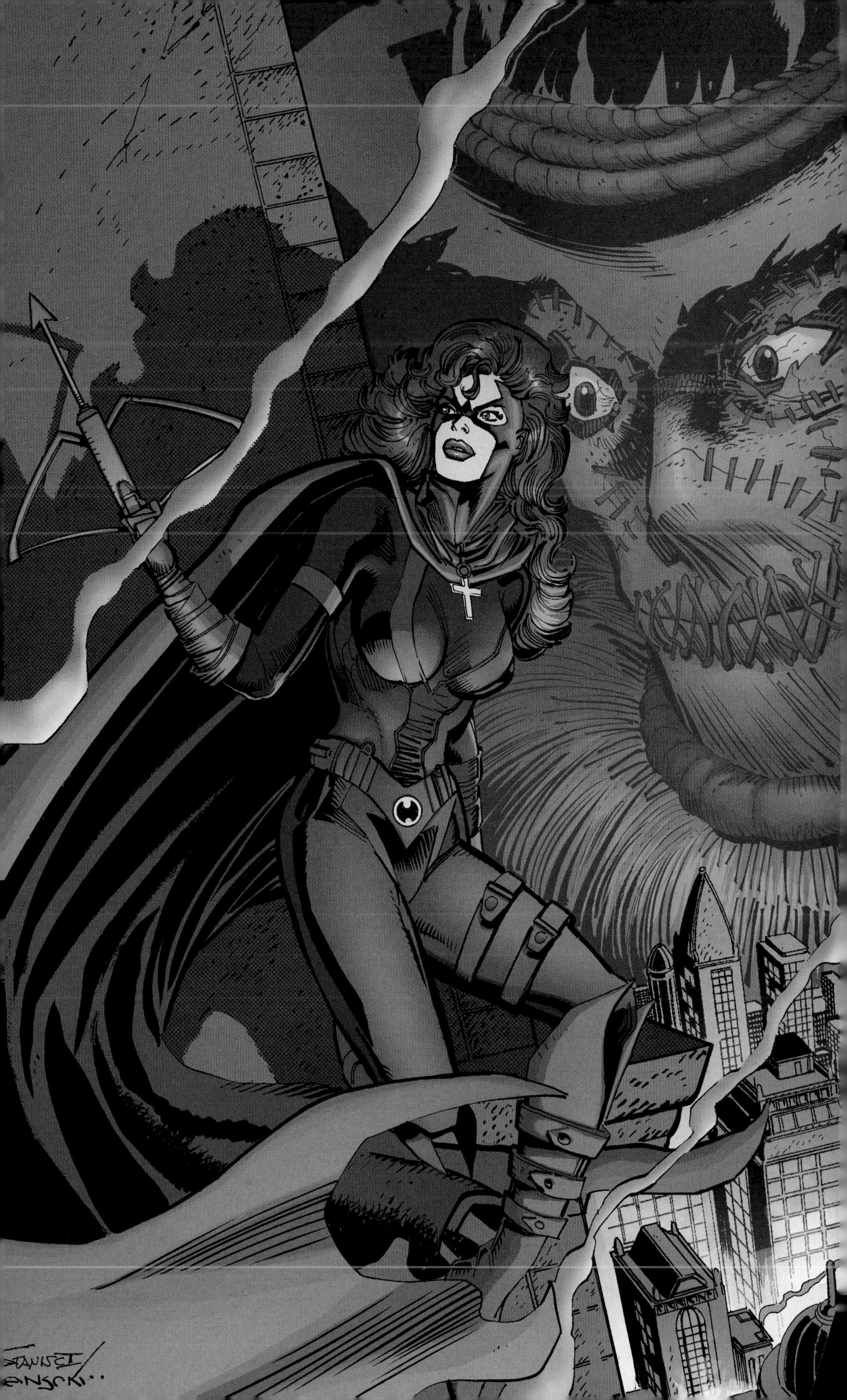

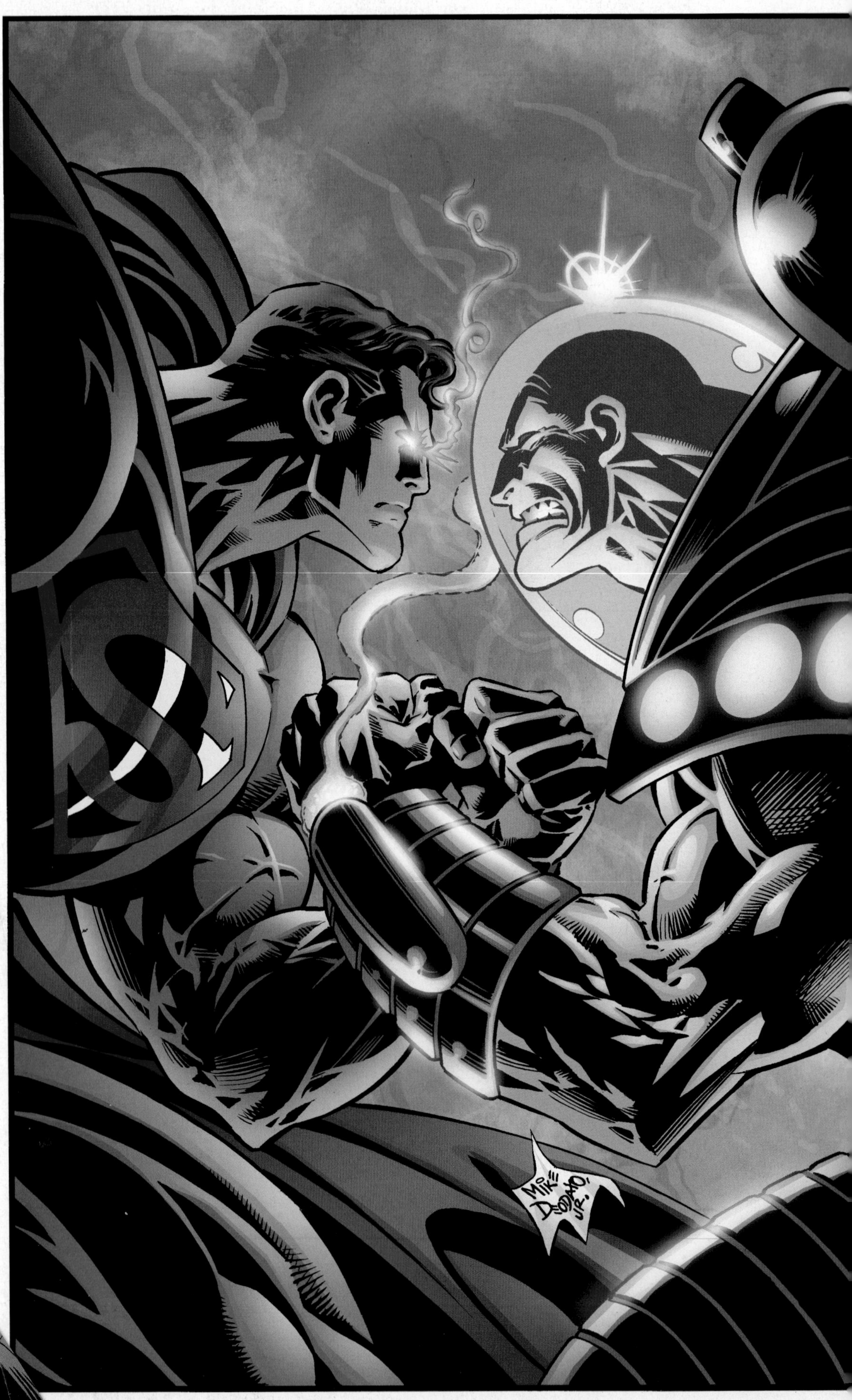

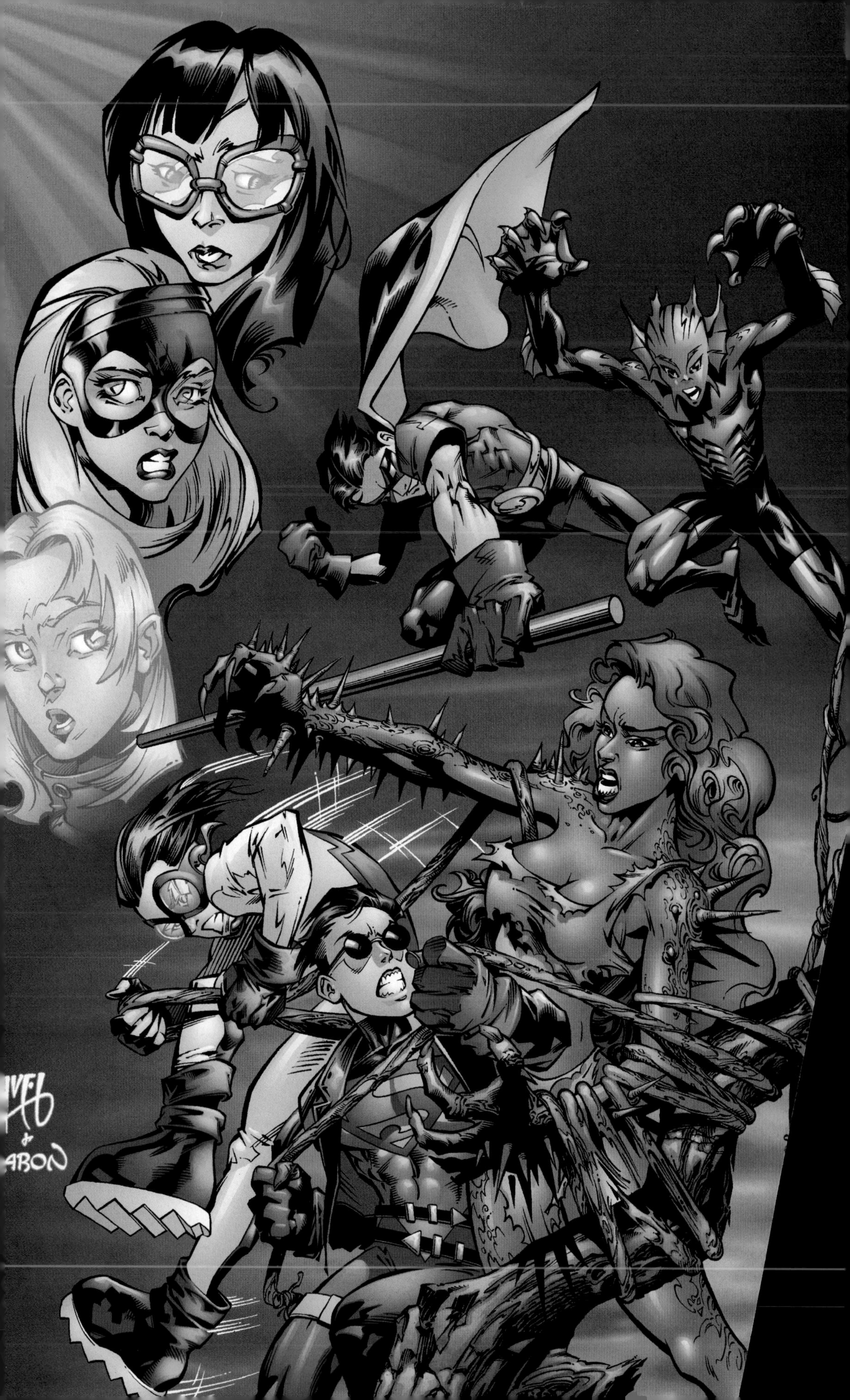

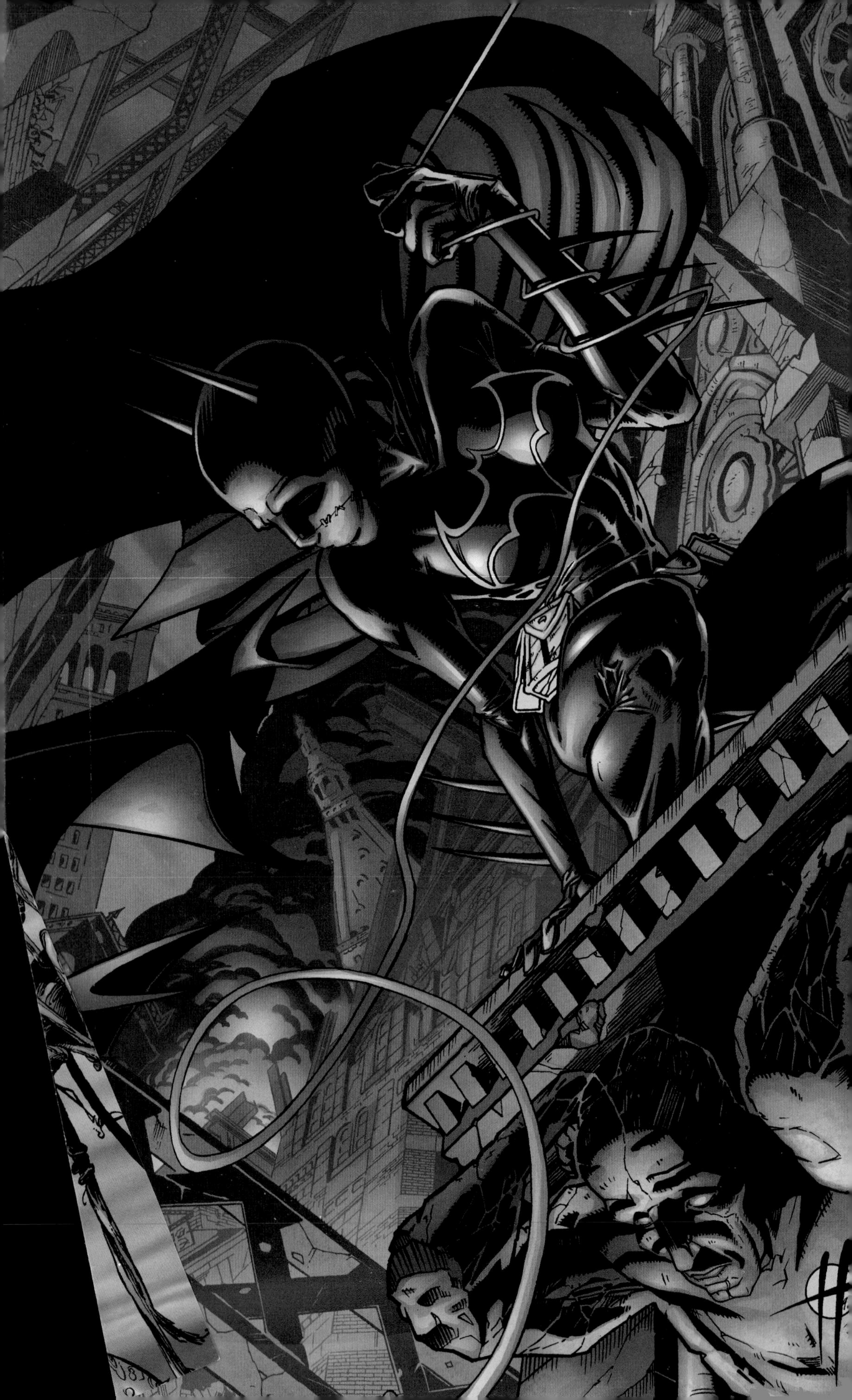